Hotel, Restaurant, and Travel Law

Karen L. Morris
Jane Boyd Ohlin
Sten T. Sliger

Kendall Hunt
publishing company

www.kendallhunt.com
Send all inquiries to:
4050 Westmark Drive
Dubuque, IA 52004-1840

Copyright © 2017 by Kendall Hunt Publishing Company

ISBN 978-1-5249-0791-4

Published in the United States of America

BRIEF CONTENTS

CHAPTER 1   Introduction to Contemporary Hospitality Law 3

CHAPTER 2   Legal Procedures: Journey of a Case Through the Courts 21

CHAPTER 3   Civil Rights and Hospitality Businesses 49

CHAPTER 4   Contract Law and the Hospitality Industry 107

CHAPTER 5   Principles of Negligence 173

CHAPTER 6   Negligence and Hospitality Practices 241

CHAPTER 7   Guests and Other Patrons 323

CHAPTER 8   Protecting Patrons' Property 343

CHAPTER 9   Rights of Innkeepers 403

CHAPTER 10   Guests' Rights 447

CHAPTER 11   Liability and the Sale of Food 487

CHAPTER 12   Liability and the Sale of Alcohol 525

CHAPTER 13   Travel Agents and Airlines—Rights and Liabilities 555

CHAPTER 14   Employment 637

CHAPTER 15   Regulation and Licensing 733

CHAPTER 16   Specialized Destinations—Casinos, Theme Parks, Spas, and Condominium Hotels 803

CONTENTS

Table of Cases xix
Preface xxiii
About the Authors xxvii

UNIT 1 Legal Fundamentals for the Hospitality Industry   1

Chapter 1 Introduction to Contemporary Hospitality Law   3
Introduction   4
What Is Law?   4
Principles of Hospitality Law   4
   Balancing Rights and Duties   5
   History of Hospitality Law   5
Sources of Law   5
   Constitutional Law   6
   Statutory Law   7
   Common Law   7
   Administrative Law   9
Attributes of Law   10
   The Role of the Judge   10
   Civil and Criminal Law   11
   Examples of Civil Law   12
   Remedies in Civil Cases   12
   Examples of Crimes   13
   Penalties and Remedies in Criminal Cases   13
How to Read a Case   14
Summary   17
Review Questions   17
Discussion Questions   18
Application Questions   18
Websites   19

Chapter 2 Legal Procedures: Journey of a Case Through the Courts   21
Introduction   22

The Parties and Proof   23
Commencing the Lawsuit   24
    The Complaint   24
    The Summons   29
    Service of Process   29
    Responses to the Complaint   30
    Responses to the Answer   31
    Summary Judgment   33
    Forum Non Conveniens   33
Pretrial Procedure   34
    Discovery   34
    Pretrial Conference   35
The Trial   36
    Types of Trials—Jury and Bench   36
    Jury Selection   37
    Opening Statements   38
    The Case-in-Chief   38
    The Plaintiff 's Rebuttal Case   39
    Summation   39
    Charging the Jury   39
    Jury Deliberations   40
    The Verdict   40
    The Judgment   40
Appeal   41
    Grounds for Appeal   41
    Appellate Courts   41
Alternative Dispute Resolution   42
Interpreting a Case Citation   43
Summary   44
Preventive Law Tips for Managers   45
Review Questions   46
Discussion Questions   46
Application Questions   47
Websites   48

Chapter 3 Civil Rights and Hospitality Businesses   49
Introduction   50
The Civil Rights Act of 1964   52
    Scope of the Civil Rights Act of 1964   53
    Lodging for Transients   53
    Dining Facilities   54
    Places of Entertainment   54
    Jurisdiction Through Interstate Commerce   55
    Remedies   57
Enforcing the Act   57
    Establishing Jurisdiction   57
    Racial Discrimination   59
    National Origin Discrimination   64
    Language Discrimination   65
    Religious Discrimination   67

Broad Enforcement Through the Unitary Rule 67
Exempt Establishments 68
    "Mrs. Murphy's Boarding House" 68
    Private Clubs 68
    Assailing "Private-in Name-Only" Clubs 70
    Scrutinizing Admission Policies 72
Extending Civil Rights Protection 77
    State Civil Rights Laws 77
    The Americans with Disabilities Act 78
    Age Discrimination 93
    Gender Discrimination 93
    Sexual Orientation Discrimination 95
Rights of Proprietors 96
    Permissible to Remove a Disorderly Person 96
    Reasonable Rules of an Establishment 98
    Retaliatory Exclusion 100
    Ejection of Objectionable Persons and Trespass 101
Summary 102
Preventive Law Tips 102
Review Questions 104
Discussion Questions 104
Application Questions 105
Websites 105

Chapter 4 Contract Law and the Hospitality Industry 107
Introduction 108
The Elements of a Contract 109
    Capacity to Contract 110
    Mutuality: Offer and Acceptance 110
    Legality 113
    Consideration 113
    Illusory Contracts 114
    Proper Form (Written; Oral) 116
    Genuine Assent 122
Ambiguous Terms/Trade Usage 125
    Conditions 129
Contracts Formed on the Internet 130
Breach of Contract 132
    Compensatory Damages 132
    Punitive Damages 139
    Clauses Limiting Damages 140
    Specific Performance 140
Contracting for a Room 141
Overbooking and Breach of Reservation Contract 141
    Damages Allowed for Overbooking 142
    Damage to Goodwill 147
    Breach by a Guest 152
Intentional Interference with Contractual Relations 160
Catering and Convention Contracts 162
Summary 165

Preventive Law Tips 165
Review Questions 167
Discussion Questions 168
Application Questions 169
Websites 170

UNIT II Negligence 171

Chapter 5 Principles of Negligence 173
Introduction 174
Negligence 175
    Elements of a Negligence Case 175
    Reasonable Person Standard 178
    Summary of the Elements of Negligence 185
    Legal Status of Plaintiff 187
    Duty Owed to Invitees 187
    Open and Obvious Exception 189
    Duty Owed to Licensees 191
    Duty Owed to Trespassers 194
    Minority Position 196
    No Special Duty Owed to Others 196
    No Duty Owed on Property Not Owned or Maintained by the
       Hospitality Facility 198
Negligence Doctrines Generally Favoring the Plaintiff 198
    Res Ipsa Loquitur 198
    Children and the Reasonable Person Test 203
    Attractive Nuisance Doctrine 206
    Negligence Per Se Doctrine 207
    Obligations Beyond Regulation 211
    Strict or Absolute Liability 211
    Strict Products Liability 212
    Respondeat Superior 213
    Nondelegable Duties 216
    Duty to Aid a Person in Distress 217
    Duty of Business Owners to Aid Invitees in Danger 218
Negligence Doctrines Generally Favoring the Defendant 224
    Contributory Negligence and Comparative Negligence 224
    Assumption of Risk 227
    Comparative Negligence and Assumption of Risk 231
Summary 234
Preventive Law Tips 235
Review Questions 237
Discussion Questions 238
Application Questions 238
Websites 239

Chapter 6 Negligence and Hospitality Practices 241
Introduction 242
Duty Owed Guests in Hotel Rooms 242
    Cleanliness of Hotel Rooms 243
    Beds, Chairs, and Other Seats 243

Windows, Window Fixtures, and Screens 245
Electrical and Heating Hazards 246
Animals and Insects 246
Bathroom Appliances and Hot Shower Water 250
Duty Owed Guests and Others in Public Areas 255
Lobby 255
Elevators 255
Doors 258
Hallways 261
Stairways, Steps, and Their Coverings 262
Duty Owed Guests in Restaurants and Dining Rooms 265
Slippery Floors 266
Foreign Substances on the Floor 266
Constructive Notice 269
Importance of Enforcing a Policy of Frequent Floor Cleaning 272
Miscellaneous Matters Relating to Floors 272
Hanging Mirrors in Dining Rooms 274
Ceilings 275
Menu Boards on Ledges 275
Hanging Televisions 276
Serving Flambé Foods 276
Serving Hot Liquids 279
Duty Owed Guests Outside 280
Outside Door Service 280
Grounds 281
Sidewalks 282
Outdoor Ramps and Parking Lots 284
Miscellaneous Outdoor Circumstances 284
Outdoor Sporting Facilities 284
Outdoor Lighting Requirements 287
Duties Owed to Guests in Swimming Areas 288
Exercise Reasonable Care 289
Remove Hazards 293
Comply with Statutory Requirements 293
Maintain Safety Equipment 294
Control Boisterous Conduct of Guests 295
Inspect for Glass in Pool Area 295
Oceanfront Properties 296
Waterfront Risks Created by a Hotel 297
Restrict Use or Warn of Hazards in the Water 298
Inspect Lake Bottoms for Hazards 298
Special Duties 299
Injuries Caused by Fire 299
Security 302
Medical Care 311
Summary 313
Preventive Law Tips 313
Review Questions 318
Discussion Questions 318
Application Questions 319
Websites 320

UNIT III   Relationships with Guests and Other Patrons   321

Chapter 7 Guests and Other Patrons   323
Introduction   324
Who Qualifies as a Guest?   324
Intent of Parties   326
    Registration   326
    Delivery of Property   329
Guests' Illegal Acts   332
Termination of a Guest-Innkeeper Relationship   334
Landlord-Tenant Relationship   334
    Factors to Consider When Determining Whether a Person Is a Tenant   336
Summary   339
Preventive Law Tips   339
Review Questions   340
Discussion Questions   341
Application Questions   341

Chapter 8 Protecting Patrons' Property   343
Introduction   344
Risks to Property in the Hotel   344
    Hotel Theft   345
    Keycards and Keys   345
    Guests' Insurance   345
    Absolute Liability for Guests' Goods   346
    Exceptions to the Absolute Liability Rule   347
    Prima Facie Liability Rule—Minority View   347
Limited Liability—Modern Limitations on the Absolute Liability Rule   347
    Providing a Safe   349
    Posting Notice of Availability of Safe   353
    Posting Notice of Hotel's Limited Liability   357
    What Property Belongs in the Safe?   358
    Theft During Checkout   359
    Hotel Guest in Hotel Restaurant   359
    Door Locks and Window Fastenings   360
Clothes and Other Personal Property   360
    Checkrooms   361
    Baggage Room   361
    Merchandise Samples   361
    Property in Transit   363
    Property Not Covered by Limiting Liability Statutes   363
Fire   363
Estoppel: Loss of Limited Liability   364
    Implying Greater Liability   364
    Misrepresenting Risk   364
Hotel's Negligence   366
    Comparative Negligence   368
    Nevada's Limiting Statute   370
Liability During Checkin and Checkout   371
    Guest Status   371
    Liability at Checkin   371

Liability After Checkout 373

Bailment 375
    Effect of Bailment on Liability 377
    Bailment for the Sole Benefit of the Bailor 379
    Bailment for the Sole Benefit of the Bailee 379
    Mutual-Benefit Bailment 380
    Proof of Negligence in Bailment Cases 382
    Items Inside Bailed Property 386
    Rules Particular to Bailment of Cars 387
    Liability for a Patron's Property in a Restaurant, Bar, or Cloakroom 391
    Checkrooms 394
    Concessionaires 396

Summary 397
Preventive Law Tips 397
Review Questions 399
Discussion Questions 400
Application Questions 401
Websites 402

Chapter 9 Rights of Innkeepers 403
Introduction 404
Right to Exclude Nonguests 404
Refusing Lodging to a Would-be Guest 407
    The Consequences of Wrongful Refusal 408
    Age 408
Selecting Accommodations for a Guest 409
Changing a Guest's Accommodations 410
    Entering a Guest's Room 410
Evicting a Guest 411
    Failure to Pay the Hotel Bill 412
    Overstaying 412
    Persons of Ill Repute 413
    Intoxication and Disorderly Conduct 415
    Disorderly Conduct 415
    Contagiously Ill Guests 418
    Breaking House Rules 418
    Business Competitors 421
    The Process of Eviction 422
    Evicting a Hotel Tenant 429
Refusing a Diner 429
Statutory Protection for the Hotelkeeper 432
    The Innkeeper's Lien 432
    Defrauding the Hotelkeeper or Restaurateur 434
    Fraudulent Payment 438
    False Arrest 439
Summary 441
Preventive Law Tips 441
Review Questions 443
Discussion Questions 444
Application Questions 444
Websites 445

Chapter 10 Guests' Rights 447

Introduction 448
Right to Occupy Assigned Room 449
Right to Privacy in Guest Room 449
Protection Against Illegal Searches 455
  Report by Innkeeper of Illegal Activity 456
  Search Warrant 457
  Warrant Exception—Consent to Search 458
  Effect of Termination of Occupancy on Privacy Rights 458
  Warrant Exception—Disturbing the Peace 460
  Emergency Situation 462
  Room Registered to Another 462
  Search of Items Mislaid by Guests 463
  Unclaimed Lost Property 464
Protection Against Insults 464
Protection Against False Arrest 467
Protection Against Credit Card Fraud and Identity Theft 471
Rights Concerning Rates and Fees 474
  Right to Advance Notice 475
  Extraneous Fees 475
  Telephone Charges 476
Proper Handling of Mail, Packages and Facsimile Correspondence and
  Internet Access 477
  Internet Access 480
Summary 481
Preventive Law Tips 481
Review Questions 482
Discussion Questions 483
Application Questions 484
Websites 484

UNIT IV Special Topics 485

Chapter 11 Liability and the Sale of Food 487

Introduction 488
Adulterated Food 488
  Warranty of Merchantability 488
  Merchantable Food 489
  Objects in Food 489
  Trend Toward the Reasonable/Expectation Test 493
  Raw Shellfish 496
  Other Grounds for Breach of Warranty of Merchantability 499
  Class Action 499
  Hot Beverages 500
  Foodborne Illnesses 503
  Proof Problems Establishing Causation 504
  Privity of Contract 507
  Strict Products Liability 508
  Statutory Violations 509
  Negligence 509
  Choice of Action 509
  Customers with Allergies 509

      Hazard Analysis Critical Control Point System 512
      Hand-Washing by Food Preparers 512
   False Food Claims 512
      Truth-in-Menu Laws 513
      Obesity and Accuracy in Advertising 514
      Trans Fats 515
      Food Labeling 515
      Kosher Foods 517
   Smoking Restrictions 518
   Safety Concerns Particular to Food Preparation 519
      Food Preparation 520
      Risks Associated with Donated Foods 520
   Summary 521
   Preventive Law Tips 521
   Review Questions 522
   Discussion Questions 523
   Application Questions 524
   Websites 524

Chapter 12 Liability and the Sale of Alcohol 525
   Introduction 526
   Alcoholic Beverages and the Hospitality Industry 526
      License to Sell Liquor 526
      Illegal Sales 527
      Sales to Underage Patrons 528
      Sales to People Who Are Visibly Intoxicated 530
      Proving Visible Intoxication 531
      Sales to Known Habitual Drunkards 532
   Alcohol Vendors' Liability Under Common Law 532
   Alcohol Vendors' Liability Greatly Increases Under Dram
      Shop Acts 533
      Alcohol Vendor's Liability to the Patron 534
      Alcohol Vendor's Liability to Third Parties 536
      Alcohol Vendor's Liability to Passengers in Patron's Car 538
      Two Licensees Serving One Patron 540
      Apportionment of Liability Among Defendants 541
      Apportionment of Liability Where Plaintiff Is Negligent 541
      States Without Dram Shop Acts 541
   Liquor Liability Insurance 542
      Dram Shop Liability on Some Employers for Office Parties 542
   Strategies to Avoid Liability 544
   Miscellaneous Alcohol Regulations 545
      Alcohol Sales in Hotel Guest Rooms 545
      Age of Alcohol Servers 545
      Restrictions on Alcohol Sales on Sunday and Christmas 546
      BYOB Clubs 546
      Warnings to Pregnant Women 546
      Prohibition of Illegal Gambling 547
      Prohibition of Disorderly Conduct 547
      Maintenance of Prescribed Records 547
      Restrictions on the Type of Alcohol Sold 547
      Limitations on Sales Promotions 547

Prohibition on Celebrity Endorsements 548
Proximity to School, Church, and Parks 548
Alcohol-Free Teen Events 548
Sexually Explicit Entertainment 549
Summary 550
Preventive Law Tips 550
Review Questions 551
Discussion Questions 552
Application Questions 552
Websites 554

Chapter 13 Travel Agents and Airlines—Rights and Liabilities 555
Introduction 556
The Makeup of the Travel Industry 557
    Agency Law 557
    Tariffs 562
Remedies for Small Damages 563
    Small Claims Court 563
    Class Action Suits 564
The Rights of the Traveler 564
    Right to Know Fare in Advance 564
    Baggage Claims—Domestic and International 564
    Airplane Security 576
    Regulation Forbids Interference with Screening Process 579
    Traveling with Animals 579
    Personal Injury Onboard International Flights 580
    Refunds on Tickets 581
    E-Tickets 582
    Rights of Travelers with Disabilities 582
    Travel Insurance 587
Special Rights of Airlines 587
    Right of Airlines to Cancel Scheduled Flights 587
    Established Checkin Time Requirements 589
Rights of Airline Captains 589
Overbooking 596
    Priority Rules for Seating 597
    Punitive Damages for Overbooking 600
    Overbooking on International Flights 600
    Punitive Damages on International Flights 602
    Prohibition on Lengthy Delays on Tarmac 602
Additional Legal Issues Involving Airlines 603
    Lack of Documentation for International Travel 603
    Liability for Negligence 605
Liabilities of Travel Agents and Charter Tour Companies 605
    Liability for Own Actions 606
    Duty to Investigate Third-Party Suppliers 609
    Recommending Travel Insurance 612
    Liability for Breach of Contract by Third-Party Service Suppliers 616
    No Liability for Third-Party Suppliers' Negligence 620
    Disclaimers by the Travel Agent 621
    Errors and Omissions Insurance for Travel Agents 622

Credit Card Fraud   622
Rental Cars   623
    Overbooking   623
    Accidents in Rental Cars   624
    Rental of a Car Known to Be Defective   626
    Unauthorized Drivers   627
    Age Discrimination with Car Rentals   630
Summary   631
Preventive Law Tips   631
Review Questions   633
Discussion Questions   634
Application Questions   635
Websites   635

Chapter 14 Employment   637
Introduction   638
Fair Labor Standards Act   638
    Minimum Wage   638
    Overtime Pay   641
    Time Worked   644
    Split and Partial Shifts   644
    Equal Pay for Equal Work   644
    Retaliatory Discharge   645
    Restrictions on Child Labor – Hours   646
    Restrictions on Child Labor – Tasks   646
    Enforcement of the FLSA   647
    Family and Medical Leave Act   647
    At-Will Employment   648
Illegal Job Discrimination   649
    Title VII of the Civil Rights Act of 1964   649
    Filing a Complaint   650
    Remedies   651
    Defense of Bona Fide Occupational Qualification   653
    Defense of Business Necessity   653
    Prohibited and Permitted Interview Questions   654
    Race   656
    Reverse Discrimination   662
    National Origin   663
    National Origin and Accent Discrimination   667
    Religion   668
    Reasonable Accommodations   669
    Hostile Work Environment   672
    Gender   673
    Gender-Differentiated Grooming Standards   676
    Sexual Harassment   679
    Pregnancy   689
    Retaliatory Discharge   698
    Mixed Types of Discrimination   699
Americans with Disabilities Act   705
    Essential Functions   705

Reasonable Accommodation 706
Undue Hardship 709
Preference Not Required 709
    ADA Impacts on Application Process 710
    Drugs and Illnesses 711
    Past Disabilities and Caregivers 712
    Pursuing an ADA Case 714
    Inability to Perform Essential Elements 715
    Not Disabled 716
Mandatory Verification of Employment Status 716
    Immigration Reform and Control Act 716
Résumé Fraud 721
Occupational Safety and Health Administration 721
Unions 722
National Labor Relations Act 722
    National Labor Relations Board 723
Emerging Issues in Employment Law 723
    Negligent Hiring 723
    Employee Use of Social Media 723
    Handling Employee Personal Data 723
    Miscellaneous Issues 724
Summary 725
Preventive Law Tips 725
Review Questions 728
Discussion Questions 729
Application Questions 730
Websites 731

Chapter 15 Regulation and Licensing 733
Introduction 734
Regulation of the Marketplace 735
    Trademarks and Service Marks 735
    Copyrights Basics 746
    Illegal Satellite Reception 747
    Music Performances 750
    Artwork 757
    Antitrust Problems 758
Application of the Rule of Reason 762
Franchising 765
    Nature of the Franchise Relationship 766
    Benefits to the Franchisee 767
    Benefits to the Franchisor 767
    Fraud and Breach of Contract by the Franchisor 769
    Tying Arrangements in Franchises as an Antitrust Issue 770
    Termination of a Franchise 774
Regulation of Hotel and Restaurant Internal Affairs 776
    Guest Register 776
    Room Rates 777
    Price Gouging 779
    Mandatory Recycling 779

Licensing and Zoning 780
 Licensing 780
 Principles for Granting Licenses and Permits 781
 License Fees 786
 Consequences of Operating without a License 787
 Revocation or Suspension of a License 788
 Zoning 792
 Variance 795
Summary 796
Preventive Law Tips 796
Review Questions 799
Discussion Questions 799
Application Questions 800
Websites 801

Chapter 16 Specialized Destinations—Casinos, Theme Parks, Spas, and
     Condominium Hotels 803
Introduction 804
A Short History of Gambling 804
 Gambling Today 805
Gaming Issues 806
 Resolution of Gaming Issues 806
 Casino Owes No Duty to Inform Patrons of Laws Relevant to Gambling. 807
 Exclusion of Card Counters Permissible 807
 Slot Machines 808
Contracts and Gambling Debts 812
 Compulsive/Problem Gamblers 814
Torts Involving Casinos 816
 Negligence 816
 Strict Liability 820
 Criminal Activity at Casinos 820
 False Imprisonment 822
 Trademark Infringement 823
 Copyright Infringement 824
Casinos and Dram Shop Act 825
Riverboat Casinos and the Jones Act 826
 The Jones Act 826
 Rough Waters 828
Casinos on Native American Reservations 829
 Sovereign Authority 829
 Application of Tribal Sovereignty to Lawsuits Against Native American Tribes 829
 Lawsuits Against Casino Employees 834
 Indian Gaming Regulatory Act 835
Internet Gambling 836
Theme Parks 837
 Introduction 837
 Crowd Control 837
 Amusement Rides 838
 Other Attractions 840
 Admission Discounts 841

Season Passes   842
Hotel Spas   842
   Licensing   843
   Sanitation and Nails   843
   Wet and Slippery Floors   844
   Effect of Liability Waivers   844
   Property Stolen from Lockers   845
   Massages   846
   Tanning Booths   846
Condominium Hotels   847
   Common Areas   847
   Amenities   847
   Unit Rentals   847
   Advantages   848
   Contracts   848
   Future   848
Summary   849
Preventive Law Tips   849
Review Questions   852
Discussion Questions   853
Application Questions   854
Websites   855

Glossary   857
Index   875

TABLE OF CASES

1-1   Viscecchia v. Allegria Hotel   15
2-1   Stern v. Four Points by Sheraton Ann Arbor Hotel   26
2-2   Clark v. Starwood Hotel & Resorts Worldwide, Inc.   27
2-3   Wenzel v. Marriott International, Inc.   33
3-1   Sherman v. Marriott Hotel Services, Inc.   62
3-2   Hernandez v. Erlenbusch   65
3-3   Daniel v. Paul   70
3-4   U.S. v. Lansdowne Swim Club   74
3-5   Kalani v. Castle Village, LLC   75
3-6   Rodriguez v. Barrita, Inc.   82
3-7   Rodgers v. Chevy's Restaurants, LLC   86
3-8   Boemio v. Love's Restaurant   90
3-9   Alexis v. McDonald's Restaurants of Massachusetts, Inc.   97
3-10   Feldt v. Marriott Corporation   99
4-1   University Hotel Development, L.L.C. v. Dusterhoft Oil, Inc.   112
4-2   Lederman Enterprises, Inc. v. Allied Social Science Associates   115
4-3   BBQ Blues Texas, Ltd. v. Affiliated Business Brokers, Inc.   118
4-4   Adams v. H&H Meat Products, Inc.   119
4-5   Filet Menu, Inc. v. C.C.L. & G., Inc.   122
4-6   Southern Hospitality, Inc. v. Zurich American Ins. Co.   125
4-7   Las Palmeras De Ossining Restaurant v. Midway Center Corp.   128
4-8   Casino Resorts v. Monarch Casinos, Inc.   129
4-9   Casino Resorts, Inc. v. Monarch Casinos, Inc.   133
4-10   Ibiza, Inc. v. Samis Foundation   134
4-11   Wyndham International, Inc. v. Ace American Insurance Co.   137
4-12   Dold v. Outrigger Hotel   142
4-13   Vern Wells et al. v. Holiday Inns, Inc.   144
4-14   Rainbow Travel Services, Inc. v. Hilton Hotels Corp.   148
4-15   Leo's Partners, LLC v. Ferrari   151
4-16   Freeman v. Kiamesha Concord, Inc.   153
4-17   2625 Building Corp. (Marriott Hotel) v. Deutsch   155
4-18   National Ass'n of Postmasters of U.S. v. Hyatt Regency Washington   157
4-19   Melo-Tone Vending, Inc. v. Sherry, Inc.   161
5-1   Ordonez v. Gillespie   176

5-2   Shadburn v. Whitlow   180
5-3   Palace Bar, Inc. v. Fearnot   182
5-4   Smith v. West Rochelle Travel Agency, Inc.   183
5-5   Willing v. Pinnacle Entertainment   185
5-6   Montes v. Betcher   188
5-7   Hudechek v. Novi Hotel Fund Limited Partnership   190
5-8   Steinberg v. Irwin Operating Co.   192
5-9   David Hanson v. Hyatt Corp.   195
5-10   Callender v. MCO Properties   197
5-11   Jones v. GMRI, Inc.   200
5-12   Parks v. Steak & Ale of Texas, Inc.   201
5-13   Frelow v. St. Paul Fire & Marine Insurance Co.   204
5-14   First Overseas Investment Corp. v. Cotton   208
5-15   Scott v. Salerno and GNOC Corp., d/b/a Bally's Grand Hotel & Casino   214
5-16   Baker v. Fenneman & Brown Properties, LLC and Southern Bells of Indiana, Inc.,
          all d/b/a Taco Bell   218
5-17   Fish v. Paul, d/b/a Horseshoe Motel   220
5-18   Campbell v. Eitak, Inc. T/D/B/A Katana   222
5-19   Ball v. Hilton Hotels, Inc.   228
5-20   Demarco v. Ouellette   230
5-21   Eldridge v. Downtowner Hotel   232
6-1   Copeland v. The Lodge Enterprises, Inc.   247
6-2   Sheridan Holiday Inn v. Poletis   252
6-3   Sheppard v. Crow-Barker-Paul   260
6-4   Fields v. Robert Chappell Association, Inc.   264
6-5   Kesselman v. Lever House Restaurant   267
6-6   Anderson v. American Restaurant Group   269
6-7   Demaille v. Trump Castle Associates   271
6-8   LaPlante v. Radisson Hotel Co.   273
6-9   Bank of New York v. Ansonia Associates   275
6-10   Young v. Caribbean Associates, Inc.   276
6-11   Kurzweg v. Hotel St. Regis Corp.   280
6-12   Eisnaugle v. McDonald's   281
6-13   Turner v. Holiday Inn Holidome   289
6-14   Audi v. Rest-All-Inn   292
6-15   Mihill v. Ger-Am Inc.   297
6-16   Taboada v. Daly Seven, Inc.   306
7-1   Wallace v. Shoreham Hotel Corp.   325
7-2   Langford v. Vandaveer   327
7-3   Adler v. Savoy Plaza Inc.   330
7-4   Freudenheim v. Eppley   331
7-5   Olley v. Extended Stay America-Houston   335
8-1   Zaldin v. Concord Hotel   349
8-2   Carlson v. BRGA Associates, LLC   351
8-3   Searcy v. La Quinta Motor Inns, LLC   354
8-4   Paraskevaides v. Four Seasons Washington   355
8-5   Fennema v. Howard Johnson Co.   364
8-6   Bhattal v. Grand Hyatt-New York   367
8-7   McReynolds v. RIU Resorts and Hotels   369
8-8   DeLema v. Waldorf Astoria Hotel, Inc.   372

8-9	*Salisbury v. St. Regis-Sheraton Hotel*	373
8-10	*Spiller v. Barclay Hotel*	374
8-11	*Augustine v. Marriott Hotel*	377
8-12	*First American Bank v. District of Columbia*	380
8-13	*Value Rent-A-Car, Inc. v. Collection Chevrolet, Inc.*	383
8-14	*Proliance Insurance Co. v. Acura*	384
8-15	*Ellerman v. Atlanta American Motor Hotel Corp.*	388
8-16	*Waterton v. Motor Inc.*	390
8-17	*Kuchinsky v. Empire Lounge, Inc.*	392
8-18	*Shamrock Hilton Hotel v. Caranas*	393
8-19	*Conboy v. Studio 54, Inc.*	395
9-1	*People v. Thorpe*	405
9-2	*Nixon v. Royal Coach Inn of Houston*	409
9-3	*Morningstar v. Lafayette Hotel Co.*	412
9-4	*Raider v. Dixie Inn*	414
9-5	*Forte v. Hyatt Summerfield Suites, Pleasanton*	416
9-6	*Kelly v. United States*	419
9-7	*Hennig v. Goldberg*	420
9-8	*Raider v. Dixie Inn*	423
9-9	*Westin Operator, LLC v. Groh*	424
9-10	*Hopp v. Thompson*	426
9-11	*Durand v. Moore*	430
9-12	*State of Utah v. Leonard*	436
10-1	*Perrine v. Paulos*	449
10-2	*Campbell v. Womack*	451
10-3	*Carter v. Innisfree Hotel, Inc.*	453
10-4	*People v. Ouellette*	459
10-5	*People v. Henning*	460
10-6	*Berger v. State*	463
10-7	*Bertuca v. Martinez*	467
10-8	*Lewis v. Ritz Carlton Hotel Co., LLC*	468
10-9	*Federal Trade Commission v. Wyndham orldwide Corp.*	472
10-10	*State of New York v. Waldorf-Astoria*	475
10-11	*Berlow v. Sheraton Dallas Corp.*	478
11-1	*Webster v. Blue Ship Tea Room, Inc.*	491
11-2	*Coulter v. American Bakeries Co.*	495
11-3	*Bergeron v. Jazz Seafood & Steakhouse, and Louisiana Dept. of Health*	497
11-4	*Oubre v. E-Z Serve Corp.*	502
11-5	*Brown v. City Sam Restaurants, Inc.*	504
11-6	*Foster v. AFC Enterprises, Inc.*	505
11-7	*Thompson v. East Pacific-Enterprises, Inc.*	510
12-1	*Kirchner v. Shooters on the Water, Inc.*	534
12-2	*Rodriguez v. Goodlin*	537
12-3	*Goss v. Richmond*	539
12-4	*Barnes v. Cohen Dry Wall, Inc.*	542
13-1	*Rottman v. El Al Israel Airlines*	558
13-2	*Vermeulen v. Worldwide Holidays, Inc.*	561
13-3	*Fontan-de-Maldonado v. Lineas Aereas Costarricenses*	562
13-4	*Lourenco v. Trans World Airlines, Inc.*	567
13-5	*Kodak v. American Airlines*	570

13-6   Mohammed v. Air France   572
13-7   United States v. Marquez   577
13-8   Tallarico v. Trans World Airlines, Inc.   583
13-9   Johnson v. Northwest Orient Airlines   588
13-10   Zervigon v. Piedmont Aviation, Inc.   590
13-11   Al-Qudhai'een v. America West Airlines, Inc.   594
13-12   Goranson v. Trans World Airlines   597
13-13   Weiss v. El Al Israel Airlines, Ltd.   601
13-14   Burnap v. Tribeca Travel   606
13-15   Josephs v. Fuller (Club Dominicus)   609
13-16   Wilson v. American Trans Air, Inc.   613
13-17   Odysseys Unlimited, Inc. v. Astrol Travel Service   616
13-18   Musso v. Tourlite International, Inc.   618
13-19   Drummond v. Walker   624
13-20   Travelers v. Budget Rent-a-Car Systems, Inc.   627
14-1   Padilla v. Manlapaz, Barrio Fiesta Restaurant, et al   639
14-2   Carter v. Thompson Hotels   657
14-3   Clements v. Fitzgerald's Mississippi, Inc.   662
14-4   Mejia v. New York Sheraton Hotel   665
14-5   Equal Employment Opportunity Commission v. Red Robin Gourmet Burgers, Inc.   669
14-6   Jesperson v. Harrah's Operating Co., Inc.   676
14-7   Gregg v. Hay-Adams Hotel   684
14-8   Crist v. Dorr to Door Pizza   692
14-9   Rivera-Aponte v. Restaurant Metropol #3, Inc.   696
14-10   EEOC v. Marion Motel Associates   698
14-11   EEOC v. Hacienda Hotel   700
14-12   Arevalo v. Hyatt Corp.   707
14-13   Buffington v. PEC Management II, LLP, d/b/a/ Burger King   712
15-1   Carlo Bay Enterprise v. Two Amigo Restaurant, Inc.   738
15-2   Holiday Inns, Inc. v. Holiday Inn   743
15-3   J & J Sports Productions, Inc. v. Orellana   748
15-4   Broadcast Music, Inc. v. Quality Hotel & Conference Center   751
15-5   BMI v. Station House Irish Publ & Steakhouse, Ltd.   753
15-6   Cass County Music Company v. Port Town Family Restaurant   756
15-7   United States v. Hilton Hotels Corporation   760
15-8   Elliott v. The United Center   764
15-9   Holiday Hospitality Franchising, LLC v. Premier NW Investment Hotels, LLC   768
15-10   Queens City Pizza, Inc. v. Domino's Pizza, Inc.   771
15-11   Travelodge Hotels, Inc. v. Budget Inns of Defuniak Sprins, Inc.   775
15-12   Archibald v. Cinerama Hotels   778
15-13   Hertenberger v. City of Texarkana   782
15-14   McDonald's Corp. v. Town of East Longmeadow   784
15-15   Oronoka Restaurant, Inc. v. Maine State Liquor Commission   788
15-16   In Re Cadillac Jacks   790
15-17   Schleuter v. City of Fort Worth   794
16-1   McKee v. Isle of Capri Casinos, Inc. 810
16-2   Lundy v. Adamar of New Jersey, Inc. t/a TropWorld   817
16-3   Buzulis v. Mohegan Sun Casino   830
16-4   Star Tickets v. Chumash Casino Resort   832

PREFACE

Lawsuits are expensive, time consuming, and damaging to a business' reputation. *Hotel, Restaurant, and Travel Law: A Preventive Approach*, Eighth Edition, focuses on *prevention* as the means to minimize the number of lawsuits a hospitality establishment experiences. While it is true that good hospitality management means satisfying patrons and guests, it also encompasses protecting customers and the business from the kinds of accidents and incidents that can lead to injury and litigation. Indeed, the two concerns of good service and lawsuit prevention overlap substantially. Pleasing guests involves not just comfortable surroundings, a welcoming staff, and good food; an additional component is a safe facility that enables patrons to enjoy their time away from home without injury or harm. Most lawsuits can be prevented if management and staff are properly trained to recognize potential hazards and guard against them. Throughout the eight editions of this book, a primary objective of the authors has been to arm future hospitality industry personnel with the legal knowledge needed to enhance the guest's experience and prevent lawsuits.

Revised for Clarity and Critical Thinking

This eighth edition has been revised and updated to make hospitality law more approachable and understandable for students. This edition, like its predecessors, is an important tool for the development of critical thinking skills in managers. Those skills are needed now more than ever—to adapt to the contemporary legal environment with its frequently changing laws and regulations, high expectations by patrons, and many legal rights for employees. For example, this edition includes the following.

- **Updates for every chapter** have been added, including references to new laws, new cases, technological changes and advancements, and new factual circumstances in the hospitality industry.

- **New website references in every chapter** offer students the opportunity for expanded exposure to topics throughout the book

- **Many new subjects** have been added.

- The **case study format** has been retained; the book continues to include substantial portions of many court decisions on numerous topics. While law can be a challenging discipline for college students, the learning process is facilitated by reading real-life case examples of legal principles applied to interesting and relevant fact patterns. By studying cases, students develop an appreciation that principles of law have direct application to the day-to-day operations of a hospitality facility; and that disregard of rules can be very costly indeed. Further, using cases to teach hospitality law sharpens students' skills in understanding the rules and the nuances of the law, both of which are critical competencies in a discipline such as law where the outcome of a case depends on many variables. The case method also helps students learn to extract important information from large amounts of data. This is a necessary management skill in today's world, given that technology has made the amount of accessible information daunting, and the challenging legal environment of business makes the absence of critical information damning.

- The **end-of-chapter material** entitled "Preventive Law Tips for Managers" has been retained and, where appropriate, expanded. This feature provides a concentrated summary of the issues addressed in each chapter.

- The **text** presents plain-English explanations of essential legal concepts. Also, each chapter includes many subtopics. The effect of both is to enhance the ability of students to read and comprehend the material.

- Case questions, included at the end of many case examples, engage the reader and connect practices and principles.

- End-of-chapter questions expand review and discussion of the material and add the challenge of applying legal principles to realistic business situations.

Training Intelligent Management

The goal of this book is to enable managers to understand the law as it relates to the hospitality industry, to appreciate how a legal case proceeds in court, and to engage their lawyers more intelligently and efficiently. To operate a business effectively, managers must be able to recognize the legal ramifications of the policies and practices of their company, and be able to apply legal principles to everyday operations. Without this knowledge and ability, avoidable accidents and illegal conduct will go unabated, resulting in unfortunate and preventable lawsuits and penalties.

This book gives managers a base of expertise on which to build and includes the following:

- **Clearly defined legal terms** help students understand important principles when they are first introduced and apply those principles to factual situations.

- **Preventive Law Tips for Managers** recast the main points of each chapter as review and practical advice.

- **Lessons on risks of injury in a hospitality facility** enable managers to identify hazards and correct them, thereby protecting their guests from harm, and their employer from lawsuits.

Profiting from Real-World Experience

This book provides readers with the opportunity to profit from the experience of others through the careful study of real lawsuits, many of which resulted from mistakes of hotel and restaurant managers working in the field.

- **Case examples** detail recent or classic legal situations that led to lawsuits, as well as the outcome of the cases and the reasoning of the courts. To be selected for inclusion in the book, cases required interesting fact patterns, issues directly relevant to hospitality management, and judges' written decisions that were distinguished for their clarity. Attention in the text is focused on what the facility did wrong and how similar problems can be avoided. Managers can thus save their hotels and restaurants from disruptive and expensive lawsuits.

- **Updated coverage** strengthens understanding of technology's impact on the law; liquor liability; issues prompting disclosure of calorie, fat, and carbohydrate content of restaurant food; legal consequences of foodborne illnesses; employment and discrimination issues, including résumé fraud, the Americans with Disabilities Act, civil rights laws, and sexual harassment; plus negligence; franchise agreements; permit and license requirements; and casino, theme park, spa, and condominium hotel operations.

Organization

The eighth edition of *Hotel, Restaurant, and Travel Law* is organized in similar fashion as the seventh edition. Both contain the following four units:

- Unit 1, Legal Fundamentals for the Hospitality Industry, presents the sources and principles of hospitality law, basic court procedures, civil rights issues, and contract law.

- Unit 2, Negligence, presents the legal principles relevant to this topic and many cases that help define the scope of obligations and liability.

- Unit 3, Relationships with Guests and Other Patrons, explores the special responsibilities that hospitality businesses have to their different publics.

- Unit 4, Special Topics, addresses food and alcohol liability; legal duties of travel agents, airlines and car rental companies; employment matters; franchising; copyrights and trademarks; licensing; and laws relevant to casinos, theme parks, spas, and hotel condominiums.

Supplementary Materials

The *Instructor's Guide* contains answers to the end-of-chapter questions, answers to in-text case questions, case briefs, and PowerPoint slides. These materials will be available to faculty electronically via a website link.

ABOUT THE AUTHORS

© Ricardo Juszkiewixz

Karen L. Morris is a lawyer, judge, and professor at Monroe Community College in Rochester, New York. She is the first community college professor to receive the designation of Distinguished Professor from the State University of New York. The courses she teaches include Hotel and Restaurant Law, Business Law, Constitutional Law, Criminal Law, and Law 101. As a town judge she presides over criminal and civil cases, including lawsuits brought against hotels, restaurants, and travel agents.

In addition to writing five editions of this textbook, she has published a case-studies book for business law and a treatise on criminal law, as well as articles in various publications on topics of interest to the hospitality industry. She pens a column for *Hotel Management Magazine* titled, "Legally Speaking," and a blog for Business Law students that explains the law behind news stories of interest. She has been honored with several awards including two for Excellence in Teaching, Golden Pen, Distinguished Citizen, and Outstanding Student Club Faculty Advisory Award.

Professor Morris was the legal advisor to the New York State Restaurant Association, Rochester Chapter. She has served as President of Text and Academic Authors Association, Dean of the Monroe Country Bar Association, and President of her Faculty Governance Association. She is a past president of the Greater Rochester Association for Women Attorneys. She has also served as president of The Academy of Legal Studies in Business, Northeast Region. Her favorite volunteer activities are being a Big Sister in the Big Brother/Big Sister program, and serving lunch at a soup kitchen.

Before beginning her teaching career, Judge Morris was in-house counsel for a corporation that operates department stores throughout the United States, and thereafter was a criminal prosecutor.

She has a Juris Doctor degree from St. John's University and a Masters of Law (LL.M.) in Trade Regulation from New York University.

© Robert N. Branciforte

Jane Boyd Ohlin is an Associate Professor and the Director of Strategic Development at the Dedman School of Hospitality, Florida State University. She served as the Director of the Dedman School of Hospitality from 2008 to 2016. Professor Ohlin has a long-standing association with Florida State University, she received her Bachelor of Science degree in Hotel and Restaurant Administration there in 1979, and her Juris Doctor from Florida State University College of Law in 1986. She joined the faculty of the Dedman School in 1989.

Prior to joining the faculty at Florida State University, Professor Ohlin worked in the consulting practice of Laventhol and Horwath, Certified Public Accountants, in Tampa, Florida. Her clients were leaders in the hotel, restaurant, resort, and tourist destination business. Her area of expertise was in management consulting and litigation support. There, she gained a great deal of experience in the legal, financial, and operational analysis of many hospitality businesses.

Professor Ohlin has gained a global perspective on the hospitality industry through her teaching of university students during the summers in Leysin, Switzerland, through the International Programs delivered by Florida State University. She also teaches hospitality management to university students from around the world each summer on the campus of Florida State, through the Center for Global Engagement. Additionally, she supervises the exchange student affiliation of the Dedman School with universities offering hospitality degrees in other countries.

In addition to teaching courses in law and in service management, Professor Ohlin also conducts research focused on the legal issues faced by hospitality businesses. She currently serves as the Statewide Coordinator of University Hospitality programs for the Florida Department of Education and has served on the Advisory Board of the Florida Department of Business and Professional Regulation, Division of Hotels and Restaurants. She has been an active member of the Florida Bar since 1987. In her free time, she enjoys traveling with her family.

Sten Sliger is an Adjunct Professor at the Dedman School of Hospitality, Florida State University, where he teaches Hospitality Law. His is also a lawyer in Quincy, Florida, and the Upper Peninsula of Michigan. His clients include hotels and restaurants. His practice involves civil trial litigation, construction, real estate, wills, probate, and family law. Most of his early legal career was spent in Tallahassee, Florida, where he grew up. In 2013 he decided to dedicate most of his practice to rural communities and enjoys the small-town life of Quincy and the towns in Michigan's Upper Peninsula.

Courtesy JCPenny Portraits.

Mr. Sliger is the Chairman of the Florida High School Athletic Association, Section 1 Appeals Committee, where he decides appeals of athletes declared ineligible to participate in sports. In addition, he is on the Gadsden County Florida Chamber of Commerce Economic Development Council, and attorney for the Quincy-Gadsden County Airport Authority. Before attending law school, Mr. Sliger was a probation officer in Tallahassee, Florida, for six years.

Mr. Sliger grew up in Tallahassee, Florida, and Trout Creek, Michigan. He is a "double-Seminole" in that he received his B.S. in Criminology in 1984 from The Florida State University and his Juris Doctorate from The Florida State University, College of Law in 1994. Since 1972, Mr. Sliger has attended every Florida State home football game without missing one......Go Noles!

The authors are grateful to Norman C. Curnoyer and Tony Marshall, their predecessors as authors of earlier versions of this book. Both men were giants in the field of Hospitality Law.

Acknowledgments

The authors would like to express their appreciation to the reviewers who enhanced the book immeasurably.

Dedication

We dedicate this book to students of Hospitality Law who hold the future of the hotel and restaurant industry. Our goal as authors has always been to facilitate your learning process. Please know that you inspire us with your intellectual curiosity, and passion for the hospitality field. We are honored to contribute to your education, and we wish you great success as you prepare to embark on an exciting career.

Karen Morris
Jane Ohlin
Sten Sliger
Authors, *Hotel Restaurant and Travel Law, 8th Edition*

UNIT I

Legal Fundamentals of the Hospitality Industry

CHAPTER 1

Introduction to Contemporary Hospitality Law

LEARNING OUTCOMES:

- Appreciate the special attributes of law that differentiate it from other disciplines
- Understand that law can be defined in a variety of ways and why each is accurate
- Clarify what constitutes hospitality law
- Learn the four sources of our law
- Understand how to read a judge's written decision in a case, including what elements to extract and why

KEY TERMS

administrative agency	Congress	issue	rape
administrative law	constitutional law	law	reasoning
assault	contract	legislative process	regulations
casebooks	criminal law	legislature	stare decisis
case decision	damages	legislators	statute
cases	decision	negligence	statutory law
civil law	delegated powers	ordinance	theft of services
common law	facts	precedents	trademark
compensatory	fraud	probation	infringement
damages	interstate commerce	punitive damages	

Introduction

You are about to embark on an exciting study. Law is a unique and contemporary discipline with many applications to our everyday lives. As you read the various court cases in this book you will sometimes applaud a judge's decision and at other times you will be perplexed at the outcome. But above all you will be fascinated and engaged as you study hotel, restaurant, and travel law.

This first chapter will introduce you to some basic principles of law including its sources, some of its attributes, and important legal definitions. The chapter will also teach you how to extract important information as you read the cases.

What Is Law?

law
Rules, enforceable in court, requiring people to meet certain standards of conduct.

Law has many definitions, including (1) a set of rules used by judges when deciding disputes; (2) a body of rules to which people must conform their conduct; and (3) a form of social control. The common denominator in all of these definitions is that law consists of rules that require people to meet certain standards of conduct and are enforceable in court.

Principles of Hospitality Law

Hospitality law covers a wide range of law applied primarily to restaurants, bars, places that offer lodging to the public (referred to collectively as hotels or inns), travel agents (including online services as well as in-person), and airlines. Much of this body of law also applies to recreational facilities such as casinos, amusement parks, theaters, nightclubs, and sports facilities.

As you study hospitality law you will notice that the various lawmaking branches of government try to balance the interests of travelers with those of business proprietors. We will conduct an in-depth study of the legal rights and duties of the hotel guest and restaurant patron, as well as those of the innkeeper and restaurateur. While these rights and obligations are quite complex, at the basic level they require the hotel or restaurant owner to provide patrons a safe place in which to lodge or eat, and the customer must act within acceptable bounds and pay for the services received. The duty of the travel agent is to provide travel services, and the responsibility of the traveler is to pay. Often the interests of service providers and patrons conflict. The law provides an organized set of rules to resolve these conflicts.

History of Hospitality Law

The early history of hospitality law is not a proud one. It is based on a very low opinion of innkeepers that was apparently justified by their unethical behavior. In fourteenth- and fifteenth-century England, innkeepers were believed to associate with robbers and even to help thieves steal from guests. To counteract innkeepers' supposed illegal activities, early laws pertaining to inns and taverns were stringent and usually favored the guests.

A quotation from a book entitled The Inns of the Middle Ages by W. C. Firebaugh illustrates the need at that time for strict laws to protect patrons:

> [I]n the eyes of the law, the innkeeper, the pander and others of like standing were on the same footing. … In past ages, the tavern and innkeeper have been guide, philosopher, and friend to all the evil reprobates in his neighborhood.

Today, innkeepers are in a different class and enjoy a respectable reputation. Nonetheless, as you progress through this book you will encounter remnants of these rigid laws.

Another factor that contributed to the harshness of hospitality laws in the early years was the limited number of inns and the resulting monopoly enjoyed by innkeepers. When competition is virtually nonexistent, unscrupulous businesspeople may be motivated to take advantage of the situation. The law was the guest's primary protection. Today, of course, inns are no longer few and far apart. On the contrary, there is a great deal of competition in most locations. This circumstance has affected changes in the law.

Sources of Law

Our law comes from four main sources: the Constitution, statutes, common law (also called case law), and administrative law. The following material explains each of these.

consitutional law
The law embodied in the federal constitution, prescribing the organization and powers of the federal government, and defining rights of the people.

delegated powers
Those powers expressly allocated to the federal government in the Constitution.

interstate commerce
Business affecting more than one state, as opposed to business done between two parties in the same state.

legislative process
The process by which the federal government, as well as other units of government, adopts laws.

Congress
The primary law-making body of the federal government.

Constitutional Law

The law embodied in the U.S. Constitution is called constitutional law. It prescribes the organization of the federal government, including the executive, legislative, and judicial branches, and defines the powers of the federal government. As you will recall from your studies of early American history, the 13 original states were suspicious of a strong federal government. Having just overthrown England, the states wanted significant limitations on the authority granted to the central government. As a result, the federal government's authority is limited to the delegated powers, which are those powers expressly allocated to the federal government in the Constitution. All other authority is left to the states. Examples of delegated powers include development of a system of money and regulation of interstate commerce. Interstate commerce is business affecting more than one state, as opposed to business done between two parties in the same state.

The process by which the federal government and other units of government (e.g., states, counties, and cities) adopt laws is called the legislative process. The Constitution defines the method by which Congress, the primary lawmaking body of the federal government, adopts laws. The legislative process is described in greater detail in Chapter 2.

The Constitution establishes important rights, called civil rights, such as equal protection under the law, freedom of speech, and freedom of religion. We will study more about civil rights in Chapters 3 and 14.

The Constitution also authorizes the federal government to enter treaties with other countries. Some of these treaties affect travel to locations outside of the United States. We will study one of these treaties in Chapter 13. Another treaty addresses international protection of a copyright, which is the exclusive right to reproduce certain types of works such as art, literature, musical compositions, and software. We will study this treaty in Chapter 15.

Broad Wording

The Constitution declares broad principles of law and provides very little detail. For example, the Constitution states that we have the right of free speech. What types of speech are protected? Do we have the right to publish false information about another person? Does free speech include the right to yell "fire" in a crowded theater? The Constitution provides no clarification on these issues. We need additional sources of law to resolve them.

The Constitution also provides the right of religious freedom. Suppose you are hired to work part time as a food server on Thursday through Sunday evenings.

You thereafter choose to become a very religious Jew and refuse to work on the Sabbath (Friday night and Saturday). If you are terminated from your job because you cannot work on those days, has your right to religious freedom been violated? The Constitution does not answer this question. Instead, it establishes broad, foundational principles. Additional sources of law, discussed in the next three subsections, provide the details.

Statutory Law

The second source of law in the United States is statutory law. Statutory law is law promulgated by a legislature and generally agreed to by the executive (president, governor, or mayor). Legislators are lawmakers elected to office by the citizenry. We elect legislators at the federal level (members of the House of Representatives and the Senate), the state level (state legislators), and the local level (county legislators and city or town council members). When federal or state legislators adopt a law it is called a statute. When local legislators adopt a law it is often called an ordinance.

Common Law

The third source of law in the United States is common law. This consists of legal rules that have evolved not from statutes, but from decisions of judges, and also from customs and practices that obtained their authority from the test of time. Historically, this body of law was called common law because it was intended to be common or uniform throughout the country. Common law has been modified gradually as habits have changed and as new inventions have created new wants, conveniences, and methods of doing business.

Precedents

A feature of a common-law system that distinguishes it from other legal systems is its reliance on case decisions. A case decision is an interpretation of the law applied by a judge to a set of facts in a given case. The case decision becomes a precedent—a basis for deciding future cases. If another judge later must decide a case with a similar issue (a related set of facts and legal questions), the judge will examine the precedent for help in deciding the case. Unless there is a good reason not to follow precedent, the judge will decide the latter case consistent with the earlier case. This process of following earlier cases is called stare decisis, which is Latin for "the matter stands decided." The purpose of stare decisis is to give some uniformity to the law. Because judges are expected to follow precedent, you can anticipate that the case law you study today will remain in effect indefinitely until a court decides that a good reason exists to change it.

Sometimes circumstances suggest that a prior decision is no longer appropriate. Perhaps the judge made a bad decision in the first case, or societal forces have changed, suggesting a different outcome would be more in tune with the times. Under these circumstances a judge is not bound by stare decisis to follow the prior judge's decision. Rather, the judge can decide the case differently and may even

statutory law
Law passed by legislatures.

legislature
A law-making body whose members are elected to office by the citizenry.

legislators
An elected law-maker.

statute
A law adopted by the federal or state legislature.

ordinance
A law adopted by a local governmental body.

common law
Legal rules that evolved in England from decisions of judges and from customs and practices that were intended to be common or uniform for the entire English kingdom.

case decision
An interpretation of the law applied by a judge to a set of facts in a given case.

precedent
A court decision that becomes a basis for deciding future cases.

stare decisis
The principal that courts will follow precedents whey they are applicable.

© Jeff Zehnder/Shutterstock.com

adopt the opposite position. The new decision then becomes the precedent for subsequent judges addressing the same issue.

For example, the U.S. Constitution provides that we all have the right to equal protection under the law. What does that mean? In 1896 the highest court in our country, the U.S. Supreme Court, determined that racial segregation was consistent with the constitutional mandate of equal protection; facilities could be separate provided they were substantially equal. The case was Plessy v. Ferguson.[1] Applying the doctrine of stare decisis, other courts throughout the country followed that ruling whenever a segregation issue arose. Almost 60 years later, in Brown v. Board of Education,[2] the Supreme Court reversed Plessy and held the exact opposite, that the separate-but-equal doctrine is inconsistent with the equal-protection clause of the Constitution. The case was the legal death knell of segregation. Why did the court not follow precedent? It explained in the decision that circumstances and knowledge developed since Plessy had established that separate-but-equal worked to deprive people of color of the range and quality of opportunities available to whites, and was thus inherently unequal. Therefore, the precedent was no longer acceptable.

In cases where judges are confronted with issues that have not been previously resolved, and thus no precedents exist, the judges will use their best judgment to determine the case after considering the facts, relevant social factors, other cases that may not be directly on point but are analogous, and any other factors that may be helpful. Thereafter, that decision will be a precedent for subsequent cases.

The common law has survived because, when coupled with stare decisis, it provides consistency to our law. Additionally, its foundations are sufficiently flexible to develop and adapt to changes over time, including social movements and technological advances.

Relationship Between Statutes and the Constitution

Occasionally a statute may be found to conflict with the U.S. Constitution. In these circumstances the statute is declared void, because the Constitution is the supreme law of the United States. For example, in Roe v. Wade,[3] a pregnant woman challenged the legality of a state statute that prohibited doctors from performing abortions. The woman claimed it violated her constitutional right to privacy. The court agreed and declared the statute void. That decision is now precedent in other cases in which a state may seek to outlaw abortions.

---

[1] 163 U.S. 537 (1896)

[2] 347 U.S. 483 (1954)

[3] 410 U.S. 113 (1973)

In another case, a town had an ordinance limiting to one the number of political signs residents could display on their lawn. People who wished to show their support for more than one candidate objected, claiming the law violated their right to free speech. The court agreed and held the restriction to be unconstitutional and therefore void.

Relationship Between Statutes and Common Law

To some extent statutes and common law are intertwined. Sometimes statutes are ambiguously worded. If such a statute is relevant in a lawsuit, the judge in the case must interpret the law; that is, the judge will determine its meaning. The judge's decision in that case will become precedent for future cases.

For example, causing physical injury to someone while using a dangerous instrument is a felony under a New York statute. The term "dangerous instrument" is defined as an article that, under the circumstances in which it is used, is readily capable of causing death or serious physical injury. A defendant in a case caused injury to his victim by beating him with a cane. The judge had to determine whether the cane was a dangerous instrument. Consistent with stare decisis, the judge first checked whether any other cases with the same issue had been decided previously. If so, the judge would have likely followed that prior decision. Research revealed that no earlier case existed. Therefore, the judge analyzed all the facts and circumstances, and reviewed the statute defining a dangerous instrument. He then determined that the cane qualified. This decision now is precedent for subsequent cases that involve the same issue.

Sometimes statutes are adopted to modify the common law. For example, common law once imposed absolute liability on innkeepers for lost or stolen property of guests. Thus, if a thief took a guest's property while the guest was at the inn, the innkeeper was almost always liable. This reflects the early history of hospitality law when innkeepers were reputed to be unsavory. In 1850, Massachusetts became the first state to change this common-law rule and substitute a statute that limited the liability of innkeepers for lost property. New York followed in 1853, and all states now have such a statute. We will study these laws in Chapter 9.

administrative law
Regulations adopted by administrative agencies.

administrative agency
A governmental subdivision charged with administering legislation that applies to a particular industry.

Administrative Law

The fourth source of law is administrative law. Administrative law refers to laws that define the powers, limitations, and procedures of administrative agencies. An administrative agency is a governmental subdivision charged with administering legislation that applies to a particular industry. Administrative agencies have many different names, including departments, commissions, bureaus, agencies, councils, groups, services, and divisions. Agencies exist at all levels of government, but are generally part of the executive branch. Examples of administrative agencies include the following:

- Food and Drug Administration, which oversees food and pharmaceutical businesses

- Federal Communications Commission, which oversees the communications/broadcasting industry

- Consumer Product Safety Commission, which polices the safety of consumer products

regulations
Laws adopted by administrative agencies.

Some agencies are authorized to adopt laws relevant to the industry they administer. For example, the Occupational Safety and Health Administration not only investigates and enforces statutes addressing safety in the workplace, but also passes laws on the topic. Laws adopted by administrative agencies are called regulations to distinguish them from laws passed by legislators. Unlike legislators, the people who govern administrative agencies are not elected; rather, they are appointed by elected officials.

Attributes of Law

Law is dynamic, always changing to adjust to societal transformations, yet also striving to remain constant enough not to disrupt the legal order that has developed. Law can be both an exciting and difficult field to study. It is not a discipline with clear-cut rules whose applications to factual situations are easy and obvious. Reasonable people can disagree on how and whether a particular rule of law applies in a given case. Confusion may result from the fact that different judges have decided seemingly similar cases differently or do not agree on the interpretation of a statute. Sometimes the law on a particular topic may be unclear because it is in a developmental stage. For example, the law relating to new technological advances takes time to crystallize. Law is further complicated by the fact that it can vary from state to state. Because of these challenges, the study of law can be both difficult and very rewarding.

The Role of the Judge

The role of the judge in our legal system is very significant. As we have seen, the judge both "makes" the law in cases where no precedent or statute exists, and interprets the law in cases where a statute applies. We will see that some judges, called appellate judges, also review decisions of other judges. The words judge and court are frequently used interchangeably.

© Matt Benoit/Shutterstock.com

Civil and Criminal Law

There are numerous classifications of law. One classification is civil law and another is criminal law. The differences are as follows:

1. In civil law a wrong usually is done to an individual. In criminal law the wrong is considered to be inflicted on society as a whole and involves violation of a criminal statute.

2. The objective of a civil lawsuit is compensation for an injury. The objective of a criminal case is punishment of a wrongdoer.

3. The party who commences the lawsuit in a civil case is the injured person. The title of the case includes that person's name and the name of the person being sued. Thus, the title of a civil case initiated by the female coauthor of this textbook against one Mindy Sanders would be Karen Morris v. Mindy Sanders. On the other hand, the party who undertakes a criminal case is society-at-large, usually referred to as "The State of …," "The People of the State of …," or "The Commonwealth of …." Thus, a Massachusetts criminal case might be titled The Commonwealth of Massachusetts v. John Doe.

4. In a civil case the person who is suing hires and pays for his or her own lawyer. In a criminal case, society (e.g., The People of the State of California) is represented by a lawyer paid by the government. The title frequently used for that attorney is district attorney and/or prosecutor.

civil law
Law applicable to legal wrongs other than crimes.

criminal law
The law applicable to criminal cases.

Examples of Civil Law

The following are examples of civil law.

contract
An agreement between two or more parties that is enforceable in court.

© Matt Benoit/Shutterstock.com

Contracts

A contract is an agreement between two or more parties that is enforceable in court. If one person fails to abide by the agreement, the other can sue for breach of contract. Unlike statutes, which are laws made by legislatures, and unlike common law, which is law made by judges, contracts represent "law" made by individuals. Businesses in the hospitality industry enter numerous contracts on a regular basis, including contracts with guests for hotel rooms and contracts by restaurants with food vendors. We will study more about contracts in Chapter 4.

Torts

negligence
Breach of a legal duty to act reasonably that is the direct (or proximate) cause of injury to another.

A tort is a violation of a legal duty by one person that causes injury to another. (Breaches of contractual duties, however, are not considered torts.) Included among the various torts are the following:

trademark infringement
Use of another company's business name or logo without permission.

- Negligence, which means breach of a legal duty to act reasonably, is often defined as carelessness. For example, a hotel is negligent if it fails to fix a broken railing on steps in a prompt manner. We will study negligence in Chapters 5 and 6.

fraud
The tort of intentionally misleading others resulting in financial loss for those who were deceived.

- Trademark infringement is the use of another company's business name or logo without permission. For example, a restaurant infringes a trademark if it adopts the same name used by another restaurant in the same vicinity without the other restaurant's approval. We will study this tort in Chapter 15.

damages
The remedy sought by the injured party in a civil case.

- Fraud is an intentionally untruthful statement made to induce reliance by another person. For example, if a resort represents in its advertisements that it has a golf course, but in fact it does not, and a guest opts to stay at the hotel because of the claimed golf facilities, this is fraud. We will revisit this tort in a number of contexts throughout the book.

compensatory damages
Money awarded in a lawsuit to reimburse the plaintiff for expenses incurred from an injury caused by defendant.

Remedies in Civil Cases

The remedy sought by the injured party in a civil case is damages, meaning money. Two main types of damages exist—compensatory and punitive. The term compensatory damages refers to money awarded to the plaintiff to compensate for injuries.

Compensatory damages include past and future out-of-pocket expenses, such as medical bills and lost wages. Compensatory damages can also include pain and suffering, meaning physical distress or mental anguish; loss of enjoyment of life, meaning inability by the plaintiff to continue to engage in those activities that brought joy or fulfillment before the injury; loss of consortium, meaning loss of the companionship and sexual relations of a spouse; and loss of services, meaning loss of the aid, assistance, and companionship of another person, such as a parent. The exact amount awarded to a plaintiff is determined by a jury or, in a nonjury case, the judge.

Punitive damages, also called exemplary damages, is money awarded in excess of compensatory damages. Punitive damages are awarded to a plaintiff not for reimbursement of a loss, but to punish or make an example of the defendant. They are awarded only in cases where the defendant's wrongful acts are aggravated by violence, malice, fraud, or a similar egregious wrong.

punitive damages
Money awarded to a plaintiff over and above compensatory damages to punish defendant for particularly reprehensible conduct.

Examples of Crimes

There are many different crimes. A few that impact the hospitality industry follow:

- Theft of services is the use of services such as cable television or a hotel room without paying and with the intent of avoiding payment. We will study theft of services in Chapter 10.

- Assault is intentionally causing physical injury to another person. In Chapter 7 we will discuss the unfortunate circumstance of assaults occurring in bars as a result of lax security.

- Rape is forcible sexual intercourse against the victim's will. In Chapter 7 we discuss cases involving rapes occurring in hotel rooms.

theft of services
A crime committed by using services, such as a hotel room, with the intent of avoiding payment.

assault
The tort of intentionally putting someone in fear of harmful physical contact, and the crime of intentionally causing physical injury.

rape
Sexual intercourse that is against the victim's will.

Penalties and Remedies in Criminal Cases

The possible penalties for committing a crime include community service, fines, probation, jail, and in some states, death. Probation is a system whereby criminal offenders remain out of jail but are supervised by a probation officer. What punishment will be applied in a given case is determined in part by statute and in part by the judge. The applicable statute will provide a range of sentences available to the judge. For example, in New York the range of sentences for theft of services includes a jail sentence of up to one year, a fine up to $1,000, probation for three years, and unlimited community service. The judge must decide in each case what sentence within the allowable range is appropriate for the particular defendant. The sentence will vary depending upon the facts of the case, the circumstances and criminal record of the perpetrator, and the impact of the crime on the victim.

probation
A system whereby some criminal offenders remain out of jail but are supervised by a probation officer.

© Zimmytws/Shutterstock.com

How to Read a Case

Judges' decisions are customarily issued in written form and may be recorded in books used for legal research. These written decisions are called cases, and the books in which they are published are called casebooks. These cases are part of the common law. You will read many cases in your study of hospitality law. Although at first they may seem hard to understand, you will soon develop the skill necessary to read them with a high level of comprehension. To understand a case you should attempt to identify four elements as you read it:

casebooks
Books that publish judges' decisions.

1. The facts

2. The issue

facts
Objective information about circumstances that exist and/or events that have occurred.

3. The judge's decision

4. The reasoning supporting the decision

issue
A legal question that parties to a lawsuit submit to the judge for resolution.

The facts are those circumstances that gave rise to the lawsuit. The issue is the legal question that the parties have asked the judge to resolve. The decision is the judge's response to the issue. The reasoning is the basis and rationale for the decision. After reading the case, consider its implications as a precedent for stare decisis. The decision, although involving unknown parties, informs hospitality managers how the law will likely be applied to their own situations. This enables innkeepers and restaurateurs to predict how the law will be interpreted and to prevent legal disputes before they arise. By understanding the implications of cases, the manager or owner can modify company policies and actions to conform to the law.

decision
A judge's determination in a case as to which party should win and which should lose.

reasoning
The explanation why a judge decides a case.

The following is an example of a case. This book contains many case examples, of which Case Example 1-1 is the first. As you read it, identify the four elements as you come to them. Then compare your findings with the analysis that follows the case.

CASE EXAMPLE 1-1

Viscecchia v. Allegria Hotel

117 F.Supp.3d 243, 2015 WL 4602729 (NY, 2015)

Plaintiff Richard Viscecchia, Jr. brings this action against his former employer, the Allegria Hotel, alleging employment discrimination on the basis of gender.

On or around June 18, 2009, plaintiff began working for the Allegria Hotel as a line cook. Throughout the course of his employment, plaintiff had long hair. The Hotel's hair policy reads in relevant part as follows: Hair must be clean, trimmed, well brushed, and neat at all times. Extreme styles, flowers, colored ribbons, beaded, braided, or streaked hair is not permitted. Color should be maintained at neutral tones. Men's hair must be above the shirt collar. Hotel management directed plaintiff to cut his hair because it was "too long." Plaintiff asserts that he complained to the Hotel that its policy on hair length was unlawfully discriminatory toward men.

On or around October 1, 2013, the Hotel's Human Resource Department issued plaintiff a written warning instructing him to cut his hair in accordance with the Hotel's policy, and notifying him that noncompliance could result in disciplinary action, including potential termination. Human Resources gave plaintiff until October 15, 2013, to comply with the warning. Plaintiff states that, at the time he received the warning, the Hotel employed females with long hair in comparable positions in the kitchen, who were not similarly reprimanded for violating the hair policy and continued to work at the Hotel. Plaintiff did not comply with the Hotel's warning and was terminated on or around October 16, 2013.

Plaintiff asserts that defendant's policy was discriminatorily applied to Plaintiff because he is a man and the policy was not equally applied to women.

Title VII of the Civil Rights Act of 1964 makes it unlawful for an employer "to discriminate against any individual with respect to his compensation, terms, conditions, or privileges of employment, because of such individual's race, color, religion, sex, or national origin."

Plaintiff argues that defendant's policy is "inherently discriminatory" because it prescribes different hair lengths for men and women. Defendant contends that dismissal is warranted because, under Title VII, "it is well established that employers can prescribe different grooming standards for male and female employees, including those standards concerning hair length." The court agrees.

Courts have consistently concluded that employer grooming codes requiring different hair lengths for men and women were not intended to be covered by the Civil Rights Act because they bear such a negligible relation to the purpose of Title VII, which was to promote equal opportunity. Hairstyles, specifications, dress-codes, and other grooming polices . . . do not affect an individual's opportunity to obtain employment. One's personal appearance and dress is sufficiently within one's control such that it is easily alterable, while Title VII aims at policies that specifically discriminate on the basis of immutable characteristics that are a fundamental aspect of that person.

Accordingly, to the extent that plaintiff grounds his gender discrimination claim on the fact that the Hotel's hair length policy requires short hair for men but not for women, any claim under Title VII solely based on such a theory of liability fails as a matter of law, and does not survive a motion to dismiss. Defendant's motion to dismiss is granted.

Now let us analyze the four elements and their implications. The important facts are that the plaintiff's employer had a hair policy, its requirements varied for males and females, and the plaintiff's hair length violated the policy. Additionally, the Civil Rights Act prohibits discrimination based on gender. The issue is whether the hotel's hair policy violates the prohibition against discrimination based on sex. The decision is no. The reasoning for that conclusion is that the Civil Rights Act was intended to protect against unchangeable aspects of a person. Hairstyles can easily be modified.

When reading a case, it is instructive to consider the implication of the decision on the hospitality industry. The implication of the hair decision is that hotels and restaurants can legally adopt hair and grooming policies that vary according to gender and reflect acceptable gender-specific grooming practices.

Summary

Law is at once an exciting and challenging study.

Our law comes from four sources—the Constitution, statutes, common law, and administrative law. The rule of stare decisis encourages judges to decide cases consistent with precedent, unless good reason to deviate exists. The objective of this rule is to achieve consistency in the law while not foreclosing change when necessary.

Numerous classifications of law exist, including civil and criminal. Civil law involves wrongs against individuals, whereas criminal law involves wrongs against society.

When reading legal cases, the four main elements to identify are the facts, the issue, the decision, and the reasoning. Students should also consider the implications of each case for the hospitality industry.

Review Questions

1. How is law defined?

2. In what country did common law originate?

3. What is a precedent and how is it related to stare decisis?

4. What is a tort? Name two torts.

5. Identify three types of injuries for which compensatory damages can be awarded in a civil case.

6. What is a crime? Name two crimes.

7. According to common law, who was liable when a guest's property was stolen from a room at an inn?

8. What changes have been made to the common law concerning liability to a hotel when a guest's property is stolen?

9. What is the difference between common law and statutory law?

10. Name four differences between civil and criminal law.

11. Under what circumstances can a judge deviate from stare decisis?

12. What are the differences among the following: statutes, ordinances, and regulations?

13. When reading a case, what are the four elements to look for?

Discussion Questions

1. Why did the lack of competition between inns in earlier times contribute to the development of laws that favored guests rather than innkeepers?

2. In what way does stare decisis enhance the stability of the law?

3. In what way is the common law able to adapt to changes in society?

4. If no precedent exists in a case, what factors will the judge use to decide the issue presented in the case?

5. Name two roles of a judge discussed in this chapter.

6. Identify three factors a judge will consider when sentencing a defendant in a criminal case. How will each of those factors impact the sentence?

Application Questions

1. Natalie, who is married with two children, was injured at a hotel because of its negligence. She broke her leg and suffered a back injury. As a result, she was bedridden for five weeks, missed work during that time, and experienced considerable pain. What type(s) of damages should she be able to collect from the hotel? What type(s) will she probably not be able to collect?

2. The defendant in a criminal case has been found guilty of stealing a pack of cigarettes from a hotel store. The applicable statute authorizes the judge to sentence the defendant to a maximum of one year in jail, fine him up to $1,000, and/or place him on probation for one year. The defendant is 23 years old and is unemployed. He has no prior convictions. If you were the judge, what do you think might be an appropriate sentence in this case? Why?

3. A statute defines the crime of disorderly conduct as using profanity in a public place. A defendant, while standing on his porch, yelled obscene comments at a passerby. The defendant was charged with this crime. As a defense, he denied that the porch was a public place. What is the issue in this case that the judge must decide? If a precedent exists, what effect will that have on the decision? What do you think the decision should be? Why? If the defendant claims that the statute is unconstitutional because it infringes his right of free speech, who decides that issue?

Websites

Websites that will enhance your understanding of the material in this chapter include:

www.uscourts.gov This site is the official site of the federal court system and includes information about the courts, answers to frequently asked questions, and links to other legal sources.

www.supremecourtus.gov This is the official site of the U.S. Supreme Court. It contains profiles of each Supreme Court judge, past and present; an archive of the court's decisions; and the history of the court.

www.oyez.com Another site about the U.S. Supreme Court, this one contains pictures and short biographies of each justice, a virtual tour of the court building, information about recent cases, and descriptions of pending cases.

www.fda.gov This is the official site of the Food and Drug Administration, which is responsible for, among other assignments, protecting the public health by ensuring the safety and security of the nation's food supply. The site provides information about disease outbreaks caused by food, recalls of food products, labeling requirements, dietary supplements, food safety, nutrition, and much more.

CHAPTER 2

Legal Procedures: Journey of a Case Through the Courts

LEARNING OUTCOMES:

- Familiarize students with the various stages of a lawsuit
- Understand the concept of jurisdiction
- Learn the purpose and content of each pleading in a lawsuit: complaint, answer, and reply
- Comprehend the purpose for discovery and how it is conducted
- Know how jurors are selected and the circumstances for which a potential juror can be removed
- Learn the components of a trial
- Understand the appeal process
- Appreciate the role of alternative dispute resolution methods
- Decipher case citations

allegations	counterclaims	interrogatories	pleadings
alternative dispute	criminal case	judgment	rebuttal
resolution	cross-examination	judgment NOV	remitter
answer	default judgment	jurisdiction	reply
appeal	defendant	jury trial	service of process
appellate court	deliberations	litigants	settlement
arbitration	deposition	mediation	subject matter
briefs	direct examination	motion	jurisdiction
bench trial	discovery	motion for summary	summary jury trial
case-in-chief	diversity of	judgment	summation
charge to the jury	citizenship	opening statement	summons
citation	for cause	parties	trial
civil case	hung jury	peremptory	verdict
claim	in personam	challenges	voir dire
complaint	jurisdiction	plaintiff	

© Ppictures/Shutterstock.com

Introduction

Conflicts can be resolved in a variety of ways. Some will grow into lawsuits and be heard in court. Others will be settled either before or after a lawsuit is begun. In settling a case, the injured party may compromise and accept less than he originally sought. Still other cases are resolved through alternative dispute resolution methods whereby a person other than a judge listens to both parties' positions and then either makes a determination concerning the merits or assists the parties in developing a mutually acceptable solution.

A **claim** is a demand for a remedy, usually money, to compensate for a perceived wrong. When a claim is asserted against a hospitality establishment, or if the establishment has a claim against an individual or a business, a decision must be made on how to proceed. Should the claim be settled? Should it be pursued in court? Is some form of alternative dispute resolution the best option? In answering these questions the owner or manager of the establishment must consider the merits of the claim, the cost in both time and money required to pursue the case, and the effect of the decision on future, similar cases. The costs include attorney's fees (which likely will be hundreds of dollars an hour), court fees (charged for the services of the court), expert witness fees, and the time of employees to oversee the case, work with the lawyer, and testify. These expenses are minimized if the case is settled early. Another factor that may impact the decision on how to handle a case is the preference of the insurance company of the party being sued. Often a hotel or restaurant's insurance contract authorizes the insurance company to determine whether to settle the case or pursue it.

The decision on how to proceed with the claim will vary from case to case as the relevant factors are weighed. A very small percentage of cases goes to trial. Most cases are settled earlier in the process, due in large part to the costs involved. The decision on how to proceed may be the most important strategic decision in the case.

This chapter will acquaint you with fundamental legal procedure and describe what takes place throughout the various stages of a claim pursued in court. The chapter will also explain different methods of alternative dispute resolution. Because most cases involving hospitality facilities are civil cases and not criminal ones, the procedural rules discussed in this chapter relate to civil proceedings. The procedural rules applicable to criminal cases are similar in some respects, and differ in others.

The Parties and Proof

Although the procedure for pursuing a case through the courts varies from state to state, certain practices are common. The **parties** to a lawsuit are the individuals engaged in a conflict. They are also referred to as **litigants.** A party may be a person, a business, or a governmental body. The **plaintiff** is the party who initiates the lawsuit. The plaintiff usually has suffered an injury or loss, and believes the defendant is responsible. The **defendant** is the party the plaintiff sues.

To be successful in the lawsuit the plaintiff must prove the following:

1. The defendant violated the law.

2. The plaintiff suffered an injury or loss.

3. The cause of the plaintiff's injury or loss was the defendant's violation of the law.

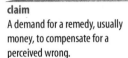

claim
A demand for a remedy, usually money, to compensate for a perceived wrong.

parties
The individuals in conflict in a lawsuit; the plaintiff and defendant.

litigants
The parties to a lawsuit.

plaintiff
The party who commences a lawsuit seeking a remedy for an injury or loss.

defendant
The party who is sued by the plaintiff in a lawsuit.

The system of justice employed in the United States is an *adversary system*. It is based on the premise that when a lawsuit develops between two parties, it will best be resolved if each party to the dispute vigorously asserts its position before an independent judge who ultimately determines the outcome.

Commencing the Lawsuit

The lawsuit is begun by serving or filing a complaint and a summons.

The Complaint

complaint
The initial pleading filed in court in a civil lawsuit alleging defendant engaged in illegal conduct and seeking compensation.

allegation
Unproven assertions.

jurisdiction
The authority of a court to hear a case, as determined by the legislature.

subject matter jurisdiction
A court's power to decide cases of a particular category.

The **complaint** is a document issued by the plaintiff that contains **allegations.** These are unproven statements that, when combined, constitute one or more claim(s) against the defendant. The complaint informs the defendant of the basis for the plaintiff's claims. Depending on the law of the state where the case is pursued, lawsuits are commenced by either filing the complaint with the appropriate court and/or serving the complaint on the defendant. A complaint consists of three parts:

1. A statement showing the jurisdiction (authority) of the court

2. Details about why the plaintiff is suing the defendant

3. A claim for relief (usually a request for money)

Figure 2-1 shows a sample complaint.

Statement of Jurisdiction

Jurisdiction is the authority of a court to hear a case. No single court has the power to decide all kinds of cases. The statement of jurisdiction in the complaint must set forth facts that demonstrate that the court designated by the plaintiff has the authority to decide the case. The assertion must establish two types of jurisdiction: *subject matter* and *in personam*.

Subject Matter Jurisdiction

Subject matter jurisdiction is a court's power to decide cases of a particular category. For example, the United States Bankruptcy Courts have the power to decide only cases involving bankruptcy (a legal procedure in which a debtor seeks relief from debts). If a catering patron with a large outstanding bill petitions the court for bankruptcy protection from its creditors, the Bankruptcy Court will hear and decide the case. However, that court normally does not have the authority to hear cases involving contract disputes between a hotel and its employees or claims that a restaurant supplier sold unhealthy food. A court's subject matter jurisdiction is determined by legislators.

SUPREME COURT OF ALBANY COUNTY STATE OF NEW YORK

Nancy Lauter,
  Plaintiff,
    v.   **COMPLAINT**
Randshire Hotel, Inc.
  Defendants.

Plaintiff, complaining of the defendant, alleges as follows:

1. This is a civil action seeking damages for negligence.

2. This court has jurisdiction based on defendant's operation of a 120-room hotel in Albany, New York.

3. Plaintiff lives in Detroit, Michigan.

4. On June 14, 20__, plaintiff was a guest in defendant's hotel. While plaintiff was walking through the hotel lobby carrying an expensive vase she had bought in a nearby antique shop, the heel of her shoe became caught in a hole in the lobby rug. Plaintiff lost her footing and fell.

5. Defendant was negligent in permitting a hole to exist in the lobby rug.

6. As a result of the fall and due to defendant's negligence, plaintiff suffered serious physical injuries and the vase was broken. Plaintiff paid $29,000 in hospital and doctor bills for her injuries; she lost $13,000 in wages while bedridden during her recuperation; and the vase was worth $3,500.

WHEREFORE, Plaintiff demands judgment in the amount of $45,500 with interest, costs, and disbursements plus any additional relief as to the court may seem just and equitable.
DATED: September 12, 20__

By _____
Maria Rodriquez, Esq.
Attorney for Plaintiff
25 Main Street West
Albany, New York 12204
518-555-1606

FIGURE 2-1 A complaint is a formal document that details allegations by the plaintiff against the defendant. Those allegations form the basis for the lawsuit.

In Personam Jurisdiction

Another type of jurisdiction is **in personam jurisdiction,** which means authority of a court over the defendant. For a state court to have in personam jurisdiction over the defendant, the latter must either be a resident of the state or have significant contacts with the state. If, for example, a resident of New York sued a restaurant in South Dakota, claiming that the restaurant served the New Yorker rancid food, New York would not have in personam jurisdiction over the restaurant be-

in personam jurisdiction
The authority of a court to determine a case against a particular defendant.

cause it has no contacts with the state of New York. To pursue the lawsuit the plaintiff would have to sue in South Dakota.

An example of a sufficient contact to establish in personam jurisdiction would be a tour company with its principal place of business located in one state and a sales office located in another. Both states could exercise in personam jurisdiction over the tour company.

An issue that has arisen with the advent of the Internet is whether a business located in one state that has a website accessible by residents of other states is thereby subject to in personam jurisdiction in the other states. For example, in one case a jazz club in New York City sued a jazz club located in Missouri claiming the latter had infringed the former's trademark, "The Blue Note." The suit was brought in New York. The Missouri club denied that the New York court had in personam jurisdiction since the club's only involvement with New York was a website accessible by New York residents. The site contained general information about the club in Missouri, a calendar of events, and a number to call for charge-by-phone ticket orders available for pickup at the Missouri club's box office on the night of the performance.

The court held that the website alone was insufficient to permit New York to exercise jurisdiction over the Missouri club. Had computer users been able to buy goods from the site that were thereafter shipped into New York, the outcome might have been different. Subsequent cases continue to draw a line between "passive" websites that merely provide information and "active" websites through which a consumer can purchase items and have them shipped into the state. Only the latter can be the basis for in personam jurisdiction. As the Internet has continued to develop, most sites are of the latter type and thus expose the company owning the site to the possibility of being sued anywhere in the country. Recently courts seem to be revisiting this issue suggesting that something more than an interactive website may be needed to confer jurisdiction. This area of law is in a state of flux.

CASE EXAMPLE 2-1

Stern v. Four Points by Sheraton Ann Arbor Hotel

19 NYS3d 289 (NY, 2015)

. . . Plaintiff, a New York resident, alleges that, while in New York, she reserved a room at the Sheraton Inn Ann Arbor in Ann Arbor, Michigan using an interactive website maintained by Starwood Hotels and Resorts Worldwide, Inc. for Sheraton hotels. During her stay at the Sheraton Inn hotel, which was then owned by defendant ZLC, plaintiff tripped over a walkway in the hotel lobby and fractured her knee. Defendant moved to dismiss. In support of its motion the hotel submitted evidence that it had no other hotels and no bank accounts, real estate, or other contacts with New York.

Although ZLC's participation in the interactive website for Sheraton hotels may demonstrate that it transacted business in New York, the relationship between ZLC's website activities and plaintiff's negligence action arising from an allegedly defective condition on the premises in Michigan is too remote to support the exercise of jurisdiction.

Since plaintiff has not shown that facts may exist to support the exercise of personal jurisdiction over ZLC with respect to her claim arising from a trip and fall accident in Michigan, ZLC's motion to dismiss was properly granted.

Federal Jurisdiction

Each state, as well as the District of Columbia and Puerto Rico, has its own system or network of courts, as does the federal government. Federal courts have jurisdiction to hear several types of cases: lawsuits that involve the U.S. Constitution, a federal treaty, or a federal law (called *federal question* lawsuits); and lawsuits that involve **diversity of citizenship,** meaning that the plaintiff and defendant are from different states or one is from a different country, and the amount of money in controversy exceeds $75,000. All other types of cases are heard in state court. The following case illustrates the amount in controversy requirement when diversity of citizenship is the basis for jurisdiction.

diversity of citizenship
Plaintiff and defendant are residents of different states; one of several criteria for federal court jurisdiction.

CASE EXAMPLE 2-2

Clark v. Starwood Hotels & Resorts Worldwide, Inc.

2015 WL 6163166 (Fl, 2015)

[Plaintiff Clark commenced this case in a state court. Defendant Starwood Hotels sought to transfer the case to federal court] Clark alleges that she was injured as a result of the Defendants' negligence when she tripped over a misplaced parking bumper in a parking lot they controlled.

Diversity jurisdiction exists where the suit is between citizens of different states and the amount in controversy exceeds $75,000. Clark does not dispute that the parties to this matter are diverse [from different states]. However, she contends that Starwood has not shown that the amount in controversy exceeds $75,000.

Clark's complaint does not provide specifics as to the amount of damages she allegedly sustained or even the precise injury or injuries she allegedly suffered. Instead, she simply seeks to recover damages [quoting from the complaint] "in excess of Fifteen Thousand Dollars ($15,000)." When a complaint does not claim a specific amount of damages, federal jurisdiction will exist if it is facially apparent from the complaint that the amount in controversy exceeds $75,000.

Although Starwood contends that a fair reading of the Complaint indicates that the amount in controversy exceeds the sum of $75,000, the pleading provides nothing to substantiate this contention. Starwood points to only one item as supporting its belief that the amount in controversy has been met: correspondence received from Clark's attorney indicating that Clark had suffered a fractured ankle and four metatarsal fractures as a result of her accident and asserting that she was being treated by an orthopedic surgeon. However, the correspondence does not include a monetary amount—such as, for example, a settlement demand or a recitation of medical bills incurred to date—or anything else that would suggest that the amount in controversy exceeds $75,000.

Starwood has not satisfied its burden of demonstrating that the jurisdictional threshold has been met in this case.

See Figure 2-2 for an illustration of a typical state court system and Figure 2-3 for an illustration of the federal court system.

The Basis for the Claim

The complaint must explain to the defendant and the court the circumstances comprising the plaintiff's claim. The complaint therefore needs to contain allegations (unproven claims) detailing the reasons why the plaintiff is suing.

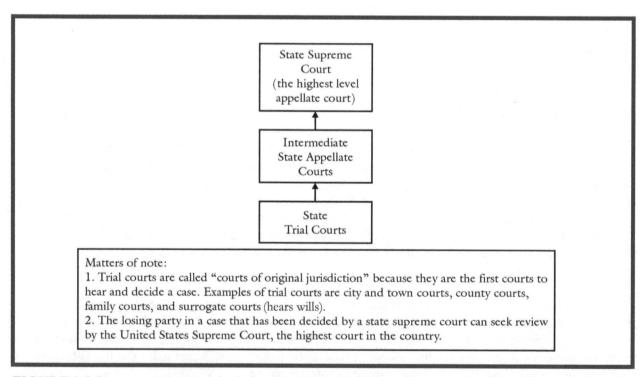

FIGURE 2-2 State court systems include courts of original jurisdiction and courts of appeal. This diagram reflects the system adopted in most, but not all, states.

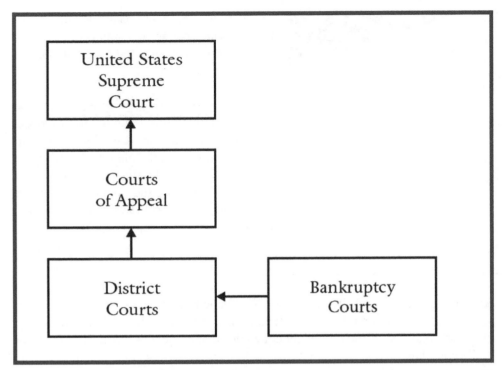

FIGURE 2-3 Federal courts hear two categories of cases: those dealing with federal questions, and those involving diversity of citizenship and a minimum of $75,000 in controversy.

The Claim for Relief

The complaint must tell the defendant and the court what the plaintiff wants from the defendant. Plaintiffs in civil cases customarily seek relief in the form of an award of money.

The Summons

A **summons** is a document ordering the defendant to appear (participate in the case) and defend the allegations made against him. It is served with the complaint. Among other things, it informs the defendant of the time within which he must respond to the complaint and the consequences of failing to do so. A sample summons is provided in Figure 2-4.

Service of Process

Delivery of the summons and complaint to the defendant is known as **service of process.** The summons and complaint are collectively called *process*. In most states these documents are filed with the court, after which a specially appointed agent of the court serves them on the defendant. In other states, they are served on the defendant before they are filed with the court. To serve a corporation requires delivery of the documents to an officer, director, or other official designated by the company. Delivery to any other employee is insufficient. Thus, where a plaintiff served the

summons
A document ordering the defendant to appear in a lawsuit and defend the allegations made against him.

service of process
Delivery of the complaint to the defendant. The method for doing so is prescribed by law, and is designed to ensure defendant receives notice of the lawsuit.

summons and complaint on the defendant corporation's attorney for labor and employment, and he was not a designated recipient, the service was invalid.[1]

If the documents are properly served and the defendant fails to provide a timely response, the defendant loses the case by default. In such circumstances, the plaintiff is entitled to a **default judgment**—that is, a court order summarily declaring the plaintiff the winner of the lawsuit due to the defendant's failure to defend.

Responses to the Complaint

default judgment
A judgment entered in favor of a plaintiff when the defendant fails to appear in court.

After being served with the complaint, a defendant must do one of two things in response to avoid a default judgment: either file motions addressed to some defect in the complaint or, if the defendant concludes that no defects exist, file an answer to the complaint.

SUPREME COURT OF ALBANY COUNTY STATE OF NEW YORK

Nancy Lauter, Plaintiff,
      v.   **SUMMONS**
Randshire Hotel, Inc., Defendants.

YOU ARE HEREBY SUMMONED and required to appear in the Supreme Court of Albany County located at 1000 Ridge Road, in the City of Albany, County of Albany, State of New York, by serving an Answer to the annexed Complaint upon Plaintiff's attorney at the address stated below, within thirty days after service of this Summons and Complaint is complete. Upon your failure to so answer, judgment will be taken against you for the relief demanded in the annexed Complaint, together with the cost of this action.

DATED: September 12, 20__

By _____
Maria Rodriquez, Esq.
Attorney for Plaintiff
25 Main Street West
Albany, New York 12204
518-555-1606

FIGURE 2-4 The summons is given to the defendant with the complaint. Delivering the summons and complaint to the defendant is called service of process.

---

1 *Burch v. Bellagio Hotel & Casino*, 2015 WL 5545018 (Nev. 2015).

Preliminary Motions

A **motion** is a request to a judge for relief that is made while a lawsuit is ongoing. For example, motions may consist of a request for an extension of time, a request to clarify the allegations in the complaint, or for a dismissal of the lawsuit because the court lacks jurisdiction. Motions are usually made in writing.

After a motion has been filed with the court, attorneys for both the plaintiff and defendant appear at a hearing and argue their respective sides. The judge then either grants or denies the motion. The case proceeds in accordance with the ruling. For example, if the defendant makes a successful motion to dismiss because the court lacks jurisdiction, the case ends. The plaintiff may, however, file the case again in another court that *does* have jurisdiction. If the defendant makes a successful motion for clarification of the complaint, the case will continue, but the plaintiff will need to supplement the complaint with explanatory information.

Another preliminary motion relating to the pleadings is that the pleading is too long. Rules require that a pleading contain a "short and plain" statement of the claim showing entitlement to relief. In a case where the complaint contained 163 paragraphs and much repetition, the court said in its decision that the "outsized complaint calls to mind an address by the former Lord Chancellor of England, in the course of which he related that: in the reign of the Stuarts there was one counsel who had offended the court by preparing a needlessly long and prolix pleading on parchment. He was ordered to have his pleadings taken, a large hole to be cut in the middle, he was to have his head pushed through it, and he was to attend the first day of the term of every court with his head through the pleadings."[2]

motion
A request to a judge for interim relief that is made while a lawsuit is ongoing.

The Answer

If the case is not dismissed on motion, the defendant must serve an **answer** on the plaintiff and the court within the permissible time period, which is defined by statute and varies from state to state. The answer fulfills the following purposes: it admits or denies the allegations made by the plaintiff in the complaint; it sets forth any defenses the defendant may have to the plaintiff's claim; and it states any claims the defendant may have against the plaintiff (called **counterclaims**). A sample answer is provided in Figure 2-5.

Failure to serve an answer in a timely manner will result in a default judgment in favor of the plaintiff. Stated differently, the defendant will automatically lose as a result of inaction.

answer
The pleading issued by the defendant in response to plaintiff's complaint.

counterclaims
Claims the defendant asserts against the plaintiff in an Answer.

Responses to the Answer

Motions Directed to the Answer

After the defendant files an answer, the plaintiff is entitled to make motions relating to it. For example, the plaintiff may move for a more definite statement if the

---

2 Brooklyn Downton Hotel, LLC v. NY Hotel & Motel Trades Council, AFL-CIO, 2015 WL 779441 (NY, 2015).

SUPREME COURT OF ALBANY COUNTY STATE OF NEW YORK

Nancy Lauter, Plaintiff,

v.   **ANSWER**

Randshire Hotel, Inc., Defendants.

Randshire Hotel, Inc. Defendants.

The Defendant, answering the Complaint:

1. Admits the allegations contained in paragraphs one and two.

2. Denies knowledge and information sufficient to form a belief as to the allegations contained in paragraph three.

3. Concerning paragraph four, admits that Plaintiff was a guest in Defendant's hotel on June 14, 20___; and denies each and every other allegation contained therein.

4. Denies each and every allegation contained in paragraphs five and six.

COUNTERCLAIM:

5. Following the injury plaintiff was taken to the hospital by ambulance.

6. Due to plaintiff's abrupt departure, she failed to pay her hotel bill and has declined to do so since, despite several requests.

WHEREFORE, Defendant demands judgment dismissing the complaint against it, and awarding defendant $145 on its counterclaim.

DATED: October 8, 20___

By _____

Leon Trombley
Attorney for Defendant
423 Monroe Street
Albany, New York 12210
518-240-4851

FIGURE 2-5 The answer is the defendant's response to the complaint.

answer is vague, or may move to strike all or part of the defendant's answer if the information is redundant or immaterial.

reply
A pleading issued by plaintiff if and only if defendant's answer contains a counterclaim.

Reply

If—and only if—the answer contains a counterclaim, the plaintiff must issue a **reply**. The sole purpose of this document is to relay the plaintiff's response to the allegations in the counterclaim.

Summary Judgment

The complaint, the answer, and the reply are known as **pleadings**. Once the pleadings have been filed and all motions relating to the pleadings have been made and ruled on by the judge, either party may make a motion for judgment on the pleadings. Such a motion, called a **motion for summary judgment,** asks the judge to decide the case in favor of the moving party without the need for a trial. This motion asserts that the opposing party's pleading has not raised any genuine issue in the case. If the motion is granted, the case is over, subject to the losing party's right to appeal. If the motion is denied, the case continues.

Forum Non Conveniens

Sometimes the court chosen by the plaintiff for the lawsuit is inconvenient for defendant's witnesses or otherwise creates an undue hardship on the defendants. In those circumstances, the defendant can ask the court to issue an order transferring the case to a more convenient court. A typical example is a hotel guest from out-of-state who injures himself at the inn, returns to his home state after the hotel stay, and sues from that state of residence. In such circumstances the court will review numerous factors to decide on an appropriate forum. Factors that will be considered are discussed in Case Example 2-3.

pleadings
Documents setting out plaintiff's claim and defendant's defense. The pleadings include a complaint, an answer, and if the answer contains a counterclaim, a reply.

motion for summary judgment
A request to a judge by one of the parties for a judgment without the necessity of a trial.

CASE EXAMPLE 2-3

Wenzel v. Marriott International, Inc., 2015 WL 6643262 (NY, 2015)

[Plaintiffs, husband and wife, are residents of New York State. They vacationed at a resort in Aruba. While there, the wife suffered an injury. After plaintiffs returned to their home in New York, they sued the resort in a New York court.]

Plaintiffs—Appellants Patti and Michael Wenzel appeal from a November 17, 2014, order entered by the United States District Court for the Southern District of New York granting the defendants-appellees motion to dismiss the case on forum non conveniens grounds. . .

The decision to dismiss a case on forum non conveniens grounds lies wholly within the broad discretion of the district court and may be overturned only when we believe that discretion has been clearly abused. . . . we conclude that the district court did not abuse its discretion when it dismissed this case on forum non conveniens grounds.

In reaching its conclusion, the district court considered the three relevant factors necessary to make such a decision: (1) the degree of deference accorded to the plaintiff's choice of forum; (2) the adequacy of the alternative forum proposed by the defendants; and (3) the balance of the private and public interests in the forum choice. As for the first factor, generally, a plaintiff's choice of forum is entitled to greater deference when the plaintiff has chosen the home forum. Here, as the district court correctly reasoned, although the Wenzels live in New York and Patti Wenzel was treated for her injuries there such that their choice of New York deserves some level of deference, the deference owed to their choice is nevertheless limited by the fact that the lawsuit lacked a substantial connection to New York, as the alleged negligence and injury occurred in Aruba.

On the second factor, the district court concluded that Aruba provided an adequate alternative forum for the plaintiffs' suit. We agree. The Wenzels argue that Aruba is an inadequate forum because tort cases there are decided by judges [with no option for a jury trial], pretrial discovery is more limited, and the potential [financial] recovery is less than if the case proceeded in the United States. Yet, in reality none of these factors demonstrate that Aruba constitutes an inadequate forum. Some inconvenience or the unavailability of beneficial litigation procedures similar to those available in the federal district courts does not render an alternative forum inadequate, nor does the fact that a plaintiff might recover less in an alternative forum render that forum inadequate. . . . Aruba represents an adequate alternative forum.

As for the third factor, . . . First, the fact that the premises, equipment, employees, and other sources of proof relevant to establishing liability are, with the exception of Plaintiffs themselves, located entirely in Aruba demonstrates that the private benefits support trying the case in Aruba. Second, the public interest such as the busy docket of the U.S. court plaintiff selected, the difficulty of applying foreign law, and the importance of the hotel and tourism industry to Aruba support Aruba as the forum. . . . We affirm the dismissal of the case on the grounds of forum non conveniens.

Pretrial Procedure

Once the pleadings have been filed and, if necessary, clarified pursuant to a motion, the parameters of the legal dispute become apparent. Both parties know the general framework of the adversary's position.

To win a lawsuit, a party must convince a jury that her version of the facts is the more probable one. So, the second stage of the suit is devoted to the collection of evidence with which to convince the jury.

Discovery

discovery
The pretrial process by which each side obtains evidence known to the other side.

If justice is to be done, all facts and evidence must be equally available to both parties. The law does not permit one party to hoard evidence and surprise his adversary at trial when it may be too late to prepare a response. Rather, the law facilitates each side's obtaining evidence and information available to the other. This is done through **discovery,** the process by which each side obtains evidence known to the other side.

Discovery usually occurs after the filing of the complaint and answer and before the trial. Discovery may include one or more of the following: (1) written questions called **interrogatories,** or oral questions called a **deposition** posed by one party to the other party or to a witness; (2) inspection of physical evidence that may be relevant to a case, such as a hotel elevator that allegedly malfunctioned; (3) review of documents or other evidence held by the adverse party or by a potential witness, such as the inspection record of the elevator; and (4) if the mental or physical condition of one of the parties is in issue (e.g., if a guest claims to have broken her hip when she fell in defendant's restaurant), a physical or mental examination of the injured party by a doctor of defendant's choosing.

A plaintiff or defendant who proceeds to trial without undertaking discovery forfeits a valuable opportunity to obtain information about the other party's case and is therefore at a significant disadvantage.

Pretrial Conference

After discovery is completed, the judge and the opposing lawyers meet to prepare for the trial. The judge normally utilizes this opportunity to encourage the parties to reach a **settlement**—that is, a resolution of a dispute without a trial. Usually, when a settlement is attained, the plaintiff agrees to accept less than the amount sought in the complaint and the defendant agrees to pay part, but not all, of the plaintiff's claim.

Although the parties may settle a case at any time, the period following discovery is particularly advantageous. Through discovery the parties have learned the strengths and weaknesses of their position and that of their adversary, and can realistically assess the chances of success at trial. A weak case will often prompt a party to seek a settlement. If the parties do not settle, the case proceeds to trial.

interrogatories
Formal written questions submitted to the opposing party in a lawsuit as part of the discovery proceedings.

deposition
Pretrial questioning of a witness under oath.

settlement
A resolution of a dispute without a trial.

© Ralf Kleemann/Shutterstock.com

The Trial

trial
The process whereby the parties present evidence and the judge or jury decides the issues.

After the preliminaries of serving the pleadings and gathering evidence, the attorneys present the case to an impartial *tribunal*, which may be either a judge or a jury. This tribunal must weigh the evidence and render a verdict as determined by the evidence and the law. This process, in which the parties present evidence and the judge or jury decides the issues, is called a **trial.**

Just as rules regulate the pretrial process, other laws regulate the trial. These rules are designed to resolve the dispute in an orderly fashion. The following trial procedure sequence is generally followed in all states:

1. Selection of the jury

2. Opening statements

3. Plaintiff's case-in-chief

4. Defendant's case-in-chief

5. Plaintiff's case in rebuttal

6. Summation

7. Judge's charge to the jury

8. Jury's deliberations

9. Verdict

10. Judgment

Types of Trials—Jury and Bench

jury trial
A case tried by a jury.

bench trial
A trial in which the judge rather than a jury decides the outcome.

A case may be tried by a jury (this is called a **jury trial**) or by the judge (this is called a **bench trial**), depending on the wishes of the parties.

In a criminal case, the determination of whether to have a jury is made exclusively by the defendant. In a civil case, if either the plaintiff or the defendant wants a jury, the case will be tried by a jury. Only if neither party desires a jury will the case be tried without one.

Here are some factors a party might consider when deciding whether to choose a jury trial.

1. *Will a party be presenting technical evidence?* For example, the proof in an embezzlement case against a restaurant manager may include analysis of many checks and financial records. The proof in a case involving injuries caused by a faulty hotel escalator may require extensive evidence about its mechanical operations. Jurors may be inexperienced listeners and "tune out" technical testimony. An experienced judge on the other hand, has had a lot of opportunity to perfect listening skills and thus can be expected to absorb complicated testimony.

2. *Will a party's case benefit from emotional appeals?* For example, a child who became a paraplegic as a result of a dive in a hotel pool will evoke sympathy. Conventional wisdom suggests a jury is more apt to be swayed by emotional appeals than a judge because jurors have not experienced many lawsuits, whereas judges are exposed daily to difficult and heartrending cases. A judge is therefore more likely to be objective in evaluating the case.

3. *Is there anything about the case that may evoke distaste in a jury for a party or his or her position?* If so, the objectivity expected from a judge may make a nonjury trial a good choice. For example, a defendant charged with a gruesome murder in a restaurant parking lot may choose a bench trial on the theory that a jury may be repulsed once the testimony is presented.

Jury Selection

If the case is to be tried before a jury, the trial begins with the examination of prospective jurors, a process called **voir dire.** Prior to the date set for trial, a group of people are randomly selected as potential trial jurors from a large jury pool. The pool may consist of registered voters, utility subscribers, licensed operators of motor vehicles, registered owners of motor vehicles, state and local taxpayers, recent high school graduates, people who have volunteered to serve as jurors, or persons in such other categories as are specified in state law. Those selected are notified that they are to appear at the courthouse on a given day. The trial jurors are chosen from this group.

Most judges start the voir dire by asking potential jurors general questions, such as whether they know or are acquainted with either the plaintiff or defendant, their attorneys, or the judge. Jurors who answer affirmatively will be questioned as to whether that familiarity will interfere with their ability to decide the case objectively. When the judge has concluded general questioning, the attorneys ask more detailed questions.

An individual's eligibility to serve as a juror may be challenged by either attorney **for cause** when, among other reasons, a juror expresses an inability to render an impartial verdict because of prior knowledge of the parties or the facts in the case, bias, or some other disqualifying reason. If the judge agrees that the juror is not suitable, the juror will be dismissed for cause. The attorneys also can make a limited number of **peremptory challenges,** which permit dismissal of potential jurors without a stated cause. A litigant would use this option when no basis exists to remove a potential juror for cause but, for a variety of reasons, the plaintiff or defendant is uneasy about the person's suitability.

voir dire
Process of examination of randomly selected prospective jurors to determine who will serve as jurors.

for cause
Grounds to remove a potential juror from the jury due to some disqualifying circumstance such as familiarity with the case or the parties, bias, or inability to speak English.

peremptory challenges
Process during voire dire which allows each attorney to dismiss a limited number of potential jurors without a stated cause.

© iQoncept/Shutterstock.com

Opening Statements

The **opening statement** is a presentation to the jury outlining the proof a lawyer expects to present during the trial. Each lawyer has an opportunity to make an opening statement before any evidence is presented. The opening statement is the first exposure the jury has to the specific facts of the case.

opening statement
A presentation to the jury at the beginning of a trial outlining the proof a lawyer expects to present during the trial.

The Case-in-Chief

direct examination
The questioning of a witness by the attorney who called the witness to the stand.

After the opening statements, the plaintiff presents its evidence. Testimony is presented one witness at a time through a process of direct examination and cross-examination. The party who calls a witness will question that person first. This questioning is called **direct examination.** The purpose of direct examination is to elicit pertinent information to help prove the party's claim. Next, opposing counsel questions the same witness, called **cross-examination.** The objective of cross-examination is to discredit the witness. This may be done by showing that the witness was intoxicated or impaired by drugs when she observed the facts about which she is testifying. Alternatively, the witness may be shown to have committed perjury in a prior proceeding, or to be a close friend or relative of one of the litigants.

cross-examination
Questioning of a witness called by the opposing side that typically seeks to discredit the witness.

case-in-chief
That part of a trial where each party presents his evidence.

Once cross-examination is concluded, the party who originally called the witness may ask additional questions, called *redirect examination*, after which the opposing party will have an opportunity to recross.

After the plaintiff has called all its witnesses, the defendant presents its **case-in-chief** in the same manner as the plaintiff.

The Plaintiff's Rebuttal Case

When the defendant has concluded its case, the plaintiff can present evidence in **rebuttal.** Suppose, for example, the plaintiff has sued a hotel for injuries sustained when the elevator malfunctioned. He claims the hotel failed to inspect it properly. The hotel defends the case by introducing into evidence inspection records that indicate the elevator had been examined and serviced at frequent intervals. The plaintiff, in its rebuttal case, may present evidence showing that the records had been altered and, in fact, the elevator had not been inspected for a long period of time. Or the plaintiff may rebut by proving that the inspector was not trained or is otherwise unqualified for the job.

Summation

After the cases-in-chief and the plaintiff's rebuttal, the attorneys summarize the case for the jury, called **summations** or closing statements. Summations allow the attorneys to review for the jury the contentions of their respective sides and to demonstrate how the evidence supports each position. In many states, the plaintiff presents a summation first, followed by the defendant. The plaintiff then gets a last opportunity to respond to the defendant's closing argument. In other states, the defendant gives a summation first, followed by the plaintiff.

Charging the Jury

After the summations, the judge informs the jury of the law applicable to the case. This is called the **charge to the jury.** For example, in a case that involves a question of negligence, the judge will charge (instruct) the jury on the law of negligence and explain what that term means. The judge will inform the jurors that unless they find, from the evidence presented in court, that the defendant was negligent within the legal meaning of that word, they cannot return a verdict for the plaintiff. In effect, in the charge the judge gives the jury a short course on the principles of law applicable to the case.

rebuttal
Opportunity at trial for plaintiff to present evidence to contest defendant's evidence.

summation
Closing statements at a trial made by attorneys, that summarize the case for the jury.

charge to the jury
The procedure at trial where the judge informs the jury of the law applicable to the case. The charge occurs after the summations.

© hafakot/Shutterstock.com

Jury Deliberations

deliberations
The process undertaken by a jury to examine, review, and weigh the evidence to decide on a verdict.

Once the jury has heard the evidence and the applicable law, it retires to a jury room for **deliberations,** which are detailed discussions that may result in a verdict. The jury first makes findings of fact. This means that, notwithstanding contradictory evidence, the jury must determine what happened in the case. For example, a jury may be called upon to determine whether the food served at a restaurant caused the plaintiff's illness. As fact finder, the jury has a large degree of discretion in deciding what evidence to believe and what evidence to discredit. When the jury has decided what actually happened, it considers whether, based on the law as relayed to them by the judge in the charge, the defendant has violated the law. For example, if the food served at the restaurant did cause the plaintiff's injuries, does the law impose liability on the restaurant under the particular circumstances of the case? Thus, two separate processes take place during jury deliberations: determination of the facts and determination of how the law applies to those facts.

verdict
A jury's decision in a case.

The Verdict

hung jury
A divided jury unable to reach a verdict.

The **verdict** is the jury's decision in a case. In most states, to have a verdict the jury must reach a unanimous decision that the defendant is either liable or not liable. In some states agreement by most but not all of the jurors is sufficient. If fewer than the necessary number of jurors are in agreement, the jury is **hung** and the judge will declare a mistrial. In this event the case can be tried again with a new jury at the discretion of the plaintiff.

judgment
The official decision of a judge about the rights and claims of each side in a lawsuit.

The Judgment

judgment notwithstanding the verdict (judgment NOV)
A rare circumstance where a trial judge reverses the decision of a jury.

A **judgment** is the official decision of a judge about the rights and claims of each side in a lawsuit. A verdict is not binding on the losing party until the court has entered judgment on the verdict. Basically, this means that the attorney for the losing party will have a chance to challenge the verdict after it is issued by the jury and before the judge issues a judgment. The attorney may pursue any one or more of the following procedures after the verdict and before the judgment:

remitter
A ruling by a judge that the amount of money awarded by the jury is unreasonably high.

1. Request that the jury be polled to ensure that the necessary number of jurors are in agreement.

2. Ask for **judgment notwithstanding the verdict (judgment NOV),** which is an order from the trial judge reversing the jury's decision. This is rarely granted because the justice system has great respect for the jury process and a jury's verdict.

3. Request a new trial on the grounds of an erroneous ruling of the judge during the trial, or a prejudicial statement improperly heard by the jury, or an improper charge by the judge.

4. Seek a **remitter,** which is a ruling that the amount of money awarded by the jury was unreasonably high.

If the trial judge denies these motions, a judgment on the verdict is entered.

Appeal

An **appeal** is the process by which a litigant can claim that a trial judge committed an error, and a request that a superior court correct the mistake.

Grounds for Appeal

Appellate courts have the authority to review the handling and decision of a case tried in a lower court. Many events at a trial occur rapidly. The decisions a judge makes during trial must, by necessity, be made without much time for studied consideration. For this reason, mistakes may be made. These mistakes may entitle a party to an appellate court review of the proceedings at the trial. Appeals occur in a calm and reflective environment, removed from the passions and speed of the trial.

Appellate Courts

Appellate courts—courts that hear appeals—are very different from trial courts. In appellate courts there are no juries. Whereas a trial court consists of one judge, an appellate court may consist of three to nine judges. To reverse the results of a trial, the vote of a majority of these judges is necessary. To appeal, the attorneys first submit **briefs,** or written arguments. Briefs attempt to convince the appellate court that the trial judge was right or wrong, depending on the position of the party submitting the brief. At some point after submission of the briefs, the case is scheduled for oral argument, at which time the attorneys argue their positions in person before the court. The judges have the opportunity to ask questions. The court subsequently issues its decision in a written opinion justifying its conclusions.

appeal
A review by one court of the decision of another court, initiated by the party who lost in the prior court.

appellate court
A court with the authority to review the decisions of other courts.

brief
Documents submitted to a court by plaintiff and defendant that contain the arguments in favor of each party's position.

© blurZA/Shutterstock.com

The appellate court can do any of the following:

- Affirm the decision of the lower court, in which case the judgment stands

- Reverse the decision of the lower court and order a new trial

- Order that the case be dismissed

Normally, each party has a right to appeal to at least one appellate court. However, the right to an appeal to the highest appellate court—the state supreme court in most state court systems or the U.S. Supreme Court in the federal court system—is restricted. The party seeking to appeal must demonstrate that his case falls into one of the limited categories for which appeal to the highest appellate court is permitted by law. Even if this can be established, the highest appellate court has discretion on whether to review the case. For example, the U.S. Supreme Court hears fewer than 1 of every 100 cases seeking that court's review.

Alternative Dispute Resolution

alternative dispute resolution
Alternatives to trial. These include, for example, arbitration and mediation.

arbitration
The process of dispute resolution by an arbitrator chosen by the parties to decide the case.

mediation
The process in which litigants settle their dispute out of court by mutual agreement with the aid of a third person called a mediator.

summary jury trial
A trial heard by a jury without witnesses; sometimes used in federal courts to save time and money. The jury renders a nonbinding decision and the law requires the parties to negotiate their dispute after the jury rules.

The cost to pursue or defend a lawsuit can be very high due to attorney fees, court costs, witness fees, and the parties' time away from work. In civil cases, a number of alternatives to trial exist, called **alternative dispute resolution** (ADR). They are usually quicker, less formal, and less expensive than a trial. More and more, litigants are choosing ADR. Some courts are even requiring it.

Methods of ADR include arbitration, mediation, and summary trials. **Arbitration** is a process in which a dispute is submitted for resolution to an *arbitrator*, an objective third party who may or may not be a lawyer. An informal hearing is held at which evidence is presented. After the hearing is completed, the arbitrator decides who should win the case. With few exceptions, an arbitrator's decision cannot be appealed. The parties pay a fee for the services of the arbitrator.

Mediation is a process in which a *mediator* facilitates discussion and negotiations between the parties to the dispute in an informal setting. Unlike an arbitrator, the mediator does not have the authority to impose a decision; rather, the mediator assists the parties in reaching a settlement of their dispute. The parties pay a fee for the services of the mediator.

Summary jury trials are used primarily in federal courts. The lawyers summarize their arguments and evidence to an informal jury without using witnesses. The jury renders a nonbinding decision, which is intended to facilitate settlement discussions. The parties thereafter negotiate a resolution to their dispute. Since no witnesses are used, the process is much faster than a trial. If the negotiations do not result in a settlement, either side can demand a trial.

The high cost of trials in both money and time suggests the trend toward ADR will continue.

Interpreting a Case Citation

Throughout the book you will encounter case citations. A **citation** is a reference to a legal authority such as a court decision, a statute, or a treatise. A case citation will appear as follows: 42 NY3d 777 (2017). Each part of the citation provides important information to aid the reader in locating the case in a law library. The middle section (NY3d) refers to a set of books that contains case decisions written by judges. "NY3d" is the third edition of a set containing cases from the highest court in New York.

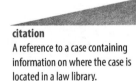

citation
A reference to a case containing information on where the case is located in a law library.

Books in sets are numbered sequentially. The first number in a citation identifies the volume in which the case is located within the set. The second number in the citation identifies the page within the volume on which the case begins.

Concerning the citation 42 NY3d 777 (2017), the case begins on page 777 of the 42nd volume in the New York Third set of books.

The date in parenthesis identifies the year in which the case was decided. Thus, in the referenced example, the court issued its ruling in 2017.

As another example, consider the following federal Court of Appeals citation: 702 F.3d 73 (1st Cir. 2016). The case begins on page 73 of the 702nd volume of the set of books entitled *Federal Reporter, 3rd Series*. The term *1st Cir* means First Circuit, which tells the reader the geographical region in which the court is located. The United States is divided into 12 circuits for purposes of federal courts of appeal. To assist your understanding of the material, throughout this book the authors will include in *Federal Reporter* citations the state in which the case originated rather than the circuit.

Summary

Claims can be resolved by lawsuits, settlement, or alternative dispute resolution methods. Which procedure to pursue in a given circumstance is an important question that should be decided only after careful review of the case.

The stages of a lawsuit include pleadings, pretrial procedures, trial, and appeals. The purpose of the pleadings is to identify the factual issues in the case. The function of pretrial procedures is to eliminate surprises at trial. The objective of the trial is to determine the facts of the case and how the law applies to the facts. The reason for an appeal is to provide an opportunity to correct an erroneous ruling.

The specific steps in a lawsuit are as follows:

COMMENCING THE LAWSUIT
    Complaint
        Statement of jurisdiction
        Basis for the claim
        Request for relief
    Summons
    Service of process
    Responses to the complaint
        Preliminary motions
        Answer
        If no answer, default judgment in favor of plaintiff
    Response to the answer
        Motions directed to the answer
        Reply
    Summary judgment motion
    PRETRIAL PROCEDURE
        Discovery
        Pretrial conference
    THE TRIAL
        Selection of the jury
        Opening statements
        Plaintiff's case-in-chief
        Defendant's case-in-chief
        Plaintiff's rebuttal
        Summations
        Charge to the jury
        Jury deliberations
        Verdict
        Judgment
    APPEAL

Alternative dispute resolution methods include arbitration, mediation, and summary jury trials. These options are quicker and less expensive than lawsuits.

Preventive Law Tips for Managers

If You Are the Plaintiff

- *Involve a lawyer early in the process.* Pursuing a lawsuit involves technical rules of procedure and evidence. A good case can be lost if procedural or evidentiary errors are made. Consult an attorney as early as possible if you are planning to commence a lawsuit. Your lawyer will advise you whether you have a good basis to sue and will guide you through the legal maze.

If You Are the Defendant

- *If you receive a complaint, contact an attorney immediately.* If a defendant fails to respond he will lose by default, so action is necessary. Once the summons and complaint are served, the defendant's time to answer is limited. The sooner the lawyer is contacted the more time will be available to properly prepare the response.

Concerns for Both Plaintiffs and Defendants

- *Fully investigate the facts of the case.* Knowledge of all the relevant facts is critical to the success of a lawsuit.

- *Document well incidents that may lead to a lawsuit.* Cases are won or lost on available evidence. The more documentary proof a party presents, the greater the likelihood of convincing a jury of the merits of that party's case. Keep good records of the circumstances that may constitute the basis for a lawsuit.

- *When working with your lawyer, be forthcoming with information about the facts of the case.* For the lawyer to best represent a litigant, she needs to know as much about the facts of the case as possible. All reports and evidence should be shared with the attorney.

- *Avoid unnecessary court and trial costs—consider alternative dispute resolution.* Not every dispute should result in a lawsuit. Court cases are expensive, time consuming, and public. In appropriate situations, much time and money can be saved by pursuing an alternative dispute resolution method such as arbitration. When thinking about ADR, consider the type of case involved, the amount of money in issue, and whether the dispute is a factual or legal one. Contemplate whether your case is better pursued in a more efficient forum than a court.

- *Avoid an unnecessary trial—settle if appropriate.* In many cases settlement is a suitable resolution. After discovery is complete, the parties should have a good understanding of the strengths and weaknesses of their respective cases and thus the likelihood of success. With the resulting bargaining power that the information gives, make an earnest effort to resolve the case without the considerable expense and angst of trial.

Review Questions

1. How is a lawsuit begun?

2. What is jurisdiction?

3. What is contained in a complaint?

4. How does a complaint differ from a summons?

5. What is a counterclaim?

6. What happens if the defendant does not respond to the complaint?

7. What is the name given to the procedure for questioning prospective jurors?

8. What does the judge do when charging a jury?

9. What is a motion? Name two types of motions that might be made during a trial.

10. What is an appellate court?

11. Name two differences between a trial and an appellate court hearing.

Discussion Questions

1. What role do the pleadings play in a lawsuit?

2. What role does discovery play in a lawsuit?

3. Why, in the case of a hung jury, can the case be retried?

4. Why do most states require that the jury be unanimous for a verdict?

5. Why do different courts have different types of jurisdiction?

Application Questions

1. Shania lives in California and took a vacation, traveling by car from California to Texas. She was injured in a motel room in Arizona when the bed on which she was sleeping collapsed, causing her to fall to the floor. She suffered substantial back and leg injuries, requiring many medical treatments causing her to miss work for 10 weeks. Her medical bills totaled $36,000 and her lost wages $15,000. Shania intends to sue the owner of the Arizona motel.

   A. Can Shania bring her case in federal court? Why or why not?

   B. Can Shania commence the case in California? What additional information might you need to answer this question?

2. If you were the defendant in the following cases, would you opt for a jury trial or a bench trial? Why?

   A. A 12-year-old guest at a hotel broke her spine and became a quadriplegic as a result of a dive she took into a hotel pool. The plaintiff claims the hotel was at fault for not maintaining the water in the pool at required levels.

   B. A guest at a hotel was injured when an in-room heater exploded. To prove that the hotel was negligent in its maintenance of the device, the plaintiff will present as expert witnesses an engineer and a mechanic who specialize in heating systems. Both will testify concerning the mechanisms that operate the heater and the circumstances surrounding the malfunction at the time plaintiff was injured.

   C. Matt, a state senator, is charged with bribery. He is accused of accepting money from several bars and restaurants in exchange for his promise to vote for a bill that would reduce the drinking age from 21 to 18.

   D. A computer hacker permeated a large hotel chain's database of past and present guests' names, addresses, and credit card numbers. Many guests sued the hotel claiming it was negligent (careless) in its online security measures.

3. What information would you try to obtain through discovery in the following cases? What methods of discovery would you use to obtain that information?

   A. A child was riding on the Ferris wheel at an amusement park. Something malfunctioned and the seat in which the child was riding dropped 40 feet to the ground with the child in it. The fall seriously injured the child. Assume you are the child's parent.

   B. Inez is a guest at a hotel. She returns to the hotel after an evening out. While she is walking to her hotel room she trips in the lobby. She claims to have suffered two broken ribs, a painful injury to her back, and a broken ankle. She further claims the hotel is at fault and sues for $1,000,000. Assume you are the vice president of the hotel and responsible for overseeing legal cases.

Websites

Websites that will enhance your understanding of the material in this chapter include:

www.cnn.com/justice CNN maintains this exciting and interactive site. It includes coverage of newsworthy trials and provides information about current legal cases covered by the media.

www.findlaw.com This site contains updates on legal news and many links to sites covering a variety of legal topics including how to find a lawyer and mediation.

www.uscourts.gov This is the official site of the federal courts. It includes information about the jurisdiction of the courts, the judges, how to become a judge, jury service, right to counsel, frequently asked questions (FAQs), and much more.

www.supremecourtus.gov This is the official site of the U.S. Supreme Court. It contains great pictures of the inside of the court building, profiles of each Supreme Court Justice (past and present), an archive of the court's decisions, information about the history of the court, and much more.

www.adr.org This is the site for the American Arbitration Association, which organizes arbitrations for disputants who wish to utilize this method of alternative dispute resolution.

CHAPTER 3

Civil Rights and Hospitality Businesses

LEARNING OUTCOMES:

- Understand the objective and mandates of the Civil Rights Act of 1964, and the state laws inspired by it
- Learn what establishments are covered by the Civil Rights Act and which are not
- Comprehend the enforcement mechanisms and procedures for violations of the Civil Rights Act
- Understand the rights and limitations of hoteliers and restauranteurs to exclude and eject categories of patrons

KEY TERMS

Americans with Disabilities Act
civil rights
civil rights laws
Civil Rights Act of 1964
discrimination
injunction
interstate commerce

landmark decision
national origin
place of public accommodation
readily achievable
transients
unitary rule

Introduction

discrimination
The act of treating some people different from and less favorably than others.

Discrimination, the act of treating some people different from and less favorably than others, is manifested primarily in two circumstances:

1. Access to places of public accommodation

2. Employment

This chapter addresses the first circumstance; Chapter 14 addresses discrimination in employment.

place of public accommodation
A variety of business establishments open to the public including hotels, restaurants, bars, theaters, stores and more.

A variety of business establishments open to the public are included within the definition of a **place of public accommodation.** While the various laws that protect against discrimination define "place of public accommodation" differently, virtually all such laws include hotels and restaurants.

According to common law, a hotel with a vacancy cannot refuse accommodations to any guest desiring to stay at the inn (a few exceptions are discussed in Chapter 9). Because travelers need rooms in which to stay while they are away from home, hotel accommodations are viewed by the law as quasi-public, creating a duty on the part of innkeepers to accept all transients who come seeking a room.

The rule had its origin in earlier times when, unlike the large number of lodging facilities available in most localities today, hotels were few in number and located at significant distances from each other. If a guest was not provided with a room at one hotel, the distance to the next could be considerable. Before the advent of the car, when travel was done by horse-drawn coach, a would-be guest denied accommodations at one inn might need to travel well into the night before reaching the next. The roads were rudimentary and fraught with robbers and other dangers. The rule mandating that innkeepers with vacancies accept all guests protected people from the vagaries of nighttime travel.

Until the 1960s, the common-law rule was largely ignored in southern hotels which regularly practiced discrimination, particularly against blacks. Most wronged guests were discouraged from bringing lawsuits, in part because of the expense involved.

This common-law rule did not apply to restaurants. Before the advent of **civil rights laws**—statutes that prohibit discrimination—a restaurant owner could refuse to serve any person, including blacks and other minorities, without violating the law. Many restaurant proprietors did discriminate.

civil rights laws
Statutes that prohibit discrimination.

In the aftermath of the Civil War, Congress passed the Civil Rights Act of 1866, which contained certain civil rights protections. The intent was to implement the constitutional mandate of equal protection of the laws. Relevant to hospitality law is Section 1981, which reads as follows:

> *All persons within the jurisdiction of the United States shall have the same right in every State and Territory to make and enforce contracts ... and to the full and equal benefit of all laws ... as is enjoyed by white citizens... .*

These early civil rights protections were seldom honored or enforced prior to the passage of the Civil Rights Act of 1964 a century later.

In the 1950s discrimination based on race was, regrettably, prevalent in our country, particularly in the South. Restaurants, hotels, theaters, schools, and many other public places withheld services from blacks; they were not permitted access to facilities available to whites. Blacks were denied the right to vote and were forced to ride in the back of buses and trains. It was an unproud time in the history of the hospitality industry and the United States.

In 1954, the U.S. Supreme Court decided the landmark case of *Brown v. Board of Education of Topeka, Kansas*. (A **landmark decision** is a ruling by a judge that sets an important precedent, sometimes marking a turning point in the interpretation of the relevant law.) In the *Brown* decision, the Supreme Court declared school segregation unconstitutional. The ruling invalidated the practice of "separate but equal" accommodations, which in practice were rarely equal, and paved the way for integration of institutions open to the public.

landmark decision
A court decision that sets a precedent marking a turning point in the interpretation of law.

Despite the court's ruling, many public facilities resisted integration. In response, blacks accelerated their enduring struggle to achieve freedom and equality. Some of their methods included freedom marches publicizing the black community's discontent with public facilities that disregarded the law mandating integration; sit-ins at lunch counters during which blacks occupied stools reserved for whites; freedom rides in which blacks occupied seats on buses and trains designated for whites; and voter-registration drives during which blacks were encouraged to challenge the practice of restricting the voting rights of minorities.

The Civil Rights Act of 1964

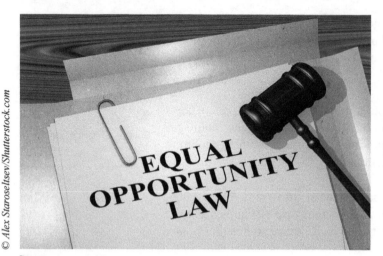

Against this backdrop Congress passed the historic **Civil Rights Act of 1964** (here after "the Act").[1] **Civil rights** are the personal rights that derive primarily from the Constitution. These include freedom of speech, freedom of contract, privacy, and due process, to name just a few. The Act as originally passed outlawed discrimination against four protected classes—race, color, religion, and national origin—in four types of establishments: hotels, restaurants, places of entertainment, and gas stations. A subsequent amendment added gender to the list of protected classes.

Civil Rights Act of 1964
A federal statute that prohibits discrimination on the basis of race, color, religion, and natural origin.

civil rights
Personal rights that derive primarily from the Constitution, for example, equal protection, free speech, freedom of contract, privacy, and due process.

The general intent and overriding purpose of the Act was to end discrimination in hospitality facilities open to the public, thereby reducing the unfairness and humiliation of racial bigotry as well as eliminating the difficulty and inconvenience discrimination created for blacks who wished to dine out or travel. The Act set the stage for eventual desegregation and a new social order. It was the death knell of Jim Crow, the name given to the unequal treatment of blacks in education, social institutions, and transportation that, until the Act was passed, had been sanctioned by either law or tradition. No longer could hotel owners refuse to provide rooms to blacks. No longer could a restaurant provide sit-down service for whites and restrict blacks to take-out service. No longer could restaurants set aside a particular room or area and shepherd all customers of color to it, keeping them separate from the white diners.

As far-reaching as the Act is, it left some gaps. For example, it did not originally cover discrimination based on gender, and it still does not protect marital status, disability, or sexual orientation. Bars are not expressly covered, nor are stores or schools. To remedy these omissions, most states have passed their own laws extending protection to groups and facilities not covered by the Act. Further, discrimination based on disability is now prohibited by the Americans with Disabilities Act, a federal law that became effective in 1992.

In addition to the Civil Rights Act of 1964 this chapter will discuss:

- What is protected by state statutes

- The Americans with Disabilities Act

- Exceptions to civil rights laws (permissible discrimination)

- Implications of these statutes for service-industry managers

---

[1] 42 U.S.C. § 2000a *et seq*

Scope of the Civil Rights Act of 1964

The Act as originally passed by Congress outlaws discrimination in places of public accommodation based on any of four factors:

- Race

- Color

- Religion

- National origin

To be illegal under the Act, the discrimination must occur in one of four types of establishments, and then only if the facility is engaged in interstate commerce. The four places covered are:

1. Lodging establishments for transient—that is, people staying temporarily (as opposed to apartment buildings)

2. Dining facilities

3. Places of entertainment

4. Gasoline stations

Interstate commerce means business transactions between people or companies from two or more states. This requirement will be explored in more detail later in this chapter.

interstate commerce
Business affecting more than one state, as opposed to business done between two parties in the same state.

The term *discrimination*, as used by the Act, means denial of access to goods, services, facilities, and accommodations on the same terms as others enjoy.

To achieve the goal of ending discrimination, courts construed the Act broadly to include within its reach the maximum number of incidents of discrimination. A single circumstance of illegal discrimination violates the Act; a pattern of discriminatory conduct is not required.[2]

The following is a discussion of the places where the Act prohibits discrimination.

Lodging for Transients

Overnight accommodations covered by the Act include, "any inn, hotel, motel, or other establishment which provides lodging to transient guests." **Transients** are people passing through a place for only a brief stay or sojourn.

transients
A person passing through a place for only a brief stay or sojourn.

Court decisions have determined that the following establishments are covered by the Act: places that rent rooms not only by the night but also weekly (but not the

---

2 *Hughes v. Marc's Big Boy,* 479 F.Supp. 834 (Wis. 1979)

more permanent relationship of landlord and tenant), YMCAs which traditionally have offered overnight accommodations, trailer parks that rent to short-term guests, and cottages at beach resorts.

Dining Facilities

The dining facilities covered by the Act are "any restaurant, cafeteria, lunchroom, lunch counter, soda fountain, or other facility principally engaged in selling food for consumption on the premises … if its operation affects [interstate] commerce." Court decisions have determined that the following establishments are included: drive-in restaurants, retail-store lunch counters, sandwich shops, lunch counters at golf courses, food facilities at hospitals, and similar establishments. On the other hand, a store such as 7-11, which sells ready-to-eat food but does not provide facilities for on-premises consumption, is not covered by the Act. Likewise, Domino's Pizza, which sells food primarily for consumption in customers' homes and not at the location where the pizza is purchased, is not covered. Vending machines are also excluded.

Places of Entertainment

The Act prohibits discrimination in "any motion picture house, theater, concert hall, sports arena, stadium or other place of exhibition or entertainment" that "affects commerce." The catch-all phrase "places of entertainment" includes both establishments that present shows for viewing by an audience, such as a sports stadium or an auditorium staging a rock concert, and establishments that provide recreational or other activities in which patrons actively participate, such as bowling alleys. Also included are health spas, beach clubs, youth football organizations, and golf clubs.

Not included as a place of entertainment is an airplane. In one case a black plaintiff claimed to have received inferior service from the flight attendant. Plaintiff alleged that her request for a pillow was ignored but the attendant provided a pillow for a white passenger. Plaintiff also claimed that she was excluded from in-flight beverage service. She reported the problem to the supervising attendant. When the supervisor confronted the allegedly offending attendant, the latter reportedly responded, "I am so tired of those uppity Niggers." Plaintiff sued, claiming discrimination outlawed by the Act. Dismissing the case, the court held that the airline was not one of the entities expressly referenced in the Act. Said the court, "[The airline] is in the transportation business, not the food service industry. Any food sales are ancillary to [the airline's] transportation business."

In another case an Iranian airline passenger was subjected to a manual search of his luggage because, per the ticketing agent, he had an Iranian passport. He sued claiming a violation of the Act. The court dismissed the claim noting that the statute clearly delineates the entities covered as places of public accommodation and they are limited to lodging facilities, eateries, places of entertainment, and vehicle service stations. Said the court, "[N]one even remotely resembles an airline, or indeed any other vehicle or mode of transportation."

Also not included are vending machines. A blind plaintiff found Coca-Cola's Glass Front Vendor type of vending machine to be inaccessible to the visually impaired. The machine does not display the availability of the products that it sells in any nonvisual manner, nor does it offer any nonvisual interface for the purchase of the products it sells. Plaintiff encountered the machine in a bus station and was unable to use it without assistance. He sued the soda company. The court dismissed the case, ruling that the coin-operated machine is not a place of public accommodation.[3] The court suggested that, had plaintiff sued the bus station, which is clearly a place of public accommodation, rather than Coca-Cola, the lawsuit may have been successful.

Note: While the law may not protect the plaintiffs in these suits, ethics and good customer relations should dictate courteous and equal treatment for all.

Jurisdiction Through Interstate Commerce

A hospitality business must affect interstate commerce to be covered by the Act. Why is this so? As we discussed in Chapter 1, when our country was formed the states were very jealous of a strong central government. The Founding Fathers had their distasteful experiences under England's autocratic rule in mind when they crafted the Constitution. As a result they gave a great deal of lawmaking authority to the states. The only powers allocated to the federal government are specifically listed in the Constitution and are called the *delegated powers*. Congress, the legislative body of the federal government, can only pass laws that address these assigned powers.

One of the areas of authority delegated to Congress is interstate commerce, which is business transacted between people or companies from two or more states. Although Congress can pass laws dealing with interstate commerce, it does not have the authority to outlaw discrimination in businesses that are purely local. Those establishments are governed by state or local law.

Hotels

Most of the guests at a hotel are travelers and some will undoubtedly be from out of state. Thus, hotels normally satisfy the requirement of affecting interstate commerce.

Restaurants

A restaurant affects interstate commerce if either it serves interstate travelers, or if a substantial portion of the food it serves was purchased from out of state.

Serving Interstate Travelers

Unlike hotels, food establishments normally do not inquire whether their patrons live in state or are residents of another state. The courts have devised certain rules

---

[3] *Magee v. Coca-Cola Refreshments USA, Inc.*, 2015 WL 6620959 (La, 2015)

to determine whether a restaurant serves interstate travelers, including the following. A dining facility located near a federal highway and a coffeeshop in a hotel have been deemed to serve interstate travelers. In one case, a restaurant in Puerto Rico argued that it was not engaged in interstate commerce, noting that it was not located at an airport or on an interstate highway. However, the restaurant was located in a primary tourist area near several large hotels. The court held that the restaurant's location was sufficient evidence that it serves interstate travelers.[4] If an eatery advertises in a magazine delivered to hotels and motels for distribution to guests, or advertises on the radio, the facility qualifies because the magazine and radio advertisements typically reach out-of-state readers and listeners.

Food Moved in Interstate Commerce

A dining facility that does not serve interstate travelers will nonetheless be covered by the Act if a substantial portion of the food it serves is imported from another state. Although the Civil Rights Act does not provide a test for determining "substantial," precedents provide guidelines. Cases have held that, where ingredients in three of four food items sold by a snack bar (hot dogs, hamburgers, milk, and soft drinks) were from out of state, the "substantial portion" test was satisfied.[5] In another case the requirement was met because 46 percent of an establishment's purchases consisted of meat bought from a local supplier who purchased it from outside the state.[6] Also qualifying as substantial was the purchase by a snack bar at a beach club of syrup from outside the state that was used in Coca-Cola beverages. Many of the purchases at the snack bar were for cold drinks, and Coca-Cola was the most popular.[7]

Places of Entertainment

A theater or stadium affects interstate commerce if it regularly presents movies, performances, exhibits, athletic teams, or other sources of entertainment that originate in other states. A theater group importing traveling shows qualifies. Golf courses that purchase out-of-state carts, pro shop inventory, rental equipment, or related items likewise qualify. Similarly, in one case the facility of a youth football association was determined to be a covered place of entertainment because all its sports equipment was manufactured outside the state.

A bar or lounge qualifies as a place of entertainment if it provides recreational facilities such as a piano, jukebox, darts, shuffleboard court, pool table, or television set. If these items are manufactured outside the state, the bar or lounge will be bound by the Act.

---

[4] *Bermudex Zeonon v. Restaurant Compostela, Inc.,* 790 F.Supp. 41 (P.R. 1992)
[5] *Daniel v. Paul,* 395 U.S. 298, 23 L. Ed. 2d 318, 89 S.Ct. 1697 (1969)
[6] *Katzenbach v. McClung,* 379 U.S. 294, 13 L.Ed.2d 290, 85 S.Ct. 377 (1964)
[7] *United States v. Lansdowne Swim Club,* 894 F. 2d 83 (Pa. 1990)

Remedies

The Act provides limited relief for people who have been denied equality of services. Money is not recoverable as a remedy under the Act (however, a mistreated plaintiff may qualify for monetary remedies under other antidiscrimination laws[8]). The possible remedies under the Act include only the following:

1. *Injunctive relief.* An **injunction** is a court order that requires a defendant to do or refrain from doing a particular act. In civil rights cases, an injunction usually orders the offending person or business to stop discriminating. Injunctive relief can include an order to alter facilities to make them readily accessible to individuals with disabilities. Where appropriate, an injunction can also require the defendant to provide an auxiliary aid or service, modification of a policy, or provision of alternative methods to deliver goods or services. It is a preventive measure that guards against future injuries rather than affording a remedy for past wrongs.

injunction
A court order forbidding a party to a lawsuit from engaging in specified acts.

2. *Reasonable attorney's fees.* A successful plaintiff is entitled to reimbursement of fees charged by the attorney. This is unusual in the law; in most lawsuits the parties pay for their own attorneys. Even a successful plaintiff is normally not entitled to collect attorney's fees from the defendant. The reason for allowing reimbursement for lawyer's fees in cases involving civil rights violations is the legislature's recognition of the importance of eradicating discrimination. By eliminating attorney's fees as a deterrent for bringing a civil rights lawsuit, victims of discrimination are more likely to pursue the wrongdoers. Recovery of attorney's fees also includes litigation expenses and costs such as fees to file a case in court, fees for transcripts, and fees for expert witnesses.

Enforcing the Act

Many facilities that had discriminated before the passage of the Act failed to comply with the new law. Some sought to challenge the Act's legality. Indeed, the constitutionality of the Act was tested immediately after its passage in two landmark cases involving recalcitrant proprietors who resisted the law.

Establishing Jurisdiction

The first case challenging the Act involved a motel. The plaintiff, a 216-room motel in Atlanta, Georgia, called the Heart of Atlanta Motel, refused to rent rooms to blacks. When charged with violating the Act, the motel claimed it was not engaged in interstate commerce and therefore application of the Act to its business exceeded congressional power. The evidence established that the motel in question did solicit guests from outside the state of Georgia through various national advertising media and that it also maintained over 50 billboards and highway signs within the state. The motel accepted convention trade from outside Georgia, and approx-

---

[8] *Wilson v. Waffle House,* 1998 WL 1665880 (Ala. 1998)

imately 75 percent of registered guests were from out of state. The court held the application of the Act to the motel was constitutional, noting that the evidence proved the motel served interstate travelers.[9]

The second test case of the Act's constitutionality involved a family-owned restaurant in Birmingham, Alabama, named Ollie's Barbecue, which catered to a family and business trade with only take-out service available for blacks. The restaurant was accused of violating the Act, and in response denied that it was engaged in interstate commerce. The restaurant purchased much of its meat and other products from out of state. The court upheld the application of the statute to the eatery, concluding that Congress acted within its power to protect and foster interstate commerce by extending the coverage of the Civil Rights Act to restaurants that either serve interstate travelers or purchase food from out of state.[10]

The hotel and restaurant involved in these landmark cases both argued that if they were required to serve blacks they would lose a substantial amount of business from whites who did not wish to dine with people of color or stay in a hotel that accommodated them. The district (lower) courts accepted this argument and barred government officials from enforcing the Civil Rights Act against the businesses. The U.S. Supreme Court, which granted certiorari in both cases and heard the appeals, rejected loss of business as a justification to avoid the mandates of the Act. The high court noted that enforcement of the Act should instead increase business by enlarging the potential clientele. Enforcement would also achieve the desirable outcome of expanding interstate commerce. As the court said,

> *A comparison of per capita spending by Negroes in restaurants, theatres, and like establishments indicated less spending, after discounting income differences, in areas where discrimination is widely practiced... . This diminutive spending, springing from a refusal to serve Negroes and their total loss as customers has ... a close connection to interstate commerce. The fewer customers a restaurant enjoys, the less food it sells and consequently the less it buys. Moreover there was an impressive array of testimony that discrimination in restaurants had a direct and highly restrictive effect upon interstate travel by Negroes. This resulted, it was said, because discriminatory practices prevent Negroes from buying prepared food served on the premises while on a trip, except in isolated and unkempt restaurants, and under most unsatisfactory and often unpleasant conditions. This obviously discourages travel and obstructs interstate commerce for one can hardly travel without eating. Likewise, it was said, that discrimination deterred professional, as well as skilled, people from moving into areas where such practices occurred, and thereby caused industry to be reluctant to establish there.*

As discussed in the following sections, the Act continues to be vigorously enforced.

---

[9] *Heart of Atlanta Motel, Inc. v. United States*, 379 U.S. 241, 13 L.Ed.2d 258, 85 S.Ct. 348 (1964)
[10] *Katzenbach v. McClung*, 379 U.S. 294, 13 L.Ed.2d 290, 85 S.Ct. 377 (1964)

Racial Discrimination

Refusing to permit anyone to enter an establishment because of race constitutes a violation of the Act. In a 1996 settlement of a Louisiana case, a Louisiana nightclub owner admitted the club discriminated against blacks. The case arose when a white woman, out for the evening with two friends—one black and one white— walked to the entrance of the nightclub to see if it was open. Meanwhile, her two friends waited in the car. When the bouncer advised her the bar was open, she and her friends parked the car and sought entry. They were then advised they would not be admitted because the club was hosting a private party. Later that evening the white woman returned to the club alone and was admitted. After she reported the incident to law enforcement, the government sent two pairs of undercover FBI agents, one white couple and one black couple, to the nightclub. The latter was denied entry while the former was admitted.

© Gustavo Frazao/Shutterstock.com

In the settlement of the case, the bar owner agreed to stop violating the Civil Rights Act of 1964, train employees in civil rights law requirements, and advertise that the bar is open to all races. Said a prosecutor involved with the case, "Over three decades ago, Congress spoke for all decent Americans by making it illegal to exclude people from [restaurants and bars] because of their skin color ... America must have zero tolerance for racial discrimination."[11]

In another case, several people of color claimed to have been victims of discrimination of the admission policies of a well-attended restaurant and nightclub called the Glass Menagerie. The plaintiffs claimed they were kept waiting in line outside the club while white people were admitted ahead of them. The plaintiffs' protests to employees were ignored. Two former doormen testified they had been instructed to discourage black customers from coming to the facility because the owner believed they did not spend as much money as white customers, they bothered white female patrons, and they were not big tippers. The court, finding that this constituted discrimination, stated,

> *The court would like to believe that these discriminatory acts*
> *occurred through shortsightedness rather than malice. The court*
> *is optimistic that voluntary corrective action will be promptly*
> *taken to eliminate all vestiges of discrimination at the Glass Me-*
> *nagerie. Even so, however, and even though the discrimination*
> *was sporadic, compelling public interests require the immediate*

---

11 1996 WL 66969 (1996); Department of Justice News Release, "Two Louisiana Nightclubs Agree with the Department of Justice to Open Their Doors to African-Americans."

issuance of injunctive relief [a court order prohibiting any further discrimination].[12]

Action by a restaurant manager in refusing to serve a group of racially mixed customers, escorting them out of the restaurant, locking the door behind them, and then allowing whites to enter likewise constitutes illegal discrimination.[13]

A restaurant in North Myrtle Beach, South Carolina, closed "for renovations" during Black Bike Week, a motorcycle festival attended mostly by blacks, yet no renovations were made. The eatery remained open during Harley Week, a similar festival held the prior week and attended by mostly white motorcycle enthusiasts. The court denied the restaurant's motion to dismiss.[14]

The Civil Rights Act was violated by a restaurant that required blacks, but not others, to prepay for their meals while the customary practice was for customers to pay after the meal had been consumed.[15] However, requiring *all* customers to prepay for their dinners does not constitute illegal discrimination, even though prepayment is contrary to normal practice.[16]

In another case the evidence was sufficient for the plaintiff to avoid summary judgment in favor of the defendant restaurant where plaintiffs, who were black patrons, were not greeted when they entered, and were ignored for a half hour while white patrons were readily greeted and seated.[17]

A court denied a hotel's motion to dismiss a discrimination case where a group of eight members of a volleyball team, all of whom were white, partied in their room and the hallway. On the same night, plaintiffs, a group of six blacks, were told the hotel had a no-party policy and allowed no more than five people in a room. The six were forced to leave and were not given a refund.[18]

A claim of discrimination against an Extended Stay of America Hotel was dismissed where plaintiff was offered a room at the defendant hotel, and the clerk recommended a nearby Holiday Inn in response to plaintiff's inquiry about availability of continental breakfast and a pool. Although plaintiffs were denied a room upon their return from examining the Holiday Inn, the clerk was then unable to access the computer system because the automatic night audit program was in process, and no racial remarks were made or racial animus evidenced.[19]

Airbnb

Airbnb is a popular website used by nonhoteliers who own or lease property and are seeking to rent all or part of it to travelers. Founded in 2008, it is used in 34,000

---

12 *U.S. v. Glass Menagerie, Inc.,* 702 F.Supp. 139 (Ky. 1988)
13 *Laroche v. Denny's Inc.,* 62 F.Supp. 2d 1375 (Fla. 1999)
14 *NAACP v. Darcy, Inc.,* 2012 WL 4473138 (S.C. 2012)
15 *Bobbitt v. Rage, Inc.* 19 F.Supp2d 512 (N.C. 1998); See also *Jackson v. Waffle House, Inc.,* 413 F.Supp. 1638 (Ga. 2006)
16 *Stevens v. Steak N Shake, Inc.,* 35 F. Supp.2d 882 (Fla. 1998)
17 *McLauren v. Waffle House, Inc.,* 178 F.Supp.3d 536 (Tex. 2016)
18 *Ross v. Choice Hotels, Inc.,* 882 F.Supp.2d 951 (Ohio 2012)
19 *Childs v. Extended Stay of America Hotels,* 2012 WL 2126845 (Minn., 2012)

cities and 191 countries. The company is valued at $25 billion. Users of the site complete a profile that includes personal information and a photo. Hosts can see the profile before agreeing to a booking.

In 2015, independent researchers found widespread discrimination by hosts against people seeking rentals who had black-sounding names such as Lakisha or Rasheed, or whose profile picture indicated a person of color. In 2016 a black person sued claiming he was denied an Airbnb rental, but the booking was accepted when he reapplied using a fake profile of a white man. He is seeking court authorization to bring the case as a class action to encompass others who have experienced similar discrimination when seeking Airbnb accommodations.

In response, Airbnb adopted new policies and procedures. It now requires that hosts not discriminate on the basis of race, color, ethnicity, national origin, religion, sexual orientation, gender identity, or marital status. It allows hosts to restrict rentals to people of the same gender as the host if and only if the host shares living space with the guest. Additionally, the site now blocks hosts from relisting a space when they have told a potential guest that it is already booked. An additional modification is that guests will soon be able to use an instant booking feature, which lets renters contract for space immediately without host approval. Plus the company plans to hire trained specialists to handle discrimination complaints, and is committed to seek more diversity within the ranks of the company's employees. Finally, it has added a new anti-discrimination team of engineers, data scientists, and researchers who will be on the lookout for discriminating patterns of host behavior.

Whites Are Also Protected

The Act protects not just minorities, but all people. This is demonstrated in a case in which a Korean restaurant refused to seat and serve plaintiff O'Connor, "a male of European descent." When O'Connor sought service, he was advised by the restaurant host that the restaurant was a private club and since O'Connor was not a member he could not enter. O'Connor returned a month later with "another white male" and was again refused service. Thereafter on two occasions of which the plaintiff was aware, Korean males who were nonmembers were seated and served at the restaurant. On other occasions, two white males and a black female sought service and were denied because they were not members.

In response to the plaintiff's lawsuit claiming a violation of various civil rights laws, the restaurant argued that only members of a racial minority are protected and therefore the white plaintiff could not sue. The court rejected this claim, holding that "a white person, just as a nonwhite," is protected by the statutes. The restaurant's motion to dismiss plaintiff's case was denied.[20]

---

[20] In *O'Connor v. 11 West 30th Street Restaurant Corp.*, 1995 WL 354904 (N.Y. 1995)

Poor Customer Service

Case law also teaches that the Civil Rights Act does not remedy all perceived wrongs. Instead, it protects only against discriminatory denial of the right to enter a covered facility and receive service. Certain indignities resulting from inferior service are not covered.

In one case the plaintiff, a black male, entered a Burger King and ordered breakfast. He was the first in line. Several white men entered the line behind him. The employee serving the food stopped waiting on the plaintiff and attended to the others. When the plaintiff complained to the assistant manager, he left his office and prepared the plaintiff's order. Upon receiving his order, the plaintiff paid and left. In this action, the plaintiff claims the delay in his service was the result of racial discrimination.

The court dismissed the plaintiff's case stating, "In the instant case, plaintiff was not denied admittance or service—his service was merely slow. While inconvenient, frustrating, and all too common, the mere fact of slow service in a fast-food restaurant does not, in the eyes of this Court, rise to the level of violating one's civil rights."[21]

In Case Example 3-1, the court similarly finds that bad service does not constitute discrimination.[22]

CASE EXAMPLE 3-1

Sherman v. Marriott Hotel Services, Inc.

317 F.Supp.2d 609 (Md., 2004)

The Plaintiff, Marcus Sherman, who is African-American, was locked out of his room at a Baltimore hotel while attending a professional conference in March 2003 when his room key became demagnetized. Unhappy with the treatment he received from hotel employees in obtaining a new key (and in later complaining about it), he filed this action for damages and injunctive relief ... pursuant to ... the Civil Rights Act of 1964... .

(T)he facts are as follows ... Plaintiff attended a professional conference at the hotel from on or about March 5 through March 7, 2003. On the evening of March 5, plaintiff worked out in the hotel gym until after 11:00 p.m. When he returned to his room from the gym, his electronic key card had become demagnetized and would not unlock the door. Plaintiff, dressed in athletic garb and sweating from his workout, went to the front desk to obtain assistance and/or a new key. At the front desk, plaintiff interacted with a white employee, Darren Kerr.

---

[21] *Robertson v. Burger King, Inc.,* 848 F. Supp. 78 (La. 1994); See also *Jackson v. Waffle House, Inc.,* 413 F.Supp. 2d. 1338 (Ga. 2006)
[22] *Callwood v. Dave & Buster's, Inc.,* 98 F. Supp. 2d 694 (Md. 2000)

It is undisputed that defendant's lock-out policy requires that a guest display identification matching the name in hotel records in order to obtain a new key. Under circumstances such as those facing plaintiff on March 5, in which the guest's identification is in his (locked) room, the policy requires that the guest be escorted to the room by hotel security to obtain the identification.

According to plaintiff, the interaction between plaintiff and Kerr at the front desk was not pleasant. Plaintiff, who alleges that it took up to 19 minutes or so for Kerr to obtain assistance from a security officer to escort plaintiff to his room, regards certain statements of Kerr ("You could have come in off the street... .") to have manifested a racially insensitive, if not racially discriminatory, attitude. In any event, an African-American security officer eventually escorted plaintiff to his room. Kerr had apparently instructed plaintiff to return to the front desk after he had produced identification to the security officer to retrieve a replacement key; however, the security officer left plaintiff in his room and returned alone to the front desk to retrieve a new key for plaintiff. The replacement key was delivered to plaintiff's room.

Apparently, plaintiff's decision to sue for damages based on the March 5 incident was made as a result of what he learned the next night during dinner with some of his professional colleagues. Specifically, plaintiff learned that a white female professional acquaintance had checked into the hotel the day before plaintiff checked in, i.e., on March 4, 2003. Later on March 4, that colleague had locked herself out of her room. When she went to the front desk for assistance, the same front desk employee who had checked her in immediately reissued an additional key to her, without demanding identification, and in violation of the hotel's written lock-out policy... .

As a matter of law, plaintiff enjoyed the benefits and privileges, on the very same terms and conditions, of the contractual relationship offered by the defendant to any prospective guest. As a matter of law, the fact that an individual employee of the hotel deviated from the undisputed policy of the hotel in respect to lock-outs (by reissuing a key to a guest who had recently checked in and who was recognized by the employee) is not remotely probative of a claim of race discrimination based on proof that such an exception or deviation from the policy was not made (by a different hotel employee) when plaintiff was locked out of his room. However unpleasant plaintiff's interactions with hotel staff on the night of his lock-out might have been, ... no reasonable juror properly instructed on the law could reasonably conclude that application of a facially neutral lock-out policy, which requires that a guest be escorted to his room for identification, as applied to plaintiff on March 5, 2003, constituted an act of racial discrimination ... Moreover, this conclusion is not remotely called into question by undisputed proof that on some occasions, whether pursuant to an unofficial or informal "policy exception," or through the ad hoc and episodic deviations from the policy by individual employees, which common sense suggests are virtually certain to occur, some guests are provided replacement keys without displaying identification. Accordingly, defendant is entitled to summary judgment.

CASE QUESTIONS

1. What facts did the Court consider to be most important in reaching its determination that the plaintiff was not discriminated against based upon his race?

2. Do you agree with the decision? Why or why not?

Proprietor's Discretion on Music Selection

In another case the plaintiff, a black patron of a dance bar, claimed the bar's owner discriminated against blacks by discontinuing rap music and playing rock-and-roll to induce black patrons to leave. Employees of the restaurant testified that the manager would tell the disc jockeys that it was "too dark in here" when it was thought there were too many blacks in the bar. In response, the disc jockeys allegedly began playing "hard rock-and-roll" music, which was not the favored music of many blacks. The court dismissed the case, noting that the manager did not refuse the plaintiff admittance to the bar or service while he was there. Said the court, "A bar's music selection cannot be grounds to find that it engages in discriminatory conduct."[23]

Refusal of Service Because Would-Be Customers Caused a Disturbance Is Not Discrimination

If a customer is refused service for reasons other than race, religion, color, or national origin, the refusal does not violate the Civil Rights Act of 1964. Three black sisters were dissatisfied with the service they received at a Burger King and left. They later returned with their mother to complain to the manager. While doing so the mother became contentious, manifested by yelling, screaming, waving her arms, and grabbing the manager's arm. To avoid further disturbance the manager called the police and refused to serve them. The mother sued for discrimination but the court rejected the claim. The manager had the right to refuse service because of the disturbance the mother caused.[24]

National Origin Discrimination

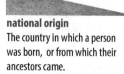

national origin
The country in which a person was born, or from which their ancestors came.

A restaurant that refuses to serve would-be customers based on national origin, or a hotel that denies a room for that reason, is engaged in illegal discrimination. **National origin** refers to the country from which one's ancestors came. For example, a person's national origin might be French, Canadian, or Puerto Rican.

To sue successfully for national origin discrimination, plaintiff must show that defendant treated plaintiff differently from others who did not share the same ethnicity. Practitioners of Falun Gong, a spiritual belief system whose members were persecuted by the People's Republic of China (hereinafter PRC), learned that the former president of PRC intended to visit Houston, Texas. They made reservations at the hotel where he was staying, causing it to overbook. By necessity, on the date of the PRC president's arrival, the hotel instituted its "walk policy" whereby it moved some guests to nearby hotels. Plaintiffs were among those transferred. The plaintiffs claimed discrimination on the basis of national origin. Denying the claim, the court noted that the former president's staff were Chinese and at least some of them too were moved from the booked hotel. Further, plaintiffs presented

---

[23] *Sterns v. Baur's Opera House, Inc.*, 788 F. Supp. 375 (Ill. 1992), dismissed on other grounds, 3 F.3d 1142 (Ill. 1993); *Phillips v. Interstate Hotels, Corp.*, 974 S.W.2d 680 (Tenn. 1998). See also *Stephens v. Seven Seventeen HB Philadelphia Corp.*, 2004 WL 1699331 (Pa. 2004)
[24] *Wells v. Burger King Corp.*, 40 F.Supp.2d 1366 (Fla. 1998)

no evidence that the hotel did not "walk" non-Chinese patrons, nor was evidence presented that the hotel offered plaintiffs unequal alternate accommodations.[25]

Language Discrimination

A person's primary language is an important part of, and flows from, his or her national origin. Therefore, discrimination based on language is often viewed as discrimination based on national origin in violation of the Civil Rights Act of 1964. Case Example 3-2 involves discrimination against Spanish-speaking bar patrons. Since the Act does not cover bars, the court could not rely on the Act to stop the tavern from discriminating. Instead, the court creatively used different federal laws that grant all citizens of the United States equal rights to enter contracts and purchase property. The proprietor in this case violated those laws by limiting the rights of the Spanish-speaking patrons to purchase beer.

CASE EXAMPLE 3-2

Hernandez v. Erlenbusch

368 F.Supp. 752 (Ore. 1973)

… At trial, a preponderance of the evidence showed the following: The setting for both cases is the same—a community of approximately 8,500 persons in which more than 2,000 Mexican-Americans have been living for at least the last four years. The plaintiffs in these cases are all U.S. citizens, most of them native born. Some two years ago, the defendants, owners of the Taffrail Tavern ("Tavern"), issued these orders to their bartenders: You are instructed to observe the following… .

11. Do not allow a foreign language to be used at the bar, if it interferes with the regular trade. If there should be a chance of a problem, ask the 'Problem' people to move to a table and turn the juke box up. (Use house money).

The rationale for this policy, as explained by its formulators and enforcers, is that the tavern has many Anglo and Chicano patrons, with attendant friction between the two groups caused by the dislike by some of the local white populace of the "foreigners" in their midst. According to the Erlenbusches, the tavern's owners, the language rule as carried out by them and their employees served everyone's interests by accommodating both Anglo and Chicano customers and ensuring peaceful continuance of the tavern business. The complaints concerning Spanish spoken at the bar allegedly stem from fear on the part of the white clientele that the Chicanos are talking about them. It was in this atmosphere ridden with mistrust and apprehension that the following incidents occurred:

On August 23, 1972, Gilberto Hernandez and Abel and Alfredo Maldonado went to the tavern where defendant Krausnick, the bartender, served them beer. While drinking, the three men began conversing in Spanish, their native tongue. Anglo customers, who were also sitting at the bar, were "irritated" and complained to Krausnick. She advised the Chicanos that if they persisted in speaking Spanish, they would have to go to a booth or leave the premises.

---

[25] *McCoy v. Homestead Studio Suite Hotels.*, 390 F. Supp.2d 577 (Tex. 2005)

Hernandez and the Maldonados took issue with these orders and an argument ensued. Krausnick poured out their remaining beer and refused to refund any money. The police were called, the plaintiffs left peacefully.

Two days later, the scene was reenacted with different plaintiffs and an additional three antagonists. Krausnick "pulled" the beers of Gonzalez, Perez and Vasquez, who were then followed out of the tavern and assaulted by defendants Salisbury, Dunn, and Clary, three Anglo regular customers. Clary was subsequently tried and convicted in state court for battering Gonzalez over the right eye with a fire extinguisher. (Gonzales was the only plaintiff who was physically struck.)

Defendant Krausnick testified that she agreed with and willingly enforced "Rule 11." Clary, Dunn, and Salisbury concurred, saying they knew of the rule and wholeheartedly endorsed it. John Erlenbusch testified he adopted the policy simply to avoid trouble and to preserve his license.

CONCLUSIONS OF LAW

… In examining the practical effect of the tavern's policy against the speaking of foreign languages at the bar, it is obvious that it amounts to patent racial discrimination against Mexican-Americans who constitute about one-fourth of the tavern's trade, regardless of an occasional visit by a customer able to speak another language. The rule's results are what count; the intent of the framers in these circumstances is irrelevant… . In the instant case, Rule 11, as intended and applied, deprives Spanish-speaking persons of their rights to buy, drink and enjoy what the tavern has to offer on an equal footing with English-speaking consumers.

Plaintiffs' rights … to the full and equal benefit of all laws and proceedings for the security of person and property as is enjoyed by white citizens have been violated. Likewise, plaintiffs have been denied their … guarantee that [a]ll citizens of the United States shall have the same right … to … purchase … personal property… . Just as the Constitution forbids banishing blacks to the back of the bus so as not to arouse the racial animosity of the preferred white passengers, it also forbids ordering Spanish-speaking patrons to the "back booth or out" to avoid antagonizing English-speaking beer-drinkers.

The lame justification that a discriminatory policy helps preserve the peace is as unacceptable in barrooms as it was in buses. Catering to prejudice out of fear of provoking greater prejudice only perpetuates racism. Courts faithful to the Fourteenth Amendment will not permit, either by camouflage or cavalier treatment, equal protection so to be profaned.

CASE QUESTION

1. What can the Erlenbusches do legally to address the friction between the Anglo and Chicano patrons?

Religious Discrimination

Similar to racial discrimination, a successful case of religious discrimination requires a showing that service was refused. Where service is offered but a requested accommodation of one's religious practices is refused for good reason unrelated to religion, the Act has not been violated.

In an Idaho case, the plaintiff was a tournament golfer and member of the Church of Jesus Christ of Latter-day Saints. Due to religious beliefs, the plaintiff did not play golf on Sunday. The club's tournaments were customarily played on Saturday and Sunday. He requested an alternate playing schedule, but the club refused. He sued, claiming a violation of the Act. The club claimed that to give the plaintiff an alternate schedule would create complications and expense, making the administration of the tournament more difficult. Among the problems would be an increased workload for the tournament marshals and umpires, a delay of the public's access to the course, and possible disruption of the practice of the lowest-scoring golfers playing at the end of the tournament, which serves economic purposes.

The court dismissed the plaintiff's action, noting that the club had "legitimate business reasons, completely unrelated to religious considerations, for scheduling its final round of play on Sunday." Further, the club had never denied the plaintiff entry to a tournament or access to the course. The court thus concluded that the club's denial of an alternate tournament date was based on the stated administrative concerns and not on hostility toward his religious beliefs.[26]

Similarly, judo competitors brought a lawsuit against judo organizations seeking to stop the latter's requirement of bowing to inanimate objects prior to matches. Plaintiffs objected to the bowing on religious grounds. Rules of the sport require that contestants bow to such items as portraits and tatami mats. The justification for such mandates include promoting fair and safe start of matches particularly where participants and officials may not all speak the same language, preserving the etiquette and traditions of judo, and promoting the unique identity of the sport. The court determined the bowing requirement did not violate the competitors' religious rights, noting that the organizations had legitimate business reasons for adopting the rule that were unrelated to religious considerations.[27]

Broad Enforcement Through the Unitary Rule

The Act covers only lodging facilities, dining facilities, places of entertainment, and gasoline stations. Other businesses, such as stores, barber shops and beauty parlors, transportation facilities, bars, and colleges are not covered (although

---

26 *Boyle v. Jerome Country Club,* 883 F.Supp. 1422 (Idaho 1995)
27 *Akiyama v. U.S. Judo, Inc.,* 181 F.Supp.2d 1179 (Wash. 2002)

discrimination in these locations are now typically prohibited by state statute). However, if a covered business is physically located within another facility not otherwise covered by the Act, such as a snack bar in a store or a food car on a train, the food facility and the store or train are *both* covered. Similarly, if a business not covered by the Act is located within a covered business, both are subject to the Act's provisions. For example, a barber shop, which is not covered by the Act, will be bound by its provisions if located within a hotel. This principle is known as the **unitary rule,** which means that if a covered facility is located within a noncovered business, or vice versa, both the covered and noncovered businesses are subject to the Act.

Exempt Establishments

The Act excludes from its coverage certain establishments, including bed-and-breakfast operations and private clubs. These businesses are not barred from discriminating by the Act.

"Mrs. Murphy's Boarding House"

The Act exempts tourist homes, known today as bed-and-breakfasts, that have five or fewer rooms and are occupied by the proprietor. This exception, sometimes referred to as the "Mrs. Murphy's boarding house clause," allows proprietors who admit transients into their home to retain discretion and control over who sleeps in their house.

Private Clubs

The Act's ban on discrimination does not apply to "private clubs or other establishments not in fact open to the public." The law recognizes that people customarily affiliate with a private club because of common interests among the members; the Act supports the perpetuation of those shared agendas. The Act does not clearly define what constitutes a private club, so the courts have interpreted the statute when the issue has been raised. It usually arises when a club claiming to be private excludes someone on the basis of race, color, religion, or national origin and that person challenges the legality of the exclusion. In considering whether a club is private, the courts examine the following:

1. Is the club selective in choosing its members? A private club usually has a limited number of members. The more selective the club is, the more likely it will qualify as a private club.

2. Are new members sought discreetly? If the club publicly advertises for members it likely is not a private club.

3. Does the club have clearly designated criteria for choosing members and do members participate in the selection process? A private club typically has specific traits it seeks to perpetuate in its members. The more specific the criteria, the more likely the club will qualify as private. Also, by participating in the selection process, members help to ensure that the interests they share with other members will continue to bind the membership in the future.

4. Do members govern and control the club's operations? A private club is usually owned and governed by its members. If the "club" is simply a business operated for profit, it will not qualify as a private club.

5. To what extent are club facilities available for use by nonmembers? The more access by nonmembers, the less likely it is a private club.

6. Is the primary purpose of the club social or business? If the primary purpose is business, it likely will not be a private club.

The following two case examples illustrate private clubs.

A bridge club (bridge is an intricate card game played with a partner; tournaments are held throughout the country) was found to be private for the following reasons:

> *[T]he club is dedicated to the promotion of bridge and other games of skill... . Club facilities are open only to members and their guests... . Prospective members must be sponsored by a current member and seconded by another member. They are subject to evaluation of their ethical reputation at the bridge table, their skill and knowledge of the game, their standards of dress and deportment, and their ability to meet their financial commitment to the Club. Members are admitted only if they are approved by the Board of Directors.[28]*

A black man was refused service by a Moose Lodge, a local branch of the national fraternal organization. He sued claiming illegal discrimination. The court held the club was private for the following reasons:

> *Moose Lodge is a private club ... It is a local chapter of a national fraternal organization having well-defined requirements for membership. It conducts all of its activities in a building that is owned by it. It is not publicly funded. Only members and guests are permitted in any lodge of the order; one may become a guest only by invitation of a member or upon invitation of the house committee.[29]*

Many clubs have sought exemption from application of the Act on the basis of being a private club. The issue in many discrimination cases is whether the defendant club is, in fact, private.

---

28 *Baptiste v. Cavendish Club, Inc.*, 670 F.Supp. 108 (N.Y. 1987); see also Davidson-Seidel v. Denver Athletic Club, 2016 WL 1046277 (Colo. 2016)
29 *Moose Lodge v. Irvis*, 407 U.S. 163, 32 L.Ed.2d 627, 92 S. Ct. 1965 (1972); see also Dalton v. Herrin, 2015 WL 1275302 (Ala. 2015)

If a club claimed by its members to be private is really a place of public entertainment, it will be subject to the Civil Rights Act, as Case Example 3-3 shows. The case also illustrates the unfortunate practice, which arose soon after passage of the Civil Rights Act, of groups forming "quickie private clubs" in an attempt to avoid serving blacks and other minorities.

CASE EXAMPLE 3-3

Daniel v. Paul

359 U.S. 298, 89 S.Ct. 1697, 23 L.Ed 2d 318 (1969)

Petitioners, Negro residents of Little Rock, Arkansas, brought this class action to enjoin respondent from denying them admission to a recreational facility called Lake Nixon Club owned and operated by respondent, Euell Paul, and his wife. The complaint alleged that Lake Nixon Club was a "public accommodation" subject to … the Civil Rights Act of 1964 … and that respondent violated the act in refusing petitioners admission solely on racial grounds. After trial, the District Court, although finding that respondent had refused petitioners admission solely because they were Negroes, dismissed the complaint on the ground that Lake Nixon Club was not within any of the [enumerated] "public accommodations" covered by the 1964 Act… .

Lake Nixon Club, located 12 miles west of Little Rock, is a 232-acre amusement area with swimming, boating, sunbathing, picnicking, miniature golf, dancing facilities, and a snack bar. The Pauls purchased the Lake Nixon site in 1962 and subsequently operated this amusement business there in a racially segregated manner.

… [T]he Civil Rights Act of 1964 enacted a sweeping prohibition of discrimination or segregation on the ground of race, color, religion, or national origin at places of public accommodation whose operations affect commerce. This prohibition does not extend to discrimination or segregation at private clubs. But, as both courts below properly found, Lake Nixon is not a private club. It is simply a business operated for a profit with none of the attributes of self-government and member-ownership traditionally associated with private clubs.

It is true that following enactment of the Civil Rights Act of 1964, the Pauls began to refer to the establishment as a private club. They even began to require patrons to pay a 25-cent "membership" fee, which gains a purchaser a "membership" card entitling him to enter the Club's premises for an entire season and, on payment of specified additional fees, to use the swimming, boating, and miniature golf facilities.

But this "membership" device seems no more than a subterfuge designed to avoid coverage of the 1964 Act. White persons are routinely provided "membership" cards, and some 100,000 whites visit the establishment each season. Negroes, on the other hand, are uniformly denied "membership" cards, and thus admission, because of the Pauls' fear that integration would "ruin the business". The conclusion of the courts below that Lake Nixon is not a private club is plainly correct—indeed, respondent does not challenge that conclusion here.

We, therefore, turn to the question whether Lake Nixon Club is "a place of public accommodation" as defined by … the 1964 Act, and, if so, whether its operations "affect commerce" within the meaning of … that Act.

Petitioners argue first that Lake Nixon's snack bar is a covered public accommodation … and that as such it brings the entire establishment within the coverage… . Clearly, the snack bar is "principally engaged in selling food for consumption on the premises." Thus, it is a covered public accommodation if "it serves or offers to serve interstate travelers or a substantial portion of the food which it serves … has moved in commerce." We find that the snack bar is a covered public accommodation under either of these standards.

The Pauls advertise the Lake Nixon Club in a monthly magazine called "Little Rock Today," which is distributed to guests at Little Rock hotels, motels, and restaurants, to acquaint them with available tourist attractions in the area. Regular advertisements for Lake Nixon were also broadcast over two area radio stations. In addition, Lake Nixon has advertised in the "Little Rock Air Force Base," a monthly newspaper. This choice of advertising media leaves no doubt that the Pauls were seeking broad-based patronage from an audience which they knew to include interstate travelers. Thus, the Lake Nixon Club unquestionably offered to serve out-of-state visitors to the Little Rock area. And it would be unrealistic to assume that none of the 100,000 patrons actually served by the Club each season was an interstate traveler. Since the Lake Nixon Club offered to serve and served out-of-state persons, and since the Club's snack bar was established to serve all patrons of the entire facility, we must conclude that the snack bar offered to serve and served out-of-state persons.

The record also demonstrates that a "substantial portion of the food" served by the Lake Nixon Club snack bar has moved in interstate commerce. The snack bar serves a limited fare—hot dogs and hamburgers on buns, soft drinks, and milk. The District Court took judicial notice of the fact that the "principal ingredients going into the bread were produced and processed in other States" and that "certain ingredients [of the soft drinks] were probably obtained … from out-of-State sources." … Thus, at the very least, three of the four food items sold at the snack bar contain ingredients originating outside of the State. There can be no serious doubt that a "substantial portion of the food" served at the snack bar has moved in interstate commerce.

The snack bar's status as a covered establishment automatically brings the entire Lake Nixon facility within the ambit of … [the] Civil Rights Act of 1964.

Petitioners also argue that the Lake Nixon Club is a covered public accommodation under [other provisions of the statute.] … These sections proscribe discrimination by "any motion picture house, theater, concert hall, sports arena, stadium or other place of exhibition or entertainment" which "customarily presents films, performances, athletic teams, exhibitions, or other sources of entertainment which move in commerce." Under any accepted definition of "entertainment," the Lake Nixon Club would surely qualify as a "place of entertainment." And indeed it advertises itself as such. Respondent argues, however, that … "place of entertainment" refers only to establishments where patrons are entertained as spectators or listeners rather than those where entertainment takes the form of direct participation in some sport or activity. We find no support in the legislative history for respondent's reading of the statute. The few indications of legislative intent are to the contrary... .

The remaining question is whether the operations of the Lake Nixon Club "affect commerce." ... We conclude that they do. Lake Nixon's customary "sources of entertainment ... move in commerce." The Club leases 15 paddle boats on a royalty basis from an Oklahoma company. Another boat was purchased from the same company. The Club's jukebox was manufactured outside Arkansas and plays records manufactured outside the state. The legislative history indicates that mechanical sources of entertainment such as these were considered by Congress to be "sources of entertainment" within the meaning of [the Act.]

Ruling of the Court: Reversed.

CASE QUESTIONS

1. Summarize the two separate grounds the court used to determine that Lake Nixon was a place of public accommodation and thus covered by the Act.

2. Can you think of any business within the hospitality/entertainment industry that is not covered by the Civil Rights Act?

Scrutinizing Admission Policies

Many cases involve clubs that claim to have sufficiently selective admission policies to qualify as a private club. In these cases the court will carefully review those policies to determine if in fact they are adequately selective.

In a Virginia case, a golf club was accused of violating the Civil Rights Act by ejecting a foursome because one golfer, who was invited to the club by a member, was black. The club defended on the ground that it was a private club and so could discriminate on the basis of race. The club's requirements for membership included

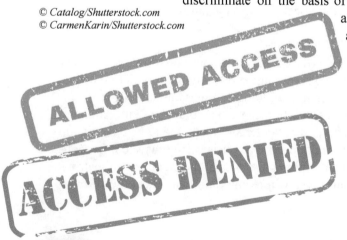

a $750 initiation fee, the signature of two members on a written application, and approval of the application by the club's board of directors. The club adopted a membership ceiling of 450. The club did not routinely investigate the background and character of its applicants, nor did it measure applicants against any moral, religious, or social standards. The evidence presented indicated that only four white applicants had been rejected in the previous 15 years. The court ruled that these admission procedures, while "official and formal," were not sufficiently selective to render the club private.

Said the court, "If only four white applicants have been denied membership [in the last 15 years], the club cannot fairly be described as truly selective about its members."[30]

Another case raised the issue of whether the Lions Club, a service organization with a worldwide membership of 313,000, was a private club. The application process for new members was as follows: They had to be sponsored by a current member; they were required to complete an application form; the club was supposed to investigate applicants' backgrounds thoroughly, but customarily no investigation was done; the board of directors then voted on the applicants; if approved by a majority of the board, applicants were asked to join. No proposed member had been rejected in 18 years. Noting that the screening process for new applicants was "cursory and operates to allow vast numbers of members," the court rejected the club's claim that it was private.[31]

A similar case involved the Jaycees, another service organization. The local chapter in question had 430 members. The club did not use any criteria for judging applicants for membership. New members were routinely admitted with no background inquiry. Not surprisingly, the court denied the club's claim that it was a private club. Said the court, "[T]he local chapters of the Jaycees are neither small nor selective."[32]

Unlike the service clubs, the Disabled American Veterans Association was found to be a private club notwithstanding a national membership that exceeds 1,000,000. One of its primary objectives is to advance the interests and work for the betterment of all wounded, injured, and disabled American veterans. It has national and regional offices that provide services to all veterans, whether or not disabled. While admission is restricted to individuals disabled in the line of duty during war time in service of the United States armed forces or its allies, entry is not otherwise subjected to review. The court weighed against the broad membership criteria and the large number of members the fact that the military experience that admits one to membership is "profoundly meaningful for almost all who go through it. It defines not simply an interest group, but a group for whom a very special social intimacy is possible. Encouragement of such intimacy is among the Disabled American Veterans Association's express purposes."[33]

Case Example 3-4 illustrates the application of the private club rules to a swimming club.

---

[30] *Brown v. Loudoun Golf & Country Club, Inc.,* 573 F.Supp. 399 (Va. 1983)
[31] *Rogers v. International Association of Lions Clubs,* 636 F.Supp. 1476 (Mich. 1986)
[32] *Roberts v. United States Jaycees,* 468 U.S. 609, 82 L.Ed.2d 462, 104 S.Ct 3244 (1984). For a similar holding, see also *Kiwanis International v. Ridgewood Kiwanis Club,* 627 F.Supp. 1381 (N.J. 1986)
[33] *Kreate v. Disabled American Veterans,* 33 S.W.3d 176 (Ky. 2000)

CASE EXAMPLE 3-4

U.S. v. Lansdowne Swim Club

894 F.2d 83 (3rd Cir. 1990)

The Lansdowne Swim Club (LSC) ... a nonprofit corporation, is the only group swimming facility in the Borough of Lansdowne, Pennsylvania. Since its founding in 1957, LSC has granted 1400 full family memberships. Every white applicant has been admitted, although two as limited members only. In that time, however, LSC has had only one nonwhite member.

The uncontroverted experiences of the following Lansdowne residents are significant. In 1976, the Allisons wrote to LSC requesting an application but LSC did not respond. Dr. Allison is black; his three children are part-black. In 1977, the Allisons twice again wrote for an application but LSC did not respond. The following year, the Allisons repeated the procedure with similar results. In 1983, the Allisons filed a timely application and otherwise qualified for membership but were rejected. The following year, the Ryans filed a timely application and otherwise qualified for membership. Nonetheless, they were rejected. Two of the Ryans' adopted children are black. The Ryans then complained to the media and picketed LSC, joined by the Allisons. In 1986, the Iverys, who are black, filed a timely application and otherwise qualified for membership. Nonetheless, they were rejected (as were the Ryans and Allisons who had again applied).

The United States alleges that LSC is a place of public accommodation ... which has engaged in a pattern or practice of discrimination by refusing membership to blacks because of their race or color, in violation of [the Civil Rights Act]... .

LSC's first argument is that it is a private club. Under [the Civil Rights Act], "a private club or other establishment not in fact open to the public" is exempt from the statute... . LSC has the burden of proving it is a private club... . Although the statute does not define "private club", cases construing the provision do offer some guidance. The district court distilled eight factors from the case law as relevant to this determination, three of which it found dispositive of LSC's public nature: the genuine selectivity of its membership process, its history, and use of its facilities by nonmembers. LSC disputes these findings.

First, the court concluded that LSC's membership process was not genuinely selective. Essential to this conclusion was the court's finding that "LSC possesses no objective criteria or standards for admission." The court identified four "criteria" for admission to LSC: being interviewed, completing an application, submitting two letters of recommendation and tendering payment of fees. We agree, and LSC apparently concedes, that these criteria were not genuinely selective. Nonetheless, LSC challenges the court's failure to consider membership approval a criterion for admission.

... [A] formal procedure requiring nothing more than membership approval is insufficient to show genuine selectivity... . In addition, LSC stipulated that the only information given to the members prior to the membership vote is the applicants' names, addresses, their children's names and ages, and the recommenders' identities. In such a situation, the court was correct to conclude that LSC "provides no information to voting members that is useful in making an informed decision as to whether the applicant and his or her family would be compatible with the existing members." Therefore, even if membership approval were considered a fifth criterion, it would not make the process any more genuinely selective in this case.

The district court also found the yields of the membership process indicative of lack of selectivity. Since 1958, LSC has granted full memberships to at least 1,400 families while denying them to only two non-black families. LSC contends that emphasizing the few instances of non-black applicant rejection "misconstru[es] the significance of selectivity. The crucial question should be whether the members exercised their right to be selective rather than the statistical results of the exercise of that right."… [F]ormal membership requirements have little meaning when in fact the club does not follow a selective membership policy… . We find the evidence of lack of selectivity convincing.

CASE QUESTION

1. What would the club need to do differently to qualify as a private club?

The Americans with Disabilities Act (ADA) will be discussed in the next section of this chapter. For our purposes here, know that the ADA outlaws discrimination in places of public accommodation against people with disabilities. Like the Civil Rights Act, the ADA includes an exemption for private clubs.

In Case Example 3-5, a mobile home park was sued for violations of the ADA relating to use of the park's clubhouse. The park claimed the building was private. The decision provides further insights on what makes a club private.

CASE EXAMPLE 3-5

Kalani v. Castle Village, LLC

14 F.Supp.3d 1359 (Calif., 2014).

Plaintiff is a wheelchair-bound resident of a mobile home park. He sues defendants under the Americans with Disabilities Act ("ADA") prohibiting discrimination based on disability in "public accommodations". Plaintiff names the clubhouse and its restroom, the sales and rental office located in the Clubhouse, and the parking lot serving the office and the Clubhouse, as non-accessible, public facilities. The parties cross-move for summary judgment. . . .

There is an Activities Committee, comprised of park residents, that plans, advertises and puts on various activities in the park. . . The Activities Committee conducted Bingo games in the Clubhouse, they were open to the general public. The Activities Committee publicly advertised the games to the general public, leaving flyers at a Senior Center, the local market and the pharmacy. In addition, a large A-frame sign was posted on the sidewalk at the entrance to the park advertising the Bingo games and inviting members of the public to attend.

The Clubhouse and its restroom were used by the public for craft sales, which was an activity that accompanied the community's twice-yearly yard sale. The yard and craft sale was run by the Activities Committee, which publicly advertises the yard sale in newspapers and as inserts to the city's water bills. The yard and craft sales were well attended by the public. During the yard sales, the public is permitted to use the restroom in the club house.

Plaintiff uses the Clubhouse to pay rent, play bingo, play cards and talk to others. . . .

The sales and rental office located in the Clubhouse was open to members of the general public who would go to the Clubhouse and to the sales and rental office to discuss buying a home or renting a space in the park. . . .

While attempting to use the "accessible" parking space, Kalani experienced difficulty transferring to his wheelchair. The parking space had excessive slope, which threatened to tip the wheelchair over, and insufficient room, which made it difficult to maneuver.

When plaintiff Kalani used the restroom in the Clubhouse, he found that there were not proper wheelchair clearances under the sink, so that he found it very difficult to use the sink. . .

Plaintiff alleges that he was denied the full and equal enjoyment of the Clubhouse and its restroom, the sales and rental office (located inside the Clubhouse), and the parking lot serving the Clubhouse and the office. . . .

Defendants assert that the mobile home park is not a public accommodation. Plaintiff does not dispute the point, because plaintiff does not assert that the mobile home park itself is a public accommodation. Rather, plaintiff asserts that the enumerated facilities physically located within the mobile home park – the Clubhouse and its restroom, the rental and sales office and the parking lot – are public accommodations, and must comply with [anti-discrimination laws].

Each is plainly included in that definition, given the undisputed facts of this case.

The Clubhouse, according to the undisputed evidence, was publicly advertised as a place for the general public to come and play Bingo. Further, the ADA includes within the definition of public accommodations: "an auditorium, convention center, lecture hall *or other place of public gathering.*" . . .

Neither the ADA nor the Civil Rights Act of 1964 defines what a "private club" is. However, an irreducible minimum is that the establishment not be open to the public at large. . . .

While the Clubhouse has "members," defendants have offered no evidence that a membership board grants or refuses membership or that the membership has any control over the Clubhouse or any ownership of it, two attributes traditionally associated with private clubs. Indeed, defendants' own evidence shows that the "members" have no control over the Clubhouse. . . .

In addition, it is undisputed that the Clubhouse housed the rental and sales office. The general public therefore were invited to come into the Clubhouse so that they could get to the rental and sales office. . . .

Plaintiff's injury is that he is being denied the full and equal enjoyment of the clubhouse and its restroom, the rental office (located inside the clubhouse), and the parking lot serving the clubhouse and the office. He has produced evidence of a defective ramp, non-compliant parking, a non-compliant restroom in the Clubhouse, all of which he personally encountered, and a laundry list of other ADA violations. . . .

In conclusion, the Clubhouse and restroom, the sales and leasing office and the parking lot – including the ramp to the Clubhouse and the accessible parking space – were operated as public accommodations. The Clubhouse is not, and never was, exempt from the ADA as a "private club."

Extending Civil Rights Protection

The Act represented a major step forward in this country's attempt to eliminate discrimination. As we have seen, however, the classes of people protected and the types of facilities covered are limited. Other federal, state, and local laws help to fill the gaps.

State Civil Rights Laws

Virtually every state has a civil rights law that, in part, duplicates the Act and, in part, expands its coverage. The differences are as follows.

Coverage

The state laws include within their coverage businesses that are purely intrastate in nature—that is, businesses not involved in interstate commerce. Remember, the Civil Rights Act of 1964 applies only to businesses engaged in interstate commerce.

Covered Facilities Expanded

Whereas the Act applies only to lodging facilities, dining facilities, gasoline stations, and "places of entertainment," most state laws encompass a large number of additional "places of public accommodation." These include bars, stores, clinics, hospitals, barber and beauty shops, libraries, schools, colleges, public halls, public elevators, public institutions for the care of neglected or delinquent children, parking garages, and public transportation.

Thus, if a store refused to sell merchandise to customers because they were Buddhist, Chinese, Hispanic, or black, the store would be in violation of the state (but not federal) civil rights act. However, where a store displayed novelties for sale that demeaned people of Polish extraction, the state civil rights act was not implicated. Said the court, "The novelty items, although offensive and in poor taste, were not communications to the effect that any of the accommodations, advantages, facilities, and privileges of the shop would be refused, withheld from or denied to any person on account of national origin."[34]

---

34 *State Division of Human Rights v. McHarris Gift Center,* 419 N.Y.S.2d 405 (N.Y. 1979)

Protected Classes Increased

As we studied, the protected classes in the Act were originally race, color, religion, and national origin. The state statutes customarily expand the categories of protected classes and frequently include gender, marital status, and disability. Some statutes and local government ordinances also outlaw discrimination on the basis of sexual orientation, thereby protecting lesbians and homosexual men. Transgendered people are protected in several states and dozens of localities. These numbers are growing.

Advertisements

Many state statutes prohibit advertisements that contain statements or suggestions, whether express or implied, that accommodations will be denied because of a protected characteristic, such as race, religion, or gender.

This issue arose in a 1974 New York State case in which female plaintiffs objected to the name and exterior sign of a bar because it implied women would not be served. The objectionable name was "Silent Woman Tavern" and the exterior sign depicted a headless woman. The owner conceded that the sign and name were intended to attract male patrons. The court refused to require the bar to remove the sign or change its name, and said,

> *The law does not prohibit appealing by signs or trade name to one sex or another. Rather, the prohibition is against displaying notice or advertisement to the effect that any of the facilities or privileges will be refused or withheld from or denied a person on account of sex... . There is nothing about the name or the exterior sign, in the form used here, that would suggest that women would be refused the use of the facilities.*[35]

Remedies

Under the Act, which is a federal law, remedies are limited and include primarily injunctive relief and attorney's fees. The state remedies are more expansive. One important redress available for violation of many state civil rights laws is damages (money), so an establishment that wrongfully denies services may be liable to pay money to the would-be patron. In addition, violation of many state civil rights laws is deemed a crime, which can result in jail and fines.

Americans with Disabilities Act
Laws that protect the rights and privileges of individuals including equal protection, right against unreasonable searches and seizures, due process, and many more.

The Americans with Disabilities Act

The **Americans with Disabilities Act** (hereinafter "Disabilities Act"),[36] a federal law passed by Congress in 1991, is a far-reaching commitment to the rights of the disabled. Its purpose is "(1) to provide a clear and comprehensive national mandate for the elimination of discrimination against individuals with disabilities; and

---

[35] *Rosenberg v. State Human Rights Appeal Board*, 45 A.D. 2d 29, 357 N.Y.S.2d 325 (N.Y. 1974)
[36] 42 U.S.C. § 12101

(2) to provide clear, strong, consistent, and enforceable standards addressing discrimination against individuals with disabilities."

The Disabilities Act prohibits places of public accommodation from discriminating against individuals on the basis of disability. The statute's definition of "places of public accommodation" is significantly broader than that in the Civil Rights Act of 1964. In addition to the hotels, restaurants, places of entertainment, and service stations covered by the latter Act, the Disabilities Act applies to bars, stores, service establishments such as barber and beauty shops, laundromats, banks, public transportation, and schools and colleges. Also covered are cruise ships including those operated under foreign flags (registered in a country other than the United States) but located in U.S. waters.[376]

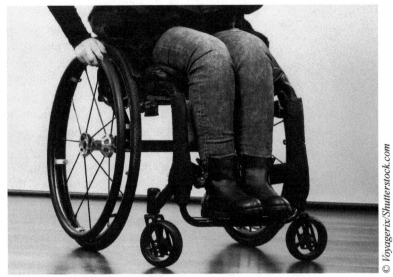

© Voyagerix/Shutterstock.com

The Disability Act defines "discrimination" as including a failure to make reasonable modifications in policies, practices, or procedures when such modifications are necessary to provide goods, services, or accommodations to disabled people. Thus the Disabilities Act requires establishments to adjust their policies and adapt their practices, within limits, to the needs of their handicapped clientele. When determining whether a specific modification is reasonable, and therefore required, courts consider the cost of the action needed, the overall financial resources of the facility, the effect on expenses and resources, the size of the business, and the type of operation.[38]

"Disabled" is defined as "a physical or mental impairment that substantially limits one or more of the major life activities of [the disabled person]." A "major life activity" refers to an activity of central importance to most people's daily lives and includes conduct such as walking, seeing, hearing, speaking, breathing, working, or caring for oneself.[39] For example, a person who uses a wheelchair or prosthetic limb may be mobile but still disabled because of a substantial limitation on the ability to walk or run.

The Disabilities Act does not apply to private clubs, which are defined in the same manner as under the Civil Rights Act of 1964.

Integrated Settings

A goal of the Disability Act is to ensure that goods, services, and facilities are provided to disabled persons in the most integrated setting possible. Thus, a restaurant

---

37 *Spector v. Norwegian Cruise Line, Ltd.,* 545 US 119, 162 L.Ed.2d 971, 125 S.Ct. 2169 (2005). Note: If, by removing barriers to enable use of the facilities by disabled passengers, the vessel fails to comply with international law relevant to safety at sea, the Disabilities Act would not apply.
38 42 USCA § 1218(9); *Wilson v. Pier I Imports,* 2006 WL 947709 (Ca. 2006)
39 42 USC § 12102(2)(A); CFR 1630.2(j); *Hubbard v. Rite Aid Corp.,* 439 F.Supp.2d 1054 (Calif. 2006); *Toyota Motors Mfg., Inc. v. Williams,* 534 US 184, 151 L.Ed.2d 615, 122 S.Ct. 681 (2002); *LaBrecque v. Sodexho,* 287 F.Supp.2d 100 (Mass, 2003)

cannot place all wheelchair-accessible tables in an isolated corner of the dining room. Instead, they must be placed throughout the dining area. Similarly, a resort that offers exercise classes could not require a wheelchair-bound patron to attend a separate class for the disabled. Instead, that guest must be permitted to join the class offered to able-bodied patrons.[40] In one case, plaintiffs complained that only six of nine poolside cabanas at a casino were accessible by wheelchair. All nine had similar amenities. On this claim the court held for the casino, noting that not all facilities in a place of public accommodation need to be accessible.[41]

In another example, a court held that not all seats at a stadium are required to accommodate wheelchairs. However, those that do must be interspersed throughout the facility. A sports arena with 33 wheelchair seats violated the Disabilities Act by locating all 33 on the same level. The Disabilities Act requires that disabled seating be dispersed throughout the stadium.[42]

Mandates Not Permitted for Disabled Guests Only

The Disabilities Act is violated if the provision of services to people with disabilities is conditional upon requirements that are not imposed on others. For example, a restaurant that requires patrons in wheelchairs to be chaperoned by a companion but seats single, able-bodied customers violates the Disabilities Act.

Modifying Rules to Accommodate the Disabled

Where the policies or practices of a place of public accommodation have the effect of discriminating against people with disabilities, the place of public accommodation must change its policies or practices unless the modification would fundamentally alter the nature of the goods or services provided. For example, a place of public accommodation may have a rule prohibiting pets, but must modify that rule by permitting entrance to a service dog.

Several cases addressed the issues associated with guide dogs for blind customers. In the first, a brewery that provided public tours of its facilities but refused to permit a guide dog to accompany a blind patron violated the Disabilities Act. Allowing the animal to accompany its owner would not fundamentally alter the nature of the brewery tour nor jeopardize safety of others.[43] Another case was based on a restaurant's refusal to allow a service dog inside. The parties settled the case with the restaurant agreeing to give full and equal access to blind people and their guide dogs, and to post the new policy conspicuously throughout the establishment. Additionally, the eatery consented to insert the statement into its policy manual for all the restaurant's employees, agents, and representatives.[44] A third case involved a Days Inn that refused to provide accommodations to a legally blind traveler with a

---

[40] *Long v. Coast Resorts, Inc.,* 32 F.Supp. 2d 1203 (Nev. 1999)
[41] *Long v. Coast Resorts, Inc.,* 267 F.3d 918 (Nev. 2001)
[42] *Independent Living Resources v. Oregon Arena Corporation,* 982 F.Supp. 698 (Or. 1997), supp'd by 1 F. Supp.2d 1159 (Ore. 1988)
[43] *Johnson v. Spoetzel Brewery,* 116 F.3d 1052 (Tex. 1997)
[44] *Fisher v. Cedar Creek Inn,* 214 F.3d 1115 (Calif. 2000)

service dog because of a no-pets policy. The court held such refusal constituted a violation of the motel's legal duty to accommodate disabled guests.[45]

A service animal is a dog that is trained to perform tasks for a person with a disability. Some but not all service animals wear special collars and harnesses. If a business is unsure that an animal qualifies as a service dog, two questions are permissible: Is this a service animal required because of a disability? and What tasks does the animal perform? The business cannot ask for documentation or certification that it is a service animal because there exists no state or national certifications.

If a dog's role as a service animal is not sufficiently proven by its owner, a hotel's refusal to provide a room or other service is not illegal discrimination.[46]

A service animal can be excluded from a facility if the animal's behavior presents a direct threat to the health or safety of others. So if the dog displays hostile behavior, it can be excluded, its status as a service dog notwithstanding.

Another modification applies to bars that have a rule requiring a customer ordering a drink to present a driver's license as proof of age. To accommodate persons with disabilities that prevent them from driving, the bar must modify the rule to accept an alternative form of identification.

Some businesses offer as an accommodation an employee who meets and assists disabled passengers to negotiate barriers. However, some courts have found this type of accommodation to be insufficient.[47]

Case Example 3-6 illustrates another circumstance that may require changes to a facility's policies.

---

[45] *Amick v. BN + KM, Inc.* 275 F.Supp. 2d 1378 (Ga. 2003)
[46] *Clavon, III v. Roscoe BK Restaurant, Inc.,* 572 Fed. Appx. 487 (Calif. 2014).
[47] *Schlesinger v. Belle of Orleans, LLC,* 2015 WL 5944452 (La., 2015).

CASE EXAMPLE 3-6

Rodriguez v. Barrita, Inc.

10 F.Supp.3d 1062 (Calif., 2014)

Plaintiff Armando Rodriguez has been physically disabled since 2006, when a car accident left him paralyzed from the waist down. Due to his paraplegia, Rodriguez uses a wheelchair for mobility.

Defendant Barrita, Inc., is the owner of the La Victoria Taqueria, a restaurant in San Jose, California. . . .

In November, 2008, Rodriguez visited La Victoria after attending a doctor's appointment in San Jose. He wanted to visit La Victoria because he remembered enjoying the restaurant prior to his accident. When Rodriguez and his brother-in-law Carlos Tovar pulled up to the restaurant, Rodriguez noticed that there was a stairway leading up to the front entrance. He further observed that there was no lift or ramp for persons in wheelchairs. Tovar went inside to see if there was an alternate entrance. At trial, Tovar testified that, while inside, he used La Victoria's restroom which he observed to be too small for an individual in a wheelchair.

Tovar returned to the car, where he informed Rodriguez that there was no alternate entrance. He also told Rodriguez that even if he could get inside, the restroom would be too small for him to use. Based on this information, Rodriguez decided to go home. He was deterred by the restaurant's barriers to access. Rodriguez persuasively testified that the experience made him feel sad, angry and frustrated. . . .

Rodriguez asserts a claim under the ADA, alleging defendants discriminated against him during his 2008 visit to La Victoria. The parties do not dispute that Rodriguez is disabled within the meaning of the statute, nor do they contest whether defendants must comply with the ADA. . . .

I. Restroom Door Barriers

La Victoria's restroom entrance poses two actionable barriers: inadequate strike-edge clearance on both the "push" and "pull" sides of the restroom door. As a result of these related barriers, individuals in wheelchairs are left with insufficient maneuvering space to open and close the door when exiting or entering the bathroom. The building, however, lacks sufficient physical space to permit defendant to bring the door's strike-edge clearance into full compliance with applicable guidelines. Due to the layout of the restaurant's interior walls and the placement of a stairway leading to the second floor, defendants cannot feasibly create adequate maneuvering space on either side of the restroom door.

Recognizing that full compliance is unworkable, Rodriguez contends that defendants must instead install an automatic door opener. Defendants reject this suggestion . . . Installation of an automatic door opener may be easily accomplished and can be carried out with minimal difficulty or expense. While such a device would not change the actual strike-edge clearance on the bathroom door, experts for both plaintiff and defendant agree that it would directly remediate the problems posed by those barriers. Defendants failed to prove that installation of an automatic door opener was not readily achievable. Accordingly, defendants violated the ADA by failing to address the restroom entrance barrier.

II. Inaccessible Entrance

La Victoria lacks an accessible entrance for individuals in wheelchairs. Rodriguez argues that removal of this significant barrier is readily achievable. Specifically, he contends that defendants could readily install a wheelchair lift at the restaurant's entrance. . . . defendants maintain that installing any lift at the entrance would simply be too burdensome and extensive of an undertaking to qualify as "readily achievable." . . .

Applicable law compels the conclusion that installation of a wheelchair lift at La Victoria is not readily achievable. As the ADA makes clear, existing, non-altered facilities only need to remove barriers where removal can be carried out without much difficulty or expense. The types of modest measures that must be taken, per the ADA Architectural Guidelines, include: installing ramps; . . . repositioning shelves; rearranging tables, chairs, vending machines, display racks, and other furniture; repositioning telephones; installing flashing alarm lights; widening doors; . . .eliminating a turnstile; installing accessible door hardware; installing grab bars in toilet stall; rearranging toilet partitions to increase maneuvering space; installing a full-length bathroom mirror; repositioning the paper towel dispenser in a bathroom; creating designated parking spaces; removing high pile, low density carpeting; or installing vehicle hand controls.

While this list is plainly non-exhaustive, none of its examples come close to the extensive construction required to build and provide an accessible path to a wheelchair lift at the entrance to La Victoria. . . .Moreover, while defendants concede that they could afford to build a wheelchair lift if required to do so, their admission does not alter the ADA's fundamental command that barrier removal is readily achievable only where it is easily accomplishable and able to be carried out without much difficulty or expense. The evidence makes clear that the proposed wheelchair lift does not meet this standard. Accordingly, under the ADA defendants are not required to remove the barrier posed by the restaurant's inaccessible entrance.

They are not, however off the hook with respect to this barrier. An entity must provide alternative methods if such methods are readily achievable. . . . The Department of Justice has explicitly recognized that offering curbside service is the sort of measure that can satisfy an existing facility's "alternative method" obligations under the statute. Here, however, the evidence does not demonstrate that La Victoria actually offers such a service. While testimony established that La Victoria provides curbside service to its patrons, the testimony did not indicate that the restaurant offers the service in a manner that is sufficiently consistent and reliable to constitute an "alternative method" under the statute. La Victoria does little to advertise the service at the restaurant or on its website. Further, the restaurant's phone number is not displayed near the sidewalk for wheel-chair bound patrons to see. Further, plaintiff persuasively testified that he was unable to place an order successfully for curbside service during a visit in 2007.

In sum, while installation of a wheelchair lift is not "readily achievable" under the terms of the ADA, defendants nonetheless violated that statute by failing to make La Victoria's cuisine available through the readily achievable alternative method of providing curbside service. Accordingly, Rodriguez is entitled to injunctive relief to ensure that defendants make their goods and services available to disabled patrons.

CASE QUESTION

1. Why does the law limit remediation to those efforts that are readily achievable?

2. How must the restaurant modify its take-out services to satisfy the Americans with Disabilities Act?

In a case against the Professional Golf Association Tours (PGA), the plaintiff was a talented golfer who qualified for tournaments. He had a degenerative circulatory disorder that prevented him from walking golf courses. The PGA sought to enforce its rule requiring competitors to walk the course. The player sought an accommodation enabling him to use a golf cart during tournaments. The PGA claimed that allowing a golfer to ride a cart fundamentally altered the nature of a PGA competition. The court rejected this argument noting that the essence of golf is shot-making, not walking. In response to the PGA's concern that walking induces fatigue, thus giving a rider an unfair advantage, the court concluded that the evidence presented established that "fatigue from walking during a tournament cannot be deemed significant." The PGA was thus required to permit the plaintiff to use a cart.[48]

If an accommodation would alter the essential nature of a business, the accommodation is not required. For example, a nightclub that regularly hosts live bands is not required to dispense with the music to accommodate a hearing-impaired patron who cannot hear his companions talk with the loud background music. Likewise, a fitness club was not required to modify the rules of tournament racquetball to permit a wheelchair player to participate. The disabled player's request to allow two bounces rather than just one would substantially alter the fundamental character of the game.

Providing Auxiliary Aids and Alternative Services

To accommodate disabled individuals, the Disabilities Act requires places of public accommodation to provide auxiliary aids and services where necessary, unless such aids or services would fundamentally alter the nature of the goods or services offered, or would result in an undue burden. For example, while a restaurant is not required to provide Braille menus for blind patrons, it will be required to provide someone to read the non-Braille menu to a visually impaired diner. Other examples include a hotel providing a hearing-impaired guest with a flashing-light device to denote emergencies, since an alarm would not be heard, and an alarm-clock mechanism that causes the bed to vibrate at a designated waking time.

---

[48] *PGA Tour, Inc. v. Martin,* 532 U.S. 661, 149 L.Ed.2d 904, 661 121 S.Ct. 1879 (2001)

Structural Modifications for Existing Buildings

The Disabilities Act contains requirements concerning accessibility of facilities. Structural obstacles often preclude access by disabled persons to buildings open to the public. For example, a second floor reachable only by steps is not available to a person in a wheelchair. Blind persons may be unable to use an elevator because they cannot determine which button to push. The requirements to remove obstacles vary depending on whether the inaccessible building is an existing one, an existing one that is being altered, or a new one under construction.

For existing buildings not undergoing renovations, the Disabilities Act requires places of public accommodation to undertake the removal of barriers if doing so is "readily achievable." **Readily achievable** is defined as "easily accomplished without much difficulty or expense." When drafting the Disabilities Act, Congress sought to protect the business community from incurring undue costs. Examples of barrier removal that are considered readily achievable include:

readily achievable
Easily accomplishable without great difficulty or expense.

- Ramping a few steps (such as those in the entryway of a building or leading to a sunken area of a dining room in a restaurant)

- Lowering telephones

- Adding raised letters and Braille markings on elevator control buttons

- Adding grab bars in bathrooms, provided only routine reinforcement of the wall is required

- Rearranging tables in a restaurant to permit wheelchair passage

© Pressmaster/Shutterstock.com

- Properly designating handicapped-accessible parking spaces

- Replacing door handles that are not easy to grasp with one hand or that require tight grasping or twisting of the wrist to operate

- Performing similar modest corrections

Where removal of a barrier is readily achievable, failure to remove it constitutes illegal discrimination. In one case a disabled patron was unable to open the entrance door of a store because of its difficult-to-use mechanism. The customer was able to gain access only with the aid of another patron who assisted in opening the door. The facility claimed that the design of the door was not a barrier because the plaintiff was able to gain access. Said the court, "This is exactly the sort of situation the [Disabilities Act] seeks to prevent: the need for a disabled person to rely upon the help of more able-bodied persons in order to go about day-to-day activities." If, however, the removal of the barrier is not readily achievable, its continued presence does not violate the Disabilities Act. For example, installation of an elevator for access to a second floor would be quite costly and would therefore not be required for existing buildings.

Case Example 3-7 illustrates the significant detail required for a plaintiff to prove that a requested barrier removal is readily achievable.

CASE EXAMPLE 3-7

John Rodgers v. Chevys Restaurants, LLC

2015 WL 909763 (Calif, 2015)

Plaintiff is a paraplegic who requires the use of a wheelchair. Plaintiff asserts that he visited the Chevy's Restaurant located in Richmond, California, on three occasions. Rodgers alleges that he encountered the following barriers during his visits: (1) lack of compliant path of travel that placed him in danger of cars backing out of parking spaces; (2) a narrow ramp with gaps and cracks that make it difficult for him to move forward and placed him in danger of losing his balance and injuring himself; (3) an uphill incline by the entrance that extended approximately 15 to 20 feet from the door to the curb, which placed him in danger of rolling off the curb; and (4) a heavy door, noncompliant tables, narrow aisles, a slope in front of the urinal, and a heavy restroom door. . . .

Plaintiff filed suit alleging that certain architectural barriers to access exist at the Chevy's Restaurant. . . .

Existing facilities must remove architectural barriers to access only where such removal is 'readily achievable'. The term 'readily achievable' means easily accomplished and able to be carried out without much difficulty or expense. The factors to be considered in determining whether an action is readily achievable include: "(A) the nature and cost of the action; (B) the overall financial resources of the facility involved in the action; the number of persons employed at such facility; the effect on expenses and resources, or the impact otherwise of such action upon the operation of the facility; (C) the overall financial resources of the covered entity; the overall size of the business of a covered entity with respect to the number of its employees; the number, type, and location of its facilities; and (D) the type of operation or operations of the covered entity, including the composition, structure, and functions of the workforce of such entity; the geographic separateness, administrative or fiscal relationship of the facility or facilities in question to the covered entity." . . . .

Plaintiff bears the initial burden of production to present evidence that a suggested method of barrier removal is readily achievable. If the plaintiff makes this showing, the burden shifts to the defendant, who bears the ultimate burden of persuasion regarding his affirmative defense that a suggested method of barrier removal is not readily achievable.

Here, plaintiff argues that: (1) there are two abrupt vertical changes on the exterior accessible route that could be filled with concrete; (2) there is no directional or informational signage along the exterior route of travel, which could be corrected by installing directional signage; (3) there is no telephone number or address posted on the tow-away sign, which could be corrected by adding this information; (4) the main customer entry/exit doors, the customer entry/exit doors to the lower seating area, and the new ADA entrance door closes in less than three seconds, which could be corrected by adjusting their pressure; (5) there is a lack of accessible seating, which could be corrected by rearranging the seating areas; and (6) less than 5% of the left and lower seating areas are accessible, which could be corrected by adding ADA compliant tables. . . .

Plaintiff has failed to meet his initial burden of production to present evidence that a suggested method of barrier removal is readily achievable. . . . Regarding these six barriers, Plaintiff fails to provide any evidence or argument concerning each of the factors that must be taken into account when determining whether removal of the barrier is readily achievable. Plaintiff has not offered any evidence on the potential cost of removing any of the identified barriers, or the impact on the restaurant's operations. . . .

Accordingly, Plaintiff has failed to establish a violation of the Disabilities Act.

CASE QUESTIONS

1. What information should the plaintiff have provided to the Court regarding whether barrier removal was readily achievable by the defendants?

Structural Requirements During Construction

The Disabilities Act does not mandate that facilities undertake major alterations or new construction. However new facilities and buildings undergoing renovation must be constructed in such a way that they can be approached, entered, and utilized easily and conveniently by people with disabilities. New construction and alterations must comply with the Disabilities Act's accessibility guidelines. These regulations contain technical standards for most aspects of a building, including entryways, door sizes, layout, bathroom construction, and more. If, however, the cost to make the new or altered building accessible would be disproportionate to the overall cost and scope of the alteration or construction, alternative methods can be pursued. The necessity of barrier removal imposed when making alterations is not triggered by minor repairs such as painting or wallpapering; more extensive remodeling is required.

For a new hotel, the Disabilities Act requires the following: All doors and doorways must be designed to allow passage by a wheelchair; bathrooms need to be sufficiently wide to allow use by people in wheelchairs; a percentage of each class of hotel rooms must be fully accessible, including grab bars in the bathroom and at the toilet; audio loops are required in meeting areas; emergency flashing lights or alarms are needed in hotel guest rooms; Braille or raised-letter words and numbers are required on elevators and signs; and handrails must be installed on stairs and ramps.

The Department of Justice (DOJ), which enforces the Disabilities Act, received many complaints from guests who reserved an accessible room but on check-in the room was either not available or not accessible. Therefore, the DOJ developed regulations requiring that reserved accessible rooms be blocked and removed from all reservation systems so they will remain available for disabled guests. If a per-

son with a disability needing a fully accessible room makes a reservation without informing the hotel of the need for such a room and, when the person arrives, an accessible room is not available, the hotel has not violated the Disabilities Act. While the hotel must make an effort to provide disabled persons accessible rooms, it can rent those rooms to nondisabled persons if an identified disabled person has not sought a reservation and other rooms are occupied.

Transportation and Telecommunications

The Disabilities Act also requires that businesses offering transportation attempt to make their facilities accessible to the disabled. A hotel that provides a hospitality van must remove barriers to its use provided removal is readily achievable.

The Disabilities Act also requires that companies offering telephone service provide telecommunication devices for the deaf that will permit a hearing-impaired person to communicate with anyone in this country who has a telephone.

Legal Action Directed at Noncompliance

Two types of lawsuits can be brought under the Disabilities Act for noncompliance. One is a private action by individuals and the other is a lawsuit by the Department of Justice, a division of the federal government headed by the Attorney General.

A private lawsuit can be brought by a disabled person who is subjected to discrimination on the basis of disability or who has reason to believe that he is about to be subjected to discrimination. For example, construction of a new hotel is being planned, but the specifications are not in compliance with the Disabilities Act. Remedies for a private lawsuit include an injunction requiring compliance with the Disabilities Act, a court order requiring alteration of facilities to comply with the Disabilities Act, or a court order requiring an auxiliary aide or service be provided, a policy be modified, or an alternate method of barrier removal be undertaken. Money as a remedy to compensate a plaintiff for any losses or for inconvenience or humiliation is not recoverable in a private suit. A successful plaintiff can, however, collect attorney's fees plus litigation expenses and costs (such as expert witness fees and court filing fees).

The second type of lawsuit can be brought only by the U.S. Attorney General, the head of the Department of Justice and the chief law-enforcement officer of the country. This type of action is pursued against a violator where a pattern or practice of discrimination exists or where the discrimination raises an issue of general public importance (where the discrimination impacts many people). In addition to the remedies available in a private action, a court in a case brought by the Attorney General may award monetary damages. Punitive damages cannot be awarded, although a court may assess a civil penalty not exceeding $50,000 for the first violation and not exceeding $100,000 for any subsequent violation. Like the Civil Rights Act of 1964, the Disabilities Act withstood constitutional challenge early in its history. Just as the courts in the *Heart of Atlanta Motel* and *Ollie's Barbecue* up-

held the Civil Rights Act, a court rejected claims by the House of Pancakes that the Disabilities Act was unconstitutional.

The court rebuffed the restaurant's claim that it was not engaged in interstate commerce, noting that the restaurant was located within two miles of two interstate highways, and within walking distance of three hotels. The court likewise repudiated the Pancake House's claim that the term *readily achievable*, used as the standard for determining when a modification must be made, was too vague to guide those bound by the Disabilities Act. The court commented that the statute provides direction by listing examples of what qualifies as readily achievable—including rearranging tables and chairs, installing small ramps, and installing grab bars in restrooms. Further, federal regulations explaining the statute clarify the term.

The Pancake House also claimed that the phrase *most integrated setting appropriate*, used by the statute to describe the goal for accommodating disabled patrons, was too vague to be enforceable. The court rejected this assertion as well, noting that the statute contains two pages of examples and explanations, and thus was sufficiently clear.[49]

Case Example 3-8 highlights the Disabilities Act's requirement that restaurants make readily achievable modifications to enable disabled patrons to utilize the establishment's facilities, including the bathrooms. Note the Court's concern with the "quality of access."

CASE EXAMPLE 3-8

Boemio v. Love's Restaurant

954 F.Supp. 204 (Cal. 1997)

This is an action based upon claims of discriminatory practices by a public accommodation...

The allegations surround Mr. Boemio's visit to the Love's Restaurant in San Diego on or about April 19, 1996. Plaintiff suffers from a medical condition which requires that he use a motorized wheelchair. On the date in question, Plaintiff attempted to use the restrooms at the premises owned and operated by Defendant and alleges that he was unable to do so because the restrooms were inaccessible

---

[49] *Pinnock v. International House of Pancakes Franchise,* 844 F.Supp. 574 (Calif. 1993)

to wheelchair users. As a result of the inaccessibility, Plaintiff alleges that he was forced to urinate in the restaurant parking lot... .

The issues at trial were whether Plaintiff could access the bathroom facilities at the premises ... Having heard the oral testimony produced by the parties, and the argument of counsel, and after reviewing the documentary evidence, the Court now makes the following findings.

1. On or about April 19, 1996 Defendant, Love's Restaurant, operated the restaurant facility in San Diego.
2. On or about April 19, 1996, Defendant's restaurant was a public accommodation as contemplated by law and required to be accessible to physically handicapped persons.
3. On or about April 19, 1996 Plaintiff, Ralph Boemio, was lawfully on the premises of Defendant's restaurant.
4. Plaintiff, Ralph Boemio, is a qualified handicapped individual as provided in the relevant sections of the Americans with Disabilities Act.
5. Plaintiff, Ralph Boemio, suffers from a medical condition which requires that he use a motorized wheelchair.
6. On or about April 19, 1996, while on Defendant's premises, Plaintiff, Ralph Boemio, attempted to use the restroom facilities, but was unable to do so because the restrooms were inaccessible to him.
7. The men's restroom at Love's Restaurant was totally inaccessible to wheelchair patrons.
8. The ladies' restroom was historically used by some disabled individuals with assistance from the restaurant staff.
9. The ladies' restroom entry door from the corridor provided a clear opening of 28 and 1/2 inches and the door from the foyer to the toilet area provided a clear opening of 28 inches, both in violation of the ADA Accessibility Guidelines (32 inches required).
10. The doorway size and configuration and layout of the corridor to the restroom prevented reasonable access to the restroom facilities on Defendant's premises.
11. As a result of the inaccessibility, Plaintiff Ralph Boemio had to urinate in the parking lot.
12. Plaintiff, Ralph Boemio, suffered actual damages in the form of mental anguish and humiliation as a result of the discrimination associated with the inaccessible bathrooms on Defendant's facility.
13. Plaintiff's actions in the parking lot were unwitnessed by third parties and unaccompanied by any mishap, injury, physical harm or property damage.

The ADA [Americans with Disabilities Act] prohibits discrimination against any individual "on the basis of disability in the full and equal enjoyment of goods, services, facilities, privileges, advantages or accommodations of any place of public accommodation by any person who owns leases or operates a place of public accommodation." A restaurant is clearly a public accommodation under the ADA... .

The remedies for an ADA violation include injunctive relief and attorney's fees. Monetary damages are not recoverable by private Plaintiffs under the ADA... .

Based upon the Findings of Fact previously set forth, it is clear that Plaintiff, as a qualified individual, has met his burden of proof with regard to the discrimination experienced in this action. While the operators and employees of Love's Restaurant made attempts to accommodate disabled individuals who needed to use the restroom on the facilities, Plaintiff was denied reasonable access in this case.

While the defense offered that with additional time, patience, and jockeying of the wheelchair, physical location and layout of the restroom access could have been achieved, this was not reasonable nor consistent with the public policy interest in providing physically handicapped persons with equal access to public facilities and warrants a finding for Plaintiff in this action. The standard cannot be "is access achievable in some manner." We must focus on the quality of access.

If a finding that ultimate access could have been achieved provided a defense, the spirit of the law would be defeated. It is clear that the legislative purpose behind these disability access laws would not support such a finding... .

The restaurant's past practice of rendering assistance to disabled persons also supports the lack of any animus toward disabled individuals in the community. On the night in question, however, the clear violation of access standards, and the practical preclusion of Plaintiff from reasonable access to the restroom facilities is undeniable. The physical location and layout of the restroom interfered with full and equal access to the Plaintiff. Plaintiff's standard sized wheelchair, and the necessary attachments and configuration are not something that present some atypical anomaly... .

Judgment is hereby entered in favor of Plaintiff and against Defendant.

CASE QUESTION

1. Why is "quality of access" a concern of the Disabilities Act?

Also constituting a violation of the Disabilities Act is failing to provide handicapped parking at a restaurant or hotel.[50] To satisfy the ADA, a facility does not need to provide disabled customers with all the options available to able-bodied patrons. Rather, the requirement is to provide at least one means of access to the services. For example, plaintiffs complained that the cashier counter at a restaurant did not have a lowered section for wheelchair accessibility. It was the practice for all patrons of the eating facility to pay the server at the table, rather than at the cashier counter. Under these circumstances, the absence of an accessible cashier did not violate the Disabilities Act. Said the court, "The plaintiff's argument that perhaps a wheelchair user might elect to pay the bill directly, rather than to the server, is without merit. The present situation provides wheelchair users the same services as those provided to and utilized by the general public."[51]

---

[50] *Boston v. Paul McNally Realty*, 216 F.3d 827 (Hawaii 2000); *Association for Disabled Americans, Inc. v. Key Largo Bay Beach, LLC*, 407 F.Supp. 2d 1324 (Fla. 2005)

[51] *Long v. Coast Resorts, Inc.*, 32 F.Supp.2d 1203 (Nev. 1999); aff'd in part, rev'd in part, 267 F.3d 1203 (Nev. 2001)

Age Discrimination

Age is a classification not protected in places of public accommodation by the Act or most state civil rights laws. Thus, it is normally not illegal to treat varying age groups differently in such places. For example, a large discount department store, concerned about the high rate of shoplifting in the electronics department, barred school-age youths from entering the store after school hours on weekdays unless accompanied by an adult. Although this amounts to treatment of young people differently from others, discrimination in places of public accommodation on the basis of age is not illegal. Similarly, a skating rink that wishes to promote a Saturday-evening session as an event for teens can exclude from the rink people who are younger or older.

While discrimination on the basis of age in places of public accommodation is generally permissible, discrimination on the basis of age in employment decisions is restricted, as we will discuss in Chapter 14.

Gender Discrimination

Another type of discrimination not outlawed by the Civil Rights Act of 1964 is discrimination based on gender. In a 1968 case, a woman was refused service at an all-male bar operated by a hotel. She was forced to leave although she was sitting quietly and not disturbing other patrons. She sued the bar, challenging its discriminatory policy. The court noted that the Civil Rights Act of 1964 did not cover gender discrimination and dismissed the case, suggesting that the plaintiff address her complaint to Congress, which has the authority to change the law, and not to the courts.[52]

Although the Civil Rights Act does not protect women in places of public accommodation, under some circumstances they can obtain redress for discrimination through the Fourteenth Amendment to the Constitution. That amendment states, "[N]or shall any *state* ... deny to any person within its jurisdiction the equal protection of the laws" (emphasis added). The operative word is state, meaning the government. The amendment does not prohibit private discrimination. How does a place of public accommodation qualify as the *state*? It qualifies only if it is subject to considerable supervision and control by the government. Is a bar or restaurant with a liquor license issued by the state subject to the necessary degree of state supervision and control, and therefore bound by the Fourteenth Amendment prohibition against unequal protection of the laws?

That question was answered in the affirmative in a New York case. Two female members of the National Organization of Women (NOW) entered the defendant establishment, a bar primarily engaged in serving beverages. They were told by the bartender that the facility did not serve women and that it had consistently adhered to this practice throughout all of its 114 years of existence. The two women sued the bar claiming illegal discrimination on the basis of the Act and the Fourteenth

---

52 *DeCrow v. Hotel Syracuse Corp.*, 288 F.Supp. 530 (N.Y. 1968)

Amendment. The court denied their Civil Rights Act claim, stating that Congress did not outlaw discrimination based on gender. Concerning the Fourteenth Amendment claim, the Court noted that a liquor licensee is restricted by state law in who it can sell alcohol to and when it can sell. Further, the licensee is subject to inspection of its premises by the State Liquor Authority, which can suspend or revoke the license. The court held this to be sufficient supervision and control to qualify the bar as an instrumentality of the state.[53]

Supplementing the Constitution, virtually all states now have state statutes that prohibit discrimination in places of public accommodation based on gender. As we have discussed, the phrase *place of public accommodation*, as used by state law, customarily covers more establishments than does the federal Act. The phrase includes almost every place open to the public, including, for example, stores and schools.

In a case involving the New York statute, a tavern refused to serve women at the bar during certain hours. The plaintiff sought a court order barring the owners from continuing that practice. Based on state law, the court granted plaintiff's request and ordered the bar to cease and desist its discriminatory practice.[54]

In another case involving Michigan's civil rights statute, the court barred the Lions Club, an all-male service organization, from denying women membership. The club had refused to accept a woman who met all membership requirements except gender.

Like the Civil Rights Act of 1964, most state civil rights acts exempt private clubs. As with the Act, the issue arises whether an establishment is public or private. The right of an allegedly private golf club to refuse to grant membership to women was at issue in a California case.[55] Plaintiff wife and her husband had a family membership at defendant golf club. When they divorced, the plaintiff was awarded the couple's membership. A rule of the club provided that family memberships "shall be issued only in the name of adult male persons … and shall not be approved for females or minors." The rule further provided that where a family membership was awarded to the wife in a divorce and the husband failed to purchase it from the wife, the board of directors of the country club could terminate the membership.

The board cancelled plaintiff's membership accordingly and the plaintiff sued based on gender discrimination. The club claimed it was a private club and so was not bound by the California state statute that prohibited discrimination by "business establishments" based on gender.

The court rejected the golf club's argument that it was a private club and held for the plaintiff wife.[56] Pivotal to the decision was the significant use of club facilities by nonmembers. While as a general rule the club's facilities were open only to members, many exceptions existed.

---

[53] *Seidenberg v. McSorley's Old Ale House, Inc.,* 308 F.Supp. 1253 (N.Y. 1969)
[54] *Rosenberg v. State Human Rights Appeal Board,* 357 N.Y.S.2d 325 (N.Y. 1974)
[55] *Rogers v. International Association of Lions Clubs,* 636 F.Supp. 1476 (Mich. 1986). See also *Benevolent and Protective Order of the Elks v. Reynolds,* 863 F.Supp. 529 (Mich. 1994)
[56] *Warfield v. Peninsula Golf & Country Club,* 896 P.2d 776 (Calif. 1995)

In another case, male bar patrons challenged a "ladies drink free" promotion that defendant bar sponsored weekly. Defendant also featured a weekly "Men's Night Out" which offered reduced drink prices and free dart games for male patrons. On other nights of the week, promotions were offered to all patrons.

The Wisconsin state statute in issue prohibited a place of public accommodation from giving preferential treatment because of gender. The court held that ladies' night promotions gave preferential treatment to women on the sole basis of gender, therefore violating the law. Said the court, "Our interpretation of [the law] does not prohibit [defendant bar] from offering a wide array of promotions in the form of reduced or no prices for food, drinks, and entertainment. It prohibits only those promotions that base price differentials on the categories specified in the statute [which include gender]."[57]

One of the bar's arguments was that, since it gave men promotional benefits on another night, ladies night was not discriminatory. The court responded, "Preferential treatment to men on other nights does not correct the violation." Had female patrons challenged the men's night promotions, the outcome would have been the same; those promotions likewise violate the law.

Gender discrimination in access to places of public accommodation is less prevalent today. Such discrimination in employment is more widespread. While the federal Act does not protect against gender discrimination in places of public accommodation, it does protect against gender discrimination in employment, as we will discuss in Chapter 14.

A related topic is breastfeeding. Forty-nine states and the District of Columbia have laws that specifically allow women to breastfeed in any public location. The only holdout is Idaho.

Sexual Orientation Discrimination

Federal law does not prohibit discrimination on the basis of sexual orientation. In 17 states and many localities, laws prevent discrimination on this ground. In these jurisdictions, gays and lesbians are entitled to equal treatment along with other protected classes. In a case from New Mexico, which has a statute prohibiting places of public accommodation from discriminating against people based on their sexual orientation, a photography company that offers wedding photography services to the general public was held to be a public accommodation. The business refused to photograph a commitment ceremony between two women. The owner stated she was personally opposed to same-sex marriages and does not photograph such weddings. In so doing the company violated the state anti-discrimination law.[58]

A few states and localities include within the protections transgender status. Numerous state courts and enforcement agencies have interpreted laws that prohibit discrimination based on sex (44 states) to include transgender people.

---

[57] *Novak v. Madison Motel Associates,* 525 N.W.2d 123 (Wis. 1994)
[58] *Elaine Photography, LLC. V. Willock,* 309 P.3d 53 (N.M. 2013)

© Freer/Shutterstock.com

Denial of access to a public restroom that is consistent with a person's gender identity may be discrimination based on sex.[59] Many state and local laws, and interpretations of laws, explicitly protect the right to use bathrooms that align with one's gender identity. However, in a few states the laws have been interpreted not to protect this right. Most states have no official guidance on the issue. Organizations advocating for transgender equality are encouraging people to bring a discrimination lawsuit if denied equal access to restrooms.

Rights of Proprietors

The law does not prohibit discrimination against categories of people not included in the protected classes. For example, no law offers protection against discrimination in places of public accommodation to people who are dressed in jeans or wearing shorts. Thus, a restaurant's policy of refusing to serve anyone in jeans is legal even though it discriminates against people wearing denim pants.

Another case involved a casino's ejection of a patron who was a counter—that is, someone who keeps track in blackjack of what cards have been played. When certain cards that tilt the odds in favor of the player remain to be played, the counter bets the house limits and frequently wins, to the chagrin of the casino.

The expelled counter challenged the casino's right to evict him. The court held the counter was not protected by the Civil Rights Act because his exclusion was not based on race, color, religion, or national origin.[60]

Innkeepers, unlike restaurateurs, have a common-law obligation to provide accommodations to all who seek them. However, even this rule has exceptions that allow an innkeeper to refuse accommodations to a guest who is unable to prove ability to pay, a guest who is disorderly, or a guest who has a contagious disease. These exceptions and others will be discussed in Chapter 9.

Permissible to Remove a Disorderly Person

Removal of a restaurant patron who is acting disorderly or is a direct threat to the health and safety of others does not violate the civil rights laws. Although the

---

59 See *Doe v. Regional School Unit 26*, 86 A.3d 600 (Maine 2014)

60 *Uston v. Airport Casino, Inc.*, 564 F.2d 1216 (Calif. 1977). Note: Updated blackjack dealer devices, where used, render counting obsolete because the dealer reuses and reshuffles the cards after virtually every hand. See also *Donovan v. Grand Victoria Casino*, 934 N.E.2d 1111 (Ind. 2010), and *Commonwealth of Pa. v. Hyland*, 2014 WL 10575193 (Pa. 2014)

unruly diner may be a member of a protected minority, ejection based on conduct does not violate the Civil Rights Act. Case Example 3-9, involving a McDonald's restaurant, illustrates this point. As you read the case, note how the customer sought to prove racial discrimination and the reasons why the court rejected that proof.

CASE EXAMPLE 3-9

Alexis v. McDonald's Restaurants of Massachusetts, Inc.

67 F.3d 341 (Mass. 1995)

… Alexis and her family, who are African Americans, entered a McDonald's restaurant, proceeded to the service counter, placed their order, and paid in advance. When the food was placed before them at the service counter, it became apparent that [their server] Alfredo Pascacio, whose native tongue is Spanish, had mistaken their order. During the ensuing exchange between Alexis and Pascacio, defendant-appellee Donna Domina, the "swing manager," intervened on behalf of Pascacio, which prompted Alexis to say: "[You] take care of the people in front of you. He's taking care of me, and we're sorting this out." Domina nonetheless persisted for several more minutes.

Ultimately, Domina said to Alexis, "I don't have to listen to you." Alexis replied, "[Y]ou're damn right you don't have to listen to me. I was not speaking to you. I was speaking to him." Domina then instructed Pascacio: "Just put their stuff in a bag and get them out of here." Turning to Alexis, Domina retorted: "You're not eating here. If you [do] we're going to call the cops." Alexis responded: "Well you do what you have to do because we plan to eat here." Notwithstanding Domina's instructions, Pascacio placed the food order on a service tray, without bagging it. The entire incident at the service counter had lasted approximately ten minutes.

After the Alexis family went into the dining area, Sherry Toham, a managerial employee, summoned defendant Michael Leporati into the restaurant. Leporati, a uniformed off-duty police sergeant, had been patrolling on foot outside the restaurant by prearrangement with the Town of Framingham, but had witnessed no part of the earlier exchange among Alexis, Pascacio, and Domina.

Upon entering the restaurant, Leporati was informed by Domina that Alexis had been yelling, creating a "scene" and an "unwarranted disturbance" over a mistaken food order, and directing abusive remarks at Pascacio. Domina informed Leporati that Alexis had argued loudly with her and another employee; that she "just wasn't stopping"; and that Alexis was still in the dining area though Domina had "asked her to leave." Finally, Domina told Leporati, "I would like her to leave."

Without further inquiry into the "disturbance" allegedly caused by Alexis, Leporati proceeded to the dining area where Alexis and her family were seated, and informed the entire Alexis family that the manager wanted them to leave and that they would have to do so. Alexis immediately asked why, denied causing any disturbance, and claimed a right to finish eating in the restaurant. When she urged Leporati to ask other restaurant customers whether there had been a disturbance, Leporati simply reiterated that the family would have to leave. …

Approximately ten minutes later, Officer William Fuer arrived, and Alexis was told by Leporati that she was being placed under arrest... .

Alexis eventually was charged with criminal trespass, a misdemeanor. Following her acquittal by a jury, Alexis and her family filed the present action ... asserting civil rights claims... . The district court granted summary judgment for the defendants... .

Alexis submitted deposition testimony of six witnesses—the five Alexis family members and Karen Stauffer, an eyewitness to the events— each of whom opined, in effect, that had Alexis been a "rich white woman," she would not have been treated in the same manner. The court found that the proffered testimony was "not supported by sufficient factual undergirding" to permit a reasonable inference that either Domina or McDonald's discriminated against Alexis on the basis of her race... . The six deponents based their inferences of racial animus on their personal observations that Domina reacted "angrily" toward Alexis and with a "negative tone in her voice," was "unfriendly," "uncooperative," "high strung," "impolite," "impatient," and had "no reason" to eject Alexis. Although these observations may be entirely compatible with a race-based animus, there simply is no foundation for an inference that Domina harbored a racial animus toward Alexis or anyone else, absent some probative evidence that Domina's petulance stemmed from something other than a race-neutral reaction to the stressful encounter plainly evidenced in the record, including Alexis's persistence (however justified)... .

As Alexis points to no competent evidence that Domina and McDonald's intentionally discriminated against her on account of her race, the district court correctly ruled that this claim should be dismissed. Disputes generally arise out of mutual misunderstanding, misinterpretation, and overreaction, and without more, such disputes do not give rise to an inference of discrimination. Accordingly, the summary judgment entered in favor of Domina and McDonald's must be affirmed... .

CASE QUESTION

1. On what basis did the court find that the restaurant was not liable for discrimination based on race?

Reasonable Rules of an Establishment

The management of a service establishment, like any other business enterprise, typically adopts rules to maintain order and express the philosophy of its management. Often these rules result in different treatment of different groups. If the rules are reasonable, applied equally, and do not result in illegal discrimination against protected classes, they are enforceable even though the result may be that some people will be treated differently than others.

In Case Example 3-10, the management of a restaurant had a rule that excluded any person who was barefoot. A woman, ejected from the restaurant because she had removed her shoes, unsuccessfully challenged the legality of the rule.

CASE EXAMPLE 3-10

Feldt v. Marriott Corporation

322 A.2d 913 (D.C. 1974)

[Appellant], about 26 years of age, and her male escort had attended a dance at a fraternity house and after leaving the dance went to a Junior Hot Shoppe, owned and operated by appellee. They went through a cafeteria line, selected and paid for some food and then sat at a table and began to eat. The manager of the shop approached the table and told appellant she would have to leave because she was not wearing shoes. [Appellant left her shoes in her escort's automobile parked near the entrance.] No sign to that effect was posted, but the manager said it was the company's policy to serve no one who was not wearing shoes. She replied she would leave as soon as she finished eating. The manager did not offer to refund her money, and she asked for no refund. [There was testimony that the manager offered to get a bag so she could take the food—a hamburger and french fries—with her.] He continued to insist that she leave, and she continued to insist she would leave only when she had finished eating. The argument continued and she finally said to the manager: "Will you, please, go to hell." He walked outside and returned with a police officer. The manager again asked her to leave, and the officer told her she would be violating the unlawful entry statute if she refused to leave after the manager had asked her to leave. She replied she would leave when she had finished eating. The officer took her arm and said unless she left he would arrest her. She arose and walked to the door and then, observing the officer behind her, began struggling with him and hit him.

Appellant was then placed in a patrol wagon, taken to a precinct station, and later taken to the Women's Detention Center. Hours later she was released on her personal recognizance and told to appear in court the next day. When she appeared in court, she was told the charge against her would be dropped and she was free to leave.

It is clear that appellant entered the premises lawfully, but it is also clear that under our unlawful entry statute … one who lawfully enters may be guilty of a misdemeanor by refusing to leave after being ordered to do so by the person lawfully in charge of the premises. Our question is whether the police officer was justified in arresting appellant when she, in his presence, refused to leave after being ordered to do so by the manager.

At common law, a restaurant owner had the right to arbitrarily refuse service to any guest. Absent constitutional or statutory rights, the common law still controls in this jurisdiction. This is not a case of racial discrimination or violation of civil rights. We do have a statute making it unlawful for a restaurant to refuse service to "any quiet and orderly person" or to exclude anyone on account of race or color; but, as we have said, there was no racial discrimination here and we do not think the requirement to serve any quiet or orderly person prevents a restaurant from having reasonable requirements as to the dress of its customers, such as a requirement that all male customers wear coats and ties, or, as here, that all customers wear shoes. Had the restaurant manager observed that appellant was not wearing shoes when she first entered the restaurant, he could have properly and lawfully refused to serve her and requested her to leave. Our question narrows down to whether the fact that the restaurant had served appellant food and received payment for it prevented the restaurant from ordering appellant to leave when her shoeless condition was observed.

The status of a customer in a restaurant, as far as we can ascertain, has never been precisely declared. It is not the same as a guest at an inn... .

The nearest analogy we have found in the reported cases to the one here is that of a patron of a theater, racetrack, or other place of public entertainment, who, after having purchased a ticket, is ordered to leave. It has been generally held that such a patron has only a personal license, which may be revoked at any time, leaving him only with a breach of contract claim [against the proprietor].

We think that is the applicable rule here. When appellant was ordered to leave, her license to be on the premises was revoked, whether legally or illegally, and she had no right to remain. Her remedy, if any, was a civil action for breach of contract... .

Our conclusion is that when appellant, in the presence of the police officer, refused to leave on the demand of the restaurant manager, the officer was justified in arresting her for violation of the unlawful entry statute... .

What should hoteliers and restaurateurs do if an individual they have asked to leave refuses to go? The best response is to call the police to handle the matter. Ideally, a confrontation like the one described in *Feldt v. Marriott Corp.* will be avoided. The rights of the proprietor in this type of situation will be discussed at more length in Chapter 9.

Retaliatory Exclusion

Often when a customer sues a hotel or restaurant she is disinclined to return to the establishment for service. In cases where a plaintiff does seek service after commencing the lawsuit, the facility is not obligated to accommodate the would-be patron.

In one case a plaintiff sued a bar claiming unspecified illegal discrimination. While that case was pending, the plaintiff returned to the defendant's bar intending to purchase drinks. She was denied admission by the doorman and informed that the reason for the exclusion was that she had sued the bar. She filed a second suit, claiming that denial of services because of her lawsuit constituted illegal discrimination. The court dismissed the action on the ground that discrimination based on retaliation for bringing a lawsuit was not a protected class. Said the court, "[A]n exclusion based on a customer's *conduct*, whether or not the customer was a member of a [protected] class, was reasonable as a matter of law."[61]

---

[61] *Gayer v. Guluch, Inc.,* 282 Cal.Rptr. 556 (1991). See also *County of Grant v. Peer,* 333 N.W.2d 734, 183 WL 161872 (Wis. 1983)

Patrons who enter the premises despite a warning not to may be guilty of criminal trespass. Even if the patrons enter the premises lawfully, they may be guilty of trespass if they fail to obey a lawful order to leave made by the owner or the owner's designee. To commit this crime, patrons must first be informed they are not welcome on the premises. For example, where an organization's meeting was restricted to members of the Board of Governors (the association's governing body), others could be legally excluded. Removal of an attendee who was not a board member and who failed to leave when asked did not constitute illegal discrimination.[62]

---

[62] *Miranda v. Resident and Directors of Georgetown College,* 818 F.Supp. 16 (D.C. 1993), aff 'd 43 F.3d 712 (D.C. 1994)

Summary

Sadly, discrimination was a practice quite prevalent in the hospitality industry before the passage of the Civil Rights Act of 1964. Today, many laws prohibit discrimination. The common law prohibits innkeepers from refusing accommodations to anyone who seeks them, unless certain exceptions apply. The Civil Rights Act of 1964 prevents hotels, restaurants, gas stations, and places of entertainment engaged in interstate commerce from refusing to provide services or accommodations on the basis of race, color, religion, or national origin. The Americans with Disabilities Act prohibits discrimination on the basis of disability and requires various accommodations for handicapped patrons. State civil rights laws fill in the gaps by preventing discrimination within the state in a large class of facilities on the grounds not just of race, color, religion, and national origin, but also gender, marital status, disability, and in some locales, sexual orientation.

We have seen in this chapter how the law can be used as a tool to deter discrimination and encourage hospitality facilities to provide their services to all equally.

Preventive Law Tips

- *Do not refuse a hotel room to anyone on the grounds of being in a protected class.* Failure to provide a room based on race, color, religion, or nationality violates the Civil Rights Act of 1964 and can result in an injunction and judgment for attorney's fees in favor of the plaintiff. Discrimination based on disability may violate the Americans with Disabilities Act. Refusal to provide a room based on gender or marital status may violate a state civil rights law and subject the innkeeper to criminal penalties. If the hotel is situated in a locality that forbids discrimination based on sexual orientation, refusal to provide a room to someone who is homosexual will result in liability. In addition to the legal penalties, discrimination contradicts the basic principle of equal opportunity upon which our country was founded, and violates a basic tenet of the hospitality industry to treat customers well and make them feel comfortable. However, if a legitimate reason exists to refuse accommodations (e.g., violation of reasonable house rules, disorderly conduct, or trespassing), an innkeeper can legally decline to provide a room.

- *Do not refuse a hotel room to anyone who shows ability to pay* unless there is a legitimate reason for the refusal (e.g., violation of reasonable house rules, disorderly conduct, or trespassing). The common law requires that hotels provide rooms for everyone requesting accommodations. Failure to provide a room to a would-be guest with the financial means to pay can result in liability.

- *Do not refuse restaurant services to someone on the grounds of race, color, religion, or nationality.* The Civil Rights Act of 1964 outlaws discrimination on these grounds; it does not prohibit a restaurant from refusing service on any other grounds. *Note:* If a legitimate reason exists to refuse accommodations

CHAPTER 3: Civil Rights and Hospitality Businesses

to a would-be patron in a protected class (e.g., violation of reasonable house rules, disorderly conduct, or trespassing), the restaurateur can legally decline to provide a table.

- *Do not refuse restaurant services to someone on the grounds of gender, marital status, or disability.* State civil rights laws customarily outlaw discrimination on these grounds, and the federal Americans with Disabilities Act outlaws discrimination against disabled persons. Failure to abide by these laws can result in civil and criminal liability. Also, local ordinances may prohibit discrimination on the basis of sexual orientation. These types of discrimination can be as hurtful to the guest and damaging to the hospitality industry as discrimination based on race, color, religion, and nationality. *Note:* If a legitimate reason exists to refuse accommodations to a would-be patron in a protected class (e.g., violation of reasonable house rules, disorderly conduct, or trespassing), the restaurateur can legally decline to provide a table.

- *Do not refuse access to places of entertainment on the grounds of race, color, religion, or nationality.* The Act prohibits discrimination in places of entertainment based on race, color, religion, or nationality. The word *entertainment*, as used by the Act, includes enterprises such as theaters and stadiums that offer entertainment to a viewing audience, as well as places where the patron actively participates in the activity such as a ranch offering horseback riding or an amusement park.

- *Do not refuse access to places of entertainment on the grounds of gender, marital status, or disability.* State civil rights laws customarily outlaw discrimination on these grounds, and the federal Americans with Disabilities Act outlaws discrimination against disabled persons. Violation of these laws can result in civil and criminal liability. Also, local ordinances may prohibit discrimination on the basis of sexual orientation. *Note:* If a legitimate reason exists to refuse service to a would-be customer in a protected class (such as violation of reasonable house rules, disorderly conduct, or trespassing), the proprietor can legally deny admission.

- *Concerning disabled patrons, eliminate barriers to accessibility if the removal is readily achievable.* Places of public accommodation are required to remove hindrances that can be eliminated easily and without a lot of expense. Barrier removal that would be costly or difficult to achieve is not required. If new construction or alterations are undertaken, more extensive obstacle removal will be required. However, accessibility is not required where the cost to remove barriers is out of proportion with the cost or scope of the alteration or construction project.

- *A private club wishing to retain that status should limit membership, develop clear selection criteria, ensure that control and ownership of the club rests with members, and refrain from widely advertising for members.* The courts have developed rules to determine which clubs are private—and therefore not bound by the Act—and which clubs are not. Unless those rules are followed closely, a club will not be deemed private.

Review Questions

1. According to the common law, to whom can a hotel refuse to provide accommodations?

2. Why did Congress pass the Civil Rights Act of 1964 (the "Act")?

3. Who is protected by the Act?

4. What facilities are covered by the Act?

5. What is interstate commerce and why is it relevant to the Act?

6. What remedies are available to a plaintiff suing for a violation of the Act?

7. Name three types of businesses not covered by the Act.

8. Identify three differences between the Act and state civil rights laws.

9. What conduct is outlawed by state civil rights laws?

10. Identify three tests used by the courts to determine whether or not a club is private.

11. What is a restaurant required to do under the Americans with Disabilities Act to remove barriers to accessibility?

12. Can a restaurant legally require that all wheelchair-bound customers eat in the same area of the dining room?

Discussion Questions

1. Many states have laws that require restaurants to prohibit smoking in their facilities. Does this constitute illegal discrimination against people who smoke? Why or why not?

2. Why do you think Congress did not include gender as a protected class in the Act?

3. Why is a successful plaintiff in most lawsuits unable to collect attorney's fees from the defendant, while a successful plaintiff suing under the Act can?

4. Why do you think the Act outlaws even single acts of discrimination rather than requiring a pattern of discriminatory conduct?

5. A train station has a snack bar located in it. What additional information would you need to know to determine if the train station is covered by the Act? Why would you need that additional information?

6. Why do you think Congress omitted many bed-and-breakfast operations from the Act (the "Mrs. Murphy's Boarding House" clause)?

7. If you were devising an expansion of the civil rights laws, would you include any additional protected classes? Who and why?

8. What distinguishes the establishments covered by the Americans with Disabilities Act from those covered by the Civil Rights Act of 1964?

Application Questions

1. Devise an operating plan for a private club that would pass muster if its status as private was challenged.

2. A community college, primarily serving residents of the local county, has a candy shop on campus. Of 20 varieties of candies it sells, only one ingredient of one variety was purchased from out of state. Is the college governed by the Act? Why or why not?

3. Identify whether each of the following constitutes illegal discrimination and explain your reasoning:
   A. A restaurant refuses to serve anyone who is Swiss.
   B. A restaurant refuses to serve someone who arrives for dinner two minutes before the kitchen closes.
   C. A restaurant refuses to serve a person in a wheelchair with a service dog because the restaurant does not allow pets in the dining area.
   D. A hotel refuses to provide a room to a couple because they are not married.
   E. A movie theater refuses to sell a ticket to someone who is carrying a weapon.
   F. A private club refuses to admit a couple because they are Protestant.
   G. A hotel refuses to provide a room to a person who is deaf because he is unable to provide proof of ability to pay.

Websites

Websites that will enhance your understanding of the material in this chapter include:

www.eeoc.gov This is the official site of the Equal Employment Opportunity Commission, the federal agency that enforces discrimination laws. Among the site's features are access to federal laws that prohibit job discrimination, information on how to file a claim, and use of mediation to settle claims.

www.aclu.org This is the site of the American Civil Liberties Union, a national organization that protects constitutional rights. The site's contents include discrimination issues.

www.usdoj.gov This is the official site of the Department of Justice. It contains information about this federal agency's law enforcement activities, including discrimination cases.

CHAPTER 4

Contract Law and the Hospitality Industry

LEARNING OUTCOMES:

- Be familiar with the elements of a contract: contractual capacity, mutuality, legality, consideration, proper form, and genuine assent
- Know the difference between a void and a voidable contract
- Understand offer and acceptance or counteroffer
- Know the three forms of consideration
- Understand the statute of frauds and the exceptions
- Know that terms of a contract should be clear and without ambiguity, and how courts resolve vague language
- Understand a breach of contract and damages received if a party breaches a contract
- Understand the duty to mitigate damages
- Understand the hotel room contract, overbooking, and breaches by the guest and the hotel
- Understand the tort of intentional interference with contractual relations

KEY TERMS

absolute	easement	offeree
acceptance	forbearance	offeror
agreement not to compete	forum selection clause	pain and suffering
antitrust laws	fraud	parol
attrition clause	genuine assent	parol evidence rule
breach of contract	goodwill	specific performance
capacity to contract	illusory	Statute of Frauds
compensatory damages	innocent misrepresentation	tort
condition	invitations to negotiate	trade usage
consideration	mitigate	unilateral mistake
contract	mutuality	valid
counteroffer	mutual mistake	voidable contract
damages	no-cause termination clause	void contract
duress	offer	

© Andrei Rahalski/Shutterstock.com

Introduction

contract
An Agreement between two or more parties which creates obligations enforceable in court.

A **contract** is an agreement between two or more parties that creates obligations enforceable in court. Examples of contracts include the following:

- A hotel agrees to buy new furniture for its lobby and in exchange agrees to pay a specified price.

- A guest agrees to rent a room for a weekend and pay the quoted rate. In exchange, the hotel agrees to reserve the room for the guest and not rent it to anyone else.

- An association agrees to hold its annual convention at a hotel and pay the specified costs. In exchange, the hotel agrees to provide rooms, banquet facilities, food, and related services.

Failure to perform the terms of a contract constitutes **breach of contract,** which in turn results in liability. For example, if a hotel contracted to purchase furniture but, after it was delivered, refused to pay, the inn would be in breach of contract. The company that sold the furniture can sue the hotel for breach of contract.

breach of contract
The failure to perform, without legal excuse, some contracted act.

Remember the definition of a contract—an agreement between two or more people that is *enforceable in court.*[1]

A contract can be in writing and signed, or it can be oral. It can even be implied, which means it can come into existence without a word ever being written or spoken. For example, assume that on your way to an 8:00 a.m. class you stop at the cleaners with a pair of slacks. You are in a hurry to get to school, and the attendant is in the back of the store reading the morning paper. He hears you enter and looks up. You put the slacks on the counter and wave. He waves back and resumes reading. The two of you have not exchanged a word; nevertheless, a contract exists requiring the cleaning company to clean your slacks and obligating you to pay the going rate.

Contracts can also be created on the Internet. Cyberspace is an increasingly popular forum for the development of business agreements.

The Elements of a Contract

Regardless of whether the contract is written, oral, or implied, certain essential elements must exist for the contract to be **valid,** meaning enforceable in court. These elements are as follows:

valid
Enforceable in court. For a contract to be valid, certain elements must exist, such as contractual capacity, mutuality, legality, consideration, proper form, and genuine assent.

- Contractual capacity

- Mutuality

- Legality

- Consideration

- Proper form

- Genuine assent

---

[1] *Del-Rena, Inc. v. KFM, Inc.*, 789 So.2d 397, 2002 WL 575139 (Fla. 2001)

Capacity to Contract

For a valid contract, the parties must have legal **capacity to contract**—that is, the ability both to understand the terms of the contract, and to appreciate that failure to perform its terms can lead to legal liability, including a lawsuit. The following groups of people are viewed by the law as having diminished mental abilities and thus lacking contractual capacity: minors (people who are not yet legal adults; those under age 18 in some states, under 19 or 21 in others); the mentally incompetent; and the very intoxicated. The contracts of all three groups are voidable.

A **voidable contract** is one that may be canceled at the option of one party (in this case, the person with the legal disability). This right to cancel, also called the right to *avoid* or *disaffirm*, applies while the disability exists and for a reasonable time after it ends—that is, after the minor reaches 18 (or 19 or 21 depending on the state), after the very intoxicated person becomes sober, or after the mentally incompetent person becomes competent (if ever). Thus, a 17-year-old girl who purchases a car can return it if she changes her mind about the purchase within certain time limits. Depending on the state, she will receive a refund of all or some of the price she paid. The reason the law allows a reasonable time after removal of the disability is to permit the person who was previously legally incapacitated to rethink the appropriateness of the contract with the benefit of newfound capability.

Certain exceptions exist to the right to cancel, the most significant being contracts for the purchase of necessities. While a minor who enters a contract for necessities can disaffirm the contract, he remains liable for the reasonable value of the goods or services he received. Necessities include food, shelter, clothing, and, depending on the minor's circumstances, possibly other items such as a car or an education. Thus a minor, who decides after enjoying a full meal at a restaurant that he wants to avoid the contract, will be liable to the restaurant for the reasonable value of the meal. The main reason for this rule is concern for the well-being of the minor. If young people could avoid payment for necessities, sellers would be reluctant to contract with even those minors who are in need of the basics.

Mutuality: Offer and Acceptance

Mutuality means that all parties to the contract are interested in its terms and intend to enter an agreement to which they will be legally bound. Mutuality is sometimes called a *meeting of the minds*. Mutuality is established by one party making an offer and the other party accepting that offer.

An **offer** is a proposal to do or give something of value in exchange for something else. For example, an offer might be phrased as follows:

"We have a room we can provide to you for the night for $89"; or

"We can cater your dinner party for 15 people with the menu you requested for $30 per person."

An **offeror** is the person who makes an offer; the **offeree** is the person to whom the offer is made.

The Offer Must Be Definite

The terms of an offer must be definite. If the terms are vague a contract may not result, either because the lack of clarity may evidence a lack of commitment to enter a contract or because the terms are too indefinite to obligate the parties to do anything sufficiently specific. For example, the following statements are too general and vague to constitute offers:

> "The rooms in this hotel range from $42 to $95 a night"; or "We cater parties of all sizes."

Rather than offers, these statements constitute what the law calls **invitations to negotiate,** which means they open discussions that may or may not lead to an offer.

Responses to an Offer

When an offer is made, the offeree has two options: Accept the offer, or reject it. An **acceptance** is an expression of agreement by the offeree to the terms of the offer. If the offeree accepts the offer, mutuality is achieved. If the other essential elements needed for a contract are present, an enforceable contract will exist. If, however, the offeree rejects the offer, the parties have not mutually agreed upon the terms and so no contract exists.

Sometimes the offeree is interested in the offer but wants to change a few terms. In such a case the offeree makes a **counteroffer,** a response to an offer that modi-

offeror
The person who makes an offer.

offeree
The person to whom an offer is made.

invitations to negotiate
Opening discussions that may or may not lead to an offer for a contract.

acceptance
Compliance by offeree with terms and conditions of offer, or an expression of agreement by the offeree to the terms of an offer.

counteroffer
Statement made by offeree to the offeror relating to the same matter as the original offer and proposing a substituted bargain differing from that proposed by the original offer.

© PORTRAIT IMAGES ASIA BY NONWARIT/Shutterstock.com

fies one or more of its provisions. A counteroffer is not an acceptance. Rather, the counteroffer is treated as a new offer. The original offeror then has the option of accepting the counteroffer, rejecting it, or making yet another counteroffer. For example, a hotel makes an offer to an association to host its annual three-day conference— including guest rooms, meeting rooms, and meals—for $675 per person based on a specified minimum number of reservations. The organization likes the location and layout of the hotel, but thinks the price is high. It responds by saying it will hold its conference at the hotel if the hotel lowers the price to $625 per person. This is a counteroffer and no contract exists unless either the hotel accepts the counteroffer or the hotel makes another counteroffer that is accepted by the association.

In Case Example 4-1, the parties discussed and considered the terms of a contract but never came to a meeting of the minds. Without that mutuality, no contract exists.

CASE EXAMPLE 4-1

University Hotel Development, L.L.C. v. Dusterhoft Oil, Inc.

715 N.W.2d 153 (N.D. 2006)

…University Hotel Development ("UHD") is a company which owns and operates the Hilton Garden Inn in Grand Forks. Loren Dusterhoft ("Dusterhoft") owns an Amoco gas station located across the street from the Hilton Garden Inn.

In 2001, UHD began planning the construction of the Hilton Garden Inn, after entering into a ground lease with the State of North Dakota to construct the hotel on the western edge of the University of North Dakota campus. The Amoco station's sewer line connected to a force main sewer line on property owned by the University of North Dakota, and under the building site for UHD's Hilton Garden Inn. Dusterhoft had a 10-year [lease] from the university for the sewer line, which ended November 6, 2001. The university and the City of Grand Forks required UHD to move the sewer lines before it could acquire a building permit [for the Hilton Garden Inn]. In 2001, UHD's managing partner and Dusterhoft discussed the sewer line relocation, but the parties did not reach an agreement on who would pay the sewer line relocation expenses. [Dusterhoft refused to pay.]

In April 2002, construction on the hotel began and the sewer lines were moved. During the construction of the hotel, Dusterhoft enjoyed uninterrupted use of the sewer line even though his lease had expired. UHD paid all costs and expenses incurred in relocating Dusterhoft's portion of the sewer line. After construction was complete, an engineering firm UHD hired calculated Dusterhoft owed UHD $43,441.28 for the benefit Dusterhoft received from the relocation and continued use of his portion of the sewer line…

UHD sued Dusterhoft for $50,000 for the costs and expenses UHD incurred in relocating Dusterhoft's portion of the sewer line, alleging … breach of contract. UHD claimed the university, Dusterhoft, and UHD agreed ... that Dusterhoft [should] pay for the benefit he received from the relocation of his portion of the sewer line...

UHD claims there were numerous communications between Dusterhoft and UHD's representatives [to that effect], and it cites letters from its former attorney and from the university's representatives to Dusterhoft as evidence...

UHD failed to establish the existence of a factual dispute about whether there was a definite, clear, and unambiguous promise by Dusterhoft to pay UHD for the benefit he received from the relocation of the sewer line. The claimed promise was not reduced to writing, and there is no written documentation of a definite, clear, and unambiguous promise. The evidence UHD presented establishes only preliminary negotiations between the university and Dusterhoft ... UHD also claims letters from the university to Dusterhoft contain evidence of the promise between UHD and Dusterhoft. These letters, however, contain evidence only of negotiations between the university and Dusterhoft, and are insufficient to raise a factual dispute about the existence of a promise between UHD and Dusterhoft. [The court therefore denied recovery to UHD; Dusterhoft did not have to pay.]

CASE QUESTION

1. What actions could UHD have taken to ensure that it would have an enforceable claim against Dusterhoft for the costs of relocating Dusterhoft's portion of the sewer line?

Legality

To be enforceable, a contract must have a legal objective. If what the parties obligate themselves to do is illegal, the contract is not just voidable, but void. A **void contract** is one that is unenforceable in court. For example, we will study in Chapter 15 that it is illegal for competing hotels to agree among themselves to all charge the same amount for a room, and it is likewise illegal for competing restaurants to agree to charge the same price for meals. This is called *price-fixing* and violates **antitrust laws,** which are laws that restrict limitations on competition. Such agreements are illegal because they guarantee that competitors will not undersell each other with the result of depriving consumers of the benefits of competition. If one hotel that is a party to such a contract deviates from the agreed price and the other hotels attempt to sue for the first hotel's failure to abide by the contract, the court will dismiss the case without the need for a trial because the contract is illegal and therefore void.

void contract
A contract that is unenforceable in court.

antitrust laws
Laws that attempt to ensure that open competition is preserved.

Consideration

For an agreement to be binding and enforceable in court there must be consideration. The word *consideration*, as used in the legal sense, means something

consideration
Something of value exchanged for something else of value.

quite different from the definition of consideration in normal parlance. In connection with contracts, **consideration** means something of value exchanged for something else of value. For example, a guest in a hotel gives the innkeeper money and in return receives the right to use a room. The consideration for the guest's payment is the right to occupy the room; the consideration for the hotel providing the room is the guest's money.

Another way to understand consideration is to recognize it as the phenomenon that distinguishes a contract from a gift. A gift transaction is one sided; one person gives something to the other and receives nothing in return. With a contract, each person gives something and each person receives something in exchange. That which is received is the consideration.

Consideration can take any of three forms:

1. A tangible item of value or a promise to give such an item (such as food or money)

2. Performance or a promise to perform (such as cleaning a swimming pool, working as a front-desk clerk, or waiting on tables)

3. **Forbearance**—agreeing to refrain from doing something you have a legal right to do—or a promise to forbear. For example, if you are injured while at a restaurant, you might promise not to sue the restaurant for your injuries if the owner agrees to pay you a satisfactory sum of money.

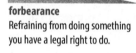

forbearance
Refraining from doing something you have a legal right to do.

Parties to a contract may exchange one form of consideration for the same form of consideration. For example, when a restaurant patron buys dinner, the customer gives money (something tangible with value) and the restaurant gives food (something tangible with value). The parties can also mix two different forms of consideration in the same contract, such as when an employee contracts to work for a hotel. The employee gives services (performance) and the hotel gives money (a tangible item of value).

Illusory Contracts

illusory
A contractual term that fails to contain a firm commitment; a promise that is so indefinite that the party making it has not in fact committed to do anything.

Sometimes the terms of the contract do not contain a firm commitment. If an apparent commitment is so indefinite that the party has not in fact promised to do anything, the promise is said to be **illusory.** An illusory promise does not constitute consideration and will not give rise to a contract. In Case Example 4-2, the court found that an alleged contract was illusory; an association scheduling its annual convention did not, in fact, agree to rent any rooms from the plaintiff hotel.

CASE EXAMPLE 4-2

Lederman Enterprises, Inc. v. Allied Social Science Associates

709 P.2d 1 (Colo. 1985)

The defendant, Allied Social Science Association (ASSA) … an unincorporated group of associations which meet together annually, contacted the Denver Convention and Visitors' Bureau in 1975 when ASSA was considering holding its 1980 convention in Denver. The Visitors' Bureau wrote to several Denver hotels, including The Regency, asking that the hotels commit to hold open a block of rooms in order to attract the ASSA convention to Denver. The Regency responded to the Visitors' Bureau, indicating it would hold 375 rooms open. This information was conveyed by the Bureau to ASSA. Thereafter, ASSA and The Regency corresponded and, on March 19, 1980, the parties signed a document prepared by The Regency, entitled "Regency Inn-Meeting/ Convention Contract." In May of 1980, ASSA mailed preregistration forms to its members informing them of the different Denver hotels available, and requesting the members to list their preferences. When the forms were returned by the members to ASSA, they were forwarded to the Visitors' Bureau which then assigned members of ASSA to the hotels in accordance with the preferences of the members.

Few of the 2,500 members who registered for the convention listed The Regency on their preference list, and none selected it as their first choice. Therefore, the Visitors' Bureau did not assign any members to The Regency. On July 21, 1980, realizing that no members would be making reservations at the Regency, the convention coordinator for ASSA wrote to the Regency stating that: "There is no need to continue to hold rooms for us… ."

The Regency filed suit against ASSA and its convention coordinator….

We agree with ASSA that The Regency's form "contract" entitled "Regency Inn-Meeting/ Convention Contract" did not, as a matter of law, constitute a reservation of rooms by ASSA… .

The "contract" between the parties specified that reservation cards had to be returned by August 4, 1980, and then stated:

> *The Regency's cut-off policy calls for all unreserved rooms within your block to be released for sale 30 days prior to arrival. All reservations received thereafter will be accepted on a space available basis only. Should you wish to guarantee any unreserved rooms past the cut-off date, please advise us in writing ... [Payment of] one night's deposit with each guest room reservation [is requested]. All reservations and agreements are made upon, and are subject to the rules and regulations of the Regency, and the following conditions: ...*

> *We require a non-refundable deposit of first night's room rate with reservation, unless your organization guarantees payment for any "no shows" in your group.*

The gist of this "contract" is that, for an ASSA member to make a reservation at The Regency, a reservation card had to be used and had to be returned to the reservation manager of The Regency by August 4, 1980, accompanied by a deposit. To say that the document itself made reservations [which is what the Regency asserts in this breach of contract case] would make meaningless the need to return reservation cards.

Other provisions in the "contract" are also inconsistent with an interpretation that it constituted a reservation of rooms at The Regency. The several references to "unreserved rooms" within the block of rooms held by The Regency would be rendered meaningless by so holding. The provision that "all unreserved rooms within your block … [will] be released 30 days prior to arrival" demonstrates that the rooms within the block had not been reserved merely by ASSA's agreement to the contract's terms.

In our view, the "contract" merely imposed upon The Regency the obligation to make available, under certain conditions, a number of rooms to ASSA; it did not obligate ASSA to reserve any rooms. ASSA's only obligation was to mention The Regency as one of the hotels where members could obtain rooms. Only if further steps were taken by the members would rooms actually be reserved.

There being no reservation of rooms under the "contract" … [ASSA did not breach the contract and therefore is not liable to The Regency].

CASE QUESTION

1. How might the wording of the Regency's "contract" have been changed so as to obligate ASSA to rent rooms from The Regency?

Proper Form (Written; Oral)

The question often arises—must a contract be in writing, or is an oral contract enforceable? The general rule (meaning some exceptions exist) is that, oral contracts are enforceable. Such contracts may, however, be difficult to prove. For example, Mrs. Gordon called the Townhouse Hotel and made a reservation for the following weekend. In contract terms, she agreed to pay for a room in consideration of the hotel agreeing to reserve one for her use and to make it available to her on the specified dates. Neither the hotel nor Mrs. Gordon reduced the contract to writing. Nevertheless, the contract is valid and enforceable. If, when Mrs. Gordon arrives at the hotel, the reservation clerk acknowledges her reservation but informs her that the hotel has overbooked and has no available rooms, the hotel will be liable to Mrs. Gordon for breach of contract. The fact that the contract was not in writing is of no consequence.

Now assume a different set of facts. Mrs. Gordon arrives at the hotel and requests her room. The hotel not only has no room for her but denies ever making a reservation in her name. Despite Mrs. Gordon's protests, the hotel holds firm to its position. In this situation Mrs. Gordon will have a difficult time proving the hotel agreed to reserve a room for her. As this scenario indicates, a good practice is to put all contracts in writing and thereby avoid the "proof problem." However, an oral contract is enforceable if it can be proved.

Contracts that Must Be in Writing: The Statute of Frauds

The rule that oral contracts are enforceable is a general rule; several exceptions exist. Certain types of contracts are not enforceable unless they are in writing. For these contracts *only*, oral agreements are *not* enforceable. The law that requires a writing for these contracts is called the **Statute of Frauds.** The name derives from the statute's objective of preventing the perpetuation of a fraud by someone claiming a contract exists when in fact none does. The statute might better be named the "Statute to Prevent Frauds."

Statute of Frauds
The law requiring that certain contracts must be written to be enforceable.

Among the types of contracts within the Statute of Frauds that must be in writing to be enforceable are the following:

easement
The privilege of using someone else's land for some limited purpose.

■ Contracts for the purchase and sale of real property, which includes land and buildings. An example is a contract to purchase a hotel. Also included within the definition of real property is an **easement,** which is the right of one person to use another person's land for some particular, limited purpose. A case example involves a restaurant owner who needed additional parking space for customers. He allegedly entered an oral agreement with an adjacent landowner in which the latter consented to allow restaurant customers to utilize his parking lot, thereby constituting an easement. Thereafter, disputes arose and the adjoining property owner installed a fence to keep restaurant patrons out. The restaurant owner sued to enforce the oral agreement. The court held the Statute of Frauds rendered the contract unenforceable because the agreement involved an interest in real property and it was not in writing.[2]

Not all contracts that are associated with the sale of real property require a writing; only those for the sale and purchase of land, buildings, or easements. In Case Example 4-3 a dispute arose about whether a contract with a real estate broker (a person who assists parties in selling and finding real estate) must be in writing.

---

2 *Payne v. Edmonson*, 1999 WL 350928 (Tex. 1999)

CASE EXAMPLE 4-3

BBQ Blues Texas, Ltd. v. Affiliated Business Brokers, Inc.

183 S.W.3d 543 (Tex. 2006)

...In a series of conversations, which began on October 11, 2002, Affiliated Business Brokers ("ABB") and BBQ Blues Texas, LTD ("BBQ") entered into an oral agreement. The parties agreed that, if BBQ found a buyer for ABB's (restaurant) business in Round Rock, Texas, ABB would pay BBQ a commission equal to 10 percent of the sales price. BBQ introduced ABB to a group that ultimately purchased the business ... for $335,000...

BBQ assert[s] that the oral commission agreement between the parties included the sale or purchase of real estate and therefore [required a writing]...

There were two separate and distinct contracts in this case: (1) the oral commission agreement between BBQ and ABB which called for a ten percent commission to be paid to ABB if they found a buyer for the restaurant, and; (2) the sales contract between the buyer and the seller of the restaurant. Regardless of the terms of the final contract between the buyer and seller of the restaurant, the jury found that BBQ breached the oral commission agreement and that the oral commission agreement did not involve the transfer of the real estate...The evidence at trial was both factually and legally sufficient to support the finding that the oral commission agreement did not involve the sale or purchase of real estate. Accordingly, we find against BBQ... [and direct that it pay AAB its commission].

The judgment of the trial court is affirmed.

CASE QUESTION

1. Which contract in this case would require a writing? Why?

Other contracts that fall within the Statute of Frauds and require a writing are the following:

- Contracts that cannot be completed within one year from when they are made. An example is a two-year employment contract for a restaurant manager.

- Contracts to pay another person's debt if that person fails to pay. For example, a hotel guest, when registering, presents the credit card of a small out-of-town company as the means for payment of the bill. The hotel, uncertain of the financial status of the company, may require that the guest agree to pay the hotel bill if the company fails to do so. This commitment by the guest must be in writing to be enforceable.

- Contracts for the sale of goods (movable, tangible objects, not services) in excess of $500. An example is a contract between a hotel and a computer store for the purchase of a $2,300 computer for the front office.

Two exceptions exist to the need for a writing for a contract for the sale of goods valued in excess of $500: (1) The seller has delivered the goods and the buyer has accepted them; or (2) the buyer paid for the goods and the seller accepted the payment. In both of these circumstances each party to the contract has evidenced the existence of the contract by his or her actions. In such circumstances a written agreement to prove its existence is needless.

The first of these exceptions to the Statute of Frauds is illustrated in Case Example 4-4.

CASE EXAMPLE 4-4

Adams v. H&H Meat Products, Inc.

41 S.W.3d 762 (Tex. 2001)

Norwick Adams ("Adams") is employed by and is the director general and a minority shareholder of Whataburger Mexico. H&H Meat Products, Inc. ("H&H") is a company that sells meat products to Whataburger franchises in the United States. Sometime in 1991 or 1992, Liborio Hinojosa ("Hinojosa"), the president and CEO of H&H, met with Adams to set up a procedure so that meat products could be sent to Mexico for Whataburger Mexico.

The procedure was as follows. Adams or an associate ordered meat products from H&H by fax or telephone. Adams instructed H&H to ship the ordered meat products to SR Forwarding, a forwarding agent [a company that would arrange for the meat to be shipped across the US-Mexico border] in Laredo, Texas. Adams also instructed H&H to invoice the meat products in the name of Proveedora de Alimentos Constratados ("PAC") because PAC had a permit to import meat products into Mexico, and Adams did not. PAC would then sell the meat to Whataburger Mexico.

This case stems from three unpaid shipments of meat that were delivered by H&H to SR Forwarding, pursuant to Adams' instructions. … H&H sued Adams for breach of contract. The trial court found in favor of Adams… .

On appeal Adams asserts that recovery by H&H is barred by the statute of frauds. Specifically, Adams contends that a contract for the sale of goods for more than $500 must be in writing, and the transactions at issue, although more than $500, were not in writing. [Texas law provides:]

> "[A] contract for the sale of goods for the price of $500 or more is not enforceable unless there is some writing sufficient to indicate that a contract for sale has been

made between the parties and signed by the party against whom enforcement is sought... A contract which does not satisfy the [writing] requirement is nonetheless enforceable with respect to goods for which payment has been made and accepted or which have been received and accepted... .

[In reference to the three deliveries in issue, the evidence established that Adams, or someone associated with Adams, ordered meat products from H&H; the meat products were delivered to SR Forwarding per Adams' instructions; and Adams received the meat products and accepted them.]

Based on these facts we hold the contract between Adams and H&H is an exception to the statute of frauds [and thus a written agreement between the parties is not required]. Judgment for H&H is affirmed.

CASE QUESTION

1. Why does the Statute of Frauds dispense with the need for a writing where the seller has delivered goods and the buyer has accepted them?

The Nature of the Writing

The required writing need not be a formal contract. A note, letter, or memorandum is sufficient. The writing should specify the identity of the parties, the subject matter of the agreement, and its essential terms. Additionally, it must have been signed by the party who is the defendant in a lawsuit to enforce the contract. Initials will suffice in lieu of a full signature. Likewise, an electronic signature is sufficient for transactions facilitated on the Internet. Among the forms an electronic signature can take are a name typed by the sender at the end of an e-mail message; a digitized image of a handwritten signature that is attached to an electronic document; or a secret code, password, or personal identification number (PIN) such as that used with ATM and credit cards.

Part Performance Exception

An exception to the writing requirement of the Statute of Frauds is the doctrine of part performance. Where the party asserting the absence of a writing as a defense has partly performed the contract, the court may construe therefrom both the existence of the contract and its terms. The need for a writing is thus eliminated.

The doctrine of part performance is illustrated in a case in which a chef was hired by a restaurant on a three-year contract. The parties prepared a written contract, but neither signed it. The chef nonetheless went to work for the restaurant and was paid pursuant to the terms of the agreement. Three months later the chef was terminated. He sued the restaurant claiming breach of the three-year commitment. The restaurant's defense was the Statute of Frauds (the agreement could not be completed within a year from its making) and the absence of a signed writing. The court held that the restaurant had partly performed consistent with the written but unsigned agreement. The court therefore concluded that the parties had a contract consisting of the terms in the writing, and held the restaurant liable for breach of contract.[3]

Parol Evidence Rule

Often in the course of negotiating a contract, many terms are added and later dropped before the ultimate agreement is reached. If the final contract is reduced to writing and is complete on its face (meaning that it addresses all of the terms that parties to that type of contract are likely to include), the parties usually intend the writing to be their full agreement. Any terms discussed by the parties but not included in the document are viewed by the law as intentionally abandoned by the parties.

One party may later try to claim that one of the terms abandoned in the negotiation process was intended by the parties to survive the writing. The **parol evidence rule** will preclude that term from becoming part of the contract. **Parol** means "oral." The parol evidence rule prevents the parties from modifying a written contract using evidence of oral agreements made prior to signing the writing. For example, assume you are negotiating to purchase a motel. In the rear of the property is an unsightly storage shed. You ask the seller to remove it and she agrees. Thereafter you prepare a written contract containing the terms of your purchase agreement, and it is signed by you and the seller. The writing does not mention the seller's commitment to remove the shed but does address all the terms that parties buying and selling a motel would customarily include. You want the shed removed, and remind the seller of the agreement, but she refuses to remove it. In this case the parol evidence rule supports the seller; she need not remove the shed. Because the agreement about its removal was reached prior to signing the contract, and because the promise to remove the shed was not included in the writing, the parol evidence rule bars the buyer from enforcing the seller's promise to remove the shed. To avoid a similar outcome, be sure to include in your written contracts *all* of the terms of your agreement.

The parol evidence rule does not apply to agreements made *after* a contract is signed. Therefore, a written contract can be modified by oral agreements made after parties sign a contract, even if those agreements vary or modify the written contract.

parol
Oral or spoken.

parol evidence rule
An evidence rule that seeks to preserve the integrity of written agreements by barring contracting parties from altering their contract with evidence of oral agreements made prior to signing.

---

[3] *Schneider v. Carlisle Corporation*, 2001 WL 400387 (Tenn. 2001)

genuine assent
Concept that the parties involved in a contract must genuinely agree to the contract terms.

duress
Threats of harm if a person does not sign a contract.

fraud
An intentional untruthful statement made to induce reliance by another person or for the purpose of misleading someone, usually for personal gain.

Another requirement for a valid contract is **genuine assent,** meaning that the parties must genuinely agree to the contract terms. If, for example, one party enters a contract, not because he truly consents to its terms, but because he was subjected to **duress** (threats of harm if he does not sign), the contract is voidable and can be disaffirmed by the party who was threatened.

Fraud and Misrepresentation

A person who enters a contract due to fraud or innocent misrepresentation can avoid the contract. **Fraud** is an intentionally untruthful statement made for the purpose of misleading someone, usually for the fraudulent party's gain. For example, you make a reservation at a hotel because the reservation clerk, under pressure to increase sales, informed you that the hotel is located on the beach at the Gulf of Mexico. The clerk knows that the hotel is not on the beach.

When you arrive at the motel on an inland canal, one mile from the Gulf of Mexico, you discover the truth. You are the victim of fraud and can cancel the reservation without liability. Likewise a hotel was held liable for fraud where it represented to a trade association that it had ample rooms to accommodate the group's annual convention, when in fact the hotel's management knew they had booked another much larger convention with overlapping dates and could not accommodate the trade association.[4]

Case Example 4-5 illustrates another example of fraud.

CASE EXAMPLE 4-5

Filet Menu, Inc. v. C.C.L. & G., Inc.

94 Cal. Rptr.2d 438 (Calif. 2000)

...Filet Menu, Inc. ("FMI") was in the printing and design business catering to the food service industry. C.C.L.&G. ("CCLG") owned and operated two restaurants of a five-restaurant chain of Mexican restaurants, the other three of which were owned by Salazar, an officer of CCLG. In the middle of 1992, FMI's salesman, Michael Klein ("Klein") made a sales solicitation call on Salazar.... .

In February 1993, Salazar signed numerous purchase orders with FMI, one to purchase 4,000 menus at $4 each, one to purchase 5 million place mats at $0.39 each, one to purchase 5 million dinner napkins at $0.39 each and one to purchase 5 million cocktail napkins at $0.09 each, the latter three items to be delivered 250,000 at a time, every 90 days.

---

[4] *Marriott Corp. v. American Academy of Psychotherapists, Inc.,* 277 S.E.2d 785 (Ga. 1981)

The facts presented to the jury revealed an elaborate, fraudulent scheme. Klein admitted that he dealt with CCLG and Salazar "with intent to defraud them purposefully." He acknowledged making numerous misrepresentations to Salazar. When Klein first solicited Salazar in August, 1992, Klein represented to Salazar, "per Mr. LeVine's [Klein's boss'] instructions on how to sell, that we were able to go into a restaurant and design a menu for them and accompanying products that would guarantee a specified increase to the bottom line, a percentage of their bottom line." [Klein guaranteed CCLG a 20 to 40 percent increase.]

Klein also told Salazar that Klein could sell him colored napkins for "a little bit more" than the white napkins they were using, though he knew he could not. [Apparently the cost for colored napkins was substantially more than for white ones.] As per instructions from LeVine, Klein told Salazar that the application Salazar signed was "a mere credit application and nothing more" needed to check references, though Klein had been told that it was more than a credit application. It was a credit application and a purchase order designed to bind the customer to terms in the ultimate transaction. The purpose of getting the customer to sign the application document was to "hook them" into the transaction. Klein was instructed by LeVine never to leave a copy of this document with the customer. Klein was also instructed by LeVine to make certain that there were distractions when the application was being signed so that the customers "don't really understand what they're signing and know what they're signing." Salazar was induced to sign the application.

With respect to the purchase of menus, Salazar said that he did not want to spend more than $4 per menu and wanted to purchase no more than 3000 menus. LeVine told Salazar at a meeting that he could work within that budget knowing that the menus would cost $7.00 to $8.88, at a minimum, but failing to disclose that to Salazar. There were numerous other misrepresentations and sharp practices employed by FMI and LeVine during the course of the transaction, elaborated upon in the trial testimony.

The jury returned a verdict which found that the contract for FMI to supply menus, place mats, dinner napkins and cocktail napkins was entered with CCLG but that CCLG's consent was induced by fraudulent misrepresentations by FMI. ...The jury also found that FMI and LeVine's misconduct was engaged in with the intent to defraud CCLG and Salazar... .

[The evidence supports the jury's verdict in favor of CCLG.] The judgment is affirmed.

CASE QUESTION

1. Identify four fraudulent statements made by Klein and LeVine and two fraudulent practices they perpetrated.

innocent misrepresentation
An untruthful statement that the speaker believes is accurate.

Another basis on which to avoid a contract is **innocent misrepresentation,** that is, an untruthful statement that the speaker believes to be accurate. For example, you arrive at a hotel on a hot summer day and find the temperature in the lobby uncomfortably warm. You ask the manager if the air conditioning is working properly. The repair person had worked on it that afternoon and informed the manager that it was fixed. Based on that statement, the manager informs you that the air conditioning was recently fixed and should be fully operational soon. Relying on the manager's statement, you contract for a room. In fact, the air conditioner is not working, as you discover a short time later when the temperature fails to cool. The manager made an innocent mistake; he had a reasonable basis to believe the information he gave you was correct. You can cancel your contract for the room and go elsewhere. The law allows a buyer of services or goods to avoid the contract in both fraud and innocent misrepresentation cases because in each the buyer has been misled.

Mistakes

Parties to a contract may make various types of mistakes in the process of negotiating and agreeing to the contract. Some of those mistakes have legal significance and others do not. Mistakes made by a buyer as to value or quality of a good being purchased will not affect the validity of the contract. For example, the manager of a restaurant purchases a desk for the receptionist, believing it is an antique made with expensive wood. The manager's belief is based on her own assessment of the desk and not on any representations made by the seller. Later the manager learns that the desk is an imitation of an antique and worth significantly less than the amount paid. The manager in this case has made a mistake in judgment as to the value or quality of the good. The contract is not affected by this mistake; the manager cannot cancel the contract. The manager should have investigated the attributes of the desk more carefully before completing the purchase.

unilateral mistake
An error made by one party to a contract as to the terms or performance expected.

Mistakes as to facts, aside from value or quality, may affect the validity of the contract. Two types of factual mistakes exist—unilateral and mutual. A **unilateral mistake** is an error made by only one party to the contract as to the terms or performance expected. A **mutual mistake** is one shared by both parties.

mutual mistake
A mistake made by both parties to a contract.

Generally, a unilateral mistake is not a basis to avoid a contract. Thus, when only one party makes a mistake as to a fact, that party cannot cancel the agreement on the basis of the mistake. For example, a guest at a resort hotel misread an advertisement concerning the Memorial Day weekend entertainment and so believed that a popular entertainer would be performing for three nights during the weekend rather than just one. Upon learning the truth he sought to cancel part of his three-day reservation. The court held that his mistake was unilateral and therefore did not support a cancellation of his reservation. Although he departed the resort before the end of the three-day weekend, he remained obligated to pay his hotel bill for the full three days.[5]

---

5 *Freemen v. Kiamesha Concord Inc.,* 351 N.Y.S.2d 541 (N.Y. 1974)

Unlike unilateral mistakes, mutual mistakes involving an important fact will enable either party to avoid the contract. For example, Theresa owns two hotels. She contracts to sell one of them to Jeff. Theresa thinks she is selling the hotel on East Main Street. Jeff thinks he is purchasing the one on Dewey Avenue. The parties in this example made a mutual mistake as to an important fact, the identity of the hotel. Since the parties never had a meeting of the minds (in legal terms, their contract lacked mutuality), either can cancel the contract without liability.

Ambiguous Terms/Trade Usage

It is important for contracting parties to state the terms of their agreement clearly and without ambiguity. If the terms are vague or confusing, the parties could end up in court disputing the meaning. Careful drafting can avoid such lawsuits. Unfortunately for the parties in Case Example 4-6, the language in their contract left room for argument as to its meaning. Thus, time and money had to be spent on a lawsuit.

CASE EXAMPLE 4-6

Southern Hospitality, Inc. v. Zurich American Ins. Co.

393 F.3d 1137 (Okla. 2004)

This case arises from the denial of insurance claims after the events of September 11, 2001… [P]laintiffs claim … their loss of business income [should be] covered by their… policy… [with Zurich American Insurance ("Zurich")]. The losses were sustained because customers canceled their visits to hotels plaintiffs operated when the Federal Aviation Administration (FAA) grounded all airplane flights in the United States…

I. Plaintiffs, who will be referred to collectively as "Southern Hospitality," manage a number of hotels throughout the United States that are highly dependent on air travel. Southern Hospitality's … revenues, and therefore Southern Hospitality's profits, plummeted following the events of September 11 because the cancellation of flights meant that Southern Hospitality's customers could not travel by air to its hotels.

Southern Hospitality filed a claim with Zurich, seeking coverage for its business income losses… One provision covers losses "caused by action of civil authority that prohibits access to the described premises."…Zurich denied the claim, contending the losses were not covered by the policy. Southern Hospitality filed the underlying lawsuit for breach of the insurance contract…

II. If language of a contract is clear and free of ambiguity the court is to interpret it as a matter of law, giving effect to the mutual intent of the parties at the time of contracting… Whether the contract is ambiguous is for the court to decide, considering the contract as a whole… The test for ambiguity is whether the language is susceptible to two interpretations on its face … from the standpoint of a reasonably prudent lay person, not from that of a lawyer… The mere fact the parties disagree or press for a different construction does not make an agreement ambiguous... In the absence of an ambiguity, the court must enforce an insurance contract according to its express terms, giving the policy's language its plain and ordinary meaning... In making this determination, we do not search for unusual or tortured meanings...

"CIVIL AUTHORITY" CLAUSE

Southern Hospitality ... contends its losses were covered by the following policy provision:

Civil Authority. We will pay for the actual loss of Business Income you sustain ... *caused by action of civil authority that prohibits access to the described premises*... This coverage will apply for a period of up to two consecutive weeks from the date of that action...

There is no dispute that the FAA's order prohibiting the flying of airplanes qualified as an "action of civil authority." Rather, Southern Hospitality argues that the words "prohibits access" apply because its customers were prevented by the FAA order from coming to its hotels by air. It does not dispute, however, that its hotels remained open for business at all relevant times. Zurich counters that the flying restrictions did not prohibit access to Southern Hospitality's hotels because the hotels themselves were accessible, and therefore the policy does not apply...

We are not persuaded [by Southern Hospitality's argument]. The plain and ordinary meaning of "prohibit" is to "formally forbid, esp. by authority" or "prevent." Oxford American Dictionary and Language Guide. "Access" means "a way of approaching or reaching or entering"... The FAA order prohibited access to airplane flights; it did not prohibit access to hotel operations.

We affirm the judgment of the district court [in favor of the insurance company].

CASE QUESTIONS

1. Do you agree with the court's narrow interpretation of the term "prohibits access"? Why or why not?

2. Do you think that the narrow definition of the term resulted in a fair and just result in this case for the hotel? For the insurance company? Why or why not?

3. How might the clause read to favor the hotel's interpretation?

In another case, a landscaping company agreed to plant and maintain a large number of trees and shrubs over a two-year period on a parcel of land. The contract required the landscaper to replace any trees that died within one year of planting, but excluded from the guarantee damages resulting from "extreme acts of nature, such as tornadoes, or excess amounts of wind." A cold wave occurred during the first year of the contract, one of the coldest ever recorded in the state. For six consecutive days the average low temperature was colder than 30 degrees below zero. Of the trees planted by the landscaper per the contract, 115 of them, with a replacement value of $52,760, were killed. The landowner claimed the landscaper was obligated to replace them. The landscaper argued that the cold wave was an extreme act of nature and thus relieved him from liability. The court determined that the contract reference to "extreme acts of nature" included only sudden and unforeseeable disasters "such as tornadoes and excess amounts of wind" and not an unexpected cold spell. The landscaper was thus required to replace the trees.[6] Had the language been clearer, the landscaper might have avoided liability.

In a Nevada case, the plaintiff was a disc jockey for the defendant hotel bar. The disc jockey had a one-year contract and the defendant reserved the right to cancel individual engagement dates. Defendant cancelled the contract with eight months remaining. Plaintiff sued for lost income. The court held that the contract's reference to individual engagement dates referred to a night now and then but did not include cancellation of the bulk of the contract. The court denied the hotel's motion for summary judgment.[7]

Sometimes when contract terms are ambiguous the court will use "trade usage" to clarify the ambiguity. **Trade usage** means practices or modes of dealing generally adhered to in a particular industry, from which an expectation arises that they will be honored in a given transaction. For example, in a New York case, the contracting parties were unable to agree on the meaning of the word *chicken*. Their contract required the seller to deliver a specified quantity of chicken to the buyer. The seller delivered stewing chickens, the least-expensive poultry. The buyer objected, claiming the word chicken, as used in the contract, required a higher grade. The dispute ended up in court. Experts in the poultry field testified (an additional expense for the seller) that various grades of chicken exist and that each is identified by a different name, except for the lowest grade, which is simply called *chicken*. Applying this custom in the industry, the court determined the seller had fulfilled its contractual obligation by delivering the bottom-of-the-line stewing chickens.[8] This case underscores the importance of careful drafting of a contract. Use of more exacting language on the part of the buyer could have resulted in purchase of the product he intended, thus saving considerable money in attorney fees and litigation expenses.

trade usage
Practices or modes of dealing that are generally adhered to in a particular industry, such that an expectation arises that they will be honored in a given transaction.

Case Example 4-7 illustrates the rule that if the wording of a contract is not ambiguous, the court will determine the parties' intent based on a practical interpretation of the language used.

---

6 *Tandem Properties v. Lawn and Landscape*, 1999 WL 185204 (Minn. 1999)
7 *Sparks v. HRHH Hotel*, 2012 WL 1970020 (Nev. 2012)
8 *Frigaliment Importing Co., Ltd. v. B.N.S. International Sales Corp.*, 190 F.Supp. 116 (N.Y. 1960)

CASE EXAMPLE 4-7

Las Palmeras De Ossining Restaurant, Inc. v. Midway Center Corp.

107 AD3d 854 (N.Y. 2013)

This is an action for a judgment declaring that the defendant breached its obligations pursuant to a lease by unreasonably delaying the repair and restoration of the subject premises subsequent to a fire. . .

The defendant is the owner of a commercial building in Ossining, NY. A portion of the building was occupied by the plaintiff's restaurant. A fire occurred at the building, causing substantial damage to the restaurant, and forcing the restaurant to close down. Thereafter, the defendant sent a notice to the plaintiff terminating its tenancy. The "fire clause" in the lease provided, in pertinent part, that the landlord may, upon requisite notice, terminate the lease if the premises are "rendered totally untenantable by fire" and the landlord decides "not to restore or not to rebuild" the premises. The lease generally defines the "premises" leased by the plaintiff as the "restaurant, bar, and adjoining space," and provides that the premises were to be "used and occupied" by the plaintiff as a "family restaurant and bar lounge."

The defendant decided not to restore or rebuild the premises but rather, to construct commercial office space in its place. Pursuant to the notice provisions of the fire clause, the defendant notified the plaintiff of its decision not to restore or rebuild the demised premises that were formerly occupied by the plaintiff's restaurant, and requested that the plaintiff vacate the premises.

Plaintiff commenced this action . . .The plaintiff moved for summary judgment. . . The defendant cross-moved for summary judgment, declaring that it properly terminated the lease and, as a consequence, was relieved of the obligation to repair and restore the premises. . . .

Interpretation of an unambiguous contract is a matter for the court [and not a jury]. In interpreting a contract, the document must be read as a whole to determine the parties' purpose and intent, giving a practical interpretation to the language employed so that the parties' reasonable expectations are realized.

Here, the terms of the lease, specifically the fire clause, are not ambiguous. The fire clause permits the defendant to terminate the lease if the premises are rendered untenantable by fire and the defendant decides not to rebuild the premises. The lease clearly defines the premises as comprising a restaurant and bar. . . .

Under the circumstances of this case the defendant's decision not to rebuild the demised premises as a restaurant and bar was reasonable, and there is no evidence of bad faith on the part of defendant. Consequently, the [lower court] should have granted the landlord's motion for summary judgment (case dismissed).

Conditions

In most contracts, the promises of the parties to perform their contractual obligations are **absolute,** meaning they must be performed or the promising party will be in breach of contract. Occasionally a contractual duty is not absolute, but is contingent upon the occurrence or nonoccurrence of a specified event. That event is called a **condition.** If the condition occurs, the contractual duty remains in effect. If the condition does not occur, the contract is discharged and the parties are not obligated to perform.

For example, a person hired to repair a hotel pool may promise to complete the work within a week, provided that a drain pump ordered from out of town arrives within two days. The prompt delivery of the pump is a condition. If the part is delivered timely, the contract requires that the pool repairs be completed within a week from when the contract was made. If the part is delivered late, the repairer is not obligated to conclude the job within the week.

Case Example 4-8 provides another illustration of a condition and its effect on a contractual duty.

absolute
Perfect or complete.

condition
An event on which a contractual duty is contingent.

CASE EXAMPLE 4-8

Casino Resorts v. Monarch Casinos, Inc.

1997 WL 793134 (Minn. 1997)

Casino Resorts, Inc. [hereinafter Casino Resorts] and Monarch Casinos, Inc. [hereinafter Monarch], executed a letter of intent in July 1993. In the letter of intent, Casino Resorts expressed an interest in acquiring certain gaming-related assets held by Monarch. The document specifically states that the contemplated transaction is subject to three conditions precedent: (1) a definitive and mutually satisfactory purchase agreement, (2) shareholder approval of the purchase agreement, and (3) approval by respective counsel. Monarch agreed that after acceptance of the letter of intent and prior to the closing date, neither Monarch nor its agent would directly or indirectly initiate or solicit any discussions or negotiations with any third party.

No purchase agreement was ever prepared or executed, and Casino Resorts never held a shareholder's meeting.

In March, 1994, approximately eight months after the execution of the letter of intent, Monarch negotiated a preliminary agreement with the Tribal Chairman of the Pokagon Band of Potawatomi Indians to provide management of its proposed gaming activities... .

[Thereafter Monarch entered into a contract with another business to sell the gaming-related assets.] Casino Resorts sued Monarch for breach of contract.... .

A condition precedent is one that must be performed before the agreement of the parties becomes operative. If the event required by the condition does not occur, there is no breach of contract because the contract is unenforceable… .

It is undisputed that none of the conditions precedent were performed; Monarch and Casino Resorts did not obtain the approval of their respective counsel, a purchase agreement was never drafted, Casino Resorts did not seek or obtain the approval of its shareholders, and a closing never occurred… .

The parties' actions constituted [nonoccurrence of a condition], which … results in a discharged [unenforceable] contract.

Contracts Formed on the Internet

Virtually every type of commercial deal can be and is pursued via the Internet, including hotel reservations, airline reservations, and purchases of restaurant and hotel supplies.

How valid are contracts entered in cyberspace? This question was baffling to lawyers and judges when the Web first became a popular means of doing business, because the law relevant to the Internet had not yet developed. Since then, legislatures and judges have strived to provide clear rules to guide Internet users. Today, as a general rule, contracts made online are as enforceable as their "land-based" counterparts. The online versions are subject to similar rules of contract law.

Many of the problems that arise with computer-generated contracts are identical to problems with traditional contracts. An example is ambiguous language, which can wreak the same havoc in an online contract as we have seen it produce in standard contracts.

© ecco/Shutterstock.com

An issue that was undetermined in the early days of the Internet was the legal effect of a "click-on acceptance." Often an Internet user is directed to indicate consent to an offer relayed online by clicking on an acceptance icon. An example is described as follows in a case involving a popular hotel reservation website: "The reservation page on the Hotels.com Web site required consumers to click on a button that said 'I Agree to the Terms and Conditions;

Book Reservation' to reserve their room. Right above the button, the terms and conditions specifically provided, 'By proceeding with this reservation you agree to all Terms and Conditions, including all terms and conditions contained in the User Agreement.' The User Agreement phrase was hyperlinked to the User Agreement pages. Additionally, the reservation page referenced the User Agreement three different times."[9]

Courts recognize these click-on acceptances as a valid means of creating a contract. In determining the enforceability of the agreement, a threshold issue is whether the computer user has access to the terms of the contract before accepting the goods or services offered on the website. If the purchase or downloading can be accomplished without the contract terms being accessible, a court will likely determine the parties have not entered a contract incorporating those terms. Thus, where defendant invited users to download free software from its webpage provided the downloader agreed to be bound by certain terms restricting the software's use, but the downloader could not have learned of the existence of the terms without scrolling down the webpage below the download button, an agreement incorporating the terms in the subsequent screen had not been formed.[10] Therefore, the downloader was not subject to the stated terms.

If, however, the user must scroll through the contract before placing an order for the goods or services, and by the terms, must accept the contract to place the order, the contract is enforceable. Thus, a term of a contract was found by a court to be valid and binding in the following circumstance: A buyer sought to purchase a seller's services online; the purchase could not be completed unless the buyer agreed to the terms of an agreement; and the electronic format of the website required the buyer to scroll through the contract in order to accept its provisions. The term in question was a **forum selection clause,** which is a provision that identifies a specific location at which any lawsuit arising out of a contract must be brought. The clause required that suits be commenced in Virginia. Plaintiff brought the action in Texas. Defendant sought dismissal of the case because of the incorrect forum. Plaintiff contested the enforceability of the online contract. The court rejected plaintiff's argument and determined the contract to be valid, including the provision requiring the case to be commenced in Virginia.[11]

forum selection clause
A clause in a contract preselecting a particular forum, such as a given state, county, court or administrative proceeding, for the resolution of a dispute.

In a Texas case, the court held that the click on "agree" button for submitting controversies to arbitration rather than court was conspicuously presented to users completing their reservations and so was enforceable.[12]

We have already seen in the discussion in this chapter about the Statute of Frauds that electronic signatures, as used with Internet communications, are sufficient alternatives to the more common form of a signature—that is, the signing of one's name at the end of a document.

---

[9] *Hotels.com L.P. v. Canales,* 195 S.W.3d 147 (Tex. 2006)
[10] *Specht v. Netscape Communications, Corp.,* 306 F.3d 17 (N.Y. 2002)
[11] *Barnett v. Network Solutions,* 38 S.W.3d 200 (Tex. 2001)
[12] *In re Online Travel Company Hotel Booking Antitrust Litigation,* 997 F.Supp.2d 526 (Tex. 2014)

Breach of Contract

Failure to perform as required by the terms of a contract constitutes breach of contract. This is a civil wrong, not a criminal one. An example of a breach of contract is provided by a case involving the purchase of a motel and its contents. The sales agreement "detailed that the motel contained 23 units … and that the air-conditioning system as well as other mechanical systems were in good operating condition and repair." A list of assets annexed to the contract included a telephone console. After the closing, the buyers discovered that the phone console was leased and not owned by sellers and thus could not be sold to buyer. Further, the air-conditioning system was leaking freon and had a defective compressor. Evidence established that the sellers were informed by their repair technician two years prior to the sale that the air conditioner had a freon leak and a broken timer on the lead compressor. Based on this the court said, "Defendants [sellers] were aware, at the time of conveyance, that the system was not in good operating condition and repair." These circumstances clearly constituted breach of contract by the seller.[13] (Note: This circumstance also constitutes fraud.)

damages
The remedy sought by the injured party in a civil case.

specific performance
A remedy for breach of contract requiring performance of the contract terms.

compensatory damages
Out-of-pocket expenses including doctor bills and lost wages, and compensation for pain and suffering, loss of enjoyment of life, loss of consortium, and loss of services.

A nonbreaching party may be entitled to a remedy of either **damages,** meaning money to compensate for resulting loss, or **specific performance,** meaning performance of the contract terms.

Compensatory Damages

The breaching party may be required to pay compensatory damages to the other contracting party (the nonbreaching party). **Compensatory damages** refers to the sum of money necessary to cover loss incurred by the nonbreaching party as a result of the breach. Stated differently, the nonbreaching party is entitled to the "benefit of the bargain," meaning that the breaching party must put the nonbreaching party in the position the latter would have been in had the contract been fully performed. For example, if a restaurant orders kitchen equipment and, following delivery, fails to pay, the supplier is entitled to compensatory damages—that is, the price of the purchased items. In a case applying the rule to a service contract, a linen company entered a three-year agreement with a restaurant owner for the leasing and cleaning of linens including the cooks' shirts, pants, aprons, and towels. The restaurateur terminated the contract early. The court awarded damages equal to the average weekly rental charge for the remaining term less costs the linen company would have incurred in servicing the contract.[14]

---

[13] *Cheng Sing Liang v. Chwen Jen Huang,* 679 N.Y.S.2d 1998 (N.Y. 1998)
[14] *General Linen Services, Inc. v. Smirnioudis,* 897 A.2d 9639 (N.H. 2006)

The nonbreaching party is generally not entitled to damages for **pain and suffering,** meaning compensation for physical pain, mental anguish, stress, or other similar injury resulting from breach of contract. Pain and suffering as an element of damages is recoverable only in cases involving negligence and other torts. We will discuss pain and suffering in more detail in Chapter 5.

pain and suffering
Compensation for physical pain, mental anguish, stress, or other similar injury resulting in breach of contract.

Requirement of Foreseeability

A plaintiff seeking to collect damages for breach of contract must prove that the damages were foreseeable to the breaching party. If the latter could not anticipate the loss, the plaintiff will not be awarded compensation.

Requirement of Reasonable Certainty

The plaintiff in a breach of contract case must prove to a reasonable certainty that she suffered a loss as a result of the breach. Some states also require that the plaintiff prove the *amount* of the loss to a reasonable certainty. For example, a resort hotel hired an unknown singer to perform in the nightclub. Due to low reservations, the hotel canceled the show, thereby breaching the contract with the performer. Unbeknownst to the hotel, the singer had arranged for a talent scout to attend the show. When the hotel breached the contract, the singer sued for loss of income that might have resulted had the scout liked the performance and agreed to promote the singer. The performer will lose the lawsuit for two reasons: (1) inability to prove reasonable certainty of the fact or amount of damages; and (2) inability to prove the hotel could have foreseen those damages.

In Case Example 4-9 the plaintiff was unable to establish any damages from defendant's breach. If a plaintiff cannot prove a loss, it will not be entitled to collect damages. The facts of this case were presented in Case Example 4-8. Reread the facts to refresh your memory.

CASE EXAMPLE 4-9

Casino Resorts, Inc. v. Monarch Casinos, Inc.

1997 WL 793134 (Minn. 1997)

...[J]udgment in favor of Monarch was also appropriate because Casino Resorts failed to demonstrate damages. The controlling principle is that damages that are speculative, remote or conjectural are not recoverable.... Uncertainty as to the amount of damages is not fatal to recovery, but a claim cannot be maintained when it is uncertain that there are any damages at all... .

Casino Resorts projects its losses based on the assumption that the letter of intent would have allowed them to develop the Pokagon Band's gaming operation. But even if that opportunity were considered a part of the agreement, the damages are still speculative. The development of any casino facilities by the Pokagon Band requires [per federal law] governmental authorizations, including a compact approved by the Governor of Michigan and ratified by the Michigan legislature. A compact was approved by the governor of Michigan in early 1996, but the Michigan legislature failed to ratify it. ... Even if the necessary state approvals are obtained, additional federal approvals, which may take as long as two years, are necessary.

Casino Resorts has failed to establish that it has sustained any loss, much less a loss that could be reasonably measured. The district court correctly concluded that the damages were too speculative, and, because proof of damages is required for the Casino Resorts' claim, [judgment for Monarch] on all claims was appropriate...Affirmed.

CASE QUESTION

1. What facts were cited by the court as proof that the damages claim was too speculative to support a recovery?

Case Example 4-10 also involves the issue of recovery of damages when a new enterprise is forced out of business because of another party's breach of contract. Unlike Case Example 4-9, the court in this case found that the existence and amount of damages were sufficiently certain to be recoverable. As you read the case, identify what facts differentiate it from *Casino Resorts* that may have resulted in the varying outcomes. Also note the importance of the expert witness in calculating damages.

CASE EXAMPLE 4-10

Ibiza, Inc. v. Samis Foundation

131 Wash.App. 1055 (Wash. 2006)

FACTS

...This appeal arises out of a dispute over a commercial lease. Ibiza, Inc. (Ibiza) leased the ground floor of the Collins Building from the Samis Foundation for a restaurant and club, also named "Ibiza" (the restaurant). The Collins Building is located at 524 Second Avenue in Seattle. A dispute between Ibiza and Samis over the installation of a heating, ventilation, and air conditioning system delayed the opening of the restaurant for 18 months. Ibiza sued Samis for breach of contract. The suit went to trial, and the jury found that Samis breached the lease.

The court awarded Ibiza $592,000 in damages for lost profits. Samis appeals the lost profits award.

On the issue of lost profits, Ibiza presented testimony from Misty Laurance, general manager of the restaurant, and Arnold Shain, an expert on the restaurant industry. Laurance testified that she created the business plan for Ibiza from the plan started by the president of Ibiza. She conducted research on the Seattle restaurant industry at a Web site run by the Washington Restaurant Association, and later received guidance and confirmation from Shain. Laurance also testified that she had visited other Seattle clubs, such as Element and Medusa, and that these visits had an impact on her pro forma for the restaurant because "I am gaining knowledge and experience from each club that I am visiting, each restaurant I am visiting, to help us be better"…

Shain testified that he has owned, operated, and developed restaurants throughout his 40-year career. For the last 12 years, he had operated his own company, the Restaurant Group, which develops, manages, and helps restaurants…

The jury found for Ibiza in its breach of contract claim and awarded $592,000 in lost profits… Samis appeals the judgment for lost profits…

ANALYSIS

In Washington, a plaintiff can recover lost profits for breach of contract only when they are proven with reasonable certainty… The usual method of proving lost profits is from profit history… But a court may allow a plaintiff to recover lost profits for a new business when a reasonable estimation of damages can be made through analysis of market conditions and a profit showing of identical or similar businesses in the vicinity, operating under substantially the same conditions… Expert testimony can be sufficient to establish lost profits…

Samis argues that Ibiza failed to establish lost profits with reasonable certainty and that the trial court should have granted judgment as a matter of law on this issue against Ibiza. We disagree. We initially note that Laurance and Shain were qualified to form an opinion and express a judgment on lost profits. A court may admit evidence in the form of expert testimony as long as the expert witness is "qualified to form an estimate and express a judgment" on lost profits… The weight to be given to an expert witness's testimony is for the trier of fact to determine…

While Laurance had not previously managed a restaurant in Seattle, she did have experience in the Portland, Oregon area. She worked for a year for the Sterling Management Group, which Laurance described as "a company that 'opened restaurants' and went into restaurants that were in trouble, that were losing money, that were having staffing issues, and went in and evaluated their business. They looked at their costs, looked at their labor, looked at the people [who] were on their team, and did an evaluation. They hired and found new staff [who] were more appropriate. We worked on the look of the restaurant. We did marketing, to gain more people coming in."

Laurance … also testified that when she developed a pro forma and business plan for the restaurant, she consulted with counselors at the Small Business Administration, conducted research on a Web site maintained by the Washington Restaurant Association, and visited other Seattle venues. Shain testified that he owned, operated, and developed restaurants throughout his 40-year career. For the last 12 years he operated his own company–the Restaurant Group–which develops, manages, and assists restaurants…

He personally handles about 15 or 18 clients, most of whom send him monthly or quarterly statements for him to review. He testified that he has "a pretty good feel for what the numbers are"…He also offered a "guesstimate" that he has consulted with 15 or 20 new restaurant owners every year for the past 12 years…

Laurance and Shain were clearly qualified to testify as expert witnesses on the subject of lost profits. Both persons had experience in the day-to-day management and financial administration of restaurants in the Pacific Northwest. Shain in particular had an extensive background in managing venues in Seattle…

The clear implication of this testimony is that venues in the Seattle area comparable to Ibiza were profitable and that Laurance's [businessplan] was accurate in projecting profits for Ibiza. While Ibiza did not describe the profits of other Seattle venues in specific dollar amounts, this is understandable given the reluctance ofrestaurants and clubs to provide proprietary information to a competitor. Indeed, Laurance testified that "[i]t is very hard to get them to give that out if I am not an employee of theirs"… The best alternative to actual profit and loss statements from nearby restaurants was the testimony of Laurance and Shain…

[W]hen a plaintiff has established that the new business would have generated profits and "the difficulty in proving their amount is directly caused by the defendant's breach, a greater liberality is permitted in making estimates and drawing inferences"… Here, the absence of profit history and the difficulty of proving the amount of lost profits are the direct result of Samis's breach of the lease agreement. Ibiza therefore must be permitted a greater liberality in estimating its profits and in drawing inferences from the industry knowledge of Laurance and Shain.

In conclusion, we affirm the trial court's judgment for Ibiza…

CASE QUESTIONS

1. Why is reasonable certainty as to damages a prerequisite for a nonbreaching party to collect damages?

2. What facts convinced the court that Ibiza's damages could be proven to a reasonable certainty?

Where a restaurant has already been in business for a period of time and has a profitable track record, damages are easier to prove. In a Missouri case the plaintiff operated a restaurant for six years, leasing space from a mall landlord. Thereafter the premises were damaged extensively by fire. The parties negotiated a new five-year lease with an option to renew and the landlord began to rebuild. Due to construction disagreements, the landlord canceled the new lease and the plaintiff successfully sued for breach of contract. Concerning lost future profits, the accountant who prepared the restaurant's financial statements testified that the business had always turned a profit. He expressed the opinion that the restaurant had a good reputation and a good location, and therefore profits could be expected in the future. Said the court, "[W]hile the claimant must demonstrate a reasonable probability of future profits, … mathematical precision is neither required nor possible. There was ample evidence here that [the restaurant] could expect profitable operations for the term of the lease." The plaintiff was thus entitled to collect lost future profits.[15]

_____

[15] *Joe Garavelli's Restaurant, Inc. v. Colonial Square Associates*, 21 S.W.3d 149 (Mo. 2000)

In Case Example 4-11 the hotel sought damages from its insurance company for lost business following the tragic events of September 11, 2001, described by the court. The hotel was unable to prove with sufficient certainty the amount of its loss. Note how the hotel's expert witness was found to be unreliable.

CASE EXAMPLE 4-11

Wyndham International, Inc. v. Ace American Insurance Co.

186 S.W.3d 682 (Tex. 2006)

Hotel owner brought action against property insurers and broker to recover over $66 million for business income loss alleged to have occurred from terrorist attacks of September 11, 2001. ...when four commercial airliners were hijacked by terrorists who flew two of those aircraft into the towers of the World Trade Center in New York City, one into the Pentagon in Washington, D.C. and one into a field outside of Shanksville, Pennsylvania. The World Trade Center was incinerated and collapsed. The Pentagon sustained extensive damage from the impact and attendant fire. Over 3000 people died as a result of the hijackings and attacks. The United States government issued orders in the face of September 11 attacks, which halted all airline service, both commercial and private, for a matter of days. Wyndham asserts these orders, and the significantly increased travel security measures, along with the reaction of the world's population, caused reservations to be cancelled and inhibited the public from using its 163 hotel and resort properties for at least the balance of September and October 2001... .

[Wyndham appeals the trial court's finding that Wyndham's damage expert was unreliable, and the court's grant of summary judgment in favor of the defendant insurance companies.]

In their motion to exclude the evidence of the expert, David Borghesi, a C.P.A. and consultant, the Insurance Companies asserted several reasons.

a. The Unreliability of Wyndham Forecasts

Borghesi bases his entire opinion on monthly forecasts of room revenues prepared by Wyndham. The insurance companies assert these forecasts are faulty and unreliable. Specifically the Insurance Companies offered evidence of the following: (1) the forecasts were prepared by employees at each of Wyndham's individual hotels, who were not required to follow any type of internal forecasting standards, did not adhere to any economic model, did not have a consistent reference point, and the forecasts were not reviewed by employees with training in forecasting; (2) Borghesi acknowledged that many of the forecasts were not accurate; (3) Wyndham's managers considered the forecasts to be accurate if they were within 5%, plus or minus, of actual revenues; (4) for the month prior to September 11, August 2001, less than 1/3 of the forecasts for the properties met Wyndham's 5% accuracy standard; and (5) Borghesi admitted he made adjustments to the forecasts as he used them in his analysis and the adjustments would yield some erroneous results.

On the other hand, Wyndham asserted: (1) Borghesi was aware of the accuracy standard of 5%, and that many of the August forecasts did not meet that standard, but he allowed for those issues in his calculations; (2) the managers at each property who made the forecasts had extensive experience in preparing such projections, used computer models which took into account economic trends that affect each property, and relied upon the forecasts to run the hotels and track their performance... .

b. The Extrapolation of Revenue Projections for Sixty-Two Properties

Wyndham claims lost business income of over $66 million for 163 of its properties. However, forecasts of revenue were created for only 101 of its properties. Borghesi testified he "extrapolated" the projections for sixty-two properties from the forecasts for the 101 properties by separating the sixty-two properties into categories by size and type of service ... Additionally Wyndham points out that the properties for which projections were extrapolated account for only 13% of the over $66 million projected loss.

The Insurance Companies contend Borghesi's extrapolation is a subjective categorization which fails to address the "myriad factors" which affect the financial experience of each hotel, including geographic location, type, and seasonality. Further, the Insurance Companies argue extrapolations are only permissible if the expert bases the analysis on a "scientifically valid mathematical formula."

These arguments are not subject to easy resolution. However the parties acknowledge the extrapolation is based upon the forecasts created by Wyndham for 101 of its individual properties. Any unreliability of those forecasts taints Borghesi's extrapolated projections, even if it is [only] 13% of the damages.

c. The Failure to Address Other Relevant Evidence

The Insurance Companies contend Borghesi improperly assumed all of the Wyndham's revenue downturn was attributable to the events of September 11th. They argue Borghesi made no effort to compensate for any issues or events which occurred subsequent to September 11 which may have affected revenues.

The Insurance Companies offered evidence that Wyndham's own 2001 Annual Report recited that business was affected during the year by the "recent economic downturn" and "decreased consumer confidence." The Insurance Companies also point to a report prepared by Wyndham's accountant which concludes 83% of decreased demand for lodging services was due to "such economic factors". Additionally, the Insurance Companies offered evidence that showed Borghesi did not consider whether events [booked at the hotel for] the post September 11 period were rebooked. They contend the revenue from those bookings was not lost, just "moved" to a later time, pointing to anecdotal evidence in the record reflecting post September 11 reservations having been moved to times later in 2001. In fact, Wyndham issued a press release dated October 2, 2001, which said, in part, that many of the bookings cancelled for the relevant period had been rebooked for a later time.

...Borghesi testified that he was aware of rebooking of cancelled reservations but did not consider them in his calculations. He also stated he did not try to "parse out" or segregate other potential causes for the decline in Wyndham's business such as the recession in the United State's economy in the third and fourth quarter of 2001. He testified that the decline in business activity in those quarters "likely" had an effect on Wyndham's results in those quarters.

We conclude Borghesi's opinion is not based upon a reliable foundation, and accordingly, is irrelevant ... [Wyndham has thus failed to prove damages; summary judgment for the Insurance Companies affirmed.]

Duty to Mitigate

A plaintiff seeking to collect damages for breach of contract must prove that it attempted to mitigate its loss. **Mitigate** means to reduce or lessen. If the plaintiff takes no steps to contain the damages and instead ignores the possibility of reducing them, plaintiff will not be able to recover any of its loss from the breaching defendant. The reason for this rule is the law's objective to avoid economic waste—that is, an unnecessary loss. Assume a motel has a contract with a snowplower to plow the motel's driveway. Following a big storm the contractor does not plow and the motel is unable to contact him. If the motel takes no steps to call another snowplower, guests might cancel reservations because they are unable to drive into the motel's parking lot. The motel may be able to avoid the resulting loss of income by locating another snowplower to do the job. If the motel does not attempt to mitigate its loss, it will not be able to collect its lost profits from the original contractor. If the motel makes a good-faith effort to hire a substitute but is unable to find someone available to plow, the original snowplower will be liable for the motel's lost profits.

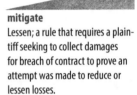

mitigate
Lessen; a rule that requires a plaintiff seeking to collect damages for breach of contract to prove an attempt was made to reduce or lessen losses.

The requirement is not that damages be actually reduced, but that the plaintiff make a reasonable effort to minimize them. In a Colorado case, a restaurant that leased space failed to pay its rent and ultimately went out of business. When the landlord sued for lost rent, the restaurant owners claimed the landlord failed to mitigate damages by attempting to locate another tenant. While in fact the space was not re-rented, the landlord established that he had hired a broker who notified existing restaurant owners that the space was available, advertised the property to the brokerage community that represents restaurant owners, sent out broadcast e-mails, placed ads in newspapers, distributed a brochure regarding the premises to restaurant operators, and posted a "for lease" sign on the premises. This was a sufficient attempt to mitigate damages and entitled the landlord to collect unpaid rent from the original tenant.[16]

Punitive Damages

As we have learned, punitive damages are a sum of money sometimes awarded to a plaintiff in excess of compensatory damages, the purpose of which is to punish the

---

[16] *CMCB Enterprises, Inc. v. Ferguson,* 114 P.3d 90 (Colo. 2005)

defendant. Punitive damages are awarded only if the defendant's actions are wanton or malicious. This type of damages is not often given in a breach of contract case.

Clauses Limiting Damages

Some contracts contain clauses stating that the parties to the contract have agreed to the amount of damages in the event of breach. For example, a hotel franchisee contracted with the defendant architectural firm to design a six-story hotel. The architectural services fee was $70,000. The agreement contained a provision stating that, in the event of negligence or breach of contract, the damages would not exceed the $70,000 fee. Due to alleged negligence by the architects in the design of the building, serious structural flaws occurred during construction that could not be remedied without demolition. There was an estimated $4.2 million in structural damages. The court found that the architectural firm was in breach of contract, but limited damages to the referenced contract clause, based upon freedom of contract.[17]

Specific Performance

Another remedy for breach of contract is specific performance, which is a court order requiring the defendant to perform the act promised in the contract. The application of this remedy is limited to contracts involving the sale of unique, one-of-a-kind items. Every parcel of real property (land) is considered unique. Therefore, in a real estate transaction, if the seller fails to execute the sale, the buyer can sue for specific performance.

---

[17] *Sams Hotel Group, LLC. v. Environs, Inc.*, 716 F.3d 432 (Ind. 2013)

Contracting for a Room

The most common contract in the hospitality business is a person making a reservation for a room. As with all contracts, a contract for a room between an innkeeper and a guest must satisfy the essential elements—contractual capacity, mutuality, legality, consideration, proper form, and genuine consent.

Most contracts for hotel rooms begin with an invitation to negotiate from a would-be guest who inquires as to room availability and price. An offer is often thereafter made by the hotel. If it is accepted, the necessary mutuality exists.

© Africa Studio/Shutterstock.com

As we have seen, if the hotel and guest are savvy, they will put their agreement in writing. Misunderstandings as to dates, duration of stay, applicable rate, and special needs of the guest are thereby avoided.

Overbooking and Breach of Reservation Contract

Wise travelers will make advance hotel reservations at their destination and at places along the route of their itinerary. The hotel reservation, once made and confirmed, constitutes a contract and binds the hotel to provide accommodations. Nonetheless, hotels sometimes overbook; in other words, they confirm more reservations than the number of rooms they have available. Experience proves that a certain percentage of confirmed guests will not use their reservations. Hotels that overbook "play the odds"—that is, they overbook by a number approximately equal to the number of people with confirmed reservations who, based on the hotel's experience, are expected not to show. If the numbers work out, everyone with a reservation who comes to the hotel will have a room. However, if the expected no-shows do appear, the hotel will not be able to accommodate everyone. For those the hotel cannot house, it will be in breach of contract and liable for damages.

For example, the Onyx Acceptance Corporation planned a holiday party as a reward for its most valued customers. The party was at the Trump Taj Mahal (hereafter Trump) in Atlantic City, New Jersey. Onyx prepared for a banquet and booked 60 rooms at a cost of $29,000. Trump represented to Onyx that the reservations were guaranteed. Trump overbooked and was short of rooms, however, and tried to remedy it by booking 26 guests at other hotels in the area and providing complimentary transportation. Onyx sought and received damages for breach of contract.[18]

---

[18] *Onyx Acceptance Corp. v. Trump Hotel & Casino Resorts*, 2008 WL 649024 (N.J., 2008).

Like any nonbreaching party, the would-be guest who is denied a room because the hotel has overbooked is entitled to collect compensatory damages. This typically includes travel expenses associated with seeking and finding alternate lodging, telephone calls necessitated by the move to let family and friends know of the changed location, and other costs that may be incurred. The overbooked hotel is well advised to assist the guest in finding a room at a second hotel. This was done by the hotel in Case Example 4-12, and may have saved it from liability for punitive damages. The issue before the court was whether the plaintiff was entitled to punitive damages.

CASE EXAMPLE 4-12

Dold v. Outrigger Hotel

501 P.2d 368 (Hawaii 1972)

…Upon arrival at the Outrigger on February 18, 1968, the plaintiffs were refused accommodations and were transferred by the Outrigger to another hotel of lesser quality because the Outrigger lacked available space. On February 19 and 20, the plaintiffs again demanded that the defendants honor their reservations, but they were again refused.

Though the exact nature of the plaintiffs' reservations is in dispute, the defendants claim that since the plaintiffs made no cash deposit, their reservations were not "confirmed" and, for that reason the defendants justifiably dishonored the reservations. Plaintiffs contend that the reservations were "confirmed," as the American Express Company had guaranteed to Outrigger a first night's payment in the event that the plaintiffs did not show up. Further, the plaintiffs claim that this guarantee was in fact the same thing as a cash deposit. Thus, plaintiffs argue that the defendants were under a duty to honor the confirmed reservations… .

An examination of the record … shows the following: …

3. In lieu of a cash deposit, the Outrigger accepted American Express Company's guarantee that it would pay the first night's deposit for the plaintiffs.

4. On February 18, 1968, the Outrigger referred twenty-nine parties holding reservations at the Outrigger to the Pagoda Hotel, which deemed these referrals "overflows."

5. On February 18, 1968, the Outrigger had sixteen guests who stayed beyond their scheduled date of departure.

6. From February 15 to 17 and 19 to 22, 1968, the Outrigger also had more reservations than it could accommodate. Plaintiff's exhibits … indicate the number of overflows and referrals … made by the Outrigger to the Pagoda Hotel on the following dates:

February 15	20 referrals	
" 16	20	"
" 17	32	"
" 19	44	"
" 20	9	"
" 21	9	"
" 22	20	"

7. Evidence was adduced that the Outrigger made a profit from its referrals to the Pagoda Hotel. Upon advance payment for the rooms to American Express, who in turn paid Outrigger, the plaintiffs were issued coupons representing the prepayment for the accommodations at the Outrigger. On the referral by the Outrigger, the Pagoda Hotel's practice was to accept the coupons [from the guests in full payment of the room] and bill the Outrigger for the actual cost of the rooms provided [which was less than the Outrigger's rate]. The difference between the coupon's value and the actual value of the accommodations was retained by the Outrigger.

The plaintiffs prevented a profit from being made by the Outrigger by refusing to use the coupons and paying in cash for the less expensive accommodations.

May Plaintiffs Recover Punitive Damages for Breach of Contract? The question of whether punitive damages are properly recoverable in an action for breach of contract has not been resolved in this jurisdiction… .

We are of the opinion that the facts of this case do not warrant punitive damages. …It has long been recognized that an innkeeper, holding himself out to the public to provide hotel accommodations, is obligated, in the absence of reasonable grounds for refusal, to provide accommodations to all persons upon proper request. …However, where the innkeeper's accommodations had been exhausted, the innkeeper could justly refuse to receive an applicant… .

We are not aware of any jurisdiction that renders an innkeeper liable on his common law duty to accommodate under the circumstances of this case. Consequently, plaintiffs are not entitled to … punitive damages… .

CASE QUESTIONS

1. Why did the court not impose punitive damages?

2. Under what circumstances do you think a court might impose punitive damages where a hotel overbooked?

In a Minnesota case the defendant hotel anticipated an overcapacity circumstance and notified registered would-be guests of a change in their hotel before their arrival. The hotel assisted them with other details of the move. Their case against the hotel was dismissed.[19]

Case Example 4-13 includes factual material about the scope and causes of overbooking. The reader should not conclude from the court's decision that a hotel can overbook with virtual impunity. Not all courts will be as sympathetic to the hotel as the court in this case seems to have been. As you read the case, take note of the following: (1) the different types of losses suffered by the plaintiff, and (2) which types of damages the plaintiff was and was not able to recover.

CASE EXAMPLE 4-13

Vern Wells et al. v. Holiday Inns, Inc.

522 F.Supp. 1023 (Mo. 1981)

This case arose out of the events which occurred when the individual plaintiffs, Vernon Lee Wells and Robert K. Hughes, traveled to San Francisco, California in July of 1976 for a convention of the National Office Machine Dealers Association (NOMDA). At that time, Wells [and Hughes were co-owners] of the corporate plaintiff, Central Office Machines. Wells planned the trip as both a business undertaking relating to the convention and as a vacation, taking his wife and son with him. The Wells family, Hughes and another co-owner of the corporation had reservations at defendant's Union Square Holiday Inn for three nights commencing July 15, 1976.

The reservations were made through the NOMDA travel coordinator in Bridgeport, Connecticut, to whom the check to cover the entire travel package cost was sent. ...Although the check to cover costs included the hotel, reservation confirmation slips sent to plaintiff's by the Housing Bureau ... indicated that no deposit had been received and that the confirmation would not be held after 6:00 p.m. unless the hotel is notified of late arrival. The Holiday Inn also sent its own confirmation slip to plaintiffs, which did not specifically indicate whether a deposit had been received but did state that these were "6 p.m. only" reservations.

On July 15, 1976, after a flight delay of approximately an hour, the plaintiffs' party arrived in the lobby of the Union Square Holiday Inn at around 3:00 in the afternoon to find a crowd waiting to check in to the hotel. After a considerable wait, and inquiries with various hotel personnel, plaintiffs were informed that no rooms were available for that night and that arrangements would be made with another hotel for one night. They were referred to the Jack Tarr Hotel, and vouchers for taxi fares to the Jack Tarr and for the return trip to the Holiday Inn were provided. Plaintiff Hughes used the vouchers but plaintiff Wells did not. Hughes returned and stayed at the Holiday Inn on July 16; Wells did not, but remained at the Jack Tarr that night and moved to the Hyatt Regency for the night of July 17, 1976.

---

[19] *McCoy v. Homestead Studio Suites Hotel* 2007 WL 444956 (Minn. 2006)

The Inn Operations Manual of defendant contains provisions for procedures for defendant's personnel to follow in the event reservations are dishonored. These include arranging substitute accommodations and paying the difference in cost if that of the substitute is higher, providing taxi fare, and other incidental expenses necessitated by the change, such as the cost of telephone calls to notify family members of a change. Such procedures appear to have been followed in plaintiffs' case. Plaintiffs received a refund of all payment made to the NOMDA convention group which was to have been applied to lodging at Holiday Inn for the nights when it was not actually used, a total of $268.40. Because Hughes and the other business associate went to Las Vegas for the last scheduled night of the San Francisco trip, plaintiffs paid, overall, $41.95 less than the amount which had been anticipated by them as payment for lodging prior to the trip. Plaintiff Wells was required to pay $16.00 for parking when he removed his rental car from the Holiday Inn garage which he would not have been charged had he been registered at the Holiday Inn, and testimony indicated that some taxi fares expended would not have been necessary if the plaintiffs had stayed at Holiday Inn.[1]

Plaintiffs contend that the dishonoring of the reservations by Holiday Inn gives rise to a claim for fraud or misrepresentation and for breach of contract. They seek actual damages in very substantial amounts, asserting (1) business losses from failure to acquire equipment at the convention for which they had a ready market, and, as to Wells (2) the triggering of a series of excruciating cluster headaches which continued for approximately two months. Punitive damages are sought under the fraud claims.

Absent a showing that defendant knowingly or willfully misrepresented a material fact to plaintiffs or intended not to reserve a room, there is no fraud. The failure to perform a contract cannot be transmuted into fraud or misrepresentation absent that intent. Although there may be a duty to disclose material facts, concealment of a remote possibility of nonperformance does not seem to be considered deceitful at common law... .

Expert testimony indicated that overbooking to some extent is a recognized and accepted practice within the hotel industry. The day that plaintiffs were refused their rooms there was a dishonor rate at that Holiday Inn of almost four percent (4%). However, the hotel's average dishonor rate was much lower, or about half the national average of one-half of one percent. Moreover, the dishonor rate is not completely attributable to the practice of overbooking, but also is affected by such unknowns as unexpected "stay-overs."...

Further, the television commercials aired by defendant, which plaintiffs testified they viewed and took into account before making the reservations, add nothing to the claim for fraud or misrepresentation. The most pertinent commercial, on the general theme "The Best Surprise Is No Surprise" depicts a traveler being rejected at the front desk of another hotel or motel by a desk clerk who denies receipt of a reservation. The message most obviously derived from the scene is that Holiday Inns are comparatively reliable in their reservation practices. There is no evidence in this case to the contrary. The reservation system described by the witnesses, particularly the "Holidex," appears to be generally efficient. The overbooking practice of Holiday Inns is fairly conservative compared with the general industry, and any slight exaggeration of the extent of reliability contained in the commercial falls within the category of mere "puffing" [an expression of opinion not made as a statement of fact and not legally binding as a promise or warranty] which is not actionable.

---

1 The additional fares total $22 as to Wells and $4 as to Hughes for a trip to Chinatown (within walking distance of the Holiday Inn).

As a general rule, the measure of damages for breach of contract is that "compensation should be equal to the injuries subject to the condition that the damages be confined to those naturally and approximately resulting from the breach and be not uncertain or speculative." [R]ecovery for breach of contract [is limited] to those damages which could reasonably be supposed to have been within the contemplation of the parties at the time they entered into the contract. The rule generally precludes such special, consequential damages as lost profits from transactions not known to the party charged with breach, in addition to barring recovery for disappointment, mental distress, and similar claims, because such items are not normally predictable by the party breaking a contract... .

[T]he Court finds that plaintiffs have failed in their proof of causation. Proof as to lost business opportunities is not adequate to support an assessment of damages with reasonable certainty. A claim for loss of anticipated profits of a commercial business may be too remote, speculative and too dependent upon changes of circumstances to warrant judgment for recovery. The Court is satisfied that a considerable amount of business is conducted at the trade show in question, and that plaintiffs had a ready market in Kansas City for various items of business equipment. However, the proof is not satisfactory as to the critical nature of the room reservation at the Holiday Inn-Union Square to acquisition of the necessary items, or that the lost room reservation seriously impeded the business activities ... Plaintiff Hughes and the third co-owner lost no appreciable time in attempting to locate desirable equipment. Plaintiff Wells appears to have been more interested in litigating than in buying. He voluntarily took time off to confer with a lawyer about the prospects of litigation... .

The Court must also be skeptical of the theory that plaintiffs could not reasonably have located suitable equipment except at the convention. Trade shows are doubtless the most convenient times to negotiate sales agreements, but it is likely that any solid prospects would have been followed up before or after the convention closed, and no showing was made why acquisitions could not be made from Kansas City after the convention, in time to satisfy the needs of the potential purchasers. The purchasers waited months and even years before buying substitute equipment. The frustrations of the trip are thus not shown to have foreclosed the market. Skepticism as to the critical nature of the NOMDA convention is increased by Wells' failure to attend the shows in 1977, 1978, or 1980.

The Court does not discount the very serious nature of Mr. Wells' problem of cluster headaches. The evidence is convincing that he suffered intermittent excruciating pain, so severe that it caused him to pace the floor at night, occasionally rolling weeping on the floor or making other attempts to block the pain, such as striking his head against the wall. Cluster headaches were shown (as the name indicates) to occur in series, the onset of which has been observed in Mr. Wells' case to be closely associated with stress, such as business pressures or overwork. ...Shortly after midnight on Friday night, July 16, Wells experienced the first in what became a new cluster of headaches. ...[T]he Court concludes that this is not recoverable under present legal standards.

It is accordingly hereby

ORDERED that judgment shall be entered in favor of plaintiff Vernon L. Wells and against defendant in the amount of Thirty-eight dollars ($38)... . It is further

ORDERED that judgment shall be entered in favor of plaintiff Robert K. Hughes and against defendant in the amount of Four dollars ($4)... .

CASE QUESTIONS

1. Why was Wells able to collect for the cab fares to Chinatown but not for the business losses from failure to acquire the desired equipment at the convention?

2. Why did the court refuse to award damages for Wells' cluster headaches?

3. The court referenced a reservation system utilized by Holiday Inns. What impact did this system have on the outcome of the case?

Damage to Goodwill

If the plaintiff in an overbooking case is not an individual, but a tour operator, it may suffer cancellations and loss of future business as a result of a hotel not honoring reservations. The tour operator thus may suffer substantial damages from loss of goodwill. **Goodwill** refers to a favorable reputation producing an expectation of future business. For example, assume you contract with a tour company for a cruise that is advertised to include a particular, upscale ship. When you arrive at the dock you discover that the boat you will be traveling on is inferior to the advertised ship. It is smaller, has fewer amenities, and is not as nicely decorated or designed. The cause of the switch was that the ship had overbooked and so your tour was bumped, through no fault of your tour operator. When you return from your trip you are not likely to recommend the tour company to your friends and, upon hearing about your experience, they will likely avoid that company in the future. The tour company has suffered injury to its goodwill.

goodwill
A favorable reputation producing an expectation of future business.

The amount of loss that a company will experience as a result of damage to its goodwill is hard to prove. We learned that a court will not grant compensation in a breach of contract case unless it is satisfied that damages are proven to a reasonable certainty. Note how the court in Case Example 4-14 addresses this potential problem.

CASE EXAMPLE 4-14

Rainbow Travel Services, Inc. v. Hilton Hotels Corp.

896 F.2d 1233 (Okla. 1990)

…[P]laintiff Rainbow Travel Service [Rainbow] won a jury verdict against the defendants for breach of contract and fraud. …The Fontainebleau Hilton is a deluxe resort hotel in Miami Beach, Florida. The hotel is operated by the defendant Hilton Hotels, Inc. ("Hilton") … Plaintiff Rainbow is a travel agency…

In the spring of 1986, Rainbow began organizing several tour packages for Oklahoma football fans who wanted to attend a University of Oklahoma versus University of Miami football game. The game was scheduled for September 26, 1986, in Miami, Florida. Rainbow initially contacted the Fontainebleau concerning the possibility of reserving hotel rooms for Rainbow's groups. After telephone calls and correspondence between the parties, the Fontainebleau sent Rainbow two contracts which called for the hotel to reserve one hundred and five rooms for Rainbow on the weekend of September 27, 1986. The second of these contracts, which is at issue in this case, provided that forty-five rooms were to be reserved for Rainbow on September 26, 1986. Rainbow executed the agreements and returned them to the Fontainebleau. In June of 1986, the Fontainebleau confirmed Rainbow's reservation by mail and requested prepayment for one night for Rainbow's groups. In response, Rainbow sent a partial payment of over $6,000. The Fontainebleau sent another confirmation in August and requested the remainder of the payment. The payments were made by checks drawn on Rainbow's account in Oklahoma.

Rainbow's president, A.J. Musgrove, went to Miami on September 24, 1986, to make sure that all arrangements had been made for his groups' stay at the Fontainebleau. One group from Rainbow arrived on September 25 and was accommodated as planned. Musgrove met with the hotel's tour representative, Livia Cohen, on September 24, twice on September 25, and again on the morning of September 26. Ms. Cohen assured Mr. Musgrove that everything was fine and that all of the reserved rooms would be available. When the Rainbow group arrived at the hotel on the afternoon of September 26, however, they were told by Hilton representatives that no rooms were available at the Fontainebleau. Hilton made arrangements for the group to stay at the Seacoast Towers, a hotel/apartment complex located about ten blocks away from the Fontainebleau. Rainbow subsequently filed this action… .

The jury found that Rainbow had sustained $37,500 in damages to its good will. Rainbow's primary witness on this issue was its president, Musgrove, who testified that he was familiar with the value of Rainbow's goodwill from his history with the company and from reviewing Rainbow's financial statements. Mr. Musgrove estimated that the incident at the Fontainebleau damaged Rainbow's goodwill in the amount of $250,000. His opinion was based in part on his observation that when customers are dissatisfied they tell others about it, meaning that a bad incident such as this one has a "rippling effect" on a business' reputation. He indicated that this is particularly true for the travel agency because it relies heavily on its reputation in the community. Additionally, Rainbow presented the testimony of witnesses who had traveled to Miami on the Rainbow tour. These witnesses stated that they were dissatisfied with Rainbow because of the hotel incident and stated they probably would not choose Rainbow again as a travel agent.

Viewing this evidence in the light most favorable to the plaintiff, we find that there was substantial evidence reasonably tending to support the jury's verdict. …Appellants argue nonetheless that the amount of damages to goodwill was so uncertain as to be speculative. The rule in Oklahoma, however, is that the prohibition against recovery of damages because the loss is uncertain or too speculative in nature applies to the fact of damages, not to the amount.

Rainbow presented evidence that Hilton accepted reservations for more rooms than were available on September 26, 1986. Hilton admitted that its policy was to book the Fontainebleau up to one hundred and fifteen per cent of its capacity, but argued that it did so based on a historic fifteen per cent "no-show" rate for guests with reservations. Hilton insisted that this policy allowed the hotel to honor almost all of its reservations. Although Hilton showed that an exceedingly high percentage of reservations were in fact honored over the course of the year, Rainbow presented evidence showing that on fifty per cent of those occasions when the hotel was operating at capacity the hotel had to dishonor reservations. Additionally, Rainbow presented evidence tending to show that Hilton was aware of a substantial likelihood that Rainbow's reservation might be dishonored. Rainbow showed that Hilton knew at least one month in advance that a large number of rooms would be closed for maintenance during September of 1986. …Additionally, Rainbow showed that on the date in question Hilton gave a block of rooms to a group from the University of Oklahoma even though the group had not reserved the rooms… .

Hilton argued strenuously … that the overbooking situation was due to factors beyond its control, such as guests extending their stay at the Fontainebleau and rooms being out of order for repairs. These explanations may have sounded rather hollow to the jury, however, in light of a portion of the Fontainebleau's policy manual which read:

Overbooked

We never tell a guest we "overbooked." If an overbook situation arises, it is due to the fact that something occurred that the hotel could not prevent.

Examples:

1. Scheduled departures do not vacate their rooms.

2. Engineering problems with a room (pipe busted, thus water leaks, air conditioning, heating out of commission, broken glass, etc.)

Always remain calm and as pleasant as possible.

In addition to the foregoing, the record contains much circumstantial evidence showing that Hilton had knowledge of a likelihood of dishonoring reservations at the time in question. The Fontainebleau was extremely busy during the week of Rainbow's visit. On September 22 and 23 for instance, the hotel was completely sold out and the Fontainebleau had to dishonor reservations. Although there were some vacant rooms on September 24 and 25, the number of vacancies was very few. Also, the "no-show" rate for reservations was much less during this period than the fifteen per cent annual average used by Hilton. Although Hilton's agent indicated to Mr. Musgrove on the morning of September 26 that his rooms would be available, theNight Clerk Summary for September 25 indicated that the hotel would be short of rooms even if fifteen per cent of the reservations for the 26th failed to show.

Some of the testimony at trial raised questions about the candor of Hilton's explanation concerning its treatment of Rainbow's reservations. Hilton said that it only became aware of a shortage of rooms after Mr. Musgrove had gone to the airport to pick up his group, yet when the group arrived back at the hotel they had already been assigned specific rooms at the Seacoast Towers. ...[W]e find substantial evidence in the record that Hilton was aware of having overbooked the hotel to such an extent as to create a substantial likelihood that Rainbow's reservation would be dishonored. Despite this, Hilton repeatedly told Rainbow that its rooms would be available and did not tell Rainbow that the group might be "bumped." Based on this and all of the evidence in the record before us, we find that a reasonable juror could find by clear and convincing evidence that Hilton recklessly made statements without knowledge of their truth, that Hilton did so with the intention that plaintiff rely on them, and that plaintiff relied on the statements to its detriment... .

[Plaintiff was entitled to recover $37,500 as compensatory damages for injury to its reputation.]

CASE QUESTIONS

1. Why is the potential for damages great when a hotel dishonors the reservations of a tour group?

2. How can a hotel damage its own goodwill by overbooking?

Another Goodwill Issue—Agreements Not to Compete

agreement not to compete
In the sale of a business, a contractual provision barring the seller from competing with the buyer in the geographical area where the company does business for a specified period of time.

When an owner of a restaurant or hotel sells the business, the sales contract customarily includes an **agreement not to compete,** which is a provision barring the seller from competing in the same geographical area for a specified period of time. This type of agreement attempts to preserve for the buyer the business's goodwill—that is, the expectation that the firm's established customers will continue to patronize the purchased business. If the seller reenters the market and competes with the buyer for the same customers, they are likely to patronize the proprietor they know, diverting business from the buyer. The agreement, called a *noncompetition clause* or an *agreement not to compete*, is generally enforceable provided the time and territory within which competition is restricted is not unduly restrictive in duration and geographical area. Case Example 4-15 illustrates a breach of such an agreement and the court's concern that the clause be reasonable in time and territory to be enforceable.

CASE EXAMPLE 4-15

Leo's Partners, LLC v. Ferrari

2005 WL 3667346 (Conn. 2005)

...On July 17, 2001, the plaintiff purchased a restaurant, then known as Leo's, from the defendant, Emmar, Inc. (Emmar) ...As part of the transaction and in exchange for $150,000.00, the plaintiff and the defendants, Emmar ... and Martin Ferrari (Ferrari), the president of Emmar, entered into a non-competition agreement (agreement)... Pursuant to the agreement, Ferrari was prohibited from engaging in the restaurant business within a radius of twenty miles of [the restaurant] for a period of ten years... Ferrari opened... [another] restaurant... [within 20 miles of Leo's] in competition with the plaintiff within the time period set forth in the agreement...

The testimony presented during the course of the trial established that [Leo's] was [a] family-style restaurant with a good reputation. The clientele was primarily local, but there were some customers who would travel a considerable distance to partake in the fare... [Ferrari's] new restaurant was known as Rooster's. Advance promotion of Rooster's indicated that a similar menu format to Leo's would be followed for breakfast and lunch... In June 2004, Ferrari was "bought out" of Rooster's. Ferrari now operates a restaurant in Guilford, which is not within the twenty-mile limitation...

The defendants, while acknowledging the violation of the agreement, claim that the agreement is unenforceable as an unreasonable restraint on trade and against public policy by virtue of its breadth and scope...

The contract between the parties is a contract in restraint of trade. The factors to be considered in evaluating the reasonableness of a restrictive covenant related to the sale of a business are that "the restraint must be limited in its operation with regard to time and place and afford no more than a fair and just protection to the interests of the party in whose favor it is to operate [the buyer], without unduly interfering with the public interest"... This court cannot, under the facts presented, find that the contract is unreasonable...

Accordingly, judgment shall enter on behalf of the plaintiff...

CASE QUESTION

1. Why do the courts consider whether the restriction at issue is "limited in its operation with regard to time and place" when determining whether a noncompetition clause is reasonable?

In a case involving the sale of a restaurant, the seller, in a noncompetition clause, agreed not to "engage either directly or indirectly as an employee, owner, partner, or agent, shareholder, director or officer of a corporation in a similar restaurant business which is directly in competition with the type of business [seller sold to buyer] within a five-mile radius" of the restaurant. Had the seller become a part owner of a competing restaurant or worked there as a chef, manager, or server, the agreement not to compete would clearly have been violated. In the referenced case the seller only did landscaping work for a competing restaurant and gave directions to another laborer at the restaurant regarding work to be done inside the building. The buyer sued, claiming breach of contract. The court ruled that because the restaurant was not in the landscaping or construction business, the seller's work did not harm the buyer's goodwill and therefore did not breach the noncompetition clause.[20]

In another case, a restaurant owner sold his pizza restaurant to a new owner. There was a noncompete clause in the contract that did not allow the former owner to have an interest in a pizza business within 12 miles for three years. The former owner opened a café in the same building as the pizza place. The court held that it was not a violation of the noncompete, because the café only served breakfast food and did not serve pizza.[21]

Breach by a Guest

Sometimes the party who fails to perform in a hotel reservation case is not the hotel but rather the guest—for example, when the latter cancels a reservation. The hotel may have a cancellation policy that permits the guest to cancel without liability until a specified number of days prior to the date of the reservation. If such a policy is not applicable, a guest who cancels a reservation may be liable for damages for breach of contract. In such a case, the same legal rules concerning remedies apply to the hotel as apply to the guest when the hotel breaches: the hotel as the nonbreaching party must try to mitigate the loss by attempting to rent the room to another guest. If the hotel is unable to relet the room, the inn is entitled to collect compensatory damages from the guest, which is commonly the agreed price for the room.

Case Example 4-16 illustrates a situation where the guest breached the contract and the hotel was entitled to damages.

---

[20] *Kladis v. Nick's Patio, Inc.*, 735 N.E.2d 1216 (Ind. 2000)

CASE EXAMPLE 4-16

Freeman v. Kiamesha Concord, Inc.

351 N.Y.S.2d 541 (N.Y. 1974)

...Plaintiff, a lawyer, has commenced this action against the defendant, the operator of the Concord Hotel (Concord), one of the most opulent of the resort hotels in the Catskill Mountains resort area, to recover the ... rate for a day charged and not refunded after he and his wife checked out before the commencement of the third day of a reserved three-day Memorial Day weekend... .

The testimony adduced at trial reveals that in early May 1973, after seeing an advertisement in the New York Times indicating that Joel Grey would perform at the [Concord] during the forthcoming Memorial Day weekend, plaintiff contacted a travel agent and solicited a reservation for his wife and himself at the hotel. In response, he received an offer of a reservation for a "three-night minimum stay" that contained a request for a $20 deposit. He forwarded the money confirming the reservation, which was deposited by the defendant.

While driving to the hotel, the plaintiff observed a billboard, located about twenty miles from his destination, that indicated that Joel Grey would perform at the Concord only on the Sunday of the holiday weekend. The plaintiff was disturbed because he had understood the advertisement to mean that the entertainer would be performing on each day of the weekend. He checked into the hotel, notwithstanding this disconcerting information, claiming that he did not wish to turn back and ruin a long-anticipated weekend vacation. The plaintiff later discovered that two subsequent New York Times advertisements, not seen by him before checking in, specified that Grey would perform [only] on the Sunday of that weekend.

After staying at the hotel for two days, the plaintiff advised the management that he wished to check out because of his dissatisfaction with the entertainment. He claims to have told them that he had made his reservation in reliance upon what he understood to be a representation in the advertisement to the effect that Joel Grey would perform throughout the holiday weekend. The management suggested that since Grey was to perform that evening, he should remain. The plaintiff refused and again asserted his claim that the advertisement constituted a misrepresentation. The defendant insisted upon full payment for the entire three-day guaranteed weekend in accordance with the reservation. Plaintiff then told the defendant's employees that he was an attorney, and that they had no right to charge him for the third day of the reserved period if he checked out. ...The plaintiff was finally offered a one-day credit for a future stay if he made full payment. He refused, paid the full charges under protest, and advised the defendant of his intention to sue them. ...This is that action.

I find that the advertisement relied upon by the plaintiff did not contain a false representation. It announced that Joel Grey would perform at the hotel during the Memorial Day weekend. Grey did actually appear during that weekend... .

The advertisement contained no false statement. It neither represented nor suggested that Grey would perform throughout the holiday weekend. The defendant cannot be found liable because the plaintiff misunderstood its advertisement... .

It must be noted that the plaintiff checked into the defendant's hotel pursuant to a valid, enforceable contract for a three-day stay. The solicitation of a reservation, the making of a reservation by the transmittal of a deposit, and the acceptance of the deposit constituted a binding contract in accordance with traditional contract principles of offer and acceptance. Unquestionably the defendant would have been liable to the plaintiff had it not had an accommodation for plaintiff upon his arrival. The plaintiff is equally bound under the contract for the agreed minimum period.

The testimony reveals that the defendant was ready, willing, and able to provide all of the services contracted for, but that plaintiff refused to accept them for the third day of the three-day contract period. These services included lodging, meals, and the use of the defendant's recreational and entertainment facilities... .

Hotels such as the one operated by the defendant have developed techniques to provide full utilization of their facilities during periods of peak demand. One such method is the guaranteed minimum one week or weekend stay that has gained widespread public acceptance. Almost all of these enterprises have offered their facilities for minimum guaranteed periods during certain times of the year by contracting with willing guests who also seek to fully utilize their available vacation time. These minimum period agreements have become essential to the economic survival and well-being of the recreational hotel industry. The public is generally aware of the necessity for them to do so and accepts the practice... .

A hotel such as the defendant's services thousands of guests at a single time. The maintenance of its facilities entails a continuing large overhead expenditure. It must have some means to legitimately ensure itself the income that its guests have contracted to pay for the use of its facilities. The minimum period reservation contract is such a device. The rooms are contracted for in advance and are held available while other potential guests are turned away. A guest who terminates his contractual obligations prior to the expiration of the contract period will usually deprive the hotel of anticipated income if that guest cannot be held financially accountable upon his contract. At that point, replacement income is virtually impossible... .

The defendant has contracted to supply the plaintiff with a room, three meals a day, and access to the use of its varied sports, recreational, or entertainment facilities. As long as these are available to the plaintiff, the defendant has fulfilled its contractual commitment....

Ruling of the Court: Judgment is accordingly awarded to the defendant... .

CASE QUESTIONS

1. What is the meaning of the court's statement in the third-to-last paragraph, "At that point, replacement income is virtually impossible"?

2. Would the decision have been different if the hotel could have rented the room to someone else? Why?

3. Why could the plaintiff not avoid the contract based on his mistake concerning when Joel Grey would perform?

If the hotel is able to relet the room for the same or higher price than the breaching guest had contracted to pay, the hotel cannot collect the agreed price for the room from the breaching guest, nor can it retain a deposit the guest might have made. Otherwise the hotel would recover twice and profit from the breach, neither of which the law permits. The hotel in Case Example 4-17 tried unsuccessfully to retain an advance payment although it had relet the room.

CASE EXAMPLE 4-17

2625 Building Corp. (Marriott Hotel) v. Deutsch

385 N.E.2d 1189 (Ind. 1979)

...[O]n December 7, 1972, Deutsch, a resident of Connecticut, made reservations by telephone for six rooms at the Marriott for the 1973 "500" Mile Race weekend (May 27, 28, 29). Marriott requested advance payment for the rooms. Deutsch complied with Marriott's demand and paid by check in the amount of $1,008 in full for the reserved rooms. At the end of March, or the beginning of April, 1973, Deutsch, by telephone, canceled the reservations and requested the return of his advance payment. Marriott refused his demand. Deutsch did not use the rooms and later brought action against Marriott to recover the $1,008 advance payment, alleging the above facts and, in addition, that Marriott had relet the rooms and was not harmed by the cancellation...

The Marriott cites *Freeman v. Kiamesha Concord, Inc.* in support of its position that it had a right to refuse to refund $1,008 to Deutsch when he canceled his reservations. However, we find the facts in the case at hand to be clearly distinguishable. In *Freeman* the guest had checked into the hotel pursuant to the contract, whereas in this case Deutsch had not. Moreover, *Freeman* involved a "last minute" checkout prior to the end of the contract period, whereas Deutsch gave the Marriott approximately two months' advance notice of his cancellation.

We do not disagree with the reasoning in *Freeman* as applied to the facts therein, and such reasoning is certainly applicable in "last minute" cancellation cases, especially at resort-type hotels. Thus, we recognize there may be instances when a guest's cancellation of reservations would not justify a refund of an advance payment. ...[T]he making and acceptance of the reservation in this case constituted a binding contract. Upon Deutsch's breach, Marriott was entitled to actual damages in accordance with traditional contract principles... .

The evidence in the record reveals that Deutsch made reservations, tendered full payment for the use of the rooms in advance, and approximately two months prior to Marriott's time for performance, canceled the reservations and demanded refund, which demand was refused. In addition, we take judicial notice [acknowledgment of a fact by a judge without the need for proof because the fact is well known and generally accepted] that the Indianapolis "500" Mile Race has the largest attendance of any single, one-day, arena-type sporting event in the world. The influx of dedicated racing fans to the Indianapolis metropolitan area in order to witness this spectacle of racing is legend. Attendant with this influx is the overwhelming demand for, and shortage of, hotel accommodations.

Therefore, we find that the facts of this case justified the trial court's conclusion that assessing Deutsch for the full amount of his room payments would cause him to suffer a loss that was wholly disproportionate to any injury sustained by Marriott. Since Marriott sustained no damage, [it is not entitled to retain any of plaintiff's money].

CASE QUESTION

1. Do you agree with the distinction made by the court between this case and *Freeman v. Kiamesha Concord, Inc.*? Why or why not?

Cancellation Clause for Organization Reserving a Large Block of Rooms

When the party canceling hotel reservations is an association that had reserved many rooms—sometimes hundreds or even thousands—for a conference, the hotel may face a substantial loss. As is the duty of any nonbreaching party, the hotel must mitigate its loss by attempting to sell the available rooms.

Many contracts between associations and hotels have a cancellation provision that identifies the obligations of each party in the event of termination of the contract. Those terms vary from contract to contract and control the liability of the canceling organization. Some cancellation provisions require that the association pay the full amount of lost revenue experienced by the hotel (the number of unsold rooms multiplied by the established group rate).[22] Other contract terms may require payment of a lesser amount such as the established group rate for only two nights, although the canceled reservations were for three,[23] or damages "equal to one night's anticipated room revenue based on single occupancy."

The specific terms of cancellation clauses for organizations reserving blocks of rooms are subject to negotiations between the association and the hotel.

Case Example 4-18 arose when an organization canceled a multi-year contract with a hotel to host the group's annual convention. The cancellation clause resulted in liability to the association.

---

[22] *Opryland Hotel v. Millbrook Distribution Services, Inc.*, 1999 WL 767816 (Tenn. 1999)
[23] *Princess Hotels International, Inc. v. Delaware State Bar Association*, 1998 WL 283465 (Del. 1998)

CASE EXAMPLE 4-18

National Ass'n of Postmasters of U.S. v. Hyatt Regency Washington

894 A.2d 471 (D.C. 2006)

...This dispute arose from a multi-year contract in which the Hyatt Regency Washington ["Hyatt"] agreed to provide blocks of rooms and other amenities for the annual leadership conference held by the National Association of Postmasters of United States ("NAPUS'). The contract, entered into in February of 2001, set specific dates for the 2002, 2003, and 2004 conferences. In each of those years, the gathering was to be held in mid-February, as it had been for many years.

After this contract was executed, a federal arbitrator... [for reasons not here relevant] ordered the U.S. Postal Service to move the 2003 and 2004 Rural Mail Count from its usual time in September to a new time in February. The dates selected by the arbitrator, February 15 through March 15, 2003, and February 14 through March 6, 2004, substantially conflicted with the dates of the 2003 and 2004 leadership conferences, which were to be held February 12–21, 2003, and February 11–20, 2004.

Because postmasters play a central role in conducting the Rural Mail Count, this newly-emerged conflict at the very least made it inadvisable to hold the leadership conferences for 2003 and 2004 on the dates previously scheduled... On February 7, 2002, NAPUS orally informed the Hyatt that there was a conflict with the 2003 and 2004 leadership conference dates. On February 8, NAPUS began exchanging e-mails with Hyatt in an attempt to identify new dates for the conference. Hyatt indicated that it would charge increased rates for the days it proposed, but NAPUS was unwilling to pay those increased rates. Unable to find dates and prices that fit, NAPUS sent a letter on February 25, 2002, terminating the contract for 2003 and 2004.

NAPUS sought a declaratory judgment absolving it of any liability for terminating the contract...

Two cancellation provisions in the contract are at the center of controversy in this case. The first of these is a "Cancellation Option." It allows either party to cancel the contract upon written notice to the other, but requires the canceling party to pay ... damages in the amount found in an accompanying graduated scale...

Hyatt claims that NAPUS' cancellation falls within this broad provision. NAPUS, on the other hand, claims that the rescheduling of the Rural Mail Count created an emergency it could not foresee and, therefore, the cancellation of the conference falls within the "For Cause" provision. The "For Cause" clause is much narrower than the "Cancellation Option," but permits cancellation without liability...

The "For Cause" clause begins by enumerating several circumstances in which the contract can be cancelled for cause: "acts of God, war, government regulation, terrorism, disaster, strikes, civil disorder, [and] curtailment of transportation facilities." NAPUS does not argue that the rescheduling of the Rural Mail Count falls within any of these specifically enumerated categories... It does contend, however, that this change of circumstances fits within the residual category included in the "For Cause" clause of "any other emergency beyond the parties' control"...

The events specifically enumerated in the "For Cause" clause of the contract are qualitatively different from the rescheduling of the Rural Mail Count. It was not a war, an act of God, or an act of terrorism; it was not a strike, civil disorder, or a curtailment of transportation facilities. This unexpected conflict of schedules was not "of the same kind" as the events listed. It would excuse the payment of … damages only if it qualifies as "any other emergency" under the residual exception. However, the word "emergency" describes an unexpected development urgently requiring a prompt response, not one where the effects will be felt in a year's time or two years' time… NAPUS learned of the rescheduling of the Rural Mail Count a full year in advance of the 2003 leadership conference and two years in advance of the 2004 leadership conference. The rescheduling of the Rural Mail Count may be an inconvenience or even make compliance with the contract inadvisable, but without an urgent need for prompt reaction, it cannot be considered an "emergency" as that term is properly understood…

We therefore conclude that the "Cancellation Option" applies and that NAPUS owes Hyatt… damages according to the graduated chart found in the contract…

CASE QUESTIONS

1. Do you agree with the court's conclusion that the rescheduling of the Rural Mail Count was not an "emergency" situation? Why or why not?

2. Do you think that the end result of this case, that the plaintiff must pay damages to the defendant, is fair? Why or why not?

3. Note that the "For Cause" clause included "curtailment of transportation facilities." Had this provision been included in the contract referenced in *Southern Hospitality, Inc. v. Zurich American Insurance Co.*, discussed earlier in this chapter (concerning lost hotel income because airline travel was unavailable), might the outcome have been different?

Attrition Clause for Organizations that Do Not Utilize All Rooms on Hold

Customarily, with a conference reservation the hotel agrees to hold a specified number of rooms for conventioneers estimated by conference planners to be needed for the sponsoring organization's attendees. The host organization's members then make reservations directly with the hotel. Occasionally, the group's estimate is significantly above the actual number of rooms rented. An **attrition clause** addresses this situation. It is a contract provision that obligates the organization to compensate the hotel if fewer than the contractual number of rooms are rented by conventioneers. The terms of the contract will control the liability of the association.

In a case involving the Women's International Bowling Conference (WIBC) and a Hyatt Regency Hotel, many fewer rooms were rented than were held by the hotel for the tournament. The hotel claimed the WIBC was liable to pay for the unused

attrition clause
In reference to a room reservation contract between an association hosting a convention and a hotel, a contractual provision obligating the organization to compensate the hotel if less than a specified number of rooms are rented by conventioneers.

rooms. The contract between the hotel and the WIBC did not contain an attrition clause. The issue had been addressed in correspondence from the WIBC to the Hyatt, which stated, "From past experience we estimate the following number of rooms will be picked up [reserved] from your block [the rooms the Hyatt was holding for WIBC] as headquarters hotel." The court held that the word *estimate* denotes that the number of rooms to be held aside by the hotel in the block was not intended as a firm commitment, but rather an approximate figure. Further, the phrase *picked up* evidences that some further action—that is, the making of a reservation by an attendee—was needed before any of the rooms held in the block would be occupied by a convention attendee. Therefore WIBC was not contractually bound to pay for rooms held by the hotel and not rented.[24]

No-Cause Termination Clause

Some contracts have a **no-cause termination clause,** which is a contract provision permitting either party to terminate the contract for any reason or for no reason at all. If the terms of the contract permit termination, ending the contractual relationship is not a breach of contract.

no-cause termination clause
A contract term that permits either party to terminate the contract for any or no reason.

An example is provided in a case involving a contract between United Airlines and a catering company for the purchase of in-flight meals. After the contract was signed, the catering company invested almost $1 million to expand its facilities to accommodate the airline's need. The contract included a no-cause termination clause that read as follows, "The term of this Agreement shall commence on May 1, 1988, and shall continue for a period of three years; provided, however, either party may terminate this Agreement upon ninety (90) days' prior written notice." After one year, the airline gave 90 days' notice and thereafter terminated the contract. The catering company sued for breach. The court dismissed the case for the following reasons: The termination clause was clear and unambiguous; no-cause termination clauses are widely utilized; and the airline abided by the terms of the provision giving 90 days' written notice.[25]

Guaranteed Reservations

Some hotel reservations are guaranteed and others are not. With a nonguaranteed reservation, the hotel is obligated to provide a room for a guest provided the guest arrives by a specified hour. If the guest does not arrive by that time, the hotel can assign the room to someone else and will not be in breach to the late-arriving guest, even if no vacancy exists. If the guest never arrives, perhaps because of a change in plans, the hotel cannot charge the guest for the room, even if the hotel was not able to sell it to someone else.

A guaranteed reservation requires the hotel to hold a room for the guest no matter how late the guest arrives. If the hotel does not have a room available for the

---

[24] *Hyatt Regency v. Women's International Bowling Congress, Inc.*, 80 F.Supp2d 88 (N.Y. 1999)
[25] *United Airlines, Inc. v. Good Taste, Inc.*, 982 P.2d 1259 (Alaska 1999)

late arriver, it will be in breach. In return for this guarantee on the hotel's part, the guest agrees to pay for the room even if she fails to arrive at all.

Sometimes hotels will include the commitment to provide a room at the hotel "or its equivalent" in their guaranteed reservation contracts. This provision would excuse a hotel from breach if it could not provide a room but secured accommodations for that guest at a nearby hotel that offered similar amenities.

Intentional Interference with Contractual Relations

tort
A civil wrong for which a court will provide a remedy in the form of damages (money).

Breach of contract can also give rise to the tort of intentional interference with contractual relations. A **tort** is a civil (noncriminal) wrong for which a court will provide a remedy in the form of damages (money). We will discuss torts in detail in Chapter 5.

To commit the tort of intentional interference with contractual relations, three elements are necessary:

1. A valid contract must exist between two parties.

2. A third party must be aware of the existence of the contract.

3. The third party must intentionally cause or induce one of the contracting parties to break the contract and do business instead with the third party.

The third party inducing the breach will be liable in damages to the contracting party who did not breach.

For example, if a particular cola company has a two-year contract to be the exclusive supplier of soda for a fast-food chain, and a competing cola company that is aware of the contract induces the chain to break the contract and purchase the competing company's beverage instead, the competing company has committed the tort; the original cola company can sue it for damages. Note that a breach of contract is inherent in interference with contractual relations cases. In the example involving the competing cola companies, the fast-food chain breached the contract with the original cola company by terminating the agreement prematurely to enable it to do business with the second company.

Case Example 4-19 vividly illustrates the tort of intentional interference with contractual relations.

CASE EXAMPLE 4-19

Melo-Tone Vending, Inc. v. Sherry, Inc.

656 N.E.2d 312 (Mass. 1995)

...Melo-Tone Vending, Inc., the plaintiff (Melo-Tone), is in the business of installing coin-operated vending machines (e.g., cigarette machines, jukeboxes, games, amusements, and pay telephones) in locations such as barrooms and restaurants. Among its accounts was Bentley's Steak House, an establishment owned by Sherry, Inc. (Sherry). ...On June 22, 1989, Melo-Tone and Sherry entered a contract under which Melo-Tone was to install at Bentley's a jukebox and two pool tables, in addition to a cigarette machine already in place. Sherry was to receive a "commission" of 22.75% on each package of cigarettes sold and 50% of the net yield from the jukebox and pool tables. For a term of eight years (i.e., until June 21, 1997), Melo-Tone would have the "sole and exclusive right" to operate vending machines in... Sherry's premises. Melo-Tone identified its machines by large green labels, bearing its name and telephone number, that were placed on the fronts of the machines.

Business between Melo-Tone and Sherry was uneventful until January, 1992, when Sherry was approached on behalf of James Indelicato, proprietor of Park Square Vending (Park Square), with a proposition about making Bentley's over into a sports bar, for which—not incidentally— Park Square's machines would replace Melo-Tone's. Sherry ... gave the word to Park Square's advance man that there was a small matter of a contract with Melo-Tone, but that did not derail the sports bar project. Late in January or early in February 1992 Melo-Tone's principal officer, Jack D. Kerner, got wind that Park Square was going to install an air hockey game at Bentley's. Kerner called Park Square and mailed to Park Square a copy of his "exclusive" contract with Sherry. Nevertheless, on February 11, 1992, Park Square moved its air hockey game machine onto the Sherry premises.

By letter dated February 18, 1992, Melo-Tone's lawyer informed Park Square that it had exclusive rights to place vending machines at Sherry's establishment and demanded immediate removal of Park Square's air hockey machine. Park Square instead added two pool tables and a cigarette machine, as well as some other machines, at Sherry's place of business. Space was a problem that Park Square solved by furnishing funds to Sherry to move Melo-Tone's machines out. On March 6, 1992, Melo-Tone brought an action against Indelicato [for wrongful interference with contractual relations], and Sherry [for breach of contract]...

As to the defendant Sherry, the plaintiff Melo-Tone stipulated dismissal well before trial. There had been a reconciliation; Melo-Tone was back in and Park Square was out. Melo-Tone's [claim for wrongful interference with contractual relations] was tried to a jury. The jury returned a verdict that the defendant Indelicato had intentionally interfered with the contractual relationship between Melo-Tone and Sherry; ...The jury set the damages at $21,000 ... Indelicato has appealed... .

To make out a case of intentional interference with a contract, a plaintiff must prove that: (1) he had a contract with a third party; (2) the defendant knowingly induced the third party to break that contract; (3) the defendant's interference, in addition to being intentional, was improper in motive or means; and (4) the plaintiff was harmed by the defendant's actions... .

[T]here was more than sufficient evidence to permit the jury to find that: (1) Sherry had entered into an eight-year contract with Melo-Tone to have Melo-Tone operate vending machines on Sherry's premises; (2) Indelicato had induced Sherry to get vending machines from him and to push Melo-Tone's out the door; and (3) Melo-Tone lost profits while its machines were excluded from Sherry's place... .

Indelicato argues that his motives were competitive and financial, not to harm Melo-Tone, and that his conduct was not improper. ... For competition and for the rough and tumble of the world of commerce, there is tolerance... .

It is one thing to lure a customer away from someone with whom it has been doing business by means of better product, service, or prices, but quite another to abet the repudiation of solemn contractual obligations of which the party interfering is well aware. Indelicato not only knew Melo-Tone's contract with Sherry still had five years to run, but also received a copy of it. Indelicato went beyond inducing Sherry to commit a breach of contract, itself sufficient to make out the tort; he abetted the breach by paying to have his competitor's machines unlawfully moved from Sherry's premises. ... The means were improper and spoke eloquently to Indelicato's purpose, although it is enough to prove either improper means or motive.

CASE QUESTIONS

1. Could Melo-Tone have won the case against Indelicato for breach of contract? Why or why not?

2. In what way could Indelicato legally compete with Melo-Tone for Sherry's business?

3. In the penultimate paragraph we learn that one of Indelicato's defenses was "the rough and tumble of the world of commerce." What is meant by this expression? Why did the court reject this defense?

4. What are the pros and cons of a lengthy contract such as the eight-year agreement in this case?

Catering and Convention Contracts

Restaurants and hotels should exercise great care when entering a catering contract to ensure the parties are in agreement on all the terms. Mistakes made at banquets or other catered affairs can cause very unhappy customers.

Given the many details involved when planning a catered event, there is virtually no excuse for not having a written contract. The items that should be included in the writing are identified in Figure 4-1.

Leaving any of these terms undecided or unclear can result in a displeased patron, lost opportunity for repeat business, and a lawsuit for breach of contract. By putting the agreement in writing and including in it the parties' understandings on all terms, the restaurant is protected against unjustified complaints from the customer after the event. If, for example, the customer objects because no ham is included on the cold-cut trays and the restaurant can point to a contract provision that lists the meats to be included and ham is not among them, the customer cannot reasonably continue to gripe. The written contract goes a long way to ensuring a successful event, goodwill with the patron, and avoidance of litigation.

Another type of contract that requires much planning and involves many details is a convention contract—that is, a contract between an organization planning a conference and the hotel at which the conference will be held. Typically,

---

CATERING CONTRACT

The following subjects should be addressed in a catering contract:
1. Names and addresses of the restaurant and the customer.
2. The date of the affair.
3. The location at which the food will be served (for example, the customer's home, a park lodge, or a specific room in the restaurant). If in the restaurant, the time limit on the use of the room, if any.
4. The shape and arrangement of the tables.
5. The type of flatware to be used—paper plates, china, or other types.
6. If the food is to be served away from the restaurant, the kitchen/cooking facilities that will be available for the restaurant staff and when they will be available.
7. If the location is away from the restaurant, whose dishes will be used—the restaurant's or the customer's?
8. The type of service ordered (buffet or sit-down).
9. The menu in its entirety.
10. If hors d'oeuvres are ordered, whether they will be served on a table, carried by servers, or a combination of both.
11. Whether the restaurant will provide liquor, and if so, what types? Will there be an open bar (guests pay no fee for drinks) or cash bar (guests pay for their own drinks)?
12. Will the restaurant provide bartenders, and if so, how many?
13. Decorations, color scheme, and theme.
14. Arrangements for a head table, if applicable.
15. Whether the restaurant will provide music or other entertainment.
16. The number of people expected; a minimum guaranteed number, if applicable; the date when the final count must be relayed to the caterer.
17. Price; amount of deposit; when payment is due; policy on gratuities.
18. Circumstances under which the price might be adjusted; for example, an increase in the costs of food, beverage, or labor, between when the contract is entered and the date of the affair.
19. Equipment to be provided by caterer.
20. Attire of servers.
21. Parking arrangements (for example, whether valet services will be provided).
22. Circumstances under which the caterer will be excused from performance, such as labor troubles, accidents, restrictions on availability of food or beverage, or other causes beyond the caterer's control.
23. Cancelation policy, including any penalties that will be charged.
24. Any other terms relevant to the particular event.

FIGURE 4-1 Recommended subjects for a catering contract

conventions held at hotels are annual gatherings of an association's members who come from a wide geographical area. The organization might be a professional association such as accountants, or a group with a common interest such as religion, athletics, or a hobby. (See Figure 4-2.)

The services offered to conventioneers by a hotel are many and varied. In addition to rooms, they can include food, banquet facilities, recreational facilities, entertainment, meeting rooms, presentation equipment such as overhead projectors, and tourist information about the area. The particular services to be provided at a given convention are subject to agreement between the sponsoring organization and the hotel. Some conventions are elaborate affairs, while others are low-cost operations. The hotel and the association must discuss what services the organization desires and can afford, and what services the hotel is willing and able to provide. Customarily, a representative from the organization will negotiate with the hotel on these matters.

The parties should prepare a written contract embodying their agreement. The terms in the contract should be specific and unambiguous to avoid later disputes.

A thorough contract will contribute greatly to a smooth flow of events during the convention. The written contract should include the terms identified in Figure 4-2.

CONVENTION CONTRACT

The following subjects should be addressed in a convention contract:

1. The name and address of the hotel, organization, and person(s) authorized to act on behalf of the organization.
2. The dates of the convention.
3. The number of guest rooms the hotel will hold for the organization's members and whether the association will be liable if all the reserved rooms are not rented by members.
4. The type of rooms (luxury, mid-priced, budget).
5. The location of the rooms (for example, main building or a wing).
6. The deadline for convention-goers to make reservations.
7. The method for convention-goers to reserve rooms.
8. Check-in and check-out procedures.
9. The number of meals to be provided by the hotel.
10. All the applicable terms identified in Figure 4-1 for catering contracts.
11. Number and location of meeting and exhibit rooms.
12. The arrangement of tables and/or chairs in meeting rooms.
13. The type of equipment to be provided in meeting rooms (for example, audio/visual equipment, including computer hookups).
14. Cancellation deadline and terms including any penalties.
15. Restrictions on posting signs and announcements in the hotel, if any.
16. Any other special services to be provided by the hotel, such as food for coffee breaks, a hospitality suite, complimentary rooms, or entertainment.
17. Any other terms relevant to the particular event.

FIGURE 4-2 Recommended subjects for a convention contract

Summary

By using contracts, a hotel or restaurant can create legally binding obligations. To be enforceable, a contract must satisfy the following essential elements: contractual capacity, mutuality, legality, consideration, proper form, and genuine assent.

Failure to perform a contractual obligation constitutes breach of contract. Overbooking by a hotel resulting in cancellation of reservations constitutes breach of contract, as does cancellation by a guest.

A party breaching a valid contract will be liable to compensate the nonbreaching party for resulting loss. The nonbreaching party must be able to prove the damages to a reasonable certainty and must attempt to mitigate.

While most oral contracts are enforceable, they may be difficult to prove. Therefore, whenever possible, contracts should be reduced to writing. This is particularly important for catering and convention contracts because of the many details involved. Well-written contracts will help achieve and maintain good relationships with patrons and avoid lawsuits.

Preventive Law Tips for Managers

- *Be sure your contracts contain the six essential elements*. To be enforceable, a contract must have six essential elements: legality, proper form, contractual capacity, mutuality, consideration, and genuine assent. If even one of these is missing, the enforceability of the contract is in jeopardy.

- *Do not enter an illegal contract*. Contracts that are illegal are unenforceable. If you agree to an illegal contract, you will not be able to sue for damages or enforce the contract. Assume your business generates toxic wastes. The law requires specific procedures for their disposal. To save money, you contract with a company to remove and dispose of those wastes illegally. You pay the company but it fails to haul away the wastes. You will not be able to regain your money; because you were a party to an illegal contract, the courts will not come to your aid.

- *For contracts covered by the Statute of Frauds, be sure to generate a writing signed by the other contracting party*. Contracts covered by the Statute of Frauds are unenforceable without a writing. The writing must be signed by the defendant, which means your priority is to get the other party's signature. Without the signed writing, you will not be able to pursue a breach of contract case. Contracts required to be in writing include contracts for the purchase and sale of real estate; contracts that cannot be completed within one year from when they are made; contracts to pay another's debts; and contracts for the sale of goods for $500 or more.

- *Reduce all your contracts to writing even if they are not covered by the Statute of Frauds*. A party can easily prove the existence and terms of a written contract. The writing indisputably establishes the terms. By contrast, an oral contract is difficult to prove. The only evidence is your word and that of the other contracting party. In a disagreement, you lack documentation to establish the truthfulness of your position. If the dispute goes to court, a judge or jury will determine which party is telling the truth. The process is cumbersome, and it is possible that the wrong person could win. A written contract avoids these problems and facilitates easy resolution of contract disputes.

- *Include in written contracts all the agreed-upon terms.* A written contract should contain the entire agreement between the parties. The parol evidence rule prevents parties from modifying a written contract with evidence of additional terms agreed upon by the parties but not included in the writing. Failure to include a term in the writing will result in that provision being unenforceable. Review your contracts carefully before signing them to ensure they are complete.

- *Use clear and unambiguous language in your contracts. Know the meaning of the contract terms.* When contract terms are unclear and a dispute results, their meaning may be determined by reference to trade usage. The application of trade usage may or may not result in terms the parties intended when they entered the contract. Avoid this problem by using language that is easily understood and not subject to multiple meanings. The wording must be intelligible to achieve your objective. Also, before working in an industry, familiarize yourself with the jargon. Use in a contract of terms with double meanings—one from normal parlance and the other from industry usage— can produce unexpected and unwanted results. If the contract is unclear, the provisions may not be enforceable.

- *Keep good records of information that might be helpful in proving the amount of damages suffered from breach of a contract.* To recover damages for breach, the nonbreaching party must prove the amount of the loss to a reasonable certainty. Maintaining good records of such matters as sales figures, occupancy rates, and cost of supplies can enhance your ability to prove your damages.

- *Mitigate damages resulting from breach of contract.* To collect damages for breach of contract, the nonbreaching party must mitigate its loss. Failure to attempt to reduce the loss may negate your right to obtain damages for a breach. Whenever someone breaches a contract with you, consider what you might reasonably do to avoid or reduce the loss, and do it.

- *If you have overbooked and cannot accommodate would-be guests with reservations, assist in locating alternate accommodations, and be sure your staff is courteous.* If you are unable to provide accommodations to a guest with reservations, you are in breach of contract. To assist the customer and defuse a potential lawsuit, be as helpful to the would-be guest as possible. At a minimum, help arrange alternate accommodations; pay for transportation to the second hotel; if the second room costs more, pay the difference; and pay for phone calls necessitated by the move, such as calls by the guest to home or office to inform relatives or colleagues of the new location. Additional courtesies may be in order—for example, a gift certificate for a discounted rate at a later date. Keep good records to establish the cause for the overbooking.

- *If requiring a minimum stay at the hotel, be sure your contract with the guest clearly states the number of days required.* If your hotel is offering a special rate or event requiring a minimum stay, you will want to collect payment for the full period of the minimum stay, even in the event a guest departs early. To preclude guests from arguing that they were unaware of the minimum stay and therefore should not have to pay, the contract should clearly state the minimum number of days required and the liability of guests to pay for those days even if they choose to leave before the end of the specified period.

- *Draft detailed contracts for catering engagements.* Catering contracts involve numerous details, many of which are very important to your customer—the host of the event. To avoid misunderstandings and mix-ups, prepare a writing containing the agreement and all the details. Review the agreement prior to the affair to ensure that you provide all the contracted services and menu items.

- *Draft detailed contracts for convention agreements.* Convention contracts also involve many details and an ongoing relationship while the convention progresses from planning to execution, often a lengthy period of time. To avoid disputes and unnecessary ill will, document all decisions and agreements relating to every aspect of the convention. Review the agreement prior to the convention to ensure that you provide all the contracted services. Failure to utilize and review written contracts can foreseeably lead to dissatisfaction with the hotel's service, jeopardizing future business opportunities with the host organization. An avoidable lawsuit might also result.

- *Be watchful for developments in the law of contracts pertaining to the Internet.* Continuing changes in the law are to be anticipated given the ever-growing popularity of the Internet as a means to transact business. Keep abreast by reading industry journals, trade-association newsletters, and newspapers of general circulation.

Review Questions

1. What are the six essential elements of a contract?

2. What categories of people lack contractual capacity?

3. What is meant by mutuality?

4. What is the legal effect of an illegal contract?

5. Name three types of contracts that are unenforceable unless they are in writing.

6. Which of the following types of damages will a plaintiff in a breach of contract case be able to recover?

    A. Lost profits

    B. Pain and suffering

    C. Punitive damages

7. If a guest cancels her reservation with a hotel, how can the hotel mitigate its loss?

8. If a plaintiff in a breach of contract case is unable to determine the amount of its loss, is it entitled to recover any damages?

9. List eight items that should be included in a catering contract.

10. List eight items that should be included in a convention contract. Do not repeat any of the items you listed in response to question 9.

11. What is an agreement not to compete?

12. What is an attrition clause?

13. What is a no-cause termination clause?

14. What is a forum selection clause?

15. What are the elements of a claim for interference with contractual relations?

16. As a general rule, are contracts entered on the Internet valid?

Discussion Questions

1. Identify whether each of the following is an offer or an invitation to negotiate.

    A. Three pounds of fresh shrimp will cost $23.50.

    B. I will play the piano at your restaurant from 5:30 until 9:00 p.m. every night during October for $90 a night.

    C. I have gourmet ice cream for sale.

    D. I am thinking about selling my motel.

    E. Private swimming lessons are available at the hotel pool for $25 per half hour.

2. Why, in a breach of contract case, must the amount of the plaintiff's damages be proven to a reasonable certainty?

3. If a contract term is ambiguous, how will a court decide its meaning? How can parties to a contract avoid ambiguity?

4. Which of the following contracts must be in writing to be enforceable?

   A. A contract to hire a banquet manager for three years

   B. A promise made by a casino patron to cover the betting debts of his friend

   C. A contract to hire a musical trio to play for three weekends at a restaurant for a total of $2,400

   D. A contract to purchase three acres of land on which the buyer intends to build a restaurant

5. Why does the law require a nonbreaching party to mitigate damages?

6. Why, as a practical matter, should all contracts be in writing?

7. What determines the obligations owed to a hotel when a person or organization with a hotel reservation cancels the reservation?

8. To successfully pursue a case for interference with contractual relations the plaintiff must prove, in addition to other elements, that the defendant was aware of the existence of the contract between the plaintiff and a third person. What is the policy reason for making this a necessary element?

9. We learned that a name typed at the end of an offer or acceptance sent via e-mail is considered the equivalent of a person's signature. Why is this so?

Application Questions

1. In a telephone conversation with a sales representative of a linen company, the manager of a hotel ordered $1,000 worth of sheets. Following the conversation he wrote a memo documenting the agreement, initialed it, and sent a copy to the sales representative. A dispute arose between the parties, and the linen company sued the hotel. Does the Statute of Frauds bar the lawsuit? Why or why not? Now suppose the breaching party was the linen company. Does the Statute of Frauds bar that lawsuit? Why or why not?

2. Laurie is planning a reception for her parents' 50th wedding anniversary. She and her parents keep kosher, which means they follow dietary laws prescribed by the Jewish religion. She decided to hold the anniversary party at the Westside Party House because the manager, under pressure to increase sales, told Laurie the Party House serves kosher food. Laurie later discovers that the Party House does not serve kosher food. If she cancels her contract with the Party House and holds the party elsewhere, will she be liable to the Party House for breach of contract? Why or why not?

3. A restaurant ordered 20 cases of champagne for New Year's Eve. Delivery was due on December 29, but the seller failed to deliver. As a result the restaurant was unable to offer its New Year's Eve patrons a midnight champagne toast. The hotel sued the seller for breach of contract, claiming lost profits from both the midnight toast and future parties the angry patrons would be discouraged from hosting at the restaurant. Discuss the restaurant's chances for success in this lawsuit.

4. A contract for yard maintenance services between a hotel and a service company contains an ambiguous term. A dispute arose concerning the term because the parties to the contract interpreted it differently. A lawsuit resulted. What rules of contract interpretation will the court use to determine the meaning of the unclear term?

5. Tyshawn sold a bar he owned to Nicolette. A provision in the contract precluded Tyshawn from opening another food or beverage establishment within 10 miles of the bar for a two-year period. If Tyshawn bought and operated a Motel Six franchise within a 10-mile radius of the bar and within one year after the sale, would he be in violation of the contract? Why or why not?

6. Shania purchased airline tickets to Las Vegas online. Prior to completing the purchase she was required to initial a statement that said she had read the applicable rules and restrictions and she agreed with them. The rules were readily available for her to review by clicking on an icon. If Shania initials the statement without reading the rules, is she bound by them? Why or why not?

7. The Saaranen Hotel is in need of a copier. The owner of the hotel discusses with a copier salesperson the different models available and that he is interested in purchasing a copier. Based on the conversation, the salesperson brings a copier to the office that costs $1900 for the hotel to try out. Neither party signed a contract for the $1,900 copier. Four months later the copier company sends a $1,900 bill to the hotel. It refuses to pay. Is there a contract between the company and the hotel? Why or why not? If a contract does exist, what will the damages be?

Websites

Websites that will enhance your understanding of the material in this chapter include:

www.findlaw.com This site contains a great deal of legal information, including good material on contracts.

www.legaldocs.com This site is an electronic legal form book. Access to some of the contracts on the site requires payment of a fee, while some are offered at no cost. For some of those requiring a fee, a summarized version is available at no cost. The forms offer an understanding of the types of terms that are included in legal documents. Because these forms are standardized, they will not likely fit a particular circumstance you may have. The forms may, however, give you some ideas on what to include in a contract.

To review a variety of catering contracts, search on Google.com for banquet contracts.

UNIT II

Negligence

CHAPTER 5

Principles of Negligence

LEARNING OUTCOMES:

- Know when a hotel or restaurant is liable for its guests' injuries
- Understand torts
- Understand the compensation for guests who are injured on the premises
- Know the term negligence and the elements of negligence
- Understand the duty to act reasonably and how it applies in all negligence cases
- Describe the reasonable person standard
- Understand proximate cause
- Learn duties owed to invitees, licensees, and trespassers
- Understand negligence
- Explain negligence doctrines favoring the plaintiff: res ipsa loquitur, children and the reasonable person test; attractive nuisance doctrine; negligence per se doctrines; strict or absolute liability; strict products liability; respondeat superior; nondelegable duties; duty to aid person in distress; duty of businessowners to aid invitees in danger
- Explain negligence doctrines favoring the defendant: contributory negligence; comparative negligence; assumption of risk

---

KEY TERMS

assumption of risk
attractive nuisance
comparative negligence
contributory negligence
Good Samaritan Statutes
independent contractor
invitee
last clear chance

licensee
negligence
negligence per se
nondelegable
preexisting condition
prima facie
proximate cause
rescue doctrine

res ipsa loquitur
respondeat superior
strict liability
strict products liability
trespasser
within the scope of
   employment

© Tom Grundy/Shutterstock.com

Introduction

Guests at a hotel or restaurant can injure themselves in many ways. One might trip in the dining room. Another might suffer burns from scalding water in a shower. Yet another might drown in the pool. This chapter answers the question: When is a hotel or restaurant liable for guests' injuries? Stated differently, must the hospitality facility compensate patrons for injuries they suffer while at a restaurant or hotel?

The answer depends on whether the establishment violated a legal duty. The hotel or restaurant is not an insurer of guests' safety. This means the hotel is not liable for all injuries that occur while guests are on the premises. With few exceptions, the hotel or restaurant will only be liable when it does something wrong—that is, when the hotel or restaurant commits a tort. The term *tort* refers to many types of noncriminal wrongs done by one person that injure another (but not to breaches of contract, which we studied in Chapter 4).

If the guest who tripped in the dining room did so because the heel on her shoe broke due to shoddy workmanship, the restaurant did not do anything wrong and therefore will not be liable. Similarly, if the scalding water in the shower occurred because the guest carelessly left the knob turned to the hottest setting, the hotel will not be obligated to compensate the guest. If, however, the patron tripped on a hole in the dining room rug, or the hot water resulted from a defective plumbing system, the restaurant or hotel may indeed be liable to the guest.

Negligence

As was mentioned in Chapter 1, **negligence** is a breach of a legal duty to act reasonably that is the direct (or proximate) cause of injury to another. In nonlegal language, negligence is carelessness that causes harm. Assume the hole in the restaurant rug had been there for two weeks. Failure to repair it was careless; the restaurant could have anticipated that someone would be injured by it. As a result, the restaurant will be liable for the customer's injury.

negligence
Breach of a legal duty to act reasonably that is the direct (or proximate) cause of injury to another.

Similarly, assume the hotel had received several complaints about excessively hot water during the week before a guest was scalded, yet the hotel had not called a plumber or taken any steps to fix the problem. Failure to investigate and correct the water problem was careless; the hotel should have anticipated that someone would be harmed. As a result, the hotel will be liable to the injured guest.

The law requires that people and businesses act reasonably in attempting to prevent injuries. When someone acts unreasonably or carelessly, that person is negligent. A reasonable restaurant manager, seeing a hole in the dining room rug, would arrange for its repair to avoid an accident. A reasonable hotel employee who had been alerted about hot water problems in the hotel would investigate and correct the problem. Failure to make the necessary repairs in these examples constitutes negligence.

If the cause of a hotel guest's injury is the carelessness of an employee, the hotel will be liable to the guest. Managers and employees of restaurants and hotels should strive to act reasonably in the way they perform their duties to avoid liability for negligence. The cases in this chapter and in Chapter 6 will illustrate some of the countless injuries that can occur and may result in liability. By reading these cases, future hospitality managers will begin to appreciate dangerous situations and will cultivate a keener eye with which to survey their facilities to ensure they are in suitable condition for customers and guests.

Elements of a Negligence Case

A plaintiff suing in negligence must prove four elements. Failure to prove any one of them is fatal to the plaintiff's case. The four elements are:

1. The existence of a legal duty to act reasonably owed by the defendant to the plaintiff

2. A breach of that duty

3. Injury to the plaintiff

4. Proximate cause

This last element means the breach of duty must be the direct cause of the injury; there can be no intervening cause. Let us examine each element individually.

Existence of a Duty to Act Reasonably

Surprisingly, we do not owe *everyone* the duty to act reasonably. We owe the duty only to those people who would foreseeably be injured by our actions. A restaurant can foresee that if the leg of a chair is broken, a patron will sit on the chair and fall. Therefore, the restaurant owes a duty to its guests to repair the chair. If a restaurant or hotel cannot foresee a particular type of injury, it does not owe a duty to protect patrons against that injury, even though someone is in fact injured. Thus, where a club patron was injured when another customer intentionally bumped into her but the club had no way of knowing that the offender presented a risk to customers or had a dangerous propensity, the club was not liable to the injured patron. Similarly, where the host of a party held at a Hyatt hotel had no way of knowing that one of the guests would fight another, the host is not liable for injuries resulting from the brawl.

In Case Example 5-1, the court concluded that hotel guests could not have foreseen that their son would sexually assault a housekeeper. Therefore, the parents owed no duty to closely monitor their son's activities.

CASE EXAMPLE 5-1

Ordonez v. Gillespie

2001 WL 294553 (Tex. 2001)

...Ordonez alleged that on or about March 9, 1996 she was working as a housekeeper at a Dallas hotel. The Gillespies had rented adjoining rooms 1224 and 1225. While cleaning room 1224, Ordonez alleged she was sexually assaulted by 17-year-old Jason Gillespie, who is mentally challenged. Ordonez alleged the Gillespies acted negligently "by violating the duty which they owed her to exercise ordinary care in the care of their mentally challenged son, a minor." More specifically, Ordonez asserted the Gillespies failed to properly supervise their son, which included failing to ensure Jason would not be left alone with unfamiliar people.... The Gillespies asserted that Jason's alleged conduct was not foreseeable to his parents... The trial court granted summary judgment for the Gillespies....

Ordonez contends a duty existed because Jason's alleged sexual assault [was] a foreseeable result of the Gillespies' negligently leaving him alone in a hotel room.

Negligence consists of three essential elements: (1) a legal duty owed by one person to another; (2) a breach of that duty; and (3) damages proximately resulting from the breach. Duty is the threshold inquiry. It is the function of several interrelated factors, the foremost and dominant consideration being foreseeability of the risk. A parent's duty to protect third parties from acts of the parent's minor child depends on whether the injury to the third party is reasonably foreseeable. Foreseeability means the [defendant], as a person of ordinary intelligence, should have anticipated the dangers his negligent act created for others....

Ordonez relies on a copy of the Gillespies' hotel reservation for room 1225, which includes the notation that the Gillespies needed to be connected to their mentally handicapped son. [Evidence also indicates that] at school Jason "disrupted the class" and "got into a lot of trouble". The Gillespies put Jason in a boarding school in Massachusetts "for kids with psychological or school problems." After six or eight months he was asked to leave the facility because he had run away a couple of times and smoked in the high school. He got his GED when he was 16.

...Jason had never been detained for any type of criminal activity. It was Ordonez' burden to present some evidence that Jason's conduct was foreseeable to his parents. We conclude she failed to do so. Evidence that Jason did not like school and disrupted class is no evidence that his parents should have foreseen the possibility that he was capable of assaultive conduct. Likewise, evidence that Jason's parents considered him to be mentally handicapped is no evidence that it was foreseeable he might be a danger to others. The trial court properly granted the Gillespies' motion for summary judgment.

CASE QUESTION

1. What changes in the facts might have resulted in the Gillespies being liable?

In another case, a bridesmaid was injured at the wedding reception when several party-goers, participating in a "wheelbarrow race" (where one person walks on his hands and his partner holds his legs up while running and steering from behind) ran into her. She sued the restaurant at which the reception was held, claiming it had not adequately protected her safety. The court, noting that the race was "spontaneous and inappropriate," found the restaurant could not have anticipated the contest and thus owed no duty to protect the plaintiff from it.[1]

The owner of an amusement park has no duty to protect patrons against unforeseeable and unexpected assaults. Thus, where a patron who had just exited the roller coaster was attacked spontaneously and without warning, the park was not liable for failing to prevent the assault.[2]

Similarly, a restaurant owed no duty to protect patrons from a firecracker that was unexpectedly thrown into the establishment by an unknown person. The firecrack-

---

[1] *Lee v. Durow's Restaurant, Inc.,* 656 N.Y.S.2d 321 (N.Y. 1997)
[2] *Scotti v. W.M. Amusements,* 266 A.D.2d 522, 640 N.Y.S.2d 617 (N.Y. 1996)

er shattered a glass picture frame, propelling shards of glass that hit a diner and caused permanent injury. The restaurant could not reasonably have foreseen this type of attack, and so it had no duty to protect customers against it.[3]

Where the presence of bees could not be foreseen, an inn hosting a 50th wedding anniversary party did not owe a duty to protect the guests from being stung. A guest was stung, resulting in anaphylactic shock and cardiac arrest causing permanent quadriplegia. The circumstances included the following: In the 20 years prior to this incident no other guest had been stung; at the time of the sting the bee was isolated and not in a swarm; no hive or nest was found on the premises; and the inn was well maintained.[4] Since the injury was not foreseeable and therefore no duty was owed, the inn was not liable for the guest's injuries.

In all of these cases the lawsuits were dismissed because no duty was owed.

Breach of Duty

For a defendant to be liable for negligence, the defendant must not only owe a duty to the plaintiff to act reasonably, but must also breach that duty. A restaurant owes a duty to its customers not to serve rancid food because customers who eat it will foreseeably become ill. If the restaurant serves spoiled food, it thereby breaches that duty. Likewise, failure by a hotel to maintain floors in its building in a safe condition constitutes a breach of duty to those who utilize the premises.

Another example is where a plaintiff slipped and fell at a hotel while exiting a recessed bathtub. The plaintiff alleged that the hotel breached its duty of care by failing to install a nonslip surface floor and railings along the walls of the tub and failing to warn of the conditions. The court held that the hotel was not an insurer of the patron's safety, but it was required to use due care under the circumstances for the patron's safety. The court denied the hotel's motion to dismiss.[5]

A hotel owes its guests and the occupants of adjacent buildings a duty to maintain fire extinguishers in operable condition. Failure to do so will foreseeably cause injury in the event of a fire and so constitutes a breach of duty. In a case where a hotel fire spread to and destroyed an adjacent saloon, efforts to put out the fire were unsuccessful because of a faulty and inoperable fire extinguisher. The hotel thus had breached its duty to take reasonable measures to prevent the spread of fire and was liable to the bar for its loss.[6]

Reasonable Person Standard

Determining whether a defendant acted reasonably is not always easy. The law provides a standard to help judge whether a defendant's actions were or were not

---

[3] *Mee-Hsiang Lee v. 69 Mott Street Corp.*, 683 N.Y.S.2d 261 (N.Y. 1999)
[4] *Febesh v. Hollow Inn*, 157 A.D.2d 102, 555 N.Y.S.2d 46 (N.Y. 1990)
[5] *Pelfrey v. Governor's Inn*, 2013 WL 5771183 (Tenn. 2013)
[6] *Bartelli v. O'Brien*, 718 N.E.2d 344 (Ill. 1999)

within the bounds of the law. Though difficult to apply in some cases, it is a helpful guide. The standard is a mythical "reasonable person of ordinary prudence." The issue in each case is whether the defendant acted as a reasonable person of ordinary prudence would have acted under similar circumstances.

Sometimes this imaginary person is described in cases by judges not only as "reasonable" and "prudent" but also as "a person of average prudence," or even as "a person of ordinary sense using ordinary care and skill." All these phrases mean much the same. This reasonable person does not have bad days; he is always up to standard, a personification of a community ideal of reasonable behavior. What constitutes reasonable conduct in a given situation is determined by a jury or, in a bench trial, by the judge.

If the defendant in a lawsuit has not breached a duty, the defendant is not liable. The plaintiff has the burden of proving the defendant's wrongdoing. If the plaintiff is unable to prove that the defendant breached a duty, the plaintiff will not be able to recover money for his losses. Examine the following questions and answers between a defense attorney and a plaintiff.

Q: What caused you to fall?

A: You tell me. I don't know. My foot slipped.

Q: And you don't know why your foot slipped?

A: No.

Q: No?

Q: Did you see anything which caused you to fall?

A: No.

The court held since plaintiff did not know what caused his fall, he is unable to prove that defendant's negligence was the cause of his injury. Therefore, the defendant was not liable. A similar outcome resulted where plaintiff fell off a curb on the property of Chick-Fil-A. After learning of the fall the store's owner inspected the area where plaintiff fell. He found no irregularities, bumps, cracks, or gravel on the pavement. It was well lit and not wet. Plaintiff presented no evidence to establish that her injury was caused by the eatery's negligence. The court determined no breach of duty occurred and dismissed plaintiff's case.

Case Example 5-2 illustrates that a plaintiff in a negligence case must prove that the cause of injury was the defendant's carelessness. The plaintiff was hurt when someone fell on her at a hotel restaurant. She sued both the hotel and the person who fell on her.

CASE EXAMPLE 5-2

Shadburn v. Whitlow

533 S.E.2d 765 (Ga. 2000)

[T]he record shows that Shadburn, Whitlow, and Jewel Palmer were on their way to Ormond Beach, Florida. En route, they stopped at New Perry Hotel to eat lunch. The three proceeded up a flight of stairs to the hotel restaurant. Palmer proceeded first, followed by Shadburn. Whitlow, an elderly woman who had impaired vision due to cataracts, followed last. Palmer was waiting in line at the restaurant when she heard a noise. Turning, she saw Whitlow, who had reached the top of the stairs, fall into Shadburn who was standing in the lobby area. Shadburn was injured. Palmer and Shadburn believed Whitlow's fall was caused by loose carpeting, which they noticed at the top of the stairwell the evening after the fall; however, all three ladies testified that they were not actually certain what caused Whitlow to fall. Palmer also averred in her affidavit that Whitlow may have tripped because she may have been inebriated after sipping an unknown beverage from a cup during the trip to Perry.

The trial court properly granted summary judgment to New Perry Hotel because Shadburn failed to present any evidence that a condition on the stairs, the loose carpeting, caused Whitlow to fall. The speculation that Whitlow may have tripped on loose carpeting does not sufficiently establish causation.

On the issue of causation, as on other issues essential to a cause of action for negligence, the plaintiff, in general, has the burden of proof. The plaintiff must introduce evidence which affords a reasonable basis for the conclusion that it is more likely than not that the conduct of the defendant was a cause in fact of the result. A mere possibility of such causation is not enough; and when the matter remains one of pure speculation or conjecture, or the probabilities are at least evenly balanced, it becomes the duty of the court to grant summary judgment for the defendant.

Similarly, the trial court also properly granted summary judgment to Whitlow because there is no evidence that Shadburn's injuries were caused by an act or omission of Whitlow. There is no evidence in the record of the cause of Whitlow's fall. Shadburn can point only to speculation that Whitlow may have tripped and fallen because she was inebriated.

CASE QUESTION

1. What more would the plaintiff need to prove to establish that the defendant in this case breached a duty?

Proximate Cause

The **proximate cause** of an injury refers to its direct and immediate cause. The requirement of proximate cause to prove negligence means that the injury must have been caused by the breach of duty; in other words, there must be a cause-and-effect relationship between the unreasonable conduct and the injury. The connection also must be direct or immediate, so that a reasonable person could foresee the potential danger of the careless act. "Proximate cause is a limit on legal liability; it is a policy decision that the defendant's conduct and the plaintiff's injury may be too remote for the law to allow recovery...It is well settled that there can be no proximate cause where there has intervened between the acts of the defendants and the injury, an independent act of a third party which was not foreseeable to the defendants, which was not triggered by the defendant's acts, and which was sufficient of itself to cause the injury."[7]

> **proximate cause**
> That which, in a natural and continuous sequence, unbroken by any efficient intervening cause, produces injury, and without which the result would not have occurred.

For example, assume a hotel van driver was adjusting the radio while driving and not watching the road. He carelessly swerved up and over a curb and came to a stop near the sidewalk. A dog owner was walking her dog on the sidewalk near the van and looking up at a low-flying plane. She thus failed to see an uneven spot in the cement slabs. She fell due to the jagged edges of the sidewalk. In this example, the hotel employee was negligent and the dog walker was injured. But the negligence was not the cause of the injury, so the hotel will not be liable.

In another example, shampoo was spilled in a hotel stairwell on the landing and the right side of the first step. The spillage had not been cleaned for more than a day, constituting negligence. A guest using the stairs slipped and was injured as she descended along the right side of the stairway on the third step below the landing. The cause of her fall was a break in the heel of her shoe. Although the hotel was negligent in not cleaning the shampoo, and although the guest was injured, the guest did not trip on the shampoo and thus her injuries were not the proximate cause of the hotel's negligence. Therefore, the hotel would not be liable.[8]

Case Example 5-3 provides another illustration of the proximate cause requirement.

---

[7] *Snellgrove v. Hyatt Corp.*, 625 S.E.2d 517 (Ga. 2006)
[8] For a case with similar facts, see *Munno v. State of New York*, 698 N.Y.S.2d 107 (N.Y. 1999)

CASE EXAMPLE 5-3

Palace Bar, Inc. v. Fearnot

381 N.E.2d 858 (Ind. 1978)

...On January 3, 1974, Garlen Fearnot entered the Palace Bar for the purpose of purchasing and being served alcoholic beverages. According to testimony, Fearnot had consumed two shots of whiskey but did not appear intoxicated when, without saying anything, he abruptly left the bar and started toward the rear of the premises. Witnesses stated that Fearnot staggered as he walked, bumped against a booth and stumbled against a pinball machine as he left the front room of the bar and continued toward the rear door, which was the door he customarily used. Subsequently, the staggering Garlen Fearnot, according to conflicting testimony, either fell down the stairs or, while clutching for the handrail, slid to the landing below.

Walters, the bartender and owner-manager of the Palace Bar, watched Fearnot as he left the bar and, thinking something might be amiss because of Fearnot's past history of heart problems, followed him. According to Walter's testimony, he discovered Fearnot on the stair landing and attempted to be of assistance to Fearnot, who was slumped against the rail, by laying him down on the landing. Walters testified that he asked Fearnot if he could help to which Fearnot replied that he would be all right and to just leave him alone. Walters went back to the front of the bar where he discussed the situation with other patrons. Walters and others apparently checked repeatedly on Fearnot's condition although no one called for medical assistance at that time. Thereafter, about an hour later, Walters apparently discovered that Fearnot had lost consciousness whereupon Walters called for the fire department's emergency medical unit, which was located across the alley from the bar. The responding unit was unable to revive Fearnot who was later pronounced dead at the scene by the Greene County Coroner.

[This action was brought by Fearnot's widow claiming negligence by the bar in causing Fearnot's death.]

The Coroner ruled that upon observing the body it was his opinion that Fearnot died as a result of a natural cause which appeared to him to be a cerebral hemorrhage. He further stated that it was his opinion that the injuries from the fall could not and did not cause Fearnot's death....

Dr. Hanes Benz, an Indianapolis pathologist who performed the autopsy, attributed Fearnot's death to heart disease. He also stated that although there were bruises found on the body [from the fall], these bruises were superficial and that Fearnot did not die as a result of a fall or injury....

Evidence further showed that Fearnot experienced a variety of health problems and was, at the time of his death, on total non-service connected disability from the Veteran's Administration. He had also confided to others that he had a "bad ticker" or heart problems....

Defendant claim that Mrs. Fearnot did not prove any proximate relationship between the [bar's alleged negligent] acts or omissions and Fearnot's death. We agree with this position.... It is basic, of course, that the plaintiff had the burden of proving by a preponderance of the evidence that the defendants had a duty to the plaintiff, that the defendant's conduct failed to fulfill or conform to the requisite standard of care required to fulfill that duty and that the plaintiff sustained an injury as a result of that failure. In order for the plaintiff to carry her burden her evidence must establish that the alleged wrongful act was a proximate cause of the injury....

With these well-established rules in mind, we will examine the evidence presented by plaintiff. The Coroner came to the conclusion that the decedent died of natural causes and not from trauma.... Dr. James Benz, a physician specializing in pathology, gave his opinion that the decedent died of natural causes and not from any injuries he received in the fall.

...In sum, the total evidence is that the decedent died from natural causes and not because of any acts of defendant regardless of whether or not they may have been negligent.

Judgment for defendant.

If plaintiff falls due to defendant's negligence but her injuries constitute a **preexisting condition,** that is, a physical impairment suffered prior to the fall, defendant's negligence would not be the proximate cause of that injury. In this circumstance the hotel would not be liable.[9] If the hotel's negligence aggravated an existing injury, however, the hotel will be liable for the additional injuries it caused.

preexisting condition
A prior physical impairment, which may or may not be aggravated, in the event of injuries suffered due to negligence.

Events independent of and occurring after the defendant's alleged negligence may be the direct cause of the injury, rather than the defendant's negligence. Such an event is called an *intervening* or *superseding occurrence* and has the effect of breaking the chain of causation between the defendant's negligence and the plaintiff's injury. In Case Example 5-4, an intervening occurrence and not the hotel's negligence was determined to be the cause of the plaintiff's injury.

CASE EXAMPLE 5-4

Smith v. West Rochelle Travel Agency, Inc.

656 N.Y.S.2d 340 (N.Y. 1997)

... The plaintiffs commenced an action against all the parties who had any connection with a 1993 spring break vacation trip to the Bahamas in which their 17-year-old son, Thomas Smith, Jr. (hereinafter the decedent), participated.... During the vacation, the decedent purchased a ticket for a "booze

---

[9] *Hines v. KMart Corporation*, 2001 WL 709515 (Mich. 2001)

cruise", a sunset cruise in international waters where alcoholic beverages were sold to anyone, regardless of their age. The decedent voluntarily leapt overboard and was killed when he came in contact with the cruise vessel's propellers. The evidence indicated that the vessel was not owned or operated by the defendant...Wyndham Hotel Co., Ltd.

The parents sued Wyndham, the hotel at which the decedent was registered, arguing that since the ground handler promoted the "booze cruise" on the hotel premises during an "orientation party" at which alcoholic beverages were served, the hotel bore some liability for facilitating the sale of tickets to the cruise....

[T]he court correctly determined that, as a matter of law, the decedent's action of voluntarily jumping off a moving vessel in open waters was a superseding event which severed whatever causal connection there may have been between the occurrence of the accident and Wyndham's alleged negligence three days earlier in permitting alcohol to be served on its premises during the orientation party....

In another case illustrating a superseding occurrence, a valet parking attendant at a nightclub negligently facilitated the theft of a patron's car. Later the same night a police officer observed the stolen car and attempted to stop it. The thief fled, first in the car and then on foot. The officer fell and was injured. He sued the nightclub for negligence. The case was dismissed because the club's negligence was not the direct cause of the police officer's injury. "The conduct of the thief was an intervening cause which the nightclub was not bound to anticipate and guard against."[10]

Another example of a superseding cause of injury is provided by a case involving storage in a vat of used restaurant cooking oil pending pickup by an oil retrieval company. The vat had malfunctioned and the restaurant called for service. The repair company failed to respond in a timely manner. The restaurant continued to add used oil to the vat. A restaurant employee was injured while pouring oil into it. He was not wearing protective clothing and he used a "greasy and wobbly" ladder to reach the top of the vat. He sued the service company for negligence due to their delay in repairing the vat. The court dismissed the case, ruling that the negligence of the repair company was not the proximate cause of the employee's injuries. Instead, his own negligence was the cause.[11]

Injury

To win a lawsuit, a plaintiff must have been injured as a result of the defendant's breach of duty. The injury might be bodily harm (the legal term for this is "personal injury"), such as a broken arm or a head wound. The injury could also be property damage, such as a dented car, or it could be emotional suffering or monetary loss.

---

[10] *Poskos v. Lombardo's of Randolph, Inc.,* 670 N.E.2d 383 (Mass. 1997)
[11] *Griffin Industries, Inc. v. Foodmaker, Inc.,* 22 S.W.3d 33 (Tex. 2000)

Remember, before a hotel or restaurant will be liable to a plaintiff for negligence, all four elements must be present: (1) the existence of a duty; (2) breach of that duty; (3) proximate cause; and (4) injury. If any element is missing, the hotel or restaurant is not liable.

CASE EXAMPLE 5-5

Willig v. Pinnacle Entertainment,

2016 WL 4942332 (La. 2016)

In this case, we examine whether a casino is entitled to summary judgment as a matter of law . . . where the plaintiff tripped and fell over the protruding wheel of another patron's walker in the dining area of the casino's restaurant. We find that summary judgment is warranted under these circumstances because reasonable minds must inevitably conclude, as the trial court did herein, that the slightly protruding wheel of the patron's walker did not present an unreasonable risk of harm to the plaintiff.

The event that gave rise to this litigation occurred on January 1, 2014, at the L'Auberge Casino & Hotel in Baton Rouge. On this date, Ms. Elvera Willig went with her companions to the casino, where they played games and then dined at the casino's self-service restaurant. Ms. Willig was 73 years old at the time.

That same day, an unidentified gentleman who walked with the assistance of a walker (four-wheeled) arrived at the casino's restaurant. A casino employee directed the unidentified gentleman and his companions to a table in the dining area that was adjacent to a designated walkway that led patrons to the main pathway to reach the buffet. The unidentified gentleman chose to sit on the side of the table that was closest to the walkway. The rear wheels of his walker slightly protruded into the walkway.

Ms. Willig was able to successfully navigate past the gentleman in the walker three times as she went back and forth between the buffet and her table in the dining area. However, on her fourth trip past, as she was returning to her table with her dessert, she tripped over the wheel of the gentleman's walker and fell. Emergency responders were called to the scene and Ms. Willig was transported by ambulance to the emergency room of a local hospital. She alleges that she sustained a fractured hip as a result of her fall.

After the incident, Ms. Willig filed suit against . . . L'Auberge Hotel & Casino [hereinafter "the casino], alleging that the casino negligently failed to protect its guests from other guests; negligently sat a patron near the walkway in such a manner that the patron's walker could obstruct the walkway; and negligently failed to sit a patron who required the assistance of a walker at a location where, or in a manner in which, other patrons or guests would not trip or harm themselves on the walker.

The casino filed a motion for summary judgment seeking dismissal of Ms. Willig's claims on grounds she failed to provide evidence sufficient to satisfy her burden of proof. She must prove each of the following elements:

1. The condition presented an unreasonable risk of harm to the claimant and that risk of harm was reasonably foreseeable.

2. The merchant either created or had actual or constructive notice of the condition which caused the damages, prior to the occurrence.

3. The merchant failed to exercise reasonable care. In determining reasonable care, the absence of a written or verbal uniform cleanup or safety procedure is insufficient alone, to prove failure to exercise reasonable care. . . .

Ms. Willig opposed the motion. . . .

The walkway opening in question was 62 inches wide. . . .

After a hearing the trial court granted the casino's motion for summary judgment on grounds Ms. Willig failed to satisfy her burden of proof with respect to the unreasonable risk of harm element, explaining: I'm sorry the lady fell, but I just cannot say that there was an unreasonably dangerous condition. Having watched their surveillance video intently for quite some time, . . . I just don't believe it presented an unreasonably dangerous condition. And for that reason, I am going to grant the casino's motion for summary judgment.

Thus the trial court dismissed Ms. Willig's suit in its entirety with prejudice. From this judgment, Ms. Willig appeals.

Failure to prove any one of the three elements is fatal to plaintiff's case for summary judgment.

Ms. Willig questions the trial court's finding with respect to the first element, namely that the condition failed to present an unreasonable risk of harm to the claimant. An unreasonable risk of harm is present if the dangerous condition would reasonably be expected to cause injury to a prudent person using ordinary care under the circumstances. . . .

The surveillance video demonstrates that a casino employee led the unidentified gentleman using the walker and his companions to a table near an entry and exit point of the restaurant's dining area. . . The video evidence reflects that two wheels of the gentleman's walker slightly protruded into the walkway that led to one of the dining area's entry and exit points. However, the video evidence also reflects that individuals who traversed the walkway behind the gentleman had ample room to navigate around him. In fact, the video evidence demonstrates that Ms. Willig successfully passed behind the gentleman three times; it was only on her fourth attempt to do so that she tripped and fell. Finally, the video evidence demonstrates that the fall occurred in the carpeted dining area of the restaurant. . . Ms. Willig acknowledges in her brief that the walkway was wide enough for two persons to traverse at the same time. . . . We note that a prudent person walking through the dining area of a restaurant must necessarily be vigilant because obstacles are common in this type of area.

We cannot find that the slightly protruding wheels of the walker created an unreasonably dangerous condition, given the ample room that remained for patrons and employees to navigate around the device. Accordingly, we find . . . that reasonable minds must inevitably conclude, from the evidence before us, that the protruding wheels of the walker did not present an unreasonable risk of harm to Ms. Willig.

For the reasons assigned, we affirm the dismissal of all claims against defendant L'Auberge Casino & Hotel Baton Rouge.

Legal Status of Plaintiff

The duty of care owed by a hotel or restaurant for the safety of its patrons varies in many states, depending on the legal status of the person injured. He may be an invitee, a licensee, or a trespasser. The greatest degree of care is owed to an invitee, the next greatest to a licensee, and the least to a trespasser.

Duty Owed to Invitees

In the hospitality industry, an **invitee** is someone who comes to an establishment for the purpose for which the business is open to the public, or for a purpose directly or indirectly connected with that business. For a hotel, invitees include guests and visitors of guests. For example, the friend of a guest invited to dinner at the hotel is an invitee. Likewise, a child who attends a birthday party held at the hotel is an invitee. Thus the hotel owes the same standard of care to the visitor as to the registered guest. Where four unregistered visitors attended a party in the room of a registered guest, the visitors qualified as invitees to whom the hotel owed a duty to maintain the premises in a reasonably safe condition. The in-wall heating/air-conditioning unit in the room caught fire and killed one of the visitors. If the cause was negligence by the hotel, it would be liable.[13] If the hotel has stores or a theater ticket service in the lobby and a nonguest enters the hotel to patronize the store or purchase tickets, that person also qualifies as an invitee. For a restaurant, diners are invitees. For a bar, patrons are invitees. For all three types of establishments, employees are invitees, as is a delivery person delivering some item necessary for the business such as food or alcohol.

invitee
A person who enters a business for a purpose directly or indirectly connected with that business.

The hotel or restaurant is not a guarantor of the well-being of its patrons. Instead it owes a duty to its invitees to reasonably inspect the premises for dangerous conditions and to exercise reasonable care to eliminate them. Liability may result if and only if the business: (1) knows, or by the exercise of reasonable care would discover, a dangerous condition that presents an unreasonable risk of harm to invitees; and (2) should expect that invitees will not discover or realize the danger or will fail to protect themselves against it; and (3) fails to exercise reasonable care to protect its invitees against the danger. The necessary reasonable care (lack of negligence) encompasses both repair of and warning about the dangerous condition.

Assume that on a rainy night the floor in the entrance to a restaurant is wet and slippery. A patron entering the restaurant falls and is injured. Is the food establishment liable? The customer is an invitee, so the restaurant owes the duty to make a reasonable effort to discover the condition and eliminate it by mopping frequently, or at the very least, to warn of its presence. Failure to do so will result in liability. To determine if the restaurant is liable, we need to know how frequently it mopped the entrance. The duty to mop on a rainy day would require greater frequency than on a dry evening. If it mopped regularly, the eatery may not be liable even though the guest fell. The duty is to exercise reasonable care, not to be right there the moment drops of water gather.

---

12 *Messina v. Sheraton Corporation of America*, 291 So.2d 829 (La. 1974)
13 *Woodty v. Weston's Lamplighter Motels*, 830 P.2d 477 (Ariz. 1992)

© Andrey_Popov/Shutterstock.com

Active Vigilance Required

Note that ignorance on the part of the restaurant of the presence of the water (or other substance) on the floor and resulting slipperiness normally will not relieve the restaurant of liability. The restaurant has a duty to inspect for and to discover the wetness or other problem, and then to protect guests from resulting risks. Case Example 5-6 illustrates this point.

CASE EXAMPLE 5-6

Montes v. Betcher

480 F.2d 1128 (Minn. 1973)

On the warm Sunday afternoon of July 13, 1968, 35 year old Fernando Montes, a citizen of Nebraska, took a running dive off a short dock which served the Appellants' resort, one of the many enhancing Minnesota's beautiful lakes. He surfaced with a severely lacerated scalp and a vertebral fracture. Shortly after the incident, a jagged piece of concrete was recovered from the lake floor in the general area where plaintiff had entered the water. The concrete piece resembled the homemade boat anchors constructed by Appellants to use in the boats which frequented the boat dock.

Plaintiff, Montes, a proficient swimmer and diver, claims that he executed a flat, "racing" dive because he knew he was plunging into shallow water. The water depth was variously described to be from 27 inches to waist level. Montes testified, however, that his ultimate purpose was to grab the ankles of a friend who was standing in the water 15 feet from the end of the dock, a purpose which would require either a deep dive or a subsequent submergence.

Montes was very familiar with the swimming area, and had executed dives from the boat dock on numerous previous occasions. Never before had he encountered rocks or blocks in the water.

The Appellants, Mr. and Mrs. Betcher, citizens of Minnesota, had owned the resort since 1963. They charged $10 per day for cabin accommodations. Although the area surrounding the boat dock was perennially in use by Appellants' swimmer-patrons and although Mr. Betcher had seen swimmers jump off the boat dock, he testified that he had never made any special attempt to inspect the lake bottom for debris nor had he ever "raked" the shoreline lake bottom. Never had he erected signs warning of the dangers of diving in the shallow water or the possible presence of debris in the swimming area. Never had he placed floats in the water to discourage the intrusion of boats into the swimming and diving area; in fact there was no segregation whatsoever of swimming waters from boating waters....

Appellants...first contend that a riparian owner [an owner of waterfront property] is not responsible for the safe maintenance of property beyond the...line...that marks the boundary between Appellants' shoreline land and submerged land which belongs to the state. But even if Appellants are held responsible for the maintenance of submerged lands, Appellants contend, that responsibility extends only to the remedy of dangerous conditions known to Appellants or of which they could have acquired knowledge had they...exercised reasonable care. Since there was no evidence that Appellants knew of the presence of the cement block nor that it had been there long enough to mandate... constructive knowledge, Appellants contend [they breached no duty]....

[This argument was properly rejected.]... A resort owner who avails himself of the advantages of riparian ownership for resort purposes owes to his patrons a duty of reasonable care which includes "active vigilance" in their protection from foreseeable risks....

The jury was perfectly justified in determining that Appellants had violated this duty in any one or more of three respects: (1) their failure to warn of the dangers of diving off the boat dock; (2) their failure to periodically "rake" the swimming–diving area in search of dangerous obstructions; and (3) their failure to segregate swimming areas from boating areas.

CASE QUESTIONS

1. What is meant by *constructive notice*, as used in the fourth paragraph?

2. We are told that Montes had two or three drinks the afternoon of the accident. What effect do you think that should have on the outcome of the case?

3. What does the term "active vigilance," used by the court, in the penultimate paragraph, mean?

This case clearly establishes that, for a resort to satisfy its obligation to an invitee, it is not enough to correct dangerous conditions of which the resort is aware. The business must also regularly inspect the premises to locate and identify dangerous conditions and correct any that are found. If the hotel fails to inspect, it will be liable to invitees for injuries caused by conditions that an inspection would have revealed.

Open and Obvious Exception

Invitees must exercise some care in protecting themselves. Generally, a hotel or restaurant will not be liable for injuries caused by a condition that is "open and obvious," meaning that the dangers are so obvious that the invitee can reasonably be expected to discover them. If the hazard is open and obvious, invitees are expected to take appropriate precautions to protect themselves. For example, a patron of a Wendy's restaurant exited the building via a concrete ramp, part of which was cracked. The ramp's condition was easily visible and therefore obvious. Nonetheless, the customer tripped and fell on the cracked portion. The court denied her claim against the restaurant stating, "[I]t was a discrete hazard in an otherwise safe walkway which plaintiff could have easily avoided by stepping over it or walking around it. Because plaintiff tripped over a defect which was an open and obvious condition that could easily have been avoided, no interpretation of the evidence could render that defect an unreasonable hazard [and thus defendant is not liable]."[14]

A guest sued a hotel claiming that she was injured when she tripped over a defective or unreasonably dangerous threshold while walking into the hotel. There was no history or records showing that any other guest had tripped, stumbled, or fallen when crossing the entranceway. The evidence did not support the presence of a defective condition. Further, the court held that even if the threshold could be considered dangerous, the area was well lit and clearly visible, rendering any gap or uneven flooring open and obvious. The case was therefore dismissed.[15]

Similarly, where octogenarian restaurant customers confronted a snow pile in the parking lot and tripped when they tried to step over it rather than going around, the court denied recovery holding the open and obvious doctrine applied.[16]

Case Example 5-7 illustrates another example of an open and obvious condition for which the innkeeper was not liable.

CASE EXAMPLE 5-7

Hudechek v. Novi Hotel Fund Limited Partnership

2007 WL 466108 (Mi. 2007)

Plaintiff slipped and fell on a wet sidewalk while leaving defendant's hotel at the conclusion of a professional seminar. The sidewalk had been painted. Plaintiff acknowledged during his deposition that the painted condition of the sidewalk was readily observable. He also acknowledged that as he was exiting the hotel he observed people running from the parking lot to avoid becoming wet from rain. Plaintiff sustained head, neck and back injuries as a result of his fall. The trial court granted summary judgment to the hotel on the basis that any danger posed by the wet painted sidewalk was open and obvious. Plaintiff argues that the trial court erred....

Whether a danger is open and obvious depends on whether it is reasonable to expect that an average person with ordinary intelligence would have discovered the danger on casual inspection.... The open and obvious doctrine will cut off liability if the invitee should have discovered the condition and realized its danger.

---

[14] *Boyd v. Warren Restaurants, Inc.,* 2001 WL 753886 (Mich. 2001)
[15] *Donley v. Dost, Inc.,* 2011 WL 6817684 (Ohio 2011)
[16] *Dunbar v. Denny's Restaurant,* 2006 WL 668544 (Ohio 2006)

Plaintiff argues that the trial court erred by granting defendant's motion for summary judgment. We disagree. The undisputed evidence shows that both the painted condition of defendant's sidewalk and that it was raining at the time plaintiff exited defendant's hotel were readily observable. Plaintiff was talking to his daughter as he walked to his vehicle and was not attentive to the conditions of his surroundings. It is reasonable to conclude that plaintiff would not have been injured had he been attentive to the conditions around him, including simply watching where he was walking more closely. Thus, the trial court did not err in concluding that the condition of the sidewalk was open and obvious.

When sued for negligence, hotels and restaurants need to be alert to the possible defense that the alleged dangerous condition was open and obvious. There is, however, a circumstance in which the hotel may be liable notwithstanding that the plaintiff was injured on a condition that was openly and obviously dangerous. If the condition is also unavoidable, the hotel may be liable. For example, in a case involving a plaintiff who was attending a seminar at a hotel, the only stairwell accessing the conference room was dark. Unable to see, plaintiff fell while descending the stairs. In her lawsuit, the court refused summary judgment to the hotel not withstanding the open and obvious nature of a darkened stairwell.[17]

Duty Owed to Licensees

A **licensee** is someone who is on the premises of another by permission or acquiescence of the owner or occupier, and not by invitation. His presence does not further the defendant's business. Instead, the licensee is on the premises for his own benefit or convenience. An example is an off-duty employee who goes to the place of employment to pick up a paycheck. At that time the employee is not advancing the employer's business interests but nonetheless is on the premises with the employer's consent. Similarly, a former employee who enters the premises to meet with a current worker is a licensee.[18] A mother who accompanied her adult daughter to an employment interview was a licensee, there being no evidence that the potential employer benefited in any way by the mother's decision to accompany the daughter.

licensee
In cases of negligence, one who does not qualify as an invitee but who has been given permission by the owner or occupier to enter or remain on the property.

States define the duty owned to licensees differently. In a majority of the states, the duty owed is twofold:

1. Refrain from willfully or wantonly injuring the licensee or acting in a manner to increase peril; and

2. Warn of any latent dangers on the premises of which the property owner has knowledge.

---

[17] *Mutual Life Insurance Co. v. Churchwell,* 471 S.E.2d 267 (Ga. 1996)
[18] *Bradley v. Radisson Hotel,* 2006 WL 205114 (Ca. 2006)

Note that, for the invitee, the hotel or restaurant must inspect for dangerous conditions and either repair them or warn the invitee about them. For the licensee, the duty is less. The hotel or restaurant can dispense with the inspection. According to the rule in a majority of states, the hotel or restaurant's only duty is to warn of those dangers it knows about. Thus, the hotel or restaurant must disclose known defects but need not make any effort to determine what defects exist. Had the plaintiff in *Montes v. Betcher,* Case Example 5-6, been a licensee rather than an invitee, the resort would have satisfied its obligation and the plaintiff would have lost the case.

In states where the minority rule applies, the hospitality facility does not even owe a duty to disclose and warn of known dangers. In those states the duty owed to licensees is merely to refrain from willful or wanton injury.

Case Example 5-8 explores the circumstances under which a visitor of a hotel guest qualifies as an invitee and when he is treated as a licensee.

CASE EXAMPLE 5-8

Steinberg v. Irwin Operating Co.

90 So.2d 460 (Fla. 1956)

...Appellant, Essie Steinberg, accompanied two friends to the Cadillac Hotel operated by appellee. The purpose of the mission was to enable one of the friends to deliver a message to a registered guest at the hotel. Inquiry at the desk revealed that the registered guest was not in. Thereupon, Mrs. Steinberg and her friends decided to explore various lounges and other rooms adjacent to the lobby. This was done for their own diversion. They first went into a "TV Room." They didn't like the program then showing. They then apparently attempted to enter an adjoining "Movie Room." This room was dark except for the light cast by the movie screen and projector. The floor level of the "Movie Room" was four inches lower than the floor level of the "TV Room." Claiming that she did not see the difference in level, Mrs. Steinberg fell and suffered injuries. She filed a complaint seeking compensation for damages resulting from the alleged negligence of appellee. The alleged negligence was the difference in the floor level....

Appellant contends that at the time of the alleged injury, Mrs. Steinberg was an invitee of the hotel. They seek recovery on the theory that the hotel was obligated to furnish its invitees with reasonably safe premises.

Appellee contends that Mrs. Steinberg was merely a licensee. They assert that the only duty owed to her was to refrain from willfully or wantonly injuring her.

There is no doubt that a registered guest of a hotel is a business invitee and is entitled to receive the degree of care applicable to invitees. We are of the view that one entering a hotel to communicate with a registered guest is entitled to receive and enjoy the same degree of care. This rule is subject to the limitations hereafter expressed.... [B]y the very nature of the business, the operator of the hotel is bound to anticipate that a registered guest is apt to have business and social callers. The invitation to such callers arises by operation of law out of the relationship between the hotel and its registered guests. The operator of the hotel should provide reasonably safe ways of ingress and egress for those legally entering and leaving the place pursuant to the implied invitation implicit in the relationship between hotel operator and registered guests.

However, this implied invitation is not without its limits. The invitation to enter the hotel to visit a guest is circumscribed by the rule that it extends only to appropriate usage of the means of ingress and egress, such as the lobby, elevator, hallways, and room area rented to the guest.

It would be stretching the doctrine of implied invitation beyond justifiable limits to hold that such invitation extends to all of the private or semipublic rooms of the hotel. When the visitor crosses the boundaries of the invitation, he ceases to be an invitee. His status then changes to that of a licensee or even a trespasser. He is entitled to the status of an invitee only to the extent justified by the implied invitation.

In this case, it is perfectly clear that Mrs. Steinberg enjoyed the status of an implied invitee when she entered the hotel lobby. This status continued so long as she used the facilities of the hotel reasonably included within the invitation. When, for her own pleasure and convenience, she crossed the bounds of the invitation on her own initiative, sought entertainment in the "TV Room," and later in the "Movie Room," she became at most a licensee. While she was in this status, the hotel owed to her only the duty to refrain from willfully or wantonly injuring her. The record is clear that there was no willful or wanton injury.

Ruling of the court: The judgment [for the hotel operator] is affirmed.

CASE QUESTIONS

1. What change of facts would be necessary to make Mrs. Steinberg an invitee at the time of her injury?

2. If Mrs. Steinberg was an invitee, what duty would the hotel have owed to her?

A Tennessee court dealt with the issue of the status of a guest's visitor. A young man drowned while he was visiting his fiancée, who was a guest at the defendant's motel. Neither could swim. They entered the motel pool together at a time when no one else was in it. He was either walking or standing in the water when he suddenly started to struggle and sank beneath the surface. His survivors sued the hotel for negligence.

The case hinged on whether the deceased was an invitee. A sign at the end of the pool read, "Motel Guests Only." The lower court held that the visitor ceased to be an invitee upon entering the pool and that the motel from that time on owed him only the minimum duty owed to a trespasser. The appellate court reversed, saying that a visitor of a hotel guest is in fact an invitee of the hotel provided the visitor has not exceeded the bounds of the invitation to visit extended by the guest. In this case the visitor was invited by the guest to join her in the pool; thus, the hotel owed the deceased a duty to exercise reasonable care in the maintenance of the pool.[19] Contrast this situation with the case where the hotel guest invites a visitor to lunch and when the meal is through bids him farewell. On his own initiative and unaccompanied by the hotel guest, he utilizes the pool. While in the pool, this visitor is beyond the parameters of the invitation to visit extended by the hotel guest and therefore is not an invitee of the hotel.

In a case discussed earlier in this chapter, the Elks (a service club) requested that the wife of the newly elected Exalted Ruler (the equivalent of president) come to the organization's headquarters to assist in the preparations for her husband's installation dinner. While helping to set the tables, she entered the kitchen seeking matching china. While there, she fell due to a sizable crack in the floor and suffered substantial injuries. In her lawsuit against the association, the question arose as to whether she was an invitee or a licensee when she entered the kitchen. The court first addressed her status when she entered the building. Since she had been invited to the premises by Elks members, she qualified as an invitee. She remained an invitee when she walked into the kitchen since "it was reasonable to expect as part of her functions that day that she would need to go into the kitchen."[20]

Duty Owed to Trespassers

trespasser
One who enters a place without permission of the owner or occupier.

The least duty is owed to a **trespasser**—a person who enters a place without the permission of the owner or occupier. Someone who enters a restaurant after it is closed for the night without the owner's permission is a trespasser. If an employee who has been fired and ordered not to return to the hotel nonetheless enters the premises, he too is a trespasser. A landowner or possessor does not owe a duty to safeguard a trespasser from injury caused by conditions on the land. Some states impose a duty not to willfully or randomly injure a trespasser, and other states impose this duty only when the trespasser's presence is known or reasonably foreseeable. A trespasser's presence would be known or foreseeable where neighborhood children regularly use for snowmobiling vacant land that is located adjacent to, and owned by, a hotel and the hotel is aware of this use.

Case Example 5-9 illustrates the application of the rule to trespassers.

© Brian Guest/Shutterstock.com

---

[19] *Kandrach v. Chrisman*, 473 S.W.2d 193 (Tenn. 1971)
[20] *White v. Waterbury Lodge*, 2001 WL 477381 (Conn. 2001)

CASE EXAMPLE 5-9

David Hanson v. Hyatt Corp.

554 N.E.2d 394 (Ill. 1990)

[P]laintiff was not a registered guest at defendant's hotel. He entered the pool area sometime after 9:30 p.m. through a gap/hole in a fence surrounding the pool. It was dark, and the lights around the pool area were off.... [H]e dove into Hyatt's pool and sustained injuries which rendered him a quadriplegic; he was 19 years old at the time of the accident.... Hanson argues that he properly alleged the element of duty...based upon Hyatt's "implied invitation" to him to enter upon its premises "for the purpose of inspection and use of its restaurant, gift shop, meeting rooms, lobbies, and swimming pool," as a licensee or invitee. The implied invitation concerning his use of Hyatt's swimming pool is specifically based on the allegation that the pool "was not fully enclosed and was open to access by the public at large...."

Hanson was required to allege facts to support a relationship which imposed a duty on Hyatt to protect him from his injury....

A [business operator] has a duty to exercise reasonable care for the safety of an invitee. The duty owed to a licensee or trespasser is not to willfully and wantonly injure him and to use ordinary care to avoid injuring him after he is discovered in a place of danger.

Hanson...appears to define an implied invitation as a failure by Hyatt to take reasonable steps to secure access to the pool area, presumably by closing up a hole in the fence through which he entered on the date of the accident...We find this argument without merit...[T]o be upon premises by an implied invitation means that the person is there for a purpose connected with the business in which the owner of the premises is engaged. Here, Hanson simply failed to allege facts to support a position that he was using Hyatt's swimming pool for a reason connected with Hyatt's business... Plaintiff is a trespasser. Judgment for the hotel.

CASE QUESTION

1. Why do you think the duty imposed on businesses vis-à-vis trespassers is significantly less than for invitees?

In another case, a plaintiff was hungry late one night and left his house to walk to Hardee's Restaurant. He took a shortcut through a parking lot of a then-closed Burger King. After arriving at Hardee's, he discovered he had forgotten his wallet. On this return trip he decided to see if there was any food in the Burger King dumpster. It was shielded on three sides by brick walls that were close to eight feet tall, and on the fourth by a set of wooden hinged gates. In an attempt to enter the dumpster area, the plaintiff jumped up on one of the brick walls, which then collapsed, severely injuring him. Unbeknownst to the plaintiff, the wall had been damaged a month earlier by a trash truck and had not been repaired. Employees had been alerted not to touch the wall. The plaintiff sued Burger King, which in turn argued that the plaintiff was a trespasser and therefore Burger King owed him no duty to keep the wall safe. Agreeing with Burger King, the court stated, "[A] trespasser...assumes the risk of injury from the condition of the premises.... While a possessor of land may not intentionally set booby traps with the design of causing injury, the possessor owes no duty to adult trespassers for conditions on the premises."[21]

A patron filed a complaint against a casino alleging assault, battery, intentional infliction of emotional distress, false imprisonment, defamation, and negligence stemming from the trespasser's removal from the casino. The patron had been drinking in the casino when he began harassing a woman and was asked to leave. The customer tried to reenter the casino and became involved in a scuffle with security. The Court held that the casino was entitled to summary judgment because security only used reasonable force in performing a citizen's arrest. The court stated that the patron became a trespasser once the casino had asked him to leave and he thereafter tried to reenter.[22]

Minority Position

Some states have abolished the distinction between licensees, invitees, and trespassers and the duties owed to each. Instead, in those states the occupier of land owes a duty of care to all three. However, even in these states the standard of reasonable care may vary with the circumstances of the visitor's entry on the premises.

No Special Duty Owed to Others

What about people who do not qualify as invitee, licensee, or trespasser? In most cases, no duty is owed. In Case Example 5-10, the innkeeper had no relationship with the injured party and therefore owed no duty of care.

---

[21] *Cochran v. Burger King Corp.*, 937 S.W.2d 358 (Mo. 1996)
[22] *Smock v. Peppernill Casinos, Inc.*, No. 3:11-cv-00094-RCI-VPC (Nev. 2012)

CASE EXAMPLE 5-10

Callender v. MCO Properties

885 P.2d 123 (Ariz. 1994)

...On March 26, 1988, appellant John Scott Callender was boating with friends on Lake Havasu.... They steered the boat toward the beach at the Crazy Horse Campground. Two women occupants of the boat got out to retrieve an inflatable raft they had left at the beach. The young women attempted to row the raft out into the water. When Callender saw that they were having difficulty, he dived from the boat into the water to assist them. During the dive, however, he struck his head on the bottom of the lake, broke his neck, and was rendered a quadriplegic.

At the time of Callender's accident, the State of Arizona owned the land along the Lake Havasu shore where the Crazy Horse Campground was located. The federal government owned and controlled the lake itself.... Appellees Ray and Marie Totah... operated the Crazy Horse Campground. Callender filed a civil action... alleging that the defendants failed to adequately warn that it was unsafe to dive in the water near the Crazy Horse Campground.... In response, the Totahs pointed out that Callender's accident occurred between 20 and 50 feet offshore from the campground premises, Callender had not been a guest of the campground, nor had he ever been on the premises nor docked at the campground. Finally, they argued that the lake's waters and subsurface were owned by the United States Department of the Interior and that Crazy Horse had no legal interest in those waters. The Totahs thus argued that they had no duty to Callender.

Callender argued in response that because the Totahs reasonably could foresee that patrons of the campground and nonpatrons in the company of patrons would approach the Crazy Horse beach by boat and might dive from the boats, the Totahs had a duty to act reasonably to warn people of the risk of diving....

The campground was a business enterprise. A business invitee "is a person who is invited to enter or remain on the land for a purpose directly or indirectly connected with business dealings with the possessor of the land."...Callender was not an invitee of the Totahs. He did not enter the campground before the accident nor did he use any of the campground services or its dock. He was not attempting to enter the campground at the time of the injury. There simply was no relationship between Callender and the campground that would have imposed a duty of care on the Totahs for his benefit... .

The trial court correctly granted summary judgment for the Totahs after finding they had no duty to warn Callender of the dangers of diving in waters offshore from the campground. We therefore affirm the trial court judgment in favor of the Totahs.

CASE QUESTION

1. How would the liability of the Totahs for the accident have been different if Callender had been a camper at the campground and had been within the campground's beach area at the time of his diving accident? Why would the liability have been different?

In another case, a motel owner rented a room to the proprietor of a used car lot located next door. In the middle of the night, the motel owner was awakened by noises from two unauthorized men on the used car lot. The motel owner called the used car lot owner and informed him of the intruders. The lot owner shot at the intruders from the motel room. One intruder was killed; the other was wounded. The intruders sued the motel owner, among others. The owner contested liability. Since the intruders were not guests of the motel or otherwise connected with it, the court found no duty was owed and entered judgment for the motel.[23]

No Duty Owed on Property Not Owned or Maintained by the Hospitality Facility

A hotel or restaurant is generally not liable for injuries that occur to patrons on property not owned or maintained by it, even if the property is near the hotel or restaurant's facility. Thus, a restaurant was not liable to diners who were assaulted in a parking lot located behind the restaurant but not owned or maintained by it. The court specifically noted that the restaurant did not own, pave, snowplow, clear, or patrol the area where the assault occurred.[24]

Negligence Doctrines Generally Favoring the Plaintiff

Numerous legal doctrines are associated with negligence. In any negligence case one or more of these doctrines may apply and affect the outcome. Some doctrines favor the plaintiff by making the plaintiff's case easier to prove. Others benefit the defendant. We will examine first those that benefit the plaintiff, and then those that favor the defendant.

Res Ipsa Loquitur

In many negligence cases, the plaintiff has difficulty proving the necessary elements. Evidence to prove that the defendant was negligent does not always exist, even though the facts of the case may strongly suggest the defendant was negligent. The legal doctrine of res ipsa loquitur aids the plaintiff in such situations. It applies to cases in which the circumstances hint the defendant was negligent but no proof of specific acts of negligence exists. In such cases, the doctrine of **res ipsa loquitur,** which means "the thing speaks for itself," frees the plaintiff from the burden of proving the specific breach of duty committed by the defendant.

In a classic example of res ipsa loquitur, the plaintiff was walking by a flour factory when, for an unexplained reason, a barrel of flour fell out of a window and injured the plaintiff. Because he was not inside the factory at the time of the incident, the plaintiff could not prove why the barrel fell from the window. Nevertheless, the occurrence is such that it likely would not have happened without negligence on the

res ipsa loquitur
"The thing speaks for itself" (Latin). The doctrine that frees the plaintiff from the burden of proving the specific breach of duty committed by the defendant. It applies where an accident would not normally happen without negligence and the instrumentality causing the injury was in the defendant's exclusive control.

---

[23] *Fedie v. Travelodge Intern, Inc.,* 782 P.2d 739 (Ariz. 1989)
[24] *Mankowski v. Denny's, Inc.,* 1997 WL 525083 (Oh. 1997)

part of someone inside the factory. In such a case, the doctrine of res ipsa loquitur creates an inference that the defendant was negligent and allows the plaintiff to proceed with the lawsuit without having to prove through witnesses or otherwise the specific negligent acts of the defendant.

Elements

To use the doctrine of res ipsa loquitur, the plaintiff must prove the following three elements:

1. The plaintiff's injury was caused by an accident that would not normally have happened without negligence.

2. The thing causing the injury (in the referenced case, the barrel of flour) was within the exclusive control of the defendant.

3. The plaintiff did not provoke the accident.

Opportunity to Rebut

Where the doctrine applies, the defendant does not automatically lose. Rather, the defendant has an opportunity to rebut the inference that it was negligent. If the defendant can prove that the cause of the accident was some factor other than its own negligence, the defendant will not be liable.

First Element—Accident Suggestive of Negligence

The first element of res ipsa loquitur, that the accident would not normally have happened without negligence by the defendant, is illustrated in a case where a light fixture fell from the ceiling onto the plaintiff. Said the court, "We cannot say that a light fixture falling from the ceiling of a business is the sort of event which ordinarily happens if those who have the management and control exercise proper care." In Case Example 5-11 against a restaurant involving an object in a meatball, the court held this first element was missing.

CASE EXAMPLE 5-11

Jones v. GMRI, Inc.

551 S.E.2d 867 (N.C. 2001)

On 11 November, 1994 Loretta Jones was injured when she bit into a meatball at an Olive Garden Restaurant owned by GMRI, Inc. ("defendant") in Pineville, North Carolina. Plaintiff filed a complaint on 10 November 1997 against defendant and Rich Products Corporation which allegedly supplied or manufactured the meatball asserting claims of negligence...

[P]laintiff presented the testimony of a friend who was present at the restaurant the day of the incident, themselves, and three physicians. Plaintiffs' evidence tended to show that when plaintiff Loretta Jones attempted to take her first bite of the meatball, she bit down into an unidentified metal object. At that time, she experienced an "incredible stabbing pain in her tooth and her jaw" caused by a broken tooth. Because she was startled , she "sucked in and immediately sucked down the food" and the object. On cross-examination, plaintiff testified that she cut the meatball into eight pieces prior to taking the bite, and that she did not detect any foreign object in the meatball at that time.

Defendant presented evidence tending to show that most of the restaurant's meatballs come into the store frozen and in sealed bags. The restaurant does a visual inspection of the sealed bags of meatballs and sends back those that do not meet the inspection. The meatballs are put into the freezer at the restaurant until needed, then put into a plastic holding container and placed in a refrigerator. The meatballs, which are slightly larger than a golf ball, are then mixed with a tomato sauce, heated, and served whole. Restaurant personnel testified that they do not poke or slice the meatballs, other than to check the temperature with a probe... . The defendant presented the following evidence on the issue of whether it exercised due care: (1) the restaurant removes whole, already formed, meatballs from the sealed bags, defrosts and reheats them, (2) the restaurant does not slice or cut into the meatballs because that would alter the nature of the dish, but (3) the restaurant does probe some of the meatballs with a thermometer to check the temperature. The evidence also showed that plaintiff cut the meatball into eight pieces prior to eating it and did not discover the object... .

The jury awarded plaintiff no recovery... .

Plaintiff's evidence at trial established that she was injured after biting into a piece of meatball. She offered no evidence showing defendant's breach of a duty or standard of care. [The evidence suggests if anyone may have been negligent it would be the manufacturer and not the restaurant. Thus, this was not the type of incident that would not happen without the negligence of the restaurant. Therefore,] the doctrine of res ipsa does not apply.

Second Element—Exclusive Control by Defendant

The second element of res ipsa loquitur is that the instrumentality causing the injury must have been in the exclusive control of the defendant prior to the accident. If exclusive control is missing, the party who was careless in the maintenance of the item causing the injury may not be the defendant, but rather someone else with access.

This element of exclusive control can be difficult to establish. In Case Example 5-12 the court rejected plaintiff's attempt to utilize res ipsa loquitur because the element of exclusive control was lacking.

CASE EXAMPLE 5-12

Parks v. Steak & Ale of Texas, Inc.

2006 WL 66428 (Tex. 2006)

...In his petition, appellant alleged the following: he and his son ate at a Steak & Ale restaurant; he returned to his table from the restroom after eating his meal; he sat down in his chair, which collapsed forward; and he fell forward, hit his chin on the table, and jammed his right wrist into the wall. Appellant further alleged that he sustained severe injuries to his neck and wrist that required surgical intervention. There were no witnesses to this incident other than appellant's ten-year old son.

The restaurant manager, Greg Lacy, inspected the chair and noted that the front right leg of the chair had broken off where the leg connects to the frame. This type of chair, according to Lacy's testimony, is approximately five feet high, measured from the floor to the top of the back of the chair, and weighs about seventy-five pounds. Lacy stated in his deposition testimony that this type of chair is sturdy. He further testified that if the fabric of a chair tears or becomes loose, he has it repaired, but that if anything happens to the chair'[s] structure, he destroys it. He stated that he had approximately 22 of these high-backed chairs in the restaurant and that he had not had to replace any of them in the two years he had been general manager of the restaurant.

Appellant testified at his deposition that a friend took him to the Cy-Fair Hospital emergency room the day after the incident at Steak & Ale because appellant was experiencing pain and a severe headache. Appellant was instructed to go home and rest. Appellant testified that, although the doctor told him nothing had been broken, appellant continued to experience discomfort and pain and was not able to work. A few weeks later, appellant visited his family practitioner and a hand specialist. Approximately eight months later, appellant filed this suit against Steak & Ale... Appellant relies on res ipsa loquitur to establish a presumption of negligence and to provide a presumption that the chair was unreasonably dangerous...

To rely on res ipsa loquitur to establish negligence, a plaintiff must show (1) that the character of the injury is such that it would not have ordinarily occurred without negligence, and that the instrumentality causing the injury was under the management and control of the defendant...

The chair at issue in this case was in the dining room of a restaurant. It was undoubtedly used by many people each day and was therefore not under the sole control of the restaurant. Thus, it is possible that the chair was broken or damaged by someone not employed by the restaurant... Accordingly, appellant has not [proven that the doctrine of res ipsa loquitur is applicable.]

CASE QUESTION

1. Why do you think the law requires exclusive control by the defendant for res ipsa to apply?

Note: The eatery may however have been negligent in its maintenance of the chair. To succeed in the lawsuit plaintiff will have to prove that fact; he cannot rely on res ipsa loquitur. The same result occurred for the same reason in cases involving the following facts: a stool at a casino that slid out from under the plaintiff as she was attempting to mount it;[1] a door check that fell from a door frame of the front door of an apartment building landing on plaintiff;[2] and a defective swing that fell on a playground, injuring a child.[3]

---

[1] *Nickel v. Hollywood Casino*, 730 N.E.2d 1212 (Ill. 2000)
[2] *Gonzalez v. Trump Village Section 4, Inc.*, 2002 WL 31940750 (N.Y. 2002)
[3] *Sinto v. City of Long Beach*, 736 N.Y.S.2d 700 (N.Y. 2002)

Another case with a similar holding involved a customer at a Pizza Hut who was injured while using the ladies room. As she entered the room, the door came off its hinges and struck her in the head. Since patrons regularly utilize the bathroom, the court held the restaurant did not have sufficient exclusive control of the door to apply the doctrine of res ipsa loquitur.[25]

A different outcome resulted in another case involving a door. Plaintiff was injured when an interior automatic door closed on her while she was entering a hotel. The inn disputed the application of res ipsa loquitur on the ground that the public regularly utilized the door and so the hotel did not have exclusive control. Plaintiff established that the mechanisms that failed were the control box, the motor that operated the door, and the motion detector. She further proved that only the hotel had access to these items. Said the court, "The appropriate target of inquiry is whether the broken component itself was generally handled by the public, not whether the public used the larger object to which the defective piece was attached." Plaintiff was thus able to benefit from res ipsa loquitur.[26]

In another case, the plaintiffs were sleeping in a double bed in a room in the defendant's hotel when plaster fell from the ceiling and injured them. The plaintiffs sued the hotel, but were unable to prove exactly how the hotel was negligent. The court held that the doctrine of res ipsa loquitur applied because ceilings do not normally fall and the maintenance of the ceiling was under the exclusive control of the hotel.[27] Likewise, where a plaintiff was injured when a ceiling fan fell on her at a Ground Round Restaurant, res ipsa loquitur could apply.[28]

---

[25] *Thompson v. Pizza Hut of America, Inc.*, 691 N.Y.S.2d 99 (N.Y. 1999)
[26] *Stone v. Courtyard Management Corp.*, 353 F.3d 155 (N.Y. 2003)
[27] *Day v. Sheehan*, 2001 WL 577178 (Conn. 2001)
[28] *Pappalardo v. NY Health & Racquet Club*, 718 N.Y.S.2d 287 (N.Y. 2000)

Third Element—Plaintiff Did Not Provoke the Accident

The third element requires that the plaintiff did not provoke or cause the accident. Revisiting the barrel-of-flour case, if the plaintiff had been throwing rocks up to the window from which the flour fell and the rocks had dislodged the barrel causing it to fall, the plaintiff would not be able to use res ipsa loquitur.

In a case involving a health club located on the second floor of a building in New York City, the plaintiff had completed a set of repetitions on a leg curl machine and stepped back to tie his shoe. In doing this, per plaintiff's testimony, his buttocks "brushed against" a large, five-foot glass window, which simultaneously exploded, causing him to fall to the street. The court held the window likely failed because it was brushed by the plaintiff's derriere. The plaintiff, having thus provoked the glass to break, could not benefit from res ipsa loquitur.[29]

Children and the Reasonable Person Test

Children do not comprehend dangers obvious to more mature persons. Nor are children able to weigh cause and effect accurately. Unlike an adult, children cannot be expected to recognize risks and take appropriate precautions. Instead, children act upon childish instincts and impulses.[30] This impacts the duty imposed by law *on* young people as well as the duty owed by adults *to* children. The law excuses a young child from negligent acts; a person injured by a young person's conduct is not entitled to compensation. Similarly, the duty imposed on adults to act reasonably is usually greater when young children are involved.

For example, a hotel was liable to a six-year-old child who was injured when she inadvertently ran into glass panels that constituted a major portion of a wall in her hotel room. Although the glass panels were properly installed, "those who invite children to go upon their premises are required to exercise a relatively higher degree of care for their safety than to adults." To avoid liability, the hotel should have placed markings on the glass to indicate its presence, or constructed guards around the panels.[31] Another option would have been to eliminate the glass panels from the building's design.

Another case reaffirms the heightened duty owed to children. A hotel was negligent when a youngster was struck by a car as he ran onto a public highway that separated two parts of the hotel. Because of the inn's layout, a guest who wanted to use all of the facilities would be required to cross the highway. The hotel attracted a significant number of Orthodox Jews and, to accommodate their needs, transformed the game room into a place for services on Sabbath mornings. The plaintiff, age five, and his Orthodox Jewish family were assigned a room on the opposite side of the highway. After services one Saturday, the boy "darted" onto the highway where he was hit by a passing car. The court noted that "The risk of injury to

---

29 *McCleod v. Nel-Co Corp.,* 112 N.E.2d 501 (Ill. 1953)
30 *Bragan v. Symanzik,* 687 N.W.2d 881 (Mich. 2004)
31 *Waugh v. Duke Corporation,* 248 F. Supp. 626 (N.C. 1966)

young children crossing the road is entirely foreseeable under these circumstances." Thus, the defendant had a duty to take reasonable steps to alleviate that risk.[32]

Query: What specific precautions might the hotel have taken?

While a proprietor of a hospitality facility owes an enhanced duty to protect the safety of children, some young people may have a duty to act reasonably to protect themselves from harm. The existence and extent of that duty depends on the age and circumstances of the child and on the relevant facts. Case Example 5-13 discusses these issues in relation to a 10-year old boy who was injured in a restaurant.

CASE EXAMPLE 5-13

Frelow v. St. Paul Fire & Marine Insurance Co.

631 So.2d 632 (La. 1994)

On December 30, 1990, a Sunday afternoon at about 2:00 p.m., James Papillion, ten years old, was having lunch at Western Sizzlin' Steakhouse in Lake Charles with his mother, brothers, and sisters. James had just been to the salad bar with his mother and sister and was carrying his salad plate back to his family's table. His sister was right behind him. James's mother, Carolyn Frelow, had already returned to the table.

James and his sister chose the most direct route between the tables back to their own table, a fairly straight path. This route took them past a recently vacated booth which was being cleaned by Michael Bruce, a busboy. On the other side of the aisle was an occupied table. As James proceeded to pass this point, at a fast walk, he tripped over Bruce's foot, which was sticking into the aisle as he leaned into the booth he was cleaning. James reeled and hit his back on the corner of a table, then fell onto the floor face down. His salad plate fell on the back of his head.... His mother had previously admonished James for running in the restaurant, before they had gone to the salad bar....

Carolyn Frelow, James's mother, testified at trial that James complained of headaches and a backache for a week after the accident. Carolyn gave him Tylenol for the headaches. Then, the following Sunday, James developed a severe headache during church which caused him to break into a cold sweat.... [He was treated by a chiropractor for three months after which,] he was asymptomatic.

The trial judge found James Papillion was negligent for walking too fast and Bruce was negligent for obstructing James's path after he saw James approaching. The court apportioned 40 percent fault to James and 60 percent to Bruce [See the discussion on comparative negligence later in this chapter]....

An owner of a business who permits the public to enter his establishment has a duty to exercise reasonable care to protect them. This duty extends to keeping the premises safe from unreasonable risks of harm or warning persons of known dangers. When the presence of small children is expected, the duty increases....

---

[32] *Kellner v. Lowney,* 761 A.2d 421 (N.H. 2000)

[W]e find that Bruce did have a duty to Western Sizzlin' customers to use reasonable care not to obstruct the aisles so that customers could travel freely between the food service stations and the tables. A reasonable man would realize that he may trip someone if he extends his leg into an aisle in a self-service restaurant....

A patron is charged with using reasonable care for his own safety and must see and avoid obvious hazards. However, a child is not held to the same standard of care as that of an adult; rather, the test is whether the child, considering his age, background, and inherent intelligence, indulged in gross disregard of his own safety in the face of known, understood, and perceived danger.

It is well settled that a child of nine or ten years of age may be capable of negligence. However, in determining the negligence of a child, the actions of the child must be judged by his maturity and capacity to evaluate circumstances. The degree of caution expected of a nine or ten-year old boy varies with the circumstances of each case. In the case before us, an apparently normal, average ten-year old boy was carrying a plate of salad through a restaurant to the table where his family was sitting. The testimony of all eye witnesses, including Michael Bruce, the busboy, was that James was walking fast, but not running.

The defendants would have us assess 100 percent fault to James for walking too fast, for not watching where he was going, and for not taking a different route to his table. However, we are discussing a ten-year old boy who was trying to carry a plate of salad from the salad bar to his table without spilling it. We do not believe that a ten-year old child generally has sufficient experience to discern the best possible route by which to negotiate a crowded self-service restaurant while carrying a plate of food; many adults find this difficult. The route he did take led directly to his family's table. The trial judge found this was a reasonable route and we agree.

However, we do not believe that the danger inherent in walking too fast in a self-service restaurant while carrying a plate of food is beyond the understanding of a normal 10 year old boy. Moreover, James had already been admonished by his mother not to run in the restaurant. The trial judge found that James's conduct was negligent. We cannot say the trial judge was clearly wrong.

CASE QUESTIONS

1. What is the standard of care an adult must exercise for his own safety? How does that differ from the standard of care a child is expected to exercise?

2. The judge noted that the restaurant was self-service. What impact does this have on Bruce's negligence?

Room Furnishings

A hotel must anticipate dangers and use reasonable care to protect against them when furnishing a room that will be occupied by children. A court upheld a jury verdict of $56,000 awarded to an 8-month-old infant who fell from an adult bed against hot radiator pipes in a hotel room where no baby crib was furnished. The hotel had at least one crib available when the family arrived at the hotel, but the clerk did not offer or give it to the plaintiffs. The court ruled that the jury could properly hold a hotel negligent for failing to provide a baby bed while maintaining exposed hot radiator pipes in the hotel room. The court said that a hotel owes its guests a "duty to provide articles of furniture that may be used by them in the ordinary and reasonable way without danger."[33] The negligence in the facts of this case was not in the exposed pipe in the room, but the failure of the hotel to provide a bed suitable for the infant given the existence of the exposed pipe. Heed this case and be proactive, particularly with young guests.

Attractive Nuisance Doctrine

As we have discussed, a landowner generally owes no duty to a trespasser other than to refrain from causing him willful injury. There is an exception to this rule for child trespassers called the *attractive nuisance doctrine*.

attractive nuisance
A potentially dangerous object or condition of exceptional interest to young people.

This doctrine is an outgrowth of the law's recognition of youngsters' limited capability to detect danger and protect themselves from risk. An **attractive nuisance** is a potentially dangerous object or condition of exceptional interest to young people, such as a swimming pool, a large empty box (like one in which a refrigerator might be delivered), a snow pile suitable for sliding created by a plow, and equipment or ditches at a construction site. If an attractive nuisance exists on the property, the owner or occupier is required to exercise reasonable care to protect children from associated risks. Thus, a hotel with a swimming area would be well advised to install a tall fence with a lock to prevent children from using the pool when it is closed or unattended (this is often required in many states by statute). A restaurant that purchased a new freezer should discard the box only after removing all tacks and other sharp items and flattening it.

The elements of an attractive nuisance are the following:

1. A condition exists that is attractive to children and is likely to cause them injury.

2. The owner or occupier of the land knows or should know of the condition.

3. Due to the child's immaturity, he does not appreciate the danger.

When these elements exist, the owner or occupier must take reasonable steps to eliminate the danger.

---

[33] *Seelbach, Inc. v. Cadick*, 405 S.W.2d 745 (Ky. 1966)

Some states have abolished the concept of attractive nuisance in circumstances where the risk should be obvious to the child. These states hold that certain risks are so obvious that even children are expected to exercise caution when confronting them, relieving the property owner from liability. In an Idaho case, a six-year-old boy fell four feet to the ground from the deck of a stationary boat used as a playhouse on the defendants' property. His parents sued the property owners to recover for the child's broken arm. The court held for the defendants on the ground that the fall was not caused by a hidden defect in the boat and that the danger of falling should have been apparent to the boy. Said the court,

> From the time they are born, all children realize the danger of falling and instinctively clutch at something when they feel that danger is near. While the instinct to climb is practically universal, and it is carried on in a venturesome spirit, a consciousness of the risk of falling is always present.[34]

There is no fixed age at which a child does and can be expected to realize a particular risk. A jury must decide in each case whether the child plaintiff could appreciate the danger. In a Michigan case a berry farm open to the public provided an amusement known as a "Jacob's Ladder" (a ladder made of rope with wooden plank rungs designed to twist and sway and be difficult to climb). Plaintiff fell off this device and broke both wrists because of insufficient padding on the ground below. The court denied defendant's motion for summary judgment and instead directed that the case proceed to trial so the jury could determine whether defendant should have perceived the risk and protected himself from it.[35]

Negligence Per Se Doctrine

Negligence per se describes conduct that violates a law or ordinance designed to protect the safety of the public. Under the majority view, such acts are treated as negligence without any need for further proof of breach of duty. When applicable, this doctrine is of great help to the plaintiff because he does not have to prove that the defendant failed to act as a reasonable person. Instead, the plaintiff need only prove the existence of the law or ordinance and the defendant's violation of it. (Of course, as with any negligence case, plaintiff must also establish the extent of the injury, and proximate cause between the violation and the injury.)

negligence per se
When a defendant has violated a law or ordinance designed to protect the safety of the public.

Under the minority view, noncompliance with the safety law or ordinance is not conclusive on the issue of the defendant's breach of duty, but is some evidence of such a breach. In some states, such noncompliance is **prima facie** evidence of negligence, which means it alone is sufficient evidence if unrebutted to support a judgment for the plaintiff.

prima facie
Evidence that alone is sufficient if unrebutted to support a judgment for the plaintiff.

The reasoning supporting the majority position on the negligence per se doctrine is that the proprietor of an establishment has a duty always to comply with legal mandates designed to protect patrons. This legal duty applies even when the owner is unaware of the existence of the safety laws. Innkeepers and restaurateurs are

---

[34] *Daniels v. Byington*, 707 P.2d 476 (Id. 1985)
[35] *Bragan v. Symanzik*, 687 NW2d 881 (Mich. 2004)

expected to stay current on both new laws applicable to their business and changes in existing laws. Sources of this information include trade journals and presentations at trade association meetings. In addition, a business can request a lawyer to perform a legal audit in which the attorney will examine the business and its compliance with applicable laws and advise the owner of any deficiencies.

Case Example 5-14 illustrates the application of the majority view of negligence per se in a case against a hotel that was woefully deficient in its compliance with safety laws relating to swimming pools.

CASE EXAMPLE 5-14

First Overseas Investment Corp. v. Cotton

491 So.2d 293 (Fla. 1986)

...Cleophus Cotton and his wife were guests at the Monte Carlo Hotel (hotel). Mr. Cotton went swimming in the shallow end of the hotel pool. The pool water was extremely cloudy as the pool attendant had that morning dumped a bucketful of soda ash into it to "sweeten" the pH. The pool attendant testified that the pool's soda ash feeder was inoperable, hence his practice of dumping the soda ash directly into the pool. Expert testimony was offered that soda ash should never be dumped directly into a pool and that a bucketful was ten to twelve times more than is needed. Soda ash increases turbidity [muddiness, thickness, darkness] and makes the water cloudy until completely filtered. The pool attendant testified that he had no training in first aid or in the use of lifesaving apparatus. He further testified that the pool's filtration system was inoperable. The pool did not have lifesaving apparatus such as a shepherd's hook, an elevated lifeguard's chair, or first aid equipment.

Michael Wolfe testified that he observed Mr. Cotton swimming in the shallow end of the pool. Mr. Wolfe turned away from the pool for about 60 seconds and when he looked back, Mr. Cotton was gone. Mr. Wolfe went to the side of the pool and looked for Mr. Cotton, but did not see him. He asked another hotel guest, Daniel Jones, if he had seen Mr. Cotton. Mr. Jones indicated that he had not seen him. Mr. Wolfe told the pool attendant that he thought Mr. Cotton was in the pool. The pool attendant and Mr. Wolfe stood at the edge of the pool and looked for Mr. Cotton, but still did not see him. Subsequently, Mr. Wolfe and Mr. Jones began swimming the length of the pool at the bottom, looking for Mr. Cotton. They testified that they did not find Mr. Cotton on the bottom until they were practically on top of him. They then brought him up to the side of the pool. Mr. Jones ran down the beach to get a lifeguard. A lifeguard was located by Mr. Jones. The lifeguard attempted to resuscitate Mr. Cotton, but his efforts were unsuccessful, as were the efforts of a fire rescue squad which arrived at the scene shortly after the lifeguard.

Mr. Wolfe testified that twelve to twenty minutes elapsed between the time he first started looking for Mr. Cotton and the time resuscitation efforts were first made. According to expert testimony, there was a high probability of Mr. Cotton's survival if he had been rescued within four to five minutes after disappearing. It was plaintiff's contention that Mr. Cotton would have been rescued within four to five minutes and would not have drowned if the hotel had complied with the following Florida Department of Health and Rehabilitative Services (HRS) rules:

Rule 10D5.66(3)

All items of equipment designed for recirculation, filtration, disinfection, and pool water treatment, shall be kept in service at all times and shall be properly maintained to perform the functions of the units and protect the swimming pool water from contamination.

Rule 10D5.68(6)

Clearness—At all times the pool water shall be sufficiently clear so that the main drain or drains are clearly defined when viewed from the pool deck.

Rule 10D5.81(1)

All owners, managers, and/or other attendants in charge of a public swimming pool shall be responsible for supervision and safety of the pool. The attendant, if provided, shall be in full charge of bathing, shall have authority to enforce all rules, and shall be trained in first aid and the use of lifesaving apparatus.

Rule 10D5.81(2)

Lifesaving apparatus—All swimming pools shall be provided with a shepherd's hook securely attached to a one piece pole not less than sixteen (16) feet in length, and at least one (1) eighteen (18) inch diameter lifesaving ring with sufficient rope attached to reach all parts of the pool from the pool deck. Lifesaving apparatus shall be mounted in a conspicuous place and be readily available for use. Pools greater than fifty (50) feet in length shall have multiple units with at least one shepherd's hook and one (1) lifesaving ring located along each of the longer sides of the pool.

Rule 10D5.81(3)

Lifesaving chairs—One elevated lifeguard chair...platform shall be provided for pools having over two thousand (2,000) square feet up to four thousand (4,000) square feet of pool water surface area. One additional lifeguard chair or platform shall be provided for each two thousand (2,000) square feet, or major fraction thereof, of pool water surface area above four thousand (4,000) square feet. The lifeguard chair(s) or platform(s) shall be located to allow a clear and unobstructed view of the pool bottom in the area of surveillance.

Rule 10D5.81(6)

First aid equipment and materials—Each pool shall have available first aid equipment and materials sufficient for use in connection with injuries which may occur in the pool or on the pool deck.

Plaintiff contended that Mr. Cotton would not have drowned if the pool's filtration system had been operating properly; the water in the pool had been clear; an elevated lifeguard chair had been in place affording a clear and unobstructed view of the pool; there had been lifesaving apparatus and first aid equipment available and the pool attendant had been trained in the use of lifesaving apparatus and first aid.... The well established rule is that it is "negligence per se" for a defendant to violate a statute which establishes a duty to protect a particular class of persons from a particular type of injury. This applies to violations of HRS rules as well....

We find that all of the HRS rules at issue obligated the hotel to protect a particular class of persons (guests using the pool), from a particular type of harm (drowning). All of the rules were designed to ensure a clear view of swimmers in distress and/or the capability of saving them from drowning....

[Judgment for plaintiff.]

CASE QUESTIONS

1. What class of persons was the pool maintenance laws designed to protect? Why do these people need protection?

2. How did the plaintiff prove proximate cause in this case?

A building owner who fails to comply with elevator safety and inspection rules will face liability for negligence per se if the elevator malfunctions and people are injured. A plaintiff was injured when an elevator dropped past the ground floor (despite buttons pushed for lobby exit), struck bottom, and rebounded to the third floor. The building elevators experienced numerous malfunctions in the days leading to the incident. State statutes required building owners to maintain elevators in a safe condition. The court held negligence per se applied to this circumstance.[36]

Another application involves a restaurant/bar that permitted loud music to emanate from its premises. This caused excessive noise and vibration to permeate the plaintiff's condominium located directly above the restaurant. Extensive testimony at trial by police officers and experts established that noise level readings were taken in the plaintiff's unit and they substantially violated the limits allowed by ordinance. The jury's verdict was for the plaintiff and it was upheld on appeal based on negligence per se.[37]

Negligence Per Se and Proximate Cause

For a restaurant or hotel to be liable under negligence per se, it is not enough that the establishment violated the law. As we discussed, the violation must be the proximate cause of the plaintiff's injury. If it is not, the hotel or restaurant will not

---

[36] *Golden Shoreline Limited Partnership v. McGowan*, 787 So.2d 109 (Fla. 2001)
[37] *Peck v. Rattlesnake Ventures, Inc.*, 1998 WL 846100 (Conn. 1998)

be liable. In a Georgia case two hotel guests, Sanders and Truett, had an altercation. Shortly after the fight Sanders went to Truett's room and knocked on the door. When Truett opened it, Sanders shot him. Contrary to statute, the door opened outward instead of inward. Truett sued the hotel, claiming negligence per se. The court rejected the claim because no connection existed between the direction in which the door opened and the injury.[38]

Obligations Beyond Regulation

Suppose a hotel fully complies with a statute but the requirements of the law are inadequate to protect the guests. Can that hotel be found negligent for failing to do more than the law requires? The answer is "yes" and here is why. The hotel has a duty to exercise reasonable care to protect guests from injury. If satisfying the law falls short of reasonable care, the hotel must do more than what the statute requires. Failure to provide that added measure of safety will result in liability for negligence, not negligence per se. Thus, where a hotel complied with the local fire safety codes that did not require smoke alarms, and guests were seriously injured in a fire due in part to the absence of alarms, the hotel was liable for negligence. Said the court, "Compliance with the appropriate regulations is not conclusive evidence of due care. If the defendants knew or should have known of some risk that would be prevented by reasonable measures not required by the law, they were negligent if they did not take such measures."[39]

How does an innkeeper or restaurateur know what is required to satisfy the due care obligation if compliance with statutory mandates is not enough? The level of care required will be determined in part by standards followed in the industry as well as by technological advances. Proprietors must stay abreast of new and state-of-the-art products and techniques, and should always be asking, "What new practice or procedure can I be performing and what new devices might I be utilizing to enhance the safety of my patrons?"

Strict or Absolute Liability

Normally defendants are not liable unless they do something wrong. If a patron trips and falls in a restaurant solely because the heel on her shoe broke, the restaurant will not be liable for any injuries sustained in the fall. Since the restaurant was not negligent it did not breach any duty owed to the customer.

One exception does exist. If applicable, a defendant will be liable even though it violated no duty and did nothing wrong. That exception is sometimes called *strict liability* and sometimes *absolute liability*. **Strict liability** imposes liability for injury caused by an ultra-hazardous activity without regard to fault or wrongdoing by the party engaging in the dangerous conduct. An example of an ultra-hazardous activity is using explosives. The doctrine of strict liability imposes liability for resulting injuries even if the defendant took every precaution and was not negligent.

strict liability
Also called absolute liability; the doctrine that imposes all the risks of an ultra-hazardous activity upon those who engage in it.

---

[38] *Truett v. Morgan*, 266 S.E.2d 557 (Ga. 1980)
[39] *Miller v. Warren*, 390 S.E.2d 207 (W.Va. 1990)

The principle supporting this rule is that the ultra-hazardous activity could have been outlawed because of the danger it creates. However, despite its potential for harm, the ultra-hazardous activity has a useful purpose. In such circumstances, in lieu of outlawing the activity, the law imposes liability for the activity on the party who engages in it, without regard to fault.

Suppose Jake purchases an old office building in the downtown section of a sizable city intending to destroy the building with dynamite and build a 10-story luxury hotel. He plans the dynamiting for a Sunday morning when very few people are downtown. He constructs a tall barricade-like fence around the building to prevent people from entering the site and to protect against any debris hitting a passerby. Nonetheless, due to the explosion, a small piece of the building is propelled over the fence and hits a pedestrian. According to normal negligence rules, Jake would not be liable; he satisfied the duty to exercise reasonable care to prevent injury. But under strict liability, freedom from negligence is not a defense. Because dynamiting is a very hazardous undertaking, he will be liable to the injured passerby.

Strict Products Liability

strict products liability
The doctrine that imposes liability on the seller of a defective product without regard to negligence.

In recent times, the doctrine of strict liability has been extended significantly to apply to sellers of defective products. This application of strict liability is called **strict products liability** and imposes liability on the seller of a defective product without regard to negligence. A product is defective for this purpose if it is designed or manufactured improperly or if it contains inadequate warnings of the dangers it presents. For example, suppose a chef buys a toaster for a restaurant. When he plugs it in and turns it on, it explodes causing injury. The store that sold the toaster is strictly liable; the chef does not have to prove negligence. If the toaster was defective when the manufacturer sold the toaster to the store, the manufacturer too will be liable in strict products liability. The chef need only prove that the toaster was defective when the defendant sold it. A restaurant patron who breaks a tooth on an unidentified object in a cheeseburger can sue the restaurant for strict products liability.[40] If the object was in the meat when the restaurant purchased the hamburger from its supplier, the restaurant or the guest could also sue the supplier.

Liability in these circumstances is a matter of social policy and based on three objectives. First, by reason of the retail seller's continuing relationship with its distributor, the seller is in a position to exert pressure for improved safety of its products. Second, a seller of goods assumes a special responsibility to its customers, who expect the seller to stand behind its goods.[41] The third objective is to spread the cost of damages suffered by individuals from defective products. The expenses associated with an injury may be an overwhelming burden to an individual, whereas manufacturers and retailers can purchase insurance and allocate the cost over all their sales.[42]

---

[40] *Rudloff v. Wendy's Restaurant of Rochester, Inc.*, 821 N.Y.S.2d 358 (N.Y. 2006)
[41] *Gunning v. Small Feast Caterers, Inc.*, 777 N.Y.S.2d 268 (N.Y. 2004)
[42] *Jiminez v. TM Cobb Company*, 98 Cal.Rptr.2d 587 (Ca. 2000), aff'd 58 P.3d 450 (2003)

Note that the product causing the injury must be defective for strict products liability to apply. Sometimes a product causes injury for reasons other than a product flaw. For example, the person injured may have misused the product, as where a guest in a hotel room used an iron while wearing the clothes he was ironing. When doing so, he burned himself. Since the hotel guest was using the iron improperly, neither the manufacturer nor the seller will be liable.

Restaurants and hotels can either benefit or be hurt by strict products liability. If they buy products that are defective and incur a loss as a result, they can sue the seller without the need to prove negligence. Thus, where a Hunan restaurant sustained significant damage from a fire because the fire suppression system it had purchased malfunctioned and failed to extinguish the flames, the manufacturer of the system may be liable in strict products liability.[43] Similarly, the manufacturer of a deep-fat fryer that did not adequately provide protection against boiling oil spills may be liable in strict products liability to a scalded restaurant employee.[44]

Restaurants and hotels can also be sued in strict products liability if they sell defective products, such as rancid tuna salad in the dining room or a bag of chips with a tack in it in the gift shop. If the product was defective when it was delivered to the hospitality facility, the restaurant or hotel can sue the manufacturer if the hotel or restaurant is sued by a customer or guest.

Respondeat Superior

In general, an employer is liable for the acts of its employees done in furtherance of their jobs. Thus, employers are liable to their customers, guests, and other invitees for the negligence of their employees. If a bellhop negligently drops a suitcase on a guest's foot, the innkeeper will be liable for the resulting injuries. If a waiter carelessly spills hot coffee on a customer, causing burns, the restaurant will be liable.

This legal responsibility of the employer for the acts of its employees is called **respondeat superior,** which means "let the master (employer) answer." Stated differently, the employer is vicariously (through a substitute) liable for the employee's wrongful conduct. The doctrine is founded on the theory that an employee is an agent of the employer; whenever an employee is performing the duties of his job, he is acting on behalf of the employer. The law in effect renders acts of the employee those of the employer.

respondeat superior
"Let the master (employer) answer" (Latin). The liability of the employer for the acts of its employees.

Several explanations exist for this rule. It encourages employers to exercise caution and care in the selection and training of employees. This liability should thus have the desirable effect of limiting the number of injuries occurring from employee errors. Another rationale for the doctrine is that it increases the injured party's chances of receiving compensation, as the employer usually has more resources than does the employee.

---

[43] *Chiang v. Pyro Chemical, Inc.,* 1997 WL 330622 (Conn. 1997)
[44] *Bullock, Inc. v. Thorpe,* 52 S.W.3d 201 (Ga. 1987)

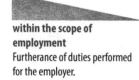

within the scope of employment
Furtherance of duties performed for the employer.

Notwithstanding respondeat superior, an employer is not liable for every negligent act of its employee. For example, the employer is not liable for negligent acts committed by the employee at home or school during the employee's off-duty hours. The employer is liable only if the employee's negligent act occurred **within the scope of employment,** which means in furtherance of duties performed for the employer.

In Case Example 5-15, the negligence clearly occurred while the employee was acting within the scope of his employment.

CASE EXAMPLE 5-15

Scott v. Salerno and GNOC Corp., d/b/a Bally's Grand Hotel & Casino

688 A.2d 614 (N.J. 1997)

Salerno, while operating an automobile owned by Pauline N. Marchese (Marchese), was involved in an accident with an automobile owned and operated by plaintiff Denise Rae Bishop Scott (Scott) in Atlantic City, New Jersey. At the time of the accident, Salerno was valet parking automobiles for Bally's as an employee....

Bally's was legally responsible for the acts or omissions of Salerno... Marchese gave Bally's permission to park her automobile. At the time of the accident, the automobile was being driven by Salerno, as agent for Bally's, for the very purpose for which it was given to Bally's. Bally's was responsible for the acts of Salerno....

Acting Outside the Scope of Employment

Sometimes an employee might be on duty but act outside the scope of his employment. Several assault cases illustrate this situation. A McDonald's employee, either on a break or at the end of his shift, cut in the customer line to order a drink. An argument ensued between the employee and a customer who objected. It escalated into a fistfight in which the customer was injured. He sued McDonald's restaurant, asserting respondeat superior. The restaurant denied that the employee was acting within the scope of his employment. The court agreed and dismissed the case stating, "When the altercation occurred, [the employee] was in the process of ordering a drink for himself. He was not cleaning, nor was he performing any of his job duties, or in the process of performing any task for his employer.... Standing in line and placing an order was not one of his job duties...even if he was 'on the clock' when the fight started."[45]

---

[45] *Montgomery v. McDonald's Corporation,* 2001 WL 705520 (Ill. 2001)

A similar outcome occurred in another case involving a McDonald's dispute. The grill worker was apparently quite unhappy when a customer threw a straw wrapper into a garbage can that was being used to hold Happy Meal toys. The cook emerged from the rear of the restaurant and assaulted the customer, who thereafter sued the eatery based on respondeat superior. The court dismissed the case, finding that a grill worker's job responsibilities do not include any contact with customers.[46]

In another fight case, several members of a Steak & Ale Restaurant kitchen staff came to the aid of a woman who was believed to be a victim of abuse by her boyfriend. The kitchen workers attacked the boyfriend in the restaurant parking lot. He sued the restaurant, relying on respondeat superior. Denying the claim, the court said, "[T]he duties of the kitchen staff were limited to activities within the kitchen, and they had no authorization to employ physical force against any party for any reason. Furthermore, the kitchen staff had no duties to maintain security on the premises....The test of liability is not whether the act was done during the existence of the employment, but whether it was done within the scope of the actual transaction of the master's business for accomplishing the ends of his employment."[47]

Depending on the facts, a fight may be included within an employee's scope of employment. A Burger King supervisory employee was attempting to resolve a refund request from a customer complaining about her order. During the discussion, the customer accused the worker of harassing her son in school, a matter unrelated to the food complaint. The employee became angered and swung his fists into a stack of trays. One of the trays rebounded and hit the customer in the face. She sued Burger King, which denied that the employee was acting within the scope of his employment. The court noted that although the actions may have been mingled with personal motives, they occurred during a discussion involving work responsibilities. The court referred the matter for a jury trial to address whether the fight occurred within the scope of the employee's job.[48]

In another case, a housekeeper for an Adam's Mark Hotel was given keys for the supply rooms at the beginning of each shift and was required to return them at the end. One day he forgot to return the keys, which fact he did not realize until after arriving home from work. He drove back to the hotel to return the keys. On his return home he negligently caused an accident, seriously injuring the plaintiff, who suffered permanent brain damage. The jury awarded damages and determined the housekeeper was not acting in the course of his employment. As a result, the hotel was not liable to pay any of the damages. The court referenced the rule that generally an employee is not within the course of his employment while driving his own car to and from his place of work. Further, a hotel supervisor testified that employees occasionally went home with the keys by mistake. Such action had never resulted in an "advisory" (a warning) or in other disciplinary action. The court thus affirmed the jury's determination that the housekeeper was not acting within the scope of his employment at the time of the accident.[49]

---

[46] *Yono v. Coolidge #1, Inc.*, 2001 WL 716928 (Mich. 2001)
[47] *Waters v. Steak & Ale of Georgia, Inc.*, 527 S.E.2d 592 (Ga. 2000)
[48] *Reynolds v. L&L Management, Inc.*, 492 S.E.2d 347 (Ga. 1997)
[49] *Soto v. Adam's Mark Hotel*, 52 S.W.3d 201 (Tex. 2000)

Independent Contractors

independent contractor
One who contracts to do work for another, but who maintains control of the method of accomplishing the work. Also, someone hired by another to perform a given task according to methods and procedures that are independent from the control of the hiring party. An independent contractor is distinguished from an employee.

While an employer is liable for the acts of its employees committed in the scope of employment, a company is generally not liable for the acts of independent contractors it hires. An **independent contractor** is someone who contracts to do one or more specific projects for someone else and maintains control of how the work is done. A few examples of independent contractors follow.

In one case a casino called a limousine service to transport a patron. While en route to the patron's destination, the limousine driver caused a car accident that resulted in serious injuries to the patron. The latter sued the casino for his damages. The court determined that the limousine service was an independent contractor and therefore the casino was not liable.[50]

A nightclub was sued by a patron who was injured when a member of the band playing that night broke a beer bottle on the customer's face. The case was dismissed because the band member was an independent contractor and therefore the bar was not liable for his actions.[51]

Determining whether a worker is an employee or independent contractor is often not easy. There exists no definitive rule for deciding the status of a worker. Additional factors to consider include the following:

- Who (as between the employer and worker) supplies the tools and the place of work (if the employer, the worker is more likely to be considered an employee)

- Length of time for which a person is hired (the longer the engagement, the more likely the worker will be deemed an employee)

- Method of payment—whether by time or by the job (if by time, it is more likely the worker will qualify as an employee)

- Whether or not the work being performed is part of the regular business of the employer (if so, the more likely the worker will be considered an employee)

- Intentions and beliefs of the parties concerning their relationship[52]

Nondelegable Duties

nondelegable
A duty that cannot be assigned

An exception exists to the general rule that an employer is not liable for the acts of an independent contractor. Normally, the duty imposed on a hospitality facility to keep the premises reasonably safe for guests is **nondelegable,** meaning it cannot be transferred (or delegated) to another. For policy reasons, the employer is not permitted to avoid liability on the ground that an independent contractor failed to properly perform the work. The rule is intended to motivate the hotel or restaurant to monitor carefully the work of the independent contractors it hires. Examples of

---

[50] *Robinson v. Jiffy Executive Limousine Co.,* 4 F.3d 237 (N.J. 1993)
[51] *Stevens v. Spec, Inc.,* 637 N.Y.S.2d 979 (N.Y. 1996)
[52] Restatement Second of Agency, a compilation of recommended rules of agency law.

nondelegable duties include parking lot maintenance and guest safety. Thus, a hotel may be liable to a guest who slips and falls on the sidewalk due to the failure of a snow removal service hired by the hotel to sufficiently clear the snow.[53] Similarly, a hotel that hires an independent contracting service to provide security for its premises remains liable to a guest who is criminally attacked because the security service is negligent in the performance of its duties.[54]

Another nondelegable duty for a hotel is the obligation to use effective pest control methods. If a licensed extermination company is hired by a hotel to spray the facility, the inn will be liable if the service fails to do its work properly and a guest is bitten, even though the company is an independent contractor. In an Oklahoma case a Days Inn guest who was bitten by a brown recluse spider while she slept would be entitled to recover against the hotel if she could prove the extermination contractor was negligent.[55]

Where liability is imposed due to a nondelegable duty, the responsible hotel or restaurant may be entitled to compensation from the negligent independent contractor.

Duty to Aid a Person in Distress

If someone in need calls out to you for help, are you legally obligated to offer assistance? If you fail to respond, will you be liable for resulting injuries to the person in trouble? The answer to both questions is generally *no*. The law does not impose a legal duty on individuals to rescue someone in trouble. Indeed, courts have denied damage claims in the following situations:

- A man who watched while a young woman drowned, even though he could easily have gone to her aid

- A man who failed to warn a neighbor's child he saw hammering on a tube of gunpowder

In each case, the moral duty was plain enough, but the courts agreed that moral responsibility is a matter of conscience and not of law.

If a person does come to the aid of another, the law imposes a duty on the rescuer to exercise reasonable care. While no liability would have resulted had the rescuer chosen to do nothing, liability will result if a rescue attempt is done negligently.[56] The reason for this rule is the expectation that, had the rescuer not attempted to help, someone else with requisite skills would likely have offered to assist. Once others observe that a person in need is being tended to, they are less likely to come forward to help.

---

53 *Wood v. Chalet Susse International,* 1995 WL 317058 (Conn. 1995)
54 *Security Services Corp. v. Ramada Inn, Inc.,* 665 So.2d 268 (Fla. 1996)
55 *Copeland v. The Lodge Enterprises, Inc.,* 4 P.3d 695 (Ok. 2000)
56 *Pacello v. Wyndham International, Inc.,* 2006 WL 110 2737 (Conn. 2006)

The law in most states requires business owners to lend a hand under certain circumstances. These include situations where the proprietor's lack of care would aggravate the harm. For example, in one case a drunk customer of a commercial fishing pier passed out on the dock, rolled over into the water and drowned. A lawsuit was begun by his estate claiming the pier operator should have assisted the man to safety. The court agreed, holding that the proprietor could not legally ignore the man but rather owed a duty to take some action to safeguard him.[57]

Thus, a business open to the public owes a duty to its patrons to aid them if they are in danger while on the premises. The rationale for this duty is that the proprietor is deriving economic benefit from the presence of the customer, and ensuring that invitees are safe is a cost of doing business. This rule is discussed in Case Example 5-16.

CASE EXAMPLE 5-16

Baker v. Fenneman & Brown Properties, LLC and Southern Bells of Indiana, Inc., all d/b/a Taco Bell

793 N.E.2d 1203 (Ind. 2003)

...Aaron Baker entered the Taco Bell store in Newburgh, Indiana, to purchase a soft drink. Upon entering the store, Baker felt nauseous, but he continued to the counter, where he ordered a drink. Baker handed the cashier money for the drink and suddenly fell backward. Baker's head hit the floor, and he was knocked unconscious and began having convulsions...A doctor determined Baker fell because he experienced vasovagal syncope... Vasovagal syncope is [a] form of syncope (fainting) that occurs as a part of a normal physiologic response to stress (often emotional stress). The individual becomes lightheaded, nauseated, flushed, feels warm and then may lose consciousness for several seconds...

Baker and defendants ("Taco Bell") disagree regarding whether Taco Bell rendered assistance to Baker. Baker claims that when he regained consciousness, he was staring at the ceiling, he had no idea what was going on, and he did not know where he was. He claims that no Taco Bell employee called for medical assistance or helped him in any way. Taco Bell claims that the cashier walked around the counter to Baker, where she waited for his convulsions to stop, and then she asked Baker if he was okay and if he needed an ambulance. The employee claims Baker said he was fine and he did not need an ambulance, so she walked back around the counter.

What happened next is undisputed. Moments after Baker stood up, he fell again. This time, Baker fell forward and was knocked unconscious. The fall lacerated his chin, knocked out his four front teeth, and cracked the seventh vertebra of his neck. when Baker regained consciousness, he was choking on the blood and teeth in his mouth. Baker stumbled out of the store to a friend, who contacted Baker's fiancé to take him to the hospital...

Baker claims Taco Bell had a duty to assist him and that it breached that duty by failing to provide assistance to him. Taco Bell argues it had no duty to assist Baker...We believe Baker is correct....

---

[57] *Starling v. Fisherman's Pier, Inc.*, 401 So.2d 1136 (Fl. 1981)

Review of decisions from a number of other jurisdictions suggests we should interpret Indiana law to impose a duty in this situation...[and] public policy suggests Taco Bell had a duty to provide reasonable care in this situation. When a storeowner opens his property to the public, he does so because he hopes to gain some economic benefit from the public... Social policy dictates that the storeowner, who is deriving this economic benefit from the presence of the customer, should assume the affirmative duty [to help customers who become ill as] a cost of doing business...

Accordingly, the duty that arises is a duty to exercise reasonable care under the circumstances. A high school student employed at Taco Bell would not be expected to provide the type of first aid an emergency room doctor would provide, as such an expectation would not be reasonable... A restaurant whose employees are reasonably on notice that a customer is in distress and in need of emergency medical attention has a legal duty to come to the assistance of that customer. However, a restaurant does not have a duty to provide medical training to its food service personnel, or medical rescue services to its customers who become ill or injured through no act or omission of the restaurant or its employees. A restaurant in these circumstances meets its legal duty to a customer in distress when it summons medical assistance within a reasonable time. Moreover, as a practical matter, we fail to see the logic in Taco Bell's position that it should have no duty to aid in these types of situations. First, we find it unlikely customers would patronize a business that left another customer who was ill or injured lying on the floor of the business simply because the business was not responsible for the customer's illness or injury.

Second, imposing on a business a duty to provide reasonable care even when the business is not responsible for an illness or injury will rarely force a business to act in circumstances in which it should not already have been acting. For example, if, as Taco Bell asserts, a business has no duty to assist if it is not responsible for the instrumentality, then... if a customer's face is turning blue, an employee should determine before providing assistance whether the person is choking on a food item from the business, in which case the employee must offer assistance, or whether the person is having a heart attack or choking on a food item purchased from a third party, in which case the employee need not offer assistance. By implementing policies and procedures that allow their employees to assist injured persons only when the business causes the illness or injury, a business might risk liability claims caused by an employee's failure to act, or failure to act promptly, when an illness or injury *was* in fact caused by an instrumentality of the business. Consequently, we are not placing a duty on businesses that they should not have already assumed.

In sum...Taco Bell had a duty, as a business that invited members of the public to enter its facility, to provide reasonable assistance to Baker even though Taco Bell was not responsible for Baker's illness. Consequently, we hold Taco Bell had a duty to take reasonable action...to give...aid to Baker after he fell and to care for [him] until [he could] be cared for by others.

CASE QUESTIONS

1. Do you agree with the court's determination that Taco Bell should provide reasonable assistance to Baker even though Taco Bell was not responsible for his illness? Why or why not?

2. What is the public policy underlying the court's decision?

In another case, an intruder entered a hotel room and bound, gagged, and raped the guest. He then left, threatening to return and kill her. Still bound, she managed to kick the phone receiver off the hook and call the front desk. The operator was slow to respond and waited a while before calling the police. The court ruled the hotel was negligent for failing promptly to respond to the guest's call for help.[58]

Limitation on Duty to Invitees

A business owner's duty to aid a patron in distress is not absolute. If the guest who is in danger is being cared for by others who appear competent to render the necessary assistance, the hotel or restaurant is relieved from the duty to offer aid. Case Example 5-17 illustrates this point.

CASE EXAMPLE 5-17

Fish v. Paul, d/b/a Horseshoe Motel

574 A.2d 1365 (Me. 1990)

Gretchen Fish, individually and a personal representative of the estate of her son, Mark Colvin...argues that [defendant motel owners] are liable for their failure to help Colvin, a guest who became ill at their motel....

The plaintiff alleges the following: On August 13, 1987, Colvin, who was 18 at the time, traveled with two companions, Steven Fahsel and Frederick Wood, from Bangor to Old Orchard Beach to attend a concert. After the concert, the three rented a room in Saco at the Horseshoe Motel, owned by the Pauls. During the night the three drank a substantial quantity of alcohol. The next morning an employee of the motel saw Fahsel and Wood carrying Colvin, who was semiconscious, to a waiting car. After placing Colvin in the rear seat, Fahsel and Wood started back toward Bangor. On I95 near Etna, the car overheated and stopped. A police officer stopped and called an ambulance for Colvin, but he was pronounced dead on arrival at St. Joseph's Hospital in Bangor. The complaint sought compensatory damages....

We have recognized the general duty of a business proprietor to exercise reasonable care to prevent injury to business invitees.... We also recognize that in certain circumstances the relationship between a guest and an innkeeper may give rise to a duty to render aid in case of illness or injury.... [H]owever... the innkeeper "is not required to give any aid to one who is in the hands of apparently competent persons who have taken charge of him, or whose friends are present and apparently in a position to give him all necessary assistance." The defendants contend that...the presence of Colvin's friends already rendering aid relieves the motel of any obligation to do so.... We find the defendants' argument persuasive.... We conclude that the facts alleged are not sufficient to state a claim against the [motel owners].

CASE QUESTION

1. Why in Case Example 5-15 did the proprietor owe a duty to aid a customer in distress while in this case the proprietor was relieved of that duty?

---

[58] *Boles v. La Quinta Motor Inns*, 680 F.2d 1077 (Tex. 1982)

Statutory Protection for Good Samaritans

While requiring rescuers to act reasonably, the law also recognizes that the conditions available to the rescuer in an emergency may be far from ideal and often even crude. For example, roadside treatment immediately following a car accident involves conditions drastically different from the sterile environment of an operating room. The law affords the rescuer protection from liability resulting from these less-than-ideal conditions. This is accomplished through **Good Samaritan Statutes,** which are laws that protect a person who reacts in an emergency situation by trying to help an injured person or someone in peril. According to these statutes, the rescuer will not be liable for any injuries caused in the attempt to render assistance if the means used were reasonable in relation to the emergency conditions at the scene. Many such statutes further provide that the rescuer is not liable for ordinary negligence, but only for gross negligence (excessive negligence). The purpose of these statutes is to encourage volunteer aid to persons in danger by limiting the rescuer's fear of potential liability.

A related principle, called the **rescue doctrine,** benefits a rescuer who is injured while administering aid. It provides that a person who negligently creates a hazard that injures another person is liable for injuries to a rescuer who assists the injured person. This principle is demonstrated in a Pennsylvania case. A defective television in a guest room caused fire to a hotel. The defect in the set was known to a hotel employee who failed to remove it. Leaving the set plugged in was negligent. A guest at the hotel repeatedly rescued other guests from the hotel during the fire. He did not return from his final rescue attempt. His family sued the hotel. The court ruled the inn was liable based on the rescue doctrine. Explained the court, "Danger invited rescue.... The wrong that imperils life is a wrong to the imperiled victim; it is a wrong also to his rescuer."[59]

> **Good Samaritan Statutes**
> Laws that protect people who, in an emergency situation, try to help a sick or injured person or someone in peril.

> **rescue doctrine**
> This rule of law recognizes that "danger invites rescue." The doctrine holds that a person who, through his negligence, jeopardizes the safety of another person, may be liable to a third person (the rescuer) who attempts to save the person at risk and suffers injuries in the process.

Rule in Choking Situations

A classic emergency at a restaurant occurs when a piece of food becomes lodged in a person's airway, blocking off all air to the lungs. Such a situation presents a grave condition because a person with a blocked airway will become unconscious in about one minute, will suffer irreversible brain damage in about four to five minutes, and will die usually within a few minutes of the onset of brain damage. These situations occur with sufficient frequency as to be recognized as a significant problem in the restaurant industry.

Nonetheless the law does not require a restaurant to administer first aid to a choking patron. Instead, the restaurant's only duty is to summon medical assistance for the hapless diner. If the eatery calls 911, it will be free from liability. If a restaurant chooses to administer aid to a choking patron and does so negligently, the restaurant will be liable in many states.

To encourage restaurants to attempt to save the afflicted person's life, some states have enacted statutes that both encourage restaurants to be ready to offer aid in the

---

[59] *Altamuro v. Milner Hotel, Inc.,* 540 F.Supp 870 (Pa. 1982)

event of a choking incident and also protect restaurants from liability when employees do offer first aid. A typical law requires that every restaurant and cafeteria in the state display prominently a poster showing the proper first-aid procedures to use in assisting a person who has a blocked airway and is choking. This procedure is called the Heimlich maneuver and is a relatively simple method of first aid that requires no apparatus or medical knowledge. The presence of the poster ensures that instructions are readily available in the event of an emergency. The legislation does not require anyone to administer this procedure; as we studied, no duty exists upon restaurateurs or their employees to render assistance to the choking victim other than to call 911 or an ambulance. If, however, restaurant owners, their employees, or patrons assist the choking person in accordance with the instructions on the poster, they will not be liable if the choking person is injured, except in cases of gross negligence. If the rescuer deviates from the poster's directions, liability may result.

Despite the mandate that the poster be exhibited, some state statutes provide that the restaurant cannot be held liable for injuries to or the death of the choke victim if the poster is not displayed.

Case Example 5-18 illustrates an application of the law concerning the limited duty of a restaurant to aid a choking victim.

CASE EXAMPLE 5-18

Campbell v. Eitak, Inc. T/D/B/A Katana

893 A.2d 749 (Pa. 2006)

...On March 25, 2002, Christopher Campbell ("Campbell"), was a patron at [the restaurant of] Appellee, Eitak, Inc, t/d/b/a Katana ("Katana")... a Japanese restaurant in Wilkes-Barre [Pennsylvania]. On that day, Campbell ordered chicken teriyaki as part of his lunch meal. When Campbell swallowed the first bite of the chicken, it became lodged in his throat, rendering him unable to breathe for approximately thirty seconds...During this period of time, he walked to the cashier counter, advised an employee that he was having difficulty breathing, and asked that she call 911. Takeshi Ei, one of the restaurant's owners, was standing nearby and suggested that Campbell attempt to dislodge the chicken by drinking water...Campbell went into the men's room, cupped his hands, and drank "a couple of handfuls" from the sink faucet...

Mr. Ei entered the restroom and asked how Campbell was doing. When Campbell replied that he was not feeling better, Mr. Ei asked if Campbell wanted a call placed to 911. When Campbell responded affirmatively, Mr. Ei left the restroom... When Campbell emerged from the restroom approximately five minutes later, he was informed that 911 had been called...He returned to the restroom, and remained there until an ambulance arrived...

Campbell explained to the EMTs that he was having difficulty breathing and talking due to the piece of chicken lodged in his throat... The EMTs provided oxygen and transported Campbell to a local hospital...Following [surgery], it was determined there was a tear in Campbell's esophagus. He was then transported by helicopter to the University of Pennsylvania Hospital in Philadelphia where he underwent surgery to repair the esophageal tear...

Campbell filed suit against Katana, alleging negligence for failure to have policies and procedures for responding to a choking emergency. He also alleged negligence for failure to have personnel trained in performing the Heimlich maneuver, and for failure to administer appropriate first aid. In response, Katana asserted that the duty of care owed to Campbell was satisfied by summoning emergency rescue personnel, and that the restaurant had no further duty...

Campbell presents one issue for our consideration: Whether the... defendant was negligent in its failure to properly respond to plaintiff's choking emergency...

A restaurant whose employees are reasonably on notice that a customer is in distress and in need of emergency medical attention has a legal duty to come to the assistance of that customer. However, a restaurant does not have a duty to provide medical training to its food service personnel, or medical rescue services to its customers who become ill or injured through no act or omission of the restaurant or its employees. A restaurant in these circumstances meets its legal duty to a customer in distress when it summons medical assistance within a reasonable time...

In absence of any legislative pronouncement, we hold that the prompt summoning of medical assistance satisfies a restaurant's duty to a patron who is choking. By calling 911 within minutes of Campbell's reported distress, Katana discharged its duty to Campbell as a matter of law...

CASE QUESTIONS

1. Under what circumstances might the restaurant have been liable?

2. Why do you think the court does not require restaurants to train their employees in medical procedures?

Courts recognize that restaurants would be strapped with a considerable burden if required to train employees to provide medical assistance or first aid. The courts seem intent on not imposing that responsibility. Said a Wyoming court,

> *We are concerned that a specific requirement of first aid, rather than aid in the form of a timely call for professional medical assistance, would place undue burdens on food servers and other business invitors.... Courses in first aid techniques require both time and money. Annual recertification classes are required in CPR and the Heimlich maneuver. Because employee turnover in the food service industry is high, continual training efforts might be required to provide a staff capable of providing first aid. This duty would apply to every food server, regardless of size.... The only persons expected to perform*

rescue techniques regardless of circumstances are the professional medical responders called for just that purpose. Whether that call is made within a reasonable time is the appropriate factual issue for jury consideration.[60]

Negligence Doctrines Generally Favoring the Defendant

The following doctrines benefit the defendant by shifting some or all of the responsibility for an injury to the plaintiff.

Contributory Negligence and Comparative Negligence

In some situations where a plaintiff is injured, not only is the defendant negligent but the plaintiff is as well. For example, assume that a plaintiff who trips on a hole in a restaurant's rug was wearing a high-heeled shoe she knew had a loose heel. The plaintiff fell due to both the loose heel and the hole. What effect does the plaintiff's negligence in wearing the shoe have on the lawsuit against the restaurant? Does the restaurant's duty to keep the premises reasonably safe give the plaintiff immunity from the consequences of her own inattention?

The impact on the lawsuit of the plaintiff's negligence depends on the applicable state's law. Each state follows either the rule of contributory negligence or the rule of comparative negligence.

Contributory Negligence—the Minority Rule

contributory negligence
The rule followed in some states that prevents a plaintiff from collecting damages if the plaintiff's negligence contributed to the injury.

According to the rule of **contributory negligence,** if the plaintiff 's carelessness contributed to the injury, the plaintiff cannot successfully sue a negligent defendant. Instead, the case will be dismissed. The defendant will not be liable for the plaintiff's damages and the plaintiff must absorb the full loss associated with the injuries. This is true regardless of how slight or insignificant the plaintiff's negligence may have been. While contributory negligence used to be the rule in most states, today only a few follow it—Alabama, Maryland, North Carolina, Virginia, and the District of Columbia.

An example of the application of this rule involves a Girl Scout leader who escorted four Scouts to a McDonald's restaurant. The leader directed the girls to sit at a table and she alone placed the order. While in line, she noticed a low, unpainted wooden platform positioned partially beneath the counter overhang. The platform was a bridge that allowed young customers to climb to a level where they could be seen and served by the cashier. When the scout leader's order was ready, she picked up the tray, and as she turned to walk to the dining area she tripped over

---

[60] *Drew v. Lejay's Sportsmen's Cafe, Inc.,* 806 P.2d 301 (Wyo. 1991)

the wooden structure and fell, injuring her hip and shoulder. Her resulting lawsuit was dismissed based on contributory negligence. Said the court, "Although an argument may be made that defendant was negligent in placing the platform so that it was partially hidden by the counter overhang, plaintiff's contributory negligence [in failing to avoid the structure after having observed it] would necessarily defeat any verdict in her favor."[61]

The reason for the trend away from the contributory negligence rule is that the all-or-nothing effect of this rule is now considered unduly harsh to the plaintiff.

Comparative Negligence—the Majority Rule

According to the rule of **comparative negligence,** a plaintiff's negligence will not totally defeat the lawsuit. Instead, the jury will allocate liability between the plaintiff and the defendant depending on their relative degree of culpability. For example, the jury might find that the restaurant patron who knew her heel was broken was 30 percent responsible and the restaurant that failed to repair the hole in the rug was 70 percent responsible. The plaintiff collects from the defendant that percentage of plaintiff's damages equal to the percentage of liability attributed to the defendant. In the example, the plaintiff must absorb 30 percent of the loss but can collect 70 percent from the defendant.

comparative negligence
The rule followed in most states that apportions damages according to the comparative contribution of the negligence of the parties. A jury will allocate the liability between the plaintiff and the defendant depending on their relative degree of culpability.

In another example, a hotel guest was raped by an intruder to her room. She had fastened the chain lock on the door, but failed to activate the doorknob lock. The hotel had improperly installed the chain lock so that, once the door was unlocked and cracked open slightly, the chain lock could easily be lifted out of its slot and the door opened. The attacker was thus able to enter the plaintiff's room. The guest sued the hotel for her damages. The court concluded that each was partially responsible for the incident and allocated liability between them. The written decision on the case did not report the actual percentages attributed to each.[62] What percentage would you assign to the hotel? Why?

In another case, the plaintiff entered a restaurant, saw that all the tables were occupied, noticed a couple vacating a table in an adjacent room, and began proceeding toward that table, watching it as she walked. Her attention was so diverted that she did not see a chair in the aisle in which she was walking. She tripped over it and suffered injuries. A manager came to her aid. Upon learning the cause of her fall, he said he had instructed servers "an hour ago to move this damn chair." In plaintiff's lawsuit the court found she was negligent for failing to watch where she was walking, and the restaurant was also negligent for failing for an hour to remove the chair from a passageway. The court determined the plaintiff and the restaurant were each 50 percent responsible.[63]

Another comparative negligence case involved a restaurant disc jockey who spun records from an elevated platform. Upon leaving for the night, and with his arms

---

61 *Allsup v. McVille, Inc.,* 533 S.E.2d 823 (N.C. 2000)
62 *Ledbetter v. Concord General Corp.,* 665 So.2d 1166 (La. 1996)
63 *Morace v. Melvyn's Restaurant, Inc.,* 719 So.2d 139 (La. 1998)

loaded with 45 to 50 pounds of equipment, he stepped across a 19-inch gap to a set of stairs leading to the back door. Unbeknownst to the disc jockey, the stairs were movable. As he placed his foot on the top step, the stairs slipped out from under him, causing him to fall and suffer a back injury. At trial his expert witness testified that the steps should have been either fixed or of a sufficient weight to prevent their easy movement which the expert opined would be 120 pounds. The actual weight of the movable steps was only 40 pounds. The court found the disc jockey was negligent for carrying so much heavy equipment while dismounting from the elevated stage and the restaurant was negligent for using such lightweight movable steps. The court allocated 39 percent of the negligence to the plaintiff and 61 percent to the restaurant. The disc jockey was thus able to collect only 61 percent of his loss.[64]

In a "pure system" of comparative negligence, the plaintiff will collect the appropriate share of his damages regardless of the percentage of fault attributed to him. Some states that follow the comparative negligence rule provide that, for the plaintiff to recover, the percentage of liability allocated to the plaintiff must be less than that assigned to the defendant (i.e., a maximum of 49 percent assigned to the plaintiff). This is known as the "less than" rule. Other states allow the defendant to recover if his percentage of fault is equal to or less than the defendant's (i.e., a maximum of 50 percent assigned to the plaintiff). A few states follow a "slight–gross" system in which the plaintiff can recover only if his share of the fault is slight and the defendant's share is gross.

The Doctrine of Last Clear Chance—Tempered by Comparative Negligence

While the contributory negligence doctrine greatly benefits defendants by barring plaintiffs from suing, in certain circumstances plaintiffs can use the doctrine of **last clear chance** to support their cases. Ordinarily, a plaintiff who is negligent in a state that follows the contributory negligence rule will be denied recovery against a negligent defendant. But if the last clear chance doctrine applies, the defendant will be liable for failing to prevent the injury even if negligent acts of the plaintiff initially put the plaintiff in peril.

The doctrine, alternatively called the *subsequent negligence rule,* requires exactly what its name implies: that the defendant actually had a last clear chance following the plaintiff's negligent act to avoid infliction of an injury on the plaintiff.

Four elements must be established before the doctrine will come into play:

1. The plaintiff has been negligent.

2. As the result of this negligence, the plaintiff is in a position of peril that cannot be escaped by the exercise of ordinary care.

3. The defendant knew or should have known of the plaintiff's peril.

last clear chance
Used by plaintiffs in certain negligence cases to support their argument that the defendant should be liable for failing to prevent the injury, even if negligent acts of the plaintiff initially put the plaintiff in peril.

---

[64] *Michalopoulos v. C&D Restaurant,* 764 A.2d 121 (R.I. 2001)

4. The defendant had a clear chance, by the exercise of ordinary care, to avoid the injury to the plaintiff, but failed to act.

For example, a plaintiff seeking to retrieve her parked car in the rain ignored a crosswalk and ran across four lanes of road, dodging traffic while jaywalking. The defendant was a motorist in the fifth lane of traffic. He observed the plaintiff traversing the road, but nonetheless hit her. The plaintiff admitted her negligence, but asserted that the defendant had ample time to take reasonable steps to avoid the accident. The plaintiff claimed the defendant was thus liable under the last clear chance doctrine. The jury agreed and awarded a verdict to the plaintiff which was upheld on appeal.[65]

If any one of the four elements is absent, the doctrine of last clear chance will not apply.

Most states that have adopted the comparative negligence rule have abolished the last clear chance doctrine. The reason is as follows: "To give continued life to [last clear chance] would defeat the very purpose of the comparative negligence rule— the apportionment of damages according to the degree of mutual fault."[66]

In a case involving a parking lot accident, an elderly handicapped woman fell when she stepped off the sidewalk onto a blue-painted tire stop that, unknown to her, was not affixed to the pavement. The court assessed the circumstance as follows, "While it is clear that [defendant restaurant] created the risk of harm by placing an unanchored tire stop in the handicapped area of its parking lot, [plaintiff] was in a position to avoid the accident simply by walking around the out-of-place, unanchored tire stop that she clearly saw before she stepped on it." If the doctrine of last clear chance applied, the court would have referenced it and decided the case in favor of the restaurant. Instead the court continued, "Under these circumstances, we assess 10 percent of the fault to [the plaintiff] and 90 percent to [the restaurant]."[67]

Assumption of Risk

Another legal doctrine with an application that has changed considerably in those states that follow the rule of comparative negligence is **assumption of risk**. Historically, and currently in states that follow the contributory negligence rule, the doctrine benefits the defendant and applies in cases where the plaintiff voluntarily engages in conduct known to present a risk of injury. If the plaintiff is injured as a result of that risk, the plaintiff, according to the doctrine, cannot successfully sue for the loss. Instead, the plaintiff is said to have assumed the risk—that is, accepted the chance that injury might occur and impliedly agreed not to sue if it does.

assumption of risk
A doctrine that holds a plaintiff may not recover for injuries received when he voluntarily exposes himself to a known risk.

---

[65] *Zaharavich v. Clingerman*, 529 So.2d 978 (Ala. 1988)
[66] *Spahn v. Town of Port Royal*, 486 S.E.2d 507 (S.C. 1997)
[67] *Leonard v. Ryan's Family Steak Houses, Inc.*, 939 S0.2d 401 (La. 2006)

To establish assumption of risk, the defendant must show that the plaintiff:

- Had knowledge of the risk

- Understood the risk

- Had a choice of either avoiding the risk or engaging in conduct that confronted the risk

- Voluntarily chose to take the risk

Case Example 5-19 illustrates an application of the assumption of risk doctrine.

CASE EXAMPLE 5-19

Ball v. Hilton Hotels, Inc.

290 N.E.2d 859 (Ohio 1972)

It appears from the record that the plaintiff, a resident of Michigan, went to Cincinnati, Ohio, on May 27, 1967, with a reservation to stay at the defendant's hostelry, known as the Terrace Hilton Hotel.

Upon arrival at the hotel, she was informed by the defendant's doorman that there was a downtown area electric power failure and there was no lighting or elevator service in the hotel. The hotel lobby and registration desk were on the eighth floor of the hotel building. The plaintiff checked her baggage with the doorman and then inquired about the use of restroom facilities.

In response to her request, the doorman advised plaintiff the restroom was downstairs; that it would be quite dark on the staircase due to the electric power failure; that plaintiff would not be able to see the doors to the restrooms; and that the doors to the restrooms were located to the right at the bottom of the stairway. The doorman gave the plaintiff a small lighted candle, and she proceeded down the darkened stairway, moving slowly and carefully groping along the handrail.

After arriving at the platform portion of the stairway [apparently the halfway point of the flight of stairs], plaintiff [apparently believing she had reached the bottom of the stairs] began to grope about for the restroom door and, while so doing, she fell to the bottom of the stair steps and received personal injuries.

In her complaint against the hotel, plaintiff alleges that her personal injuries and resulting damage were directly and proximately caused by the negligence of the defendant in inducing her to enter a hazardous, darkened area of the hotel facility....

Before the defendant would be entitled to a judgment on the theory of assumption of the risk, it must be proven that plaintiff had full knowledge of a condition; that the condition was patently dangerous; and that she voluntarily exposed herself to the hazard created....

[P]laintiff was told that the electric power in the downtown area had failed and there was no light or electric power in the defendant's hotel; that it was dark in the stairway leading to the hotel restrooms; that plaintiff had full knowledge of the darkness when she walked down the stairway with a small lighted candle; and that she moved slowly and carefully as she descended the stairway.

Since it appears there is no genuine issue of any material fact, the trial court correctly determined the plaintiff assumed the risk of her injury and damage when she proceeded into the darkened area of the premises in question....

Ruling of the Court: Judgment affirmed for defendant.

CASE QUESTION

1. Identify the elements of assumption of risk and state the particular fact(s) in *Ball* that satisfy each element.

Participants in sporting activities are considered to assume the obvious and inherent risks associated with the sport. A plaintiff was injured while participating in a timed obstacle course at a company picnic held at a resort owned by defendant Ramada. The first obstacle of the course was mounting a slide backwards. In the process the plaintiff fell from the ladder portion of the slide. The court held for Ramada, as the dangers associated with the activity were obvious and therefore the plaintiff assumed the risk.[68] If, however, the reason the plaintiff fell was because a step on the ladder had rotted and weakened, Ramada would be liable because this was not a normal risk of the activity and the plaintiff therefore did not assume it.

In Case Example 5-20 the doctrine of assumption of risk was applied to an injury that occurred on a nightclub dance floor.

---

[68] *Coleman v. Ramada Hotel Operating Co.*, 933 F.2d 470 (Ill. 1991)

CASE EXAMPLE 5-20

Demarco v. Ouellette

2005 WL 2170557 (N.Y. 2005)

This personal injury action is brought by plaintiff Lisa DeMarco against individual defendant Timothy Ouellete, and corporate defendant... The Culture Club NYC, LLC (the "Club")...

Plaintiff now claims that the... Club is responsible for her injury because it... operated an inherently dangerous "tiered" dance floor...

On the evening of June 20, 2003, plaintiff and a friend, Gina Giarratana, arrived at the... Club between 9 and 11 o'clock... Both had been to the Club on several previous occasions. As the evening wore on, the two danced and socialized, consuming approximately two drinks each between the time they arrived and 2 a.m. the next morning. There is no evidence that plaintiff was intoxicated when she arrived at the Club, and plaintiff testified that she remained sober throughout the evening, most of which she spent with Giarratana on the Club's "tiered" dance floor...

The "tiered" nature of the dance floor can be described as follows. There is a "bottom" level, which is flush with the main floor of the club, but readily distinguishable by embedded lights... This bottom level is roughly square, is constructed of wood, and can accommodate approximately 40–45 dancers... Sitting on top of the bottom level, and entirely contained within it, is a "second" level... Relative to the bottom level, this second level is significantly smaller in square footage—it can accommodate between 15 and 25 people—and is reached by climbing a step of approximately one foot... Like the bottom level, the second level is "lit up", and is otherwise distinguished by a colored band running its perimeter... The "third" or "top" level sits on top of the second level, and is similarly constructed, with a light-colored band running its perimeter... It has the smallest square footage of the three levels, and can hold approximately 6 people...

Plaintiff's injury occurred on the second level of the dance floor in the following manner. According to plaintiff, she and Giarratana were dancing just after 2 a.m. when an unidentified male patron bumped into her, causing her to lose her balance and fall straight back...Plaintiff testified that when she landed on the ground, her legs were beneath her as if she was "kneel[ing] down on the floor," with the top of her feet facing down...In a sort of "domino" reaction, the unidentified patron also fell down, landing on top of plaintiff with her left leg still trapped under her. Plaintiff's ankle fractured under the added weight... Realizing that she had been seriously injured, plaintiff yelled for the man to get off her, which he did without delay...

There is no dispute that plaintiff's injury was accidental. Plaintiff remembered that between six and eight people fell at the same time she did, including Giarratana...

[T]hirty minutes after plaintiff was escorted out of the Club, Giarratana drove her to a hospital in Bayonne, New Jersey... Hospital records show that plaintiff checked in to the emergency room at 3:07 a.m... They also indicate that an X-ray was taken at about the same time, and that plaintiff was diagnosed with an oblique fracture to her left anklebone. After being told that the injury would require surgery, plaintiff was admitted to the hospital… Surgery was performed the next afternoon, during which pins and plates were placed on the ankle… .

Plaintiff now brings this lawsuit to recover for her injuries… .

Plaintiff… argues that the Club was negligent because the "tiered" nature of the dance floor was inherently dangerous…

[T]his claim…fails because plaintiff clearly assumed the risk of any inherent danger…. [T]he doctrine of assumed risk rests on the common sense proposition that, "by engaging in a sport or recreational activity, a participant consents to those commonly appreciated risks which are inherent in and arise out of the nature of the sport [or activity] generally and flow from such participation."…Here, there is no dispute that plaintiff was aware that the dance floor was tiered; she had patronized the club on several prior occasions and had spent much of the evening in question on the dance floor. Under similar circumstances, where a plaintiff was aware of the condition of which he or she complained, New York courts routinely apply the doctrine of assumed risk to preclude negligence claims based on a theory of inherent danger…This Court will do likewise…

For the foregoing reasons, defendant's motion is GRANTED.

CASE QUESTIONS

1. What facts did the court rely upon in making its determination that the plaintiff assumed the risk of any inherent danger?

2. Under what different circumstances might the court have found that the plaintiff did not assume the risk?

Comparative Negligence and Assumption of Risk

Most states that have adopted the comparative negligence rule have abolished assumption of risk as a bar to recovery in tort lawsuits. Instead, assumption of risk is treated as another factor for the trier of fact (jury or judge) to consider when making a comparative negligence allocation of liability. Thus, in some cases where assumption of risk fits the facts, the defendant's negligence may nonetheless be a partial cause of the injury. In such a case, an apportionment of fault between the plaintiff and defendant will be made. "Thus, there is no arbitrary bar to recovery and no sweeping exemption from duty accorded a defendant."[69]

---

[69] *Auckenthaler v. Grundmeyer,* 877 P.2d 1039 (Nev. 1994)

In Case Example 5-21, rowdy crowds spurred the plaintiff to expose himself voluntarily to significant risks. The assumption of risk rule was applied and the doctrine constituted a bar to the plaintiff's recovery. As you read the case, consider whether the outcome would have been different if comparative negligence had been used.

CASE EXAMPLE 5-21

Eldridge v. Downtowner Hotel

492 So.2d 64 (La. 1986)

[O]n February 7, 1978, Mardi Gras day, plaintiff was the guest of a patron of the Downtowner in the French Quarter. While on the second floor balcony of the hotel, he observed various individuals on other balconies toying with the crowds below by exposing their breasts or "mooning" the crowds by exposing their bare buttocks. Spurred on by the wild atmosphere in the Quarter, plaintiff climbed on the balcony railing and mooned the crowd. While on the railing plaintiff fell to the street below and was seriously injured.

Plaintiff filed suit for 1.75 million dollars arguing that Downtowner was negligent in failing to have a protective screen or a uniformed guard on the balcony to prevent just such accidents as occurred herein....

The record reflects that plaintiff's fall resulted solely from his own conduct. Plaintiff was not pushed off the railing, and he was neither enticed nor encouraged by defendant to sit on the railing. Moreover, the railing was not defective. It is clear, therefore, that plaintiff's fall was in fact caused by his own want of skill, that is, exercising bad judgment by sitting on the railing and in losing his balance. Thus, the question becomes whether Downtowner had a duty to protect plaintiff from his own conduct.

[A] "visitor assumes the obvious, normal or ordinary risks attendant on the use of the premises and owners are not liable for injuries to a visitor when those injuries result from a danger which he should have observed in the exercise of reasonable care." Here the risk of harm was that of falling while sitting on a railing on a second floor balcony. Such a risk is an obvious and reasonable risk of harm which the defendant had no duty to protect against.

But plaintiff argues that because of the wild atmosphere of Mardi Gras and the fact that traditionally women would expose themselves from the balconies, defendant should have foreseen that an accident was likely and was under an obligation to protect plaintiff from himself. We find no merit in this argument.... [A]bsolutely no evidence was offered at trial demonstrating that anyone had ever fallen from the balcony during Mardi Gras or even that people sat on the balcony railings....

For these reasons we hold that the trial court was not required to charge the jury that the defendant had a duty to protect patrons from the type of conduct engaged in by the plaintiff herein....

CASE QUESTIONS

1. What was the particular risk of injury that the plaintiff assumed in this case?

2. The plaintiff claimed the hotel owed him a duty to provide either a protective screen or a uniformed guard on the balcony. Do you agree? Why or why not?

Ignorance of Risk Negates Application of Assumption of Risk

The assumption of risk doctrine will not apply if the plaintiff is unaware of the risk. For example, a newly hired bartender at a restaurant was assigned the duty of stocking the bar. This task required that he bring beer and liquor up to the first floor from the basement. A coworker suggested he use the dumbwaiter. The bartender had never used the device before and had not been instructed on its use. Believing it would facilitate the stocking process, he employed it. He loaded the dumbwaiter, closed the door, and pressed the start button. He then went upstairs to meet it. He waited several minutes, but there was no indication it had arrived. Deciding to investigate, he opened a service access panel into the dumbwaiter shaft. He saw moving cables and believed the dumbwaiter was descending from the first floor to the basement. He put his head sideways into the panel to look into the shaft. Only then did he realize that the dumbwaiter's path continued up to the second floor and it was then above him. Before he could pull his head out, the dumbwaiter struck his face and jaw. He sued the restaurant, which asserted the defense of assumption of risk. The court refused to apply it noting that the plaintiff was a new employee, had never used the dumbwaiter before, and had not been given any instructions. When he put his head in the shaft, he was not aware that it extended up to the second floor.[70]

---

[70] *Lang v. The Red Parrot, Inc.,* 746 A.2d 142 (R.I. 2000)

Summary

Hotels and restaurants face substantial liability for negligence. If a customer is injured by a restaurant or hotel's failure to act reasonably, the business will be obligated to compensate the customer.

For a successful negligence case, a plaintiff must prove four elements: (1) the existence of a duty to act reasonably owed by the hotel or restaurant to the plaintiff; (2) a breach of that duty; (3) injury to the plaintiff; and (4) proximate cause, meaning the plaintiff's injury was caused by defendant's breach of duty. To avoid liability for negligence, hotels and restaurants must constantly be vigilant to ensure they are exercising reasonable care to protect the safety of their patrons. In states that continue to recognize varying standards of duty depending on the status of the injured party, for invitees the hospitality facility must inspect the premises, remove any risks of injury that exist, and make the premises reasonably safe. For licensees, the facility must disclose any known defects and refrain from causing willful or wanton injury. For trespassers, the facility's only duty is to refrain from causing willful or wanton injury. In states that no longer recognize the differences between an invitee, licensee, or trespasser, a varying duty of care is owed to all three. Various legal doctrines are associated with negligence. Those that aid the plaintiff are:

- *Res ipsa loquitur*, which means "the thing speaks for itself" and relieves the plaintiff of the need to prove specific acts of negligence

- *Higher duty of care owed to children* because of their relative lack of judgment and experience

- The *attractive nuisance doctrine*, which obligates occupiers of land to exercise reasonable care to protect trespassing children

- *Negligence per se*, which in most states eliminates the need for a plaintiff to prove negligence where the defendant violated a safety law

- *Strict liability*, which renders a defendant liable without fault under limited circumstances

- *Respondeat superior*, which obligates an employer to compensate persons injured by the negligent acts of its employees

- The *doctrine of last clear chance*, which applies in states that follow the contributory negligence rule and holds that, even if a plaintiff is negligent, a defendant may be liable if he knew of the plaintiff's peril and had an opportunity to prevent the injury but failed to do so.

The legal doctrines related to negligence that aid the defendant include:

- *Assumption of risk*, which, in contributory negligence states, relieves a defendant from liability for injuries incurred by a plaintiff when the plaintiff voluntarily engages in conduct known to present risks of injury

- *Contributory negligence*, which relieves a defendant from liability if the plaintiff is at all negligent. This doctrine is followed in only four states and the District of Columbia

- *Comparative negligence*, which lessens a negligent defendant's liability if the plaintiff is also negligent (This doctrine results in only partial liability on the defendant.)

- *Good Samaritan statutes*, which restrict exposure to liability for rescuers who come forward in an emergency to assist a person in distress

- *Choking laws*, which relieve a restaurant from liability for failing to perform the Heimlich procedure on a choking patron provided only that the restaurant summon emergency assistance

Preventive Law Tips for Managers

- *Always anticipate dangers that may exist at a hotel or restaurant and take the necessary action to eliminate the risks.* Hotels and restaurants are obligated to use reasonable care to protect their patrons from injury. Failure to do so will result in liability. Managers and employees should always be alert to conditions that may present risks. Upon discovery of any such conditions, fix them promptly. If removal of the condition is not immediately feasible, warning notices should be conspicuously posted.

- *Make frequent inspections of the premises so that dangerous conditions can be detected.* Undetected and uncorrected dangers increase the risk of injury to patrons. The purpose of regular and thorough inspections is to discover problems before they lead to injury. Once uncovered, they can be corrected and injury avoided.

- *Promptly repair dangerous conditions.* Elimination of dangerous conditions decreases the chances that guests will be injured. Reasonable care should be taken to ensure that the repair process does not itself generate injury. For example, while washing a floor following a spill, housekeeping should post a sign cautioning passersby that the floor may be slippery.

- *Train employees on how to detect dangerous conditions, and include inspections and reporting in their job responsibilities.* The better trained employees are, the more likely they will uncover unsafe conditions. The more employees are responsible for identifying safety risks, the less likely accidents are to occur.

- *Carefully examine facilities used by children.* The duty of care owed to youngsters takes into consideration their lack of judgment and thus requires more on the part of the hotel or restaurant than the duty owed to adults. Since children cannot be expected to take precautions for their own safety, hotels and restaurants must be especially careful to ensure facilities likely to be used by them are suitable. Play areas, toys, pinball machines, highchairs, cribs, and similar items must be maintained in a condition safe for youngsters.

- *Be alert to attractive nuisances, and take precautions to protect youngsters from related dangers.* An attractive nuisance is a condition on property that is appealing to children and likely to attract them, even though the property owner or occupier does not invite them. While hotels and restaurants do not ordinarily owe much duty to trespassers, if businesses tolerate a condition that is likely to attract children, they must maintain that condition in a way that neutralizes associated dangers. Failure to do so may result in liability.

- *Stay current on laws that relate to your business and comply with them.* Failure to abide by applicable safety laws may result in liability based on negligence per se. In such cases, plaintiffs are not required to present proof of negligence. Instead, the plaintiff need only prove the existing law and the defendant's failure to comply (plus proximate cause). To avoid overlooking statutes that relate to the hospitality industry, diligently read trade journals, regularly consult with a knowledgeable attorney, and become active in a trade association.

- *Do not rely on compliance with statutes alone to protect your business from lawsuits; in addition, exercise reasonable care to protect patrons from injury.* Compliance with statutes alone may not relieve the hotel from liability. Instead, compliance with laws may be only the beginning of what is required to avoid liability. Analyze risks associated with the establishment and determine what action, in addition to that required by statute, is necessary to eliminate those risks.

- *Carefully choose the suppliers of goods that your hotel or restaurant resells, such as food and gift-shop inventory.* The rule of strict products liability enables a buyer of defective goods to sue the seller whether or not the latter was negligent. All the plaintiff must prove is that the product was defective when sold and the defect caused injury. To minimize the number of incidents of rancid food in restaurants and defective products in shops, be discriminating in the suppliers from whom inventory is purchased. Check references and reputation, inspect the merchandise when it is delivered, and verify the supplier's financial viability. If you are sued, you may be able to pursue the supplier in strict liability. A supplier who is no longer in business will be of little value in this regard.

- *Select employees carefully and train them well.* An employer may be liable for the acts of its employees based on the rule of respondeat superior. Much potential liability can be avoided by conducting thorough background checks on employees to ensure their suitability, by verifying their qualifications for the job, and by providing in-depth training to secure their compliance with company rules, policies, and expectations.

- *Aid patrons in need of assistance.* Many states now require a hotel or restaurant to come to the aid of a guest in need. If a hotel guest calls the front desk seeking help for an illness or assault, respond quickly. Delay in reaction time can result in liability. Train front-desk personnel on how to handle emergency phone calls. Instruct restaurant and hotel employees on first aid and who to call in the event of an emergency.

- *Prominently display the required poster showing first-aid procedures, including the Heimlich maneuver.* The Heimlich maneuver is a procedure that can dislodge food on which a diner is choking. Posters that illustrate the maneuver and contain directions on how to administer it are available, and in some states are required. By prominently displaying the poster, the information required to assist a patron in trouble is readily available whenever needed. However, in most states, statutes relieve a restaurant from a duty to apply the Heimlich maneuver. Promptly summoning medical assistance may be sufficient legally as a response to a choking patron.

Review Questions

1. What does *negligence* mean?

2. Who or what is the reasonable person?

3. Identify the four elements of a negligence case.

4. Which two elements of a negligence case must have a cause-and-effect relationship?

5. What is res ipsa loquitur?

6. If the assumption of risk doctrine applies in a case, who wins—the plaintiff or the defendant?

7. What is the difference between comparative negligence and contributory negligence? Which rule have most states adopted?

8. What duty of care is owed by innkeepers to guests who are children? Does the duty differ at all from the duty owed to adults? If so, how does it differ?

9. What is an attractive nuisance? What are some examples of an attractive nuisance?

10. What differentiates negligence per se from ordinary negligence?

11. What is the difference between an invitee, a licensee, and a trespasser?

12. What does the following statement mean: "The appellate court affirmed the judgment entered for the plaintiff by the trial court."?

Discussion Questions

1. In which of the following cases would res ipsa loquitur apply? Why?

   A. The plaintiff was driving his car on hotel property and hit an obstacle in the road.

   B. The plaintiff was sitting at the desk in her hotel room writing postcards when the ceiling light fixture fell on her head and injured her.

   C. The plaintiff tripped in a restaurant.

2. You are a manager at a restaurant. Your restaurant is sued by a customer who fell while at your establishment. What does the element of proximate cause require the plaintiff to establish? How might you dispute proximate cause?

3. The plaintiff was a guest at a hotel with a golf course. While playing a round of golf he tripped on a large hole in the ground and was injured.

   A. Did the plaintiff assume the risk? Why or why not?

   B. What is the effect of the assumption of risk doctrine in a state that has adopted the rule of comparative negligence? Why?

4. Under what circumstances does a hotel or restaurant have strict liability? What can a business do to protect itself against this type of liability?

5. What is the significance of the doctrine of respondeat superior to a hotel or restaurant?

6. How might the duty of care owed by a hotel or restaurant differ depending on whether the plaintiff is an invitee, a licensee, or a trespasser? How might the outcome of a case vary depending on the status of the plaintiff? What is the rationale for such different results?

Application Questions

1. The plaintiff, while about to descend a flight of stairs from a second-story restaurant, was engaged in conversation with a companion and failed to survey the steps. An obstacle on the second step caused her to slip and fall, resulting in injuries. The state in which the restaurant was located adopted the rule of comparative negligence. What impact will her negligence have on her lawsuit against the restaurant? Explain fully.

2. Assume in question one that the applicable state rule was contributory negligence rather than comparative negligence. What impact would that have on the outcome of the case?

3. A customer at a pizza parlor ate a piece of pizza with a tack in it. Did the customer assume the risk of the tack's presence? Why or why not? What other negligence doctrine(s) might apply?

4. The Drumlin Hotel has a pond on its property. During the winter the pond freezes and neighborhood children come to play on it. One day in late March the ice was thin and a child fell through and suffered from exposure and frostbite. Will the hotel be liable for the child's injuries? Why or why not? What additional information do you need to decide this case? Discuss the issues thoroughly.

5. At a bowling banquet one of the diners started to choke on a steak. He was assisted to the bathroom by several of his bowling friends and in the process passed by you as manager. You do not assist him personally, but you do call the police and an ambulance. They respond in three minutes. The choking diner is taken to a hospital, where he dies. His wife is now suing your restaurant for $1 million. What defenses are available to the restaurant?

6. Identify the legal status (invitee, licensee, or trespasser) of each of the following.
   A. A hotel guest.
   B. A person who comes to the hotel to meet a friend who is a guest of the hotel.
   C. A person who enters the hotel restaurant only to use the bathroom.
   D. A person who enters the hotel to attend a meeting being held in a room rented for the day by her employer.
   E. A person who enters the hotel to buy a gift in the lobby gift shop.
   F. A person who enters the hotel to take a shortcut through the building.
   G. A person who enters the hotel to rob a guest.
   H. A patron of a restaurant who left his coat and returns the next day to retrieve it.

Websites

Websites that will enhance your understanding of the material in this chapter include:

www.findlaw.com This site contains updates on legal news and many links to sites covering a variety of legal topics, including personal injury (negligence) cases.

www.nolo.com This site provides articles and information on numerous legal topics relevant to this chapter, including personal injury and independent contractors. Once on the home page, click on the desired topic from the list on the left side of the screen.

www.expertpages.com This site provides listings of expert witnesses and consultants on a large variety of topics, including accidents and injuries, food and restaurant industries, lighting and illumination, premises liability, casinos, amusement parks, and many more.

CHAPTER 6

Negligence and Hospitality Practices

LEARNING OUTCOMES:

- Understand the duty owed to guests in hotel rooms
- Understand the duty owed to guests and others in public areas of hospitality businesses
- Understand the duty owed to guests in restaurants and dining rooms
- Understand the duty owed to guests using outside facilities of hospitality businesses
- Understand the duty owed to guests in swimming areas
- Understand the duty to exercise reasonable care to provide for guests' safety in the circumstances of fire, security, and medical treatment

KEY TERMS

constructive notice   insurer
expert witness

Introduction

In Chapter 5 we learned what types of conduct constitute negligence. We also learned about various legal doctrines that apply to negligence cases. In this chapter we will examine a variety of cases in which an injured plaintiff claimed a hospitality facility acted negligently. In some of the cases the plaintiff was able to prove that the hotel or restaurant was liable; in others, the facility won.

insurer
One who is generally obligated to compensate another for losses.

We know that a business owner owes to invitees a duty of reasonable care, including the duty to inspect the premises, discover dangerous conditions such as a hole in the lobby rug, and correct them. This legal duty, however, does not make a hospitality business an **insurer,** one who is generally obligated to compensate another for all losses. Hotels and restaurants are liable only when they are negligent. This chapter discusses the precautions a proprietor must take regarding the following areas and items in hotels and restaurants: the lobby, guest rooms, furniture, windows, bathroom appliances, elevators, doors, hallways, stairways, dining rooms, grounds, sports facilities, and swimming pools. Also addressed are legal issues associated with security, fires, and medical service.

Duty Owed Guests in Hotel Rooms

Numerous circumstances in guest rooms can lead to liability if a hotel fails to exercise reasonable care. These situations include the level of cleanliness; the condition of the furniture, windows, lighting, and heating; bathroom appliances; and the presence of insects or animals.

Cleanliness of Hotel Rooms

Guests expect a clean room when they register. If a guest room is not cleaned well, liability can result. In a New Jersey case, the plaintiff was assigned to a hotel room that recently had been vacated by other guests. The room was very messy. Wastebaskets had not been emptied and the floor was covered with lint and cigarette ashes. The plaintiff reported the condition to the front desk and then left for a few hours to allow housekeeping time to clean. When the plaintiff returned, the bed linens had been changed and clean towels placed in the bathroom, but the other problems had not been remedied. The plaintiff retired for the night. In the morning while answering a knock on the door she stepped on a needle that snapped after breaking the skin. She received medical attention but her foot became infected. The plaintiff sued the hotel for negligence and was awarded $2,500 compensation. The court stated that the proprietor of a hotel is required to use due care to have rooms thoroughly cleaned before reassignment. Because the hotelkeeper failed in the performance of this duty, the hotel was liable for resulting injuries.[1]

Beds, Chairs, and Other Seats

Courts have generally permitted recovery for injuries caused by defective beds and furniture. In an early case, the hotel room was equipped with a bed that would fold up so as to leave the bed in an upright position when not in use (a "Murphy bed"). The top of the bed was heavy, weighing about 300 pounds. After sleeping in the bed all night, and as the plaintiff was about to leave it in the morning, "the top or upright portion of the bed fell forward upon him, crushing his head down upon his breast and inflicting severe injury." The plaintiff sued the hotel. The testimony presented by the plaintiff stopped short of identifying the exact defect in the bed that caused it to fall down and entrap him. He was able to use res ipsa loquitur and won the case.[2] Murphy beds are sometimes used today to enhance the size of a room during the day when the bed is not needed for sleeping. The mechanisms should be inspected regularly to ensure proper functioning.

A hotel was liable where a guest was injured on a piece of the metal bed frame that protruded out from the bed by about three inches. The guest had not seen it because it was covered by a bedspread. An award in this case for punitive damages was upheld on appeal because the hotel had a new owner who failed to adequately inspect upon purchase, failed to consult the incident reports which included many bed frame problems, and failed to inquire of the prior owner's general manager about the condition of the hotel. Further, metal sticking out from the bed frames was a common problem because the support rails on which the box spring sat were five inches longer than the box spring.[3]

In one case the thermostat for the air conditioner in a motel room was located 6′9″ above the floor. Plaintiff, a woman, used the dressing-table stool to reach the

---

[1] *Nielson v. Ritz Carlton Restaurant and Hotel*, 157 A. 133 (N.J. 1931)
[2] *Lyttle v. Denny*, 71 A. 841 (Pa. 1909)
[3] *Nettles v. Forbes Motel, Inc.*, 182 So.2d 572 (La. 1966)

knob to adjust the temperature. As she was standing on the stool it collapsed, causing her to fall and suffer injuries. She sued the motel for negligence. It denied liability and argued that the plaintiff knew the stool was not intended for that use. The court rejected this defense and held for the plaintiff, saying the hotel should have foreseen the particular misuse involved here, given the height of the airconditioner control. Further, the testimony revealed that the stool had been improperly assembled by the hotel and the legs on several other stools at the hotel had come loose, necessitating repairs. Despite this reoccurring problem, the hotel had failed to inspect the remaining stools for soundness.[4]

Furniture used by guests is sometimes abused or just wears out. To what extent should a hotel be liable when such furniture breaks and a guest is hurt? The cases hold that the hotel or restaurant must regularly inspect the furniture and discard any that is no longer suitable. Failure to do so will result in liability.

In one case the webbing on a chair seat was missing. The hotel covered the seat with a cushion. When a guest sat on the chair the cushion collapsed, causing him injury. The court held the hotel was liable to the guest because it breached its duty to provide the guest with premises that are reasonably safe for use and occupancy.[5] The same result was obtained where injury was sustained when a bed in the defendant's hotel collapsed while the plaintiff was sitting on it with one foot raised, removing his socks. The court said, "There was evidence from which a jury might find that the bed was defective and that such defect could, or should, have been discovered by a reasonable inspection."[6] In another case, the plaintiff was seated in the defendant's restaurant attending a meeting when his chair collapsed, injuring him. The court held the restaurant was negligent for failing to properly maintain the chair.[7]

A casino escaped liability for a collapsing bar stool used by a patron to play video poker. Immediately prior to the fall the plaintiff, who weighed 350 pounds, was leaning back on the stool so that two of the four stool legs were off the ground. An expert witness testified that the reason for the fall was the plaintiff's leaning back on the stool. The jury held for the casino, finding that it was not negligent. The verdict was upheld on appeal.[8]

A casino stool was also involved in another case in which a slot-machine player attempted to mount the seat. In the process the stool slipped, causing the player to fall and sustain injuries. The player sued the casino and attempted to benefit from res ipsa loquitur. The court, however, refused to apply the doctrine reasoning that the casino did not have exclusive control of the chair. Rather, many customers use it daily. The plaintiff could proceed with his lawsuit but could not use res ipsa loquitur.[9]

---

[4] *Shiv-Ram, Inc. v. McCaleb*, 892 So.2d 299 (Ala. 2003)
[5] *Gary Hotel Courts, Inc. v. Perry*, 251 S.E.2d 37 (Ga. 1978)
[6] *Palagano v. Georgian Terrace Hotel Co.*, 181 S.E.2d 512 (Ga. 1971)
[7] *Gresham v. Stouffer Corp.*, 241 S.E.2d 451 (Ga. 1978)
[8] *Hagenet v. Jackson Furniture*, 746 So.2d 912 (Miss. 1999)
[9] *Nickel v. Hollywood Casino*, 730 N.E.2d 1212 (Ill. 2000)

In a case involving a sports bar, the plaintiff was injured when metal bleachers he was sitting on collapsed. The bleachers had been installed four months earlier for use by patrons while watching sporting events on a big-screen television. Testimony established that the bleacher manufacturer's assembly instructions called for metal cross-bracing to be installed across the back of the bleachers in an *X*. Instead, the metal supports had been fastened in a vertical position. The cause of the bleachers' collapse was the improper installation. Although the bar had hired an independent contractor to install the bleachers, the duty to install them safely was a nondelegable duty. Therefore, the bar was liable for the resulting injuries.[10]

In a case involving a KFC restaurant, a diner, attempting to sit at a table while holding his tray, fell and injured himself when the bench collapsed. Expert testimony suggested that the cause of the collapse was either faulty construction of the bench by the restaurant in using inappropriate, inflexible screws to attach the bench to its frame, or failure to occasionally check for loosening bolts that would have been evident by simply jiggling the bench with one's hands. Summary judgment entered by the trial court in favor of the restaurant was therefore reversed on appeal and a trial ordered.[11]

Regular inspections for broken or defective furniture will help reduce these types of incidents. Catering and other departments regularly handle portable chairs and tables that are exposed to much wear and tear, making loose screws, nuts, bolts and brackets predictable. Setup crews should watch for needed repairs and carry a screwdriver and wrench. When an item of furniture needing repair is discovered, it should be immediately removed from service until the repairs are completed.

Windows, Window Fixtures, and Screens

The same duty to inspect for defects and remedy them exists in regard to windows and screens. A plaintiff on a riverboat casino was knocked to the floor by fallen decorative woodwork that framed a window. The woodwork and window had been negligently maintained. In these circumstances, the casino was held liable.[12] In another case the plaintiff-guest in the defendant hotel was trying to close a window when it shattered, injuring her arm. Testimony showed that the putty around the window pane was old and decayed, a defect that could have been ascertained by reasonable inspection. The hotel was liable for the oversight. In another case, a window shade fell on a guest and injured her, resulting in the application of res ipsa loquitur and liability on the hotel.[13]

Inspecting fixtures on a regular basis can protect a hotel from liability. Although a child pushed through a window screen in a hotel room and fell out, the evidence showed no visible defect in the screen. Despite inspection, neither the child's parents nor the hotel had found any problems with the screen before the accident. The hotel was therefore not liable to the injured child. Remember, a

---

[10] *Otero v. Jordan Restaurant Enterprises*, 922 P.2d 569 (N.M. 1996)
[11] *Bishop v. KFC National Management Co.*, Inc., 473 S.E.2d 218 (Ga. 1996)
[12] *Morris v. Players Lake Charles*, Inc., 761 S.2d 27 (La. 2000)
[13] *Hotel Dempsey Company v. Teel*, 128 F.2d 673 (Ga. 1942)

hotel is not an insurer of its guests' safety; it is only liable when it fails to exercise reasonable care.

Electrical and Heating Hazards

Electrical and heating devices must be maintained in good working order. An early case on point has not been modified through the years. In that case, the plaintiff suffered a shock when she turned on an electric light in her hotel room. The court held that the injury was occasioned by the hotel's lack of reasonable care in maintaining and inspecting the electrical equipment in the room, and so the hotel was liable.[14]

As with all negligence cases, if the party responsible for an electrical problem cannot be identified, liability will not result. In a case involving an incident at the Miami International airport, the plaintiff, a United Airlines employee, was on a coffee break and noticed a "puff of smoke" coming from a room on Concourse F. He entered the unlocked room to investigate and was burned by an exploding electrical panel. The explosion resulted from a loose connection in a high-voltage panel that caused the panel's circuit breakers to melt and slowly burn, exhausting the oxygen in the room and resulting in a flash explosion when the door was opened. A construction company had been doing work in the room and had a duty to lock the door upon leaving. The United employee sued the construction company. The evidence established that keys to the room had been distributed to numerous airport and nonairport personnel, and no evidence established that the construction company had left the door unlocked. The court concluded that the wrongdoing in the case was leaving the door unlocked and evidence failed to identify who was responsible. Said the court, "without proof of wrongdoing, liability cannot attach." Judgment was for the construction company.[15]

Animals and Insects

The duty of reasonable care owed by hotels and restaurants to their customers applies also to injuries from animals or insects. If a guest is injured by an animal or an insect and the hotel or restaurant's negligence led to its presence, liability will result.

A hotel guest was bitten by a rat while lying in bed at a hotel. Evidence showed that numerous rat holes existed in the baseboard of the room prior to this event. The defendant claimed that it had taken all necessary precautions by employing a cleaner and a competent exterminator, and by routinely inspecting the room. The jury held for the plaintiff, apparently relying on the failure of the hotel to discover and remove the rat holes.[16]

Case Example 6-1 addresses the equally unpleasant thought of spiders in a hotel room. To help you understand this case, let us review the concept of summary

---

[14] *Reid v. Her*, 174 N.W. 71 (N.D. 1919)
[15] *Johnson Construction Management, Inc., v. Opez*, 902 So 2d 206 (Fla. 2005)
[16] *Williams v. Milner Hotel Co.*, 36 A.2d 20 (Conn. 1944)

judgment. Once a case is begun defendants often move for summary judgment, claiming that the plaintiff has failed to raise any factual issues on which the defendant could be held liable. If there are no such issues, there would be nothing for a jury to decide and so the judge dismisses the case without the need for a trial. Summary judgment represents a substantial victory for the defendant and a total loss for the plaintiff. In Case Example 6-1 the court was determining whether or not to grant summary judgment.

CASE EXAMPLE 6-1

Copeland v. The Lodge Enterprises, Inc.

4 P.3d 695 (Okla. 2000)

In November of 1992, Joyce Kathleen Copeland ("Copeland") was working as a pharmaceutical sales representative. While on a business trip, she spent the night as a paying guest at the Days Inn Motel in Muskogee, Oklahoma, a roadside hotel owned by the Lodge Enterprises, Inc., and operated by Sharon Andrews ("defendants"). Sometime during the night, she was allegedly bitten by a brown recluse spider. Copeland alleged the spider bite caused her to suffer severe, permanent, and disfiguring injuries... . The plaintiff and her husband bring this action alleging that defendants were negligent in failing to provide Copeland with safe premises, free of "varmints, critters and harmful insects" or in the alternative, to warn of their presence. Copeland sought damages for injuries, and her husband for loss of services, society, companionship and consortium.

Defendant moved for summary judgment, arguing that (1) they fulfilled their duty of care owed to invitees to maintain the premises in a reasonably safe and suitable condition, (2) their duty of care did not encompass protecting Copeland from injury from the bite of a brown recluse spider because the particular risk of harm from the presence of a brown recluse spider was not foreseeable; (3) they were not the insurers of the safety of motel guests; and (4) their conduct did not create or worsen any risk of harm, but rather prevented or lessened any such risk.

In support of their motion, defendants submitted copies of monthly invoices from Admiral Pest Control Co ("Admiral") showing a continuous program of pest control services at the Days Inn from August 1989 through February 1993, including the time period in which Copeland suffered her injury. Defendants also tendered portions of Sharon Andrews' deposition. Andrews, who was the Days Inn manager at the time of Copeland's injury, testified that she was trained in motel management, including pest control, she had engaged Admiral to spray the motel premises for insects and other pests, she had given Admiral oral instructions that all pests were to be eliminated from the property, she sometimes personally watched as the pest control chemical was applied, she had terminated the services of the previous extermination company because it had failed to eradicate a roach infestation, she had never had to call Admiral because of a problem with any type of spider, and she had never received any complaints from customers other than Copeland about the presence of spiders.

Andrews also testified in her deposition that on Monday or Tuesday morning after Copeland's incident the previous Wednesday, she and Admiral's exterminator searched for spiders in the room in which

Copeland had stayed as well as several other rooms. Although no spiders were found, they nonetheless sprayed the rooms. According to her deposition, the Days Inn received two or three annual, unannounced inspections by the Oklahoma Department of Health and had not been cited for any deficiencies during her tenure as manager.

In response, plaintiffs offered an affidavit from a licensed, experienced exterminator, who stated that (1) brown recluse spiders are common and indigenous to eastern Oklahoma, and (2) if reasonable care were exercised in the pest control treatment of a facility, brown recluse spiders would be eradicated. Plaintiffs also tendered a letter of apology from defendant Andrews *acknowledging that Oklahoma is known for spiders*. Finally, plaintiffs offered copies of certain rules of the Oklahoma State Department of Health pertaining to lodging establishments, which condition licensure to operate a motel on compliance with the state's health and safety regulations. On this record, the trial court entered summary judgment for the defendants, and plaintiffs appealed.... We now reverse.

...The elements of negligence are: (1) a duty owed by the defendant to protect the plaintiff from injury, (2) a failure properly to exercise or perform that duty, and (3) an injury to plaintiff proximately caused by the defendant's breach of that duty. Plaintiff's licensed exterminator's affidavit speaks to the elements of duty and breach of duty by raising an issue of material fact as to the liability of defendants for the alleged negligence of their extermination contractor. This provides a sufficient evidentiary basis to defeat defendants' quest for summary judgment.

An innkeeper in Oklahoma continues to have a status-based, common-law duty of care to a guest. This duty remains unaltered by inspection and licensing statutes enacted under the police power of the state. The owner or operator of a motel is not an insurer of his guests' personal safety. Often described as a duty to maintain the premises in a reasonably safe and suitable condition, the innkeeper's common-law responsibility applies only to defects or conditions which are in the nature of hidden dangers, traps, snares, pitfalls, and the like—things which are not readily observable. The duty is fulfilled when reasonable care is taken to prevent the invitee's exposure to dangers which are more or less hidden, not obvious.

Although a hirer ordinarily cannot be held liable for the negligence of an independent contractor, the rule of non-liability does not apply where the hirer contracts for the performance of a duty imposed by law. Hence, while an innkeeper may hire an independent contractor to perform the [innkeeper's] nondelegable duty, he may not pass off to an independent contractor the ultimate legal responsibility for the proper performance of that duty. Under the nondelegable duty rule, an innkeeper may be held vicariously liable for an independent contractor's failure to exercise reasonable care *even if the innkeeper has himself exercised due care*.

The duty of an innkeeper to provide a reasonably safe premises encompasses the duty to use effective measures of pest control.... The improper or ineffective application of pest control agents creates a foreseeable risk of harm to motel guests from the presence of what may otherwise be eradicable pests. Insects, arachnids, and other undesirable creatures in a motel room... can pose a hidden, unexpected danger to unsuspecting motel guests.

Because the innkeeper's duty of care to invitees is nondelegable, the duty to use effective measures of pest control encompasses not only the motel's own actions or missions, but also those of an independent contractor/ exterminator with whom the motel contracts to perform the services.

The affidavit of the licensed exterminator offered by plaintiffs in the case under review raises a disputed fact issue as to whether the Days Inn's extermination contractor might have been negligent in the performance of the pest control services. Where a genuine disputed issue of material (on the merits) exists, disposition of a case by summary judgment is erroneous. Plaintiffs are entitled to a jury's consideration of this dispositive issue.

CASE QUESTIONS

1. What is meant by the following statement in the beginning of the eighth paragraph: "An innkeeper in Oklahoma continues to have a status-based, common-law duty of care to a guest"?

2. What facts presented in the case might establish that the hotel used reasonable care to keep spiders and insects out of the hotel?

3. What facts presented in the case will favor the plaintiff's argument that the hotel failed to exercise reasonable care to eliminate spiders?

In another case the plaintiff-guest at the defendant hotel was awakened by a burning and stinging sensation on her right arm caused by an insect bite. The critter that stung or bit the plaintiff was not known or identified, nor was it known where the bug came from, how long it had been in the room, or the conditions under which it had entered. The plaintiff claimed res ipsa loquitur applied, but the court disagreed stating that to permit the jury in this situation to draw an inference of lack of due care on the part of the hotel would have been mere conjecture. Only if the plaintiff can prove lack of due care on the part of the hotel, and proximate cause between that negligence and the inset bite, will the hotel will be liable.[17]

The plaintiff-guest in a Louisiana case was stung by bees while showering, causing him to fall and injure his left wrist. Upon examination he discovered beehives were located outside the window of the room. The plaintiff sued the hotel. The manager admitted knowing of the existence of the hives but had not received reports of bees inside any rooms. The court held that if a hotel is on notice of the existence of beehives on or near its building, it should foresee that bees might enter the premises and sting a guest. The hotel was negligent for failing to remove the hives and for failing to warn guests of the bees' presence. The hotel was thus liable for the plaintiff's injuries.[18]

Sometimes insect or animal bites occur despite careful action on the part of the hotel. If the inn was not negligent, it will not be liable. In Chapter 5 we studied *Febesh v.*

---

[17] *Cunningham v. Neil House Hotel Co.*, 33 N.E.2d 859 (Ohio 1940)
[18] *Brasseaux v. Stand-By Corp. d/b/a Plantation Inn*, 402 So.2d 140 (La. 1981)

Elcejay Inn Corp., in which the court held a restaurant was not liable to a guest who suffered a bee sting at an outdoor reception. No prior incidents of bee stings had occurred at the eatery and the outdoor area was sprayed for bees at least once a day.

In Hawaii a guest was bitten by a brown recluse spider. The plaintiff sued the hotel for premises liability. The hotel kept good records of the treatment of insects. In addition, the hotel employees were trained to spot and report any pest activity. The court also reviewed the maintenance logs and there was no evidence of guests' complaints. The plaintiff did not offer any evidence that there was a prevalent spider problem. The court held that no reasonable jury could find that the resort had any actual knowledge of any specific dangerous condition on the property regarding pests. The case was thus dismissed.[19]

In an appropriate case, assumption of risk will apply. At a ranch in Texas a horse rider was injured when the horse bucked, causing her to fall. An investigation disclosed that the horse at the time was bothered by "fire ants all over his back legs." Prior to beginning the ride, the owners of the ranch told plaintiff that he had been battling fire ants all summer. The court held that "The unpredictability of a horse's reaction to another animal is an inherent risk of an equine activity." Therefore the ranch was not liable.

Bathroom Appliances and Hot Shower Water

Many problems involving bathroom fixtures and plumbing can be avoided if housekeeping personnel are instructed to examine the bathroom fixtures routinely, and turn on the water in the shower and sink and let it run a bit. If fixtures appear cracked or broken, or if the water temperature rises substantially, maintenance should be called to inspect and make necessary repairs.

Water Faucets

Several cases have originated in hotel bathrooms involving defective appliances and plumbing systems. In a Kentucky case, the guest, while turning on the water faucet in his hotel room, cut his hand when the porcelain faucet broke into pieces. The guest sued the hotel. The evidence established that the hotel failed to make regular inspections of the plumbing fixtures, and the hotel had "mysteriously" lost the shattered faucet fragments. Therefore the hotel lost the case.[20]

In another lawsuit, the plaintiff was injured by the faucet on a bathroom sink when the spigot "spun around and came back very quickly and with extreme force" hitting the plaintiff's fingers, causing injury. The force of the impact was such that a diamond and an emerald on the plaintiff's ring were knocked out of their setting. The parties were unable to determine the cause of the incident. The facts did not suggest that the defect could have been discovered by inspections of the sink's hardware; therefore, the building owner was not liable to the plaintiff for her injuries.[21]

---

19 *Lackey v. Disney Vacation Development*, 101 F.Supp.3d 849 (Ariz. 2015)
20 *Brown Hotel Co. v. Marx*, 411 S.W.2d 911 (Ky. 1967)
21 *Lonsdale v. Joseph Horne Co.*, 587 A.2d 810 (Pa. 1991)

Showers

In addition to bathroom sinks, showers can malfunction, leading to injuries. Excessively hot water has generated a number of negligence cases. In one from New Jersey, the plaintiff, a hotel guest, turned on the shower water and set it at a comfortable temperature before entering. While he was in the shower rinsing off and without touching the controls again, very hot water came gushing out unexpectedly. The plaintiff jumped back, hit the back of the tub, and fell, suffering injuries. The court applied res ipsa loquitur and held for the plaintiff, noting that the sudden gush of water suggested a malfunction and negligence on the part of the hotel, which had exclusive control of the water heating system, pipes, and plumbing devices.[22]

Routine inspections can save a hotel from liability. In a Massachusetts case, a guest sustained injuries when she slipped and fell in her bathroom at the defendant's motel while trying to shut off the hot water on a shower fixture. The knob had failed to respond. The evidence established that the fixture was brand new; the motel owner had inspected the shower handles daily and had no difficulty in turning them.

The owner was thus unaware of any defect in the fixture and in the exercise of due care would not have discovered any problem. As you should expect given these circumstances, the court held the motel was not negligent.[23]

Hand Bars and Grips

Proper maintenance of a bathroom requires inspection and repairs of hand railings and other grip devices. Lack of attention to these mechanisms can result in liability.

Case Example 6-2 illustrates an example of liability that can result from failing to properly care for hand bars.

---

22 *Wolfe v. Chateau Renaissance*, 357 22d 282 (N.J. 1976)
23 *Bearse v. Fowler*, 196 N.E.2d 910 (Mass. 1969)

CASE EXAMPLE 6-2

Sheridan Holiday Inn v. Poletis

954 P.2d 1353 (Wyo. 1998)

Andrew Poletis sued the owner of the Sheridan Holiday Inn, John Q. Hammons, Inc., for injuries Poletis sustained while a guest at the hotel. Following a jury verdict in favor of Poletis, the Holiday Inn moved for a judgment notwithstanding the verdict. Holiday Inn now appeals the court's denial of its motion. We affirm....

Poletis and his family, on vacation from their home in Michigan, checked into the Sheridan Holiday Inn on the night of July 25, 1993. The next morning when Poletis was showering, he grasped the hand bar to lower himself into the bathtub. As he lowered himself, the bar came out of the wall and Poletis fell, hitting his lower back on the tub.... Dr. Meengs examined Poletis and reviewed his spine x-ray. Dr. Meengs concluded that Poletis suffered from a low back strain or contusion as a result of the fall, and he instructed Poletis to work on a gentle exercise program to stretch and strengthen the area. Poletis visited Dr. Meengs two other times due to continuing back pain and discomfort. Both times Dr. Meengs advised Poletis to continue his stretching and strengthening program as long as the pain and discomfort continued, and to use anti-inflammatories to keep any pain under control.

Poletis brought suit against Holiday Inn, alleging the hotel's negligence resulted in injuries to his back. The case was tried to a six-person jury. The jury found in favor of Poletis and awarded him $75,000.

An innkeeper must use ordinary care to keep the property in a reasonably safe condition for the purpose for which the property was reasonably intended. It was for the jury to determine, based on the evidence presented and with the background of ordinary human experience, whether Holiday Inn exercised ordinary care to keep the property in a reasonably safe condition.

Negligence and proximate cause are never presumed from the happening of an accident, and mere conjecture cannot form the basis of liability. Poletis testified at trial that the bar came out of the wall when he put his weight on it. He stated that the wall where the bar came out was "punky soft" and that there was mold. Mrs. Poletis testified that when she came into the bathroom she saw Poletis lying in the tub, with the bar in his hand, with the screw still in it. She stated that the "crumbled wall was all over the place" and tiles were missing. She described the wall where the bar detached as being "crumbly and rotted" and "mushy." Holiday Inn maintains that because there was no evidence of Holiday Inn's failure to maintain or inspect the bar, or that the bar was improperly installed or the wall improperly constructed, Poletis did not show that Holiday Inn violated its duty.

The mere fact that the bar came out of the wall, causing Poletis to fall, is not sufficient to show that Holiday Inn breached its duty to keep the hotel room in a reasonably safe condition. However, Poletis and his wife both testified that the wall was mushy, crumbly and rotted where the bar came out. From this testimony, a jury could reasonably infer that the condition of the wall had occurred over a significantly long period of time and that Holiday Inn, in the exercise of reasonable diligence, should have discovered and fixed the problem... . The jury could infer, based on common knowledge and ordinary human experience, that moisture had to have been accumulating behind the tiles for more than a short time for the wall to assume that appearance....

Damages

The jury awarded Poletis $75,000 in compensatory damages. Holiday Inn contends that the verdict is grossly excessive, arguing that Poletis only showed $400 in medical expenses actually incurred, no past or future wage loss, no future medical expenses, and very little evidence of pain and suffering.

...[T]he amount of money to be awarded rests almost totally within the discretion of the jury. Appellate courts are reluctant to interfere with the jury's decision unless the award, by its excessiveness or inadequacy, denotes passion, prejudice, bias or some erroneous basis.

At trial the jury heard testimony from Poletis and his wife of the ongoing effects of the injury. Poletis testified that he experiences a great deal of pain in his back and legs when he sits for long periods in the car or stands for several hours, both of which are requirements for his job as a salesman. He testified that he can no longer run without aggravating his back. Mrs. Poletis testified that her husband is not able to walk with the family anymore because he gets sore. She stated that when he rides his bike it alleviates the pain, but that activity takes time away from the family. She also testified that he must sometimes rearrange his work schedule to avoid long-distance driving if his back is too achy or sore.

The jury also heard Dr. Meengs's deposition testimony that Poletis could perform normal functions of daily living, but had to curtail more strenuous physical and recreational activities which he enjoyed. Dr. Meengs testified that, in his opinion, Poletis' pain was real, not feigned. Dr. Meengs also stated that although exercise alleviated the symptoms, Poletis was likely to continue to experience pain and discomfort.

Taken together, the evidence amply supports the $75,000 awarded by the jury, and we find no evidence that passion or prejudice influenced the award.

CASE QUESTIONS

1. The court stated, "The mere fact that the bar came out of the wall, causing Poletis to fall, is not sufficient to show that Holiday Inn breached its duty to keep the hotel room in a reasonably safe condition." Why not? What more is needed?

2. How does a jury determine the appropriate amount of damages?

Another case had the opposite results, when a guest fell in a hotel bathtub and sustained injuries. She sued claiming negligence for the hotel failing to place grab bars in the bathtub, failing to place antislip measures inside the tub, and failing to warn guests of the slippery conditions. The court held that the inherent nature of a wet bathtub is an open and obvious condition and so an innkeeper has no duty to warn or otherwise address.[24]

Bathroom Doors

Bathroom doors can create problems if their maintenance is overlooked. Broken hinges can cause a door to fall on a patron. Broken latches or locks can result in accidents. In one case, a plaintiff entered the only available stall in a store bathroom which was laid out, like many bathrooms in the public areas of hotels, with multiple stalls. She discovered that the latch to lock the door was missing. She closed the door and placed her pocketbook on the floor of the stall in front of the door so that anyone looking at the outside of the stall would see that it was occupied. She was in the process of rearranging her clothing when a woman opened the door to the stall forcefully and caused it to hit plaintiff's head. As a result, the plaintiff suffered injuries and sued the store. The maintenance manager established that the store cleaned and restocked the restroom daily and performed more comprehensive cleanings weekly that would have revealed the broken latch. There had been no prior broken latches at the store. The court held that, given the store's reasonable maintenance schedule and the lack of similar incidents, the store could not have foreseen the risk and therefore was not liable for the plaintiff's injuries.[25] Had the store been less vigilant, it likely would have been liable.

In-Room Hot Tubs and Whirlpools

Some hotel rooms sport hot tubs or whirlpools for guests' pleasure. Like all appliances, if not properly maintained and utilized, they can cause accidents and injuries. However, most guests are aware that hot water can cause burning and scalding and so they know they must take precautions to avoid such injuries.

A couple was celebrating a birthday and reserved a hotel room with a whirlpool. The celebration began with some friends at the hotel lounge. During the course of the evening, two of the celebrants went to the plaintiffs' room and filled the whirlpool bathtub with hot water. They covered the whirlpool with balloons and returned to the lounge to continue the party. Later when the plaintiffs returned to their room they stepped into the whirlpool without testing the temperature of the water. Due to its heat they suffered burns over portions of their bodies requiring hospital treatment. In the lawsuit the hotel proved that the heaters in the whirlpool complied with applicable temperature specifications and warnings set by the American National Standards Institute. The plaintiffs each acknowledged that they were aware that hot bathwater could cause scalding. That acknowledgment renders the risks open and obvious, eliminating any duty

---

[24] *Dille v. Renaissance Hotel Management Co., LLC.,* 2012 WL 2396666 (Mo. 2012)
[25] *Parks-Nietzold v. J.C. Penney,* Inc., 490 S.E.2d 133 (Ga. 1977)

on the part of the hotel to warn guests. Instead, the plaintiffs needed to take precautions to protect themselves against scalding, which they failed to do. The court thus held for the hotel.[26]

Other concerns with hot tubs and whirlpools include safety devices to facilitate entering and exiting. Where a guest in a whirlpool fell while using a plastic handle affixed to the wall which broke as he attempted to lift himself from the tub, the court refused to grant summary judgment for the hotel based on defective design. It is of interest that soon after the accident the hotel removed all the plastic handles and substituted them with heavy-duty metal ones.[27]

Duty Owed Guests and Others in Public Areas

This section deals with a hotel's public areas, such as the lobby, stairs, elevators, bars, doors, and dining rooms. These cases also apply to restaurants.

Lobby

Because the lobby is the most frequently used public area of a hotel, special precautions should be taken. Frequent and regular inspections should be made to ensure the walkways are not blocked by suitcases or similar items, the rugs have no bumps or holes on which people might trip and fall, the furniture is in good condition and able to hold anticipated weight, no intruders are bothering guests, debris is picked up and the lobby is generally in good order. When hotel employees are repairing or cleaning the floors or furniture, they should place barriers around the work area to protect guests from related harm.

Elevators

Elevators are an indispensable part of most hotels. Guest rooms are usually located on upper floors. Hotels often position restaurants and bars above the lower floors to take advantage of the view or for efficiency of space utilization. As a result, elevators are in great demand and accidents occasionally occur. The causes range from failing to level the elevator with the floor when a guest is exiting, to malfunctioning elevators that plunge down the shaft out of control.

In general, a hotelkeeper who operates an elevator is obligated to use at least ordinary care in its maintenance and operation. In some states, a high degree of care is required.

---

[26] *Severn v. Fifth Season Inn*, 1998 WL 254444 (Tex. 1998)
[27] *Enstrom v. Garden Place Hotel*, 811 N.Y.S.2d 263 (N.Y. 2006)

Self-Service Elevators

Virtually all elevators today are automatic (also called self service). These are designed to operate by buttons controlled by passengers without a human operator. Guests of all ages and aptitudes who may have little familiarity with elevators use them. The manufacturer or contractor installing an automatic elevator, as well as the owner and those under contract to service or inspect it, must act with care.

A hotel guest stumbled while exiting a self-service elevator because the car stopped below the floor level. The guest sued. At trial the guest presented an expert witness who testified that the cause of the misleveling was carbon dust buildup in the elevator's motor generator. The jury determined the hotel was negligent in its maintenance of the device and the verdict was upheld on appeal.[28] We learn from this case that businesses with elevators should ensure that their maintenance program includes regular cleaning of the system's components.

Where an elevator headed for the ground floor dropped past that floor, struck bottom, and rebounded to the third floor, causing injuries, a lawsuit resulted. The plaintiffs were patrons in the elevator at the time of the incident. They proved that the elevator had a history of recent malfunctions. Within the preceding six days the service company had been called three times, and the day before the accident the elevator had been stuck between floors, trapping people inside. Although a service call had been made just hours prior to the rebound incident, an award of summary judgment for the building owner was reversed and the case was referred to a jury to determine liability.[29] Similarly, where a hotel elevator "plunged approximately 18 floors to the elevator pit below," several construction workers who had been renovating the hotel were injured. Evidence established that in the days prior to the accident the hotel had received reports of multiple incidents of malfunctioning. The court on appeal reversed the lower court's grant of summary judgment in favor of the hotel and referred the case to trial to determine liability.[30]

Elevator Maintenance Is a Nondelegable Duty

The duty to maintain an elevator in reasonably safe condition is a nondelegable duty. Thus, if a hotel hires a maintenance company and it negligently overlooks a problem that leads to an accident and injury, the hotel will be liable to injured guests, although the negligent party was not the hotel but rather the elevator service company.

A woman entered a self-service elevator on the building's third floor, intending to go to the ground floor. When the doors shut the elevator plummeted and came to an abrupt stop below the first floor, causing injuries to the passenger. The building owner will be liable if the cause of the injury can be traced to the owner's negli-

---

28 *Dowden v. Otis Elevator Company*, 2001 WL 824406 (Mich. 2001)
29 *Golden Shoreline v. McGowan*, 787 So.2d 109 (Fla. 2001)
30 *DiPilato v. Park Central Hotel*, 795 N.Y.S.2d 518 (N.Y. 2005)

gence or to negligence on the part of a repair or maintenance company it may have hired. Liability for the latter would be based on the owner's nondelegable duty to keep the premises safe.[31] Note: While the hotel will be liable to the guest, the hotel can sue the maintenance company for the money the inn had to pay the guest.

Freight Elevators

Freight elevators are customarily maintained at a lower level than are elevators used by guests. This circumstance not only creates added risks to employees who use the freight elevators, but may also result in injury to guests who somehow find their way to the service elevators. Others, too, are at risk. For example, an emergency medical technician (EMT) responded to a call at a restaurant located within a hotel. He was escorted by a hotel employee via the freight elevator to the kitchen area where the distressed employee was located. The EMT determined he needed additional supplies in his car and sought to exit the kitchen. He could not locate his escort and so he attempted to operate the freight elevator himself, which resulted in injuries. Its operation was more complicated than a typical self-service elevator, and no instructions were posted.[32] Care should be taken to maintain freight elevators in a safe condition and restrict access to trained employees.

Supervision of Maintenance

Safety risks result when elevators are being repaired. Precautions must be taken. For example, when an innkeeper leaves the door to an elevator open or unlocked, which sometimes happens when an elevator is undergoing repairs, a guest might fall into the well and suffer injury. This type of accident will probably result in a finding of negligence against the hotel. It can easily be avoided by roping off the area around the elevator and displaying warning signs.

Escalators

Like stairs, escalators need maintenance attention. Injury can result if an escalator is not working properly or is overcrowded; if running or horseplay is permitted while riding; or if dents, holes, or other damage to the steps develop and go unattended.

Three escalator cases, all involving casinos, are instructive on the factual circumstances that can lead to accidents. In one, the escalator stopped suddenly, throwing the plaintiff forward causing injuries. The apparent problem was defective installation.[33] In another case, the plaintiff fell and injured her knee while on an allegedly overcrowded escalator. The plaintiff was unable to prove any previous problems involving pushing or tripping on the device. No one had reported any problems with the escalator prior to the incident. Based on these facts, the

---

[31] *Gaffney v. EQK Realty Investors*, 445 S.E.2d 771 (Ga. 1994)

[32] *Young v. Interstate Hotels and Resorts*, 906 A.2d 857 (D.C. 2006)

[33] *Lupkus v. Otis Elevator Co.*, 2000 WL 486936 (Conn. 2000)

court dismissed the case, holding that the plaintiff failed to show the defendant was negligent.[34] In the third case the plaintiff was injured when another rider located two people in front of her fell backward onto the passenger behind her who then fell on plaintiff. No evidence was presented to establish that the escalator malfunctioned. Said the court, "Now, it's possible that the woman could have fallen through some defect in the escalator. It's also possible that she could have fallen through some negligent act on her part. It also could have been that she just lost her balance. Accidents sometimes do happen without negligence... A fact finder cannot conclude that negligence by the defendant was the most likely reason for the tumble." The court thus entered summary judgment in favor of the casino and escalator maintenance company.[35]

The operating mechanisms of escalators are not the only concern of the facility in which an escalator is located. An escalator's railings and access areas should be inspected and any dangerous conditions corrected. A restaurant may be liable where it failed to remove a screw protruding one inch from the railing of an escalator, causing injury to a patron.[36]

Doors

The duty of restaurateurs and innkeepers to exercise due care to keep the premises reasonably safe also applies to doors. Development of and adherence to a maintenance plan can save a hospitality facility from liability. A plaintiff in the ladies' room of a Pizza Hut was struck in the head and upper body by a door to a stall that came off its hinges as she pulled it toward her to close it. The eatery sought summary judgment, claiming that the plaintiff could not establish that the restaurant had actual or constructive notice of the defective condition of the door. Said the court, Pizza Hut "failed to demonstrate reasonable maintenance of the bathroom facility" and thus failed to convince the court that it lacked constructive notice of the unsafe condition of the door.[37] The court thus refused to grant summary judgment for the eatery. Additionally, in this case plaintiff sought unsuccessfully to benefit from res ipsa loquitur. The court however refused to apply that doctrine because the restaurant did not have sufficient exclusive control of the door to rule out the possibility that the problem was caused by someone other than the restaurant's employees.

Crowded Doorways

Under ordinary circumstances hotels and restaurants need not have a door attendant; but, if they are aware that an extraordinary crowd will be gathering, a duty exists to employ an attendant to ensure the safety of patrons entering and leaving. An illustrative case arose from the circumstance that the Hotel Astor was the traditional Army team headquarters on the day of the Army-Notre Dame football game, an event that attracts a lot of people. In the early evening of gameday the hotel lobby was congested with people in a "gay, hilarious and carousing mood." The plaintiff, a 63-year-old

---

[34] *Hilton Hotels v. Fleming*, 774 So.2d 174 (La. 2000)
[35] *Vasil v. Trump Marine Hotel and Casino and Otis Elevator Co.*, 2006 WL 941764 (N.J. 2006)
[36] *Anderson v. Market Street Developers*, Ltd., 944 S.W.2d 776 (Tex. 1997)
[37] *Thompson v. Pizza Hut*, 691 N.Y.S.2d 99 (N.Y. 1999)

woman, entered the hotel through the revolving door on her way to a banquet hosted by the hotel and sponsored by the Danish Society. As she had almost completed her entrance, suddenly "there was an awful rush" and several "young fellows" chasing each other inside the hotel lobby ran into the same compartment of the revolving door the plaintiff was in and gave it a hard push. As a result, she was struck by a part of the door and suffered a fractured hip and other injuries.

The hotel was held liable because it should have foreseen the large, rowdy crowd generated by the football game; thus, it should have provided a door attendant to help control the crowd's ingress and egress.[38] If an unruly crowd is not foreseeable, an innkeeper or restaurateur cannot be held liable for the unexpected conduct of its patrons.

Automatic Doors

Automatic doors are very common, providing the public access to an abundance of facilities on a daily basis. Malfunctioning automatic doors can injure an un-suspecting patron in a variety of ways. To avoid this kind of injury, hospitality facilities should make regular examinations of the doors' mechanisms and promptly repair any defect discovered.

A 94-year-old woman attempting to enter a hotel in Las Vegas was partly through the doorway when the automatic doors unexpectedly closed on her, knocking her down and causing injury. The plaintiff's expert witness testified that automatic doors should receive thorough mechanical inspections at least every six months, and they should be inspected weekly to determine if they are working properly. The hotel's chief engineer testified that the hotel did not have a regular maintenance or inspection program for the doors. A jury found the hotel liable and the verdict was upheld on appeal.[39]

Note that the plaintiff in that case was 94 years old and therefore arguably needed more time than the average person to get through the door. She might also have been more susceptible than most people to serious injury in this type of accident. Do these facts lessen the hotel's liability? The answer is no. Hotels and restaurants invite people of all ages and circumstances to their establishments and must anticipate that some guests are more injury-prone than others. Hospitality facilities owe a duty to exercise reasonable care to protect the safety and well-being of *all* their patrons, regardless of physical abilities or frailties.

Sliding-Glass Doors

Another popular door used in many hotels and restaurants is the sliding glass door. Without careful maintenance, the glass can shatter, causing injury to those nearby. Case Example 6-3 illustrates this scenario.

---

38 *Schubert v. Hotel Astor*, Inc., 5 N.Y.S.2d 203; aff'd 281 NY 597 (N.Y. 1938)
39 *Landmark Hotel & Casino, Inc. v. Moore*, 757 P.2d 361 (Nev. 1988)

CASE EXAMPLE 6-3

Sheppard v. Crow-Barker-Paul

968 P.2d 612 (Ariz. 1998)

...Tarik Sheppard ("Tarik")—then 15 years old— was playing in a basketball tournament in Scottsdale, Arizona. The members and coaches of Tarik's team were registered guests at the Safari Hotel. Tarik was injured on the hotel premises when his teammate, Melvin Johnson, closed the sliding glass door to his hotel room, number 249, as Tarik was about to enter. The parties...do not dispute that the door shattered into pieces of glass, severely lacerating Tarik's arms.

Tarik's father, Daniel Sheppard ("Sheppard"), brought this suit against Safari. Because Tarik was a minor at the time, Sheppard asserted Tarik's claim for personal injuries and his own claim for the cost of necessary medical treatment for his son.

Safari denied liability and alleged Tarik's comparative fault. The case proceeded to a trial by jury and concluded in a $445,000 verdict in Sheppard's favor; the jury assigned Safari 100% of the fault....

As background, in 1956, when the Safari Hotel was built, the Arizona laws neither required safety glass nor proscribed plate glass in hotel sliding doors. As of July 1, 1974, the Arizona Legislature made it unlawful to install any form of glass other than safety glass in hazardous locations in public buildings, including hotel and motel sliding doors. The statute does not impose a statutory duty to retrofit pre-1974 installations with safety glass. [The glass on Tarik's door was annealed (plate) and not safety glass.]...

Safari had a common-law duty to avoid subjecting its guests to a foreseeable and unreasonable risk of harm. The trial court defined this duty to the jury in the following instructions:

The duty of a hotel like defendant to its guests is to maintain its premises in a reasonably safe condition. Defendant is required to use ordinary care to inspect for, warn of, safeguard against or remedy a dangerous condition of which Defendant has notice.

Safari seeks judgment notwithstanding the verdict contending that Sheppard introduced no evidence that Safari had pre-accident notice of any unreasonably dangerous condition in Tarik's room. We disagree.

Actual knowledge of the dangerous condition is not required. The duty to inspect arises when the owner has reason to suspect a defect.

Sheppard introduced substantial evidence to establish that Safari had reason to suspect a defect. Arthur Freedman, Sheppard's expert witness, testified from a review of hotel records that the glass doors in the east building [where Tarik's room was located] were breaking with regularity and that Safari had already replaced 11 of the 58 door panes in that building in the 21 months before Tarik's accident. The jury could reasonably have inferred that, in the course of Safari's cleanup and replacement effort, the Safari management had abundant opportunity to discover that its guests were exposed to the danger of annealed glass doors.

Moreover it was undisputed that Tarik's friend Melvin Johnson had reported a malfunction of the door in Room 249. This testimony, coupled with Freedman's testimony, permitted the jury to conclude that Safari should have known before the accident that a door containing annealed glass was unstable within its track. That door was the single entrance and exit for Room 249. Upon such evidence the jury could properly have concluded that Safari had reason to suspect a dangerous condition and that it breached its common-law duty to use ordinary care to inspect for, warn of, safeguard against, or remedy that condition.

CASE QUESTIONS

1. What maintenance procedures should be followed for sliding glass doors?

2. How might the hotel have avoided liability in this case?

3. In 1974, when the legislature imposed the duty of safety glass, why do you think the lawmakers did not require immediate replacement of non-safety glass doors?

Hallways

Hallways are often heavily traveled. Improper maintenance of these spaces can result in liability for negligence. An alert manager will inspect to ensure they are properly cleaned, warning signs are utilized during repairs and cleaning, and rugs are free from holes.

A hole in a rug can trap a shoe heel and result in someone falling. A bulge in a carpet can easily lead to a trip-and-fall accident resulting in injuries and liability.[40]

Is a casino liable when a guest is hurt from a fall in a hallway caused by over-crowding? A plaintiff was walking through a crowded walkway in the midst of numerous gaming tables. Unexpectedly, someone extended his leg and the plaintiff tripped over it. She sued the casino for failing to safely manage the crowds. The court, holding for the casino, differentiated between the facts of this case and a circumstance in which there is only one available route and it is congested. In the latter circumstance, the premises owner may be liable if it fails to protect the customer. However, in a more open setting such as a restaurant, casino, or mall where many hallways and aisles exist, the patron has some responsibility to ensure a safe route. Said the court, "[A]ny one avenue of travel available to a customer

---

[40] *Carrasquillo v. Holiday Carpet Service, Inc.,* 615 So.2d 862 (Fla. 1993)

may at any moment become temporarily congested so as to require the patron to change his route or to slow his movement to the point of stopping altogether as a precaution against unexpected collisions with other customers." The plaintiff thus lost the case.[41]

Stairways, Steps, and Their Coverings

Guests are entitled to assume that steps and passageways are clear of dangerous impediments and otherwise reasonably safe. Because stairways in a hotel or restaurant constitute a potential danger to guests, hotelkeepers must do all of the following to avoid liability: see that steps are properly constructed; keep them in good repair; install railings; avoid leaving items on the steps; provide adequate lighting; if the step is located in an unexpected place, use some means to alert patrons of the step's presence (e.g., different color carpet or a strip of white paint at the end of the step); and if the step is carpeted, maintain the carpets in good and safe condition.

Building codes provide numerous safety specifications for stairways. Deviations that cause injury to guests will likely result in liability. Examples of code mandates are requirements of uniform height for all steps, a maximum permissible height, railings on both sides of a stairway, height of the railings, width of the stairwell, and lighting. When the elevation is inconsistent, unsuspecting users may trip and fall. In a case involving a woman who fell on internal hotel steps that were of various heights, including one that exceeded the code's maximum, the building owner was denied summary judgment. Defendant argued that the uneven height of the step was open and obvious, precluding liability. The court however held that differences in riser heights might not be readily noticed by someone using the stairs and thus the open and obvious doctrine did not defeat plaintiff's claim.[42]

© Cunaplus/Shutterstock.com

---

[41] *Green v. Harrah's Casino*, 774 So.2d 1174 (La. 2000)
[42] *Smith v. Basin Park Hotel, Inc.*, 350 F.3d 810 (Ark. 2003); See also Mac International Savannah Hotel v. Hallman, 595 S.E.2d 577 (Ga. 2004)

CHAPTER 6: Negligence and Hospitality Practices

Another case involved a staple embedded in the carpeting in a hotel conference room. A disc jockey, hired to play for a wedding reception being held in the room, hurt her knee while kneeling to plug electrical cords for her equipment into an outlet. The staple pierced her left knee through the cartilage down to the bone. She sued the hotel claiming it was negligent in the maintenance of the carpet. The hotel night janitor testified that during the week leading up to the injury he had discovered numerous staples while vacuuming because they made a "clinking noise" in the appliance. He attributed them to construction done for a "Queen of the Universe" pageant held in the room a week earlier. Each night since that event he had picked up fewer and fewer staples. He was eventually satisfied that he had picked up all the staples in the room because he no longer heard the clinking noise. The court determined the hotel used reasonable care to remove the staples and dismissed the case.[43] Remember, an innkeeper is not an insurer of guests' safety. Rather, an innkeeper's duty is to act carefully to make the premises reasonably safe. The court determined the hotel had met this standard.

Another issue with stairs that can result in liability for negligence is inadequate lighting. A plaintiff was attending a concert and needed to use the bathroom, requiring that she descend a flight of stairs from the balcony. There was "no light whatsoever," causing the plaintiff to fall and break a leg and shoulder. The concert hall's motion for summary judgment was denied. The court ruled that a jury might well determine that the concert hall was negligent.[44]

The plaintiff in a New York hotel case tripped on a short flight of four steps leading to her room. The hotel was found negligent on several grounds: The lighting was poor, no handrail existed; no warning of the stairs was provided; and the use of the same carpeting on the foyer, stairway, and corridor created an illusion of one level and no stairs. The fact that no previous accident had occurred during the four years since the hotel was built did not constitute a defense.[45]

In Case Example 6-4, the plaintiff's heel became wedged in a gap on a step that the hotel should have discovered and corrected.

---

[43] *Richardson v. Sport Shinko*, 880 P.2d 169 (Hawaii 1994)
[44] *McGowan v. St. Antoninus Church*, 2001 WL 331931 (Ohio 2001)
[45] *Orlick v. Grant Hotel and Country Club*, 331 N.Y.S.2d 651 (N.Y. 1971)

CASE EXAMPLE 6-4

Fields v. Robert Chappell Association, Inc.

256 S.E.2d 259 (N.C. 1979)

…Plaintiff was a registered guest in defendant's motel. She left her room intending to go to the motel office. It was necessary for her to turn to her right and go down a flight of steps. She looked down the steps and saw nothing unusual, except that she saw that the left side was obstructed by the protruding metal handle of a hook that is used to clean swimming pools. She, consequently, did not hold the handrail but moved more to her right towards the wall. There was no handrail on the right side of the step. She fell forward but did not fall all the way down the flight of steps because her foot was caught. She had to pull her shoe loose from the step to get up. There was a deep gash in her leg. She yelled for assistance, and some of the other motel guests gave her first aid before she was taken to a hospital emergency room. After she had been taken to the hospital, another guest went to the stairs where plaintiff had fallen. The stairs were concrete with a metal strip along the front edge of the step. This guest testified that the steps were bloody. She found a piece of plaintiff's shoe heel, the heel cap, wedged between the metal strip and the concrete part of the step. There was a gap between the metal strip and the concrete. Part of the concrete was missing. The witness described it as "a crumbling or an erosion as opposed to a crack." There were similar gaps on several of the steps but on the step where plaintiff's shoe heel had been lodged, the gap was somewhat larger. There was also an eroded area on the top of that step about four inches long that extended back about two inches. It was easier to observe this defect from below than when one looked down the steps from the top. The guest took plaintiff's shoe heel to the motel office and explained what had happened.

Defendant called only one witness, the motel manager. She testified that she was not present on the day the accident occurred. She further testified that the stairs were 13 years old at the time plaintiff fell and that no repairs had been made after the accident. The motel, including the stairs, was regularly inspected every three months. She had participated in these inspections and had not observed any defects in the steps "prior to the time Mrs. Fields fell, nothing that would be noticeable enough to think you would fall, you know, you might see a crack here or there." She admitted, nonetheless, that the cracks were wide enough to receive the heel of a shoe… .

The legal principles that arise on the evidence may … be simply stated. The defendant motel operator was not an insurer of the safety of plaintiff, its invited guest. It was, however, required to exercise due care to keep the premises in a reasonably safe condition so as not to expose plaintiff unnecessarily to danger, and to warn her of any hidden perils. It is liable to plaintiff for any injury proximately caused by a breach of that duty.…

The evidence all but compels the conclusion that plaintiff fell on defendant's stairs because the heel of her shoe unexpectedly became wedged in a crevice near the front edge of one of the stair steps. Plaintiff was proceeding in a careful and prudent manner, and the crevice was almost imperceptible to one proceeding down the steps. The wearing away of the concrete and resulting gap between the metal strip and the rest of the step did not occur suddenly. Defendant knew of the condition, should have known that it was dangerous, and yet allowed it to continue to exist without doing anything to warn its guests of the danger. Defendant, thereby, unnecessarily and unreasonably exposed plaintiff and its other guests to a danger that resulted in injury to plaintiff.

[Judgment for plaintiff.]

1. How could the hotel have avoided the injury and liability in this case?

Movable Steps

A hotel or party house will likely have one or more sets of movable steps to provide access to platforms and stages. Like other steps, the movable variety must also comply with relevant safety codes and be properly maintained.

A restaurant disc jockey, after completing his evening's work, sought to dismount the elevated platform that constituted his work station. While carrying approximately 45 pounds of equipment, he stepped across some 19 inches from the platform to a set of stairs leading to the back door. As he placed his right foot on the top step, the stairs moved out from under him. He landed on the floor and struck his back against the elevated platform. Before he fell he was unaware that the stairs were movable. They weighed 35 to 50 pounds and were not affixed to the wall or the floor. The smooth, wooden base of the stairs sat on a smooth, wooden floor with a polyurethane finish. The disc jockey sued the restaurant. His expert witness testified that the unattached and movable stairs violated the building code because the regulations require that stairs be either fixed or, if movable, weigh approximately 120 pounds. Also, the elevated platform where the disc jockey sat was in violation because it lacked a permanent stair or step. The restaurant, having failed to provide the disc jockey with a reasonably safe means to exit the elevated platform, was negligent and therefore liable for a portion of the injuries (comparative negligence applied).[46]

Indoor Ramps

Sometimes ramps are used in lieu of stairs, often for the purpose of facilitating use of the premises by customers in wheelchairs. Poor construction of ramps also can result in liability. For example, the layout of a bar required that customers use a ramp to reach the back room where the bathroom was located. The ramp was made of wood that, per an expert witness, was likely to shrink, crack, and move over time. A patron fell on her way to the lavatory when her high-heeled shoe became stuck in a gap in the wood, causing serious knee and back injuries. The jury decided the case in favor of the plaintiff, and the verdict was affirmed on appeal.

Duty Owed Guests in Restaurants and Dining Rooms

Restaurateurs and hotels with restaurants have a duty to exercise reasonable care to avoid conditions relevant to restaurants that can result in injury. Those conditions include slippery floors, foreign substances on floors, overcrowding of tables and chairs, hanging mirrors, and flambé dishes.

---

[46] *Michalopoulos v. C&D Restaurant*, 764 A.2d 121 (R.I. 2001)

Accidents caused by slippery floors are not infrequent in dining rooms, banquet halls, and bars.

Highly polished and waxed floors are the cause of many slippery-floor cases. For example, a plaintiff slipped while walking on a polished floor at a banquet. The hotel proved that the floor was waxed only twice a year, the latest being three months before the accident, and the floor was inspected on the day of the banquet and the morning after by the banquet director and found not to have been overwaxed, not unduly slick, and in its normal condition. The court held for the hotel; the plaintiff failed to prove the hotel was negligent.[47]

Before applying wax or polish on a floor, be sure the type being used is appropriate for the particular floor and the application is done consistently with the directions that accompany the product.

Floors are made from a variety of materials, many of which have their own cleaning and maintenance protocols. In a case involving a Macaroni Grill restaurant, the eatery had three sets of floor-cleaning instructions, one applicable to outside concrete floors, one for stained and sealed inside concrete floors, and a third for tile floors. Plaintiff, who was on crutches, fell in the entryway. She sued, claiming the restaurant had utilized the wrong cleaning procedure. The manager testified that proper procedures were used. The court determined that, even if there were cleaning errors, there was no direct evidence of any resulting accumulation of cleaning substances in the entryway that might have created a dangerous condition. Therefore the court awarded summary judgment to the restaurant.[48]

Other conditions will also result in slippery floors and possible liability. A 17-year-old guest of a defendant hotel was severely injured when she slipped on a wet spot on a wooden walkway at the rear of the lobby. The evidence established that the floor where the fall occurred was dangerously worn, smooth, and therefore slippery, and the entire area was inadequately lighted. This, according to the court, was ample evidence that the hotel had negligently maintained the premises.[49]

Some floor materials are inherently slippery, such as marble. Use of these materials does not generally create liability when a patron trips on them unless the floor was improperly constructed or is out of repair.[50]

Foreign Substances on the Floor

Many slippery-floor accidents in a dining room, restaurant, or snack bar result from a foreign substance on the floor. As with all negligence cases, the restaurant is not liable unless it failed to exercise reasonable care.

---

[47] *Mitchell v. Baker Hotel of Dallas, Inc.*, 528 S.W.2d 577 (Tex. 1975)
[48] *Spaude v. Macaroni Grill*, 2006 WL 330105 (Minn. 2006)
[49] *194th St. Hotel Corp. v. Hopf*, 383 So.2d 739 (Fla. 1980)
[50] *Portanova v. Trump Taj Mahal*, 704 N.Y.S.2d 380 (N.Y. 2000)

On a rainy day a restaurant patron, who admitted that he was not watching where he was going, slipped on water near the entrance. An employee had repeatedly mopped the floor in the foyer area to combat the effects of patrons dripping rainwater. The court held that the restaurant was not negligent. It had diligently cleaned the front entrance area throughout the day and the plaintiff failed to pay attention to his surroundings.[51] The outcome was different in Case Example 6-5, which involved spilled water.

CASE EXAMPLE 6-5

Kesselman v. Lever House Restaurant

816 N.Y.S.2d 13 (N.Y. 2006)

Plaintiff and her husband were dining at defendant restaurant. Shortly after the main course, she proceeded to the restroom. To get there patrons had to walk down a large hallway. The hallway floor was dark, wide and shiny. Runners (carpets with rubber backing) had been placed on the floor but did not cover the entire width of it. The hallway was crowded with waiters and restaurant staff, mostly moving in the opposite direction of plaintiff.

Shortly after reaching the very beginning of the hallway, plaintiff was forced to walk to her left, onto the bare floor, to avoid several waiters who were working at a station located on the right side of the hallway. As she stepped off the runner, she slipped on a wet substance on the floor and fell, sustaining injuries.

Plaintiff thereafter commenced this action, alleging she fell and sustained injuries as a result of a dangerous and defective condition existing on defendant's premises…

To establish negligence in this type of slip-and-fall case, a plaintiff must demonstrate, inter alia, that the defendant breached its duty to the plaintiff by creating a dangerous condition… defendant failed to establish that it did not create the wet condition which caused this plaintiff to slip and fall.

The evidence submitted by plaintiffs demonstrates that the hallway leading to the restaurant's restrooms was heavily utilized by waiters and other restaurant employees, as well as patrons utilizing the restroom. At the time of the incident, it was crowded with approximately 20 people, many of whom were moving in… opposite directions. Most of these were waiters… Water and hot beverage service was located in this hallway, as well as waiter stations. Significantly, plaintiff had to alter her path to the restroom as a result of waiters using one of these stations. The food from the kitchen was hand-carried to the dining room through this hallway. A small sink used to fill pitchers with water and ice was located near the waiter stations.

The floor in the hallway was made of terrazzo, a material that becomes very slippery when wet. Defendant's manager testified at his deposition that since the hallway was heavily traveled, slippery material such as food and drinks might fall to the floor based on its intended use. As a result, runners

---

[51] *Sivira v. Midtown Restaurants*, Corp., 753 So.2d 492 (Miss. 1999)

were placed in the hallway for added safety to create a secure path to avoid a slick condition in the event of accidental spills. These runners, however, did not cover the entire width of the hallway and had gaps between them.

Plaintiff testified that after she fell, she noticed the bottom and seat of her pants were wet, and that it was more than mere dampness...

Given the fact that this hallway was a "center of activity for restaurant staff," it is permissible to draw the inference that defendant's employees created the wet condition that caused plaintiff to slip and fall. The restaurant has thus failed to demonstrate entitlement to summary judgment.

CASE QUESTION

1. What might the restaurant have done differently to avoid liability in this case? Often key in this type of case is whether the eatery was aware or should have been aware of the existence of the substance on the floor.

Sometimes proof that the restaurant was aware of the problem is easy. Where an unsafe condition is reoccurring, the restaurant is on notice. For example, a restaurant that served Jell-o shots in paper cups was aware that customers routinely discarded the cups on the floor. A customer who slipped on one of the cups while dancing sued the restaurant for her injuries. The court held the defendant was 80 percent responsible for failing to correct a known dangerous condition.[52]

Even if the existence of an unsafe condition is known to the restaurant, if the circumstance is open and obvious and customers can be expected to observe the condition and take precautions, the restaurant will not be liable.

Lone Star Steakhouse restaurants serve peanuts to patrons and encourage them to throw the shells on the floor. A diner who had been at a Lone Star facility for two hours tripped on the shells while exiting a restaurant and was injured. The restaurant was not liable. The court held the presence of peanut shells on the floor was open and obvious, and the eatery had no reason to anticipate that the customer would not see them.[53]

Query: Why was the plaintiff allowed to collect in the Jell-o shot case and not in the peanut-shell case, given that both involved obvious debris on the floor?

---

[52] *Endres v. Mingles Restaurant, Ltc.*, 706 N.Y.S.2d 32 (2000)
[53] *Johnson v. Lone Star Steakhouse & Saloon*, 997 S.W.2d 490 (Ky. 1999)

CHAPTER 6: Negligence and Hospitality Practices

Answer: In the Jell-o shot case, the dirtied floor was used for dancing, an activity during which patrons' attention is diverted from the condition and circumstances of the ground. The court apparently felt that the dancer's opportunity to observe the debris on the floor was less than in the case involving a restaurant patron who was eating dinner for two hours. Also, some states are more inclined to temper the open and obvious doctrine by applying comparative negligence when the doctrine is used.

Constructive Notice

Sometimes a plaintiff cannot prove that the restaurant had actual notice of a condition. In such cases, the plaintiff can nonetheless win the case if she can show that the facility should have known of the problem, called **constructive notice**. A restaurant or hotel has constructive notice of a problem when the condition has existed for a sufficiently long period of time that the facility should have discovered the problem in the ordinary course of monitoring the premises.

Case Example 6-6 illustrates a number of the principles relevant to floors that we have discussed.

constructive notice
Information or knowledge of a fact imputed to a person by law because he or she could have discovered the fact by proper diligence or because the situation was such as to put upon such person the duty of inquiry.

CASE EXAMPLE 6-6

Anderson v. American Restaurant Group

2000 WL 1665693 (Wash. 2000)

Carolyn Anderson suffered injuries when she slipped and fell while running across the bathroom floor at the Black Angus restaurant… The Black Angus lounge sponsored a series of scavenger hunts "as an entertainment/promotional device for the patrons." During the scavenger hunt, participants sat in chairs on the dance floor. As the disc jockey called out each object, the participants moved throughout the restaurant to locate the required item. The last participant to return to the dance floor with the item for that round was eliminated, and the game continued until only one person remained. On the night in question Anderson went to the Black Angus with two friends and participated in one of the scavenger hunts. When she and three others were the only remaining participants, the DJ announced "toilet paper" as the next required item, and Anderson dashed to the women's restroom nearest the lounge. According to Anderson, she slipped and fell as she ran across the bathroom floor… She glanced back after falling and noticed there was water on the floor.

She also realized there were wet spots on her jeans in the knee area and below, and concluded the wet floor had caused her fall. As she stood up, Anderson was in some pain but able to walk. She took a piece of toilet paper from inside one of the bathroom stalls and returned to the dance floor. She remained in the game and ultimately finished second. She did not file an incident report or notify management until five months later when she advised the restaurant's general manager that she had had three surgeries on her right knee as a result of the fall, and re-injured her back…

[W]e hold that Black Angus' decision to host and invite customers to participate in the scavenger hunt gave rise to a duty to inspect for and remedy or warn participants about water on the bathroom floor. Black Angus knew or should have known that scavenger hunt participants would run through the bathrooms to look for toilet paper, and it had a duty to inspect and maintain the bathrooms in a manner consistent with that knowledge.

Given this duty, a reasonable jury could find that Black Angus breached its duty of reasonable care... It is always foreseeable that there may be water slopped on the floor. The Restroom Checklist that Black Angus used states the obvious: A wet floor is a safety hazard and keeping the bathroom floors clean and dry is a basic safety consideration. Accordingly, a jury could conclude that by not ensuring the bathroom floor was clean and dry up to and including the moment it challenged the scavenger hunt participants to get a piece of toilet paper as fast as possible, it breached its duty of care. And a jury could conclude that Black Angus should have expected that patrons darting into the bathroom would not discover or realize the danger of a wet floor because they would be focused elsewhere and in a hurry. For these reasons, summary judgment was inappropriate.

CASE QUESTION

1. What could the restaurant have done to avoid liability?

How frequently must a facility inspect? There is no definitive time period. Remember that a restaurant is not an insurer of diners' safety. It is not responsible for wiping up fallen food the moment it drops. Such would not be feasible. Rather, the restaurant is liable only if it fails to exercise reasonable care. If the restaurant regularly inspects the floor for spilled or dropped substances and cleans the floor when necessary, the eatery will not be liable even though someone trips and falls. The cases are instructive in defining what is reasonable.

A plaintiff who slipped on a scoop of ice cream dropped by another customer two to four minutes prior to the fall was unsuccessful in her lawsuit against the proprietor for damages because there was insufficient time to discover the unsafe condition.[54]

While dining in a Burger King, a plaintiff slipped on a puddle of water three to four feet away from the self-service beverage center. The restaurant proved that 10 minutes prior to the accident an employee had inspected the area and found no water on the floor. The court determined that the restaurant acted reasonably and so granted summary judgment in its favor.[55]

Where a person slips on ice, the size of ice at the time of the fall may be a telltale sign of the amount of time water has been allowed to remain on the floor without being wiped up, as illustrated in Case Example 6-7.

[54] *Schnuphase v. Storehouse Markets*, 918 P.2d 476 (Utah 1996)
[55] *Dwoskin v. Burger King Corp.*, 671 N.Y.S.2d 494 (N.Y. 1998)

CASE EXAMPLE 6-7

Demaille v. Trump Castle Associates

725 N.Y.S.2d 40 (N.Y. 2001)

Plaintiff brings this action to recover for personal injuries sustained on October 2, 1994, when she slipped and fell on one of several puddles of partially melted ice on a marble floor in Trump Plaza Hotel in Atlantic City.

To constitute constructive notice, a defect must be visible and apparent and it must exist for a sufficient length of time prior to the accident to permit defendant's employees to discover and remedy it. The evidence established that plaintiff fell when she and a friend walked from their room into the elevator lobby, which had a marble floor and was adjacent to the room where the ice machine was located. Circumstantial evidence of defendant's constructive notice of a dangerous condition was provided by the uncontroverted trial testimony of plaintiff and her friend regarding the size of the puddles and the size of the partially-melted ice cubes, relative to the size of those produced by the ice machine, as well as by the deposition testimony of an individual who entered the elevator lobby shortly after plaintiff fell.

The circumstantial evidence was sufficient to permit the jury to draw the necessary inference that the ice had been spilled a sufficient length of time prior to the accident such that defendant's employees should have discovered and remedied the condition.

In another circumstantial evidence case, the outcome was different. A plaintiff was in a Walmart store walking in a busy aisle near the cafeteria. She slipped and fell on a piece of macaroni. She testified the macaroni had mayonnaise in it and was contaminated with a lot of dirt, including footprints and cart track marks. The court refused to find the store negligent, holding instead that soiled macaroni on the floor of a heavily traveled aisle is not evidence of the length of time it was on the floor. The court noted that no analysis was done of the dirt on the pasta to determine if it was dried or otherwise evidenced the food's presence on the floor for a considerable length of time.[56]

In another case with a similar issue, the judge ruled more liberally. A plaintiff who fell at an Outback Steakhouse on dirty mashed potatoes was entitled to present her case to a jury. The court in this case said, "The soil on the potatoes may have been caused by plaintiff stepping on them when she fell, or by them being on the floor for a period of time sufficient to create constructive notice," establishing a factual issue for a jury.[57] These cases are hard to reconcile. Sometimes different results merely reflect varying opinions of different judges on how the law should be applied to particular facts.

---

[56] *Wal-Mart Stores, Inc. v. Gonzalez*, 968 S.W.2d 934 (Tex. 1998)
[57] *Colon v. Outback Steakhouse of Florida, Inc.*, 721 So.2d 769 (Fla. 1998)

A restaurant may be able to establish that it exercised reasonable care and thus was not negligent where it enforces a policy of frequent inspections of the floor to ensure it is free from spilled foods or beverages. A restaurant was saved from liability for a diner's fall on a lasagna noodle because of the restaurant's cleaning policy. The owner testified that the restaurant had adopted and strictly followed a comprehensive cleaning policy. Employees were required to sweep and clean the floor after ever meal and mop with a sterilizing solution at night. All employees were trained and required to watch for objects on the floor at all times and remove any that they saw. Based on these procedures, the court found no basis to assume that the restaurant had constructive notice of the fallen food.[58]

Similarly, judgment was entered against a plaintiff who fell in a restaurant on a lemon peel because of the restaurant's policy and practice that all wait staff inspect for foreign substances on the floor and pick up any that are found. In addition a busboy was always assigned to check constantly for debris during meal periods.[59] Similarly, in another case, a country and western dancer slipped and fell at a restaurant while "spinning and twirling around the dance floor," resulting in a broken ankle. Testimony from the restaurant established that it had a strictly enforced policy that drinks were not allowed on the dance floor, employees monitored the dance area to ensure patrons did not enter it with drinks, and any spills that did occur were immediately cleaned. This testimony contributed to the appellate court's reversal of a jury verdict in favor of the plaintiff.[60]

To help avoid liability, hospitality facilities should develop floor maintenance policies designed to achieve floors that are safe for customers' use. But a policy alone will not suffice to avoid liability. Strict adherence to the policy is necessary for a hotel or restaurant to establish it exercised reasonable care when sued by a guest who trips on an object on the floor. Where a restaurant has a policy of floor-cleaning procedures that ensures safe, nonslippery floors, but the restaurant fails to adhere to the policy, an inference may be drawn that the restaurant was negligent.[61]

Miscellaneous Matters Relating to Floors

Other circumstances involving a restaurant floor can cause injury. A couple was dancing in the pavilion area of a casino. The dance area was designated by ropes and a row of potted plants on saucers placed just inside the ropes. While slow dancing, the plaintiff tripped on one of the saucers and broke her wrist. In her lawsuit against the casino she was able to rebut its defense that the condition was open and obvious. The saucers were the same color as the carpet and thus not easily visible.[62]

---

[58] *Solomon v. Monjuni's Restaurant*, 768 So.2d 799 (La. 2000)
[59] *Kauffmann v. Royal Orleans, Inc.*, 216 So.2d 394 (La. 1968)
[60] Ochlockonee Banks Restaurant, Inc. v. Colvin, 700 So.2d 1229 (Fla. 1997)
[61] *BBB Service Co. v. Glass*, 491 S.E.2d 870 (Ga. 1997)
[62] *Creel v. St. Charles Gaming Co*, 707 So.2d 475 (La. 1998)

Placement of Chairs and Tables

Overcrowding in a restaurant or banquet hall can create a dangerous condition.

If tables in a dining room are so close together that walking between them is difficult, a diner may foreseeably be injured. A plaintiff who tripped on another diner's coat belt because of the proximity of the tables survived a summary judgment motion by the restaurant.[63] While exceeding the maximum number of diners that can comfortably be accommodated in a restaurant may be appealing from a profit vantage point, it can lead to damages that easily negate any additional money the extra diners might generate. Case Example 6-8 helps answer the question: How close is too close to place the tables?

CASE EXAMPLE 6-8

LaPlante v. Radisson Hotel Co.

292 F.Supp. 705 (Mich. 1968)

. . .Simply stated, the question is whether a jury may find a hotel negligent where the hotel, in hiring itself out to stage a banquet for 1,200 paying guests in one of its banquet rooms, allegedly set the banquet tables so close to each other as to leave inadequate aisles and room between seated guests, causing the plaintiff to trip over a chair when attempting to leave the room and thereby injuring herself.

[T]he plaintiff, a semiretired school teacher, 67 years of age, was a guest at the defendant's hotel for the purpose of attending the national convention of a professional education sorority of which she was a member. The convention meetings and related banquets were all held at the defendant hotel.

On August 10, 1967, the convention staged its final banquet, and the plaintiff was in attendance....

Long tables, seating twelve to eighteen persons each, were placed at preset distances apart, which the defendant claims was forty-two inches, though the jury could find from evidence the plaintiff introduced that the actual distance between tables was somewhat less. Further, there was evidence that on at least at some of the tables, the chairs were back to back to those at the next table. . .

There was testimony that waitresses were unable to move down the aisles between the long tables, and at the table at which the plaintiff was seated, the plates of food were passed down by the waitresses from person to person from the end of the table. The hotel manager testified this was not a good practice, and he did not permit it, if discovered. . .The banquet began at 8:00 p.m., and the plaintiff came to the hall and selected a seat about in the middle of one of the long tables. Several hours later, at approximately 11:15 p.m., before the banquet program was over and while the lights were dimmed, with a spotlight on the head table . . . the plaintiff decided to leave the banquet hall to meet her son-in-law as prearranged. Moving sideways, she negotiated a path between chairs as the various

---

[63] *Hopkins v. Fire Mountain Restaurants, Inc.*, 2006 WL 2548864 (Mo. 2006)

people moved in toward the table to accommodate her. The jury could find that not realizing the position of the final chair, and believing she had negotiated herself to the main aisle, plaintiff caught her foot on the leg of that last chair and tripped and fell, injuring herself. Based on this evidence and the medical testimony as to the extent of her injuries, the jury awarded plaintiff the sum of $3,500. . . .

The defendant contends that since there was no violation of any statute or ordinance pleaded [or] proved, the burden was on the plaintiff to show by expert testimony or otherwise the standard of care to which the defendant's conduct should have conformed. . . .

The issue becomes one of whether a jury should be permitted, without expert testimony, to draw upon their own knowledge, background, and common experience to determine what the standard of care should be and, hence, whether any departure therefrom occurred.

Certainly the nature of the case is not scientifically complicated nor technical. While some training and experience in catering and hotel management may be a necessary prerequisite to the handling of a banquet for 1,200 people, the court is of the view that such training or background is not [indispensable] to the ability to determine what is unreasonable crowding and what is not. The lay juror, knowing no more than the next person about catering procedures, could determine from the evidence in this case whether or not the tables were too close for safety. . . .The rule of evidence applied in determining the appropriateness of opinion "expert testimony" is whether the subject involved is so distinctively related to some science, profession, business, or occupation as to be beyond the ken of the average layman. Here the court is not convinced that expert testimony was required or would necessarily have been helpful to the jury. . . .

The jury could find that the hotel reasonably could foresee that during a banquet commencing at 8:00 p.m. and lasting until after 11:00 p.m., a number of people would leave the hall to go to the restrooms or for other purposes; that with a program in progress, the lights might well be dimmed and vision made more difficult; and that with the crowded or overcrowded conditions, such a fall as occurred might be anticipated . . . .

Ruling of the Court:. . . Judgment for plaintiff.

CASE QUESTIONS

1. Do you agree that the injuries in this case were foreseeable by the hotel? Why or why not?

2. Do you agree that an expert witness was not necessary in this case? Why or why not?

Hanging Mirrors in Dining Rooms

Large plate-glass mirrors in a dining room are another factor that can cause injury. A restaurant must be vigilant to ensure such mirrors remain securely attached. In an Indiana case, a wall mirror measuring 3.5 by 7 feet fell on a guest and severely injured her. She sued the restaurant claiming res ipsa loquitur. The court upheld the application of that doctrine to this case because the mirror was under the restaurant's exclusive control and the injury would not have occurred if proper maintenance of the mirror had been exercised.[64]

Ceilings

Improperly built or supported ceilings create another condition that can cause significant injuries and give rise to liability. Case Example 6-9 illustrates this point.

CASE EXAMPLE 6-9

Bank of New York v. Ansonia Associates

656 N.Y.S.2d 813 (N.Y. 1997)

...On May 12, 1990, the ceiling collapsed in the croissant shop located in a West Side [of New York City] landmark building. One patron, Miriam Rosa Toigo was killed, and a number of others were injured; 13 plaintiffs in all have commenced suit. The defendants included owners of the premises, architects, contractors, builders and others...

Evidence established, and both sides' experts agreed that the ceiling which caused the plaintiffs' injuries was a disaster waiting to happen. This is because suspended from the plaster ceiling above the croissant shop were ducts weighing 600 pounds, air conditioners weighing over 200 pounds, a sprinkler system weighing over 1000 pounds, and a hung acoustical tile ceiling, none of which were attached to any structural support other than the plaster ceiling. There was testimony from which it could be found that the owners had numerous opportunities to discover and remedy this dangerous condition over the years. There was also testimony of warning signs such as falling chunks of plaster, and falling debris.

There was more than ample evidence supporting the jury's finding of negligence.... .

Menu Boards on Ledges

Restaurants are well advised not to place items on ledges near tables where customers sit. The risks created by such circumstances are illustrated by a case involving a wood-framed chalkboard menu. The restaurant rested the menu board on a ledge immediately above one of the seats at a table. When the server approached the table, he removed the board from the shelf and walked around the table to show each customer the menu. The waiter then returned the board to the ledge. While the diners were waiting for their meal to be served, the chalkboard fell and struck the

---

[64] *Deming Hotel Company v. Prox*, 236 N.E.2d 613 (Ind. 1968)

plaintiff in the head. The court, noting that the restaurant controlled the placement of the menu board and the tables and chairs, held that a jury could reasonably determine that the restaurant failed to meet its duty to use reasonable care.[65]

Hanging Televisions

Sports bars and some restaurants display televisions for patrons' entertainment. One restaurant installed sets in all four corners of the dining area, each resting on a platform hung from the ceiling and supported on all four corners by a plastic link chain. A server was hit while cleaning a corner table when one of the televisions fell. He sued the restaurant's builder for negligent construction. The plaintiff's expert witness, a mechanical engineer, testified that the platforms holding the TVs were not properly supported, noting that the plastic chains were clearly marked with warnings by the manufacturer that they were not to be used for hanging overhead loads. The jury determined that the restaurant was negligent.[66]

Serving Flambé Foods

Flaming dishes such as cherries jubilee and baked Alaska add an element of excitement to a menu and a dining room. As the Case Example 6-10 tragically illustrates, they also add an element of danger and must be handled with great care. Particularly note the facts that constituted the server's negligence and, in the latter part of the decision, the court's discussion on calculating damages.

CASE EXAMPLE 6-10

Young v. Caribbean Associates, Inc.

358 F.Supp. 1220 (V.I. 1973)

This is a tort and breach of warranty action tried by the court without a jury. [*Breach of warranty* means that a guaranty made by a seller of goods has been broken.] A father and his 10-year-old son seek recovery for mental anguish suffered by the father and bodily injuries suffered by the son brought about in unusual circumstances. The son, Francis Howard Young, was staying with his parents at the defendant, Caribbean Beach Hotel. On New Year's Eve, 1969, the family was having dinner in the hotel dining room. At the end of the meal, the son volunteered to go through the dessert serving line to bring a cherries jubilee for his father. As the son reached the head of the serving line, the waiter in charge of flaming and serving the cherries jubilee found it necessary to kindle the flames by adding more rum to the chafing pan. He took a bottle of 151-proof rum, which was stoppered with a narrow "slow pour" spout, and proceeded to pour the rum directly into the pan. As he did so, the spout either

---

[65] *Everett v. Peter's La Cuisine*, 739 So.2d 1015 (Fla. 1999)
[66] *Ross v. Paddy*, 532 S.E.2d 612 (S.C. 2000)

dropped out or was popped out by an internal combustion in the rum bottle, and a quantity of volatile rum gushed out. An abnormally high flame resulted that reached out to touch the boy, setting his shirt on fire. The boy suffered severe burns and has undergone considerable treatment for skin and flesh grafts and plastic surgery. The complaint requests $200,000 compensatory damages for the son and $19,912 medical expenses for the father. The complaint [bases] recovery principally upon negligence of all defendants [the hotel, the serving waiter, and Sears, Roebuck & Company which sold plaintiff the shirt he was wearing], but the breach of warranty... allegations were aimed primarily at Sears, Roebuck & Company, the vendor of the allegedly highly flammable boy's shirt... .

The father's right to recover his expenditures for medical expenses and the son's right to recover compensatory damages for his bodily injuries are clear. The hotel is, at the very least, accountable for its serving waiter's negligence in using an improperly stoppered bottle, which permitted the "slow pour" spout either to fall out or pop out, thereby discharging a large quantity of volatile rum. Moreover, as the evidence tended to show, the hotel's serving waiter was negligent in the first place in pouring the rum directly from the bottle and not from an intermediary bowl or pitcher. An experienced maitre d'hotel and chef testified that to pour directly from a bottle was to invite the flame to catch onto the stream of rum and leap from the chafing pan to ignite the vaporous gases inside the bottle, blowing out the cork and turning the bottle into a veritable "flame thrower" or "blowtorch," capable of throwing a flame 10 to 15 feet. Although I need not decide that this in fact did happen, I do find that it was negligent to pour directly from the bottle and not from an intervening bowl or wide mouth pitcher....

I further find that the negligence of the hotel and its serving waiter was the sole and proximate cause of plaintiff's injuries. The hotel for a time relied in part on the theory that the boy's shirt was itself highly flammable as evidenced by the vigor with which it burned, and that this was an important intervening cause of the holocaust that developed. With this theory in mind,... the hotel [sued] Sears, Roebuck & Company.... At the trial, however, a written statement of the waiter was produced that indicated that a substantial quantity of the rum had gushed directly onto the boy's shirt. This itself would be more than enough to support the combustion, no matter what the flammability of the shirt fabric might be. [The alleged flammability of the shirt was thus not the proximate cause of the plaintiff's injury.] The... complaint against Sears was therefore dismissed.... The action then proceeded against the serving waiter and the hotel alone. I also find that the boy was not guilty of contributory negligence. Although there was some testimony indicating that he was warned to stand back, the warning would have been, at the very best, an insufficient caution to a normal boy of plaintiff's age.

With the question of liability settled, I must now address myself to the matter of damages. The father's medical expenses, and reasonably related outlays, have totaled some $12,352.08 to date. In addition, some further surgery will be needed in order to minimize the burn scars on the boy's face and body. Although it is difficult for the medical experts to estimate the costs of these future contemplated operations, the uncontroverted estimate given at trial of $6,000 appears reasonable. The father's total [medical] damages would therefore come to approximately $18,352.08.

The most important and troublesome issue of damages is the award of compensable damages that must be granted to the son for his pain, suffering, permanent disfigurement, and the effect thereof upon his psyche and social adjustment. That his pain was considerable is unquestioned. The boy was on fire for more than several seconds before any one of the astonished bystanders came to his rescue. Before falling to the floor, he tried desperately to tear his shirt off. Finally, after perhaps a full half minute of time, one of the waiters came to his rescue with a tablecloth to snuff out the fire. An ambulance was called and soon the boy and his father were taken to the hospital emergency room.. ..

At the Washington Hospital Center, several skin grafts were performed by Dr. Fry. On June 17, the boy was again admitted to the hospital for several injections of steroids into the hypertrophic scarred areas. Hypertrophic scarred areas are scars that are thickened and raised from the healthy, normal skin. There was hospitalization again in October 1970 for further operations to improve the scarred areas.

From my personal observations of the boy's scars, I would say that the scars on his right cheek and beneath his chin are unsightly, as are the scars on his chest and on the backs of both hands. The scar underneath the chin is actually a keloid [a thick scar resulting from excessive growth of fibrous tissue] and is red in color. There are two keloid formations on the chest. There was an attempt to remove one by excision, but the result was a scar worse than the one removed.

The doctor obtained skin for the skin grafts from the boy's left and right thighs. These areas are approximately six inches long and two and-a-half inches wide. These are called "donor sites" that will eventually become less noticeable, but... they may always appear as "patches."

The medical testimony was generally that the boy received second and third degree burns over 30 percent of his body's surface. The boy has no injuries to his organs, nor to his eyes. He can make a fist and move his fingers in the normal way. In sum, he has no physical disabilities. The doctors are of the opinion that the scars and keloid on the face and chest areas can be further improved by a combination of excision and injections. One doctor opined that surgery can make noticeable improvements and improve the boy cosmetically. However, there would have to be between three and five hospitalizations to achieve this improvement. The medical consensus is that time alone will show improvement on the scarred areas and that within a few years much of the scars should become less noticeable....

It is no easy undertaking to make a judicial pronouncement that a certain damage award will fully compensate the boy for his pain, suffering and disfigurement... . I award the boy $80,000 and the father $18,352.08....

CASE QUESTION

1. How might the result have been different if the plaintiff were an adult rather than a 10-year-old boy?

A restaurant that serves flambé dishes or does any type of tableside cooking with a flame must carefully train its employees on how to prepare the food safely, how to use the related cooking devices, and what to do in the event of a fire.

A number of cases have involved circumstances where hot tea or coffee purchased with a take-out order spilled and injured someone. Given that we all expect tea and coffee to be served hot, the question becomes how hot is too hot? In a widely publicized case involving McDonald's, a woman was burned when coffee she purchased from a McDonald's drive-through window spilled from its cup, which she had placed between her legs. The accident occurred while she was adding cream and sugar to the beverage in a parked car. She received a sizable damage recovery, which likely prompted many of the similar subsequent cases. A critical factor in her case was that the coffee she purchased was served at a higher temperature than the industry standard.[67]

The coffee industry has determined that the optimum temperature needed to release the flavor from coffee beans is 170–175 degrees Fahrenheit. This standard has been accepted by the restaurant industry and is the temperature at which customers anticipate receiving their coffee.[68]

In another case, a woman spilled in her lap coffee she purchased from E-Z Serve. The store established that the coffee was served at the industry standard temperature. The court, noting that "plaintiff clearly intended to purchase hot coffee, not tepid," and that plaintiff frequently drank coffee and so was familiar with the liquid's temperature, found that the store was not negligent and dismissed the complaint.

In another case, the plaintiff spilled on her lap hot tea she had purchased at the drive-through window of a McDonald's. She claimed the restaurant did not give sufficient warning of the risks of spilled tea. The cup in which her drink was served included the following notice in two places, "CAUTION: CONTENTS MAY BE HOT." Said the court, "The cup in question contained bold warnings cautioning the holder about hot contents. In the case at hand, the consumer had ordered hot tea. The *Oxford Encyclopedic English Dictionary* describes teas as, 'A drink made by infusing tea-leaves in boiling water.' This court holds that consumer expectations coupled with warnings on the cup established red lights to the plaintiff that the tea might be too hot for the tongue. . . . also society is thoroughly aware from childhood of the dangers of a hot liquid spill."[69]

In situations where a diner eats in the restaurant, wait personnel need to be careful both as they pour hot beverages and as they position the containers that hold them. Negligence in serving these hot drinks can result in liability. If coffee is spilled on a patron while the server is attempting to fill a cup, liability will likely result. This can be easily avoided if the server removes the cup from the vicinity of the customer while pouring. In an Ohio case a woman was scalded while eating in a Chinese restaurant when a teapot containing hot tea fell on her lap from the lazy Susan where the waitress had placed it. The woman claimed the restaurant

---

[67] *Liebeck v. McDonald's Restaurants, P.T.S., Inc.,* 1995 WL 360309 (N.M. 1994)
[68] *Oubre v. E-Z Serve Corporation,* 713 So.2d 818 (La. 1998)
[69] *Immormino v. McDonald's,* 698 N.E.2d 516 (Ohio 1998)

was aware of at least one prior similar incident and so should have put the teapot on the tabletop and not the lazy Susan. A jury entered a verdict in favor of the injured plaintiff. That verdict was upheld on appeal.[70]

From these cases we learn the importance of not overheating coffee, tea, hot chocolate, and other drinks that are customarily served hot. Heating should be done consistent with industry standards. Warnings on cups that the liquid inside is hot can assist in avoiding liability. Wait personnel should handle hot beverages with care and avoid spilling on customers.

Duty Owed Guests Outside

A variety of conditions outside a hotel or restaurant can lead to liability if reasonable care is not exercised. These include, among others, valet service, sidewalks, handicapped ramps, outdoor sporting facilities, and outdoor lighting.

Outside Door Service

When guests arrive at a hotel by car or taxi, they often stop in front of the establishment, where the door attendant takes their luggage and a valet parks the car. A hotel or restaurant is not, absent foreseeably rowdy circumstances, required to furnish door attendants or valets. If it does, however, the hotel or restaurant may be liable if these employees are negligent. This rule is illustrated by Case Example 6-11.

CASE EXAMPLE 6-11

Kurzweg v. Hotel St. Regis Corp.

309 F.2d 746 (N.Y. 1962)

Plaintiff, descending from a cab stopped in the second lane from the sidewalk in front of the Hotel St. Regis, was injured when a car nearer the curb backed up. She sued the owners of both vehicles and the hotel owner, alleging against the latter negligence of the hotel doorman. The hotel owner moved to dismiss the complaint for failure to state a claim on which relief could be granted....

It is the hotel's contention that it was under no duty by New York law to furnish a doorman, and that therefore failure of the doorman to act cannot bring an action against it. But New York has held liable a person under no duty to act who voluntarily undertakes to act and causes injury through his negligent act....[T]he complaint states a claim upon which relief can be granted....

---

[70] *Babich v. Hunan Szechwann Inn, Inc.*, 1997 WL 410720 (Ohio 1997)

When invitees use the sidewalk of a hotel or restaurant, they have the responsibility to exercise care where they walk. If they trip and fall due to an obvious obstruction or defect, the hotel or restaurant will not be responsible. For example, one case involved a wheelchair-bound restaurant patron who tried to maneuver around a trash barrel situated near the restaurant sidewalk. She recognized passage would be "at best, a tight squeeze." Because she was aware of the risk created by the barrel she was unable to recover for injuries she suffered when it forced her to fall.[71]

A guest may be charged with awareness of a condition where, prior to the accident, he had experienced the condition that caused the problem. Thus, where plaintiff guest was injured when stepping down from a curb in front of defendant's hotel, and defendant had stepped off that curb three times prior to the fall without injuring himself, the condition is rendered open and obvious, and plaintiff's case was dismissed.[72]

If, however, a defect is not obvious to patrons and the restaurateur is aware of the problem, the restaurant will be liable, as illustrated in Case Example 6-12.

CASE EXAMPLE 6-12

Eisnaugle v. McDonald's

2000 WL 33226184 (Ohio 2000)

…On a rainy morning Jill Eisnaugle, then 15, and her father stopped at the McDonald's restaurant in Jackson for breakfast. Jill walked across the parking lot and stepped up onto the tile sidewalk in front of the side entrance. Upon stepping onto the tile, Jill immediately fell. Jill twisted and broke the neck of her femur. Resetting the bone required surgery and the implantation of surgical screws… . Her doctor did not release her to full activity until nearly 19 months after the accident. The Eisnaugles filed a lawsuit against the restaurant alleging that the McDonald's negligently permitted an unsafe condition to exist. They sought damages for Jill's medical expenses, her pain and suffering, and her parents' loss of Jill's company and services.

At trial the testimony revealed that defendant franchisee leases the land and the building, and is responsible for its upkeep and remodeling. In 1990 defendant opted to change the type of sidewalk outside the restaurant from exposed aggregate (a type of sidewalk material) to tile. The franchise owner testified that he selected the tile sidewalk because it is easier and cheaper to maintain than aggregate. The Eisnaugles' expert witness tested the tile and determined that it did not comply with the Ohio Building Code, the Life Safety Code, or Americans with Disabilities Act standards for safe, slip-resistant outdoor walkways… .

The jury deliberated and determined that defendant was negligent and that defendant's negligence proximately caused Jill's accident and the resulting injuries….

---

[71] *Spagnuolo v. McDonald's*, 561 N.W.2d 500 (Mich. 1997)
[72] *Mlincek v. CC2 Tree Tenant Corp.*, 2005 WL 2035565 (Va. 2005)

On appeal the judgment affirmed.

CASE QUESTION

1. Why was the defect in the tile sidewalk not considered obvious and open?

Another potential pavement problem is the occasional step located in an unexpected place. Unsuspecting pedestrians may fail to see the step and trip unless its existence is highlighted in some way.

For example, plaintiff who had just exited a restaurant where she had eaten lunch failed to see a single step that was embedded in the sidewalk. It was located "two-thirds of the way down a long walk, and not at the entrance to any building or to a parking area or another sidewalk." No sign or warning of the step existed. She fell and severely injured her hip. The walkway was terra-cotta (reddish) and was "glaring bright" in the afternoon sun on the day in question. A single white strip 1.5 inches wide had been painted on the top of the step to catch the attention of passersby. However, the white strip was nearly worn off and was barely discernable. The restaurant sought summary judgment claiming the existence of the step was open and obvious and thus should have been visible to the guest. The court refused to grant summary judgment and instead referred to a jury the issue of whether the establishment used reasonable care in protecting its customers.[73]

The jury in this case will likely find the restaurant negligent. To avoid liability in a circumstance with an unexpected step, the facility should consider a number of precautions: painting the different levels of the step different colors; installing a warning sign; or applying a strip of paint of contrasting color at the top of the step, repainting it whenever necessary to avoid fading.

Sidewalks

Often sidewalks and paved areas deteriorate over time. Numerous cases result from guests tripping on depressions in walkways or uneven sidewalk slabs. The law in many states allows some tolerance of such defects, calling small depressions too trivial to give rise to liability. The cases give some guidance on the size of a hole that will and will not result in liability.

A ski-lodge patron fell on a crack in a sundeck pavement that had a depth of one-half inch. The court held this was too trivial a defect to impose liability.[74] In another case, a ramp located at the exit of a restaurant was elevated one-half to three-quarters of an inch above the adjacent surface. A diner tripped on the

---

[73] *Sherman v. Arno*, 383 P.2d 741 (Ariz. 1963)
[74] *Sullivan v. State of New York*, 2000 WL 1598934 (N.Y. 2000)

uneven portion of the ramp and was injured. The court refused to hold the restaurant liable due to the limited elevation.[75] A South Carolina court held that a depression in the sidewalk of one and three-fifths inches violated the building code, but nonetheless was too insignificant to raise an inference of negligence. A lawsuit filed by a woman who fell on the hole while walking to her car from a restaurant where she had just eaten was thus dismissed.[76] Similarly, a plaintiff who fell on a hole in a sidewalk that was one inch deep and six inches wide lost her case. The court held the relatively small size hole did not constitute a breach of the defendant's duty to keep its sidewalk in "reasonably safe condition" or "proper repair."[77]

© Lane V. Erickson/Shutterstock.com

In a case with a somewhat different holding, a plaintiff tripped on an elevation differential in the pavement of an amusement park measuring one-half to one and one-half inches. The court refused to grant summary judgment for the park and instead referred the matter to trial for a jury to decide whether the park should be liable.[78] Similarly, a two-inch difference in elevation between the landing of a concrete staircase and the adjoining walkway was found to preclude summary judgment.[79]

In a similar case, a plaintiff tripped and fell on broken sidewalk, as she was walking past the hotel on a clear, dry day wearing walking shoes in good condition. The location was not on the hotel's property but on a portion of the sidewalk located right in front of the entrance to the hotel's underground parking garage. The appeals court found that a property owner may be held liable for a dangerous condition on portions of a public sidewalk if they had been altered or constructed to serve a purpose for the benefit of the property owner apart from the ordinary use of a sidewalk. Here the sidewalk had been modified to match up exactly with the entrance to the driveway leading to the hotel parking garage, thus benefitting the property. The court also noted that the defect, which measured two and three-fourths by five and one-half inches was not minor nor trivial.[80]

In summary, where a patron falls on a hole in the pavement, the following will determine whether the facility can avoid liability: the size of the hole; the law of the particular state in which the fall occurred; and the presence or lack of other contributing circumstances. An advisable practice for hotels and restaurants is to avoid injury to guests by repairing pavement problems when they first appear. If, however, an accident occurs and a lawsuit is commenced, the facility should measure the depression and consider if a defense of triviality might be availing.

---

[75] *Boyd v. Country Boy Deli Delights*, 2001 WL 753886 (Mich. 2001)
[76] *Desmond v. City of Charlotte*, 544 S.E.2d 269 (N.C. 2001)
[77] *Jackson v. City of Clinton*, 595 S.E.2d 816 (N.C. 2004)
[78] *Schatz v. Herco*, 708 N.Y.S.2d 435 (N.Y. 2000)
[79] *Fasano v. Green-Wood Cemetery*, 799 N.Y.S.2d 827 (N.Y. 2005)
[80] *Mitchelson v. Sunset Marquis Hotel*, 2013 WL 5917644 (Ca. 2013)

Outdoor Ramps and Parking Lots

Other areas of concern on the grounds of a hotel or restaurant include ramps and parking lots. The establishment should inspect these areas regularly. If obstructions such as stones, wood chips, or debris are found, they should be removed immediately. Cracks and holes should be repaired. Other unsafe conditions should be eliminated.

A design defect in a handicap ramp at a hotel resulted in a drop-off of an unspecified size between the end of the ramp and the road. A guest encountered the drop-off and tripped and fell while walking to the parking lot. The court declined to find that the defect was open and obvious and thus refused to dismiss the case on the hotel's motion for summary judgment.[81] Where, however, a guest chose to use a handicapped access ramp to enter an airport because, by her own testimony, she was "lazy" and wished to avoid having to use steps, she was aware of the ramp's incline, rendering it an open and obvious condition. Having failed to establish any defective condition of the ramp, judgment was entered for the airport.[82]

Miscellaneous Outdoor Circumstances

The opportunities for guests to injure themselves at a hotel or restaurant are endless. The innkeeper must always be alert to anticipate possible dangerous conditions and ameliorate them. For example, a Marriott was liable to a guest who fell into a drain inlet located on the hotel's property.[83]

The duty to exercise reasonable care does not extend to unforeseeable risks. For example, in another case the plaintiff was a guest at a Ramada Inn that was undergoing roof repairs. He allegedly became ill when fumes from the tar pot used for the roof wafted into his room via the air conditioning. The contractor performing the remodeling work showed proof that it took appropriate precautions and that no other guest or employee had ever complained of fumes or become ill from the type of work being done. The hotel manager confirmed that no other guest had objected. The court therefore found the injury unforeseeable and entered a verdict for the hotel.[84]

Outdoor Sporting Facilities

Many resorts owe their popularity to outside activities and sports they offer. Are such resorts liable for injuries sustained by a guest while using the sporting facilities? The hotel owes to its guests a duty of reasonable care in the maintenance of all its sporting facilities. Even in states that continue to recognize the doctrine of assumption of risk (see discussion on that doctrine in Chapter 5), a guest does not assume the risk that the resort will fail to maintain the sporting facility in a condition that makes it reasonably safe for the guest. Such failure on the part of the hotel will result in liability.

---

[81] *Anderson v. Turton Development*, 483 S.E.2d 597 (Ga. 1997)
[82] *Poythress v. Savannah Airport Commission*, 494 S.E.2d 76 (Ga. 1997)
[83] *Marriott International, Inc. v. Perez-Melendez*, 855 So.2d 624 (Fla. 2003)
[84] *Spencer v. Red River Lodging*, 865 So.2d 337 (La. 2004)

Some hotels provide facilities for skiing, tennis, golf, working out, or other sports. Injuries and liability can result from infrequent inspection, careless selection of equipment, faulty assembly, or haphazard placement.

Resort hotels often offer bicycles or mopeds for their guests' use. Precautions are necessary. Regular periodic inspections should be done to ensure the bikes are in good working order. They should not be issued to a child unless the child is accompanied by a responsible adult. The bikes should be equipped with horns, reflectors, and, if used at night, lights. Any other equipment mandated by state or local law should also be provided. No more than one person at a time should be permitted to ride a bike unless it is configured for multiple users (e.g., as a tandem or with a sidecar).

Ski Hills

Many skiers are injured while on the slopes, resulting in lawsuits against the ski resorts. Many resorts will require that skiers sign releases of liability and indemnity agreements to protect against such lawsuits. A skier suffered injuries after a snowboard incident and sued the ski area. While the case was pending, and as the spouse of an employee, he applied for a free season pass for the next season. He was presented with a document titled "Release, Warnings and Disclaimers on Skiing" which he signed. It stated he released all claims "from anything which has happened up to now." Based on this release, the court dismissed the case.[85]

Colorado has a state law called the Colorado Ski Safety Act that provides immunity to ski area operators for injuries resulting from collisions between skiers. A 9-year-old skier was injured when a ski instructor allegedly struck and injured the boy. His parents sued for negligence, alleging that the instructor was skiing unreasonably fast, which caused the collision. The court held that the referenced statute covers any skier-skier collisions and so dismissed the case.[86]

© Jan Pala/Shutterstock.com

Jogging Paths

Walking and jogging are popular sports among travelers because they do not require packing a lot of equipment and are good exercise. Many hotels provide information to guests about nearby running/walking paths. Incidents of guests being injured on these trails have resulted in lawsuits against the lodging facility. Generally the inn is not liable when injury is caused by a condition on a footpath that is not on the hotel premises. In one case, a couple was enjoying a walk on a path recommended on a "Jogging, Walking, and Running Map" provided by the hotel concierge. The path was not part of the hotel premises and was maintained by the local government. As they were walking they came upon tall

85 *Dearnley v. Mountain Creek*, 2012 WL 762150 (N.J. 2012)
86 *Johnson v. Vail Summit Resorts*, 835 F.Supp.2d 1092 (Colo. 2011).

bushes and foliage that created an obstacle to their continuing along the route. They observed an apparent continuation of the path on the opposite side of the road and decided to cross. There were no traffic signs or lights at the location. As plaintiff stepped off the sidewalk she was struck by a sports utility vehicle and thrown into the bushes, suffering numerous injuries. She sued the hotel, claiming it should have known about and warned her of the condition of the path. The court denied liability, noting that the inn had no control over the path, and the dangers associated with crossing a public highway are open and obvious.[87]

In a similar case a guest was injured on a fitness trail when he fell on black ice in Maryland in January. The hotel had "absolutely no interest in or control over the portion of the fitness trail where plaintiff fell." The guest alleged that the receptionist at the Marriott where he was staying had stated that the path was "safe," and the trail was advertised in the hotel's promotional brochure. The court dismissed the case, holding that the hotel did not have a duty to inspect or maintain the trail unless it had represented to guests that it would undertake that responsibility, which the Marriott had not done. Further, the brochure which "merely makes guests aware of the nearby fitness trail" is not sufficient to create a duty to provide "up-to-the-minute factual reports on its condition." Said the court, "Advising guests about a fitness trail in the vicinity of the hotel cannot reasonably be interpreted as a representation that Marriott regularly inspected the trail each morning…" Concerning the desk clerk's statement that the path was "safe," the court held that based on that single word, plaintiff could not infer that the employee was assuring him that he need not be concerned about ice on the trail on the day after a cold, wet and windy night.[88]

Tournaments

Resort hotels are becoming a common site for sports competitions such as tennis and golf tournaments and boxing matches. Large and potentially unruly crowds can be anticipated for these events. The facility owes a duty to its patrons to provide the necessary crowd control and security to prevent injury. An unruly crowd at a boxing match at the MGM Grand Hotel in Las Vegas resulted in injury to several spectators and a lawsuit against the hotel.[89]

Lightning

When outdoor activity takes place, there is always a risk of people being struck by lightning. This raises the question of whether the premises operator is liable when injury results. The rule appears to be that there is no duty to warn invitees of the risk of being struck by lightning.[90] However, if the operator assumes the duty of alerting guests, or undertakes action that leads guests to believe a warning will issue if lightning is in the vicinity, a duty exists to act reasonably in providing warnings when warranted. In a case involving a country club, a

---

[87] *Felheimer v. Fairmont Hotels and Resorts, Inc.*, 2004 WL 2278533 (Penn. 2004)
[88] *Fagerhus v. Host Marriott Corp.*, 795 A2d 221 (Md. 2001)
[89] *Castro v. MGM Grand Hotel, Inc.*, 8 S.W.3d 403 (Tex. 1999)
[90] *Seelbinder v. County of Volusia*, 821 So.2d 1095 (Fl. 2002); *Sall v. T.S. Inc.*, 2006 WL 1713207 (Kans. 2006)

golfer was struck by lightning and was seriously and permanently injured. The golf complex had a policy in place to monitor weather and warn players to return to the clubhouse, by sounding an air horn, if dangerous conditions were predicted. Players were alerted to this policy by signage on the course and at the counter in the clubhouse. If the injured golfer can prove his allegations that the manager was negligent in monitoring the weather, resulting in late warning, the complex may be liable. Also, the court stated that if the country club could prove that plaintiff was negligent for not heeding observable weather conditions, the golf club's liability could be reduced by comparative fault.[91]

In another case a 47-year-old plaintiff was struck by lightning as she stood on a beach. The beach was operated by the county which adopted a system using whistles and orange flags to alert swimmers when a storm was approaching. Plaintiff claimed the warning was issued too late. The court disagreed. Said the court, "If any duty to warn exists, it arises from the County's having undertaken to provide warnings of lightning to beachgoers. Having undertaken this responsibility, the County was obliged to exercise reasonable care in so doing... There was no evidence offered that the lifeguards failed to exercise reasonable care in executing the procedure, merely that the procedure failed to protect plaintiff." Judgment thus issued for the county.[92]

Amusement Rides

Midway rides present potential risks that operators must address. The duty owed by the proprietor to patrons of a place of amusement is to use reasonable care to inspect and maintain the rides in a reasonably safe condition. Given that carnival rides attract children, operators must adhere to an exacting vigilance. Liability resulted in a case of a 14-year-old injured on a ride called the Swinger when the operator disregarded manufacturer's warnings by failing to use seatbelts for users and failing to immediately stop the ride when a child exhibited potentially dangerous horseplay.[93] For more on this topic, see Chapter 16.

Outdoor Lighting Requirements

Outdoor lights are an important aid at night to guests seeking to negotiate the parking lot and areas surrounding a hotel or restaurant. The high cost of energy makes it easy to understand why a hotel or restaurant might be tempted to reduce outdoor lighting. Yet even when only a few rooms are rented or business at a restaurant is slow, the inn and eatery plus any area used by patrons must be properly illuminated. An attempt to save a few dollars on lighting can lead to a guest's injury and liability. An example is the case of *Bowling v. Lewis*, 261 F.2d 311 (4th Cir. 1958). The facts were simple. As stated by the court,

> *The... plaintiff, who was vacationing with his wife and two small children at an ocean front motel, arrived on a Sunday afternoon and used*

---

[91] *Sall v. T.S. Inc.*, 2006 WL1713207 (Kans. 2006)
[92] *Seelbinder v. County of Volusia*, 821 So.2d 1095 (Fla. 2002)
[93] *Harvey v. Sons Rides, Inc.*, 2000 WL 862821 (La. 2000)

the walk [between the parking lot and the hotel] several times until the following Tuesday, when he and his family spent the early evening in an amusement area and returned to the motel when it was very dark and the walk was unlighted. The plaintiff had... 18 years' experience driving buses and had very good night vision. He remained in his car with the headlights on to illuminate the walk for his wife and children, and when they had reached the room, he turned off the headlights, waited momentarily to give his eyes an opportunity to adjust to the dark, and proceeded very cautiously along the walk but, nevertheless, tripped over a 10-inch stone in the walk.

Was the guest contributorily negligent by going to his room in the dark? The court ruled that:

A guest or lodger is deemed guilty of contributory negligence in using a dark or unlighted stairway or in using a dark or unlighted passageway, in instances where lighted stairways, or the means of providing light, are available to him. On the other hand... a guest cannot be charged with contributory negligence or assumption of risk merely because he uses a darkened stairway where the elevator is out of commission and the stairway is the only means available for passing between the room and the ground floor, or where, on instructions from an employee, he uses an insufficiently lighted hallway, but exercises care...

The plaintiff in this case was not negligent. He was using the only available means of ingress to his room. There was no one present from whom he could have requested help. He was familiar with the concrete walkway and knew its location; he and his family had used it as a means of ingress and egress several times since their arrival. He had good night vision. His wife and the children had safely proceeded along this walkway immediately before the accident. The plaintiff thus had good reason to believe that he could safely negotiate it.

Outdoor light fixtures should be inspected daily. If they are not in good working order, they should be repaired without delay.

Many facilities use electronic timers that control exterior lighting. These must be reset when daylight savings time begins and ends. If clocks are not adjusted immediately, the timing of the lights will be off by an hour and guests may not have adequate light.

Duties Owed to Guests in Swimming Areas

Countless Americans enjoy swimming, and many hotels and motels offer pools or beach areas. A swimming pool presents hoteliers with a difficult dilemma. It helps to attract business but it has high maintenance, energy, and labor costs and it exposes the hotel to another area of potential liability. Many states regulate swimming pools extensively. These requirements relate to lifeguards, required safety equipment, chemicals used for sanitation, and maintenance of the pool. Failure to abide by these laws can result in liability for pool accidents based on negligence per se. Likewise, negligence in tending to a pool or waterfront area can lead to liability. Swimming pool accidents can be caused by wet floors, unsafe diving boards, inadequate safety equipment, horseplay, inadequate supervision, or any of a variety of other factors.

Exercise Reasonable Care

Consistent with general principles of negligence, a hotel is not an insurer of guests' safety in and around a hotel pool. The hotel is only liable if it fails to exercise reasonable care. A 10-year-old girl drowned while playing in a pool with her siblings. The shallow area was roped off, but children jumped into the deep end and scurried back to the shallow area several times while playing. The deceased had been left by her father for roughly five minutes when the accident occurred. The trained lifeguard on duty did everything in his power to affect her rescue. All necessary and required safety devices for swimmers were on hand. Given these facts, the girl's parents were unable to prove that the defendant was negligent.[94] The operator of a pool must keep it in a safe condition, have safety equipment available, and, depending on the circumstances and state or local law, have qualified personnel on hand; the defendant did all of this.

An example of a facility ignoring pool safety precautions is provided in Case Example 6-13. As it illustrates, disregard of basic safety requirements can result in serious injury or death to a guest and liability to the hospitality facility.

POOL RULES

WARNING NO LIFEGUARD OR ATTENDANT IS ON DUTY

- SWIM AT YOUR OWN RISK!
- PROPER SWIMWEAR REQUIRED
- A SHOWER MUST BE TAKEN BEFORE ENTERING THE POOL.
- EXCESS BODY LOTION SHOULD BE REMOVED PRIOR TO ENTERING THE POOL.
- POOL NOT TO EXCEED____PEOPLE.
- SWIMMING ALONE IS PROHIBITED.
- CHILDREN UNDER ____ MUST BE ACCOMPANIED BY AN ADULT.
- NO GLASS CONTAINERS ALLOWED IN THE POOL AREA.
- NO FOOD OR ALCOHOLIC BEVERAGES IN THE POOL AREA.
- NO ANIMALS ALLOWED IN POOL OR ON POOL DECK.
- NO DIVING OR JUMPING IS ALLOWED
- NO HORSEPLAY.
- ALL "CUT-OFFS" SHOULD BE HEMMED.
- RUNNING & ROUGH PLAY ARE PROHIBITED IN AND AROUND THE POOL AREA.
- PERSONS WITH OPEN WOUNDS, BANDAGES, OR ANY SYMPTOM OF A COMMUNICABLE DISEASE SHALL BE PREVENTED FROM ENTERING THE POOL.
- MANAGEMENT RESERVES THE RIGHT TO DENY USE OF POOL TO ANYONE AT ANY TIME.

IN CASE OF EMERGENCY CALL 911

POOL HOURS____TO____

© TyBy/Shutterstock.com

CASE EXAMPLE 6-13

Turner v. Holiday Inn Holidome

721 So.2d 64 (La. 1999)

Krystal Turner was the 12-year-old daughter of Ms. Eliza Turner. Chosen to be a member of the Jefferson Parish Recreation Department's All-Star girl's basketball team, Krystal was taken to the Holidome in Houma [Louisiana] to participate in a basketball tournament. While there she went swimming in the Holidome's pool and drowned… .

---

94 *McKeever v. Phoenix Jewish Community Center,* 374 P.2d 875 (Ariz. 1962)

At check-in at the Holidome, Frey [the team's coach] was not informed of any rules or regulations regarding the children's use of the swimming pool. After the tournament game on Saturday, which finished at 7:00 p.m., the group went to eat. They finished at around 8:30 p.m., arriving back at the hotel at around 9:00 p.m. The pool closed at 10:00 p.m. Most of the kids went in the pool. There were a lot of people in the pool at that time, somewhere between 30 and 50... .

Frey first realized there was a problem when someone yelled for him; he turned and saw Krystal in the arms of another player. Someone began to administer CPR; Frey ran to call 911....

There was no lifeguard at the pool, nor were there any buoys or lifelines... .

Holidome has had biddy (youth) basketball teams come to stay for several years, and the manager knew there would be children using the pool. He knew there would be eight or nine groups of children from southeastern Louisiana on that particular weekend. Holidome had no regulation as to the number of people who could use the pool at one time. The manager knew that the pool rope, or life line at the deep end [which separates the shallow and deep sections of the pool and alerts swimmers that the depth is changing] had broken, but he could not remember when it happened. He knew that the pool became cloudy when subjected to heavy use, and if employees could not see the bottom, they were instructed to close the pool. Safety devices included a "shepherd's hook" (a long pole with a hook on the end), and a life ring located on the wall adjacent to the pool. A security guard employed on the night of the accident testified that there were forty or fifty children in the pool on that night and about one hundred people around the decking, at the tables, etc. There were problems with some children running and diving. The pool water started to get cloudy, and he could not quite see the bottom of the pool. There were no life lines in the pool. Both of the security guards on duty and the manager were called to different parts of the hotel for different reasons; when he returned to the pool area, the accident had taken place... .

Mr. Doky, the brother of one of the team players, testified that he swam to retrieve a ball and when walking back he stepped on something and assumed it was a toy. He looked down to see what it was but could not see to the bottom. A few seconds later, he again went to get the ball, at which time he decided to see what was in the water. At that time he found Krystal's body. This was at about six-foot depth level. He swam back to the top of the pool and because it was so loud, he had to scream a few times to get the attention of the coaches. He went back under and brought the body up, pushing her to the side of the pool... .

[Krystal's mother sued the Holidome for negligence.]

We find that Holidome acted unreasonably by maintaining its pool in an unsafe manner. The testimony establishes that Holidome never employed a lifeguard. The management of the hotel knew that a number of teams of children ages 10–12 would be staying that weekend for the tournament, and had the authority to request a temporary lifeguard, yet failed to do so. Furthermore, there was no one with water safety training assigned to monitor the safety and security of the swimmers. Management was aware from previous experience that these young guests usually use the pool area. There [were] no rules relative to pool capacity, and the pool was, by all accounts, very crowded in the evening. The surrounding area was also extremely crowded and very noisy, making it unlikely that a swimmer in distress would be readily observed. The pool had no safety rope or lifeline at the deep end of the pool, and the rope had been missing for some time. Depth markers inside the pool did not display the pool depth at seven and one-half feet, the deck marker of that depth [located on the markers, the pool] was difficult to see from inside in the pool, these markers and safety ropes Holidome had a Louisiana Sanitary Code.

Testimony also established that the water in the pool was cloudy by the time Krystal drowned, to the extent that the bottom of the pool was obscured. The effect of this is obvious because when Mr. Doby touched Krystal's body with his foot, he did not know that he stepped on the body of a child, perhaps at that point still viable [able to be resuscitated], but thought he had touched a toy. No one could see Krystal at the bottom of the pool… The whole purpose of maintaining clear water, providing a lifeguard, guarding against overcrowding, providing a safety rope and depth is to insure that there are not accidents, specifically drownings. In summary, Holidome had a duty to act in a reasonable manner, which duty is breached.

CASE QUESTIONS

1. What should the hotel have done to avoid the problems that led to liability?

2. Was the hotel liable for negligence per se? Why or why not?

The lesson from this case is that a hotel needs to monitor carefully the use of its swimming pool to ensure safety precautions are taken. If the hotel can anticipate high use of the pool, sufficient lifeguards are important. Rules concerning maximum capacity should be developed and honored. A rule should be adopted and followed requiring closing the pool when the water's clarity is compromised. Safety devices, such as the presence of a rope delineating the shallow and deep ends, should be evident and in good working order whenever the pool is being used.

In another drowning case, the plaintiff sought to establish the hotel's negligence by the fact that no lifeguard was on duty at the time of the accident. Signs were prominently posted around the pool warning swimmers of the absence of a lifeguard. A friend who had been swimming with the deceased had seen the signs and was aware no lifeguard was on duty. The applicable law did not require a lifeguard for a pool the size of the hotel's. Rescue equipment was provided poolside. The court held that, in these circumstances, the absence of a lifeguard was obvious and apparent to the deceased and thus the hotel was not liable.[95]

In the following drowning case, a hotel was sued for negligence where an emergency exit door leading to and from the pool was propped open, enabling a youngster to enter the pool area unattended. An issue in the case was proximate cause.

---

[95] *Kemp v. Charter House Inn*, 2000 WL 23180 (Ohio 2000)

CASE EXAMPLE 6-14

Audi v. Rest-All-Inn

2015 WL 7889928 (Mich. 2015)

This case arises from 32-month-old Karim Audi's drowning in the indoor enclosed swimming pool at defendant Rest-All-Inn of Oscoda, Michigan, during a weekend get-together involving approximately 35 relatives of Karim's mother, Laura. At approximately 6:00 p.m. that day, plaintiff and family members gathered and prepared food in the recreation area just outside the pool area. The hotel's surveillance video showed that Karim entered the pool area several times after 6:00 p.m. through an emergency exit door that had been propped open with a cement block. . . . Laura's cousin, Zeina Bazzi, was inside the pool area at the shallow end of the pool watching another child. Karim interacted with Zeina before he went to play with other children on the pool steps in the shallow end of the pool. Karim played on the steps for several minutes before he entered the water. Shortly after he entered the water, Karim became submerged and did not resurface. Approximately five to eight seconds after Karim went under the water, Laura entered the pool area looking for Karim. Laura briefly stood at the side of the pool before leaving the pool area and yelling to her husband that she could not find Karim. Plaintiff and a number of others then entered the pool area in search of Karim. A relative, Hayssam Bazzi, pulled Karim from the shallow end of the pool approximately three minutes after he went under the water. Hayssam performed CPR on Karim until first responders arrived. However, Karim died six days later.

Karim's father commenced this wrongful death suit alleging ordinary negligence, premises liability, and nuisance.

Plaintiff alleges that Karim was able to enter the pool area because defendant allowed an emergency exit door leading from the pool area to the outside recreation area to be propped open with a concrete block. That Karim's rescue was hindered because defendant allowed the pool water to come cloudy and that both actions violated Michigan's statutes, rules, and regulations. Plaintiff further alleged that defendant's breach of its duties was a proximate cause of Karim's injuries.

Defendant moved for summary disposition. The trial court granted the motion with respect to plaintiff's nuisance and premises liability claims, and denied the motion on the negligence claim, meaning plaintiff and the case proceeded to a jury trial. The trial court instructed the jury on the elements of negligence and provided the following instruction with respect to defendant's duty as a business: It was the duty of defendant in connection with this occurrence to use ordinary care for the safety of the plaintiff. The law recognizes that children act upon childish instincts and impulses. If you find the defendant knew or should have known that a child or children were or were likely to be in the vicinity, then the defendant is required to exercise greater vigilance, and this is a circumstance to be considered by you in determining whether reasonable care was used by the defendant.

The jury found that defendant was negligent, but that the negligence was not a proximate cause of Karim's death. The trial court entered a judgment in favor of defendant and plaintiff appeals . . .

Boiled down to its essence, plaintiff alleged that defendant failed to abate the conditions that allegedly caused Karim's death. Plaintiff alleged that defendant allowed the condition of the pool water to become cloudy and murky at the time that Karim's family was using the pool, and allowed the door to remain propped open. . . . and that defendant's staff failed to properly monitor the security cameras at the front desk. Plaintiff alleged that defendant had a duty to adequately monitor the pool area and the service door, and that defendant undertook to monitor the areas with three security cameras and a live feed to the front desk, yet failed to adequately monitor the areas when it allowed the door to remain propped open and allowed the pool to be used even though it was not in compliance [with regulations relating to clarity of pool water]. Plaintiff alleged that defendant's failure to abate these conditions in a timely manner was a proximate cause of Karim's death. Thus, the injury was alleged to have occurred because of defendant's negligence. . .

While the jury found defendant negligent, it also found that the defendant's negligence was not the proximate cause of the minor's death. . . .. [the jury's verdict in favor of defendant hotel is] affirmed.

CASE QUESTION

1. What do you think the jury determined was the proximate cause of the child's drowning?

Remove Hazards

A hotel may be liable for leaving maintenance equipment in the vicinity of the pool. In one case pool cleaning equipment, including large, heavy floats, were stored beside the pool. The evidence showed that the floats were sometimes used as playthings in the pool. The 11-year-old plaintiff-guest went swimming upon her arrival at the motel. When surfacing from a dive, she hit one of the floats and was injured. In her lawsuit against the hotel the court held for the plaintiff. The motel was negligent for failing to move the cleaning equipment to a place where it would not be easily accessible to swimmers.[96]

Comply with Statutory Requirements

Failure to comply with safety requirements imposed by statutes on pool operators can result in liability under the doctrine of negligence per se.

Diving Boards

Local governments often issue regulations applicable to pool diving boards. Failure to comply with these laws can lead to terrible consequences for both a patron

---

[96] *Tucker v. Dixon*, 355 P.2d 79 (Colo. 1960)

who is injured and for the hotel. In one case, a hotel installed a high-performance aluminum "Duraflex" board. This type of diving board propels divers a significant distance farther forward than other materials. The plaintiff, a hotel guest, used the board, was catapulted into the shallow area, and struck his head on the bottom of the pool. As a result of his injuries he was rendered quadriplegic. The court held the hotel liable based on negligence in selecting the diving board.[97]

An additional risk associated with diving boards and also pool slides is that the divers or sliders will collide with a swimmer in the pool when they hit the water. People injured in this way often sue the hotel, claiming negligent supervision of the guests using the pool.[98]

To avoid risks associated with diving boards and pool slides, many hotels have eliminated them.

Pool ladders, if not properly maintained, can also result in liability. A plaintiff who was injured while entering a pool using a ladder claimed the second rung was loose and wobbly, causing him to lose his balance and fall. The hotel's chief engineer testified that the ladder was not defective and the rung was not loose. The judge held for the hotel, but had the ladder in fact been problematic or had the trier of fact believed the plaintiff and not the engineer, the hotel would have been liable.[99]

Maintain Safety Equipment

Hotels with pools must maintain necessary safety equipment to permit rescue of a swimmer experiencing difficulty in remaining afloat. A hotel was found liable for a guest's drowning where it provided a straight pole, but not one with a hook at the end that is used to help raise a submerged swimmer to the surface. The plaintiff, a swimmer at a hotel pool, sank to the bottom. A rescuer, using the available pole that had no hook, was unable to lift the submerged swimmer from the water. Instead, the rescuer was limited to the slower process of pushing the victim to the shallow area. The swimmer was dead by the time the rescue was completed. A city ordinance required that all pools be equipped with a hooked pole. The hotel was found liable based on negligence per se.[100]

To avoid liability for this type of negligence, a business must carefully study applicable laws and regulations and do what is necessary to comply. If a hotel or restaurant is uncertain as to the meaning of a statute, clarification should be sought from an appropriate source such as the director of the governmental department responsible for enforcing the particular law or the hotel's attorney.

Additional safety equipment, such as a rescue tube (a flotation device that can support the weight of both the swimmer and the rescuer), is mandated for hotel

---

[97] *Hooks v. Washington Sheraton Corporation*, 578 F.2d 313 (D.C. 1977)
[98] *Casey v. Treasure Island Corporation*, 745 A.2d 743 (R.I. 2000)
[99] *Thomas v. Wyndham Hotel*, 2003 WL 21040288 (Ohio 2003)
[100] *Harris v. Laquinta-Redbird Venture*, 522 S.W.2d 232 (Tex. 1975)

pools in some states. Absence of the tube can result in liability. The same is true for rescue-breathing face shields or masks, which are used to perform CPR safely on victims who are aspirating blood.[101]

Control Boisterous Conduct of Guests

When boisterous conduct and horseplay are allowed in a pool area, accidents may occur. For example, a plaintiff, while swimming face-down in the defendant hotel's pool, was hit when another swimmer was thrown into the pool by a group of rowdy boys and landed on her. The hotel denied liability. The court ruled that the defendant, as an operator of a swimming pool, owed its invitees the duty to use reasonable care to eliminate unsafe conditions including halting horseplay in the pool.[102] If disorderly conduct was allowed to occur, the hotel could be liable to an injured guest for failing to stop the unruly behavior. If, however, prior to the accident, no one in the pool was acting disorderly, the hotel will not be liable. In another case a 12-year-old youth fell backward off the ladder leading to the diving board at a country club and was injured. He claimed that other children were clamoring up the ladder while he was ascending it, causing the fall. Three lifeguards were on duty and none had observed any horseplay. The court noted that the cause of the fall was as likely to be that the plaintiff lost his foothold as that supervision was lax. Therefore, the plaintiff failed to prove a breach of duty on the part of the club and the court held for the defendant.[103]

Inspect for Glass in Pool Area

Glass and other debris in swimming and wading areas pose a significant risk to pool users. If someone's foot is cut on a piece of glass at the bottom of a hotel wading pool, the hotel may or may not be liable. If the glass was dropped or placed in the pool just prior to the injury, it likely would not have been detected nor could its presence have been prevented in the exercise of ordinary care. In such a circumstance, the hotel would not be liable. However, if the plaintiff can prove the glass had been in the pool for a while, the hotel will have breached its duty to inspect the property at reasonable intervals and remove hazards.

Guard Against Additional Pool Hazards

A swimming pool requires significant vigilance on the part of the innkeeper. Additional hazards include excessive chlorine, which can lead to chlorine poisoning, and poor ventilation in the pool area, which can cause an unsafe concentration of chlorine in the air.[104]

---

101 *Glaubius v. YMCA of Norfolk*, 2003 WL 22175706 (Nebr.2003)
102 *Gordon v. Hotel Seville, Inc.*, 105 So.2d 175 (Fl. 1958)
103 *Cohen v. Suburban Sidney-Hill, Inc.*, 178 N.E.2d 19 (Mass. 1961)
104 *Lawson v. Edgewater Hotels, Inc.*, 167 S.W.3d 816 (Tenn. 2005)

Many hotels are adjacent to public beaches. These bodies of water present numerous potential dangers that can and do cause injury and death. The risks include heavy surf, riptides, underwater tows, and man-eating animals. In the cases that result from such deaths or injuries, the plaintiffs argue that the hotel breached a duty to warn of risks and to protect guests from them. Most cases hold that hotels, which neither own nor control the ocean, have no duty to warn, correct, or safeguard guests from naturally occurring dangers common to waters, even if those dangers are hidden.

A hotel guest drowned when caught in a riptide in the ocean off a public beach adjacent to the hotel. A second guest attempted to rescue the swimmer and also drowned. The survivors of both guests sued the hotel and the case was dismissed. The court held that the hotel did not owe the guests a duty to warn of the riptide or to protect them from it.[105]

In a similar case a hotel, physically separated from a public beach only by a four-lane highway, marketed its proximity to the beach and encouraged guests to use the waterfront. The hotel provided beach chairs, umbrellas, towels, and a security escort service. The hotel also furnished guests with pamphlets warning about sun exposure and crime on the beach. A guest drowned in a riptide while swimming there. His survivors sued, claiming that the hotel had a duty to disclose dangerous surf conditions. The court dismissed the complaint, holding that an innkeeper owes no duty to a guest injured or endangered while away from the premises. Providing beach accessories and warning of some risks did not create a duty to warn against hazards of the sea. The court noted, "[I]t may well have been good practice [to provide warnings] but it was not required."[106]

Given that a goal of hospitality facilities is not just to avoid liability, but also to protect guests' well-being and provide a fun, healthy getaway, a hotel near a beach should keep apprised of related risks and alert their patrons to danger.

A minority of states require a hotel to warn of risks at off-premises facilities that the innkeeper reasonably can foresee that guests will visit. A guest suffered a paralyzing injury while swimming in an ocean near his hotel. The injury ultimately caused his death. The court held the hotel could be liable if it could anticipate that the guest would visit the beach and it failed to warn of known risks. Proof that the hotel could have anticipated the guest's beach visit was facilitated at trial by a brochure issued by the hotel touting its location "overlooking the golden sands of Kamaole Beach Park."[107]

In another case, an Aruban resort located next to a public beach advertised its proximity to the beach as an enticement to potential guests. The hotel's promotional materials included pictures and descriptions of lounge chairs and tiki huts along with an invitation to enjoy water sports activities conveniently provided on

---

[105] *Poleyeff v. Seville Beach Hotel*, 782 So.2d 422 (Fla. 2001)
[106] *Darby v. Meridien Hotels, Inc.*, 2001 WL 630158 (N.Y. 2001)
[107] *Rygg v. County of Maui*, 98 F.Supp.2d 1129 (Hawaii 1999)

the premises by Unique Sports. The resort rented space to Unique Sports, which offered snorkeling and scuba diving trips. Plaintiff was a guest at the hotel and went to the beach for the day. She was provided with a lounge chair by a hotel employee, who placed the chair under a tiki hut close to the water. While the guest was asleep in her chair she was struck by a pickup truck and boat trailer operated by an employee of Unique Sports, who was transporting its boats to the water. The company's trucks and trailers traveled along the beach. No barricades or other devices separated the tiki huts from the line of travel. Unique Sports did not notify beachgoers of its vehicles' presence, route, or schedule. Plaintiff had no warning that vehicles would be approaching. The court held that the hotel created a foreseeable risk by placing tiki huts and guest chairs on the beach close to where Unique Sports drove its vehicles. The hotel thus owed plaintiff a duty of reasonable care, which it breached by failing to separate vehicular traffic from lounging guests.[108]

In another case plaintiff, a retired high school teacher, was a guest at a campground in a national park. He went bodysurfing in a swimming area in the park. A forceful, shore-breaking wave drove him headfirst into the sand, causing him to break his neck and rendering him a quadriplegic. He sued the campground, claiming it had breached its innkeeper's duty to reasonably protect guests from harm. The facts established that the defendant had a contract with the National Park Service (NPS) authorizing defendant to operate the campground only. The agreement gave defendant no control over the swimming area, access to the beach, or the beach itself. These were maintained by the NPS. Given these circumstances, the court held the campground did not owe plaintiff a duty to warn of the dangers of shore-breaking waves.[109]

Waterfront Risks Created by a Hotel

If a hotel with waterfront property erects an entertainment facility for guests utilizing the water, it must warn of any related risks and prohibit inappropriate use. In Case Example 6-15, failure to warn resulted in liability.

CASE EXAMPLE 6-15

Mihill v. Ger-Am Inc.

651 N.Y.S.2d 746 (N.Y. 1997)

Plaintiff Michael Mihill (hereinafter plaintiff) and his parents seek to recover for serious injuries sustained by plaintiff when he jumped or fell into Mirror Lake from a swing located on defendant's property. The swings were on the shore of the lake, approximately three to six feet from the water's

---

108 *Lienhart v. Caribbean Hospitality Services, Inc.*, 426 F.3d 1337 (Fla. 2005)
109 *Fabend v. Rosewood Hotels*, 181 F.Supp.2d 439 (V.I. 2002)

edge, and were intended for use by patrons of defendant's hotel. According to defendant's president, the swings were posted with a sign stating, "Do not jump from swings." [The existence of the signs was disputed by several other witnesses.] Despite the claims of defendant's president and night manager that they did not tolerate such activities, there is evidence in the record that neighborhood children used the swings to jump into the lake on a fairly regular basis. Although the water was shallow close to the shore, there was evidently a sharp drop-off 10 to 15 feet out, such that if one swung high enough before jumping, he or she would arc past the shallow area and land safely in the deeper water.

On the evening of the accident, plaintiff, then age 17, and his friend, Chad Flyte, were… on the hotel premises for the purpose of swimming in the lake. Flyte had successfully jumped from the swing into the lake, and plaintiff, who had never swum in that area before and was unaware of the depth of the water or the contour of the lake bed, had begun to swing with the same end in mind. Whether he actually jumped or—as he avers—"chickened out", and was slowing the swing to dismount when his foot caught on the ground, causing him to "flop off" the swing and into the water, is the subject of conflicting deposition testimony. Unfortunately, he apparently entered the water head first, and suffered several injuries rendering him a quadriplegic.

…Given that a dispute existed as to the presence of warning signs near the swings, and the testimony that defendants tolerated children on the swings despite the known danger, defendant's motion for summary judgment is denied.

CASE QUESTION

1.   What should the hotel have done to avoid liability in this case?

Restrict Use or Warn of Water Sports Equipment

Another potential danger for swimmers is errant surfboards and other sporting equipment that get separated from their owners. In one case a hotel provided surfboards for its guests. One swimmer who had completed his ocean dip and was about to leave the water was hit in the face with one of the hotel surfboards. The court determined that the inn acted negligently by failing to either restrict the area in which surfboards were allowed or warn bathers of the possibility of stray flotation devices.[110]

Inspect Lake Bottoms for Hazards

If a hotel invites its guests to swim in a natural body of water, the inn's duty of reasonable care requires it to inspect the bottom for dangerous objects and, if any are

---

[110] *Landrum Mills Hotel Corp. v. Ferhatovic* 317 F.2d 76 (P.R. 1963)

found, remove them. The facility should also prevent the cause of the dangerous objects—such as boats—from using the swimming area.

In a case presented in full in Chapter 5, the plaintiff, an experienced diver, dove off a pier at the defendant's lake resort. The plaintiff had dived there many times before. On the day in question he hit a jagged piece of concrete and suffered serious injuries to his scalp and vertebrae. The area was regularly used by both swimmers and boaters. The concrete obstruction was recovered, and it resembled a boat anchor. The defendant never inspected the lake bottom for debris, never raked the bottom, did not erect a warning sign to swimmers, and did nothing to discourage boaters from entering the swimming area. The jury found these omissions to be negligent.[111]

Access to the Water

A hotel with waterfront property may provide a walkway, bridge, or boardwalk between the hotel and the beach. The duty of care owed to guests includes maintaining any such walkway in a reasonably safe condition. A steel catwalk leading from the shore to a marina collapsed without warning. Liability could result if the breakdown was due to shoddy construction or maintenance.[112]

Special Duties

A hotel or restaurant's duty to exercise reasonable care to provide for guests' safety applies in the important circumstances of fire, security, and medical treatment.

Injuries Caused by Fire

Fires present very serious risks to hotels and their guests. Liability can result from inadequate fire safety equipment, delays in notifying the fire department and guests about a fire, and failing to train employees on the protocols to follow in the event of a fire.

Innkeepers' concern about fire is heightened as a result of three substantial fires in large hotels in the 1980s that led to many deaths and injuries, much property damage, and many lawsuits. In 1981, fire broke out in the MGM Grand Hotel in Las Vegas, Nevada. Eighty-four people died, almost 700 were injured, and approximately 900 lawsuits were brought against the hotel. Many of the cases were settled for considerable sums of money. In 1982, a fire occurred in the Stouffer's Inn in White Plains, New York, killing 26 people. The DuPont Plaza Hotel in San Juan, Puerto Rico was the site of a fire in 1986, killing 98 and injuring 140. The death toll was due in part to locked exits, obstructed passageways, and inaccessible fire alarms—all of which bespeak negligence.

---

[111] *Montes v. Betcher*, 480 F.2d 1128 (Minn. 1973)
[112] *Howell v. Buck Creek State Park*, 2001 WL 710113 (Ohio 2001)

Maintain Fire Safety Equipment

Most states and many localities have passed statutes and building codes listing equipment that all hotels and restaurants are required to have for fire protection.

Failure to provide the mandated equipment constitutes negligence per se, resulting in automatic liability. Required apparatus include fire extinguishers, sprinkler systems, smoke detectors, fire alarms, smoke and fire dampers, voice-communication systems in guest rooms and other public rooms, exit illumination, posted maps showing exit routes in case of fire, emergency lighting, evacuation plans, employee training, and fire escapes. To accommodate guests who are hearing impaired, alarm systems should include a visual component. Failure to provide required fire safety devices can lead to liability.

In a Kentucky case, a hotel guest died when the hotel was destroyed by fire. The deceased's survivors charged that the defendant innkeeper negligently failed to provide the hotel with either an iron stairway as a fire escape on the outside of the building or fire-fighting equipment, although both were required by statute. The court held for the survivors, stating that it is a firmly fixed rule that a person injured by a violation of a safety statute may recover from a defendant for any damages sustained based on negligence per se.[113]

Remember, compliance with statutory safety requirements does not guarantee freedom from liability. Rather, these laws set only the minimum standards for fire safety. Innkeepers should view the safety codes as only a starting point and work up from there. For example, since the fire at the MGM Grand in Nevada, the hotel has installed many fire safety devices not required by law, including a computerized alarm system and monitoring mechanisms. Despite significant cost for these initiatives, the potential loss from fire renders the cost a worthwhile investment. In addition to liability concerns, another reason exists to comply with fire-safety laws. Many states permit an official, often called a *fire marshal*, to inspect premises for violations. If warranted, the marshal is typically authorized to direct that certain remedial action be taken, such as installation of an automatic sprinkler system. If the hotel thereafter fails to act, the marshal can obtain an injunction (a court order) requiring the innkeeper to make the repairs.[114]

Train Staff on How to Respond to a Fire

When a hotel fire breaks out, the hotel has a continuing duty to exercise reasonable care to protect the safety of its guests. A hotel was found negligent where the night clerk, upon learning of a fire in the hotel, first went to the second floor to look for the fire and only after finding it called the fire department. He then returned to the lobby and attempted to turn on the fire alarm, but discovered that it did not work. Further, he testified he had not been instructed on how to use the alarm. An occupant of one of the rooms died in the fire. His estate sued the

---

113 *Pirtle's Administratrix v. Hargis Bank and Trust Co.*, 44 S.W.2d 541 (Ky. 1931)
114 *Crazy Water Retirement Hotel v. State of Texas*, 2001 WL 799946 (Tex. 2001)

hotel and won. The hotel was negligent for failing to notify the fire department immediately, failing to properly maintain the alarm, and failing to train the night clerk on how to use it.[115]

In another case where an employee failed to respond properly, the night clerk, upon learning of a fire, properly called the fire department first. However, rather than notifying guests, he then went outside to remove his truck from in front of the hotel. The family of a guest who died in the fire sued the hotel based on a statement in the death certificate which reported that the guest had survived for 10 minutes after the fire began. The jury found for the plaintiff and the verdict was upheld on appeal.[116]

Liability to Adjacent Premises

Once a fire starts, it is likely to spread if not contained. Neighboring properties are at risk. If the business where the fire originated was negligent in causing the blaze, that business may be liable to the owner of an abutting property that is damaged by the fire. A court determined that a hairdresser was negligent in causing a fire at her salon. The fire caused significant water, smoke, and fire damage to adjoining businesses, including a nearby restaurant. The salon was liable to the damaged businesses.[117]

In a similar case, a fire began in the defendant hotel and grew quickly. Hotel patrons attempted to extinguish the blaze, but were unable to do so because of "faulty and nonserviceable fire extinguishers." The fire spread to the plaintiff's saloon located next door. As a result of damage the plaintiff was unable to operate the business for seven months and incurred loss of revenue. The court, refusing to grant the hotel's motion for summary judgment, said, "It is foreseeable that, in a hotel where there are inadequate or inoperative smoke detectors and fire extinguishers, a fire could move unchecked throughout the structure to the point where it would spread to buildings immediately adjacent to it."[118]

No Liability to Firefighters—Firefighter's Rule

Firefighting is a dangerous undertaking. Unfortunately, firefighters are sometimes injured when responding to a fire call. A doctrine called the *fireman's rule* prevents firefighters from recovering tort damages for acting in their official duty even if the fire was caused by the negligence of a hotel or restaurant. The explanation for the rule is, "[The firefighters] are likely to enter at unforeseeable times, upon unusual parts of the premises, and under circumstances of emergency, where care in preparing for the visit cannot be expected and a duty to make the premises reasonably safe for them at all times would constitute a severe burden."[119]

---

115 *Parker v. Kirkwood*, 8 P.2d 340 (Kans. 1932)
116 *Burrows v. Knots*, 482 S.W.2d 358 (Tex. 1972)
117 *Deardorff Associates, Inc. v. Brown*, 2000 WL 1211078 (Del. 2000); aff'd, 781 A.2d 692 (Del. 2001).
118 *Bartelli v. O'Brien*, 718 N.E.2d 344 (Ill. 1999)
119 *Hart v. Shastri Narayan Swaroop, Inc.*, 870 A.2d 157 (Md. 2005)

Fires and Criminal Liability

Fires have the potential of causing a lot of injury and damage quickly. As a result, facilities have a duty to act reasonably in minimizing this risk. To encourage innkeepers and restaurants to take necessary precautions, the law sometimes imposes criminal liability where the hotel was reckless in its disregard of the possibility of fire. A tragic example of this occurred in 2003 at the Station nightclub in Rhode Island. One hundred people died in nightclub fire. The soundproofing foam behind the stage was flammable, a violation of the local building code. The tour manager of the band playing that night set off pyrotechnics (fireworks) that ignited the soundproofing material and started an uncontrollable fire. A stampede ensued, causing a bottleneck at the exits which resulted in the deaths and many more injuries. An investigation revealed that, had a sprinkler system been installed, it would have successfully contained the fire. Although a building code provision required that there be a sprinkler system, the nightclub was exempt because the club had been built before the regulation was enacted. The owners of the nightclub and the band's tour manager were charged with 100 counts of involuntary manslaughter. All three pled guilty and were sentenced to jail.

The lesson of this case is safety is paramount. As noted elsewhere in this chapter, compliance with laws is only the starting point of the precautions hotels and restaurants should take to avoid injuries to guests. Building codes are adopted for a reason—the safety of the public. They must be strictly complied with; deviation is not acceptable. Additional precautions are encouraged.

A house rule barring use of candles in hotel rooms may be in order. In a case with an unusual twist on the issue of liability, a guest was found guilty of the crime of Reckless burning first degree where she lit a candle in her hotel room, left for 20 minutes, and returned to find a rapidly spreading fire. The hotel suffered substantial damage. The judge ordered the guest to pay restitution to the facility in the amount of $1,355,266.97![120]

Security

Appropriately, a significant concern of hoteliers, restaurateurs, and travelers today is security. An examination of the various cases and media accounts dealing with attacks, robberies, and rapes of guests in hotel rooms or on restaurant premises justifies this concern. Personal injury, loss of life, and loss of property suffered as the result of criminal activity has cost the hospitality industry many millions of dollars in damage payments.

---

[120] *State v. Lohr*, 125 F.3d 977(Mich. 2006)

How much security does a hotel, motel, or restaurant owe to guests in the buildings or on the grounds? Said one court, "Security is a significant monetary expense for any business and further increases the cost of doing business in high crime areas that are already economically depressed. Moreover, businesses are generally not responsible for the endemic crime that plagues our communities, a societal problem that even our law enforcement and other government agencies have been unable to solve. At the same time, business owners are in the best position to appreciate the crime risks that are posed on their premises and to take reasonable precautions to counteract those risks."[121]

So what is a hospitality facility's responsibility to protect the safety of its patrons? Any business that invites the public onto its premises must take reasonable steps to guard against risk of assaultive behavior. Nevertheless, this duty does not extend to unforeseeable or unexpected criminal acts by third persons. Thus, a business with reason to anticipate the occurrence of a criminal act has a duty to protect patrons. A business will be charged with knowing criminal activity will occur where, prior to the criminal act, the perpetrator was abusive or disorderly, or where there existed a pattern of prior criminal activity that made similar or related conduct foreseeable. Thus, foreseeability is an important element in determining whether a hospitality defendant has a duty to protect patrons from criminal acts of third parties.

Foreseeability of Criminal Activity

Under what circumstances is criminal activity reasonably foreseeable, thereby creating a duty on the part of the restaurant or hotel to provide reasonable protection to customers? If the facility is in a high-crime area, or if the facility or its patrons have been the victim of criminal activity, the restaurant or hotel should, for the purpose of defining its legal duty, anticipate additional criminal activity in the future. In one case, a plaintiff was robbed and raped in a Wellesley Inn. The hotel had been the site of 56 crimes, including numerous robberies, within a two-and-a-half-year period immediately prior to the rape. The jury determined that the hotel was negligent for not providing sufficient security, and on appeal the verdict was upheld.[122] *Note:* While the hotel in this case had been the victim of many crimes, the duty to anticipate criminal activity and protect against it may be triggered by just a few or even one prior incident. If there has been a history of criminal activities at a hospitality business, it may be foreseeable that violence will occur again at the same location. In one such case a plaintiff was shot while attending an event in the defendant's nightclub. Some of the patrons had been patted down for weapons because the club had a history of violent incidents in the past. The court held that the club was on constructive notice that patrons could be injured by third persons in the club due to the history of violent acts in the past.[123]

Another circumstance that alerts a facility that criminal activity may occur is the presence of rowdy or abusive customers. In a case involving a Burger King, a family observed a group of seven teenagers who were "rowdy, obnoxious, loud, abu-

---

121 *Young v. Fitzpatrick*, 865 So.2d 969 (La. 2004)

122 *Simms v. Prime Hospitality Corp.*, 700 So.2d 167 (Fla. 1997)

123 *Baker v. Solo Nightclub, LLC*, 2013 WL 1927052 (Pa. 2013)

sive, and using foul language." The conduct continued while they all ordered and also as they proceeded into the dining area. The father of the family approached the group, identified himself as an off-duty police officer, and requested that they desist. One of the group hit him, knocking him to the ground, and then struck him in the head with a chair. At the resulting trial, the Burger King manager, arguing that an assault had not been foreseeable, testified that he had worked at the restaurant for three years and had never seen an incident where one customer hit another. The court nonetheless determined that the eatery should have anticipated the fight. Said the judges, "We hold the teenagers' unruly behavior could reasonably have been anticipated to escalate into acts that would expose patrons to an unreasonable risk of injury. . ..[T]he teenagers' behavior in the restaurant created a foreseeable risk of harm that the defendant unreasonably failed to address."[124]

An auditorium that housed a rock concert should have foreseen the increased potential for security problems when many concert-goers were unruly and openly drinking alcohol, the floor was littered with liquor bottles and pieces of glass, some patrons were smoking marijuana, and the band performed songs that encouraged the use of drugs and alcohol. One attendee who was struck and injured by a bottle thrown from the balcony sued the city that owned the auditorium. The jury's verdict for the plaintiff was upheld on appeal. The court ruled that the city had created an unreasonable risk of harm to those who attended the performance.[125]

Unpredictable Attack

If an attack occurs unexpectedly with no reason to anticipate it, the facility owes no duty to patrons to offer protection against the incident. A woman was injured when she was attacked by someone brandishing a gun when leaving a casino The woman sued the facility for failing to provide adequate security. The court granted the casino's motion for summary judgment because the casino could not have been aware of the violent nature of the unknown attacker. [126]

Nor was a rape foreseeable where the plaintiff and her attacker had engaged in conversation in a lobby bar at an Omni Shoreham Hotel; nothing he did there made her uncomfortable or suggested he might become violent; no assaults, burglaries, or thefts had occurred on the premises for 10 years; and no guests had complained about the hotel's security. In the victim's lawsuit against the hotel, the court thus granted summary judgment for the Omni.[127]

Similarly, a patron at a Denny's restaurant was injured by his companion when the two became involved in a fight. They were being loud and the manager asked them to quiet down or leave. The plaintiff stood up and was struck by the other. The plaintiff sued Denny's for breach of duty of care to maintain safe premises. Summary judgment was granted for the restaurant. The court found that the incident was not foreseeable. There had never been an assault inside the premises and

---

124 *Iannelli v. Burger King Corp.*, 761 A.2d 417 (N.H. 2000)
125 *Greenville Memorial Auditorium v. Martin*, 391 S.E.2d 546 (S.C. 1990)
126 *Sawvell v. Gulfside Casino, Inc.*, 158 So.3d 363 (Miss. 2015)
127 *Shaddy v. Omni Hotels Management, Corp.*, 2006 WL 693680 (Ind. 2006). For another case with somewhat similar facts and the same outcome see *Young v. Fitzpatrick*, 865 So.2d 1038 (La. 2004)

therefore Denny's could not have reasonably anticipated that one patron would assault another.[128]

The following facts were also determined to be insufficient evidence that an attack was foreseeable: The plaintiff was injured when an occupant of the room directly above her accidentally discharged a handgun. Although the gun owner was wanted by the police, this fact was unknown to the hotel. Further, he did not display a gun in the hotel, there were no complaints from other guests regarding suspicious behavior, and there was no unusual noise coming from his room.[129]

To review, a hospitality facility has a duty to provide reasonable protection to invitees if it can reasonably anticipate the occurrence of criminal activity.

We next will explore the amount of security that is required.

Matching Security to Circumstances

As we have studied, the duty required of an innkeeper for guests' safety is to exercise reasonable care. It is not a static, clearly defined concept. One definition will not fit all hotels in all locations at all times. The type of security that would constitute reasonable care in a relatively quiet and tranquil location with a low crime rate might be considered inadequate and therefore negligent if employed in a high-crime area with a history of muggings and unauthorized entries into guests' rooms. The appropriate level of security is thus a relative concept. The precautions necessary must be determined for each individual hotel based upon the likelihood of criminal activity.

Factors that are examined to determine if an establishment has provided adequate security include the number and type of security incidents occurring at the facility within the last few years, the community crime rate, crime rate in the immediate area and in similar businesses, industry standards, and any particular security problems posed by the establishment's layout, such as multiple buildings. Basic security measures all facilities should adopt include deadbolts locks, chain locks or other lock or safety device on the doors, a peephole on the door, bright lighting outside and in hallways, trimmed shrubbery, written guidelines on handling emergencies, and ongoing training of employees. Some hotels dispense with safety chains because they hinder management's entry into rooms in emergencies. If safety chains are used, the chain should be strong to withstand attempted forced entry. The chain locks and deadbolts should be designed so they are easy for the guest to use. They should be inspected regularly to verify they are in good condition.

Broken locks can lead to intrusions and serious injury. Singer Connie Francis was raped at knifepoint in a Long Island Howard Johnson's Motor Lodge. Her assailant gained access to the room through a sliding glass door. Said the court, "The doors gave the appearance of being locked but the testimony showed they were capable of being unsecured from the outside without much difficulty." Francis recovered

---

128 *Crill v. WRBF, Inc.*, 369 P.3d 501 (Wash. 2015)
129 *Hopper v. Colonial Motel Properties, Inc.*, 762 N.E.2d 181 (Ind. 2002)

$2.5 million in damages for her inability to continue her lucrative music career based on the hotel's failure to provide a "safe and secure room."[130]

A peephole, or one-way viewer, enables the guest to determine who is at the door before opening it. This simple device can protect guests from unknown intruders. The placement of the peephole on the door should be eye level for persons of average height, subject to lower installation for handicapped-equipped rooms designed for wheelchair-bound guests. The glass should be properly installed so that the person inside the guest room can look out and not vice versa.

In Case Example 6-16 the court refused to grant summary judgment in favor of the hotel, finding that a jury could determine that the hotel's security precautions were insufficient. The case provides further insight into how a court determines whether a hotel should have foreseen an injury to guests and taken greater precautions.

CASE EXAMPLE 6-16

Taboada v. Daly Seven, Inc.

626 S.E.2d 428 (Va. 2006)

...Daly Seven, Inc. owns and operates hotels in Virginia, including a Holiday Inn Express located in downtown Roanoke. At approximately 2 a.m. Ryan Taboada and his family arrived at the Holiday Inn Express seeking lodging for the night. Taboada had selected the hotel relying, in part, upon the hotel's representation that the hotel was a "safe, secure and reliable place to lodge." Taboada registered as a guest and was assigned a room. Taboada then returned to his vehicle in the hotel's parking lot where his wife and two children were waiting and began to unload the family's luggage. Derrick W. Smith, who was not a guest at the hotel, approached Taboada and demanded money from him. Smith then, immediately and without provocation, began to fire a weapon at Taboada. Taboada was wounded eight times, suffering severe bodily injuries. Smith took a wristwatch from Taboada's seven-year-old son and stole the family vehicle; Taboada's infant daughter was still in her seat in the vehicle at the time. Police apprehended Smith, recovered the vehicle, and rescued the infant, who was not physically harmed...

Taboada sued the hotel for negligence premised upon the innkeeper's breach of a duty of care owed to Taboada as a guest. Taboada alleged that Daly Seven had misrepresented that the Holiday Inn Express was located in a "safe" area when, in fact, Daly Seven "knew the business was a known target for repeat criminal activity including assaultive crimes on employees and guests." Taboada alleged that for the three months prior to his arrival the hotel called the Roanoke City Police Department on at least 96 occasions to report the presence of trespassers who refused to the leave the premises, the presence of suspicious persons on the premises, larcenies, disorderly persons, suspicious circumstances and suspected drug offenses, robberies, malicious woundings, shootings, and other criminally assaultive

---

130 *Garzelli v. Howard Johnson's Motor Lodges, Inc.*, 419 F. Supp. 1210 (N.Y. 1976)

acts. Taboada alleged that these facts placed Daly Seven on notice that uninvited persons regularly came upon the property and created a risk of imminent harm to guests and employees… . Taboada alleged that Daly Seven had at one time employed uniformed security guards to patrol the hotel and its parking lot during the overnight hours, but that it had discontinued this practice in favor of saving expenses. Taboada alleged that had Daly Seven continued to employ uniformed security guards, they would have been able to see the assailant prior to the attack and would have been able to stop the assailant before the assault… .

The hotel asserted that Taboada failed to allege that Daly Seven knew that criminal assaults against persons were occurring or about to occur on the premises which would have indicated an imminent probability of harm…

There is no liability when the defendant neither knows of the danger of an injury to a plaintiff from the criminal conduct of a third party, nor has reason to foresee that danger… The guest of an innkeeper entrusts his safety to the innkeeper and has little ability to control his environment. The guest relies upon the innkeeper to make the property safe and the innkeeper's knowledge of the neighborhood in taking the reasonably necessary precautions to do so. In this regard, it is reasonable for the law to impose upon the innkeeper a duty to take reasonable precautions to protect his guests against injury caused by the criminal conduct on the part of other guests or strangers, if the danger or injury by such conduct is known to the innkeeper or reasonably foreseeable…

We hold that Taboada's allegations, if proven, would be sufficient to permit a trier of fact to find that Daly Seven had breached its duty of care. Taboada alleged that, over a three-year period immediately prior to the attack upon Taboada, Daly Seven's employees had regularly contacted police 96 times to report criminal conduct including robberies, malicious woundings, shootings and other criminally assaultive acts… As a result of these repeated incidents, Daly Seven had been advised by police that its guests were at an imminent risk of harm from uninvited persons coming into or upon its property. These allegations are sufficient to support a reasonable conclusion that Daly Seven knew its property was located in a high-crime area, and that Daly Seven was on notice that its guests were in danger of injury caused by criminal acts of third parties. These allegations sufficiently support the further conclusion that the injury to Taboada from the criminal act of the third party was reasonably foreseeable.

For these reasons we decline to grant summary judgment to Daly Seven.

CASE QUESTIONS

1. What was the basis for the court ruling that the hotel was on notice that injury to guests was foreseeable?

2. What precautions might the hotel have taken to avoid liability?

In another case, the court determined that a hotel did not meet its duty to provide reasonable protection where front-desk personnel failed to notify police promptly when a guest called to report a crime in progress within the hotel. Once alerted to a security incident, hotel staff are expected to respond quickly.[131] The ruling in that case also held that, when a hotel had 1,200 rooms and was hosting a large ball, having on duty only one security officer, one room clerk, and one bellhop was insufficient to satisfy the inn's duty to provide reasonable safety precautions.

In another case, the plaintiff, after registering at a 300-room motel, went to her car to retrieve some papers. She was attacked by a stranger she had seen by the front desk when she registered. The guest was brutally sodomized and suffered serious physical and psychological injuries. Management was aware of approximately 30 criminal incidents occurring on the premises during the six months prior to the attack, yet the hotel employed only one security guard "from time to time on a sporadic basis." The victimized guest sued and won. Given the prior criminal incidents at the motel, more security precautions clearly were needed.[132]

In a case involving a Comfort Inn, the plaintiff was attacked in the hotel parking lot as she exited her car. In her lawsuit against the inn, the evidence established incidents of criminal activity had occurred within a one-mile radius of the hotel but no violent crimes had ever been committed on the premises and none had been reported at neighboring motels. The court dismissed plaintiff's case, holding that the risk of the criminal conduct against plaintiff was not foreseeable and so the inn had no duty to protect plaintiff from the criminal attack.[133]

Large Crowds

Sizeable gatherings of people can become unruly. When a large crowd gathers on a hotel's premises, the inn must exercise reasonable care to control the crowd and prevent a violent outbreak. Some examples of inadequate responses follow.

A bar in a high-crime area promoted an "End of Summer Bash" on a local radio station that broadcast from the tavern's parking lot, thereby attempting to attract a large crowd. The establishment did not provide a doorman or other security measures such as bouncers or additional waitstaff. This was insufficient protection under the circumstances. The facility was therefore liable to a patron who was hit by another customer.[134]

Likewise, a crew of 14 security guards at a rock concert attended by six thousand people was held to be insufficient to manage the crowd.[135]

In another case, a hotel faced liability for having an inadequate number of security guards to control a large, unruly crowd in a lobby. The guards had requested au-

---

131 *Nordmann v. National Hotel Co.*, 425 F.2d 1103 (La. 1970)
132 *Orlando Executive Park v. PDR*, 402 So.2d 442 (Fla. 1981)
133 *Jai Jalarem Lodging Group, LLC v. Leribeus*, 225 S.W.2d 238 (Tex. 2006). See also *Luong v. Tran*, 2006 WL 1679722 (Ga. 2006)
134 *Jeffords v. Lesesne*, 541 S.E.2d 847 (S.C. 2001)
135 *Greenville Memorial Auditorium v. Martin*, 391 S.E.2d 546 (S.C. 1990)

thorization from hotel management to summon the police to assist with crowd control but the request was denied. A resulting fight was arguably foreseeable. The hotel's summary judgment motion was thus denied.[136]

The same outcome occurred where a party in a hotel room became very noisy; groups of youths were passing through the lobby alerting the front desk clerk of the sizeable number of attendees; the only hotel employees on duty were the front desk clerk, who was only 19, and a mildly retarded maintenance worker; neither had received training in hotel safety or security; and when the host of the party reported to the clerk that the party was out of control and someone had a gun, a call was not made to 911 until 10 minutes later.[137]

Adequate Security Can Eliminate Liability

If a hotel or restaurant takes adequate security precautions and a guest is nonetheless attacked, the facility will not be liable. Thus, a case was dismissed against a hotel at which the plaintiff was the victim of a vicious assault, robbery, and rape on her honeymoon.[138] Said the court:

> [I]t would be incorrect for this court to say the mere fact of a rape is conclusive evidence that security at the Inn was unreasonable. To do such would be to hold the Inn as an insurer of its guests' safety.
>
> ...There can be no doubt that armed guards in every building, 24 hours a day, would have provided the guests with more protection than the security system employed by Islander Inn. However, it must be remembered that the Inn's function was as a luxury island motel, not a prison. In considering the reasonableness of the security, the court must take into account the purpose and function of the business.
>
> Based on the lack of criminal activity on the premises in the past, one uniformed guard during the nighttime hours is reasonable security for a guest at the motel. The motel is relatively small with 190 total guest rooms. One trained guard could adequately patrol the premises....
>
> The Islander Inn, as a whole, was operated and supervised reasonably. The Inn obviously felt a need to protect its guests from criminal attacks by third persons, and measures were taken to ensure their safety. The measures were reasonable. The rape incident was a truly unfortunate and horrible experience, but the defendants cannot be held responsible. For this court to hold otherwise would be equivalent to making all motels the insurer of their guests' safety. Therefore, it is ORDERED, that this action be dismissed.

---

[136] *Sawyer v. Wight*, 196 F.Supp.2d 220 (N.Y. 2002)
[137] *Corinaldi v. Columbia Courtyard*, 873 A.2d 483 (Md. 2005)
[138] *Courtney v. Remler*, 566 F.Supp 1225 (S.C. 1983)

In another case, a patron at a nightclub was on the dance floor when a fight broke out and a gun went off. Plaintiff was hit by a bullet and sued the club for negligence. The appellate court held that the plaintiff presented no evidence that the security measures undertaken by the club were performed in a negligent manner. The club had four to eight security guards who patted down and scanned with a metal detecting wand patrons before they could enter the club.[139] The court added that the club is not the insurer of safety by taking some precautions on behalf of invitees.

Security Personnel and Firearms

Should security personnel in a hotel carry weapons? This is a difficult question and there is no easy answer. A gun in the hands of even a well-trained guard can present dangers. If the guard is attacked and subdued, the attacker will have easy access to the firearm and may misuse it. A gun can be a very dangerous instrument in the hands of someone not well trained in its use. An unarmed security guard may be of only limited help in the event of an attack, and the hotel or restaurant that employs the guard risks civil liability for any injuries the guard incurs. Each facility needs to develop a policy that suits its circumstances.

Emergency/Disaster Plan

An effective safety program at any facility must include emergency and disaster plans identifying procedures in the event of a catastrophe such as a hurricane, fire, flood, tornado, terrorist attack, chemical or other toxic release, and related occurrences. The goal of such plans is to save lives, minimize personal injury, and reduce property damage. Emergency responders in your community (police, ambulance services, fire fighters) can provide invaluable advice when developing the plan and should be consulted.

Components of a plan include: how and where to report the emergency; evacuation procedures; a system to account for patrons and employees after the evacuation; identification of safe areas outside buildings for evacuees to go; identification of nearby shelters; a warning system; rescue and medical functions; a list of resources (police, fire, etc.) and their contact numbers; directions for on-premises emergency responders; access to emergency generators; and communication systems for emergency responders and for trapped guests. Additionally, the plan should mandate that the facility review at specified intervals its insurance coverage; examine periodically the integrity of its buildings and undertake any indicated repairs and upgrades; stockpile supplies such as flashlights, bottled water, mops, etc.; adopt and regularly verify operability of an off-premises computer backup system. Training on the components of the plan should be provided with appropriate frequency. Further, the disaster plan should address any specific needs and circumstances of the particular facility.

---

[139] *Yearwood v. Club Miami, Inc.*, 728 S.E.2d 790 (Ga. 2012)

Guests occasionally need medical care while staying at a hotel or eating in a restaurant. Is either obligated to provide the services of a doctor or other health professional? The answer is no, neither is required to offer its patrons medical services. The hotel's legal duty is to provide the guest with such first aid as it reasonably can, and summon qualified assistance usually by calling 911. If a hotel chooses to offer health services, it must exercise reasonable care in the selection of medical personnel and in the provision of the services.

To avoid potential liability if a doctor is accused of malpractice, most hotels today will not even recommend a particular doctor. Instead, the hotel might provide a list of available physicians and nearby hospitals, and require the guest to select one.

If the hotel provides or recommends a doctor or nurse, at a minimum the person should be licensed. A guest at a Hilton Hotel fell backward in his hotel room while dressing and hit his head against the wall. He became nauseous and complained to his travel companion of a headache. The latter called hotel management for a doctor and was advised that "some help" would be sent. A woman arrived within a half hour and identified herself as a nurse. After ascertaining the circumstances, she recommended the guest remain in bed for 12 hours. By the next day he was in a comatose state. He was taken by ambulance to a hospital, where surgery was immediately performed. He suffered permanent brain damage. In fact, the woman who had come to his hotel room was not a licensed nurse. While the hotel had a medical department, a physician was not on call during the evenings. Instead, the uncredentialed woman responded to medical calls "with the full knowledge and consent of the hotel management."

Expert testimony established the following: When the woman visited the guest's room the guest was exhibiting classic symptoms of a blood clot in the brain; a licensed nurse would have identified the symptoms; a nurse would have sought immediate treatment; and prompt medical care would have averted the brain damage. Said the court, while the hotel did not owe a duty to its guests to provide medical services, if it undertakes to do so, it must send a doctor "or at the very least a nurse." Judgment was rendered against the hotel.[140]

If a hotel opts to recommend medical personnel, it should ensure that the doctors are qualified in all respects, including language compatibility with the guest/patient. Clearly, a physician who cannot understand the language of her patients cannot properly treat them. A plaintiff and two friends, all English-speaking, traveled to the Dominican Republic on vacation. The plaintiff was a "well-controlled, insulin-dependent diabetic." While away, she became ill and sought assistance at her hotel from the front desk clerk. Plaintiff was referred to a clinic within the hotel complex which provided medical services to guests only, not to residents of the Dominican Republic. The doctor, whose native language was Spanish but who could communicate in English, did not understand the words *diabetic* or *diabetes*.

---

[140] *Stahlin v. Hilton Hotels Corp.*, 484 F.2d 580 (Ill. 1973)

Plaintiff died from her injuries. If the inability of the doctor to understand English contributed to the cause of death, the hotel may be at least partially liable since its employee recommended the physician.[141]

Another case involving medical care illustrates proper conduct on the part of a hospitality facility when confronted with a medical emergency. A casino patron/plaintiff had a heart attack while gambling at a blackjack table. The dealer immediately summoned security who responded quickly and, upon assessing the circumstances, called the casino medical station. A nurse from the medical station arrived at the scene within minutes and immediately instructed security to call an ambulance. She assisted three other patrons in providing CPR. When the ambulance arrived, the attendants intubated plaintiff (a procedure in which a tube is inserted into the trachea to help restore the ability to breathe), which caused him to regain a pulse. In the resulting lawsuit, the plaintiff claimed the casino violated its duty of care to him because the nurse did not intubate him prior to the arrival of the ambulance, as a result of which his heart attack was prolonged. The court held that the casino's duty was to summon aid and, until help arrived, provide "such first aid as the [facility's] employees are reasonably capable of giving." The law did not require the casino to perform an intubation.[142]

Another issue is whether facilities have a duty to keep a defibrillator on the premises and to use it when a patron is experiencing cardiac arrest. A defibrillator is a device designed to deliver an electric shock to a patient in an effort to re-start the heart. Recent progress in cardiac research has led to substantial improvements in the technology and thus the device's growing presence in places where people gather, such as hotels, airports, casinos, and sports stadiums. In several cases where plaintiffs suffered consequences from a heart attack exacerbated by the absence of a defibrillator, they sued; in one case the defendant was a hotel,[143] in another a YMCA.[144] The court in both cases determined that the law does not require the facility to have a defibrillator or to use it in an emergency.

Negligence was found where a hotel failed to call an ambulance for a guest asking for medical help. Instead, the front-desk attendant called a cab to take the guest to the hospital. The guest had explained to the attendant that he was not feeling well and asked for a medical facility on site. He was pale, sweating, and flushed white. Upon learning that the hotel lacked medical care, he decided to go to a hospital emergency room. The guest died soon after reaching the hospital. The hotel's failure to summon emergency medical help resulted in liability.[145]

Sometimes hotel staff may try to diagnose a guest's problem and suggest home remedies. Personnel should be trained not to do this. A guest whose injury is made worse by such advice may sue and is likely to win.

[141] *Gianocostas v. Rio Hotels,* 2006 WL 467557 (Mass. 2006)
[142] *Lundy v. Admar of N.J. Inc.,* 34 F.3d 1173 (N.J. 1994)
[143] *Pacello v. Wyndham International, Inc.,* 2006 WL 1102737 (Conn. 2006)
[144] *Salte v. YMCA of Metropolitan Chicago Foundation,* 814 N.E.2d 610 (Ill. 2004). See also Actuuitz v. Gulph Mills Tennis Club, 812 A.2d 1218 (Pa. 2002)
[145] *Gingeleskie v. Westin Hotel Co,* 145 F.3d 1337 (Ariz. 1998)

Summary

The potential liability faced by a hotel or restaurant for negligent acts encompasses virtually every part of the facility. To avoid liability, hotels and restaurants must be diligent in maintaining their premises in a safe condition. Liability can result from unclean rooms, broken furniture, poorly maintained windows, and unsafe electrical systems. Also exposing hotels and restaurants to lawsuits are uncontrolled rodents, deteriorated bathroom appliances, unsafe elevators, broken doors, improperly maintained ceilings, dangerous steps and escalators, slippery floors, out-of-control flambé dishes, and excessively hot drinks. Likewise, hospitality establishments will be liable for failing to properly maintain sidewalks and sporting facilities on the premises and for inadequate lighting inside and outside of buildings. A hotel offering swimming facilities must use reasonable care to protect the safety of guests who use these amenities. Similarly, precautions must be taken to avoid fire and, if fire does break out, to minimize injury to guests. Security measures consistent with the foreseeable risks are required.

If a hotel chooses to offer medical services, it must ensure that the caregiver is qualified and has proper credentials. If a guest complains of illness and expresses a need for immediate medical care, the hotel or restaurant should quickly call an ambulance.

Preventive Law Tips for Managers

- *Be sure guest rooms are thoroughly cleaned after each guest leaves and before the next guest is allowed access.* A guest has a legal right to expect the room to be in a clean and safe condition. Failure to clean it before the room is re-assigned can result in injuries to the incoming guest, as in the case where the guest stepped on a discarded needle. Inadequate cleaning constitutes negligence and if injuries result, the hotel will likely be liable.

- *Regularly inspect the furniture in guest rooms, the lobby, and other public rooms to verify they are in good repair and able to withstand expected use.* A hotel may be liable for injuries resulting from collapsing beds and chairs, weak stools, wobbly legs on desks or tables, and other furniture flaws that create risk of injury. These problems should be sought by frequent inspections, and disabled furniture should be removed from service. Failure to detect and either remove or repair the broken items constitutes negligence.

- *Anticipate likely misuses of furniture and protect against them either by providing written warnings to guests or taking other action appropriate under the circumstances.* We read about a case in which a hotel was liable when a guest fell while standing on an unsteady dressing-table stool to adjust the air-conditioner knob. While the stool was not meant for standing on, this use was foreseeable given the location of the knob almost seven feet from the floor. Be alert to similar foreseeable misuses and take appropriate steps to prevent them.

- *If furniture is purchased unassembled, be sure the assembly is done correctly and no loose screws or other dangerous conditions result.* Furniture assembly requires a certain expertise. Be sure the assembly is done consistent with accompanying instructions so that harm will not result. If an injury occurs, determine what the problem was, inspect all other like furniture still in service, and correct any similar problems.

- *Inspect windows to ensure the glass is not broken and is securely attached, fittings are in good working order, and screens, blinds, and curtains are securely affixed.* A hotel must ensure that the window fixtures in guest rooms and other public rooms are safe. The hotel can foresee that guests will be injured if window glass or fixtures are loose or otherwise unsafe. A regular regime of inspection and repair is necessary to avoid liability.

- *Maintain the heating and electrical systems in a hotel or restaurant in good repair.* The potential injuries from defects in these systems are devastating. These functions require special attention. In-house employees may not have the required skills. Frequent maintenance and check-ups by a business specializing in heating and electricity may be required.

- *Develop a plan to minimize the presence of insects, rodents and other objectionable animals on the premises.* The plan should include: (1) regular inspections for rat holes, beehives, and other telltale signs of unwanted critters; (2) hiring exterminators if needed; and (3) additional precautions required by the particular circumstances of the establishment.

- *Regularly examine the bathroom appliances and plumbing system to ensure they are in good working order.* Numerous accidents occur in the bathroom. These can result from deteriorating faucets, poorly maintained toilet seats or stall doors, and faulty plumbing. Frequent inspections will alert management to unsafe conditions that need repair or replacement. Failure to detect defects and repair them will lead to liability for the hotel or restaurant.

- *Regularly inspect the lobby and other public rooms for unsafe conditions such as walkways blocked by luggage, bumps in rugs, intruders bothering guests, and repairs in progress.* Many people regularly use the lobby. Unsafe conditions can easily cause injury. Precautions must be taken to reduce risks of injury from circumstances in the lobby and other public rooms.

- *Develop a maintenance plan for elevators including regular inspections by both in-house employees and a company specializing in elevator maintenance.* Virtually everyone in a sizeable hotel uses the elevators. A faulty elevator is likely to cause injury. As with the electricity and heating systems, the hotel or restaurant may not have the required expertise in-house. The elevator maintenance plan should include regular and frequent inspections by a company with the necessary skill to keep the elevators in good working order. Maintenance is required not just for the elevators used by guests, but also for service elevators.

- *Access to service elevators should be strictly limited.* Often a service elevator requires training for use and lacks amenities available in elevators used by guests. Access to the service elevators should be restricted to those employees who have received the necessary training. Precautions should be taken to prevent guests and customers from using the service elevators.

- *Inspect automatic doors regularly to ensure they are working properly.* Malfunctioning automatic doors will foreseeably cause injury. They should be inspected regularly and any operational problems corrected.

- *If a large, rowdy crowd is expected, increase security by the front door and in the lobby.* A boisterous crowd is likely to push, shove, and run, causing injury to others in the vicinity. If such a crowd can be anticipated, the hotel should undertake crowd-control efforts. Failure to do so will lead to liability if someone is injured by the unruly mob.

- *Check stairs for conditions that can cause injury, including deterioration, obstructions, poor lighting, lack of railings, unexpected location, and inappropriate warning.* Countless accidents occur on steps, many of them avoidable. Frequent assessment of the safety of stairways in the establishment can greatly decrease the number of incidents.

- *Inspect floors for dangerous conditions, including excessive polish or wax, worn spots, and spilled food or beverages.* Failure to detect and correct these conditions will foreseeably lead to injury and liability. Dining-room floors should be inspected before an event or meal. Service personnel should be alerted to inspect the floor for fallen food or debris throughout the meal and while diners are leaving. Regarding construction of floors, consider the slipperiness of the tile or covering when selecting and purchasing materials.

- *Do not overbook your dining room or other facilities.* Overbooking leads to crowded, unsafe conditions in which guests and patrons may trip and be injured. If your facilities cannot comfortably accommodate an event, do not accept the reservation. Clearly inform event planners of limitations on the number of attendees and hold firm to your maximum capacity.

- *Do not serve flambé dishes unless the proper serving utensils are used, emergency equipment is readily available, and your employees have been thoroughly trained on how to control and handle the flames and what to do in an emergency.* Flambé dishes, if not strictly controlled, can lead to serious injury and significant property destruction by fire. Precautions will reduce the chance of injury. Consider avoiding the problem by exploring alternatives to flambé dishes being flamed in the dining room.

- *Do not serve hot liquids that are so hot as to cause burns.* While customers expect—indeed demand—their tea, coffee, and like drinks hot, remember that customers may accidentally spill their drinks on themselves or others nearby, and servers may do the same. The temperature at which such beverages are sold should be no hotter than industry standards.

- *Instruct valets how to protect patrons from dangers presented by arriving and departing vehicles.* The unloading area of hotels and restaurants often becomes congested with people and several lanes of traffic. A car pulling out, pulling in, or backing up could foreseeably hit an arriving or departing guest. The valet and other employees who greet arriving patrons at their cars must be alert to the risks and guide both pedestrian and vehicular traffic to avoid accidents.

■ *Adequately illuminate all areas in a hotel or restaurant, and be particularly watchful of parking lots and stairs.* Many accidents occur because customers are unable to see where they are walking. Areas particularly prone to accidents due to insufficient lighting are parking lots and stairways. Once adequate lighting is installed, examine it regularly to ensure the fixtures and bulbs are fully operable.

■ *Be sure sporting facilities are designed safely and maintained properly.* Poorly designed and inadequately maintained facilities increase the risk of injury to users. A hotel owes its guests the duty to exercise reasonable care to keep the facilities in a safe condition. While guests assume the ordinary risks associated with a sport, they do not assume the risk that the facilities are hazardous.

■ *Hotels with swimming pools must provide rescue equipment including, without limitation, ropes, rings, poles, and shepherd's hooks.* Failure to provide lifesaving devices can result in a drowning that was avoidable. The equipment should be kept very close to the pool and readily accessible. It should be examined regularly to ensure freedom from defects.

■ *Conspicuously display the depth of the pool.* Clearly posting the depth of pool water can prevent accidents caused by guests diving into water that is too shallow, and by guests proceeding into water that is too deep for their abilities. The depth should be painted in large numbers and bright colors along the perimeter of the pool. Regularly verify that the depth of the water is consistent with the postings. For pools with unusual depths, such as a pool that has no deep end, prominent signage should also be used to alert unsuspecting swimmers.

■ *Provide every possible safety precaution in the pool area.* Always rope off the shallow area to alert swimmers when they are entering the deep end. Demand a current lifesaving certificate from lifeguards. Install a telephone close to the pool so that help can be summoned quickly in an emergency. Be intolerant of horseplay in and around the pool. Prevent the water from becoming cloudy by maintaining the filtration system in good repair and by use of appropriate chemicals in the proper quantity. Use underwater lights in the evening and keep them operable. Verify that the diving board is made from suitable material and is the proper length. Do not let the water in the pool become low, thereby rendering the depth markings inaccurate. Alert guests if a lifeguard is not provided. Use material that is slip-resistant for the floor of the area around the pool. Clean regularly around and in the pool to remove objects that might cause injury to bare feet.

■ *Check the statutes in your state and locality that identify pool safety mandates and strictly comply.* Failure to abide by safety laws constitutes negligence per se. The laws in different states and localities vary. Review the applicable laws with a lawyer and make arrangements to comply.

- *Take every possible safety precaution in beach areas.* Rake the sand along the beach to protect barefoot strollers from foot injuries. Rake the bottom of the water where swimmers walk and dive to remove objects they might hit. Restrict the areas in which surfboards and like paraphernalia can be used to avoid swimmers being hit by them. Post signs warning of unusual water conditions such as a strong undertow.

- *Check state and local fire-safety laws and strictly comply.* Failure to abide by fire-safety laws constitutes negligence per se. These laws often require that equipment such as fire extinguishers be maintained in good condition on the premises and that fire escapes be provided. They also mandate specifications in the construction of new buildings and additions. The laws in different states and localities vary. Review the applicable laws with a lawyer and make arrangements to conform

- *Train employees thoroughly on what to do in case of fire.* Many lawsuits requiring hotels to compensate guests injured in fires result from employees who fail to call the fire department or alert the guests in a timely manner. This problem can be remedied by thorough training and practice drills. Employees should be instructed to call the fire department immediately when a fire is reported. Their next step should be to alert guests in a manner consistent with hotel facilities and policies.

- *Exercise reasonable care to protect guests from criminal activity.* Make an assessment of the security risks at the establishment and implement a plan to address them. The assessment should include a review of recent security incidents at the hotel or restaurant and in the vicinity, as well as specific risks presented by circumstances of the particular facilities, such as multi-building layouts and outdoor access to guest rooms. The plan could include such security devices as: security guards; enhanced lighting in the parking lot, in hallways, and in other appropriate places; TV-type monitors; automatic locks on doors; chain or safety locks; special doorknobs that deter picking of locks; peepholes; door construction designed to prevent unauthorized entry; and computerized keys that change with each guest. The business should also develop an alliance with the local police for advice and back-up help.

- *Instruct employees on how to handle a phone call announcing an emergency.* In the event of an emergency, time is of the essence. If an employee receiving an emergency call does not respond timely and adequately, a patron may be severely injured and the hotel or restaurant may be liable. Adequate training of employees and prompt summoning of police can mitigate many would-be security incidents.

- *Be alert to suspicious circumstances on the premises.* Employees should be trained to watch for unusual circumstances or suspicious people on the property, such as an ex-employee who enters the premises late at night or a person in the lobby who approaches guests for no apparent reason. Depending on the circumstances the person should be observed until the suspicion fades, or the person should be asked to leave, or the police should be called.

- *If a hotel provides medical services, verify the credentials and capability of the caregiver.* A hotel will be liable if it represents to a guest that a doctor or nurse will be provided when the supposed professional is not certified. A hotel should have referral information on local doctors readily available to give to inquiring guests. Before referring a guest to a particular local doctor, the hotel should confirm the physician's qualifications and standing in the medical community. If a guest complains of illness and expresses a need for immediate medical care, call an ambulance quickly.

Review Questions

1. In what rooms of a hotel does the innkeeper's duty to exercise reasonable care apply?

2. What responsibility, if any, does an innkeeper have to maintain self-service elevators in a safe condition?

3. What risks are associated with flaming foods? What precautions should a restaurant take when serving them?

4. What precautions should a restaurant take when serving hot beverages?

5. For what safety concerns should a parking valet be watchful?

6. What responsibility, if any, does an innkeeper have to maintain sporting facilities in a safe condition?

7. Name four causes of swimming-pool accidents and state how they can be avoided.

8. Must all hotels have security guards to protect guests' safety?

9. Must a hotel have medical personnel on duty at all times?

10. Is a restaurant required to have a defibrillator readily available?

11. What is a hotel's liability for injuries occurring to a guest on an off-premises jogging trail recommended by the hotel?

Discussion Questions

1. Identify several circumstances in which liability can result to a restaurant for failing to inspect and maintain the furniture in the dining room. State how the liability can be avoided.

2. Identify several circumstances in which liability can result to a hotel for failing to inspect and maintain the windows, screens, and doors. State how the liability can be avoided.

3. Identify several circumstances in which liability can result to a restaurant for failing to inspect for and contain rodents, bugs, and animals. State how the liability can be avoided.

4. Identify several circumstances in which liability can result to a hotel for failing to inspect and maintain the bathrooms. State how the liability can be avoided.

5. Identify five circumstances in which liability can result to a hotel for failing to maintain its sporting facilities properly. State how the liability can be avoided.

6. Identify four circumstances in which liability can result to a hotel for failing to maintain its waterfront property properly. State how the liability can be avoided.

7. Identify five circumstances in which liability can result to a hotel for failing to provide adequate security. State how the liability can be avoided.

8. How should the front desk personnel at a hotel respond when a guest calls stating, "This is an emergency"?

9. What response is appropriate if a guest says "There is a fire on the second floor"?

10. What safeguards should a hotel or restaurant take to minimize liability for fires?

11. State five elements necessary for a disaster plan.

Application Questions

1. You are the banquet manager at a catering hall. The guests for a large wedding reception will start to arrive in 20 minutes. You are inspecting the premises to ensure everything is in order. What should you be looking for?

2. Jan was a guest at the Hideaway Hotel. As she was walking from her room to the hotel's restaurant for breakfast, a maintenance worker was washing the floor. Jan tripped on the wet floor and fell. What additional information do you need to know to determine if the hotel will be liable?

3. One night Joshua fell in a restaurant parking lot because the lights were dim. At the time, he was on his way to attend the anniversary reception of a close friend, which was being held in the restaurant. The hotel argued that Joshua was negligent for exiting his car in the dark. Was Joshua negligent in this case?

4. While swimming at the pool at the Browninger Resort, Ursala, age 31, was hit on the head by Tom, another swimmer, age 11, who had been engaged in

horseplay with two friends for a half hour. The lifeguard had twice requested that Tom and his friends settle down but to no avail. If Ursala sues the resort for negligence, what is the likelihood she will win? Why?

5. Juanita was sitting in the bar in a restaurant waiting to be seated for dinner. A man mistook her for someone else and, without warning, hit Juanita in the face. She was injured and sued the bar for negligence because it failed to prevent the assault. Will the hotel be liable under these circumstances? What additional facts would you like to know before deciding?

6. The Charming Motel, located in a medium-crime area, was the site of a rape eight months ago. As a result, the hotel installed monitors covering the front and back entrances and the elevators, and requested that the police increase their normal surveillance of the building during the night. Tyrone, a guest at the motel, was assaulted in his room in the middle of the night by two attackers who broke a window to gain entry. Tyrone suffered a broken jaw and the theft of $1,000. No crimes had occurred at the motel during the year prior to the initial rape and none after it until the assault of Tyrone. Is the Charming Motel liable for his injuries? Explain.

7. In one episode of the once popular television show *L.A. Law*, the door to an elevator on an upper floor at a law firm was left open while the elevator was temporarily out of order and undergoing repairs on the first floor. No warning sign was posted. One of the characters, not realizing the elevator was not waiting at the door, stepped into the shaft and fell to her death. Do these acts constitute negligence? What should the company repairing the elevator have done to avoid the accident? What could the law firm have done to prevent this accident from happening?

Websites

Websites that will enhance your understanding of the material in this chapter include:

www.findlaw.com This site contains updates on legal news and many links to sites covering a variety of legal topics including personal injury (negligence) cases.

www.experts.com Often in negligence cases an expert witness is utilized by one of the parties to explain relevant phenomena to jurors who would otherwise not have the knowledge the witness does. This site contains a listing of available expert witnesses and their field of expertise.

www.hotelbusiness.com This site provides a wealth of business information about recent news in the hotel industry, including security issues.

www.ahma.com This is the site of the American Hotel and Lodging Association, a trade organization for the hotel and lodging industry. The site addresses numerous topics of interest to the hotel industry, including guest safety.

UNIT III

Relationships with Guests and Other Patrons

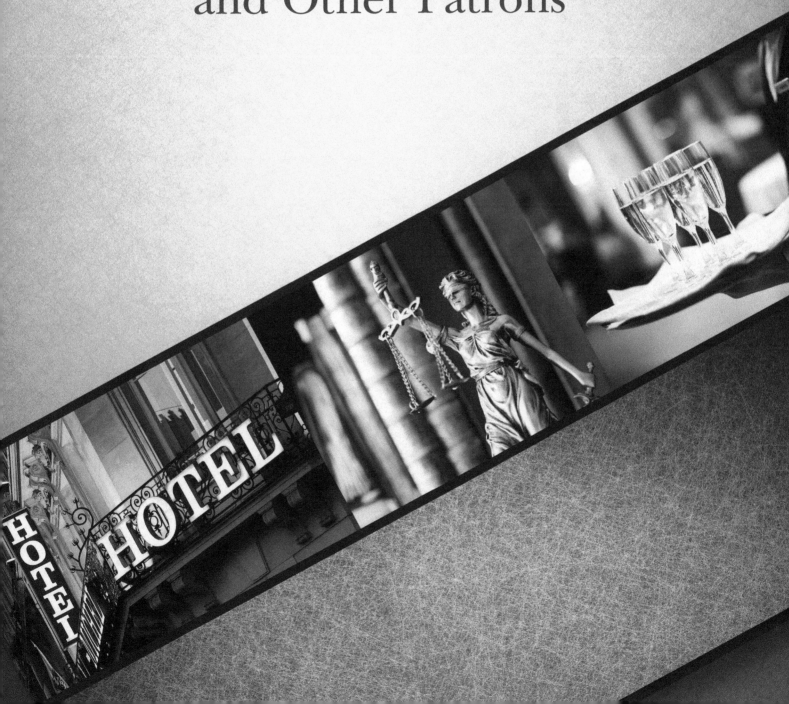

CHAPTER 7

Guests and Other Patrons

LEARNING OUTCOMES:

- Appreciate significance of whether a person qualifies as a guest
- Understand the duties owed to a guest
- Comprehend the various relationships between hotels and people who use the facilities
- Know the importance of intention of both innkeeper and guest in determining guest status
- Appreciate the circumstances that terminate innkeeper-guest relationship
- Understand distinguishing characteristics creating a landlord-tenant relationship
- Comprehend the legal significance of a landlord-tenant relationship

Introduction

An innkeeper owes certain duties to those who use the hotel's facilities. Those duties vary depending on whether the patron fits the legal definition of a *guest*. Not everyone who utilizes or seeks to utilize the facilities of a hotel or inn becomes a guest in the legal sense. Instead, they may be shoppers, restaurant customers, special event attendees, tenants, or trespassers. The list goes on. Whether or not a person qualifies as a guest has legal significance. For example, if property is stolen from a hotel, the extent of the hotel's liability depends on whether or not the property owner is a guest. We will study this in Chapter 8. A hotel owes

certain duties to guests but not to others—for example, to refrain from insulting or humiliating them. We will study this obligation in Chapter 10. As we saw in Chapter 5, a hotel owes to invitees a duty to act reasonably, and a lesser duty to licensees and trespassers. Guests are invitees. Thus, the outcome of many negligence lawsuits turns on whether or not the plaintiff is a guest.

This chapter explains who qualifies as a guest and discusses the other types of relationships that exist between a hotel and the people who use its various facilities.

Who Qualifies as a Guest?

For a person visiting an inn to qualify as a guest, the visit must be for the primary purpose for which an inn operates—rental of rooms suitable for overnight stay. As a general rule, people are not guests unless they require overnight accommodations. People who register at a hotel for rooms are guests. People who go to a hotel to pay social calls upon the guests are also treated in law as guests.[1] People who are in a hotel for some other reason do not qualify. For example, a passerby who enters the hotel to shop in a lobby store is not a guest. A person who comes to the hotel for the sole purpose of attending a banquet or reception and does not register for a room is likewise not a guest.[2] Similarly, a person attending a seminar at

---

[1] *Farnham III v. Inland Sea Resort Properties, Inc.*, 824 A.2d 554 (Vt. 2003)
[2] *Ross v. Kirkeby Hotels*, 160 N.Y.S.2d 978 (N.Y. 1957)

a hotel who does not register for a room is not a guest, nor is a person who enters a hotel merely to use the bathroom.[3]

In Case Example 7-1, a patron in a hotel cocktail lounge who was not a registered guest in the hotel claimed he was short-changed by the waiter, and then was insulted, humiliated, and embarrassed. As we will study in Chapter 11, a hotel but not a restaurant owes a legal duty to treat its customers respectfully and without insult. Thus the liability of the hotel turned on whether the patron qualified as a guest. The hotel in this case will be liable if the patron is a guest; it will not be liable if he is not a guest. As you read the case, you should be able to anticipate how the court ruled.

© Photographee.eu/Shutterstock.com

CASE EXAMPLE 7-1

Wallace v. Shoreham Hotel Corp.

49 A.2d 81 (D.C. 1946)

...The substance of the complaint is that plaintiff, in company with his wife and four friends, was a guest at the cocktail lounge of defendant's hotel; that, in payment of the check rendered, plaintiff gave the waiter a $20 bill but received change for only $10; that the waiter insisted he had received from plaintiff a $10 bill and stated publicly for all in the lounge to hear: "We have had people try this before"; that in fact plaintiff had tendered a $20 bill, which fact was later admitted by representatives of the hotel and proper change given plaintiff; that the language of the waiter indicated to those present in the lounge that plaintiff was underhanded and of low character and that his demand for change was illegal and comparable to that of a cheat or other person whose reputation for honesty is open to question; that by reason thereof plaintiff was "insulted, humiliated, and otherwise embarrassed." The plaintiff sought judgment for punitive damages of $3,000.

...The question thus presented is whether a patron of a cocktail lounge has a cause of action for humiliation and embarrassment resulting from insulting words of a waiter.

It has been held that an innkeeper owes a duty extending to a guest of respectful and decent treatment, and that the innkeeper is liable to a guest for insulting words or conduct. ...Such duty, however, rests on the peculiar relationship between innkeeper and guest.... In the instant case the defendant is an innkeeper. The complaint alleges plaintiff was a "guest" at the cocktail lounge and not a registered guest of the hotel.... One who is merely a customer at a bar, a restaurant, a barber shop or newsstand operated by a hotel does not thereby establish the relationship of innkeeper and guest.... The situation, as we see it, is the same as if the plaintiff had been the customer of any restaurant or tavern [not affiliated with a hotel] where drinks are served.

---

[3] *State v. Lowry*, 2004 WL 308105 (Ohio 2004)

[Judgment, therefore, was for the defendant.]

CASE QUESTION

1. What one fact in this case, if changed, would have resulted in the plaintiff winning the lawsuit?

Intent of Parties

The innkeeper–guest relationship is a contractual one—the parties exchange the exclusive use of a guest's room for money. An essential element of all contracts is an intention by the parties to enter a contract. Guest status can arise once the intention is formulated, even before the contract is entered. Thus, a transient becomes a guest upon entering a hotel intending to procure overnight accommodations where the innkeeper has a room available. It is not essential that the guest have already registered.

How does one determine whether the parties have formulated an intention to enter a contract? The actions of the parties usually provide the needed evidence. An example is provided by the odd fact that people sometimes come to a hotel to commit

suicide. They do so in part to distance themselves from family and friends who would likely try to discourage them. A person whose sole purpose in entering the hotel was to jump to his death from the top of their building was not considered a guest.[4] On the other hand, individuals who check into a hotel room, for the purpose of committing suicide, are considered to be guests.

A request for a room or an advance reservation is sufficient to evidence intent on the part of a would-be patron to become a guest; of course, if the innkeeper indicates a willingness to register the traveler and provide a room, this is sufficient evidence of intent on the innkeeper's part to form an innkeeper–guest relationship. A trickier issue arises when registration has not occurred or is incomplete. Judges decide these issues based on the particular facts of each case, as the following section explains.

Registration

While registration clearly evidences intent on both the guest's and innkeeper's part to develop an innkeeper–guest relationship, registration is not essential for the relationship to exist.

---

4 *Schwenke v. Outrigger Hotels Hawaii, LLP*, 227 P.3d 555 (Hawaii 2010)

In Case Example 7-2, two young males registered for a hotel room. A question arose as to whether the innkeeper intended to contract with two minor females who did not register and who, unknown to the innkeeper, accompanied the two males. One of the females was injured due to the hotel's negligence. If the females qualified as guests, the hotel would be liable for the injuries. If, on the other hand, an innkeeper-guest relationship did not exist, the girls would in these circumstances be trespassers and the innkeeper would not be liable.

© Dotshock/Shutterstock.com

CASE EXAMPLE 7-2

Langford v. Vandaveer

254 S.W.2d 498 (Ky. 1953)

[Ruth Vandaveer] was severely burned in the explosion of a butane or propane gas heater in a cabin of a motor court operated by the appellant, Clyde B. Langford.... Our present inquiry is whether the young lady was a guest.

On Sunday afternoon of January 22, 1950, four young people, C. P. Howe, Bill Nash, Ruth Vandaveer, and Myna Walker, drove to Henderson, Kentucky, from Albion, Illinois, a distance of 60 miles or more. Miss Vandaveer… 17 years old, and Miss Walker, about 15, were students in the high school at Albion and the young men worked in the oil fields near Henderson. The men went into a hotel where Howe's brother was staying, but could not procure accommodations. The party then drove to Langford's Motor Court, a short distance from the city. This was about 8:30 o'clock. The car was stopped in a well lighted place near the entrance of the office and restaurant. Howe met Langford at the door and asked for rooms for four oilmen, saying that one of them was then at work but would return early enough to get some rest before checking out time. Langford showed the cabins to the two men, lighted the heaters and explained to them how the valves worked. He and Howe returned to the office and Howe filled out a registration card, giving his address and an automobile license number and signed it "C.P. Howe and party." He filled in the figure "4," showing the number of people in the party and paid six dollars for the two rooms. Neither Howe nor Miss Walker testified. Miss Vandaveer and Nash testified he stood by the side of the automobile at all times. It is undisputed that Langford passed twice within 10 or 15 feet of the parked automobile. He says he looked at the car and could have seen anyone in it but saw no one. As the car started over to the cabins he noted that the license number was not the same as that registered and he entered the correct number on the card. (It appears that Howe had given the number of his own car instead of Nash's, which he was driving.) Miss Vandaveer testified that when Langford passed the automobile she was sitting on the edge of the back seat looking into the small mirror in front, combing her hair, and Miss Walker was on the front seat doing the same thing. Both were erect and could be easily seen.

According to Miss Vandaveer and Nash, the party entered one of the cabins and then the other, where they spent some time together. Then the boys left about 10:00 to go to work. They planned to return early enough to drive the girls back to Albion in time for school. After they had gone, she and Myna concluded to occupy separate cabins. She took No. 4 and retired about 11:00. Neither had any baggage. On the contrary, Langford and his sister testified that about 11:15 Howe came to the restaurant, ate a sandwich, drank a cup of coffee and then left with three colas. Nash testified he and Howe left the motor court about 10:00 and worked until seven the next morning. However, there is evidence that immediately following the explosion Howe was there. A man in or about the cabin was heard to say, "I told you not to do that." One of these witnesses, according to Langford, first told him of the presence of the girls on the premises.

The relation of innkeeper and guest is a mutual contractual one, and the existence of intention by both parties is an essential element. It is an exceptional case where that requisite is not clearly established, usually by implication. Ordinarily, where one holds himself out to the public as an innkeeper, and is accustomed to receive all who apply and a transient goes to the [inn] to procure accommodation and receives [same], the relationship is created. But … it is not essential that the guest shall have registered … though it may be an important circumstance in determining the status.

In the case at bar, the intention of the young lady to become a guest in the legal sense is apparent. The question is whether or not she was intentionally or knowingly *received* as such by the proprietor of the motor court. (Emphasis added.)

[A] person may not impose himself upon the proprietor and become a guest without [the proprietor's] knowledge or intention to receive [that person]. One becomes a guest only if he is received to be treated as a guest and the intention to become such must be communicated to the innkeeper or his agent. [As stated in a prior case] … "a mere guest of the registered occupant of a room at a hotel, who shares such room with its occupant without the knowledge or consent of the hotel management, would not be a guest of the hotel, as there would be no contractual relations in such case between such third person and the hotel proprietor.…"

Here we have the acceptance of four men as guests when there were in fact two men and two women.… According to the innkeeper's testimony, the young lady slipped into the cabin and occupied the room for the night without the proprietor's knowledge or consent.… [In another case,] where a registered guest, without permission from anyone representing the hotel, transferred a room to a woman, she had no right to its possession [and did not qualify as a guest].…

There is no dispute in the evidence that Howe procured the two rooms for four men. But if the proprietor of the motor court saw the young women in the car under the circumstances described and could reasonably have anticipated or understood that they would occupy the cabin, then the jury could find he accepted her as a guest and assumed the legal responsibility owing in such relationship.… Ruling of the [appeals] court: [The trial court should not have determined Vandaveer was a guest as a matter of law. Rather, the issue turns on a question of fact and should have been submitted to a jury for determination. Trial ordered.]

CASE QUESTION

1. Assume you are on the jury in this case. Based on the information available, would you hold that the plaintiff was a guest? Why or why not?

Delivery of Property

As the court in *Langford* stated, registration at the hotel is not essential for an innkeeper–guest relationship to exist. Some cases hold that a person who intends to register but has not yet done so becomes a guest by delivering luggage to a hotel employee. In such circumstances, the soon-to-be guest evidences an intent to become one by transferring possession of the suitcase to the hotel employee. The hotel's intent is evidenced by its acceptance thereof. In these situations, the responsibility of the innkeeper starts at the moment of the delivery and acceptance of the luggage.

© ESB Professional/Shutterstock.com

In one lawsuit a jewelry salesman, upon arrival at the MGM Grand Hotel in Las Vegas, checked his luggage and jewelry samples with the bellhop at the door. Thereafter he registered, went to his room, and waited for his luggage. When it arrived he discovered that some of the jewelry samples were missing. The liability of the hotel depended on whether the salesman was a guest when he gave his baggage to the bellhop. The court held the salesman became a guest at the time he made use of the hotel's luggage check service, since that service was provided specifically for guests.[5] Similarly, the innkeeper–guest relationship can begin when the traveler alights from a taxi in front of the hotel and gives the bellhop a suitcase, or steps into a hotel van or car at the airport and gives the driver the luggage, assuming a room is available at the hotel and the traveler intends to register.

In Case Example 7-3 the plaintiff left her luggage at the defendant hotel although her room reservation did not begin until the next day. Jewelry was stolen from her suitcase. The issue was whether the parties' intention to enter a contract on the following day was sufficient to render the plaintiff a guest on the day the baggage was checked. The court held it was.

© Vibrant Image Studio/Shutterstock.com

---

5 *Pachinger v. MGM Grand Hotel-Las Vegas, Inc.,* 802 F.2d 362 (Nev. 1986)

CASE EXAMPLE 7-3

Adler v. Savoy Plaza Inc.

108 N.Y.S.2d 80 (N.Y. 1951)

This is an action for the loss of jewelry and personal effects contained in a suitcase which was delivered by plaintiff to defendant for safekeeping. The claimed value of the jewelry was something over $20,000 and the claimed value of the personal effects about $3,300.

The facts are as follows: The plaintiff was accustomed to staying at the defendant's hotel whenever she visited New York and had been a guest of the hotel many times. She and her husband had requested reservations for May 15, 1946. Upon their arrival at 10 o'clock that morning, they were advised that their reservation was for the following day, but that the hotel would try to accommodate them, so they registered, hoping that a room might be assigned during the day. At the same time, they delivered their luggage to the bell captain, and it was deposited in a section of the lobby set aside for the luggage of arriving and departing guests. Plaintiff's husband attended to business during the day while plaintiff was in and out of the hotel. When both returned to the hotel in the afternoon, they found that a room was still not available, so they whiled away some time in the lounge bar and had dinner in the room of a friend who was a guest of the hotel.

All during the day defendant's manager was seeking accommodations for the couple but was unable to locate any in the hotel. He finally secured accommodations for them for the night at the Sherry Netherlands Hotel where they registered at about 8:00 p.m., taking with them two suitcases and a cosmetic case, and leaving the suitcase with the valuables and two matching cases at defendant's hotel.

When plaintiff returned to defendant's hotel the next morning to take up residence for two or three weeks and requested delivery of her luggage, the large suitcase was missing. During the night the suitcase had been delivered by the night manager of the hotel to an imposter. The circumstances of this delivery are not altogether clear as the night manager was deceased at the time of the trial. Whether there was some complicity on the part of one or more of the hotel employees, as plaintiff suggests, we are not called upon to surmise.

[One of] the questions as to the [hotel's liability for the lost] jewelry, was whether plaintiff was a guest of the hotel.

…We are prepared to rule as a matter of law on the admitted facts that plaintiff was a guest.

CASE QUESTIONS

1. Why do you think the court ruled that the plaintiff was a guest?

2. What role did her intent to rent a room play in the determination that she was a guest?

3. Suppose the plaintiff did not have reservations and the hotel was full, but she was allowed to leave her bags for the day while she looked for a room elsewhere. Would the plaintiff qualify as a guest?

When people deliver baggage to the hotel bellhop, if they do not intend to become guests of the hotel, an innkeeper–guest relationship does not exist. In a Washington D.C. case the plaintiffs had come to town to celebrate President Reagan's inauguration. Before returning home, and after checking out of their hotel, they decided to have lunch at the Jockey Club, an elegant restaurant that was part of the Fairfax Hotel, which was not the hotel in which they had stayed. When they arrived at the restaurant, they checked a briefcase and a small carry-on bag with the hotel doorman. After lunch they retrieved their bags from the doorman and discovered a jewelry pouch was missing. The liability of the hotel turned on whether the plaintiffs qualified as guests. The court held they were not, stating, "One who is merely a customer at a bar, a restaurant, a barber shop, or newsstand operated by a hotel does not thereby establish the relationship of innkeeper and guest."[6]

A person who has not yet decided whether to rent a room may, under certain circumstances, be considered a guest. The key issue is whether that person came to the hotel for the purpose of benefiting from the various services offered by the hotel to guests. This rule of law is illustrated in Case Example 7-4.

CASE EXAMPLE 7-4

Freudenheim v. Eppley

88 F.2d 280 (Pa. 1937)

…[F]reudenheim was the traveling salesman of his diamond firm, and… he was accustomed to visiting Buffalo, Detroit, Cleveland, Toledo, Chicago, Indianapolis, Cincinnati, and Pittsburgh. [If] trade justified, he stayed at hotels which had vaults for the deposit of valuables and he left his bag containing diamonds in their vaults…. Prior to 1930 he came to Pittsburgh eight or nine times a year and stayed at the William Penn [Hotel] two, three, or four days at a time, depending on trade conditions. In 1933 he was twice in Pittsburgh, received his mail at the hotel, but did not stay overnight. On every one of his trips to Pittsburgh he used the vault at the William Penn. On the morning of December 5, 1933, after visiting other cities, he arrived in Pittsburgh from Cincinnati before 7:00 a.m. After checking his personal bag at the railroad station, he went to the hotel. [He testified]: "I intended to stay here as long as I could do business here." He arrived at the hotel around 7:00 a.m., but the cashier's office, where the hotel had vaults, was not open, and the cashier, Schaller, had not arrived.

His testimony was: "I waited around the lobby until about seven-thirty and around seven-thirty I went back to the cashier's office and saw Mr. Schaller there and he greeted me. I told him I wanted a box, or he said, 'I suppose you want a box….' Whether he knew me by name, I don't know, but he knew me quite well." Continuing, the witness said: "Mr. Schaller came out of the cage, which

---

6 *Blakemore v. Coleman*, 701 F.2d 967 (D.C. 1983)

is controlled by a wire door grill there, and he brought out a couple of keys and a tag. He tore off part of the tag and gave me the bottom of it, and asked me to sign the upper part, which I did and returned it to him, and he gave me this stub bearing the same number as appears on the part bearing my signature which I gave to him. He then gave me two keys, which were attached to this little ring bearing a metal disc on which is noted the letter 'C.' He then inserted the key which was attached to this ring and opened the box—opened the door—and I put my briefcase in which my merchandise had been placed right inside that box. I closed the door and I went downstairs."

In the first place, we have the fact that Freudenheim was known to the hotel as a past guest and that there was the possibility of his lodging at the hotel if trade warranted such stay. There was, therefore, in the mind of both parties that the hotel would have Freudenheim as a guest. He was recognized by the cashier; inquiry was made whether he wanted a box; he was given the box; his merchandise was deposited;…This was a service or accommodation which the hotel had extended before and Freudenheim had enjoyed before.

Now it is clear that vault service for valuables is a customary hotel accommodation, and that it was the intention of both parties that Freudenheim should have that accommodation,… The responsibility of an innkeeper for the safety of a traveler's property begins at the moment when the relation of guest and host arises, and that relation arises as soon as the traveler enters the inn with the intention of using it as an inn, and is so received by the host. It does not matter that no food or lodging has been supplied or found up to this time of the loss. It is sufficient if the circumstances show an intention on the one hand to provide and on the other hand to accept such accommodation.

Moreover, later on, and before he left, Freudenheim, who was busy with his customers all morning and into the afternoon and took no lunch, did take his dinner in the general dining room of the hotel. It is true he did not take a room and register, but his omission to do so does not put him out of guest protection …. It is not necessary that a traveler shall register at an inn as a guest in order to become such, but it is sufficient if he visits the inn for the purpose of receiving [customary services and receives them].…

CASE QUESTION

1. How does this case expand our definition of a guest?

Guests' Illegal Acts

A question arises concerning the status of a would-be guest who registers at a hotel giving false information. In one case, the plaintiffs sought damages for personal injuries allegedly sustained when they attempted to escape a fire in the lodging house where they were staying. They had registered as husband and wife, but were not in fact married. The defendant lodging house argued that by reason of the

plaintiffs' misrepresentation, they were trespassers and not guests. Therefore, the argument went, the lodging house owed them no duty to exercise reasonable care.

The court, however, stated that without a demonstration that the plaintiffs' illegal act directly contributed to their injuries, neither false registration nor an illegal or immoral purpose in occupying a room would change their status as guests to whom the defendant owed the duty of reasonable care. Therefore, the plaintiffs qualified as guests and could pursue the case against the lodging house notwithstanding the false registration.[7]

In an older case, dated by its facts but not by the legal ruling, an unlicensed peddler staying at an inn stored his peddler's cart in the hotel stable overnight. Goods were stolen from the cart while he slept. In the peddler's lawsuit against the hotel, the innkeeper denied liability on the ground that the peddler, by selling without a license, was engaged in illegal activity. In this case, too, the court held the fact that the peddler was unlicensed was not a bar to the lawsuit because the illegal act of selling without a license did not directly contribute to the theft.[8]

A different outcome resulted, and the hotel was not liable, where a minor went to a hotel room with strangers for the sole purpose of smoking marijuana illegally. In the hotel room, she became the victim of statutory rape. Her parents sued the hotel. Following the common law, the court determined she was not a guest because the element of mutual benefit was lacking; the inn received no benefit from the girl's presence on the premises. Therefore the only duty the hotel owed to her was to refrain from willfully or wantonly injuring her. The court further ruled the fact that she was a minor was overridden by her admission that she knew the danger of going to a hotel room with strangers.[9]

---

[7] *Cramer v. Tarr, 165 F.Supp. 130* (Maine 1958)
[8] *Kimbel's Case* 168 A. 871 (Maine 1929)
[9] *Doe v. Jameson Inn*, 56 So.3d 549 (Miss. 2011)

Termination of a Guest–Innkeeper Relationship

The innkeeper–guest relationship ends when any of the following occurs:

1. The contracted time for the room has elapsed and it has not been extended.

2. The bill is not paid when due.

3. Proper notice is given to vacate the hotel.

4. A reasonable amount of time has passed since checkout.

5. The bill has been settled and paid.

Once a guest pays his bill and checks out of the hotel, termination of guest status follows closely in time.[10] The status of guest is not instantaneously terminated upon checkout, however, but continues for a reasonable period of time while the guest remains on the hotel premises.[11]

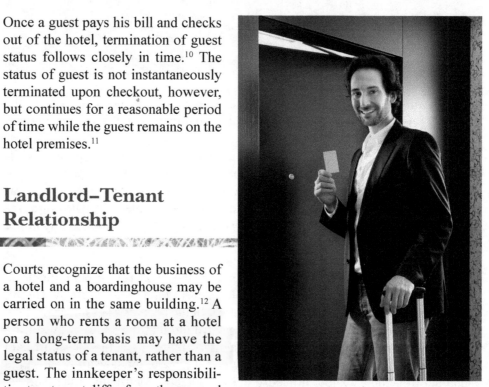

© Kzenon/Shutterstock.com

Landlord–Tenant Relationship

Courts recognize that the business of a hotel and a boardinghouse may be carried on in the same building.[12] A person who rents a room at a hotel on a long-term basis may have the legal status of a tenant, rather than a guest. The innkeeper's responsibilities to a tenant differ from those owed to a guest. To qualify as a guest, a person must be a transient; that is, his stay at the inn is temporary. An innkeeper has no duty to keep a guest indefinitely as Case Example 7-5 demonstrates.

---

10 *Garrett v. Impac Hotels 1*, LLC, 87 S.W.3d 870 (Mo. 2002)
11 *Moog v. Hilton Hotels Corp.*, 882 F. Supp. 1392 (N.Y. 1995)
12 *Gutierrez v. Eckert Farm Supply, Inc.*, 2003 WL 21500161 (Minn. 2003)

CASE EXAMPLE 7-5

Olley v. Extended Stay America – Houston

449 S.W.3d 572 (Tex., 2014).

…Jeff Olley checked into an Extended Stay America in May 2012 and stayed there with his wife and child. He stopped making payments as of April 23, 2013. On April 25, the hotel served Olley "and all other occupants [of the room]" with a termination notice requiring them to vacate the hotel by May 2. When they failed to do so, the hotel served Olley with a notice to vacate and subsequently filed a forcible detainer lawsuit [this is a quick remedy used by a property owner to oust an occupant who was initially in legal possession of the property but no longer] in justice court. The justice court awarded possession of the hotel room and money damages to the hotel. Olley appealed to the county court.

The county court awarded possession of the hotel room and monetary damages to the hotel. It moved for a temporary restraining order (TRO) to restrain Olley from returning to the hotel based upon his aggressive behavior in the courtroom. The county court granted the TRO and ordered the eviction immediately.

A deputy constable executed the writ of possession the next day [this means the occupants were removed and the lock was changed]. Olley's wife was present and was allowed to retrieve the Olleys' possessions before she was escorted off the property.

Olley complains that the trial court erred in awarding possession of the premises to the hotel and issuing the temporary restraining order….

An action for forcible detainer is intended to be a speedy, simple, and inexpensive means to obtain immediate possession of property. It is a determination of the right to immediate possession. [It can be used to remove a nonpaying hotel guest but not a tenant. The procedure to remove a tenant is lengthier.]

A guest in a hotel is a mere licensee, not a tenant. No landlord-tenant relationship exists between a hotel and its guest….

© ppl/Shutterstock.com

Olley points to a registration card from the hotel that he signed, contending it is a contract allowing him to stay in the hotel room. Although the registration card included an "arrival date" and a "departure date," it did not include language indicating that Olley was a tenant. It merely included the dates Olley was authorized to occupy the room, noted that the reserved rate was guaranteed for only 60 days from check-in, and informed Olley that advance notice was required to extend his stay, subject to availability.

The registration card also included the following statements: "I am aware that failure to meet my payment and other obligations will result, at a minimum, in the immediate termination of my stay."…

The hotel's general manager testified that a guest may leave before the anticipated departure date on the registration card without incurring a penalty. [In contrast, a tenant who leaves before the end of a lease is responsible to pay the rent through the end of the lease term.] We conclude that the registration card did not establish that Olley has a potentially meritorious claim of right to possession of the property.

Olley also argues that he has the right to possess the room because he offered to pay after he fell behind on payments. He contends the hotel rejected his offer. …Olley's argument is misplaced. An innkeeper has no duty to accept late payment and keep a guest indefinitely.

We conclude Olley has not shown an arguable right to possession of the hotel he and his family previously occupied.

Case Questions

1. What was the effect of the language in the registration card?

2. Should innkeepers have a duty to keep guests indefinitely?

Factors to Consider When Determining Whether a Person Is a Tenant

If the person is staying on a permanent basis, he is a tenant. Whether a hotel patron is a tenant or a guest is determined from the following factors:

- The terms of the contract between the parties. For example, use of the terminology *landlord* and *tenant* rather than *innkeeper* and *guest* suggest the customer is a tenant.

- The extent of control or supervision of the patron's room maintained by the proprietor. The more control and supervision is retained by the hotel, the more likely the patron is a guest.

- The rental rate interval (e.g., daily, weekly, or monthly). The shorter the interval, the more likely the patron is a guest.

- Length of occupancy. The longer the occupancy, the greater the suggestion the patron is a tenant.

- Incidental services offered. For example, frequent housekeeping and room services are often associated with guests but not tenants.

- Whether the room has cooking facilities. Those are more frequently associated with a landlord–tenant relationship than with an innkeeper–guest relationship.

- The kind of furnishings in the room and who owns them. Whereas hotel rooms virtually always are furnished, rooms intended as apartments are less likely to be furnished.

None of these factors alone determines the legal relationship; the more the circumstances resemble a landlord–tenant relationship, the less likely an innkeeper–guest relationship exists.

Several cases help explain how these factors are applied. In the first, a plaintiff had an 11-month written lease for a room at a hotel. His rent included housekeeping and telephone services. He was a tenant and not a guest.[13]

In another case the person in question had lived at the inn for two months, all his belongings were there, and the inn was his sole residence. He, too, was a tenant and not a guest.[14]

In the second case, a patron at a licensed hotel occupied a room that was 12 feet by 15 feet, and contained a bed and sink. Toilet and bathing facilities were located down the hall and shared with others. Cooking facilities were not provided. Rent was paid weekly. The patron occupied the room for three and one-half months, during which time he had no other residence. When he registered, he was required to sign a hotel registration card. He did not make any special arrangements with the hotel concerning the duration of his occupancy.

The issue of whether he was a guest or a tenant arose when he was two weeks late with his rent. The legal method of evicting a guest is different from and easier than that for tenants, as is discussed in Chapter 9. The hotel used the easier method applicable to guests. The patron argued that he was a tenant and therefore the eviction was invalid. The court determined the relationship was innkeeper and guest, stating,

> *[A]ny unilateral intention on the part of the plaintiff to remain at the hotel indefinitely or to make it his home of which [the hotel] had*

---

[13] *Chawla v. Horch d/b/a Master Hotel,* 333 N.Y.S.2d 531 (N.Y. 1972)
[14] *Gutierrez v. Eckert Farm Supply, Inc.,* 2003 WL 21500161 (Minn. 2003)

no reasonable notice, would not be determinative in ascertaining what contractual arrangements existed between the parties....

The three-month duration of plaintiff's occupancy of the room was not so extended that the trial court was obliged to view it as "permanent". In conjunction with...the operation of the premises as a licensed hotel, the rudimentary nature of the accommodations furnished, without cooking, bathing or toilet facilities in the room, is some indication that only a temporary living arrangement was intended.[15]

---

[15] *Bourque v. Morris*, 460 A.2d 1251 (Conn. 1983)

Summary

The legal duties owed by an innkeeper to guests are different from those owed to nonguests. A threshold issue in many lawsuits against hotels is whether the plaintiff was a guest in the legal sense. The outcome of the case may depend on the resolution of that issue.

The easiest-to-identify guest is one who has registered for a room on a temporary basis. By registering, the guest has evidenced an intention to utilize overnight accommodations and the hotel has evidenced an intention to provide the guest a room. The definition of *guest* has been expanded to include people who mistakenly come to the hotel a day earlier than the first day of their reservations and utilize baggage-check services in the interim; people who are in the process of checking in or out; and regular overnight patrons who, on a day in question, utilize the hotel safe although unsure if they will stay in town overnight, but who intend to stay at the hotel if they do decide to remain. While the class of guests has expanded, still necessary is an intention by the guest to use the hotel's accommodations and intention by the hotel to provide the guest a room on a temporary basis.

A hotel guest should be distinguished from a tenant, whose use of a room is of a longer duration than a guest's. The obligations of an innkeeper to a guest differ from those of a landlord to a tenant.

Preventive Law Tips for Managers

- *Recognize that the innkeeper has special obligations to guests.* For this reason, the innkeeper must know who qualifies as a guest and who does not.

- *Keep in mind that the following categories of people may qualify as guests*:

    - A person who arrives at the hotel and registers for a room;

    - A person who arrives at a hotel, intends to register, and gives luggage to the bellhop who accepts it, assuming the person has a reservation or the hotel has rooms available;

    - A person who arrives at the airport, enters a hotel courtesy van, and gives the driver the luggage which the driver accepts, assuming the traveler intends to register and the hotel has a room available;

    - A person who arrives at the inn, has reservations for the following day, intends to register as soon as a room is available, and leaves luggage with the bellhop who accepts delivery of it; and

- A regular guest of the hotel who arrives without a reservation and, as per prior dealings with the inn, intends to stay the night if business warrants it, and the hotel has a room available for rent

- *Illegal activity on the part of guests may not affect their status as guests.* A person injured at a hotel who registers using false information or engages in illegal activity in the room is not thereby any less a guest for purposes of obligations owed by the innkeeper, unless the illegality was the direct cause of the injury that underlies a lawsuit.

- *The innkeeper–guest relationship terminates when certain events occur.* Those events include passage of the contracted time for the guest to occupy the room; the bill is not paid when due; proper notice is given to vacate; or a reasonable time has passed following checkout.

- *A tenant is not a guest.* The circumstances of a tenant vary from those of a guest in numerous ways, including that the duration of a tenant's stay usually exceeds that of a guest's; the proprietor's right to enter the room of a guest to clean or otherwise tend to the room usually exceeds that for a tenant; the room rates of a guest are usually calculated on a daily or weekly amount, whereas the rates of a tenant are usually weekly or monthly; and a tenant's room will customarily have kitchen facilities included, whereas a guest's room is less likely to have them.

Review Questions

1. What role does registration for a hotel room play in the formation of the innkeeper–guest relationship?

2. Under what circumstances can a person who has not registered at a hotel be considered a guest?

3. What is the significance of someone qualifying as a guest?

4. Does a person who is attending a half-day seminar at a hotel without registering for a guest room qualify as a guest?

5. When does an innkeeper–guest relationship terminate?

6. What are some factors that distinguish a guest from a tenant?

Discussion Questions

1. Which of the following qualify as guests?

   A. A patron of a hotel gift shop who works in an office nearby.

   B. A person who has a reservation at a hotel and, upon arriving at the airport, enters the hotel's hospitality van and hands her luggage to the driver, who accepts it.

   C. A person who registers for a room for two weeks.

   D. A resident of the area in which a hotel/resort is located who takes tennis lessons twice a week from the professional on the hotel premises.

2. What is the significance of someone qualifying as a guest?

3. Under what circumstances might a guest's illegal activity on hotel premises affect the liability of the hotel for injuries to that guest?

4. The Mandarin Hotel provided rooms on a nightly, weekly, and monthly basis. Ryan rents a room by the week. What additional information would you need to determine whether Ryan is a guest or a tenant?

5. At what point in the hotel check-in process do you think a person should first be deemed a guest? Why? How does your answer compare to the decisions in the cases in this chapter?

Application Questions

1. Sarah is having her wedding reception at the local Marriott hotel. Her parents contracted with the hotel for the use of a banquet room and catering facilities. Sarah and her then-husband will leave immediately after the reception for their honeymoon in another state. Some out-of-town guests will be staying at the hotel overnight. Who is a guest of the hotel? Why do the others not qualify?

2. Andrea flew from her home in Miami, Florida, to New York City. She planned to meet a friend at the airport for dinner. While waiting for the friend, she noticed a hospitality van from the hotel at which she had reservations for that evening. She gave her luggage to the driver so she would not have to worry about her suitcase during dinner. Does Andrea qualify as a guest?

3. Alishia had reservations to stay at the Islander Inn for a week. After she was there for three nights, she received a call advising that her father was quite ill. She immediately left the inn and returned home. For what period of time was Alishia a guest? When did she cease being a guest?

4. Nick made reservations at the Peaceful Valley Resort near a ski center. Before the trip, he hurt his foot working out on a stepper machine and was unable to ski. He told his friend, who decided to go skiing in Nick's place. When the friend arrived at the hotel, he explained the circumstances to the hotel proprietor, who agreed to rent the room to the friend. Was Nick ever a guest of the motel? Why or why not? Does the friend qualify as a guest? Why or why not?

CHAPTER 8

Protecting Patrons' Property

LEARNING OUTCOMES:

- Comprehend the risks to guests' property in the hotel
- Understand the limitations on the absolute liability rule, and the requirements to benefit from them
- Appreciate the concept of estoppel and its loss of limited liability
- Know the role of hotel negligence in loss of limited liability
- Understand liability during checkin and checkout
- Learn about bailments and the responsibilities they impose

KEY TERMS

absolute liability	bailor	merchandise samples
act of God	concessionnaire	mutual-benefit bailment
bailee	conspicuous	prima facie
bailment	constructive bailment	prima facie liability rule
bailment for the sole benefit of the bailee	equitable estoppel	public enemy
	infra hospitium	strict liability
bailment for the sole benefit of the bailor	limiting liability statutes	
	limiting statutes	

Introduction

Hotel guests bring a variety of personal property to hotels, including money, jewelry, computers and other electronic devices, clothing, sports equipment, and cars. Business travelers may bring merchandise samples or inventory for sale. Hotels often provide safes for such property, but guests may choose not to use them. Sometimes property may be left in the lobby, a restaurant, the pool area, other rooms in the hotel, or in a guest's car parked in a hotel parking lot. Occasionally, guests' property is stolen. Additionally, consumer's personal information may be stolen. Protection of personal information will be discussed in Chapter 10. This chapter will discuss the liability of a hotel or restaurant when property disappears.

Risks to Property in the Hotel

Hotel theft is a problem the hospitality industry has not fully solved. The liability of the innkeeper for losses has lessened over time. Whereas the law long ago imposed full responsibility on the innkeeper for personal property stolen from the premises, states today have chosen to relieve the hotelier of a significant portion of that liability. While the hotel has a duty to protect guests by maintaining the premises in a safe condition, the duty does not extend to protecting or warning guests with respect to the unforeseeable criminal acts of third parties.[1]

---

1 *Heimberger v. Zeal Hotel Grp., Ltd.*, 42 N,E.3d 23 (Ohio 2015)

Hotel Theft

Unfortunately, hotel thefts are not rare. Hotel crime is an industry-wide problem. Most hotel thieves are professionals seeking money, jewelry, debit cards, or credit cards. They often register as guests in the hotel they plan to burglarize or pretend to be employees. The many tricks of the hotel thief include offering money in exchange for confidential information from housekeepers, bartenders, or other hotel personnel. These thieves generally do not carry a weapon; if surprised in the act, they may convincingly feign drunkenness or claim an innocent mistake has taken place.

© Zdorov Kirill Vladimirovich/Shutterstock.com

Hotels have developed numerous strategies to stem the increase of hotel thefts, including increasing the number of security personnel; hiring trained professionals; warning guests to lock their rooms and put their valuables in a hotel safe; installing closed-circuit televisions to monitor hallways; installing electronic lock devices for guest rooms, which are changed for each guest using the room, thereby preventing access by retained keys; instituting tighter security checks on employees; restricting access to elevators leading to guest rooms to people displaying room keys; and, in small hotels, installing electronic lobby doors that can be opened only by the desk clerk when a guest is recognized.

Alliances between the police and hotel security staff can enhance efforts to reduce crime. For example, large, urban police departments often have a hotel unit that concentrates on crimes committed at city hotels. The officers in the unit and the security forces at hotels communicate frequently to share information and alert each other to potential problems. Issues discussed include new methods of committing theft, and the latest methods of detection and prevention.

Keycards and Keys

Most hotels today have abandoned the use of traditional keys and instead use electronic keycards, which have a magnetic strip. These devices allow the hotel to change the code that opens the door every time a new guest occupies the room. Smartphone apps allow keyless entry to hotel rooms. These uses of technology have greatly improved security in hotel rooms when compared to the frequent duplication of keys seen in the past.

Guests' Insurance

Many people are not personally insured against the loss of their valuables. Therefore if their property is stolen while they are at the hotel, they are likely to sue the hotel seeking compensation. If a traveler whose property disappears does have insurance coverage and recovers the loss from the insurance company, the hotel is not relieved from liability. Normally the guest's insurance policy provides that the insurance company is subrogated (substituted) to the legal rights of the guest. This means that the insurance company can sue the hotel to recover the money the insurance company paid to the guest. If the hotel was liable for the loss, the insurance company will collect.

In another case, the hotel's insurance coverage for guests' stolen property varied depending on whether the hotel had "care, custody or control" of the property when the theft occurred. If so, the insurance coverage was limited to $250,000. If the hotel did not have "care, custody or control," the insurance company was liable for up to $1 million. This type of coverage for hotels was not unusual. A guest's valuable, worth at least $1 million, were stolen from an in-room safe. The amount of the loss was not contested by the hotel or the insurance company. An issue arose as to which insurance coverage amount should apply. The court determined that guests' property, while maintained in an in-room safe, is in the "care, custody or control" of the hotel. The court reasoned that the hotel fully controls the security arrangements for property left in a hotel room, and the hotel also controls access to the room. Therefore, the insurance company was liable only for $250,000.[2]

strict liability
Also called absolute liability; the doctrine that imposes all the risks of an ultra-hazardous activity upon those who engage in it.

infra hospitium
Meaning "within the inn." This doctrine states that under common law hotels were liable as insurers for guests' property on the hotel premises.

Absolute Liability for Guests' Goods

In prior times and according to common law, hotelkeepers were liable for any loss of guests' property occurring on hotel premises. This doctrine was called **absolute** or **strict liability** and applied to guests' property that was **infra hospitium,** literally meaning "within the inn." Thus, if property was stolen or otherwise disappeared from the hotel, the innkeeper was liable to reimburse the guest even if the innkeeper did nothing wrong. This strict rule originated several centuries ago when inns were not always safe and the innkeeper was often the culprit. The rule contributed in no small measure to an increase in the level of safety associated with travel because innkeepers sought ways to protect their guests' valuables and thereby avoid liability. The reputation of the hotel industry has improved substantially since those early days. We will see shortly that the rule of absolute liability has likewise been modified.

---

2 *Liberty Mut. Ins. Co. v. Zurich Ins. Co.*, 402 Ill. App. 3d 37, 341 Ill. Dec. 363, 930 N.E. 2d 573 (2010).

Almost every rule of law has exceptions, and the outdated rule that held the innkeeper absolutely liable for guests' goods was tempered by three exceptions:

1. Loss was attributed to what the law calls an **act of God,** which includes earthquakes, lightning, snowstorms, tornadoes, and floods.

2. Loss was caused by a public enemy, which includes terrorist and wartime activities.

3. Negligence occurred by the guest, such as leaving luggage unattended in the lobby.

act of God
A happening not controlled by the power of humans, but rather from the direct, immediate, and exclusive operations of the forces of nature.

Prima Facie Liability Rule—Minority View

Six states have adopted a rule that modifies the common law absolute liability rule as follows: Hotelkeepers are liable for property loss only if the loss occurs through their negligence; if the innkeeper can prove that the loss resulted from some other cause, for example, if the goods are stolen by robbers without the aid or negligence of the innkeeper, the innkeeper is not liable. This is called the **prima facie liability rule.** If, however, the innkeeper cannot prove that it is free from negligence, the innkeeper will be liable for the loss. The six states that have adopted this rule are Illinois, Indiana, Maryland, Texas, Vermont, and Washington.

prima facie liability
A rule that states that hotelkeepers are liable for property loss only if the loss occurs through their negligence; if the loss results from some other cause, the innkeeper is not liable.

Justification for the rule was stated in an early case from Indiana:

> *Innkeepers, on grounds of public policy, are held to a strict accountability for the goods of their guests. The interests of the public, we think, are sufficiently [served] by holding the innkeeper prima facie liable for the loss or injury of the goods of their guests; thus throwing the burden of proof upon [the innkeeper], to show that the injury or loss happened without any fault whatever on his part, and that he exercised reasonable care and diligence.[3]*

Limited Liability—Modern Limitations on the Absolute Liability Rule

As hotels grew in size and the number of travelers increased, the difficulty of safe-guarding property increased. Current law recognizes that the absolute liability rule is unnecessarily burdensome to modern-day hotels and innkeepers. All state legislatures have adopted statutes to limit significantly hotelkeepers' liability for guests' property losses, provided the hotels follow specific procedures. The result of these statutes is that a hotel that complies with the mandated rules will

---

[3] *Laird v. Eichold,* 10 Ind 212 (Ind. 1858)

face liability of only a few hundred dollars, even if guests' property valued at many thousands of dollars or more is stolen.

While the details of these statutes vary from state to state, certain common provisions exist, as follows:

- The hotel must provide a safe for use by guests to protect their property.

- The hotel must post notices announcing to guests the availability of the safes.

- The hotel must post notices announcing that the hotel's liability for guests' property is limited.

- The maximum recovery allowed to a guest for stolen or lost property is prescribed by statute and is usually substantially less than the value of the missing property. For example, a statute may specify that the maximum liability will be $1,000 regardless of the value of the lost property. If a hotel complies with the statute and a guest's $50,000 ring is stolen, the hotel will be liable to the guest for only $1,000.

In essence, limited liability statutes provide that if a hotel proprietor provides a safe or safe deposit box for the storage of valuables and posts conspicuous notice that a safe is available, a hotel guest who fails to use the safe or safe deposit box cannot hold the hotel responsible if his valuables are later lost or stolen. Alternatively, if the guest utilizes the safe, the hotel owner will be liable only for the limited amount provided in the statute. In a New York case a guest left several thousand dollars in cash and checks in his hotel room and they were stolen while he was at dinner. The hotel had properly posted notices that safes were available and the hotel's liability was limited. The guest could not recover from the hotel for the loss because he had failed to store the items in the safe.[4] If the guest had locked the items in the safe and they were stolen, the hotel would have been liable to the guest, but only for a limited amount of money.

To qualify for the reduced liability, the hotel must fully comply with the statute's mandates. Courts interpret them very strictly. If the innkeeper deviates from the requirements of the statute in any manner, the common law rule will apply and the innkeeper will have unlimited liability. Thus, innkeepers must be careful to provide the mandated safe, post the necessary notices in the required places, and otherwise rigorously comply with the applicable state statute.

limiting liability statutes
Laws that restrict an innkeepers' liability for property loss in exchange for strict statutory compliance by the innkeeper. Also called limiting statutes.

In this chapter, the laws that restrict innkeepers' liability will be called **limiting liability statutes** or **limiting statutes.** Each of the requirements for limited liability outlined above will be discussed separately.

---

[4] *Beam v. Marriott Corp.,* 655 N.Y.S.2d 566 (N.Y. 1997)

Providing a Safe

Almost invariably, the limiting liability statutes require that the innkeeper provide a "proper safe" for guests' valuables. In the past, hotels uniformly provided a safe or safe deposit boxes in a central location, usually in the vicinity of the front desk. A popular alternative today is for hotels to provide individual safes in each guest room.

In Case Example 8-1, the hotel provided a central safe but it was not available late in the evening when the plaintiff sought to deposit two diamond rings. What impact do you think that fact had on the hotel's liability? See if your answer agrees with the judge's decision.

© Maxx-Studio/Shutterstock.com

CASE EXAMPLE 8-1

Zaldin v. Concord Hotel

421 N. Y.S.2d 858 (N.Y. 1979)

Plaintiffs, registered guests, bring suit on a theory of absolute liability for the loss of two valuable diamond rings that disappeared from their hotel room. In its answer, the defendant hotel pleaded [New York's limiting liability statute] by way of defense. Asserting that the hotel's vault was not available to guests at the time they attempted to place the jewelry there for safekeeping, plaintiffs moved for... judgment.... [W]e hold that a hotel may not claim the limitations on liability afforded it by [the limiting liability statute] at times when it fails to make a safe available to its guests.

[The limiting liability statute] reads: "Whenever the proprietor or manager of any hotel shall provide a safe... for the safekeeping of any money, jewels, ornaments, bank notes, bonds, negotiable securities, or precious stones, belonging to the guests... and shall notify the guests or travelers there of by posting a notice stating the fact that such safe is provided... in a public and conspicuous place and manner in the office and public rooms... and if such guest or traveler shall neglect to deliver such property... for deposit in such safe, the proprietor or manager... shall not be liable for any loss of such property, sustained by such guest or traveler by theft or otherwise."... The statute goes on to limit a hotel's liability for property so deposited with it, whether the loss is sustained "by theft or otherwise," to a sum not exceeding $500.

...It is agreed that on Friday afternoon, the plaintiffs William and Shelby Modell, accompanied by their daughter [Anna Zaldin] and son-in-law, checked into the defendant's large resort hotel. No one disputes but that the hotel provided a safedeposit vault for the use of its guests and that shortly after the plaintiffs' arrival, the daughter requested and was assigned one of its boxes. Plaintiffs allege that she then placed two diamond rings belonging to her mother in the box and that late the following afternoon, she withdrew them from the box for her mother to wear while attending the Saturday evening festivities sponsored by the hotel.

Sometime after midnight, however, upon the conclusion of the hotel's nightclub performance and before retiring, when the Modells and their daughter attempted to redeposit the jewelry, a hotel desk clerk informed them that the vault was closed and that they would have to retain possession of their valuables until it was opened in the morning. The defendant concedes that it would not allow guests access to the vault between the hours of eleven in the evening and eight in the morning. The Modells claim they thereupon secreted the jewelry in their room only to find, upon arising at about 9:00 a.m., that the chain lock with which they had secured the room had been cut from the outside and the rings were missing. They promptly notified the hotel and police of what they took to be a theft.

In now applying the statute to this factual framework, we first remark on the obvious: The statute's wording is plain.… [W]hen, as here, a statute is free from ambiguity… we must do no more and no less than apply the language as it is written.

Thus read, the statute offers the innkeeper an option: "Provide" a safe for your guests and sharply restrict your liability; or, feel free to do absolutely nothing about a safe and continue the risk of exposure to open-ended common law liability. But, whichever choice you make, since the statute is in derogation of [deviates from] the common law rule, to obtain the benefit of the more circumscribed liability… you must conform strictly to its conditions.

The statute fixes no time when a safe may or must be provided. Nor does it mandate availability around the clock.… These matters are left entirely up to the hotel. The statute makes no effort to evaluate cost or convenience. Neither does it distinguish between large and small inns, between those that cater to the large convention and those that cater to the individual patron, between those that come alive at night and those that do so in the day, between those that have a wealthy clientele and those that do not. The legislative formula is uncomplicated. It says, straightforwardly, that "whenever" a safe is provided, the liability limitations shall be applicable. Conversely, at those times when an innkeeper chooses not to provide a safe for the use of its guest, he cannot claim the statutory protection… . More specifically, nowhere does [the limiting liability statute] suggest that an innkeeper may provide a safe part of the time and yet gain the benefit of the exemption all the time.… [Judgment for plaintiffs.]

CASE QUESTIONS

1. Did the hotel violate any law by closing the safe during the night?

2. What was the consequence of failing to make the safe available at all hours?

In another case, several guests wanting to deposit jewelry in the hotel safe waited for the night clerk for up to 40 minutes in the early morning hours. Without success they went to bed, taking their valuables with them. Following a theft that night from their room they sued the hotel. The court held the hotel was liable for the full loss because the front desk was unattended and therefore access to the safe was unavailable.[5]

---

[5] *Durandy v. Fairmont Roosevelt Hotel, Inc.,* 523 F.Supp. 1382 (La. 1981)

An interesting situation arises when guests choose to put their valuables at risk in the hotel room. Case Example 8-2 demonstrates the legal outcome associated with such decisions.

CASE EXAMPLE 8-2

Carlson v. BRGA Associates, LLC

84 F. Supp 3d 1333 (Ga. 2015)

...On November 5, 2012, Plaintiffs Arthur and Arlene Carlson were traveling from one home in New Jersey to another home in Florida. Having stayed at the Brunswick Park Hotel before, they decided to stop there for the evening once again. After arriving at the hotel, Plaintiffs checked in and took their luggage and dog to their room. Among the luggage was a backpack in which Mrs. Carlson carried about 95% of all the jewelry she owned.

Once they were in the room, Mr. Carlson began to inspect a safe that the hotel had provided guests to secure their valuables. However, the Carlsons ultimately elected not to pursue use of the safe. While Mr. Carlson did spend some time trying to open the safe after Plaintiffs first checked into their room, he was unable to do so. Rather than contact the front desk to ask for assistance with the safe, Plaintiffs decided that Mrs. Carlson would simply take her backpack of jewelry with her to dinner.

Plaintiffs then fed their dog and tried to place it in its crate so they could leave for dinner. However, the dog did not want to stay in the crate and became upset. After Plaintiffs got the upset dog in its crate, they left the room so quickly that Mrs. Carlson forgot to take her backpack with her. Mrs.

Carlson says this oversight was an "accident" as her usual custom is to keep her jewelry bag on her person when she travels.

Mrs. Carlson realized she had left her backpack in the room when she and her husband were at the hotel elevator on their way out of the hotel. Mrs. Carlson wanted to go back to the room but her husband replied, "No, we're going to dinner. The dog will get upset again, don't go back." Mrs. Carlson responded, "If there's anything missing, it's going to cost you a hell of a lot of money." Mr. Carlson, knowing that all of Mrs. Carlson's jewelry was in the backpack, concluded the conversation by saying, "What can happen in 45 minutes?" The couple then walked to a restaurant for dinner, where Mrs. Carlson spent the meal worrying about the jewelry.

When the Carlsons returned to their room after dinner, Mrs. Carlson immediately went to her backpack to check the jewelry. She opened the bag and noticed that almost all of her jewelry, expect for a few pieces, was gone. She became very upset.

Similar thefts had occurred at the hotel 13 months before the theft of the Carlsons' jewelry. However, no one was aware of any thefts of any items from the hotel rooms for more than a year prior to the Carlson incident. The prior thefts all occurred when the hotel was managed by a different company....

Plaintiffs sued the hotel and management company arguing that each failed to take appropriate remedial measures to mitigate the risk of burglaries. Defendants raise Plaintiffs' assumption of the risk as an affirmative defense....

A defendant asserting the assumption of the risk defense bears the burden of proving that the plaintiff 1) had actual knowledge of the danger; 2) understood and appreciated the risks associated with such danger; and 3) voluntarily exposed himself to those risks....

Here, Plaintiffs had actual knowledge of the danger that Mrs. Carlson's jewelry could be stolen while they were out to dinner. Plaintiffs specifically stopped at the elevator before they left the building to discuss the possibility of a theft.... Plaintiffs' knowledge was not of some vague possibility of criminal activity, but rather of the specific risk that someone would enter their room without authorization and steal Mrs. Carlson's jewelry.... there was no deception here that caused Plaintiffs to assume a different risk than the one that actually transpired.... Plaintiffs in this case knew of the specific danger that someone could enter their hotel room while they were gone and steal the jewelry that was not locked away. Furthermore, Plaintiffs' conversation before leaving the hotel about the risk of theft, which Mr. Carlson concluded by asking "what can happen in 45 minutes?" shows that Plaintiffs "tested the danger" until the assumed risk came to pass. There was no pressing reason for Plaintiffs not to go back to the room to get the jewelry and take it with them to dinner – a precaution that Plaintiffs acknowledge would have prevented their loss. Plaintiffs weighed the risk of theft against the inconvenience of disturbing their dog and delaying their meal for a few minutes, and they chose to head to dinner rather than secure the jewelry. In light of their informed and calculated decision, Defendants cannot be held liable when Plaintiffs tested the risk of theft and that risk came to pass.

Plaintiffs have argued that they did not assume the risk of theft because they, unlike Defendants, were unaware of the prior thefts that had occurred on the property more than a year before and thus did not have a full appreciation of the risk they took by leaving the jewelry in the hotel room…. Plaintiffs argue that both Defendants had a superior knowledge of the risk of theft in their hotel room that Plaintiffs themselves did not enjoy. Therefore, Plaintiffs contend, they did not assume the risk of theft….

There are at least two reasons why this Court will not adopt this theory.

First, such "knowledge balancing" unduly shifts the focus of the assumption of the risk analysis from the plaintiff's knowledge to the defendant's…The parties' relative knowledge of the risk is not relevant in assessing Plaintiffs' assumption of the risk.

Second,… the presence of a safe in Plaintiff's room should have indicated to them that theft of personal belongings was a conceivable risk….

Here, Mrs. Carlson's exact fears came true. She meant to keep her jewels with her so they would not be stolen from the hotel room. She recognized the risk she ran if she proceeded to dinner, but she elected to accept that risk so as not to disturb her dog. There is no evidence to the contrary. Her appreciation of the risk and warning to her husband are plain, palpable and prescient.

Defendants' motion for summary judgment is granted.

CASE QUESTIONS

1. What was the significance of prior burglaries taking place?

2. What was the relevance of the conversation held between Mr. and Mrs. Carlson at the elevator prior to leaving the hotel?

Another issue is the theft-resistant qualities of the safe. If a safe is not adequate to withstand theft or fire, the hotel may not be able to benefit from the limiting statutes. Innkeepers are well advised not to scrimp on the purchase of safes.

Posting Notice of Availability of Safe

Virtually all limiting statutes require posting of one kind or another. "Posting" means displaying a sign that calls the guests' attention to the availability of a safe and the fact that, by law, the hotel's liability for valuables is limited. Each state's statute identifies the places where the notice must be posted and what the notice must state. The required locations and contents vary from state to state. Typically, notice must be posted at the registration desk, on the check-in form, and in guest rooms.

Failure by a hotel to comply strictly with the posting requirements will result in loss of the limited liability. The law applied in such a case will be absolute liability as imposed by common law. If the relevant state statute mandates posting in three locations, compliance with two out of the three is not good enough. This principle is illustrated in Case Example 8-3.

In a similar case, liability for $35,000 worth of jewelry was at stake. The limiting liability statute required the hotel to post notices "in the office and public rooms" (such as the lobby) and in the guest rooms. Although the hotel properly posted in the guest rooms, it failed to post in all of the public rooms. Therefore, the hotel was strictly liable and forced to pay the $35,000.[6]

Omitting the required posting in public places was likewise the hotel's downfall in Case Example 8-4, resulting in liability in excess of $1 million.

CASE EXAMPLE 8-3

Searcy v. La Quinta Motor Inns, Inc.

676 So.2d 1137 (La 1996)

Plaintiff checked into the La Quinta Inn.... She left the room and returned 45 minutes to one hour later, unlocked the door, and found her suitcase practically empty, with some of her things scattered around the room....

A notice was posted by the hotel in the registration area which read, "This property is privately owned and operated. The management reserves the right to refuse service to anyone for lawful and legitimate reasons. Safety deposit boxes are available at the front desk and money, jewelry and documents or other articles of value should be deposited for safekeeping. Unless deposited, the motel assumes no responsibility for any loss or injury to such articles." The writing was very small.... [The relevant Louisiana statute states that the hotel is liable for $500 if the guest is informed of a safe and uses the safe, and then the guest's property disappears. The statute also states that the guest has the right to negotiate with the hotel manager a special written agreement in which the hotel would have greater liability.]

The notice posted in the registration area clearly only advises guests that the hotel is not responsible for the protection of personal property. This notice is totally inadequate. It does not contain either the complete text of the applicable Louisiana statute or the gist of the text. The correct notice was posted in the guest room and apparently was also contained on the check-in slip. However literal compliance with the statute requires that the notice also be placed in the registration area. The hotel did not comply with the statute.... Judgment is rendered in favor of the plaintiffs in the amount of $4,938.95.

---

6 *Insurance Co. v. Holiday Inns, Inc.*, 337 N.Y.S.2d 68 (N.Y. 1972)

CASE EXAMPLE 8-4

Paraskevaides v. Four Seasons Washington

292 F.3d 886 (D.C. 2002).

Thelma and Christine Paraskevaides, together with their insurance company, American Home Assurance Company, brought suit against Four Seasons Washington after $1,000.000 worth of their jewelry was stolen from a convenience safe located in their hotel room. The Four Seasons defended on grounds that their liability was limited by District of Columbia law [limiting liability statute]... Because the Four Seasons failed to comply fully with the Innkeeper Statute... we reverse [the decision that was made in favor of the hotel]...

The Paraskevaides checked into the Four Seasons Washington ("the Four Seasons") in Washington, DC. They brought with them close to $1,200,000 worth of jewelry to wear to various political functions around the city. The Paraskevaides stayed in a suite that consisted of two bedrooms adjoined by a living room. Each bedroom and the living room contained a "convenience safe" that was located in the back of a closet and accessible via keys provided by the hotel. The Paraskevaides placed their valuables (i.e. jewelry, travel documents, traveler's checks, etc.) in the bedroom safes rather than the safety deposit boxes that were provided by the hotel and located near the hotel's reception area.

The Paraskevaides left their hotel room with their room and safe keys. Upon returning to their suite, they discovered that their room had been entered (although not forcibly) and that their bedroom safes were open and empty. Both hotel security personnel and the Washington Metropolitan Police Department were notified, but the items were never recovered...

[The court next quoted the Washington, DC limiting liability statute, which states that, if a hotel provides a "suitable" safe and "displays conspicuously in the guest and public rooms" of the hotel a copy of the statute, its liability for loss of property will be limited to $1000.]

On the back wall of each bedroom closet in the Paraskevaides' suite that contained a convenience safe, the Four Seasons had posted a notice that explained the hotel's limited liability... . These disclaimers were only located on the back walls of closets that contained convenience safes; they were not posted anywhere else in the hotel.

The hotel had also placed a disclaimer sticker that summarized the hotel's limited liability on the door of each safe itself... .

The Four Seasons asserted an affirmative defense of a statutory limitation of liability... .

Under the general common law doctrine of infra hospitium, an innkeeper is strictly liable for loss or damage to a guest's property "unless the property is lost or destroyed by an act of God, the public enemy, or fault by the guest." Many jurisdictions, however, have limited an innkeeper's common law liability to his guests through statutory enactment... . In limiting a hotel's liability, these statutes deviate from the general common law and must therefore be strictly construed. The plain language of the statute states quite clearly that a hotel must "display conspicuously in the guest and public rooms of the hotel a printed copy" of the limiting statute (or summary thereof). It is undisputed that the Four Seasons only posted a copy of the limiting statute in the guest rooms of the hotel, thereby failing to post notices in any of the hotel's "public rooms". The Four Seasons nonetheless contends that its posting of the "summary of the statute and the accompanying disclaimer notice was sufficient to place the Paraskevaides on notice of the liability limitations provided by the Innkeeper Statute... " Perhaps the Paraskevaides had notice; perhaps not. But whether they did is irrelevant to our disposition of this case. The statute says what it says: a hotel must "display conspicuously in the guest and public rooms of the hotel a printed copy" of the statute in order to limit its liability to guests. The Four Seasons undoubtedly displayed a copy or summary of the statute in its guest rooms. It may even have done so "conspicuously," although that remains unclear. What is clear is that the Four Seasons did not display, conspicuously or otherwise, a copy or summary of the statute in its public rooms. Therefore, when we strictly construe this statute, as we must, we conclude that the Four Seasons failed to comply fully with the statute's requirements for limiting its liability to the Paraskevaides... .

If a hotel provides a suitable depository [safe] but does not post the statute in the guest and public rooms—in effect, if a hotel only complies with part of the statutory requirements—then the statute does not apply. Because the Four Seasons failed to post a copy or summary of the statute in its public rooms, we hold that the Four Seasons cannot rely on the statute to limit its liability to the Paraskevaides... .

The Four Seasons Hotel made a very expensive mistake: Rather than facing liability for the limited amount provided by statute of $1,000, it exposed itself to liability for the full value of the plaintiff's loss—in excess of a million dollars. The lesson is clear: Familiarize yourself with your state's limiting liability statute and comply with it exactly.

In yet another case where the hotel learned the hard way of the need to comply strictly with the posting requirements, a guest's suitcase containing $500,000 in jewelry and $8,000 in cash was stolen. The inn had displayed the necessary notice on the registration card but not in the guest rooms, rendering the hotel ineligible for the statute's limits on liability.[7]

One aspect of the decision provides some consolation to the innkeeper. The jury found the guests were contributorily negligent, allocated 40 percent liability to them, and reduced their recovery accordingly. Rather than the hotel being liable for the full $350,000 loss, the plaintiff's award was reduced to $210,000. Had the hotel complied with the notice requirements, its liability would have been reduced by the relevant state statute to the much lesser amount of $2,000.

While strict compliance is required in most states, a few states are more forgiving. For example, Kentucky has enacted a statute that provides,

> [A]ll statutes of this state shall be liberally construed with a view to promote their objective and carry out the intent of the legislature...

---

[7] *Ippolito v. Hospitality Management Associates,* 575 S.E.2d 562 (S.C. 2003)

Kentucky's limiting statute requires hotels to post notice in the office and public rooms of the inn. A hotel posted notice only on the doors in each of the guest rooms; it failed to post notice in the hotel office or public rooms. The Kentucky court held the innkeeper had sufficiently complied with the statute. This decision was based on the quoted statute.[8]

Conspicuous Posting

Most limiting liability statutes require that the posted notice be **conspicuous,** meaning that the notice must be displayed in such a way that people are likely to see it.

conspicuous
Out in the open; easily seen.

If, for example, the posted notice in a lobby is obscured by the branches of a decorative tree or a banner announcing a special event, the notice would not be conspicuous. If the print is not easily readable, the notice likewise is not conspicuous. In one case, the hotel placed the notice under the glass on a dresser table in a hotel room. The notice was two and one-half inches square and was displayed among promotions describing the hotel and its features. In determining the notice was not conspicuous, the court stated that a guest who glanced at the total display of printed material on the dresser would likely assume its general import was advertising.[9]

In another case, a court strongly suggested that posting notice on the inside of the closet in a motel room was not conspicuous.[10]

Some hotels print the information required to be posted on registration cards or on the register in which arriving guests sign their names. This is generally not a permissible substitute for mandated posting elsewhere.

If the only notice of limited liability is posted near the room-key drop-off, where guests would see it only after their stay was completed, the conspicuous posting requirement likely has not been met.[11]

Posting Notice of Hotel's Limited Liability

It is not enough for a hotel to post conspicuously the availability of a safe. Virtually every state's limiting statute requires that the posted notice also inform guests that the hotel's liability is limited. Without that notice, guests are led to believe that if valuables are deposited in the safe, the guest will be protected for the full value of the deposited items. Absent notice of limited liability, the common-law rule will apply and the hotel will be fully liable.

This principle is illustrated in a case in which a Days Inn hotel was sued for $142,834.00—the value of jewelry stolen from a safe located in a guest's room. A sign was located on the front check-in desk that read, "Because We Care: For

---

8 *Roth v. Investment Properties,* 560 S.W.2d 831 (Mo. 1978)
9 *North River Insurance Company v. Tisch Management, Inc.,* 166 A.2d 169 (N.J. 1960)
10 *Fennema v. Howard Johnson Co.,* 559 So.2d 1231 (Fla. 1990)
11 *Moog v. Hilton Waldorf-Astoria,* 882 F.Supp. 1392 (N.Y. 1995)

your safety and convenience, a SAFEKEEPER [a type of safe] is provided for you in the privacy of your room to secure and protect your valuables." Also located at the front desk was another posted sign that stated, "The hotel is not responsible for loss of valuables left unprotected. A personal safe with contents insurance in case of forced entry is located in each room." When the plaintiff returned to her room one night she observed that the SAFEKEEPER had been forcibly removed from the wall and floor. In the ensuing lawsuit, the court held the hotel liable for the full value of the jewelry—$142,834.00—because the inn failed to inform the guest of limits to its liability.[12]

In another case, $10,000 of a guest's money stored in a hotel safe was stolen. The posted notices said, "We have safe deposit boxes that are available for you without charge. We will appreciate your cooperation." A note on the registration card read, "Money, jewels and other valuables must be placed in the safe in the office, otherwise the management will not be responsible for any loss." The hotel sought the benefits of limited liability. The court held that the notices led guests to believe that if they deposited their valuables in the safe, no limitation of liability applied. The hotel was ordered to pay the full $10,000 loss.[13]

Languages Other than English

If a hotel can anticipate guests who speak languages other than English, the hotel is well advised to post notices written in those other languages in addition to English. By so doing, the hotel avoids an argument by non–English-speaking guests that they had not been provided notice of the availability of a safe or of the hotel's limited liability.

What Property Belongs in the Safe?

© Dimj/Shutterstock.com

Not all property brought to a hotel by a guest is appropriate for a safe. If it is not and the property is stolen, the hotel may have no liability. Most state statutes require the following property to be deposited in the safe: money, jewels, ornaments, banknotes, bonds, negotiable securities, precious stones, and other articles of similar value. However, ambiguities exist. For instance, are cufflinks "ornaments"? How much money may guests keep in their rooms outside of the safe? Must they put a watch in the safe?

A court ruled that cufflinks valued at $175 were not ornaments and a watch is neither a

---

[12] *Days Inn v. Tobias Jewelry, Ltd.,* 751 So.2d 711 (Fla. 2000)
[13] *Depaemelaere v. Davis,* 351 N.Y.S.2d 808 (N.Y. 1973), 363 NYS2d 323 (N.Y. 1974)

jewel nor an ornament;[14] it is instead a timepiece, an article of ordinary wear used daily by most travelers of every social class. A gold money clip was likewise found not to be jewelry.[15] However, in a case in the state of Washington involving an expensive watch, the court treated it as more than a timepiece and the result was different. The guest left his $3,685 watch on a nightstand and went out to dinner. When he returned, the watch was gone. The court ruled that the watch should have been deposited in the safe. Since it was not, the hotel was relieved of all liability.[16]

Gambling chips were determined to be included within the list of valuables that the statute requires to be stored in a safe. In a New Jersey case a high-stakes gambler won $76,000. Before retiring to his hotel room he converted his winnings into $25,000 cash, 10 chips of $5000 each, and a $1000 chip. He left the cash and chips on the dresser when he went to bed and they were stolen during the night. Defendant sought recovery from the hotel which asserted as a defense the limiting statute. The court denied recovery noting that the hotel had properly posted the necessary notices of both the availability of the safe and the hotel's limited liability. While gambling chips were not expressly included within the statute's list of items that should be kept in the safe, they can be exchanged for cash and so were included within the statute's catch-all phrase, "and other articles of similar value."[17]

In a New York case the president of a design company was a guest at a Sheraton hotel that was hosting a convention when belongings were stolen from her room. Among the missing items were orders for the design company's services which the guest had obtained during the convention, and the president's business cards. The hotel asserted as a defense the limiting liability statute. The court held the stolen items did not constitute any of the types of property covered by the statute—"money, jewels, ornaments, banknotes, bonds, negotiable securities or precious stones."[18]

Theft During Checkout

Consider the circumstances where a guest is in the process of checking out of the hotel. She has already retrieved her valuables from the safe and, while settling her account with the hotel, her jewelry is stolen. In a case addressing this circumstance, the court held that the hotel would not be liable. Said the court, "A hotel guest who fails to use the safe deposit box cannot hold the hotel responsible if his or her valuables are later lost or stolen.... The hotel's freedom from liability is not altered by the fact that the loss occurred as the guest was preparing to leave the hotel."[19]

Hotel Guest in Hotel Restaurant

An interesting case involved a hotel guest whose purse was stolen in the hotel restaurant. In the purse were cash and valuables. The guest sued the hotel and lost

---

14 *Federal Insurance Co. v. Waldorf Astoria Hotel*, 303 N.Y.S.2d 297 (N.Y. 1969)
15 *Chase v. Hilton Hotel Corp.*, 682 F.Supp. 316 (La. 1988)
16 *Walls v. Cosmopolitan Hotels, Inc.*, 534 P.2d 1373 (Wash. 1975)
17 *GNOC Corp. v. Powers*, 2006 WL 560687 (N.J. 2006)
18 *Susan Faris Designs, Inc. v. Sheraton New York Corp.*, 2000 W.L. 191689 (N.Y. 2000)
19 *Moog v. Waldorf-Astoria*, 882 F.Supp. 1392 (N.Y. 1995)

because, said the court, even in the restaurant she retained her status as hotel guest since the eatery was owned and operated by the hotel. The limiting statute precluded the guest from recovering for lost cash and valuables that were not placed in the safe.[20]

Door Locks and Window Fastenings

Some states' limiting statutes require a hotel seeking to benefit from limited liability to maintain suitable locks and bolts on doors and fastenings on windows. The reason for this requirement is that these devices help deter in-room thefts.

Clothes and Other Personal Property

What about property not required to be placed in a safe, such as clothes, sporting equipment, inexpensive watches, or merchandise samples? Does a hotel have unlimited liability as to those items? The generally applicable answer is no. Most states have a statute that limits the hotel's liability for these items as well.

The typical limiting statute restricts a hotel's liability for damage or loss of a guest's apparel and other personal property, such as a camera, to a specified maximum; for example, $500. The amount may vary from the hotel's maximum liability for lost money and jewels required to be in the safe. Where, however, the loss or damage to clothes and other personal property is caused by negligence on the part of the hotel, in most states the hotel is not entitled to the benefit of the limiting statute and will be liable for the full amount of the guest's loss.

© Sorowat.c/Shutterstock.com

---

20 *Summer v. Hyatt Corp.*, 266 S.E.2d 333 (Ga. 1980)

The limiting liability statute in Florida treats clothes and personal property a bit differently. Florida's statute relieves the hotel from any liability for loss caused to guests' clothes and personal property unless the hotel was negligent. If it is negligent, the hotel's liability is limited to $500. The application of this provision is illustrated by a case in which two guests sharing a hotel room in Florida discovered that the lock on the door to their room was broken. They called the front desk and requested it be repaired. The hotel sent a repairman, but he negligently went to the wrong location. The room of the guests with the broken lock was burglarized and property was stolen. In the lawsuit that followed, the guests sought reimbursement for the full value of their loss, which significantly exceeded $500 each. The court held the hotel was negligent and so it had some liability to the plaintiff-guests. Based on the Florida limiting statute, the maximum liability was $500 to each.[21]

Checkrooms

Some states' limiting statutes differentiate between clothing lost or damaged in the lobby, hallways, and guestrooms, on the one hand, and property lost in a checkroom. While many provisions of limiting statutes may apply only to hotels, those laws that have a separate section for checkrooms may also cover restaurants because both hotels and restaurants typically have a coat-check area. Later in this chapter we will look closer at the rules applicable to checkrooms.

Baggage Rooms

Most states' limiting statutes restrict a hotel's liability for loss or damage caused to guests' property while stored in a baggage or storage room. The hotel's liability will be limited to a specified maximum amount, such as $100. If, however, the loss or damage to property stored in the baggage room is caused by negligence on the part of the hotel, the statutes customarily provide that the hotel is liable for the full amount of the guest's loss.

Merchandise Samples

The term **merchandise samples** refers to goods for sale brought to a hotel by a salesperson-guest. Even in common-law days, the strict liability rule governing an innkeeper's liability for guests' property recognized a distinction between items brought to the hotel for personal use and property brought for commercial purposes. The unlimited liability rule applied only to the former and not inventory for sale.

merchandise samples
Samples of goods for sale brought to a hotel by a salesperson-guest.

In an early U.S. Supreme Court case, a salesman sued a hotel to recover for the theft of his samples. The court held for the hotel, saying:

> *Although Fisher [the salesman] was received by the defendants into their hotel as a guest, with knowledge that his trunks contained articles having no connection with his comfort or convenience as a mere traveler or wayfarer, but which, at his request, were to be*

---

[21] *Southernmost Affiliates v. Alonzo*, 654 So.2d 1066 (Fla. 1995)

placed on exhibition or for sale in a room assigned to him for that purpose, [the innkeeper] would not, under the doctrines at common law, be held to the same degree of care and responsibility, in respect to the safety of such articles, as is required in reference to baggage or other personal property carried by travelers. The defendants, being owners or managers of the hotel, were at liberty to permit the use of one of the rooms by Fisher for such business purposes, but they would not, for that reason and without other circumstances, be held to have undertaken to hold and safely keep them.[22]

Many limiting liability statutes provide that innkeepers have no liability for damage to or loss of merchandise samples unless the innkeeper receives written notice that the samples are in the hotel and acknowledges in writing that a guest has such property and its value. If the guest gives the necessary notice and the hotel makes the required written acknowledgment, the statutes customarily limit the hotel's liability. Strict compliance with the statute is mandatory if the guest seeks to hold the hotel liable. A plaintiff had manufactured a prototype (working model) of a new product and used the prototype to demonstrate the benefits to be offered by the finished product. The plaintiff rented a room at the defendant's hotel for display of the model to potential customers. The hotel had orally agreed to "plug and seal" the room where the model was being displayed to prevent overnight entry and removal of the model. The hotel had also orally agreed that it would order its employees not to enter or clean the room during the night. The next morning the plaintiff discovered the room had not been sealed; it had been cleaned, and the model was missing.

The plaintiff claimed the hotel was liable for $87,000, the value of the prototype, because the hotel had breached its agreement with him. The hotel denied liability, arguing that the prototype was a merchandise sample within the meaning of the limiting statute and the plaintiff failed to give written notice of the presence of the model. The court agreed with the hotel; the plaintiff lost the case.[23]

Some states' limiting statutes require that a guest who keeps merchandise samples in his room to inform the hotel of the value of the merchandise. Without that notification, the hotel is not liable if the property is stolen. For example, a dealer in the business of buying and selling baseball cards attended a baseball card show. He took with him five briefcases full of cards. While out to dinner one night, he left the cards in his room at a Marriott hotel. When he returned he discovered that all of his inventory had been stolen. In the resulting case against the hotel, the evidence was undisputed that the dealer failed to declare to any employee of the hotel the value of the cards. Therefore, the hotel was not liable.[24][25]

---

[22] *Fisher v. Kelsey,* 121 U.S. 383 (1887)
[23] *Associated Mills, Inc. v. Drake Hotel, Inc.,* 334 N.E.2d 746 (Ill. 1975)
[24] *Beam v. Marriott Corp.,* 655 N.Y.S.2d 566 (N.Y. 1997)

Property in Transit

Occasionally, hotel personnel will take possession of guests' suitcases or other property before the guest arrives at the hotel. For example, a guest arriving at the airport may take the hotel shuttle bus to the hotel and give the driver his luggage. Without a limiting statute, the hotel would have unlimited liability in this circumstance. In a New York case predating that state's limiting statute, a bellhop was sent to pick up a guest's trunk at the railroad station. The hotel employee made a stop while returning from the station and left the bag unattended. The trunk was stolen, along with its contents, which consisted of expensive furs and dresses valued at $10,000. The guest sued the hotel for the full value of the lost property and won, based on common law unlimited liability.[25]

Today, most states have limiting statutes that restrict a hotel's liability for guests' property while in transit. For example, currently in New York, liability in this circumstance is limited by statute to $250. These statutes customarily provide that if the loss is due to the hotel's negligence, the hotel's liability is unlimited.

Property Not Covered by Limiting Liability Statutes

The limiting liability statutes do not cover all property that might be stolen or disappear in or around a hotel. These statutes apply only to property of hotel guests; they do not cover property of nonguests. The limiting statutes also do not apply to cars.

The liability of a hotel or restaurant for cars, property of nonguests, and property of restaurant patrons is based primarily on the law of bailments, discussed in detail later in this chapter.

Fire

Just as the innkeeper was liable at common law for virtually all losses to guests' property occurring at the hotel, the innkeeper was likewise liable where the loss was caused by fire. This was true even if the innkeeper was not responsible for starting the fire.

Consistent with the statutory limitations on innkeepers' liability that we have been studying in this chapter, most states have passed laws limiting or eliminating the hotel's liability for damage caused by fire where the fire was not the result of the hotel's negligence. If, however, a fire is caused by the hotel's failure to exercise reasonable care, the hotel will be fully liable for the resulting loss.

---

[25] *Davidson v. Madison Corp.,* 247 N.Y.S. 789 (N.Y. 1931); aff 'd, 257 N.Y. 120 (N.Y. 1931)

Estoppel: Loss of Limited Liability

equitable estoppel
A legal principle that precludes a person from claiming a right or benefit that might otherwise have existed because that person made a false representation to a person who relied on it to his or her detriment.

Hoteliers or their agents may make comments to a guest that result in the hotel losing the benefits of a limiting liability statute. This is known as the doctrine of **equitable estoppel,** a legal principle that precludes a person from claiming a right or benefit because that person made a false representation to another person who relied on the untruthful statement to his detriment.

Implying Greater Liability

An example of estoppel is the following. A desk clerk at a hotel tells a guest that the hotel maintains safe deposit boxes that she can use free of charge to safeguard her valuables. The clerk further tells the guest that if she deposits the jewelry in one of the boxes, there will be no limit on the hotel's liability if the jewelry is stolen. As a direct result of the clerk's statement, the guest places her jewelry in a safe deposit box. The jewelry disappears without explanation. The guest sues the hotel for the full value of the jewelry; the hotel asserts the limiting liability statute as a defense. The guest claims that the desk clerk orally modified the terms of the statute and that the guest incurred the loss only because she relied on the clerk's representation. The hotel will likely be estopped from denying liability for the full loss.

Now assume one change of the facts in that scenario. When the hotel clerk informs the guest about the safes, the clerk tells the guest that if the jewelry is stolen from the safe, the hotel's liability will be limited according to statute. Under these circumstances, the hotel will be entitled to the benefit of limited liability.

Misrepresenting Risk

The principle of estoppel will also be imposed if the innkeeper or an employee misleads a guest into believing that property can be left safely at a particular place in the inn, causing the guest to disregard posted directions for safekeeping property. The hotel in Case Example 8-5 was estopped for this reason.

CASE EXAMPLE 8-5

Fennema v. Howard Johnson Co.

559 So.2d 1231 (Fla. 1990)

The material facts of this case are undisputed. In August, 1985, plaintiffs Robert J. Fennema and his wife Kimberly A. Fennema came to Dade County, Florida from the state of Washington so that Robert Fennema could become a university professor at Florida International University. They traveled to Dade County in a Chevrolet Camaro and a rented 24-foot U-Haul truck which, in turn, towed their 1970 Toyota Land Cruiser; they placed all their possessions in the U-Haul truck. Mr. Fennema drove the U-Haul truck, and Mrs. Fennema drove the Camaro. Upon their arrival in Dade County, they stopped at a Howard Johnson Motor Lodge located at 1430 South Dixie Highway, Coral Gables, Florida, at approximately 6:00 p.m. on August 10, 1985. This lodge was owned and operated by defendants H. William Prahl, Jr. and Robert A. Prahl, under a franchise from the defendants Howard Johnson Company.

Mrs. Fennema went into the motel office and registered for her and her husband. She specifically advised the registration clerk that they had a Toyota Land Cruiser towed by a large U-Haul truck with nearly all their personal belongs in it; she asked where would be a safe place to park this vehicle. The clerk directed her to park the vehicle in a particular area of the motel parking lot behind a building where presumably it would be safe from vandalism or theft. Mrs. Fennema conveyed this information to Mr. Fennema who, in turn, parked the vehicle in the place designated by the clerk. Although there had been numerous incidents of criminal activity including motor vehicle thefts on or about the grounds and parking lot of this motel, the plaintiffs were not provided with this information nor warned of the risks of leaving their vehicle in the lot. The Fennemas thereafter spent the night in the motel without incident, and, the following day, went for a drive in the Camaro. When they returned to the motel at 3:00 p.m. that afternoon, they discovered that the U-Haul truck with all of its contents and the attached Toyota Land Cruiser had been stolen by unknown third parties from the place in the parking lot where the clerk had told them to park it for safekeeping.

Plaintiffs brought a negligence action… against defendant innkeepers for the property loss sustained as a result of the above theft in the amount of $177,000. They alleged that the defendants were negligent in failing to warn the plaintiffs that there had been criminal activity in the motel parking lot, and that defendants failed to take other steps to warn their guests and/or to prevent criminal activity from occurring in the parking lot. Plaintiffs also claimed that defendant Howard Johnson, as owner, departed from a standard of care nationally advertised by it, that all defendants knew the parking lot was dangerous, and that, as owners, lessees and operators of the motel, they had an obligation at a minimum to warn their guests. Defendant filed an answer denying any liability for the theft loss and setting up various affirmative defenses, including that plaintiffs' recovery was limited by… Florida's limited liability statute.…

Plaintiffs [argue that]… the statute had no application to their vehicle and its contents under the circumstances of this case.…

It is settled in Florida that "[a]n innkeeper owes the duty of reasonable care for the safety of his guest" (person and property)… and that an innkeeper's knowledge, as here, of prior criminal activity on or around the grounds of his inn imposes a duty to take adequate security precautions for the safety of his guests and their property.… With respect to any damage to or loss of a guest's property, however, an innkeeper's negligence liability is specifically limited by… [Florida's limiting liability statute]—provided a copy of that statute is posted "in the office, hall, or lobby or another prominent place of such public lodging… establishment.… "

It does not follow, however, that an innkeeper may, under all circumstances, rely on the… statute to limit his liability even if the statute is properly posted at the inn. [W]e conclude that an innkeeper is estopped to rely on the innkeeper's limitation of liability statute if he personally misleads his guest into believing that the latter's property may be safely placed at a particular location in the inn, as this causes a guest to disregard whatever posted statutory procedures there might be for safeguarding a guest's property generally.…

[I]n our view, the defendant innkeepers are estopped to invoke whatever protection… [the limiting liability statute] may afford. This is so because the defendant's motel clerk affirmatively misled the plaintiffs into believing that their motor vehicle and its valuable contents were safe if parked at a particular location in the motel parking lot. Mrs. Fennema specifically informed the motel registration clerk concerning the valuable contents of the plaintiffs' motor vehicle and asked where would be a safe place to park the vehicle; the clerk, in turn, directed the Fennemas to park their vehicle at a particular spot in the motel guest parking lot behind a building where presumably the vehicle would be safe. Plaintiffs had every right to believe and did believe that their vehicle would be safe at that location; they parked their vehicle in the exact spot as directed and later the vehicle was stolen from the spot.

Having affirmatively misled the plaintiffs that it was, in effect, safe to leave their vehicle and its contents at this location in the motel parking lot, the defendant innkeepers are in no position to claim the limited liability protection…. Plaintiffs had every right to rely on defendant's affirmative assurance of safety for their property and to believe that these personal assurances of safety overrode whatever statutory procedures might exist for safeguarding guests' property…. [T]he defendants, by their conduct, are estopped to rely on the protection of the subject statute because they, in effect, misled the plaintiffs into disregarding the procedure stated in the posted statute as being unnecessary, given the motel's personal directive which they followed for safeguarding their property….

CASE QUESTIONS

1. What was the representation made by the hotel that enabled the guest to involve the doctrine of estoppel?

2. What was meant by the court's statement, "Plaintiffs also claimed that the defendant Howard Johnson, as owner, departed from a standard of care nationally advertised by it"? What was the significance of that statement on the outcome of the case?

The court in another case with similar facts likewise held that a hotel, whose clerk affirmatively misled a guest into believing his belongings would be safe in the car, would be estopped from seeking the protection of a limited liability statute.[26]

Hotel's Negligence

As we have learned, most limiting statutes do not protect an innkeeper in situations where the loss of guests' property is due to the hotel's negligence. Case Example 8-6 illustrates this principle.

---

[26] *David v. Prime Hospitality Corp.*, 676 So.2d 1049 (Fla. 1996)

CASE EXAMPLE 8-6

Bhattal v. Grand Hyatt-New York

563 F.Supp. 277 (N.Y. 1983)

...Plaintiffs, residents and citizens of India, registered as guests in defendant's Grand Hyatt Hotel in Midtown Manhattan on July 19, 1981 and were assigned Room 2946. Following the customary practice in first-class hotels in this City of the sort operated by defendant, plaintiffs turned over to the bell captain various pieces of personal luggage, which are now said to have contained valuables of great significance, and this luggage was duly transferred by defendant's employees to plaintiffs' assigned hotel room.

Plaintiffs did not request that any of their valuables be placed in the safe depository provided by the hotel....

Shortly after arriving at their room with the luggage, plaintiffs left the hotel for luncheon with friends, locking their door with a key provided by defendant. On returning [early] the same evening, plaintiffs discovered that their luggage and the contents thereof were missing... .

Apparently defendant's front desk relies heavily on computer support, and as a result of computer error, employees of defendant transported plaintiffs' luggage from plaintiffs' room to JFK International Airport, along with the luggage of aircraft crew members of Saudi Arabian nationality, who had previously occupied Room 2946. In other words, the computer omitted to notice that the room had been vacated and relet to plaintiffs, and hotel employees responding to computer direction, included plaintiffs' luggage along with the other luggage of the departing prior guests. This is not to suggest that the Grand Hyatt-New York is a hotbed house, but apparently it was operating at 100 percent occupancy with no lost time between the departure of the Saudi Arabian aircraft crew members who had previously occupied the room, and the arrival of plaintiffs.

Needless to say, plaintiffs' luggage departed for Saudi Arabia and has not since been seen. A missing pearl is always a pearl of the finest water, and accordingly plaintiffs demand damages in the amount of $150,000... .

The [case] presents the question of whether [the limiting liability] statutes limit the liability of an innkeeper in a case where the innkeeper, by his own agents, intentionally and without justification, took custody and control of plaintiffs' luggage and contents, without plaintiffs' authorization, and intentionally, although inadvertently, caused the luggage to be transported to Saudi Arabia. The Court concludes that the statutes do not extend so far as to protect the innkeeper under these facts... .

Here, defendant's employees entered plaintiffs' locked room, without plaintiffs' permission or knowledge, and removed their luggage, commingled it with the luggage of the Saudi Arabian aircraft crew members and placed it on a bus headed for Kennedy Airport. The Court infers that if the luggage was not stolen at Kennedy Airport, it arrived in Saudi Arabia and was eventually stolen by a Saudi thief who still had the use of at least one good hand. In this instance, the intentional acts of the defendant clearly constituted conversion [unauthorized exercise of ownership over goods] under New York law.

... New York [limiting liability laws] were adopted in the middle of the 19th century to relieve an innkeeper from his liability at common law as an insurer of property of a guest lost by theft, caused without negligence or fault of the guest.... These statutes and the cases cited thereunder by the defendant extend to the situation where there is a mysterious disappearance of valuable property, either as a result of a theft by an employee of the hotel—or a trespass or theft by an unrelated party, for whose acts the innkeeper is not responsible. The statutes are also intended to protect the innkeeper from the danger of fraud on the part of a guest in a situation where the property said to have disappeared never existed at all, or was taken or stolen by or with the privity of the guest.

The reason for limiting a hotel's liability... is to protect against just such a situation. When a hotel room is let to a guest, the innkeeper has lost a large measure of control and supervision over the hotel room and its contents. While housekeeping and security staff can enter the room at reasonable hours and on notice to any persons present therein, essentially, for most of the time at least, property of a guest which is present in a hotel room can be said to be under the exclusive dominion and control of the hotel guest, rather than the innkeeper.

...In this case... employees of defendant, acting within the scope of their employment and relying on the accuracy of the employer's computer, intentionally converted the luggage of the plaintiffs by removing it from plaintiff's room and delivering it to an aircraft bound for Saudi Arabia. [The limiting statute does not limit the liability of the hotel in this case. Rather, the hotel is liable for the full value of the loss.]

CASE QUESTION

1. What would have been the outcome of the case if the luggage had been stolen by a thief through no fault of the hotel?

Comparative Negligence

Consider a circumstance when the hotel and the guest are both negligent and the guest's loss is due to the combined negligence. What liability does the hotel have? At least in states that have adopted the comparative negligence rule, the hotel's liability will be reduced by the percentage of responsibility for the loss attributed to the guest. In one case, the plaintiff brought to the defendant's hotel a coin collection valued at $34,973. The plaintiff placed the collection in a dresser drawer in his guest room under some garments. Two days later, he discovered the collection was missing. The jury determined that both the hotel and the guest were negligent (the facts supporting the determination that the hotel was negligent were not provided). It allocated to the guest 49 percent of the responsibility for the loss. The guest recovered only 51 percent of his damages.[27]

---

[27] *Vasilios Nicholaides v. University Hotel Associates,* 568 A.2d 219 (Pa. 1990)

In an interesting twist, a plaintiff who suffered a loss in her hotel room attempted to hold the travel agent responsible for failing to warn her about the hotel's key system. Case Example 8-7 illustrates.

© Antonio Guillem/Shutterstock.com

CASE EXAMPLE 8-7

McReynolds v. RIU Resorts and Hotels

880 N.W. 2d 43 (Ne., 2016)

......In February, 2011, Jeannette L. McReynolds traveled to a resort in Puerto Vallarta, Mexico. The trip was an all-inclusive vacation package arranged by two companies, Ultimate Cruise and Vacation, Inc. and The Mark Travel Corporation, doing business as Funjet Vacations (collectively – the companies).

When McReynolds checked into the hotel in Mexico, she received a key to the safe in her room, and she began storing her jewelry and cash in the safe. A few days later a traveling companion told her that she should not keep her room key in the same bag as her safe key, because her room number was engraved on her room key. He told her that she should keep them separate because of their sitting down at the beach, going in the water and how unattended her beach bag was. After receiving this advice, McReynolds continued to use the safe and began to hide the safe key in her room. She did not consider keeping the safe key on her person or giving it to another person for safekeeping, and she did not ask the companies for recommendations regarding where to keep the key.

Near the end of her stay, McReynolds left her room and stowed eight pieces of jewelry and some cash in the safe. She hid the safe key inside a purse and hid the purse inside a drawer in her room before she left. When McReynolds returned, she discovered that the safe key was missing and that the safe was locked. Hotel staff used a drill to open the safe, which was empty. There were no signs that entry into the room was forced.

Hotel staff reported the theft to the police, but McReynolds never recovered the items taken from the safe. She claims that the jewelry taken was valued at $63,985 and that $560 in cash was also taken.

When McReynolds returned from the trip, she contacted an employee of the companies. That employee told her that the other hotel at the resort "included a credit card key system as opposed to the antiquated room key system" used at the hotel where McReynolds stayed.

McReynolds filed a complaint in district court and named as defendants the companies and the local and corporate owners of the hotel. Her lawsuit was based on negligence....

McReynolds claimed that the companies were negligent in failing to warn of the "defect in the key system of the hotel." According to McReynolds, a key system in which the key displays the room number does not comply with the international hotel industry's standard. She claimed the companies should have warned her of "this industry standard violation."

Regarding her breach of contract claim, McReynolds claimed that she contracted with the companies for her hotel room and that they breached their duty under the contract to provide her with a secure room free from criminal acts. She did not point to any language in any contract to support this argument.

The companies moved for summary judgment.... The court granted summary judgment for the companies on both of McReynolds' theories of recovery. She filed this timely appeal....

The threshold inquiry in any negligence action is whether the defendant owed the plaintiff a duty. A "duty" is an obligation, to which the law gives recognition and effect, to conform to a particular standard of conduct toward another. If there is no duty owed, there can be no negligence.

This court has never considered whether a travel agent owes a duty to disclose pertinent information to its clients....Under agency principles, travel agents do not owe a general duty to warn travelers of general safety precautions, but they do owe a duty to use reasonable efforts to give the [traveler] information which is relevant to affairs entrusted to him....

However, courts in other jurisdictions also agree that travel agents and tour operators do not owe a duty to disclose information about obvious or apparent dangers. It appears well settled in other jurisdictions that an agent's duty to warn travelers of dangerous conditions applies to situations where a tour operator or travel agent is aware of a dangerous condition not readily discoverable by the plaintiff. It simply does not apply to an obvious dangerous condition equally observable by plaintiff....

In the instant case, we conclude that the companies did not owe a duty to warn plaintiff about the hotel's key system, because any dangers it may have posed were obvious in view of the nature of the hotel's key system....

CASE QUESTION

1. The plaintiff claimed the companies owed her a duty to inform her of the key system. Do you agree? Why or why not?

Nevada's Limiting Statute

Nevada, well-known for its casinos and related tourist attractions, is very protective of its innkeepers. The state's limiting liability statute is quite different from that found in most other states. Its limitation of liability (maximum $750) applies even if the hotel is not only negligent, but grossly negligent.

Liability During Checkin and Checkout

Should there be a period of time while guests are checking in and out of a hotel that the statute does not apply? When guests first enter a hotel and have not yet completed the registration process, they have not had time to access the safe. When they are packing and preparing to check out, they will likely remove their valuables from the hotel safe. Generally, when goods are stolen or disappear during checkin or checkout, courts have found the limiting statutes applicable and the hotel not liable for the full loss.

Guest Status

If the person whose property disappears during checkin or checkout is a hotel guest at the time of the loss, the limiting statute applies. In two cases the owner of the missing property was found to be a guest; thus, recovery was limited.

A guest of the Hilton hotel in New Orleans inadvertently left two rings in her hotel room after washing her hands. She checked out of the hotel that day and did not realize the rings were missing until she was partway home. She immediately called the hotel and an investigation was made. The rings, valued at $10,000, were never found. Like most limiting statutes, Louisiana's applied only to guests. The owner of the rings sued the hotel for their value, claiming the innkeeper–guest relationship had terminated before the loss occurred and thus the limiting liability statute should not apply. The court ruled the loss occurred when she left the rings in the room, which happened while she was still a guest. Therefore, the hotel was only responsible for $500, the maximum provided by the applicable limiting statute.[28]

In another case a jewelry salesman had been a guest at the hotel for several days. On the last day of his stay he attended a sales presentation to which he took $150,000 worth of diamonds. After the presentation, he returned to his room to pack and took the diamonds with him. A few minutes before leaving his room, he was beaten and robbed of all the diamonds. He sued the hotel, claiming the limiting statute should not apply since, at the time of the theft, he was about to leave. The court disagreed and ruled the statute was applicable. The salesman should have deposited the diamonds in the safe before he went to his room to pack.[29]

Liability at Checkin

When during checkin do the limiting liability statutes take effect? The following examples inform us that the statutes take effect almost immediately upon entry to a hotel by a guest who intends then to register. Although timing may not have enabled a guest to yet utilize the safe, the limiting liability statute's benefit to the hotel is nonetheless in effect.

---

[28] *O'Rourke v. Hilton Hotels Corp.,* 560 So.2d 76 (La. 1990)
[29] *Pacific Diamond Co., Inc. v. Hilton Hotels Corp.,* 149 Cal. Rptr. 813 (Ca. 1978)

In a Nevada case a jewelry salesman, upon arrival at the MGM Grand Hotel in Las Vegas, checked his luggage and jewelry samples with the bellhop at the door. He told the bellhop that the samples were valuable. After checking in and going to his room, his luggage was delivered but one case of jewelry samples worth $19,000 was missing. The salesman sued the hotel for the value of the jewelry. The plaintiff argued that he was not a guest at the time he gave the luggage to the bellhop since he had not yet registered and therefore the limiting liability statute should not apply. The court held that the innkeeper–guest relationship was established when the plaintiff checked his luggage with the bellhop. Therefore, the salesman could only recover the limited statutory amount, which in this circumstance was $750.[30]

CASE EXAMPLE 8-8

DeLema v. Waldorf Astoria Hotel, Inc.

588 F. Supp. 19 (N.Y. 1984)

Plaintiff Jose Maria Berga de Lema, a Brazilian resident, arrived in New York. His luggage consisted of three suitcases, an attaché case, and a cylindrical bag. The attaché case and the cylindrical bag contained jewels. Plaintiff says the jewels in the case exceeded $300,000 in value. Plaintiff went from JFK Airport to the Waldorf Astoria Hotel ("the Hotel"), maintained by defendant, where he had a reservation.

Plaintiff handed over the three suitcases to hotel staff in the garage. He then ascended to the lobby, carrying the attaché case and cylindrical bag, and first encountered an assistant manager, Mr. Baez, sitting behind a desk with a sign proclaiming his title. Plaintiff told Baez he had a reservation. Baez rang a bell and summoned a room clerk, Mr. Tamburino, to assist plaintiff. Plaintiff carried the case and bag from Baez's desk to a place at the counter opposite Tamburino, and put them on the floor.

While plaintiff was filling out the reservation form, paying $300 in cash as an advance, and Tamburino was filling out a receipt for that amount, a blond woman jostled plaintiff, apparently creating a diversion. When plaintiff next looked down, he discovered that the attaché case was gone. The case and its contents have never been recovered. This suit followed.

Both parties recognize that the case is governed by [New York's limiting liability statute]… The courts have not lost sight of the legislature's original purpose: to benefit hotel owners…. it is the duty of the guest to make the deposit [into the safe]… This rule may be inconvenient to guests but the statute was not intended for their benefit. It was manifestly enacted for the protection of the hotelkeepers.

It is clear that under this rule, the plaintiff's claim for damages at large fails. By virtue of plaintiff's advance reservation, his occupancy of a room at the Waldorf was in the definite contemplation of both parties. At the time of the loss, plaintiff was in the process of actually registering. These circumstances are sufficient to bring about the relationship of guest and hotel keeper. In consequence, the Hotel may claim the benefit of the statute's limited liability. It is also common ground that the Hotel maintained an appropriate safe or safety deposit boxes, and that the requisite notices called for by the statute were given.

---

[30] *Pachinger v. MGM Grand Hotel-Las Vegas, Inc.,* 802 F.2d 362 (Nev. 1986)

In many cases, guests retain their status after checkout, and limiting liability statutes still apply. A plaintiff was in the hotel lobby in the checkout line, having just removed from the hotel safe her jewelry valued at $72,000. While she waited for her turn to check out, someone grabbed the jewelry from her possession and it was never recovered. The court held she was still a guest and so the limiting statute applied. Therefore her recovery was restricted to $500. In response to the plaintiff's argument that application of the statute in her case was unjust, the court suggested she address her argument to the legislature, which alone has the power to change the statute.[31]

In Case Example 8-9, the court held that guests who had checked out of a hotel retained their status as guests for purposes of the limiting statute where they left their luggage in the hotel's luggage room while they went shopping for the day.

CASE EXAMPLE 8-9

Salisbury v. St. Regis-Sheraton Hotel

490 F.Supp. 449 (N.Y. 1980)

On the morning of November 22, 1978, Mr. and Mrs. Roger Salisbury concluded a three-day stay at the St. Regis-Sheraton Hotel in New York. While Mr. Salisbury paid the bill and surrendered their room key, Mrs. Salisbury checked their luggage with a bellhop in the lobby. The couple was to spend the day in town and return for the luggage that afternoon. Mrs. Salisbury did not inform the hotel when she checked the luggage that one of their pieces, a cosmetic case, contained jewelry and cosmetics worth over $60,000 and did not ask that the case be kept in the hotel's safe... .

When the Salisburys returned to the hotel to retrieve their luggage at about 4:30 that afternoon, the cosmetic case containing the jewelry was missing. Mrs. Salisbury sued to recover the value of the case and its contents.

It is undisputed that posted conspicuously in the public areas of the hotel was a notice informing guests that the hotel provided a safe for the safekeeping of their valuables, and notifying them of the provisions of the [limiting liability statute] of the New York General Business Law... .

The question, then, is whether Mrs. Salisbury ceased to be a "guest" within the meaning of the limiting liability statute when she checked out of the hotel, even though she arranged to have the hotel hold her luggage for the day... . The lost luggage was not stored with the hotel for a lengthy period, but simply held for the day as an accommodation to departing guests... .

It is not uncommon for a hotel to hold luggage for a few hours after guests check out as an accommodation to them. This would appear to be one of the services that a hotel performs for its guests in the normal course of its business, and there is no reason why it should be deemed to alter the otherwise existing legal relationship between them. Accordingly, we conclude that the limiting liability

---

[31] *Nagashima v. Hyatt Wilshire Corp.*, 279 Cal.Rptr. 265 (Calif. 1991)

statutes are fully applicable in the circumstances of this case and preclude any recovery against the hotel for the loss of Mrs. Salisbury's jewelry and limit any recovery for the loss of the case and its other contents to $100.

CASE QUESTION

1. On what basis did the court determine that the plaintiffs were still guests at the time of the loss?

At what point in the check-out process does a guest cease to be a guest for purposes of a limiting liability statute? According to Case Example 8-10, a guest is no longer considered a guest if she has checked out of the hotel and given luggage to a bell-hop to place in the vehicle in which the guest will depart the hotel.

CASE EXAMPLE 8-10

Spiller v. Barclay Hotel

327 N.Y.S.2d 426 (1972)

Plaintiff, a guest of the Barclay Hotel, sued for the value of the property, primarily wearing apparel and jewelry, lost on the steps of the hotel while she was in the process of leaving.

Plaintiff testified that after her two bags were brought to the lobby floor, she asked a bellboy to take them to the cab area and to watch them while she checked out. When she came to the cab area, only one of her bags was there and the bellboy was not present. A search failed to disclose the missing bag or its contents.

No directly contradictory testimony was presented. A representative of the hotel did testify to a telephone conversation in which plaintiff allegedly gave a different version of the event and described the personal property as business samples. However, I accept as substantially accurate plaintiff's trial testimony as to the property that was lost and the manner in which it was lost... .

The claim for the items of lost jewelry presents a troublesome problem. [New York's limiting liability statute] excludes recovery by a hotel guest for loss of, among other categories enumerated, jewels, ornaments, and precious stones where the hotel provides a safe for such items, gives appropriate notice of that fact, and the guest does not use that facility. It was conceded that the hotel maintained such a safe and had posted the required notice... .

What seems to me decisive here is that [New York's statute] was not designed to apply to a loss occurring under the circumstances of this case. [New York's statute] clearly contemplates a procedure for safeguarding the specified categories of property during a guest's stay at a hotel. Its provisions do not seem to me to be reasonably applied to a loss that takes place when a guest is about to leave, has gathered together her property preparatory to an imminent departure, and is arranging for the transfer of luggage to a vehicle for transportation.

Although that situation presents some conceptual difficulties, I am satisfied that the sensible and fair approach is to consider a loss occurring at that point in time neither in terms of the provisions of [New York's limiting statute], nor in terms of the traditional common law liability of innkeepers, but rather on the basis of the presence or absence of actual negligence... .

Having found that the loss here resulted from the negligence of a hotel employee, acting within the scope of his employment, I hold that plaintiff is entitled to recover the value of the lost jewelry... .

CASE QUESTIONS

1. On what ground did the court find the hotel liable for the full value of the jewelry?

2. If the missing property had been merchandise samples, what would the outcome of the case likely have been?

Bailment

Another basis of potential liability for a hotel when a guest's property is lost or stolen is the law of bailment. A **bailment** is a transfer of possession of personal property from one person to another, with the understanding that the property will be returned. The person transferring possession of the property is called the **bailor;** the person receiving possession is the **bailee.** For example, if a guest leaves a shirt with room service for ironing, the guest is the bailor, the hotel is the bailee, and the arrangement is a bailment. Other examples of bailment include hotel guests who give their car and keys to a valet (the guest is the bailor and the hotel is the bailee); a hotel that rents projection equipment from a rental company for use by conference attendees (the rental company is the bailor and the hotel is the bailee); and a diner at a restaurant who leaves her coat with a coatroom attendant (the diner is the bailor and the restaurant is the bailee).

The essential elements of a bailment are:

1. *Personal property.* Bailments involve only movable, tangible objects such as cars, clothing, sporting equipment, and the like. Bailment does not apply to real property (land and buildings), nor to a liquor license which is not personal property but rather a privilege to engage in the sale of alcohol.[32]

> **bailment**
> A transfer of possession of goods or personal property from a person in possession of the property to another with the understanding that the property will be returned.

> **bailor**
> The owner of goods or personal property who transfers such property to a bailee.

> **bailee**
> The person receiving possession of goods or personal property.

---

[32] In Re *The Ground Round, Inc. and Abboud v. The Ground Round, Inc.,* 326 B.R.23 (U.S. Bankruptcy Crt. 2005)

2. *Delivery of possession.* Possession of the personal property must be transferred to the bailee.

3. *Acceptance of possession by the bailee.* The bailee must knowingly accept possession of the bailed property.

4. *Bailment agreement.* Part of every bailment is an agreement, express or implied, by the bailee to return the bailed goods to the bailor.

If a bailment exists, the bailee is expected to return the goods at the end of the bailment period or otherwise comply with directions from the bailor. Provided the bailee does so, it has no liability. In a Rhode Island case a jeweler gave jewelry to a Westin Hotel with directions that it be given to a certain guest at the inn. The Westin complied. Therefore, the hotel was not liable when the jewelry subsequently disappeared.[33]

Assume a hotel lent its hospitality van to another hotel during a week when the first hotel was closed for renovations and the second hotel expected a high demand for van services. The parties agreed that the second hotel would return the van at the end of the week. A bailment was thus created. Assume further that the second hotel/bailee thereafter sold the van rendering return of it impossible. The bailee thereby breached the bailment agreement and will be liable to the first hotel/bailor for the value of the vehicle.[34]

Consider the example of a restaurant patron who leaves her coat with a hat-check person. The coat is personal property; possession has been given to the attendant; and an implied agreement exists that the hat-check attendant will return the coat when the patron (bailor) is ready to leave.

Let us change the facts a bit. Suppose the patron enters the restaurant, removes her coat, and hangs it on an unattended coat rack near the table where she is sitting. Does a bailment exist? The answer is no. Although the coat is personal property, the restaurant has not accepted possession since no one on behalf of the restaurant physically took possession of the coat.

In a case involving a health club, a member left his expensive Rolex watch and $400 in cash in a secured locker in the men's locker room while he worked out. When he returned he discovered the lock had been pried open and his valuables removed. He sued the health club claiming the club was liable as a bailee. The court determined the member had not delivered the items to the club, nor had the latter accepted the watch and money. Therefore, no bailment had been created.[35]

Does a bailment exist when you park your car at a parking lot? The answer is—it depends. A critical factor is whether or not you leave your key with a parking lot attendant. In most circumstances, if you park the car and take the key with you, the law holds that you have not delivered possession to the lot attendant because he

---

[33] *Don-Lin Jewelry Co., Inc. v. The Westin Hotel Co.,* 877 A2d 621 (R.I. 2005)
[34] For a case with similar facts, see *Hickman v. Cole,* 1999 WL 254379 (Oh. 1999)
[35] *Sisters of Charity of the Incarnate Word v. Meaux,* 122 S.W.3d 428 (Tex. 2003)

does not have the ability to move the car. If, however, you leave the key, a bailment exists. We will discuss bailment of cars in more detail later in this chapter.

Effect of Bailment on Liability

The existence or nonexistence of a bailment directly affects liability. If no bailment exists, neither does liability. For example, if you leave your coat on an unattended coat rack in a restaurant and it is stolen during your meal, the restaurant is not liable. Because the restaurant was not a bailee, it is not responsible for the coat. Case Example 8-11 illustrates this point. Also note the court's determination that the limiting liability statute was not applicable to the property involved in this case.

CASE EXAMPLE 8-11

Augustine v. Marriott Hotel

503 N.Y.S.2d 498 (1986)

Plaintiff attended, for a fee, a dental seminar at the Marriott Hotel. The seminar sponsor rented a banquet room, furnished with seats, from defendant.

At the request of the sponsor, defendant furnished a movable coat rack, placing it outside the [seminar] room, in the public lobby.

Plaintiff placed his coat on the rack before entering the seminar. At the noon recess, plaintiff exited the seminar room, but found that the rack had been moved a distance down the lobby and around a corner, near an exit.

Unfortunately, his cashmere coat was missing. He then commenced this action in the Small Claims Part of this court.

Under the common law an innkeeper was an insurer of property, infra hospitium [within the hotel facility], of his guests, and liable for the loss thereof or damage thereto unless the loss was caused by negligence of the guest, act of God, or the public enemy.

By statute, such liability has been limited... .

The relationship of guest on the part of plaintiff, and that of hotel keeper on the part of defendant, vis-à-vis each other never arose. The occupancy by plaintiff of a private [guest] room was never contemplated by the parties.

Plaintiff was a patron of the seminar sponsor, who rented facilities from defendant. The status of plaintiff was like that of a wedding guest of individuals who rent banquet facilities from a hotel... .

Therefore, the New York limiting statutes is in no way applicable to the facts presented here.

The relationship of bailor and bailee never came into existence because plaintiff did not entrust his coat to defendant. Not only was there never a delivery to defendant, but defendant never was in actual nor constructive custody of plaintiff's coat.

The sole question remaining is whether defendant owed a duty to plaintiff to provide a guard for the coat rack. Defendant placed the rack in a position near the door to the seminar room, at the request of the seminar sponsor. This created not only an opportunity but an implied invitation on the part of the sponsor, to patrons of the seminar to use the rack.

However, there was no evidence to indicate that users of the rack were led to believe either by the sponsor or by defendant that there would be a guard for the rack. Under the circumstances presented, it was clear that there was merely a rack available for those who wished to use it. Defendant did not lull plaintiff into a sense of security, by which there was created a duty to provide a guard.

There being no duty on the part of defendant, there can be found no breach of duty upon which to underpin a finding of [liability].

Furthermore, a reasonable man would have wondered about the safety of his coat which he hung on a rack in a public lobby of a hotel...

The claim must be dismissed.

CASE QUESTIONS

1. Why was the limiting liability statute not applicable in this case?

2. Why did the court determine a bailment had not been created?

This case illustrates the principle that if no bailment exists, no liability exists. If, on the other hand, a bailment for property not subject to limiting liability statutes does exist, the bailee is not automatically liable. A bailee is liable only if it fails to exercise the amount of care required by law in tending to the bailed goods. The requisite care varies depending upon the type of bailment. Bailments are classified into three types:

1. For the sole benefit of the bailor

2. For the sole benefit of the bailee

3. For mutual benefit

The required level of care differs for each classification. The duty in each circumstance is discussed below.

Bailment for the Sole Benefit of the Bailor

A **bailment for the sole benefit of the bailor** exists when the bailee receives no benefit from the bailment. For example, a Caribbean hotel is located on the predicted path of a hurricane. Hoping to avoid damage to its computers, the hotel removes them and stores them with another hotel located outside the expected path of the hurricane. Under the circumstances, the second hotel does not charge a fee to hold the items. The first hotel, the bailor, benefits from this arrangement. The second hotel, the bailee, does not.

bailment for the sole benefit of the bailor
The bailee receives no benefit from the bailment.

In a bailment such as this, entered for the sole benefit of the bailor, the bailee is obligated to exercise only a slight degree of care over the bailed goods. Stated differently, the bailee is liable only for gross (extreme) negligence.

Bailment for the Sole Benefit of the Bailee

A **bailment for the sole benefit of the bailee** exists where the bailor lends property to the bailee and receives nothing in return. For example, assume that your restaurant is catering four parties this weekend. You are in need of extra serving dishes. A friend owns a restaurant in the business district that is closed on weekends. She agrees to lend you serving dishes for the weekend at no cost. You benefit from this arrangement but your friend, the bailor, does not.

bailment for the sole benefit of the bailee
The bailor receives no benefit from the bailment.

In this type of bailment, entered for the sole benefit of the bailee, the bailee is required to take great care of the property and exercise a degree of care higher than a reasonable person ordinarily exercises in connection with her own property. To avoid liability, you should ensure the serving dishes are utilized only by trained wait staff to avoid breakage, and that they are securely stored when not in use to avoid theft.

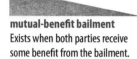

mutual-benefit bailment
Exists when both parties receive some benefit from the bailment.

A **mutual-benefit bailment,** also called a bailment for hire, is one in which both parties receive some benefit from the bailment. Examples of this type of bailment include a traveler renting a car, and a restaurant leasing a tent in which to stage a wedding reception. In the first example, the traveler (bailee) receives the use of the car, and the car rental company (bailor) receives money. In the second example, the restaurant (bailee) receives the use of the tent, and the leasing company that owns the tent (bailor) receives money. In mutual-benefit bailments, the bailee's duty is to exercise ordinary care over the bailed goods. The difference in the duty owed in a mutual-benefit bailment and a bailment for the sole benefit of the bailor is illustrated in Case Example 8-12.

CASE EXAMPLE 8-12

First American Bank v. District of Columbia

583 A.2d 993 (D.C. 1990)

…First American Bank employed Ronald Armstead as a courier whose duties included making deliveries between the bank's various branch offices and the main office. One afternoon, at approximately 4:20 p.m., Armstead parked the bank's station wagon near the entrance of Branch 13 on 7th Street, N.W., in violation of "No Parking Rush Hour Zone" signs, which were in clear view of Armstead. Four locked bank dispatch bags, marked as such, which Armstead had just picked up from four different branches, were in the rear luggage compartment of the station wagon and in plain view of anyone looking into the vehicle. The dispatch bags contained checks and other valuable documents.

Armstead had received tickets for illegal parking at this particular spot on at least five prior occasions and had been warned against future violations by traffic enforcement personnel. Traffic enforcement personnel had counseled Armstead to park across the street during rush hour to avoid being ticketed or towed. Armstead, who had received numerous parking tickets during his employment with the bank, would simply give the parking tickets to a supervisor for payment. The bank did not reprimand or discipline Armstead, nor did it dock his pay, for the parking tickets.

Within a short time after Armstead entered Branch 13, a parking control aide approached the bank's station wagon and began writing up a ticket for illegal parking. Almost immediately thereafter, a tow truck owned by Transportation Management, Inc. (TMI) arrived at the scene. While the parking control aide was completing the ticket and the tow truck operator was simultaneously preparing to tow the car, one of the employees at Branch 13 alerted Armstead that the bank's vehicle was being towed. Armstead, carrying a dispatch bag, ran out to the vehicle and told the tow truck operator that, as the driver of the vehicle, he was prepared to drive the vehicle away immediately. When the tow truck operator ignored his request to return the vehicle, Armstead asked that he be allowed at least to remove the dispatch bags from the vehicle. The tow truck operator, however, also ignored this latter request, and instead entered the truck and began to drive away with the bank's vehicle in tow. The… form filled out by the tow truck operator indicated that the doors, trunk, and window of the bank's station wagon were locked when it was towed from 7th Street. When the tow truck operator arrived at the

Brentwood impound lot at 4:45 p.m., the dispatch bags were still inside the luggage compartment of the vehicle. The tow truck operator observed the District's lot attendant test all the doors and the rear gate of the vehicle. The lot attendant found them all locked and so certified on the same form.

One and a half hours later, the bank's supervisor of mailroom couriers paid for the vehicle's release and retrieved it from the impoundment lot. The bank supervisor found the driver's door unlocked and one dispatch bag missing. There were no signs of forced entry, nor were there signs of the tape which is customarily affixed to car doors at the impoundment lot. The dispatch bag was never found, nor have the police identified or apprehended anyone who may have removed it from the vehicle. The value of the checks and other papers contained in the dispatch bag was determined to be $107,561.... First American brought suit against the District of Columbia and TMI for breach of bailment...

The trial court ruled that the District and TMI were gratuitous bailees [bailment for the sole benefit of the bailor] and therefore liable only for gross negligence. The trial court further ruled that First American [was not] grossly negligent.... We reverse on the bailment issue.

There is no dispute here that TMI and the District had sufficient possession and control of the bank's vehicle to establish a type of bailment.... The question we must resolve is whether the bailment was gratuitous or for hire. A bailee that takes possession of goods solely for the benefit of the owner is a gratuitous bailee and liable only for gross negligence, willful acts or fraud.... In contrast, a bailee that receives compensation for its services is held to a standard of ordinary care... .

A bailment for hire [mutual benefit bailment] relationship may be created even in the absence of an explicit agreement.... All that is required is the existence of a mutual benefit... .

The District and TMI actively took possession of the bank's vehicle with the expectation of deriving benefit therefrom. In addition to furthering its interest in insuring the smooth flow of traffic, the District tows and stores illegally parked vehicles for compensation. Likewise, TMI is under contract with the District for the purpose of towing illegally parked vehicles to impoundment lots. Owners of vehicles, on the other hand, receive the direct benefit of having their vehicles safeguarded in the city's impoundment lot until they are ready to retrieve them. As users of the District's roads and highways, they also benefit indirectly from the District's practice of towing illegally parked vehicles that impede the flow of traffic... .

We hold, therefore, that the District and TMI are held to the standard of ordinary care when they tow and impound illegally parked vehicles... .

In view of the foregoing, we remand this case [for a trial] for a determination of whether the city and TMI exercised ordinary care in safeguarding the bank's vehicle and its contents.

Duty of Bailor in Mutual-Benefit Bailment

In a mutual-benefit bailment, the bailor has responsibilities as well as the bailee. The bailor is obligated to warn the bailee of any defects in the bailed property that might result in injury to the bailee or interfere with use of the property. This is a form of strict liability; the bailor is liable for failing to disclose defects even if it is unaware of their existence. For example, Jerry rented a car for one day. While he was driving the vehicle, the steering gear broke causing an accident in which he was injured. Jerry had not been warned by the bailor that the steering mechanism was defective, and he sued for injuries. The bailor responded that it did not know of the defect. Notwithstanding the bailor's lack of knowledge, it is responsible for any loss or injury suffered by the bailee as a result of a defect in the bailed goods. A company in the business of leasing goods, such as a car-rental company, should make regular and frequent inspections of its inventory. To avoid liability, it must correct any problems discovered or alert the bailee of potential risks.

A case from Louisiana is illustrative. It involved the rental of a freezer that was represented as having the capacity to quick-freeze a specified number of shrimp per hour. Gulf American, a processor of shrimp, leased the freezer and discovered it could not process the advertised number of shrimp. Instead, the appliance malfunctioned and the frozen shrimp were "extremely dehydrated, white, and sometimes came out in clumps of two or three." Gulf American sued the lessor of the freezer for damages. The court held that the lessor, by failing to disclose the freezer's defects, breached its duty as bailor. It was liable to Gulf American for its damages.[36]

Proof of Negligence in Bailment Cases

A bailor does not usually monitor the bailee while the latter is in possession of the bailed goods. Therefore, when the goods are lost or stolen, a bailor would typically have difficulty in proving that the bailee failed to exercise the required degree of care. Because of this, bailment law does not require the bailor to prove that the bailee was negligent. Instead, a bailor need only prove delivery of the bailed property to the bailee, acceptance by the bailee, and either a failure by the bailee to return the bailed property, or return of the property in a damaged condition. Such proof establishes a **prima facie** case, that is, a case sufficient to warrant a judgment for the plaintiff if the defendant does not contradict it with other evidence. With such proof, a presumption arises that the bailee was negligent (failed to use reasonable care); the bailee will lose the case unless it presents evidence to dispute the presumption of negligence or proves that the loss or damage occurred from a cause other than its own negligence. If the bailee can establish either of those circumstances, it will not be liable for the loss. Application of the presumption and an example of a successful rebuttal is illustrated in Case Example 8-13.

prima facie
Such evidence as will suffice to establish a cause of action until contradicted and overcome by other evidence.

---

[36] *Gulf American v. Airco Industrial Gases,* 573 So.2d 481 (La. 1990)

CASE EXAMPLE 8-13

Value Rent-A-Car, Inc. v. Collection Chevrolet, Inc.

570 So.2d 1376 (Fla. 1990)

Value Rent-A-Car (Value)… left its car in Collection Chevrolet, Inc.'s (Collection) care for repairs. When Value returned to pick up the car, the car and its keys had disappeared. Collection reported the car's disappearance to the police. The police subsequently recovered the car, stripped and heavily damaged.

Value brought suit against Collection for negligence arising from the disappearance of its car. Collection denied having been negligent.… Value rested its negligent bailment case upon the stipulation of the parties that: (1) Value delivered the car to Collection; (2) Collection had exclusive possession and control of the car; and (3) Collection failed to return the car to Value. Collection presented testimony about the extensive security measures that existed at the area from where the car was taken. No witness for Collection was able to explain how the car and its keys were removed from Collection's lot. [Value seeks a] verdict based on the general rule that a bailee who has sole, actual, and exclusive possession of the goods is presumed to be negligent if he cannot explain the loss or disappearance of the goods. The trial court [held that] Collection had established due care in its storing of the car, that the evidentiary presumption of negligence had vanished, and that the burden of establishing Collection's negligence had shifted to Value… .

Value contends the trial court erred in ruling that the presumption of Collection's negligence, as bailee of the car, vanished, where Collection was unable to explain the loss or disappearance of the car. Collection asserts that proof of its due care overcame the presumption of negligence. Collection further argues that theft of the car was the only logical explanation for its disappearance because the car had been recovered by the police, stripped and vandalized.

As Value correctly argues, and Collection agrees, the well-settled rule in bailment cases is that:

[A] bailee who has the sole, actual, and exclusive possession of goods is presumed to be negligent if he cannot explain the loss or disappearance of the goods, and the law imposes on him the burden of showing that he exercised the degree of care required by the nature of the bailment… .

This presumption, however, is a vanishing presumption. Once the bailee introduces evidence of its due care, the presumption of negligence vanishes and the case is decided by the trier of fact [jury] without regard to the presumption… .

In this case, the presumption, which was enveloped in a protective bubble, burst, when Collection presented evidence of its due care, that is, its extensive security measures, and the only logical inference from the evidence presented was that the car had been stolen… .

A ruling that the presumption continues even though the bailee has presented evidence of its due care, would effectively result in the bailee becoming the insurer of the bailed goods. This is not the rule in Florida. Florida agrees with the weight of authority that a bailee is not an insurer of the bailed goods and if the bailee is not negligent or at fault, the risk of loss by theft is on the bailor.…

Accordingly, the... judgment [for Collection] is affirmed.

CASE QUESTION

1. On what basis did Collection Chevrolet rebut the presumption of evidence?

If the bailee is unable to prove it acted reasonably in caring for the bailed property, the bailee will be liable for any resulting loss or damage. An application of the presumption is illustrated in a case involving valet parking. The plaintiff gave the key to his car to a hotel bellboy with directions to park the vehicle in the hotel parking lot. After going off duty, the bellboy returned to the lot and, without authorization, took the car out for a joyride. Unfortunately, he was in an accident and the car was destroyed. The court held that the hotel was liable for the damage. When the car was originally delivered to the bellboy, a mutual-benefit bailment was created between the plaintiff and the hotel. The hotel was required to return the property to the bailor (plaintiff) when he requested it. Since the hotel was unable to do that, a presumption arose that the hotel was negligent. The presumption arose even though the plaintiff did not prove negligence on the part of the hotel. Had the hotel been able to prove that it exercised reasonable care, it would not have been liable. However, it was not able to prove freedom from negligence. Therefore, the court ordered the hotel to reimburse the plaintiff for his loss.[37]

Case Example 8-14 illustrates another circumstance where a bailee was unable to prove it acted reasonably.

CASE EXAMPLE 8-14

Proliance Insurance Co. v. Acura

2001 WL 766894 (Oh. 2001)

... [O]n June 31, 1999, Gallagher delivered a car to Lindsay Acura to have repairs or maintenance performed on it, thereby creating a bailment contract. Contrary to the bailment, Lindsay Acura failed to return the car to Gallagher in an undamaged condition at the termination of the bailment. Instead, the vehicle was stolen and damaged in an amount approximately $6,700. Without his car, Gallagher was required to rent a replacement car at a cost of $500. The cost to repair the vehicle was $6,600.26. Proliance, Plaintiff's insurance company, paid plaintiff the amount of his loss and sued Acura for reimbursement....

---

[37] *Dispeker v. The New Southern Hotel Co.,* 373 S.W.2d 904 (Tenn. 1963)

William Lytle, Lindsay Acura's service manager, [had] considerable familiarity with the typical operation of a dealership's service/parts department, including the one at Lindsay Acura.

Lytle stated that he was aware that on or about June 13, 1999 Kevin Gallagher's 1998 Acura automobile was stolen from the Lindsay Acura dealership lot. Gallagher left his vehicle when the dealership was closed by using what is commonly referred to as the "night drop" or "early bird" drop. He parked his vehicle on the dealership lot and would have placed the keys to his car in an envelope that would have been dropped in the "early bird" slot.

…[E]very new car dealership had a similar procedure and Lindsay Acura's is the same or similar in construction to those used at other dealerships. Lytle also stated that before the incident with Gallagher, Lindsay Acura never had a similar problem with a car left by a customer in that manner… .

In describing the premises, Lytle stated the lot was fully lighted and the level of security taken by Lindsay Acura in its "early bird" service is commensurate with the level of security customarily employed by new car dealerships in the area… .

Proliance responded to Lytle with Kevin Gallagher who stated… When he returned to Lindsay Acura the next day, he observed that the door "which held the slot for the early bird drop off was about one inch above the floor. Keys are placed in envelopes and dropped into the slot and land on the floor. "When my car was finally recovered, the envelope which had contained the keys to my car was inside the car."

The parties had a mutual benefit bailment. Lindsay Acura failed to return the car in an undamaged condition. Accordingly, the burden shifted to Lindsay Acura to set forth evidence explaining its failure to redeliver the bailed property. Lytle claims that although the car was stolen from the lot, the theft happened despite Lindsay Acura providing all the typical security found in new car dealerships throughout the area. Proliance responds by asserting that the theft occurred because a gap in Lindsay Acura's door negligently allowed the thief to pull the envelope from under the door and steal the vehicle. Proliance thus has come forward with evidence that counters Lindsay Acura's evidence and allows an inference of Lindsay Acura's negligence in the theft of Gallagher's car… .

In the final analysis, Proliance met its initial burden of making a prima facie case for failed bailment. Lindsay Acura claimed it exercised ordinary care as required by its obligations as a mutual-benefit bailee. Proliance responded with evidence which, if believed, identifies the negligence of Lindsay Acura that allowed the theft. Accordingly the trial court improperly granted summary judgment to Lindsay Acura.

CASE QUESTION

1. Why was Lindsay Acura's rebuttal of the inference of negligence not sufficient to save it from liability?

In another bailment case, an employer operated a service garage for cars and large machines. It required that employees furnish their own tools. For the convenience of the employees and employer, the latter allowed workers to leave their toolboxes at the garage. Two employees' tools were stolen from the employer's storage area. The court found the employer accepted the plaintiff's tools for storage, and thus a bailment occurred. The failure of the employer to return the tools to the workers constituted a prima facie case of breach of the bailment agreement. The burden of proof then shifted to the bailee to establish that it exercised reasonable care. There was testimony that the office door had a deadbolt lock, the garage door had a lock placed in the roller guide track so that the door could not be lifted, and some windows were covered with security bars. However, the window broken on the night of the theft did not have bars. That window measured four feet by eight feet in size and was four feet from the ground in an unlighted area. Further, the premises had no security system. The court ruled in favor of the employees stating, "Although there was evidence that appellant exercised some care, it was reasonable to conclude that appellant failed to exercise due care."[38]

Items Inside Bailed Property

Is a bailee liable when valuable property is located inside the bailed property and its presence is unknown to the bailee? For example, suppose you put a valuable ring in the pocket of your leather coat, which you leave with a hat-check attendant at a restaurant. You do not inform the attendant of the presence of the ring. The attendant took a coffee break, during which the coats were unattended. While the attendant was gone your coat was stolen. The restaurant will be liable for the value of the coat because it was negligent for leaving the garments unattended. Will the restaurant also be liable for the value of the lost ring?

© *spaghettikk/Shutterstock.com*

The answer becomes obvious if you apply the elements necessary for a bailment. The bailee must knowingly accept possession of the property. In this example the hat-check attendant knowingly accepted possession of the coat. But did he knowingly accept possession of the ring? The answer, of course, is no; he did not even know of its existence. Therefore, the restaurant was not a bailee of the ring and will not be liable for its loss.

Similarly, when you park your car in a parking lot and leave the key with an attendant, a bailment of the car is created. If you have a valuable camera in the trunk but fail to inform the attendant of its existence, no bailment is created as to the camera. If the car is stolen due to the attendant's negligence, the parking lot will be liable to you for the value of the car. The outcome is quite different for the camera. Since no bailment of it existed, the parking lot is not liable for its loss.

---

[38] *Templeton v. DiPaolo Truck Services, Inc.*, 2001 WL 584310 (Oh. 2001)

In a case involving the bailment of a car, the plaintiff checked into a hotel, removed clothing from the back seat of the car, and then delivered the car and key to an employee of the hotel for parking. The bell captain had observed the guest remove a cosmetic case from the trunk and from where he was positioned could not see anything else in the trunk. He asked if there was any more personal property in the car, but the guest did not respond. The car was then parked by a hotel employee in a nearby garage. A few days later when the plaintiff checked out, the hotel was unable to deliver his car or its contents, nor could it account for its disappearance. The car was located some time later, but drums claimed by the plaintiff to have been in the trunk were missing. The plaintiff sued the hotel for the loss, claiming the hotel was a bailee and therefore liable to him.

The court determined a bailment existed between the plaintiff and the hotel as to both the car and any contents the hotel employees knew about. An employee would be aware of property in a car if the guest pointed it out or it was in plain view. Here, however, there was no evidence to show the hotel employee knew that drums were in the trunk. Therefore, there was no bailment of the instrument, and the hotel was not liable.[39]

One exception exists. Most cases hold that, although a bailee may not have known of specific property in a car, a bailment of that property will nonetheless exist if the bailee could reasonably anticipate that the property would be in the vehicle. For example, a country-club bailee should reasonably anticipate that the trunk of a car might contain golf clubs, tennis rackets, and sportswear.[40] Likewise, a bailee should reasonably expect that the trunk of a car might contain spare tires and jacks, but not massage equipment such as a portable massage-therapy table, massage oils, a portable cassette player, massage-therapy tapes, and sheets and towels.[41]

Rules Particular to Bailment of Cars

A hotelkeeper or restaurateur who takes care of a patron's car assumes a great responsibility. The value of an automobile can range from as low as a few hundred dollars to over $100,000. The limiting statutes do not apply to cars. Public parking lots often attempt to limit their liability for stolen or damaged cars by claiming on signs and parking receipts that they are not liable. Because of the quasi-public nature of the hospitality industry, hoteliers are not allowed to do so; they are not permitted to limit their liability for loss or damage to bailed property caused by their own negligence. Therefore, such disclaimers of liability on signs or receipts are not effective. Case Example 8-15 clearly illustrates this point.

[39] *Dumlao v. Atlantic Garage, Inc.*, 259 A.2d 360 (D.C. 1969)
[40] *Jack Bowles Services, Inc. v. Stavely*, 906 S.W.2d 185 (Tex. 1995)
[41] *Klonis v. Carroll*, 1991 WL 188693 (Tex. 1991)

CASE EXAMPLE 8-15

Ellerman v. Atlanta American Motor Hotel Corp.

191 S.E.2d 295 (Ga. 1972)

Plaintiff, a guest at a motor hotel operated by the defendant, placed his automobile in the defendant's parking facility. He was required by the defendant to leave the ignition key with the defendant's employee, and the latter parked the vehicle in an area unknown to plaintiff. At the time, plaintiff was given a claim check which plaintiff admitted reading. It provided in part as follows: "Liability. Cars parked at owner's risk. Articles left in car at owner's risk. We reserve privilege of moving car to other section of lot. No attendant after regular closing hours." Prior to delivering the ignition key and the car to the attendant, the plaintiff removed a raincoat from the interior, placed it in the trunk of the car, and kept the trunk key. When plaintiff checked out of the hotel, his car was found missing. The car and its contents have never been recovered. Plaintiff's suit sought to recover the value of the items of personality contained in the trunk that he alleged were allowed to be stolen through the defendant's negligence. Plaintiff had been paid by his insurance company for the loss of the automobile... .

The defendant contends that the depositing of the automobile with the defendant's attendant under these circumstances does not give rise to a bailment relationship because of the disclaimer of liability printed on the claim check given to plaintiff. He relies upon our decision in [a previous case] as controlling. As we view this issue, [that case] is not in point. [It] dealt with an ordinary parking lot. This case involves a parking facility operated by a motel as a part of its service, and this creates the relationship of innkeeper and guest... .

It is recognized that an ordinary bailee by contract may limit or completely exculpate himself from any liability for loss or damage to the bailed property as a result of his own simple negligence.

However, an innkeeper is not an "ordinary" bailee. Many courts and texts have described an innkeeper as a "professional" bailee.... Unlike an "ordinary" bailee, the "professional" bailee is often precluded from limiting by contract liability for his own negligence as violative of public policy. The reasoning utilized is that the public, in dealing with innkeepers, lacks a practical equality of bargaining power and may be coerced to accede to the contractual conditions sought by the innkeeper or else be denied the needed services. We think that both the principle precluding the limitation of liability and the reasoning underlying it are sound... [A]ny... contract purporting to... exculpate the innkeeper is contrary to the public interest and policy and cannot be enforced.

CASE QUESTION

1. The court distinguishes between a hotel parking facility and a public parking lot. Why does the court make this differentiation?

A hotel with a parking lot or garage that takes possession of guests' car keys must establish effective security procedures and systems to avoid liability. The high cost of cars dictates the importance of proper management and planning.

An example of negligence on the part of a hotel when acting as bailee is leaving the ignition key in a parked, unattended car, unless the parking lot is carefully monitored at all times. Also, leaving in a place easily accessible to patrons a board or other device on which car keys are kept constitutes negligence. Easy access to car keys facilitates the thief's job. A much better practice is to place all the keys in a specified location accessible only to authorized employees.

Significance of a Car Key

We have discussed car bailments as involving transfer of the key. Customarily, if a person parks a car in a lot and retains the key, in the eyes of the law he has not delivered possession of the vehicle to the lot owner and therefore no bailment exists.

A case in Tennessee expanded, at least in that state, the circumstances under which leaving a car in a parking lot will be viewed as a bailment. A guest at a Hyatt Regency parked his car in the hotel parking garage, taking with him his key and a ticket received when he entered the garage. Upon his return, he discovered the car was missing. It was never recovered. The owner sued the hotel for his loss. Without a bailment, the hotel would not have been liable. Although the driver did not leave the key with the attendant, the court determined a bailment existed based on the particular facts of the case.

Entrance to the garage in question was made via a single entryway controlled by a ticket machine. A lone exit was controlled by an attendant in a booth located just opposite the entrance and in full view therefrom. The hotel hired security guards, two of whom were on duty most of the time. They wore a distinctive uniform so as to be easily identifiable and patrolled the hotel buildings and grounds. The guards were instructed to make rounds through the garage, although not at specified intervals. Finding from the facts that a bailment had been created, the court said, "Appellee's vehicle was not driven into an unattended or open parking area. Rather it was driven into an enclosed, indoor, attended commercial garage which not only had an attendant controlling the exit but regular security personnel to patrol the premises for safety."[42]

This case is not widely followed by other states. Most other states require in cases involving parking lots that a transfer of the car key to the lot attendant occur for a bailment to exist. Case Example 8-16 is more typical of the rules applied to bailment of cars.

---

[42] *Allen v. Hyatt Regency-Nashville Hotel*, 668 S.W.2d 286 (Tenn. 1984)

CASE EXAMPLE 8-16

Waterton v. Motor Inc.

810 NYS2d 319 (2006).

In this Small Claims action the Court must determine the standard of liability to apply to an innkeeper when a guest's automobile is vandalized while parked in a garage on the premises.

Claimant Viola W. Waterton and her husband, Andy Henry, took a room at Defendant's Linden Motor Inn. They knew the facility and had been guests before. When they arrived, they parked Claimant's 1990 Honda Accord in the belowground garage on the premises, checked in at the front desk, and retired to their room.

There was no gate or other barrier controlling entry to or exit from the garage, and no attendant or security guard. They paid no separate fee to park in the garage, did not register the vehicle with the front desk, and retained the keys. There was no discussion at all with the desk clerk about the vehicle, nor any discussion about the hours that the desk would be attended. At the front desk, however, there was a monitor that showed the interior of the garage, obviously through a security camera. Ms. Waterton and Mr. Henry denied seeing any sign in the garage that purported to disclaim or limit the Motor Inn's responsibility for any loss of, or damage to, the vehicle or its contents while parked in the garage.

…The following morning, when they returned to the car, they found that it had been vandalized, that installed audio-visual equipment had been removed, and that some "expensive" items left in the car, including a video camera, had been stolen. Claimant presented receipts totaling $1,322.45 representing the cost of parts and repairs to the vehicle and the cost of the stolen items.

At common law an innkeeper was an insurer of goods delivered into his or her custody by a guest, and so was absolutely liable for the loss or destruction of such goods "unless caused by the negligence or fraud of the guest, or by the act of God or the public enemy." The "infra hospitium" concept, with its associated rule of innkeeper liability without fault, had its origins in considerations of public policy. The traveler was particularly exposed to depredation and fraud. He was compelled to repose confidence in a host. By mid-nineteenth century the days of violence, which in early times required this protection to the traveler, had passed away and [state legislatures] enacted a series of statutes to restrict the innkeeper's exposure. The common law rule has been abandoned in favor of the traditional negligence standard of reasonable care under the circumstances… .

The court finds and concludes that there was no bailment of Claimant's automobile or its contents… . There were no assurances, or even any discussion, that would have led Claimant and her husband to reasonably expect that Defendant was undertaking care and custody of the vehicle. The circumstances were similar to the typical park-and-lock transaction, except here Claimant maintained even more control over the vehicle because there were no barriers to access to, or removal of, the car at her will. Unlike the presence of a security guard, a security camera evidences no dominion and control over the vehicle by Defendant.

Even without a bailment, however, Claimant may recover if she has proved that Defendant was negligent in failing to take reasonable protective measures against reasonably foreseeable criminal activity on the premises, and that Defendant's negligence caused her loss. To establish foreseeability, the criminal conduct at issue must be shown to be reasonably predictable based on the prior occurrence of the same or similar criminal activity at a location sufficiently proximate to the subject location. Claimant presented no evidence that theft or vandalism in the garage was reasonably predictable, and the presence of security camera is, in itself, insufficient. Claimant and her husband were familiar with the area, but were not concerned about leaving items, which they characterized as "expensive", in the vehicle overnight.

Assuming duty, Claimant must also establish the failure to exercise ordinary care. Proof that the damage occurred by vandalism, without more, does not suffice to establish the absence of reasonable care.

There was insufficient evidence for the Court to conclude that Defendant's clerk failed to use reasonable care in monitoring any activity in the garage.

CASE QUESTIONS

1. What circumstances were missing that led the court to determine a bailment did not exist?

2. What additional factors would the plaintiff have had to prove to establish negligence by the hotel?

Similarly, a hotel was not liable for a stolen car left in the hotel parking lot where the car's owner retained the key. The hotel avoided liability notwithstanding the car was left as part of a promotional "Park and Fly" package, offering guests one night's accommodation, free transportation to the airport, and parking for up to two weeks.[43]

Liability for a Patron's Property in a Restaurant, Bar, or Cloakroom

The only portion of many limiting liability statutes that apply to a restaurant or bar covers no-fee checkrooms where the customer is given a receipt for the checked property. In all other circumstances, the only basis for liability for lost property in a restaurant or bar is bailment. As Case Example 8-17 illustrates, if a bailment does not exist and the patron did not receive a receipt, the bar is not liable.

© joyfull/Shutterstock.com

---

[43] *Garrett v. Impac Hotels 1*, LLC, 87 S.W.3d 870 (Mo. 2002)

CASE EXAMPLE 8-17

Kuchinsky v. Empire Lounge, Inc.

134 N.W.2d 436 (Wis. 1965)

Kuchinsky entered the Empire Lounge as a customer and hung his coat on a clothes tree near his table. His coat was stolen while he ate.... The rule... is that before a restaurant keeper will be held liable for the loss of an overcoat of a customer while such customer takes a meal or refreshments, it must appear... that the overcoat was placed in the physical custody of the keeper of the restaurant or his servants, in which cases there is an actual bailment... .

In [another case], the plaintiff was a guest at a luncheon held at the defendant's hotel. She hung her mink jacket in an unattended cloakroom on the main floor across from the lobby desk. After the luncheon and ensuing party, the plaintiff went to the cloakroom to retrieve her jacket and discovered it was gone. The court held that no negligence had been established against the defendant and stated: "...In any event, we do not feel that it is incumbent upon a hotel or restaurant owner to keep an attendant in charge of a free cloakroom for luncheon or dinner guests or otherwise face liability for loss of articles placed therein. The maintenance of such rooms without attendants is a common practice, and where the proprietor had not accepted control and custody of articles placed therein, no duty rests upon him to exercise any special degree of care with respect thereto... ."

Ruling of the Court: [Complaint dismissed]

In another case, a diner whose coat had fallen off his chair was directed by the waitress to hang it in an unattended cloak room. The coat was stolen from the room and the patron sued. The court held the restaurant was not liable because the coat had not been delivered to or accepted by the restaurant and so a bailment was never created.[44]

constructive bailment
Bailment created by law rather than by the parties agreeing.

If a bailment does exist, the hotel or restaurant will be liable if it fails to exercise the necessary care. In Case Example 8-18, the restaurant learned this rule of law the hard way. The case also illustrates a **constructive bailment,** which is a bailment created by law as a result of special circumstances rather than by agreement between the parties. A constructive bailment, like a mutual-benefit bailment, requires the bailee to exercise reasonable care of the bailed goods. In this case, a constructive bailment was created where a restaurant patron mistakenly left her purse by her table when she departed and it was found by an employee.

---

[44] *Black Beret Lounge and Restaurant v. Meisnere,* 336 A.2d 532 (D.C. 1975)

CASE EXAMPLE 8-18

Shamrock Hilton Hotel v. Caranas

488 S. .W2d 151 (Tex. 1972)

…Plaintiffs, husband and wife, were lodging as paying guests at the Shamrock Hilton Hotel in Houston on the evening of September 4, 1966, when they took their dinner in the hotel restaurant. After completing the meal, Mr. and Mrs. Caranas, plaintiffs, departed the dining area leaving her purse behind. The purse was found by the hotel busboy who, pursuant to the instructions of the hotel, dutifully delivered the forgotten item to the restaurant cashier, a Mrs. Luster. The testimony indicates that some short time thereafter, the cashier gave the purse to a man other than Mr. Caranas who came to claim it. There is no testimony on the question of whether identification was sought by the cashier. The purse allegedly contained $5.00 in cash, some credit cards, and 10 pieces of jewelry said to be worth $13,062. The misplacement of the purse was realized the following morning, at which time plaintiffs notified the hotel authorities of the loss.

Plaintiffs filed suit, alleging negligent delivery of the purse to an unknown person and seeking a recovery for the value of the purse and its contents… .

[W]e find that there was indeed a constructive bailment of the purse. The delivery and acceptance were evidenced in the acts of Mrs. Caranas' unintentionally leaving her purse behind in the hotel restaurant and the busboy, a hotel employee, picking it up and taking it to the cashier, who accepted the purse as a lost or misplaced item. The delivery need not be knowingly intended on the part of Mrs. Caranas if it is apparent that were she… aware of the circumstances (here the purse being misplaced), she would have desired the person finding the article to have kept it safely for its subsequent return to her.

As stated above, the evidence conclusively showed facts from which there was established a bailment with the Caranases as bailors and the hotel as bailee. The evidence also showed that the hotel, as bailee, had received Mrs. Caranas' purse and had not returned it on demand. Such evidence raised a presumption that the hotel had failed to exercise ordinary care in protecting the appellees' property. When the hotel failed to come forward with any evidence to the effect that it had exercised ordinary care… the appellees' proof ripened into proof by which the hotel's primary liability was established as a matter of law.

Further, this bailment was one for the mutual benefit of both parties. Appellees were paying guests in the hotel and in its dining room. Appellant hotel's practice of keeping patrons' lost personal items until they could be returned to their rightful owners, as reflected in the testimony, is certainly evidence of its being incidental to its business, as we would think it would be for almost any commercial enterprise that caters to the general public. Though no direct charge is made for this service, there is indirect benefit to be had in the continued patronage of the hotel by customers who have lost chattels and who have been able to claim them from the management.

Having found this to have been a bailment for the mutual benefit of the parties, we hold that the appellants owed the appellees the duty of reasonable care in the return of the purse and jewelry, and the hotel is therefore liable for its ordinary negligence.

Ruling of the Court: [J]udgment for plaintiff.

In another case also ostensibly involving forgotten property, the plaintiff guest placed in his room a paper bag filled with $9,000 in cash and left the hotel temporarily. The housekeeper found the money while cleaning the room. Seeing no personal effects of the guests in the room, she wrongly assumed he had checked out. Consistent with hotel procedure for lost property, she gave the money to her immediate supervisor, who in turn gave it to the general supervisor. He absconded with the money, which was never recovered. The general supervisor had been employed by the hotel for three years and had in that time been given items of value to turn into the office on several occasions. He had consistently done so until the incident in question. The guest sued the hotel; it denied liability for the full $9,000, based on the limiting statute. The plaintiff argued the hotel should be liable, notwithstanding the statute, on a bailment theory since it took possession of the money for safekeeping. The court hedged on whether the law of bailment should supersede the limiting statute, but stated that even if bailment law applied, the hotel was not negligent and therefore would not be liable because the housekeeper and her supervisor gave the money to the proper person and that person had always acted responsibly with regard to guests' valuables in the past. The court further held the hotel was not liable for the general supervisor's theft of the money on a respondeat superior theory since, when he stole the money, he was acting outside the scope of his employment. Instead, the hotel's liability was limited by the statute.[45] A significant factual difference between this case and Shamrock is that in Shamrock the bailee of the purse was negligent; in this case the court held the bailee was not.

Checkrooms

Many hotels, restaurants, clubs, concert halls, museums, and other public businesses have checkrooms available to safeguard guests' valuables. A bailment is created between the customer who leaves property with a checkroom attendant and the facility. The attendant on duty accepts patrons' garments or other property and issues a receipt as proof that the property was delivered and accepted. In many states, the limiting liability laws cover attended checkrooms and baggage rooms. If applicable these statutes limit the facility's liability for losses occurring there. In New York, for example, the maximum liability for a checked item is $200.

If the coatroom is unattended, the limited liability statute is not applicable. Since typically no bailment arises when a coatroom is unattended, the hotel or restaurant will customarily have no liability for property lost or stolen there.

Case Example 8-19 involves Studio 54, a once-famous upscale New York City disco. The case addresses three issues: (1) the liability of a discotheque when a coat is missing from the coatroom; (2) the effect of a sign in a coatroom purporting to limit liability for lost articles; and (3) the method for calculating damages when a coat is missing. The case also discusses many of the issues we have studied—bailments, limiting liability statutes, and conspicuous notice. This case again highlights the courts' requirement of strict compliance with limited liability statutes. As we have seen repeatedly in this chapter, unless all the terms of the statute are satisfied, the limitation of liability is not applicable.

---

[45] *Gordon v. Days Inn*, 395 S.E.2d 876 (Ga. 1990)

CASE EXAMPLE 8-19

Conboy v. Studio 54, Inc.

449 N.Y.S.2d 391 (1982)

The issue that I must decide is whether the [New York limiting liability statute] provides a monetary haven for a discotheque… .

On January 23, 1982, the claimant, his wife and a group of friends convened for a party at Studio 54 (Studio) in Manhattan. Studio, licensed by the New York City Department of Consumer Affairs as a cabaret, is a discotheque, where patrons dance to recorded music usually played continuously on high-fidelity equipment.… Often a psychedelic light show accompanies the music and provides background and impetus for the free-spirited patrons who pay $18 per person to dance to the deafening and often overwhelming disco music played continuously on the sophisticated sound system… .

No food is sold or served here—not even a single peanut or pretzel to accompany the alcoholic and soft drinks available for purchase.

The Conboy party checked their coats, 14 in all, with the coatroom attendant. They received 7 check stubs after paying the 75¢ charge per coat. A bailment of the coats was created.

After their evening of revelry, they attempted to reclaim their coats. Mr. Conboy's one-month-old, $1,350 leather coat was missing. It has not been found and accordingly, he has sued Studio for $1,350.

Under traditional bailment law, once the goods were delivered, the failure of the bailee (Studio) to return them on demand created a prima facie case of negligence. The burden of coming forward with evidence tending to show due care shifted to Studio. Studio did not come forward with any evidence to meet this burden. Mr. Conboy is entitled to a judgment.

Studio, relying on [New York's limiting liability statute], contends that its liability is limited to $75. Its argument is incorrect…

The statute offers innkeepers and restaurant proprietors who comply with it a reduction of the innkeeper's common law insurer-liability as to guest's property deposited with them.

That being said, it need only be noted that the statute offers its protection to restaurants, hotels and motels, not discotheques which appear to be modern-day versions of dance halls.

Simply put, a discotheque may qualify as a restaurant but there is no logic in giving it that classification unless one of its principal activities is the furnishing of meals. Certainly, Studio should not be classified as a restaurant, because it serves no food… .

The limitations on liability set forth in the statute are therefore not applicable here… .

Studio claims however that their liability may nevertheless be limited by the posting of a sign in the coatroom. The sign states: "Liability for lost property in this coat/check room is limited to $100 per loss of misplaced article."...

[T]he posting of the sign [is not] a useless act, for it may still function as a common-law disclaimer. To bind Conboy to this limitation, I must find however that he had notice of the terms of the disclaimer and agreed to it. Studio did not establish that the sign was posted in a conspicuous manner. I hold that Conboy is not bound by the posted disclaimer of liability.

As to damages, Conboy is entitled to the "real value" of the coat. Real value, especially with respect to used clothing or household furnishings that are lost or damaged is not necessarily its market value which presumably would reflect a deduction for depreciation. In fact, the real value may be measured by the price paid when new for the lost or damaged goods.

One commentator has offered a reason that the strict market value approach is not favored:

No judge buys his clothing second hand and none would expect any owner to replace his clothing in a second hand store. Hence no judge expects to limit the cost of replacing clothing to a market no one should be expected to use.

I therefore hold that Conboy may be compensated on a basis that will permit him to replace the very same coat purchased new—$1,350.

Judgment for claimant in the sum of $1,350.

CASE QUESTIONS

1. Why did the limiting liability statute not apply in this case?

2. Why did the disclaimer sign hung by Studio 54 not relieve the discotheque from liability?

3. If Conboy's coat was three years old rather than one month, do you think the court would have awarded him its full value of $1,350? Why? Alternatively, why not?

Concessionaires

concessionaire
An independent contractor who provides a service to a hotel's guests.

Often a hotel or perhaps a restaurant will contract with a **concessionaire** (an independent contractor) to operate the checking facilities (luggage and coats). Usually the concessionaire pays the hotel a fee in exchange for the business opportunity. Such an arrangement saves the hotel from having to manage and staff the checking operations. Several plaintiffs whose checked property was not returned from concessionaires have argued that the concessionaire is not entitled to the benefits of the limiting statutes because those statutes were designed to protect only innkeepers and restaurateurs. Courts have accepted this argument and denied the concessionaire limited liability.[46]

---

46 *Aldrich v. Waldorf Astoria Hotel, Inc.*, 343 N.Y.S.2d 830 (N.Y. 1973); *Jacobson v. Belplaza Corp.*, 80 F.Supp. 917 (N.Y. 1949)

Summary

The liability of hotels and restaurants for their guests' and patrons' property has appropriately changed over time. The common law imposed unlimited liability on inns and food establishments. Most states have since passed limiting statutes that significantly reduce this liability.

For money, jewels, and securities, limiting statutes typically require that hotels provide safes and post notices in prescribed places announcing the availability of the safes and the hotel's limited liability. The specifics of these statutes vary from state to state. Only if the hotel strictly complies with the statutory requirements will it benefit from limited liability. Less than complete compliance may result in full liability.

For other property a guest brings to a hotel, such as clothes or sporting equipment, limiting statutes provide limited liability for hotels unless the loss is caused by the hotel's negligence. If it is, the hotel will typically be liable for the full value of the missing property. An exception is the state of Nevada, which limits the liability of innkeepers even when they are negligent.

For property not covered by the limiting statutes, the liability of a hotel or restaurant is based on laws regarding bailment. If no bailment exists, the business is not liable for loss or theft of property. If a bailment does exist, the hotel or restaurant will be liable for the loss only if it failed to exercise the requisite degree of care for the bailed goods. The level of care required varies depending on whether the bailment is for the sole benefit of the bailor, the sole benefit of the bailee, or a mutual-benefit bailment. If the hotel or restaurant renders the care required, the establishment will be free from liability even though property is stolen or otherwise disappears.

Preventive Law Tips for Managers

- *Identify the specific requirements of your state's limiting liability statute and follow them exactly.* The limiting statutes relieve a hotel from common-law strict liability. The statutes are generally not applicable unless the hotel strictly follows their mandates. Most states' statutes require that the hotel provide a safe and post notice conspicuously in specified places announcing the availability of the safe and the hotel's limited liability. To qualify under the statutes, a hotel safe must be secure and capable of withstanding burglary attempts. It should be available to guests twenty-four hours a day. Anything less jeopardizes the relief from full liability provided by the statutes.

    The posted notices must not only inform the guest of the safe's availability, but must also state that if goods are lost or stolen from the safe, the hotel's liability will be limited. The notices must be posted each and every place the statute requires. For example, if the statute mandates posting by the registration desk, in the lobby, and in guest rooms, posting in less than all three locations is inadequate in most states and will not protect the hotel from unlimited liability. The notice must also be conspicuous, meaning easily seen and easy to read. For example, a notice hidden behind decorations or signs in the lobby or in a nonobvious place in a guest room will not satisfy the statute. In these circumstances, the hotel will be liable for the full value of the lost property.

Individual states may have additional requirements. For example, some states require "suitable" locks or bolts on the doors of guest rooms and "suitable" fastenings on windows. Check your state statute carefully and make sure your establishment is in full compliance. Loss through inadvertence or carelessness of the very significant benefit offered by these statutes can impact a facility's financial success and can easily be avoided by vigilant monitoring.

■ *Train appropriate employees how to use the safe.* If a guest is unable to place valuables in the safe because staff does not know how to operate it, the safe is not "available" to the guest as required by statute and the hotel will have unlimited liability. Employees should be well trained on use of the safe and the importance of its being available around the clock. If an employee does not correctly operate the safe or fails to follow hotel procedures for its use, thefts may be facilitated.

■ *Instruct employees about the hotel's limited liability and the importance of their not overstating that liability.* The consequence of an employee exaggerating a hotel's liability for property stored in a safe may be that the hotel has unlimited liability. The only way to avoid the principle of equitable estoppel from curtailing the limiting statutes' applicability is by ensuring your employees do not misstate the hotel's liability. Training and frequent reminders about the benefits of the statutes and what constitutes appropriate comments to guests about liability should minimize this potential problem.

■ *Adopt procedures to limit thefts of property from the safe.* While the limiting liability statutes remove much of the liability a hotel would otherwise have when property is missing from a safe, such incidents are costly to the hotel in terms of good customer relations. Efforts should be made to minimize this loss. Security measures concerning the safes should be reviewed and updated regularly. The number of employees with access to the safes should be limited (but not too limited because guests must have access around the clock for limited liability to apply). Tight control should be maintained of keys to the safes and records that identify their contents. Passcode protected safes eliminate concerns about safe keys. Other security measures appropriate to the particular circumstances of your establishment should be instituted.

■ *Regularly review procedures followed in checkrooms to minimize chances of theft.* Many thefts in hotels and restaurants occur in the baggage checkroom or the coat-check area. Access to these rooms should be limited. Attendants should be instructed not to leave unless another attendant is available. They should be trained always to require a receipt or other proof of ownership before returning goods. The checkrooms should be equipped with security devices to enable attendants to notify security unobtrusively if a theft is in progress.

- *Develop and strictly enforce procedures for parking guests' cars.* Employees assigned to parking customers' cars should be screened for driving abilities and criminal records for theft and crimes relating to driving, such as driving while intoxicated and reckless driving. Their training should stress the importance of driving patrons' cars carefully. The establishment should have procedures for handling car keys designed to avoid loss or theft. The hotel should maintain adequate insurance to cover its potential liability for violation of its duties as a bailee.

- *If the coat room is unattended, hang a sign stating the hotel is not liable.* The sign alerts the customer that the establishment will not cover the loss and the patron leaves the goods at his or her own risk. This may motivate the customer to take extra precautions to avoid the disappointment of a loss.

- *Adopt procedures enabling the hotel or restaurant, when acting as bailee, to prove it exercised reasonable care.* The law of bailment creates a presumption of negligence on the part of the bailee if the bailor can prove delivery of property, acceptance by the bailee, and damage to or loss of the property. The bailee can rebut the presumption of negligence by showing it used reasonable care while in possession of the goods. Procedures for ensuring safekeeping should be developed and enforced so that the hotel can prove it exercised reasonable care.

- *If a concessionaire operates the checkrooms, the contract should require safety procedures be utilized and insurance be obtained.* A careless concessionaire can damage a restaurant or hotel's reputation. A guest is hardly ever aware that a service is being offered by someone other than the hotel or restaurant. When a guest's property is stolen while checked, the guest views the wrongdoer as the hotel, not the concessionaire. The hotel thus has a public relations interest in ensuring that concessionaires do not engage in conduct likely to alienate patrons. The hotel should be vigilant to ensure the concessionaire's practices maximize security and minimize theft. The contract should require that specified security procedures be followed and also that the concessionaire purchase insurance to cover the potential for unlimited liability.

Review Questions

1. According to common law, what is the innkeeper's liability for a guest's lost or stolen property?

2. What is a limiting liability statute?

3. What two key facts must be included in a notice posted pursuant to most limiting liability statutes?

4. Which of the following types of property are covered by limiting liability statutes that require hotels to maintain a safe?

   A. Jewelry

B. Cash

C. A laptop computer

D. Diamond cufflinks

E. Expensive ski equipment

F. Clothes

5. What is the consequence of a guest failing to put valuables in a safe?

6. What is estoppel? What is its relevance to a hotel's liability for lost property?

7. At what point in the checkin process does a limiting liability statute become effective?

8. What is a bailment?

9. What is the difference between a bailment for the sole benefit of the bailor and a bailment for the sole benefit of the bailee?

10. What is a mutual-benefit bailment?

11. If you leave a watch with the jeweler to be repaired, who is the bailor and who is the bailee?

12. Does a bailment exist between a hotel and a guest when the guest goes out for the evening and leaves property in the guest room?

Discussion Questions

1. Describe two possible circumstances in which a hotel that provides a safe to its guests fails to satisfy the statutory requirements for a safe.

2. The Mandolin Hotel posts the notice required by the limiting statute in the bathroom of guest rooms on the inside door of the medicine cabinet. Has the hotel posted the notice conspicuously? Why or why not? Suppose the notice is placed in an informational booklet about the hotel, which is placed on the desk in each guest room. Is this conspicuous posting? Why or why not?

3. Erika ate dinner at the Cypress Restaurant. After dinner she paid the cashier and went home without realizing she had left her purse at the restaurant. What liability does the restaurant have if the cashier does not notice the purse and it is stolen? What liability does the restaurant have if the cashier takes possession of the purse intending to notify Erika that it is at the restaurant?

4. John did not use the in-room safe in the closet of the hotel. He decided to tuck his wallet and cellphone into his shoe left in the hotel room under the bed. He went to swim in the hotel pool and when he returned to his room, his wallet and cellphone were missing. What is the responsibility of the hotel?

5. Compare the liability of a hotel and a concessionaire for coats checked in a cloakroom.

6. Jesse left his coat with an attendant in the coat-check area of a restaurant. In his coat pocket was a cell phone. Does a bailment exist for the phone? Why or why not?

Application Questions

1. A limiting statute requires that a hotel post the necessary notice in the registration area, in the hotel lobby, and in the guest rooms. If a hotel posts the notice in the registration area and in guest rooms but fails to post in the lobby, will the hotel be entitled to limited liability? Why or why not?

2. Nicole arrives at a hotel and informs the desk clerk that she has with her a large amount of cash. She expresses concern for its safety, and the clerk recommends she place it in a hotel safe deposit box. When she hesitates, he assures her that the money will be protected and further, even if it does become lost the hotel will be fully liable. Relying on this assurance, she deposits the money in the safe deposit box. When she sought to retrieve the money it had disappeared and has not been recovered. Is the hotel entitled to limited liability under these circumstances? Why or why not?

3. Cameron is a computer salesperson. He is staffing a booth at a computer expo and has brought with him approximately $30,000 worth of laptops. What must he do vis-à-vis the hotel to obtain maximum protection for the equipment? What if he fails to do so?

4. Julia is talking to the front-desk clerk and is in the process of checking out. While she is reviewing the bill, someone steals her briefcase, which was on the ground near her feet. The briefcase had in it various documents she needed for work, a spare pair of glasses, and a necklace with diamonds in it. Will the hotel be liable for the loss of any of these items? Why or why not?

Websites

Websites that will enhance your understanding of the material in this chapter include:

www.nolo.com/lawcenter/faqs Once on this site, click on *Consumer & Travel*, then scroll down to *Hotels and Other Accommodations FAQ*. Several questions and answers address legal issues associated with guests whose property was stolen from a hotel or whose car was damaged while parked at a hotel.

www.palmersecurity.com This is one of numerous vendor sites that promote hotel safes for installation in guest rooms.

www.hotellawyer.com/ This site covers legal, safety, and security solutions for the hotel, food and beverage, private club, meeting, event, and corporate travel industries.

CHAPTER 9

Rights of Innkeepers

LEARNING OUTCOMES:

- Know the right to exclude nonguests
- Understand when a would-be guest can be denied services
- Understand the rules relevant to selecting accommodations for a guest and changing a guest's accommodations
- Comprehend when a prospective diner can be refused service
- Learn when an unwanted patron can be evicted and how to execute the eviction.
- Know statutory protections for the hotel operator including criminal laws for bidding fraudulent payments

---

KEY TERMS

assault	evict	libel
battery	excessive force	lien
criminal possession of stolen property	false arrest	privilege
	forgery	slander
defamation	issuing a bad check	theft of services
defraud	larceny	trespass

Introduction

This chapter focuses on the innkeeper's rights including room selection; entry into guests' rooms; eviction of guests; and pursuing a nonpaying guest.

While patrons are the lifeblood of hotels and restaurants, an unruly or belligerent customer can interfere with the enjoyment of other patrons and damage the reputation of the business. Hotels and restaurants may not want to serve such people.

In this chapter we will explore the circumstances under which a hotelkeeper or restaurateur can refuse a would-be customer accommodations or a meal or evict a guest. The chapter also discusses how to evict and how not to evict. Overzealous action can lead to a lawsuit accusing the proprietor of negligence, assault, false arrest, defamation, or false imprisonment.

Occasionally guests are discontented with their room. We will learn in this chapter that the innkeeper owes no legal duty to guests to accommodate their room preferences. Sometimes patrons do not pay their bill or pay by fraudulent means. The law arms hospitality proprietors with various methods to secure payment, including the criminal charges of theft of services, possession of stolen property, forgery, or issuing a bad check; and the innkeeper's lien and civil lawsuits for breach of contract. This chapter discusses these legal rights and remedies.

Right to Exclude Nonguests

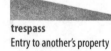

trespass
Entry to another's property without right or permission.

Generally, innkeepers and restaurateurs extend an implied invitation or license to all, including nonguests, to enter their facility. Therefore, the public's presence on the premises does not constitute **trespass**, which is a legal wrong consisting of entering or remaining unlawfully on the premises. This implied license for nonguests can be revoked by the innkeeper at any time. Persons entering a hotel who are not guests and do not intend to contract for a room are required to leave the premises if asked. Thus, where two people somehow were able to occupy a guest room at a hotel although they had not rented the room, they were "simply trespassers" and the hotel was entitled to demand their departure.[1] Similarly, a restaurateur can ask a person to leave who is not intending to eat or drink, but rather is just lingering, loitering, or otherwise "hanging out." Likewise, a casino can exclude anyone so long as the reason is not discriminatory or unlawful.[2] A person who has been requested to leave and fails to do so after being given a reasonable opportunity becomes a trespasser.[3] The operator may use reasonable force to evict a trespasser, but only after the trespasser has been asked to leave and refuses. The amount of force that can be used is limited by law. Only that amount of force that is reasonably necessary to remove the trespasser is permitted. Any additional force constitutes **excessive force,** which subjects the hotelier or restaurateur to liability; the trespasser will be able to sue the business for injuries that result.

excessive force
Unnecessary force; more than is required to defend oneself.

When ejecting troublesome customers, the best practice, if time permits, is to call the police. Officers are trained on how to effectuate the removal of a troublesome patron. In Case Example 9-1, the defendants were charged with the criminal violation of disorderly conduct for proselytizing door-to-door at a hotel. The innkeeper wisely sought the assistance of the police to remove the defendants.

CASE EXAMPLE 9-1

People v. Thorpe

101 N.Y.S.2d 986 (N.Y. 1950)

Defendants are charged with the offense of disorderly conduct in violation of ... the Penal Law. They are members of a religious group known as Jehovah's Witnesses. Each of these defendants asserts that he is a minister of the gospel and preaches from door to door under the direction of the Watchtower Bible and Tract Society, Inc., a corporation established by law for religious purposes.

Defendants entered the Endicott Hotel located at 81st Street and Columbus Avenue, New York City, at 10:30 a.m. on Saturday morning, February 4, 1950. Defendant Thorpe proceeded to the second floor and defendant VanDyk to the top floor of the hotel. Each went from door to door down the hotel corridors, knocking to gain the attention of the hotel guests, and, upon the door being opened, sought to impart to each person thus approached the religious doctrines advocated by the Jehovah's Witnesses. Literature was tendered by the defendants consisting of a book, booklet, and magazine. Contributions, if not actively solicited, were certainly encouraged and, in any event, were admittedly accepted.

Defendants continued their mission until halted by the hotel manager. They conducted their activities as quietly as possible and seemingly without undue annoyance of the hotel residents. When the

---

[1] *Foster v. State*, 2002 WL 31109928 (Tex. 2002)
[2] *Slade v. Caesar's Entm't Corp.*, 373 P.3d 74 (Nev. 2016)
[3] *Taylor v. State*, 836 N.E.2d 1024 (Ind. 2006)

hotel manager learned of their presence, he asked defendants summarily to desist. The defendant Thorpe explained that he considered it his constitutional right to preach from door to door, which was, he claimed, established as an appropriate method of preaching in accordance with the tenets of his faith. Defendants refused to leave the hotel, whereupon a police officer was summoned who, upon arrival, informed defendant Thorpe that the hotel management had a right to insist that the defendants' activities stop and that they forthwith leave the hotel. Defendant replied that he had a right to stay there and, admittedly, told the officer then in uniform, "If I was to leave, he would have to put me under arrest."

In the meantime, the hotel manager located defendant VanDyk pursuing his activities on one of the upper floors. He was requested to leave the hotel. Defendant VanDyk thereupon went down to the hotel lobby with the manager, the police officer, and defendant Thorpe, who had been escorted by the policeman to the street. The hotel manager admonished defendants that they could not return to the hotel.... Defendants insisted that it was their right to preach in the hotel and, admittedly, "returned shortly to the hotel with the intention of resuming their preaching activity."...

It is urged that a conviction will result in abridgement of the liberties of press and worship guaranteed by the United States Constitution.

It was long ago held that "from the very nature of the business, it is inevitable" that a hotel owner "must, at all reasonable times and for all proper purposes" have "control over every part" of the hotel, "even though separate parts thereof may be occupied by guests for hire."... The hotel management rightfully may exercise control designed to serve the convenience, comfort, or safety of guests and their property. A person who is not a guest "has in general no legal right to enter or remain" in the hotel against the will of the management.

The hotel management may guard against the possible dangers and annoyances of trespassers or unsolicited visits, and to that end it may, and it is common knowledge that it usually does, exclude all uninvited visitors from the private hotel corridors and from gaining access to the private accommodations of the hotel guests, regardless of whether the one excluded is actually engaged in an otherwise lawful mission, be it commercial, political, or religious.

It was entirely proper for the hotel management to enforce that policy here. That some or even many of the hotel guests may not have found the preaching activities of the defendants objectionable did not deprive the hotel manager of the right to compel observances of such policy... .

Greater vigilance is normally demanded and expected of a hotel in the adoption of measures designed to serve the comfort, convenience, and especially the privacy of its guests, as well as their safety and the safety of their property.

The hotel manager, hence, rightfully halted the defendants' preaching activities and justifiably summoned police aid in ejecting them from the hotel. After they were ejected, and notwithstanding that they were admonished not to return to the hotel by the police officer, the defendants, nonetheless, did return for the express purpose of proceeding with their activities, announcing that they proposed to do so unless arrested... . Defendants' conduct, "at the very least, was such that it tended to disturb the public peace and quiet and to occasion a breach of the peace. That, under our cases, is sufficient... ."

Ruling of the Court: The defendants are found guilty.

Since the decision in the *Thorpe* case in 1950, Congress has enacted the Civil Rights Act of 1964, which we studied in Chapter 3. The act renders hotels and restaurants places of "public accommodation" and as such they cannot discriminate against persons because of race, color, religion, or national origin. Could Thorpe successfully argue today that he was denied equal access to the hotel because of religion in violation of the Civil Rights Act? The answer would be no, provided the hotel barred all door-to-door solicitors and not just religious proselytizers. The reason the hotel evicted Thorpe was not his religion, but rather his action of engaging in door-to-door solicitations inside the hotel. Excluding all persons who seek to solicit a hotel's guests does not constitute illegal discrimination and protects guests from unwanted disturbances.

Refusing Lodging to a Would-Be Guest

A general rule is that a hotel cannot refuse accommodations to anyone seeking them. A hotel with vacancies must provide accommodations for all who seek them, with limited exceptions. This is true regardless of the hour of the guest's arrival.

The reason for this rule is steeped in history. In olden days, the means of travel was horse and buggy, the number of hotels was very limited, and thieves were prevalent along the roads in the night. If a traveler was refused accommodations at one hotel, he might not arrive at the next hotel until very late or be forced to travel throughout the night. He would thus be exposed to considerable risk.

Several exceptions to the general rule exist that allow a hotelkeeper to refuse to provide a room. For example, if a hotel has no vacancies it may refuse a would-be guest. "No vacancies" can exist even though some rooms are not occupied, provided those rooms are legitimately out of service, as where they are being painted, refurbished, or repaired, or the unoccupied rooms are being held for reservations. A hotel that refuses accommodations to someone seeking a room and later the same day accepts a different guest will have to explain its actions if challenged by the person who was turned away, or by a governmental agency that enforces civil rights laws. Without a good explanation, the hotel may be liable for violation of its general duty to provide accommodations to all who seek them or for discrimination.

The hotelkeeper can also refuse persons who are criminals, intoxicated, disorderly, unclean (not bathed) and unkempt, or suffering from a contagious disease. The explanation for the innkeeper's right to exclude these categories of people is the hotelier's duty to protect the well-being of its guests. Would-be guests who meet the referenced descriptions may cause existing guests disruption, injury, or disease. The courts have also allowed innkeepers to refuse persons of bad reputation because of the effect such guests may have on the stature of the hotel. Likewise, the innkeeper can deny a room to a prospective guest who is not able or willing to pay in advance a reasonable price for a room covering the duration of the intended stay. For example, if a person seeks an available room for five days, but can only prove ability to pay for one, the innkeeper must provide him with a room for one night but need not accommodate him thereafter. If the would-be guest cannot show means to pay for even one night, the innkeeper can legally refuse to provide that person a room.

© MintImages/Shutterstock.com

A hotel can also refuse to accommodate guests with firearms, explosives, or pets. In recent years, all states have adopted statutes that forbid refusing services to a person with a seeing-eye dog (one who has been trained to accompany and provide services for people who are blind). Many of these statutes have been expanded to include service animals that aid sighted but otherwise disabled people. The Americans with Disabilities Act, a federal law discussed in Chapter 3, likewise requires a hotel to accommodate seeing-eye dogs and other service animals.

The Consequences of Wrongful Refusal

What are the consequences of wrongfully refusing a guest? The excluded guest can sue the hotel for damages, which may include additional expenses of staying elsewhere. If the refusal is based on race, color, religion, sex, or disability, most state statutes have penalty clauses requiring the hotel to pay a fine for the wrongful exclusion in addition to any damages suffered by the would-be guest. The remedy under the federal civil rights law is an injunction barring further illegal discrimination.

Age

Age is not a protected class in places of public accommodation under federal civil rights laws or most state laws. Therefore, restaurateurs can refuse to serve a young person if so inclined. While most restaurants would have little motivation to refuse service to a child accompanied by an adult, they may be less willing to serve a table full of young people, perhaps because of concern for rowdiness or inability to pay. A few jurisdictions have statutes prohibiting discrimination against young people in places of public accommodation. An example is Washington, D.C. (D.C. Code §2–1402.31).

The innkeeper is in a situation different from the restaurateur. The innkeeper has a common-law duty to provide accommodations to anyone seeking them, except people within the exceptions just discussed in the section entitled, "Refusing Lodging to a Would-be Guest." Thus, a young person is entitled to hotel accommodations unless an exception applies.

In Chapter 4 we learned that a minor can cancel a contract and, in many states, avoid partial or even full payment. Is an innkeeper at risk for not being paid when a room is rented to a minor? The answer is no, for two reasons. First, as we studied, although minors may cancel their contracts, they remain liable for the reasonable value of necessities they receive. Food and shelter are normally considered necessities. Further, parents are liable for necessities furnished to their minor children. Thus, if the minor refuses to pay, the hotel can pursue the minor's parents.

Selecting Accommodations for a Guest

The determination of which room will be assigned to a guest has always been the innkeeper's prerogative. All hotel rooms are different from each other, even though they may be furnished identically and be of the same or similar size. In many instances, the room location is important to a guest—its view, proximity to the lobby, the floor it is on, or other factors affect its appeal. While a hotel might be well advised to accommodate guest preferences for purposes of customer satisfaction, guests have no legal recourse if denied their preference. Case Example 9-2 illustrates this rule.

CASE EXAMPLE 9-2

Nixon v. Royal Coach Inn of Houston

464 S.W.2d 900 (Tex. 1971)

... On December 4, 1968, Virginia Key Nixon was twenty-eight years of age, married, and in the employ of General Electric Company of Dallas as a systems analyst. On this particular day her work required her to come to Houston. She drove her automobile from Dallas to Houston and, arriving after it was dark, checked into the Royal Coach Inn alone at approximately 8:30 p.m. A motel employee directed her to the room to which she was assigned, which was some distance away from the main desk. After depositing her luggage in her room, she left the hotel to eat outside the motel area. Approximately one hour later, she returned to the motel, parked her car in the parking lot in the rear of the motel, and entered the building. She ascended the stairs and, while in the process of unlocking the door to her room, was attacked by an unknown assailant. She testified that though she did not lose consciousness, everything went black, and then she started screaming. It was at this time that she saw an unidentified man running down the hall in the direction of the main desk. Her screams brought no assistance, but she was able to reach the office switchboard through the phone in her room. Individuals came to her assistance in response to her phone call.

In her original petition, appellant [Nixon] alleged that appellee [the motel] was negligent [for] "... (1) billeting a single woman in a remote room in a desolate area of the motel."

An innkeeper is not an insurer of the safety of its guests. An innkeeper's responsibility to his guests is limited to the exercise of ordinary or reasonable care. We are cited to no authority that requires an innkeeper to assign any guest to a particular room or to any particular part of a hotel or motel. Nor has our attention been directed to any part of the record that would indicate that the appellant was in fact billeted in a remote or desolate area of the motel....

Ruling of the Court: The judgment of the trial court is affirmed for the defendant.

Good customer relations may influence room-assignment decisions. For example, some guests are superstitious and wish to avoid the thirteenth floor. Others may request an ocean view. If a guest asks for a particular floor or view, the hotel is not legally obligated to honor the request, but may seek to do so in an effort to please the patron. If a guest's request is based on a disability, such as a desire to be in a room near an elevator because of difficulty walking, the Americans with Disabilities Act, studied in Chapter 3, requires the hotel to make reasonable efforts to accommodate the guest.

Changing a Guest's Accommodations

Once a room is assigned to a guest, can an innkeeper require the guest to change rooms? Only two cases have been reported on this issue and both allow the innkeeper to change the room. In one, the plaintiff-guest sued the defendant hotel for trespassing and taking his goods from the room he was originally assigned and moving them to another room. The court said the hotelkeeper has the right to select the room for the guest and, if expedient, to change it.[4] This ruling was followed in another case in which the court held that an innkeeper would not be liable for moving a guest "if he offered plaintiff proper accommodations in lieu of the room previously assigned to him."[5] Further, the hotelkeeper does not become a trespasser while transferring the guest's belongings. It is not good policy to change a room or move a guest's possessions without notice and permission. Recognizing that room changes are disruptive to the guest, they should be avoided unless the reasons are compelling. If a switch cannot be prevented, the preferred approach would be to inform the guest of the impending change and provide an explanation.

Entering a Guest's Room

Most courts hold that when guests are assigned a room, they are to be the sole occupants during their stay. The innkeeper retains the right of access only for such reasonable purposes as may be necessary in the conduct of the hotel such as nor-

---

[4] *Doyle v. Walker,* 26 U.C.Q.B. 502 (Canada, 1867)
[5] *Harvey v. Hart,* 42 So. 1013 (Ala. 1906)

© boscorelli/Shutterstock.com

mal maintenance and repair, imminent danger, nonpayment, and when entry is requested by the guest (e.g., room service).

When imminent danger exists, an innkeeper or the police may enter a guest's room to address the emergency circumstance.[6] Thus, entry was permitted where a woman fell to her death directly below a particular hotel room which "was the only place she could have come from." The possibility existed that others in the room were in grave danger.[7] Indeed, emergency conditions, if known to the innkeeper, impose a duty to enter a guest's room to eliminate the danger. Failure to do so can result in liability.

We saw in Chapter 6 that, where an innkeeper is aware of a rape or assault occurring in a hotel room, the hotelier has a duty to enter the room promptly and provide aid to the guest. Likewise, where guests were throwing water-filled pillowcases and laundry bags out of the window of their room, causing injury to pedestrians below, the hotel had a duty to stop the offending conduct and had the right to enter the guest room if necessary to end the behavior.[8]

Evicting a Guest

Under certain circumstances an innkeeper has the right to withdraw hotel privileges and evict a guest, provided no more force is used than is necessary.[9] To **evict** means to remove someone from property. The following are grounds for eviction.

eviction
Legal removal of someone from property.

---

[6] *People v. Love,* 84 N.Y.2d 917, 620 N.Y.S.2d 809 (N.Y. 1994)
[7] *Mark v. State,* 2002 WL 341979 (Ala. 2002)
[8] *Connolly v. Nicollet Hotel,* 95 N.W.2d 657 (Minn. 1959)
[9] *Bertuca v. Martinez,* 2006 WL 397904 (Tex. 2006)

A guest's right to occupy a hotel room ends when the guest stops paying.[10] Failure to pay one's hotel bill is grounds for eviction. The eviction is ordinarily carried out by asking the guest for the amount due and requesting the guest to leave by a certain hour if the bill is not paid. If the guest fails to pay after such a demand, the hotel may evict. Thus, a hotel was entitled to remove a guest who had occupied her room for some time, was delinquent in payment for the room, meals, and telephone calls, and refused to pay after the request was duly made.[11] The reason the law gives the hotel this remedy is to allow the innkeeper to rent the room to someone else who has the ability to pay, thereby producing income for the inn.[12]

In Case Example 9-3, the guest refused to pay for food he received at the hotel restaurant. In response, the hotel thereafter refused to serve him in the restaurant, which action was upheld by the court.

CASE EXAMPLE 9-3

Morningstar v. Lafayette Hotel Co.

211 N.Y. 465 (N.Y. 1914)

The plaintiff was a guest at the Lafayette Hotel in the city of Buffalo.... He...purchased some spare-ribs, which he presented to the hotel chef with a request that they be cooked for him and brought to his room. This was done, but with the welcome... [food] there came the unwelcome addition of a bill or check for $1, which he was asked to sign. He refused to do so, claiming that the charge was excessive. [Remember, the year was 1914. A dollar was worth much more then.]

That evening he dined at the [hotel] cafe, and was again asked to sign for the extra service, and again declined. The following morning, Sunday, when he presented himself at the breakfast table, he was told that he would not be served.... He remained at the hotel till Tuesday, taking his meals elsewhere, and he then left. [He thereafter sued the hotel claiming it wrongfully refused to serve him.] An innkeeper is not required to entertain a guest who has refused to pay a lawful charge....

Overstaying

Occupying a room beyond the agreed time is grounds for eviction. The contract for a room is for a definite time, be it one or several days, a week, or longer. When the period is over, the hotel has met its obligation under the contract with the guest to rent the room and the guest's right to occupy the space ends.[13] If requested by the hotel, the guest must leave. If the guest fails to depart, the contract is breached

---

[10] *People v. Gutierrez*, 2004 WL 1468751 (Calif. 2004)
[11] *Sawyer v. Congress Square Hotel, Co.*, 170 A.2d 645 (Maine 1961)
[12] *People v. Lerhinan*, 455 N.Y.S.2d 822 (N.Y. 1982)
[13] *Laney v. State*, 842 A.2d 773 (Md. 2004)

and the guest becomes a trespasser. The hotel can then do one of two things: either assume that a new contract exists on a day-to-day basis, obligating the guest to pay in advance the daily room rate, or, if the hotel has made other commitments for the room, evict the guest. A good practice that most innkeepers have adopted when the vacancy rate is low is to print or stamp the date of departure on the registration card and on a copy given to the guest with an oral reaffirmation of the departure date. This helps to ensure that both the hotel and guest have the same understanding of the duration of their relationship.

Three states—Hawaii, Louisiana, and North Carolina—as well as Puerto Rico have passed statutes that codify this common-law position and make a holdover guest a trespasser. For example, Hawaii's statute specifies: "Any guest who intentionally continues to occupy an assigned bedroom beyond the scheduled departure without the prior written approval of the keeper shall be deemed a trespasser." This modifies the common law slightly in that the statute does not require the innkeeper to request overstaying guests to leave prior to evicting them.

North Carolina's statute requires the innkeeper to issue a written statement specifying the time period during which the guest may occupy a room and have the guest initial it. At the end of the stated period, the innkeeper automatically has the right to lock the former guest out of the room. The statute denies the former guest the right to enter to reclaim any personal property and permits the innkeeper to remove it. The statute also authorizes the innkeeper to use reasonable force in preventing the lodger from reentering the room.

Puerto Rico requires the innkeeper to call the police to physically remove a holdover.

In the states that do not have statutes specifically covering the rights of innkeepers with regard to overstays, innkeepers should proceed with caution when evicting the guest so as to reduce the possibility of lawsuits. Later in this chapter we will examine preferred methods to execute an eviction and the possible grounds for lawsuits that can develop if the ejection is done inappropriately.

Persons of Ill Repute

People with reputations for engaging in criminal activity or other types of disruptive conduct may be inclined to engage in troublesome behavior at a hotel and so can be denied a room. In Case Example 9-4, the court upheld a hotel's right to evict a guest because she was a prostitute. Read carefully the description of the method used by the hotel for the eviction and the court's decision on the acceptability of that method.

CASE EXAMPLE 9-4

Raider v. Dixie Inn

248 S.W. 229 (Ky. 1923)

Appellant, Thelma Raider, applied to the Dixie Inn, at Richmond, for entertainment, and paid her board and lodging for a week in advance, saying that her home was in Estill County and she had come to Richmond, at the expense of her mother, to take treatments from a physician. At the end of the week she paid in advance for another week, and so on until the end of a month, when she went downtown, and on returning was informed by the proprietor and his wife, who are appellees in this case, that she no longer had a room at that hotel, and remarked to her that no explanation was due her as to why they had requested or forced her removal. Alleging that she was mortified and humiliated by the words and conduct of the proprietors of the hotel, appellant, Raider, brought this action to recover damages in the sum of $5,000. Appellees answered, and denied...harsh or improper conduct on the part of the proprietors of the hotel, but admitted that they had required appellant to vacate her room and to leave the hotel, and gave as their reason for so doing that she was a woman of bad character, recently an inmate of a house of prostitution in the city of Richmond, and had been such for many years next before she came to the Inn, and was in said city a notoriously immoral character, but that appellees did not know her when she applied for entertainment at their hotel, but immediately upon learning who she was and her manner of life had moved her belongings out of the room into the lobby of the hotel, and kindly, quietly, and respectfully asked her to leave; that they had in their hotel several ladies of good reputation who were embarrassed by the presence of appellant in the hotel and who declined to associate with her and were about to withdraw from the hotel if she continued to lodge there; that appellant had not been of good behavior since she had become a patron of the hotel... .

...As a general rule a guest who has been admitted to an inn may afterwards be excluded therefrom by the innkeeper if the guest refuses to pay his bill, or if he becomes obnoxious to the guests by his own fault, is a person of general bad reputation....

It appears, therefore, fully settled that an innkeeper may lawfully refuse to entertain objectionable characters, if to do so is calculated to injure his business or to place himself, business, or guests in a hazardous, uncomfortable, or dangerous situation. The innkeeper need not accept any one as a guest who is calculated to and will injure his business... . A prizefighter who has been guilty of law breaking may be excluded... . Neither is an innkeeper required to entertain... persons of bad reputation... drunken and disorderly persons... one who commits a trespass by breaking in the door... one who is filthy or who subjects the guests to annoyance... . It therefore appears that the managers of the Dixie Inn had the right to exclude appellant from their hotel upon several grounds without becoming liable therefor... .

The petition...did not state a cause of action in favor of appellant against appellees.

Judgment [in favor of the hotel] affirmed.

What constitutes an objectionable character is a debatable question, and a hotelier relying on this ground for eviction should proceed carefully. The decision in *Raider v. Dixie* upholding the innkeeper's right to remove a prostitute might not be followed today unless the guest was practicing the illegal trade in the hotel or otherwise disturbing other guests.

Intoxication and Disorderly Conduct

Intoxication alone is not an adequate reason in most states for eviction. However, a hotel has the right to evict a person who is intoxicated and disturbing other guests.[14] There must be a disturbance of the peace, disorderly conduct, threat to other guests, damage to the room, or some other similarly unsavory conduct.

Thus a hotel was entitled to evict a guest who yelled complaints and accosted the hotel clerk after she told him he owed money for his phone bill.[15] In some circumstances, not only does the hotel have the right to remove a disruptive guest, but it may violate a duty to other guests if it does not do so. For example, if the intoxicated person threatens the well-being of other guests, a hotel may be negligent if it fails to remove the disorderly person.

Disorderly Conduct

A sober person engaged in disorderly conduct can likewise be evicted. Said a Texas court, "When a guest is obnoxious for some reason, he may be forcibly removed without resort to legal process, provided no more force is used than necessary...There is no...law which, regardless of his conduct or behavior, allows a person to stay in a hotel room merely because the rate for the room has been paid."[16] An interesting exam-

---

14 *In re John Haskin*, 807 N.E.2d 43 (Ind. 2004); *Olsen v. State*, 663 N.E.2d 1194 (Ind. 1996); *Poroznoff v. Alberti*, 401 A.2d 1124 (N.J. 1979)
15 *People v. Weaver*, 16 N.Y. 3d 123 (N.Y. 2011)
16 *Bertuca v. Martinez*, 2006 WL 397904 (Tex. 2006)

ple involving unusual disorderly conduct concerns a television station that sent a camera crew to a restaurant that had been cited for health code violations. The instructions given the crew were to enter unannounced "with cameras rolling," apparently in an effort to catch unsanitary practices on film. The television team entered as directed with bright lights glaring. Some diners hid under the table, others left without paying their bills, and those waiting to be seated departed without purchasing a meal. The restaurant ordered the crew to leave and sued for damages on the grounds of trespass. A verdict in the restaurant's favor for $1,200 was upheld on appeal.[17]

In Case Example 9-5, the plaintiff was a guest in the hotel. He was acting erratically in the hotel lobby and telling everyone that his life was in danger. The police were called and after their hour-long attempt to coax him out of his room was unsuccessful, and he refused to speak with the police, he was detained by law enforcement for a mental health evaluation. The plaintiff sued the hotel claiming wrongful eviction, false imprisonment, negligent infliction of emotional distress, assault, battery, and civil rights violations. The court determined, however, that a hotel cannot be held liable for false imprisonment either for its communication to the police or for the conduct of the police in detaining guests. The court dismissed the plaintiff's claims and granted summary judgment for the defendant.

CASE EXAMPLE 9-5

Forte v. Hyatt Summerfield Suites, Pleasanton

2012 WL 6599724 (Calif. 2012)

…Plaintiff, his wife, and his four children checked into the Hyatt Summerfield Suites in Pleasanton, California, early in the morning. After spending a few hours in the room, Plaintiff returned to the lobby of the hotel at around 10:00 a.m. to ask where he could find breakfast for himself and his family. The clerk at the front desk assisted him and then watched as Plaintiff began to distribute copies of a newspaper called Badger Flats Gazette, which Plaintiff self-publishes, to other hotel guests in the lobby. According to the clerk, Plaintiff also spoke with several hotel guests about the newspaper and told them that his life was in jeopardy.

After Plaintiff left the lobby, the front desk clerk telephoned the hotel's manager, Veronica Villa, to report that several guests had complained about Plaintiff's behavior. Villa then called Plaintiff's room to discuss what had happened in the lobby. Before she could ask Plaintiff to provide his version of events, however, plaintiff began telling Villa that his life was in danger and she needed to call the Los Banos police. He then began to shout and told Villa that if he was killed, it would be her fault.

---

[17] *Le Mistral, Inc. v. Columbia Broadcasting System*, 402 N.Y.S.2d 815 (N.Y. 1978)

Villa claims that she then told Plaintiff that she was going to call the Pleasanton police to have him removed from the hotel. In any event, Villa called the police after she finished speaking with Plaintiff.

Soon afterward, at approximately 11:00 a.m., Pleasanton Police Department Officers Nicely and Lashley arrived at the hotel. Villa told the officers about Plaintiff's erratic behavior in the lobby and on the phone and expressed her concerns about him staying at the hotel. The officers agreed to stand by as she attempted to remove plaintiff and his family from the hotel. When the three of them arrived at Plaintiff's hotel room, however, Plaintiff refused to come outside to speak with them. Instead, he began yelling at them through the door and window of the hotel room and telling them to contact the Los Banos police department. He told the officers they were in trouble, bolted the door to the room, and refused to let them enter. He alleges that the officers attempted to break down the door.

Over the next ninety minutes, Officers Nicely and Lashley—as well as several other PPD officers who later joined them at the hotel—spoke with Plaintiff through the hotel room door in an effort to get him to leave. Plaintiff refused all requests to exit the room and at several points screamed at the officers. He refused PPD's offers for medical support despite telling the officers that he had been injured and his daughter might need medical attention. Throughout the standoff, he continued to talk about the Los Banos police and the purported death threats he had received the previous month. At one point, PPD officers called the Los Banos police and learned that a restraining order had been issued against Plaintiff for threatening statements that he had made about the town's mayor.

The PPD officers concluded that Plaintiff posed a danger to himself and his family; they therefore decided to detain him for a mental health evaluation. When Plaintiff finally left his room, two officers placed him in a control hold and onto a gurney for transport to a nearby medical center....

One year after the incident at the hotel, Plaintiff filed this lawsuit for wrongful eviction... Defendants now move for summary judgment.

Wrongful Eviction

Plaintiff alleges a tort claim of wrongful eviction against the hotel and police officers. To survive summary judgment on this claim, he must first provide evidence to support an inference that he was a person in peaceable possession of real property.

Plaintiff has failed to present any such evidence. California courts have long recognized that hotel guests do not have a possessory interest in their hotel rooms. The guests in the hotel are not tenants and have no interest in the realty; they are mere licensees and the control of the rooms, halls and lobbies remains in the proprietor. For this reason, courts typically reject wrongful eviction claims asserted by hotel guests....

Plaintiff contends that this principle should not apply here because Hyatt houses "permanent residents" in addition to its temporary guests. Courts have expressly rejected this argument in the past. As the Court of Appeal recognized, "It is a matter of common knowledge that hotels, in addition to guest rooms, sometimes contain apartments which include kitchen facilities and are designed and intended for occupation of persons or families for living purposes. Under such circumstances, the entire hotel building would not necessarily be denominated an apartment house where it is designed and used primarily for the accommodation of [transient] guests."

In short, a hotel does not grant *all* of its guests a possessory interest in their rooms merely by granting such an interest to certain, individual tenants.

Plaintiff also argues that his wrongful eviction claim should survive because Defendants repeatedly used the word "eviction" to describe their efforts to remove him from the hotel. Defendants' imprecise term "eviction," however, does not endow Plaintiff with property rights that he would not have otherwise had. Because Plaintiff provides no other evidence to show that he had a possessory interest in his hotel room, Defendants are entitled to summary judgment on his wrongful eviction claim.

Interestingly, disorderly conduct does not require a public inconvenience, annoyance, or alarm if there was proof that the conduct recklessly created a risk of such disruption, and nearby guests were sleeping in a hotel. Thus, a man yelling at his wife in a hotel parking lot qualified as disorderly conduct.

Contagiously Ill Guests

According to common law, hotel operators have the right to evict a guest who contracts a contagious disease that is easily spread. The reason for this rule is protection of other guests from illness. When removing a sick patron, the innkeeper should use great care to avoid aggravating the guest's condition, which generally means the innkeeper should summon the assistance of a doctor or an ambulance if the condition warrants.

According to the Americans with Disabilities Act (ADA), which became effective in 1992 and was discussed in Chapter 3, a debilitating contagious disease may constitute a disability. The act bars innkeepers and restaurateurs from withholding their services if a reasonable modification can be made to accommodate the disability. Arguably, if the disability is a contagious disease, the innkeeper can exclude the guest notwithstanding the ADA because to provide them a room would expose many others to the illness, jeopardizing their well-being. In ADA terms, providing accommodations to a guest with a contagious disease, like the flu, gastroenteritis, measles, etc., that is spread easily would likely fall outside the realm of a reasonable accommodation and therefore is not required of the hotel.

Breaking House Rules

Hotels are legally entitled to adopt reasonable rules to ensure order and safety on the premises and to prevent misconduct that can offend guests or bring the hotel into disrepute. Such rules, often called house rules, might for example include prohibitions against walking in the lobby in a wet bathing suit, having pets in guest rooms (other than seeing-eye dogs or service animals, which by statute must be allowed), or horseplay by the pool. An innkeeper can evict a guest for failing to comply with a house rule.[18] Such rules should be posted in conspicuous places, including guest rooms. All house rules concerning the use of a pool should also be displayed poolside.

Persons Not Registered

When a person is not or has never been a guest of the hotel, the innkeeper can evict that person for violating house rules or even without cause. In Case Example 9-6, a hotel had a rule prohibiting unregistered guests in the building above the lobby. A nonguest was ordered to leave the inn because she was suspected of engaging in prostitution in guests' rooms, which were located on floors above the lobby. She challenged the hotel's right to evict her. The court upheld the hotel's authority to bar from the premises those people who fail to abide by its rules.

CASE EXAMPLE 9-6

Kelly v. United States

348 A.2d 884 (D.C. 1975)

...Between the months of January and March 1974, appellant was seen by the chief of security at the Statler Hilton Hotel on approximately five occasions. He first noticed her in the hotel bar speaking with a guest with whom she later went upstairs. On one occasion when she was in the lobby all night, a police officer assigned to the vice squad told the hotel's security officer that appellant was a prostitute and showed him a copy of her criminal record and her mug shot.

On March 18, hotel security officers again noticed appellant in the hotel. At that time she was once more observed going upstairs with a guest. After about an hour in the guest's room, she came out of the room alone. She was stopped by the hotel security officers and informed of the hotel policy of not allowing any unregistered guests above the lobby. She was also told of the conversation with the police vice squad officer and was read a "barring notice" [a notice that orders someone to remain off the premises, disregard of which constitutes the crime of unlawful entry which is a violation of law similar to trespass. The notice said: You are hereby notified that you are not permitted entry in the Statler Hilton Hotel, 1001 Sixteenth Street, Northwest. In the future, if you return to the Statler Hilton Hotel and gain entry, you may be subject to criminal prosecution for unauthorized entry.] Furthermore, she was told that if she returned to the hotel, she would be arrested and charged with unlawful entry.

On August 19, security officers were called to the fifth floor of the hotel. They waited outside one of the rooms until appellant emerged with two male companions. She was then placed under arrest.

---

[18] *McClean v. University Club,* 97 N.E.2d 174 (Mass. 1951)

Appellant...argued that the [unlawful entry] statute [quoted below] was not applicable to a hotel and accordingly a hotel could not issue a valid barring notice... .

It is a general rule that.. .

[Where a person does] not enter the hotel as a guest nor with the intention of becoming one, [it is] his duty to leave peaceably when ordered by the [innkeeper] to do so, and in case of his refusal to leave on request, [the innkeeper] was entitled to use such force as was reasonably necessary to remove him... .

It necessarily follows that if a hotel has the right to exclude someone, and he or she receives appropriate notice of his exclusion, that person's subsequent presence in the hotel is without lawful authority. Thus he or she is subject to arrest for the crime of unlawful entry. The unlawful entry statute of Washington, D.C. provides:

Any person who ... being [in or on any public or private buildings] without lawful authority to remain therein or thereon shall refuse to quit the same on the demand of... the person lawfully in charge thereof, shall be deemed guilty of a misdemeanor.

In the instant case, appellant concedes that she was warned not to return to the hotel. She also admits that she was in the hotel on the evening of August 19, 1974. Consequently, under the authorities cited above, with which we agree, her entrance into the hotel was unlawful...

Appellant's other grounds for reversal, namely that the hotel policy was unreasonably and discriminatorily applied and that the government's evidence was insufficient, are without substance. Ruling of the Court: ...judgment...for the defendant.

As illustrated in Case Example 9-7, the rights of a guest are not assignable— that is, they cannot be transferred. Therefore, a registered guest who prepaid and leaves early cannot give another person the right to occupy the room.

CASE EXAMPLE 9-7

Hennig v. Goldberg

68 N.Y.S.2d 698 (N.Y. 1947)

...Defendants were innkeepers, and plaintiff occupied a room in their hotel.... [D]efendants, in [plaintiff's] absence, changed the lock of the room which she occupied, so that upon her arrival at the hotel in the early morning of February 20, 1946 and again in the early afternoon of February 25, 1946 she was unable to gain admittance. [She sued the hotel for forcible entry.]

... Furthermore, I find that plaintiff occupied the room—which had been assigned to one Bihovsky, who had dwelt in it for some time and had paid the February 1946 rent in advance in full—without permission from defendant or anyone representing the hotel, that she had not registered as a guest, and that the permission to use the room which she had obtained from the guest Bihovsky gave her no lawful right to the room and did not even put her in possession inasmuch as Bihovsky's rights as a guest were not assignable or transferable.

...Obviously [the relevant statute] was never intended to make it necessary for an innkeeper to resort to court proceedings... to remove from his inn, or from a room in his inn, one who came in without his permission, express or implied. This is simply a case in which defendants found plaintiff in a room in which she did not belong and changed the lock so that she could not again gain access to that room. In so doing defendants were within their strict legal right, although I think it probable that they acted as they did because they wished to rent the room to someone who would pay a daily rather than a monthly rate.... [Defendants] acted lawfully and are not answerable in damages to plaintiff.

Judgment may be entered in favor of defendants dismissing the complaint....

Business Competitors

If business competitors come to a hotel seeking accommodations, they cannot be refused. But a business competitor who comes to a hotel to solicit customers or to recruit employees can be enjoined, meaning the hotel can obtain a court order barring competitors from continuing such solicitations. In an early case a hotel maintained a livery business supplying its guests with horses. The defendant, a competitor in the livery business, likewise supplied horses to the hotel's guests using the hotel's property to make its business arrangements with the guests. The hotel, seeking to exclude the competitor from transacting business on hotel property, sued. The court granted an injunction prohibiting defendant from taking any of its horses onto the plaintiff's property. Said the court,

> Has an innkeeper the right to refuse a competitor access to his premises, for the purpose of competition, when the presence of the latter is requested by one of the former's guests?... [I]t has never been held that [innkeepers] must furnish their private facilities for the use of a competitor in business. Cases involving the same general principles as the one at bar have frequently arisen, and it has been held almost invariably that the owner of the premises is within his rights in excluding a competitor therefrom.[19]

Suppose a hotel offers food and room services and a guest orders food to be delivered to the hotel by a competitor. Can the hotel refuse admittance to the competitor, making the delivery impossible? The answer seems to be, yes.

---

[19] *Champie v. Castle Hot Water Springs Co.*, 233 P. 1107 (Ariz. 1925)

© Gabriel Georgescu/Shutterstock.com

If the hotel chooses to grant permission to the competitor to carry on business at the inn and allow the competitor access to the hotel's guests, the hotel can charge a fee for that privilege.

Suppose the hotel does not offer food. Can the inn select one or a few exclusive food preparers and exclude others from doing business on the premises? The answer is yes. The hotel has a legitimate interest in protecting the level of service provided. As we have studied, the hotel has a duty to exercise reasonable care for the well-being of its guests. The hotel also has a rightful interest in maintaining its reputation, which could be adversely affected by allowing unknown or substandard food providers on the premises.

The Process of Eviction

Evicting someone from a hotel or restaurant for cause is proper. It should be carried out with reasonable care; no harsh words or force should be used unless absolutely necessary. A wrongful eviction can result in liability, not only for physical injuries, but also for mental and emotional distress.[20]

How to Evict

Evictions must be handled with reasonable care for the person being forced to leave the premises. Ideally, physical force and harsh words can be avoided. Good practice requires the innkeeper or restaurateur in the first instance to inform the person being evicted that she is no longer welcome on the premises and should

---

[20] *Lopez v. City of New York*, 357 N.Y.S.2d 659 (N.Y. 1974)

leave. If the person asks the basis for the eviction, she should be told. If the person declines to leave, the innkeeper or restaurateur should repeat that the person's license to remain on the premises has been withdrawn and a second request to leave should be made.

The following portion of a case discussed earlier in this chapter demonstrates an appropriate method.

© g-stockstudio/Shutterstock.com

CASE EXAMPLE 9-8

Raider v. Dixie Inn

248 S.W. 229 (Ky. 1923)

Plaintiff says that she is advised that these defendants (the Dixie Inn) had a legal right to remove her, and that she does not question that right, but that she was removed as a guest for hire from said Dixie Inn at a time that was improper and in a manner that was unduly disrespectful and insulting, and that she was greatly mortified and humiliated thereby, and suffered indignity because of the wrongful manner in which she was removed from said Dixie Inn as herein set out and complained of.

[T]he only remaining question is: Did they do so in a proper manner, or did they employ unlawful means to exclude her? The allegations of the petition show she was not present at the time they took charge of her room and placed her belongings in the lobby of the hotel, where they were easily accessible to her; that when she came in they quietly told her that they had taken charge of her room, but gave no reason for doing so. We must believe from the averments of the petition that very little was said, and that the whole proceeding was very quiet and orderly. As they had a right to exclude her from the hotel, they were guilty of no wrong in telling her so, even though there [may have been] other persons present in the lobby at the time they gave her such information, which is denied.

CASE QUESTION

1. What specific actions of the hotel staff likely convinced the court to rule in favor of the hotel?

When executing an eviction, the facility has a duty to exercise reasonable care for the patron's well-being. For example, if someone is removed from the premises because of rowdiness due to intoxication, the person may need assistance to avoid hurting himself or others. The hotel must take reasonable action to protect against such injuries. The next case illustrates a violation of that duty and the liability that can result.

CASE EXAMPLE 9-9

Westin Operator, LLC v. Groh,

347 P.3d 606 (Colo. 2015)

.. On Saturday, March 3, 2007, Jillian Groh registered as a guest at the Westin at the Tabor Center in Denver. Groh checked in with two friends, and each of them received their own keys. They visited several downtown nightclubs. At 2:00 a.m. the women returned to the hotel and brought five to eight additional people back to their room. The hotel room had a mini-bar with alcohol, but no one in the group consumed the alcohol. No other guests complained about the noise although there were multiple rooms occupied nearby. The Westin security guard, however, noticed the group and summoned another security guard and also the guest service manager. At 2:45 a.m., a heated confrontation between the Westin's security guards and the occupants of the room ensued. Some members of Groh's group became boisterous and argumentative. Ultimately, hotel security told everyone except the registered guests to leave the premises. Groh refused to stay without her friends. The Westin conceded it evicted Groh as well.

At least one person told the security guard that everyone in the group was "drunk," that the "whole purpose" of renting the room was to allow them to drink without driving, and that they could not leave because, "We are drunk. We can't drive." While these discussions occurred, several members of the group left separately and were not involved in the following events. The security guards escorted Groh and the remaining members of the group outside. Police officers happened to be on the hotel premises investigating a separate, unrelated incident, but the Westin employees did not seek police intervention with Groh or her friends.

Groh called her brother for advice, and he told her to call a cab. She ignored his advice. Video footage showed two taxis in the vicinity at the time of the eviction. No taxi was visible at the time the group exited the hotel, but a police car was parked at the hotel entrance. There is no indication that any member of the group saw a taxi. One person testified he looked for a cab but did not see one. That person also asked if the group could wait in the lobby while they called a taxi because it was freezing outside. The security guard refused his request, blocked the door to prevent re-entry, and told him, "No, get the f*** out of here." A second person testified she did not see any taxis in front of the hotel at any time when they exited the building. A third person testified that he did not know there was a cab stand outside the Westin.

The Westin's security guard watched the group walk to the nearby parking garage. At 3:20 a.m., seven people loaded into Groh's P.T. Cruiser, designed to hold up to five passengers. Only the driver, Angela Reed, wore a seatbelt.

At 4:00 a.m., they were involved in an accident on Interstate 225, fifteen miles from the Westin. Reed, whose blood alcohol content was above the legal limit, was driving seventy-five miles per hour in a fifty-five mile-per-hour zone. She rear-ended a Ford Expedition traveling well below the speed limit and illegally towing another vehicle with a flat tire in the right-hand lane. One passenger in Groh's car was killed. Others were badly injured. Groh sustained traumatic brain injuries.

Through her parents, Groh sued the hotel for negligence, premises liability, breach of contract and negligent hiring and training. The Westin was granted a motion for summary judgment by the trial court. The court of appeals initially upheld the summary judgment order, but then, granted Groh's petition for rehearing, and held that a hotel has a duty to evict a guest "in a reasonable manner", and reversed the summary judgment order with respect to Groh's claims of negligence and negligent hiring and training. Westin appealed.

For the first time, the supreme court examines the duty of care a hotel owes to a guest during a lawful eviction. Based on the special relationship that exists between an innkeeper and a guest, the supreme court holds that a hotel that evicts a guest has a duty to exercise reasonable care under the circumstances. This requires the hotel to refrain from evicting an intoxicated guest into a foreseeably dangerous environment. Whether a foreseeably dangerous environment existed at the time of eviction depends on the guest's physical state and the conditions into which he or she was evicted, including the time, the surroundings and the weather. In this case, genuine issues of material fact preclude summary judgment on Groh's negligence-related claims. The court concludes that the [Dram Shop] Act does not apply because it is undisputed that the Westin did not serve alcohol to Groh. Consequently, the supreme court affirms the judgment of the court of appeals and remands for further proceedings.

CASE QUESTIONS

1. How might the outcome have been different if the mini-bar alcoholic beverages had been consumed?

2. Would the decision have been different if the hotel hailed a taxi for Groh and her friends and they refused to enter the cab?

If, following a request that a patron leave, he refuses to comply, the hotel may have only two choices: call the police or use force. If time permits, the preferable method is to call the police. If force is used, the person may become agitated and injury may result to an employee or to customers. The police are specially trained to handle such situations. If the person who was asked to depart is out of control and delay until police arrive is not feasible, the courts have consistently held that the hotelkeeper may forcibly remove the guest, provided that no more force is used than is reasonably necessary to effectuate the removal or defend against harm. The eviction of a hotel guest must be for one of the previously stipulated reasons—nonpayment, overstaying, intoxication coupled with disorderly conduct, contagious illness, or breaking house rules. If an eviction from a hotel is prompted by personal animus, or race, color, national origin, religion, gender, disability, or marital status, the hotel may be held liable for wrongful eviction.

Hotel and restaurant employees should be carefully instructed on how to evict a guest. Remember, an employee's actions are attributed to the employer for liability purposes per the legal principal of respondeat superior. In all situations, forceful

assault

The tort of intentionally putting someone in fear of harmful physical contact, such as making a fist in a way suggestive of an imminent punch.(Compare to battery.) Also, the crime of intentionally causing physical injury to another person.

battery

The tort of causing harmful physical contact to a person, such as punching someone. (Compare assault.)

eviction should be a last resort. Efforts to convince the person to leave peaceably should always be attempted first.

Excessive Force

Unnecessary force in the course of an eviction can lead to liability for the torts of assault or battery. In tort law, **assault** means intentionally putting someone in fear of harmful physical contact, such as making a fist in a way suggestive of an imminent punch. The tort of **battery** means causing harmful physical contact to a person. Intentionally hitting someone in the face is an example of the tort of battery. Battery occurs where a hotel or restaurant owner or employee grabs a patron and pushes him or her out of the premises without good cause, resulting in injury.[21]

In Case Example 9-10, the hotel owner was liable to a patron for battery based on action taken in the course of a wrongful eviction.

CASE EXAMPLE 9-10

Hopp v. Thompson

38 N.W.2d 133 (S.D. 1949)

This is an action to recover damages for assault and battery. Defendant [Appellant] owns and manages the Thompson Hotel in Sisseton. On the evening of June 21, 1946, plaintiff [Respondent] entered the hotel and a fracas occurred in which both parties were injured. Plaintiff brought the action to recover his damages and defendant filed an answer denying liability. Defendant also pleaded a counterclaim for the damages which he claims were sustained by him. The jury returned a verdict for plaintiff in the sum of $10,249 upon which judgment was entered and defendant appealed.

The first question presented is the sufficiency of the evidence to justify the verdict of the jury. Respondent testified that he entered the hotel in response to the invitation of a guest; that appellant, without just cause, ordered him to leave the hotel; that he started to leave, as ordered, when appellant assaulted and beat him with a piece of iron pipe thereby causing unconsciousness, severe cuts and bruises on his scalp and body, and injuries to his brain. His claim to damages consists of hospital and physicians' expense, loss of time, pain and suffering, both present and future, besides exemplary and punitive damages.

Appellant denied all of these contentions of respondent. He testified that respondent was a stranger to him and was not a guest at the hotel. That when respondent entered the hotel it was about 11 o'clock in the evening which was closing time; that respondent started to go upstairs and as he did so appellant repeatedly asked him who he was and what he wanted, to which respondent made no reply; that

---

21 *Jones v. City of Boston*, 738 F.Supp. 604 (Mass. 1990). Also constituting battery would be the unlikely circumstance of a hotel connecting a tank of adulterated water to a guest room. A delusional guest made such a claim but was unable to prove it. *Wang v. Lam*, 2003 WL 1890486 (Calif. 2003) (unpublished).

appellant then told respondent to come down and go home; that respondent still refused to go and thereupon appellant tapped him lightly on the shoulder and told him to get out; that respondent did not leave as ordered and that appellant told him that appellant would call an officer; that when appellant picked up the telephone receiver respondent assaulted him and took the receiver from him. At this time appellant says he picked up a short piece of pipe, tapped respondent on the shoulder with it and again ordered him to leave and that respondent still refused to go; that a scuffle ensued in which appellant hit respondent on the shoulder and respondent grabbed appellant by the neck with both hands; that during this time appellant struck respondent on the back of the head with the pipe; that the parties were on the floor part of the time; that appellant called for help, which came, and then the struggle ended. Appellant contends that he struck respondent only to subdue him and that he used no more force than he thought was necessary for that purpose.

It is the general rule that an innkeeper gives a general license to all persons to enter his hotel. Consequently, it is not a trespass to enter an inn without a previous actual invitation, but, where persons enter a hotel or inn, not as guests, but intent on pleasure or profit to be derived from [interaction with its guests], they are there, not of right, but under an implied license that the landlord may revoke at any time.... The respondent did not enter the hotel as a guest nor with the intention of becoming one, and it was his duty to leave peaceably when ordered by the landlord to do so, and in case of his refusal to leave on request appellant was entitled to use such force as was reasonably necessary to remove him... .

Here respondent denies that he refused to leave when ordered to do so. He also denies that he knowingly assaulted or beat appellant. He testified that he walked toward the desk, then turned to go out, and that the next thing he remembered he was standing outside on the street covered with blood. This record presents a substantial conflict in the evidence. The jurors are the exclusive judges of the weight of the evidence and the credibility of the witnesses and therefore this court could not substitute its judgment for the verdict... .

The judgment [in favor of Respondent/ Plaintiff] is affirmed.

CASE QUESTIONS

1. The jury believed the guest's version of the facts. Based on that version, what did the hotel manager do wrong? How should he have handled the situation?

2. Why did the appellate court refuse to substitute its own opinion for that of the jurors?

Verbal Abuse

Evictions can be carried out verbally without the use of force, or statements by hotel employees might accompany forceful eviction. In either circumstance, untruthful comments can lead to liability. In a Mississippi case, an eviction for cause was handled very badly. The plaintiff-guest paid the room rent for her husband, daughter, and herself weekly. The rent was current for one more day when the plaintiff tried to pay for an additional week. Her money was refused and she was told to vacate her room by the manager, who said in an angry voice, loud enough for others in the lobby to hear, "We do not want you here." The plaintiff was also locked out of her room. She was embarrassed and distressed over the alleged damage to her reputation.[22] The plaintiff had recently been a witness in a case against the corporation that owned the hotel. The manager of the hotel later admitted to the plaintiff that he had been ordered to evict her because of her involvement in that case.

The plaintiff sought punitive damages which, as the court said, are only awarded if the defendant committed a wrongful act, intentionally, willfully, and with gross disregard of the plaintiff's rights. The court determined that the manager spoke to the plaintiff, as quoted above, with intentional malice and in gross disregard of the plaintiff's rights, and awarded the plaintiff punitive damages.

As this case illustrates, statements made about the person being evicted can lead to a lawsuit, not only for wrongful conviction but also for defamation or slander. **Defamation** is the tort of making false and demeaning statements about a person to a third person. **Libel** refers to written defamatory statements; **slander** refers to oral defamatory statements. To avoid this liability, hospitality personnel should always treat patrons respectfully. Good customer relations notwithstanding, a more recent case suggests that, where the grounds for the removal of a patron are in dispute, some leeway is given to the hotel or restaurant to verbalize the basis for the eviction without liability for defamation. This allowable margin to state the basis for the eviction is called in law a **privilege**, meaning an ability to communicate alleged wrongful acts without fear of a lawsuit for statements believed to be true but ultimately determined to be false. For example, a bar customer was accused by a female patron of inappropriately touching her. Based on this accusation the offending customer was asked to leave and was barred from returning. He sued on several grounds, one of which was defamation. The court held "ejection from a bar and prohibited re-entry are not slander." Thus the bar was not liable for comments made during the customer's ejection.[23]

In a case involving a Jack in the Box drive-through customer who proferred a $100 bill for his food, the employee at the window believed it was counterfeit and called the police. Based on the employee's report, an officer arrested the customer but later learned the bill was legitimate. The court dismissed the patron's case for defamation against the eatery, finding that the employee's statement to the police, while false, was privileged. Said the court, "[V]ital to our system of justice is that there be the ability to communicate to police officers the alleged wrongful acts of others without fear of civil action for honest mistakes."[24]

defamation
The tort of making false written statements about someone to a third person when those statements subject the former to ridicule or scorn.

libel
Written defamation.

slander
The tort of making defamatory statements orally, as opposed to in writing.

privilege
An ability to communicate alleged wrongful acts without fear of a lawsuit for statements believed to be true but ultimately determined to be false.

---

[22] *Milner Hotels, Inc., v. Brent*, 43 So.2d 654 (Miss. 1949)
[23] *Lopez v. Howth, Inc.*, 2002 WL 31677202 (Mass. 2002)
[24] *Kennedy, III v. Sheriff of East Baton Rouge and Jack in the Box*, 935 So.2d 669 (La. 2006)

Remember that a requirement for proof of defamation is that the untruthful statement be relayed to a third party. This element became an issue in a case where a church youth group was denied a room at a hotel because the hotel's chief operating officer believed the group's members would make too much noise. They sued the hotel for defamation. The court denied the claim, noting that the only people who heard the comments were the plaintiffs themselves, thus the requirement that defamatory statements be made to a third person was missing. Further, hypothetical statements predicting future behavior are too nebulous to constitute defamation.[25]

These aforementioned cases, involving either excessive force or verbal abuse, underscore the importance of affecting an eviction properly.

Evicting a Hotel Tenant

When considering an eviction, a hotel must distinguish between a guest and a tenant (see Chapter 7 for the distinction). While a guest can be removed for the reasons identified in this chapter, a tenant cannot be evicted without a court proceeding.[26] Due to the relative longevity of a tenant's occupancy of an apartment, a tenant is considered by law to have a greater interest in the apartment than a guest has in a hotel room. That greater interest prevents a hotel/landlord from evicting the tenant without a court order. The law in most states provides a summary proceeding (a quick legal procedure) for this purpose that enables the landlord to obtain the eviction order within a few weeks, provided grounds for eviction can be proven in court.

Refusing a Diner

A restaurant not associated with a hotel has more leeway than a hotel to exclude people. We studied that an inn, as a general rule, must provide a room to anyone who seeks accommodations. Under common law, a restaurant, unless it was part of an inn, had the right to select its customers and to refuse any person. Today, absent a state statute that changes the common law, the restaurant has the right to accept some customers and reject others. However, federal and state civil rights laws prohibit discrimination on the basis of race, color, national origin, religion, gender, marital status, and disability. Thus, a restaurant cannot refuse service on these grounds but can refuse service on other grounds.

In a Washington D.C. case, the appellant entered a restaurant at which he had previously worked, sat at a table to have dinner with his friends, and was conducting himself in a proper manner. He was notified by the night manager that he would have to leave because his name was on a list of undesirables. The appellant failed to leave. The police were called and the appellant was arrested for trespass. He defended on the ground that the restaurant was open to the public and so he had a

[25] *Rockgate Management Co., v. CGU Insurance, Inc.,* 88 P.3d 798 (Kans. 2004)
[26] *Stonebrook Hillsboro, LLC v. Flavel,* 69 P.3d 807 (Or. 2003); *Williams v. Alexander Hamilton Hotel,* 592 A.2d 644 (N.J. 1991)

right to be there. The court rejected his defense in favor of the restaurant's common-law right to refuse service to a guest, even "arbitrarily."[27]

Although a restaurant can refuse service, it cannot in the process use excessive force. In Case Example 9-11, an overzealous bouncer at a club was found liable for battery. The case also is instructive on the doctrine of respondeat superior, which we studied in Chapter 5.

CASE EXAMPLE 9-11

Durand v. Moore

879 S.W.2d 196 (Tex. 1994)

...Lewis was a doorman at Durand's nightclub when he assaulted a customer waiting to enter the club. Durand complains that Lewis was not acting in the course and scope of his employment when the assault occurred [and therefore Durand is not liable under respondeat superior].

On April 19, 1991, Craig Lewis, an employee of Durand, was assigned to the front door of the club. His job included checking IDs, enforcing the dress code, and coordinating the admission of customers into the club.

That night or early morning April 20, Michael Moore and Lawrence Ward went to the club. The club was filled to capacity, and both men waited in line for customers to leave. However, doorman Lewis did not admit customers into the club in waiting-line order. Instead, he selected several persons from the line behind Moore and Ward. Ward, and then Moore, left the line and complained to Lewis. Ward turned away and walked toward his car, but Moore remained and continued the discussion with Lewis. There was conflicting testimony whether Moore and Ward were loud and abusive and whether Durand personally quieted them down just before the assault.

Without provocation, Lewis grabbed a tall cocktail glass filled with a drink and struck Moore on the side of the head shattering the glass. While Moore struggled to restrain Lewis and ward off further attack, Lewis struck Moore several more times with a flashlight. Ward returned and attempted to break up the struggle, but Lewis struck him in the face with the flashlight, breaking Ward's nose. Ward retreated as Durand and others pulled Lewis and Moore apart. Ward called the police. An ambulance arrived, and Moore and Ward received first aid. Ward was later treated at a hospital. Moore declined treatment. Moore sued Durand and Lewis. Lewis defaulted. After a bench trial, the court found Durand liable under respondeat superior. Durand appeals.

In general, to impose liability upon an employer for the tort of his employee under the doctrine of respondeat superior, the act of the employee must fall within the scope of the general authority of the employee in furtherance of the employer's business and for the accomplishment of the objective for which the employee is hired... .

---

[27] *Drew v. United States*, 292 A.2d 164 (D.C. 1972)

When an employee commits an assault, it is for the trier of fact to determine whether the employee ceased to act as an employee and acted instead upon his own responsibility... .

It is not ordinarily within the scope of a servant's authority to commit an assault on a third person... .

The nature of the employment may be such as necessarily to involve at times the use of force as where the employee's duty is to guard the employer's property and to protect it from trespassers so that the act of using force may be in furtherance of the employer's business, making him liable even when greater force is used than is necessary.

The master who puts the servant in a place of trust or responsibility, or commits to him the management of his business or the care of his property, is justly held responsible when the servant through lack of judgment or discretion, or from infirmity of temper, or under the influence of passion aroused by the circumstances and the occasion, goes beyond the strict line of his duty or authority and inflicts an unjustifiable injury on a third person... .

[T]here was evidence that Lewis had the responsibility to control the admittance of customers into the club. There was evidence that Lewis admitted, ahead of Moore and Ward, two spendthrift customers who had "paid the light bill last month." Lewis' assault of Moore immediately followed their discussion of why Lewis was giving preferential treatment to certain customers. We find that this evidence was probative that Lewis' assault of Moore was overzealous enforcement of the criteria and procedures used to select waiting customers for admittance into the club....

[The evidence was sufficient to support the verdict against Durand. Judgment affirmed.]

CASE QUESTION

1. How might the situation in this case have been handled to avoid liability?

In another case involving an assault by security employees at a club, the employer was held responsible for employees' use of unreasonable force. The plaintiff patron had too much to drink and was evicted. The bouncer escorted the plaintiff to the front door, took from him the drink he had just purchased, and discarded it. The plaintiff attempted to push the bouncer away, but was seized by two other employees who shoved the plaintiff out the front door. While the plaintiff's arms were pinned by the two workers a third employee, the head doorman, repeatedly hit the plaintiff in the face with his fists. A jury found the employees used excessive force and were acting within the course of their employment. A verdict was issued in the plaintiff's favor against the club. The decision was affirmed on appeal.[28]

---

[28] *Country Road, Inc. v. Witt,* 737 S.W.2d 362 (Tex. 1987)

In a case involving the related circumstance of removing a store patron, the court provided a somewhat helpful description of whether or not respondeat superior will apply, characterizing the issue as "whether the [employee]'s alleged actions were an overzealous misuse of his authority [in which case the employer will be liable] or were utterly unrelated to his duties [in which case the employer will not be liable]."[29]

A court interpreted the definition of the tort of battery broadly in a Texas case, ruling in favor of a restaurant customer. The manager of a restaurant snatched a black patron's dinner plate just as the latter reached the buffet because the manager refused to serve African Americans. The patron chose to sue the restaurant for battery rather than discrimination. The jury found that the manager "forcibly dispossessed plaintiff of his dinner plate" and "shouted in a loud and offensive manner." The court ruled that this conduct constituted battery stating, "Under the facts of this case, we have no difficulty in holding that the intentional grabbing of plaintiff's plate constituted a battery. The intentional snatching of an object from one's hand is as clearly an offensive invasion of his person as would be an actual contact with the body."[30]

In this case, the plaintiff also could have sued for discrimination on the basis of race in violation of the federal Civil Rights Act of 1964 and state antidiscrimination laws. Why did the plaintiff sue for the tort of battery, rather than violation of civil rights laws? One reason may be that the remedy for a violation of the federal civil rights law is not monetary; it is instead an injunction that prevents the wrongdoer from continuing the discrimination. The remedy for a battery case is compensation (money) for the resulting injuries.

Statutory Protection for the Hotelkeeper

Statutes in most states provide protection to the innkeeper and restaurateurs against patrons who seek to avoid payment. The hotel lien gives an innkeeper the right to retain the personal property of a nonpaying guest. Fraud and theft of services statutes authorize innkeepers and restaurateurs to pursue criminal charges against those patrons who receive services but intentionally fail to pay. The innkeeper's lien and fraud statutes are discussed in more detail in the next few sections.

The Innkeeper's Lien

lien
A security interest in real or personal property for the satisfaction of a debt.

A **lien** is a security interest in the property of someone who owes money. If the debtor fails to pay, the lien entitles the creditor to take possession of the debtor's property, sell it, and apply the proceeds to the unpaid debt. For example, if you borrowed money from a bank to buy a car, the bank probably has a security interest (lien) on your car. If you fail to repay the loan in a timely manner, the bank will likely enforce its lien by repossessing your car, selling it, and applying the proceeds to reduce the outstanding balance on your loan.

---

[29] *ANA, Inc. v. Lowery,* 31 S.W.3d 765 (Tex. 2000)
[30] *Fisher v. Carrousel Motor Hotel, Inc.,* 424 S.W.2d 627 (Tex. 1968)

The innkeeper's lien originated in early common law when credit cards were not yet invented. The lien's purpose was to protect innkeepers from dishonest guests who failed to pay their bills. The lien authorizes the innkeeper to take possession of a nonpaying guest's property that is at the hotel, sell those possessions, and apply the proceeds toward the unpaid bill. At common law, the innkeeper could sell the property without first obtaining a court order. Today many states require by statute that the hotel, prior to enforcing the lien, obtain a court ruling that the guest is in fact delinquent.

Impact of Credit Cards

In the age of credit cards, the lien has only limited application. Currently, most hotels make a copy and charge guests' credit card upon check in. If the guest later departs without settling the bill, the hotel will charge the bill to the credit card; thereby, the hotel is assured of payment. Some states, such as New York, have repealed the innkeeper's lien.

Applicable Property

To what property does the lien apply? Courts have held that most property a guest brings to the hotel is covered by the lien. Innkeepers' liens have been held valid on such diverse items as a portable piano, valuables in a safe deposit box, and cars.[31] Covered property is not limited to articles necessary for travel; merchandise samples of traveling salespeople may be subject to the lien. Coverage does not, however, extend to a person's necessary apparel and certain personal jewelry such as wedding rings. Those items are exempt and the guest is entitled to retain them. Also, the goods of one's spouse are not subject to the innkeeper's lien when the indebtedness is solely that of the other spouse.[32]

When innkeepers have a lien on the personal property of a guest, the innkeeper's right to possession is superior in the law to that of the guest. If the guest attempts to remove the property from the hotel, he can be charged with theft.

Applicable Charges

Items on a guest's bill to which the lien applies include the guestroom charge, service charges for delivery of a guest's baggage to and from the hotel, valet service, room service, and the like. However, the innkeeper cannot enforce the lien where the services were rendered by an independent contractor, such as the owner of one of the shops in the lobby, or by a doctor whose services the guest needed while at the inn. Nor can the independent contractor enforce the lien; it is particular to the innkeeper.

---

31 *Chesham Auto Supply v. Beresford Hotel,* 29 Times L.R. 584 (1913)
32 *Geobel v. United Railways. Co. of St. Louis,* 181 S.W. 1051 (Mo. 1915)

Termination of the Lien by Payment or Sale

An innkeeper's lien terminates when the bill is paid. The hotelkeeper must then return to the guest any property seized pursuant to the lien. If payment is not made, the innkeeper can sell the property and use the proceeds to satisfy the bill, as well as expenses associated with the sale, including advertising and storage of the goods pending sale. Many states mandate the procedure to be followed when goods subject to the lien are sold. The objective of these statutes is to ensure, for the benefit of the guest, that the sale generates the most money possible. A typical statute requires the innkeeper to publish notice of the sale in a local newspaper at least two weeks prior to the sale date, including a description of the goods to be sold. The goal is to notify as many people as possible and stimulate their interest in purchasing by the description of the goods. The innkeeper is further required to send notice of the sale to the nonpaying guest. This allows the guest one last opportunity to pay the bill and retrieve the possessions before the sale occurs.

Following the sale, the innkeeper retains from the proceeds the amount of the unpaid bill and expenses incurred in arranging and advertising the sale. Any surplus must be paid to the guest. If the innkeeper cannot locate the guest, the extra money can be paid to a designated public official, such as the chief fiscal officer of the city in which the sale occurred. That person is required to hold the money until the guest retrieves it. The hotel is thus saved from having to keep track of the excess money indefinitely.

Not an Exclusive Remedy

The innkeeper's lien is not an exclusive remedy. The hotelier can also sue the guest for breach of contract. Remember that a contract exists whenever a guest registers for a room: The inn agrees to provide a room and the traveler agrees to pay.[33]

Defrauding the Hotelkeeper or Restaurateur

defraud
To cheat or trick; intentionally misrepresenting an important fact intending for someone to rely on the misrepresentation who thereby suffer damages.

All states and the District of Columbia have passed criminal statutes that seek to protect the innkeeper and restaurateur from guests who attempt to **defraud** by leaving without paying. These statutes criminalize nonpayment where the perpetrator sought services with the intention of avoiding payment. The name given to the crime varies from state to state. It may be called theft of services, larceny, or fraud. Many of the statutes provide varying penalties depending upon the amount and value of the goods or services received by the absconder. For example, in Massachusetts, a defendant who receives food, entertainment, or accommodations in excess of $100 faces a maximum jail sentence of two years. In New York, theft of services from a hotel or restaurant is punishable by imprisonment up to one year and a fine up to $1,000 without regard to the value of the services stolen. As evidenced by the penalties, states view this type of crime quite seriously.

---

[33] *Zimmerman v. Dominion Hospitality*, 2004 WL 51016 (Mo. 2004)

A difference between **larceny** and **theft of services** is that the former involves theft of property (tangible items) and the latter involves receipt of services without payment in circumstances where the provider expects to be paid. Failing to pay a restaurant for food can result in a larceny charge because food is property whereas failure to pay for the use of a hotel room would result in charges of theft of services because occupying a guestroom does not constitute property. Thus, a defendant who stayed at an Embassy Suite hotel for several months billing the charge to a business account that never paid was not guilty of larceny for the hotel bill.[34]

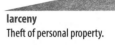

larceny
Theft of personal property.

theft of services
A crime consisting of the use of services, such as a hotel room, with the intent of avoiding payment and the act of failing to pay.

Intent to Defraud

Remember that a criminal case is quite different from a civil case, as discussed in Chapter 1. In a civil case, the plaintiff seeks compensation. Inadvertent or unintended action by the defendant can lead to liability if the plaintiff thereby suffers a loss. A criminal case can result in a variety of penalties, including jail time and the resulting loss of freedom. To justify penalizing the defendant requires that he act with a criminal mental state, which usually means "intentionally." A person acts intentionally when his conscious objective is to engage in the illegal conduct.

For example, a defendant planned a surprise party for his wife at a restaurant. As required by the contract he prepaid the bill, using a check for payment. He asked the proprietor to wait five days before cashing it because the defendant anticipated a paycheck in the interim, and the owner agreed. Two days after giving the check and one day before the party, the defendant stopped payment (directed his bank not to pay the check when the restaurateur sought payment). The party was held and approximately 50 to 70 guests attended. Finding the defendant guilty of the crime of defrauding a restaurant, the court said his intent to deceive was established by his accepting the entertainment while concealing the fact that he had stopped payment on the check written to cover the cost.[35]

Likewise, a patron was guilty of theft of services where he ate at a restaurant and signed the bill with a false name, thereby charging the meal to an account on which he did not have authorization to sign.[36]

Consider the circumstances of a restaurant patron who places her purse on the floor while dining and it is stolen. Assume she has no other money with her and will be unable to pay her bill. She is not guilty of a crime because her inability to pay was not by design. However, she remains liable to the restaurant for the cost of her dinner. If she fails to pay once her financial situation is settled, the restaurant could bring a civil action to collect the funds.

Similarly, a court found the element of intent to defraud missing in a case where the defendant moved into a hotel following a flood, anticipating payment for the room by the Red Cross Relief Fund. After accumulating a bill in excess of $1,000, the defendant learned she was not eligible for money from the fund. She moved

---

[34] *People v. Perry,* 836 N.E.2d 387 (Ill. 2005)
[35] *Morton v. Commonwealth,* 1999 WL 1129728 (Va. 1999)
[36] *Minkler v. Chumley,* 747 So.2d 720 (La. 1999)

out of the hotel and failed to pay. She was charged with the crime of defrauding an innkeeper. The court dismissed the case, finding absent the element of intentionally misrepresenting her eligibility for Red Cross reimbursement.[37]

To establish a defendant's guilt of a crime such as theft of services, the prosecutor must prove two elements at trial: (1) the defendant obtained services such as lodging without paying for it, and (2) the defendant intended to avoid payment. Proving a defendant's intentions is often difficult, as illustrated in Case Example 9-12.

CASE EXAMPLE 9-12

State of Utah v. Leonard

707 P.2d 650 (Utah 1985)

The defendant, Steven Charles Leonard, appeals from his jury conviction of theft of services.... He argues that the evidence was insufficient to support the verdict...

On February 10, 1981, the defendant checked into the Tri-Arc Travel Lodge in Salt Lake City.... He paid for the first night's lodging in cash. On February 11, 1981, he again paid his full hotel bill in cash. After the payment on the 11th, no more payments were made. By February 14th, the accumulated bill for the defendant's room was over $100. When the defendant did not respond to the hotel's requests for him to contact the desk to pay the accumulated bill, his hotel room was locked. On February 15th, the defendant and another male, James Borland, reported to the front desk supervisor that they were locked out of their room. Defendant promised to pay the outstanding $352.40 owed on the hotel and restaurant bills that were in his name the following day when he could go to his credit union for the necessary money. The defendant was let back into his room.

The following day the resident hotel manager called the defendant's room. The person who answered the phone responded to the defendant's name and promised to pay the bill. Instead the defendant and Borland vacated the room. The defendant was arrested shortly thereafter and charged with theft of services... .

The defendant was convicted of obtaining services by deception.... [The relevant statute] provides: "A person commits theft if he obtains services which he knows are available only for compensation by deception, threat, force, or by any means designed to avoid the due payment therefore."

Fraudulent intent is the gravamen of the offense of theft of services. Without [the requirement of] proof of a criminal state of mind, the law would imprison people for mere failure to pay a debt, a practice not sanctioned in this or any other state of this nation.... The rule is that a person who in good faith accepts the benefit of services for which he plans to pay later cannot be convicted of theft even though he subsequently does not recompense the provider of services. The remedy in such case is a civil suit for breach of contract. Obviously, however, a defendant's denial of a fraudulent intent at the time of receiving the services is not binding. As is often the case, circumstantial evidence may speak louder than words.

---

[37] *Louis v. Commonwealth,* 578 S.E.2d 820 (Va. 2003)

The defendant made an implied promise to pay for the lodging and services provided the nights of February 12th, 13th, and 14th. However, the implied promise to pay and the subsequent failure to pay the bill, standing alone, are legally insufficient to show the elements of deception...the prosecution must prove fraudulent intent by more than just a mere failure to pay. Some additional evidence is required to sustain a finding of fraudulent intent. In short, a conviction cannot be sustained merely on proof that a person acquired lodging and failed to pay for it.

Numerous types of circumstantial evidence may show fraudulent intent. For example, circumstantial evidence that a defendant had no money and no prospect of acquiring sufficient money when it was time to pay might be sufficient, as would express false promises, or deception as to the identity of the renter. However, evidence that establishes no more than a breach of an express or implied contract is not sufficient to prove the crime of theft of services, and a jury should be so instructed.

[Defendant's conviction was thus reversed.]

CASE QUESTIONS

1. Why is failure to pay an outstanding bill not sufficient, standing alone, to establish fraudulent or criminal intent?

2. What additional evidence would have been necessary in this case to establish a fraudulent or criminal intent?

A court reached a different result for good cause in a case where the defendant secretly left the hotel without informing the management of his departure. Additionally he left his luggage in the room in an apparent attempt to mislead the hotel about his status. When he left he owed the bills that had accumulated for room, board, long-distance telephone calls, and related items. The statute in Wisconsin, where the incident occurred, provides that a crime is committed if a person who "had obtained food, lodgings or accommodations at any hotel, motel...intentionally absconds without paying for it." The defendant was found guilty at trial. The appellate court found sufficient evidence to support defendant's conviction.[38] The defendant's attempts to mislead the innkeeper plus the extent of the bills strongly suggested the defendant intended to avoid payment.

To aid the prosecutor, the criminal law in many states creates a presumption of an intent not to pay when a hotel or restaurant customer leaves without paying. In these states, once the prosecutor proves that the defendant received food or accommodations without paying, a presumption arises that the defendant intended to avoid payment. The defendant is then given an opportunity to present evidence to rebut the presumption. If the defendant fails to do so, the evidence of nonpayment together with the presumption is sufficient for conviction.

---

38 *State v. Croy,* 145 N.W.2d 118 (Wis. 1966)

Evidence sufficient to rebut such a presumption was present in a Texas case. A father and his three children were diners in the Grubsteak Restaurant. Two of the children's spaghetti dinners were cold and the pasta stuck together. The father and the other child complained about their food as well. The waitress had the dinners recooked but they still were not satisfactory. When the bill was brought to the table, the father requested an adjustment. The waitress left to talk to the cook and did not immediately return. The father, apparently exasperated, left his card at the cash register with the following note on the back. "Call me when you decide. Residence: 937–5300." The restaurateur immediately had the patron arrested for theft of services. At trial, the cook admitted that whoever prepared the spaghetti did not wash and separate it to keep it from sticking. The customer was convicted in a bench trial, but the conviction was reversed on appeal.[39] The appellate court stated,

> *While the customer might be colored irritable and impatient and inconsiderate for not waiting to settle the dispute, we cannot conclude he "absconded" [an element of the crime in the state involved; meaning he intentionally left without paying]. He left his name, business address and telephone number of his business and residence.... [W]e cannot conclude that the evidence is sufficient to establish the requisite intent to commit the offense.*

Fraudulent Payment

Additional statutes also protect the innkeeper and restaurateur from conniving patrons. Most states criminalize the act of knowingly issuing a bad check. A bad check is a check for which the maker has insufficient funds in the bank, or a check written on an account that has been closed. If a customer pays for dinner or a room with a bad check and knows the check is bad (the knowledge constitutes the required criminal mental state), the restaurant or hotel can pursue the patron on criminal charges. Although the statutes vary from state to state, the crime is typically a misdemeanor subjecting the customer to fines of up to $1,000 and a jail term of up to one year.

criminal possession of stolen property
Act of knowingly taking possession of stolen property with intent to benefit someone other than the owner.

In addition, patrons who pay their bills with a credit card they know is stolen and who sign the card owner's name on the receipt are likely committing the crimes of possession of stolen property and forgery. The crime of **criminal possession of stolen property** is committed when a person knowingly possesses stolen property with intent to benefit herself or someone other than the card's owner. A defendant who was in possession of stolen hotel banquet supplies and equipment from a Crowne Royal Plaza Hotel was found guilty of this crime.[40] Another example is provided by a defendant who posed as a Red Cross worker in the days immediately following the terrorist attack on the World Trade Center on September 11, 2001. He stole credit cards and other property from a hotel damaged in the attack. His conviction for criminal possession of stolen property was upheld on appeal.[41]

---

[39] *Manley v. State*, 633 S.W.2d 881 (Tex. 1982). See also *Carlton v. Nassau County Police Dep't.*, 761 N.Y.S.2d 98 (N.Y. 2003)
[40] *People v. Adams*, 779 N.Y.S.2d 275 (N.Y. 2004)
[41] *People v. Abarrategui*, 761 N.Y.S.2d 632 (N.Y. 2003)

Forgery is the unauthorized alteration, completion, or making of a written instrument, such as a debit or credit card receipt or a check, with intent to defraud or deceive. Most states designate forgery and criminal possession of stolen property as either high-level misdemeanors or felonies.

Hotels and restaurants may also be the victims of thefts of such items as hair dryers, courtesy bathrobes, flatware, glasses, towels, and the like. To avoid this type of theft, some hotels nail or otherwise affix radios and televisions to the desks and dressers in guest rooms. If a guest does steal property, she is liable for the crime of larceny, which is either a misdemeanor or a felony depending on the state involved and the value of the goods stolen. Many hotels have taken a different approach. They will encourage guests to take items from the room and will post the price associated with each item indicating the amount that will be charged on the guests' account assuming the guest intended to purchase the item.

False Arrest

When a hotel or restaurant believes it is the victim of one of these crimes it should proceed cautiously. Overreaction can result in liability to the guest for **false arrest**—the tort of intentional and unprivileged detention or restraint of another person. When an incident occurs, if time permits, the restaurant or hotel manager should call the police rather than handling the matter in-house. When officers arrive, the manager will explain the basis for believing a crime has occurred. The police will then assume the investigation.

A hotel was found not liable for false arrest where the front desk clerk called the police who detained the plaintiff for two hours. In that case when the plaintiff registered the clerk observed that he was very rude and angry. The clerk copied his driver's license, contrary to hotel policy. When he went to his room she called the police, concerned for the well-being of other guests. She shared the information on the license with the officers. His name, date of birth, and general description were identical to a man wanted for narcotics trafficking in Florida. The police came to the hotel, interviewed the plaintiff, handcuffed him, and detained him for two hours. Fingerprints eventually established that the plaintiff was not the wanted man. The plaintiff sued the hotel. The court dismissed the charges, holding that an inn is not liable for false arrest where its employees do not detain a guest but merely provide information to the police who thereafter detain the person.[42]

A similar decision clearing the hotel from liability occurred where hotel security heard glass breaking and the TV on high volume in plaintiff's room and so called police. Officers knocked and announced themselves but plaintiff refused to respond. The police thereafter broke the door and arrested defendant on charges that were eventually dismissed. Plaintiff's case for false arrest against the hotel was dismissed because the hotel had ample reason to call the police and the responding officer, not hotel personnel, made the decision to arrest.[43]

forgery
The unauthorized alteration, completion, or making of a written instrument with intent to defraud or deceive.

false arrest
Intentional and unprivileged detention or restraint of another person.

---

[42]*Roberts v. Essex Microtex,* 46 S.W.3d 205 (Tenn. 2001)
[43]*Bertuca v. Martinez,* 2006 WL 397904 (Tex. 2006)

If, however, the suspect is likely to escape pending the arrival of police, the hotel or restaurant may want to act on its own. Again, prudence is advised. In many states, hotels and restaurants will be liable for detaining a person unless that person has in fact committed a crime. Therefore, hotel or restaurant management should not restrain a person unless the manager is quite sure the individual did in fact engage in criminal activity.

Summary

The law gives the innkeeper numerous rights. Among them is the exclusive right to determine what room will be assigned to which guest, and, if necessary, to switch the room during the guest's stay at the hotel.

A restaurant can refuse to serve anyone for any reason except race, color, national origin, religion, gender, marital status, and disability. A hotel, however, must provide accommodations to all who seek them. A hotel nonetheless can evict guests who fail to pay their bill, are unruly, ill with contagious diseases, break house rules, or stay beyond their scheduled departure date. When evicting a guest, the hotel should attempt to avoid the use of force, but if force does become necessary, no more force should be used than is necessary to effect the eviction.

If a hotel guest fails to pay the bill, the hotel may be able to enforce an innkeeper's lien against the guest's property at the inn. If a restaurant patron or hotel guest attempts to leave without paying, the business can press criminal charges for theft of services, larceny, or fraud. If the guest pays with a stolen credit card or bad check, the guest can be prosecuted for possession of stolen property, forgery, or issuing a bad check. Theft of hotel or restaurant property can result in prosecution for larceny.

Preventive Law Tips for Managers

- *Do not refuse accommodations to a guest unless one of the permissible reasons for refusing accommodations exists.* The common-law rule provides that a hotel may not refuse accommodations to a guest. With few exceptions, anyone seeking a room is entitled to one. A hotel can legally refuse to provide a room only if the prospective guest is unable to pay, intoxicated, disorderly, suffering from a contagious disease, unclean, a known criminal, accompanied by a pet (other than a service animal), or in possession of a firearm or explosives. The hotel can also deny accommodations if it has no vacancies. Absent one of these circumstances, the hotel must provide rooms for all who seek them.

- *Do not change a guest's room unless absolutely necessary, and then only after informing the guest and requesting cooperation.* The law allows an innkeeper to change a guest's room. Guests are foreseeably troubled and inconvenienced by such moves and so room changes should be avoided whenever possible. If a room change does become necessary, the best practice is to inform the guest and request cooperation. In addition to winning goodwill, such an approach can cushion anger generated by a surprise relocation.

- *Do not enter a room assigned to a guest except for maintenance, imminent danger, nonpayment, or upon request.* When guests are assigned a room, they are the sole occupants for the duration of their stay; the innkeeper is not free to come and go in the room. The permissible reasons for hotel staff to enter are limited to cleaning, repairs, emergencies, or when requested by the guest, as when room service is called.

- *Do not evict a guest unless the ground is one recognized by law: inability to pay, overstaying, bad reputation, disorderly, contagious disease, or breaking house rules.* Generally, once a guest is granted a room, she is entitled to occupy it during the scheduled stay and the hotel cannot expel her. A few exceptions exist; these are the ones enumerated above in italics. In those circumstances, a hotel can evict a guest. Eviction for any other reason can lead to liability.

- *When evicting a patron, do so with reasonable care taking into consideration all circumstances and do not use any more force than is necessary.* When evicting a customer, the innkeeper or restaurateur should attempt to avoid the use of force. If appropriate, the patron should be invited to leave peaceably. If the patron refuses and repeated urging does not change his mind, and if circumstances permit, the innkeeper or restaurateur should summon the police. If circumstances do not permit, the patron can be physically removed from the premises, but the facility can use only that amount of force as is reasonably necessary to effect the removal. Use of a greater amount of force can result in liability for battery.

- *When making an eviction, do not make derogatory remarks to the guest.* Insulting commentary during an eviction is inappropriate and serves only to worsen an already difficult situation. If the comments are false and overheard by passersby, the hotel may be liable for slander. If a guest wants to know why she is being evicted, she should be told the reasons without additional comment. Whenever possible, the encounter at which the innkeeper or restaurateur informs the guest of the eviction should occur in an office or private room where others cannot hear. The innkeeper will be well advised to have an additional employee present who can testify later, if necessary, concerning the propriety of the eviction process. It is reasonable to assume others will film the encounter on their cell phones and post the video online. The video may be admitted as evidence in a court proceeding as well.

- *Hotels cannot evict long-term boarders who qualify as tenants without a court order.* To evict a tenant, the hotel/landlord must pursue a lawsuit for eviction. The law provides a summary (quick) proceeding for this purpose. Eviction without a court order violates a tenant's rights and may lead to liability.

- *Restaurants should not refuse to serve a diner on the basis of race, national origin, color, religion, marital status, gender, or disability.* A restaurant, unlike a hotel, is not legally obligated to serve all who seek service. With the exceptions enumerated, the restaurant can refuse to serve anyone it chooses. Liability under civil rights laws will result if the restaurant discriminates on any of the prohibited grounds.

- *A hotel should not sell property subject to an innkeeper's lien without complying with the specific requirements of the relevant state law.* While the law in many states permits an innkeeper to sell property subject to an innkeeper's lien, each state has specific rules concerning the required method of sale, notice to the nonpaying guest, and related matters. Determine the applicable state law before selling guests' property, and comply with it.

- *Train employees to detect stolen debit and credit cards, forgeries, counterfeit money, and bad checks.* Unfortunately, some hotel and restaurant patrons attempt to avoid payment by use of stolen debit and credit cards, forgeries, counterfeit money, bad checks, or simply failing to pay the bill. To help reduce the number of such incidents, employees should be trained to recognize these occurrences. Police are usually willing to conduct an employee training session on these issues.

- *Before pressing criminal charges, be sure the evidence supports a finding of a wrongful act and a criminal mental state.* To prove someone guilty of a crime involving fraud against a hotelier or restaurateur, the prosecutor must prove beyond a reasonable doubt that the defendant committed a wrongful act and had the required criminal mental state (intentionally or knowingly, depending on the crime). If the evidence suggests an innocent explanation for nonpayment, such as the patron's wallet was stolen while at the restaurant, criminal charges should be avoided. Wrongfully accusing someone of a crime can result in liability.

Review Questions

1. Under what circumstances can a hotel refuse to provide accommodations to someone seeking a room?

2. What precautions should a hotel take before moving a guest to another room?

3. Under what circumstances can an innkeeper enter a room assigned to a guest?

4. Can a hotel refuse to allow competing businesses to solicit its guests or employees on its premises? Why or why not?

5. Name five legal grounds for eviction of a guest from a hotel.

6. How much force can a hotel use when evicting a guest?

7. What are the consequences to a hotel of using excessive force when evicting a guest?

8. Under what circumstances can a restaurant refuse to provide dinner to a would-be guest?

9. What is the difference between the torts of assault and battery?

10. What benefit does an innkeeper's lien provide to an innkeeper?

11. If a district attorney is prosecuting a defendant for theft of hotel services, what are the elements of the crime that the prosecutor must prove?

12. What acts constitute the crime of issuing a bad check?

Discussion Questions

1. Juanita and Victoria, both waitresses at Nino's Restaurant, were having a dispute. Juanita made a gesture suggesting she was about to throw a glass at Victoria. Victoria was frightened and ran from the room. Has Juanita committed any tort? If so, which one? What are the elements of that tort?

2. What is required of an innkeeper who is enforcing an innkeeper's lien?

3. What are the differences between a hotel's right to refuse to provide a room to a would-be guest and a restaurant's right to exclude?

4. Can a hotel operator adopt a house rule prohibiting pets on the premises? Where should the rule be posted? What right does a hotel have if a guest violates the rule and brings a dog to the room?

5. What rights does a hotel operator have to restrict possession of a firearm on the property?

6. What rights does a hotel operator have in instituting a house rule requiring a person be age 21 or over to rent a hotel room?

Application Questions

1. Benjamin was drinking at a hotel bar. He became intoxicated and left the bar around 10:00 p.m. While walking through the hotel lobby, he stopped a woman seated on a couch and tried to engage her in conversation. She requested that he leave, but he failed to go. This encounter was observed by a security guard. What action should the guard take? Discuss various possibilities.

2. Chris operates a restaurant. His girlfriend recently broke up with him so she could date another man. The "other man" sought to eat dinner at the restaurant. Chris refused to seat him. Is Chris legally entitled to deny service to the man? Why or why not?

3. Alex and Jeff walked into a corner grocery store at 1:55 a.m. to buy beer. At 2:02 they took their selections to the cash register. The clerk refused to sell the beer because the law in the town prohibits alcohol sales after 2:00 a.m. Alex, refusing to take no for an answer, left money on the counter and told the clerk, "Here's $20 for the beer and an extra $5 for your trouble. If there's any prob-

lem we're staying at the Hampton Inn down the street, room 312." Based on their prior purchases of beer elsewhere, Alex and Jeff believed $20 was generous and would more than cover the cost. Unknown to them, the actual cost of the beer was $25. Have they committed the crime of larceny? Why or why not?

4. Several diners at the Olympia Restaurant have complained of stolen coats in the last few days. Vanessa, a regular customer known to the manager, entered the store with a coat that resembled the description of one of the stolen coats. The manager detained the customer pending an investigation. Was the manager's action in detaining the customer legal? Why or why not?

5. Barry is a guest at the Midway Inn. He paid his bill with a stolen credit card and signed the name of the credit card owner on the receipt. Identify all the crimes that Barry has committed in this transaction.

Websites

Website that will enhance your understanding of the material in this chapter include:

www.ahma.com This is the site of the American Hotel and Lodging Association, a trade organization for the hotel and lodging industry. The site addresses numerous issues of interest to hotel proprietors and managers including those studied in this chapter.

www.Hotelnewsnow.com This site provides current information on items of interest to hotel operators including topics studied in this chapter.

CHAPTER 10

Guests' Rights

LEARNING OUTCOMES:

- Comprehend the right of the guest to occupy the assigned room
- Appreciate the right to privacy in the guest room
- Know the developing right of guests to expect a hotel to intervene if evidence of human trafficking exists
- Know the guest's right to protection against illegal searches
- Understand the guest's right to protection against insults
- Comprehend the guest's right to protection against false arrest
- Appreciate the guest's rights against credit card fraud and identity theft
- Know guests' rights concerning disclosure of rates and fees
- Understand the guest's right to proper handling of private information, mail, packages, and facsimile correspondence
- Know guests' rights concerning access to their personal Wi-Fi networks

KEY TERMS

exclusionary rule	intentional infliction of emotional distress
false arrest	probable cause
identity theft	search warrant

Introduction

The law endows guests with a variety of rights. If an innkeeper violates any of these rights, liability can result.

Among the rights guests have are the following:

- The right to occupy hotel rooms without disruption

- The right to privacy in guest rooms, including the right to restrict access by the innkeeper, police, and others

- The right to be treated respectfully and not be insulted or humiliated by hotel staff

- The right to be free from false arrest or detention without cause

- The right to be free from credit card fraud, identity theft, and other criminal activity committed by hotel staff

- The right to be informed of fees and charges before they are imposed

- The right to have hotel employees process guests' mail properly.

The extent of these rights will be discussed in this chapter.

Right to Occupy Assigned Room

A guest assigned a room in a hotel has the right to occupy the room without disruption from the innkeeper.[1] An exception to this rule is where the innkeeper has legal grounds to remove the guest, as discussed in the previous chapter. An innkeeper who wrongfully excludes a guest from the room will be liable to the guest for damages.

The hotel in Case Example 10-1 violated a guest's right in this regard.

CASE EXAMPLE 10-1

Perrine v. Paulos

224 P.2d 41 (Cal. 1950)

Two young women were evicted by defendants from a hotel in Los Angeles. Returning from work one evening, they found padlocks on their rooms. They could not get to any of their personal belongings or clothing. They could not find other accommodations and had to sleep in their automobiles for three nights. Then, on demand of their counsel, they were permitted to again occupy their rooms.

The case was tried by the court, with judgment for plaintiffs for $500 each for general damages; and $500 more each, exemplary [punitive] damages....

The evidence establishes without contradiction that defendants owned the hotel and that plaintiffs were guests.

At common law, innkeepers were under a duty to furnish accommodations to all persons in the absence of some reasonable grounds....

An innkeeper who refuses accommodations without just cause is not only liable in damages, but is guilty of a misdemeanor. In such cases, exemplary [punitive] damages may be assessed. In this case, no showing whatever was made by defendants in excuse or in justification of their treatment of plaintiffs. Defendants just locked them out.

Ruling of the Court: The judgment is affirmed....

Right to Privacy in Guest Room

A guest has the right to occupy the room without intrusion by the innkeeper or any unauthorized person. However, there are five situations when the innkeeper is authorized to enter the guest room. They are:

---

[1] *People v. Faureau,* 661 N.W.2d 584 (Mich. 2003)

1. Normal maintenance (including housekeeping) and repair

2. Imminent danger

3. Nonpayment

4. When requested to enter by the guest, such as to respond to a guest's room service order

5. When the rental period has expired and the guest has no basis to believe it has been extended

In a case involving nonpayment, the hotel discovered on the second day of a guest's stay that the credit card the guest presented as her means of payment had been stolen. The manager went to the guest's room to resolve the issue and knocked several times. When the guest failed to respond, the manager opened the door with a master key and found her in the room. The guest objected to the intrusion on privacy grounds. The court held that an innkeeper who reasonably believes he has been defrauded relating to payment may enter a hotel room and ask the occupants to leave.[2] In a case where the guest stayed beyond the end of the rental period, the guest had asked for a late departure. The hotel allowed her to remain an extra two hours. When the later time came and went, the guest was still packing. She became belligerent when the manager went to her room and advised her she needed to leave. The manager summoned the police who entered the room to confront the defendant and regain control of the room. While there, the officer observed drug paraphernalia and found forged checks in a search. The guest claimed this search violated her right of privacy and so the evidence should be suppressed. The court refused to exclude the evidence, holding that a guest's expectation of privacy normally ends upon the termination of rental period.[3]

The guest's right to privacy obligates the innkeeper to take steps not only to prevent unauthorized employees from entering the guest's room, but also to prevent entry by unauthorized would-be visitors. Without authorization from the guest, even the guest's spouse is not entitled to access. In Case Example 10-2, the court affirmed the propriety of the hotel's caution in this regard.

---

[2] *People v. Satz,* 71 Cal.Rptr.2d 433 (Calif. 1998); see also *People v. Gutierrez,* 2004 WL 1468751 (Calif. 2004)
[3] *State v. Loya,* 18 P.3d 1116 (Utah 2001)

CASE EXAMPLE 10-2

Campbell v. Womack

345 So.2d 96 (La. 1977)

Plaintiff, Elvin Campbell, is engaged in the sand and gravel business. Since the nature of his business often requires his absence from his home in St. Francisville, Mr. Campbell generally obtains temporary accommodations in the area in which he is working. For this purpose, Mr. Campbell rented a double room on a month-to-month basis at the Rodeway Inn in Morgan City, Louisiana. The room was registered in Mr. Campbell's name only. From time to time, Mr. Campbell would share his room with certain of his employees; in fact, he obtained additional keys for the convenience of these employees. It also appears that Mr. Campbell was joined by his wife on some weekends and holidays, and that they jointly occupied his room on those occasions. However, Mrs. Campbell was not given a key to the motel room. On one such weekend, Mrs. Campbell, arriving while her husband was not at the motel, attempted to obtain the key to her husband's room from the desk clerk, Barbara Womack. This request was denied, since the desk clerk found that Mrs. Campbell was neither a registered guest for that room, nor had the registered guest, her husband, communicated to the motel management his authorization to release his room key to Mrs. Campbell. Plaintiffs allege that this refusal was in a loud, rude, and abusive manner. After a second request and refusal, Mrs. Campbell became distressed, left the Rodeway Inn, and obtained a room at another motel. Mr. Campbell later joined his wife at the other motel and allegedly spent the weekend consoling her. Shortly thereafter, suit was filed against the Rodeway Inn and desk clerk, Barbara Womack....

The motel clerk was under no duty to give Mrs. Campbell, a third party, the key to one of its guests' rooms. In fact, the motel had an affirmative duty, stemming from a guest's rights of privacy and peaceful possession, not to allow unregistered and unauthorized third parties to gain access to the rooms of its guest....

The additional fact that Mrs. Campbell offered proof of her identity and her marital relation with the room's registered occupant does not alter her third-party status; nor does it lessen the duty owed by the motel to its guest. The mere fact of marriage does not imply that the wife has full authorization from her husband at all times and as to all matters.... Besides, how could Mrs. Campbell prove to the motel's satisfaction that the then present marital situation was amicable? This information is not susceptible of ready proof....

In another case the hotel was less diligent. A battered wife sought shelter in a Holiday Inn against her husband's abuse. Upon arrival, she informed the front desk that her husband had beaten her, requested that no calls be put through to her room, and no one be informed of her presence at the inn. Her husband, however, convinced the hotel manager not only to unlock her door for him, but also to cut the safety chain when she refused to unhook it. While in the presence of the manager, the husband stated he was going to kill his wife. Later that day, he beat her so severely she died in her sleep from her injuries. Her sister sued the hotel, among others. The hotel claimed it was not liable and sought summary judgment. The court denied

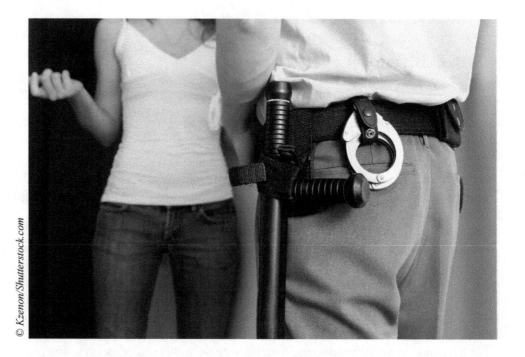

© Kzenon/Shutterstock.com

the motion and referred the matter to a jury.[4] While the outcome of the jury trial is unreported and therefore unknown, this case illustrates that disregard of the innkeeper's duty to protect the privacy of its guests can have grave consequences and can result in liability for the hotel.

Not all states impose liability for disclosure of a guest's room number where harm by disclosing it is not foreseeable. In an Indiana case, the hotel gave a woman's room number to a man who represented himself to the front-desk clerk as the guest's brother who was seeking to help the guest with supposed car trouble. He was in fact her estranged husband. He went to her hotel room, found her there with a date, and attacked him. The court held the attack was unforeseeable and therefore the hotel was not liable for the resulting injuries.[5]

Peeping Toms

Another privacy issue involves individuals creating peepholes through which they observe guests in their hotel rooms. Such conduct intrudes on guests' right to privacy. Case Example 10-3, which received much media coverage, details how this phenomenon can occur.

---

[4] *Thetford v. City of Clanton,* 605 So.2d 835 (Ala. 1992)
[5] *Ellis v. Luxbury Hotels, Inc.,* 716 N.E.2d 359 (Ind. 1999)

CASE EXAMPLE 10-3

Carter v. Innisfree Hotel, Inc.

661 So.2d 1174 (Ala. 1995)

Paul Carter and Wendy Carter sued Innisfree Hotel, Inc. ("Innisfree") [a management corporation that managed the Travelodge Hotel] [and others] alleging various claims arising out of an alleged "peeping Tom" incident during their stay at the Birmingham Civic Center Travelodge Hotel. The trial court entered a summary judgment in favor of all defendants. The Carters appeal from the summary judgment as it relates to Innisfree....

On February 25, 1993... the Carters [traveled to attend a concert and] decided to rent a room for the night at the Birmingham Civic Center Travelodge. They checked into Room 221 that afternoon, and, after purchasing fast food, went back to their room to eat and relax. While in the room, they heard knocking and scratching sounds, which appeared to emanate from behind a wall near the bathroom; the wall was covered by a mirror. However, they assumed that the sounds were from a neighboring room. They conducted their private marital activities that afternoon, including sexual intercourse, without regard to the strange noises. Wendy was undressed in front of the mirror for nearly two hours that afternoon, while applying her makeup and fixing her hair in preparation for the concert. Before the concert, while Paul was brushing his teeth in front of the mirror, he noticed two scratches in the mirror at eye level. He did nothing about the scratches at that time. The Carters went to the concert as they had planned.

After the concert, Paul again looked into the mirror and saw the scratches. He then removed the mirror and found two round, dime-sized scratches on the back of the mirror. Upon closer inspection, Paul found a large hole in the wall behind where the scratches were placed on the mirror. There was a hollow space approximately 1.5 feet wide between the Carters' wall and the wall of the adjoining room, which allows for maintenance workers to repair wiring and plumbing pipes. After looking at the hole closely, the Carters noticed a hole in the wall of the adjoining room that was covered by the mirror in that room. There was black electrical tape stuck onto the mirror of the other room; when Wendy pulled the tape off, the Carters discovered scratches on that mirror as well....

Paul then telephoned the police and asked them to investigate; they were not able to identify the alleged "peeping Tom." After the police left, the Carters checked out of the hotel and drove back to Huntsville. Paul testified that he has suffered chronic nervousness and sleeplessness since the incident. Wendy testified that she and Paul have had strains in their marriage resulting from nervousness and paranoia she has suffered due to the incident....

Nora Wood, a manager employed by Innisfree, stated that she inspects the Travelodge's rooms on a daily basis but said she did not know of the holes and scratches until the Carters complained about them.

The Travelodge customer who rented the adjoining room during the Carters' stay testified that he did not spy on the Carters. However, the record does not indicate whether he was absent from his room during the time the noises occurred. The record indicates that security guards, maintenance workers, housekeepers, and management personnel employed by Innisfree all have access to master keys that open the hotel rooms.

Invasion of Privacy

... Because the scratched mirror and the hole in the wall of Room 221 that gave a secret viewing access into Room 221 from the adjoining room, a jury could find a wrongful intrusion into the Carters' right to privacy, and a jury could reasonably infer that the intrusion arose through the actions of Innisfree's agents, who have control over the hotel. The Carters need not prove the actual identity of the "peeping Tom," nor need they demonstrate actual use of the spying device, although, as we have already stated, a jury could reasonably infer from the evidence that the mirror and hole had been used to spy on them. There is no need for the Carters to establish that they saw another's eyes peering back at them through their mirror.... There can be no doubt that the possible intrusion of foreign eyes into the private seclusion of a customer's hotel room is an invasion of that customer's privacy.... Even if it is proven that a third party, someone other than an agent of Innisfree, caused the holes and scratches, Innisfree may be held liable for the invasion of the Carters' privacy. It had an affirmative duty, stemming from a guest's right of privacy and peaceful possession, not to allow unregistered and unauthorized third parties to gain access to the room of its guests....

Negligence/Breach of Contract

... A jury could reasonably conclude from the evidence that Innisfree, through reasonable inspections, could have prevented the scratched mirrors and the holes behind those mirrors.... The jury could conclude that Innisfree had a contractual obligation to the Carters, its customers, to provide them with security, which, at the least, would mean a room free from fear that they were being viewed through their mirror. The jury could also find that Innisfree negligently failed to fulfill this duty, by allowing viewing access to the Carters' room through its failure to inspect the wall and to replace the scratched mirror. The trial court erred in entering the summary judgment for Innisfree on these claims....

An important fact in *Carter* was that the hotel could have discovered the scratched mirrors through reasonable inspections of the hotel's premises. Interestingly, scratches were ultimately found on the back of mirrors in thirteen other guest rooms in the hotel and six additional rooms had holes cut into the wall behind those mirrors to enable cable wiring. In another case involving "peeping Tom" holes discovered by guests in the bathroom mirror, no evidence existed that the hotel's employees knew or could have known of the installation or use of the spying device. The hotel was thus not liable for violating its duty of privacy.[6]

In a highly publicized case, further demonstrating the need for hotel operators to be vigilant in preventing individuals from spying on guests, the perpetrator was a voyeur, a person who likes to spy on others engaged in private behavior. He called the Nashville Marriott at Vanderbilt University where Erin Andrews, a well-known

---

[6] *Cangiano v. Forte Hotels, Inc.,* 772 So.2d 879 (La. 2001)

reporter for ESPN and host of the popular *Dancing with the Stars* TV show, was scheduled to stay. When he called to confirm she was staying at the hotel, he requested the room next to hers. After he checked into the room he removed and modified the peephole into her room so that he gained full visibility of her room. He proceeded to film her through the altered peephole while she was changing her clothing. He then posted the video online where it was seen by millions of people. She sued the hotel and also the perpetrator.

The civil case was presented before a jury which awarded her damages in the amount of $55 million in 2016. The case was also prosecuted criminally. Barrett, the perpetrator, pled guilty to interstate stalking and was sentenced to twenty-seven months in federal prison.[7]

It is clear the front desk staff must never reveal the room number of guests. During check-in, rather than verbally state the room number, the clerk instead should write the room number on the key card protective holder. Additionally, requests to stay next to or adjacent to a guest should be vetted to make sure there is not an ulterior motive. Housekeeping and other staff should be trained to notice unusual conduct or indications of spying behavior that may be present in the hotel.

Human Trafficking

A federal law and some state laws prohibit hotels from profiting from human trafficking. Guests have a developing right to expect hotels to intervene when evidence of such activity exists on the premises. Offending hotels face both criminal and civil liability. Conduct of guests that would alert innkeepers that such activity may be occurring on the premises include the following: men lingering in the hall near a room, regular refusal of housekeeping services, checking into the hotel with few or no personal belongings, paying for the room with cash or a prepaid card, frequent requests for new linens, towels, and restocking of the refrigerator, a suspected victim being treated aggressively, a suspected victim exhibiting fear and anxiety. If human trafficking is believed to be occurring, police should be consulted.

Protection Against Illegal Searches

Sometimes guests engage in illegal activity in a hotel room. For example, a guest might be hiding stolen property, storing drugs, harboring a kidnap victim, or committing rape. Or a guest might, while in his room, engage in conduct that is bothersome or threatening to other guests. In these and related circumstances, a guest's right to privacy may conflict with the interests of the innkeeper and police to enter and search a room as part of an investigation. The particular facts of each case determine whose rights and interests are given priority.

---

7 *Andrews v. Marriott Int'l,* 2017 WL 603387 (Ill. 2017)

©Bennian/Shutterstock.com

As we discussed earlier in this chapter, the innkeeper and hotel employees are not permitted to enter a guest's room at will. Rather, they must have a legal basis to go in. Permissible grounds include cleaning the room, nonpayment, consent of the guest, conduct in a room that disturbs other guests, and an emergency.

If a hotel employee, in the course of legally entering a guest's room, finds evidence of illegal activity, what action should the hotel take? Permitting criminal activity to proceed unabated may endanger other guests in violation of the innkeeper's duty to exercise reasonable care to protect their safety. Tolerating unlawful conduct may also jeopardize the hotel's license to carry on business, as we will discuss in Chapter 15.

The hotel should report the illegal activity to the police. Is the hotel violating any rights of the guest by informing the police? The answer is no, provided the hotel employee was legally in the guest's room when the wrongful conduct was discovered.

In a Florida case a member of the hotel housekeeping crew discovered, while cleaning, automatic rifles under the bed and some marijuana in an ashtray. She reported her findings to her manager, who reported them to the police. The hotel did not violate any obligation owed to the guest by making the report to the police.[8]

If a guest discards property in a wastebasket in the guestroom, the property is considered to be abandoned and no privacy rights to that property remain. A hotel did not violate a guest's rights where housekeepers gave to police trash bags removed in the ordinary course of cleaning from a guest's room. The bag contained evidence of the crime of money laundering.[9]

A guest also loses privacy rights if he damages property in the guest room. An innkeeper can enter the room of a guest who is "smashing things" in the room without violating the guest's right to privacy.[10] Likewise, a guest who is engaging in loud and disruptive conduct in the room loses his expectation of privacy; the innkeeper can legally enter.[11] In these circumstances, the guest should anticipate that the hotelier will need to investigate to protect the interests of other guests and the hotel, and so the guest's privacy rights are diminished.

---

8 *Engle v. State,* 391 So.2d 245 (Fla. 1980)
9 *Ohio v. Duncan,* 719 N.E.2d 608 (Ohio 1998)
10 *McCary v. Commonwealth,* 548 S.E.2d 239 (Va. 2001)
11 *State v. Perkins,* 588 N.W.2d 491 (Minn. 1999)

Absent an emergency or disruptive behavior, police cannot search an occupied hotel room unless they have either permission from the guest or a search warrant. Concerning permission, the police cannot legally search a guest's room on the strength of permission given by the hotel manager or owner alone. The guest's right to privacy requires the *guest's* permission for the police to make a consensual search. Without the *guest's* approval and assuming no emergency or disruptive behavior, the police must obtain a **search warrant**, which is an order from a judge commanding a police officer to search a designated place for evidence of criminal activity. If a search is made of a hotel room without the guest's permission and without a search warrant, the search invades the guest's privacy. Before issuing a search warrant, a judge must be satisfied that the police have probable cause to believe the search will uncover evidence of a crime. **Probable cause** consists of facts sufficient for a reasonably prudent person to believe that evidence of a crime is located in the place the police want to search. A suspicion or hunch is not enough.

The warrant requirement provides a buffer between individuals and the police that helps ensure that people's privacy rights are not violated. The **exclusionary rule** holds that evidence obtained in a warrantless search (assuming no consent, emergency or disruptive conduct) will not be admissible in court. Instead, the evidence is suppressed; the prosecutor will not be able to use such evidence to help prove the defendant's guilt. In such circumstance, the criminal charges placed against the defendant are typically dismissed unless the police have other evidence.

In the *Engle* case, discussed previously in this chapter, the police searched the hotel room for the weapons and the marijuana without first obtaining a search warrant. The defendant asked the court to suppress the evidence, and the court did so. Similarly, where a hotel manager permitted police to search a hotel room occupied by a guest without the latter's permission and without a search warrant, a gun found in a backpack in the room was suppressed and the criminal action against the guest was dismissed

Would the *innkeeper* be liable in either of these cases if the police, relying on information provided by a hotel employee, made an illegal search without a warrant? The answer is no. The hotel is not liable for the acts of the police; they are not employees or agents of the hotel. Thus, while the search without a warrant constitutes an invasion of the guest's privacy, the hotel cannot be held liable for that wrong.

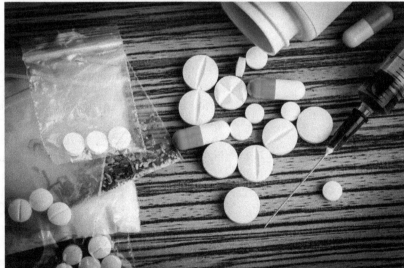

© FabrikaSimf/Shutterstock.com

search warrant
An order from a judge commanding a police officer to search a designated place for evidence of criminal activity.

probable cause
A reasonable ground for belief in certain alleged facts; facts sufficient for a reasonably intelligent and prudent person to believe the defendant committed a crime or that evidence of a crime is located in the place the police want to search.

exclusionary rule
The rule that holds evidence obtained in consequence of a warrantless search is not admissible in court.

Consent is an exception to the requirement that the police obtain a search warrant. If a guest voluntarily agrees to permit the police to enter the room and search it, the police are entitled to do so. Any evidence they find will not be suppressed.

For the consent to be valid, the person agreeing to the search must have the authority to give consent. Clearly, a guest has the authority to consent to a police search of his own room. An innkeeper does not have that authority.

Suppose the guest is not in when the police arrive seeking permission to search. If they ask the innkeeper for approval and he consents, is the search valid? The answer is no. During the time a room is assigned to a guest, neither the innkeeper nor any employee of the hotel has the authority to consent to a search. If the police make a search of a guest's room relying only on consent granted by the innkeeper or a hotel employee, any evidence found will be suppressed. Will the hotel be liable to the guest? If the guest suffers a loss, a court would likely find the hotel liable for violating the guest's privacy.

Effect of Termination of Occupancy on Privacy Rights

As we have seen in this chapter, the guest's right to exclusive use of the room ends if the guest fails to pay as agreed or if the occupancy period expires. In these circumstances, the right to occupy the room reverts from the guest to the innkeeper, who is then entitled to enter the room, prepare it for the next visitor, and remove any remaining property of the guest. Such property is considered abandoned and so no privacy rights apply. Thus, if any evidence is found by hotel staff in the room while preparing it for the next guest and the police are called, they can search without a warrant and the evidence will not be suppressed.[12]

Just as the guest's right to occupy the room ends, so too does the guest's expectation of privacy. A hotel guest has no reasonable expectation of privacy in a room after the rental period has expired.[13] This rule applies even if the guest remained physically present in the room after checkout time.[14] In a New York case the guest was two weeks overdue in payments, so the innkeeper entered the room and removed the belongings. The hotel manager discovered liquor and tools that had been stolen from the hotel. He called the police, who investigated without a warrant. The guest was arrested the next day. His attempt to suppress the evidence was denied because, at the time the incriminating items were discovered, he no longer had the exclusive right to occupy the room and thus, in the eyes of the law, had no expectation of privacy.[15]

In that case the hotel waited two weeks before ending the occupancy of the room by the nonpaying guest. In Case Example 10-4 the police entered the room soon after checkout time on the last day for which the hotel had received payment.

---

12 *United States v. Procknow*, 784 F. 3d 421 (Wis. 2015)
13 *People v. D'Antuono*, 762 N.Y.S.2d 198 (N.Y. 2003)
14 *United States v. Davies*, 2005 WL 2088591 (Tenn. 2005)
15 *People v. Lerhinan*, 455 N.Y.S.2d 822 (N.Y. 1982)
16 *People v. Gutierrez*, 2004 WL 1468751 (Ca. 2004)

CASE EXAMPLE 10-4

People v. Ouellette

2006 WL 1688183 (Mich. 2006)

Defendant was convicted of possessing and aiding in the concealment of stolen property worth $20,000 or more.... He appeals. We affirm. In early May of 2004 four houses in the Monroe area were broken into, and jewelry was stolen from each. On May 11, 2004 Derek Cole, then manager of Donovan's Pub, a bar connected to the Travel Inn in Monroe, contacted the police because he believed that defendant and his friend Marc Sanders were using counterfeit money in the bar. Cole testified at trial that the police "took Sanders and defendant out of the bar" and added that it later turned out the money was not counterfeit. They were taken into custody... both had Travel Inn hotel keys at the time. The officer contacted the prosecutor to determine whether a search warrant was needed for the Travel Inn hotel room shared by the suspects. The officer testified that the prosecutor informed him it was not required after checkout time on the last day paid for by the room's occupants.

The officers went to the Travel Inn and waited until checkout time so that defendant and Sanders would no longer have an expectation of privacy in the hotel room, then got the inn's owner's consent and searched the room assigned to defendant. During the search the officers found some items of jewelry and a pawn slip from a Detroit jewelry store. The items of jewelry were later identified by various victims of the break-ins as property stolen from their homes. Several employees of the hotel and the bar testified that they either saw defendant and Sanders attempting to sell jewelry, or that they were solicited to purchase jewelry themselves. One employee noted that an unidentified patron had told her defendant tried to sell her a 14-karat gold necklace for only $40. Cole and an employee of the inn searched room 117 after the police searched it. They found some items of jewelry and turned them over to the police; these items were also later identified as stolen in the Monroe break-ins....

Defendant argues that the trial court erred when it denied his motion to suppress the fruits of the searches of the hotel room. We disagree....

Generally, materials seized and observations made during an unconstitutional search may not be introduced into evidence. However, the right to challenge a search is not automatic. Rather, a person needs a special interest in the area searched or the article seized. The test is whether a party challenging a search had a reasonable expectation of privacy in the object or area of the intrusion. Generally, an occupant of a hotel or motel room is entitled to Fourth Amendment protection against unreasonable searches and seizures. However, even if a hotel guest plans to continue occupying his room, if he has failed to pay the next day's rent, he does not have a legitimate expectation of privacy in the hotel room or in any article therein because his rental period has expired or been lawfully terminated....

Here, room 117, in which defendant and Marc Sanders stayed, was paid for until noon (checkout time) of May 12, 2004. The owner of the hotel told Monroe police officers that neither defendant nor Sanders had a right to room 117 after 12:00 p.m. on May 12, 2004. The officers waited until after 12:00 p.m. on May 12, 2004 and then got the hotel owner's consent to search room 117. The warrantless search of the room was proper because neither defendant nor Sanders had an expectation of privacy in the hotel room at the time it was searched by the police.... [The evidence found during the search was therefore admissible.]

In a related case, a guest who used a stolen credit card to pay for her hotel room was not occupying it legally and so lacked an expectation of privacy. Evidence found in the room consisted of equipment and paraphernalia used in forging checks and creating false documents, including boxes of checks in different names, templates for checks and driver's licenses, and a false identification card. All of the evidence was thus admissible in the resulting criminal case.[16]

Warrant Exception—Disturbing the Peace

Suppose a condition in a guest's room is disturbing to other guests. A hotel employee enters the room to quell the disruption and discovers evidence of a crime. Is this an illegal search requiring suppression of the evidence? The answer is no. The innkeeper has a duty to protect guests from interference by others. The innkeeper is thus entitled to enter a room where a disturbance is occurring. Any evidence in plain view found by the innkeeper while legally in the guest's room will not be suppressed. Further, when faced with conduct by one guest that is disturbing to others, the innkeeper can solicit the assistance of police who can in this circumstance enter a guest's room without the guest's permission and without a search warrant. This rule of law is explored in Case Example 10-5.

CASE EXAMPLE 10-5

People v. Henning

96 Cal.Rptr. 294 (Calif. 1971)

Sometime after 10:00 p.m. (the curfew hour), on the evening of December 25, 1969, the desk clerk of Hillside Inn called the police department asking assistance concerning a disturbance in one of its rooms. An officer responded. He was told that a guest had complained about a disturbance at room 109, where a group of juveniles and adults were pounding on the door demanding admittance. The officer and a hotel employee went to the room. No one was then present in the outside hall, but inside "a very loud radio" was turned on. The officer knocked on the door repeatedly and called the name of the defendant Henning, to whom the room was registered. There was no response whatever, and there was no diminution of the radio's sound output. At the officer's request, the hotel employee unlocked the door. The officer again knocked on the door, with a similar lack of response from within. The door was then pushed slightly ajar. The officer testified, "At that time I could see in, and I could see the lower half of a male's body extended in a prone position over the end of the bed fully clothed." The man was lying face down. Fearful that the man was in trouble, the officer entered to "check on his welfare." Upon the entry, in plain sight on the floor, on a table, and protruding from the prone man's pocket, the officer saw a portion of the narcotics and dangerous drugs that were later the subject of Henning's motion to suppress. The man partially on the bed was Henning, who appeared to be in a deep sleep.

From this evidence, it could reasonably be concluded that the officer entered Henning's room with consent of the hotel employee; that the initial purpose of the entry was to silence a loud radio that was annoying the hotel's guests; and that upon seeing Henning prone and in an unusual position on the bed, an additional purpose developed—concern for the man's safety. It may clearly be inferred that the officer at no time prior to the entry had a purpose to arrest anyone or to search the room. And he may reasonably be considered as an agent of the hotelman, who understandably did not wish, unattended, to risk a hostile confrontation in silencing a source of annoyance to the hotel's guests.

We have no hesitancy in concluding that a hotelkeeper himself may enter a rented, but presently unoccupied, room when reasonably necessary to quiet a "very loud radio" that is presenting a substantial annoyance to other guests. Indeed, it has been held that an innkeeper is under an obligation not to harbor persons dangerous to the peace and comfort of those for whose comfort he is bound to provide...to protect his patrons from annoyance...and to exercise proper care for the safety and tranquility of the guest.

It seems most reasonable for the hotel people to have called upon a police officer for assistance, rather than risk violence in pursuit of their duty of care for the nighttime comfort, tranquility and quiet of their guests. If so, then it was equally reasonable for the police officer, on request and with their consent and under the facts before us, to assist in such an undertaking.

The additional purpose of the officer, upon observing the condition of Henning within the room, was clearly without Fourth Amendment or other fault. Reason tells us, and valid authority holds, that an entry is proper when a police officer reasonably and in good faith believes such entry to be necessary in order to render aid to a person in distress....

[A] reasonable inference could be, and was, properly drawn by the court that the officer acted only in aid of the hotel management late at night to quell a disturbance—a loud radio—in the room....

[W]e must conclude that there was substantial evidence in support of the superior court's order denying Henning's motion to suppress evidence.

CASE QUESTION

1. If the radio had not been playing loudly, would the evidence have been suppressed?

© Marcos Mesa Sam Wordley/Shutterstock.com

Emergency Situation

Another circumstance under which an innkeeper is permitted to admit police into a guest's room is where reasonable grounds exist to believe that the guest is in distress and in need of assistance. If the police see evidence of a crime in plain view while in the room, it is admissible in court against the guest. In an Arizona case the police were called to a hotel in response to a report of a disturbance. Guests in one room had been awakened by pounding on the door of the adjacent room. When the police arrived, two people were outside the room where the disturbance occurred. They explained they were trying to wake their friend, who had been drinking heavily earlier in the evening. No response was made to the officer's knocking. He obtained a key from the innkeeper and entered. The occupant was unconscious on the bed. His pulse was weak. An ambulance was called. The police found drugs in plain view on the table in the room. In the resulting criminal case charging the guest with possession of drugs, he claimed the police entry into the room was unauthorized and therefore the drugs should be suppressed. The court rejected this argument, holding that the police can enter the hotel room of a guest in an emergency where the occupant is in need of imminent aid or reasonably believed to be in such need.[17]

In another case the hotel called the sheriff because of a strong chemical odor, described as an "ammonia smell typical of the process for manufacturing methamphetamine," emanating from one of the rooms. The court stated that "it is generally known that the chemicals and chemical reactions involved in manufacturing methamphetamine create significant health and safety risks." The court determined the situation constituted a threat of imminent injury justifying the sheriff deputy's entry into the room without a warrant. Evidence found in the room supporting a charge of criminal possession of drug paraphernalia was thus admissible at trial.[18]

Room Registered to Another

A person who is not a registered guest does not have a right of privacy in a hotel room. Similarly, a guest's right to privacy applies only to the room she occupies. In a case involving murder, the defendant was originally arrested for stealing his girlfriend's fur coat. When he was searched the police discovered a key to room 234 at a nearby hotel. The police obtained a search warrant for the room and found a corpse under the bed. The defendant's attempt to challenge the search was rebuffed by the court because, although he was a registered guest at the hotel, the room where the body was located was not the room registered to him.[19]

In another case a male and female were in a hotel room that neither had rented. The police were called by the innkeeper, who was seeking to remove the occupants. The police entered the room without a warrant and found cocaine. In the resulting criminal action the defendant claimed the illegal drugs should be suppressed. The court stated, "No notion of privacy that society respects could arise from defendant's uninvited takeover of a motel room."[20]

---

[17] *State v. Wright*, 607 P.2d 19 (Ariz. 1980)
[18] *Delong v. Commonwealth of Kentucky*, 2005 WL 2573401 (Ky. 2005)
[19] *People v. Zappulla*, 724 N.Y.S.2d 433 (N.Y. 2001)
[20] *Foster v. State of Texas*, 2002 WL 31109928 (Tex. 2002)

A related privacy problem involves mislaid or forgotten luggage of a guest. Can an innkeeper who finds a guest's mislaid briefcase open it to help determine the true owner? The answer is yes. In such a case, the owner's right to privacy must yield to a reasonable search of the briefcase by the manager to determine the owner. Further, if the innkeeper fails to verify ownership of the briefcase and by mistake gives it to someone other than the owner, the innkeeper will be liable for breach of its duty as bailee, as discussed in Chapter 8. Case Example 10-6 illustrates the various issues that can arise in this situation.

CASE EXAMPLE 10-6

Berger v. State

257 S.E.2d 8 (Ga. 1979)

The assistant manager of the Hyatt Regency Hotel was given a briefcase that had been found in the main lobby. It was closed but not locked. It was not an unusual occurrence to find several misplaced briefcases each day in the hotel. He opened the briefcase to find if it contained any identification of its owner. It contained a wallet, a large amount of "business papers," and "bundles of money." Two men who inquired about the briefcase were directed to his office. One man, the defendant, stated that it was his briefcase. The manager asked him if he had any personal identification. The defendant told him his identification was in the wallet in the briefcase. The manager stated that it was hotel policy that identification must be made from the person and not from the lost object, and "if the person can't identify themselves, obviously we can't give it out." The manager was particularly concerned about this item because of the large amount of cash it contained. Both men were getting "agitated" and "a bit loud."

Police officers Derrick and Cochran were employed by the hotel as security personnel while they were off duty. Officer Derrick received a call over his "beeper" and was directed to report to the assistant manager's office. Officer Derrick testified that when he arrived, the assistant manager briefed him on the situation, and he identified himself to the defendant and asked him if the briefcase was his. The defendant stated that it was. Officer Derrick asked defendant if he had "any identification, driver's license or anything like that." The defendant said it was in the briefcase.... According to Officer Derrick, the briefcase was unlocked and the top was mostly down. He opened up the case, pulled out the billfold and left the briefcase open. Officer Derrick asked the defendant to write out his signature for comparison purposes. "As I was looking at the signatures on the driver's license and... the signature on the piece of paper, the case was right in front of me, and I noticed there was a bag of what I thought was marijuana inside the case in the back of it...and [the defendant] saw me see the marijuana...that's when he said... "I don't want you to search the briefcase...."

The defendant testified that when he was asked for identification by the assistant manager, he took his wallet out of the briefcase and told the manager what was in it, and at that time the officers came in. He stated the briefcase was closed and the wallet was in his hand. When asked for identification, he showed Officer Derrick his driver's license, and he signed his name to let the officer make a comparison. He testified that Officer Derrick said: "...yeah, that's you all right... but that doesn't prove this is your briefcase I am going to have to look in it.... It was closed. I said I would prefer that you [the officer] do not look in it." Although [the defendant] repeated his request [that the officer] not look in the briefcase, the officer opened it and searched through the briefcase until he found the marijuana, cocaine, and $7,000 in cash. [Defendant tried to suppress the money and drugs on the ground that the search was illegal.] The court denied the motion to suppress. Defendant brings this appeal.

Defendant argues that... [he] had a reasonable expectation of privacy in his briefcase that was protected by the Fourth Amendment....

Innkeepers of this state have a statutory liability to guests for property coming into their possession....It is not an unauthorized search for hotel management personnel, including security personnel, to open unlocked items found on their premises in an attempt to determine ownership so that the lost or misplaced property can be returned to its proper owner.

In the instant case, the incriminating evidence came into possession of the law enforcement authorities inadvertently and unmotivated by any desire to locate incriminating evidence We find nothing unlawful about a police officer opening an unlocked, lost, or misplaced item to determine ownership. The marijuana was then in plain view, and the officer was authorized to confiscate the contraband....

Ruling of the Court: Judgment affirmed. [The drugs found in the briefcase were admissible against the defendant in his trial for illegal possession of controlled substances.]

CASE QUESTION

1. Why was the search of the briefcase not a violation of the defendant's constitutional right against unreasonable searches?

Unclaimed Lost Property

What is the responsibility of an innkeeper or restaurateur when lost property is found and no one claims it? Many states have statutes that prescribe a procedure for disposing of such items. Typically, the proprietor is required to inform the police of the finding or deposit the property at the police station. When owners of lost property realize items are missing, they often do not know where they misplaced them. Police headquarters provide a central, easily located place for owners to pursue their property. Failure of the facility to notify the police or deposit the property may constitute a crime. See, for example, New York Personal Property Law §252.

Protection Against Insults

Though the use of insulting and abusive language is objectionable and can evoke anger, the courts have been slow to regard it as a basis of civil liability as between individuals. Most states do not recognize abusive language, without more, as a tort. However, if the language is beyond abusive and qualifies as outrageous, it may constitute the tort of **intentional infliction of emotional distress**. For this tort, the comments must consist of more than mere insults indignities and annoyances. The words must be "so extreme in degree, as to go beyond all possible bounds of decency and to be regarded as atrocious and utterly intolerable in a civilized community."[21] In addition, for a successful lawsuit, the plaintiff must have suffered severe or extreme emotional distress. Lawsuits typically fail because the challenged conduct is not sufficiently outrageous.

Some courts have allowed recovery for a lower threshold of abusive language in cases where an innkeeper and guest are involved. The reason is that the innkeeper, carrying on a business of a public nature, is expected to extend to guests respectful and decent treatment, and to refrain from conduct that would interfere with patrons' comfort or humiliate and distress them. In an early case on point the court said,

> *One of the things that a guest for hire at a public inn has the right to insist upon is respectful and decent treatment at the hands of the innkeeper and his servant, so that is an essential part of the contract, whether express or implied. This right of the guest necessarily implies an obligation on the part of the innkeeper that neither he nor his servants will abuse or insult the guest or indulge in any conduct or speech that may unnecessarily bring upon him physical discomfort or distress of mind.[22]*

A plaintiff was entitled to damages based on defamation where he entered a Big Boy Restaurant and was "repeatedly and loudly accused" by the assistant manager of leaving the restaurant the day before without paying for his meal. At the time of the assistant manager's accusation, there were other patrons in the restaurant whose attention was drawn to plaintiff. A manager determined that the assistant manager was mistaken; plaintiff had paid his bill.[23]

No similar duty is owed to a nonguest. In a Kentucky case the plaintiff, who was not registered at the hotel, was waiting in the lobby for her brother, who was attending a banquet. The hotel detective approached the plaintiff and, in a rude and menacing manner, told her erroneously that no such meeting was going on in the hotel and ordered her to leave. Fearing bodily harm, she left. A few minutes later, she returned and went directly to the room where the meeting was in progress. The court ruled that although the detective's manners were rude and highly objectionable, "bad manners are not actionable." The court stated, "[A]ppellant was at most a mere licensee, [a status with less rights than a guest] and that if she had been requested in a proper manner to leave the lobby and had failed to do so, reasonable force could lawfully have been used to eject her."[24]

intentional infliction of emotional distress
A tort in which the offending conduct must be outrageous or so extreme as to go beyond all possible bounds of decency, and be regarded as atrocious and utterly intolerable in a civilized community.

---

21 *Vinson v. Linn-Mar Community School District,* 360 N.W.2d 108 (Iowa 1984)
22 *DeWolf v. Ford,* 86 N.E.527 (N.Y. 1908)
23 *Burden v. Elias Brothers Big Boy Restaurants,* 613 N.W.2d 378 (Mich. 2000)
24 *Jenkins v. Kentucky Hotel Co.,* 87 S.W.2d 95 (Ky. 1935)

If a hotel or restaurant employee's comments to a guest are not only false but also outrageous, the facility might be liable for intentional infliction of emotional distress, a tort.

Conduct was sufficient to withstand a summary judgment motion where the plaintiffs had received a letter from a Columbia Business School professor who was conducting a study on the reaction of restaurants to consumer complaints. In the letter, which was sent to thirteen highly rated New York City restaurants, the teacher stated that he and his wife had eaten at the restaurant the night before, that she had become ill due to food poisoning, and he expected the restaurant to "respond accordingly." The restaurateurs alleged that they were extremely upset, especially in view of the extraordinarily competitive nature of the restaurant business and the critical importance of reputation. They claimed to have suffered "enormous emotional distress, guilt, fear of loss of individual jobs and business, and fear of loss of reputation." The court noted that a food poisoning claim could conceivably "destroy a restaurant's viability as a business in such a highly competitive trade. Once a restaurant's reputation is tainted, it is hard to undo the damage. The possibility of a forced closing of a restaurant could very likely affect the physical and emotional well-being of the restaurateurs involved, especially those who have invested all their savings and energy into the business."

One owner involved said, "The restaurant was turned upside down to try and find out how this could have happened. Much food on hand in our kitchen was destroyed, at a cost of thousands of dollars. Vendors were notified and told to check their entire inventory. Staff members were all put on notice that if this were ever to be traced to a particular person, that individual would not only be fired, but would probably never work in this field again. My life's work would go out of business, or be reduced in its reputation to a second rate establishment." Another owner went into a serious depression and sought psychiatric care.[26]

In another case, polite treatment of a guest helped to save the hotel from liability. A clerical error resulted in a hotel checking the plaintiff out of his room one day before his reservation was to expire. Another guest was soon thereafter given possession of the room. When the plaintiff returned to the hotel in the early morning hours, he was unable to occupy his room. He sued for "indignity, abuse and humiliation." According to the plaintiff's testimony, the desk clerk was not discourteous or abusive. Said the court, "[I]t is difficult to find any degree of humiliation in an incident which unfolded in a deserted hotel lobby at 3:00 a.m. witnessed by a solitary and apologetic desk clerk.... It is the publicity of abusive language that causes the humiliation." The plaintiff's case was thus dismissed.[27]

25 *Speed v. Northwest Airline, Inc.*, 2000 WL 34030833 (Iowa 2000)
26 *164 Mulberry Street Corp. v. Columbia University*, 771 N.Y.S.2d 16 (N.Y. 2004)
27 *Pollock v. Holsa Corp.*, 454 N.Y.S.2d 582 (N.Y. 1982)

Protection Against False Arrest

Neither a hotelkeeper nor a restaurateur is under any duty to prevent the arrest of a guest by police officers who are seemingly acting within their authority. This rule is illustrated in Case Example 10-7.

CASE EXAMPLE 10-7

Bertuca v. Martinez

2006 WL 397904 (Tex. 2006)

On September 29, 2000, Gonzalez checked into a room at the Hampton Inn in Laredo, Texas. Because he was in the process of studying for his Texas Import/Export examination, he requested the front desk not to disturb him after 9:00 p.m. That evening, at sometime past 10:00 p.m., Gonzalez's mother, Julie Bertuca, attempted to call Gonzalez in his hotel room. After being unable to contact him, she called the front desk, requesting that somebody check on her son's well-being. The hotel dispatched David Martinez, the security guard on duty, to check on Gonzalez in his room. Martinez knocked on Gonzalez's hotel room door several times. Gonzalez did not open the door or acknowledge Martinez's presence. Martinez did, however, hear the sound of breaking glass coming from inside the room. He could also hear the television set because it had been turned up to a high volume.

When Martinez returned to the front desk, he explained what had happened to the hotel's staff and told them that he suspected Gonzalez was causing damage to the room and that he was concerned for Gonzalez's and the other guests' safety and well-being. In response, the hotel staff called the police. When two police officers responded to the call, Martinez escorted them to the door of Gonzalez's hotel room where they found a disconnected telephone lying on the floor [outside the room] along with one or two broken beer bottles. The officers knocked on the door and announced that they were with the Laredo Police Department and that they wanted to check on Gonzalez's well-being. Gonzalez refused to open the door. After failed attempts to open the door with a key and with the permission of the hotel, the officers broke down the door and entered the room. An altercation then allegedly arose between Gonzalez and the officers. Gonzalez was handcuffed and arrested for criminal mischief and resisting arrest. Criminal charges were brought against Gonzalez. Because restitution was paid to the hotel by Gonzalez, the charges were dismissed. Subsequently Gonzalez brought a civil action against the hotel for false arrest.

There is no evidence of instigation [of the arrest by the hotel]. The hotel personnel never requested or directed the police officers to arrest Gonzalez. After Gonzalez refused to answer his mother's call, she asked hotel staff to check on him. When the hotel security guard knocked on Gonzalez's room, Gonzalez did not answer the door, and the guard heard breaking glass coming from inside the room. Thus, the hotel had ample reason to call for the police to investigate Gonzalez's well-being. Once the police officers forcefully broke into Gonzalez's room, Gonzalez became aggressive. Thus, the police officers had probable cause to arrest Gonzalez. Because there is no evidence of instigation, the trial court did not err in dismissing Gonzalez's claim.

false arrest
Intentional and unprivileged detention or restraint of another person.

If the arrest is due to a false statement by the hotel, restaurant, or their agents, the establishment could be liable. In a Nebraska case a hotel employee falsely told a police officer that a guest had breached the peace, which led to the guest's arrest. She successfully sued the hotel for **false arrest,** which is the unauthorized restraint of a person.[28]

CASE EXAMPLE 10-8

Lewis v. Ritz Carlton Hotel Co., LLC,

712 S.E.2d 91 (Ga. 2011)

In May, 2006, Lewis checked into the Ritz Carlton Hotel in Atlanta to attend graduation ceremonies at Morehouse College. He was met at the airport by his friend, Patillo. After he and Patillo checked into the hotel, they went to the hotel's club lounge where Lewis ordered a drink and began talking loudly on his cellphone. Other patrons complained to the staff. When he went to the bar for another drink, the bartender refused to serve him because Lewis appeared to be intoxicated. Lewis continued to request to be served. Another guest told Lewis to "leave it alone." Lewis told him to "sit his ass down" and stay out of his business.

According to the concierge, Lewis made his point using "racially charged" language. Other guests departed the lounge. Celestin, the hotel manager, was called by security to the club lounge. She asked Lewis to lower his voice and later asked him to leave the lounge and go to his hotel room. He refused to leave the lounge immediately as requested, but he did eventually return to this room.

Shortly afterward, Lewis heard a knock on his door. His friend allowed a police officer and the hotel manager to enter the room. According to Lewis, the officer told him "[y]ou're either voluntarily like leaving the hotel, or I am arresting you." Lewis asked to give his side of the story, and when the officer was not interested Lewis told the officer "since you're taking that attitude, do what you think should happen." Lewis refused to comply with several requests to leave and the officer arrested him and charged him with criminal trespass. According to Patillo, the officer repeatedly insisted that Lewis get his belongings and leave the hotel before the officer arrested Lewis.

The arresting officer deposed that he was dispatched by Ritz Carlton, where he spoke with managers who complained of an unruly guest who refused to leave. He accompanied management and hotel security to Lewis's room, where he asked Lewis to leave the hotel. Lewis protested that he had done nothing wrong, and after Lewis refused to comply with several requests to leave, the officer arrested him and took him to jail on charges of criminal trespass. Lewis's accusation for criminal trespass was subsequently nolle prossed [dismissed] with the notation "lack of probable cause."

Lewis sued the hotel and hotel manager for false imprisonment and malicious prosecution. The state court granted the defendant's summary judgment and Lewis appealed.

Lewis contends that material issues of fact remain for a jury on his claim of false imprisonment. We disagree. The essential element of false imprisonment is an unlawful detention. The overall legality of the warrantless arrest, including both probable cause and exigent circumstances, "is the decisive factor." If Lewis's detention was unlawful, the issue becomes whether Ritz Carlton and Celestin caused the arrest.

---

[28] *Nensen v. Barnett,* 134 N.W.2d 53 (Nebr. 1965)

"The party need not expressly request an arrest, but may be liable if his conduct and acts procured and directed the arrest." Lewis challenges the legality of his arrest ....on two grounds. First....that the hotel management could not evict him ......without advance notice [and] that a jury should consider whether his eviction by a police officer amounted to a criminal trespass warning. We find both these arguments lack merit. A hotel keeper may evict a guest without advance notice for cause, including failure to pay the bill, lack of reservations, failure to abide by the rules of occupancy or "other action by a guest." Thus a hotel manager is entitled to terminate a room rental agreement without prior notice for, among other things, "creating a disturbance in the hotel." Celestin, as the hotel manager, was accordingly authorized to evict Lewis for cause and was not required to give.....advance notice.

We also conclude the officer's instruction to Lewis constituted a criminal trespass warning. A person commits the offense of criminal trespass when he or she knowingly and without authority: Remains upon the land or premises of another person.....after receiving notice from the owner, rightful occupant, or upon proper identification, an authorized representative of the owner or rightful occupant to depart.... [L]ewis's refusal to leave the hotel when instructed to do so by a police officer, in the presence of management, the "facts and circumstances [were] sufficient for a prudent person to believe [Lewis] committed the offense of criminal trespass." Further, exigent circumstances authorized the warrantless search. Accordingly, no issue of material fact remained as to the probable cause and exigent circumstances which authorized Lewis's arrest on the charge of criminal trespass, and the trial court correctly granted summary judgment to Ritz Carlton and Celestin on Lewis's false imprisonment claim.

We also find that the trial court properly granted summary judgment to Ritz Carlton and Celestin on Lewis's claim of malicious prosecution. To establish malicious prosecution, Lewis was required to show, among other things, that Ritz Carlton and Celestin lacked probable cause to accuse him of criminal trespass. ...[T]he undisputed evidence established such probable cause. His sole argument, without citation to supporting authority, is that a material issue of fact exists because the nolle prosequi stated that there was a lack of probable cause. The nolle prosequi was entered by the solicitor, and consented to by a state court judge. "Nolle prosequi is the State's formal action on its decision not to further prosecute an [accusation]." Assuming that the solicitor's decision to nolle pros the accusation is comparable to a dismissal of criminal charges, which may be considered as non-conclusive evidence of a lack of probable cause in a malicious prosecution action, we cannot conclude that the nolle pros, in itself, is sufficient to create an issue of material fact given, among other things, Lewis's own testimony as to the events that led to his arrest. Judgment affirmed.

CASE QUESTIONS

1. The manager chose not to tell Lewis that she was going to call the police, instead the police were summoned without his knowledge. Was this a good idea or should he have been informed in advance? Why or why not?

2. Would the outcome have been different if Lewis left the hotel room immediately upon the first request to do so by the police officer?

3. What was the effect of the nolle prosequi in the determination of whether malicious prosecution by the hotel and general manager had taken place?

A hotel or restaurant also commits the tort of false arrest or imprisonment when it detains a person illegally. *Only* if the person actually has committed a crime can the establishment legally detain him.

A plaintiff, accompanied by her aunt, entered the defendant's restaurant and proceeded through the crowded facility up one flight of stairs to the ladies' lounge. As the aunt did not desire anything to eat, the plaintiff went alone downstairs to the dining area and was served. Upon receiving her bill, she returned to her aunt and together they walked toward the door to leave. As they passed the cashier's desk, the plaintiff paid for the food she ate. As they started to leave the restaurant, the cashier called them back by ringing a bell and beckoning the plaintiff. The cashier questioned the plaintiff as to why the bill covered only one meal. She explained that her aunt had not eaten in the restaurant and again started to leave. The cashier commanded her to wait. The head waiter and then the manager were summoned. The plaintiff and her aunt were asked to accompany the headwaiter to the rear of the restaurant for questioning, where they were detained and questioned for twenty-five minutes. The plaintiff's truthfulness was openly and repeatedly challenged, such that if the plaintiff had left the restaurant before being exonerated, "her departure might well have been interpreted by the lookers-on as an admission of guilt." Finally, the cashier approached the plaintiff, who was then with the manager, and said he (the cashier) had mistakenly mixed up the plaintiff's check with someone else's. The plaintiff was then allowed to leave.[29]

Like many states, Massachusetts, the state in which the case occurred, authorizes a restaurant to detain a person if it has reasonable cause to believe she did not pay money owed, provided the detention lasts for only a reasonable amount of time and is carried out in a reasonable manner. If, however, the person is detained without reasonable cause or for an unreasonable amount of time or in an unreasonable manner, she is entitled to recover for damages. In the case involving the plaintiff and her aunt, the court determined the detention was based on inattention and carelessness of the cashier, which falls short of the necessary standard of reasonable cause. Therefore, the restaurant was liable to the plaintiff.

This case underscores the principle that a hotel or restaurant cannot with impunity interfere with its patrons' freedom of movement without good cause. To avoid liability, the hospitality facility needs reasonable grounds to believe the patron has acted illegally.

A court found a casino had the necessary probable cause to detain the plaintiff employee in an incident involving a $100 token. The plaintiff was part of a hard count team, meaning he serviced slot machines. His duties included removing coin buckets from the machines, replacing them with empty bins, placing the buckets on a cart, taking them to the hard count room, and counting them. The team included eight employees and four security guards. Plaintiff discovered a $100 token that had fallen into the tray rather than the bucket. Instead of collecting the $100 token for the count or alerting a security guard as the casino required, plaintiff approached a patron, told him about the coin, and watched him retrieve the $100

---

[29] *Jacques v. Child's Dining Hall Co.*, 138 N.E. 843 (Mass. 1923)

token and cash it. After plaintiff finished the count he located the patron who shook plaintiff's hand and in the handshake passed a $20 bill.

Security became suspicious, reviewed the videotape that records the removal of money from machines, and confirmed the appropriation of the money. Soon thereafter plaintiff was detained and questioned. The sheriff was called and plaintiff was arrested for petit larceny. The charges were eventually dismissed and plaintiff sued the casino for false arrest. The court dismissed the claim determining that the following facts constituted probable cause. "Plaintiff knew when he saw the token fall into the tray that it wasn't 'finder's keepers,' that it was casino property just like the hundreds of other tokens he had collected in his job as a hard count team member. But instead of reporting the coin to the nearby auditor or the nearby security or to management, he determined to take it for his own use through the involvement of an intermediary, the fortunate casino customer whom he alerted about the coin."[30]

Protection Against Credit Card Fraud and Identity Theft

Guests frequently pay their hotel and restaurant bills with a credit card. They expect employees with access to their credit card number to use it for official purposes only—to complete the payment transaction. Occasionally an employee misuses the information and makes unauthorized purchases charged to the customer's account. Or the employee might utilize the card number to engage in **identity theft**, which means obtaining personal financial information about the debit or credit card holder and illegally using that information for the thief's economic gain. For example, the wrongdoer might transfer money from the hotel guest's bank accounts to the employee, accumulate large amounts of debt on the person's credit card, or obtain loans in his name.

© serpeblu/Shutterstock.com

identity theft
Obtaining personal financial information about a credit card holder without authority to do so and illegally using that information for the thief's economic gain.

Such unauthorized transactions constitute crimes and may subject the employee to civil liability for fraud as well as criminal prosecution for larceny (theft), forgery, and criminal possession of stolen property. The hotel or restaurant employing the wrongdoer may also be liable if it failed to institute procedures designed to prevent such occurrences. Yet again, we see the importance of good management and supervision of employees.

---

[30] *Croft v. Grand Casino Tunica, Inc.*, 910 So.2d 66 (Miss. 2005)

In addition to credit card fraud internally, hospitality operators are obligated to secure their computer systems to protect against data breaches of confidential information. Several cases were recently filed seeking class action status for consumers affected by the more than 500 million account holders of Yahoo whose private information was stolen as part of a massive data breach in 2014. The cases claim that Yahoo "intentionally, willfully, recklessly, or negligently" failed to protect their computer systems and also failed to inform users that their data "was not kept in accordance with applicable, required, and appropriate cybersecurity protocols, policies and procedures."[31]

The Federal Trade Commission has authority under the Federal Trade Commission Act's prohibition against unfair and deceptive acts and practices to regulate failure of companies to maintain reasonable and appropriate data security for consumers' sensitive personal information. The seriousness of security was demonstrated when the Federal Trade Commission filed suit against Wyndham Worldwide Corp. in 2012 alleging unfair and deceptive trade practices, in violation of the Federal Trade Commission Act. The FTC claimed the hotel company misrepresented security measures to prevent breaches by computer hackers. The lawsuit alleged Wyndham acted with "an unfair and deceptive" lack of protection in storing information. Three attacks on the hotel company and its franchisees, beginning in 2008, resulted in theft of 500,000 credit card numbers followed by attacks that breached an additional 119,000 accounts.

The Federal Trade Commission claimed Wyndham failed to take common and well-known security measures, presented in Case Example 10-9. Wyndham was faulted for not requiring complex passwords, and for implementing a network setup that failed to separate corporate and hotel systems. Additionally, the company used "improper software configurations" that led to sensitive payment card information being stored without encryption.

CASE EXAMPLE 10-9

Federal Trade Commission v. Wyndham Worldwide Corp.

10 F.Supp.3d 602 (N.J. 2014)

The Federal Trade Commission (the FTC) brought this action against Wyndham Worldwide Corporation alleging that Wyndham violated Section 5(a) of the Federal Trade Commission Act which prohibits acts or practices in or affecting commerce that are unfair or deceptive and are likely to cause substantial injury to consumers.

...Wyndham Worldwide is in the hospitality business. At all relevant times, Wyndham Worldwide controlled the acts and practices of the following subsidiaries: Hotel Group, Hotels and Resorts, and Hotel Management. Through these three subsidiaries, Wyndham Worldwide franchises and manages hotels and sells timeshares....

---

31 Bartiromo, Maria. "Class-Action Suits filed after Yahoo Data Breach", *USA Today*, September 26, 2016.

Hotels and Resorts licensed the Wyndham name to approximately 75 independently-owned hotels under franchise agreements. Similarly, Hotel Management licensed the Wyndham name to approximately 15 independently-owned hotels under management agreements.

Under these agreements, Hotels and Resorts and Hotel Management require each Wyndham-branded hotel to purchase—and configure to their specifications —a designated computer system that, among other things, handles reservations and payment card transactions. This system, known as a "property management system," stores consumers' personal information, including names, addresses, email addresses, telephone numbers, payment card account numbers, expiration dates and security codes.

The property management systems for *all* Wyndham-branded hotels are part of Hotels and Resorts computer network and are linked to its corporate network....

The Federal Trade Commission (FTC) alleges that, since at least April 2008, Wyndham failed to provide reasonable and appropriate security for the personal information collected and maintained by Hotels and Resorts, Hotel Management, and the Wyndham branded hotels. The FTC alleges that Wyndham did this by engaging in a number of practices that, taken together, unreasonably and unnecessarily exposed consumers' personal data to unauthorized access and theft.

As a result of these failures, between April 2008 and January 2010, intruders gained unauthorized access—on three separate occasions—to Hotels and Resorts' computer network, including the Wyndham-branded hotels' property management systems. The intruders used information stored there, including customers' payment card account numbers, expiration dates, and security codes. And, after discovering the first two breaches, Wyndham failed to take appropriate steps in a reasonable time frame to prevent the further compromise of Hotels and Resorts' network.

The FTC further alleges Wyndham's failure to implement reasonable and appropriate security measures exposed consumers' personal information to unauthorized access, collection and use that has caused and is likely to cause substantial consumer injury, including financial injury, to consumers and businesses. Defendants failure to implement reasonable and appropriate security measures caused, for example, the following: the three data breaches described above, the compromise of more than 619,000 consumer payment card account numbers, the exportation of many of those account numbers to a domain registered in Russia, fraudulent charges on many consumers' accounts, and more than $10.6 million in fraud loss. Consumers and businesses suffered financial injury, including, but not limited to, unreimbursed fraudulent charges, increased costs, and lost access to funds or credit. Consumers and businesses also expended time and money resolving fraudulent charges and mitigating subsequent harm.

Given these allegations, the FTC brought this action seeking a permanent injunction to prevent future violations of the FTC Act, as well as certain other relief...

Hotels and Resorts argues that the FTC's authority to prosecute unfair practices does not cover data security....The Court rejects this argument....

Next, Hotels and Resorts argued that, even if the FTC has sufficient authority, it would violate basic principles of fair notice and due process to hold Hotels and Resorts liable without rules, regulations or other guidelines explaining what data-security practices the Commission believes is forbidden or required....the court is not persuaded by Hotels and Resorts' position....Indeed, the proscriptions [embodied by the phrase unfair trade practices] are flexible, to be defined with particularity by the myriad of cases from the field of business....particularly given how quickly the digital age and data-security world is moving....

Hotels and Resorts proclaims that an unfair practice must, by statute, cause or be likely to cause substantial injury to consumers, which Hotels and Resorts denies....

The FTC's allegations, however, permit the court to reasonably infer that Hotels and Resorts' data security practices caused theft of personal data, which ultimately caused injury to consumers...For instance, the FTC alleges that Defendants failed to employ commonly-used methods to require user IDs and passwords that are difficult for hackers to guess and did not require the use of complex passwords for access to the Wyndham-branded hotels property management systems and allowed the use of easily guessed password.... Similarly, the FTC alleges that Defendants failed to adequately inventory computers connected to Hotels and Resorts' network so that Defendants could appropriately manage the devices on its network. And the FTC correspondingly alleges that, since Defendants did not have an adequate inventory of Wyndham-branded hotels' computers connected to its network—they were unable to physically locate those computers and therefore, Defendants did not determine that Hotels and Resorts network had been compromised until almost four months later.

Likewise, the FTC alleges that Defendants failed to use readily available security measures to limit access between and among the Wyndham-branded hotels' property management systems, such as firewalls. And this aligns with the FTC's allegation that intruders were able to gain unfettered access to the property management system servers of a number of hotels because Defendants did not appropriately limit access between and among the Wyndham-branded hotels' property management systems.

Finally, the FTC alleges that this failure to implement reasonable and appropriate security measures exposed consumers' personal information to unauthorized access, collection and use and has caused and is likely to cause substantial consumer injury, including financial injury, to consumers and businesses....

As set forth above, the court DENIES Hotels and Resorts' motion to dismiss.

CASE QUESTION

1. In what ways did Wyndham's actions fall short of required precautions?

Rights Concerning Rates and Fees

Legal mandates and good practice require that room rates and other fees be disclosed to guests before the costs are incurred. Further, a hotel cannot impose charges for services not provided.

Right to Advance Notice

Guests have a right to know, prior to contracting for a room, the fees and charges a hotel will impose. Many states require that rates be posted in each room, and signs containing prices not be misleading.

Extraneous Fees

Guests had the right not to be charged for services they do not receive. For example, a statute in New York provides that "no charge or sum shall be collected or received by any hotelkeeper for any service not actually rendered." Contrary to this statute, the Waldorf Astoria charged all guests a 2% fee for "sundries" (miscellaneous items), which covered messenger services that some guests used and others did not. The legality of the fee was successfully challenged by the New York State Attorney General, the chief legal officer of the state. The court's decision appears in Case Example 10-10.

CASE EXAMPLE 10-10

State of New York v. Waldorf-Astoria

323 N.Y.S.2d 917 (N.Y. 1971)

Petitioner brings this special proceeding...to permanently enjoin and restrain the respondents from conducting and transacting their business in a persistently fraudulent and illegal manner, and to direct restitution to all consumers of the amount charged for services not rendered...pursuant to [statute]....

The General Business Law does require every hotel to post "a statement of the...charges by the day and for meals furnished and for lodging." It further provides that "No charge or sum shall be collected or received by any such hotelkeeper or innkeeper for any service not actually rendered."

Between December 2, 1969 and May 21, 1970 the respondents did add to each bill of each customer a 2 percent charge for sundries....

Respondents argue that there was no violation of the General Business Law because it only prohibits charges "for any service not actually rendered" and that message services in fact were rendered. However, even respondents admit that all of their customers did not receive special, costly messenger service. They contend that 77 percent did receive such service but admit that 23 percent did not. None of their customers received any explanation or itemization of the charge for sundries. All of them were charged this 2 percent during the period in question....

The business of an innkeeper is of a quasi public character, invested with many privileges and burdened with correspondingly great responsibilities....The charge for message services delineated as sundries was fraudulent and unconscionable. Accordingly, petitioner's application is granted to the extent that respondents are permanently enjoined from engaging in the fraudulent and illegal acts and practices complained of herein.

The amount of money to be refunded is admitted. The petitioner, by its Bureau of Consumer Frauds and Protection, investigated the records of the respondents and claims that the 2 percent charge for sundries during the period in question involved 64,338 customers and amounts to $113,202.83. Frank A. Banks, vice-president and manager of respondent, in an affidavit of June 10, 1971, states that during the period in question transient room sales amounted to $6,329,484. The 2 percent charge would therefore be over $126,000. However, the exact amount is not important, as the respondents are ordered to refund to each and every customer during the period in question all charges for unexplained sundries. These refunds are to be made within 60 days of the date of service of the judgment herein with notice of entry. Within 30 days thereafter canceled vouchers or copies thereof will be exhibited to the petitioner....

CASE QUESTION

1. What alternate arrangements for payment of the fee might the hotel have made to avoid liability for returning the money?

Many hotels charge a mandatory resort fee, a cost added to the room price for various services that guests may or may not use. Those services typically cover pool use, gym access, towel service, WiFi, and more.

In response to consumer complaints about resort fees and misleading advertising on prices of hotel rooms, legislation has been introduced in Congress, entitled Truth in Hotel Advertising Act of 2016. The Act is intended to prohibit hotels from advertising a room rate that fails to disclose all mandatory fees. It also gives the Federal Trade Commission authority to enforce the prohibition, and state attorneys general the power to bring a civil action in federal court against violators.[32] The Act would not however outlaw resort fees. Apparently the prohibition on such charges is viewed differently in recent times, and the objection by consumers has not been sufficiently strong to deter imposition of the fees.

As an alternative pricing method, a hotel can provide optional complimentary services, such as breakfast, without charging the guest an additional fee. Instead, the cost to the hotel is incorporated into the room rate. The room fee remains constant regardless of whether the guest chooses to utilize the additional service. Since guests who do not use the service are not charged an extra fare, this arrangement is permissible.[33]

Telephone Charges

Telephones are a staple in most hotel rooms. Cell phones notwithstanding, failure to provide a telephone in the room may violate the innkeeper's duty to exercise reasonable care to protect guests' safety and to provide adequate security.

---

[32] S.2599-114th Congress (2015-2016).
[33] For an example of this type of pricing, see *Nashville Clubhouse Inn v. Johnson*, 27 S.W.3d 542 (Tenn. 2000).

A telephone may be the only source of fast communication with the front desk in an emergency situation. It might be used to give instructions to guests trapped in their rooms during a fire, or to summon help by a guest who suddenly takes ill and is unable to leave the room.

In the past, the charges that hotels could impose on guests for phone service were severely restricted by both state and federal regulation. More recently, most states have eliminated regulations that limited the surcharge that hotels can impose on local and intrastate calls, thus providing hotels with a source of revenue. In states where surcharge regulations still exist, innkeepers are bound to conform to them and may not impose a surcharge greater than that allowed by the state regulatory authority. In states where the regulations have been withdrawn, only competition limits the fees charged. Many guests are irritated by the amount of the fee and the lack of uniformity in the amount; the charges vary significantly from hotel to hotel. Some states, including New York, now have a "truth-in-dialing act" that requires the hotel to display a sign conspicuously on or "in the immediate vicinity of" the phones in the room advising guests that the hotel will impose a fee when calls are made on the hotel's phone. The purpose of these laws is to protect hotel guests from surprise charges and secret surcharges. The advent of cell phones has significantly reduced revenues for hotels from in-room phone calling.

Proper Handling of Mail, Packages, and Facsimile Correspondence and Internet Access

Hotel guests often receive letters, packages, and faxed documents at the hotel. Sometimes these items arrive at the hotel. Sometimes mail arrives after guests depart. In either case, guests have a right to have these items handled properly by the innkeeper. Delivery services such as United Parcel Service, FedEx, the United States Postal Service, and retailers discharge their obligations when they deliver the items to the hotel in good condition. The innkeeper should develop rules for processing them. The hotel may be liable to the intended recipient for negligent handling of the package if something is mistakenly delivered to the wrong person. An example of procedures that fulfill the hotel's responsibility to guests include the following:

1. When a package is received for a guest, a notice is placed in the guest's room informing him of receipt by the hotel of the package.

2. The "call" light in the guest room is illuminated, alerting the guest to call the front desk.

3. The package is not released unless the person claiming it exhibits identification.

In a case where the hotel deviated from the above procedures, the claimant exhibited a room key instead of identification and the hotel gave the package to that person. The hotel later discovered that person was not the addressee. The inn was liable to the intended recipient for negligent handling of the parcel.[34]

A related issue involves facsimile communications. If the hotel provides a facsimile machine for guests to use, procedures should be established to ensure guests can send and receive faxed documents reliably.

Case Example 10-11 illustrates the problems a hotel can encounter if proper procedures are not followed. The innkeeper agreed to refuse delivery of a package expected by a departing guest. Unfortunately, a hotel employee accepted delivery and stored the package. The hotel was found to be a bailee (see discussion on bailments in Chapter 8) with a duty to exercise reasonable care.

CASE EXAMPLE 10-11

Berlow v. Sheraton Dallas Corp.

629 S.W. 2d 818 (Tex. 1982)

Berlow, a designer and manufacturer of jewelry, frequently authorized her parents (the Soifers) to represent her in showing and selling jewelry to fashionable department stores. In January, 1978, Berlow authorized the Soifers to show 10 pieces of jewelry in Dallas. Berlow arranged to have a package containing the jewelry delivered by United Parcel Service (UPS) to her parents at the hotel. The package was marked "insured" on the outside and showed Berlow's return address. The package did not arrive at the hotel during the four-day stay of the Soifers. During their stay, each of the Soifers asked frequently about it at the front desk and, before checking out, the Soifers informed front desk personnel that this was a very important package, although they deliberately refrained from telling them the contents or value of the package. They asked that the hotel refuse delivery of it, and personnel at the front desk agreed to refuse its delivery. Agreeing to and subsequently refusing delivery of packages upon the oral instructions of guests to front desk attendants was standard procedure for the hotel. Contrary to its agreement, however, when the package arrived the hotel took delivery of it, stored it at the front desk for a month, and then turned it over to the United States Post Office (USPO) without postage, marked "Return to Sender." This, too, was standard procedure for the hotel in dealing with packages stored at the front desk. No attempt was made to determine if the Soifers had been recent guests at the hotel, nor to contact Berlow. The package was lost. At trial, Berlow testified that the fair market value of the jewelry was $10,231.

[T]he jury found that the hotel was negligent in its acceptance, care, and handling of the package, and that this negligence both increased the risk of loss of the package and was the proximate cause of the loss. The jury refused, however, to find the hotel grossly negligent.... Additionally, the jury found that the hotel did not substantially perform its agreement to refuse delivery of the package by delivering it to USPO and that Berlow's loss was suffered because she relied on the hotel's promise to refuse the package. Finally, the jury found that the hotel, acting as a reasonable and prudent person, should have foreseen that the package contained property of substantial dollar value. The jury awarded Berlow $10,231, the fair market value of the jewelry....

---

[34] *Bottoms & Tops International, Inc. v. UPS & Marco Polo, Inc.*, 610 N.Y.S.2d 439 (N.Y. 1994)

The hotel argues that the bailment of the package was merely gratuitous and, as a gratuitous bailee, it can be held liable only for gross negligence. Because we find for reasons explained below that the bailment of the package was a bailment for mutual benefit and not a gratuitous bailment, the hotel was liable for its ordinary negligence....

In order to constitute a bailment there must be a contract, express or implied, delivery of the property to the bailee, and acceptance of the property by the bailee. Uncontroverted evidence showed that the hotel, rather than refusing delivery, took possession of Berlow's package and stored it on the premises, under lock and key, for one month. Assuming custody of the package in this manner established an implied contract to bail the package. Delivery of the package and acceptance of it by the hotel were stipulated; thus bailment of the package was established as a matter of law.

That the bailment was one for mutual benefit and not merely gratuitous was also established as a matter of law. A bailment is for the mutual benefit of the parties, although nothing is paid directly by the bailor, where property of the bailor is delivered to and accepted by the bailee as an incident to a business in which the bailee makes a profit. The Soifers were paying guests at the hotel. It is not unusual for patrons to have packages delivered to them at a hotel, and, in this case, the evidence showed that the practice occurred frequently enough that the hotel developed standard procedures for dealing with packages. Although no direct charge was made, the price paid for the room also included the incidental services provided by the hotel. This provided consideration for the implied agreement to bail Berlow's package and established a bailment for mutual benefit as a matter of law.

Having entered into a bailment for mutual benefit, the hotel became liable for its ordinary negligence. The jury found that the hotel was negligent in its acceptance, care, and handling of the package, and there was some evidence to support this finding. The evidence showed that the hotel violated its own standard procedure, as well as its express agreement with the Soifers, to refuse delivery of packages when requested to do so. The evidence also showed that the package was stored for one month, during which the hotel made no attempt to contact the Soifers or Berlow, then delivered it to USPO without postage. This raises some evidence upon which the jury could find the hotel negligent.

[T]he hotel argues that, as a matter of law, it was not negligent. According to the hotel, because the package was delivered to USPO for return to Berlow, the liability for any loss rested with USPO as a subsequent bailee and not with the hotel. We do not agree. While the evidence showed that Berlow's package was lost while in the custody of USPO, it also showed that the hotel gave the package, which was insured when delivered to the hotel by UPS, to USPO without insurance or postage. This was evidence of negligence by the hotel, sufficiently strong to require submission of the issue to the jury. The hotel, therefore, did not establish its non-negligence as a matter of law.

There was also some evidence to support the jury's finding that the hotel's negligence was a proximate cause of Berlow's loss.... [B]ecause the package was given to USPO without postage, the jury could find that the hotel should have reasonably foreseen that the package would never reach Berlow.

Likewise, there was some evidence to support the jury's finding that it was foreseeable that the package contained property of substantial dollar value.... [T]he jury could find it reasonable for the hotel to foresee that guests would bring or deliver items of value to the hotel....

Because there was some evidence on each element of recovery on Berlow's theory that she and the hotel entered into a bailment for mutual benefit, the trial court erred in granting the hotel's motion for judgment notwithstanding the verdict; thus judgment should be rendered for Berlow....

[J]udgment rendered in favor of Berlow for $10,231.

CASE QUESTION

1. Assume that the hotel employee with whom the Soifers made arrangements for return of the package was not on duty when it arrived or had been terminated before it was delivered. What procedures might the hotel have instituted to ensure the Soifers's wishes were nonetheless honored?

Internet Access

Many consumers purchase cellular data plans to enable internet access at any time and any location. A federal law prohibits disabling or interfering with cellular or wireless networks. In 2014, the Federal Communications Commission (FCC) fined Marriott $600,000 because it blocked guests' and exhibitors' personal WiFi networks during an event held at the Grand Opryland Resort and Convention Center in Nashville and then charged exhibitors and others up to $1,000 per device to access the hotel's wireless network. As a consequence, Marriott is prohibited from blocking guests' WiFi at all of the hotels it owns and manages and must file a compliance plan with the FCC every three months for three years. Said the FCC Enforcement Bureau Chief, "It is unacceptable for any hotel to intentionally disable personal hot spots while also charging consumers and small businesses high fees to use the hotel's own Wi-Fi network. This practice puts consumers in the untenable position of either paying twice for the same service or forgoing internet access altogether."

Summary

Guests have a variety of rights which innkeepers must honor or risk liability for their breach. Those rights include the right to occupy the guest room without disturbance; the right against unauthorized police searches; the right against insulting treatment by hotel employees; the right to be free from unlawful arrest or restraint by the hotel staff; the right to disclosure of information concerning fees and charges for the room, phone and other services; and the right to proper handling of written communications and packages.

Preventive Law Tips for Managers

- *Protect the confidential information of the guest.* Ensure all personal information is maintained in a secure manner. Do not verbally disclose the room number of the guest. Follow through on requests made by others to have rooms adjacent to another guest to ensure it is in accordance with the wishes of all concerned.

- *Do not disrupt a guest's occupancy of the room except for good and exceptional cause.* A guest has the right to occupy the hotel room without interference from the innkeeper. Once a room is assigned to a guest, the innkeeper can enter only for normal maintenance, imminent danger, nonpayment, disruption of other guests, and when requested by the guest. Entering the room at other times or forcing a guest out of a room without cause entitles the guest to damages from the hotel.

- *If police ask you for permission to search the room of a current guest who is not in arrears in payment, remind the officer that you do not have legal authority to consent to a search.* A police officer in pursuit of a defendant may not know or recall in the heat of an investigation that an innkeeper lacks authority to consent to a search of a guest's room. If police request authority to search an occupied room, ask to see the warrant. If the officer does not have one, remind him that by law an innkeeper does not have the authority to consent to a search (unless one of the exceptions apply) and any evidence obtained will be suppressed. In response, most officers will apply for a warrant.

- *Do not give lost or mislaid property to someone claiming to be the owner without verifying that person's identity and ownership.* An innkeeper has a duty to exercise reasonable care in tending to lost or mislaid property. If a hotel gives the merchandise to someone other than its rightful owner, the hotel may be liable to the owner. To avoid that happening, the innkeeper should require proof of ownership before giving the goods to someone claiming to be the owner.

- *Train employees to be polite and respectful of guests; stress the importance of avoiding insulting or abusive language, and false statements.* Offensive or humiliating comments made by a hotel employee to a guest can result in liability for the hotel. Employees should be trained to address guests respectfully and avoid insulting comments and untruthful accusations.

- *Train employees on how to handle a suspected theft properly.* Guests have the right not to be falsely accused of illegal conduct by hotel staff. Employees should be taught proper procedures for handling suspicious activity. The protocol might include any of the following, depending on the circumstances: contacting the manager or other supervisory employee; investigating further; and contacting the police.

- *When investigating suspected criminal activity, do it confidentially, informing only those who need to know, and do it reasonably, with minimal disruption to the guest.* Conducting an investigation improperly can lead to liability. The investigation should be done promptly. The treatment of the suspect during the investigation should be respectful and reasonable. The investigation should be no broader than necessary to determine the truth or falsity of the suspected activity.

- *Do not impose any charge on a guest's bill for services not utilized by the guest.* A guest can legally be charged only for those services that he utilized while a guest at the hotel. Additional charges are not permitted. The hotel's billing procedures should be reviewed to ensure guests are not charged for unused services. Resort fees appear to be an exception to this rule.

- *Disclose information concerning the fees for in-room telephone use.* Most hotels charge a fee for the use of phones located in hotel rooms. The fees vary and guests are often uncertain as to the amount of the charges in a given hotel. Some states require that information identifying the charges be disclosed in writing near the phone. Compliance with these statutes is necessary to avoid fines. In states that do not statutorily require disclosure of this information, good practice calls for its disclosure. Unpleasant disagreements at checkout are thereby avoided.

- *Develop procedures to ensure that mail and packages addressed to guests and prior guests are properly handled, and follow those procedures carefully.* A hotel may be liable when mail, packages, or facsimile messages sent to guests or prior guests are not delivered to the addressee. The hotel should adopt procedures for handling the mail or package to ensure it reaches the intended recipient. Those procedures should include (1) maintaining a record of the guest's home address; (2) determining the proper method of forwarding the mail or package to a prior guest (U.S. mail, overnight mail service, etc.); (3) providing funds for postage and insurance; and (4) developing rules for proper handling during the period between receipt of the mail by the hotel and forwarding it to the guest.

Review Questions

1. What obligation, if any, does a hotel have to refrain from using abusive or insulting language when addressing a guest?

2. Under what circumstances can an innkeeper enter a guest's room without consent?

3. What constitutional rights are at risk when the police search a hotel room for evidence?

4. If a police search violates a constitutional right, what happens to any evidence that is seized in the search?

5. Who has authority to issue a search warrant?

6. What must a police officer prove in order to obtain a search warrant?

7. Who has the authority to consent to a search of a hotel room that has been assigned to a guest? Who does not have that authority?

8. What obligation does the hotel have with regard to storing the private information of others in a secure manner?

9. What restrictions does a hotel have concerning the fees it charges?

10. What obligation, if any, does a hotel have concerning mail, packages, and facsimile messages received by the hotel and addressed to guests?

11. What restrictions apply regarding the ability of a hotel to require use of the hotel's wireless network?

Discussion Questions

1. According to the exclusionary rule, incriminating evidence found during an illegal search cannot be used against the defendant. Often, without that evidence, the defendant will be acquitted. What is your opinion about the exclusionary rule?

2. In what way does a guest's expectation of privacy vary depending on whether he is still a guest or has checked out? Why does the expectation of privacy vary in these two circumstances?

3. Why can a hotel employee look into a mislaid briefcase before returning it to a guest who claims ownership of it? Why does this not violate the owner's right of privacy?

4. You are the assistant manager of a hotel. You have been assigned the task of devising procedures for handling mail and packages delivered to the hotel for guests, both current and past. What are the legal issues you will need to address and what procedures will you recommend?

5. What is the difference between defamation and intentional infliction of emotional distress?

Application Questions

1. Jan and Craig are friends and are both guests at the Morbury Hotel. While they were in the lobby after returning from a stroll through downtown, the hotel manager stopped them and loudly accused them of failing to pay their breakfast bill. There were many people in the lobby who overheard the exchange, including Jan and Craig's business associates with whom Jan and Craig were traveling. Both Jan and Craig were embarrassed and annoyed. They had in fact paid for their breakfast. Has the hotel violated any obligation owed to Jan and Craig? Why or why not? How should the hotel have handled the matter?

2. Connor and his wife are guests at a hotel, having reserved a room for three days. On the second day and while Connor was supposed to be attending a business meeting, he was arrested for sale of illegal drugs. The police immediately went to the hotel and received from the innkeeper permission to search the room. During the search the police found illegal drugs and drug paraphernalia. Can these items be used against Connor at trial? Why or why not? Does the hotel have any liability to Connor in this circumstance? Why or why not?

3. Joanne was a guest at the Billet Hotel. As she was checking out she was surprised to discover that she was charged for a service she had utilized at the hotel but had thought was offered for free. The hotel had not informed her previously that a fee would be imposed. She was angry and demanded to see the manager. Is the hotel legally entitled to collect these fees? What should the hotel have done to avoid this problem?

Websites

Websites that will enhance your understanding of the material in this chapter include:

www.privacyrights.org This site belongs to the Privacy Rights Clearinghouse and offers information about financial privacy of consumers.

www.ftc.gov This is the site of the Federal Trade Commission, an agency of the U.S. government. Its mission is to protect consumers. This site addresses such issues as privacy, identity theft, credit card fraud, and travel.

www.landmarkcases.org On this site you can obtain information about search warrants including when the police must have one and when a warrant is not necessary.

www.congress.gov This site provides access to current legislative activities.

www.govtrack.us This site allows for tracking of the activities of the U.S. Congress.

www.ftc.gov This site includes news and alerts, consumer protection details, and antitrust information.

UNIT IV

Special Topics

CHAPTER 11

Liability and the Sale of Food

LEARNING OUTCOMES:

- Understand the warranty of merchantability with the foreign/natural and reasonable/expectation tests
- Know cases involving raw shellfish, hot beverages, and foodborne illnesses
- Understand the choice of actions: breach of warranty of merchantability, strict products liability, statutory violations, negligence
- Know how the hospitality industry handles patrons with food allergies
- Understand false food claims with the Truth in Menu Laws
- Comprehend food labeling and its application to restaurants
- Learn restrictions on the use of the word kosher
- Understand smoking restrictions in bars and restaurants
- Understand the safety concerns for food preparation

KEY TERMS

class action	privity of contract
foreign/natural substance test	reasonable/expectation test
kosher	strict products liability
merchantable	Uniform Commercial Code (UCC)

Introduction

Studies suggest that one out of every three meals is eaten away from home. If restaurants serve unhealthy food, a serious health risk results. To encourage safe practices, the law imposes liability on restaurants that serve tainted food or make claims about the food that are not truthful.

A restaurant has a duty to provide reasonably safe premises for its patrons. Disregarding this duty can result in liability for damages.

This chapter will examine the laws applicable to the sale of food and the duty of a restaurant to protect the safety of its patrons.

Adulterated Food

A diner who is served food that causes illness has three possible grounds on which to sue: breach of warranty of merchantability, strict products liability, and negligence. A discussion of each of these causes of action follows.

Warranty of Merchantability

Uniform Commercial Code (UCC)
A set of rules designed to simplify and modernize the law governing the sale of goods, including food.

The **Uniform Commercial Code (UCC)** is a set of rules designed to simplify and modernize the law governing the sale of goods, including food. Virtually all states and the District of Columbia have adopted the UCC. It imposes, in all contracts for the sale of goods where the seller is a merchant, an implied warranty that goods, including food, are "merchantable."[1] A restaurant qualifies as a merchant for purposes of the warranty. **Merchantable** means the goods are fit for their ordinary purpose and are at least of average quality. For example, if you order a breakfast burrito and then bite into it, and you discover a nail in it, the burrito is not merchantable.

This warranty of merchantability is implied in all contracts for the sale of goods made by a merchant; it exists even if the parties never mention it in their negotiations. The warranty renders manufacturers and sellers of food virtual insurers that the food is safe to eat. The basis for imposing this liability is public policy for protection of consumers.

merchantable
An implied warranty that refers to the sale of goods, including food, and establishes a standard of average quality and requires that the goods be fit for their ordinary purpose.

Merchantable Food

Food, to be merchantable, must be fit for human consumption—that is, it will not make you ill when you eat it. To pass muster, food does not have to be nutritious or taste great; it merely must be eatable. Inappropriate objects in food will render it unmerchantable. Food infected with harmful bacteria or a virus breaches the warranty, as does spoiled as well as undercooked food.

Objects in Food

A pizza served with a tack in it is not merchantable. The restaurant that served the pizza will be liable to a customer injured by the tack based on breach of the warranty of merchantability.

Foreign/Natural Test

In some states, whether an object found in food constitutes a breach of warranty is determined by the **foreign/natural substance test.** This test is considered by restaurateurs more business friendly than the reasonable/expectation test. The foreign/natural doctrine provides that a food producer is not liable for anything found in the food product that naturally exists in the ingredients.[2] If the object is foreign—that is, unrelated to the components or ingredients of the product—the warranty is breached. If, however, the object is natural, the warranty is not breached.

foreign/natural substance test
A test that holds that the presence of an object natural to a food product does not breach the warranty implied in its sale. (The presence of a foreign object is a breach of warranty).

An example of a foreign object is a piece of glass. A plaintiff swallowed pieces of glass lodged in ice cream while eating a banana split. Not surprisingly, she won her lawsuit against the restaurant.[3] Other examples of foreign objects found in food include an unwrapped condom in chicken salad,[4] a shish kabob stick in a Tex-Mex egg roll,[5] a toothpick in a piece of prime rib,[6] "something sharp and hard" in a

---

[1] UCC 2–314. (This is a typical UCC citation. The numeral "2" identifies which of the UCC's nine articles is referenced. The number following the dash refers to a section within the referenced article.)
[2] *Newton v. Standard Candy Co.*, 2008 WL 752599 (Nebr. 2008)
[3] *Deris v. Finest Foods, Inc.*, 198 So.2d 412 (La. 1967)
[4] *Chambley v. Apple Restaurants, Inc.*, 504 S.E.2d 551 (Ga. 1998)
[5] *Arenas v. The Cheesecake Factory Restaurants*, 907 So.2d 1184 (Fla. 2005)
[6] *Thomas v. HWCC-Tunica, Inc.*, 915 So.2d 1092 (Miss. 2005)

pumpkin muffin,[7] mold in a Coke,[8] and grain and wood shavings in a "ready-to-cook" turkey carcass.[9]

A case illustrating the application of the foreign/natural test to a natural object involves a plaintiff who was injured by a chicken bone while eating chicken pot pie in a restaurant. The court held the defendant was not liable. Although chicken bones are not expected in a pot pie, they are natural to chicken.[10] Similarly, chicken-bone slivers in chicken soup and nutshell pieces in nut breads are natural substances and, so, under the foreign/natural test, do not violate the warranty of merchantability.

Likewise bone fragments were found to be natural to a sausage, egg, and cheese bagel sandwich.[11] The court stated, "Bones which are natural to the type of meat served cannot legitimately be called a foreign substance, and a consumer who eats meat dishes ought to anticipate and be on his guard against the presence of such bones." The plaintiff attempted to distinguish her claim by arguing that a customer could not have reasonably guarded against the presence of a pig's bone in a "melted conglomeration" sandwich (sausage, egg, and cheese). The court rejected this argument stating, "We find that there is no difference between a 'melted conglomeration' sandwich, pot pie, beef stew, or a cherry pie because these foods, by their very nature, obscure the ingredients therein." Judgment was thus entered for the restaurant.

Reasonable/Expectation Test

© Charoenkrung.Studio99/Shutterstock.com

reasonable expectation test
A test that examines whether an object found in food ought to have been anticipated by the consumer. If so, its presence in the food does not constitute a breach of the warranty.

An alternate test applied by a majority of states is the **reasonable expectation test,** which examines whether an object found in food ought to have been reasonably anticipated by the consumer. The reasonable expectation test relies on "widely shared standards that food products ought to meet."[12] If the object should be expected, its presence in the food does not constitute a breach of the warranty. Instead, the diner, when eating, should be on the alert for the object. If, on the other hand, its presence is not reasonably anticipated, it does constitute a breach. Under this test, more circumstances are likely to constitute breach of the warranty than under the foreign/natural test because some objects may be natural but are nonetheless unexpected. The reasonable/expectation test is more patron-friendly than the foreign/natural substance test. Examples include the chicken bone in the chicken pot pie and the nutshell pieces in the nut bread. Other examples are a pit in a maraschino cherry used as a garnish,[13] a piece of bone in a barbecue pork sandwich,[14] and a pit from a date contained in a date muffin.[15]

7 *Schafer v. JLC Food Systems, Inc.,* 695 N.W. 2d 570 (Minn. 2005)
8 *Hagan v. Coca-Cola Bottling Co.,* 804 So.2d 1234 (Fla. 2001)
9 *Ruggiero v. Perdue Poultry Company,* 1997 WL 811530 (N.Y. 1997)
10 *Mix v. Ingersoll Candy Co.,* 59 P.2d 144 (Calif. 1936)
11 *Parianos v. Bruegger's Bagel Bakery,* 2005 WL 78114 (Ohio 2005)
12 Restatement (Third) of Torts §7
13 *Williams v. Roche Brothers Supermarkets, Inc.,* 1999 WL 788509 (Mass. 1999)
14 *Norris v. Pig'n Whistle Sandwich Shop, Inc.* 53 S.E. 2d 718 (Ga. 1949)
15 *Phillips v. West Springfield,* 540 N.E.2d 1331 (Mass. 1989)

The outcome of the application of the reasonable expectation test is not always clear because reasonable people might disagree about what should be anticipated. See if you agree with the judge's decision in Case Example 11-1. *Note:* While most cases cite precedent as support for a judge's decision, you will enjoy the fact that this case cites the cookbook author Fannie Farmer.

CASE EXAMPLE 11-1

Webster v. Blue Ship Tea Room, Inc.

198 N.E.2d 309 (Mass. 1964)

… On Saturday, April 25, 1959, about 1 p.m., the plaintiff, accompanied by her sister and her aunt, entered the Blue Ship Tea Room operated by the defendant. The group was seated at a table and supplied with menus.

This restaurant, which the plaintiff characterized as "quaint," was located in Boston on the third floor of an old building on T Wharf, which overlooks the ocean.

The plaintiff, who had been born and brought up in New England (a fact of some consequence), ordered clam chowder and crabmeat salad. Within a few minutes she received tidings to the effect that "there was no more clam chowder," whereupon she ordered a cup of fish chowder. Presently, there was set before her "a small bowl of fish chowder." She had previously enjoyed a breakfast about 9 a.m. that had given her no difficulty. The fish chowder contained haddock, potatoes, milk, water, and seasoning. The chowder was milky in color and not clear. The haddock and potatoes were in chunks (also a fact of consequence). She agitated it a little with the spoon and observed that it was a fairly full bowl.… It was hot when she got it, she… stirred it in an up and under motion. She denied that she did this because she was looking for something, but it was rather because she wanted an even distribution of fish and potatoes. She started to eat it, alternating between the chowder and crackers which were on the table with… [some] rolls. She ate about 3 or 4 spoonfuls then stopped. She looked at the spoonfuls as she was eating. She saw equal parts of liquid, potato, and fish as she spooned it into her mouth. She did not see anything unusual about it. After 3 or 4 spoonfuls she was aware that something had lodged in her throat because she couldn't swallow and couldn't clear her throat by gulping and she could feel it. This misadventure led to two esophagoscopies at the Massachusetts General Hospital, in the second of which, on April 27, 1959, a fish bone was found and removed. The sequence of events produced injury to the plaintiff that was not insubstantial.

We must decide whether a fish bone lurking in a fish chowder, about the ingredients of which there is no other complaint, constitutes a breach of implied warranty under applicable provisions of the Uniform Commercial Code… As the judge put it in his charge, "Was the fish chowder fit to be eaten and wholesome?… [N]obody is claiming that the fish itself wasn't wholesome.… But the bone of contention here—I don't mean that for a pun—but was this fish bone a foreign substance that made the fish chowder unwholesome or not fit to be eaten?"

The plaintiff has vigorously reminded us of the high standards imposed by this court where the sale of food is involved… and has made reference to cases involving stones in beans… trichinae in pork…and to certain other cases, here and elsewhere, serving to bolster her contention of breach of warranty.

The defendant asserts that here was a native New Englander eating fish chowder in a "quaint" Boston dining place where she had been before; that [f]ish chowder, as it is served and enjoyed by New Englanders, is a hearty dish, originally designed to satisfy the appetites of our seamen and fishermen; that this court knows well that we are not talking of some insipid broth as is customarily served to convalescents. We are asked to rule in such fashion that no chef is forced "to reduce the pieces of fish in the chowder to minuscule size in an effort to ascertain if they contained any pieces of bone." "In so ruling," we are told (in the defendant's brief), "the court will not only uphold its reputation for legal knowledge and acumen, but will, as loyal sons of Massachusetts, save our world-renowned fish chowder from degenerating into an insipid broth containing the mere essence of its former stature as a culinary masterpiece." Notwithstanding these passionate entreaties we are bound to examine with detachment the nature of fish chowder and what might happen to it under varying interpretations of the Uniform Commercial Code.

Chowder is an ancient dish pre-existing even the appetites of our seamen and fishermen…. The word "chowder" comes from the French chaudiere meaning a "cauldron" or "pot." In the fishing villages of Brittany…faire la chaudiere means to supply a cauldron in which is cooked a mess of fish and biscuit with some savoury condiments, a hodge-podge contributed by the fishermen themselves, each of whom in return receives his share of the prepared dish. The Breton fishermen probably carried the custom to Newfoundland, long famous for its chowder, whence it has spread to Nova Scotia, New Brunswick, and New England….Our literature over the years abounds in references not only to the delights of chowder but also to its manufacture. A namesake of the plaintiff, Daniel Webster, had a recipe for fish chowder that has survived into a number of modern cookbooks and in which the removal of fish bones is not mentioned at all. One old time recipe recited in the New English Dictionary study defines chowder as "A dish made of fresh fish (esp. cod) or clams, stewed with slices of pork or bacon, onions, and biscuit." Cider and champagne are sometimes added. Hawthorne speaks of "…[a] codfish of sixty pounds, caught in the bay, [which] had been dissolved into the rich liquid of a chowder." A chowder variant, cod "Muddle," was made in Plymouth in the 1890s by taking "a three or four pound codfish, head added. Season with salt and pepper and boil in just enough water to keep from burning. When cooked, add milk and piece of butter." The recitation of these ancient formulae suffices to indicate that in the construction of chowders in these parts in other years, worries about fish bones played no role whatsoever. This broad outlook on chowders has persisted in more modern cookbooks. "The chowder of today is much the same as the old chowder.…" The all-embracing Fannie Farmer states, in a portion of her recipe, [that] fish chowder is made with a "fish skinned, but head and tail left on. Cut off head and tail and remove fish from backbone. Cut fish in 2-inch pieces and set aside. Put head, tail, and backbone broken in pieces, in stewpan; add 2 cups cold water and bring slowly to boiling point.…" The liquor thus produced from the bones is added to the balance of the chowder.…

Thus, we consider a dish that for many long years, if well made, has been made generally as outlined above. It is not too much to say that a person sitting down in New England to consume a good New England fish chowder embarks on a gustatory adventure which may entail the removal of some fish bones from his bowl as he proceeds. We are not inclined to tamper with ageold recipes by any amendment reflecting the plaintiff's view of the effect of the Uniform Commercial Code upon them. We are aware of the heavy body of case law involving foreign substances in food, but we sense a strong distinction between them and those relative to unwholesomeness of the food itself, e.g., tainted mackerel [on the one hand]…and a fish bone in a fish chowder [on the other]. Certain Massachusetts cooks might cavil at the ingredients contained in the chowder in this case in that it lacked the heartening lift of salt port. In any event, we consider that the joys of life in New England include the ready availability of fresh fish chowder. We should be prepared to cope with the hazards of fish bones, the occasional presence of which in chowders is, it seems to us, to be anticipated, and which, in the light of a hallowed tradition, do not impair their fitness or merchantability…We are most impressed by Allen v. Grafton, 170 Ohio St. 249, 164 N.E.2d 167, where in Ohio, the Midwest, in a case where the plaintiff was injured by a piece of oyster shell in an order of fried oysters. Mr. Justice Taft (now Chief Justice) in a majority opinion held that "the possible presence of a piece of oyster shell in or attached to an oyster is so well known to anyone who eats oysters that we can say as a matter of law that one who eats oysters can reasonably anticipate and guard against eating such a piece of shell…"

Thus, while we sympathize with the plaintiff who has suffered a peculiarly New England injury….

Judgment for the defendant.

CASE QUESTION

1. The court's decision was based in part on its belief that people who eat fish chowder anticipate and expect that it will contain occasional bones. Do you agree? Do you think the decision would have been different if the plaintiff came from Nebraska?

In a similar case, the court, relying on *Webster*, ruled that an occasional piece of clam shell in a bowl of clam chowder should be reasonably expected. The court therefore decided in favor of a grocery store that sold a can of clam chowder to the plaintiff, who injured a molar when she bit down on a piece of shell while eating the soup.[16]

Trend Toward the Reasonable/Expectation Test

In judging the merchantability of food, courts recently have been favoring the reasonable/expectation rule over a strict application of the foreign/natural test. The reason for this is, at least in part, because even the presence of natural substances can sometimes render food unfit. A Florida court explained it well as follows.

> *The reasoning applied in [the foreign/natural] test is fallacious because it assumes that all substances which are natural to the food in one stage or another of preparation are, in fact, anticipated by*

---

16 *Koperwas v. Publix Supermarkets, Inc.,* 534 So.2d 872 (Fla. 1988)

the average consumer in the final product served. It does not logically follow that every product which contains some chicken must as a matter of law be expected to contain occasionally or frequently chicken bones or chicken-bone slivers [just] because chicken bones are natural to chicken meat and both have a common origin. Categorizing a substance as foreign or natural is not determinative of what is unfit or harmful for human consumption. A nutshell natural to nut meat can cause as much harm as a foreign substance, such as a pebble, piece of wire or glass. All are indigestible and likely to cause the injury.[17]

The plaintiff in the Florida case was eating maple walnut ice cream when she suffered punctured gums and fractured teeth from the presence of a walnut shell in the ice cream. The court held the shell, although a natural substance, could not be reasonably anticipated and thus its presence violated the warranty of merchantability.

In a case from New York, a movie theater patron broke a tooth on an unpopped popcorn kernel. The court held that until such time as the same bio-engineers who brought us seedless watermelon are able to develop a new strain of popping corn where every kernel is guaranteed to pop, we will just have to accept partially popped popcorn as part and parcel of the popcorn popping process. The patron should reasonably anticipate unpopped popcorn kernels in their popcorn.[18]

In a case from California, a patron, while dining at a pizza restaurant, bit into a whole olive in an antipasto salad and broke a tooth. California uses the reasonable/expectation test so the inquiry was whether an ordinary customer would expect to find whole olives containing pits in the salad. The court held for the restaurant and explained that a certain kind of olive salad comes with whole olives which by their nature, have a pit.[19]

In a case from the state of Washington, the plaintiff ordered a crab-melt open sandwich, which consisted of a toasted English muffin topped with shredded crab meat, melted cheese, and chopped parsley. The plaintiff bit into the sandwich and swallowed a one-inch piece of crab shell. Surgery was necessary to remove the shell from the plaintiff's esophagus. If Washington followed the foreign/natural test, the shell would have been deemed natural and the restaurant would not have been liable. But the state adopted the reasonable expectation rule. The court held that diners would not reasonably anticipate the shell and so its presence constitutes a breach of the warranty of merchantability.[20]

In another case the plaintiff purchased from a convenience store a cup of coffee that contained a considerable amount of coffee grounds. She became ill when she drank the beverage and inadvertently swallowed some of the grounds. She sued the store. Had the court applied the foreign/natural test, it would have dismissed the case. Instead, the court applied the reasonable/expectation test and referred

---

[17] *Zabner v. Howard Johnson's, Inc.*, 201 So.2d 824 (Fla. 1967)
[18] *Kaplan v. American Multi-Cinema, Inc.*, 873 N.Y.2d 234 (N.Y. 2008)
[19] *Foor v. Amici's East Coast Pizzeria*, A129689 (Calif. 2011)
[20] *Jefferies v. Clark's Restaurant Enterprises, Inc.*, 580 P.2d 1103 (Wash. 1978)

the case to trial, leaving it to a jury to decide whether the coffee grounds should reasonably have been anticipated.[21]

In a case involving candy, the plaintiff bit into a Katydid, a chocolate-covered pecan-caramel candy, and broke a tooth on a hard pecan shell embedded in it. Again, had the court applied the foreign/natural test, the case would have been dismissed. Instead, the court applied the reasonable/expectation test and denied the manufacturer's motion to dismiss.[22]

Consider a case in which the state applies the reasonable/expectation test and the object found in the food is foreign. In most such cases, the object will be unexpected, so the food vendor will be liable for breach of warranty. For example, human blood would not be expected in biscuits and gravy purchased from a restaurant. A plaintiff found blood when she opened the styrofoam container in which her takeout breakfast was delivered. An investigation revealed that the preparer had not sufficiently bandaged a cut on her arm.[23] Likewise, two AA batteries would not be expected at the bottom of a Diet Coke can. Their presence constituted a breach of the implied warranty of merchantability. A verdict in the consumer's favor in the amount of $554,000 was upheld on appeal.[24]

Case Example 11-2 also illustrates this point.

CASE EXAMPLE 11-2

Coulter v. American Bakeries Co.

530 So.2d 1009 (Fla. 1988)

… The uncontroverted evidence presented at trial revealed that appellant had purchased doughnuts manufactured by appellee and sealed in their original package. She opened the package in her automobile and in the course of driving to her destination consumed several pieces of one doughnut by breaking them off with her fingers and popping them into her mouth. Because of an abscessed tooth and sore jaw, instead of chewing the doughnut with her teeth, appellant would sip milk through a straw allowing the doughnut to dissolve in her mouth. In fact, it was the dissolving nature of the doughnut which had prompted appellant to purchase that particular product. Shortly after she began consuming the doughnut, she felt something stick in her throat and immediately ceased ingestion. It was later discovered through x-rays the same day that appellant had consumed a piece containing a metal wire [that] caused her subsequent injury.

A complaint was filed alleging breach of implied warranty in that the doughnuts were unfit for human consumption.…

---

[21] *Johnson v. C.F.M., Inc.*, 726 F.Supp. 1228 (Kan. 1989)
[22] *Jackson v. Nestle-Beich, Inc.*, 589 N.E.2d 547 (Ill. 1992)
[23] *Flagstar Enterprises, Inc. v. Davis*, 1997 WL 564475 (Ala. 1997)
[24] *Vamos v. Coca-Cola Bottling Company of New York, Inc.*, 627 N.Y.S.2d 265 (N.Y. 1995)

In a breach of an implied warranty action based on the presence of a harmful substance in food, the test of whether the presence of the harmful substance constitutes a breach of implied warranty is whether the consumer can reasonably expect to find the substance in the food as served....

Applying the foregoing to the instant case, there was simply no evidence that appellant could have expected to find a wire in the doughnut.... [J]udgment in favor of appellant.

Sometimes an object is not natural to a product but nonetheless is associated with that product. A court may determine such items should be reasonably expected by the diner. Another example is a pearl in oysters. A diner broke his tooth when he bit down on a pearl in an oyster po'boy sandwich but was denied recovery in his lawsuit against the restaurant. The court, noting that a pearl "will occasionally" be found within an oyster, stated that the plaintiff should have reasonably anticipated the possible presence of the pearl.[25]

Raw Shellfish

Raw shellfish in its natural habitat often accumulates bacteria that are seldom harmful to healthy people but can be unsafe and even deadly to those with compromised immune systems. *Vibrio vulnificus* occurs naturally in saltwater environments. Whenever it is present in water where an oyster lives, the oyster will contain the bacteria. Generally, it is only dangerous to persons with chronic health problems, gastric disorders, liver diseases, and immune disorders. Proper cooking will kill the bacteria present in oysters. Whether the bacteria should be reasonably anticipated was the issue in a Delaware case. The plaintiff suffered a serious illness from eating raw shellfish that contained bacteria. Expert testimony established that most people who eat that type of bacteria suffer only minor digestive tract discomfort. However, if the diner has a compromised immune system or liver disease, he will suffer a more severe reaction. The plaintiff had a liver condition and sued the restaurant for breach of warranty of merchantability. Expert testimony established that the bacteria are common in the waters off North America and are known to be taken in by filter-feeding organisms such as clams. The court thus found that one who eats raw clams should expect the presence of substances that are indigenous to clams in their natural state, including the bacteria at issue in this case.[26]

Many states require that restaurants conspicuously post warnings that ingestion of raw oysters may be hazardous to one's health.

25 *Porteous v. St. Ann's Cafe & Deli*, 713 So.2d 454 (La. 1998)
26 *Clime v. Dewey Beach Enterprises, Inc.*, 831 F.Supp. 341 (Del. 1993)

The oyster warning must be provided wherever oysters are offered within the establishment. If there is a separate bar area where oysters can be ordered without a menu, the oyster warning consumer advisory must be provided within the sight of these customers, also. Menu advisories are not required, but it would be a good idea to include the warning on the menu as well.

A case in Ohio involved a man who died as a result of contracting *Vibrio vunificus* after eating raw oysters. The menu contained the required warning. The Court held that no liability could have been imposed on the restaurant for inadequate warning because the menu contained a warning directly below the oyster entrees.[27]

In Case Example 11-3 the sufficiency of the warning was at issue.

CASE EXAMPLE 11-3

Bergeron v. Jazz Seafood & Steakhouse, and Louisiana Department of Health

64 So.3d 255 (La. 2011)

This appeal arises from a suit for damages filed by Godfrey Bergeron seeking recovery for injuries resulting from the consumption of raw oysters at Jazz Seafood & Steakhouse. . . .

On July 23, 2001, Godfrey Bergeron ate approximately one dozen raw oysters in the oyster bar at the Jazz Seafood & Steakhouse (hereinafter "Jazz") in Kenner, Louisiana. Approximately two to three days later, Mr. Bergeron became very ill and was admitted to the Medical Center of Southwest Louisiana. Mr. Bergeron was diagnosed with a vibrio vulnificus infection, a flesh-eating bacterial infection, which he contracted from ingesting raw oysters that contained the vibrio vulnificus bacteria. As a result of the infection, Mr. Bergeron required an extensive hospital stay, incurred significant medical expenses, and sustained permanent damage to his nerves and skin.

Mr. Bergeron and his wife instituted this action for damages against Jazz and the Department of Health (hereinafter "DHH"). Specifically with regard to Jazz, the plaintiffs alleged that Jazz was obliged by the Louisiana sanitary code to, but did not, post a warning to susceptible persons of the dangers of eating raw oysters, and alternatively, that any warning which it posted was inadequate and was hidden or so inconspicuous that it was inadequate. With regard to DHH, the plaintiffs alleged that DHH had an affirmative duty to cause restaurants, such as Jazz, to post warnings about the dangers of eating raw oysters and that DHH failed to perform its duty.

DHH moved for summary judgment alleging that it could not be held liable to the plaintiffs for any damages suffered as a result of eating raw oysters because it had complied with its obligation to enforce the sanitary code with regard to Jazz, and therefore, DHH sought dismissal from these proceedings. . . . The trial court granted DHH's motion for summary judgment and dismissed the plaintiffs'

---

[25] *Woeste v. Washington Platform Saloon & Restaurant*, 836 N.E. 2d 52 (Ohio 2005)

claims against it with prejudice . . .This court affirms the trial court's grant of summary judgment in favor of DHH. . . .

The evidence submitted by DHH established that the oyster warnings were posted or displayed at Jazz in the oyster bar where Mr. Bergeron ordered the oysters—the "point of sale"—in accordance with the sanitary code and that DHH fulfilled its duty to enforce the sanitary code by performing routine inspections of Jazz to ensure its compliance with the sanitary code. While the evidence submitted by Jazz indicated that Mr. Bergeron and his dinner companions did not *see* (or take *notice* of) the warning signs pertaining to oysters, this evidence was insufficient to establish that the signs were not present at the oyster bar or that the inspections by DHH to ensure compliance with the sanitary code were improper or deficient. . . .

After a hearing the trial court dismissed plaintiffs' claim that Jazz failed to post a warning of the dangers of eating raw oysters as required by the Louisiana Sanitary Code and limited plaintiff's sole remaining cause of action against Jazz to [apparently quoting from plaintiff's complaint] "the allegation that the warnings found to have been posted by Jazz on the date of the accident at the point of sale as mandated by the Sanitary Code were allegedly inadequate due to clutter and/or interference."

Jazz seeks dismissal of plaintiffs' sole remaining claim based on the inadequacy of the posted warning. Jazz contends the evidence showed that the warning signs posted at the time of sale were "clear, visible and unambiguous." Thus, Jazz contended, it was entitled to dismissal of plaintiffs' claims. . . Plaintiffs contend that the trial court erred in granting Jazz's motion for summary judgment. . . .

Due to the growing number of cases of vibrio vulnificus infections arising from the consumption of raw oysters, in 1991, DHH published a rule requiring mandatory oyster warnings. The rule requires all restaurants that sell or serve raw oysters to provide clearly visible warnings about vibrio vulnificus at the point of sale . . .

The duty of a restaurant under this provision is to warn the public by displaying "clearly visible messages at the point of sale" with language dictated by the statute. . . .

Jazz also presented the testimony of DHH Inspector Francis who testified that he routinely inspected Jazz Seafood four times a year, including approximately a week after Godfrey Bergeron purchased and consumed the raw oysters, and that Jazz was never cited with failure to comply with the official notice to post warning. Inspector Francis further testified that he is familiar with the term "sign pollution" and that during the five years he inspected Jazz Seafood, he did not have any problem noticing the warning signs displayed at the bar at Jazz Seafood. He testified that sign pollution was not a factor in this case and that the bar did not contain numerous signs that would distract one from the warnings posted in accordance with the sanitary code provisions. . .

Jazz also presented the affidavit of David Bowman, the general manager of Jazz. Bowman stated that as general manager, he was responsible for posting the warnings cautioning customers of the dangers of consuming raw shellfish as required by DHH. Bowman stated that he personally prepared the warning signs which appeared on the menus and walls of the restaurant. He further identified and attached to his affidavit one of the signs, which were prepared on 8.5 by 11 sheets of paper [and contained the exact wording mandated by the statute].

Bowman stated that he posted the signs at various points in the restaurant, which he identified in an attached diagram, including, in particular, a sign posted at the front of the bar on the corner post facing where Godfrey Bergeron indicated that he was seated. Bowman further testified that he was never made aware of any DHH inspections as they were all unannounced and spontaneous.

Jazz also submitted the deposition of Edward W. Karnes, Ph.D, plaintiffs' expert in this case who explained that competing signage or information is detrimental to the visual attraction of the sign and that from a human factor standpoint, it would not be unlikely or unreasonable for a person to fail to read a sign when competing information is present. Although Dr. Karnes testified that there were competing signs at the hostess station and at the bar from the view of the hostess station, he conceded that if the signage appeared as shown to him in a photo taken from the location where Bergeron was seated when he purchased and consumed his oysters, there was no problem with the visual presentation. . . .

Thus, Jazz contends, the evidence established that Bergeron's position at the oyster bar was two seats away from a very large warning sign that was clearly visible at the point of sale pursuant to the requirements of the sanitary code . . .

On review of the evidence set forth, . . . we agree that Jazz was entitled to judgment in its favor, dismissing plaintffs' claim. Affirmed.

Other Grounds for Breach of Warranty of Merchantability

Foreign or unexpected objects in food are not the only basis for liability based on the sale of food. Other grounds include rancid or spoiled food, adulterated or contaminated food, improper handling and preparation including time and temperature abuse that result in unwholesome fare, or significantly burned food. Thus, a restaurant was liable where a plaintiff bit into a cheeseburger that "splintered off [apparently due to it being greatly overcooked], causing a piece of severely burned cheeseburger to become lodged in his esophagus" requiring an emergency esophagoscopy to remove the burned burger.[28] If the food is unfit, regardless of the cause, the warranty of merchantability is breached.

Class Action

A restaurant's failure to properly handle or prepare food could result in not just one customer becoming ill, but in some cases many. If numerous people are made sick from the same unhealthy food, they may be able to ease the expense of the lawsuit by bringing a **class action**.[29] This is a proceeding pursued on behalf of many people who are injured by the same cause, and whose cases raise common legal issues. Due to the decreased expense and relative ease of participating in a class action suit, potential plaintiffs who might not otherwise sue will assert their claim, thus expanding the liability exposure of the defendant. In a Florida case, the complaint alleged that several hundred people contracted salmonella poisoning or other gastrointestinal ailments as a result of unsanitary and unsafe practices at the defendant's restaurant. The court authorized those who became ill to pursue the

class action
A lawsuit brought by a group of persons who are similarly situated.

---

28 *Morin v. Troymac's, Inc.*, 2000 WL 670040 (Conn. 2000)
29 *Farrenholz v. Mad Crab, Inc.*, 2000 WL 1433956 (Ohio 2000). But another court with similar facts disallowed the class. See *Peet v. The Sweet Onion, Inc.*, 2005 WL 624895 (Mich. 2005)

case against the restaurant as a class action.[30] Likewise, a class action was authorized among patrons of a restaurant who dined at the establishment during a three-day period and subsequently became ill from food poisoning.[31]

Where, however, the facts pertaining to members of the would-be class vary, a class action is not appropriate. An example is provided in a case involving an icecream store chain that significantly understated the calories and fat content of its products. A misled customer sought to formulate a class consisting of all patrons who purchased food products from the chain during a specified time period. The court rebuffed the plaintiff noting that members of the would-be class had diverse reasons for using the product, only one of which was nutritional and health value. Others chose the ice cream for taste, convenience, or some other reason, and so were not injured by the misrepresentations.[32]

© Stefano Cavoretto/Shutterstock.com

Hot Beverages

Food establishments need to exercise caution when serving hot beverages. An elderly woman won a multimillion-dollar verdict against McDonald's after she was scalded by spilling hot coffee on her lap. A judge on appeal significantly reduced the amount of the verdict, but the fast-food restaurant nonetheless was forced to pay the plaintiff for her injuries. A key fact that influenced the outcome of the case related to the temperature of the beverage. McDonald's at the time maintained coffee sitting in a pot at a temperature significantly higher than the industry norm. Had the facts been otherwise, the plaintiff would likely not have been successful in her case. Numerous similar lawsuits followed involving not only coffee, but also hot tea and other hot beverages.

Most courts today recognize that coffee is customarily served hot and is intended to be consumed hot. Further, the average person knows that hot coffee can cause burns. As we studied in Chapters 5 and 6 (which discuss negligence), there is no duty to warn where the danger is obvious. Therefore, plaintiffs seeking compensation for injuries resulting from spilled coffee are usually not successful unless they can show that the coffee was served at too high a temperature or the cup and lid were designed such that the possibility of injury was increased. Thus, a woman who was burned from hot chocolate that was served at a customary temperature in a suitable cup with a lid was denied recovery.[33]

In another McDonald's case, the patron filed a lawsuit based on injuries he sustained when three large cups of coffee that he ordered from McDonald's drive-thru fell out of a cup holder. There was no evidence that the coffee served was too hot. Plaintiff had coffee from this McDonald's before, so he is presumed to know about

[30] *McFadden v. Staley,* 687 So.2d 357 (Fla. 1997)
[31] *Farrenholz v. Mad Crab, Inc.,* 2000 WL 1433596 (Ohio. 2000)
[32] *Gentile v. Stay Slim, Inc.,* 819 N.Y.S.2d 848 (N.Y. 2006)
[33] *Martinelli v. Custom Accessories, Inc.,* 2002 WL 1489610 (Mass. 2002)

the inherent danger of hot coffee. Accordingly, McDonald's had no duty to provide additional warnings to the plaintiff, a regular coffee drinker. The Court stated "the world in which we live is an imperfect one, one in which accidents will happen due to no one's negligence. The present case represents such instance. The growing tendency of the victims of accidents and their attorneys to always attempt to find a reason to blame someone else to obtain compensation is disturbing where any reasonable person should recognize that the injury was not another person's fault."[34]

In another case plaintiff, while sitting in a car, accepted from a co-worker a tray with five cups of coffee that had just been purchased. The tray had only four cupholders. When the tray was passed to plaintiff the co-worker warned her that the tray was "very flimsy" and "very wobbly." Nonetheless plaintiff carried the tray on her lap. As the co-worker drove the car over a speed bump the cups fell and the contents burned plaintiff. The court denied recovery notwithstanding the ineffective tray, finding that plaintiff knew of the risk caused by the coffee being hot and the tray being flimsy, and so she assumed the risk by holding the tray on her lap.[35] Similarly, a seller of hot tea was not liable where plaintiff was injured when the water spilled as she lifted the lid. The seller utilized two cellulose cups to serve the tea—one inside the other. The court refused to fault the seller, noting "Double cupping is a method well known in the industry as a way of preventing a cup of hot tea from burning one's hand."[36] A plaintiff injured from hot water was denied a remedy against the manufacturer of the hot water dispenser where the appliance emitted steam. The court noted that steam is generally known to indicate hot water which in turn is generally known to cause burns if spilled on skin.[37]

To avoid liability in this type of case and/or to protect patrons from injury, a restaurant should take several precautions. The temperature at which the drink is served should not be higher than industry standards. Automatic tea and coffee makers can be preset to serve the drink at a safe-to-dispense temperature. Lids should be provided for carry-out cups. If hot beverages are served at a buffet, diners should have the option of putting a cap on the cup to avoid spilling while returning to their seats. However, at least one court has found that the failure of a coffee seller to provide lids did not result in liability. Instead, the court determined that injuries usually result from the negligence of the beverage drinker or the inadvertent involvement of a third party who, for example, might have jostled the drinker.[38]

If tops are provided, they should have a lift-off tab so customers can add sugar, cream, or other customary additives without having to totally remove the cap. Waitstaff should avoid placing hot beverages near a child. A Pizza Hut was liable for negligence where a waitress placed hot dipping sauce within reach of a three-year-old who spilled it and suffered burns. In a comparative negligence allocation, the court attributed 70 percent of fault to the restaurant and 30 percent to the parents for "lack of due diligence in their supervision" of their young son.[39] Finally, if the drink is extremely hot, warn the customer either orally when the beverage is served, or

34 *Triche v. McDonald's Corporation d/b/a McDonald's Restaurant*, 164 So.3d 253 (La. 2014)
35 *Bernath v. People Success, Inc.*, 619 S.E.2d 378 (Ga. 2005)
36 *Fung-Yee Ng v. Barnes and Noble, Inc.*, 764 N.Y.S.2d 183 (N.Y. 2003)
37 *Kessel v. Stansfield Vending, Inc.*, 714 N.W.2d 206 (Wisc. 2006)
38 *Kessel v. Stansfield Vending, Inc.*, 714 N.W.2d 206 (Wisc. 2006)
39 *Lavergne v. America's Pizza Co., LLC*, 838 So.2d 845 (La. 2003)

in writing by placing a notice on the cup. McDonald's and virtually all dispensers of hot beverages now place such a warning on cups. McDonald's states, "Caution: Contents Hot." Cups at Starbucks, the coffee chain, state, "Careful, the beverage you are about to enjoy is extremely hot." Both notices alert the customer to be cautious.

Case Example 11-4 illustrates a number of principles relevant to liability associated with hot beverages.

CASE EXAMPLE 11-4

Oubre v. E-Z Serve Corp.

713 So.2d 818 (La. 1998)

…Plaintiff sued E-Z Serve [a convenience store] for burns she sustained from spilling in her lap, while riding in a car, a cup of hot coffee just purchased from E-Z Serve.

The record shows that plaintiff was a passenger in the back seat of a car driven by her husband. They stopped at an E-Z Serve in LaPlace where her husband and another passenger went inside to purchase breakfast. Plaintiff received a hot dog and a cup of coffee. The group left the E-Z Serve, driving a short distance away when, for unknown reasons, plaintiff spilled the coffee in her lap. She was wearing cotton sweat pants at the time, which she alleged trapped the hot coffee and produced a serious second-degree burn on her thigh.

Plaintiff alleged that the coffee was unreasonably hot, that E-Z Serve failed to warn consumers that the coffee was unreasonably hot, and other acts of negligence….

E-Z Serve's evidence included an affidavit from Glen Blackwell, who was employed by Standard Coffee Services as Manager of Field Services. He stated that he had 16 years as a technician and supervisor in Standard's repair shop, and that he was familiar with the operation and repair of the Bunn-O-Matic, the same brand of machine that E-Z Serve used to brew and serve coffee. He stated that the brewing process starts with water being heated in a tank, controlled by a thermostat. The brewing water then exits a spray head at the top of the brewing funnel. Customarily, the temperature of the water at the time it exits the spray head is 195 degrees Fahrenheit, plus or minus 5 degrees. This is the temperature at which the oil and flavor is released from the coffee in the brewing funnel. The brewed coffee drips into a decanter or beaker through the bottom of the brewing funnel. Customarily the coffee has cooled approximately 5 degrees from the temperature of the water at the top of the spray head. Immediately after the coffee has finished dripping into the beaker and the brewing cycle is complete, its temperature is customarily between 175–185 degrees Fahrenheit. The warming plate under the coffee decanter maintains the coffee's temperature at approximately 175 degrees, which is the temperature determined by the coffee industry as the one at which optimum flavor is retained. The temperature of the coffee will continue to decline over time stabilizing at approximately 155 degrees Fahrenheit….

E-Z Serve noted that it is customary to serve coffee hot, because the heat is needed to release the flavor from the beans, and consumers desire to purchase their coffee hot, not tepid….

The fact that the coffee was hot enough to cause injury if not properly handled does not mean that it was defective or negligently served. Where, as here, a product by its very nature had a dangerous attribute, liability is imposed only when the product has an attribute not reasonably contemplated by the purchaser or is unreasonably dangerous for its intended use. Since plaintiff clearly intended to purchase hot coffee, plaintiff must present evidentiary facts establishing that the coffee served by defendant was defective or unreasonably dangerous, or negligently served…. Plaintiff did not refute defendant's evidence of the accepted standard of coffee temperature, nor did she produce any evidence that her cup of coffee was super-hot or hotter than normal. Moreover, the record shows that plaintiff was a frequent user of coffee, that she had purchased coffee from E-Z Serve before the incident, and has done so since.

Accordingly judgment for defendant.

CASE QUESTION

1. Given that the plaintiff was injured by the temperature of the coffee, why was the seller not liable?

Foodborne Illnesses

Restaurants must take precautions to protect against spreading foodborne illnesses. These are illnesses caused by consuming foods or beverages contaminated with any of a variety of bacteria, viruses, or parasites. Usually proper handling will eliminate the risks. Failure of a restaurant to follow safeguards can result in liability if a diner becomes ill from eating improperly prepared food.

Some of the more common foodborne infections are caused by salmonella or *E. coli*. Salmonella is a type of bacteria that causes typhoid fever and other intestinal infec-

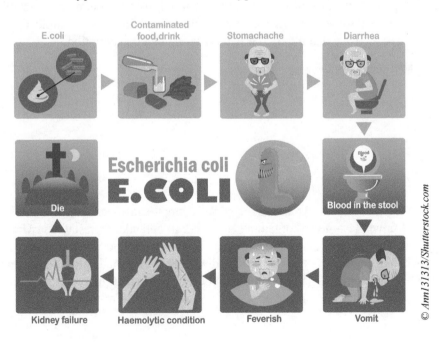

tions. It is often found in uncooked eggs, poultry, and meat. Proper sanitation and cooking will greatly reduce the risk of salmonella infection. *E. coli*, also a bacterium, is another risk in many foods, especially uncooked or undercooked beef. Not only is the beef itself a potential problem, but if the workspace where infected meat is handled is not properly cleaned, other food prepared on the same counter may also become contaminated. Chipotle Mexican Grill had an outbreak of *E. coli* that put twenty-two people in the hospital and left 38 more ill. It was not known whether it was related to contaminated vegetables or beef. Produce such as spinach, sprouts, and lettuce have been responsible for a number of *E. coli* outbreaks across the country.

Trichinosis is an illness caused by eating raw or undercooked pork and wild game products infected with the larvae of a species of worm called trichinella. Infection from pork was once quite common, but is now relatively rare due to strict legislation prohibiting the feeding of raw meat garbage to hogs, and public awareness of the danger of eating raw or undercooked pork. Today, cases of trichinosis are more commonly associated with raw or undercooked game meats. Proper cooking eliminates the risk.

Restaurants should ensure that their chefs and kitchen staff have adequate training in food safety. It is critical that foods be properly prepared to protect diners' health and avoid liability.

Proof Problems Establishing Causation

An ill plaintiff in a breach of warranty action must prove that the food purchased at the defendant's establishment was the cause of the sickness. If a person eats in a restaurant or buys takeout food and later becomes ill, those facts alone are not sufficient proof that the food from the restaurant caused the illness. The food that made the plaintiff sick may have originated in the plaintiff's refrigerator or a different restaurant or a friend's house where the plaintiff may have eaten close in time to the onset of the illness. Additionally, the sickness may have been caused by something other than bad food. To win the case, the plaintiff must prove that food purchased from the defendant's establishment was unwholesome and was the cause of the illness. In Case Example 11-5, the plaintiff failed to prove that the food was unfit for human consumption.

CASE EXAMPLE 11-5

Brown v. City Sam Restaurants, Inc.

666 N.Y.S.2d 409 (N.Y. 1998)

…We agree with the court [of original jurisdiction] that it is mere speculation to attribute plaintiff's flulike symptoms to his consumption of unwholesome or contaminated lobster at defendant's restaurant where it is undisputed that plaintiff had eaten other foods earlier that day, that he had a known food allergy to some shellfish, that no one else in his dinner party became sick, and where his own medical evidence was inconclusive as to the cause of his symptoms.…Plaintiff would not be able prove that his symptoms were caused by ingestion of contaminated lobster, such being an essential element to this lawsuit.

Complaint dismissed.

CASE QUESTIONS

1. What is the significance of the fact that the plaintiff had a known food allergy to some shellfish?

2. What is the significance of the fact that no one else in the plaintiff's dinner party became ill?

In Case Example 11-6 the plaintiff was able to overcome the difficulties of proof and identify his illness as food poisoning and the defendant restaurant's food as the cause.

CASE EXAMPLE 11-6

Foster v. AFC Enterprises, Inc.

896 So.2d 293 (La., 2005)

On June 3, 2002 the Plaintiff John Foster, Jr., awoke and ate his standard breakfast of grits, bacon and eggs before leaving for his maintenance job. He testified that, between 11:00 and 11:30 a.m., he and a co-worker went to Church's Fried Chicken for lunch, where he ordered three pieces of chicken, French fries, and a cold drink. Mr. Foster further testified that he returned to work to eat his meal, finished his workday, and returned home in the afternoon. According to Mr. Foster, he did not eat anything else after lunch because he began vomiting and having stomach pains at approximately 7:00 p.m. that evening. His stomach pains and vomiting persisted until his wife took him to a hospital emergency room during the early morning hours of June 4.

Mr. Foster was admitted into the emergency room complaining of abdominal pain, nausea, and vomiting…. While in the emergency room Mr. Foster vomited a green liquid with food particles. Despite treatment in the emergency room, doctors were unable to control Mr. Foster's vomiting and he was admitted to the hospital. In his assessment Dr. Lubbos diagnosed Mr. Foster with "gastroenteritis that is most likely secondary to food poisoning with vomiting that is responding to conventional therapy."… Dr. Lubbos discharged Mr. Foster on June 4 with a final diagnosis of gastroenteritis with food poisoning. Mr. Foster testified that after returning home he continued to have stomach pains and feel nauseated and could not return to work for approximately three or four days.

Mr. Foster filed suit alleging that he "was advised that he was diagnosed with food poisoning" and "that the sole cause of his condition was the faulty preparation of the food prepared by the employees of defendant." Following a bench trial, the trial court found in favor of Mr. Foster. The defendants appealed.

To meet his burden of proof in a food poisoning case, the plaintiff must prove that the deleterious condition existed in the product when it was purchased. The plaintiff must further prove the existence of a relationship between the illness and the consumption of the food. In fulfilling this burden of proof, it is not necessary for the consumer to negate every conceivable cause but he must show that it is more likely than not that the food's condition caused the injury of which he complains. The courts have never compelled a plaintiff to produce an actual analysis of the food consumed in order to establish its unwholesome condition.... Rather, the courts have been willing to infer the deleterious nature of the food consumed from the circumstances surrounding the illness. In all of the cases in which there has been successful recovery, the plaintiff has shown that the food was consumed by him, and that no other food which might reasonably be assumed to have caused the illness had been consumed within a number of hours before or after the consumption of the suspect product.

The plaintiff has also had medical opinions to the effect that it was probable that his illness was caused by the consumption of the particular product involved.... Furthermore, Mr. Foster does not have to establish that other people became ill from eating the chicken. Mr. Foster explained that the only other food he ate that day was his usual breakfast items. It was after he consumed the chicken that he fell violently ill. Dr. Lubbos testified that Mr. Foster had never had any stomach problems before. Dr. Lubbos explained that his diagnosis of food poisoning was based on the symptoms of abdominal pain, nausea, and vomiting and the history provided by Mr. Foster.

The trial court stated in its written reasons for judgment for plaintiff that "considering the testimony of the parties and Dr. Lubbos' diagnosis at the time he first examined plaintiff, the Court finds that it is more probable than not that plaintiff's condition was the result of food-poisoning."

Based on the entirety of the evidence, we cannot say that the trial court was clearly wrong in its decision that Mr. Foster met his burden of proving that the chicken he received at the defendant's place of business was served to him in a deleterious condition and that the consumption of that chicken actually caused his injuries.... His own treating physician released him from the hospital with a diagnosis of food poisoning as the most probable cause of his sudden stomach illness. There was also an absence of evidence that Mr. Foster had ever suffered any stomach problems either before or after this incident. Therefore, we find that the trial court could conclude that more probably than not Mr. Foster's condition was caused by chicken from Church's contaminated with food poisoning that he had eaten before he got sick.

In response all Church's offered was an affidavit that no one else made a claim that they had gotten sick that day from the chicken. It could have been that no one reported their illness or that Mr. Foster was the only person served from a particular batch of chicken that somehow got contaminated. Furthermore, there was no evidence or testimony that this was not food poisoning.

For the reasons set forth in this opinion the judgment of the trial court is affirmed.

CASE QUESTION

1. What evidence was critical to the court's determination that plaintiff suffered food poisoning caused by chicken eaten at Church's?

In a case in which the plaintiff alleged flulike symptoms from the presence of a worm in a can of string beans purchased at a grocery store, the court dismissed the complaint due to the plaintiff's failure to prove the cause of her illness was the worm. Said the court, "The mere fact that the plaintiff became nauseous about one-half hour after consuming some of the contents of the can is insufficient [to avoid dismissal of the complaint]. There are many different causes of nausea, vomiting and stomach distress, which the plaintiff experienced. Moreover, the report of the plaintiff's own examining physician, in describing her visit to his office the day after the alleged incident, makes no reference to the incident."...[40]

Similarly, a diner at a Kentucky Fried Chicken (KFC) noticed that his chicken "smelled kind of funny" and "didn't taste right." A day and several meals later, he developed severe abdominal pains. A doctor stated that his condition was consistent with improperly cooked poultry or meat but "chicken was at the top of the list" of culprits. The plaintiff had eaten bacon since his KFC meal. The trial court dismissed the case, ruling that the proof of proximate cause between the chicken and the illness was insufficient. The appellate court reversed and ordered that the case proceed to trial so that a jury could decide whether the evidence of proximate cause connecting the two was sufficient.[41]

Privity of Contract

Under common law, a direct contractual relationship was required between the plaintiff and the defendant in a breach of warranty action. The relationship between parties to a contract is called **privity of contract.** If you go into a store and purchase a can of corn and the corn is adulterated and makes you ill, you will be able to sue the store because you were in privity of contract with it. If, however, you ate the corn as a guest at a wedding reception held at a restaurant, you are not in privity of contract with the restaurant and so your right to sue the restaurant may be questioned.

privity of contract
A contractual relationship that exists between two parties.

All states have relaxed the requirement of privity to some extent. An example is provided by a case in which a hotel guest invited a friend to lunch at the hotel. The friend was injured by a piece of glass in a roll. The bill for the meal was paid by the hotel guest. When the friend sued the hotel, it denied liability on the ground she was not in privity of contract with the hotel. The court rejected this argument, holding that the hotel, by accepting the plaintiff's order, impliedly contracted with her even though she did not pay the bill.[42] Another state with a more rigid approach to privity might have held against the plaintiff.

When the UCC was adopted, the states were in disagreement about how much to relax the privity rule. To accommodate all positions, the UCC contains three different rules concerning privity; each state selects the one it prefers. The most restrictive option limits the benefits of the warranty to the buyer, the buyer's family, and the buyer's household guests. The broadest alternative covers any person who may reasonably be expected to consume the food.[43]

---

[40] *Valenti v. Great Atlantic & Pacific Tea Company,* 615 N.Y.S.2d 84 (N.Y. 1994)
[41] *McCarley v. West Quality Food Service,* 960 S.W.2d 585 (Tenn. 1998)
[42] *Conklin v. Hotel Waldorf Astoria,* 161 N.Y.S. 2d 205 (N.Y. 1957)
[43] UCC 2-318

strict products liability
The doctrine that imposes liability on the seller of a defective product without regard to negligence.

To bypass the privity requirement, most states have adopted a related cause of action called **strict products liability** that is based in tort law rather than contract; thus, privity is not required. To sue in strict products liability, a plaintiff must prove only three elements:

1. The defendant sold a product in a defective condition, such as food that was unhealthy;

2. The plaintiff was injured; and

3. The injury was caused by the defect.

An example is a hamburger purchased at a restaurant that contained a hard piece of plastic, causing the customer to choke and become ill.[44]

While strict products liability may seem a lot like breach of warranty of merchantability, the former eliminates the requirement of privity and enhances a plaintiff's chances of success in a lawsuit based on defective food.

For example, a restaurant unknowingly bought eggs contaminated with salmonella. The presence of the salmonella deemed the eggs defective. An employee of the restaurant ate some of the eggs and became ill. The employee could sue the supplier for strict products liability although the employee was not in privity with the supplier.[45]

For the purposes of a lawsuit in strict products liability, food is defective if it is adulterated, contains foreign or unexpected objects, or is otherwise not fit for human consumption. If a diner becomes ill from food, but the cause is inherent in the food, poses no threat to most people, and the restaurant took precautionary measures to protect diners from the illness, the food will not be considered defective. For example, a patron of a Louisiana restaurant died from eating oysters that contained a rare bacterium that poses no threat to a healthy person but can be lethal to someone with a weakened immune system. His family sued the restaurant based on strict products liability. The evidence established that the bacteria were in the oysters when they were harvested from the sea and have no effect on the large majority of the population. Also, the restaurant took many precautions to prevent contamination of the oysters. Restaurant employees carefully stocked and refrigerated the oysters, and restaurant personnel used approved sanitary procedures for shucking them. Similarly, the supplier followed state regulations, purchasing oysters only from licensed fishermen who harvested from state-approved oyster beds. Based on these facts, the court held the oysters were not defective and therefore the restaurant was not liable in strict products liability.[46]

---

[44] *Williams v. McDonald's of Torrington,* 1997 WL 276308 (Conn. 1997)
[45] *Bacci Restaurant v. Sunrise Produce Co.,* 1995 WL 774387 (Conn. 1995)
[46] *Simeon v. The Sweet Pepper Grill,* 618 So.2d 848 (La. 1993)

Statutory Violations

Various state statutes require restaurateurs to follow specified mandates in the preparation of food. For example, in Case Example 11-3, a state law required that restaurants warn patrons of known risks associated with food products. Violations can result in liability to customers who become ill, fines imposed by the state, and in circumstances where the violation creates serious risks of injury, temporary or permanent closure of the business.[47]

Negligence

An additional basis for suing a restaurant that serves unhealthy food is negligence. In these cases an injured diner claims that the restaurant was careless while preparing the food and that inattentiveness led to the meal being tainted. For example, a restaurant that served a glass of water to a diner was liable for negligence where the water was contaminated with detergent due to an employee's carelessness, and the guest became ill as a result.[48]

Similarly, a restaurant would be liable in negligence if a food preparer, after handling tainted meat on a kitchen surface, failed to clean the space adequately before preparing another food product on the same surface, causing contamination of the second item.

Choice of Action

A diner who is served defective food may have several bases on which to sue: breach of warranty, strict products liability, statutory violation, and negligence. How does the plaintiff determine on which ground(s) to sue? In some states a statute limits the plaintiff to one cause of action. Absent such a law, the plaintiff should include in the complaint all theories that are possibly applicable, hoping to prove at least one. For example, a restaurant diner who found a roach on his pizza sued the restaurant and referenced breach of warranty, strict products liability, and negligence causes of action is his complaint.[49] If at trial plaintiff is able to prove more than one ground for recovery, he will nonetheless collect only once for his damages.

Customers with Allergies

Restaurant patrons frequently request that certain ingredients be eliminated from their food. Some of these requests are prompted by allergies. Servers should be trained to view these requests seriously and relay them to the food preparers. If a restaurant fails to honor such requests and the customer suffers an allergic reaction from having eaten the offending food, the restaurant may be liable. In one case, a child's mother sent back a serving of ice cream because it contained nuts, to which the child was allergic. The restaurant merely scraped off the nuts and squirted some

---

[47] *Bergeron v. Jazz Seafood & Steakhouse*, 64 So.3d 255 (La. 2011)
[48] *Waddell v. Shoney's, Inc.*, 664 So.2d 1134 (Fla. 1995)
[49] *Cooke v. Pizza Hut, Inc.*, 1994 WL 680051 (Del. 1994)

fresh whipped cream on top and returned the ice cream to the customer. The child ate the ice cream and went into anaphylactic shock from the residue of the nuts.

When food is rejected by a patron due to allergies, wise policy mandates that substitute food be served and that it be presented on a clean dish. If only the offending ingredient is removed and the balance of the food is returned to the customer on the same plate, the residue although small in amount, may be sufficient to cause an allergic reaction.

Some states have requirements for posting awareness of food allergies. The restaurants should prominently display in the staff area a poster relative to food allergy awareness. The poster shall include, but not be limited to, information regarding the risk of an allergic reaction and included on all menus a notice to customers of the customer's obligations to inform the server about any food allergies.

American Airlines, in its airline magazine, posts a warning regarding nut allergies. Even though the airline does not serve peanuts as a snack, it even warns the passengers that other served foods may contain peanut oil and that other passengers may bring peanuts or other nuts on board. They encourage fliers to take all precautions to prepare for the possibility of exposure.

Case Example 11-7 illustrates the situation where a customer fails to alert the restaurant about an allergy. In such case the restaurant is not liable if the guest suffers an allergic reaction. It is the duty of the guest to inform the server of any allergies that the guest may have. As you read this case, note the serious health condition an allergic reaction can trigger.

CASE EXAMPLE 11–7

Thompson v. East Pacific-Enterprises, Inc.

2003 WL 352914 (Wash. 2003)

…Debra Thompson, a registered nurse, was diagnosed with a peanut allergy when she was eight years old. She was aware that exposure to even a trace amount of peanut could trigger an allergic reaction. Thompson had experienced allergic reactions after eating in restaurants and she had previously been hospitalized because of an allergic reaction to walnuts. On the evening in question, Thompson and her co-worker, Peggy Riley, decided to order food from Genghis Khan, a restaurant, to be delivered to the ir place of employment. Thompson did not consult a menu before ordering. Although in her deposition Thompson stated that she always tries to make restaurant personnel aware of her allergies and tries to ascertain what is contained in food she orders, Thompson did not ask Riley to make these inquires. Riley placed the order over the telephone for several dishes, including almond chicken for Thompson. When Riley placed the order, she did not ask the Genghis Khan employee about the ingredients of the almond chicken dish nor did she make any special requests.

When the order was delivered, Thompson ate a piece of the almond chicken. She immediately felt the onset of an allergic reaction. She took the medication she had in her possession to arrest the symptoms, but they continued to worsen and she was taken to the emergency room for treatment.

Upon arrival in the emergency room, Thompson lost consciousness and went into anaphylactic shock. She suffered respiratory arrest and had a heart attack. She was stabilized and discharged from the hospital after nine days. Thompson's treating physicians diagnosed her with "anaphylaxis, felt secondary to peanuts."

Thompson and her family members filed suit against Genghis Khan Restaurant. Genghis Khan's owner, manager and head cook stated that the orders from that day revealed no special requests for Riley's order. He also described the restaurant's recipe for almond chicken, which does not call for peanuts.

Thompson submitted a declaration from a physician stating that peanut allergy is a common allegy that affects approximately two million people in the United States, and is probably the most common cause of death caused by allergic reaction. She also submitted a declaration of Jon Alberts, an owner of an Asian restaurant. Alberts expressed the opinion that it is "common knowledge" in the restaurant industry that many people are allergic to peanut and peanut products. Alberts described the procedures used in his restaurant to prevent peanut and peanut products from contaminating other dishes.

Thompson's primary argument on appeal is that Genghis Khan's menu should have warned that the almond chicken entree might contain trace amounts of peanut due to cross-contamination and the failure to give such a warning rendered the product not reasonably safe.

[The court rejected Thompson's arguments and decided in favor of the restaurant noting] Thompson did not inform the restaurant of her allergy....

We affirm the trial court's decision to grant Genghis Khan's motion for summary judgment....

CASE QUESTIONS

1. Do you agree with the decision? Why or why not?

2. Would the outcome have been different if Thompson had advised Genghis Khan of her allergy to peanuts? Why or why not?

3. Do you think restaurants should be required to ask patrons if they have food allergies? Why or why not?

The Food and Drug Administration (FDA) is a federal agency that oversees the food industry. Its objectives include promoting public health by ensuring foods are safe, wholesome, sanitary, and properly labeled. Among the FDA's undertakings is a Food Code, which is a set of model ordinances that provides guidance on standards and practices for the achievement of food safety in restaurants and other segments of the food industry.

An important component of the Food Code is the Hazard Analysis Critical Control Point (HACCP) system, a quality assurance scheme to identify and minimize spoilage and contamination problems during food manufacturing and service. HACCP focuses on managing risks at each of ten operating activities, also known as control points, common to all food service establishments.[50] Such a system requires food producers and servers to systematically look at hazards that can cause spoilage or contamination and identify how to avoid them. Among the control methods utilized are cooking, refrigeration, packaging, monitoring, and employee handwashing. The implementation of an HACCP quality control system is recognized as an essential element of managing the operations of a food-service facility. Adopting and complying with such a system helps prevent and mitigate legal liability for defective food. Books are available that explain the program in detail and should be a part of a restaurateur's library.

Hand-Washing by Food Preparers

Employee hand-washing is a critical control point (CCP) in food safety and prevention plans. The reason is this: If food handlers (cooks and servers) come to work when they are not well, their illness may be transferred to customers. One illness transferable in this way is hepatitis, which infects the liver. It can be spread by a food preparer inadequately washing his hands after using the restroom and before handling food. If an infected employee is discovered, public officials will likely become involved and a public announcement will be made to encourage at-risk patrons to seek treatment.

In addition to harming a customer, negative publicity about an eatery can seriously hurt its business. To safeguard against this, management should ensure that employees are knowledgeable about proper hand-washing procedures and compliant with them. Signs in bathrooms should remind employees to cleanse their hands properly after using the facilities.

False Food Claims

Restaurants often make various claims about the food they sell. These representations may refer to health or nutritional benefits, methods of preparation, or other

---

[50] The ten points are menu planning, purchasing, receiving, storing, issuing, preparing, cooking, holding, serving, and cleaning/maintenance.

attributes. The law requires that such representations be truthful. False claims can lead to prosecution.

Truth-in-Menu Laws

Both federal and state laws require accuracy in representations made by restaurants about the food they serve. Federal laws regulating menu descriptions apply only to items that are advertised with a nutrient or health claim such as "low fat" or "heart healthy." If these terms are used, the associated food product must satisfy the statute's definition. For example, to qualify as "low fat," the serving size of the food product must contain no more than three grams of fat. Notwithstanding the limited scope of federal regulations, many restaurants strive for accurate menu descriptions out of concern for state laws, quality assurance, and consumer confidence. Most states have laws seeking to eliminate misleading food advertisements and labels. Some states have laws that specifically outlaw untruthful statements on menus. Other states have general statutes that bar "unfair trade practices" that have been interpreted to apply to fraudulent food claims. Controversies can result from omitting ingredients, mistaking a product's origin, misdescribing a dish, or inaccurately identifying the cooking method. For example, orange juice made from concentrate cannot be promoted as "fresh." Syrup promoted as "made in Vermont" must have been made in Vermont. This is because the public perceives that syrup from Vermont has attributes that enhance the taste and are not present in syrup originating elsewhere. Likewise, Maine lobster is considered sweeter than like crustaceans caught elsewhere. If a lobster was not caught in Maine, it cannot be advertised as Maine lobster.

Sometimes when the name of a food product references a geographical place, that location does not denote place of origin and can be used regardless of where the food was made. For example, the word *Swiss*, when used with cheese, describes the type of cheese and not the country in which it is made. Similarly the name *Kentucky Fried Chicken* does not suggest that the chicken was raised in Kentucky, nor does French dressing indicate the condiment's country of origin.

In a lawsuit involving another type of misleading food claim, Kentucky Fried Chicken was forced to rename its "Lite and Crispy" chicken "Skinfree Crispy" and pay a fine of $25,000. Whereas the term *lite* usually suggests reduced calories, KFC's "Lite and Crispy" chicken was virtually identical in calories to the original recipe.

Fish or other products that have been frozen cannot be sold as "fresh." Florida has truth in menu laws that make it illegal to advertise one species of fish and then serve another. Grouper is a popular fish in seafood restaurants in Florida, but many times other fish are served in its place. The penalties can be imposed on the fisherman, exporters, importers, and distributors. Ultimately, it is the restaurant that will also bear strict liability.

Inaccurate cooking methods stated on a menu should be corrected. A fastfood chain was challenged by a consumer watchdog agency for using the word "grilled" to describe a chicken sandwich. In fact, the chicken patties were precooked in a steam oven and the brown marks, which inferred searing of the meat on a grill, were applied by a machine called a heat-and-control rotary brander. The patties were then frozen and transported to restaurants, where they were thawed and cooked in a two-sided hot plate. In response to the inquiry the chain discontinued using the term "grilled" in connection with the product.

Inaccurate weights of meats served at restaurants is another problem. Steaks may be on the menu at a certain weight, but the restaurant is basing their menu weight on the weight of the meat plus the juices. The customer expects the meat to weigh the advertised amount.

A growing number of people are vegetarians. Fast-food chains have attempted to attract these diners by providing vegetarian offerings. What constitutes "vegetarian" has been the subject of some dispute. One chain offered a Garden Veggie Pita labeled as a vegetarian meal in the company's nutritional brochure. The item was made with gelatin, a by-product of beef. When questioned, the chain explained that its suppliers had represented the product as vegetarian and so the misrepresentation was an "honest mistake." The chain removed the reference to vegetarian in the nutritional brochure.

To comply with the law and avoid customer displeasure, restaurants must pay close attention to accuracy in product descriptions. Failure to serve what is advertised would be a breach of warranty. There may also be statutory fines for each instance. This could give rise to a class-action suit.

Obesity and Accuracy in Advertising

Obesity is often described as an epidemic in this country. The incidence of obesity among adults has increased significantly in recent years and is currently estimated as 30 percent of United States adults 20 years of age or older.[51] For children and teens aged 6–19, 16 percent are overweight. Being overweight or obese increases the risk of many diseases and health conditions, including coronary heart disease, stroke, type 2 diabetes, sleep apnea and respiratory problems, some cancers (breast, colon, and endometrial), and more. Additionally, obesity is often accompanied by poor self-esteem. A lawsuit against McDonald's brought by the parents of several youngsters sought to impose liability on the restaurant chain for the "weight gain, obesity, hypertension, and elevated levels of LDL cholesterol" experienced by the plaintiffs, allegedly as a result of eating McDonald's food. Plaintiffs claimed they were misled to believe the fast food meals were healthful. The allegations underlying plaintiffs' claim were threefold:

1. The combined effect of McDonald's various promotional representations created the false impression that its food products were nutritionally beneficial and part of a healthy lifestyle if consumed daily.

---

[51] National Center for Health Statistics

2. McDonald's failed to adequately disclose that its use of certain additives and the manner of its food processing rendered certain of its foods substantially less healthy than represented.

3. The restaurant reneged on its promise to provide nutritional information to its New York customers.

McDonald's claimed in response that virtually everyone understands that hamburgers and French fries can cause obesity.

The court agreed that the risks of obesity were "open and obvious to a reasonable consumer" and dismissed the case.[52] Nonetheless, in response, many restaurants and other food providers have taken steps to ensure that healthy options and nutritional information are available at their establishments. For example, McDonald's has eliminated supersizing and added salads and fruit to its menu. All fast food establishments developed brochures to disseminate nutritional information about its products.

Fast-food establishments are not the only businesses catering to customers' health. For example, many school systems hve removed soft drinks to help reduce childhood obesity.

Efforts by Congress to pass a bill protecting eateries from obesity-related lawsuits have not been successful. However, more than half the states have adopted laws protecting the restaurant industry form such lawsuits.

Trans Fats

New York City has adopted legislation that precludes the use of trans fats by restaurants. Additional localities have adopted or are considering such bans. Numerous major food companies have done the same. Studies show that people living in areas that adopted the bans on transfats had fewer hospitalizations for heart attack and stroke compared to residents in areas without restrictions. The Food and Drug Administration issued a regulation requiring food manufacturers to label the trans fat content of their products.

Food Labeling

As the public has become more concerned about health issues, including cholesterol and saturated fat intake, health claims have become a significant factor in consumers' choice of food products. Food producers have tried to capitalize on customers' interests in healthy foods. Too frequently, manufacturers have stretched the truth or made claims they could not substantiate.

An example of questionable claims is an advertisement for margarine, a product with a significant fat content, saying it is a "headstart to a healthier heart" and

---

[52] *Pelman v. McDonald's Corp.,* 396 F.3d 508 (N.Y. 2005)

"does your heart good." Similarly, advertisers have overused and misused words such as "light," "low-calorie," "low fat," and "low sodium."

The federal labeling law is known as the Nutrition Labeling and Education Act of 1990 (the "Act"). The FDA has promulgated regulations to enforce the Act. Some applications apply to packaged foods only, and some to food served in restaurants. The latest are expected to become effective in 2018. Both are discussed in the following sections.

Application to Packaged Foods

Mandatory nutritional labels are required for all packaged goods and they must contain the information specified in the following list, which enumerates what the Act requires:

1. Standardization of serving sizes. This is significant because information such as fat grams and calories are based on serving sizes. Before the effective date of the Act, food purveyors used varying serving sizes, making comparison shopping difficult. Companies often used an artificially small serving size, making the nutritional information such as calories and fat grams look unjustifiably attractive to health-conscious consumers.

2. Regulation and standardization of the use of words such as *light, cholesterol-free*, and *low calorie*

3. Mandatory labeling of fat content by weight, specifying both total fat and saturated fat

4. Mandatory labeling of fiber content by weight

5. Mandatory labeling of the content of the following as percentages of the United States Recommended Daily Allowance (RDA): total fat, saturated fat, cholesterol, sodium, carbohydrates, and fiber

6. Limitations on health claims. The statute specifies the permissible representation of the relationship between foods and disease avoidance. It permits only claims that the food "may" or "might" reduce the risk of disease and precludes statements that suggest a guaranteed reduction of risk.

Application to Restaurants

Many restaurants previously exaggerated the nutritional value of their food items. To address this, special regulations were promulgated for restaurants. Whenever a restaurant makes a claim about the nutritional content (e.g., "low sodium" or "light") or the healthfulness of a food product (e.g., "fiber helps to prevent cancer"), the restaurant is required to provide to patrons upon request the same information as is required to be on a label of a food package. As initially adopted, these regulations did not apply to health and nutritional-content claims made on menus, but rather only those made on signs, placards, or posters in the restaurant.

The menu exclusion was challenged in court by a public-interest consumer group. It noted that almost half the American food dollar is spent on food consumed away from home, and argued that restaurant menus often contain misleading or false representations about the nutritional and health value of the food. The court held the exclusion of menus from the regulations was unauthorized. As a result, all restaurants that make health or nutritional-content claims on their menus must provide the mandated nutritional information.[53]

However, the information was not required to be included on the menu. Instead, the information needed only to be available "upon request." Some restaurants provide fliers, brochures, or handbooks with calorie, fat gram, and related information, even in the absence of a request, which are popular with certain customers. Other restaurants may orally provide the information when asked by a customer.

How do restaurants determine the nutritional content of their food? The regulations provide that restaurants can rely upon information from nutrient databases, cookbooks, and analyses, "or other reasonable bases that provide assurance that the food or meal meets the nutrient requirements for the claim."[54]

Further, if a restaurant uses as descriptors of its menu items any terms defined by the Act or regulations, the restaurant must comply with those definitions. Thus, if a restaurant promotes a menu item as "light," that item must meet the standard for that term as developed by the FDA.

Recently, the FDA promulgated menu-labeling regulations. These regulations apply to restaurants and similar retail food establishments with twenty or more locations operating under the same name and serving substantially the same menu items. These eateries are required to post "clearly and conspicuously" calorie information for standard menu items and provide guests with additional nutrition information upon request. In addition, a statement regarding recommended calorie intake must be included.

Kosher Foods

Kosher is a designation referring to food prepared consistent with Jewish religious requirements. For example, those mandates specify the method of slaughter of animals that produce meat and the time within which processing must occur following slaughter. The requirements also prohibit eating certain foods, such as pork and shellfish, regardless of the method of slaughter or preparation. Thus, for example, lobster, crab, and scallops are prohibited. Additionally, dairy and meat products cannot be served at the same meal.

kosher
A designation referring to food prepared consistent with Jewish religious requirements.

The preparation of kosher food is supervised by a rabbi (Jewish clergy) or his or her designee. Without the rabbi's verification that the food has been properly prepared to merit the designation of kosher, it cannot be advertised as such.

When food is labeled as kosher, the label suggests the food has been prepared in accordance with religious requirements. People who "keep kosher"—that is, eat

---

[53] *Public Citizen, Inc. v. Shalala*, 932 F. Supp. 13 (D.C. 1996)
[54] 21 C.F.R. Section 101.10

only food that is kosher—have a right to expect that a restaurant advertising kosher food will serve food prepared as required by applicable rules.

Laws in most states prohibit advertising food as kosher unless it is. Promoting nonkosher food as kosher violates these laws. Many states treat such conduct as criminal, subjecting wrongdoers to potential jail terms and fines.

Smoking Restrictions

Many states and localities have adopted laws that restrict or prohibit smoking in many public buildings, including restaurants and bars. Typically trade associations of restaurants and bars have lobbied vigorously against these laws, fearing they would affect a reduction in business. The antismoking laws are based on findings that breathing secondhand smoke, which contains carcinogens, is a significant health hazard for nonsmokers as well as smokers. Secondhand smoke consists of exhaled smoke from smokers and from smoldering cigarettes, cigars, or pipes, which smoke is then inhaled by others. This smoke contains many of the same harmful chemicals that a smoker inhales. Secondhand smoke can kill and cause irritation. It is estimated to cause approximately 3,000 lung cancer deaths in nonsmokers annually. Secondhand smoke can also cause heart disease, stroke, headaches, and nausea. It can exacerbate asthma and respiratory infections. The more a person is exposed to secondhand smoke, the greater the risk. The danger applies to customers of restaurants and bars, and even more so to service employees at these establishments. The latter are customarily exposed to significant amounts of secondhand smoke throughout their work shifts.

Typically, laws that restrict but do not prohibit smoking require that a restaurant designate a nonsmoking area and allocate a certain percentage of seating capacity to it, such as 70 percent. An issue in one case was whether a restaurant could include in the calculation of total square footage of the dining area a room designated for private parties and only intermittently available for public dining. If the room was included in the calculation, the permissible smoking area would be enlarged. The court held that such a room can be included.[55] In Florida stand-alone bars with no more than 10 percent revenues from food sales may allow smoking for its patrons.

Some statutes prohibit smoking in the restaurant area but permit it in an accessory bar, and/or prohibit drifting of smoke from a designated smoking area into a nonsmoking area.[56] Some restaurants, when cited for violating a smoking regulation, have challenged the regulation's validity on constitutional grounds. Generally these statutes have been upheld as appropriate means to protect public health.[57]

In another case, a restaurant association (an organization of restaurant owners) successfully challenged a city ordinance that banned smoking altogether because the ordinance was more restrictive than the related state statute. The state legis-

---

[55] *Bleiburg Restaurant, Inc. v. NYC Dept. of Health,* 658 N.Y.S.2d 574 (N.Y. 1997)
[56] See, for example, Arizona Code § 11–19 (A)(5)
[57] See, for example, *Taverns for Tots, Inc. v. City of Toledo,* 341 F.Supp.2d 844 (Ohio. 2004); *Tucson v. Grezafel,* 23 P.3d 675 (Ariz. 2001)

lature had adopted a statute permitting smoking in a portion of restaurant dining areas. The court held that the state statute controlled and the conflicting local ordinance was unenforceable.[58] Some states, however, allow local governments to adopt stricter restrictions than state law provides.

In localities where smoking is permitted in a portion of a restaurant, the space is usually defined as a percentage of the dining area. Restaurants often want to maximize the permissible smoking section to accommodate their smoking patrons. An avid cigar smoker challenged New York City's antismoking law, one of the toughest in the nation as it relates to cigars. He claimed no reliable scientific study had ever established that secondary cigar smoke was harmful. A court rejected his claim, finding sufficient basis for the position that secondary cigar smoke subjected nonsmokers to health risks.[59]

In some states there are exceptions that include casinos, private clubs, and cigar bars. As of January 2014, ten states (Alabama, Alaska, Kentucky, Mississippi, Missouri, Oklahoma, South Carolina, Texas, West Virginia, Wyoming) had not enacted statewide bans on smoking. Many colleges and universities prohibit smoking anywhere on campus.

Customers with illnesses such as asthma who find it particularly difficult to tolerate secondhand smoke have sued restaurants whose policies permit smoking. These cases have been limited in number because so many restaurants are now required by law to prohibit smoking. The cases that have been pursued are based on the Americans with Disabilities Act, which we studied in Chapter 3. They have been decided on a case-by-case basis and their outcome depends on the impact of prohibiting smoking on the facility's business. The greater the impact, the less likely the court will require that smoking be prohibited. Similarly, cases have been pursued by servers whose health is impacted by customers smoking. As with disabled customers, whether the restaurant is required to modify the smoking policy for employees depends on the impact on business a smoking prohibition would have. See the Chapter 14 discussion on employment and the Americans with Disabilities Act.

Generally, the enforcement mechanism for smoking regulations is the county board of health, and the penalty is a fine of several hundred dollars.

Safety Concerns Particular to Food Preparation

Some aspects of food service present particular safety risks to employees. The restaurateur has a duty to exercise reasonable care to minimize these risks.

---

[58] *Michigan Restaurant Association v. City of Marquette,* 626 N.W.2d 418 (Mich. 2001)
[59] *Beatie v. City of NY,* N.Y.L.J. (N.Y. Aug. 7, 1996)

Food Preparation

Kitchen areas are inherently dangerous. Most of the equipment can cause serious injuries if misused, such as meat cutters, grills, deep-fat fryers, knives, and stoves. In Chapter 6 we discussed the hazards associated with flaming foods, which can cause injury to employees and customers. Another danger is dropped food, which can result in slip-and-fall cases.

A direct relationship exists between the quality of an accident-prevention program and the frequency and severity of accidents. Managers must devise policies to encourage safety in the food-preparation process. Employee training is imperative.

Risks Associated with Donated Foods

A restaurant with unused food may be motivated to give it to a charitable organization. Often food is donated because it is near the recommended last day of use or it is left over from an event for which large amounts of food were prepared. In either circumstance, the donated food may be at risk for spoilage. Good intentions will not relieve the restaurant from liability for rancid or defective food. Food served beyond the recommended last date of use may be spoiled. Prepared food that has been displayed for awhile may have deteriorated without timely refrigeration or other preservation measures. Good managers will verify the condition of the food before it is donated to employees or people in need.

The Good Samaritan Food Donation Act is a federal law that protects good faith donors from civil and criminal liability should the donated food later cause harm to the recipients. The donor may still be liable if there was gross negligence or intentional misconduct by the donor. Most states have passed similar good samaritan laws that provide protection against liability for good faith donors. The purpose of these laws is to encourage restaurants, grocery stores, and others to donate healthy food that would otherwise go to waste.

Summary

Various laws protect patrons of restaurants against dangers of adulterated and mis-labeled food. These laws include the implied warranty of merchantability, strict products liability, and negligence.

Claims made about food—including health or nutritional benefits, methods of preparation, and other attributes—must be accurate and comply with any statutory definitions. Labeling laws mandate disclosure of certain nutritional information.

Food preparation and service present particular safety issues that should be addressed. These include proper use of equipment, safeguards related to service of hot beverages, adequate training on the preparation and service of flambé dishes, and precautions to avoid dropped food.

Preventive Law Tips for Managers

- *Inspect food carefully before it is served to ensure it is fit for human consumption.* A restaurant that serves inedible food will be liable for breach of the warranty of merchantability. Liability will result, even if the restaurant is not aware that the food is unwholesome. To minimize the chances of serving unhealthy food, all food should be carefully inspected before it is used as an ingredient in a recipe and before it is served. Any unfit food should be removed, including adulterated food, foreign objects, and natural objects that a customer may not expect that can cause injury.

- *Cook pork and game meats thoroughly to destroy the parasite that causes trichinosis.* Those products, when uncooked contain a parasite that can cause the life-threatening disease of trichinosis. The parasite is killed upon proper cooking. To ensure restaurant patrons are not exposed to the risk of the disease, all pork and game meats should be thoroughly cooked before serving.

- *Be sure all claims made about food offered at a restaurant are accurate.* The law requires that only truthful claims be made about food offered to restaurant patrons. Descriptions on menus such as "fresh," "made in Vermont," or "zero cholesterol" must be truthful. If a restaurant uses words that are standardized by regulations of the Food and Drug Administration (FDA) pursuant to the Nutrition Labeling and Education Act, such as light or low-calorie, the food item must meet the FDA standards. If food is promoted as kosher, it must meet the requirements mandated for that designation.

- *If a hotel recommends food from a restaurant not operated by the hotel, it should inspect the restaurant periodically to verify that sanitation, food preparation, and management standards are being met.* A guest injured by food from a restaurant promoted by a hotel may have a cause of action against the hotel if the latter has not assessed the operational practices of the restaurant on a regular basis. To protect itself from liability, a hotel that encourages its guests to dine in a particular restaurant should satisfy itself periodically that the restaurant is worthy of the endorsement.

■ *Comply with smoking restrictions imposed on hospitality facilities.* Most states and many localities have adopted smoking restrictions that require restaurants to either ban smoking or set aside a certain percentage of seating capacity for use by nonsmoking diners. Know the law in your area and do whatever is necessary to comply.

■ *Attempt to reduce the effects of secondhand smoke.* Secondhand smoke can become an issue to customers and employees with respiratory illnesses or those with a general concern about their health. Lawsuits may be pursued under the Americans with Disabilities Act. Methods to reduce the effects of secondhand smoke, such as specially designed ventilation systems, should be investigated and seriously considered.

■ *Adopt procedures for use and maintenance of kitchen appliances to minimize injuries to employees.* Kitchens, by necessity, contain many potentially dangerous appliances and utensils including stoves, grills, meat cutters, knives, and deepfat fryers. Procedures should be adopted for their use and maintenance to ensure maximum safety. Other components of a good risk-reduction plan are employee training and frequent monitoring of kitchen operations by managers.

■ *Develop and strictly follow a Hazard Analysis Critical Control Point System.* Such systems help to ensure that food served at restaurants is safe and wholesome by promoting development of prevention methods directed at hazards that can cause spoilage or contamination. Components of any such system for restaurants should include training and enforcement relating to good handwashing procedures.

■ *Follow all relevant labeling laws.* Both long standing and recent regulations promulgated by the Food and Drug Adminstration pursuant to the Nutrition Labeling and Education Act mandate disclosure of various nutritional information. Additionally, the Act restricts the use of certain terms—such as light and low calorie—unless the product conforms to standardized definitions. Compliance with all related rules is required.

Review Questions

1. What states have adopted the Uniform Commercial Code?

2. What does the warranty of merchantability guarantee?

3. What is the difference between the foreign/natural test and the reasonable/ expectation test?

4. What disease can be contracted by eating uncooked pork or game meat?

5. What bacteria can be found in oysters harvested in warm waters?

6. What does "privity of contract" mean? How does it impact a lawsuit involving the warranty of merchantability?

7. What is strict products liability?

8. What is meant by "truth in menu"?

9. What impact does the 1990 Nutrition Education and Labeling Act have on restaurants?

10. What is kosher food?

11. Why do some states limit smoking in restaurants?

12. What safety precautions are necessary to avoid injuries occurring to employees in a restaurant kitchen?

Discussion Questions

1. If you are the manager of a restaurant, would you prefer that the foreign/ natural test or reasonable/expectation test apply? Why? Is it reasonable to believe that a plaintiff who is successful under the foreign/natural test would always be successful under the reasonable/expectation test?

2. Do you agree with the decision in *Webster v. Blue Ship Tea Room, Inc.* involving the bone in the fish chowder? Why or why not? Do you think that different states could have different reasonable expectations for the reasonable/expectation test?

3. Dan ate breakfast at a restaurant known as Pam's Breakfast Shop. He later became ill. Are these facts sufficient to establish that Pam's Breakfast Shop sold unwholesome food? Why or why not? If not, what more is needed?

4. Must a plaintiff suing for breach of the warranty of merchantability show that the defendant was negligent? Why or why not?

5. What differentiates strict products liability from the warranty of merchantability?

6. What steps should a restaurant manager take to ensure that the menu contains no inaccurate statements?

7. Sam ate a dozen oysters at a restaurant and became very ill. He brought a lawsuit against the restaurant. Sam had a history of liver problems. What facts must he establish to be successful in this case?

Application Questions

1. Mandy, manager of a cafeteria at a large corporation, purchased a new freezer for the kitchen. It operated at a temperature a few degrees above the setting. Is the freezer merchantable? Why or why not?

2. A hotel chain and a well-known hamburger fast-food chain are negotiating a contract that would authorize the hotel to use the fast-food chain's name on the hotel's room-service menu to promote the sale of hamburgers. What terms will the hamburger company want to include in the contract? Why? What terms will the hotel want included? Why?

3. Blatnik's Restaurant served Andrew coffee. Andrew spilled the coffee on his legs and was injured. The cup did not have a warning stating that the coffee was hot. Will Andrew be successful in his lawsuit against the restaurant?

4. Look at a menu. Identify all the words whose meanings might be disputed by a diner who ordered the item and was disappointed.

5. An outdoor patio at a restaurant was the site of a post-football game party for the local high school. The restaurant, anticipating many hungry fans, prepared large quantities of picnic food (hot dogs, hamburgers, macaroni salad) and, at the appointed time, displayed it buffet style. Unfortunately, rain began in the middle of the game. As a result, many spectators left the game and so the crowd for the post-game party was much smaller than anticipated. Much of the buffet food was not eaten. The restaurant owner wants to donate the leftovers to a shelter for homeless people. What legal issues should the restaurant consider before making the donation?

Websites

Websites that will enhance your understanding of the material in this chapter include:

www.FDA.gov This is the official site of the Food and Drug Administration, the federal agency that oversees food products. Included on the site is information about food-borne illnesses, allergy risks from undeclared ingredients of food products, and food labeling, to mention but a few.

www.restaurant.org This is the site of the National Restaurant Association, a trade organization for restaurant owners and managers. Among the issues addressed are food safety and handling and how to elect pro-restaurant legislators.

www.nraef.org This is the official site of the National Restaurant Association Educational Foundation. This site provides information and training on such topics as safe service of food and regulatory requirements for restaurant safety.

CHAPTER 12

Liability and the Sale of Alcohol

LEARNING OUTCOMES:

- Appreciate the extent of the regulation of alcohol sales
- Know the categories of people to whom alcohol sales are prohibited
- Understand the consequences of selling alcohol illegally
- Familiarize with the Dram Shop Act and the liability for violation
- Learn the role of liquor liability insurance
- Know strategies to avoid liability
- Familiarize with miscellaneous liquor regulations

KEY TERMS

dram shop act   visibly intoxicated
liquor liability insurance

© Boule/Shutterstock.com

Introduction

The government has long been concerned about the sale of alcohol, and for good cause. If a vehicle is operated by a driver who has been drinking, his ability to operate and control the car is diminished. This causes many accidents, some fatal, others resulting in serious injury. In recent years, more than 17,000 deaths and 254,000 injuries occur annually as a result of alcohol-related traffic accidents. In an attempt to limit this type of bloodshed, each state highly regulates (restricts) the sale of liquor. Regulations include limitations on who can sell (a liquor license is required), who can buy, and even the days and times liquor can be sold.

Alcoholic Beverages and the Hospitality Industry

Restaurants and bars have various goals concerning the sale of alcohol, some of which are conflicting. On the one hand, hospitality facilities view liquor as a moneymaker. Many customers regularly have one or more drinks and the income from those sales can be substantial. On the other hand, restaurants and bars have significant motivation to moderate their promotion of alcohol. When enforcing liquor laws, the government shows no leniency; liquor laws are strictly enforced. Violation of these regulations can result in substantial liability. Potential consequences include revocation of the license to sell liquor, which may result in the business being forced to close; jail time; fines; legal fees; and payment for injuries and property damage in a civil suit. With these penalties at stake, an alcohol establishment is well-advised to strictly follow the law.

An additional concern for sellers of alcohol is that intoxicated persons are frequently belligerent and cause disturbances that interfere with other patrons. This may prompt customers to leave, resulting in lost business. If a fight results and another patron is injured, the bar may be liable.

License to Sell Liquor

No business can sell alcohol without first obtaining a liquor license from the state in which the bar or restaurant is located.

To obtain a license to sell alcohol, a restaurant or bar must apply to the appropriate government agency within the state. The agency will typically have a name like The Alcoholic Beverage Control Board or Liquor Licenses and Control. In most states, to qualify for a license the applicant must prove he has not abused liquor in the past, whether as a consumer, a seller, a driver, or otherwise; has not been convicted of a felony; and is otherwise of good character.

Applicants typically are required to answer questions such as: Have you ever been denied a liquor license? Have you ever had a liquor license suspended or revoked for a liquor law violation? Have you ever been convicted of a crime? Do you have any criminal charges pending? Are you currently on probation? Have you ever had any state-issued licenses suspended or revoked, including a driver's license? Additionally, applicants will be required to identify all their employers and residence addresses for the five years prior to the license application. The applicant will also be required to swear to the truth of his responses under penalty of perjury. If the information is false, the applicant will be guilty of a crime and face jail and fines.

A liquor license, once granted, may be revoked or suspended by the state if the licensee violates the liquor laws. For example, in a Pennsylvania case, the Plaintiff Club XS filed for a liquor license renewal application and the liquor control board denied the renewal due to two adjudicated citations and thirty-seven incidents of disturbance at the club or on nearby property. The disturbances included public intoxication, assaults, drugs, weapons, and other illegal activities. The club challenged the denial in court. The Court held that the plaintiff did not take substantial and timely steps in response to the problems taking place at the club and so affirmed the ruling to deny renewal.[1]

Liquor licenses may also be denied based upon the location of the business. A city council's denial of a liquor license was held to be not arbitrary or capricious where a bed and breakfast seeking the license was located in a residential area across the street from a park used by families.[2]

Illegal Sales

In most states, sales are prohibited to people under age 21, people who are visibly intoxicated, and known habitual drunkards.

You may think that the law imposes liability only on customers who wrongfully imbibe; for example, the underage drinker. This is a misconception. Because the effects of alcohol are potentially so dangerous, the law strives to motivate not just the consumer, but also the server, to comply strictly with the law. Therefore, a restaurant or bar that wrongfully provides alcohol to a person not legally entitled to drink, risks harsh penalties. Punishment can include suspension or revocation of a liquor license, civil liability for injuries caused by the patron who was wrongfully served, and criminal liability for serving underage patrons, which could result in jail and a fine. Great care should be taken to avoid illegal sales.

---

[1] *Club XS, Inc. v. Pennsylvania Liquor Control Board*, No. 123 C.D, 2011 (Pa. 2012)
[2] *Biggs v. City of Birmingham*, 91 So.3d 708 (Ala. 2012)

Virtually every state outlaws serving alcohol to people under age 21. Individuals in this age range often try to finagle their way into a bar to be served. A licensee (a bar or restaurant with a liquor license) must develop and strictly enforce rules and procedures to ensure that proper proof of age is obtained before alcohol is served. It is the responsibility of the bar or restaurant to ask for an acceptable form of identification. Management must determine what type of identification will be acceptable. Among the recommended forms are a state-issued driver's license, a state-issued nondriver identification card, a military identification card, or a passport. To verify age the bouncer should check the provided documentation for signs of tampering or alteration; check that the photo matches the patron, and ensure that the patron matches the descriptive information provided such as color of hair, eyes, height, weight, and age. The bouncer might also query would-be patrons about information on their identification documents. For example, the enforcer might ask would-be customers their middle name and verify that it matches the one on the identification card. Another trick for a bouncer is to ask the would-be patron to provide his or her horoscope sign.

Some states use underage informants to find bars that are serving to underage customers. In the state of Washington, the Washington State Liquor Control Board determined that a nightclub had allowed an underage person into an area off limits to persons under the age of 21. The liquor enforcement officers sent an underage investigative aid to attempt to enter the club using his own identification card. The club contested the finding asserting the compliance check was a search requiring a warrant, and that the Board entrapped the club. The Court rejected the club's claim of a search, noting that the club did not have privacy interests that were violated by the Board.[3]

Fake Identification Cards

Management should frequently reinforce to employees the importance of confirming customers' age in the effort to minimize incidents of underage service. In many states it is illegal for people under 21 to misrepresent their age or present false identification. In such states, young people presenting fake IDs, or otherwise claiming to be older than they are, face fines and in some states more serious penalties. State statutes often provide a defense to a charge of serving someone under 21 where the young person displayed to the licensee an authentic-looking identification card with a photograph "apparently" issued by a governmental entity, and the licensee had implemented a written policy requiring government-issued identification.

Purchases for Underage Drinkers

Sometimes a person of legal age purchases alcohol and gives it to someone under age. Is the licensee liable in these situations? The answer is, it depends. If the

---

[3] *Dodge City Saloon, Inc. v. Washington State Liquor Control Board,* 271 P.3d 363 (Wash. 2012)

licensee had no reason to know that the underage person would gain access to the alcohol, the seller will not be liable. For example, in an Alabama case a male over age 21 bought beer from a convenience store. After exiting the store and proceeding beyond the sight of the sales clerk, he gave some of the beer to his underage friend, who was driving. A car accident resulted, and the injured party sued the convenience store. The court held the store was not liable due to the absence of evidence that the store employees knew or should have known that the purchaser would share it with an underage person.[4]

If, however, the circumstances are such that the licensee should have known that an adult purchased the beverages for a minor's use, the sale may be illegal. In one case, a minor asked his adult neighbor to purchase beer for him. The neighbor agreed and together the two went to a beer distributor. An employee of the distributor approached the car and the adult neighbor placed the order. After the beer was put in the car, the employee sought payment. The neighbor looked at the minor, who took money from a mug he was holding and handed it to the neighbor, who in turn gave it to the employee. Apparently, the amount was insufficient because the employee sought additional money and again the neighbor looked to the minor, who withdrew additional money from the mug. After leaving the store and consuming the beer, the minor climbed an electrical transmission tower, came into contact with a high-voltage line, was burned, and fell 100 feet to the ground, resulting in serious injury. He sued the beer distributor for damages. Pennsylvania, where the case occurred, renders a licensee liable to a minor if the minor is served alcohol and is injured as a result. The court dismissed the case, holding that the sale by the beer distributor was made to the neighbor and not the minor. However, on appeal, the dismissal was reversed and the case was referred to trial on the basis that a jury might determine that the beer distributor should have known the actual purchaser was the minor.[5]

---

[4] *Jones v. B.P. Oil, Inc.*, 632 So.2d 435 (Ala. 1994)
[5] *Thomas v. Duquesne Light Co.*, 595 A.2d 56 (Pa. 1988)

This case instructs us that licensees must be alert to circumstances where an apparent purchase by an adult is in reality an illegal purchase by someone underage. Failure to detect such unlawful buys when the facts suggest an underage person is the actual purchaser can result in liability and loss of license. Bars, restaurants, and all licensees must always be vigilant. Some grocery stores have instituted the practice of asking for the identification from everyone in a grocery shopping group and refusing to sell alcohol if anyone in the group is too young to buy.

Academic Exception

Some state laws that prohibit underage drinking include an exception for an academic course in which tasting alcohol is required for instructional purposes. Part of your curriculum may include, for example, a course on bartending.

Sales to People Who Are Visibly Intoxicated

visibly intoxicated
A person whose appearance or actions indicate that he is intoxicated. Sale of alcohol to people who are visibly intoxicated is illegal and can result in Dram Shop liability.

Sale of alcohol to people who are **visibly intoxicated** is illegal. For a sale to qualify as illegal, the buyer's appearance or actions must indicate he is intoxicated. Absent proof that a patron is noticeably intoxicated, service of alcohol to him is not illegal.[6] If evidence of visible intoxication is presented at a trial or hearing and the bar or restaurant is unable to refute it, the bar will be responsible for the illegal sale.[7]

A factual determination of intoxication cannot be made solely on the basis of how much alcohol a person has consumed, as the effects of alcohol differ greatly from person to person. Thus, the fact that a patron had four alcoholic drinks within an hour is insufficient by itself to establish visible intoxication.[8] Where a driver in a car accident had a blood alcohol level two hours after the collision of 0.21, more than twice the legal limit, and the accident occurred soon after he left the bar, an expert witness extrapolated that he was visibly intoxicated when he was at the bar.[9] The bar's motion for summary judgment was thus denied.

In a Michigan case, plaintiff was assaulted in the parking lot of the defendant's hotel. Plaintiff claimed the hotel was liable based on the dram shop act. This is a law that holds sellers of alcohol liable when they serve someone who is visibly intoxicated and who then causes injury to another. The law is discussed in more detail later in this chapter. Plaintiff proved that the assailant drank between twelve and fifteen beers at the defendant's establishment over the course of six to seven hours. The court rejected this testimony as sufficient proof the attacker was visibly intoxicated, a necessary element in a dram shop case. The court held that visible physical manifestations of intoxication are required. Plaintiff failed to provide such evidence.[10]

---

[6] *Wilder v. Nickbert, Inc.*, 678 N.Y.S.2d 766 (N.Y. 1998)
[7] *Smith v. Blue Mountain Inn, Inc.*, 680 N.Y.S.2d 386 (N.Y. 1998)
[8] *Adamy v. Friday's*, 92 N.Y.2d 396 (N.Y. 1998)
[9] *Roy v. Volonino*, 694 N.Y.S.2d 399 (N.Y. 1999)
[10] *Mindykowski v. Olsen & CWB Property Management, Inc. & Alpena Hotels, LLC.*, 854 N.W.2d 711 (Mich. 2014)

Although intoxication is sometimes difficult to detect, that may not be a defense to a charge of illegal sale. Bartenders and wait personnel are expected to be familiar with indicia of intoxication. Servers must be trained to identify them. These indicia include slurred speech; bloodshot, glassy, or watery eyes; flushed face; and poor coordination, which is often evidenced by difficulty in performing such acts as handling money, lighting a cigarette, removing a credit card from a wallet, standing without swaying, or walking without staggering or stumbling. Evidence of intoxication can also include being overly friendly, boisterous, loud, argumentative, aggressive, crude, or annoying to other customers, to mention only some.[11] Good training videos developed by the National Restaurant Association and the American Hotel and Motel Association are available to instruct bartenders and wait personnel on how to recognize intoxication. Instructional materials also cover such topics as how to control the dispensing of alcoholic beverages, how to manage customers' consumption, how to prevent service to underage or intoxicated patrons, how to prevent an intoxicated customer from driving, and what to do if those efforts fail. In addition to initial employee training, frequent refresher programs are an important component of alcohol-service training. Staff meetings provide a good opportunity to reinforce the message that alcohol must be served responsibly, and to remind servers of the various indicia of intoxication. Some states, such as Maryland, have laws that require all establishments that serve alcohol to be certified in an alcohol awareness training program.

Errors in who a licensee serves not only put at risk the license to sell alcohol but also can lead to liability for injuries caused by the wrongly served patron. We will discuss this liability in the section of this chapter on dram shop acts.

Proving Visible Intoxication

Visible or noticeable intoxication can be proven at trial in several ways. The first is by the indicia of intoxication discussed previously in this chapter. Various people may have observed the customer becoming intoxicated, including the bartender, waitstaff, other customers, or the police. These folks will become witnesses for the prosecution.

---

[11] *Dollar v. O'Hearn,* 670 N.Y.S.2d 230 (N.Y. 1998)

The second way to prove noticeable intoxication involves the use of a device that measures the alcohol in a person's blood. The result is called the BAC (blood alcohol content). The easiest, least invasive, and most frequently used device is called a breathalyzer. If the BAC is 0.08 or higher, the person is legally intoxicated. Expert witnesses may have relevant testimony in circumstances where a customer, after leaving the bar, is arrested for driving while intoxicated and submits to a breathalyzer test. If the amount of time between when the person left the bar and when the test occurred is known, expert witnesses can extrapolate backwards using the breathalyzer results to determine the person's level of intoxication while still in the restaurant.[12]

Other factors that may aid in proving that a bar served a patron illegally include failure by the tavern to train its employees about alcohol consumption and intoxication indicators, absence of an employer policy identifying how much liquor can be served to a customer, and rotation of wait personnel in the course of an evening so that no one server keeps track of the amount a particular patron drinks.[13]

Sales to Known Habitual Drunkards

Sale of alcohol to known habitual drunkards is prohibited. A habitual drunkard is someone who regularly imbibes alcohol and frequently becomes intoxicated. A licensee who serves a known habitual drunkard risks losing his license and may be liable for injuries caused by such person.

Alcohol Vendors' Liability Under Common Law

An issue that has long troubled liquor licensees is potential liability for injuries caused by a customer who is served alcohol illegally.

Under common law, in most states the licensee was not liable for damages caused when it served alcohol to someone who was under 21, visibly intoxicated, or a habitual drunkard, and that person was injured or caused injury to another. Thus, if a wrongfully served customer left a bar, drove a car, and on the way home caused an accident in which he or someone else was injured, the bar was not liable. According to this common-law rule, the cause of the injuries was the *consumption* and not the *sale* of the liquor. The injured person, if other than the operator, could sue only the drunk driver. If the wrongfully served customer was injured, he had no remedy. The bar or restaurant that sold the alcohol to the driver was not liable.

As the number of alcohol-related accidents grew, most states found the common-law rule unsatisfactory. Said one court, "With today's car of steel and speed it becomes a lethal weapon in the hands of a drunken imbiber. Accidents involving drunk drivers are commonplace. The resulting affliction of bodily injury to an unsuspecting public is also of common knowledge."[14]

---

[12] *Adamy v. Ziriakus*, 92 N.Y.2d 396 (N.Y. 1998)
[13] *Copeland v. Red Dog Saloon and Café*, 996 P.2d 931 (Okla. 1999); rev'd on other grnds, 79 P.3d 1128 (Okla. 2003)
[14] *Ohio Casualty Insurance Co. v. Todd*, 813 P.2d 508 (Okla. 1991)

The law came to recognize that a party able to prevent alcohol abuse is the licensee—that is, the bar or restaurant. The common law rule, by excusing the bar from liability, did nothing to encourage the server to prevent patrons from abusing alcohol.

Another weakness of the common-law rule was that many intoxicated persons who caused injury had little money with which to compensate those they injured. The owner of a restaurant or bar was more likely to have insurance and assets.

Alcohol Vendors' Liability Greatly Increases Under Dram Shop Acts

Over time, public policy came to demand more responsibility from the dispenser of alcohol, resulting in legislation in many states called **dram shop acts** (*dram shop* is an outdated term for a bar). These acts impose liability on a restaurant or bar for certain injuries resulting from illegal sales. The objectives of dram shop acts are to discourage proprietors from selling alcohol illegally and to afford compensation to victims whose injuries emanate from the unlawful sale of alcohol.

Dram Shop Act
A statute that holds sellers of alcohol liable when they wrongfully serve someone who then causes injury to a third person.

The potential liability is significant. Some illegal sales have resulted in verdicts that have financially ruined the bar or restaurant involved. In a few states the amount of damages that a plaintiff can collect from a licensee is capped at a specific amount on the theory that the major share of responsibility for the injury should fall on the intoxicated driver.

The following quote from a decision in a case explains well the rationale for holding the bar or restaurant liable.

> *When alcoholic beverages are sold by a tavern keeper to a minor or to an intoxicated person, the unreasonable risk of harm not only to the minor or the intoxicated person but also to members of the traveling public may readily be recognized and foreseen; this is particularly evident in current times when traveling by car to and from the tavern is so common-place and accidents resulting from drinking are so frequent. ...*

The hazards of travel by cars on highways are a national problem. A drunken driver is a threat to the safety of many. It is understandable that early cases did not recognize any duty of an innkeeper to the traveling public because a serious hazard did not exist. (Presumably because at one time cars were not yet invented, and once they were, initially they were not accessible to many people and did not have the speed potential of today's vehicles.) It is a well-established, sound principle of legal philosophy that the common law is not static. Under the skillful interpretation of our courts, it has been adapted to changing times and conditions of our civilization....

The increasing frequency of serious accidents caused by drivers who are intoxicated is a fact well known to those who sell and dispense liquor. This lends support to those cases which have found the automobile accident to be "the reasonably foreseeable" result of furnishing liquor to the intoxicated driver.[15]

Liability of the bar or restaurant is not restricted to car accidents. Any injury caused by the wrongfully served patron will suffice, including, for example, those resulting from fights.

Alcohol Vendor's Liability to the Patron

Today, when a licensee makes an illegal sale and the person improperly served (as distinct from a third person) is injured, is the licensee liable to the patron? The answer varies, depending on the state. In most states, dram shop acts do not impose liability for injuries to wrongfully served customers. In those states, the act imposes liability only for injuries to a third person. One court explained the reason as follows, "In our view, a rule which allows an intoxicated individual to hold a tavern owner liable without regard to his own actions in continuing to consume alcohol promotes irresponsibility and rewards drunk driving."[16] In the referenced case, a bar patron drank to excess and was injured in a car accident he caused while driving home. The court affirmed a jury verdict in favor of the bar. In a Michigan case, the plaintiff was injured in a single vehicle accident while driving home from the defendant's bar. She claimed that, prior to the accident, she was served alcohol even though she was visibly intoxicated. The court dismissed the case on the grounds that neither common law nor the state dram shop act imposed liability on a licensee for injuries to a wrongfully served patron.[17]

In Case Example 12-1 the parents of a man who drowned sued the bar based on the Ohio dram shop law.

CASE EXAMPLE 12-1

Kirchner v. Shooters on the Water, Inc.

856 N.E.2d 1026 (Ohio 2006)

This appeal rises out of the drowning death of plaintiff Paul M. Kirchner's son, Paul C. Kirchner in the Cuyahoga River. The incident occurred at approximately 2:15 a.m. next to the premises of Shooters on the Water ("Shooters"). Kirchner was 20 years old at the time of his death.

Prior to arriving at Shooters on the night in question, Kirchner and his friends attended a Hawaiian luau party at a private home. Approximately 40 to 50 guests were at the party. Kirchner and his friends remained at the party for several hours drinking beer and vodka Jell-O shots.

---

[15] *Rappaport v. Nichols,* 156 A.2d 1 (N.J. 1959)
[16] *Tobias v. Sports Club, Inc.,* 474 S.E.2d 450 (S.C. 1996)
[17] *Jackson v. PKM Corp.,* 422 N.W.2d 657 (Mich. 1988)

While at the party Kirchner and his friends decided to go to Shooters. They left the party and drove to Shooters at approximately 1:15. Shooters is a restaurant/bar located on the west bank of the Flats in downtown Cleveland, Ohio....

When the young men arrived at Shooters, they walked to the back entrance where they believed they had a better chance of getting into the bar since numerous members of their group, including Kirchner, were under the legal drinking age. The entire group managed to gain entry into Shooters despite their underage status.

Kirchner was at Shooters for approximately one hour prior to the incident. According to his friends, Kirchner drank beer, mixed drinks, and shots. At approximately 2:15 a.m. Kirchner and his friends made plans to leave Shooters. However Kirchner told his friends that he was going to urinate off the dock of Shooters, into the Cuyahoga River. Kirchner's friends observed Kirchner walk to the end of the dock, lean against a pole, and begin urinating. Shortly thereafter, Kirchner fell into the river. Kirchner's friends ran to the end of the dock and after seeing no sign of their friend, jumped in after him. The U.S. Coast Guard arrived and eventually recovered Kirchner's body from the river. He was pronounced dead at 4:40 a.m. The coroner's toxicology report indicated that Kirchner had a blood alcohol level of .24, which is three times the legal limit for operating a motor vehicle in Ohio....

[Plaintiff claimed the bar and its owner should be liable based on the state's Dram Shop Act.] We conclude that a patron that has become voluntarily intoxicated is not the type of innocent third party that the Dram Shop laws were designed to protect. Therefore we must affirm the grant of summary judgment in favor of Shooters and its owner....

In another case, the plaintiff was allegedly served at the defendant's bar after reaching a visibly intoxicated condition. While intoxicated, he fell from his stool and permanently injured his leg, requiring the use of a brace and crutches. His action against the bar was dismissed because neither Maryland's dram shop act nor common law permits the patron to sue the licensee.[18]

The plaintiff in a Mississippi case was attending a medical technician's convention at the defendant hotel where she allegedly was served alcohol after becoming visibly intoxicated. She fell over a railing 30 feet to the lobby floor. Her action for damages against the hotel was likewise dismissed.[19]

Minority Rule

A minority of states allow a wrongfully served patron to sue a licensee for resulting injuries, some based on particulars of the state's dram shop law and others based on negligence. An example of dram shop liability is provided by a Texas case in which the plaintiff was illegally served alcohol. While driving home she crashed into a telephone pole and was seriously injured. The bar was found liable.[20] In a Colorado

---

[18] *Fisher v. O'Connor's, Inc.*, 452 A.2d 1313 (Md. 1982)
[19] *Cuevas v. Royal D'Ibervilee Hotel*, 498 So.2d 346 (Miss. 1986)
[20] *Salzar v. Giorgio's*, 53 S.W.3d 412 (Tex. 2001)

case, the bar was held responsible on a negligence theory. The plaintiff, the decedent's relative, claimed the deceased was served at the defendant's restaurant when he was visibly intoxicated and then drove his car off a mountain road and was killed. In holding that the plaintiff could sue the restaurant, the court explained,

> *We have stated before that a reasonable person would foresee that an inebriate will act without prudence, control or self-restraint. We agree that voluntary [intoxication] is a self-indulgent act. We also note that a person who voluntarily consumes alcohol to the point of intoxication is at the very least partially responsible for his injuries. However, the fact that the patron has acted in an unacceptable manner should in no way lessen the equally unacceptable conduct of a tavern owner. One who stands behind a bar and serves drink after drink to a visibly intoxicated customer engages in behavior which is as opprobrious as that of the customer. ... Insulating tavern owners from liability does not send the message that they, as well as their patrons, must be accountable for their actions.[21]*

Note: In states that allow the wrongfully served driver to sue, the bar can assert the defense of comparative negligence (Chapter 5), thereby requiring the jury to allocate the relative liability for the accident between the tavern and the intoxicated patron, and reducing the bar's liability accordingly.

Regardless of whether a particular state holds the bar liable to the drinker, a licensee that makes an illegal sale of alcohol faces fines and license suspension.

Alcohol Vendor's Liability to Third Parties

Although licensees in most states will not be liable to a wrongfully served patron injured from the alcohol, the bar may be held liable to others who are injured from the patron's intoxication. For example, if a licensee serves a visibly intoxicated customer who, while driving home, hits another car causing injury to the other car's driver, the licensee will be liable to that driver. A visibly intoxicated patron drove from the premises of the licensee and collided with another car, killing one person and seriously injuring another. The court held that the licensee would be liable to the deceased's estate and the person injured.[22] Similarly, if the wrongfully served patron leaves the bar, drives a boat, and causes an accident and injury to others, the bar may be liable.[23]

Another application of the dram shop act is the circumstance where a bar patron who was served too much alcohol engages in a fight and injures a third person. An example involves an intoxicated customer who threw an ashtray at the bartender but missed and instead hit another customer. Assuming proof that the contentious drinker was served while visibly intoxicated, the bar will be liable for the injuries caused by the ashtray based on dram shop liability.[24]

---

[21] *Lyons v. Nasby*, 770 P.2d 1250 (Colo. 1989)
[22] *Grayson Fraternal Order of Eagles v. Claywell*, 736 S.W.2d 328 (Ky. 1987)
[23] *Koehane v. Lakefront Pier Restaurant, Inc.*, 676 N.Y.S.2d 363 (N.Y. 1998)
[24] *Smith v. Blue Mountain Inn, Inc.*, 680 N.Y.S.2d 386 (N.Y. 1998)

Dram shop liability also applied where numerous guests at a private function held at a hotel were wrongly served alcohol and thereafter, while dancing, one fell causing a "chain reaction." It ended with the plaintiff, who was involuntarily pulled onto the dance floor, being knocked down and suffering a broken wrist.[25]

The potential liability under dram shop acts is significant. To protect against this liability, tavern keepers should do everything possible to avoid illegal alcohol sales. Employee training is critical. If an error is made and a patron is wrongfully served, the barkeeper should discourage the customer from driving home. Funding a cab or car service may be well worth avoiding the risk of dram shop liability. Many restaurants and bars contract with companies that provide rides home to intoxicated patrons and in some circumstances drive the customer's car home as well. This eliminates much of the reason customers resist a ride home.

The practice of managers overseeing service decisions made by bartenders and wait personnel can help to limit liability. In one case involving a proceeding to revoke a restaurant's liquor license, beer had allegedly been served to a visibly intoxicated customer. The manager had observed the customer's condition and immediately removed the bottle of beer. Based on these facts, the court found for the restaurant. Similar prompt action in a dram shop case might also save the licensee from dram shop liability by avoiding an accident.

For a plaintiff to be successful in a dram shop lawsuit, she must be able to establish that the hospitality establishment served alcohol illegally. If plaintiff is unable to provide evidence of this fact, the case will be dismissed. This is illustrated in Case Example 12-2.

CASE EXAMPLE 12-2

Rodriguez v. Goodlin

2006 WL 23 90218 (N.J. 2006)

Ruben Almeida stabbed David Rodriguez in Sherlock's Lounge & Liquors, a tavern in Atlantic City. Rodriguez sued Sherlock's for injuries he sustained in the assault....

No evidence is extant from which a jury could reasonably conclude that Almeida appeared intoxicated when he was served the alcoholic beverages. Without proofs, plaintiff has no cause of action under the New Jersey Licensed Alcoholic Beverage Server Fair Liability Act, commonly known as the dram shop law, for injury resulting from the sale of alcoholic beverages. That Rodriguez considered Almeida to be drunk [at the time of the altercation] would not permit a jury, without speculating, to reasonably conclude that Almeida was served while visibly intoxicated.

[Plaintiff's case was therefore dismissed .]

---

[25] *Dollar v. O'Hearn*, 670 N.Y.S.2d 230 (N.Y. 1998)

CASE QUESTION

1. Why was plaintiff's opinion that his assailant was intoxicated when he hit plaintiff not sufficient evidence of the attacker's intoxication for purposes of dram shop liability?

In another case the driver of a car purchased a six-pack of beer from the defendant's store having not consumed any alcohol or intoxicating substance that day. Later the driver was responsible for a two-car collision that caused injury to the other driver. The court said the injured driver could not prevail against the store unless "it was apparent to the provider that the individual being sold alcoholic beverages was obviously intoxicated to the extent that he presented a clear danger to himself and others. Appellants concede they cannot make this showing." The case against the store was therefore dismissed.[26]

In a limited number of states the dram shop act contains a provision limiting the licensee's liability to cases where the bar or restaurant knows that the patron will soon be driving a motor vehicle.[27] In such a state a court refused to impose dram shop liability where the bar was located in a strip mall "and accessible by foot or by car," some patrons arrived or departed on foot or by taxi, and employees testified "they had no information suggesting that [the patron who caused a car accident] was going to drive away" from the establishment.[28]

Alcohol Vendor's Liability to Passengers in Patron's Car

Often when injury results from a car accident, the injured party is a passenger in the patron's car. In most states, whether or not the bar will be liable to the passenger depends on whether the passenger procured alcohol for the wrongfully-served driver. If the passenger purchased alcohol for the driver or encouraged the latter to drink more than he could tolerate, most states will not impose dram shop liability on the bar. However, if the passenger did not contribute to the driver's intoxication, the bar or restaurant may be liable for the passenger's injuries. In Case Example 12-3, the court discusses the circumstances under which a passenger's lawsuit against the licensee will and will not succeed.

---

[26] *Tankersley v. New York Brothers Investments, Inc.*, 195 S.W.3d 797 (Tex. 2006). See also *Jackson v. Walker*, 2006 WL 2422561 (Ohio 2006)

[27] See for example Georgia statutes, OCGA Section 51–1–40(b)

[28] *Baxley v. Hakiel Industries, Inc.*, 633 S.E.2d 360 (Ga. 2006)

CASE EXAMPLE 12-3

Goss v. Richmond

381 N.W.2d 776 (Mich. 1985)

Plaintiff alleged in his dram shop action that defendant Le-Rob, a licensed seller of alcoholic beverages, illegally sold intoxicating liquor to a visibly intoxicated person, defendant Robert Richmond. Richmond allegedly drove his automobile off the road and struck a tree. Plaintiff was a passenger in the Richmond automobile and suffered serious injuries.

Plaintiff testified that he and Richmond purchased pitchers of beer in "rounds," each taking turns buying pitchers. The trial court held that buying such "rounds" amount to buying drinks for defendant Richmond. The court held that, by doing so, plaintiff was a non-innocent party under the dram shop act and was thus precluded from proceeding under the act.…

Plaintiff argues that his participation in bringing about the injury-producing intoxication should not bar recovery.…

The objective of the Legislature in enacting the dram shop act was to discourage bars from selling intoxicating liquors to visibly intoxicated persons and minors and to provide for recovery under certain circumstances by those injured as a result of the sale of intoxicating liquor.… To permit one who has been an intentional accessory to the illegality to shift the loss resulting from it to the tavern owner would lead to a result we believe the Legislature did not intend. A person who buys drinks for an obviously intoxicated person, or one whom he knows to be a minor, is at least as much the cause of the resulting or continued intoxication as the bartender who served the consumer illegally. In short, barring recovery by a wrongdoer by holding that the wrongdoer is not among those to whom the Legislature intended to provide a remedy advances both purposes of the act, to suppress illegal sales and to provide a remedy for those injured as a result of the illegality.

Plaintiff next argues that the "innocent party" doctrine as applied in this case denies him equal protection of the laws. Plaintiff claims that, because he could recover if he and defendant Richmond, instead of buying "rounds," would each have purchased their own pitchers and drank side by side, the "innocent party" doctrine as applied in this case creates an arbitrary distinction between persons of the same class.…

The material question when a defendant claims a plaintiff is not an "innocent party" under the dram shop act is whether the plaintiff actively participated in the intoxicated person's inebriation.…

We do not find the distinction between persons who purchase "rounds" and those who merely accompany the allegedly intoxicated person to be arbitrary. A person who purchases a pitcher of beer knowing that the allegedly intoxicated person will drink therefrom is a more direct participant in the other's intoxication and more directly encourages the other's intoxication than a mere drinking companion. Buying in "rounds" conceivably sets the pace at which the allegedly intoxicated person will consume alcohol and conceivably encourages the allegedly intoxicated person to consume his "fair share."

[Judgment for the licensee] Affirmed.

In another case, the intoxicated driver's passenger was killed when the car missed the entrance of a bridge and crashed into a wall. The passenger's estate was denied recovery against the bar in which the two had been drinking because the passenger had, on several occasions during the evening, obtained glasses of beer for the driver. Further, the passenger had purchased alcohol he and the driver drank while in the car.[29]

The plaintiff passenger in a New York case had bought "at least one drink" for the driver. The one drink was found to be enough to preclude the plaintiff's dram shop action against the bar.[30]

In another case the companion of an intoxicated driver was a passenger in the car and was killed in a one-car collision caused by the alcohol. No evidence was presented that the passenger had furnished alcohol to the driver. The passenger's estate was therefore able to sue the bar at which the driver had been wrongfully served.[31]

Interestingly, where a passenger who did not buy alcohol for the driver knows when he enters the car that the driver is intoxicated, some states have determined that the act of riding with the inebriated motorist is itself negligent, impacting recovery if an accident occurs. These states apply a comparative negligence apportionment of liability (discussed in Chapter 5) between the bar and the passenger. Thus, the passenger will have to absorb a percentage of his damages equal to the percentage of liability attributed to him.[32]

Other states hold that knowledge by the passenger of the driver's inebriation does not limit the passenger's right to sue or recover. Said a court in a state adopting this view, "While a plaintiff may properly be alleged to have assumed the risk of the reckless or wanton operation of a vehicle by a driver that he knew or should have known was intoxicated, he cannot be held to have assumed the risk that a seller of alcoholic beverages continued to serve such beverages to a person known to be intoxicated."[33]

Further, in some states the dram shop act expressly excludes the restaurant or bar from liability to a passenger in the customer's car, whether or not the passenger contributed to the driver's intoxication and whether or not the passenger knew the driver was inebriated.

Two Licensees Serving One Patron

More than one bar or restaurant may be liable in a given case. For example, if a visibly intoxicated person is served first at one bar and then at a second one, both will be liable to a third person injured by the patron. The injured person cannot, however, recover twice for the same injuries. Instead, the liability will be allocated

---

29 *Pollard v. Village of Ovid*, 446 N.W.2d 574 (Mich. 1989)
30 *Prunty v. Keltie's Bum Steer*, 559 N.Y.S.2d 354 (N.Y. 1990)
31 *Griffin Motel Co. v. Strickland*, 479 S.E.2d 401 (Ga. 1997)
32 *Terwillinger v. Kitchen*, 781 A.2d 1201 (Pa. 2001)
33 *Buzon v. Ballard & Kane, LLC.*, 2005 WL 2435834 (Conn. 2005)

between the two bars. If, however, the drinker was not visibly intoxicated until he arrived at the second bar, the first bar will not be liable.

Apportionment of Liability Among Defendants

The injured party in a dram shop case will likely sue both the bar and the intoxicated driver. In some states comparative negligence applies in this circumstance,[34] enabling the restaurant or bar to reduce its liability by the percentage of liability attributed to the drinking driver. The jury will be asked to allocate the liability between the defendants. Each will pay that percentage of the plaintiff's damages equal to the percentage of liability attributed to him. If, for example, the intoxicated operator of the vehicle was found 75 percent responsible and the bar 25 percent, the bar would be liable for only 25 percent of the damages suffered by plaintiff. The driver would be liable for the remaining 75 percent.

Apportionment of Liability Where Plaintiff Is Negligent

Where the person injured by the illegally served drinker negligently contributed to the cause of the accident, the injured person's recovery will be reduced accordingly. As in a comparative negligence case, the jury will allocate a percentage of the liability to the plaintiff. His recovery against the bar will be reduced by that percentage.[35]

In an Oklahoma case liability was apportioned between plaintiff and defendant as well as between the defendant bar and driver. The bar was found 43 percent responsible, the intoxicated driver 50 percent, and the plaintiff 7 percent. Plaintiff's damages totaled $300,000. He was thus entitled to collect $129,000 ($300,000 x 0.43) from the bar.[36]

States without Dram Shop Acts

A few states do not have dram shop acts. Some have created a negligence cause of action for holding the licensee liable when an illegally served patron causes injury to a third party. Other states protect the tavern owner from liability for injuries caused by illegal sales. In those states, alcohol servers are immune from civil liability. An example of a state without a dram shop law is Nevada, where Las Vegas, the most popular United States tourist destination, is located. In those states, people injured by a wrongfully served customer will not be able to collect from the liquor licensee for their injuries;[37] only the customer who caused the injury will be liable.

---

[34] See for example *Idaho Department of Labor v. Sunset Marts, Inc.*, 91 P.3d 1111 (Idaho 2004)
[35] *Steak and Ale of Texas, Inc. v. Borneman*, 2001 WL 1548958 (Tex. 2001); *Dowell v. Gracewood Fruit Co.*, 559 So.2d 217 (Fla. 1990); *McGill v. McAninch Corp.*, 202 WL 984619 (Kan. 2002)
[36] *Copeland v. Tela Corporation*, 79 P.3d 1128 (Ok. 1999), rev'd on other grounds, 79 P.3d 1128 (Ok. 2003)
[37] See for example *Bland v. Scott*, 112 P.3d 941 (Kan. 2005)

Liquor Liability Insurance

liquor liability insurance
Insurance purchased by
a liquor licensee to cover Dram Shop liability.

A licensee can purchase insurance to cover dram shop liability. This insurance is often called **liquor liability insurance** or dram shop insurance. The cost is based on numerous factors, including the volume of alcohol sold by the licensee, prior incidents of illegal sales, the nature of the establishment, and the hours it is open.

Some states require that liquor-license applicants have either liquor liability insurance or a liability bond to cover liability.

Dram Shop Liability on Some Employers for Office Parties

Beware the company Christmas party! An area of potential liability for employers involves supplying alcohol at company events. Some states hold the host company liable to someone injured by an illegally served attendee at the event.[38] Case Example 12-4 illustrates this type of liability.

CASE EXAMPLE 12-4

Barnes v. Cohen Dry Wall, Inc.

2005 WL 2122313 (S.C. 2005)

The sole issue is whether we will impose third-party liability on a social host who knowingly and intentionally serves alcohol to guests aged 18, 19, and 20, that is, persons who are minors for purposes of alcoholic beverage control laws.

Orin Feagin was a 19-year-old employee of petitioner Cohen Dry Wall, Inc. (Company) when he attended the Company's 1998 Christmas party. There was evidence that, despite Company's preparty warning that Feagin would not be served at the party and its attempt to enforce this decision at the party, Feagin in fact consumed Company-supplied alcohol while there. Although Feagin exited the party with a group of people including a designated driver, he drove himself to his girlfriend's place of employment.... After leaving his girlfriend's work, Feagin was involved in a two-car accident, which killed him and the passenger in the other car.

The passenger's personal representative (Respondent) sued both Company and Feagin's estate. . . .

Issue: Whether social hosts who knowingly and intentionally serve alcoholic beverages to a guest aged 18 to 20 owe a duty to a third party injured or killed by the guest in an alcohol-related accident.

Analysis: ...In South Carolina, persons under 21 "are incompetent by reason of their youth and inexperience to deal responsibly with the effects of alcohol." Imposing liability on social hosts encour-

---

[38] See for example, *Raymond v. Duffy,* 2005 WL 407655 (Conn. 2005); *O'Connor v. Gaspar,* 2005 WL 914441 (Mass. 2005)

ages them to be more vigilant about who is consuming alcohol at their gatherings, and thus promotes our public policy which prohibits the use of alcohol by incompetent and inexperienced youth. We find that this policy is served by the extension of social host liability to third parties injured or killed in an alcohol-related accident by a guest under 21 years of age who has consumed alcohol knowingly and intentionally provided to him by the host. Before the injured person can recover damages from the social host, he must present evidence not only that the host knowingly and intentionally provided the minor with alcoholic beverages, but must also establish a causal connection between the alcohol consumption and his injuries.

Conclusion: The decision of the Court of Appeals holding that a social host may be liable to a third party injured by an underage guest who has consumed alcohol provided by the host, is affirmed.

In a California case, the annual holiday party was sponsored by the defendant hotel for its employees. The hotel allowed each employee to have two drink tickets for beer or wine and no other alcohol. Nonetheless, some of the employees were also drinking whisky from liquor supplied by the hotel. An employee left the party with some co-workers who all went to the employee's house. About twenty minutes later, that employee drove a co-worker home and had a car accident killing the passenger of the other vehicle. The employee driver had a registered blood alcohol content of 0.16 and was convicted of vehicular manslaughter. The victim's family sued the hotel for wrongful death. The court held that the defendant hotel may be found liable for its employee's actions as long as the proximate cause of the injury occurred during the scope of employment, a legal term meaning actions in furtherance of the employer's business. A jury will determine if the employee driver appeared intoxicated and whether the drinking occurred during the scope of employment. The court said that it was irrelevant that the accident occurred after the employee driver arrived home safely and then went out again, the hotel could nonetheless be found liable.[39]

Other states relieve the sponsoring company from social host liability[40] and hold responsible only liquor licensees engaged in the commercial enterprise of selling and serving alcohol.[41]

Companies planning events at a restaurant or bar are well advised to negotiate terms in their contracts obligating the licensee to supervise the liquor service, follow responsible alcohol dispensing procedures, serve alcohol only to those legally entitled to drink, purchase liquor liability insurance, and hold the company harmless (compensate the company) for any liability incurred as a result of alcohol at the function. Hospitality facilities may resist the "hold harmless" provision. The inclusion of such a term in a restaurant or bar's contract not only increases the facility's potential liability, but may also increase the facility's insurance premium.

---

[39] Purton v. Marriott International, Inc., 218 Cal.App.4th 499 (Calif. 2013)
[40] *Bland v. Scott*, 112 P.3d 941 (Kan. 2005)
[41] *McGee v. Alexander*, 37 P.3d 800 (Ok. 2001)

Strategies to Avoid Liability

As we have seen, liability for illegal alcohol sales can lead to money verdicts against a bar or restaurant, revocation of the liquor license, and criminal charges. This liability must be taken very seriously by all licensees. We have already discussed important steps to help reduce liability. These include employee training and refresher courses, oversight of sales by a supervisor, and providing transportation home to intoxicated customers. Other practices that can contribute to reduced risk of liability include the following:

- Adopt internal written policies and rules concerning alcohol sales, publish them in an employee newsletter, and post them near the employee lounge or the time clock.

- Encourage groups of customers to select a designated driver.

- Provide free nonalcoholic drinks to the designated driver.

- Educate employees about liquor liability laws and strategies for refusing service to visibly intoxicated patrons.

- Have a written policy stating what employees should do when confronted with a patron who has had too much alcohol. Train employees about the policy and have them sign a copy periodically to reinforce it.

- Post signs that inform customers of their responsibilities. Suggested wordings:

  WARNING! No person will sell or give away any alcoholic beverage to any person under age 21 or who is visibly intoxicated. To do so would violate the law.

  WARNING! It is a violation punishable under law for any person under the age of 21 to present any written evidence of age that is false, fraudulent, altered, or not actually his own for the purpose of attempting to purchase alcohol.

- Post signs of taxi companies with phone numbers near the entrance so that intoxicated patrons can call for a ride home.

- Encourage responsible drinking in marketing and advertising.

- Employ a system to determine the amount of alcohol served in each drink sold. Use measuring devices instead of free pouring.

- Mandate that supervisors *must* support employees who discontinue service to a patron who is believed to be intoxicated.

- Have a limit on the number of drinks that will be served to a patron during happy hour.

- Promote alternatives to liquor, such as bottled waters and distinctive coffees and teas. Train service personnel to offer guests both a wine menu and a water/coffee/tea menu, or combine the two. Treat bottled waters the same way as bottled wines in all aspects of sales and service. Consider the possibility of a special "house" water or other nonalcoholic drink carrying the licensee's name and logo.

- Offer "minidrinks"—drinks that contain less alcohol than the norm—at a lower price. With proper promotion, frozen drinks with just a touch of alcohol can be fun and appealing.

- Offer nonalcoholic wine and beer which, as the name suggests, contain no alcohol.

- For specialty drinks that contain more than the normally expected one to one-and-a-half ounces of liquor, state the quantity of alcohol on the beverage menu to alert customers.

- As a last resort, if an intoxicated patron insists on driving home after being warned, inform the police. An arrest of the customer will remove him from the road, prevent a possible accident, and save the bar from dram shop liability.

Miscellaneous Alcohol Regulations

Various statutory mandates apply to licensees, depending on the state involved. States have gone to great lengths to control the sale of alcoholic beverages. The purpose of these laws is to foster and promote temperance in the consumption of alcohol, and respect for and compliance with the law. They are enforced by a state agency authorized to issue, suspend, and revoke liquor licenses. The name given to that agency varies from state to state, and will be referred to here as the liquor authority. The penalties for failing to abide by these laws include suspension or revocation of the liquor license and fines. Remember, these regulations vary from state to state.

Alcohol Sales in Hotel Guest Rooms

Many hotel licensees sell alcohol through vending machines or other mechanical devices in guest rooms. Access to the liquor is restricted by means of a key or magnetic card. The prohibition against illegal sales applies to these devices. The innkeeper must not provide the key or magnetic card to anyone who is under 21, visibly intoxicated, or a habitual drunkard.

Age of Alcohol Servers

Most states specify a minimum age (usually 18 or 19) for certain workers in establishments that serve alcoholic beverages. No one under that age can be on the waitstaff or sell, dispense, or handle alcoholic beverages. Lower minimum age requirements apply to dishwashers or busboys. The objective of these regulations is to limit the exposure to alcohol of young people.

Restrictions on Alcohol Sales on Sunday and Christmas

In many locations, alcohol cannot be sold on Sunday before noon. Also, sales for off-premises consumption, such as purchases from a liquor store, may be prohibited all day. The objective of these laws is to further the recognition of a sabbath day.

Numerous states prohibit sales on part or all of the Christmas holiday. For example, in Michigan, the sale of alcoholic beverages must end on Christmas Eve by midnight and may not begin again until noon on Christmas Day. Previous to this law being enacted in 2010, alcohol could not be sold after 9 p.m. on Christmas Eve and the bars and retailers were restricted from selling any alcohol until 7 a.m. on December 26.

BYOB Clubs

Some states allow restaurant or bar customers to bring their own alcohol into the establishment. Some of the businesses will charge a corkage fee for glasses or ice, others do not have corkage fees. What if a customer becomes intoxicated on the alcohol that he brings into the establishment and later is involved in an automobile accident? Would the establishment be liable to an innocent injured party? An Illinois gentlemen's club was not allowed to serve alcohol, but allowed patrons to bring their own alcohol into the club. It charged for glasses, ice, soda, and other mixers. An intoxicated patron drove from the premises and killed a pregnant driver, her unborn baby, and the passenger in his own vehicle. The decedents' families brought a wrongful death suit under the Illinois Dram Shop Act and common-law negligence. The Illinois Supreme Court held that the dram shop act did not apply because the bar did not sell alcohol to the patron. The Supreme Court held that common-law negligence did apply, because the bar's bouncers ejected the patron from the bar and the valet at the bar brought the intoxicated patron's vehicle to him and encouraged him to drive off. The club settled the lawsuit for $1 million.[42]

Warnings to Pregnant Women

Licensees must display a sign close to where alcohol is dispensed stating the following: "Government Warning: According to the Surgeon General, women should not drink alcoholic beverages during pregnancy because of the risk of birth defects." The objective of this law is to alert and remind pregnant women about the risks to the fetus from drinking alcohol.

---

[42] Simmons v. Homatas, 925 N.E.2d 1089 (Ill. 2010)

Prohibition of Illegal Gambling

In most states, a licensee cannot permit its bar or restaurant to be used for illegal gambling. The objective of this law is to prevent illegal conduct from occurring where alcohol is sold, and also to prevent would-be gamblers from making betting decisions, which could negatively impact their financial circumstances, while their judgment is compromised by alcohol. The betting game of Texas Hold 'Em has become very popular, prompting an interest on the part of bar managers to host tournaments. By holding such an event a bar would be permitting gambling and thus risking revocation of its alcohol license and fines.

Prohibition of Disorderly Conduct

A licensee cannot permit disorderly conduct, such as fighting, solicitation for purposes of prostitution, lewd or indecent sexual acts or performances in the bar or restaurant, or other criminal activity. Concerning fights, the New York State Alcoholic Beverage Control Board stated in an announcement that a bar's license had been suspended, "Nightclub owners that cannot maintain control of their establishments will lose the privilege of holding a liquor license…[43] Bar owners who run unruly establishments will not be tolerated."[44] The objective of this law is to maintain peace and order by minimizing the disorderly and illegal conduct that may occur where alcohol is served.

Maintenance of Prescribed Records

A licensee is required to maintain records of its suppliers, documenting the extent of its daily alcohol purchases and information about the vendor. The objective of this law is to permit the liquor authority to track liquor purchases and sales, and determine the volume of sales of particular licensees.

Restrictions on the Type of Alcohol Sold

States usually offer various types of liquor licenses, including licenses for on-premises consumption, the type a restaurant would likely have; licenses for off-premises consumption, which a liquor store would have; licenses authorizing the sale of beer and wine only; licenses authorizing sales of alcohol for one day only; and other categories. A licensee with a limited right to sell must abide by the limitations. For example, a licensee with a wine and beer license cannot sell mixed drinks.

Limitations on Sales Promotions

The licensee may be restricted from utilizing specials such as "two for one" and novelties such as gifts or prizes in the sale of alcohol. The purpose of these laws is to encourage moderation in the intake of liquor. Because of antidiscrimination

---

[43] "Liquor Authority Suspends License of Club Hush," Media Advisory, October 20, 2006
[44] "Last Call for Bronx Bar," Media Advisory, October 5, 2006

laws, bars are restricted from having a "ladies' night" or "men's night" during which drinks are offered at a reduced price to one gender but not the other. Many bars disregard this prohibition. One reason may be that few people are motivated to sue because of these promotions.

Prohibition on Celebrity Endorsements

The licensee may be forbidden from displaying signs that suggest athletes or other celebrities recommend drinking alcohol. The purpose of these laws is to discourage overindulgence.

Proximity to School, Church, and Parks

In most jurisdictions, a licensee cannot be located within a certain distance (prescribed by statute or ordinance) from the entrance of a school or place of public worship. The objective is to protect the well-being of students, and the sanctity and tranquility of churches. In Alabama, the court upheld a city council's denial of a liquor license where the bed-and-breakfast seeking the license was located in a residential area across the street from a park used by families.[45]

Alcohol-Free Teen Events

Bars or restaurants planning an alcohol-free teen event are required in some states to notify the state liquor authority prior to holding such an activity. The purpose of this law is to enable the authority to investigate the event and verify that no alcohol is served.

Alcohol Inhaling Devices

Alcohol inhaling devices enable consumers to inhale alcohol vapors. These devices, called AWOLs (Alcohol Without Liquid), mix alcohol with gas to produce a mist of alcohol that is inhaled by the user. The alcohol travels directly to the bloodstream, and so an AWOL is able to cause a dangerously fast intoxication. The device resembles an asthma inhaler and can be used for virtually all types of alcohol including wine, vodka, and martinis. Many states including California, Florida, New York, Pennsylvania, and Ohio have banned AWOLs. Penalties for selling, possessing, or allowing the use of such devices include revocation of a liquor license and fines up to $10,000.

---

[45] Biggs v. City of Birmingham, 91 So.3d 708 (Ala. 2012)

Sexually Explicit Entertainment

Some bars provide nude or sexually explicit dancers. Many municipalities and their residents seek to discourage these businesses because of their impact on the community. Adult entertainment often attracts prostitutes, generates rowdiness, insults many people's morals, and discourages families from living nearby. The mechanisms used by governments to deter these establishments are regulations or ordinances that restrict these businesses' operation and locations. Among the regulations towns have adopted are prohibitions on total nudity; limitations on the hours of operation for sexually oriented businesses; prohibition of specific sexually explicit dance movements; and requirements that such businesses be located outside residential areas.

Courts have determined that nude or nearly-nude dancing is a form of speech that conveys eroticism. As such, it is entitled to some protection by the constitutional right to free speech. Adult entertainment businesses often challenge governmental restrictions, claiming they are unconstitutional and therefore void. To pass constitutional muster, the restrictions must further an important government interest unrelated to suppression of free expression (such as protecting public health and safety), and must not be broader than is necessary to achieve the stated government interest. Among permissible regulations are the requirement that dancers wear minimal clothing such as a G-string or panties; a limitation on the hours of operation, provided the limitation does not unreasonably confine the times the business can be open; and restrictions on the geographical areas within the town where an adult entertainment business can be located, provided some locations exist where the adult entertainment business can operate.

Summary

Businesses that dispense alcohol must have a valid liquor license and should avoid sales to patrons who are visibly intoxicated, underage, or known habitual drunkards. Illegal sales can result in revocation of a liquor license, criminal sanctions, and dram shop liability, requiring the licensee to compensate a third person injured by the patron. In some states, the licensee might also be liable to compensate the illegally served patron.

Employee training programs addressing service of alcohol and identification of intoxicated drinkers are necessary to help limit liability. This in-service training should be reinforced with frequent refresher courses. Dram shop insurance should also be considered.

Each state has adopted various regulations relating to the sale of alcohol. Liquor licensees should determine the applicable laws and strictly comply.

See Table 12-1 for a listing of additional alcohol-related laws by state.

Preventive Law Tips for Managers

- *Comply strictly with state restrictions on serving alcoholic beverages to avoid loss of a liquor license.* A restaurant or bar cannot serve alcohol without a license from the state. In most states, serving the following people is illegal: a visibly intoxicated person, someone under age 21, and a habitual drunkard. If a licensee does not strictly comply with these laws, the state can suspend or revoke the license. Most states are unyielding in their enforcement of the alcoholic beverage control laws. Stringent compliance is the only way to preserve a liquor license.

- *Another reason for avoiding illegal sales is dram shop liability.* Dram shop acts, adopted by most states, render a bar or restaurant liable when a person is injured by someone to whom the licensee sold alcohol illegally. To avoid this potentially financially devastating liability, the licensee should do all of the following: do not sell to persons in the prohibited categories; train employees on how to manage alcohol sales, how to detect if someone is intoxicated, and how to handle requests for alcohol from customers who cannot legally be served; reinforce employee training regularly; offer alternatives to alcohol such as bottled waters, fancy coffees and teas, or "minidrinks" containing less alcohol; and provide a ride-home service for patrons who appear incapable of driving safely.

- *Train employees on detecting intoxicated drinkers.* Dram shop liability is based in part on serving customers who are already intoxicated. To assist employees in making the assessment of intoxication, training programs should be provided and regularly reinforced.

- *Train employees to identify underage patrons.* Serving customers who are too young to drink legally can result in revocation of a liquor license, criminal liability, and civil liability. To avoid errors by service staff in determining age, provide training on how to determine a customer's age and how to review identification documents for possible unauthorized alterations.

- *Underscore to employees management's commitment to avoid serving alcohol illegally.* Employees will take the lead from management directives and attitudes. Supervisors, managers, and owners must evidence at all times a commitment to avoid service to those who are intoxicated, underage, or habitually drunk.

- *Develop a policy for dealing with customers who have been served too much alcohol.* Plan for the possibility of a customer becoming intoxicated at your bar by identifying methods you will use to assist the patron in getting home safely. Instruct your employees on how to handle such a customer.

- *Determine what additional regulations your state imposes on licensees and comply with them.* States have adopted various restrictions and regulations for its liquor licensees. Examples of such regulations include a minimum age for wait personnel in licensed restaurants and bars; required warnings to pregnant women about the effect of alcohol on the fetus; and prohibition of illegal gambling and disorderly conduct at licensed premises.

Review Questions

1. The law prohibits the sale of alcohol to certain categories of people. Identify those categories. What penalties do states impose for illegal sales?

2. What is meant by dram shop liability?

3. When a patron who is visibly intoxicated continues to drink at two different licensees and then is in a two-car accident injuring the driver of the second car, which licensee is liable to the driver of the second car?

4. Identify three strategies for limiting dram shop liability.

5. What behaviors might alert wait service personnel that a patron is visibly intoxicated?

6. Identify five regulations some states impose on liquor licensees.

7. What factors determine the price of liquor liability insurance?

8. What constitutional right impacts laws effecting sexually explicit entertainment?

Discussion Questions

1. In most states, a patron who is illegally served alcohol and thereafter injured as a result cannot sue the licensee who made the illegal sale. A third person injured by the patron can sue the licensee. What is the rationale for distinguishing between the two?

2. Raj is a server at a bar. A customer orders a beer. Raj knows he has served the customer several beers already. What factors should Raj consider in determining whether to serve the customer another drink?

3. From the previous question, if Raj determines that the customer is intoxicated, how might Raj both refuse to provide another beer but nonetheless appease the patron?

4. Why might a municipality not want a business in town that provides adult entertainment? What can the municipality do and not do when regulating such businesses?

Application Questions

1. Jerry had been drinking all evening at the Bonger Bar and became visibly intoxicated. The bartender continued to serve him. Thereafter, Jerry left the Bonger Bar and, still visibly intoxicated, went to Gordon's Restaurant, where he had another drink. While driving home from Gordon's, Jerry drove his car in the wrong lane and crashed head-on with another car. Both Jerry and the driver of the other car suffered serious injuries. Both sued Gordon's and Bonger Bar. Who is liable to whom?

2. A bartender at the Rascal Café, which is located in a state with a drinking age of 21 and a dram shop act, served a female who was 19 years old. She had only one drink. Due to the effects of the alcohol, she failed to stop at a red light and hit a pedestrian who was crossing the street. Is the Rascal Café liable to the pedestrian for the injuries? Why or why not?

3. Assume in the previous question that no one from the Café asked the patron for proof of age. What penalty might the Café face and why?

4. David and Shep celebrated David's bachelor's party at Jarvis' Gentlemen's Club. The club was not allowed to serve alcohol but allowed its customers to bring their own alcohol into the club. It supplied glasses and ice for a minimum charge. David and Shep later got into Shep's car and were involved in a two car accident, killing the other driver. Will the club be liable under the dram shop act or for negligence? Why or why not?

TABLE 12-1 Alcohol-related legalities by state

States	Minimum BAC Constituting DWI	Dram Shop Act	Mandatory Server Training	Sobriety Check-points Permitted*
Alabama	.08	yes	no	yes
Alaska	.08	**	yes	no
Arizona	.08	yes	no	yes
Arkansas	.08	yes	no	yes
California	.08	**	no	yes
Colorado	.08	yes	no	yes
Connecticut	.08	yes	no	yes
Delaware	.08	no	yes	yes
District of Columbia	.08	**	yes	yes
Florida	.08	**	no	yes
Georgia	.08	**	no	yes
Hawaii	.08	**	(some islands have)	yes
Idaho	.08	**	no	no
Illinois	.08	yes	no	yes
Indiana	.08	yes	yes	yes
Iowa	.08	yes	no	no
Kansas	.08	no	no	yes
Kentucky	.08	yes	no	yes
Louisiana	.08	**	yes	yes
Maine	.08	yes	no	yes
Maryland	.08	no	yes	yes
Massachusetts	.08	yes	no	yes
Michigan	.08	***	no	no
Minnesota	.08	yes	no	no
Mississippi	.08	**	no	yes
Missouri	.08	**	no	yes
Montana	.08	**	yes	no
Nebraska	.08	no	no	yes
Nevada	.08	no	no	yes
New Hampshire	.08	yes	no	yes
New Jersey	.08	**	no	yes
New Mexico	.08	yes	yes	yes
New York	.08	yes	no	yes
North Carolina	.08	**	no	yes
North Dakota	.08	yes	no	yes
Ohio	.08	yes	no	yes
Oklahoma	.08	**	no	yes
Oregon	.08	yes	yes	no

Pennsylvania	.08	**	no	yes
Rhode Island	.08	yes	yes	no
South Carolina	.08	**	no	yes
South Dakota	.08	no	no	yes
Tennessee	.08	**	yes	yes
Texas	.08	**	no	no
Utah	.08	**	yes	yes
Vermont	.08	yes	yes	yes
Virginia	.08	no	no	yes
Washington	.08	**	yes	no
West Virginia	.08	yes	no	yes
Wisconsin	.08	**	yes	no
Wyoming	.08	**	no	no

* A sobriety checkpoint is a police roadblock requiring all vehicles traveling through the checkpoint to submit to momentary inspection by the police. If violations are discovered the motorist is typically ticketed. If the police observe indicia of intoxication when the driver is stopped for the checkpoint, an arrest for driving while intoxicated may result.

** *Limited Application.* The state has a dram shop act but it application is limited. For example, it may apply only to service of alcohol to minors.

Note: While many states used to have a minimum BAC of 0.10 they changed to 0.08 in response to a federal law that authorized the federal government to withhold a portion of a state's federal highway funds beginning in 2004 if the state had not adopted a 0.08 BAC.

Websites

Websites that will enhance your understanding of the material in this chapter include:

www.azliquor.gov This is the site of the Arizona Department of Liquor, Licenses, and Control, the governmental agency that issues liquor licenses to appropriate applicants and monitors licensees' sales. Each state has a similar agency which also has a website that can be easily accessed by an online search. Included in the Arizona site are state laws, information on the process to obtain a liquor license, advice on training servers, and frequently asked questions and their answers.

www.nhtsa.gov This is the site for the National Highway Traffic Safety Administration, a bureau of the U.S. Department of Transportation. The site contains information about all aspects of highway safety including much information about drinking and driving.

www.Madd.org This is the site of MADD (Mothers Against Drunk Driving), a nonprofit organization whose mission is to stop drunk driving, support victims of the crime of driving while intoxicated, and prevent underage drinking.

CHAPTER 13

Travel Agents and Airlines— Rights and Liabilities

LEARNING OUTCOMES:

- Understand the makeup of the travel industry
- Appreciate small claims court and class actions
- Comprehend the rights of travelers
- Appreciate the special rights of airlines
- Understand the rights of airline captains
- Learn the concept of overbooking
- Understand liabilities of travel agents and charter tour companies
- Know liabilities of rental car companies

KEY TERMS

agency	errors and omissions insurance	principal
agent		small claims court
class action suit	e-tickets	tariff
credit card fraud	independent contractors	travel insurance
disclaimer	Montreal Convention	Warsaw Convention
	negligent entrustment	

Introduction

At one time the American travel industry catered primarily to three categories of travelers: the wealthy, businesspeople, and government officials. This is no longer the case. U.S. citizens have developed one of the highest per capita incomes in the world. As a result, travel is now within the reach of many. As the travel industry has grown to serve more people, it has become more complex and the problems inherent in arranging travel also have grown.

There was an Alka-Seltzer television commercial in which a vacationing couple is seen sitting beside a swimming pool in a state of extreme agony. As the camera retreats, it becomes obvious that their vacation paradise is undergoing extensive construction and earth removal. The man shouts over the roar: "I asked the travel agent, 'Where can we go for a little peace and quiet?' He says, 'Mr. Fields, I've got just the place! A peaceful little cottage in the heart of the Mellow Mountains.'" The sounds of construction increase. "My head…my stomach…I need some Alka-Seltzer."

The travel industry felt so maligned by the ad that they pressured Alka Seltzer's advertising agency to change the commercial. (Note the power of concerted action.) But the picture it presented was not entirely fictional. Sometimes promised amenities do not materialize.

Travel agents do not just sell tickets; the travel agent also dispenses travel information and advice on all aspects of a trip, including the best way to get to your destination, where to stay, where to eat, and what to anticipate en route and upon arrival. Most travelers put their trust in the travel agent and expect to be notified of important information or risks affecting their trip. Unfortunately, the facts of many lawsuits against agents suggest that trust is sometimes misplaced.

The consumer rights movement has had a large impact on the travel industry. Travelers are very aware that they may be entitled to compensation when their travel plans go awry. Many disappointed travelers seek recompense in court via litigation against the travel agent or against one of the many third-party suppliers (e.g., hotels and tour companies) that make up the travel industry.

This chapter discusses the rights of the traveler and the liabilities of the travel agent and the airlines when travel plans fail.

© Olga Gavrilova/Shutterstock.com

The Makeup of the Travel Industry

The travel industry generally is composed of the following four groups:

1. Suppliers of travel services, such as hotels, resorts, airlines, and other types of transportation

2. Travel wholesalers that combine the services offered by suppliers into "package tours"

3. Travel agents who sell both package tours and services of individual suppliers

4. Travelers

To fully comprehend this chapter, you need to know a bit about two topics: agency law and tariffs. An introduction to each follows.

Agency Law

In some cases in this chapter the issue arises whether the travel agent is a legal representative of the supplier of travel services (such as a hotel, airline, or bus company) or, in the alternative, a legal representative of the traveler. The legal term used for a legal representative is *agent*. The term is used in a more formal and legal way than the term *travel agent*. The latter term refers to an individual who advises travelers on most aspects of taking trips. While confusing, know that a travel agent sometimes is the legal representative (agent) of the traveler and sometimes is the legal representative (agent) of a travel service provider such as a hotel or airline. The outcome of a case against a travel agent or service provider is often determined by whether the travel agent acted as the agent (legal representative) of the traveler or of the service provider.

Agency is a related term that means a relationship in which one person acts for or represents another based on authority voluntarily given by that other person. Such

agency
A relationship in which one person (the agent) acts for another (the principal) based on authority voluntarily given.

principal
A person who authorizes an agent to act on his or her behalf and controls or directs the method used by the agent in performing authorized tasks.

agent
A person authorized by a principal to act on the principal's behalf under the principal's direction.

relationships involve two parties: a principal and an agent. The **principal** is the person who authorizes someone else (an agent) to act on his behalf. The principal typically controls the method used by the agent to do the authorized tasks. The **agent** is the person so authorized, the one who represents or acts for the principal consistent with the principal's directions. A classic example of a principal/agent relationship is an employer (principal) and employee (agent). By using agents, a principal can conduct multiple business transactions simultaneously in different locations and thus greatly expand the principal's business.

When an agent acts on behalf of a principal and within the scope of the authority given by the principal, the latter is legally bound by (liable for) the agent's acts, and the agent is not.

CASE EXAMPLE 13-1

Rottman v. El Al Israel Airlines

849 N.Y.S.2d 431 (N.Y. 2008).

Jerry Rottman has brought this Small Claims action against defendant El Al Israel Airlines ("El Al") for breach of contract for bumping him from its flight and not arranging alternative transportation. El Al denies liability.

Rottman purchased airline tickets through a travel agent for travel between Baltimore, Maryland and Israel on March 29, 2007. The agent booked Rottman on an American Airlines flight that left Baltimore/Washington International Airport ("BWI") at 1:50 p.m. and arrived at John F. Kennedy Airport at 2:50 p.m. Rottman was booked on El Al's 5:05 p.m. flight to Israel.

Rottman testified that after arriving from Baltimore on the American Airlines flight, he proceeded to the El Al terminal. There was a long security line. He went to the front of the line and showed his ticket to airport personnel. He was told that he was too late to make the flight. He was directed to another line, and the El Al representative advised him that all flights were overbooked and that he had only a 10% chance of getting on a flight to Israel before the start of Passover. Rottman testified further that he had no knowledge of El Al's time requirement protocols for check-in.

Rottman was able to reserve a seat on a Swissair flight that left New York for Tel Aviv on April 1, 2007. He paid $2,945.40 for the one-way ticket. Rottman testified that he incurred additional expenses of $340.00 for lodging, transportation and food as a result of the three-day layover.

Peter Ninger, an employee of El Al, testified on behalf of defendant. He had no personal knowledge of the facts. His testimony was based on El Al's computer records regarding claimant's reservation. The flight was called for check-in at approximately 4:00 p.m. Rottman had not checked in. At this time, the flight was closed for check-in. Rottman was deemed a "no show" and forfeited his seat on the flight. Ninger conceded that the 5:05 flight was overbooked by 17 seats.

Moreover, Ninger stated that Rottman did not comply with a condition of the contract which required passengers to check in at least three hours prior to departure. This requirement was in El Al's "system". A copy of the computer page was introduced in evidence. Mr. Ninger testified that claimant could not have made the flight. He needed to check in at El Al by 2:15 p.m. The flight from BWI did not arrive until 2:50 p.m. He testified further that travel agents were authorized to sell tickets for El Al flights; were independent agents; and were required to follow El Al's rules.

Claimant has failed to establish that El Al breached its contract by overbooking the flight and not offering him alternative transportation. Rottman arrived at the El Al terminal less than an hour before departure. By this time, the flight was closed, and El Al properly refused him passage.

However, the court's inquiry does not end here. The ticket issued by the travel agent to Rottman made it impossible for him to comply with El Al's rule requiring a minimum of three hours for check-in. Defendant's position is that it is not responsible for the travel agent's issuance of Rottman's ticket.

Liability in this case rests on whether the travel agent who issued Rottman's ticket is an agent of the airline or an independent contractor. The Restatement of Agency suggests that airlines and travel agents stand in a principal/agent relationship.

Here, the travel agent who was bound by El Al's rules pertaining to the sale of tickets was acting as the agent of the airline when it sold Rottman the ticket for travel to Israel. The principal, El Al, is responsible for the agent's error in writing a ticket for the first leg of the journey that did not comply with the airline's rules. As a result of the error, Rottman was required to pay an additional $2,045.40 for a one-way ticket. He is awarded the cost of the ticket. The claim for damages relating to additional expenses Rottman states he incurred is dismissed for failure of proof.

Ordered that the Clerk of the Court enter a judgment in favor of claimant and against defendant in the sum of $2,945.40 with interest from April 1, 2007, together with costs and disbursements as taxed by the Clerk.

When an agent acts outside the parameter of delegated authority, the principal is not bound and the agent may be liable for fraud (deception) for misrepresenting his authority. Thus, where a travel agent has not been authorized by an airline to sell its tickets, but the travel agent sells tickets on the airline's flights notwithstanding, the airline is not required to honor the tickets. The travel agent will be liable to the traveler for losses incurred.

Agency law requires that the agent disclose to the agent's client the identity of

© Puhhha/Shutterstock.com

the principal so that the client can investigate the reputation or credit of the principal if the client is so inclined. Thus, where a travel agent is acting as an agent of a tour operator when selling a trip, the travel agent must inform the client of the tour operator's identity. If the agent fails to disclose either the identity of the principal or the fact that the agent is acting for another party, the client can legally assume the agent is acting on his own behalf. In this circumstance, the agent will be liable as a principal. A New York case illustrates this point. Ten plaintiffs sued a travel agent in Small Claims Court for three days of lost touring time and other inconveniences suffered during a trip to Israel, caused by the agent's poor planning and failure to make reservations. When planning the trip, the travel agent disclosed that he was acting as an agent for a travel wholesaler, but did not disclose the latter's identity. In the lawsuit the travel agent argued that, since he was acting as an agent of the wholesaler, the wholesaler and not the agent should be liable. The court held the travel agent was liable and the wholesaler was not because the travel agent failed to disclose the identity of the wholesaler to the plaintiffs.[1]

In another case with a similar holding, newlyweds were advised on their honeymoon departure day that the wholesaler of their trip had gone bankrupt. Fortunately, the wholesaler had paid for the couple's airline tickets; unfortunately, the wholesaler had not paid for the hotel. The bride and groom opted to take the trip and pay anew for their accommodations. Upon their return, they sued the travel agency that arranged the trip. The agent claimed the wholesaler alone should be liable. The travel agency had not informed the couple that it was acting as an agent for a wholesaler or the identity of the wholesaler (the principal). As a result, the travel agency was liable.[2]

At first blush it may seem unfair to hold the travel agent liable in these circumstances. However, if the travel agent does not disclose the principal (the tour company), the travelers cannot verify the principal's reputation, history, or financial circumstances, and therefore rely totally on the recommendation of the travel agency.

independent contractor
One who contracts to do work for another, but who maintains control of the method of accomplishing the work. Also, someone hired by another to perform a given task according to methods and procedures that are independent from the control of the hiring party.

An agency relationship must be distinguished from that of an independent contractor. Independent contractors may or may not be agents acting on someone else's behalf, depending on the facts. **Independent contractors** are people who contract to do work for someone else, but are engaged in an independent business for themselves. The only part of the work controlled by the party who hires an independent contractor is the outcome. Independent contractors furnish their own supplies and equipment, pay their own expenses, set their own hours of work, and are paid fees or commission, not a salary. Thus, an independent contractor relationship was found when a tourist booked a trip to Sandals resort and went on a horseback ride. After the tourist sat on the horse, an employee of the horseback riding business slapped the horse hard on the backside causing the horse to run, injuring the tourist. The court determined the horseback riding business was not an agent of the travel company because the travel company had no control over the means by which the horseback riding provider conducted its business. Furthermore, the provider of horseback riding excursions was wholly responsible for maintenance of animals, equipment, and vehicles; hiring and supervising its own employees; and the overall operation of its business.[3]

---

[1] *Siegel v. Council of Long Island Educators, Inc.*, 348 N.Y.S.2d 816 (N.Y. 1973)
[2] *Van Rossen v. Penney Travel Services, Inc.*, 488 N.Y.S.2d 595 (N.Y. 1985)
3 *Johnson v. Unique Vacations*, 498 Fed. Appx. 892 (Fla. 2012).

The acts of independent contractors who are not agents will not bind travel-service providers who hire the independent contractor.

Case Example 13-2 illustrates principles of agency law.

CASE EXAMPLE 13-2

Vermeulen v. Worldwide Holidays, Inc.

922 So.2d 271 (Fla. 2006)

Klaas Vermeulen sued Worldwide Holidays, Inc., a travel agency, for injuries he sustained in a vehicular accident in Peru.

…Vermeulen is a travel consultant with twenty-two years experience. He called Worldwide to book a cruise to the Galapagos Islands the day before his departure. The next day he called Worldwide to book a tour in Peru. When he asked how he would get his tickets, Worldwide told Vermeulen that someone from Chasquitur, the local Peruvian tour operator, would meet him upon his arrival to give him his tickets.

Worldwide does not set the rates charged for Chasquitur's services. Worldwide has no employees in Peru and does not control Chasquitur's operations. All of Worldwide's employees work in South Miami, Florida. Worldwide does not employ anyone who also works for Chasquitur. Worldwide does not operate tours; it sells packages operated by others. All in-country services are provided by the tour operator, not by Worldwide.

On April 24, 1996 Vermeulen was met at the Peru airport by a Chasquitur employee. The employee did not identify herself as an employee of Worldwide nor was she wearing a Worldwide logo or uniform. Vermeulen did not know who this employee worked for and had no evidence that she was a Worldwide employee or agent. The Chasquitur employee escorted Vermeulen to a van for a trip from the airport to the train station. The van was not marked with a Worldwide logo, nor did the driver identify himself as a Worldwide employee.

While the driver was driving the van, Vermeulen claims that the driver rear-ended another vehicle. Vermeulen alleges that he was thrown inside the vehicle, and that he, the driver and another passenger suffered injuries. Vermeulen testified that it was not until after the accident that he learned that the driver and van were provided by Chasquitur.

Vermeulen sued Worldwide for personal injuries that occurred during the accident.

…Vermeuelen claims that Worldwide is liable because Chasquitur's employee was negligent and Chasquitur was Worldwide's agent. The record reflects that Worldwide and Chasquitur were operating independent of each other. The standard for determining whether an alleged agent is an independent contractor is the degree of control exercised by the employer or owner over the alleged agent. There is no evidence on this record that Worldwide had the right to control Chasquitur in any way. On the contrary, the record reflects that Worldwide did not intend for Chasquitur to be its agent. Worldwide and Chasquitur are in different businesses; Worldwide sells cruises and tours operated by others; and Chasquitur operates in-country tour services. The pricing for Chasquitur's tours was established by Chasquitur, not Worldwide. Furthermore, Worldwide did not pay Chasquitur a wage or split profits with Chasquitur. Chasquitur charged Worldwide's customers a fixed amount for each tour. Worldwide and Chasquitur maintained completely separate offices, employees and equipment. In sum, the evidence indicates that Chasquitur was not acting as Worldwide's agent.

For the agency relationship to exist, there must be some affirmative evidence of ownership, operation or control. Mere allegations of agency are not enough to create a principal/agent relationship between a travel agent and a tour operator....

We affirm summary judgment in favor of Worldwide.

Tariffs

tariff
A rule or condition of air travel that binds the airline and passengers. Tariffs are developed by airlines and approved by the federal Department of Transportation.

The tariff system is referenced in many cases in this chapter. A **tariff** is a rule or condition of air travel that binds the airline and passengers. Tariffs cover such items as limitations on an airline's liability for damaged baggage, procedures for filing a claim, rules for reservations and checkin times, limits on the airline's liability for schedule changes and flight delays, and personal injury liability limitations. Travelers are bound by tariffs even though they do not know about them and do not expressly agree to them. Tariffs are developed by the airlines and must be approved by the Department of Transportation.

Tariffs on file with the Department of Transportation, if valid, control the services provided by the airlines. Some of these tariffs contain very one-sided language favoring the airline. Copies of tariffs are available upon request at airports, although few passengers are aware of this and few ask to see them. Tariffs conclusively and exclusively govern the rights and liabilities between an airline and traveler.

Case Example 13-3 provides insights into the role of tariffs in travel law.

CASE EXAMPLE 13-3

Fontan-de-Maldonado v. Lineas Aereas Costarricenses

936 F.2d 630 (P.R 1991)

The appellant, Ms. Enriqueta Fontan de Maldonado ("Fontan"), is an American citizen who lives in Puerto Rico. She planned a vacation in Costa Rica and booked a ticket, through a travel agent, to fly on a Costa Rican airline, Lineas Aereas Costarricenses, S.A. ("the Airline"). An employee of the

Airline, she alleges, told her travel agent that she need take only her birth certificate, not her passport. But, because she did not take her passport, her return journey became a nightmare, with officials in Panama (where she had intended a stop-over) refusing to accept her, the Airline shunting her from one country to another, and her eventually spending the night on the floor of a Venezuelan airport. She sued the Airline, claiming that its bad advice about the travel documents amounted to negligence. The Airline replied that the ticket says such documents are the traveler's, not the Airline's, responsibility and that its tariff holds it free of liability for bad advice about which documents are needed. ...

The relevant provision in the Airline's tariff says that passengers "shall comply with all...travel requirements of countries to be flown from, into, or over," and that the Airline "shall not be liable for any... information given by any employee... to any passenger in connection with obtaining necessary documents... or for the consequences to any passenger resulting from his/her failure to obtain such documents. ..." As required by law... the Airline has filed its tariff with the Department of Transportation, which regulates the rates and services of international airlines serving the United States. Fontan concedes that if this tariff provision is valid, she cannot prevail. Tariff provisions are binding on a passenger, even if the passenger did not actually know of them....

Remedies for Small Amounts of Damages

The amount of damages suffered by a traveler whose plans have gone awry is not always large. The cost of a lawsuit may discourage such travelers from suing the party responsible for the disruption, whether that party was the travel agent, airline, or travel service supplier. Two developments reduce the cost of suing and therefore encourage would-be plaintiffs to sue, thereby increasing liability exposure in the travel industry. These developments are small claims court and class action lawsuits.

Small Claims Court

Many travel cases are brought in **small claims court**, a forum that encourages people to act as their own advocates without a lawyer. To aid that process, small claims court dispenses with formal rules of evidence and procedure that govern trials in other courts. The maximum amount of money a plaintiff can seek is relatively small and varies from state to state, but is customarily $3,000 to $5,000.

small claims court
A forum that dispenses with formal rules of evidence and procedure that govern trials in other courts.

Because rules of procedure and evidence are relaxed, and because lawyers are not necessary, many plaintiffs who might be deterred from suing by the complexities and expense of a typical lawsuit decide instead to pursue their case in small claims court. As a result, businesses, including those in the hospitality industry, have a much greater exposure for their shortcomings than if small claims courts did not exist.

class action suit
A legal device in which many people who have suffered losses from the same cause sue the defendant jointly.

A **class action suit** is a legal device in which many people who have suffered losses from the same cause sue the defendant jointly. It is a financially attractive option for plaintiffs because the cost of the lawsuit is spread among many plaintiffs instead of just one. An example is provided by a class action case that was pursued on behalf of many people who purchased a vacation package from Club Med. The complaint alleged that the seller had promoted the accommodations as luxurious, but instead they lacked electricity, air conditioning, hot and cold running water, and operable toilets.[4]

In another case, the judge granted permission for a class action. The plaintiffs claimed that the defendants—Club Islandia, two Long Island travel agencies, a Long Island tour organizer, and a New York tour wholesaler—misrepresented the nature and quality of accommodations at a Jamaican resort and sued for fraudulent misrepresentation and breach of contract. The class was comprised of 400 people who took three separate charter tours during a three-week period. Said the court, "[C]lass action relief may well be necessary to vindicate the rights of members of the class, whose individual claims are otherwise too small (under $500) to warrant independent litigation against the impressive legal strength of the defendants."[5]

This case is significant in the hospitality industry for a reason in addition to allowing the class to sue jointly rather than requiring each traveler to shoulder independently the cost of a lawsuit. By defining the class as including travelers on three separate charter tours, rather than limiting the class to just one, the potential liability for the travel industry defendant is increased.

The Rights of the Traveler

When travel plans do not turn out as represented and purchased, the law is quite supportive of the traveler and provides a remedy in many circumstances.

Right to Know Fare in Advance

The Department of Transportation requires airlines to display the full cost of an airline ticket, including all mandatory airline charges, governmental taxes, and user fees, in online postings and other advertising. This requirement extends to online travel agencies as well as airline websites.

Baggage Claims—Domestic and International

A tariff provides that when travelers hand their baggage to an airline to have it transported to their destination, they are entering into a contract with the airline.

---

[4] *King v. Club Med, Inc.,* 430 N.Y.S.2d 65 (N.Y. 1980)
[5] *Guadago v. Diamond Tours and Travel, Inc.,* 392 N.Y.S.2d 783 (N.Y. 1976)

This contract binds the airline to deliver the baggage to the destination and to restore it to the traveler upon arrival. If the airline fails to deliver the luggage at the destination, it has breached its contract. Under normal contractual circumstances, the traveler would be entitled to recover from the airline the value of the lost baggage and its contents. However, because of the frequency of loss or delayed delivery by the airlines, they would suffer a significant financial burden if travelers were able to recover the full value of lost property in every case. Therefore, tariffs have been adopted to protect the airline from unlimited liability.

While less than 0.70 percent (seven-tenths of one percent) of luggage transported by airlines is misrouted, this number exceeds 600,000 annually. The airlines report that 75 percent of those lost bags are reunited with their owners within 12 hours, and an additional 20 percent are delivered within five days. The remaining 5 percent, most of which are lost and never returned to the traveler, still amounts to a significant number at 30,000. The concept of limiting the airline's liability for this lost luggage is similar to the limiting liability statutes applicable to innkeepers when guests' property is lost or stolen, which we studied in Chapter 8. One set of laws for limiting liability applies to international flights and another to domestic flights. Both will be reviewed in this chapter. In both, passengers are entitled to compensation only for a portion of their lost property; compensation for emotional stress is not permitted, nor are punitive damages.

International Flights

Before 2003, international flights were governed by the **Warsaw Convention**, an international treaty that set limits of liability for lost, stolen, damaged, or misdelivered baggage. The terms of the convention remain relevant for any remaining cases that originated prior to the effective date of the newer convention. Also, understanding the newer agreement is facilitated by familiarity with the Warsaw

Warsaw Convention
An international treaty that sets limits of liability for lost, stolen, damaged, or misdelivered baggage.

© PhotonCatcher/Shutterstock.com

Convention. Under that convention, the limitation on liability for checked luggage on international flights was $9.07 per pound up to 44 pounds, or about $400; the limit for carry-on baggage was $400. Passengers were informed of the limitation on the airline ticket. See Figure 13-1 for an example of a notice.

FIGURE 13-1 Limitation of liability stated on the back of an airline ticket.

ADVICE TO INTERNATIONAL PASSENGERS ON LIMITATIONS OF LIABILITY

Passengers on a journey involving an ultimate destination or a stop in a country other than the country of departure are advised that a treaty known as the Warsaw Convention may apply to the entire journey, including any portion entirely within a country. For such passengers, the Warsaw Convention, including special contracts of carriage embodied in applicable tariffs, governs the liability of the carrier for death of or injury to passengers. The names of carriers who are party to such special contracts are available at all ticket offices of such carriers and may be examined on request.

NOTICE OF BAGGAGE LIABILITY LIMITATIONS

Liability for loss, delay, or damage to baggage is limited unless a higher value is declared in advance and additional charges are paid. For most international travel (including domestic portions of international journeys) the liability limit is approximately $9.07 per pound for checked baggage (maximum 70 pounds, or $640, per checked bag), and $400 per passenger for unchecked baggage. For international travel to which the Montreal Convention applies, liability for loss, delay, or damage to baggage is limited to approximately $1,375 per passenger for checked and unchecked baggage. For travel wholly between U.S. points the limit on the airline's baggage liability is $2,800.

CARRIER RESERVES THE RIGHT TO REFUSE CARRIAGE TO ANY PERSON WHO HAS ACQUIRED A TICKET IN VIOLATION OF APPLICABLE LAW OR CARRIER'S TARIFFS, RULES OR REGULATIONS.

Explained one court, "The remedial system provided by the Warsaw Convention is designed to protect air carriers against catastrophic, crippling liability by establishing monetary caps on awards and restricting the types of claims that may be brought against the carriers, while accommodating the interests of injured passengers by creating a presumption of liability against the carrier...."[6] In exchange for limited liability, the airline is presumed to be responsible when luggage is missing or lost; the passenger does not need to prove that the airline was negligent. The airline can rebut this presumption if it can show it took all possible precautions to avoid the loss. Further, passengers have the option of purchasing insurance to cover loss in excess of the convention's maximum.

---

[6] *King v. American Airlines, Inc.,* 284 F.3d 352 (N.Y. 2002)

Case Example 13-4 provides some background about the Warsaw Convention. The value of the plaintiff traveler's lost property considerably exceeded $400. As you read the case, note the requirements with which the airline had to comply to avail itself of the limited liability.

CASE EXAMPLE 13-4

Lourenco v. Trans World Airlines, Inc.

581 A.2d 532 (N.J. 1990)

… On January 24, 1988 plaintiffs and their two minor daughters were passengers on T.W.A. flight 33 from Nassau, Bahamas to J.F.K. Airport in New York City. The flight was cancelled due to technical difficulties. The Lourencos and their children were later flown to Miami, Florida on Bahamas Air. The group then boarded a Pan American flight to J.F.K.

Their luggage, last seen in Nassau, was shipped separately and lost. It was delivered to plaintiff's home three days later. Plaintiffs allege the luggage was broken into and that $9,232.59 worth of jewelry and other valuables is missing.

Plaintiff Mario Lourenco, is an employee of T.W.A. Neither he nor his wife made a special declaration of the value concerning the contents of their luggage. Plaintiffs did not request special handling of the baggage or purchase special insurance covering the full value of their possessions. …Defendant did not state the weight and number of pieces of luggage on plaintiffs' ticket or baggage check. The total weight of the items missing is stipulated as less than (50) fifty pounds.

T.W.A. argues that its liability is limited by the Warsaw Convention.…The Convention is an international treaty that limits the liability of airlines for death, injury, property damage or loss and delay. It applies to all international transportation of persons, baggage or goods performed by aircraft for hire. The carrier is liable for loss or damage to any checked baggage occurring during transportation by air, including the period baggage is in the charge of the carrier whether in an airport or on an aircraft. Liability is limited to $9.07 per pound of lost baggage, except in cases of willful misconduct. The parties agree the baggage was in international flight and is governed by the Warsaw Convention.

In return for limited liability, the air carrier is presumed liable to a passenger unless the carrier can show that it had taken all necessary measures to avoid damages, or that it was impossible for it to take such measures.

The Convention permits an airline to limit its liability if the provisions of Article 4 are complied with. Article 4 of the Convention states:

1) For the transportation of baggage, other than small personal objects of which the passenger takes charge himself, the carrier must deliver a baggage check.

2) The baggage check shall be made out in duplicate, one part for the passenger and the other part for the carrier.

3) The baggage check shall contain the following particulars:

   (a)   The place and date of issue;

   (b)   The place of departure and of destination;

   (c)   The name and address of the carrier or carriers;

   (d)   The number of the passenger ticket;

   (e)   A statement that delivery of the baggage will be made to the bearer of the baggage check;

   (f)   The number and weight of the packages;

   (g)   The amount of the value; …

   (h)   A statement that the transportation is subject to the rules relating to liability established by this convention.

4) The absence, irregularity, or loss of the baggage check shall not affect the existence or the validity of the contract of transportation which shall nonetheless be subject to the rules of this convention. Nevertheless, if the carrier accepts baggage without a baggage check having been delivered, or if the baggage check does not contain the particulars set out at (d), (f), and (h) above, the carrier shall not be entitled to avail himself of those provisions of the convention which exclude or limit his liability.

The Warsaw Convention is binding on a passenger if the passenger has notice of its provisions. Notice, ordinarily printed on the airline ticket, gives the passenger an opportunity to declare that the value of his baggage is in excess of standard limits. The passenger can then pay a supplementary fee to cover the excess and increase his potential recovery to the declared value. The passenger is also free to make a special contract with the airlines or purchase insurance.

Plaintiffs received written notice of the Convention's applicability. The defendant did not, however, write down on the baggage check the number of pieces or weight of plaintiffs' luggage as required by subsection (3)(f) of Art. 4. The parties agree that defendant complied with all other provisions of Art. 4.

What are the consequences to an airline if it does not strictly comply with subsection (3)(f) of Art. 4? The cases demonstrate a considerable split in authority.

The courts in the State of New York generally hold that when the claim check or ticket does not indicate the number and weight of the packages, the carrier cannot avail itself of the limitation [of liability].

The weight of federal authority, however, holds that the carrier's failure to record the number and weight of a passenger's luggage is a technical and insubstantial omission.…

The economic interest of passengers to be adequately compensated for lost baggage competes with the airline's interest in controlling costs and curtailing litigation. The Convention's limits on liability have been criticized as unconscionably low. Nations in the Third World have complained that the limits of liability are too high. Compromises have been reached in setting the present limits; …The economic policy choice, however, is not for this Court to make.

As an international treaty the Warsaw Convention remains "the supreme law of the land." It is not for Courts to "indulge in judicial treaty-making," or to decide if the U.S. Airline Industry, no longer in its infancy, still needs special protection. The Court's function is to construe the Convention, determine its meaning and apply it fairly. Whether the treaty is construed strictly or liberally, the polestar should be to effectuate its evident purpose. There is populist appeal in subjecting the airlines to unlimited liability for lost baggage. This is not, however, the evident purpose of the Treaty....

This Court holds that the failure to record the weight and number of plaintiffs' luggage on the baggage check is a technical and insubstantial omission and should not deny defendant the benefit of the limitation of liability provisions of the Warsaw Convention....

The difficulty presented by the instant case is that the plaintiffs' luggage was lost, found and returned; with jewelry and other valuable items missing.

The Treaty bases damages on weight, not the actual value of the lost baggage. A pound of jewelry, or for that matter clothing, is obviously worth more than the $9.07 allowed. The plaintiffs were well aware of the worth of their jewelry, and the modest recovery permitted under the Convention for lost baggage, before they checked their luggage with the airline. They chose to run the risk of its loss without benefit of insurance or special declaration. Since the Court has decided that the Warsaw Convention's limitations of liability apply and the plaintiffs have stipulated that the missing items weighed fifty (50) pounds or less, it follows that defendant's liability is limited to a total of $453.50.

CASE QUESTIONS

1. On what principle did the court base its decision that the Warsaw Convention's limitation of liability applied?

2. What options were available to the plaintiffs to avoid the convention's limitation on liability?

The limitation of liability also applied in a case involving the lost luggage of a marketing director for a sporting goods company. The contents included 1,500 T-shirts and 120 pairs of soccer shoes. The company sought damages in the amount of $15,728; the court held the company's recovery was restricted by the limitation of liability in the Warsaw Convention.[7]

Under the Warsaw Convention, if the airlines failed to issue a baggage check and luggage was lost or stolen, the airline was unable to benefit from the convention's limitation of liability ($634.90 per suitcase). This rule is vividly demonstrated in Case Example 13-5.

---

[7] *Abbaa v. Pan Am*, 673 F.Supp. 991 (Minn. 1987)

CASE EXAMPLE 13-5

Kodak v. American Airlines

805 N.Y.S.2d 223 (N.Y. 2005)

In this small claims action plaintiffs' claim for damages resulting from the defendant's failure to deliver two pieces of luggage on an international flight is governed by the Warsaw Convention. That Convention applies rather than the subsequent treaty commonly referred to as the Montreal Convention... since the acts giving rise to the instant suit took place prior to the effective date of the Montreal Convention. Under the Warsaw Convention, an international air carrier's liability for baggage claims is limited to a specified amount. Defendant claims that plaintiffs' recovery is limited to the sum of $634.90 per piece of luggage, for a total of $1,269.80.... Plaintiffs argue that defendant may not invoke the limitation of liability provision because defendant failed to comply with the Warsaw Convention.

Article 4 of the Warsaw Convention req uires the carrier to deliver...a baggage check which sets forth specified particulars including notice of the limitation of liability provisions of the Warsaw Convention and provides that "if the carrier accepts baggage without a baggage check having been delivered, or if the baggag e check does not contain the particulars required, the carrier shall not be entitled to avail itself of those provisions of this convention which exclude or limit his liability."

...An air carrier's failure to prove delivery of the passenger ticket precludes it from invoking the Convention's limitation of liability. In the instant case, defendant failed to prove delivery of the baggage check.... Accordingly it was error for the court below to conclude that plaintiffs' remedy is limited to the limitations of the contractual agreement with defendant.... Instead, the measure of plaintiffs' damages for the loss of their personal property is athe actual value of such property taking into account the original cost and relative newness and the extent, if any, to which it has deteriorated or depreciated through use, damage, age, decay or otherwise."

In another case a traveler's bags were damaged in flights from the United States to Italy and back. The airline failed to issue a receipt for his luggage. Therefore, the Warsaw Convention's limitations on liability did not apply.[8] Defendant raised an interesting question on damages. The damaged luggage consisted of three pieces of a five-piece set. Plaintiff sought compensation for the full cost of replacing the set. The court refused to award more than the damaged pieces were worth.

Grounds for Loss of the Warsaw Convention's Limited Liability

Failure of the airlines to comply strictly with various provisions of the convention can result in loss of the limited liability. A Washington, D.C. case followed the line

---

[8] *D'Arrigo v. Alitalia,* 745 N.Y.S.2d 816 (N.Y. 2002) Of note, the flight involved in this case was due in the air on September 11, 2001 en route from Italy to Newark. Because of the events of that day, the flight was required to return to its place of departure, Milan, Italy. Defendant was not able to provide a return flight home for plaintiff until five days later.

of cases referenced in Case Example 13-4, which holds that the airline, by failing to provide on the baggage claim stub the weight of a passenger's luggage, loses the convention's limitation of liability. The case involved the loss of five pieces of luggage belonging to a family traveling from Washington, D.C. to Santo Domingo.[9]

Willful Misconduct

Another factor that will bar an airline from the advantages of the Warsaw Convention's limited liability is "willful misconduct," which was explained in a case where plaintiffs exited a plane during a stopover in Rio de Janeiro, Brazil. The plane was continuing to New York. The plaintiffs' luggage was not unloaded. The plaintiffs, New York residents, were at the beginning of an 18-day trip and had with them only the clothes they were wearing. Despite the plaintiffs' urgent requests during the layover that airline personnel search the baggage compartment for the plaintiffs' suitcases, the airline refused. It claimed the search would have taken an hour and it did not want to delay the departure of the flight. The airline's lost-and-found agent assured the plaintiffs their luggage would be returned to Rio de Janeiro within two days. However, the plaintiffs' itinerary required they leave Rio de Janeiro the next day. The plaintiffs' luggage was never recovered. They sued for the full value of their belongings; the airline claimed the Warsaw Convention's limitation of liability applied. The court found the airline's refusal during the stopover to attempt to locate the plaintiffs' luggage was willful misconduct and therefore the convention's limitation of liability did not apply. Said the court, "[The airline personnel's] callous disregard for plaintiffs' plight and willful renunciation of its contractual obligation to its passengers [to safely transport and deliver luggage] was motivated by selfish economic interest and justifies a finding of willful misconduct under the provisions of the Warsaw Convention." The court, however, rejected the plaintiffs' claim for damages based on physical inconvenience, discomfort, and mental anguish.[10]

Damaged Baggage

Occasionally, a traveler's luggage will be damaged during transport. To obtain recovery for damaged baggage requires that the traveler strictly follow the prerequisites identified in the tariffs. One such requirement is that notice be given to the airline within a specified number of days after receipt of the damaged luggage. Failure to give timely notice is fatal to the lawsuit. In a Pennsylvania case Pan Am transported the plaintiff's mother's body from Pennsylvania to Nigeria. The casket arrived late; upon arrival the body and casket were damaged. Per the applicable tariff, damage complaints were required to be reported within two weeks. Plaintiff waited two months.[11] The plaintiff's lawsuit was thus dismissed.

If the airlines misled a passenger about the time limits for filing a complaint, failure to comply with time requirements for written notice to the airlines will not result

---

[9]*Rodriquez v. American Airlines*, 193 F.3d 526 (D.C. 1999)
[10] *Cohen v. Varig Airlines*, 405 N.Y.S.2d 44 (N.Y. 1978)
[11] *Onyeanusi v. Pan Am*, 952 F.2d 788 (Penn. 1992)

in dismissal of a case. For example, a disabled passenger on an international flight checked his wheelchair as baggage and it was damaged during the flight. While he gave prompt oral notice of the damage, his written notice was given beyond the applicable time period but only because the airline gave him incorrect information. Although the notice was late, the lawsuit was not time-barred.[12]

The Montreal Convention

Montreal Convention
An international treaty effective in 2003 that controls many aspects of lawsuits against airlines for injuries and losses caused in the process of international airline travel.

Since 2003 the **Montreal Convention** has controlled many aspects of lawsuits against airlines for damages and injuries caused in the process of international airline travel. Among the changes are the following:

1. A maximum recovery for damage to property in the approximate amount of $1,400

2. Calculation of the amount of damages awarded for property loss based on the law of the state or country where the action is commenced

3. Relaxation of the requirement that an airline issue a baggage check with prescribed contents

4. Elimination of the loss of limited liability if the airline fails to comply with the documentation requirements (compare this with Case Example 13-5)

5. Introduction of a requirement that airlines maintain adequate insurance to cover their potential liability

6. Authorization for a plaintiff to bring a lawsuit at the place of his residence (under the Warsaw Convention this was not always possible)

Case Example 13-6 illustrates some of these rule changes.

CASE EXAMPLE 13-6

Mohammed v. Air France

816 N.Y.S.2d 697 (N.Y. 2006)

On August 10, 2004 Wali Mohammed flew Air France from New York to Nigeria to participate in a religious ceremony that, he testified at trial, could be fairly characterized as an "ordination". Over a period of seven days, ten people, including Mr. Mohammed, produced a number of religious artifacts from iron, wood and other materials that were not purchased but "came from the land". When Mr. Mohammed left Nigeria on August 28, he placed a box containing the artifacts in the possession of Air France. During a stopover in Paris, apparently for security reasons Mr. Mohammed was asked to

---

[12] *Dillon v. United Air Lines, Inc.,* 162 F.Supp.2d 380 (Pa. 2001)

identify the box and open it for inspection. When he arrived in New York, however, the box did not arrive with his flight, and he has not seen it or any of its contents again.

Because Mr. Mohammed's property was lost (apparently) during international travel, Air France's liability for the loss is controlled by the Montreal Convention.... The damages legally cognizable under the Convention are those cognizable under New York law. New York law does not recognize recovery for mental suffering and emotional disturbance as an element of damages for loss of a passenger's property. Generally the measure of a passenger's damages for loss of personal property is the actual value of such property taking into account the original cost and relative newness and the extent, if any, to which it has deteriorated or depreciated through use, damage, age, decay or otherwise. The actual value is the real value to the owner and of the loss by being deprived of the property, not including, however, any sentimental or fanciful value the owner may for any reason place upon it.

The real value to the owner is determined by considering all of the circumstances in a rational way and assessing damages through the exercise of good sense and judgment. The owner's own estimate of the value of personal belongings and household items may be credited but for more uncommon items some demonstrated expertise of the owner may be necessary ...

Among other things, Air France contended that in no event could Mr. Mohammed's damages exceed $1,437.58, the maximum permitted under the Montreal Convention....

Mr. Mohammed provided no evidence of value other than his own estimate of $5,000, the jurisdictional limit of Small Claims Part. But that estimate was supported by no demonstration of expertise, nor any evidence of the value of comparable objects, either functional, such as the drums, or ornamental or decorative. Even assisted by the Court's questions, Mr. Mohammed did not provide testimony as to materials and labor that could support valuation based upon the cost of creation and reproduction.

In short, accepting that the religious artifacts were both irreplaceable and unique, the Court has no basis for making an award that is not inadequate or excessive. At most, then, the Court can only make an award of nominal damages.

Judgment is awarded to Mr. Mohammed for $10, with disbursements.

CASE QUESTIONS

1. What more might Mr. Mohammed have provided to the court to establish the value of the items in question?

2. Why do you think Mr. Mohammed did not present the necessary evidence?

Domestic Flights

Neither the Warsaw Convention nor the Montreal Convention applies to domestic flights. Limits of liability for lost luggage on domestic flights (those that begin and end within the United States) are covered by tariffs, which, as we have seen, are developed by the airlines and approved by the Department of Transportation. By law, since 2004, the lowest maximum liability an airline can include in its tariff is $2,800. As with international flights, airlines must offer passengers the option of purchasing insurance coverage above the tariff's maximum.

Security Checkpoints

Before boarding a flight, passengers are required to pass through a security checkpoint in the airport consisting of metal detectors, x-rays of carry-on luggage, wanding of some travelers, and sometimes a "puffer" or sniffing machine that blows a puff of air on the passenger and then determines if the odor of explosives is present. During the check, the passenger is separated from his bags as the carry-on luggage is placed on a conveyor belt and passed through x-ray detection equipment. An interesting case involved a passenger who grabbed the wrong carry-on baggage after proceeding through the security screening process. Upon discovering the mixup he reported it to the airlines, but his baggage was never returned. He sued the airline in small claims court seeking the value of his lost goods. The airline claimed that, since it was required by law to perform the security checks, it should not be held liable for property lost during the process. The court determined the value of the passenger's lost property was $950 and ordered the airline to pay, stating that while the airlines are required to conduct security screenings they also have a duty to safeguard passengers' hand baggage during those checks.[13] Said the court,

> *The traveling public is warned not to pack valuables in checked luggage which is stored within the aircraft's freight and luggage compartments during the flight's duration. Accordingly, valuables are encouraged to be packed in hand baggage intended to be carried aboard the plane to be kept within the passenger's view and control. Yet, the passenger and his hand baggage are separated as both go through the required security measures. The passenger, indeed, is placed in a catch-22 situation in need of a safe place to carry his traveler's cheques, credit cards, travel and business documents, identification, airline tickets, eyeglasses and jewelry....*
>
> *Thus, the security system of an airline should operate in such a manner that it is accountable to the public for the return of hand baggage....*

The airline in this case had hired an independent security company to perform the security checks. The airline's contract with the security company contained a provision that required the latter to "indemnify and hold harmless" (compensate) the airline for any liability the latter incurred from the security checks. As a result, the security company was required to reimburse the airline for the $950 awarded

---

[13] *Tremaroli v. Delta Airlines*, 458 N.Y.S.2d 159 (N.Y. 1983)

to the plaintiff. Note the effectiveness of an "indemnity and hold harmless" clause in a contract.

In another factually similar case, but one where the loss exceeded the maximum recovery permitted by tariff, the plaintiff's recovery was limited. The alarm sounded when the plaintiff went through the metal detector at the security checkpoint. She was "briefly inspected" and then permitted to continue to the airplane. By then, her purse was no longer on the conveyor. A search was unsuccessful. She sued the airlines for the value of jewelry contained therein—$431,000. The court held the airline's liability was limited by its tariff amount of $1,250.[14]

In a case involving an international flight, the plaintiff's carry-on bag likewise disappeared as she passed through the security checkpoint. She claimed it contained jewelry with a wholesale value of approximately $100,000. She was limited in her recovery to the $400 limitation of the then applicable Warsaw Convention.[15]

Today, screening at some airports is performed by private companies rather than the Transportation Security Administration (TSA). A person who is injured or whose property is lost or damaged during the screening process may file a claim. The Federal Tort Claims Act governs the processing of the claim and establishes the rights of the claimant. The resolution of the claim may take six months or more, depending on whether law enforcement is involved. Settlements may be denied without sufficient proof of the loss. An interesting study determined that between 2010 and 2015, $3 million was paid in claims that airport security screeners damaged, lost, or stole luggage or items inside. Settlements were reached in 15,000 cases, nearly one-third of all claims filed. Each day, 2.5 million pieces of baggage are screened by agents. Additional risks for theft take place as luggage is transported through the airport on conveyor belts and carts to the airplane.

The TSA uses undercover surveillance to oversee operations and prevent theft. Approximately 1 in every 20 bags is opened when scanning equipment identifies a suspicious item. Additional use of video monitoring of screening areas is being addressed. Half of all claims are denied due to lack of evidence that an item was damaged, lost, or stolen. The issue of theft came to light during a 2011 report by the Government Accountability Office (GAO) that found TSA inspectors received incomplete and inadequate background checks that missed disqualifying criminal information. Today, applicants are thoroughly vetted.

The claimant must provide proof of the damage, the cost associated with the loss, and negligence attributed to the screening agency within 24 hours or so of the event. Today, the industry average is approximately three pieces lost, damaged, delayed, or stolen per 1,000 passengers according to the Department of Transportation. Video monitoring and improved tracing technology is essential to managing this issue successfully.[16]

---

[14] *Wackenhut Corp. v. Lippert,* 609 So.2d 1304 (Fla. 1993)
[15] *Dazo v. Globe Airport Security Services,* 268 F.3d 671 (Del. 2001)
16 Penzenstadler, N., Ptacek, R. (2015, July 2). Lost, stolen, broken: TSA pays millions for bag claims USA Today investigation finds. *USA Today.*

Other Applications of the Lost Baggage Tariff

Another plaintiff was likewise restricted to the maximum recovery stated in the tariff. The airline transported cremated remains from Georgia to Puerto Rico, and held them in its warehouse pending retrieval by the family. Before they arrived, the box containing the remains disappeared.[17]

Airplane Security

Federal law has long required that commercial airlines refuse to transport any prospective passengers who do not submit to a search of their persons and possessions for dangerous weapons, explosives, and other destructive devices prior to boarding an aircraft, as part of a nationwide anti-hijacking program.[18]

The surprise attack on September 11, 2001, on the Pentagon in Washington, D.C. and the World Trade Center in New York City prompted significant expansion of airport security measures. Three hijacked commercial planes filled with passengers en route from New York and Boston to the West Coast were flown into the referenced buildings by extremists on a suicide terrorist attack. Congress and the airline industry responded with increased security measures to help prevent further incidents. These enhanced precautions were directed at three areas of concern: (1) keeping terrorists away from airports; (2) at airports, detecting hijackers to prevent their access to planes; and (3) preventing unauthorized entry into cockpits.

Among the changes adopted were federal standards for airport security applicable throughout the country; federalization of airport baggage screeners and other security personnel; additional x-ray screenings of luggage; body pat-downs; multiple identification checks to occur at the ticket counter and the departure gates; security checkpoints throughout the airport; regular monitoring of all aspects of airport security systems to ensure standards are being met; training for pilots on carrying guns and responding to attacks; enhanced training for flight attendants as first responders in on-board emergencies; hiring of federal marshals to fly on airlines at random to repel hijack attacks; installation of impenetrable doors for the cockpit; and new training protocols for security personnel.

Prohibitions were imposed on bringing the following items into the passenger cabin in carry-on luggage or on a traveler's person: knives, metal nail files, lighters, loaded firearms, other weapons, poisons, infectious materials, golf clubs, bats, pool cues, ski poles, hockey and lacrosse sticks, items of similar shape and hardness, instruments with retractable blades, and scissors and other cutting or piercing instruments of any kind.

Passengers may not carry on liquid and gel products in excess of three ounces in any one container unless these products were purchased in the airport after the passengers have been screened by security. Additional screening is conducted on

---

[17] *Cubero Valderama v. Delta Air Lines, Inc.*, 931 F.Supp. 119 (P.R. 1996)
[18] 49 U.S.C. § 44902; *U.S. v. Davis*, 482 F.2d 893 (Calif. 1973)

laptop computers. Travelers are typically limited to one carry-on bag and one personal bag, such as a purse or briefcase.

Only ticketed passengers are allowed beyond x-ray security checkpoints, with two exceptions. The two exceptions are parents with children who will be traveling alone, and certain attendants of disabled passengers. Both can obtain a special pass from the ticket counter authorizing them to escort the child or disabled person to the gate area.

All passengers aged 18 or over must carry government-issued photo identification at all times in the airport and on the plane. Parking is now prohibited in a 300-foot zone around terminals. Due to these heightened security procedures, passengers are advised to arrive at the airport at least 90 minutes prior to their flight.

The breadth of these new safety measures and proposals evidence the heightened concern for safety aroused by the terrorist attacks.

Travelers dislike these screening measures for a variety of reasons. First, it is inconvenient to remove shoes, belts, and other items of clothing. Second, the security process takes time, which can be quite annoying for a passenger who is running late for a flight. Additionally, the screening process can expose illegal drugs, resulting in arrest. The TSA allows certain passengers, who meet prescreening approval, to pass through security with less scrutiny.

Case Example 13-7, from the state of Washington, explains well the circumstances of an airport security screening.

CASE EXAMPLE 13-7

United States v. Marquez

410 F.3d 612 (Wash. 2005)

…Marquez attempted to board a domestic flight to Anchorage from Seattle. After checking in for his flight, he proceeded to the Transportation Security Administration (TSA) security checkpoint where he was diverted to Checkpoint B, the "selectee lane." A passenger chosen for the selectee lane is subjected to more thorough search procedures regardless of whether or not the x-ray luggage scan reveals something suspicious or the walkthrough magnetometer sounds an alarm. The primary additional procedure involves a full-body wanding with a handheld magnetometer that uses technology similar to, but more sensitive than, the walkthrough magnetometer. According to testimony, a passenger is randomly selected for the selectee lane either by the airlines at the time of check-in or by TSA employees stationed at the security checkpoint entrance when the passenger presents his or her identification and boarding pass. [Concerning the decision to select Marquez for Checkpoint B], there was no showing that the decision was supported by any articulable reason other than completely random selection.

Once in line, Marquez took off his coat and shoes and placed them on the x-ray scanner conveyor belt along with his carry-on luggage. He walked through the magnetometer and was instructed to sit down in the screening area. At this point, TSA screener Peterson, who was in charge of wanding the passengers in the selectee line when Marquez passed through, retrieved Marquez's personal items from the x-ray belt. Petersen then approached Marquez and began to scan his person with the handheld magnetometer, screening Marquez's feet first, then having him stand up to screen the rest of his body. However, the wand "alarmed" when it passed over Marquez's right hip. Petersen testified that he understood TSA policy to require him to determine the cause of the alarm. Thus, Petersen informed Marquez that he had to touch Marquez's hip in order to ascertain what had triggered the alarm. Marquez denied Petersen permission to touch his hip, and swatted Petersen's hand away when he tried to touch the area. Nonetheless, Petersen felt a "hard brick type of thing" and, on the basis of his experiences in the military and his TSA training, Petersen feared that the object might be explosives. After swatting Petersen's hand away, Marquez continued to protest Petersen's subsequent attempts to determine the source of the alarm, telling Petersen that the wand must have been triggered by a metal rivet on his pants, and that there was no need to look any further. Petersen persisted as well, telling Marquez that he needed to determine what set off the wand, and Marquez continued to refuse, repeating that it was "just a rivet ".

Petersen called for his supervisor. Marquez was becoming increasingly agitated and, upon arrival, the supervisor recommended that he "calm down a little bit" because they had to "get through this if Marquez wanted to fly." Both Petersen and his supervisor again attempted to obtain Marquez's permission to continue with the wanding and determine the source of the alarm, but Marquez refused. Ultimately, after entering a private screening room and in response to the supervisor's repeated requests to determine what caused the wand to alarm, Marquez quickly pulled down his pants, revealing "bricks of stuff in his crotch area… with a pair of spandex leggings over the top." Port of Seattle Police were summoned, and an agent from the Drug Enforcement Agency also responded. The officers searched and questioned Marquez and then retrieved four wrapped bricks of cocaine from his person….

[Defendant was convicted of possession with intent to distribute cocaine. He claimed that the search violated his right against unreasonable searches. The court rejected this argument.]

Recognizing that the United States Constitution affords us a right against unreasonable searches and seizures, you may wonder why airport screenings do not amount to illegal searches. The legal underpinning of the screenings is implied consent. That is, the traveler, by choosing to utilize air transportation, impliedly agrees to the screening process. An interesting question is whether a person in the position of Marquez could withdraw the consent upon being selected for the more thorough search. In a case from Hawaii the court answered this question in the negative. It said that once a person began the screening process, he could not thereafter revoke his consent to secondary screening.[19]

---

[19] *U. S. v. Aukai*, 440 F.3d 1168 (Hawaii 2006)

Regulation Forbids Interference with Screening Process

A federal regulation prohibits interfering with, assaulting, threatening, or intimidating screening personnel in the performance of their screening duties. The rules specifically permit good-faith questions from individuals seeking to understand the screening of their person or property.[20]

A man whose plane was departing shortly set off the alarm as he walked through a metal detector during screening. He was directed to step aside and wait for a screener with a hand-wand. The passenger, anxious to catch his plane, complained that the process was "bullshit" and, as he waited, became more belligerent. "Shit, man, can't you get someone over here" and "This is fucking bullshit." The screener responded, "Mr. Rendon, you do not have to use profanity," to which the would-be passenger commented, "I have a First Amendment [free speech] right to say what I want." He further commented that the screener should be in a different line of work, that the screener should live in a bubble, and that it was a free country and he could say what he wanted. His conduct continued to escalate as did the swear words. In response the screener shut down his line to deal with the man and called over his supervisor. Thereafter the police were called and Mr. Rendon was charged and ultimately convicted of violating the referenced federal regulation. The court rejected the defendant's contention that his statements were protected by freedom of speech, noting that the wrongful conduct was not the content of his comments but rather the interference with the screener's work.[21]

Traveling with Animals

For purposes of determining an airline's liability for mishandling pets, animals are treated the same as suitcases. This was the holding in a case in which the plaintiff's pet dog died while in the custody of the airline on a domestic flight. The plaintiff sued not only for the value of the dog (it was an expensive breed), but also for compensation for the emotional disturbance she suffered as a result of the dog's death, and for punitive damages. The court dismissed the claims for mental suffering and punitive damages, noting that these types of damages are not recoverable where an airline mishandles a traveler's property. Concerning compensation for the value of the dog, the court held recovery was limited to $500 by applicable tariffs. The dog was classified as the plaintiff's personal property and, for compensation purposes, was the equivalent of an inanimate piece of luggage.[22]

We have seen that a passenger can purchase insurance from the airlines to cover the value of property in excess of the maximum provided in the Warsaw or Montreal Convention for international flights, or the airline's tariffs for domestic flights. Could a dog owner purchase insurance with the airline to cover the value of the dog so as to increase the amount of her recovery in the event of the animal's death? Based on the previous case holding that the dog has the same status as luggage, it would follow that the airline would be obligated to sell insurance to cover the dog as it is for other baggage.

---

[20] 109 C.F.R. §1640
[21] *Rendon v. Transportation Security Administration,* 424 F.3d 475 (Ohio 2005)
[22] *Young v. Delta Airlines, Inc.,* 432 N.Y.S.2d 390 (N.Y. 1980)

In another case the plaintiff's golden retriever died as a result of heat stroke caused during a flight delay that resulted from mechanical difficulties. The delay was in Arizona on a June day when the temperature was 115 degrees Fahrenheit. The dog had been maintained in the airplane's baggage compartment, which was unventilated. The court denied recovery to the plaintiff for emotional distress and loss of companionship of the pet. The plaintiff also sought recovery for pain and suffering *of the dog*. The facts established that, upon removal from the baggage compartment, "the [deceased] dog's face and paws were bloody; there was blood all over the crate; and the condition of the cage evidenced a panic effort to escape." Notwithstanding the dog's apparent distress, the court rejected this claim as well. The tariff restricted recovery to the value of the dog.[23]

Damage calculations for lost pets under the Warsaw Convention similarly exclude emotional damages. A California case involved an airline passenger who traveled from Toronto, Canada to San Francisco with five cats. One of their crates was damaged en route and the cat traveling inside it, named FU, was missing and never found. In the lawsuit the owner sought the value of the cat, emotional damages, and punitive damages. The court rejected this measure of loss and instead, consistent with the convention, awarded $9.07 per pound. The court calculated that the feline (dubbed by the court as "FU the Flying Feline") and its crate weighed 25 pounds for an award of $226.75.[24]

In-cabin pet travel is allowed on many airlines. Domesticated cats, dogs, rabbits, and household birds are typically allowed to be carried on board in addition to carry-on baggage and are subject to a service charge, typically of $125 each way. The animal must be carried in a hard or soft-sided kennel with dimension restrictions.

Personal Injury Onboard International Flights

Accidents that occur onboard a plane and cause physical injury to a passenger are covered by the Warsaw and Montreal Conventions. As with damage to or loss of luggage, the airline's liability for personal injury is limited by those conventions. The maximum amount recoverable under the Warsaw Convention was $75,000. Where a woman suffered personal injuries during a flight when a drink cart struck her knees while she slept, her recovery was limited by the convention.[25]

Another case involved a disabled plaintiff who checked his motorized wheelchair as baggage during a flight. Upon arriving at his destination, the plaintiff discovered the chair had been damaged en route. Two days later the plaintiff was injured when the chair malfunctioned from the flight damage and hit a wall. In the resulting lawsuit, the plaintiff argued that since he was not injured onboard the aircraft, the limitations on liability of the Warsaw Convention were not applicable. The court held that the convention was applicable because the accident that caused the injury was the damage to the wheelchair and that occurred onboard.[26]

---

[23] *Gluckman v. American Airlines*, 844 F.Supp 151 (N.Y. 1994)
[24] *Sysotski v. Air Canada*, 2006 WL 581093 (Calif. 2006)
[25] *Price v. KLM-Royal Dutch Airlines*, 107 F.Supp.2d 1365 (Ga. 2000)
[26] *Dillon v. United Air Lines, Inc.*, 162 F.Supp.2d 380 (Penn. 2001)

The Montreal Convention increases the liability of airlines for death or personal injury to passengers to approximately $140,000 per passenger. If the death or injury was due to the carrier's negligence, the liability is unlimited in amount.

Refunds on Tickets

Sometimes circumstances entitle a traveler to a refund on airline tickets, but getting that refund can be difficult.

The plaintiffs in a New York case purchased round-trip tickets from the Comet Travel Agency for the itinerary of New York-London-Amsterdam-Copenha-genStockholm-London-New York. The plaintiffs paid Comet for the tickets and Comet in turn paid the airline, British Overseas Airway Corporation (BOAC). The airline thereafter cancelled the Stockholm leg of the trip. The plaintiffs returned their ticket directly to BOAC and sought a refund of $86, which the airline did not deny was due. However, consistent with a practice adopted by many airlines, BOAC sought to make refund payments directly to the travel agent (Comet) and deduct therefrom the travel agent's commission for the cancelled portion of the trip. The plaintiffs objected, seeking payment of the refund directly from BOAC.[27] The court sided with the plaintiffs and stated that once the travel agent paid the fare to the carrier, the traveler has a valid claim for restitution against the carrier. While the travel agent was an agent for the plaintiffs when purchasing the tickets, once the travel agent had completed the ticket purchase, all authority to act for the customer ended. Therefore, Comet was not authorized to accept refund money on the plaintiffs' behalf, and so the court ordered the airline to pay the full refund to the plaintiffs directly.

In another case, the plaintiff was the victim of fraud perpetrated by the travel agent, Peters. He sold the plaintiff a trip for six to Israel, which supposedly included airfare and hotel. The plaintiff paid the travel agent more than $8,000, in return for which Peters delivered to the plaintiff six TWA airline tickets issued on blank ticket forms. Thereafter, the travel agent disappeared without paying TWA for the tickets. The travel agent had been an authorized agent of TWA until two weeks prior to the plaintiff's ticket purchase, but then TWA had revoked the agency. The airline thus refused to honor the tickets. The plaintiff sued TWA. The court, noting that TWA was not a party to the fraud, held for the airline; the plaintiff was not entitled to a refund from TWA.[28]

Remember, when an alleged agent is not authorized to act for the purported principal (TWA in this case), that principal is not bound by the acts of the agent. Further, the alleged agent may be liable for fraud. Here the plaintiff could sue Peters for fraud. Unfortunately, the plaintiff will likely have difficulty finding him.

---

[27] *Levine v. British Overseas Airways Corp.*, 322 N.Y.S.2d 119 (N.Y. 1971)
[28] *Antar v. Trans World Airlines, Inc.*, 320 N.Y.S.2d 355 (N.Y. 1970)

E-Tickets

Today, electronic tickets (**e-tickets**) are stored in the reservation system of the airline and eliminate the need to print an airline ticket. Passengers must check in with positive identification showing a photo of the passenger. Checked baggage must be cleared through the boarding procedure as well.

Some travelers prefer to print their e-ticket or validation email at or prior to arriving at the airport. Others rely on the apps on their cellphones for boarding. Travelers check in via kiosks or with individual ticket agents on duty.

Rights of Travelers with Disabilities

Vinogradov, the great Russian philosopher, said that social change can only be made by legislating the change. In the United States, this maxim is constantly being proved. The school desegregation and other civil rights cases of the 1950s and 1960s stand as examples of this rather dismal truth. See Chapter 3 for a discussion of the civil rights laws relating to disabled patrons as applied to hotels and restaurants. When we examine the transportation industry, we see that the airlines and other carriers were likewise slow to accommodate persons with disabilities.

Prior to 1986, few laws impacted the decision of commercial airlines and other forms of transportation on whether to provide transportation to persons with disabilities. When a carrier decided to deny transportation, the reason usually given was simply that planes, trains, and buses were not equipped to transport such persons.

The Americans with Disabilities Act (ADA) became effective in 1992, and The Air Carrier Access Act (ACAA) in 1986. The ADA is discussed at length in Chapter 3. The ACAA was adopted to prevent what Congress called the "humiliating and degrading" practices of airlines. It states that, "[N]o air carrier may discriminate against any otherwise qualified handicapped individual, by reason of such handicap, in the provision of air transportation." What effect do these statutes have on the approximately 57 million Americans who have disabilities?

The law is quite clear that persons with disabilities now have a legal right to use the airlines if they can meet minimum requirements concerning mobility that are designed to ensure personal and public safety. Refusing service to people who meet these minimum criteria will result in liability, as evidenced in Case Example 13-8.

CASE EXAMPLE 13-8

Tallarico v. Trans World Airlines, Inc.

881 F.2d 566 (Mo. 1989)

Polly Tallarico, who is fourteen years old, has cerebral palsy, which impedes her ability to walk and talk. She generally uses a wheelchair, but is able to move about on her own by crawling. Although Polly is able to speak only short words, she is able to hear and understand the spoken word. She communicates by use of a variety of communication devices such as a communication board, a memo writer and a "Minispeak."

On November 25, 1986, the day before the Thanksgiving holiday, Polly arrived at Houston's Hobby Airport intending to fly to St. Louis, Missouri, unaccompanied. When the TWA ticket agent, Richard Wattleton, learned that Polly intended to fly alone he contacted Lynn Prothero, acting TWA station manager, and asked for directions as to how he should handle the situation. Wattleton had learned from the limousine driver assisting Polly that she could not speak or walk. Wattleton … [informed Prothero] that Polly could communicate by use of a communications board. From this information, Prothero determined that Polly would not be allowed to fly unaccompanied and informed Wattleton of her decision. This decision was apparently made on the basis of Prothero's conclusion that Polly could not take care of herself in an emergency and could not exit the plane expeditiously. As a result of this decision, Polly's father had to fly to Houston to accompany Polly to St. Louis.

The Tallaricos brought suit alleging that TWA violated the ACAA by denying Polly the right to board the plane because of her physical handicaps. The jury found for the Tallaricos, awarding damages in the amount of $80,000. The district court entered judgment notwithstanding the verdict on the issue of damages, reducing the award to $1,350, which is equivalent to the Tallaricos' actual out-of-pocket expenses.

… The ACAA states that "[n]o air carrier may discriminate against any otherwise qualified handicapped individual, by reason of such handicap, in the provision of air transportation."…

[A] "qualified handicapped person" is a handicapped individual (1) who tenders payment for air transportation, (2) whose carriage will not violate Federal Aviation Administration regulations, and (3) who is willing and able to comply with reasonable safety requests of the airline personnel, or if unable to comply, who is accompanied by a responsible adult passenger who can ensure compliance with such a request. …

The evidence at trial showed that Polly had tendered payment for air transportation, that her carriage would not violate any FAA regulations (in fact she had flown alone before), and that she was capable of complying with the reasonable safety requests of airline personnel. The evidence demonstrated that Polly is able to crawl on her knees or her hands and knees, that she has normal intelligence, and that she is capable of communicating her needs. Polly has a variety of ways of communicating including the use of communication boards which contain the letters of the alphabet and some short phrases; a memo writer; an electronic typewriter-like device; and a "Minispeak," a portable computer with an electronic voice attached. Polly is able to fasten her own seat belt as well as put on an oxygen mask. In addition, Polly's mother testified that she was confident that Polly could crawl to the bathroom (and, presumably, an exit) on the plane if necessary. ...

The jury awarded the Tallaricos $80,000. The district court then granted judgment n.o.v. in favor of TWA as to $78,650 of the damages award. The court concluded that there was insufficient evidence to support the total award and that as a matter of law, the award was not sustainable. The court determined that $1,350 of the award was compensation for out-of-pocket damages as a result of TWA's refusal to allow Polly to board and the remainder was damages for emotional distress. ...

In this case the proof of the emotional distress which Polly suffered after TWA denied her boarding came from the testimony of her mother, her father, the assistant director for Polly's school and the driver who was with Polly when the incident occurred. Theodore Sherwood, the driver who took Polly to the airport, testified that Polly was with him when he was told she would not be allowed to board the aircraft. He stated he noticed that Polly was getting disturbed as she listened to his conversations with TWA employees. Sherwood also testified that he felt it necessary to call Polly's school to see if someone there could talk to Polly and calm her down because after the incident she was crying and upset about what had happened. Polly's father testified that Polly was very angry and upset about the incident. In addition, he stated that since the incident Polly has seemed more withdrawn, quiet and reserved. Polly's mother also testified that Polly was upset about what happened and that Polly was anxious about the situation and concerned about having to fly back to Houston after the Thanksgiving holiday. Susan Oldham, the assistant director of Polly's school, testified that prior to the incident Polly was very outgoing and socialized well with the other students. After the incident, Ms. Oldham testified, Polly seemed more withdrawn and would spend large amounts of time by herself in her room after school was over. Ms. Oldham stated that when she asked Polly if something about her trip home had upset her, Polly replied that what had happened had made her feel badly and had hurt her feelings.

We find that sufficient evidence was presented to support the jury's award of $80,000. Consequently, we reverse the district court's judgment n.o.v. ...

We agree with the district court that the Tallaricos failed to present sufficient evidence to support an award of punitive damages and similarly do not reach the question of whether punitive damages would be allowed under the ACAA.

CASE QUESTION

1. How could TWA have avoided the liability in this case? Include in your answer not just changes in their handling of the plaintiff's situation, but also steps to avoid liability in future cases involving passengers with other types of disabilities.

Similar discrimination issues were raised in two cases from other states. One involved a woman who was reliant on medical oxygen at all times and sued when the airline refused to provide medical oxygen during a flight.[29] The other involved a woman who claimed the airline should provide a wheelchair enabling disabled passengers to traverse the aisle of the plane to use the facilities.[30] Both courts held that individuals claiming disability discrimination cannot originate their case in court but rather must begin the case in an administrative proceeding. Specifically, the relevant statute provides that an aggrieved traveler can file a claim with the Secretary of Transportation and is entitled to a hearing before an administrative law judge. Remedies available include an order compelling compliance with the ACAA, revocation of an airline's air carrier certificate (thereby terminating the airline's business), and imposition of a fine up to $10,000. If the airline fails to comply, the Department of Transportation can initiate an enforcement lawsuit in federal court or can ask the Department of Justice to bring a civil suit.[31]

If an airline has adopted a tariff requiring a companion for a disabled person and a rational reason exists for that requirement, the tariff will be enforceable. This was illustrated in a New Jersey case in which the plaintiff used a wheelchair for mobility. He sought to purchase a round-trip ticket from Alitalia Airlines from New Jersey to Italy. The airline refused to sell him a ticket for that flight unless he bought a second ticket for an attendant or companion to fly with him. Alitalia had a tariff requiring an attendant for passengers who use wheelchairs if the flight exceeds three hours. The rationale was that Alitalia wanted to ensure disabled passengers would be able to move expeditiously to an exit in the event of an emergency. The plaintiff purchased a more expensive ticket on another airline that permitted him to fly alone and sued Alitalia, claiming damages and seeking a modification of the tariff. The court dismissed the plaintiff's case, concluding that the airline's policy sought to ensure the safety of passengers and thus "had a very real and rational relation to the services to be provided."[32]

Other provisions of the ACAA include the following requirements: Air carriers must design terminals to accommodate people with disabilities; airlines must provide fully accessible services in all existing airport facilities; airlines cannot require passengers with assistive devices to undergo special security procedures if the person using the aid clears the system without activating it, but airlines are entitled to examine assistive devices they believe may conceal a weapon; airlines must allow passengers with disabilities to store canes and other assistive devices close to their seat, and cannot count that equipment toward a person's limit of carry-on luggage; if space in the baggage compartment is insufficient to accommodate all travelers, priority must be given to wheelchairs and other assistive devices; and personal mobility equipment stored during flight in the airplane's baggage compartment must be among the first items removed from the compartment upon arrival at the destination.

---

[29] *Boswell v. Skywest Airlines, Inc.,* 361 F.3d 1263 (Utah 2004)
[30] *Love v. Delta Airlines,* 310 F.3d 1347 (Ala. 2002)
[31] 49 U.S.C. §§49106 and 41110
[32] *DeGirolamo v. Alitalia-Linee Aeree Italiano,* 159 F.Supp.2d 764 (N.J. 2001)

Disclosing Need for Assistance

Travelers with disabilities must make known their needs to the airlines. Travel providers need not guess what the needs of a person with disabilities are. Failure to ask for help may preclude recovery for resulting injuries. In an Arizona case the plaintiff had severe arthritis, which made walking very difficult and required the use of two canes. When his connecting flight was cancelled, he was rerouted, requiring him to change terminals, a distance of one-and-a-half miles. He requested a wheelchair, which was provided. A skycap pushed him in the chair from his plane to the bus stop where he would catch the bus to the new terminal. Upon arrival at the bus stop, the plaintiff was told, "This is where you get off. This is where the bus stop is." The plaintiff exited the chair without help and without request for further assistance. In the waiting area, all seats were occupied. The plaintiff stood in pain for 20 minutes until the bus arrived. He refused the offer of an elderly woman to relinquish her seat to him. The bus was not handicapped accessible. He entered it with difficulty but without requesting assistance.

Soon thereafter, the plaintiff suffered a heart attack. He sued the airline, claiming the attack was caused by the lack of assistance in making the terminal change. The court held for the airline, noting that applicable laws and regulations "do not force air carriers to provide unrequested assistance to handicapped individuals.... Furthermore, it is a violation of [applicable laws] to force handicapped individuals to accept services they do not request ...." Addressing the requirements of the Americans with Disabilities Act, the court noted that the airport had two wheelchair-accessible shuttle vans available 24 hours a day, seven days a week. They could be summoned by passengers from special phones located at ground transportation areas or by airport personnel upon request by a disabled passenger. Because the plaintiff failed to request help, his claim against the airline was dismissed.[33]

Service Animals

Trained service animals are allowed in-cabin to accompany disabled passengers. A service animal cannot be in the aisle. It should sit in the floor space immediately in front of the disabled passenger. Approved in-cabin kennels are allowed for smaller service animals. Exit row seating is not available for service animals.

Emotional Support and Psychiatric Assist Animals

Qualified passengers with a disability may travel with emotional support or psychiatric assist animals. Typically, advance notice to the airline is required and documentation must be verified prior to arrival. Without verification, the pet may be required to be transported as a pet, with pet fees charged.

---

[33] *Adivtori v. Sky Harbor International Airport,* 880 F.Supp. 696 (Ariz. 1995), aff 'd 103 F.3d 137 (1996)

Travel Insurance

To protect against financial losses associated with trip cancellations, injuries, and other mishaps that can occur while on a trip, travelers can purchase **travel insurance**. The types of risks covered by travel insurance vary, but can include losses resulting from (1) trip cancellations or interruptions due to war or terrorism, supplier default (e.g., a hotel goes bankrupt and cancels room reservations), or sickness, injury, or death of the insured, an immediate family member, or a traveling companion; (2) trip delays due to natural disasters, quarantine, transportation cancellations (plane, train, bus, ship), injury, or stolen or lost passport, visa, or money; (3) medical expenses for an injury or illness incurred on a trip; or (4) loss or damage to baggage.

travel insurance
Insurance that may be purchased to protect against financial losses associated with trip cancellations, injuries, and other mishaps that can occur while on a trip.

Travel insurance can be purchased through a travel or insurance agent. Given the significant costs of many trips, travelers are well advised to consider purchasing this insurance.

Special Rights of Airlines

Because of the nature of air travel, and the ever-present dangers associated with adverse weather conditions, hijacking, terrorism, and passenger safety, certain rules apply to airlines only.

Right of Airlines to Cancel Scheduled Flights

Many airline flights are cancelled each day, usually with a bona fide reason. Still, with each cancellation many travelers' schedules are disrupted. A great deal might depend on the traveler getting to the destination on time.

In normal contract situations, cancellation would constitute a breach of the airline's contractual duty to transport the passenger to the designated destination, and liability would result. However, there are conditions under which the airline is not bound to fly. In such cases, cancellation of a flight will not result in liability. One of those conditions is mechanical problems with the aircraft. An airline will not be liable for breach of contract where it cancels a flight due to mechanical problems.[34] Another circumstance in which cancellation of a flight will not result in liability is poor weather. This is illustrated in Case Example 13-9.

© Ekaterina Pokrovsky/Shutterstock.com

---

[34]*Dillon v. United Air Lines, Inc.,* 162 F.Supp.2d 380 (Pa. 2001)

CASE EXAMPLE 13-9

Johnson v. Northwest Orient Airlines

642 P.2d 1067 (Mont. 1982)

On December 12, 1979, plaintiff bought a round trip Missoula-Billings ticket from Northwest. On December 22, 1979, plaintiff's scheduled return date, Northwest issued the plaintiff a boarding pass for the Billings-Great Falls-Missoula-Spokane flight. But weather conditions at take-off time, 9:50 a.m., prevented Northwest from landing in Missoula. Therefore, all Missoula passengers were placed on a Billings-Helena flight and were then taken by bus from Helena to Missoula. Plaintiff was offered a check for $29.70, the savings on his alternative transportation. The check was returned several months later, after this suit was initiated.

Plaintiff alleges he arrived home eight hours late because of the flight cancellation. He earned $153,000 in 1979, working 3,000 hours at $50 an hour. As an insurance agent, he claims his weekends are particularly lucrative, earning him more than $100 an hour for ten hours a day. He is seeking $1,000 damages for the loss of a ten-hour day and $122 refund for his plane fare. ...

The [lower] Court determined there were no material issues of fact and that Northwest was entitled to judgment as a matter of law.

Did weather conditions in Missoula prevent the plane from landing? Northwest needs three miles of visibility to land in Missoula. Common sense dictates that only the weather conditions existing prior to take-off, 9:50 a.m., are pertinent. In this case, plaintiff's own exhibit from the National Weather Service shows there was only one and one-half miles of visibility at 9:52 a.m. Therefore, weather clearly prevented Northwest from landing in Missoula.

Did Northwest have a legal right to cancel the Billings-Missoula flight in light of the poor weather? Civil Aeronautics Board regulations govern rights and liabilities between airlines and passengers and cover this issue. Those regulations authorize airlines to cancel flights when necessary. Therefore, Northwest acted within its legal authority in canceling the Billings-Missoula flight.

Did Northwest have a right to refuse plaintiff a seat after a boarding pass had been issued? As noted above, the flight was properly cancelled due to adverse weather. [A] Civil Aeronautics Board Tariff does not require advance notice to be given of flight cancellations. Therefore, Northwest properly excluded plaintiff, even after a boarding pass had been issued.

[W]e believe there are no material issues of fact and that Northwest is entitled to judgment as a matter of law.

CASE QUESTION

1. Why do you think the law relieves an airline from liability for breach of contract when a flight is canceled due to weather conditions?

Prior to deregulation of the airline industry, airlines were required by law to put passengers of cancelled flights onto the next flight out, even if it was on another airline, at no additional cost to the passenger. Today, airlines are not required to do so. All passengers should check flight status online. Any necessary rebooking can be handled online or by communicating with the gate agent or main ticketing area of the airport.

In a small claims case involving cancellation of a flight due to mechanical problems with the aircraft, the court held the airline was not liable for breach of contract. The airline had a tariff stating that where the airline deemed cancellation of a flight to be reasonably necessary for the safety of its passengers, it could cancel without liability. The airline thereafter provided the plaintiff with an alternative itinerary using scheduled flights of other airlines. Due to these circumstances, the original airline was not liable to the passenger when the second airline canceled the flight due to bad weather.[35]

When a flight is canceled, substantially delayed, or rescheduled, the passenger has the right to reroute at no extra cost or to receive a full refund, even on a nonrefundable ticket under the Department of Transportation requirements. The airline policies may vary, however, regarding the definition of a "substantial" delay or schedule change. The federal rules require domestic airlines and foreign airlines flying into the United States to file "Customer Service Plans" which outline the airline's promises with regard to various issues, including delays, cancellations, and diversion event. Contracts and service plans typically call for meal vouchers when a delay extends beyond a normal meal time and for hotel accommodations in the event of an overnight delay. Implementation varies by airline.

Some airlines will provide a transfer to another airline if that carrier can get the passenger to the destination. Other airlines state they may provide a transfer for the passenger, but the airline retains the right to make the decision. Others offer a seat on their own next-available flight as the only option. Neither customer service plans nor contracts for carriage require specific compensation for when an airline fails to meet its commitment.

Established Checkin Time Requirements

The Airline Deregulation Act (ADA) permits airlines to establish checkin time requirements and deny boarding to passengers who fail to comply with checkin time limits.[36]

Rights of Airline Captains

Passengers in flight are confined in the aircraft for the duration of the trip. If anyone on the plane seeks to jeopardize the safety of the passengers—by hijacking, terrorist acts, assault, or otherwise—the option of calling the police is not avail-

---

35 *Dillon v. United Airlines, Inc,* 162 F.Supp.2d 380 (Pa. 2001)
36 A.P. Keller, Inc. Cont'l Airlines, Inc., No. 14-10-00917-CV, 2011 WL 5056241 (Tex. App. Oct. 25, 2011)

© Alexey Y. Petrov/Shutterstock.com

able. The result is that the occupants of the plane can readily be placed at risk, as this country observed only too clearly when terrorists flew hijacked planes into the Pentagon and both towers of the World Trade Center in New York City. To address this peril, the law gives pilots significant latitude in deciding to remove a ticketed passenger from the plane prior to takeoff. Federal legislation, called the Federal Aviation Act, states that an air carrier "may refuse to transport a passenger or property the carrier decides is or might be inimical to safety." Such a refusal cannot give rise to a claim for damages unless the carrier's decision was arbitrary or capricious. When the pilot and/or airline is sued for removing a traveler, the court will make an objective assessment of the carrier's decision, taking into account all the circumstances surrounding the determination including the facts known at the time, the time constraints under which the decision was made, and the general security climate in which the events unfolded. Additionally, the pilot is entitled to rely on a flight attendant's representations that a passenger is disrupting the attendant from performing her safety-related duties; the pilot is not required to pursue further inquiry of the circumstances.[37]

Case Example 13-10 addresses the extent of the pilot's authority to remove travelers who are suspected of being hijackers.

CASE EXAMPLE 13-10

Zervigon v. Piedmont Aviation, Inc.

558 F.Supp. 1305 (N.Y. 1983), aff'd w/out opinion, 742 F.2d 1433 (1983)

Eight plaintiffs, who were removed from an airplane owned and operated by defendant, Piedmont Aviation, Inc., ("Piedmont"), which was about to depart from Tampa, Florida, to New York City, were each awarded $7,500 damages by a jury. Piedmont now moves for judgment notwithstanding the verdict ("nov").

The Plaintiffs allege that their involuntary removal was discriminatory and in violation of [the law]. Piedmont justified its action upon the ground that in the opinion of the captain of the airplane plaintiffs' continued presence thereon (1) "would or might be inimical to the safety of [the] flight," and (2) presented the possibility that they "would cause disruption or serious impairment to the physical

---

[37] 49 U.S. §4490 2(b)

comfort or safety of other passengers or [the] carrier's employees," as provided under Piedmont's tariff filed with the Civil Aeronautics Board....

A trial court may correct a jury verdict only if after so viewing the evidence it is convinced that the evidence is so strong and overwhelming in favor of the prevailing party that reasonable and fair-minded persons, in the exercise of impartial judgment, could not render a verdict against it.

The issues must be considered against the totality of the facts as they existed at the time the captain took his action. His decision cannot be viewed in isolation separate from events that preceded it but in proper perspective as of the time of their occurrence and in relationship to one another. Whether a captain properly exercised the power to remove a passenger... "rests upon the facts and circum-stances of the case as known to the [captain] at the time [he] formed [his] opinion and made [his] decision and whether or not the opinion and decision were rational and reasonable and not capricious or arbitrary in the light of all those facts and circumstances." The fact that the safety and well being of many lives are dependent upon his judgment necessarily means that the captain is vested with wide discretion. "This is understandable when one considers that an airline usually must make such deci-sions on the spur of the moment, shortly before takeoff, without the benefit of complete and accurate information." Thus, " the reasonableness of the carrier's opinion...is to be tested on the information available to the airline at the moment a decision is required. There is correspondingly no duty to conduct an in-depth investigation into a ticketholder's potentially dangerous proclivities."

We thus consider the evidence against the applicable law. The eight plaintiffs and their band boy left LaGuardia Airport, New York City, on the morning of March 28, 1981, on a Piedmont airplane for Tampa, where they were to perform at a dance concert that evening. They were ticketed to return to New York the next morning at 7:05 on Piedmont Flight 372. After completing their performance, and following a brief stopoff in the early hours of the morning at a hotel, they arrived at the Tampa airport where they waited in an embarkation room preparatory to boarding the 7:05 a.m. plane. While there and waiting to enplane, the group, by their loud and boisterous manner, attracted the attention of Mr. Luis Ramos, another passenger. Mr. Ramos and his wife heard one of the group say to another in Spanish "when we arrive in the capital they will ask us for our experience on this flight," which Mr. Ramos regarded as unusual.

After the passengers were seated on the plane, it left the gate and readied for the takeoff. The mem-bers of the musical group were seated generally in the same area in the rear of the plane. However, before reaching the runway, the band boy assaulted a stewardess by grabbing her hand, twisting it and she screamed. She was visibly shaken and reported the incident and her concern about the group to the captain, George Sturgil, who immediately called airport security and returned to the gate, where he ordered the band boy removed from the plane. Following the band boy's removal, the plane again taxied for the takeoff. It returned a second time to the gate, however, to remove a bass instrument that erroneously was thought to belong to the band boy. While the plane was at the gate for the second time, Mr. Ramos, who had observed the band boy being taken off the plane by a police or security officer, said to a passenger seated next to him, Mr. Herbert Hill, that the band boy "belong[ed] to a group of musicians, like eight or ten, who were talking in the waiting room. And one of them said to another, 'when we arrive in the capital, they will ask us about our experience on this flight.' "Hill understood Ramos to say "[W]on't the people be surprised when we get to the capital with this aircraft." The use of the word "capital" suggested to Hill that the plane would not land as scheduled, and "rang a bell" in his head that it was Havana, Cuba, where the plane would be forced to land. Thereafter, Hill signaled a stewardess and at his request Ramos repeated the statement to her. She then apprised the captain of it, who immediately left the cockpit and went to where Hill and the Ramoses were sitting. Ramos then repeated his story to the captain. Captain Sturgil returned to the cockpit and ordered the removal of the plaintiffs. Mr. and Mrs. Ramos and Mr. Hill all testified that the overheard statement made them apprehensive that a highjacking to Cuba was in the making.

There can be no doubt that as a matter of law the captain's decision was reasonable and appropriate. The facts known to him provided a sufficient basis for concluding that plaintiffs' continued presence on the aircraft would or might be inimical to the safety of the flight. From the totality of circumstances, the captain was completely justified in believing that there existed a potential highjack threat. As commander of the aircraft, he was charged with the responsibility for the one hundred persons aboard: both passengers and crew alike. If he had decided otherwise, and continued the flight with the plaintiffs on board, his inaction might well have subjected the flight and passengers to grave danger. Indeed, with the information conveyed to him and the prior incident of an assault upon a crew member, if the captain had not taken the action he did he may well have faced a charge of dereliction of duty. Overall, his decision to remove the plaintiffs, therefore, was both reasonable and prudent. There is not the slightest basis to the charge that the action was not taken in good faith. The contention that he should have questioned each member of the group before ordering their removal is unrealistic. He had sufficient indicia of conduct centering about the members of the group that "would or might be inimical to the safety of [the] flight" to warrant forthwith action. He did not have to tempt fate so that the prospect of hijacking became reality.

Moreover, the captain's action was justified under the terms of the tariff filed with the Civil Aeronautics Board. The information conveyed to him by the flight attendant as to the conduct of the group was sufficient to alert him to the "possibility…that [the plaintiffs] would cause disruption or serious impairment to the physical comfort and safety of other passengers." Therefore, the Court grants defendant's motion and sets aside the jury's verdict. The complaint is dismissed and a verdict directed in favor of the defendant. So ordered.

CASE QUESTION

1. Why does a pilot need the authority to remove passengers from a flight?

In a similar case the airline was sued by passengers of Iraqi descent, alleging the airline discriminated against them on the basis of their race, color, or national origin, in violation of the Airline Deregulation Act. The court held the pilot's decision was not arbitrary or capricious and that with respect to removal of allegedly suspicious or threatening passengers, the captain is entitled, and must be able, to implicitly rely on information relayed to him by his flight crew, assuming it is reasonable and believable. The flight attendants are the captain's eyes and ears in the passenger area of the plane, while the pilot is in the cockpit. Additionally, the flight attendants' identification of seven passengers of Iraqi descent for police questioning after the captain returned the plane to the gate following reports of suspicious behavior was not arbitrary or capricious, even though only three of the passengers engaged in suspicious behavior, where the flight attendants believed that all seven passengers were traveling together.[38]

In another case a pilot evicted from a plane the famous opera singer Jessye Norman. She had missed a connecting flight and boarded a later plane. She attempted to use an onboard phone to notify contacts of the change in her arrival time. She discovered that the telephone was out of order and so requested the flight attendant to ask the cockpit crew to call or radio her contact. The attendant informed Norman that such a call would be contrary to policy but he would inquire. When five minutes later he had not yet relayed her request to the crew, she became distraught and an angry exchange occurred. After a stopover the attendant refused to continue to work the flight unless Norman was ousted. The pilot ordered her removed based on the following: the attendant's description of her as unruly and therefore a safety threat; the unavailability of other attendants; a safety regulation barring the flight from flying without a minimum number of attendants, which the flight would lack without the attendant in question; and impending bad weather that jeopardized the flight if takeoff was further delayed. The court determined the pilot did not act arbitrarily in ordering Norman's eviction and dismissed her claim for damages.[39]

In a New York case a pilot properly evicted a passenger whose conduct was described as follows: She was "yelling loudly and generally behaving in a rude, disruptive, and inconsiderate manner. She cut in front of other passengers who were waiting at the boarding gate information counter and interrupted Gate Agent Osorio who was assisting another passenger." Osorio claims plaintiff yelled at him and used "foul and shocking" language during the encounter. In addition, plaintiff was observed drinking alcoholic beverages in the airport bar prior to boarding the plane. Once plaintiff got on the plane, passengers and flight attendants heard her shouting "free booze!" They also claim she was being disruptive, out of control, and appeared intoxicated. Osorio and passengers stated that plaintiff smelled of alcohol."[40]

Another case involving an unruly passenger likewise resulted in judgment for the airline. Removal resulted because the passenger was irate, refused to follow directions, abandoned her luggage at the doorway of the plane and declined to move it, and attempted to make an unauthorized entry into the first-class section.[41]

Since the attacks of September 11, 2001, airline personnel have been, understandably, particularly wary of any attempt by a passenger to access the cockpit. Such was the circumstance in Case Example 13-11.

---

38 *Al-Watan v. Am. Airlines, Inc*, 658 F. Supp. 2d 816 (Mich. 2009)
39 *Norman v. Trans World Airlines, Inc.*, 2000 WL 1480367 (N.Y. 2000)
40 *Ruta v. Delta Airlines, Inc.*, 322 F.Supp.2d 391 (N.Y. 2004)
41 *Rubin v. United Airlines, Inc.*, 117 Cal. Rptr. 109 (Calif. 2002)

CASE EXAMPLE 13-11

Al-Qudhai'een v. America West Airlines, Inc.

267 F.Supp.2d 841 (Ohio 2003)

...Plaintiffs are Saudi Arabian citizens residing in Arizona with their wives and children on F-1 student visas. Plaintiffs are studying to receive doctoral degrees. Some of the defendants are the America West employees who served as pilots and flight attendants on Flight 90. Plaintiffs planned to attend a series of events and lectures at the Saudi Cultural Attache in Washington, D.C. on November 19, 1999, however plaintiffs did not make reservations for the flight until 9:00 p.m. on November 18, 1999. On November 19, 1999 plaintiffs were issued boarding passes and boarded America West Flight 90 from Phoenix, Arizona to Washington, D.C. with a layover in Columbus, Ohio. Prior to departure, plaintiff Al-Qudhai'een asked flight attendant DeCampo if he could [arrange for] plaintiff Al-Shalawi to sit in the empty seat next to him. Plaintiff was instructed that he would have to wait until the plane was airborne. Ignoring DeCampo's instruction, Al-Qudhai'een decided to get up from his seat and tell Al-Shalawi to come sit next to him. Plaintiff Al-Shalawi then remained in his seat for the duration of the flight and did not do anything that defendants considered suspicious.

The only time plaintiff Al-Qudhai'een got up during the flight was to use the bathroom. Plantiff decided to go to the first-class bathroom because people were waiting to use the bathroom at the rear of the airplane. Flight attendant Asada observed Al-Quadhai'een walk straight to the cockpit door and pull on the handle. Plaintiff now denies that he ever touched the cockpit door. Plaintiff claims that before he even reached the first-class bathroom, he was told by flight attendant Asada that the first-class lavatory was reserved for first-class passengers only and he would have to use the bathroom at the rear of the plane. Plaintiff used the bathroom at the rear of the airplane and then returned to his seat and remained there for the remainder of the flight.

Although plaintiff now denies that he touched the cockpit door or even got close to the first-class bathroom, plaintiff did state to the FBI later that day that he may have inadvertently touched the door to the flight deck due to its close proximity to the handle of the forward lavatory. Additionally, a first-class passenger, Renato Fernandez, observed Al-Qudhai'een walk directly to the cockpit and try to get into the cockpit.

After plaintiff used the bathroom at the rear of the plane, flight attendant DeCampo searched the bathroom. He also searched under the seat originally assigned to Mr. Al-Shalawi, but did not find anything. Plaintiffs also noted that no other passengers on Flight 90 had their seats searched, nor were the bathrooms searched after other passengers used them.

Although plaintiff claims to have returned to his seat after using the bathroom, flight attendant DeCampo states that Al-Qudhai'een approached him after returning from the bathroom and asked a series of questions related to the flight. DeCampo recalls that plaintiff asked how long the plane would be on the ground in Columbus and whether they would be on the same plane going to Washington, D.C. After some discussion between the flight attendants regarding plaintiffs' behavior, they decided to inform Captain Patterson that plaintiff had asked similar questions about the flight to two different flight attendants, plaintiff disobeyed the flight attendant's order to remain in his seat, and plaintiff attempted to get into the cockpit. Flight attendant DeCampo also mentioned to Captain Patterson that plaintiffs were Arab and plaintiffs believe that defendants relied on this information to justify the allegation that plaintiffs were hijackers.

Captain Patterson was concerned with the report by the flight attendants and believed that the circumstances posed a security threat to the flight. Therefore, he notified America West's Dispatch and relayed his concerns. Captain Patterson provided plaintiffs' names and seating information and suggested that when they arrive they should be met by security to determine [plaintiffs'] intent and examine their luggage. When the plane arrived in Columbus, Captain Patterson was instructed by airport security to taxi at a remote parking area away from the terminal. When the plane stopped, airport security boarded the plane, handcuffed plaintiffs and escorted them off the plane, and then interrogated them for four hours, while the rest of the passengers were able to continue on to their destinations. After being questioned by the FBI, plaintiffs were advised that they were not under arrest and were free to leave. America West apologized to plaintiffs and upgraded them to first-class for their flight to Washington, D.C ....

Plaintiffs filed their complaint alleging defendants violated their civil rights. ...Defendants argue that pilots have broad discretionary authority to request investigatory assistance from law enforcement authorities and/or remove any passenger the pilot decides is or may be inimical to safety ....A captain of an airplane is entitled without further inquiry to rely upon a flight attendant's representations that a conflict with a passenger might distract the flight attendant from performing his or her safety-related duties.

Taking into account all the circumstances known to Captain Patterson at the time he made the decision to radio America West for assistance and the fact that he is entitled to rely on the information provided to him by his crew despite any exaggerations or false representations, the Court finds as a matter of law that Captain Patterson's decision to remove plaintiffs from the airplane and to request a search of their baggage was not arbitrary or capricious. Defendants are therefore entitled to summary judgment on all of plaintiff's claims against them.

CASE QUESTION

1. Why do you think the pilot is entitled to rely on statements from the crew "without further inquiry"?

To summarize, the law gives the pilot considerable leeway in making decisions to remove passengers in order to protect the safety of the other travelers onboard. Only if the decision is made arbitrarily or capriciously will the airline face liability.

Overbooking

Because many people make airline reservations and then do not appear for the flight, airlines will frequently and deliberately overbook a flight. This practice ensures that the plane will fly as close to full capacity as possible. Airlines are not the only travel service suppliers that overbook; hotels also do it, as we discussed in Chapter 4.

A problem arises, of course, when there are fewer no-shows than expected. The result is insufficient seats on the plane (or rooms in a hotel) to accommodate everyone with a confirmed reservation. In such instances, the airline will "bump" some passengers, denying them transportation.

The Department of Transportation (DOT) requires airlines to ask for volunteers to give up their seats voluntarily, in exchange for compensation, before bumping anyone involuntarily. The airline may or may not provide additional amenities such as a hotel room, free meals, and transfers between hotel and airport. Airlines can negotiate mutually acceptable compensation. Generally, airlines offer a voucher for a free trip at a later date.

Each airline is required by the DOT to give all involuntarily bumped passengers a written statement describing their rights and explaining how the carrier decides who boards and who does not. The denied passengers are frequently entitled to compensation depending on the price of their ticket and length of delay. If the airline provides substitute transportation that gets the passenger to the final destination within one hour of originally scheduled arrival time, no compensation is required. If the arrival time is between one and two hours (or one and four hours

on international flights), the airline must pay the passenger an amount equal to 200 percent of the one-way fare to the final destination that day, with a $650 maximum. If the substitute transportation gets the passenger to their destination more than two hours later (four hours internationally), or if the airline does not make any substitute travel arrangements for the bumped passenger, the compensation doubles to 400 percent of the one-way fare, with $1,300 as the maximum.

If the ticket does not indicate the fare, as in the example of a ticket based on frequent-flyer points, the compensation for being denied boarding involuntarily is based on the lowest cash, check, or credit card payment charged for a ticket in that class on that flight. Passengers involuntarily bumped can choose to keep their original ticket to use on another flight. They can make their own travel arrangements and request an involuntary refund for the ticket. If the bumped passenger paid for optional upgrades or checked baggage, and the passenger did not receive the benefit of those on the substitute flight or was required to pay for them a second time, the airline that bumped the passenger involuntarily must refund that amount to the passenger.

Priority Rules for Seating

When overbooking occurs, the law specifies how a determination will be made as to who will be denied seating. The airlines must first ask for volunteers who agree to wait for a later flight, usually in exchange for free airline tickets for a subsequent trip. Thereafter, the airline must apply its priority rules, which all airlines must develop and file with the Department of Transportation. Some airlines, after inquiring if any passengers are willing to give up their seats, will choose to involuntarily bump passengers who were the last to check in or the passengers with the lowest fares. This process is explained in Case Example 13-12.

CASE EXAMPLE 13-12

Goranson v. Trans World Airlines

467 N.Y.S.2d 774 (N.Y. 1983)

This small claim is based on TWA's bumping of the plaintiff, Arlene Goranson, from her scheduled flight to London as part of a vacation tour for which she had contracted. The Court holds TWA liable for bumping as a common law breach of contract and awards compensatory damages in the amount of $1,500....

Plaintiff, Arlene Goranson, contracted with TWA for a flight to London as part of a tour to Great Britain and other places in Europe that was leaving on April 18, 1982. She is an intelligent woman having a genuine interest in gardening and is a member of various horticulture associations. She therefore had a special personal interest in visiting the Savill Gardens, which was scheduled as part of the tour. She saved for this trip and waited many years before taking it. She selected TWA because of its representations as to reliability and responsibility. One of many such representations in TWA's brochures promoting the tour read:

Remove Uncertainties the TWA Way

Have you ever been stranded at an airport because you couldn't get on a plane? Have you ever had to travel miles out of your way to catch a "bargain" flight? If not, think about it. It's not the best way to begin a carefree vacation. Consider: *with TWA there are no charter risks, no standby blues or airport gambles. Every flight is scheduled, carrying with it the TWA reputation of reliability. You know in advance exactly where you'll fly from and when.* Maybe you'll pay a few dollars more for peace of mind, but don't you think it's worth it? [Emphasis by TWA]

When she arrived at JFK Airport on the evening of the scheduled departure date, TWA was unable to provide her with the previously confirmed space due to overbooking. Reliability and peace of mind, promised to her, vanished except for the printing in the advertisements.

She could not obtain transportation to London for two days and she arrived in London on the following Monday, missing the first two days of her tour which included the Savill Gardens. She asked permission from TWA during the tour to return to London at the end of the tour to see the places that she missed. However, TWA refused this proposal. She was required to return to the United States with the remaining passengers as scheduled. TWA offered to pay her $400 being the maximum set forth in the [Civil Aeronautics Board–CAB] regulations, but she refused and brought this small claims action for $1,500.

The two issues presented are: (1) whether TWA was liable because of overbooking and subsequent bumping as a simple common law breach of contract; and (2) whether the amount of damages is exclusively governed by, and cannot exceed that allowed by, CAB regulations.

In 1976, Justice Powell, in *Ralph Nader v. Allegheny Airlines, Inc.*, 426 U.S. 290, 294, 96 S.Ct. 1978, 1982, 48 L.Ed.2d 643 (1976), discussed the necessity of overbooking and the airlines contention that it was a desirable practice:

Such overbooking is a common industry practice, designed to ensure that each flight leaves with as few empty seats as possible despite the large number of "no-shows"— reservation-holding passengers who do not appear at flight time. By the use of statistical studies of no-show patterns on specific flights, the airlines attempt to predict the appropriate number of reservations necessary to fill each flight. In this way, they attempt to ensure the most efficient use of aircraft while preserving a flexible booking system.…At times the practice of overbooking results in oversales, which occur when more reservation-holding passengers than can be accommodated actually appear to board the flight. When this occurs, some passengers must be denied boarding ("bumped"). The chance that any particular passenger will be bumped is so negligible that few prospective passengers aware of the possibility would give it a second thought. …

The CAB's current policy embodied in its Oversales Regulations, however, is (1) to allow oversales, (2) to leave it to the carrier to ensure that bumping is minimized, (3) to provide a regulated amount or minimum compensation to the aggrieved passenger, and (4) to recognize the passenger's optional right to recover damages in a court of law.

The inconsistency of the CAB's approval of the bumping practice, along with the implied recognition that it is a breach of contract, has proven to be troublesome.

Under CAB regulations, in the case of "deliberate overbooking," the airline must now follow a defined procedure....It must first request volunteers who are willing to relinquish their reserved space in return for compensation and second, it must arrange for comparable transportation for a passenger denied boarding.

The airline may then deny boarding to a passenger in accordance with its own boarding priority rules. The airline, however, must then provide compensation for those involuntarily denied boarding. The amount of this compensation as set forth in the tariff varies for each case, but the maximum is $400.

This Court now concludes that when TWA refused to provide plaintiff passage on the plane that she had tickets for—when she was "bumped," and when TWA did not provide plaintiff with the first two tour days she contracted for, in each instance, there was a common law breach of contract for which there is a traditional state court remedy.

Accordingly, TWA is liable for overbooking and bumping as simple common law breach of contract and plaintiff Arlene Goranson is awarded actual compensatory damages without regard to TWA's tariff or to any CAB regulation.

With respect to the damage issue, courts have held that damages may consist of a wide variety of elements, including expenses for substitute or alternate transportation, meals, compensation for humiliation, outrage and inconvenience. ...

Plaintiff's actual damages are related to her loss of two days of traveling and vacation in England where she had intended specifically to see the Savill Gardens and related attractions. She is therefore entitled to recoup these two days in England, with TWA paying her expenses as damages.

The Court therefore calculates her damages as the cost of round trip air transportation to London ($800), ground transportation to and from airports for the round trip ($100), hotel and meals for 3 days in England ($400) and tour expenses ($100). This totals $1400. Plaintiff is also entitled to recover for her extreme inconvenience, aggravated by TWA's refusal to allow her to return to England at the end of the tour to see the attraction she missed on her first 2 days. Since the Court's small claim jurisdiction is only $1500, only $100 additional can be allowed for inconvenience.

Judgment is therefore entered for Plaintiff for $1500 plus costs.

CASE QUESTION

1. What should the airline have done in this case to minimize the loss to the plaintiff?

In another case the airline was liable for failing to follow its priority rules. The plaintiff was denied seating on his confirmed fight because it was overbooked. The airline used a first-come first-served basis to determine who would be bumped. However, the applicable tariff required priority be given based on the time and date the passenger booked the reservation. The boarding agent testified that had he used the first-come, first-served method, the time needed for the record check would have delayed the flight several hours. The plaintiff nonetheless won the case.[42] The basis for the airline's liability was its disregard of its own priority rules as stated in its tariff. Clearly the airline needed to review the suitability of its regulation.

Punitive Damages for Overbooking

To avoid liability for punitive damages when a passenger is bumped, airlines should assist the traveler in arranging alternate transportation. The bumped plaintiff referenced above also sought punitive damages based on the following additional facts. The plaintiff originally rejected alternate flights offered by the airline because they would have caused him to miss a rehearsal for a wedding in which he was the best man. He thrice demanded a charter flight to his destination. The ticket agent finally responded, "I don't know when you're going to get it through your thick head we're not going to charter you a flight."

The court refused to award punitive damages, finding no malice on the part of the airline. Instead, the court termed the agent's statement "a reaction obviously provoked by [plaintiff's] repeated unreasonable requests for a charter flight." The court further noted, "Although he missed the rehearsal, plaintiff performed flawlessly as groomsman." An important point in the airline's favor on the issue of punitive damages was that it assisted the plaintiff in securing alternate travel arrangements.

Punitive damages were awarded in a case involving bus transportation. The defendant bus company failed to honor the plaintiffs' confirmed bus tickets home from an overnight trip to Atlantic City because the bus was oversold. The defendant also failed to help the plaintiffs find alternate means of transportation. The plaintiffs found a ride on an alternate bus company and sued the defendant for compensation for their expenses home, reimbursement for their ticket on the defendant's bus, and punitive damages. The court held for the plaintiffs on all counts, stating that the defendant's failure to assist the plaintiffs in "secur[ing] some safe alternative means of transportation is not to be countenanced, and shows a reckless and willful disregard towards the plaintiffs in derogation of their contract for safe passage."[43]

Overbooking on International Flights

Overbooking on international flights is governed by the Warsaw and Montreal Conventions, discussed previously in this chapter. Bumping is covered by the convention, which permits a maximum recovery of $400. Thus, a law student who missed

---

[42] *Smith v. Piedmont Aviation, Inc.,* 567 F.2d 290 (Tex. 1978)
[43] *Bottenstein v. Connecticut American Bus Lines,* 509 N.Y.S.2d 248 (N.Y. 1986)

the bar exam (the test a law student must pass to become a lawyer, which is given only twice a year) because she was not allowed seating on her flight from India, was awarded only $400.[44]

Numerous plaintiffs diverted from their itinerary by overbooking have attempted to bring various tort and breach of contract actions against the responsible airlines. These efforts have been rejected by the courts because the Warsaw and Montreal Conventions are intended to be exclusive remedies notwithstanding the limited recovery available. Case Example 13-13 illustrates this point.

© Matej Kastelic/Shutterstock.com

CASE EXAMPLE 13-13

Weiss v. El Al Israel Airlines, Ltd.

433 F.Supp.2d 361 (N.Y. 2006)

…Essentially, plaintiffs purchased two round trip tickets for transportation from New York's John F. Kennedy Airport (JFK) to Jerusalem's Ben Gurion Airport …. Plaintiffs arrived at JFK and passed through security in sufficient time to catch their flight, but as the result of overbooking plaintiffs were bumped from their contracted departure. El Al placed plaintiffs on a standby list to enable them to obtain available seats on a subsequent departure, and plaintiffs paid $100 to upgrade their seats to business class on the future flight. Plaintiffs spent two days in the airport on standby status, during which time they allege that they suffered physical and emotional fatigue and exhaustion from walking from place to place required to comply with the airline's standby procedures, and were treated in a "wanton, oppressive, indifferent, and uncaring" manner by the airline's employees. Finally, unable to acquire seats on any El Al flight, plaintiffs purchased tickets on another airline. Subsequently, plaintiffs filed this action seeking recovery in tort for, as stated in the complaint, "Physical and emotional suffering and great inconvenience during those two days for which the airline induced the passengers to remain at the airport."…

Unfortunately, bumping passengers and then making them wait in airport terminals for extended periods of time is a common occurrence. Plaintiffs were not held against their will, but remained in the terminal on a standby list, meaning defendant was engaged, at least slightly, in providing a service to plaintiffs. …Despite the fact that the ultimate goal of obtaining transit for plaintiffs was not fulfilled, El Al was performing services for plaintiffs…

---

[44] *Minhas v. Biman Bangladesh Airlines,* 1999 WL 447445 (N.Y. 1999)

The court dislikes bumping as much as any passenger with a schedule to keep or a life to live. Keeping passengers waiting in a terminal for two days is certainly terrible customer service. However, even assuming that plaintiffs' allegations are true,… plaintiffs merely allege the sort of rude, indifferent, and uncaring treatment that is all too common in customer service businesses. Plaintiff's tort action is preempted by [relevant federal law including the Montreal Convention].

Likewise, a traveler whose trip was prolonged when an airline cancelled his flight from Ghana to the New York was limited in his recovery to the provisions of the conventions. His claim for additional money based on breach of contract and damages was thus dismissed.[45] In another case a family of four with first-class tickets was relegated to coach because first-class was oversold. Vacancies in coach were so limited the family was unable to sit together. The court determined these occurrences were not "out of the ordinary or unexpected" and recovery was limited by the conventions. The case was therefore dismissed.[46]

Punitive Damages on International Flights

A passenger who is refused seating on an oversubscribed international flight is not entitled to punitive damages due to the limitations of liability provided in the Warsaw and Montreal Conventions.

Although protected from punitive damages, the airline is well advised to assist the customer in arranging replacement travel plans.

Prohibition on Lengthy Delays on Tarmac

In response to highly publicized incidents involving passengers who were stranded on aircraft for very lengthy periods, the Department of Transportation enacted rules which prohibit U.S. airlines operating domestic flights from allowing an airplane to sit on the tarmac for more than three hours without deplaning passengers. Exceptions are allowed only for safety or security or if air traffic control advises the pilot that returning to the terminal would disrupt airport operations. U.S. carriers operating international flights arriving or departing from the United States must specify, in advance, their own time limits for deplaning passengers, with the same exceptions in effect.

Adequate food and potable drinking water must be provided to passengers within two hours of delay on tarmac and bathrooms must be in working order. Medical attention, if needed, must be provided as well.

---

[45] *Paradis v. Ghana Airway Ltd.*, 348 F.Supp.2d 106 (N.Y. 2004)
[46] *Sobol v. Continental Airlines*, 2006 WL 2742051 (N.Y. 2006)

Additional Legal Issues Involving Airlines

Airlines are occasionally sued on additional grounds, including failure to verify that international travelers possess the necessary documentation for entry into their country of destination, failure to advise such travelers of the needed documents, wrongful rejection of identification documentation, and in-flight acts of negligence.

Lack of Documentation for International Travel

When people travel to countries other than their place of residence, certain documents are often required for entry. These may include a passport and a visa. The airline tariffs provide that the traveler and not the airline is responsible for determining what documents are required and for securing them. Occasionally, a passenger who lacks the necessary documentation and is thus refused entry into the country of destination will attempt to blame the airline for not verifying that the traveler possessed the needed documentation. These cases uniformly result in a verdict for the airlines.

In one case, the plaintiff traveled from Taiwan to Atlanta, Georgia. Upon arrival at the international port of entry, the plaintiff was deported because he had not obtained an entry visa required by the United States. The plaintiff faulted the airline for permitting him to board without first assuring that he had obtained the proper documentation for entry into the United States. Because applicable tariffs place solely on the passenger the duty to ensure compliance with various international laws, the plaintiff's case was dismissed.[47]

© NicoElNino/Shutterstock.com

---

47 *Williams v. Northwest Airlines,* 163 F.Supp.2d 628 (N.C. 2001)

In a similar lawsuit a plaintiff was permitted to board a plane in Puerto Rico and flew to Turkey. Upon arrival, she was taken into custody by Turkish officials because she did not have the necessary visa to enter the country. Following her ordeal she sued the airline, claiming it should have informed her of the visa requirement. Again, the airline's tariff placed the requirement of securing the necessary travel documents on the passenger, and relieves the airline from advising the passenger concerning necessary documentation. Therefore, the case was dismissed.[48]

If the airline undertakes to verify proper documentation and refuses passage to a ticketed traveler who lacks a needed visa, the airline will not be liable for failure to provide transportation. In a Massachusetts case the plaintiff, although ticketed, was not allowed to board his flight because he did not have the required visa for his destination. The airline refunded the cost of the ticket. The plaintiff sought damages for "unreasonable psychological traumatic experiences." The court dismissed the case, finding that the airline's tariff permitted it to deny boarding to a passenger whose travel documents were legally insufficient.[49]

Wrongful Rejection of Identification Documentation

A passenger heading from Nigeria to the United States was denied boarding after review of his passport due to a "security problem." The traveler was told by security personnel that he should report to the American Embassy in Nigeria. The would-be passenger arranged for the eight-hour trip to the American Embassy and, in due course, was informed that there was no problem with his passport. He returned to the airport, boarded a flight, and arrived at his destination almost a week later than planned. He was a "busy surgeon" and had been forced to cancel all surgeries, procedures, and consultations for that week. He sued the airline for lost income and emotional injury. The court dismissed the claim for emotional injury as such injury is not compensable per the Warsaw (and Montreal) Conventions. The airline's motion to dismiss the claim for financial loss was denied because the conventions permit compensation from the airline for out-of-pocket loss caused by a delay in air transportation.[50]

Wrong Destination

Passengers are responsible for ensuring their tickets accurately state their intended destination. A passenger seeking round-trip transportation to Brazzaville, Republic of Congo, accepted tickets printed with the destination of Douala, Cameroon. Rerouting was necessitated to reach Brazzaville, resulting in a late arrival and lost business. The traveler sued the airline, but the case was dismissed. The court held that the ticket evidences the parties' intent as to the transportation services to be provided by the airlines. If the destination is misidentified the traveler must initiate action to affect the necessary changes.[51]

---

[48] *Aquasviva v. Iberia Lineas Aereas de Espana,* 902 F.Supp. 314 (P. R. 1995)
[49] *Chukwu v. British Airways,* 915 F.Supp. 454 (Mass. 1996)
[50] *Ikepeazu v. Air France,* 2004 WL 2810063 (Conn. 2004)
[51] *Fondo v. Delta Airlines, Inc.,* 2001 WL 604039 (N.Y. 2001), aff'd 25 Fed.Appx. 82 (2002)

Airlines, like other hospitality businesses, are liable for negligence that causes injury to a guest. Examples of the type of negligent acts that have resulted in lawsuits against airlines include (1) failing to properly latch the door of a serving cart that swung open on takeoff and struck a passenger's knee; (2) improper monitoring by flight attendants of overhead luggage racks, resulting in a suitcase falling on a passenger's head;[52] (3) failing to monitor during flight an 11-year-old female passenger participating in the airline's "unaccompanied minor" program, enabling a passenger in an adjacent seat to molest her;[53] (4) inadvertently serving an in-flight passenger with a heart condition alcohol in his cranberry juice, allegedly exacerbating his heart problem;[54] and (5) failing to prevent employees from using passenger luggage to transport drugs and controlled substances illegally into the United States, which allegedly resulted in an airline passenger whose luggage was so conscripted being incarcerated for nine months.[55]

Liabilities of Travel Agents and Charter Tour Companies

Travel agents play a key role in the travel industry, although their influence has decreased significantly with the advent of home computers and the access they give to flight information and airline reservations. While in the past travel agents functioned as mere ticket dispensers, today they are information specialists on whose expertise a portion of the traveling public relies.

In this section we will examine the parameters of the retail travel agent's liability in day-to-day business conduct. This liability is based on the travel agent's own actions, those of the agent's employees, and under certain circumstances, those of third-party suppliers that a travel agent recommends to clients.

© The World in HDR/Shutterstock.com

---

[52] *Charas v. Transworld Airlines, Inc.*, 160 F.3d 1259 (Calif. 1998)
[53] *Garza v. Northwest Airlines, Inc.*, 305 F.Supp.2d 777 (Mich. 2004)
[54] *Scale v. American Airlines*, 249 F.Supp.2d 176 (Conn. 2003)
[55] *Singh v. North American Airlines*, 426 F.Supp.2d 38 (N.Y. 2006)

A travel agent is not an insurer that all aspects of a trip are safe. Nor can the agent be expected to "divine and forewarn of an innumerable litany of tragedies and dangers inherent in foreign travel ... [A] travel agent cannot reasonably be expected to guarantee that a traveler will have a good time or will return home without having experienced an adverse adventure or harm."[56] However, like any other business-person, the travel agent will be held liable to clients for wrongful acts, including torts such as negligence and fraud. The reason for this liability is that travel agents present themselves as experts in making travel arrangements and customers rely on that expertise. Travel agents must exercise reasonable care in making a client's travel arrangements and must not intentionally mislead a client.

Provide Accurate Information

If the travel agent gives false or incomplete information, the traveler may experience great inconvenience and possibly injury. In such a case the travel agent may be liable. In Case Example 13-14, both the travel agent and the airline misled the plaintiff traveler. Both were required to compensate the plaintiff.

CASE EXAMPLE 13-14

Burnap v. Tribeca Travel

530 N.Y.S.2d 926 (N.Y. 1988)

In this small claims case, the court has been asked to decide when a ticket is a ticket. It all began when Mr. Boston and Ms. Burnap purchased two round-trip tickets from Tribeca Travel agency for Paris, back in August of 1987. The travel agency booked them on Continental Airlines departing on September 16, 1987 and returning from Paris on September 26, 1987.

Perhaps it did not bode well for their trip that the tickets did not arrive until September 15, 1987, but nevertheless they took off at the scheduled time on September 16, 1987.

Once in Paris they called to confirm their return flight three days before (Sept. 23) and they arrived at the airport on September 26, 1987 for their return flight in what they thought was a timely fashion, i.e., since the tickets indicated the departure time was 11:00 a.m. they arrived about 10 minutes before 10:00 and were informed that the flight had been rescheduled for 10:00 a.m. and that given customs and security they could not make the flight. Since both Mr. Boston and Ms. Burnap had obligations in New York and Continental had no other flights that day, they purchased two one-way tickets to New York on American Airlines.

---

[56] *Krautsack v. Anderson*, 768 N.E.2d 133 (Ill. 2002)

Once back in New York, they wrote to Tribeca Travel requesting that they be reimbursed for the return tickets they had bought from American Airlines and Tribeca refused. Mr. Boston and Ms. Burnap sued Tribeca, and Tribeca in turn sued Continental Airlines....

[T]hrough its president, Larry Handel, Tribeca Travel denied responsibility. Mr. Handel testified that the time of the return flight from Paris had been changed by Continental Airlines on September 5, 1987. Mr. Handel indicated that he wrote the ticket himself on September 4, 1987. He acknowledged however that the ticket was not delivered until September 15, 1987. When asked why the ticket was not altered to reflect the change in time between September 4 (when it was written) and September 15 (when it was hand delivered) Mr. Handel had a number of explanations which are presented here, not necessarily in the order argued. The first of those was that the change occurred over a holiday week-end (Labor Day). The second was that he did not have a computer on which to receive notice of the change. Third, he stated that the cost of the tickets ($440) was substantially less than the market price (over $1,200). Finally Mr. Handel argued that anyone who travels nowadays must count on delays and problems and that they must learn to take it in stride. Hence this decision since it seems clear to the Court that no monetary award alone will sufficiently indicate to the travel agent that while travel delays and hassles these days are more the rule than the exception, that he has some obligation to prevent them where he is responsible.

Following Mr. Handel's testimony Mr. Stuart Pollack, the General Manager of Continental Airlines, testified that Continental had rescheduled the time of the return flight from Paris to New York on September 4, 1987. As was their standard procedure for such changes (or "Ques" as they call them), the change was relayed by computer to Tribeca travel agents on September 5, 1987. He offered into evidence a computer printout with an accompanying explanation of the various codes contained in it which indicated that the information concerning the change in flights had been sent to the Continental Reservations Agents in Paris. When questioned about why Mr. Boston and Ms. Burnap had not been told of the time change when they called to reconfirm their flight in Paris, he responded that the code on the printout indicated that the travel agent had already been notified and therefore there was no need to tell them.

Neither the airline nor the travel agent acknowledge any responsibility for the failure to notify Boston and Burnap. Mr. Handel [president of Tribeca] implied that the purchase of a ticket at a bargain rate creates less of a contract than if it is purchased at full rate.

Mr. Handel seems to view the purchase of an airline ticket as no different from buying a subway token: Caveat emptor [let the buyer beware] and if the train comes, get on it quick! These arguments notwithstanding, the courts have recognized that the purchase of an airline ticket creates a contract between the parties. Here the travel agent held himself out as being in the business of selling tickets. Both claimants responded and purchased tickets. Clearly part of the contract created by the purchase is being able to rely on the date and times of flight departures as they are given on the ticket. The travel agent claims that he had no computer in his uptown office and therefore did not receive the transmission from Continental Airlines indicating that they had changed the time of departure. This is no defense since he had a computer in his other office and more importantly, he had an obligation to inform the passengers who purchased tickets and relied on him to provide them valid and proper tickets in exchange for the requested fare. Nor can Continental Airlines be viewed as blameless. They sent the information to Paris and failed to notify Boston and Burnap when they called to confirm....

However, Tribeca and Continental are both liable to claimants. Continental must pay claimants for the balance of the tickets paid for that were unused because claimants were not informed of the scheduled change. Judgment is awarded against Continental, in the amount of $440.

Tribeca Travel bears greater responsibility since it drew up the ticket but never corrected it to reflect the actual departure time. Since the claimants' return tickets cost $1,384 and Continental is liable for the unused half of the tickets, judgment is awarded against Tribeca Travel in the amount of $944. [The difference between the cost of the return tickets and the amount Continental was required to pay.]

CASE QUESTIONS

1. What should Tribeca Travel Agency have done to avoid liability?

2. What could Continental Airlines have done to avoid liability?

3. Why do you think Tribeca Travel Agency was ordered to pay more than Continental Airlines?

In another case involving misfeasance by a travel agent, the latter issued airline tickets to a client for travel from New York City to Calcutta, India. The agent handwrote on the tickets "confirmed." In fact, the travel agent knew the client was "wait listed" (meaning the client's name was placed on a waiting list without a confirmed reservation). When the client arrived for the flight he was denied a seat and sued the agent. The court held for the plaintiff, finding the agent had breached the duty of care and awarded the plaintiff both the cost of the tickets and money for emotional distress.[57]

© Pikoso.kz/Shutterstock.com

[57] *Das v. Royal Jordanian Airlines*, 766 F.Supp. 169 (N.Y. 1961)

Travel agents regularly recommend hotels, charter companies, tour operators, restaurants, tourist attractions and more. Agents have a duty to their customers to do the following vis-à-vis these service providers: investigate their operations, locate material information about them that is reasonably available, and disclose that information to the agents' customers. Travelers are legally entitled to expect that travel services recommended by a travel agent will be reliable and suitable. Failure of a travel agent to adequately investigate can lead to liability, as the agents in Case Example 13-15 and the cases following it learned the hard way.

CASE EXAMPLE 13-15

Josephs v. Fuller (Club Dominicus)

451 A.2d 203 (N.J. 1982)

This is an action by John and Regina Josephs against a resort known as Club Dominicus and a travel agency known as Richard's Travel Service, brought because defendant's resort accommodations were substandard.

It is uncontested that defendant Richard's Travel Service (Richard's) recommended and arranged for plaintiffs to spend their vacations at Club Dominicus in the Dominican Republic, and that the accommodations provided by Club Dominicus were far below standard.

It appears, further, that Richard's is independent from Club Dominicus except for the commissions received for booking vacations.

Richard's moved for dismissal at the end of plaintiff's case on the ground that plaintiff had not proved any facts upon which liability of a travel agent could be based. (It should be noted that defendant Club Dominicus is not involved at this point of the litigation because it is in default for failing to answer the complaint.) [So Club Dominicus automatically loses its part of the case by default judgment.]

Richard's argues that it was simply an agent for a disclosed principal and, as such, owed no duty to plaintiffs. The only party owing any duty to plaintiffs [according to Richard's] was the disclosed principal, Club Dominicus, and that party is the only one liable for a breach.

For the reasons enunciated herein, Richard's motion [to dismiss] is denied.

Defendant is mistaken in its contention that because it was paid by Club Dominicus it was the agent of Club Dominicus only, and since its principal was disclosed to the plaintiffs, it owed no duty to the plaintiffs. ...

Defendant's position is that, even if it was negligent in booking a vacation at a resort about which it knew nothing, it is not liable because it owed no duty to the plaintiffs. This is clearly wrong.

Since defendant's commissions were paid by Club Dominicus, those commissions would not be earned without plaintiff's patronage. The pecuniary benefit bestowed on defendant by plaintiff forms the basis of a legal duty.

As a travel agent, [defendant] owed a certain duty to [its customers]. A travel agent is a special agent, akin to a broker, which engages in a single business transaction with the principal.

[I]t would seem absurd to hold that defendant Richard's had no duty to acquire any knowledge of the facilities it was booking. Plaintiffs could well have made their own arrangements, choosing a resort at random. But rather than risk a substandard vacation, they took advantage of the service offered by defendant. As it turned out, defendant had little or no more knowledge than the plaintiffs.

This court, therefore, holds that when a traveler relies on the recommendations of a travel agent and suffers damage because of accommodations so totally unacceptable that any reasonable travel agent would have known not to make such recommendations, the travel agent is liable.

A travel agent was liable when a hotel he recommended to a customer was "closed, chained and guarded" upon the traveler's arrival. Said the court, "A travel agent has a duty to his customer to not only use reasonable care in making travel reservations, but also in confirming them prior to the date of the trip."[58] Another travel agent who failed to investigate the viability of a tour operator was liable to a would-be traveler who paid for a trip to Israel that did not materialize because the operator went out of business.[59]

A traveler sued her agent because she was dissatisfied with the quality of the three-star hotel accommodations arranged by the agent. The customer's discontent included that the wash basin was equipped with separate hot and cold faucets rather than a single faucet to allow the water to be mixed, towels and bed linens were changed only twice during the week rather than daily, the room was dirty, and she was visited by roaches and a mouse. There was no evidence that the travel agent knew or had reason to know of the unsanitary condition. The court concluded the travel agent was not liable for failing to discover or disclose the condition of the faucet or the frequency with which linens are exchanged. However, the court did hold the agent liable for not discovering the unsanitary condition that led to mice and roaches. In determining the amount of damages the court noted, "The fact that plaintiff did not document with any photographs the conditions that she described, despite her conversations from London with her son, the attorney, suggests that the conditions were not the worst." The court ordered defendant to pay $120.[60]

A travel agent was liable to his customer where the agent failed to confirm that a tour, advertised as including two meals a day, in fact included the meals. After the client paid $1,032 for two people and the agent sent the money to the tour operator minus the agent's commission, the agent learned the trip did not include the meals.

---

[58] *Barton v. Wonderful World of Travel, Inc.*, 502 N.E.2d 715 (Ohio 1986)
[59] *Grisby v. O.K. Travel*, 693 N.E.2d 1142 (Ohio 1997)
[60] *Shiuko v. Good Luck Travel, Inc.*, 763 N.Y.S.2d 906 (N.Y. 2003)

Thereafter, upon the agent's representation to the customer that the trip could be canceled with a full refund, the customer chose to cancel rather than pay an additional $300 for the meals. In fact, the money already paid was not refundable, so the customer lost $1,032. He sued, and the court held that the travel agent was liable for this amount based on breach of contract and negligent performance of his duties. Said the court, "Defendant's contractual obligation included verifying and confirming that such tour with the enumerated components and was actually available at the stated price before he sold it."[61]

In another case, the travel agent was found liable for failing to investigate sufficiently the status of a charter company with which he made reservations for the plaintiff and her four children. The plaintiff's trip to Puerto Rico occurred without incident. When she and her family arrived at the airport ready to board the flight home, she learned the air carrier had gone out of business. She sued the travel agent, seeking the cost of the tickets she purchased from another airline for the flight home. Said the court, "There was no testimony of efforts made [by the travel agent] to assure the performance [by the charter company] and no evidence that the travel agent provided the [traveler] with information about any risks associated [with a charter]." The court held the travel agent was liable for the cost of the return-flight tickets because it failed to ascertain the reliability of the charter company it recommended.[62]

Similarly, a travel agent was found liable for having insufficiently researched a tour operator it recommended. The tour company went bankrupt, resulting in the loss of a client's vacation money. The court ordered the travel agent to compensate the traveler for the loss.[63]

The death of a college student on a Mexican party train led to a lawsuit by her parents against the tour operator that arranged the itinerary, transportation, and lodging. The student was killed on an unsafe platform while walking from one train car to another. Three prior deaths of college students had occurred on the party train, a fact known to the tour operator but not disclosed to the tour participants. The court refused to dismiss the lawsuit against the tour operator. While the court noted that a travel agent or tour operator cannot be "reasonably expected to divine and forewarn of an innumerable litany of tragedies and dangers inherent in foreign travel," the court nonetheless found that the tour operator in this case may have violated its duty to disclose available information.[64]

A hotel guest, who booked her hotel room through a travel company, slipped and fell in a puddle on the bathroom floor and broke her leg. She sued her travel agent and the court dismissed the case. The court stated that a travel agent is emphatically not an insurer, and owes no duty to warn of or protect every potential incident that may come to pass during an overseas trip. The court concluded that it would not impose a duty on travel agents to warn of specific dangers that are unknown and inherent in the destinations to which their clients frequent. A leaky shower is

61 *Pellegrini v. Landmark Travel Group*, 628 N.Y.S.2d 1003 (N.Y. 1995)
62 *Rodriguez v. Cardona Travel Agency*, 523 A.2d 281 (N.J. 1986)
63 *Douglas v. Steele*, 816 P.2d 586 (Okla. 1991)
64 *Maurer v. Cerkeunik-Anderson Travel, Inc.*, 890 P.2d 69 (Ariz. 1994)

an inherent danger, and its foreseeability in the hotel room was not established and so consequently the travel agent would not be bound to predict or forewarn of the condition.[65]

The clear lesson from these cases is that travel agents must investigate the third-party suppliers they recommend to ensure continued existence and ability to provide the contracted services. Failure to do so can result in liability.

Recommending Travel Insurance

Travel agents are well advised to suggest travel insurance to their customers. Such insurance compensates the would-be traveler for the cost paid for the vacation if the trip is canceled for certain reasons, including bankruptcy of the travel provider. Having recommended the purchase of travel insurance can assist a travel agent's defense when sued by a customer whose plans were frustrated by a defunct supplier. In a New York case, the plaintiffs traveled to St. Croix. Partway through their two-week prepaid vacation, both the airline and a subsidiary that made plaintiff's hotel arrangements went bankrupt. The plaintiffs had to pay anew for the hotel and their flight home. They sued the travel agent for the money they double-paid. Unlike the rulings in the cases you just read, the court held the travel agent was not liable to the plaintiff for the airline's bankruptcy.[66] Facts in this case distinguish it from the two prior cases. The agent was aware that the financial condition of the airlines was questionable and had so informed the plaintiffs prior to booking the trip. They chose to continue their travel plans nonetheless. An additional factor noted by the court as a basis for finding no liability was the travel agent's repeated recommendation that the plaintiffs purchase travel insurance, which they declined. The recommendation was included with a written confirmation the agent sent to the plaintiffs of their itinerary, and again with the tickets.

Sometimes a travel agent will investigate recommended suppliers and find them in good order. Nonetheless, while the traveler is at the supplier's facility something unexpected occurs and the traveler's trip is disrupted. In these circumstances, the agent will not be liable. By researching the premises, agents satisfy their duty to their clients and avoid liability. In Case Example 13-16, travelers accused a tour operator of failing to properly investigate the hotel accommodations provided on the tour. The tour operator, however, had researched the hotel and so was not liable.

---

65 *Schwartz v. Hilton Hotels Corp.*, 639 F.Supp.2d 467 (N.J. 2009)
66 *Creteau v. Liberty Travel, Inc.*, 600 N.Y.S.2d 576 (N.Y. 1993)

CASE EXAMPLE 13-16

Wilson v. American Trans Air, Inc.

874 F.2d 386 (Ind. 1989)

… American Trans Air (American) is a charter tour operator headquartered in Indianapolis, Indiana.

It regularly plans and operates tours to the Cayman Islands. Participants in these tours are offered accommodations at the Holiday Inn Grand Cayman International Beach Resort (Holiday Inn Grand Cayman), operated by Humphreys (Cayman) Ltd, under a franchise agreement with Holiday Inns, Inc. American sometimes sponsors two or three trips to the Cayman Islands per month and has included, as an option, accommodations at the Humphreys hotel in its tours since at least 1976. One employee of American always accompanies the tours to the Caymans and stays with the tour group at the Humphreys hotel.

Mr. and Mrs. Wilson participated in an American tour to the Cayman Islands in October 1984. They chose to stay at the Humphreys hotel. On October 30, Mrs. Wilson was assaulted by an intruder entering her second-floor hotel room through a balcony door while she was asleep. The intruder attempted to rob and rape Mrs. Wilson, and she suffered bodily injuries during the attack.

The majority of participants in these tours apparently do not choose to purchase an optional "ground package" that includes accommodations at a local hotel (in this case, Humphreys). However, promotional materials for this trip did include references to accommodations at the Holiday Inn Grand Cayman. In addition, brochures, rate cards, and other promotional material are provided to American by Humphreys at American's request. The Wilsons also assert that, since 1978, American has published advertisements for 131 tours specifically offering accommodations at the Humphreys hotel.

American did conduct basic research regarding its tours. It attempted to gain information about the political stability and climate of the destination country. It apparently did not inquire into guest safety and security at the hotel. The Wilsons allege that there was substantial criminal activity involving guests at the Humphreys hotel in the months preceding the attack on Mrs. Wilson, but American disclaims any knowledge of such activity.

The Wilsons maintain that American is liable to them because it breached its duty as a charter tour operator to investigate proposed accommodations for safety and to warn prospective patrons of any dangerous conditions discovered during the investigation. The Wilsons submit that this duty arises out of contractual language contained in American's travel brochure, the federal regulations governing charter tour operators, and tort law.

The Wilsons ground their contract argument in the following language found in the advertising newsletter that American distributed to potential customers:

Responsibility of American Trans Air: This tour program is planned and operated by American Trans Air, Inc.…as *principal* and tour operator…American Trans Air is responsible for making all arrangements for transportation, provided that *in the absence of negligence on the part of American Trans Air*, the responsibility does not extend to any assumption of liability for any personal injury or property damage arising out of or caused by any negligent act on the part of any hotel, other air carrier or anyone rendering any of the services or accommodations being offered in connection with this Public Charter. …

The Wilsons…note that the contract states that American is the principal and is responsible for any negligent act of its own with respect to the accommodations offered in connection with the tour. The Wilsons assert that this duty required American to make some reasonable investigation into the safety of any accommodations that it promoted and recommended and to warn prospective patrons of any danger at the hotel that might affect them.

We cannot accept the Wilsons' contention. … [W]e note that a charter tour operator, as the principal responsible to tour participants for all the services and accommodations offered in connection with the charter tour, cannot disclaim liability for injuries arising out of its own negligence. A charter tour operator, as principal, employs independent contractors such as airlines and hotels to provide transportation and accommodation services to its patrons. Although a principal generally cannot be held liable for the torts of an independent contractor, [the] law does allow a principal to be held liable for the torts of a hired independent contractor when the consequences of the principal's own negligent failure to select a competent contractor caused the harm upon which the suit is based. This negligent selection theory would allow liability to be imposed upon American for its own negligence as principal, liability that it did not disclaim under its contract and cannot disclaim under the applicable federal regulation. Although the Wilsons' allegation that American breached a duty to investigate the safety and security of the hotel accommodations that it included in its tour package can be construed as a claim based on negligent selection theory, their claim cannot survive. American chose Humphreys to provide the hotel accommodations in its tour package. Humphreys operated a Holiday Inn. The hotel was located on Seven Mile Beach on Grand Cayman Island, British West Indies—a British Crown Colony. There is nothing in the record that indicates that the Holiday Inn Grand Cayman was located in a high-crime area, that the hotel experienced more safety and security problems than other resort hotels on the island, or that the level of criminal activity involving guests at the Holiday Inn Grand Cayman was unusually high for a large beach resort. In addition, American stated that, in considering guest safety and security at hotels included in its tour packages, it "rel[ied] on the general reputation" of the hotels involved. American also knew that Humphreys had security guards on the premises, and it had received no notice of any guest complaints regarding safety and security at the Holiday Inn Grand Cayman. An officer of American had visited the island and engaged in face-to-face negotiations over rates and payment policies with representatives of the hotel. Under such circumstances, American had no duty to make specific inquiries into guest safety or security at the Holiday Inn . .…

The judgment of the district court [in favor of American] is affirmed.

CASE QUESTIONS

1. On what principle did the court base its decision?

2. Based on the court's holding, how does the liability of a tour operator for a guest's safety compare with that of an innkeeper?

Security Incidents

If the travel agent is aware of security issues associated with a hotel or other service provider the agent recommends, the agent should disclose that information to the traveler. The latter can then make an informed decision on whether or not to utilize the service. Failure to reveal such information may expose the agent to liability. For example, vacationers in Jamaica were robbed and one was raped at gunpoint. Among the parties sued was the travel agent who made the

arrangements for air travel and lodging. The court, noting that a travel agent is not an insurer or guarantor of its customers' safety, stated that the agent is not obligated to investigate safety factors of lodging accommodations unless requested by the customer to do so. However, the court also stated that "where the agent has knowledge of safety factors or where such information is readily available, a travel agent has the duty to inform the customer of those factors."[67] Based on the court's somewhat conflicting statements, travel agents are well-advised to make inquiry of recommended destinations to ensure their relative safety.

A more definitive statement declaring that travel agents and tour operators are not liable when guests are attacked in hotel rooms is provided in a Rhode Island case. The plaintiffs were assaulted in their hotel room in St. Kitts. They sued the tour operator who arranged their trip. The court stated, "Courts nationwide routinely hold travel agents and tour operators innocent for the negligent acts of third party providers of services such as hotels .... Travel agents are not guarantors of the happiness or safety of the tourists to whom they sell tickets. In the instant case the tour operator does not own, manage, operate or control the hotel at which plaintiffs' injuries occurred. Accordingly, the court finds that there is no reasonable possibility that the tour operator could be held liable to plaintiffs for the injuries."[68]

Duty to Disclose

The travel agent's duty to investigate and disclose is based in significant part on the services for which the traveler engaged the agent. If the agent was contacted merely to arrange for airline tickets, ground transportation, and hotel accommodations, but was not consulted on selection of a destination or hotel, the travel agent owes no duty to provide information about the destination or hotel the client selects. Thus, where a customer chose to visit a specific hotel in Mexico and was injured when he dove into the pool that was shallower than anticipated, the agent was not liable for failing to inform the swimmer that swimming pools in Mexico are uni-

© Aleksandar Tasevski/Shutterstock.com

---

[67] *Creteau v. Liberty Travel, Inc.,* 600 N.Y.S.2d 576 (N.Y. 1993)
[68] *Gabrielle v. Allegro Resorts Hotel,* 210 F.Supp.2d 62 (R.I. 2002)

formly of a shallow depth and do not have depth markings.[69] However if the agent acts as more than a ticket agent and also recommends the destination, promotes a particular hotel, or otherwise encourages the client to try various services at the destination, the agent has a duty to use reasonable efforts to obtain and inform the client of important, relevant information.

Liability for Breach of Contract by Third-Party Service Suppliers

When a customer purchases a trip from a travel agent and the trip does not materialize as portrayed, the agent may be liable for breach of contract.

In Case Example 13-17, the travel agent was found liable to a client for breach of contract where the client's vacation was spoiled by the wholesaler's failure to reserve hotel rooms.

CASE EXAMPLE 13-17

Odysseys Unlimited, Inc. v. Astrol Travel Service

354 N. Y.S.2d 88 (N.Y. 1974)

Following an earlier practice, in the summer of 1972 the Paterson and Majewski families began to plan a joint vacation over the Christmas holiday. In doing so they relied upon Astral Travel Service ("Astral") an agency with which they had previously dealt. They looked forward to spending a few days with their five children in the Canary Islands, of course not anticipating the discomfort, inconvenience and disappointment they would suffer....

Astral (a retail travel agent) suggested to Dr. Paterson and Mr. Majewski a package tour prepared by Odysseys (a wholesale agency). The tour, entitled "Xmas Jet Set Sun Fun/Canary Isle," was scheduled to depart December 26, 1972 by jet for Tenerife, Canary Isles,... staying at the "deluxe Semiramis Hotel" and returning on January 1, 1973 by jet. Majewski and Paterson accepted this trip costing $1,375.90 and $1,706.80 respectively and made their down payments to Astral. Astral withheld its commission and forwarded the balance along with the reservations to Odysseys who in turn confirmed the reservations to Astral....An information sheet...furnished details of the trip and referred to the accommodations at the "Five-Star Hotel Semiramis."

On December 26, 1972 the group flew off to the Canary Islands. They arrived at the airport in Tenerife at about dawn and waited about two hours...before they were taken to the Hotel Semiramis. At this point the passengers had been en route some thirty hours. While at the airport they saw Mr. Newton, President of Odysseys, who accompanied the group tour. (The inference may reasonably be drawn that he went along because he anticipated the difficulties which were shortly to be encountered.) Two hundred fifty weary but expectant guests arrived at the Semiramis and were presented with a letter from the hotel...advising them that there were no accommodations available to their group. Dr. Paterson confronted Mr. Newton with this letter and the latter acknowledged that there

---

[69] *Schneider v. Suntrips, Inc.*, 2003 WL 21153746 (Calif. 2003)

was no space available and that he was looking for others. For about four hours, two hundred fifty people (including baggage) were in the lobby of the Semiramis until they were divided into groups and directed to other [hotels]. The Paterson and Majewski families were brought to the Porto Playa Hotel which was not fully ready for occupancy because it was under construction and without the recreational facilities and conveniences available at the Hotel Semiramis. Portions of the Porto Playa Hotel were enclosed in scaffolding. Paterson and Majewski testified that work was done in their rooms, water supply uncertain, electric connections incomplete, etc., etc. throughout their stay.

The court is convinced that prior to the group's departure Mr. Newton was aware that there were no reservations at the Semiramis Hotel for his charges. He testified that on either December 18th or 19th, 1972 he knew of the overbooking at the hotel....In his letter of January 12, 1973 addressed to tour members, Mr. Newton confirms the fact that he had been aware of some "problem with overbooking by that hotel" (Semiramis Hotel) and states that his agent "had the foresight to have arranged for alternate accommodations".... [T]he reservations for the tour were not confirmed and, therefore, the hotel was not obligated to accommodate the members of the group. ...

Majewski and Paterson sue in contract and negligence seeking recovery of their payments for their trip and for their ordeal. Their claims spring from a breach of contract by Astral for its failure to furnish the hotel accommodations agreed upon. Majewski and Paterson are entitled to recover from Astral for the breach of contract. Damages in the usual breach of contract action should indemnify a party for the gains prevented and losses sustained by the breach; to leave him in no worse, but put him in no better, position than he would have been had the breach not occurred....However, when a passenger sues a carrier for a breach of their agreement concerning accommodations the [i]nconviences and discomforts which a passenger suffers...are to be considered in the assessment of the damages....

The agent should be held responsible to: (a) verify or confirm the reservations and (b) use reasonable diligence in ascertaining the responsibility of any intervening 'wholesaler' or tour organizer. Because the contract was violated and the accommodations contracted for not furnished, a more realistic view for awarding damages to Majewski and Paterson would include not only the difference in the cost of the accommodations but also compensation for their inconvenience, discomfort, humiliation and annoyance.

Odysseys attempted to mitigate the damages to Majewski and Paterson by offering proof as to the difference in value between what they received (at a four-star hotel) and what was agreed upon (a five-star [hotel]). However, this evidence is without force because the hotel at which they stayed was under construction, its recreational facilities were non-existent and its location was not nearly as desirable as that of the Semiramis. The proverbial expression about a picture being worth a thousand words has particular application to Exhibits [presented by plaintiffs] to reveal what Majewski and Paterson expected and what they found. Paterson and Majewski are entitled to the return of the total sum each paid for the trip as damages to them and their family for the inconvenience and discomfort they endured. ...

On Astral's cross-claim against Odysseys for breach of contract, concerning the Majewski and Paterson claims...Astral is entitled to a judgment against Odysseys in the amount of $2,452.70 less $308.30 which Astral retained as its commission, because Odysseys failed to perform its contract and it was Odysseys which was responsible for the fate which befell Majewski and Paterson.

© Roy Pedersen/Shutterstock.com

At first it may seem unfair that the travel agent is liable to the client for the dereliction of the wholesaler. But remember, the party who dealt face-to-face with the client and who arranged the travel itinerary was the travel agent; the client likely had no direct dealings with the wholesaler, and the client may not even know how to contact the wholesaler. Also, imposing liability on the travel agent will motivate the agent to verify that the travel wholesaler is making the necessary plans and reservations for the booked tour. Further, the travel agent is not without a remedy. Note in the last paragraph of the case, the judge said that the travel agent was able to collect from the wholesaler the money the agent was required by the court to pay the client. Thus, the liability ultimately rests with the party at fault, the wholesaler. However, if the wholesaler goes bankrupt or has discontinued business and cannot be located, the travel agent will bear the loss. This fact should motivate travel agents to investigate the tour operators with whom they do business.

Not every traveler makes arrangements through a travel agent or airline office. Some travelers use charter companies that offer reduced rates for those who do not mind traveling without a lot of frills. The charter company is liable, too, if it breaches its contract to provide transportation. This is illustrated in Case Example 13-18.

CASE EXAMPLE 13-18

Musso v. Tourlite International, Inc.

500 N.Y.S.2d 969 (N.Y. 1986)

When Thomas Wolfe wrote *You Can't Go Home Again* it is clear he had no reference to Mr. Musso, the plaintiff in this case. On the other hand, given what happened to Mr. Musso, he undoubtedly felt the sentiments of Wolfe's title during the events.

Mr. Musso's travels began with his decision to purchase charter airline tickets from Tourlite Inc. to pay a visit to Italy, from whence he came. He bought round trip tickets for himself and his wife and they flew to Rome with no incident.

Mr. Musso was aware of the rules of the charter which required a confirmation of the return flight at least 72 hours prior to departure (which he complied with, and there is no dispute as to the fact that this was done). He was also required to arrive at the airport three hours in advance of the flight.

Mr. Musso testified that he and his wife arrived at the airport for their return flight on August 3, 1985 at 10 a.m. The flight was scheduled to depart at 1 p.m., but when he inquired at the information counter, Mr. Musso was informed that the flight was delayed until 3 p.m. The person at the booth instructed him to get on line at about 1:30 p.m. Mr. Musso remained at the airport and joined the line at 1:30 as he had been instructed. There was only one line for charter flights. When he finally arrived at the front he was told by the person behind the counter that while they had his reconfirmed reservation, the plane was full and that it was ready to leave, and that he would therefore not be able to board it. Later, he was told by a representative of the charter company (Tourlite) that he might be able to catch the following week's charter. Upon hearing that Mr. Musso, who from his description remained calm in the face of being told that he had no flight home, decided that he would make other arrangements. He rented a car, drove into Rome where he checked into a hotel overnight, and bought two Alitalia tickets to New York for the following day.

Once he returned to New York, Mr. Musso sued Tourlite, the charter company, in Small Claims Court for the cost of the airline tickets. ...

The rights of an airline passenger are provided for in regulations, which establish the obligations of airlines. While the flight here was not on a scheduled airline, and was booked through the charter company, it is clear that the purchase of airline tickets creates a contract between the purchaser and the provider of service. Tourlite agreed to bring Mr. Musso and his wife to Italy and back providing they complied with certain conditions. As the facts indicate Mr. Musso fulfilled his end of the bargain—he reconfirmed, he appeared promptly for departure, but was told there was no room for him on the plane.

Tourlite, in its defense, offered the testimony of the Director of Customer Service, Hans Elsevier. Mr. Elsevier, who was not present in Rome at the time these events occurred, testified that on the day in question, the flight manifest [a list of a plane's passengers] indicated twenty-seven vacant seats. He stated that while Tourlite had a representative present, the seating for the plane is done by a "handling agent." The manifest also indicated that the Mussos were confirmed on the flight in question. He said that a representative of Tourlite was stationed in front of the counter to assist passengers with difficulties. However, Mr. Musso testified that he had not encountered any such person although he had looked for someone. Mr. Elsevier admitted that he had no idea why Mr. Musso had not been permitted to board the plane.

None of the arguments advanced by defendant Tourlite relieves it of its contractual responsibility to the plaintiff here. The testimony indicated Mr. Musso complied with his part of the contract by reconfirming. He appeared at the airport, and waited on line. Since Mr. Elsevier was not present at the time of these events it is difficult to accept his hearsay testimony that a representative of Tourlite was there and was assisting those on line.

Mr. Musso is therefore entitled to recover from Tourlite the cost of his Alitalia airline tickets ($1,100) and the additional cost for the rental car ($55) that he needed to go back into Rome to spend the night, together with interest from August 1985.

Travel agents and tour operators are not guarantors that third-party suppliers will act without negligence. Rather, agents and tour operators are not liable to travelers when the latter are injured at recommended facilities due to the supplier's carelessness.

Travel Agents

Travel agents are not liable for the negligence of a hotel, resort, or other service provider booked by the agent for a client. Thus, the agent who made reservations for a customer at a Club Med resort was not liable to the vacationer who suffered injuries due to the resort's negligence.[70] Likewise, a bed-and-breakfast reservation service was not liable to a customer who fell at a facility because the steps lacked railings.[71] Similarly, where a traveler on a European bus tour sustained injuries due to the negligence of the bus company, the travel agency that arranged the tour was not liable for the injuries.[72] A travel agent was not liable when the hotel's key system did not meet industry standards resulting in theft of the traveler's jewelry from an in-room safe.[73] Nor was the agent responsible where the client, who purchased a vacation package to Mexico that included lodging and meals, was injured in a jet skiing accident in Mexico. The court noted that the agent did not book the jet skiing excursion and did not own or control the company that operated it. Liability was avoided even though the traveler had asked whether Mexico was a safe destination and was not told of a Consular Information Sheet from the United States Department of State that included a warning about jet skiing in Mexico.[74]

Tour Operators

Tour operators organize trips and arrange for various services such as transportation, accommodations, local transportation, and tickets for events and destinations. They do not customarily provide the services to the tour participants. Tour operators, like travel agents, are not liable for negligence of third-party suppliers. While touring Morocco a plaintiff's bus stopped to permit tourists to observe camels wandering about the desert. As the plaintiff stepped from the bus to the ground she slipped on loose sand causing a broken ankle. She sued the tour operator and bus company, claiming they were both negligent for not having disclosed to her the danger of exiting the bus. The tour operator denied liability because it did not own the bus, did not employ any of the tour personnel who served the plaintiff in Morocco (the bus company owned the bus and employed the guides), and did not possess knowledge of the existence of the alleged dangerous condition. The court agreed and dismissed the claim against the tour operator for the reasons stated.[75]

In another case, the plaintiff was injured when the jet ski he rented from his hotel malfunctioned. His claims of negligence against the tour operator and the travel

---

[70] *Stein v. Club Med Sales, Inc.*, 658 N.Y.S.2d 639 (N.Y. 1997)
[71] *Manes v. Coats*, 941 P.2d 120 (Alaska 1997)
[72] *Dorkin v. American Express Co.*, 351 N.Y.S.2d 190 (N.Y. 1974)
[73] *Reynolds v. RIU Resorts & Hotels.*, 880 N.W.2d 43 (Neb. 2016)
[74] *Yurchak v. Atkinson and Mullen Travel, Inc.*, 2006 WL 3076675 (Pa. 2006)
[75] *Davies v. General Tours, Inc.*, 774 A.2d 1063 (Conn. 2001)

agent were dismissed since neither owned the skis or controlled the rental personnel.[76] The proper defendant would be the hotel, which managed the ski rental operation and hired the staff. Likewise, neither the travel agent nor the tour operator were liable when customers vacationing in Cancun, Mexico, fell 15 feet because their hotel room balcony collapsed without warning due to the hotel's negligence.[77] In another case a tour operator responsible for coordinating transportation, hotel accommodations, and certain special events was not liable when a tour participant took a "booze cruise" and was served too much alcohol, which caused him to leap overboard to his death.[78]

Nor was a tour operator responsible where a traveler, staying at a hotel the tour operator recommended, was injured due to a faulty window. Said the court, "Tour operators do not have a duty to tour participants to insure the non-negligent performance of hotel services by independent contractors."[79]

Tour operators are also not liable for suppliers' contract breaches. Thus, where a tour operator organized a tour that included a charter flight and the flight was canceled for unexplained reasons, the tour operator was not liable.[80]

Neither are tour operators generally liable when a tour participant is injured during sightseeing at an attraction on the tour, assuming the sight is not under the control of the tour operator. A plaintiff, while a member of a tour offered by the defendant, fell near her lodge while visiting the Grand Teton National Park in Moran, Wyoming. The tour operator claimed it was not responsible for any dangerous condition on which the plaintiff tripped, nor did it have control over the area surrounding the inn and therefore it should not be liable. The plaintiff argued that since the tour operator selected the tour sites and provided supervision, it had a duty to warn of foreseeable risks such as rocky slopes and steep trails. The court rejected the plaintiff's position and held that a tour operator has no duty to warn or protect tour participants from a possible hazardous condition that may exist on the property of others.[81]

Disclaimers by the Travel Agent

Travel agents frequently insert disclaimers in their written materials. A **disclaimer** is a term in a contract that attempts to avoid all liability on the part of one party to the contract. The effectiveness of disclaimers in limiting the liability of travel agents is questionable. The courts have not looked favorably on attempts by travel agents to relieve themselves from liability for negligence or other wrongful conduct, and have usually limited the enforceability of disclaimers. Such clauses are often invalidated under various legal theories including insufficient notice to the customer, lack of specificity in the language, inequality of bargaining power, and, perhaps most important, offensiveness to public policy. However, a disclaimer that

disclaimer
A term in a contract that attempts to avoid all liability on the part of one party.

---

[76] *Chimenti v. Apple Vacations*, 2000 WL 33401822 (Mich. 2000)
[77] *DiBiase v. Oasis International*, 2001 WL 1200324 (Conn. 2001)
[78] *Smith v. West Rochelle Travel Agency, Inc.*, 656 N.Y.S.2d 340 (N.Y. 1997)
[79] *Saachi v. TNT Vacations*, 2001 WL 291950 (N.H. 2001)
[80] *Carley v. Theater Development Fund*, 22 F.Supp.2d 224 (N.Y. 1998)
[81] *Loeb v. Tauk Tours*, 793 F.Supp 431 (N.Y. 1992)

does not seek to avoid liability for the travel agent's action but rather clarifies that the agent is not, by law, liable for actions of service providers, will be enforced.[82]

Whether using a disclaimer or other language in a contract, a travel agent is well advised to include information that defines the relationship between all the parties involved and properly sets out what liabilities attach to each. In this way travel agents can make clear to clients that suppliers of travel services are not agents of the travel agent and so the travel agent generally is not liable if the supplier does any of the following: is negligent, breaches a contract, or otherwise disrupts the client's travel plans. Such explanatory material enhances the client's understanding of the relationships involved and may aid the travel agent in avoiding a lawsuit.

Know that providing information about limitations of liability will not relieve travel agents from their own negligence or wrongful conduct.

Errors and Omissions Insurance for Travel Agents

errors and omissions Insurance
Insurance that covers the cost of defending a lawsuit and any adverse judgment resulting from failure to fulfill one's obligation to a client.

Mistakes and poor judgment can happen in any business, although with good management their occurrence should be limited. A travel agent or tour operator can purchase **errors and omissions insurance** to cover its loss when mistakes are made. The objective of this type of insurance is to minimize for the agent or tour operator the financial effects of errors made by them or their staff.

While many types of insurance coverage are available, errors and omissions insurance covers the cost of defending a lawsuit and any adverse judgment resulting from failure to fulfill one's obligation to a client. Insurance, however, should not be used as an excuse for poor management techniques or shoddy business practices. Clients are entitled to better, and with each lawsuit the travel agent's reputation and business will suffer and the cost of the insurance is likely to escalate.

Credit Card Fraud

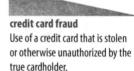

credit card fraud
Use of a credit card that is stolen or otherwise unauthorized by the true cardholder.

Many sales of airline tickets are made over the Internet or on the phone. Facilitated by e-tickets, such transactions can be completed without the need for the agent and buyer to ever meet face-to-face. These long-distance transactions, while good for business volume, provide ample opportunity for unscrupulous customers to commit **credit card fraud.** Travel agents must be vigilant to avoid being victims.

If the credit card used in a ticket transaction is stolen or its use is otherwise unauthorized and the true cardholder denies the charges after reviewing the monthly bill, the travel agent may be financially responsible for the sale. In a typical travel fraud scheme, the buyer orders airline tickets by phone and is quite willing upon request of the agent to send by fax or mail any identification documents requested—for example, copies of credit cards, a passport, authorizations, or a birth certificate. They all appear real, but the travel agent has no way to authenticate them. When the documents later turn out to be counterfeit or used without authority and

---

[82] *Bailey v. U.S.,* 289 F.Supp.2d 1197 (Hawaii 2003)

the true owner denies liability, the travel agent has no way to locate the supposed customer and may be liable for the cost of the ticket.

The way to protect against liability when the true cardholder refuses payment is to have an imprint of the actual credit card and the cardholder's signature. While Internet and phone transactions are consummated regularly in commercial transactions without an imprint or signature, travel agents accepting credit cards without in-person contact must be aware of the risks and act cautiously to avoid being the victim of fraud.

Rental Cars

The car-rental business is an important component of the travel industry, as it provides travelers with mobility and relieves them from reliance on public transportation. However, car rentals present potential problems for travelers and the rental companies, including overbooking issues and liability for accidents.

Overbooking

A traveler who flies into a strange city expecting a car to be waiting and discovers the rental company cannot fill the reservation will not be happy. A few states have enacted consumer protection laws that deal with unfilled car-rental reservations. These laws state that if a company fails to provide a car to a customer with a confirmed reservation, the company may be subject to a fine. Each rental company has a contingency plan for unfilled reservations. Most have adopted a compensation policy for travelers whose car reservations cannot be filled and who rent a car from another company at a higher price. The amount the rental companies will pay is the difference between their contract price and the higher price the customer pays to the other company.

In a small claims case, claimant alleged Hertz failed to honor his reservation for a rental car in New York City for the Thanksgiving holiday weekend. Hertz personnel informed him they had overbooked. Two hours later they offered to reduce his charge by $25 if he would go to Hoboken or Hackensack, New Jersey, where they could not guarantee a car would be available. Alternate transportation was not available. The plaintiff did not incur any out-of-pocket expenses, but he missed the holiday with his family. The court determined the claimant was entitled to actual damages for breach of contract, but denied damages for mental anguish as they are not recoverable in a breach of contract action. The court futher held that actual damages include inconvenience, delay and uncertainty, which "are worth something even in the absence of out-of-pocket costs." The court thus awarded the plaintiff $500.[83]

---

83 *Crawford v. Hertz*, 984 N.Y.S.2d 266 (N.Y. 2014)

negligent entrustment
Providing a product for use by another, knowing that person is likely to use the product in a dangerous manner.

When a rental car is involved in an accident while a customer is driving, questions arise as to whether the rental company is liable to people injured. Generally, the rental company is not liable. An exception is the circumstance where it negligently entrusts the vehicle to a lessee. **Negligent entrustment** means providing a product (in this circumstance, a car) for use by another person knowing that person is likely to use the car in a dangerous manner. For purposes of negligent entrustment claims, a rental car company can only be charged with constructive knowledge of a renter's driving incompetence based on facts that are openly apparent and readily discernable, with no duty to investigate the renter's criminal background or driving history.[84] A car-rental company is liable for negligent entrustment only when it has reason to know the lessee is incompetent to drive the car. If it has such knowledge and the lessee is in an accident, the car-rental company may be liable for the damages. As Case Example 13-19 illustrates, the law gives considerable leeway to the rental company.

CASE EXAMPLE 13-19

Drummond v. Walker

643 F.Supp. 190 (D.C. 1986), aff'd 861 F.2d 303 (1988)

This action arises out of a car accident which occurred early in the morning on August 6, 1984. Plaintiff alleges that defendant Kenneth Scott, while driving a car rented from defendant Americar, fell asleep at the wheel and struck a guardrail on Route 70 near Hagerstown, Maryland. Plaintiff, a passenger in the car, suffered facial injuries in the accident.

Scott did not actually execute the rental agreement for the car. Defendant Charlene Walker rented the car for Scott on August 2, 1984, because Scott lacked the appropriate identification and credit necessary to rent the car. When Walker rented the car, the Americar manager gave the keys to Scott, who drove the car away from the Americar lot. Walker never took possession of the car.

In...her complaint, plaintiff alleges that Americar is liable for her injuries by virtue of Americar's negligent entrustment of the car to Scott. She contends that the entrustment was negligent because Scott lacked proper identification and did not possess a credit card. Plaintiff further suggests that Americar was negligent in entrusting the car to Scott whom they knew to be slightly under 21 years of age. Americar has a policy of not renting to drivers under 21 years.

Even if Americar's employees knew that Scott would be driving the car, that he lacked proper identification and credit, and that he was under 21 years of age, such knowledge would still be insufficient to establish a prima facie case of negligent entrustment. One liable for negligent entrustment is:

---

84 *Hall v. CAMRAC, LLC.,* No HHDX04CV126027530S, 2013 Conn. Super. LEXIS 2821, (Super. Ct. Dec. 10, 2013).

[o]ne who supplies, directly or through a third person, a chattel for the use of another, whom the supplier knows or has reason to know to be likely because of his youth, inexperience, or otherwise, to use it in a manner involving unreasonable risk of physical harm to himself and others ...

Generally, negligent entrustment of a vehicle to an incompetent driver is imposed only where the owner entrusts the vehicle to one whose appearance or conduct is such as to indicate his incompetency or inability to operate the vehicle with care. In order to impose liability in other cases, where the incompetency of the driver is not apparent to the owner of the vehicle at the time of entrustment, it must be affirmatively shown that the owner had at that time knowledge of facts and circumstances which established the incompetency of the driver.

The negligent entrustment rule is considered a harsh rule because it imposes liability on an owner for the negligence of a driver over whose conduct the owner is unable to exercise the slightest degree of supervision or control. Its application has, therefore, been held limited to situations where the owner had knowledge that the driver did not know how to drive, was physically or mentally incapable of operating a motor vehicle, was intoxicated or who had the habit of becoming intoxicated, or was a minor with a record of reckless driving.

In order for defendant American to be liable for negligent entrustment it would have to be established that defendant Scott belonged "to a class which is notoriously incompetent to use [cars] safely" and that his incompetency was the proximate cause of plaintiff's injury. None of the facts presented by plaintiff, even if known by American, would indicate that Scott belonged to a notoriously incompetent class. The fact that Scott was under the age of 21, or lacked adequate identification or credit does not reflect directly on his ability to operate a car competently. American would not be on notice by virtue of these facts that Scott was not a safe driver. Therefore, [the cause of action based on negligent entrustment] must be dismissed. ...

Consequently, this action is dismissed.

CASE QUESTION

1. Why was the car-rental company able to avoid liability in this case?

A similar issue arose in a Hawaii case. Here, too, the court held the rental company had not negligently entrusted the vehicle. Yoshiko Ono, a Japanese national with a valid Japanese driver's license, rented a car from the defendant, Dollar Rent A Car. While driving the car, she lost control of it and struck the plaintiff's vehicle. The plaintiff sued Dollar claiming it negligently entrusted the vehicle to Ono. Plaintiff argued that Ono, as a foreign citizen, was presumably unfamiliar with local driving and traffic laws. The court rejected the plaintiff's claim and held for Dollar. In the opinion, the court identified the types of circumstances that constitute negligent entrustment. Said the court,

Plaintiff does not allege Ono was intoxicated or otherwise physically or mentally impaired when Dollar turned the car over to her. Additionally, there is no proof that she appeared unusually young or inexperienced. Finally, plaintiff has made no showing that Ono rented cars from Dollar on other occasions, thereby putting Dollar on notice of her alleged incompetence as a driver... [F]oreign citizenship alone cannot constitute notice of a driver's incompetence.[85]

Renting to someone who the lender knows does not have a valid license does not constitute negligent entrustment unless the lender also has knowledge that the driver is incompetent behind the wheel.[86] Nor does negligent entrustment apply where a car-rental company had intended but failed to place the renter on a "Do Not Rent" list. The reason the company intended to restrict her rental privileges was that she had a record of returning cars late and not making timely rental payments. She was inadvertently permitted to rent and the car was in an accident. Since the late returns and nonpayment do not bear on competency to drive, renting the car to her did not constitute negligent entrustment.[87]

Permitting a renter to drive with a dog in the vehicle, whether leashed or unleashed, is not considered negligent and will not lead to liability for negligent entrustment where the dog does not display any signs that it would be an unusually difficult to drive with[88] (e.g., it does not evidence significant behavioral problems).

The concept of negligent entrustment also applies to airplanes. A court refused to dismiss a lawsuit against a company that rented a private plane to a graduate of its pilot training school. The pilot caused an accident killing several people. The pilot told the rental company that he intended to fly the plane to a high-altitude airport. Such airports present special problems for pilots and require special training. The rental company had not trained the pilot to take off or land at high-altitude airports. Because of the risks of mountain flying it is the custom in the rental industry to require pilots who wish to fly to high-altitude destinations to submit to a "mountain checkout" to ensure they are competent at take-offs and landings. The lending company rented the airplane to the pilot without requiring the testing and knowing the pilot had never received high-altitude training.[89]

Rental of a Car Known to Be Defective

Another circumstance that can give rise to liability on the part of the car-rental company is knowingly renting a vehicle that has mechanical problems. In a New York case the plaintiff was forced to make an emergency stop on the side of a busy unlighted highway because the car he rented malfunctioned. While so situated, he was hit and killed by a passing truck. The rental company was aware at the time it leased the car to the plaintiff that it had a history of overheating and leaking engine coolant. The court refused to dismiss the case and instead referred it for a jury trial.[90]

---

[85] *Nielson v. Ono and Dollar Rent-A-Car,* 750 F.Supp 439 (Hawaii 1990)
[86] *Whitcomb v. El Cajon Ford,* 2003 WL 21513484 (Calif. 2003)
[87] *Francis v. Crawford,* 732 So.2d 152 (La. 1999)
[88] *Zamora v. Castle Auto Sales,* 2004 WL 3001041 (Calif. 2004)
[89] *Hubbard v. Pacific Flight Services, Inc.,* 2005 WL 2739818 (Calif. 2005)
[90] *Betancourt v. Manhattan Ford Lincoln Mercury, Inc.,* 621 N.Y.S.2d 522 (N.Y. 1994)

A customer rented a car and then was involved in a rollover accident. He sued the rental-car business alleging defective design of the car. It was not equipped with optional side curtain airbags, which the driver alleged would have prevented him from being ejected from the car in the rollover accident. The car-rental agency purchased the car from a reputable manufacturer. The court held the rental company was thus entitled to rely on the manufacturer's reputation in assuming the car was not defectively designed. Further, it was not obvious upon inspection that, without side curtain airbags, the car was defectively designed.[91] Therefore, the rental company did not breach its duty to provide a safe car in good working order.

Unauthorized Drivers

A problem that car-rental companies often confront is use of the rented vehicle by unauthorized drivers. Authorized operators include the lessee and anyone else the rental company approves in writing. Everyone else is an unauthorized driver. Virtually all car-rental contracts include a provision forbidding operation of the rental car by an unauthorized driver, as well as a provision stating that insurance coverage applies only to authorized drivers. If a traveler rents a car and allows a friend to drive who has not been approved, the friend is an unauthorized driver. If the friend is in an accident with the car, the rental company's insurance will not cover the collision. The traveler who rented the car will be liable to the rental company for damage to the car. The traveler, in turn, may be able to recover from the friend. Travelers who rent cars can avoid these problems by ensuring the vehicles are driven only by authorized drivers.

In Case Example 13-20, a question arose whether the driver was authorized. Take note of the court's unwillingness to interpret the contract to include an implied (unwritten) term that would allow as permissible drivers people who are not expressly authorized by the rental company but who are granted permission to drive by an authorized driver. Thus, a valet was not an authorized driver even though he parked a rental car with the permission of the authorized driver.

CASE EXAMPLE 13-20

Travelers v. Budget Rent-a-Car Systems, Inc.

901 F.2d 765 (Hawaii 1990)

The facts are not in dispute. In October 1985, while vacationing on the island of Maui in Hawaii, Albert Mellon rented a car from Budget Rent-A-Car. The rental agreement stated that Budget would provide liability insurance for Mellon and any other authorized driver. Budget was self insured.

---

91 *Noveck v. Avis Rent A Car Sys.*, LLC, 446 Fed. Appx. 370 (N.Y. 2011)

Several days after renting the car, Mellon and his wife drove to Mama's Fish House, a local restaurant of some renown. On arrival, Mellon turned the rental car over to Brent Jones, a valet parker in Mama's employ. The Mellons partook of piscine fare; Mr. Mellon had the mahi-mahi, Mrs. Mellon the shrimp.

After a satisfying dinner, Mellon dispatched Jones to retrieve the car. Jones drove the car to the restaurant entrance, where—while still seated behind the wheel—he opened the passenger side door for Mrs. Mellon. As Mrs. Mellon stood beside the open door, Jones got out of the car. The car lurched backward. The open door struck Mrs. Mellon, dragged her along the ground and caused numerous injuries.

The Mellons filed suit against Mama's and Jones. That suit was settled when Travelers Insurance, Mama's insurer, tendered its full policy limit of $300,000. Budget, as owner and insurer of the car that struck Mrs. Mellon, also paid her $15,000 pursuant to Hawaii's no-fault insurance statute. Travelers then instituted the present suit seeking a declaration that Budget must also indemnify [reimburse] Travelers…because the valet used the car with Mellon's permission.

…The district court held that, because Jones did not have Budget's permission to drive the car, he was not insured by Budget. Consequently, the court granted…judgment in Budget's favor.

Travelers appeals.…

To allow Travelers to recover from Budget on the basis of the rental agreement would require an act of interpretive legerdemain [trickery or magic]; the language of the contract could not be clearer. The rental agreement provides liability coverage "only for Renter and any Authorized Driver…for bodily injury…arising from use or operation of Vehicle as permitted by this Agreement." As to what is permitted by the agreement, it states explicitly that the:

Vehicle shall not, under any circumstances, be used or operated by any person: (a) Other than Renter or any Authorized Driver which shall by definition include only the Additional Driver shown on the reverse side hereof, and any driver who is a member of Renter's immediate family, his employer, his employee, or his partner provided such driver has Renter's prior permission and is a qualified, licensed driver of at least 21 years of age, …

Brent Jones is neither the Renter nor an Authorized Driver as provided by the rental agreement. Under the plain terms of the contract Budget provides no coverage for the accident at Mama's Fish House. …

Travelers… asks us to read into the rental agreement an implied term providing liability coverage to anyone who drove the car with Mellon's permission. The company points to cases from other jurisdictions that have found such an implied term.…

For one thing, an implied term providing liability coverage to anyone other than the renter or an authorized driver would be directly contrary to the express language of the contract. It is elementary contract law that a court will only supply a term where the contract does not address the dispute between the parties.… Where the language of a contract is clear and addresses the issue before the court, the court may not interpret the contract by supplying an implied term.... The Budget-Mellon rental agreement is definite and unambiguous on this point; the contract excludes insurance coverage for the events at Mama's parking lot. There is no occasion to supply an implied term, and that should be the end of the matter as far as Hawaii contract law is concerned.

Travelers nonetheless points to cases from other jurisdictions...According to these courts, car rental companies must expect that some renters will allow other people to drive the rental car in violation of the agreement. Therefore, the rental companies are deemed to have consented to the breach. ...

To recite such reasoning is to criticize it. The idea that a party may not rely on a contract term because the other side can be expected to violate it cuts at the very heart of contract law. Contracts enable parties to define their mutual rights and responsibilities; they are useful only insofar as each side can count on being able to hold the other to the terms of the agreement. If a contract provides anything at all, then, it is the reasonable expectation that the parties will fulfill their obligations, either voluntarily or under judicial compulsion. For a court to deny enforcement of a contract term because breach is foreseeable defeats the purpose of having a contract, effectively withdrawing that particular issue from regulation by mutual assent....

The rule Travelers advocates is also dangerous because it adds a heaping measure of uncertainty where certainty is essential. Insurance companies, like other commercial actors, need predictability; they write their contracts in precise language for that reason, and they calculate their premiums accordingly. When insurance contracts no longer mean what they say, it becomes exceedingly difficult to calculate risks. Insurance companies can predict with a fair degree of accuracy the risks involved when a car "may only be used or operated by an Authorized Driver." Just how many other risks will some court find foreseeable and inevitable? Increasing uncertainty through judicial meddling raises insurers' costs of doing business; inevitably those costs are passed on to customers. ...[Judgment for Budget] Affirmed.

CASE QUESTION

1. Why was the court so adamant in the penultimate paragraph not to read into the rental contract an implied provision that would extend coverage of the car-rental company's insurance to unauthorized drivers?

In a Michigan case a man who rented a car from National Car Rental gave his brother permission to drive the vehicle although he was not listed as an authorized driver on the rental contract. The sibling fell asleep while driving and collided with another vehicle, causing injury. The person hurt sued National and its insurance company, both of whom denied liability because the brother was not an authorized driver. The court dismissed the lawsuit against both defendants for that reason.[92]

---

[92] *Allstate v. MacDonald*, 2006 WL 2060398 (Mich. 2006)

In another unauthorized-driver case, the 17-year-old brother of the car renter took the vehicle without permission. He was intoxicated at the time. He caused an accident that killed his passenger. The passenger's family sued the car-rental company claiming negligent entrustment. The court denied recovery on the grounds that the rental company did not entrust the car to the brother, and further the company could not foresee that the brother would gain access to the car or be in an intoxicated state.[93]

Age Discrimination with Car Rentals

Many car-rental companies have refused to rent a car to a person who is under age 25. The reasons given for the refusal are high accident rates and high insurance premiums for this age group. The law in some states upholds the right of a rental company to refuse to rent to people under 25.[94] The law in other states prevents car-rental companies from refusing to rent a car to someone who is at least 18 years of age, provided insurance coverage is available. Most such states provide that any additional insurance costs imposed by law because of the age of the driver can be passed on to the driver. While some car-rental companies continue to resist making rentals to those under 25, a case in New York upheld the state law requiring rentals to be made to customers who are at least 18.[95]

---

[93] *Watson v. Enterprise Leasing Company,* 757 N.E.2d. 604 (Ill. 2001)
[94] *Lazar v. Hertz,* 82 Cal.Rptr.2d 368 (Calif. 1999)
[95] *People v. Alamo Rent-a-Car,* 664 N.Y.S.2d 714 (N.Y. 1997)

Summary

Airline passengers have certain rights when they travel, including the right to compensation, albeit limited, when an airline loses luggage; the right to rerouting assistance from an airline when flights are canceled; and the right of travelers with disabilities to access planes for transportation.

Travel agents must exercise reasonable care in making a client's travel arrangements and must not intentionally mislead. A travel agent may be liable for giving false or incomplete information and for failing to investigate third-party suppliers for financial viability and for suitability of facilities. A travel agent will not generally be liable for the negligence of third-party suppliers such as hotels, tour guides, and restaurants.

A tour operator is generally not liable for the negligence of a third-party provider over whom the operator has no supervisory control. A tour operator may, however, be liable when third-party suppliers fail to provide promised accommodations.

Car-rental companies provide an important service to travelers. These companies are liable if they negligently entrust a car to a driver they know or should know is incompetent, or if they rent a car they know or should know is not roadworthy. A car-rental company will not be liable for an accident caused by an unauthorized driver of the rented vehicle.

Preventive Law Tips for Managers

- *If employed by an airline, regularly review your company's system of baggage control to minimize the number of suitcases that are misrouted.* Failure to deliver luggage to a passenger's destination breaches the airline's contract with the traveler to transport the luggage, as well as the passenger, to the destination. Although the law provides limited liability, thereby sparing airlines from the need to compensate passengers for the full value of their loss, reimbursement at the limited liability rates can be costly. Further, loss of passengers' luggage generates bad will and may cause loss of future business. Taking precautions to minimize the incidents of misdirected luggage will save the company from unnecessary lawsuits and liability.

- *If employed by an airline, do not mislead passengers concerning the whereabouts of lost luggage.* Intentionally giving passengers false information about the whereabouts of their suitcases can lead to loss of limited liability. Be truthful and accommodating when passengers inquire about misplaced baggage.

- *If employed by an airline, be sure your company's rules and facilities for transporting pets protect the well-being of the animal.* An airline may be liable for injury to pets in flight. While critters are considered the equivalent of baggage for airline liability purposes, entitling the airlines to limited liability, animals have needs that suitcases do not. Those needs should be met to the fullest extent possible.

- *If a flight is canceled, the airline should offer assistance to passengers in making alternate arrangements.* The law recognizes that bad weather and other circumstances can present safety issues for air travel, and the airline will not be liable for breach of contract where circumstances dictate cancellation of a flight. However, the law also recognizes that passengers' travel plans will be disrupted by such a cancellation and so imposes on the airlines a duty to aid passengers in locating alternate flights. Failure to assist displaced passengers can lead to liability.

- *If employed by an airline or as a travel agent, accord patrons with disabilities the rights provided under the Americans with Disabilities Act and the Air Carrier Access Act.* These Acts generally require that handicapped persons be given access to places of public accommodation, including travel agents' offices and air transportation. The law also requires that airlines make necessary accommodations for disabled passengers, provided they are able to travel without presenting a risk to themselves or others.

- *In the event of overbooking, the airline should offer assistance to passengers in making alternate arrangements to reach their destinations.* The law recognizes that overbooking will occur on occasion as a result of the airlines' attempts to run their operations as efficiently as possible. To avoid liability to bumped passengers, the airlines should assist them in finding alternate transportation. Also, when determining who to bump, the airline should follow its priority rules and tariffs.

- *If engaged as a travel agent, double-check the times of your clients' flights and give accurate information.* If a travel agent gives incorrect information about the times of a flight or fails to update a client about a change in departure time, the travel agent may be liable for the clients' inconvenience and costs for alternate travel. Diligence in verifying information can avoid this problem.

- *If engaged as a travel agent, do not misrepresent a client's status on a flight.* If a travel agent informs a client that he has a confirmed seat, when in fact the client is on the waiting list, the travel agent may be liable for inconvenience and added expenses caused to the client by the misrepresentation. The travel agent should always give the client only truthful information.

- *If engaged as a travel agent, investigate thoroughly any travel wholesaler you recommend to a client.* A travel agent may be liable to clients for the failure of a travel wholesaler to provide the intended trip if the agent did not adequately investigate the wholesaler. The agent may also be liable to the client on breach of contract theory when the wholesaler fails to perform in whole or part. Although in such cases the travel agent may be able to obtain compensation from the wholesaler, bad will is generated by the unhappy clients. Further, if the wholesaler has gone out of business, compensation may not be obtainable. A thorough check into the wholesaler's business operations, experience, financial status, and past tours can help ensure reliability by the wholesaler and freedom from liability for the travel agent.

- *If engaged as a travel agent, investigate thoroughly any travel services you recommend to a client.* A travel agent may be liable to clients for the nonperformance or substandard performance of any travel service or accommodation suggested by the agent. Before recommending a hotel, bus, train, limousine service, sightseeing tour, or other service, the agent should familiarize himself with the company's services and reliability to ensure they are suitable for the client.

- *If employed in the car-rental business, regularly review your procedures to ensure the number of unfilled reservations is kept to a minimum.* When a car-rental company overbooks its fleet and is unable to accommodate customers with reservations, it is in breach of contract and liability will follow. To minimize this occurrence, frequent review of procedures should be undertaken.

- *If employed in the car-rental business, do not rent a car to someone who is obviously incompetent to drive.* A car-rental company will be liable for negligent entrustment where it rents a car to someone who obviously is incapable of driving lawfully. The car-rental company should require renters to produce a valid driver's license. If the would-be renter appears intoxicated or high on drugs, the rental company should decline to provide a vehicle. If it rents to someone it should have known was not qualified and that person is in an accident with the car, the rental company may be liable for resulting injuries.

- *If employed in the car-rental business, inspect your fleet of cars regularly for mechanical problems.* If a car develops a mechanical problem, remove it from service until the matter is fully repaired. A car-rental company that rents a vehicle known to contain mechanical problems may be liable if an accident results. To avoid this liability, inspect the cars regularly and repair any problems found to exist.

Review Questions

1. Name the four groups that comprise the travel industry.

2. What differentiates small claims court from other courts?

3. If an agent acts with authority for a principal, who is legally bound by the acts of the agent?

4. What is the difference between an agent and an independent contractor?

5. What is a tariff?

6. What is an airline's responsibility when it takes custody of a passenger's luggage?

7. What are the rules related to obligations of the airlines to involuntarily bumped passengers?

8. What are the rules concerning extended delays on the tarmac?

9. What two treaties have bound the United States and other countries on matters involving international plane flights? Which treaty is in effect now?

10. Why should a travel agent be familiar with the places he recommends?

11. What is a disclaimer, and how do the courts treat travel agents' disclaimers?

12. What obligation, if any, does an airline have to passengers when it cancels a flight due to bad weather?

13. Under what circumstances can a pilot remove a person from a plane and refuse to provide him or her with transportation?

14. What is the consequence of a person representing himself as an authorized agent when in fact the "agent" has not been authorized by the principal to act?

15. What is errors and omissions insurance?

16. What laws protect the rights of passengers with disabilities?

17. What is negligent entrustment?

18. What is required of car rental agencies in providing safe cars to drivers?

Discussion Questions

1. How does the availability of small claims courts increase the potential liability of the travel industry?

2. How does one distinguish between an agent and an independent contractor?

3. What do you think is the policy reason supporting class action lawsuits? How do they increase the potential liability of the travel industry?

4. A travel agent has made arrangements through a travel wholesaler for a client's tour. The wholesaler fails to make hotel reservations and as a result the client must stay in an inferior hotel. Is the travel agent liable? Why or why not?

5. How might airport security checks be modified to ensure that passengers and their carry-on luggage do not become separated?

6. Identify at least five enhanced safety precautions airlines have recently adopted.

Application Questions

1. Theresa is a pilot for ABC Airlines. Does either Theresa or the airline qualify as a principal or an agent? If so, which qualifies as which? Why?

2. Melanie contracted with a travel agent for the purchase of a charter trip to England. The travel agent made the necessary arrangements with the charter company. The agent recommended a one-day side trip, which the client agreed to purchase. While the client was on the side trip, she was injured because a step on the company's bus was rusted. Further, the airline overbooked the client's return flight, which resulted in a two-day delay in the client's arrival home. What potential liability, if any, does the travel agent have in these circumstances?

3. Salvatore had confirmed reservations on a flight from New York City to Boston. The airline overbooked the flight. How should the airline determine whether or not Salvatore will get bumped? Why should it use that method?

4. Referring to the facts in question 3, assuming that Salvatore is bumped, what responsibility, if any, does the airline have to him?

5. Tyrone was struck by a car while jogging on the sidewalk. The car was a rental car. Under what theory might Tyrone attempt to hold the car-rental company liable for his injuries? What would he need to prove to establish his case? How could he prove that?

6. Ariel and Jeremy were passengers on a plane that was about to take off. They were loud and rowdy, and were overheard to say, "This is the big one." Passengers in adjoining rows became alarmed and summoned the flight attendant. She asked Ariel and Jeremy to settle down and they became angry and more boisterous. What rights do the attendant and the pilot have in this circumstance? Why?

Websites

Websites that will enhance your understanding of the material in this chapter include:

www.faa.gov This is the official site of the Federal Aviation Administration. Topics covered include airport and airplane safety, and security advice for air travelers.

www.Findlaw.com This site offers information on many legal topics, including various airline issues.

www.restaurant.org This is the site of the National Restaurant Association, a trade organization for restaurant owners and managers. One of the issues addressed on the site is class action abuse and reform.

www.ftc.gov This is the site of the Federal Trade Commission whose mission is in part, consumer protection. The site contains information about telemarketing travel fraud ("Hello. You have been specially selected to receive our SPECTACULAR LUXURY DREAM VACATION offer"), vacation prize promotions on e-mail, and travel advisories.

www.nsarco.com/emotional_support This site provides information on service animals and the legal rights of their owners.

www.transportation.gov/access-advisory-committee This site provides information on the 2017 recommendations of the Advisory Committee on Accessible Air Transportation[96] which is charged with recommending rules for airline accessibility.

www.faa.gov This is the site of the Federal Aviation Commission. Its mission is to ensure the safety of the airline industry.

---

[96] Appointed by the Department of Transportation.

CHAPTER 14

Employment

LEARNING OUTCOMES:

- Understand the mandates of the Fair Labor Standards Act including minimum wage, overtime pay, equal pay for equal work, and child labor laws
- Learn about the Family and Medical Leave Act
- Comprehend at-will employment
- Know Title VII of the Civil Rights Act of 1964
- Be aware of prohibited and permitted interview questions
- Understand the Americans with Disabilities Act
- Become familiar with the Immigration Reform and Control Act
- Understand the torts of resume fraud and negligent hiring
- Learn about the Occupational Safety and Health Administration
- Be aware of employees' union rights
- Understand the importance of staying current on ever-changing employment laws

---

affirmative action
at-will employment
back pay
bona fide occupational qual-
    ification (BFOQ)
business necessity
collective bargaining
collective bargaining
    agreement
comparable worth
disability
disparate impact

disparate treatment
Equal Employment
    Opportunity Commission
    (EEOC)
equal pay for equal work
essential functions
Fair Labor Standards Act
    (FLSA)
glass ceiling
hostile environment sexual
    harassment
illegal alien

immigrant
negligent hiring
pretext
protected classes
quid pro quo sexual
    harassment
retaliatory discharge
reverse discrimination
sexual harassment
undue hardship

© wavebreakmedia/Shutterstock.com

Introduction

The employer-employee relationship is fertile ground for lawsuits against the employer. These cases seek to enforce employment laws and can take one of two forms, either a lawsuit by the employee or by the government against an employer.

Employment law is far-reaching and affects employees' wages; and prohibits discrimination on the grounds of race, religion, color, national origin, gender, pregnancy, age, disability, union membership, and in some locales, sexual orientation. The law also requires the employer to verify worker eligibility for employment in the United States. We will study each of these topics in this chapter.

Fair Labor Standards Act

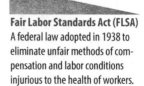

Fair Labor Standards Act (FLSA)
A federal law adopted in 1938 to eliminate unfair methods of compensation and labor conditions injurious to the health of workers.

The **Fair Labor Standards Act (FLSA)** is a federal law adopted in 1938, and still effective today, to eliminate unfair methods of compensation and labor conditions injurious to the health and efficiency of workers. It mandates minimum wages, one-and-one-half pay for overtime work, equal pay for equal work, and restrictions on child labor. The Act has been amended and updated numerous times since its original passage.

Minimum Wage

The FLSA requires that, with few exceptions, employers involved in interstate commerce pay employees at least the minimum wage set by Congress. The minimum wage is increased from time to time as Congress sees fit. Since July 2009, the federal minimum wage has been $7.25 an hour. States may adopt a minimum wage higher but not lower than Congress. If they do so, employers in those states must pay the higher amount set by the state.

Many fast-food workers have advocated for a $15 minimum wage. Some states and locales have passed laws increasing the minimum wage incrementally over several years, eventually reaching $15.

If an employer fails to pay minimum wage, employees can sue for unpaid wages. A delinquent employer will be directed by the court to remit all unpaid wages.[1]

Maintainence of Records

Employers are required to keep accurate records of the hours each employee works and the wages paid. In 2015 Papa John's Pizza in New York City was found guilty of paying hundreds of delivery workers less than minimum wage and failing to maintain sufficient records of wages and hours. The franchisee involved paid $2.2 million as compensation and penalties.

Low Sales Exception to Minimum-Wage Requirement

Excepted from the minimum-wage requirement are employers with less than $500,000 in annual sales. Case Example 14-1 illustrates this rule.

CASE EXAMPLE 14-1

Padilla v. Manlapaz, Barrio Fiesta Restaurant, et al

643 F.Supp.2d 298 (N.Y., 2009)

. . . Plaintiff was employed as a waitress at Barrio Fiesta Restaurant from October 2003 through May 2006. Her duties included purchasing supplies. . . On November 21, 2007 Plaintiff initiated this action alleging that while employed at Barrio Fiesta, Defendants violated the Fair Labor Standards Act of 1938. . . Plaintiff alleges that Defendants failed to pay her both the federal minimum wage and overtime wages in violation of applicable law. Both the minimum and overtime wage sections of the FLSA provide coverage for every "employee who is engaged in commerce . . .or is employed in an enterprise engaged in commerce . . . ."

---

[1] *Li v. Iron Sushi*, 2017 WL 1194733 (N.Y. 2017)

The FLSA is applicable if an employer is an "enterprise engaged in commerce." [Per the wording of the statute] Enterprise coverage applies when an employer, inter alia, grosses at least $500,000 in annual sales. . . . For Plaintiff's claims to ultimately succeed on a theory of enterprise liability, she will have to prove that Barrio Fiesta grossed more than $500,000 annual sales during the relevant time period.

In another case, the court had to decide whether a hotel and adjacent restaurant were two separate businesses, each of which fell below the threshold amount for FLSA coverage (then $362,500 in annual sales), or one business subject to the Act. Ruling that the two businesses should be treated as one, the court noted that the two buildings were physically connected. Also, while the two businesses had separate owners, the owners are husband and wife; therefore, the real property is owned jointly by the couple and neither business pays rent. Further, the establishments shared a phone, laundry facilities, advertising, and managers.

If two businesses are not in close proximity, but rather separated by several miles, the outcome may be different. Additional factors to consider include:

- whether the units share a common business purpose and whether the activities performed by each unit are related;

- operational autonomy (for example, whether the units have separate records and bookkeeping); and

- whether each unit has dedicated employees not shared by the other.[2]

None of these factors is determinative. A case involved two ski resorts separated by six miles. The two resorts had a common owner, marketed their operations as one enterprise, and shared accounting, management, and other personnel. Said the court, "Common ownership and a close functional and economic relationship between physically separated units of a business are not sufficient to make such combined units a single establishment, particularly where, as here, the geographic separation is substantial."[3] In another case two businesses were under common control but did not share a common business purpose. They were treated as two separate entities for purposes of the Fair Labor Standards Act.[4]

Tips Exception to Minimum-Wage Requirement

Another exception to the minimum-wage requirement applies to employees who routinely receive more than $30 per month in tips on the job. For those employees, an employer can credit workers with $5.12 toward the minimum wage, and pay tipped

---

2 *Chao v. Double JJ Resort Ranch*, 375 F.3d 393 (Mich. 2004)
3 *Chessin v. Keystone Resort Management, Inc.*, 184 F.3d 1188 (Co. 1999)
4 *Nelson v. Long Lines, Ltd.*, 335 F.Supp.2d 944 (Iowa 2004)

employees only $2.13. However, the credit cannot exceed the tips actually received by the employee. Thus, for the restaurant to take advantage of the tip credit and pay the server only $2.13 per hour, the waiter must regularly and customarily receive more than $30 per month in tips. In those states that have adopted higher minimum-wage laws, the amount the employer must pay after applying the tip credit will be higher.

Under federal law, tip pooling among tipped employees, including wait personnel, counter help, bus help, and bartenders, is permitted for purposes of the employer utilizing the tip credit to reduce an employee's pay below minimum wage.

Seven states have adopted laws that do not allow tip credits to reduce the minimum wage an employer must pay. Those states are California, Washington, Oregon, Nevada, Alaska, Montana, and Minnesota.

Often tipped employees are required to spend part of their time engaged in tasks that do not generate tips. For example setting tables, cleaning up, rolling silverware, making coffee, and acting as hostess. An employer can take the tip credit, and therefore pay less than minimum wage, for time an employee spends doing jobs related to the tipped occupation but which do not themselves generate tips, provided time spent on such tasks does not exceed 20 percent of the employee's time at work.

Youth Minimum-Wage Exception to Minimum-Wage Requirement

An employer can pay a wage below minimum to a limited class of young employees. Called the youth minimum wage,[5] the amount is $4.25 per hour. The application of this exception is limited. The only employees to whom this wage applies are workers under age 20 and then only for the first 90 calendar days of employment (consecutive days, not work days) with each employer. Thereafter, the employer must pay the full minimum wage. Employers are prohibited from displacing employees to hire young people at the training wage.

Overtime Pay

The FLSA requires that certain employees who are paid on an hourly basis and who work more than 40 hours in one week be paid at least one-and-one-half times their regular pay for the hours in excess of 40. For example, if a receptionist at a restaurant is paid $8 per hour and works 45 hours in one week, the employer must pay $12 per hour for the last five of those hours.

Exempt Employees

The statute contains an exemption to the overtime and minimum-wage requirements for executive, administrative, and professional employees. Employers often

---

[5] This used to be called Training Wage. The name changed because 16–19-year olds in their first 90 days of employment with a particular employer qualify for the reduced minimum wage regardless of whether they are in training.

seek to avoid overtime pay for employees by designating them as within the exempt categories. Employees denied overtime pay may contest their classification. A discussion of the exemptions follows.

Two general rules apply: (1) To qualify, an employee must pass a salary test and a duties test (job titles are not controlling); and (2) employees paid an hourly wage are nonexempt regardless of their duties.

Executive Employees

To qualify as an executive employee for the purposes of exemption from overtime pay, all of the following tests must be met:

1. The employee must be compensated on a salary basis (as opposed to an hourly wage) at a rate of not less than $455 per week.

2. The employee's primary duty must be managing the business or a department or other business subdivision.

3. The employee must regularly direct the work of at least two full-time employees or their equivalent (e.g., one full-time and two half-time employees).

4. The employee must have the authority to hire or fire other employees or have significant input in those decisions.[6]

A chain restaurant claimed its lowest-level manager, whose job title was Associate Manager, was in an executive position and therefore exempt from overtime pay. The job, an entry-level position, included work that regular crew members do (preparing pizzas, salads, and other food, running the cash register, waiting on customers, cleaning), which tasks were described by the company as "learning by doing," and studying company manuals to prepare for management tests. Associate Managers performed little or no supervision of other employees, were not in charge of a restaurant, and did not supervise shifts. Not surprisingly, the court held that the position of Associate Manager was not an executive position.[7]

Similarly, the Luigi Q Italian Restaurant labeled the chef an executive employee and did not pay him overtime. The chef sued. The evidence established that he did not hire, fire, or make promotion recommendations. The court therefore found the chef was wrongly classified and entitled to overtime.[8]

In contrast a second assistant manager at McDonald's was responsible for interviewing and hiring crew members, training, ensuring product quality, verifying that food safety checks are completed, deciding how much food will be produced on his shifts, performing or giving input on crew members' performance reviews, sending crew members home if the restaurant was overstaffed or for disciplinary

[6] U.S. Dep't. of Labor Fact Sheet #17B, Exemption for Executive Employees under the FLSA.
[7] *Dole v. Papa Gino's of America, Inc.*, 712 F.Supp. 1038 (Mass. 1989)
[8] Solis v. Luigi Q Italian Restaurant, 938 F.Supp.2d 380 (N.Y. 2013).

reasons, and dealing with customer complaints. His claim for overtime was denied; he was determined to be a "bona fide executive."[9]

Administrative and Professional Employees

In addition to executive employees, administrative and professional employees are also exempt from the overtime and minimum-wage requirements of the FLSA. To qualify for the administrative employee exemption, the employee must satisfy all of the following criteria:

1. They must be compensated on a salary or fee basis at a rate of at least $455 per week.

2. They must have as a primary duty the performance of office or nonmanual work directly related to the management or general business operations of the employer or the employer's customers.

3. The employee's primary duties must include the exercise of discretion and independent judgment with respect to matters of importance.

To qualify for the professional employee exemption, workers must satisfy both of the following tests:

1. They are compensated on a salary or fee basis in a minimum amount of $455 a week.

2. Their primary duty is the performance of work requiring advanced knowledge in a field of science or learning customarily acquired by a prolonged course of specialized intellectual instruction.

---

9 *Stubbs v. McDonald's Corp.*, 2006 WL 1722267 (Kans. 2006)

New regulations issued by the Department of Labor sought to expand the number of workers who were entitled to overtime pay by raising the threshold wage from $455 per week ($23,600 annually), to $913 per week ($47,476 annually). The new rules were scheduled to take effect on December 1, 2016. However, as this book goes to press the rules are on hold. A federal judge issued an injunction (a court order requiring a litigant to refrain from doing something) postponing the effective date pending further legal proceedings.

Time Worked

The FLSA identifies what constitutes time worked for purposes of determining the number of hours for which an employee is entitled to hourly pay and for determining whether an employee has worked overtime. In addition to time spent on job-related tasks, the following are counted as time worked: coffee and snack breaks; meetings to discuss daily operations problems; rest periods of 20 minutes or less; travel from job site to job site or to customers; required training; and clearing a cash register or totaling receipts after regular work hours. However, time spent waiting in line for a mandatory security check of bags, backpacks, and briefcases when leaving work is not counted as time at work.[10]

Split and Partial Shifts

An employee with a split shift (e.g., a server who works lunch and dinner with a few hours off in the middle of the afternoon) is entitled to payment only for the hours worked and not for the hours off in the middle of the separated work time. However, some states require "spread of hours" pay. This means extra wages if a split shift extends the workday beyond a specified number of hours, for example, ten. Likewise, if an employee is sent home partway through a shift because of lack of work, in most states the employee is not entitled to payment for the time he did not work. Eight states and Washington, D.C., mandate that employees who are obligated to report to work but are sent home early must be paid at least half a day's pay.

Some employers utilize "on-call scheduling" where employees are required to be available for possible shifts but must check by phone, text, or email before coming to work to learn whether their services are needed or not. This significantly disrupts workers' ability to plan their workday and schedule other commitments. Advocacy groups are seeking legislation to mandate advance notice of schedules and payment for minimum hours on days when an employee's shift is canceled.

Equal Pay for Equal Work

A 1963 amendment to the FLSA, called the Equal Pay Act (EPA), requires that men and women who do the same job, or do jobs that require equal skill, effort, and responsibility, be paid the same or according to the same pay schedule, a practice

---

10 *Friekin v. Apple, Inc.*, 2014 WL 2451598 (CA., 2014).

known as **equal pay for equal work**. An issue that often arises when an employee claims a violation of the EPA is whether jobs are the same. The test is whether they have a "common core" of tasks; or, stated differently, whether much of the work involved is very similar. Comparable generalized responsibilities are not sufficient, nor are similar titles. Although the act protects both men and women, most lawsuits invoking the EPA have involved situations where a woman was paid less than a man.

Comparable Worth

The EPA applies only when two people are doing the same job, or jobs that require the same skills and responsibility. Sometimes men and women work at jobs that are quite different and one is paid more than the other, yet the value of their work to the employer is equal. **Comparable worth** refers to jobs requiring different skills and responsibilities that have equal value to the employer. Courts have rejected the argument that comparable worth requires equal pay. If adopted, courts would be required to evaluate the worth of different jobs and rank them according to their relative values, something courts seem ill-equipped and unwilling to do. Advocates of equal pay for jobs of comparable worth argue that the concept would address the undervaluation of jobs traditionally associated with women, a circumstance that is not addressed by the EPA.

In 1989, comparable worth was again rejected in a federal case.[11] The employer (the State of Michigan) had done its own market studies and was aware of wage disparities in its pay system between jobs predominantly filled by males and different jobs of comparable worth filled by females. The plaintiffs, female state employees, claimed that by perpetuating such a system the employer discriminated against female workers. In denying the plaintiffs' claims, the court stated,

> *Laws prohibiting unequal pay are] not a substitute for the free market, which historically determines labor rates. . . . Mere failure to rectify traditional wage disparities that exist in the marketplace between predominantly male and predominantly female jobs is not actionable.*

Given this precedent, few comparable-worth cases have since been brought.

Retaliatory Discharge

If employees believe they are being paid unfairly and complain or commence a lawsuit under the FLSA, the employer is often irritated and sometimes antagonistic toward them. The EPA addresses this circumstance by prohibiting an employer from discharging or otherwise discriminating against such employees.[12] Thus, where a restaurant discharged a manager for complaining about the restaurant's break policy and nonpayment of overtime compensation, the discharge was retal-

equal pay for equal work
A rule of law that requires that men and women who do virtually the same jobs be paid according to the same pay schedule.

comparable worth
The idea that men and women should earn equal pay for jobs requiring comparable skills and responsibility, or are of comparable worth to the employer.

---

[11] *International Union v. Michigan,* 886 F.2d 766 (Mich. 1989).
[12] 29 U.S.C. § 215(a)(3)

iatory and violated the FLSA. The court awarded the terminated manager in excess of $52,000 for unpaid overtime, back pay, and other compensatory damages.[13]

Restrictions on Child Labor—Hours

Many employees in hotels and restaurants are young people, often high school or even junior high students. The FLSA provides a minimum age for employees, restricts the number of hours younger employees can work, and limits the tasks they can perform. The goal of the FLSA is to provide young people with nonhazardous working conditions, and hours that do not interfere with their schooling or health.

The minimum work age is 14; an employer cannot legally hire a person younger than that. During the school year, an employee who is 14 or 15 cannot work more than 18 hours a week, not more than 3 hours on a school day, and cannot begin work earlier than 7:00 a.m. or end later than 7:00 p.m. During vacation, that same employee can work up to 8 hours a day but cannot exceed 40 hours a week. The workday cannot begin earlier than 7:00 a.m. or end later than 9:00 p.m. No federal law restricts the number of hours a 16- or 17-year-old can work.

Some states have additional, stricter rules that further limit the hours young people can work. For example, in New York, 16- and 17-year-olds are limited to 4 hours of work per day except for Fridays, Saturdays, and Sundays when they can work 8 hours. The maximum number of hours a week they can work while school is in session is 28, and if the employer wants them to work beyond 10:00 p.m., parental permission is necessary, as is verification from the school that the employee's academic standing is satisfactory.

Restrictions on Child Labor—Tasks

The federal law as well as some state laws limit the types of work young employees can do. These limitations are intended to protect young people's safety. For example, under the FLSA a worker under the age of 18 cannot operate meat grinders, meat-slicing machines, meat- and bone-cutting saws, or power-driven knives used for meat processing. Also prohibited are dough mixers, batter mixers, bread slicing and wrapping machines, and cake-cutting band saws and other power-driven equipment. Young workers are also barred from delivering messages, food, or other goods (room service) between the hours of 10:00 p.m. and 5:00 a.m. As an example of a related state law, an employee in New York under age 16 cannot paint the exterior of a building.

The need for such laws is exemplified by a case in which a 17-year-old kitchen worker at an Italian restaurant lost part of his arm while cleaning a pasta machine, a task prohibited for workers under 18. Somehow the machine activated and severed the young employee's arm at the elbow.[14]

---

[13] *Brown v. Pizza Hut of America, Inc.*, 113 F.3d 1245 (Okla. 1997)
[14] The restaurant was Violi's in upstate New York. See New York Daily News, May 17, 2014.

An employee whose rights under the FLSA have been violated has two options in pursuing the case: (1) File a claim with the Wage and Hour Division of the United States Department of Labor, an agency charged with overseeing enforcement of laws that protect employees; or (2) commence a lawsuit against the employer seeking damages and attorney fees. Additionally, if the employer's actions are willful, the employer can be criminally prosecuted by the United States Justice Department, a branch of government charged with prosecuting federal crimes. Penalties for criminal offenses include fines and jail.

The maximum fine for violations of the child labor provisions is $10,000 for each employee who is the subject of a violation. The same fine applies to retaliatory discharges. Employers who willfully or repeatedly violate the minimum-wage or overtime pay provisions may be required to compensate the wronged employee for double the amount of unpaid back pay, plus attorney's fees and court costs, and are subject to a civil penalty of up to $10,000 for each violation.

Family and Medical Leave Act

The Family and Medical Leave Act (FMLA) addresses a problem that employees often face—obtaining time off from work to care for sick children or other close family members. The FMLA, effective in 1993, entitles eligible employees to take up to 12 weeks of unpaid leave per year for childbirth, adoption, foster placement, or to care for a child, spouse, or parent who has a serious health condition, or for the employee's own serious health situation. To be eligible, an employee must have been employed for at least 12 months before the leave commences and have worked at least 1,250 hours during the 12-month period immediately prior to the leave. A restaurant employee who had worked for only 10 months prior to an injury was not eligible for a FMLA leave.[15]

Not all employers are covered by the FMLA. To be covered, employers must carry on their payroll 50 or more employees for each working day for each of 20 or more weeks in the year.

A bill has been introduced in Congress to mandate that the leave be paid. The bill has not been adopted.

Upon returning from the leave, an employee must be reinstated to the position held before the leave or to a comparable position with equivalent pay, benefits, and other terms of employment. In a case involving the executive housekeeper at a hotel, her position was filled while she was on leave. Upon her return she was offered the job of food and beverage manager at the same salary and benefits. She argued that the position was not equivalent. The court disagreed, noting that both involved supervisory duties and both had the same goal of customer service.[16]

---

[15] *Banat v. Pop Restaurants*, 2005 WL 97397 (Tex. 2005)
[16] *Oby v. Baton Rouge Marriott*, 329 F.Supp.2d 772 (La. 2002)

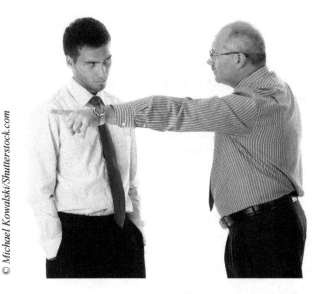

© Michael Kowalski/Shutterstock.com

Once an employer becomes aware that a worker qualifies for the leave, the employer must provide workers with notice of the FMLA rights. Failure to do so can result in liability for damages and lost benefits.

If upon return from a leave the employee is unable to perform the tasks of his job, the employer is not obligated to reinstate him to that job. A kitchen employee with the title of "fourth man assembler" fell at his home and suffered a neck and back injury. He took a FMLA leave to recover. Upon his return to work it was undisputed that he was physically unable to resume all the duties of his position. He was offered a new job of "salad expediter." He declined because it paid less and, in his opinion, came with less prestige. He was thereafter fired. He sued for violation of the FMLA. The court entered judgment for the restaurant. The fact that the employee could not perform the duties of his previous job excused the restaurant from reinstating him.[17]

The FMLA prohibits retaliation against an employee who exercises his rights under the Act. However, an employee whose violation of company rules is discovered during his leave can be terminated for violation of the rules. Thus an employer acted legally for terminating an employee on leave upon discovering significant incidents of company credit card cellular phone abuse.[18]

Likewise, an employer can refuse to rehire an employee seeking to return from an FMLA leave where the worker's job has been eliminated while she was away. A singing bartender took an FMLA leave due to throat and lung issues resulting from dust and debris kicked up during renovations at the hotel. While she was on leave, the employer made a strategic decision to update the look and feel of the bar and change its theme, ending the feature of singing servers. When she was ready to return and was not rehired, she sued claiming the employer was retaliating because she took the leave. The court disagreed and dismissed the case, upholding the inn's right to eliminate for good cause positions of workers on leave.[19]

At-Will Employment

at-will employment
The rule of law that provides that an employment contract between an employer and an employee that is indefinite in duration can be terminated by either party for any reason or no reason at any time without liability.

In many states, employment arrangements between employers and employees are considered "at-will." **At-will employment** means the employment contract between an employer and an employee is indefinite in duration and can be terminated by either party for any reason or no reason at any time without liability. If, however, a written employment contract exists between the employer and employee, and if the contract contains a provision stating that an employment arrangement will exist for a specified period of time, early termination can result in liability. A management trainee was terminated for making a profane statement to a fellow employee and for other miscon-

17 *Morro v. Resorts Casino Hotel*, 2015 WL 3991144 (N.J. 2015).
18 *Johnson v. Houston's Restaurant, Inc.*, 167 Fed. Appx. 393 (Tex. 2006)
19 *Jarjoura v. Erikson, Inc.*, 266 F.Supp.2d 519 (Tex. 2003)

duct. He sued the hotel claiming breach of his employment contract. That contract did not contain a provision stating his employment would last for a specific time period. The court held that the employment relationship was at will, enabling the hotel to terminate it at any time without obligation to the trainee. His lawsuit was thus dismissed.[20]

Illegal Job Discrimination

Notwithstanding an employer's right to terminate an employment contract based on the at-will doctrine, an employer cannot discriminate against workers on the basis of race, skin color, religion, gender, pregnancy, national origin, disability, age (if the employee is at least 40 years old), or union membership. These categories are called **protected classes.** In some locales, discrimination on the basis of sexual orientation is likewise illegal.

protected classes
Groups of people with a common characteristic who are legally protected from discrimination based on that characteristic. A few examples include race, color, religion, and national origin.

Discrimination in employment is the basis for many lawsuits. These cases are based on the Civil Rights Act of 1964, the Civil Rights Act of 1991, and the Americans with Disabilities Act, all of which have greatly enhanced employees' rights. These lawsuits underscore the need to treat all employees and applicants fairly.

Other statutes also prohibit discrimination. For example, discrimination against U.S. citizens employed abroad by U.S. companies is prohibited by the Civil Rights Act of 1991. Discrimination on the basis of age is prohibited by the Age Discrimination in Employment Act. The Genetic Information Nondiscrimination Act bars unequal treatment because of genetic information. Such data are used to determine if someone has an increased risk of developing a disease, disorder, or condition. Employers are prohibited from requesting, requiring, or purchasing genetic information about employees, and from making employment decisions using genetic information. The referenced acts are federal laws. State statutes prohibit discrimination on grounds similar to the federal statutes. Many encompass additional protected classes, including marital status and arrest and conviction record.

Title VII of the Civil Rights Act of 1964

The statute that outlaws most grounds for discrimination is the federal Civil Rights Act of 1964, Title VII. It reads, in relevant part, as follows:

> *It shall be an unlawful employment practice for an employer (1) to fail or refuse to hire or to discharge any individual or otherwise discriminate against any individual with respect to his compensation, terms, conditions, or privileges of employment, because of such individual's race, color, religion, sex, or national origin.*[21]

The statute prohibits discrimination not only in hiring and firing but also in promotion, access to training, discipline, work assignments, shift assignments, vacation time, and more. A purpose of the Civil Rights Act is to prevent and remediate invidious discrimination in the workplace.

---

[20] *Parker v. John Q. Hammons Hotels, Inc.*, 914 F.Supp. 467 (N.M. 1994)
[21] 42 U.S.C. § 2000e-2(a)

disparate treatment
Intentional discrimination based on race, color, religion, gender, or national origin.

disparate impact
Neutral employment practices that unintentionally result in unequal treatment.

Equal Employment Opportunity Commission (EEOC)
An agency of the Federal government that is authorized to both develop policy and enforce Title VII mandates against discrimination.

A restaurant violates Title VII, for example, by hiring only males as wait personnel and refusing to hire females, as would a hotel that refuses to hire anyone who is Norwegian or any other specific nationality. Often acts of discrimination are not as obvious as these examples. Instead, the discrimination can be very subtle and therefore difficult to detect as well as prove. Title VII outlaws both **disparate treatment** discrimination, which is intentional discrimination based on considerations of race, color, religion, gender or national origin, and **disparate impact** discrimination, which involves neutral practices that result, often unintentionally, in unequal treatment. For example, an employer's no-beard policy was found to discriminate against black males because they suffer in substantially greater numbers than white males from a skin disorder that makes shaving difficult. In enforcing the no-beard policy, the employer had not intended to restrict employment opportunities for black males, but the effect of the rule was to do exactly that.[22]

Title VII covers employers with 15 or more employees. It created the **Equal Employment Opportunity Commission (EEOC),** a federal government agency that is charged with enforcing Title VII's mandates. Sometimes the status of a manager or close relative of an owner is unclear—are they employers or employees? If the number of employees in a business is close to the threshold of 15, this assessment may determine whether Title VII applies. A court addressing this issue noted that even highly placed employees who lack the inherent right to participate in the governance of the business are as subject to the control of the business principals as any other employees. To effectuate the purpose of the Civil Rights Act—to ameliorate discrimination in the workplace—such persons should be considered to be employees.[23]

Filing a Complaint

Before a Title VII action can be brought in federal court, a discrimination charge must be filed with the EEOC, which has regional offices throughout the country. The reason for the requirement of initial recourse to the EEOC is Congress' intention that the principal administrative mechanism to resolve employment discrimination claims is that agency. Said a court, "The EEOC should have the first opportunity to investigate the alleged discriminatory practices to permit it to perform its role in obtaining voluntary compliance and promoting conciliation efforts."[24] If successful, the EEOC's involvement in a case will avoid the need for a lawsuit.

The EEOC has specific rules and procedures for filing a claim, and strict time limits within which cases must be pursued. Generally, an employee must file a claim with the agency within 180 days after the alleged discriminatory act. Thereafter, an EEOC staff attorney or investigator will meet with the employee and make an initial assessment of whether the claim is supported by the facts and whether it should proceed. If the EEOC determines there is no reasonable basis to believe the charges are true, the agency will decline to pursue the claim. The employee can nonetheless proceed with a lawsuit in court against the employer. If the EEOC

---

[22] *Bradley v Domino's Pizza*, 939 F.2d 610 (Neb. 1991)
[23] *Smith v. Castaways Family Diner*, 453 F.3d 971 (Ind. 2006)
[24] *Makousky v. Wing King Three, Inc.*, 2005 WL 3481538 (Fla. 2005)

finds grounds to prosecute the claim, it will prepare a complaint, forward it to the employer, and then meet with the employer in an effort to reach a resolution.

Due to a large caseload, the EEOC has a sizable backlog and cannot fully investigate every claim. If the agency fails to act on a claim within 180 days of filing, the employee can request a right-to-sue letter authorizing the worker to file a lawsuit in federal court against the employer notwithstanding inaction by the EEOC. Once the employee receives a right-to-sue letter, he has only 90 days to file the lawsuit. If the employee waits more than 90 days to begin the case, it will be untimely and the court will dismiss it. A woman who was a cook and waitress at a Waffle House alleged illegal discrimination and filed a claim with the EEOC. It issued a right-to-sue letter. She began the lawsuit 114 days later. The court dismissed the case as untimely. Plaintiff argued that she should be granted additional time because she had moved and failed to notify the EEOC of her new address, resulting in late receipt of the right-to-sue letter. The court refused to allow an equitable tolling of the time restriction since she was at fault for not informing the agency of her move.[25]

Remedies

The remedies available to a successful plaintiff in a Title VII case are substantial. Until 1991, the remedies were limited to the following:

- An injunction, which is a court order precluding the employer from continuing the offending conduct

- A court order requiring the employer to adopt a policy forbidding discrimination and mandating implementation of the policy

- Attorney's fees, thereby relieving the plaintiff of this substantial expense

- Back pay, if the plaintiff suffered a loss of income due to the discrimination

Back pay refers to the difference between (a) the amount of money the plaintiff would have earned in the absence of discrimination, which might include increased salary that would have accompanied a promotion that plaintiff was denied or salary that was lost due to wrongful termination; and (b) the amount of money the plaintiff earned as the victim of discrimination. This might include plaintiff's salary without the raise plaintiff should have received, or pay earned in alternate employment, or, if the plaintiff did not seek another job, what she could reasonably have earned had she looked for employment.

back pay
An item of damages in an employment discrimination case consisting of pay the plaintiff would have earned but for a wrongful termination.

Prior to 1991, compensatory and punitive damages were available in discrimination cases only for plaintiffs who could prove *intentional* job discrimination based on race or skin color. Compensatory damages include, in addition to back pay, the following: front pay (lost earnings where reinstatement is not feasible), future monetary losses, emotional pain and suffering, mental anguish, and other nonmonetary losses.

---

[25] *Soggins v. Hillcrest Foods, Inc.*, 339 F.Supp.2d 702 (N.C. 2004)

The categories of plaintiffs to whom a judge can award compensatory or punitive damages in a Title VII case was significantly expanded by the Civil Rights Act of 1991,[26] although intentional discrimination (as opposed to disparate impact) remains a prerequisite. The act authorizes compensatory and punitive damages as a remedy for plaintiffs seeking redress, not only from intentional discrimination based on race or skin color, but also from intentional discrimination based on gender, religion, or national origin. Note that age discrimination is not included; a plaintiff in such a case is still not entitled to compensatory or punitive damages.

Plaintiffs in cases involving intentional discrimination on the basis of race and skin color can collect unlimited damages. The Civil Rights Act of 1991 places a cap on the amount an employer will be obligated to pay (exclusive of back pay) in any one suit involving gender, religion, or national origin. The amount is based on the number of employees an employer has. For employers with 15 to 100 employees, the maximum is $50,000; for those with 101 to 200 employees, $100,000; 201 to 500, $200,000; and for those with more than 500, the maximum is $300,000. These caps do not apply to back pay awards; those are limited only by the amount of pay lost.

Punitive Damages

Punitive damages can be awarded only in those circumstances in which the employee can show that the employer engaged in illegal discrimination "with malice or with reckless indifference to the federally protected rights" of the employee. This requires proof of evil motive or intent, or callous indifference of the sort that calls for deterrence and punishment over and above that provided by compensatory awards. This was illustrated in a case involving an employer who recruited 52 men from India, obtained illegal visas, paid them less than minimum wage, provided substandard housing and food, significantly restricted their nonwork activities, and repeatedly threatened and demeaned them. Punitive damages were awarded as punishment for the employer's malicious and willful conduct, and as a deterrent to other employers.[27]

An Asian cocktail waitress at a Reno, Nevada, casino was denied a medical leave for which she qualified and thereafter was terminated because the medical issue rendered her incapable of performing her job. The Employee Services Manager's confusion about the worker's eligibility arose in part out of a misclassification of the employee's status as a part-time worker by the previous owner of the casino. Said the court, "[N]egligent decision making and poor communication among managers may properly give rise to compensatory liability under Title VII, but they do not, without more, warrant punishment." The waitress was thus awarded compensatory damages but not punitive.[28]

Expert Witness Fees

Another remedy authorized by the Civil Rights Act of 1991 is compensation for expert witness fees. This is an important addition because most discrimination cas-

---

[26] 42 U.S.C. §1981
[27] *Chellen v. John Pickle Co. Inc.*, 446 F.Supp.2d 1247 (Okla. 2006)
[28] *Ngo v. Reno Hilton Resort Corp.*, 140 F.3d 1299 (Nev. 1998)

es require one or more expert witnesses, such as a specialist on gender stereotyping in a gender discrimination case. Each expert witness must spend time reviewing the case, researching particular issues, preparing for trial with the plaintiff's attorney, and testifying. As a result, their fees are typically quite high.

Defense of Bona Fide Occupational Qualification

A **bona fide occupational qualification (BFOQ)** relieves an employer from liability for disparate treatment (intentional) discrimination where selection of an employee based on gender, religion, age, or national origin is reasonably necessary for the normal operation of the employer's business. This defense is construed narrowly by the courts. To qualify, two elements are necessary: (1) the job in issue must require a worker of a particular gender, religion, age, or national origin; and (2) such requirement must be necessary to the essence of the business' operation. An example of a BFOQ is hiring only women to model women's makeup or women's bathing suits.

Another example of a BFOQ is embodied in a rule promulgated by the Federal Aviation Administration that requires pilots who reach age 60 to retire. In an age discrimination lawsuit brought by a 60-year-old pilot who wished to continue flying for Federal Express, the court determined that, "At some age everyone reaches a level of infirmity or unreliability that is unacceptable in a pilot in air transportation. That age will vary from person to person but cannot yet be predicted in a specific individual." The court thus determined that being younger than 60 was a BFOQ for pilots and did not constitute discrimination based on age.[29] In a job where safety is not as significant an issue as it is with pilots, a mandatory retirement age of 60 does not constitute a BFOQ and will likely constitute illegal discrimination. For example, a mandatory retirement age of 62 for directors of an employee-benefits consulting firm was found to constitute age discrimination and not to qualify as a BFOQ.[30] Note that BFOQ is *not* a defense to a claim of racial discrimination.

Defense of Business Necessity

Business necessity may relieve an employer of liability for disparate impact (unintentional) discrimination. If a neutral selection criterion has a disparate impact on a protected class, but constitutes a business necessity, the requirement will not violate the Civil Rights Act of 1964. **Business necessity** means that the criterion has an obvious relationship to job performance. An example of a business necessity is speaking fluent English for a person with a job requiring communication with English-speaking people. Some job applicants from countries other than the United States may not meet this job requirement. The employer can, for that reason, exclude them from consideration. Like a BFOQ, business necessity is defined narrowly, thereby minimizing the number of potential employees who can be eliminated from consideration.

bona fide occupational qualification (BFOQ)
A job qualification that legally discriminates on the basis of race, religion, national origin, or gender because (1) excluded classes cannot perform the job effectively, (2) such inability is factually supported, and (3) the job classification is reasonably necessary for the normal operation of the business.

business necessity
A criterion for job applicants that has an obvious relationship to the job.

---

[29] *Coupe v. Federal Express Corporation*, 121 F.3d 1022 (Tenn. 1997)
[30] *EEOC v. Johnson & Higgins*, 887 F.Supp.682 (N.Y. 1995).

© g-stockstudio/Shutterstock.com

To help ensure that employers do not discriminate against protected classes in the hiring process, the law bars employers from asking certain questions at employment interviews. Permissible questions relate to the job the candidate is seeking. Prohibited questions ask for information relating to a candidate's possible membership in a protected class. The ban applies to all aspects of the hiring process, including the application form, the interview, and questions contained in any testing materials the employer may utilize.

Prohibited Questions

Race

- What is your race?

National Origin

- What is your nationality? What country are you from? What is your native language?
- What country are your parents from? In what country were you born?
- Your name is unusual. Where is it from?

Citizenship

- Are you a United States citizen?
- Where are you a citizen?

Age

- How old are you?
- What is your date of birth?
- When did you graduate from high school?

Marital Status

- Are you married? Engaged? Divorced?
- What is your spouse's name?
- With whom do you live?

Children

- Do you have children? How many?
- What childcare arrangements have you made? Are you using birth control?
- Are you pregnant?
- Do you plan to have a family? If so, when?

Religion

- What religion do you practice?
- With which church/synagogue/mosque are you affiliated? What religious holidays do you observe?

Disabilities or Medical Conditions

- Do you have any disabilities? Have you ever been hospitalized?
- Have you had a major illness in the last five years?
- How many days were you absent from work because of illness last year? Have you ever been treated for a mental condition?
- Are you taking any prescribed medication?
- Have you ever been treated for drug addiction or alcoholism?

Arrest Record

- Have you ever been arrested?

In summary, if a question is not job related, it should not be asked.

Permissible Questions

National Origin/Citizenship

- Are you legally authorized to work in the United States?

© Photographee.eu/Shutterstock.com

Age

- Can you meet the minimum age requirements for this job as set by law? Are you at least 18 years old? If hired, can you provide proof that you are at least 18 years old?

Marital Status

- Would you be willing to relocate?
- Would you be willing to travel as needed for the job? Would you be willing to work overtime if necessary?

Religion

- We often work holidays and weekends. Is there anything that would prevent you from doing so?

Disability

- Are you able to lift a 50-pound weight and carry it 100 yards, which is required by this job?

- Are you able to perform the essential functions of the job? (This question assumes the interviewer has thoroughly described the job.)

- Can you demonstrate how you would perform the following job-related functions: ...?

Arrest Record

- Have you been convicted of any of the following crimes? (The crimes listed must be reasonably related to the job.)

A developing trend, known as "ban the box," prohibits employers from inquiring about an applicant's criminal history on an employment application and instead, requires the inquiry be postponed until later in the application process. Additionally, many state laws require employers to consider whether the conviction is time-related, the amout of time passed since the conviction, mitigating circumstances, and evidence of rehabilitation.

Race

As we have seen, race is one of the grounds on which Title VII outlaws discrimination. The statute's main objective concerning race was to eliminate discrimination against blacks. Sadly, racism against people of color pervaded our society and mandated this remedial legislation. Its application, however, is not restricted to any one racial or minority group. In the words of the U.S. Supreme Court, the prohibition against discrimination in employment on the basis of race bars "discriminatory preference for any racial group, minority or majority." Additional examples of racial groups include Hispanic, Asian, Native American, Caucasian, and Eskimo.

The outlawed discrimination includes not only refusals to hire, resistance to promote, and unjustified firings, but also all other types of discrimination, such as refusal to allow an employee to wear an Afro-American hairstyle, and terminating a white employee for associating with a black colleague.

An African American front office manager of a Wyndham Hotel established a prima facie case of discrimination based on events that followed the elimination of her position in a reorganization. Two days later a front desk supervisor position opened and plaintiff applied, but the hotel hired a white woman. Defendant failed to offer a nondiscriminatory reason for its decision. The court therefore denied the hotel's motion to dismiss the case.[31]

---

[31] *Davis v. Valley Hospitality Services LLC*, 372 F.Supp.2d 641 (Ga. 2005)

An interesting application of Title VII is found in a case in which the plaintiff was a black attorney. Her supervisor, while unhappy with her work, was advised by the department manager not to relay his dissatisfaction to her but rather to "let it ride" to avoid charges of racial discrimination. The plaintiff thereby missed the opportunity to improve her performance through constructive criticism and counseling from her supervisor. The plaintiff was terminated when the department manager, in a cost-cutting effort, was forced to terminate the two lowest-rated employees. The court held that the employer's failure to provide feedback and constructively develop the plaintiff's job skills was motivated by race and thereby violated Title VII.[32]

An employer can defend against a claim of discriminatory firing by establishing a legitimate, nondiscriminatory reason for the termination. A charge of discrimination made by an African-American hotel engineer was dismissed in Case Example 14-2 because the employer could establish misconduct on the employee's part, thus justifying the termination.

CASE EXAMPLE 14-2

Carter v. Thompson Hotels

943 F.Supp.2d 830 (Ill., 2013)

Kelly Carter filed this lawsuit against Thompson Hotels ("the hotel") alleging race discrimination and retaliation while employed at [defendant hotel] Chicago location, in violation of the Civil Rights Act of 1964. Presently before the court is the hotel's motion for summary judgment on plaintiff's amended complaint. For the reasons that follow, the hotel's motion for summary judgment is granted. . .

I. Carter's Employment Duties at the Hotel

Carter, who is African-American, began working for the hotel as an engineer in 1999. The events at issue occurred during the summer and fall of 2010. During this period, the hotel employed six full-time engineers, of whom Carter was the most senior. The engineers' job duties included performing maintenance and repairs within the hotel. Engineers performed many of the same duties although their individual areas of skill and experience differed. Carter's skill was in heating, ventilation, and air conditioning (HVAC). In addition, Carter worked on kitchen equipment and ice machines. . . . . .

The hotel applied "progressive discipline," starting at counseling, proceeding to verbal warning, written warning, final written warning, and termination.

II. Carter's Work Performance History

In March, Carter received a performance review . . . that stated his job performance needed improvement . . . The review explained Carter's quality of work as below average. . . .On August 16 Carter received a written warning for attendance issues.

---

[32] *Vaughn v. Texaco*, 918 F.2d 517 (La. 1990)

III. The Dishwasher Incident

Also in August . . . Carter examined the dishwasher twice because it was not working. . . . He was unable to make the repair. A less experienced engineer ultimately fixed the dishwasher by tightening a loose screw.

IV. Ice Machine Incident

In October Carter was working on a broken ice machine and incorrectly concluded that the cause of the problem was a defective controller. He was unable to fix it. . . . The next day another engineer fixed the problem in approximately 30 minutes. Carter acknowledged that he did not perform the repair correctly. The hotel issued Carter a written warning for failing to make an acceptable effort to complete the task. . .

Carter made several comments to his boss that she considered disrespectful. She issued Carter a verbal warning. On October 27, the hotel gave Carter a letter informing him that his work performance needed to improve and offering to help with that process. The letter also stated that it was "not too late to turn things around." . . . On November 11, after Carter failed to replace a guest room lamp, the hotel . . . terminated Carter's employment stating, "Your performance over the last few months has deteriorated substantially. We have warned you repeatedly . . . Such unsatisfactory job performance can no longer be tolerated."

On December 20, Carter filed a charge with the EEOC alleging discrimination and retaliation. . . He alleged that the hotel discriminated against him based on race by subjecting him to discriminatory discipline and terminating his employment. Carter proceeds under the familiar indirect method of proof set out in *McDonnell Douglas Corp. v. Green.* Under that approach, to demonstrate a prima facie case of discrimination Carter must show that 1) he is a member of a protected class; 2) he was meeting the hotel's legitimate expectation; 3) he suffered an adverse employment action; and 4) similarly situated employees outside of his protected class were treated more fairly.

Carter satisfied the first element because he is African American. . . . During August through October, the hotel issued Carter six warnings related to his job performance. It issued two additional warnings for behavior. He was given a final warning after the October 27th incident. . . . Plainly, the number of performance-related warnings issued to Carter exceeded each of the engineers with whom he compares himself. The record reflects that white engineers received comparable discipline for infractions as did Carter. . . .

To succeed in the lawsuit, Carter must demonstrate that the hotels' reason for his termination was pretextual . . . by showing that the defendants' proffered explanation is unworthy of credence. . . . Carter claimed the hotel had failed to communicate with him about his job performance. [But Carter] had ample notice of the employment policies and expectations, having received an employee handbook when he was hired, and further information from the head engineer about expectations of the job of engineer. Carter was given numerous disciplinary warnings that set out an Action Plan describing expectations and what Carter needed to do to improve his performance in the future. . . . Carter was uncooperative. . . .

In short, Carter has failed to carry his burden of demonstrating that he was meeting the hotel's legitimate expectations. Nor does he present sufficient evidence of pretext to call the honesty of the hotel's reasons for termination into question. Accordingly, the hotel's motions for summary judgment with respect to [the race discrimination claim and his retaliation claim] are granted.

In a Pennsylvania case an African American female assistant manager of a Burger King eatery was terminated. She claimed the basis was discrimination. The employer proved the reason was that she left the safe unlocked and unattended, a serious violation of company policy. Further, Burger King established that a white manager was also terminated after he too neglected to lock the safe in his eatery. Summary judgment was granted in favor of the restaurant.[33]

A claim of discriminatory and retaliatory termination by a Pakistani service shift supervisor at an Old Country Buffet was rejected where he had a poor job performance record and was guilty of repeated acts of insubordination.[34] Unsatisfactory job performance was proven by another employer in response to an Iranian Muslim worker's claim that his termination two months after the World Trade Center terrorist attacks was discriminatory.

A history of failing to "adhere to and properly enforce Food Safety procedures in his restaurant" resulted in the termination of an African American McDonald's manager. His lawsuit for racial discrimination was dismissed. One of his complaints was that, because of his race, he had been temporarily transferred to a restaurant in a predominantly black neighborhood. The transfer did not result in loss of pay or position to plaintiff. The court held that the temporary transfer did not violate his rights. Plaintiff also argued that other, Caucasian managers with similar violations were not terminated. Proof of this claim would establish discrimination. The evidence, however, revealed that the food safety violations in those cases were the employees' first such violation; plaintiff had previously been cited for several such violations.[35]

In another case won by the employer, the basis for the discharge was "economic conditions" and plaintiff, an African American manager/trainee at Arby's, had the least seniority.[36] In another case, a bartender at the Adams Mark Hotel in Philadelphia proved a prima facie case. He was black; he had been employed for six years, and had received good reviews, thus establishing that he was qualified for the position; but he was discharged and replaced by someone who was Caucasian. The hotel claimed the firing was due to the plaintiff misappropriating hotel property by providing a "free drink" to a former hotel employee in violation of a well-established hotel policy. If the hotel can prove this allegation, the plaintiff, to win, would need to present evidence showing that the hotel's explanation is a pretext, meaning either that it is untrue or that it was not the motivating factor for the discharge.[37]

One way a plaintiff can show that the employer's claimed explanation for a termination was not in fact the reason is by showing that other employees who committed similar violations were not discharged. For example, assume the plaintiff in the previous case could show that other nonminority bartenders violated the same rule and were nonetheless retained. The hotel's justification for the plaintiff's

---

[33] *Cheaton v. Burger King Corp.*, 2006 WL 435732 (Pa. 2006)

[34] *Khan v. OCB Restaurant Co.*, 2006 WL 297177 (Md. 2006)

[35] *Hartzol v. McDonald's Corp.*, 437 F.Supp.2d 805 (Ill. 2006)

[36] *Jenneh v. Endvest, Inc.*, 64 Fed. Appx. 814 (N.Y. 2003)

[37] *Williams v. Adam's Mark Hotel*, 51 F.Supp.2d 637 (Pa. 1999)

termination would thus be exposed as pretextual. In a New Jersey case, an African American casino dealer was terminated for rude and discourteous treatment of a customer. He was able to show a few situations involving white employees who committed similar infractions but were not terminated. In response, the hotel established that of 15 employees fired within 5 years of the plaintiff, 12 were terminated for inappropriate conduct toward a patron. Eight of those were Caucasian employees. The court determined that the plaintiff's discharge was justified and for nondiscriminatory reasons.[38]

An African American manager of McDonald's established a prima facie case of race discrimination by showing that she was denied a pay raise while four white managers of stores owned by the same proprietor were given increases. The owner rebutted the claim by showing that the plaintiff's overall work rating was "needs improvement," while the managers given a raise were rated "good." These facts would constitute a defense to the discrimination charge. However, the plaintiff responded that the employer's argument was a pretext because the nonminority managers also underperformed on most or all of their goals and still received a "good" rating and a salary increase. If the plaintiff is able to prove this allegation, she will likely have established that the employer's explanation is pretextual and the probable reason for the difference in treatment was racial discrimination.[39]

Racially Hostile Work Environment

Also constituting discrimination based on race is the creation or tolerance by an employer of a racially hostile work environment. An employment atmosphere that permits racially derogatory comments, jokes, and conduct has been determined to

© michaeljung/Shutterstock.com

---

[38] *Jason v. Showboat Hotel & Casino*, 747 A.2d 802 (N.J. 2000)
[39] *Colterr v. McDonald's Restaurants*, 35 F.Supp.2d 824 (Kans. 1999)

CHAPTER 14: Employment

significantly and adversely affect the psychological well-being of an employee. For a plaintiff to prove a racially hostile work environment, he must show evidence that he was subjected to pervasive or severe harassment stemming from racial animus.

A police officer alleged a hostile work environment based on 12 racially hostile comments and jokes made during his 20-month tenure. The incidents included a comment by his supervisor that the plaintiff officer had to accept the fact that he was working with racists and should not be so sensitive. In the officer's lawsuit against the police department, the court determined these incidents would amount to a hostile environment and so denied the police department's motion to dismiss.[40]

A racially hostile environment was found in a case in which an African American plaintiff established numerous incidents of racial slurs. These included:

- An instructor in a stress-management session at the employer's facility offered an example of a stressful situation as being in a bar patronized mainly by blacks.

- One of the plaintiff's supervisors stated in the plaintiff's presence that certain African American murder suspects looked like "apes or baboons" and another supervisor was present and laughed.

- On Halloween, a co-worker said to the plaintiff and others, "all you spooks have a nice Halloween" and plaintiff's co-workers turned to look at plaintiff when the remark was made.

- During a training seminar, one co-worker made repeated references to "Arnold Schwarzenigger" and another commented that an unidentified Caucasian had "some nerve bringing his brown-skinned wife to the party."

- A co-worker called the plaintiff "nigger."

- Two co-workers distributed a copy of a racially offensive joke that included use of the word "nigger."[41]

The lesson from these two cases is that employers have an obligation to ensure the workplace is tolerant and accepting of all races.

A single incident or a few disparaging comments is usually not enough to prove a hostile environment. An African American second assistant manager at McDonald's was unable to establish a racially hostile work environment where he overheard a derogatory comment, although not directed toward him, plus McDonald's management requested plaintiff to transfer to an inner-city restaurant because management wanted a "strong African American presence" there. Additionally,

---

40 *Schwapp v. Town of Avon*, 118 F.3d 106 (Conn. 1997)
41 *Armenakis v. Top Notch Family Restaurant*, 2006 WL 1660589 (Ind. 2006)

plaintiff was assigned the undesirable closing shift for part of his seven years employment with defendant, and plaintiff was once asked to work on his day off picking up trash.[42] Likewise, a hostile work environment did not exist where a black waitress' boss once called her a "nigger bitch" in a "failed attempt at a joke."[43]

To escape liability for permitting a hostile work environment, it is not enough for an employer to have on record a policy prohibiting such conduct. The employer must take steps to train employees about the policy and must enforce it.

If the work environment is demeaning, but for reasons other than race, a plaintiff will not be able to prove discrimination. An African American male manager/trainee at Arby's alleged that his supervisors were impolite, sarcastic, antagonistic, and rude. There was no evidence of "racially charged comments" and the record reflected that the supervisor was equally unpleasant to Caucasian employees. The trainee's charge of unlawfully hostile work environment was therefore dismissed.[44]

Reverse Discrimination

reverse discrimination
Discrimination (differential treatment) against members of a dominant or majority group such as white people and males.

Typically in a race discrimination case the plaintiff is affiliated with a race in the minority. Sometimes, however, a person of a majority race, which in the United States is Caucasian, sues based on race discrimination. This type of claim is called **reverse discrimination**. In Case Example 14-3 plaintiff proved reverse discrimination.

CASE EXAMPLE 14-3

Clements v. Fitzgerald's Mississippi, Inc.

128 Fed. Appx. 351 (Miss. 2005)

Douglas Clements, a white male, was, until December 7, 2001, the head of human resources for Fitzgerald's Mississippi-based casino. On that date, the ownership of the facility passed from Fitzgerald's to Barden Mississippi Gaming, LLC ("Barden"). Barden's owner and sole shareholder is Don Barden, a black male. Despite an agreement between Fitzgerald's and Barden that a certain group of Fitzgerald's employees would be hired by Barden on that date—a group that the parties concede includes Clements—Barden refused to hire Clements. At the time of his "firing," Clements had been in the employ of Fitzgerald's for 2 years, and had 14 years of experience in the human resources field. Clements was replaced at his position with Tami Tolliver, a black female. Tolliver's husband, Kevin Tolliver, was also hired by Barden to be its Slot Director. Neither Tolliver had the requisite experience for their respective positions.

---

[42] *Stubbs v. McDonald's*, 2006 WL 1722267 (Ky. 2006)

[43] *Richardson v. N.Y. Dept. of Correctional Services*, 180 F.3d 426 (N.Y. 1999)

[44] *Jenneh v. Endvest, Inc.*, 64 Fed.Appx. 814 (N.Y. 2003); see also *Schmitz v. M&M MARS*, 73 Fed. Appx. 238 (Del. 2003) in which the court stated, "When a manager treats employees of different gender and races in the same manner even if offensive, it is not actionable under Title VII... [Plaintiff] simply failed to establish that the manager's mistreatment of him was racially motivated."

Clements brought this Title VII action against Barden alleging that he [Clements] was the victim of racial discrimination in connection with an adverse employment action. At a bench trial the district court found the following relevant facts: that during a February 2001 meeting between Clements and key Barden officials, Chief Operating Officer Michael Kelly and Don Barden, both Kelly and Barden thought that Clements was "bland" and "boring"; that Clements was told in October, 2001 that he would lose his job "because of Barden Gaming's desire to 'diversify'"; that Don Barden publicly stated that "if you look at our wall of managers here you'll see all white males...so we're gonna have more women as managers and more African-Americans as managers." The court ruled that, as a matter of law, because of the contract between Fitzgerald's and Barden, Barden was legally obligated to provide employment to Clements, making any reason given not to hire the plaintiff illegitimate. The court determined that Barden was liable to Clements for the unlawful "firing," and awarded Clements roughly $32,000 in backpay, $20,000 in emotional damages, and $260,000 for punitive damages. Barden appeals that decision....

Barden argues that its refusal to hire Clements was proper because it was based on Barden's conclusion that Clements was "bland" and "boring." Moreover, Barden contends that Clements was not qualified because...he had no degree in human resources.

It is uncontested that Barden replaced Clements, a manager with over 14 years of experience, with someone with objectively less experience. Moreover, it is uncontested that Clements was, under the Fitzgerald/Barden contract, to be hired by Barden.

[The court found no error of law and upheld the verdict, including the punitive damages.]

In an unsuccessful reverse discrimination case, a white male guest services representative at a Colorado Red Roof Inn claimed reverse discrimination when he was terminated. The hotel responded that he was fired because he repeatedly violated the hotel's policies on payment and check acceptance. The court dismissed the case noting that plaintiff failed to present evidence that the inn discriminated against whites or that minorities were disciplined differently from him.[45]

National Origin

National origin, another protected class, refers to the country where people were born or from which their ancestors came. A refusal to hire workers of, for example, Spanish ancestry violates Title VII. National origin discrimination was established in a case involving the Westin Tucson Hotel. The plaintiff was a Nigerian-born black man who was employed in the hotel's laundry. He tried six times unsuccessfully to transfer to other jobs for which he was qualified, primarily in the accounting department. When he asked about his status, he was told by the head of housekeeping, "Go back to Africa where you came from. We don't have any job for you here"; and by the Director of Human Services, you "should go to a black

---

[45] *Lyons v. Red Roof Inns, Inc.*, 130 Fed. Appx. 953 (Colo. 2005). See also *Tarshis v. Riese Organization*, 66 Fed. Appx. 238 (N.Y. 2003)

business to find a job." The court awarded the plaintiff employment in the accounting department of the hotel, back pay, and attorney's fees.[46]

If a plaintiff is unable to prove national origin prejudice on the part of the employer, the employee will likely not win a discrimination lawsuit. A Puerto Rican credit manager at a newly opened hotel was terminated soon after receiving a raise and a letter of commendation. She claimed the basis for her discharge was discrimination based on national origin. The hotel countered that the termination was due to poor job performance. The court ruled for the hotel. In its decision, the court identified various circumstances to consider when assessing whether national origin discrimination has been proven. The court stated, "Here plaintiff offers no evidence that [the hotel] fired Puerto Ricans in greater proportion than non-Puerto Ricans, engaged in a pattern of firing Puerto Ricans and replacing them with non-Puerto Ricans, or adopted corporate policies discriminatory toward Puerto Ricans. There is no evidence of statements by [the hotel's] management or officers indicating a bias against Puerto Ricans, and no evidence that [the hotel's] evaluation of her performance was infected by stereotyped thinking or other types of unconscious national-origin bias."[47]

A Nigerian employee who was terminated claimed the basis was national origin discrimination. As evidence of discrimination he referenced numerous statements by the employer including: (1) "Provide proof of your legal residence in the United States" and (2) "You are difficult to understand, particularly when you become excited." The court found neither of these statements sufficient to establish evidence of discrimination. Concerning the first, an employer is required by federal law to obtain proof of legal residence. (See the discussion on the Immigration Reform and Control Act later in this chapter.) The meaning and intent of the second statement is unclear and could refer to the plaintiff's speed, tone, or volume of speech. Absent further evidence to suggest the comment was a veiled reference to the plaintiff's national origin, it does not support an inference of discrimination.[48]

Employer tolerance of ethnic slurs or jokes by employees or supervisors may constitute a hostile work environment based on national origin. An example is provided by an Oklahoma case which involved an employer who recruited 50 men from India to work in Tulsa. The hostile work environment was characterized by abusive language, demeaning job assignments, and threats and intimidation based on their Indian ethnicity. The workers were regularly referred to as "Indian animals," "Indian donkeys," "Indian bastard," and other obscenities, "Indian dogs," "dirty and lazy." Threats to deport the workers and to inflict physical injury on them were prevalent. The court not surprisingly held the employer liable.[49]

Fluency in English

Employers often prefer to hire an employee who is fluent in English. People from other countries may not speak or understand English well. Refusal to hire someone whose English is faltering may constitute illegal discrimination on the basis of national origin.

---

[46] *Odima v. Westin Tucson Hotel*, 53 F.3d 1484 (Ariz. 1994)
[47] *Feliciano de La Cruz v. El Conquistador Resort*, 218 F.3d 1 (P.R. 2000)
[48] *Okumabuo v. McKinley Community Services, Inc.*, 2001 WL 709457 (Ill. 2001)
[49] *Chellen v. John Pickle Co., Inc.*, 2006 WL 1478516 (Okla. 2006)

However, as discussed earlier in this chapter, if the ability to speak English is a business necessity for the job, an employer who refuses to hire an applicant not well versed in English is not discriminating illegally. An example of English fluency being a business necessity is a job that requires communication with English-speaking patrons, such as wait personnel in restaurants or a hotel concierge. A plaintiff, a black male of Haitian origin, was a purchasing clerk for a Sheraton Resort. His duties included delivering supplies to many of the departments at the resort. His inability to understand English resulted in misdelivery of supplies and at least one employee having to obtain her own supplies. The plaintiff was terminated from the clerk position and offered a lesser-paying job in housekeeping. He sued the hotel, claiming national origin discrimination. The court held for the Sheraton, determining that the plaintiff's termination "rested on proper concerns of business necessity.... [T]he employer took the contested employment action for a legitimate nondiscriminatory reason."[50]

If fluency in English is not required for the job, as is the case for housekeeping personnel at a hotel or dishwashers at a restaurant, refusal to hire based on poor language skills would be illegal.

In Case Example 14-4, the hotel refused to promote a Hispanic employee because of her limited capacity to speak English. The court denied her claim of illegal discrimination, finding the hotel's requirement of fluent English was a business necessity.

CASE EXAMPLE 14-4

Mejia v. New York Sheraton Hotel

459 F.Supp. 375 (N.Y. 1978)

This is an employment discrimination case pursuant to Title VII of the Civil Rights Act of 1964....

Plaintiff alleges in her complaint that she was discharged on June 24, 1975 from her position as a chambermaid with the Sheraton Hotel on account of her Spanish surname and the fact that her primary language was Spanish, and that two years earlier she was denied a promotion to a front office cashier position for the same reasons.

The defendants deny any discriminatory purpose or effect of their conduct and assert that... the reason why plaintiff was not promoted to the front office cashier position which she sought was that she was not qualified by reason of the paucity of her English language ability and her lack of familiarity with office procedures. The facts established herein are the following.

Plaintiff is a female Dominican national who came to the United States in about 1970 as the holder of a visa entitling her to become employed in this country. Her education and schooling occurred abroad in a Spanish school and she never had any education in the English language until she arrived in this country. The plaintiff was employed as a chambermaid in the housekeeping department of the Sheraton Hotel from on or about October 29, 1970 to on or about June 24, 1975. During her employment, whatever ability she possessed to understand, speak and write English she acquired through courses that she had taken in English at New York University during a period of three months after her arrival here.

---

50 *Stephen v. PGA Sheraton Resort, Ltd.*, 873 F.2d 276 (Fla. 1989)

The defendant [is] New York Sheraton Hotel....

Commencing in April 1973 the plaintiff enrolled in an Industry Training Program, a program jointly sponsored by plaintiff's Union and the city's hotel industry to train hotel employees for positions within the hotel industry....A week after her training she applied for a position as a front office cashier. Such a job was never tendered to her....

In 1974 there was an opening in the cashier's department and plaintiff spoke to the manager but she was told that she would have to learn to speak better English because the position required a greater aptitude than the plaintiff possessed. ...The management found that the plaintiff's language barrier was a stumbling block to a front office post for the plaintiff, a post that would necessarily bring her in contact and communication with the guests of the hotel....

Following her discharge, plaintiff resorted to the EEOC charging that she was discriminated against because...of her national origin and was not promoted because she was Spanish....

The evidence in the case established beyond peradventure of doubt a serious past and current inability on the plaintiff's part to articulate clearly or coherently and to make herself adequately understood in the English language. She continued taking English courses after her discharge in the summers of 1975, 1976 and 1977 with minimal improvement. Her instructor's latest report card for the 1977 session recites that she was a poor student and definitely should not go on to [the next] level as she could not do the written work and that pronunciation was also a problem.

...Plaintiff's exhibition on the witness stand emphasized the current existence of an English language deficiency that made it quite difficult for the Court, the reporter and counsel to understand what she was saying in her testimonial responses.

The requirement of the hotel for greater English proficiency than the plaintiff can exhibit was significantly related to successful job performance and did not operate to exclude minority applicants at a higher rate than applicants who are not of that minority group. There is no doubt that the plaintiff was not sufficiently qualified to be placed in a position in the front office cashier's department. The defendants found her not acceptable for such employment in a legitimate, nondiscriminatory manner....Plaintiff's Hispanic origin... formed no part of defendant's refusal to place her in the front office cashier's department. Business necessities precluded a person of plaintiff's qualifications from being placed in the front office cashier type occupation in a large public hotel. The Sheraton Hotel employs about 650 persons, more than a third of whom are of Hispanic origin....Although plaintiff cannot be faulted for her eagerness to advance from the position of a chambermaid to the front office of the hotel, the evidence conclusively shows that she was never sufficiently qualified and therefore was not eligible for the position she sought in the defendant's front office....

Accordingly, the complaint herein is dismissed....Judgment for defendant.

CASE QUESTION

1. Why was fluency in English important in the job the plaintiff sought? Why was it less important for her job as a chambermaid?

A person from another country may be knowledgeable about English but speak with an accent. Said one court, "Accent and national origin are inextricably intertwined." The law in this area is very important to managers in the accommodations industry, where so many employees are foreign born.

A plaintiff who has been discriminated against solely because of his accent may be a victim of illegal discrimination based on national origin. A Lebanese American employee proved national origin discrimination was the reason he was denied a promotion. His supervisor's explanation, rejected by the court, was that the tasks required of the higher-paying position included supervising white employees, and they would not take orders from plaintiff, particularly because he had an accent.[51]

A native of Ghana attempted to prove a hostile work environment based in significant part on a comment by his supervisor that he should learn to speak English with an American accent because co-workers found it difficult to understand him when he spoke. On another occasion his supervisor told him, "Now they have you doing all the dirty assignments that we do not want." The court denied the claim finding the comments not sufficiently serious or pervasive to be actionable. Said the court, "Not all harassing workplace conduct is sufficient to establish a hostile work environment. To be actionable, the harassment must be sufficiently severe or pervasive to alter the conditions of the victim's employment and create an abusive working environment." The two comments of which plaintiff complained were insufficient.[52]

An employer can, however, refuse to hire a job applicant based on an accent if it materially interferes with job performance. A high school teacher was denied tenure (a permanent teaching position) because students complained her accent was difficult to understand. She sued the school district, claiming discrimination on the basis of national origin. The court found for the school district stating, "Unlawful discrimination does not occur when a plaintiff's accent affects his ability to perform the job effectively."[53] Similarly, where the accent of a Vietnamese mailroom clerk was so strong that other employees could not understand her and organizational productivity was diminished, her termination was justified and did not constitute illegal discrimination based on national origin.[54]

But if the accent does not interfere with the ability to perform the job, the employer cannot refuse to hire or promote or otherwise discriminate on that basis. A bank employee was denied a promotion to loan officer because of his accent. The court determined that his accent would not have interfered materially with his performance. The judgment in the plaintiff's favor, which was upheld on appeal, included back pay, lost future pay, expert witness fees, attorney's fees, compensation for emotional distress, and expenses for medical and psychiatric treatment necessitated by the discrimination.[56]

---

[51] *Abouri v. Florida DOT*, 408 F.3d 1338 (Fla. 2005)
[52] *Obeng-Amponsah v. Rorh, Inc.*, 2002 WL 31518852 (Calif. 2002)
[53] *Forsythe v. Board of Education, Hays, Kansas*, 956 F.Supp. 927 (Kans. 1997)
[54] *Bishop v. Hazel & Thomas*, 151 F.3d 1028 (Va. 1998)
[55] *Xieng v. People's National Bank of Washington*, 844 P.2d 389 (Wash. 1993)
[56] *EEOC v. Beauty Enterprises, Inc.*, 361 F.Supp.2d 11 (Conn. 2005)

In a California case a preliminary question was whether the employee's linguistic expert witness should be permitted to testify. The court allowed the testimony over the employer's objection that the testimony was irrelevant and unreliable. Employee plaintiffs claimed disparate impact discrimination stemming from an English-only workplace rule. The witness' testimony is instructive on the effect of English-only work rules and included: where job duties constitute routine manual labor, the language required for job performance is minimal; restrictive language rules impede a person's ability to learn a second language and thus prolong dependence on a foreign language; native speakers of a language other than English would improve their English proficiency if they were allowed to first learn their jobs in their native language; the English-only rule impedes safety because it slows an employee's reaction time during an emergency; and an English-only rule stigmatizes linguistic minorities and harmfully affects their ethnic identity.[55]

The courts may also look at the severity of a defendant's comments in a ruling on national origin employment discrimination. A Pakistani employee sued his employer Holiday Inn, claiming national origin discrimination and hostile work environment. The employee claimed that during 12 years he worked for Holiday Inn, the hotel chain referred to him as "You are the Pakistani, right" or "You Pakastani" on ten occasions, and once called him "stupid Pakistani." The court held that this was not sufficiently pervasive or severe to constitute illegal harassment.[57]

Religion

An employer cannot discriminate against a person based on religion, including all aspects of religious observance and practice. This rule can sometimes present difficulties for employers. For example, some workers celebrate the Sabbath in such a way that work is precluded. Some celebrate it on Saturday and others on Sunday. Various religious holidays occur throughout the year. Accommodating religion-based requests for days off can complicate an employer's work schedule.

© Billion Photos/Shutterstock.com

Must an employer oblige employees' requests for days off to celebrate religious holidays? An employer has an affirmative duty to attempt to accommodate the religious observances and practices of its employees. If, however, the employer can demonstrate that such an accommodation would cause undue hardship to the business, it can refuse to grant the days off. Stated differently, an employer who is unable to reasonably satisfy the religious needs of an employee can escape liability if it can show it made a good-faith attempt to accommodate those needs or that to do so would cause undue hardship.

57 *Kowavi v. Intercontinental Hotels Group Resources, Inc.*, 2013 WL 4737328 (Calif. 2013)

In a Washington, D.C., case, the plaintiff, a Moroccan-born Muslim working at defendant hotel, filed a complaint alleging that hotel personnel discriminated against him on the basis of religion when he was not permitted to do his job as a dry cleaning valet on certain floors while an Israeli delegation stayed on two of those floors. The plaintiff claimed that his supervisor told him, "You know how the Israelis are with Arabs and Muslims." The plaintiff obeyed the rules but complained he was deprived of tips from not being able to work those two floors. The court denied the claim for discrimination and said the deprivation of tips was de minimus.[58]

Reasonable Accommodations

Reasonable accommodation requires an employer to give unpaid time off for religious holidays if the employer can reasonably dispense with the employee's services on the days in question. Further, if paid leave is allowed for other purposes, unpaid leave for religious holidays may not qualify as a reasonable accommodation. Further, an employer is required to accept schedule changes prompted by religious observance and arranged by the employees unless there is a good reason not to permit the substitution, as where the alternate worker lacks necessary skills to do the job. Another reasonable accommodation an employer might provide is a means of communication among employees to facilitate their finding substitutes, such as a bulletin board in the employee break room. In Case Example 14-5 an employee of a Red Robin Gourmet Burgers, Inc. convinced the court that his tattoos were religious based and therefore the restaurant was required to accommodate them, notwithstanding a no-tattoo and body piercing policy.

CASE EXAMPLE 14-5

Equal Employment Opportunity Commission v. Red Robin Gourmet Burgers, Inc.

2005 WL 2090677 (Wash. 2005)

Plaintiffs Equal Employment Opportunity Commission and Edward Rangel filed suit against Rangel's former employer, Defendant Red Robin Gourmet Burgers, Inc. alleging religious discrimination in violation of Title VII of the Civil Rights Act of 1964. Red Robin terminated Rangel when he refused to cover his tattoos, allegedly obtained for religious reasons, in violation of Red Robin's dress code policy.

. . . Rangel practices Kemetecism, a religion with roots in ancient Egypt, or "Kemet." With an interest in joining the priesthood, Rangel obtained two tattoos, encircling his wrists, which are less than a quarter-inch wide. Written in Coptic, the tattoos translated in English state, "My Father Ra is Lord. I am the son who exists of his father; I am the Father who exists of his son." Rangel received the tattoos during a religious ceremony after undergoing a rite of passage involving communal prayer, meditation, and ritual. The tattoos allegedly represent his servitude to Ra, the Egyptian god of the

---

58 *Arafi v. Mandarin Oriental*, 867 F.Supp.2nd 66 (D.C. 2012)

sun, and his commitment to his faith. Rangel believes that intentionally covering them is a sin, while incidentally covering them, such as when wearing a long-sleeve shirt or gloves, is not a sin. Covering the tattoos is permissible during the month of Mesura, when Rangel believes Ra died and was reborn. Covering his wrists (and thereby his tattoos) during that time represents his grief and servitude to Ra.

Rangel began working in December 2001 for Red Robin as a server. Upon being hired he signed Red Robin's "Uniform/Appearance" policy which provides in part, "body piercings and tattoos must not be visible." Rangel, as well as other servers, worked with their tattoos uncovered for about six months when the assistant manager told him to cover his tattoos. Rangel alleges that he explained the religious significance of his tattoos to the manager, who allowed him to continue working with the tattoos uncovered.

A month later at an orientation a Red Robin general manager and senior regional operations director approached Rangel about his tattoos, telling him to cover them. Rangel gave a lengthy explanation about his faith, his reasons for having the tattoos, and his belief against covering them. The manager suggested Rangel cover the tattoos with wrist bands or bracelets (contrary to Red Robin policy which limits jewelry to two rings and earrings), Rangel refused and was escorted out. . . .

Title VII prohibits employers from discharging an employee based on the individual's religion. Broadly defined, "religion" includes all aspects of religious observances and practice, as well as belief, unless the employer demonstrates it is unable to reasonably accommodate an employee's religious observance or practice without undue hardship on the conduct of the employer's business.

The parties strongly dispute whether Rangel possesses a bona fide religious belief against intentionally covering the tattooed name of Ra (his Creator) on his wrists...Rangel explained that he based his belief on both scripture and Egyptian history. Further, he answered repeated questions about his reasons for covering his tattoos during Mesura and the distinction that exists for him between incidentally and intentionally covering his tattoos...Rangel's testimony, along with his decision to sacrifice his job rather than cover his tattoos, is sufficient to demonstrate a bona fide religious belief.

The burden now shifts to Red Robin to show that it made a good faith effort to reasonably accommodate Rangel, or that accommodating him would result in undue hardship....An accommodation that results in more than a *de minimis* cost to the employer, such as additional costs arising from lost efficiency or higher wages, constitutes an undue hardship. Employers must support a claim of undue hardship with proof of actual imposition on coworkers or disruption of the work routine. Here, Red Robin asserts that allowing Rangel to work with his tattoos visible would have resulted in undue hardship....

The court finds that plaintiffs have brought sufficient evidence to demonstrate that a genuine issue of fact exists regarding whether Rangel's proposed accommodation constituted undue hardship. Rangel worked for six months at Red Robin before being asked to cover his tattoos. There is no evidence in the record that any customers complained about his tattoos, or any other employee's tattoos, during this time. The small size of Rangel's tattoos (less than a quarter-inch) and the little-known language in which they are written (Coptic) suggest that few customers noticed or understood Rangel's tattoos. Moreover, although Red Robin submitted a customer study suggesting that Red Robin seeks to present a family-oriented and kid-friendly image, Red Robin fails to present any evidence that visible tattoos are inconsistent with these goals generally, or that its customers specifically share this perception. Hypothetical hardships based on unproven assumptions typically fail to constitute undue hardship....

The court is unmoved by Red Robin's final, slippery-slope argument that allowing Rangel to work with his tattoos uncovered would force it to allow whatever tattoos, facial piercings or other displays of religious information an employee might claim, no matter how outlandish, simply because an employee claimed a religious exemption. Determining whether an undue hardship exists depends on the facts of each case, and the mere possibility that there would be an unfulfillable number of additional requests for similar accommodations by others cannot constitute undue hardship. Thus, the court finds that Red Robin has failed to bring forward sufficient evidence to demonstrate that it is entitled to summary judgment.

CASE QUESTIONS

1. What specific facts influenced the court's decision?

2. Can you think of a circumstance where a court might decide a case against a server claiming a religious exemption from a tattoo prohibition policy?

In another case an employer had a dress code policy that included a prohibition on facial jewelry. Plaintiff claimed to be a member of the Church of Body Modification. Her interpretation of the group's goals included requiring that her piercings be visible and precluding removal of her facial jewelry, which included eyebrow rings. The employer suggested that she cover them during working hours with a band-aid or replace the rings with a clear plastic retainer. Plaintiff refused and was fired. She sued claiming religious discrimination. The court decided the case in favor of the employer. The judge had suspicions about whether the Church of Body Modification was an actual religion but based its decision on a different reason. The court held that the employer had offered the worker a reasonable accommodation of her religious practice—a Band-aid or a retainer. Said the court, "The employee has a duty to cooperate with the employer's good faith efforts to accommodate. Title VII does not require [the employer] to grant [the employee's] preferred accommodation, but merely a reasonable one."[59]

Before an employer is required to make a reasonable accommodation of an employee's religious practices, the employee must establish that the religious foundation for the requested accommodation is bona fide. A Muslim banquet waiter who had been employed by a hotel for 14 years appeared for work one evening with a one-eighth inch beard (two to five days' growth) in violation of the hotel's rules. When asked by a supervisor about the facial hair, the waiter responded, "It is part of my religion." The hotel, concerned about its reputation, refused to let the waiter

---

[59] *Cloutier v. Costco Wholesale Corp.*, 390 F.3d 126 (Mass. 2004)

work. Three months later, the waiter shaved his beard. He sued the hotel claiming religious discrimination. The court rejected his claim, finding that his assertion that an accommodation of his beard was mandated by his religious beliefs was not made in good faith. The court noted that the waiter had worked without a beard for 14 years, he did not explain why he had not worn a beard previously (for example, he might have claimed he was a recent convert), and the fact that he shaved off the beard three months later undercut his claim of religious necessity.[60]

In another case, a store salesperson took an unauthorized leave to go on a religious pilgrimage in late October. The employer had a policy prohibiting all leaves during the two-month busy season immediately prior to Christmas, including the period of the plaintiff's religious sojourn. She explained the timing of her trip by saying, "I felt from deep in my heart that I was called. I had to be there at that time." Nonetheless she failed to complain about the alleged discrimination until after she learned her plane ticket was nonrefundable. Her companion testified at trial that they decided to go on the pilgrimage because they thought it would be "interesting to go on." Upon the employee's return, she was terminated. She sued claiming religious discrimination. The court ruled for the employer, stating that to claim she is entitled to an accommodation, she needed to establish that the timing was part of a bona fide religious belief. Said the court, "Title VII does not protect secular preferences."[61]

A manicurist and a skin specialist sought a day off without pay to observe Yom Kippur, a Jewish holy day, which fell on a Saturday, the busiest day in the salon business. The employer, noting that the employees already had customers booked for appointments on the day in question, denied the request. Neither employee came to work on Yom Kippur and both were terminated from their jobs. They sued, claiming discrimination based on religion. The employer was unable to show that it tried to accommodate the employees' religious practices or that it would suffer an undue hardship by granting the day off. The employer was thus liable for religious discrimination.[62]

In the hospitality industry, Saturdays and Sundays, the days on which many religious observances fall, are busy and therefore important business days. Accommodating employees who need these days off on a regular basis may cause a hardship to employers. Factors that can support a claim of undue hardship by an employer include lack of availability of substitute employees, lost efficiency to the operation caused by the absence of the observant employee's skills, costs necessarily incurred by employers such as paying a premium to encourage other employees to work on the weekend, and lost patronage.

Hostile Work Environment

A court rejected a claim of hostile work environment by a Muslim based on two "inappropriate and offensive" comments; one was a dinner invitation to get pork chops, where the person extending the invitation knew that Muslims do not eat pork,

---

[60] *Hussein v. Waldorf-Astoria Hotel*, 134 F.Supp.2d 591 (N.Y. 2001)
[61] *Tiano v. Dillard Department Stores*, 139 F.3d 679 (Ariz. 1998)
[62] *EEOC v. Ilona of Hungary, Inc.*, 108 F.3d 1569 (Ill. 1997)

and the other was a reference to sexual prowess. Said the court, "Teasing, offhand comments, and isolated incidents (unless extremely serious) will not amount to discriminatory changes in the terms and conditions of employment" as needed to establish a hostile work environment.[63] Similarly a court held for the employer on a claim of hostile work environment asserted by a "brown-skinned" Muslim from Pakistan where the supervisor over a four-year period yelled at the plaintiff on multiple occasions, twice threatened a criminal investigation, issued a letter of reprimand, issued a letter of counseling, and issued a memorandum of proposed suspension. The court depicted these circumstances as "isolated incidents of a nasty supervisor."[64]

Gender

Title VII outlaws discrimination in employment on the basis of gender. An employer cannot refuse to grant women or men a benefit of employment based on their gender. For example, paying men more than women for the same job responsibilities, based only on gender, constitutes illegal discrimination.

Hiring only one gender for a particular job generally constitutes discrimination. For example, a restaurant cannot hire only males as servers. The EEOC brought a discrimination action against Joe's Stone Crab Restaurant, a well-known Florida eatery, that did exactly that. In the decision the court stated, "While women have predominated among Joe's owner/managers, as well as among the laundering, cashiering and take-away staff [bussers], women have systematically been excluded from the most lucrative entry-level position, that of server." The court thus held the restaurant's hiring practices violated Title VII.[65] Now both men and women fill the ranks of servers at the restaurant.

A related case involved Hooters, a 425-restaurant chain that operates in 46 states and 19 foreign countries, with a theme of scantily clad women. At Hooters such women performed most jobs involving customer interaction, working as wait personnel, bartenders, and receptionists. Males were hired only as managers or kitchen help. The company was charged with gender discrimination in a class action lawsuit brought by males who had applied for wait jobs and had either been refused on the basis of their gender or hired to work in lesser-paid kitchen jobs. The case was settled for $3.75 million and a commitment by Hooters to hire males as bartender assistants, greeters at the door, and in a new "staff position" responsible for clearing tables and bringing condiments to the table. As part of the settlement, the wages for the staff position will be more than what bussers customarily make, and employees filling the staff position will share in tips. In exchange for expanding job opportunities for males, the principal server position remains female-only. Had the case proceeded to court, Hooters would likely have been directed to modify its theme to permit male waiters.

In another case, a hotel that refused to hire women as bartenders "patently offended" Title VII.[66]

---

63 *Williams v. Arrow Chevrolet, Inc.*, 121 Fed. Appx. 148 (Ill. 2005)
64 *Baloch v. Norton*, 355 F.Supp.2d 246 (D.C. 2005)
65 *EEOC v. Joe's Stone Crab, Inc.*, 136 F.Supp 1311 (Fla. 2001); aff'd, 296 F.3d 1265 (Fla. 2002)
66 *Krause v. Sacramento Inn*, 479 F.2d 988 (Calif. 1973)

An airline that required women flight attendants to be single but hired married men for the same position acted illegally.[67]

An employer cannot use the argument that a particular job is dangerous as a basis to hire only men. An objective of Title VII is to permit each woman to make the decision for herself whether she chooses to incur the risks associated with certain jobs. The U.S. Supreme Court held that an employer discriminated illegally when it excluded women of childbearing age, but not men of a similar age, from jobs requiring exposure to lead, which had the potential to damage both male and female reproductive systems.[68]

The protection against gender discrimination is not limited to females, but also protects males. A male guest-service agent at a Pennsylvania Sheraton Hotel had a basis to sue when he was able to show that his reassignment to a phone operator position was motivated by considerations of gender.

Proving that an employer's discriminatory acts are based on gender can sometimes be difficult. A male housekeeping manager terminated at defendant hotel was unable to prove gender was the cause. The plaintiff asserted that female managers earned more than he did, and received greater wage increases. The court dismissed his claim noting that, of eleven housekeeping managers, he was one of the highest paid, only two female housekeeping managers earned more than he did. The court noted that some of the female hotel employees did receive greater wage increases, but plaintiff was not similarly situated because he had disciplinary issues and infractions in his record which the women did not.[69]

Statements made by management that women in general are simply not competent to perform a particular job are classic examples of evidence that helps to establish a gender discrimination case. The following comments, made by an employer who was hiring for the position of collections manager, helped to prove a case of gender discrimination: "Women cannot get tough enough with customers and collect the money," and "This job requires a man to do it."[70]

In another case, a discharged female sales representative attempted unsuccessfully to establish that her termination was due to gender discrimination. One of the circumstances she cited as allegedly proving discrimination was her supervisor's scheduling a lunch meeting at a Hooters restaurant. The court, while referring to the meeting site as "grossly unprofessional," found the meeting locale insufficient to support a discrimination verdict.[71]

Competency Required

To establish a case of discrimination for failing to hire or promote based on gender, plaintiffs must establish that they are qualified for the position they seek. An

---

[67] *Sprogis v. United Air Lines, Inc.*, 444 F.2d 1194 (Ill. 1971)
[68] *International Union, United Automobile Workers v. Johnson Controls, Inc.*, 499 U.S. 187, 111 S.Ct. 1196 L.Ed.2d 158 (1991)
[69] *Rosario v. Hilton Hotels Corp.*, 2012 WL1292881 (N.Y. 2012)
[70] *Davis v. Sheraton Society Hill Hotel*, 907 F.Supp. 896 (Fla. 1995)
[71] *Haynes v. W.C. Caye & Co.*, 52 F.3d 929 (Ga. 1995)

employer can refuse to hire or promote a person who lacks the skills necessary to perform a job adequately. A plaintiff, the assistant general manager of the defendant motel, sought promotion to general manager. When the position was assigned to a man, she sued for gender discrimination. The court decided the case in favor of the hotel, finding that the plaintiff was not qualified for the position. In making that determination, the court referenced testimony that established that the plaintiff was occasionally tardy for work, failed to alert off-site management of excessive absences of the general manager, and "was reluctant to perform tasks over and above her regular job duties."[72]

Glass Ceiling

Glass ceiling refers to artificial barriers that have held women and minorities back from promotion to management and decision-making positions in business. To address the underrepresentation of women and minorities, the Civil Rights Act of 1991 established a Glass Ceiling Commission to study the manner in which businesses fill management positions.

© fizkes/Shutterstock.com

The report, issued in 1995 and, regrettably, still relevant today, concluded that substantial barriers exist for women and minorities at the highest levels of business. The commission found that white males hold the vast majority of all senior-management positions at the level of vice president or higher. Major contributors to this circumstance include persistent bias, negative stereotypes, prejudice concerning women and racial minorities, and inadequate laws. Among the commission's recommendations for removing these barriers are the following:

1. Chief executive officers must demonstrate commitment to diversity.

2. Affirmative action should be used as a tool to ensure equal opportunity to compete for upper-management positions. **Affirmative action** refers to employment programs designed to remedy discriminatory practices in hiring.

3. Senior managers and directors should be sought from nontraditional sources and backgrounds.

4. Businesses should prepare minorities and women for senior positions (e.g., provide training and mentoring).

5. Businesses should provide training to sensitize employees about gender, racial, ethnic, and cultural differences.

---

[72] *EEOC v. Marion Motel Associates,* 763 F.Supp. 1334 (N.C. 1991)

6. Recognizing that women are still primarily responsible for home and family, companies should adopt policies that accommodate the balance between work and family.

Companies should review their policies and practices, and modify them where needed to facilitate the achievement of diversity and the advancement of all segments of the workforce.

Gender-Differentiated Grooming Standards

A number of cases involve male employees who were fired for failing to comply with grooming standards imposed on men but not women. The plaintiffs in these lawsuits claim the personal appearance regulations discriminate on the basis of gender. The law is now clear that minor differences in an employer's appearance rules for men and women that reflect customary modes of grooming for one sex but not the other do not violate Title VII. In a New York case, a male employee was fired because his hair was longer than his shirt collar. Women at the hotel were allowed to wear their hair longer. He sued claming that the different requirements constituted sex discrimination. The court rejected this argument and stated that the law is well established that different grooming requirements for men and women do not constitute sex discrimination.[73]

The objective of Title VII is to equalize employment opportunities. Discrimination based on gender characteristics that are unchangeable is prohibited, but discrimination based on factors of personal preference that an employee can modify does not illegally restrict employment opportunities. Thus, a prohibition against men wearing earrings while women are permitted to do so does not violate the discrimination laws.[74] Said the court, "[A]n employer is permitted to exercise legitimate concern for the business image created by the appearance of its employees." In Case Example 14-6 a female employee objected to a requirement that women workers wear makeup.

CASE EXAMPLE 14-6

Jesperson v. Harrah's Operating Co., Inc.

444 F.3d 1104 (Nev. 2006)

Plaintiff Darlene Jespersen worked successfully as a bartender at Harrah's Reno casino for 20 years and compiled what by all accounts was an exemplary record. During Jespersen's entire tenure with Harrah's, the company maintained a policy encouraging female beverage servers to wear makeup. The parties agree, however, that the policy was not enforced until 2000. In February 2000, Harrah's implemented a "Beverage Department Image Transformation" program at 20 Harrah's locations, including its casino in Reno. Part of the program consisted of new grooming and appearance stan-

---

[73] *Tavora v. New York Mercantile Exchange*, 101 F.3d 907 (N.Y. 1996)
[74] *Capaldo v. Pan American Federal Credit Union*, 43 E.P.D. § 37,016 (N.Y. 1987), aff'd, 837 F.2d 1086 (N.Y. 1987)

dards, called the "Personal Best" program. The program contained certain appearance standards that applied equally to both sexes, including a standard uniform of black pants, white shirt, black vest, and black bow tie. Jespersen has never objected to any of these policies. The program also contained some sex-differentiated appearance requirements as to hair, nails, and makeup.

In April 2000, Harrah's amended that policy to require that women wear makeup. Jespersen's only objection here is to the makeup requirement. The amended policy provided in relevant part:

> All Beverage Service Personnel...must be well-groomed, appealing to the eye, be firm and body toned, and be comfortable with maintaining this look while wearing the specified uniform...

The program, called "Personal Best" included the following:

> Beverage Bartenders and Barbacks will adhere to these additional guidelines:
> Overall Guidelines (applied equally to male/ female):
> Jewelry—tasteful and simple jewelry is permitted; no large chokers, chains or bracelets.
> No faddish hairstyles or unnatural colors are permitted.
> Males: Hair must not extend below top of shirt collar. Ponytails are prohibited.
> No colored fingernail polish is permitted.
> Eye and facial makeup is not permitted.
> Females: Hair must be teased, curled, or styled every day you work. Hair must be worn down at all times, no exceptions.
> Nail polish can be clear, white, pink or red color only. No exotic nail art or length.
> Makeup (face powder, blush and mascara) must be worn and applied neatly in complimentary colors. Lip color must be worn at all times.

Jespersen did not wear makeup on or off the job, and in her deposition stated that wearing it would conflict with her self-image. She felt it interfered with her ability to perform as a bartender. Unwilling to wear the makeup, and not qualifying for any open positions at the casino with a similar compensation scale, Jespersen left her employment with Harrah's. She filed this action alleging that the "Personal Best" policy discriminated against women by subjecting them to terms and condition of employment to which men are not similarly subjected, and requiring that women conform to sex-based stereotypes as a term and condition of employment.

Harrah's argued that the policy created similar standards for both men and women, and that where the standards differentiated on the basis of sex, as with the face and hair standards, any burdens imposed fell equally on both men and female bartenders...

Jespersent testified that when she wore the makeup she felt very degraded and very demeaned. In addition, Jespersen testified that it prohibited her from doing her job because it affected her self-dignity and took away her credibility as an individual and as a person....

This case involves an appearance policy that applied to both male and female bartenders, and was aimed at creating a professional and very similar look for all of them. All bartenders wore the same uniform. The policy only differentiated as to grooming standards.

...We are dealing with requirements that, on their face, are not more onerous for one gender than the other. Rather, Harrah's Personal Best policy contains self-differentiated requirements regarding each employee's hair, hands and face. While individual requirements differ according to gender, none on its face places a greater burden on one gender than the others. Grooming standards that appropriately differentiate between the genders are not facially discriminatory. We have long recognized that companies may differentiate between men and women in appearance and grooming policies....When an employer's grooming and appearance policy does not unreasonably burden one gender more than the other, that policy will not violate Title VII.

Jesperson did not submit any documentation or any evidence of the relative cost and time required to comply with the grooming requirements by men and women. As a result, we would have to speculate about those issues in order to then guess whether the policy creates unequal burdens for women. This would not be appropriate.

Having failed to create a record establishing that the "Personal Best" policies are more burdensome for women that for men, the court below correctly granted summary judgment to Harrah's.

Concerning the sex stereotyping claim, we are beyond the day when an employer could evaluate employees by assuming or insisting that they matched the stereotype associated with their group... We respect Jespersen's resolve to be true to herself and to the image that she wishes to project to the world. We cannot agree, however, that her objection to the makeup requirement, without more, can give rise to a claim of sex stereotyping under Title VII... This is not a case where the dress or appearance requirement is intended to be sexually provocative and tending to stereotype women as sex objects. Jespersen, in contrast, was asked only to wear a unisex uniform that covered her entire body and was designed for men and women...

We emphasize that we do not preclude, as a matter of law, a claim of sex-stereotyping on the basis of dress or appearance codes. This record, however will not support such a claim. There is no evidence of a stereotypical motivation on the part of the employer. This case is essentially a challenge to one small part of what is an overall apparel, appearance, and grooming policy that applies largely the same requirements to both men and women.

CASE QUESTIONS

1. Are you surprised by the court's decision? Why or why not?

2. What more would Jespersen have had to prove for her case to have been successful?

An employer cannot require one sex to wear a uniform and not the other where both are doing the same job. A bank that required female tellers as well as office and managerial employees to wear uniforms while permitting men to work in customary business attire was liable for sex discrimination. The court explained the defendant had several options: permit women to wear "appropriate business attire"; require the male employees to wear uniforms; or make uniforms optional for both men and women. Said the court, "Title VII does not require that uniforms be abolished but that defendant's similarly situated employees be treated in an equal manner."[75]

Sexual Harassment

Sexual harassment is a form of sexual discrimination and constitutes a violation of Title VII. Sexual harassment includes two types of illegal action: (1) unwelcome sexual advances or requests for sexual favors in return for job benefits; and (2) verbal or physical conduct of a sexual nature that creates an intimidating, hostile, or offensive work environment. The former is called **quid pro quo sexual harassment**; the latter, **hostile environment sexual harassment.**

Quid Pro Quo Sexual Harassment

This type of sexual harassment applies where an employee is forced to submit to unwelcome sexual advances as a condition for receiving a job benefit—such as hiring, a promotion, a raise, or continuation as an employee. Examples of quid pro quo sexual harassment include firing a female worker who rejects her supervisor's sexual advances;[76] threatening to terminate an employee if she ceases to have intercourse with the boss;[77] promising to promote an employee who agrees to perform sexually;[78] denying a woman a promotion and/or training opportunities because she rejects her boss's advances;[79] threatening to write disparaging reviews concerning an employee's job performance unless she engaged in sexual intercourse;[80] demoting a female employee for the same reason;[81] and conditioning the grant of a two-week leave of absence for a female employee on her performing oral sex on her supervisor.[82]

Hostile Environment Sexual Harassment

This type of sexual harassment addresses the circumstance where harassing conduct of a sexual nature permeates the workplace. The offending behavior could be taunting, lewd jokes, touching or brushing up against the victim, comments about a person's appearance or their sexual practices, sexually suggestive comments or noises, repeatedly asking an employee out on a date when the invitee has indi-

sexual harassment
Unwelcome sexual advances, requests for sexual favors, and other verbal or physical annoying actions of a sexual nature occurring in the workplace.

quid pro quo sexual harassment
Unwelcome sexual advances or requests for sexual favors in return for job benefits.

hostile environment sexual harassment
Verbal or physical conduct of a sexual nature that creates an intimidating, hostile, or offensive work environment.

---

[75] *Carroll v. Talman Federal Savings & Loan Association*, 604 F.2d 1028 (Ill. 1979)
[76] *Sparks v. Pilot Freight Carriers, Inc.*, 830 F.2d 1554 (Ga. 1987)
[77] *Armenakis v. Top Notch Family Restaurant*, 2006 WL 1660589 (Ind. 2006)
[78] *Wu v. Best Western Lighthouse Hotel*, 2001 WL 492475 (Calif. 2001)
[79] *Henson v. City of Dundee*, 682 F.2d 897 (Fla. 1982)
[80] *Virgo v. Sheraton Ocean Inn*, 2001 WL 1136052 (Tenn. 2001)
[81] *Carrero v. New York City Housing Authority*, 890 F.2d 569 (N.Y. 1989)
[82] *Nichols v. Frank*, 42 F.3d 503 (Ore. 1994)

cated a lack of interest, obscene gestures, giving personal gifts, and like conduct. Common patterns of victims' reactions to sexual harassment include distraction, inability to work, anger, anxiety, depression, sleeping problems, and other physical ailments.

An employer who creates or condones a sexually hostile work environment risks liability for gender discrimination. To qualify as sexual harassment the conduct must be sufficiently severe or pervasive to alter the conditions of the victim's employment and create an abusive working environment. To determine whether a hostile work environment exists, the court looks to the totality of the circumstances including the frequency of the discriminatory conduct, its severity, its offensiveness, and whether it interferes with an employee's work performance.

An example of a hostile work environment is one in which female employees are exposed to persistent lewd remarks and ubiquitous pinups.[83] Said the court, "Pornography on an employer's wall or desk communicates a message about the way he views women, a view strikingly at odds with the way women wish to be viewed in the workplace." Another example of a hostile work environment includes a situation in which an employee was confronted with unwelcome sexual advances on five separate occasions.[84]

In another case, the following clearly constituted a hostile environment: Male employees grabbed at the female plaintiffs, commented extensively on their physical attributes, showed them pornographic photos and videotapes, offered them money for sex, favored other employees who had affairs with them, and speculated aloud as to the plaintiffs' sexual prowess.[85]

The actions enumerated are typical of the types of conduct that underlie sexual harassment hostile environment claims. Also constituting hostile environment sexual harassment is the following circumstance: A waitress' supervisor, on at least a dozen occasions, bumped into her from behind and rubbed against her or ran his hands over her buttocks at the pie cooler or in other behind-the-counter spaces; he inquired about her sex life; and he led other employees to believe he was having an affair with her.[86]

In another case an employer's motion for summary judgment was denied where the following incidents of sexual harassment occurred over 16 months: The owner/supervisor made five to ten comments about plaintiff waitress' breasts, he grabbed her rear end three to five times, and on one occasion he exposed himself and asked for oral sex.[87]

Casual or isolated incidents of discriminatory conduct such as a few sexual comments or slurs will not constitute a hostile environment. However, conduct less severe than that in the referenced cases may cross the threshold and result in liabil-

---

[83] *Robinson v. Jacksonville Shipyards, Inc.*, 760 F.Supp. 1486 (Fl. 1991)
[84] *Phillips v. Taco Bill Corp.*, 83 F.Supp.2d 1029 (Mo. 2000)
[85] *Splunge v. Shoney's, Inc.*, 97 F.3d 488 (Ala. 1996)
[86] *Knabe v. Big Boy East*, 114 F.3d 407 (Tenn. 1997)
[87] *Carballo v. Log Cabin Smokehouse*, 399 F.Supp.2d 715 (La. 2005)

ity. Factors to consider include the frequency of the harassing conduct, its severity, whether it is an offensive utterance or is physically threatening or humiliating, and whether it unreasonably interferes with an employee's work performance. The court will look at the "totality of the circumstances" in making its decision.

Frequency of Offending Conduct

Customarily, to qualify as sexually harassing conduct, the objectionable behavior in hostile environment cases occurs repeatedly over a period of time. Simple teasing, offhand comments and isolated incidents (unless extremely serious) will not normally amount to actionable sexual harassment. "Vulgar and sexually suggestive" comments occurring on almost a daily basis for two months made by a male restaurant manager at a Steak and Ale to the female "second-in-charge" was sufficient.[88] However, one incident can qualify if it is sufficiently hostile and abusive. Thus, sexual harassment occurred where a male supervisor traveling for business with a female subordinate engaged in sexual conversation, appeared at her hotel door barely clothed, entered the room uninvited, sat on her bed, touched her thigh, and attempted to kiss her, all of which were unwelcome.[89]

The plaintiff, a waitress at a Georgia Waffle House, alleged she was harassed by the cook and a supervisor. She claimed the restaurant was aware of the harassment, but kept the cook and supervisor. The allegations included grabbing her buttocks on several occasions and making sexual comments on a regular basis. There was video of the plaintiff kissing and joking around with the cook. The trial court found for the restaurant, holding that the waitress did not prove that the harassment was severe enough. The court noted she did not utilize the employee hotline until 10 months after the alleged harassment began.[90]

Same Gender Sexual Harassment

In most cases alleging sexual harassment, the offending employee is male and the victim is female. That fact notwithstanding, sexual harassment can also be perpetrated by a female against a male. Prior to 1995, a question existed whether sexual harassment could also occur between two males or two females. The U.S. Supreme Court resolved the issue, holding that sexual harassment can occur between two people of the same gender.[91]

The complainant, a male, was working with a drilling crew of eight men on an oil platform in the Gulf of Mexico. On several occasions, he was forcibly subjected to "sex-related, humiliating actions" by a male supervisor in the presence of the all-male crew. Complainant was also physically assaulted and threatened with rape. Protests to other supervisory employees prompted no remedial action. He sued and two courts dismissed his lawsuit holding that same gender sexual harassment was not actionable. The high court reversed those decisions stating, "When the work-

---

[88] *Deel v. Metromedia Restaurant*, 2006 WL 897606 (Fla. 2006)
[89] *Moring v. Arkansas Department of Correction*, 243 F.3d 452 (Ark. 2001)
[90] *Guthrie v. Waffle House, Inc.*, No. 10-15090 (Ga. 2012)
[91] *Oncale v. Sundowner Offshore Services, Inc.*, 523 U.S. 75, 118 S.Ct. 998 (La. 1998)

place is permeated with discriminatory intimidation, ridicule, and insult that is sufficiently severe or pervasive to alter the conditions of the victim's employment and create an abusive working environment, Title VII is violated." The genders of the perpetrator and of the victim are without significance.

Sexual Orientation-based Sexual Harassment

In a case involving MGM Grand Hotel in Las Vegas, an openly gay man who worked as a butler on a floor reserved for the rich and famous was the victim of sexually harassing conduct based on the harassers' animus toward his sexual orientation. The harassing conduct, which came from his supervisor and male co-workers, included whistling and blowing kisses at him, calling him "sweetheart" and "muneca" (Spanish for doll), telling crude jokes and giving sexually oriented gifts, forcing him to look at naked men having sex, caressing, hugging, and poking fingers in his anus through his clothing. The hotel sought summary judgment on the grounds that claims of discrimination based on sexual orientation are not recognized under the Civil Rights Act. The court denied the motion, noting that the conduct was of a sexual nature and was severe and pervasive, thus constituting exactly what Title VII outlaws. Said the court, "Whatever else those attacks may, or may not, have been 'because of' has no legal consequence. So long as the environment itself is hostile to the plaintiff because of his sex, why the harassment was perpetrated (sexual interest? misogyny? personal vendetta? misguided humor? boredom?) is beside the point...Title VII prohibits offensive physical conduct of a sexual nature without regard to the sexual orientation—real or perceived—of the victim."[92]

Sexual Stereotyping and Sexual Harassment

Sexual harassment resulting from failing to conform to a sexual stereotype is another form of illegal sexual harassment. A woman who sought partnership in an accounting firm was denied because she was "macho," in need of "a course in charm school," "a lady using foul language," and had been a "tough-talking somewhat masculine hard-nosed manager." She was advised by her firm that she should "walk more femininely, talk more femininely, dress more femininely, have her hair styled and wear jewelry." The court held she was being penalized for failing to comply with the stereotypes associated with women and that constituted illegal discrimination based on gender.[93]

Somewhat similarly, a waiter employed by Azteca Restaurant Enterprises, Inc., which operates a chain of restaurants in Washington and Oregon, was discriminated against because he was effeminate. The barrage of derogatory comments regularly directed at him by co-workers and his supervisor included taunts for walking and carrying his tray "like a woman," and for having feminine mannerisms; referring to him as "she" and "her," and as a "faggot" and a "fucking female whore." Said the court, "At its essence, the systematic abuse directed at Sanchez reflected a

---

[92] *Rene v. MGM Grand Hotel, Inc.*, 305 F.3d 1061 (Nev. 2002)
[93] *Price Waterhouse v. Hopkins*, 490 US 228, 109 S.Ct. 1775, 104 L.Ed.2d 268 (1989)

belief that Sanchez did not act as a man should act. Discrimination is barred on the basis of sex stereotypes. That rule squarely applies to preclude the harassment here."[94]

© SpeedKingz/Shutterstock.com

Unwelcome Conduct

A critical factor for sexual harassment is that the activity must be unwelcome by the employee and this fact must be known by the harasser. If the conduct is desired, it is not harassment.

Consent alone does not establish that the conduct is welcome. An employee may begrudgingly consent to unwelcome acts because of fear of losing a job or promotion. In a U.S. Supreme Court case, a bank employee agreed to have sexual relations with a bank vice-president because she feared losing her job if she refused. The encounters continued for a period of years. She later sued the bank for sexual harassment. The bank defended in part by claiming the relationship was voluntary. The court, significantly, differentiated between "voluntary" and "unwelcome." It stated, "The correct inquiry is whether respondent by her conduct indicated that the alleged sexual advances were unwelcome, not whether her actual participation in sexual intercourse was voluntary." The appellate court referred the case back to the court with original jurisdiction to determine whether the acts were unwelcome. Note that the court did not rule that the long-term aspect of the relationship merited a presumption or inference that the sexual conduct was welcome. Rather, a sexual relationship between a supervisor and a subordinate employee is suspect for being unwelcome regardless of its duration.[95]

In some circumstances, the unwelcome nature of the conduct can be implied from the nature of the activity, such as coerced (nonvoluntary) sexual intercourse. In other circumstances, the conduct's offensiveness will be less clear and the employee must relay that it is not appreciated. If a supervisor asks an employee out on a date for the first time, the request is normally not sexual harassment even if the employee refuses. If, however, following the refusal, the supervisor continues to invite that employee on dates, the repeated requests may constitute sexual harassment.

An employee need not verbalize the unwelcome nature of sexually suggestive conduct; consistent demonstration through action is sufficient notification. A court held that an employee adequately relayed the unwelcome nature of her boss's advances where, on several different occasions, she failed to respond to his sexual innuendos, changed the subject when he suggested intimacy between them, and pulled her hands away when he reached for them across a restaurant table at lunch.[96]

---

[94] *Nichols v. Azteca Restaurant Enterprises, Inc.*, 256 F.3d 864 (Wash. 2001)
[95] *Meritor Savings Bank v. Vinson*, 477 U.S. 57, 106 S.Ct. 2399, 91 L.Ed.2d 49 (1986)
[96] *Chamberlin v. 101 Realty, Inc.*, 915 F.2d 777 (N.H. 1990)

Employer Liability—Quid Pro Quo Sexual Harassment

Employers such as hotels and restaurants often attempt to avoid liability by claiming that a supervisor's harassing conduct should not be attributable to the employer. The liability of an employer depends in part on the type of sexual harassment involved. For quid pro quo sexual harassment (where a supervisor conditions a job, job benefits, or the absence of a job detriment on an employee's submission to sexual conduct), the harasser's employer is liable. The theory of the employer's liability is respondeat superior—that is, the employer is liable for the wrongful acts of an employee (the supervisor) done in furtherance of the employee's job responsibilities (granting job benefits or detriments).

Employer Liability—Hostile Environment Sexual Harassment

In a case where a supervisor creates a hostile environment, the employer is presumed liable but an affirmative defense exists. The employer can escape liability if it satisfies three elements constituting the defense: (1) no adverse employment action was taken against the employee (e.g., the worker was not fired or demoted); (2) the employer exercised reasonable care to prevent and correct promptly any sexually harassing behavior (e.g., the employer has in place an anti-harassment policy with a complaint procedure, the employer investigates complaints it receives, and the employer takes appropriate corrective action); and (3) the plaintiff unreasonably failed to take advantage of preventive or corrective opportunities provided by the employer to avoid harm (e.g., the employee did not report the harassing conduct to the company representative designated to receive such complaints).[97]

Case Example 14-7 illustrates appropriate response by an employer to a sexual harassment complaint. As a result, the employer escaped liability.

CASE EXAMPLE 14-7

Gregg v. Hay-Adams Hotel

942 F.Supp. 1 (D.C. 1996)

...Plaintiff Debra Denise Gregg is currently employed as an Assistant Pastry Chef at the Hay-Adams Hotel in Washington, D.C. She was hired as such in June of 1993 and has remained in this position since that time. She alleges that within a few months of her hiring, the Executive Chef of the Hotel, Patrick Clark, began to make suggestive remarks toward her, culminating in unwelcome physical contact....

On April 14, 1994, some eight months after the harassment allegedly began, Gregg complained about Clark to Payroll/Personnel Assistant Toya Roberts. Independently, another coworker, Victoria Dade, also complained about Clark to Roberts that very day. There had never been a sexual harassment complaint by any hotel employee prior to this date.

---

[97] *Burlington Industries v. Ellereth*, 524 U.S. 742, 118 S.Ct. 2270 (1998) and *Faragher v. Boca Raton*, 524 U.S. 775, 118 S.Ct. 2275 (1998)

Still on April 14, 1994, Roberts reported the complaints to Human Resources Director Jeffrey Lea, who instructed Roberts to prepare a memorandum regarding the charges—which she delivered to him the next day. In the memo, Roberts reported, among other things, that she told Gregg she would assist her and urged Gregg to take down notes concerning the events.

On Friday morning, April 15, 1994, Lea met with Urs Aeby, the General Manager of the hotel, who then ordered an immediate investigation of the complaints. Aeby then met with each of the two women to inform them that all appropriate steps would be taken to provide them a harassment-free workplace, and he further assured them that they would not be subject to retribution. Statements were taken from Gregg, Dade, and several other employees who might have knowledge of the events. Clark was told generally about the allegations but not about who had made them.

On April 26, 1994, less than two weeks after the complaints, Aeby issued Clark a "formal and final written warning." The letter stated that the investigation revealed behavior "verging on harassment" and that even with respect to unsubstantiated allegations, Clark had "shown a serious lack of judgment." The letter further warned him that any retributive acts could be punishable by termination of employment.

There have been no subsequent sexual harassment accusations since the April 14, 1994 charges....

Gregg attempts to place liability on the employer by arguing that the hotel "violated its expressed company policy regarding sexual harassment to refrain from sexually discriminating against plaintiff by allowing its agents and employees to make sexual advances towards plaintiff and by creating an intimidating hostile and offensive work environment." Gregg neither alleges, nor has evidence to suggest, that the employer actually knew or had reason to know of the harassment [prior to Gregg's complaint], nor that the Hotel approved of it....When a company, once informed of allegations of sexual harassment, takes prompt remedial action to protect the claimant, the company may avoid Title VII liability.

Turning to the issue of whether the hotel actually did respond in an appropriate and timely fashion to Gregg's complaint, the court finds that defendant did so, and to a degree which would remove it from any Title VII liability.

It is undisputed that the Hotel took the following actions:

1. When Gregg reported her complaints to the Payroll/Personnel Assistant, Sonya Roberts, she immediately carried the news to the Human Resources director.

2. Gregg (and another woman who complained) was assured that she would be helped.

3. Within a week of the allegations, four interviews, plus statements by complainants were taken to confirm or disaffirm the charges.

4. The General Manager of the Hotel notified Clark of the allegations, and personally assured Gregg that sexual harassment would not be tolerated.

5. Clark was issued a "formal and final warning," placed in his personnel file, on April 26, 1994, less than two weeks after the complaint was made.

6. The warning to Clark stated that further behavior would result in the immediate termination of his employment.

7. Clark was also threatened with termination should he retaliate against those who complained about him.

8. Clark apologized to Gregg.

9. The Hotel re-issued its sexual harassment policy, ran seminars on sexual harassment (with mandatory attendance for all employees), and Gregg was told to report any further harassment or retaliation directly to the Human Resources Director or the General Manager.

10. A new Human Resources Director, Graciela Lewis, made several visits to the kitchen to ensure the working environment was comfortable there.

11. Gregg admits there was no further harassment after April 14, the date of her first and only complaint to the hotel.

These steps are substantial enough both in action and effect to negate Title VII liability....

CASE QUESTION

1. What is the lesson of this case concerning on how an employer who receives a sexual harrassment complaint should respond?

In a case involving a manager at a Steak and Ale restaurant, the court determined that the restaurant exercised reasonable care to prevent sexual harassment. The restaurant's efforts included the following. The topic was discussed at employee orientation. A booklet entitled, "Sexual Harassment in the Work Place" was distributed to all employees. It described prohibited conduct and included the complaint procedure for reporting sexual harassing conduct. The employee handbook provided a hotline telephone number and the number of Steak and Ale's human resources department for employees to make complaints.[98] In the same case the court also concluded that the employer promptly addressed allegedly harassing behavior. Within three days of filing a complaint with corporate headquarters an investigation was begun. Representatives from headquarters arrived three days later and interviewed 15 employees at the restaurant. On the ninth day following the complaint the harasser was terminated. Said the court, "Under these facts, the court

_____

[98] *Deel v. Metromedia Restaurant Services*, 2006 WL 897606 (Fla. 2006)

is satisfied that Steak and Ale has demonstrated that it exercised reasonable care to correct promptly sexually harassing behavior."

Importance of Remedial Action

An employer who fails to take appropriate and effective remedial action will face liability. In a case involving an Adam's Mark Hotel, the banquet manager reported to the general manager incidents of sexual harassment by a supervisor. The general manager issued a warning to the supervisor, but the harassing conduct continued. The banquet manager then complained to the Director of Personnel who took no action. The banquet manager next complained to the Director of Food and Beverages who told her to "get over it" and "work around" the supervisor. Two other employees also complained about sexually harassing conduct by the same supervisor, but no corrective action resulted. The banquet manager ultimately quit her job and sued the hotel for sexual harassment. She won her case and was awarded $400,000 in compensatory damages, $55,000 in back pay, and $187,000 for attorney's fees and litigation expenses. The hotel's indifference led to this avoidable expensive result.[99] The moral of this case is that an employer should promptly address all sexual harassment complaints by investigating the charges and taking appropriate remedial action.

In another case a cocktail waitress was raped by her supervisor. Thereafter he continued to make sexual advances, find excuses to brush up against her, and touch her unnecessarily. She reported the incidents to management. The restaurant did not have a sexual harassment policy nor a written procedure for investigating complaints of sexual harassment. Not only was no disciplinary action taken against the harasser, but he was allowed to continue supervising the waitress. Not surprisingly the court found this response insufficient. The employer was thus unable to benefit from the defense of having exercised reasonable care to prevent sexual harassment and having taken prompt action to stop it once uncovered.[100]

Also insufficient was a response by management consisting only of a handful of spot checks in the two weeks immediately following a complaint. No investigation of the complaint was made, no discussions with the alleged perpetrators were pursued, no demand was made that the unwelcome conduct cease, and no threats of serious discipline for continuation of the objectionable behavior issued. Although the manager did tell the targeted employee to inform him if the conduct recurred, this wrongly places "virtually all of the remedial burden on the victimized employee."[101]

Sexual Harassment by Co-Workers

An employer may be liable for sexual harassment, not only when supervisors initiate the harassment, but also when co-workers harass an employee. For an employer to be liable for sexual harassment administered by nonsupervisory co-workers,

---

[99] *Ellis v. Adam's Mark Hotel*, 229 F.3d 1151, 2000 WL 1234350 (Tenn. 2000)
[100] *Benjamin v. Anderson*, 112 P.3d 1039 (Mont. 2005)
[101] *Nichols v. Azteca Restaurant Enterprises, Inc.*, 256 F.3d 864 (Wash. 2001)

the employer must be aware of the harassment, as where it is occurring openly and blatantly, or where the harassed employee reports it to a superior.

Sexual Harassment by Customers

An employer who condones or tolerates a sexually hostile work environment created, not by supervisors or co-workers, but by customers, may also be liable to the employee. The reasoning for this rule is that the employer ultimately controls the conditions of the work environment and has a duty to protect employees from abuse. Thus, a Pizza Hut restaurant was liable where the manager denied a waitress' request not to be assigned to customers who had made sexual comments when she served them previously. After she seated them, one grabbed her hair and she again asked her supervisor to be relieved of their table. When he refused and she served them beer, one pulled her to him, grabbed her breast and put his mouth on it. She was awarded compensatory damages and attorney fees. To avoid liability, the manager should have honored her request to be reassigned, insisted that the customers cease their abusive conduct, or require that they leave the restaurant.[102]

In another case involving sexual harassment by patrons, a Las Vegas casino cocktail waitress reported harassing comments by customers to her boss who did nothing in response. The casino defended its inaction by claiming that inappropriate comments, sexual or otherwise, by patrons is inevitable in a job that requires constant contact with the public, particularly in a city that is a "fun" destination where people sometimes drink to excess and often lose more money than they should. The court clearly rejected this defense. Said the court, "[E]mployers are liable for failing to remedy or prevent a hostile or offensive work environment of which management-level employees knew or in the exercise of reasonable care should have known."[103]

An employer that takes prompt and substantial action to protect employees from customer harassment will avoid liability. In one such case, a professional mime performed for Circus Circus Casino in the character of a life-size children's wind-up toy. She was sufficiently convincing in this role that casino patrons occasionally tried to touch her to determine if she was human. When the mime discussed her concerns about this circumstance with her supervisor, he assigned a large man dressed in a clown costume to accompany her when she performed. Further, a sign was prepared for her to wear that read, "Stop: Do not touch." Further, other casino employees were alerted to call security if they saw that she was being harassed and to direct customers not to touch her. Thereafter, a customer touched the mime despite another employee warning the customer three times not to do so. The mime sued the casino, claiming it did not take sufficient precautions to protect her. The court disagreed, finding the casino took reasonable and sufficient steps to protect the mime from customer harassment.[104]

In another case involving harassment by customers, an employer was held liable where it forced an employee to wear a sexually provocative uniform that the em-

---

102 *Lockard v. Pizza Hut, Inc.*, 162 F.3d 1062 (Okla. 1998)
103 *Powell v. Las Vegas Hilton Hotel & Casino*, 841 F.Supp. 1024 (Nev. 1992)
104 *Folkerson v. Circus Circus Hotel & Casino*, 107 F.3d 754 (Nev. 1997)

ployer could reasonably foresee would subject the employee to sexual harassment by customers.[105] Indeed, it did subject her to such conduct. Employers such as bars and casinos, who require waitresses to wear short skirts and low-cut tops, may incur liability when the scant clothing foreseeably provokes harassing behavior by the clientele.

Outside Scope of Employment

If the sexual harassing conduct occurs outside work hours and away from the place of employment, the conduct is considered to be outside the scope of a supervisor's employment responsibilities and the employer will not be responsible. Thus, an employer was not liable where an applicant for a bartending position was raped by the front end manager in his home after the two had shared a few drinks in the bar unrelated to the job application process. Said the court, "The alleged rape occurred after hours and off of the employer's premises."[106]

Policies and Complaint Procedures

To limit occurrences of sexual harassment, employers should develop a company policy clearly establishing that sexual harassment will not be tolerated. The policy should be posted and published to all employees. It should include a complaint procedure that authorizes employees to file complaints with a high-level employee *not* in their line of supervision. Complaints should be treated seriously and investigated thoroughly. When warranted, appropriate and prompt remedial action should be taken, including the following:

- In a quid pro quo case, changing the work site of the harasser, terminating the harasser, and denying him or her a promotion and raise;

- In a hostile environment case, mandating that the objectionable conduct stop (such as requiring that pinups be removed and lewd comments cease), penalizing those who caused the hostile environment through adverse job action, and requiring employee training about sexual harassment.

Pregnancy

Female workers who become pregnant have historically been subject to termination, even though they are able to perform their job responsibilities. Pregnant employees now have legal protection against discrimination on the basis of pregnancy. Part of Title VII, called the Pregnancy Discrimination Act (PDA), makes it unlawful for an employer to treat pregnancy, childbirth, or medical conditions relating to pregnancy and childbirth less favorably than other disabilities, unless justified by business necessity.[107] The basic principle of the PDA is that women

---

[105] *EEOC v. Sage Realty Corp.*, 507 F.Supp. 599 (N.Y. 1981)
[106] *Paugh v. P.J. Snappers*, 2005 WL 407592 (Ohio 2005) [104] 42 U.S.C. § 2000e
[107] 42 U.S.C. § 2000e

who are pregnant or affected by related conditions must be treated the same as other applicants and employees; adverse job action can only be based on the inability to work. A woman is therefore protected against such practices as being fired or forced to take a leave of absence because she is pregnant. Terminating a pregnant employee because of concern for her health or the employer's potential liability constitutes illegal discrimination based on pregnancy. Thus, a restaurant was denied summary judgment in a lawsuit brought by a pregnant waitress where the owner of the eatery expressed concern for the server's health and the restaurant's liability, and also stated that she was a good waitress, was well liked in the restaurant, and he wanted to give her a good recommendation.[108]

Pregnancy discrimination includes reneging on a promised promotion from manager of catering to director of catering and sales because the employee became pregnant.[109] Women who are pregnant and able to perform the tasks associated with their job must be permitted to work on the same conditions as other employees. A restaurant that terminated a pregnant waitress was denied summary judgment where the server's employment was ended within a month after disclosing her pregnancy. The manager had said to her, "You are getting big, getting too big, you're getting too big, we have to get you out of here."[110]

If the pregnancy becomes disabling and the woman is not able to work for medical reasons, she must be accorded the same rights, privileges, and other benefits as other workers who are disabled. An employer cannot terminate a pregnant woman whose doctor requires her not to work if the employer allows workers with other disabilities to take a leave of absence. This is an important right for a pregnant worker since, with a leave of absence, the employee preserves her right to the job, seniority, and benefits. If the employee is terminated and later rehired, she loses the seniority and benefits she accumulated prior to the termination.

---

108 *Carballo v. Log Cabin Smokehouse*, 399 F.Supp.2d 715 (La. 2005)
109 *Newman v. Deer Path Inn*, 1999 WL 1129105 (Ill. 1999)
110 *Buffone v. Rosebud Restaurants, Inc.*, 2006 WL 1843366 (Ill. 2006)

In circumstances where an employer is imposing adverse job action on all employees, the employer can include the pregnant woman among those affected. For example, if the pregnancy coincides with a slowdown in the employer's business during which the employer is cutting hours of all employees—as, for example, a summer resort in the fall—the employer can legally cut the pregnant employee's hours as well.

Business Necessity

If an employer can show that a business necessity renders pregnant employees unfit, the employer can require pregnant workers to take a leave of absence pending wellness following birth.

In a case involving business necessity, an airline's policy of removing flight attendants from the work roster as soon as their pregnancy became known was challenged by a pregnant stewardess. The court upheld the airline's policy, noting that fatigue and nausea often accompany pregnancy and could render a flight attendant unable to perform job responsibilities in an emergency, risking the safety of passengers. Although different women have different physical reactions to pregnancy, the airline would not be able to predict which pregnant stewardesses would suffer from ailments and which would not. Therefore, the policy of not allowing pregnant stewardesses to work satisfied the business necessity exception and did not constitute illegal discrimination.[111]

Reinstatement After Giving Birth

Reinstatement policies for employees returning to work after giving birth must be the same as for employees returning to work after absences due to other temporary disabilities. The EEOC has declared that an employer cannot prohibit an employee from returning to work during a specified length of time after childbirth. Instead, individualized determinations of the time needed for recovery should be made in the same manner adopted for other disabilities.

If an employee is terminated long after a pregnancy leave, she will have difficulty proving that the pregnancy was the cause of her termination. During a female employee's pregnancy she endured comments such as, "Shouldn't you get out of here, you look like you're ready to pop" and "I don't want you to wobble around anymore." For more than eight months after returning from her leave she experienced no similar comments. She was thereafter terminated and claimed a violation of the PDA. The court dismissed her case noting there was "very little evidence of improper behavior by [the employer] relating to her pregnancy after she returned from maternity leave. Essentially, a plaintiff who was not pregnant at or near the time she was terminated must demonstrate that the effects of her pregnancy continued to exist at the time she was terminated, either in actual fact or in the thoughts and actions of those responsible for firing her."[112]

In Case Example 14-8, the defendant proved that a pregnant worker's marked decline in the performance of her job duties was the reason for her demotion and not the fact that she was pregnant.

---

[111] *Levin v. Delta Air Lines, Inc.*, 730 F.2d 994 (Tex. 1984)
[112] *Solomon v. Redwood Advisory Co.*, 183 F.Supp.2d 748 (Pa. 2002)

CASE EXAMPLE 14-8

Crist v. Dorr to Door Pizza

2015 WL 4574949 (Colo. 2015)

Ms. Narelle Crist ("Plaintiff") brings this action against her former employer, Dorr to Door Pizza, under Title VII of the Civil Rights Act of 1964, alleging that she was discriminatorily demoted and fired because she was pregnant. Before this Court is Defendant's Motion for Summary Judgment. For the reasons stated below, Defendant's motion is granted. . . .

Plaintiff worked at Double D's Sour Dough Pizza ("Double D's"), a chain of pizza restaurants owned by Defendant, which in turn is owned and operated by Ted and Cyndi Dorr. Plaintiff began her employment at Double D's as a delivery driver and shift runner. She was promoted to assistant manager, and was promoted again to general manager of Defendant's Louisville, Colorado restaurant. As manager, Plaintiff's duties included all operations of the restaurant, including supervising staff, making food and taking orders. She generally worked around sixty-eight to seventy-two hours per week. Ted Dorr described Plaintiff's performance up until July, 2011 in very positive terms, that Plaintiff "was very good at doing things, someone who could do it all, or a lot of it by herself" and "was an awesome one-man team" However, Plaintiff found the job to be stressful due to the long hours and from issues she would encounter dealing with customers.

On July 26, 2011, Plaintiff informed Ted and Cyndi Dorr that she was pregnant with her second child. . . . Shortly after she became pregnant, Plaintiff began experiencing difficulties with her pregnancy in the form of morning sickness and migraines. Plaintiff believed these ailments were being exacerbated by the stress she was experiencing in her job.

On August 6, 2011, Plaintiff left the restaurant for about two hours during her shift, placing a "shift runner" in charge of the restaurant who was not trained or approved to act as a manager. Shortly before she left the restaurant, Plaintiff sent a text message to Ted Dorr stating that she was having a very bad day and needed to take a couple hours away from the store. Mr. Dorr set a meeting with Plaintiff for later that day when she returned to the restaurant. However, Plaintiff again left the restaurant before the meeting occurred and left a note explaining that she was forced to leave due to "overwhelming stress."

Plaintiff had a meeting with Ted and Cyndi Dorr the following day to discuss her performance. At that meeting, Plaintiff expressed that she was "stressed out" and "unhappy" at Double D's due to the long hours she was working. At the meeting, the Dorrs gave Plaintiff an option to change her position to make it less stressful, which Plaintiff declined.

Plaintiff had another meeting with Ted Dorr on August 12, 2011. During the meeting Plaintiff described that she was having very bad morning sickness and also having trouble sleeping. She also stated that the long days working as a manager were hurting her. Mr. Dorr explained to Plaintiff that she was an important part of Double D's team and they discussed reducing Plaintiff's hours and other ways to make her job less stressful. Following this meeting, the Dorrs became more concerned with Plaintiff's health and her ability to perform her job as manager. Plaintiff complained to Cyndi Dorr on numerous occasions regarding the health problems she was experiencing as a result of her pregnancy and work-related stress. Plaintiff reported experiencing debilitating headaches and the nausea she was experiencing required her to temporarily leave her shift on numerous occasions so that she could vomit.

On August 18, 2011, Plaintiff again sought to leave the restaurant during her shift, texting Cyndi Dorr that she needed a break because her head was hurting. Later that day Cyndi Dorr met with Plaintiff and discussed reassigning Plaintiff to work as a shift runner instead of working as a manager. Although it is disputed as to whether this change in position was offered to Plaintiff as a choice or whether it was involuntary, it is not disputed that Plaintiff expressed that she would not be happy with that change. Defendant contends that, even as a shift runner, Plaintiff would have received the same hourly wage that she received while working as a manager, but that this position would entail fewer hours and fewer responsibilities than what Plaintiff had as a manager. Following that discussion, Cyndi Dorr made the schedule for the following week and did not include Plaintiff on the schedule, either as shift runner or as manager.

The next day Plaintiff went to the restaurant, dropped off her uniform and picked up her last pay check, although it is disputed as to why Plaintiff took this action. Plaintiff claims that she was sent a text message telling her to bring in whatever Double D's property she had in her possession, which Plaintiff interpreted to mean that her position had been terminated. Defendant claims that Plaintiff was never told that her position was terminated. . . .

Plaintiff's claim falls under the Pregnancy Discrimination Act (PDA) which makes it unlawful to discriminate against any individual with respect to terms, conditions, or privileges of employment based on the employee's sex. The PDA states that the terms "based on the Employee's sex" include, but are not limited to, on the basis of pregnancy, childbirth, or related medical conditions . . .

Congress intended the PDA to provide relief for working women and to end discrimination against pregnant workers. . . .

A pregnancy discrimination claim is analyzed in a three-step process. The plaintiff has the initial burden of establishing a prima facie case of discrimination showing that 1) she is a member of a protected class (in this case, that she is pregnant); 2) she satisfactorily performed the duties required of the position; 3) she suffered an adverse employment action. . .

The burden of production then shifts to the defendant, who is then tasked with the burden of articulating a legitimate, nondiscriminatory reason for its action. Should the defendant articulate such a reason, the burden of persuasion moves back to the plaintiff who is then required to show that defendant's explanation for its action was merely pretext. . . .

Defendant claims plaintiff was merely offered the position of shift runner on a temporary basis, and at the same rate of pay, in order to accommodate the problems she was experiencing. Further, Plaintiff was not included on the schedule because she had not yet informed Cyndi Dorr whether she wanted to work as shift runner or as manager.

Even if Plaintiff's pay would have remained the same in her new position as shift runner, Plaintiff's reduced hours and responsibilities would be sufficient to constitute an adverse employment action.

The court finds that Plaintiff sustained her burden of establishing prima facie case of discrimination.

Therefore the Court must analyze whether Defendant is able to show that it had a legitimate non-discriminatory reason for its employment action and whether Plaintiff is able to show that Defendant's proffered reason is mere pretext. Here, Plaintiff is unable to show that Defendant's actions were not based on the significant issues she was having in the performance of her job. . . .

Defendant would be able to sustain its burden of offering a legitimate, nondiscriminatory reason for any employment action that was taken against Plaintiff: that Plaintiff had shown a marked decline in the performance of her duties as manager of the restaurant due to stress and had even left the restaurant without adequate supervision on one occasion. Plaintiff in turn is required to show that the reason offered by Defendant is mere pretext.

Plaintiff argues that there was a significant shift in Ted and Cyndi Dorr's treatment towards her immediately following the announcement of her pregnancy and that this temporal connection shows that the catalyst for Plaintiff's demotion and eventual termination was her pregnancy. . . .

However, Plaintiff's argument ignores the fact that immediately following the announcement of her pregnancy, Plaintiff had shown a marked decline in the performance of her job duties. . . it appears from the evidence that the primary causal factor behind Defendant's employment action was the clear job performance deficiencies that occurred in the same time frame as Plaintiff's pregnancy. . . It is far from pretext to say that a manager's abandonment of her post to an underling is legitimate grounds to terminate her employment.

Plaintiff is therefore unable to meet her burden of showing that the reason offered by Defendant to explain its employment action was mere pretext.

Based on the foregoing, Defendant's motion for summary judgment is granted. [Case dismissed.]

Abortion Issues

An issue of abortion rights was raised in a case involving a busser at a Holiday Inn who became pregnant and informed her manager and fellow staff members. She also discussed with them that she had not ruled out the possibility of an abortion. According to the Food and Beverage Director, "We have a very Christian staff in that restaurant, who were very offended by [the busser's discussion of a possible abortion]." The busser was disciplined for creating an "uproar" among the staff and advised if she spoke of an abortion again at work she would be terminated. She ultimately was fired based on her "pondered abortion." The court held that discharging an employee on the basis of a statement that she is considering an abortion, has had one, or intends to have one, constitutes illegal pregnancy discrimination. The court also determined that the busser had adequately presented a claim of religious discrimination since her belief that abortion was morally permissible, as opposed to the beliefs of Christian employees who objected to abortion, was identified as the cause of staff uproar and contributed to her termination.[113]

---

[113] *Turic v. Holiday Inn*, 85 F.3d 1211 (Mich. 1996)

Age

As medical developments have expanded life expectancy, the American work force has aged and issues of age discrimination arise with greater frequency and take on heightened importance. An employer may prefer a 25-year-old for a wait job over a 60-year-old. Can the employer fire or refuse to hire the older person? The answer is no; if an employer opts not to hire or fires the older worker because of age, the employer will be liable for age discrimination. A federal law called the Age Discrimination in Employment Act (ADEA)[114] bars an employer from discriminating against an employee on the basis of being 40 years of age or older. The ADEA makes it unlawful for an employer to refuse to hire, discharge, or otherwise discriminate with respect to compensation or conditions of employment because of a person's age. The purpose of the ADEA is "to promote employment of older persons based on their ability rather than age; to prohibit arbitrary age discrimination in employment; and to help employers and workers find ways of meeting problems arising from the impact of age on employment."

International House of Pancakes was denied summary judgment in an age discrimination claim by a 67-year-old applicant for a waitress job. Supervisors had commented "She's too old." "That old lady? We don't want her here. You've got to be kidding me" and "She wouldn't fit into the harmony of the younger wait staff." The hiring manager attempted to evade her, canceling an appointment, leaving the restaurant to go to the bank while she was on hold for him, and misrepresenting that he had offered her a job and then terminated her when she failed to appear for the first shift of which she had not been informed.[115]

The ADEA attempts to balance the needs of seasoned workers with those of the business community. As with all the discrimination laws, the ADEA does not mandate that an employer hire a person over 40. Rather, it requires the employer to make employment decisions based on legitimate reasons other than age, such as qualifications. Employers are allowed to terminate or not promote employees over age 40 when there is a legitimate nondiscriminatory reason based on the employee's performance.[116] A restaurant successfully thwarted a claim of age discrimination where it showed the reason for terminating a 62-year-old manager was not age but unsatisfactory performance. Written reviews of the employee documented recurring problems of understaffing, excessive use of overtime, high turnover of restaurant staff, lack of training staff, improper accounting procedures and issues with food quality.[117] Similarly, a 65-year-old employee was unsuccessful in his claim of age discrimination despite demeaning comments about age by his boss where the employee was terminated for damaging a hotel room while on company business in violation of the policies in the employee manual.[118] Case Example 14-9 underscores the right of an employer to terminate even an older employee whose behavior or performance is below expectations.

---

[114] 20 USC §§621–634

[115] *EEOC v. IHOP*, 411 F.Supp.2d 709 (Mich. 2006)

[116] *Vaughan v. Amtrak*, 892 F. Supp. 2d 84 (D.D.C. 2012)

[117] *Davis v. Valley Hospitality Services, LLC*, 372 F.Supp.2d 641 (Ga. 2005)

[118] *Rohn v. Wyndham Vacation Resorts, Inc.*, 2013 WL 588250 (Fla. 2013)

CASE EXAMPLE 14-9

Rivera-Aponte v. Restaurant Metropol #3, Inc.

338 F.3d 9 (P.R. 2003).

...Before opening [on the day in issue] Paul Rivera Aponte (Rivera) and Alberto Nogueras, a busboy at the restaurant, had an altercation, during which Rivera threw or accidentally dropped a tray full of drinking glasses on Nogueras. Nogueras was cut by the glasses and received twelve stitches at the hospital. The manager of the restaurant interviewed employees regarding the incident; after determining that Rivera was the aggressor, the manager fired Rivera later that day.

At the time of his discharge, Rivera was 55 years old and had been a waiter at Metropol for 8 or 9 years.

Rivera filed suit alleging age discrimination under the Age Discrimination in Employment Act (ADEA). That law makes it unlawful for an employer to discharge any individual because of such individual's age. In an ADEA wrongful discharge case, the plaintiff must prove that he would not have been fired but for his age...

Metropol offers a legitimate, non-discriminatory reason for discharging Rivera: Rivera assaulted and injured another employee while at work. Rivera had received a copy of Metropol's employment manual, which warns that an employee's attack, aggression, assault, or threat of aggression against a supervisor or fellow employee justifies Metropol's immediate termination of that employee. Rivera's behavior violated Metropol's rules of conduct, and the restaurant took swift disciplinary action....

First Rivera asserts that the pre-termination investigation was cursory—evidenced by the fact that Rivera was never allowed to explain his side of the story—and therefore Metropol's reason for terminating him was pretextual. Metropol responds that it determined, based on one interview and Nogueras' actual and undisputed injuries, that Rivera was the aggressor, and it sought to take swift action to deter further workplace violence. Whether a termination decision was wise or done in haste is irrelevant, so long as the decision was not made with discriminatory animus...the restaurant's reason was compelling, and our thorough review of the record reveals that Rivera lacks any evidence that the real reason for his termination was age discrimination.

Second, Rivera contends Metropol discriminated against older workers, sometimes referring to employees as "imbeciles" or "corpses." Such stray workplace remarks are generally insufficient, standing on their own, to establish discriminatory animus. Given Metropol's compelling stated reason for Rivera's termination, these stray remarks do not permit the inference that the real reason for Rivera's termination was age discrimination....

Finally, Rivera alleges that other employees were involved in altercations at work but not fired. Metropol counters that some of those incidents were unknown to supervisors, and none resulted in personal injuries requiring medical treatment. Therefore these examples fail to show disparate treatment....

CASE QUESTIONS

1. What role did the employee handbook play in the court's decision?

2. What was the significance of remarks made about older workers?

3. What was the implication of other employees involved in altercations at work not being fired?

In a highly publicized class-action lawsuit, nearly 1,000 golf club employees sued for a variety of employment issues, including age discrimination. According to court documents, Donald Trump pressured his managers for many years to fire female employees he considered unattractive and replace them with younger, more attractive women. Comments made by Trump included, "I want you to get some good looking hostesses here" and "People like to see good looking people when they come in." Older female workers were routinely rotated off their shift when Trump was scheduled to visit the property because he preferred to see younger and prettier women working at this clubs. The case was settled for $475,000 in 2013.[119]

Comments made by supervisors are often entered into evidence in age discrimination cases. For example, comments such as "Show the old-timers how it's done" and "We need to get rid of all these old clunkers" were put in an email from the supervisor to younger workers. In a lawsuit alleging the older employee was demoted and harassed because of his age, the court determined the employee could proceed under an ADEA claim and a jury could decide whether the supervisor's decision to demote the employee was discriminatory. However, the court further stated the age-related comments were insufficient to establish a hostile work environment because they were "relatively infrequent."[120]

An employer can refuse to hire older workers if it can show that youth is a legitimate business necessity. An example would be hiring young males to model fashions that are popular with teens only.

In Case Example 14-10, two hotel employees claimed that they were fired because they were each over 40 years old. An employment ad placed by the restaurant and comments made by the owner established illegal age discrimination.

---

[119] *USA Today,* Sept. 30, 2013
[120] *Parris v. Wyndham Vacations Resorts, Inc.,* 979 F.Supp.2d 1069 (Hawaii 2013)

CASE EXAMPLE 14-10

EEOC v. Marion Motel Associates

763 F.Supp. 1338 (N.C. 1991), aff'd 961 F.2d 211 (1992)

...The Plaintiff, on behalf of claimants Aileen Peterson and Effie C. Petersen, alleged that the Defendant...terminated their employment on the basis of their ages....

The evidence established that both claimants were over 40 years of age during their employment by the Defendant. Gary F. Hewitt, owner and manager of the Defendant Park Inn, testified that he was satisfied with the work of claimant Effie C. Petersen. While there was some testimony as to claimant Aileen Peterson's tardiness in reporting to work, it appears that she also generally met the legitimate expectations of Defendant. Moreover, the evidence was that Hewitt expressed his desire to replace claimants Aileen Peterson and Effie C. Petersen with younger employees. According to the testimony, although Hewitt was an experienced businessman, he caused an unlawful advertisement to be published in The McDowell News which announced vacancies in all supervisory and desk clerk positions and urged "young, energetic persons" to apply for employment at the Park Inn. Hewitt testified that when claimant Effie Petersen offered to learn additional tasks for the second shift, he replied, "You can't teach an old dog new tricks." The evidence further established that the job application used by the Defendant contained a notice regarding prohibitions under the Age Discrimination in Employment Act (hereinafter "the Act")....

The Court sent the issues covering the age discrimination claim of Aileen Peterson and Effie Petersen to the jury. The jury responded in the affirmative to the question, "[D]id the Defendant...terminate the employment of claimant Aileen Peterson and claimant Effie C. Petersen because of their age?"

The evidence was that Hewitt was an experienced businessman with knowledge of the Act. Hewitt used job application forms at the Park Inn that contained a notice regarding the Act's prohibitions. As stated above, Hewitt placed an advertisement in The McDowell News that was in violation of federal law. Moreover, the Court heard the testimony about Hewitt's age-biased comment to Effie Petersen and the circumstances regarding her departure. The Court finds that the totality of the evidence establishes a course of conduct [proving violation of the Act]....

[Judgment for plaintiff affirmed.]

Retaliatory Discharge

It is illegal for an employer to retaliate against an employee who files a complaint with the EEOC or otherwise objects to or protests an employer's violation of civil rights laws. Retaliation often takes the form of terminating the employee. Such an unlawful discharge is called a **retaliatory discharge.** For example, a plaintiff had been employed by the defendant as a poker dealer for a period of time and then quit. Thereafter, he testified against the defendant in a discrimination lawsuit brought by another employee. Subsequently, the plaintiff reapplied for a poker dealer's position at the defendant's casino. The defendant normally followed a policy of rehiring dealers who had previously worked at its casino before hiring new dealers. The plaintiff was told by the poker room manager that "I don't even know if they're gonna want to hire you back because of the involvement with the [discrimination case]." The defendant thereafter twice hired new dealers rather than the defendant. The court held these facts support a finding of retaliation.[121]

In another case a waitress was terminated five days after she complained to a manager about sexual harassment by a supervisor. The restaurant claimed that she was fired because of emotional outbursts and poor attitude. Yet the manager admitted that the waitress was "a great employee, well-liked at the restaurant," and the manager wanted to give her a good recommendation. The court refused to grant summary judgment to the employer on the waitress' claim of illegal retaliation.[122]

Another form of prohibited retaliation is writing a negative job reference for someone who files a discrimination complaint. A budget analyst for the Navy filed a complaint against her immediate supervisor alleging race and gender discrimination. She thereafter sought a position with the Army and asked the supervisor for a reference. He provided one but it was not flattering. The court concluded that the negative reference was motivated by "retaliatory animus" and thus violated Title VII.[123]

Only employees can sue for unlawful retaliation. Where the manager of a Friendly's restaurant ordered an ill employee back to work under threat of discharge, the employee's roommate complained. The roommate alleged that the manager responded by assaulting her. In the resulting lawsuit for unlawful retaliation, the complaint was dismissed because the plaintiff's roommate was not an employee.[124]

Mixed Types of Discrimination

Sometimes an employer will discriminate against a worker on more than one illegal ground. As you read Case Example 14-11, see how many illegal bases for discrimination you can find. While the case is quite long, it provides an excellent review of many of the discrimination topics we have discussed.

retaliatory discharge
Termination of an employee in response to the worker filing a complaint against the employer.

---

121 *Brady v. Sam's Town Hotel and Gambling Center*, 110 F.3d 67 (Nev. 1997)
122 *Carballo v. Log Cabin Smokehouse*, 399 F.Supp.2d 715 (La. 2005)
123 *Hashimoto v. Secretary of the Navy*, 118 F.3d 671 (Hawaii 1997)
124 *Boden v. Friendly's Ice Cream Corp.*, 2006 WL 1490099 (Pa. 2006)

CASE EXAMPLE 14-11

EEOC v. Hacienda Hotel

881 F.2d 1504 (Ca. 1989)

On May 30, 1986, the Equal Employment Opportunity Commission ("EEOC" or "the Commission") initiated this employment discrimination action against appellant defendant Hacienda Hotel ("Hacienda" or "the Hotel"), in El Segundo, California. The Commission alleged that the Hacienda, its General Manager (Frank Godoy), its Executive Housekeeper (Alicia Castro), and its Chief of Engineering (William Nusbaum), had engaged in unlawful employment practices against female employees in the Hacienda housekeeping department by sexually harassing them, terminating them when they became pregnant, failing to accommodate their religious beliefs, and retaliating against them for opposing Hacienda's discriminatory practices. Relief was sought and obtained on behalf of five current and former Hacienda maids, all but one of whom were undocumented aliens, who were alleged to have been victims of appellant's discriminatory employment practices during 1982 and 1983. We affirm.

[Facts of the case involving Teodora Castro:]

The Hotel hired Teodora Castro in June 1980. Teodora became pregnant in late 1981 and continued to work for defendant. During the course of her pregnancy, both Alicia Castro and Nusbaum made numerous crude and disparaging remarks regarding her pregnancy. Nusbaum, for example, told Teodora that "that's what you get for sleeping without your underwear;" he also asked why she was pregnant by another man and made comments about her "ass." Nusbaum often subjected her to sexually offensive remarks in the presence of Alicia Castro, who merely laughed. Alicia Castro herself told Teodora that she did not like "stupid women who have kids," and on many occasions called her a "dog" or a "whore" or a "slut."

In late 1981 and early 1982, Teodora Castro complained to Frank Godoy and Jose Ortiz, the union representative, about Nusbaum's and Alicia Castro's comments, but the situation did not improve. On June 30, 1982, Teodora Castro was terminated, as Alicia Castro admitted in her deposition and at trial, because of her pregnancy. She was rehired in November 1982, following the birth of her child.

Teodora Castro is also a Seventh-Day Adventist who observes the Sabbath on Saturdays. Prior to her termination, she had been given Saturdays off. After she was rehired in November 1982, however, Alicia Castro informed her that she would have to work Saturdays. Teodora reminded the Executive Housekeeper that she needed Saturdays off in order to observe her Sabbath, but Alicia Castro denied her request. On December 17, 1982, Alicia Castro terminated Teodora for refusing to work on her Sabbath. During this time period, another maid in the Housekeeping Department, who was less senior than Teodora, was permitted to have both Saturdays and Sundays off after she had been attacked on the way home from work while waiting for public transportation, which was inadequate on weekends.

Following her termination, Teodora immediately sought employment [without immediate success]. After another pregnancy, she finally secured new employment at another hotel in May 1984. Between May 1984 and the date of the trial, Teodora Castro earned less than she would have earned had she remained employed by the Hacienda.

[Facts of the case involving Maria Elana Gonzales:]

Maria Elana Gonzalez was a maid in the Hacienda Housekeeping Department from October 27, 1980, to September 21, 1982. Gonzalez is a Jehovah's Witness and observes her Sabbath on Sundays. In early September 1982, Gonzalez requested that she be given Sundays off in order to observe the Sabbath. Alicia Castro initially granted Gonzalez's request; two days later she changed her mind and told Gonzalez that she had to work Sundays or quit.

Gonzalez filed a union grievance complaining of Castro's refusal to accommodate her religious beliefs. Gonzalez also informed the General Manager of the Hacienda Hotel, Frank Godoy, of Alicia Castro's refusal to adjust her schedule. Godoy told Gonzalez that he would speak with Castro regarding her request. Alicia Castro subsequently told Gonzalez that because she had complained to Godoy, she would never have Sundays off and that she should be grateful that she had a job. Castro also told Gonzalez that she [Castro] was going to "make life so difficult for her that she [Gonzalez] would not know her head from her feet."

During the month of September 1982, Castro issued four disciplinary warnings to Gonzalez and terminated her on September 21, 1982. Following her termination, Gonzalez sought other comparable employment.

[Facts of the case involving Flora Villalobos:]

The Hotel hired Flora Villalobos in April of 1980. After she became pregnant in early 1982, she was regularly subjected to sexually offensive remarks from Alicia Castro and Nusbaum. Castro often called her a "dog" or a "whore," and Nusbaum told her that women "get pregnant because they like to suck men's dicks." On many occasions, Nusbaum threatened to have her fired if she did not submit to his sexual advances. Castro witnessed some of Nusbaum's behavior and laughed at his sexual remarks. On October 31, 1982, when Villalobos was approximately seven months pregnant and still able and willing to work, Castro terminated her employment because of her pregnancy. Villalobos had obtained a statement from her doctor indicating that she was able to continue working until two or three weeks before her estimated delivery date of December 28, 1982.

On February 9, 1983, Villalobos provided Castro a written statement from her doctor indicating that she was able to return to work immediately. Villalobos was not rehired until April 8, 1983. The Hotel hired two maids, one rehire and one new employee, while Villalobos was awaiting rehire.

[Facts of the case involving Leticia Cardona:]

Leticia Cardona was employed by the Hotel from May 15, 1981, to September 28, 1982. After she became pregnant in early 1982, she was subjected to sexually offensive comments by Alicia Castro and Nusbaum. In September 1982, when Cardona was six months pregnant, Castro told her that she was too fat to clean rooms and fired her on September 28, 1982. Although at trial Castro testified that Cardona was terminated for poor work performance, Castro had previously admitted in a deposition that she terminated Cardona pursuant to her practice of terminating pregnant employees. Cardona's notice of termination form, which was completed by Castro, states that she was terminated because of her pregnancy.

In December 1982, after the birth of her baby, Cardona returned to the Hotel and requested her job back, but Castro refused. Castro testified that Cardona was not rehired because she was a poor worker.

[Facts of the case involving Mercedes Flores:]

Throughout her term of employment from October 8, 1978, to March 10, 1983, William Nusbaum made sexual advances and offensive sexual comments to Mercedes Flores. Nusbaum regularly offered, for example, to give her money from his paycheck and an apartment to live in if she would "give him [her] body." He also assured her that she would never be fired if she would have sex with him. Flores claimed to have heard Nusbaum make offensive sexual comments to other maids, including complainants Cardona, Castro, and Villalobos. On one occasion, for example, she heard him say to Villalobos: "You have such a fine ass. It's a nice ass to stick a nice dick into. How many dicks have you eaten?"...

[Pregnancy Discrimination]

Alicia Castro admitted that it was her practice to terminate pregnant employees rather than permit them to take temporary leaves of absence, although she did not terminate other employees who were similarly temporarily disabled because of illness or injury. Alicia Castro specifically admitted that she terminated claimants Castro, Villalobos, and Cardona because of pregnancy.

Appellant argues that it should not be held liable for pregnancy discrimination because no one suffered any "damage" as a result of an application of the discriminatory policy. In particular, appellant contends that Teodora Castro and Villalobos were rehired following their pregnancies without loss of seniority or other benefits, while Cardona would not have been reinstated in any event because of her poor work performance....

Even if no employee suffered a "tangible loss" of an "economic nature," i.e., a loss of seniority or wages or other monetarily quantifiable employment benefit, appellant's implementation of a policy or practice under which pregnant employees were treated differently from other temporarily-disabled employees with similar capacity for work would still be a violation of both the letter and spirit of Title VII's prohibition against pregnancy discrimination. Appellant overlooks, moreover, the district court's ultimate determination that at least one of the pregnancy discrimination claimants, Flora Villalobos, actually did lose wages because of appellant's discriminatory policy....

[Religious Discrimination]

The district court found that Teodora Castro and Marie Elena Gonzalez informed Alicia Castro of their religious beliefs and requested that their schedules be adjusted such that they would have a day off on their Sabbath, that their supervisor, Alicia Castro, denied their requests, threatening them with discharge if they did not work on their Sabbath, and that Teodora Castro was actually dismissed for refusing to work on her Sabbath. These findings are clearly sufficient to establish appellees' prima facie case of religious discrimination....

[The] Hacienda made no effort whatsoever to accommodate the religious beliefs of both these women. Alicia Castro admitted that she never asked any maid if they would volunteer to work, nor did she make any effort to rearrange the schedule of the maids according to the religious needs of the employees within the housekeeping department. The record also reflects that there was at least one voluntary substitute, Teodora's sister, who was willing to work for her....

[T]he Hacienda failed reasonably to accommodate the religious practices of Teodora Castro and Maria Elena Gonzalez, and it terminated Teodora Castro because of her religion, in violation of Title VII....

[Retaliatory Discharge]

The district court found that Maria Elena Gonzalez established a prima facie case of retaliation. When Alicia Castro found out that Gonzalez had spoken with Frank Godoy, she told Gonzalez that now she would never have Sundays off and threatened to make her life very difficult. Within less than a month of her complaint to Godoy, Castro issued three written warnings to Gonzalez and fired her.

Appellant contends, however, that Gonzalez was fired for poor work performance and not for any retaliatory reasons. ... [D]uring trial, Alicia Castro testified that she fired Gonzalez for poor work performance. The court below, however, explicitly found that Alicia Castro was not a credible witness....

[Sexual Harassment Claim]

Hacienda argues that the sexually harassing conduct in which Castro and Nusbaum were proven to have engaged was not sufficiently severe or pervasive to be actionable. Appellant also contends that it could not be held liable for the acts of Nusbaum and Castro of which it had no notice. Finally, Hacienda argues that its policy against discrimination and its internal grievance procedures should shield it from liability for sexual harassment. We consider each of Hacienda's contentions in turn.

There is no dispute in this case that the acts of sexual harassment complained of occurred, and that they were unwelcome. The contested issue is whether the harassment was sufficiently "severe or pervasive" to alter the terms and conditions of the claimants' employment and to create a sexually hostile work environment. As the record reveals, Nusbaum repeatedly engaged in vulgarities, made sexual remarks, and requested sexual favors from the complainants. The complainants' direct supervisor, Alicia Castro, also frequently witnessed, laughed at, and herself made these types of comments. Castro had direct authority to hire, discharge, and discipline housekeeping employees, and Nusbaum threatened at least one of the claimants that he would have Castro fire her if she did not submit to his sexual advances. ... [W]e agree with the district court's conclusion that the complainants were subjected to severe and pervasive sexual harassment that "seriously tainted" the working environment and altered the terms and conditions of their employment. ... [that is, attempts to resolve disagreements in-house without going to court. Internal remedies might include discussion, negotiations, mediation, or arbitration.]

Appellant's remaining argument, that the complainants failed to pursue internal remedies under appellant's general nondiscrimination policy, can be disposed of quickly....Where, as here, the employer's discrimination policy does not specifically proscribe sexual harassment, and its internal procedures require initial resort to a supervisor who is accused of engaging in or condoning the harassment of which the employee complains, it would be plainly unreasonable to require discrimination claimants to exhaust such procedures as a predicate to suit. In any event, this court has held that a Title VII plaintiff need not exhaust her employer's internal remedies.

[Undocumented Aliens]

Appellant argues that the district court erred in awarding back pay to Teodora Castro, Flora Villalobos, and Maria Elena Gonzales, all of whom were undocumented alien workers [meaning an immigrant who lacks necessary immigration documents to prove they have the legal right to be employed in this country; see Mandatory Verification of Employment Status, later in this chapter] when they were subjected to appellant's discriminatory employment practices. The Hacienda also challenges the district court's calculation of the back pay awards....

The district court in this case assumed that Title VII, including its remedial provisions, applied to the undocumented aliens who were subjected by appellant to various forms of employment discrimination. It is basically undisputed that all of the employees who were awarded back pay for the Title VII violations in this case were in the United States, were not subjected to deportation proceedings, and were available for employment throughout the back pay period that could readily be calculated with certainty. Under our existing case law, then, the district court did not err in concluding that Castro, Villalobos, and Gonzalez were entitled to back pay in this case despite their status as undocumented aliens.

[Back Pay]

We turn now to appellant's arguments that the district court abused its discretion in calculating the back pay awards in this case. ...In awarding back pay, the district court is required to attempt to make victims of discrimination whole by restoring them to the position in which they would have been absent the discrimination. Title VII also requires mitigation of damages, however, by providing that "amounts earnable with reasonable diligence [by the employee]" be deducted from a back pay award. The back pay award in this case was well within the court's discretion....

[Injunctive Relief]

Appellant's final arguments challenge the district court's decision permanently to enjoin [forbid] appellant from "engaging in any employment practice which discriminates on the basis of sex, religion [or otherwise violates employment laws]." ...Appellant contends that injunctive relief ...was an inappropriate and unneeded sanction because there is no reasonable expectation that the alleged violations will recur....

Even if the individual complainants have been made whole by the [monetary] relief awarded by the district court, this court has recognized that the EEOC has a right of action [for an injunction] that is independent of the employees' private rights of action. This is because the EEOC is not merely a proxy for the victims of discrimination, but acts also "to vindicate the public interest in preventing employment discrimination." By seeking injunctive relief, the EEOC not only deters future unlawful discrimination but also seeks to protect aggrieved employees and others similarly situated from the fear of retaliation for filing Title VII charges....

An employer that takes curative actions only after it has been sued fails to provide sufficient assurances that it will not repeat the violation to justify denying an injunction. Appellant's recent efforts to train managerial employees regarding discrimination problems and the absence of further EEOC charges in recent times are encouraging and laudable; however, the district court did not abuse its discretion by awarding permanent injunctive relief on the facts of this case.

For all of the foregoing reasons, the judgment of the district court is AFFIRMED.

Americans with Disabilities Act

The Americans with Disabilities Act (ADA), which became effective in 1992, is an uncompromising proclamation of this country's commitment to equal opportunity for the disabled. The impact of this law can be understood from estimates that put the number of Americans with disabilities at 57 million. Prior to the adoption of the ADA, many employers declined to hire people with disabilities because of fears that they would be unable to perform the job or would be absent frequently or would require a lot of assistance. Such fears are based on stereotypes and should not be the basis for employment decisions. The ADA seeks to eliminate the barrier of those stereotypes for disabled persons who are able to perform on the job.

We saw in Chapter 3 the ADA's provisions requiring accessibility to places of public accommodation. In this chapter we study the ADA's employment provisions. They apply to all phases of employment including hiring, advancement, discharge, compensation, and training. To the hospitality industry, the ADA has effectuated fundamental changes in personnel policies.

In short, the ADA provides that an employer cannot refuse to hire and cannot otherwise discriminate against a disabled person who can, with reasonable accommodation if needed, perform the essential functions of a job. A **disability** is defined as a physical or mental impairment that substantially limits a person's ability to walk, see, hear, perform manual tasks, learn, work, or care for self. To qualify for ADA protection the disability must be permanent or long term. An injury to a dish washer's hand which prevented him from working but healed within a month does not qualify as a disability under the ADA.[125] **Essential functions** are the core responsibilities of a job as distinguished from marginal or incidental assignments. The ADA applies to employers with a minimum of 15 employees; it does not apply to employers with fewer than 15 employees.

disability
A physical or mental impairment that substantially limits one or more major life activities.

essential functions
As defined by the Americans with Disabilities Act, the core responsibilities of a job as distinguished from marginal or incidental assignments.

Essential Functions

In determining what functions are essential to a job, a court will consider the following: the employer's judgment as to which functions are essential; written job descriptions drafted before the job was advertised or interviewing began; and the

---

[125] *Hopkins v. Godfather's Pizza, Inc.*, 141 Fed.Appx. 473 (Ill. 2005)

amount of time on the job allocated to performing the function. Examples of essential functions in the job of a server are lifting, carrying, and lowering heavy trays.

The following are circumstances that may render a job function essential: the reason the position exists is to perform that function; only a limited number of employees are available who can perform the task; the function may be highly specialized and the reason for hiring a particular person is her expertise or ability to perform that duty.

A general manager of a Burger King was terminated due to obesity (he weighed 600 pounds), which qualified as a disability. He had always received excellent reviews evidencing that his weight did not prevent him from performing the essential functions of the job. The employer thus violated the ADA and, when sued by the employee, was liable to pay him back and future wages that he lost due to the illegal discharge.[126]

Reasonable Accommodation

If an employee with a disability is able to perform the essential functions of the job but needs a reasonable accommodation to do so, the employer may be obligated to make the adjustment. What constitutes a reasonable accommodation depends on the facts of each case. The ADA may require an employer to do any of the following: restructure the job; modify facilities to make them accessible, such as enlarging doors to make them negotiable in a wheelchair; modify work schedules; acquire equipment, such as magnifiers for the visually impaired; or modify exams and training programs for the visually impaired or learning disabled. Providing a stool to sit on while performing food preparation and hostessing duties was a reasonable accommodation to a Friendly's restaurant employee who suffered from a joint disease preventing her from walking more than 100 feet or standing for more than one minute without sitting.[127]

© Stock-Asso/Shutterstock.com

Employers are not required to provide personal use items such as hearing aids or eyeglasses. While employers have expressed concerns about the cost of accommodations, studies have concluded that over 70 percent of accommodations cost less than $500 and 50 percent cost less than $50. Additionally, some tax incentives are available for providing accommodations.

The employer's duty to provide reasonable modifications applies not only to applicants for employment, but also to employees already on staff who are or become disabled

---

[126] *Polesnak v. R.H. Management Systems, Inc.*, 1997 WL 109245 (Tenn. 1997); *Connor v. McDonald's Restaurant*, 2003 WL 1343259 (Conn. 2003)

[127] *Bearley v. Friendly's Ice Cream*, 322 F.Supp.2d 563 (Pa. 2004)

and cannot perform their original jobs without some restructuring. Reasonable accommodation in these circumstances can include, in addition to those already listed, reassigning employees to a vacant job for which they are qualified. Employers, however, are not required to invent new shifts or place disabled employees into positions for which they are not qualified.[128] If accommodations are unavailing and no alternate job is available, the employer is not required to continue the employment. This was illustrated in a case involving a bartender at the Waikiki Sheraton who tripped at work and suffered a back injury. As a result he was no longer able to do his job. His doctor identified a few jobs at the hotel the bartender could perform but none was vacant. The employee sought as an accommodation the creation of a position for him by displacing an incumbent employee. The court held this proposed accommodation was unreasonable and therefore not required of the employer. Said the court, "The ADA does not require employers to create vacancies for disabled employees."[129]

CASE EXAMPLE 14-12

Arevalo v. Hyatt Corporation

No. CV 12-7054 JGB (VBKx) (C.D. Cal. 05/13/13)

Gloria Arevalo began working as a room attendant at the Century Plaza Hotel in 1982. She cleaned guest rooms…including cleaning bathtubs, showers, toilets, sinks, walls, mirrors, counters, and floors, changing sheets and towels, making beds, dusting furniture, wiping windows, vacuuming and sweeping. Room attendants work for eight-hour shifts and may take two 10-minute breaks and one 30-minute lunch break. A room attendant stands or walks the entire time she is performing her duties and generally is expected to clean about fourteen rooms per shift.

On February 6, 2010, Arevalo fell and injured her left knee. Immediately after the injury, she did not return to work and Hyatt placed her on a leave of absence because her knee was swollen and she had to walk with crutches. On April 29, 2010, Dr. Abrams performed surgery on her left knee. Between April 29, 2010 and December 7, 2010, Dr. Abrams provided her with work status reports that stated she could not return to work in any capacity. During this time, Hyatt continued to keep Arevalo on leave of absence.

On December 7, 2010, Dr. Abrams released her to return to work with the restrictions of no prolonged standing or walking and limited squatting. He considered the restriction to mean she should not stand or walk more than 15 to 20 minutes in an hour. Hyatt's Assistant Director of Human Resources, Sara Aguilar, reviewed Dr. Abrams work status report and restrictions on December 10, 2010 and determined that she could not perform the duties of a housekeeper at that time. Instead, Hyatt offered her temporary modified duty on December 30, 2010, also known as "light duty," which she began on January 4, 2011.

128 *Jeffries v. Gaylord Entertainment, et al.,* 641 Fed.Appx. 265 (Md. 2013)
129 *Soone v. Kyo-Ya Co., Ltd.,* 335 F.Supp.2d 1107 (Hawaii 2005)

Per Hyatt's policy, light duty is not a permanent position; it is a modified temporary assignment for a maximum period of three moths for employees who have work restrictions and require accommodations. While on light duty, her duties consisted of answering phones, folding ice bucket liners and laundry bags, stocking amenities, and checking guest rooms for cleanliness.

On February 9, 2011, Dr. Abrams completed another work status report which continued to limit her to fifteen to twenty minutes of walking or standing every hour and found it was unreasonable for her to return to her room attendant duties. Based on these restrictions, Aguilar determined on March 15, 2011 that Arevalo could not return to her position as a room attendant when her light duty expired.

On March 15, 2011, Aguilar, Arevalo and Housekeeping Director, Andrew Jones, met to discuss how Hyatt could accommodate her work restrictions. Aguilar notified Arevalo her light duty assignment had expired… [and] that she could not return to her position as a room attendant because of her work restrictions. Aguilar and Arevalo reviewed a list of job openings at the hotel, but Plaintiff did not see any open jobs for which she was qualified. Aguilar placed Arevalo back on leave of absence, as she had four months…remaining. She notified Arevalo that if she remained unable to perform the duties of a room attendant or another available positon, at the end of her four months of leave, she would be terminated.

On August 2, 2011, Dr. Abrams provided an updated work status report which stated that Arevalo could return to work with the following restrictions, "no kneeling on left knee, no running, no jumping." Arevalo further understood that her restrictions as of August 2, 2011 were that she could not climb, bend her knees, jump, run, kneel, or walk for long periods of time. She believed that she could perform her job as a room attendant with these restrictions. Aguilar and Arevalo met on August 8, 2011 and Aguilar informed her that her work restrictions prevented her from returning to work as a room attendant. Aguilar notified her there were no jobs at the hotel that she was able to perform with her restrictions. On August 8, 2011, Hyatt terminated Arevalo.

At the time of her termination, she was required to use a cane to walk. Since her termination, at least three doctors have told her that she could not perform work which required her to bend her knee, walk for extended periods, jump, or lift more than twenty or twenty-five pounds. Arevalo understands she needs to have her knee replaced because it is very damaged.

Plaintiff states four causes of action. Claim one is for breach of covenant of good faith and fair dealing. Claim two alleges disability discrimination in violation of the Fair Employment and Housing Act ("FEHA") during the period of August 2 to August 22, 2011. Claim three contends that Hyatt failed to provide a reasonable accommodation to Plaintiff from August 2 to August 22, 2011 in violation of FEHA. Claim four states a claim for retaliation against Plaintiff for her assertion of her rights under FEHA. Finally, Plaintiff's fifth claim is for wrongful termination in violation of public policy.

Before the court is a Motion for Summary Judgment filed by Defendant Hyatt Corporation. Plaintiff "bears the burden of proving [she is] an employee…able to perform the essential functions of a job with or without reasonable accommodation." In determining which functions are essential, relevant evidence includes, but is not limited to, the employer's judgment as to which functions are essential, written job descriptions prepared before advertising or interviewing applicants for the job, the amount of time spent on the job performing the function, the consequences of not requiring the incumbent to perform the function, and the past and current work experience of incumbents on the job. The court finds, as a matter of law that Arevalo, who required the use of a cane at all times, could not have performed the essential duties of a room attendant, most of which required consistent unaided walking or standing, such as cleaning bathtubs, changing sheets and sweeping. Plaintiff's testimony that she could perform the essential duties of her positon with a cane is a 'bald, uncorroborated, and conclusory assertion rather than evidence," and the Court finds that it does not create a triable issue of material fact that requires consideration by the jury.

The evidence does not show that Plaintiff's condition was improving such that an additional leave would have made it likely that Plaintiff could return to work. "Reasonable accommodation does not require the employer to wait indefinitely for an employee's medical condition to be corrected." Thus, an employer would not be required to provide repeated leaves of absence (or perhaps even a single leave of absence) for an employee with a poor prognosis of recovery.

Hyatt has introduced substantial evidence to show that it is more likely than not that Arevalo's inability to perform her duties was the reason Hyatt discharged her, and has thus identified a legitimate non-discriminatory reason for its actions.

The Court GRANTS Defendant's motion for summary judgment on all five of Plaintiff's claims for relief.

Undue Hardship

If the accommodations required to enable the employee to perform the essential job functions are not reasonable, but rather impose an undue hardship on the business, the employer can legally refuse to extend employment to the disabled person. An **undue hardship** refers to an accommodation that requires significant difficulty or expense on the part of the employer, or major modification of the employer's business, taking into account such factors as the nature of the business, cost of the accommodation, and the business' resources. For example, a nightclub that features live music need not discontinue the music to accommodate a would-be waiter who is hearing impaired and unable to hear customers' beverage and food orders over the sound of a band. To eliminate music would change the format of the business and thus constitute an undue hardship.

undue hardship
An accommodation for a disabled employee that would require a significant difficulty or expense for the employer.

Preference Not Required

An employer is not required to give preference to a disabled person, but can instead hire the most qualified applicant. For example, two people apply for a hotel maintenance job. One applicant has a disability and has experience working on heating and plumbing systems, but not electrical systems. The other has no disability and has experience not only with heating and plumbing systems but also with electrical systems. The employer can hire the latter because he has better qualifications.

If the applicant with the best qualifications is the one with the disability, the employer cannot decline to hire him because of the disability. If, to enable that worker to do the job, the employer would need to make an accommodation, the employer must do so unless the employer can prove that the accommodation would create an undue hardship. For example, assume that the disability prevents the applicant from driving, and public transportation will result in his arriving at work a half hour after the beginning of the business day. As an accommodation, the employer would need to modify the hours of the position unless the altered schedule presents an undue hardship for the business.

An employer cannot make employment decisions based on inability to perform *nonessential* functions of the job. These are marginal tasks that do not qualify as essential functions. Change the facts of the maintenance hire a bit: A nonessential function of the job is occasionally answering the phone to take service calls; assume the disabled person is unable to hear and so cannot answer the phone. Does this justify the employer hiring the other applicant? The answer is no, because in this example answering the phone is not an essential job responsibility; the employer would violate the ADA by refusing to hire the disabled worker for this reason. Note: If answering the phone was an essential element of the job, the employer would need to explore possible ways to accommodate the worker's deafness. Examples might include work orders being transmitted via written notes, captioned phone, text messages, e-mail, or use of other technology.

ADA Impacts on Application Process

The ADA permeates all aspects of the hiring decision. At a pre-employment interview, an employer cannot ask job applicants about the nature of a disability. Prohibited questions include:

- Do you have a disability?

- How severe is your disability?

- What medications are you taking?

- Have you been hospitalized recently?

- How many days were you sick last year?

- Have you ever been treated for mental health problems?

The employer is permitted to inquire whether the applicant can perform the essential functions of the job, and can require the applicant to demonstrate ability to perform those tasks. Depending on the job, permissible questions might include: Can you lift and carry a 25-pound tray? Will you please demonstrate your ability to do this? Or, if the answer to the previous question is no, a follow-up question should be: Is there anything we could do to accommodate you so you could perform that task?

An employer cannot require that an applicant submit to a medical exam prior to extending a job offer. However, the offer can be conditioned on the results of a medical exam, but only if all incoming employees with the same job title are required to be examined regardless of disability. The information obtained from the test must be kept confidential and in a file *separate* from the employee's employment file. The only people entitled to see the medical report are first-aid personnel, supervisors who need the information to determine necessary restrictions and accommodations, and government officials investigating compliance with the ADA.

Drugs and Illnesses

Drug tests are treated differently from medical exams. An employer can require a test to detect illegal use of drugs as part of the application process. An applicant for employment who uses illegal drugs is not protected by the ADA. An employer can discriminate against such a person when making employment decisions. However, if a would-be employee abused drugs in the past but has since been rehabilitated or is enrolled in a supervised rehabilitation program and does not currently use the drugs, she qualifies as a person with a disability and cannot be denied employment on that ground.

An interesting issue arose in a case when a casino worker had a history of treating a chronic injury with pain medication. His employer did not allow him to use the narcotic hydrocodone while at work but did allow him to use it while off duty. While at work, he cut his finger, and in accordance with the casino's policy, he was required to submit to a drug test to check for illegal drugs in his system. Prescription drugs were exempted as ground for discipline and he was aware of this policy. Nonetheless, plaintiff refused to be drug tested and was terminated. He sued claiming the casino used the test refusal as a pretext to discriminate against him. The jury found for the worker, but on a judgment notwithstanding the verdict, (JNOV), the court reversed the jury verdict noting that the casino had safety concerns and had made accommodations for the worker.[130]

The ADA does not require a restaurateur to hire as a food handler a person with an infectious or communicable disease that may be transmitted to others through food handling. For a disease to qualify, it must be on a list developed by the Secretary of Health and Human Services that is required to be updated annually. Diseases that are on the list include hepatitis A, Salmonella typhi, Staphylococcus aureus, and Staphylococcus pyogenes. An employer can refuse to hire a would-be food handler who has these illnesses. With the list, the Secretary publishes symptoms that may indicate the presence of one of the listed diseases. The symptoms include open skin sores, boils, fever, dark urine, jaundice, and vomiting.

AIDS is not transmitted through food handling and is not on the list. Persons afflicted with AIDS and people who are HIV positive are considered disabled for purposes of protection under the ADA, provided the infection substantially limits them in a major life function. A restaurant that refuses, because of the disease, to hire a food handler with AIDS violates the ADA if the person is thereby rendered

---

[130] *Brown v. Mystique Casino*, 840 N.W.2d 726 (Iowa 2013)

disabled. In a case involving an HIV-positive applicant for a waitress job, no evidence was presented that having HIV limited her in a major life activity. Therefore her claim of disability discrimination was dismissed.[131]

Past Disabilities and Caregivers

The ADA protects not only people with disabilities, but also those with a past disability. For example, an employer cannot refuse to hire a recovered cancer patient. Also protected are those people who have a relationship with or are caregivers for a disabled person, such as a child, spouse, or parent. Although the employer may fear that an applicant with a disabled child might be absent frequently, that surmise cannot be used as a reason for rejecting the applicant. If the applicant is hired and does take excessive leave, she can be terminated for that reason. As Case Example 14-13 illustrates, when employees are not treated in the same way for violation of policies, harsher treatment can be a pretext for discrimination based on a disability.

CASE EXAMPLE 14-13

Buffington v. PEC Management II, LLP d/b/a Burger King

2014 WL 5341929 (N.J. 2014)

PEC is a franchisee of Burger King Corporation. Buffington was employed by PEC in a restaurant management capacity from December 2003 until November 2010. PEC owns and operates 34 Burger King Restaurants in Western Pennsylvania and Eastern Ohio. Keith Egyed ("Egyed") is PEC's Managing Director who has overall responsibility of operating the 34 Burger King Restaurants.

Buffington was hired as a general manager in training in December 2003. A general manager is responsible for "all aspects of the restaurant's operations and performance, such as scheduling, overseeing employees, financial matters, compliance with all Burger King Corporation and PEC standards, ordering and maintaining product and overall ensuring the smooth and profitable operation of the restaurant." The General Manager also has the authority to hire, train and terminate other restaurant level employees.

Buffington had a son, D. J. Honneffer ("D.J."), who passed away on June 18, 2011 at the age of 14 years old after a 12-year battle with cancer. D.J. had a form of cancer called rhabdomyosarcoma, which attacks muscles and bones. Over the course of D.J.'s struggle with cancer he had various relapses when the cancer would return and he would have a new tumor that would require surgery and follow-up courses of chemotherapy and radiation. It is undisputed that PEC managers knew of D.J.'s condition before or as of the time Buffington became an employee of PEC.

D.J. had a relapse in April 2010. He had surgery in July 2010, and continued to receive chemotherapy and radiation treatments following the surgery. In August 2010, the tumor that could not be removed

---

[131] *EEOC v. Lee's Log Cabin, Inc.*, 436 F.Supp.2d 992 (Wis. 2006)

grew larger. He had his last surgery for this relapse in February/March 2011. He passed away on June 18, 2011.

[Alice] Lawrence [Buffington's District Manager], noted a decline in Buffington's performance over the summer of 2010. During this time, there was an exchange of emails and memoranda among Managers regarding Buffington's performance. In her March 2010 Manager Performance Review, Lawrence gave Buffington an overall rating of "Good minus." Subsequently Buffington and Lawrence discussed a possible demotion for Buffington if she couldn't "handle the job." Still, Buffington contends that she was never documented for "Poor Work Performance."

In the meantime, in July 2010, Egyed learned that a crew member employed at the North East restaurant had been involved in a single vehicle accident while driving her vehicle to another restaurant to borrow product. As a result, Egyed directed the Human Resources Department to prepare a Memorandum dated August 16, 2010 which was hand delivered to all restaurant managers stapled to their paychecks which stated:

Please be reminded; the only employees permitted to drive for restaurant business, under any circumstances, are exclusively management employees. Absolutely no crew members are to drive for restaurant business even if accompanied by a management employee.

This policy has several different iterations in the Manager Handbook since 2003. Buffington claims she did not receive the August 16, 2010 Memorandum.

On November 7, 2010, Buffington was the only manager on duty when she ran out of product called "funnel sticks" at her restaurant. Buffington sent an off-duty crew member who had pulled up to the drive-through window, Scott Hayes ("Hayes"), on the errand to deliver tomatoes to, and obtain the funnel sticks from, the Beaver Falls Burger King. Hayes punched in on the clock and was sent on the errand in his own vehicle. During the errand Hayes was involved in a car accident where he claimed that his brakes failed and he rear-ended another vehicle. Buffington promptly reported the accident to Lawrence. Lawrence, in turn, reported the accident to Egyed on Monday, November 8, 2010.

On November 12, 2010, Lawrence, accompanied by Jenkins, met with Buffington…and informed her that she was being terminated. Lawrence presented her with a termination letter stating, "Based upon ongoing issues related to performance, your employment is being terminated effective immediately."

It is undisputed that at the termination meeting Lawence told Buffington, "the rule violation of sending Scott [Hayes] to run an errand to get product was the straw that broke the camel's back, and because of that rule violation, I had to let her go." There are other allegations that Lawrence made statements at the termination meeting such as, "We need someone whose head is there 100 percent," "We are planning on spending 400 grand to remodel the restaurant," "Now you can go spend all your time with your son," and "Please go spend some time with your son." The parties do not agree as to which allegations are accurate.

Evidence showed she performed her responsibilities as a general manager for seven years, had never received a written or oral warning during that time; had received top or middle marks on all evaluations in March 2010. She contended she was fired instead, solely because she violated the Use of Vehicles policy in the Manager's Handbook, which was a pretext for the actual discriminatory reason for dismissal. The plaintiff maintained the policy was not enforced and it was a common practice for managers to send staff on errands to other restaurants. None were ever disciplined or terminated.

Plaintiff was awarded $115,000 in front pay, $43,000 in back pay, and $70,000 in compensatory damages for her claims of discrimination based on her association with a person with a disability in violation of the Americans with Disabilities Act.

CASE QUESTIONS:

1. What was the effect of evidence other managers violated the Use of Vehicles policy?

2. Was there significance in the evaluation of March 2010?

3. Is there a better way for the defendant, in future cases, to provide evidence each manager has knowledge of the policy, since Plaintiff maintained she didn't receive the memo?

4. What is "pretext"?

Pursuing an ADA Case

The ADA encourages would-be plaintiffs to resolve their complaints through mediation rather than litigation. A person wishing to pursue a claim under the ADA can file a complaint with the Equal Employment Opportunity Commission or pursue the case in court. The potential liability a defendant faces in a lawsuit is significant and includes the following:

1. Compensatory damages, including emotional pain and suffering, mental anguish, and loss of enjoyment of life

2. Punitive damages

3. Attorney's fees

4. Expert witness fees

5. Reinstatement where an employee was wrongly terminated

6. Back pay

The ADA encourages employers to attempt reasonable accommodation by relieving them from liability for compensatory damages where they made a good-faith effort in consultation with the disabled person to identify and make a reasonable accommodation. For a plaintiff to win punitive damages, she must prove that the employer acted with malice or reckless indifference to the rights guaranteed under the ADA.

The responsibilities of employers to disabled employees and job applicants are triggered only when the disabled person is able to perform the essential functions of the job with or without reasonable accommodations. The ADA does not protect an applicant or employee who cannot perform the essential components of a job. Thus, the termination of a food server did not violate the ADA where the server suffered from panic attacks when the restaurant became crowded causing a "complete inability to function." In those circumstances, she was unable to serve food. The attacks occurred notwithstanding an accommodation made by the employer assigning the server to the least-busy workstation.[132]

Likewise, where a would-be waitress was able to lift and move no more than 10 pounds at a time and the job required lifting and moving trays, bus tubs, and garbage cans weighing 25 to 30 pounds up to 20 or more times each shift, the applicant is not protected by the Americans with Disabilities Act. Therefore the employer can refuse to hire her.[133] A housekeeping supervisor, whose job included filling in for truant housekeeping staff, was in a car accident and suffered neck and back injuries. As a result she was rendered unable to vacuum, which was an essential element of her job. She was not therefore protected by the ADA. In response to her request that her vacuuming responsibilities be assigned to other employees, the court said, "It is well settled that an employer is under no obligation to reallocate the essential functions of a position."[134]

Another case involved a kitchen worker who, due to a back injury, was no longer able to clean oven hoods, stock various products, change oil in the fryers, sweep and mop floors, pick up and carry chicken, work the grill during peak hours, and wash windows, several of which were essential elements of his job. The only accommodation that would have enabled the plaintiff to retain his job was for the restaurant to hire an additional employee to perform the tasks the plaintiff could not, or to exempt the plaintiff from performing many of his essential functions. Neither of these accommodations is reasonable and thus they are not required by the ADA.[135]

A manager at Pizza Hut faced a similar situation. Her job required that she perform tasks done by supervised employees when they were late or absent. Due to inflammatory arthritis, she was unable to lift more than 20 pounds and could not do repetitive motions with her arms. Her doctor advised that for her to continue work, the restaurant would need to hire a new employee to perform the functions of truant employees that the plaintiff was unable to perform. The court held this was not a reasonable accommodation and therefore the employer did not violate the ADA by terminating her employment.[136]

---

132 *Johnston v. Morrison, Inc.*, 849 F.Supp. 777 (Ala. 1994)
133 *EEOC v. Lee's Log Cabin, Inc.*, 436 F.Supp. 992 (Wis. 2006)
134 *Alexander v. Northland Inn*, 321 F.3d 723 (Minn. 2003)
135 *Clement v. Bojangles' Restaurants, Inc.*, 2001 WL 66317 (N.C. 2001), aff'd, 10 Fed. Appx. 237 (2001)
136 *Burnett v. Pizza Hut of America, Inc.*, 92 F.Supp.2d 1142 (Kans. 2000)

Similarly, a slot attendant at a casino suffered a neck injury deeming him unable to carry heavy items. An essential function of his job was to carry bags of coins. Termination of his employment was therefore not discrimination under the ADA.[137]

Not Disabled

If an employee is not disabled, he is not entitled to protection of the ADA. A terminated Burger King manager claimed a disability caused by knee problems. The evidence established that he mowed his yard, raked leaves, occasionally took out the trash and vacuumed, and did other duties around the house while he was working at Burger King. These activities required lifting, bending, and stooping, like his job. The court thus concluded that he was not substantially limited in a major life activity by his knee problems and therefore could not claim disability discrimination.[138]

Mandatory Verification of Employment Status

Not everyone in our country is legally entitled to work here. Citizens from other countries must have proper authorization to be legally employed in the United States. The necessary documentation proving authorization must be verified by employers.

Entrance to this country is restricted by law. While tourists are permitted to come in large numbers, only a limited number of people can enter each year for other purposes. To immigrate to the United States to attend school, work, or otherwise live here requires permission from the Immigration and Naturalization Service (INS), the government agency responsible for overseeing the immigration laws. An **immigrant** in the United States is a citizen of another country who enters this country with authorization from the INS. One who enters without the necessary approval is an **illegal alien.**

immigrant
In the United States, a citizen of another country who enters the United States.

illegal alien
One who enters the United States without the necessary authorization.

Immigration Reform and Control Act

The Immigration Reform and Control Act (IRCA),[139] is a federal law passed in 1986 that enlists employers in the effort to prevent illegal aliens from working in this country. The IRCA requires employers to verify the employment status of workers they hire. An employer must complete and retain a form called the Employment Eligibility Verification Form, commonly referred to as Form I-9. The primary purpose of this form is to verify that the individual is authorized to work in the United States. The employee must present identification and proof that he has permission from the INS to work here. The employer is required to physically examine the document(s) to determine if, in the words of the statute, it "reasonably appears on its face to be genuine." No later than three days following the date of hire (the first day of work for pay), the employer must sign Form I-9, stating under penalty of perjury that the employer has verified that the individual is not an unau-

---

137 *Van de Pol v. Caesars Hotel Casino*, 979 F.Supp. 308 (N.J. 1997)
138 *LeRoy v. Pamax Development, Inc.*, 29 Fed.Appx. 514 (Okla. 2002)
139 8 U.S.C. §§ 1324a and 1324b

thorized alien. The employee must also sign attesting to legal status. The employer must retain the form for three years following the date of hire or until one year after the employee leaves, whichever is longer. Form I-9 is shown as Figure 14-1.

FIGURE 14-1 Employment Eligibility Verification Form, commonly referred to as Form I-9

Employment Eligibility Verification	**USCIS**
Department of Homeland Security	**Form I-9**
U.S. Citizenship and Immigration Services	OMB No. 1615-0047
	Expires 08/31/2019

▶ **START HERE:** Read instructions carefully before completing this form. The instructions must be available, either in paper or electronically, during completion of this form. Employers are liable for errors in the completion of this form.

ANTI-DISCRIMINATION NOTICE: It is illegal to discriminate against work-authorized individuals. Employers **CANNOT** specify which document(s) an employee may present to establish employment authorization and identity. The refusal to hire or continue to employ an individual because the documentation presented has a future expiration date may also constitute illegal discrimination.

Section 1. Employee Information and Attestation *(Employees must complete and sign Section 1 of Form I-9 no later than the **first day of employment**, but not before accepting a job offer.)*

Last Name *(Family Name)*	First Name *(Given Name)*	Middle Initial	Other Last Names Used *(if any)*

Address *(Street Number and Name)*	Apt. Number	City or Town	State	ZIP Code

Date of Birth *(mm/dd/yyyy)*	U.S. Social Security Number	Employee's E-mail Address	Employee's Telephone Number

I am aware that federal law provides for imprisonment and/or fines for false statements or use of false documents in connection with the completion of this form.

I attest, under penalty of perjury, that I am (check one of the following boxes):

☐ 1. A citizen of the United States

☐ 2. A noncitizen national of the United States *(See instructions)*

☐ 3. A lawful permanent resident   (Alien Registration Number/USCIS Number): _____

☐ 4. An alien authorized to work   until (expiration date, if applicable, mm/dd/yyyy): _____
   Some aliens may write "N/A" in the expiration date field. *(See instructions)*

Aliens authorized to work must provide only one of the following document numbers to complete Form I-9: An Alien Registration Number/USCIS Number OR Form I-94 Admission Number OR Foreign Passport Number.

1. Alien Registration Number/USCIS Number: _____
   OR
2. Form I-94 Admission Number: _____
   OR
3. Foreign Passport Number: _____
   Country of Issuance: _____

QR Code - Section 1
Do Not Write In This Space

Signature of Employee	Today's Date *(mm/dd/yyyy)*

Preparer and/or Translator Certification (check one):
☐ I did not use a preparer or translator.   ☐ A preparer(s) and/or translator(s) assisted the employee in completing Section 1.
(Fields below must be completed and signed when preparers and/or translators assist an employee in completing Section 1.)

I attest, under penalty of perjury, that I have assisted in the completion of Section 1 of this form and that to the best of my knowledge the information is true and correct.

Signature of Preparer or Translator	Today's Date *(mm/dd/yyyy)*

Last Name *(Family Name)*	First Name *(Given Name)*

Address *(Street Number and Name)*	City or Town	State	ZIP Code

 Employer Completes Next Page

Form I-9 11/14/2016 N

Page 1 of 3

Employment Eligibility Verification
Department of Homeland Security
U.S. Citizenship and Immigration Services

USCIS
Form I-9
OMB No. 1615-0047
Expires 08/31/2019

Section 2. Employer or Authorized Representative Review and Verification

(Employers or their authorized representative must complete and sign Section 2 within 3 business days of the employee's first day of employment. You must physically examine one document from List A OR a combination of one document from List B and one document from List C as listed on the "Lists of Acceptable Documents.")

Employee Info from Section 1	Last Name *(Family Name)*	First Name *(Given Name)*	M.I.	Citizenship/Immigration Status

List A Identity and Employment Authorization	OR	List B Identity	AND	List C Employment Authorization

List A

Document Title

Issuing Authority

Document Number

Expiration Date *(if any)(mm/dd/yyyy)*

Document Title

Issuing Authority

Document Number

Expiration Date *(if any)(mm/dd/yyyy)*

Document Title

Issuing Authority

Document Number

Expiration Date *(if any)(mm/dd/yyyy)*

List B

Document Title

Issuing Authority

Document Number

Expiration Date *(if any)(mm/dd/yyyy)*

List C

Document Title

Issuing Authority

Document Number

Expiration Date *(if any)(mm/dd/yyyy)*

Additional Information

QR Code - Sections 2 & 3
Do Not Write In This Space

Certification: I attest, under penalty of perjury, that (1) I have examined the document(s) presented by the above-named employee, (2) the above-listed document(s) appear to be genuine and to relate to the employee named, and (3) to the best of my knowledge the employee is authorized to work in the United States.

The employee's first day of employment *(mm/dd/yyyy)*: _____ *(See instructions for exemptions)*

Signature of Employer or Authorized Representative	Today's Date*(mm/dd/yyyy)*	Title of Employer or Authorized Representative
Last Name of Employer or Authorized Representative	First Name of Employer or Authorized Representative	Employer's Business or Organization Name

Employer's Business or Organization Address (Street Number and Name)	City or Town	State	ZIP Code

Section 3. Reverification and Rehires *(To be completed and signed by employer or authorized representative.)*

A. New Name *(if applicable)*			B. Date of Rehire *(if applicable)*
Last Name *(Family Name)*	First Name *(Given Name)*	Middle Initial	Date *(mm/dd/yyyy)*

C. If the employee's previous grant of employment authorization has expired, provide the information for the document or receipt that establishes continuing employment authorization in the space provided below.

Document Title	Document Number	Expiration Date *(if any) (mm/dd/yyyy)*

I attest, under penalty of perjury, that to the best of my knowledge, this employee is authorized to work in the United States, and if the employee presented document(s), the document(s) I have examined appear to be genuine and to relate to the individual.

Signature of Employer or Authorized Representative	Today's Date *(mm/dd/yyyy)*	Name of Employer or Authorized Representative

Form I-9 11/14/2016 N

Page 2 of 3

LISTS OF ACCEPTABLE DOCUMENTS
All documents must be UNEXPIRED

Employees may present one selection from List A
or a combination of one selection from List B and one selection from List C.

LIST A		LIST B		LIST C
Documents that Establish Both Identity and Employment Authorization	**OR**	**Documents that Establish Identity**	**AND**	**Documents that Establish Employment Authorization**

LIST A	LIST B	LIST C
1. U.S. Passport or U.S. Passport Card	1. Driver's license or ID card issued by a State or outlying possession of the United States provided it contains a photograph or information such as name, date of birth, gender, height, eye color, and address	1. A Social Security Account Number card, unless the card includes one of the following restrictions: (1) NOT VALID FOR EMPLOYMENT (2) VALID FOR WORK ONLY WITH INS AUTHORIZATION (3) VALID FOR WORK ONLY WITH DHS AUTHORIZATION
2. Permanent Resident Card or Alien Registration Receipt Card (Form I-551)		
3. Foreign passport that contains a temporary I-551 stamp or temporary I-551 printed notation on a machine-readable immigrant visa	2. ID card issued by federal, state or local government agencies or entities, provided it contains a photograph or information such as name, date of birth, gender, height, eye color, and address	
4. Employment Authorization Document that contains a photograph (Form I-766)		2. Certification of Birth Abroad issued by the Department of State (Form FS-545)
	3. School ID card with a photograph	3. Certification of Report of Birth issued by the Department of State (Form DS-1350)
5. For a nonimmigrant alien authorized to work for a specific employer because of his or her status: **a.** Foreign passport; and **b.** Form I-94 or Form I-94A that has the following: (1) The same name as the passport; and (2) An endorsement of the alien's nonimmigrant status as long as that period of endorsement has not yet expired and the proposed employment is not in conflict with any restrictions or limitations identified on the form.	4. Voter's registration card	
	5. U.S. Military card or draft record	4. Original or certified copy of birth certificate issued by a State, county, municipal authority, or territory of the United States bearing an official seal
	6. Military dependent's ID card	
	7. U.S. Coast Guard Merchant Mariner Card	
	8. Native American tribal document	5. Native American tribal document
	9. Driver's license issued by a Canadian government authority	6. U.S. Citizen ID Card (Form I-197)
	For persons under age 18 who are unable to present a document listed above:	7. Identification Card for Use of Resident Citizen in the United States (Form I-179)
6. Passport from the Federated States of Micronesia (FSM) or the Republic of the Marshall Islands (RMI) with Form I-94 or Form I-94A indicating nonimmigrant admission under the Compact of Free Association Between the United States and the FSM or RMI	10. School record or report card	8. Employment authorization document issued by the Department of Homeland Security
	11. Clinic, doctor, or hospital record	
	12. Day-care or nursery school record	

Examples of many of these documents appear in Part 8 of the Handbook for Employers (M-274).

Refer to the instructions for more information about acceptable receipts.

If the new hire claims the necessary documents were lost, stolen, or destroyed, the person must provide a receipt evidencing a request for replacement documents within the three days. The receipt is valid in lieu of the documents for 90 days. At the end of the receipt validity period, the individual must present the replacement document to complete Form I-9. The penalty for hiring a person, knowing they are not authorized to work includes a fee that ranges from a minimum $375 per worker for the first offense to a maximum $16,000 per worker for the third offense. Failure to comply with the Form I-9 requirements fine ranges from $110 per form to $1,100 per form for the third offense. Committing or participating in document fraud ranges from a minimum $375 for each worker for first offense to $6,500 per worker for third offense. Criminal penalties up to six months in prison apply when there is a pattern or practice of violations.

When reviewing documents to satisfy the IRCA, it is the employer's responsibility to check the expiration dates. An expired document is not adequate proof of a person's status.

When the IRCA was under consideration by Congress, various minority groups feared that employers would attempt to avoid liability by refusing to hire all aliens. Although the Civil Rights Act outlaws discrimination based on national origin, it does not include noncitizens as a protected class. To prevent discrimination against immigrants who are authorized to work, the IRCA prohibits discrimination in employment based on citizenship status, which means an employer cannot refuse to hire, based on lack of citizenship, a qualified alien authorized to work. Interestingly, the IRCA provides a preference in hiring and recruiting for a U.S. citizen over an alien "if the two individuals are equally qualified."

Résumé Fraud

Misrepresentations contained in a résumé are termed *résumé fraud* or *credentials fraud*. The untruths can relate to the college attended, degrees received, prior employers, prior job responsibilities, title held, dates employed, salary history, certifications earned, and virtually any other factor contained in a résumé.

The Internet expands the opportunities for résumé fraud because it provides easy access to fake degrees, authentic-looking diplomas, and even fill-in-the-blank transcript templates. Credential falsification creates dilemmas for employers because it increases the difficulty of finding the best candidates for openings. Résumé fraud is likewise costly to employers because it results in higher employee turnover and increased training time.

Some employers are addressing the problem by utilizing in the hiring process intensive one-on-one, in-person testing of candidates for each skill required by the job and also for communication proficiencies. Also helpful in detecting embellishments of an applicant's background are thorough reference checks.

Another precaution employers should consider is including a statement at the bottom of the application form stating that the would-be employee swears to the truth of the information provided. If any data is later discovered to be false, this statement lays the foundation for a civil case in fraud or a criminal prosecution for perjury. Penalties for perjury include jail, fines, and probation. Consequences for civil fraud include reimbursement to the employer of expenses incurred as a result of the untruthful information.

Occupational Safety and Health Administration

The Occupational Safety and Health Administration, known by its acronym OSHA, is a federal agency whose mission is to ensure that workplaces in the United States are safe. OSHA enforces laws passed by Congress as well as regulations adopted by the agency that mandate safe conditions at work sites. Some states have adopted their own safety standards, which may be more stringent.

Examples of the thousands of OSHA regulations include proper labeling and storing of hazardous materials (such materials may be present in cleaning solvents and pesticides used in restaurants or hotels), mandated safety devices for meat-cutting machinery, procedures to reduce the spread of such diseases as hepatitis B and HIV through bloodborne pathogens, proper storage and placement of portable fire extinguishers, and maintenance of required first-aid devices.

The agency hires and trains inspectors who visit workplaces to investigate whether employers are complying with applicable safety rules. In addition to routine safety audits, inspections occur in response to accidents, complaints by employees or customers, and referrals from other government agencies. All employers are required to post information for employees about their workplace safety and health rights and contact information for OSHA so employees can contact the agency if they observe violations. Employers who fail to comply face substantial fines and other penalties. Trade associations of restaurants and hotels provide training and awareness materials to assist members in identifying risks, preventing accidents, and complying with OSHA regulations.

Unions

collective bargaining
A process where representatives of a union negotiate with representatives of management on terms of employment such as hours, wages, benefits, vacations, and other working conditions.

collective bargaining agreement
A contract between workers and management that is a result of collective bargaining.

Unions are organizations of workers whose mission includes negotiating for higher wages, better benefits, greater job stability, and safer workplaces. These goals are achieved in significant part by **collective bargaining,** the process whereby representatives of the union negotiate with representatives of management (the owners and operators of a company) on terms of employment such as hours, wages, benefits, vacations, and working conditions. The resulting contract between workers and management is called a **collective bargaining agreement.**

Union membership customarily enhances the bargaining power of workers because unions are acting on behalf of not just an individual but rather groups of employees. The collective bargaining agreement typically secures rights greater than provided to employees by law. For example, we have studied that the law provides that employment is customarily at will, meaning the employer can terminate an employee for any reason except illegal discrimination. Contrast that with the terms of a collective bargaining agreement, which typically restrict the employer's right to terminate absent good cause. Management, not surprisingly, usually prefers a nonunionized workplace where its control is unbridled.

National Labor Relations Act

The National Labor Relations Act (NLRA), a federal law enacted in 1935, protects employees' right to form, join, or assist a union. Congressional findings that led to the passage of the NLRA include the following: "Experience has proved that protection by law of the right of employees to organize and bargain collectively safeguards commerce from ...interruption by removing certain recognized sources of industrial strife and unrest, by encouraging practices fundamental to the friendly adjustment of industrial disputes arising out of differences as to wages, hours, or other working conditions, and by restoring equality of bargaining power between employers and employees."

Union membership is a protected class for purposes of discrimination. An employer violates the NLRA if it refuses to hire an applicant because of union activity or retaliates against a union activist by, for example, demoting, transferring, or terminating that person.

Enforcement of the NLRA is done by the National Labor Relations Board (NLRB) which, among other powers, has the authority to prevent employers from engaging in unfair labor practices. Such prohibited acts include threats, warnings, and orders to refrain from protected union action; discrimination against employees who participate in union activities; retaliation for filing a charge of an unfair labor practice with the NLRB; and refusal to negotiate in good faith with union representatives over conditions of employment.

Emerging Issues in Employment Law

Employment law is not static; new issues emerge regularly. Among the issues currently developing are those presented in this section.

Negligent Hiring

Failure to perform reference checks and criminal checks on a new hire can result in liability to the employer. **Negligent hiring** is a cause of action that holds an employer responsible when an employee harms a customer or another worker, and a background check would have revealed a propensity for aggressive or assaultive conduct. The liability may apply even when the rogue employee is acting outside of his job description. Employers should develop an efficient and effective reference and criminal checking system, and abide by it.

negligent hiring
Failure by an employer to investigate the background of a job applicant prior to hiring.

Employee Use of Social Media

The use of social media is becoming increasingly popular as a means for employees to express their satisfaction or discontent with their employers, and to report circumstances occurring inside companies. Among the potential problems for businesses include the possibility of disclosure of the company's trade secrets; inclusion of defamatory words, pictures, or videos that damage the reputation of the brand; invasion of another's privacy rights; and publication of information that undermines the company's media and communications department. Employers should develop policies regarding use of social media by employees that protect the interests of the business.

Handling Employee Personal Data

In the normal course, employers accumulate much personal data about their employees including addresses, photos, social security numbers, date of birth, ethnicity information, and some medical records. The law is becoming increasingly restrictive of an employer's use, dissemination, and method of disposal of this information. Employers should regularly consult with their legal advisors to ensure compliance with ongoing changes in the law.

Antonio Guillem/Shutterstock.com

Miscellaneous Issues

New employment issues develop frequently. Current examples include the following. As the population ages, many employees will continue to work past the traditional retirement age. The law changes periodically regarding visa requirements for employers who rely on seasonal workers. The legal use of marijuana for medical and recreational purposes has greatly expanded in recent years. Also, the laws with regard to an individual's right to carry weapons have expanded. Marriage laws have changed across the nation. Technology improvements will lead to changed expectations among job applicants and employees. All of these developments impact employment law. Hospitality employers will need to stay current on developments in these areas.

Summary

Employment laws cover virtually every aspect of the employer–employee relationship. The Fair Labor Standards Act mandates minimum wages, one-and-one-half pay for overtime work, equal pay for equal work, and restrictions on child labor. The Family and Medical Leave Act entitles qualified employees to unpaid leave to care for a child, spouse, or parent, or for the employee's own illness.

The Civil Rights Act of 1964, Title VII, prohibits discrimination on the basis of race, color, religion, and national origin. Gender was added as a protected class in 1991. Other laws prohibit discrimination on the basis of pregnancy, age (over 40), disability, marital status, arrest record, lack of citizenship, and union activity.

The Immigration Reform and Control Act requires employers to verify the employment status of employees, primarily to prevent illegal aliens from working in this country.

Employers are also required to follow safety regulations to help protect employees from workplace injuries.

Employers should keep current on ever-changing laws impacting the rights of employees and employers.

Preventive Law Tips for Managers

- *Unless your business is exempt, pay your employees the applicable minimum wage.* The Fair Labor Standards Act (FLSA) imposes an obligation on employers to pay a minimum wage. Effective July, 2009, the federal minimum wage is $7.25. State governments can increase the minimum wage. Some exceptions to the federal minimum wage apply, including employers whose annual sales are less than $500,000, and employees who receive part of their pay in tips.

- *Pay employees one-and-one-half times their hourly wage for hours they work in excess of 40 per week.* The FLSA requires time-and-a-half pay for time worked in excess of 40 hours in any given week. This rule does not apply to qualifying managerial, administrative, or professional employees.

- *Utilize the same pay scales and ranges for male and female employees who perform the same job.* The Equal Pay Act, a provision of the FLSA, requires equal treatment in pay for men and women who do the same jobs.

- *Do not hire anyone under age 14.* The FLSA prohibits the employment of young people under age 14.

- *If you hire young workers, review the applicable restrictions on their hours and duties and abide by them.* The FLSA and laws in many states restrict both the hours certain teenage employees can work and the types of tasks they can perform. Do not assign these workers to illegal hours or prohibited responsibilities. Determining permissible working hours can be confusing because they differ by age groups and change for school days, weekends, and holidays. Careful attention to the various restrictions is required to avoid fines, risks to young workers, and unwanted negative publicity.

- *Do not discriminate on the basis of race.* Race is a protected class. Employees should not be treated differently because of their race. Racial groups include African Americans, Caucasians, Asians, Native Americans, Eskimos, and Native Hawaiians.

- *Do not discriminate on the basis of national origin.* National origin is a protected class. Employees should not be treated differently because of their country of origin.

- *Do not discriminate on the basis of accent or inability to speak English unless mastery of the language is a job necessity.* Generally, discrimination against a person who cannot speak English well or who speaks with an accent constitutes discrimination on the basis of national origin. If, however, performance of the job requires the ability to speak and understand English well, someone who cannot understand the language or who cannot be understood is not qualified. Failure to hire that person would not be illegal discrimination.

- *Do not discriminate on the basis of religion.* Religion is a protected class. Employees should not be treated differently because of their religion. If an employee needs a modified work schedule to comply with religious observances, the employer is required to make a reasonable effort to accommodate the employee. If accommodation would cause the employer undue hardship, the employer can refuse to oblige the employee's religious needs and will not be liable for religious discrimination.

- *Do not discriminate on the basis of gender.* Gender is a protected class. Employees should not be treated differently because of their gender.

- *Do not tolerate sexual harassment.* Sexual harassment is a form of gender discrimination. Managers should be vigilant to prevent quid pro quo and hostile environment sexual harassment.

- *Do not treat pregnancy or childbirth differently from other disabilities.* The Pregnancy Discrimination Act, which is part of Title VII, requires that pregnant employees be treated the same as other employees. An employer cannot treat pregnant employees less favorably than employees with other temporary disabilities in regard to opportunities to continue to work, making arrangements for the leave, or reinstatement after a leave.

- *Take steps to ensure your work site is free from illegal discrimination.* Develop and strictly enforce an anti-discrimination policy. Sponsor training sessions for all employees on what constitutes illegal discrimination and underscore the company's intolerance of it. Identify one or more persons with whom employees can file complaints and include someone outside the line of employees' supervision, such as a representative of the personnel department. When a complaint is made, react to it promptly by investigating thoroughly and taking appropriate corrective action. Consult the employee who complained before initiating remedial action.

- *Do not discriminate against employees who are 40 years of age or older.* The Age Discrimination in Employment Act (ADEA) renders people age 40 or older a protected class. An employer cannot treat them differently because of their age. A preference for youth is an illegal basis on which to make job decisions unless youth is a business necessity.

- *Abide by the Americans with Disabilities Act (ADA).* Do not discriminate on the basis of disability. The ADA outlaws discrimination against disabled applicants or employees who are able, with or without accommodations, to perform the essential functions of the job. Examples of reasonable accommodations include enlarging doors to accommodate wheelchairs, and modifying schedules to coincide with public transportation. People protected by the ADA include not only those with disabilities, but also those with a past disability and those responsible for the care of a disabled person.

- *Do not make employment decisions based on nonessential functions of a job.* An employer who refuses to hire a qualified disabled person because that person is unable to perform nonessential job functions has violated the ADA.

- *Accurately write job descriptions so they include all essential functions of the job.* Job descriptions are one source of information for identifying the essential functions of a job. To ensure applicants are qualified with or without accommodations to perform the essential functions, and to ensure applicants are not excluded because of inflated descriptions of job responsibilities, the job description should accurately describe the duties of the job.

- *When interviewing a job applicant, do not ask questions about medical conditions or disabilities.* The employer can inquire whether an applicant can perform the essential functions of the job and can ask the applicant to demonstrate the ability to do so. Questions about the person's medical condition, disability, medication, or hospital stays violate the ADA.

- *If employees become disabled, attempt to find them other jobs within the company that they are qualified to perform.* The ADA requires that employers attempt to reassign an employee who becomes disabled while employed.

- *Do not require an applicant to submit to a medical exam prior to offering that person a job.* The ADA precludes an employer from mandating a pre-offer medical exam. A job offer, once made, can be conditional on the results of a medical exam provided all incoming employees are required to submit to such exam.

- *Keep information obtained from a medical exam confidential.* This information cannot be kept in an employee's employment file, but instead must be kept in a separate file. The only people entitled to review it are first-aid personnel, supervisors who need the information to determine necessary restrictions and accommodations, and government officials investigating compliance with the ADA.

- *If your business is accused by an employee of illegal discrimination, investigate promptly and take any needed remedial action.* Whenever a complaint is made, your attorney should be consulted on how best to handle it. Timely corrective action may rectify illegal discrimination and mitigate the outcome.

- *Do not discharge employees or take other adverse job action against them because they complained about illegal discrimination or filed a complaint with the EEOC.* Such a discharge or adverse action is retaliatory and is itself illegal discrimination.

- *Verify the employment status of each employee you hire within three days of the date of employment.* The Immigration Reform and Control Act (IRCA) seeks to minimize the number of illegal aliens employed in this country. Employers are required to examine their worker's employment documents to verify authorization to work in the United States. Any employee who cannot produce the necessary proof within 21 days of employment must be terminated.

- *Do not discriminate against immigrants who are authorized to work in this country.* The IRCA prohibits an employer from refusing to hire a qualified alien on the ground she is not a citizen.

Review Questions

1. What statute imposes a minimum-wage requirement on employers?

2. Name two exceptions to the minimum-wage requirement.

3. How much is an employee entitled to be paid for working in excess of 40 hours a week?

4. Name five protected classes for employment purposes.

5. What is Title VII?

6. To what do the initials EEOC refer?

7. Name four remedies available for a Title VII violation.

8. What must a plaintiff prove to establish a retaliatory discharge?

9. Name two racial groups other than African Americans and Caucasians.

10. Under what circumstance can an employer refuse to hire an applicant who speaks only minimal English?

11. In the category of age, who is included within the protected class under federal law?

12. What are the two types of sexual harassment? Provide an example of each.

13. Name five types of activity that can constitute sexual harassment.

14. In what ways can an employee relay that sexually harassing conduct is unwelcome?

15. What does the Pregnancy Discrimination Act outlaw?

16. To what aspects of employment does the Americans with Disabilities Act apply?

17. What is the difference between essential functions of a job and nonessential functions?

18. What is the significance of a task being deemed essential or nonessential?

19. Can an employer require a disabled applicant to submit to a medical exam before making a job offer?

20. What does the Immigration Reform and Control Act require of an employer? What is the penalty if the employer fails to comply?

21. Why do employers customarily prefer that their employees not unionize? Why do many employees choose to join a union?

Discussion Questions

1. What is the difference between the legal concepts of equal pay and comparable worth?

2. What do you think prompted the laws that impose a minimum age for employment and restrict the hours a young employee can work?

3. Why do you think Congress placed a cap in the Civil Rights Act of 1991 on the amount of compensatory damages a court can award to a plaintiff in most civil rights cases?

4. Why are minor differences in grooming rules for male and female employees acceptable?

5. The dining room manager of a restaurant is hiring servers. A person who walks with a limp applies. The manager is concerned about the applicant's ability to handle the physical demands of the job. What can the manager ask the applicant during the interview, and what can the manager not ask?

6. What defense is available to an employer accused of violating the Pregnancy Discrimination Act? Give an example. Why do you think the legislature included this defense in the statute?

7. What is retaliatory discharge? Why is it illegal?

8. If an employee is assaulted at work by a co-worker, under what theory might the employer be liable? What is the justification for holding the employer liable per that theory?

Application Questions

1. An employer has an aversion to red hair. She refuses to hire anyone with that color hair. Is this illegal discrimination? Why or why not?

2. Lee is opening a Thai restaurant. He refuses to hire anyone who was not born in Thailand as chef, dishwasher, or wait personnel. Is this illegal discrimination against applicants of other nationalities? Why or why not?

3. Marti is an observant Jew and celebrates eight religious holidays that do not coincide with legal holidays. Does Title VII require that her employer give her time off for these holidays? Why or why not?

4. Allison's boss continually makes sexually suggestive comments to her and often brushes against her when she is in his office. She has asked him to stop but he continues. She reported his conduct to the vice president for personnel. He felt she was exaggerating the facts and did not investigate or take any action.

   a. Is the company Allison works for liable for sexual harassment under these circumstances? Why or why not?

   b. What should the vice president have done?

5. Kyle, who is deaf, has applied for a job as a bookkeeper at the Brookside Hotel. The bookkeeper is required to maintain financial records of the business and prepare financial reports for management. The information is obtained primarily from guest invoices, bills, and receipts. Most of the required reports are submitted in written form. The bookkeeper is also required to attend two staff meetings a week at which the general manager orally informs the staff of developments at the hotel. The general manager frequently consults informally with the bookkeeper concerning financial matters.

   a. What accommodations could the hotel make to enable Kyle to handle the job responsibilities?

   b. Will the hotel be obligated to make those accommodations or can it refuse to hire Kyle because of his disability? Why?

6. The Bystone Restaurant, a 25-table family restaurant with a strong business of take-out ice cream, has advertised for a manager. Among the applicants are a woman in a wheelchair with a bachelor's degree in restaurant management and two years of experience as an assistant manager at a similar restaurant, and a man with a master's degree in restaurant management and five years of experience, three as an assistant manager and two as a manager. What is the employer's obligation to the disabled applicant?

7. The Nimark Hotel is hiring a business manager. Of all the applicants, the two most qualified are a citizen of the United States and a citizen of France who is legally authorized to work in this country. According to the Immigration Reform and Control Act, if the two are equally qualified, which one should be offered the job? Why?

8. What risks must an employer address concerning employee blogs?

Websites

Websites that will enhance your understanding of the material in this chapter include:

www.dol.gov This is the federal Department of Labor's site. It contains information on a variety of labor-related issues, including minimum pay, overtime pay, tips, occupational safety and health regulations, the Family and Medical Leave Act, and workplace injuries. The site also contains a list of state labor departments and their addresses, phone numbers, and websites.

www.restaurant.org This is the site of the National Restaurant Association, a trade organization for restaurant owners and managers. Among the employment issues it addresses are tip reporting, new legislation impacting rights of workers, and career information.

www.eeoc.gov This is the site of the Equal Employment Opportunity Commission, the federal agency that enforces discrimination laws. Among the site's features are access to federal laws that prohibit job discrimination, information on how to file a claim, and use of mediation to settle claims.

www.ada.gov This site provides information on the Americans with Disabilities Act and offers guidance. It is created by the U.S. Department of Justice, Civil Rights Division.

www.adata.org/factsheet/accessible-lodging This site provides information and training on the Americans with Disabilities Act.

www.oshadefenseleague.com This is the site of a safety and regulatory consulting firm that provides services in the area of OSHA compliance, workers' compensation claims reduction, and loss control. The site contains compliance guides, safety plans, and information about compliance products.

www.findlaw.com This site contains updates on legal news and links to sites covering many legal topics, including immigration laws and rights of employees.

www.uscis.gov This is the site of the United States Citizenship and Immigration Services (USCIS), a branch of the Department of Homeland Security. USCIS oversees immigration and naturalization policies. The site contains much information about immigration.

CHAPTER 15

Regulation and Licensing

LEARNING OUTCOMES:

- Understand basic laws relating to trademarks, copyrights, and patents
- Learn about antitrust rules
- Know the benefits and drawbacks of franchises
- Comprehend the legal rights and responsibilities of a franchise owner
- Be aware of laws requiring maintenance of a guest registry
- Be knowledgeable about mandated posting of room rates, and consequences of price-gouging
- Understand the process of obtaining and maintaining necessary licenses for the operation of a hospitality business
- Become familiar with zoning laws

KEY TERMS

administrative remedies must be exhausted	group boycott	secondary meaning
ASCAP	license	service mark
antitrust laws	merger	territorial division agreements
BMI	monopoly	territorial restrictions
copyright	per se violations	trademark
dissolution	police power	trademark infringement
divestiture	price discrimination	treble damages
due process	price-fixing agreements	tying arrangement
encroachment	prospectus	variance
exclusive dealing contracts	public domain	vertical price fixing
franchise	resale price-maintenance agreement	victualler's license
franchisee	royalty	zoning
franchisor	rule of reason	

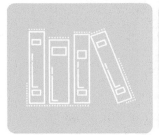   

REGULATIONS

REGULATIONS   **COMPLIANCE**   **LAW**   **PROCEDURE**

Introduction

The law regulates various aspects of the hotel and restaurant business. Throughout this book we have seen numerous circumstances in which the law significantly impacts the manner in which a hotel or restaurant is operated. In this chapter we will see even more examples, including the law of trademarks, copyrights, anti-competitive activities, franchising, registration of guests, rates charged for rooms, recycling, licensing requirements, and zoning.

Regulation of the Marketplace

Trademarks and Service Marks

Various aspects of successful businesses are sometimes emulated by other companies desiring to trade on the familiar name, style, and image portrayed to the public. The reason for this is obvious. If you decided to open a fast-food restaurant specializing in hamburgers, you would likely make considerably more money if you called it McDonald's rather than, say, Karen's Hamburgers. However, the name McDonald's, when used in the fast-food industry, is a trademark, which means the owner has the exclusive right to its use. If you use the name without the owner's permission, you will be illegally infringing on McDonald's trademark.

A **trademark** is any word, name, symbol (such as the Nike "swoosh"), or device adopted and used by a manufacturer or merchant to identify its goods and distinguish them from products sold or manufactured by others. A **service mark** is similar to a trademark except that it identifies services rather than goods. A company can obtain a trademark or service mark in its name or logo simply by using it in connection with its business. The company can also register the mark with the federal Patent and Trademark Office located in Washington, D.C., which notifies other potential users that the name has been appropriated. The ownership of the mark, however, is acquired by use alone and is unaffected by failure to register. When two companies are using the same name, the test to determine who has the superior right to the name is who used it first.

© Wolfilser/Shutterstock.com

A business or individual who adopts another's trademark or service mark in connection with a similar product or service in the same market area without permission will be liable for trademark infringement. For example, Burger King has a trademark on the name "Chicken Tenders" for battered and fried chicken breast pieces. A defendant who sold a chicken breast meat product under the same name was thereby liable for **trademark infringement.**[1]

The law on trademarks and service marks is found in the Lanham Act, a federal statute that prohibits promoting goods or services by one person under the guise that they are the products or offerings of another. The statute states:

trademark
Any word, name, symbol, or device adopted and used by a manufacturer or merchant to identify its goods and distinguish them from goods sold or manufactured by others.

service mark
Any word, name, symbol, or device adopted and used by an organization to identify its services and distinguish them from services provided by others.

trademark infringement
Use of another company's business name or logo without permission.

---

[1] *Burger King Corporation v. Pilgrim's Pride Corporation*, 934 F.Supp. 425 (Fla. 1996)

[A]ny person who shall affix, apply, or annex, or use in connection with any… services… a false designation of origin, or any false description or representation, including words or other symbols tending falsely to describe or represent the same… shall be liable to a civil action by any person… who believes that he is or is likely to be damaged by the use of any such false description or representation.[2]

Proving Infringement

To prove a trademark infringement case, the plaintiff must show two things: (1) ownership of a distinctive mark or name, and (2) defendant's use of a similar mark or name is likely to cause confusion as to the source of the products or services. The test for infringement is whether the second user's adoption of the name is confusingly similar to the original user—that is, will consumers be diverted by the name from doing business with the first user and do business with the second instead? The more alike are the names and products being offered by the two companies, the more probable a trademark infringement will exist.

Similarity in names and services was the basis for a finding of infringement in an Illinois case. The trademark owner used the name "Delta" in its hotel, motel, and restaurant business. A new restaurant sought to use the name "The Delta Café." The court noted the similarity of the services offered by each party (restaurant operation) and also that the dominant element in the cafe's name (Delta) was identical to the trademarked name.[3]

Another infringement lawsuit was brought against a restaurant named "Cafe Renaissance" that opened in the same city as an existing cafe with the exact same name. The court found infringement notwithstanding that the plaintiff cafe was open only for breakfast and lunch, occupied only 240 square feet, and had a large take-out service, whereas the defendant was a 4,000 square-foot dinner-only restaurant that also provided entertainment.[4] A hotel named Econo Studios Inn & Suites was found to infringe on the trademark of Econo Lodge Inn & Suites.[5] On the other hand, a court rejected Econo Lodge's infringement claim brought against a hotel named "Econotel" located directly across the street from an Econo Lodge.[6]

The script used to promote a name can add to the likelihood of confusion. In an Illinois case the court ruled illegal the use of the word *Americana* by a Chicago hotel company that adopted that name without permission from a luxury hotel that had a trademark on the same name. Said the court, "Not only did the defendant pirate the name, but it also adopted plaintiff's fanciful presentation of the name in all details, namely, 'americana' all in lowercase letters with a white line extending through the first *a* and a five-point star as the dot over the *i*."[7]

---

[2] 15 USC § 1125(a)
[3] *In Re Dixie Restaurants, Inc.*, 105 F.3d 1405 (Ill.1997)
[4] *Cicone v. Cafe Renaissance, Inc.*, 2000 WL 1725483 (R.I. 2000)
[5] *Choice Hotels v. Zeal*, 135 F.Supp.3d 451 (S.C. 2015)
[6] *Choice Hotels v. Kaushik*, 147 F.Supp.2d 1242 (Ala. 2000)
[7] *Tisch Hotels, Inc., v. Americana Inn, Inc.*, 350 F.2d 609 (Ill. 1965)

Likelihood of Confusion

The required element of likelihood of confusion can be proven in one of two ways: (a) by showing actual confusion—that is, would-be customers who were misled; or (b) by evidence establishing a strong potential for confusion. Difficulties in obtaining evidence of actual confusion make its absence in a case not dispositive and generally not noteworthy. An eight-factor test is used to determine likelihood of confusion and includes the following: (1) strength of the mark (how long it has been used; how much advertising has been done; how familiar consumers are with the name); (2) likeness of the goods of the first user and alleged infringer; (3) similarity of the marks used by each; (4) evidence of actual confusion; (5) marketing done by the parties of the marks; (6) degree of care exercised by consumers when purchasing the item (confusion is less likely where buyers exercise care and precision in their purchases, such as for expensive or sophisticated items); (7) defendant's intent in adopting the mark; and (8) likelihood plaintiff will expand its operations.[8]

Likelihood of confusion was found in an Oregon case brought by the well-known coffee-seller Starbucks. Defendant used the name "Sambuck's Coffeehouse" for a business that sold coffee and related products. Starbucks sued. The court noted the defendant's name was very similar to Starbucks's, the defendant's products were competitive with Starbucks's, and the marketing channels used by the two companies were the same. Further, because coffee is a low-priced item, consumers exercise only limited attention to the business name, increasing the possibilities for confusion. The evidence at trial established that defendant had adopted the name knowing of plaintiff's trademark and intending to mislead the public. For all of these reasons the court determined that defendant infringed Starbucks's trademark.[9]

Penalties

Penalties for infringing a trademark include an injunction prohibiting further infringement, return of profits diverted from the trademark owner, and fines. The effects of an injunction are illustrated in a Connecticut case. The Marathon Oil Company of Ohio had registered the name "Gas Town" as a trademark. Eighteen months later, a corporation with 200 service stations in New England, New York, and Louisiana used "Gas Town" as the name for its stations. The Marathon Oil Company sued for trademark infringement. A federal court issued an injunction barring the second corporation from using the name and ordered it to remove the Gas Town signs from its 200 stations. The infringer thus had to abandon its investment in promoting the name Gas Town, and had to pay for new signs and for advertising to introduce the public to its new name—no small expense.[10]

A plaintiff in a trademark infringement case is entitled to collect damages for losses incurred as a result of the infringement. If plaintiff is unable to prove the amount of its loss, plaintiff may be entitled to *statutory damages*—a sum of money defen-

---

[8] *Automotive Gold, Inc., v. Volkswagen of America, Inc.*, 457 F.3d 1062 (Ariz. 2006)
[9] *Starbucks Corp. v. Lundberg*, 2005 WL 3183858 (Ore. 2005)
[10] *Gas Town, Inc. of Delaware v. Gas Town*, 331 F.Supp. 626 (Conn. 1971)

dant must pay authorized by statute rather than based on plaintiff's actual loss. The purpose of statutory damages is both to compensate the plaintiff and deter defendant from future wrongdoing. The statute provides a range the court can order; the court determines the amount in a given case.

Prior to adopting a trade name, a business can and should conduct a trademark search on a registry maintained by the U.S. Patent and Trademark Office. The registry, accessible by computer, will disclose whether the desired name is already in use.

Case Example 15-1 illustrates the application of many of these rules.

CASE EXAMPLE 15-1

Carlo Bay Enterprise, Inc. v. Two Amigo Restaurant, Inc.

2014 WL 6886053 (Fla., 2014)

Plaintiff Carlo Bay Interprise, Inc. (Carlo Bay) is the owner and operator of Club Prana, a Latin-themed bar, nightclub, and restaurant in Ybor City. In furtherance of this venture, Carlo Bay owns the federal and state service marks for CLUB PRANA. Carlo Bay also owns the name "Club Prana," under which it operates its business.

Carlo Bay contends that Defendants used its "Prana" name in relation to their nightclub and restaurant—Prana Restaurant and Lounge—without authorization or permission from Carlo Bay. Carlo Bay avers that Prana Restaurant & Lounge utilizes the same business model as that of Club Prana, specifically, Prana Restaurant & Lounge is a Spanish-themed bar, nightclub, lounge, and restaurant located in Sarasota, Florida, less than an hour away from Club Prana. Carlo Bay submits that it sent Defendants two letters requesting that they cease and desist their unauthorized use of its Prana name. Nevertheless, Defendants continued to operate Prana Restaurant & Lounge.

Carlo Bay initiated this action against Defendants for trademark infringement. . . . Defendants failed to timely respond to the complaint. Carlo Bay filed for entry of default judgment against Defendants. . . .

The federal statute that proscribes trademark infringement reads in relevant part: "Any person who shall, without the consent of the registrant, use in commerce any reproduction, counterfeit, copy or colorable imitation of a registered mark in connection with the sale, offering for sale, distribution or advertising, of any goods or services on or in connection with which such use is likely to cause confusion, or to cause mistake or to deceive shall be liable in a civil action by the registrant for the remedies hereinafter provided" (15 USC 114[1][a]).

Thus, to succeed on a trademark infringement claim, a plaintiff must prove that: 1) its valid mark was used in commerce by the defendant without consent, and 2) the unauthorized use was likely to cause confusion, to cause mistake, or to deceive.

Carlo Bay provides that it is the registered owner of the CLUB PRANA mark. Furthermore, Carlo Bay has produced a certificate of registration issued by the United States Patent and Trademark Office which serves as prima facie evidence of the validity of the registered mark and of Carlo Bay's ownership and exclusive right to use this mark in commerce. . . . Carlo Bay never consented to Defendants' use of the mark; in fact, Carlo Bay sent Defendants two letters requesting that they cease and desist their unauthorized use of its Prana name.

Proof of likelihood of confusion is the sine qua non in actions for trademark infringement. Determination of likelihood of confusion requires analysis of the following seven factors: 1) type of mark, 2) similarity of mark, 3) similarity of the products or services the marks represent, 4) similarity of the parties' retail outlets and customers, 5) similarity of advertising media used, 6) defendant's intent, and 7) actual confusion. . . .

In this case, Carlo Bay has sufficiently alleged that Defendants' Prana Restaurant & Lounge is likely to cause consumer confusion. In particular, with respect to the third factor, Carlo Bay alleges that Defendants operate a Latin-themed restaurant, bar, lounge and club, that uses the name "Prana." Carlo Bay submits that Defendants have intentionally used the "Prana" name to deceive or confuse the public at large in an attempt to use Plaintiff's well established name and reputation. Thus, there is a strong likelihood of confusion in the present case because consumers may associate Plaintiff's Club Prana with the Prana Club and Restaurant operated by Defendants.

In regards to the fourth factor, Carlo Bay further contends that both establishments cater to the same clientele, which could lead consumers to believe that Defendants' establishment is related or affiliated to Carlo Bay's business. Specifically, Carlo Bay submits: The use of said name, by Defendants, has caused massive confusion, mistakes and deception. Plaintiff's CLUB PRANA is a popular night club and restaurant in Tampa, Florida that has been operating in business for over 13 years. Defendants have and are marketing via radio stations, festivals and Facebook in Tampa and targeting patrons in the same marketing area as Plaintiff's CLUB PRANA. Patrons are highly confused and under the impression that Defendant's business is another location of Plaintiff's CLUB PRANA.

This contention is supported by the fact that Carlo Bay's Club Prana is located in Tampa, Florida while Defendants' Prana Restaurant & Lounge is located less than an hour away in Sarasota, Florida. Therefore, the likelihood of confusion is apparent. Accordingly, Carlo Bay has met its burden as to its claims for trademark infringement under Federal and Florida law. . . .

Carlo Bay seeks an award of $2,000,0000 against Defendants, noting that Defendants willfully and without any regard for the rights of Carlo Bay, continued to infringe on the Registered Mark of Carlo Bay, despite the issuance of multiple cease and desist letters. . . .

In determining an appropriate award of statutory damages, the Court must strike a balance between permitting a windfall for the plaintiff and emphasizing to the defendant that the trademark laws and court proceedings are not mere incidental costs to doing business in the profitable counterfeit trade. The court finds Carlo Bay's request for $2,000,000 in statutory damages vastly inappropriate in this case. . . .

The Court is mindful that Defendants have chosen to default rather than to cooperate in providing particular records from which to assess the value of the infringing business. Additionally, the Court finds that Defendants' infringing conduct was indeed willful. These considerations warrant an award above the statutory minimum. . . .

The Court finds that statutory damages in the amount of $30,000 is an appropriate, just, and reasonable award.

ORDERED: Enter Judgment in favor of plaintiff in the amount of $30,000.

Geographic Proximity

Remember, the test for infringement is likelihood of confusion. Absent a likelihood of confusion, no infringement exists. If the trademark owner and second user do not compete in the same markets, the public is unlikely to confuse one for the other. In such circumstances, the use of the mark by the newcomer may not be illegal. A plaintiff in a case operated a chain of restaurants under the name "Steak & Brew." He attempted to prevent the defendant, which operated a restaurant named "Beef & Brew," from using the word *Brew* in its name. The defendant operated only one restaurant, which was in Rock Island, Illinois; the closest restaurant in the plaintiff's chain was 100 miles away. The facts in the case established that the defendant had innocently adopted the name without knowledge of the plaintiff's use, and that "Steak & Brew" was unknown in the Rock Island, Illinois area. The court stated that ordinarily the use and registration of a trademark will bar a subsequent business from using the same name. However, when two parties employ the same mark on goods of the same class, but they operate in remote and separate markets, the second user may legally continue to use the name.[11] An exception to this rule is a situation where it appears that the second adopter has selected the mark to benefit from the reputation of the first user or to forestall the expansion of the first user's business.

Similarly, two companies independently and concurrently developed several restaurants under the name "John Q's." The plaintiff, with a restaurant in Cleveland, could not prevent the defendant from opening one in Cincinnati, 240 miles away. The plaintiff failed to present evidence that the restaurant in Cincinnati would be patronized by customers of the Cleveland restaurant, or any other evidence that confusion would result. Further, there was no evidence that the defendant attempted to deceive the public or capitalize on the plaintiff's name.[12]

Sometimes even businesses in close proximity can coexist with comparable names. In a Pennsylvania case the court determined that a restaurant named "Positano Coast by Aldo Lamberti" (Positano Coast) did not violate the trademark of "Positano Ristorante" notwithstanding that the two eateries were located within nine miles of each other. The court noted that the term *Positano* is geographic and therefore more difficult to protect than a fanciful (made-up) word. Positano Ristorante had not advertised the name much, thus limiting the number of people who knew of the restaurant and who might confuse it with Positano Coast. Twenty other restaurants across the country use the term Positano in their name. The evidence established only vague, limited anecdotal incidences of customer confusion. Further, 90 percent of Positano Ristorante's business consisted of repeat customers, none of whom had been diverted by Positano Coast.[13]

A different outcome resulted in a case in which plaintiff opened a "gastropub," essentially a bar with high-quality food options, in San Diego, California, named Duck Dive. The facility is located very close to San Diego's Pacific Beach, and

---

[11] *Steak & Brew, Inc., v. Beef & Brew Restaurant, Inc.*, 370 F.Supp. 1030 (Ill. 1974)

[12] *Stouffer Corp. v. Winegardner & Hammons, Inc.*, 502 F.Supp. 232 (Ohio 1980)

[13] *Lamberti v. Positano Ristorante*, 2005 WL 627975 (Pa. 2005)

derives its name from the surfing term "duck dive," which is a method of diving beneath a breaking wave with a surfboard. Defendants opened the "Duck Dive Gastropub" in Malibu, California, two and a half hours by car from San Diego. Press reports and multiple patrons confused the gastropubs for each other. Said the court, "The test of trademark ownership is priority of use. The first to use a mark is deemed the senior user and has the right to enjoin junior users from using confusingly similar marks in the same industry and market or within the senior user's natural zone of expansion. The fact that others may use the terms 'Duck Dive' with respect to art, clothing, or even food services thousands of miles from Plaintiff's establishment has no bearing on Plaintiff's ability to obtain trademark protection in its industry and market, within which Plaintiff is undisputedly the senior user of the Duck Dive mark." Thus, plaintiff was entitled to preliminary injunction, an interim remedy that suggests the plaintiff's case is strong.[14]

Descriptive Terms

Another reason the court found no infringement in the Steak & Brew case is that the word *brew* is descriptive and in common use. Therefore, it is not subject to exclusive appropriation. Ordinarily a company cannot gain trademark rights in a word that is part of the English language and commonly used. Such a word could achieve trademark protection only upon proof that it attained a **secondary meaning,** that is, the public identifies the term or phrase with the company using it. Thus, for example, Kentucky Fried Chicken could not prevent another restaurant from using the word *chicken* or *fried chicken* in its name. However, the public has come to recognize the phrase *Kentucky Fried Chicken* as the former name of a chain of fast-food restaurants. Therefore, no other company could name itself Kentucky Fried Chicken.

secondary meaning
A doctrine of trademark law that affords protection to an otherwise unprotectable mark when the mark, through advertising and other promotions, has come to be associated in the public's mind with a particular producer.

Public Domain

According to trademark law, a valuable trademark may be lost if the word becomes a part of the language—that is, used in common speech. When this happens, the word becomes part of the **public domain,** meaning it has become so commonly used that it loses its trademark protection. Over the years, this has happened to such notable trademarks as Aspirin, Frisbee, Rollerblade, Kleenex, Linoleum, Escalator, Cellophane, and Kerosene. In each instance, what began as a trademark ended as a frequently used word in normal parlance. Doubtless, the English language has been enriched, but the manufacturer is the poorer—penalized, ironically, because its product became too popular.

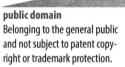

public domain
Belonging to the general public and not subject to patent copyright or trademark protection.

How does the law determine that a trademark has gone into the public domain? While the point in time is rarely clear, the main prerequisite is that the public has come to consider the word as the generic name for the thing itself, rather than as an indication of a specific manufacturer or that manufacturer's specific product. For example, a court held that "Toll House," at one time a trademark for a cookie made by Nestlé, was no longer entitled to trademark protection because so many

---

14 *Duck Dive v. Heydari*, 2014 WL 1271220 (Calif., 2014).

consumers used that term to describe a kind of cookie rather than a specific cookie made by Nestle.[15] For the same reason, "Shredded Wheat" lost its status as a trademark.[16]

Trademark Registration

We have seen that a trademark can be registered with the federal Patent and Trademark Office. Although registration is not necessary for trademark protection since rights accrue from mere use of a name, registration helps to discourage unauthorized use and makes a trademark infringement case easier to prove. Additionally, registration helps to protect the mark from infringement nationwide.

The process of registration includes submission of various documents to the Patent and Trademark Office; publication of the proposed mark by that office to alert others with similar names; opportunity for objection to registration by others who might already be using the same or a similar name; and, if there is no objection, or if there is but the applicant convinces the Patent and Trademark Office that it is nonetheless entitled to registration, issuance of a registration certificate that completes the registration process.

Once a trademark is registered, the owner should include with the name, usually after the last letter, the following insignia: ® (the capital letter "R" in a circle). This alerts the public that the word is a registered trademark and cannot be used by others. Most states have registration procedures that protect a business' name on a statewide basis. The process is easier and less expensive than federal registration. Which registration is appropriate depends on the geographical area in which the business anticipates using the name. If the company's owners foresee opening other similar businesses with the same name in more than one state, or if they anticipate franchising the operation (see discussion later in this chapter on franchising), federal registration should be pursued.

One case that encompasses many trademark principles is *Holiday Inns, Inc. v. Holiday Inn,* presented as Case Example 15-2. The defendant, who was not associated with the well-known Holiday Inn chain, was the first user of the name "Holiday Inn" in Myrtle Beach, South Carolina. It undertook a course of action calculated to associate itself in the public eye with the plaintiff, the owner of the trademark in the remainder of the country, intentionally misleading the traveling public. The case contains historical background on a venerable company in the hotel industry, states the test of what constitutes trademark infringement, and discusses the rights of the traveling public not to be deceived. As the case suggests, the plaintiff Holiday Inn chain was, at the time of the case, and continues to be one of the biggest and most prominent hotel chains in the industry.

---

[15] *Nestle Co., Inc. v. Chester's Market, Inc.*, 571 F.Supp. 763 (Conn. 1983), rev'd on other grounds, 756 F.2d 280 (1985)

[16] *Kellogg Co. v. National Biscuit Co.*, 305 U.S. 111, 59 S.Ct. 109 (1988)

CASE EXAMPLE 15-2

Holiday Inns, Inc. v. Holiday Inn

364 F.Supp. 775 (S.C. 1973)

This action is brought by the plaintiff, Holiday Inns, Inc.… the largest company in the restaurant and lodging business in the United States, hereinafter referred to as "the Chain." The suit is for… service mark infringement against the defendant Holiday Inn, a South Carolina corporation that operates a motel and restaurant at Myrtle Beach, South Carolina, under the name of Holiday Inn. This defendant has counterclaimed, alleging [trademark] infringement and unfair competition, and seeks cancellation of certain of plaintiff's [trademark] registrations… .

This matter was heard before the court without a jury… [T]he court makes the following finding of facts:

1. The plaintiff Holiday Inns, Inc …is a corporation… founded in 1952 and since that time has grown to the point that it is now the largest factor in the restaurant and lodging business in the United States.… The Plaintiff's principal business is providing restaurant and lodging services operating under the name Holiday Inn. These services are provided either through company owned facilities or facilities franchised by the Chain. At present the Chain has a facility in almost every major city in the United States, including 33 in the State of South Carolina. The Chain presently owns or franchises approximately 1,300 facilities in the United States.

2. The Chain's original concept was to establish a network of motels and restaurants spanning the entire country upon which the traveling public could rely in obtaining satisfactory services. The facilities affiliated with the Chain are readily recognizable, with quality controls exercised by the Chain and many similar services available at all facilities, such as free use of baby cribs, no charge for children under 12 when sleeping in the room with the parent, kennels for pets, etc.

3. The Chain had developed and prominently displays on each facility a large sign, generally referred to as the "great sign." This sign is one of the major features by which travelers generally identify a motel as belonging to or affiliated with the Chain. This sign is quite large, but in some cities smaller versions are used in order to comply with local zoning restrictions. The sign has a green background with the name HOLIDAY INN in large distinctive script lettering, a large star at the top and smaller stars by the name HOLIDAY INN, a large orange arrow starting at the bottom of the sign and running in a sort of semicircle with the point indicating the location of the facility. There is always an attraction panel near the bottom of the sign.…

5. In the promotion of its services, the plaintiff also uses certain slogans, one of which is YOUR HOST FROM COAST TO COAST.…

7. The above registered service marks of plaintiff are well known to the American traveling public. They have been extensively used and advertised in promoting plaintiff's services and the services of its franchisees. Numerous advertisements have appeared in magazines, newspapers, on radio and television and billboards, as well as a house magazine and a directory of member facilities of which more than ten million are printed and distributed each year.…

8. The defendant Holiday Inn was incorporated in 1960 (Emphasis Added)....

10. The defendant's facility grew over the years to its present 87 units....

12. The plaintiff first learned of defendant's facility in 1956 when a franchisee of plaintiff, who was constructing a motel facility in Myrtle Beach, received a letter from defendant's lawyer objecting to the proposed usage of HOLIDAY INN within the Myrtle Beach area. Plaintiff's franchisee obtained permission from plaintiff to operate the facility within the plaintiff's system under the name HOLIDAY LODGE. This facility has been operated continuously since 1956.... A great sign was erected in front of the facility presenting the words HOLIDAY LODGE in large script lettering above the words HOLIDAY INNS OF AMERICA SYSTEM....

15. In 1968 the defendant's general manager ordered a sign constructed and placed in its parking lot immediately across the street from its facility. He requested the sign maker to design a sign which would resemble, but not exactly duplicate, the plaintiff's "great sign" and delivered to the sign maker one of plaintiff's brochures to use as a guide.... [T]he signs are so similar that the traveling public would be easily confused and upon seeing defendant's sign would conclude that it was a franchisee of plaintiff or affiliated with it. The colors of the two signs are almost identical. The use of stars, the big arrow, the attraction panel, and the script of Holiday Inn are so similar that the court can only conclude that defendant erected his sign with the intent and purpose of infringing the rights of the plaintiff and unfairly competing with it....

23. Confusion has developed as a result of the similarity of names and there have been mix-ups in bills, letters, reservations, deliveries, etc....

26. ...[C]onfusion has been deliberately and systematically nurtured by the defendant in an effort to profit from the national recognition and goodwill of the plaintiff....

Conclusions of Law

2. Upon review of the evidence the court is compelled to conclude that the defendant's course of conduct proves it guilty of...service mark infringement....

3. The test for trademark infringement... is whether... imitation of the registered mark is "likely to cause confusion, or to cause mistake, or to deceive." The test is to be applied with regard to the effect of the marks on an ordinary purchaser having an indefinite recollection of the mark to which he has been exposed on a previous occasion. [T]he sign erected by the defendant in 1968 is substantially identical to the plaintiff's "great sign" and although differences are obvious when pictures of the two signs are compared side by side, the effect of the defendant's sign was obvious and was likely to cause confusion, mistake or to deceive the public....

4. The script form in which defendant presents its name Holiday Inn is substantially identical to the distinctive script used by plaintiff.... Although there may be slight differences in the location of the stars, the overall effect is such as is likely to cause confusion, mistake and to deceive the public.

5. Defendant's slogan, YOUR HOST ON THE COAST and YOUR HOST WHILE AT MYRTLE BEACH, differs from the plaintiff's slogan, YOUR HOST FROM COAST TO COAST, and if these

slogans alone were the basis of the plaintiff's complaint, this court would not find them to be an infringement. However, when considered with the other acts of the defendant... the court must conclude that the use of these slogans by the defendant was an effort to trade upon the goodwill of the plaintiff and represent an infringement of its protected mark, YOUR HOST FROM COAST TO COAST.

6. Although intent is not a necessary element of trademark infringement, there can be no question of defendant's intent to infringe upon the plaintiff's marks....

7. The plaintiff's [trade]marks are famous throughout the United States and are becoming well known in many other countries. Great effort and expenditure of funds by the plaintiff have not only built up its successful business but have created in the mind of the public strong recognition of its name and service marks.... These property rights of the plaintiff are entitled to broad protection....

10. The defendant has asserted and this court finds that it is the prior user of the name Holiday Inn in Myrtle Beach, South Carolina.... The defendant is entitled to continue the use of the name Holiday Inn within the city limits of Myrtle Beach, South Carolina, but this court will not prevent the plaintiff from operating its facilities now known as Holiday Lodge... in Myrtle Beach....

Now, Therefore, It Is Ordered, Adjudged and Decreed:

1. The defendant [is] hereby perpetually enjoined and restrained from:

   a. Using either directly or indirectly a script identical to or any colorable imitation of plaintiff's script Holiday Inn on the outside of its building, on any billboards or on any advertising material.

   b. Using directly or indirectly its version of plaintiff's "great sign" or any colorable imitation thereof.

   c. Using directly or indirectly the slogan YOUR HOST WHILE AT MYRTLE BEACH or YOUR HOST ON THE COAST or any colorable imitation thereof.

   d. Using directly or indirectly any sign, script, slogan or star design, color combination or other indicia of plaintiff that suggests or tends to suggest a connection with the plaintiff.

2. The defendant shall have ninety (90) days from the date of this order to comply and defendant's attorney within such time shall submit to the court evidence of compliance.

3. The defendant has the right to continue using the name Holiday Inn within the town of Myrtle Beach, South Carolina....

And it is so ordered.

Trademarks and the Internet: Cybersquatting

For trademark purposes, the Internet is viewed as an extension of the real world and not a separate universe. Thus, the owner of a trademark in real time also owns rights to the name in cyberspace.

The Venetian Casino Resort owned 15 trademark registrations using the term Venetian and Venetian Casino. An interloper registered the domain name "venetiangold.com" and six other domain names that included the word Venetian and Venetian Casino, which he linked to a website offering worldwide casino-type gaming services on the Internet. The resort sued. The court held for the casino, noting that the domain names reserved by defendant were confusingly similar to the resort's trademarks; Internet users could mistakenly conclude defendant's sites were endorsed by the casino; and defendant evinced a bad faith intent to profit from the resort's marks.[17]

Copyright Basics

copyright
The exclusive right of a creator or other copyright owner to reproduce and license (authorize) the reproduction of the following literature, art, music, drama, sculpture, choreography, motion pictures, computer software, and other audiovisual works including broadcasts of sporting events.

A **copyright** is the exclusive right of an author or other copyright owner to reproduce and license (authorize) the reproduction of literature, art, music, drama, sculpture, motion pictures, computer software, and other audiovisual works including broadcasts of sporting events.

Generally, the copyright is initially owned by the creator of the work. The rights associated with a copyright are separate from the work itself. Indeed, the artist can sell the work but retain the copyright. For example, a restaurant owner who

enzozo/Shutterstock.com

---

17 *Venetian Casino Resort, LLC v. Venetiangold.com*, 380 F.Supp.2d 737 (Va. 2005)

purchases a copyrighted painting but not the copyright can display the picture but cannot, for example, reproduce it onto placemats without permission of the copyright owner. Normally, the copyright owner will charge a fee for the permission, thus enabling the owner to benefit repeatedly from the creative talent utilized in the work. If, however, the artist sells the copyright, the purchaser becomes the copyright owner and can reproduce the work without further authorization.

A copyright comes into existence automatically when the work is created. Prior to March 1, 1989, the law required the copyright owner to place a copyright notice on the work when it was first made available to the public in order to retain the copyright. Failure to include the notice resulted in loss of the copyright. The required notice consisted of three parts: (1) the letter "c" in a circle ©, (2) the name of the copyright owner, and (3) the year of first publication. Due to a change in the law, the copyright notice is no longer necessary, although it is strongly recommended to discourage unauthorized copying.

Illegal Satellite Reception

An area of copyright law that has been the subject of much litigation in the hospitality field is the use of satellite dishes to receive and exhibit audiovisual programming without the permission of the program's copyright owner. Such use infringes on the copyright of the programs. In one case a Holiday Inn was sued for copyright infringement by various cable stations including Home Box Office, Inc. (HBO), ESPN, Showtime, and The Movie Channel, Inc. The hotel had installed a satellite system enabling it to receive copyrighted programming without paying for it and without anyone's permission. The Holiday Inn in turn offered to its guests the opportunity to view the programming in their rooms for a fee. No part of the proceeds was paid to the cable stations. The stations claimed the interception and exhibition of the copyrighted programs without permission constituted copyright infringement. The court agreed and issued an injunction against the hotel requiring it to stop.[18]

© arogant/Shutterstock.com

Another case involved the satellite interception by several bars of a blacked-out football game. The National Football League (NFL) customarily contracts with the television networks for the broadcast of its games. The contract typically states that if a game is not sold out 72 hours before the start, it cannot be broadcast within 75 miles of the home team's field. (This rule was suspended by the NFL for the 2015-16 season. Future application of the rule is uncertain.) The defendant bar owners used satellite dishes to receive transmissions of the blacked-out games without the approval of the NFL, which owned the copyright. The bar owners were thus able to exhibit the blacked-out games to their patrons. The NFL sued the bars. The court held the unapproved exhibition of the copyrighted games constituted an unauthorized reproduction of the work and copyright infringement. The court issued an injunction against the bars.[19]

18 *Home Box Office, Inc. v. Corinth Motel, Inc.*, 647 F.Supp. 1186 (Miss. 1986)
19 *National Football League v. McBee and Bruno's, Inc.*, 792 F.2d 726 (Mo. 1986)

Another basis on which to pursue a business that exhibits television programming without authority is the Communications Act, a federal law that prohibits the interception of cable or satellite transmissions without authority from the sender of the transmission.

Pay-for-view programming requires viewers to pay a fee to obtain access to a show. As illustrated in Case Example 15-3, a bar or restaurant that receives access without payment of the fee and enables its customers to view the programming does so illegally.

CASE EXAMPLE 15-3

J&J Sports Productions, Inc. v. Orellana

2013 WL 3341001 (Calif., 2013)

On November 9, 2012, Plaintiff filed its complaint against Defendant alleging unlawful interception, receiving, and exhibiting of "Manny Pacquiao v. Juan Manuel Marquex III WBO Welterweight Championship Fight Program (the "Program"), which was telecast on November 12, 2011. Plaintiff was the exclusive commercial distributor of the program.

Restaurant Santa Fe is a Mexican restaurant in the rural community of Pixley in Tulare County [California]. It has an estimated capacity of 80 to 100 patrons. On the evening of the broadcast, more than 75 people were present. The restaurant had two televisions, both of which were playing the fight. One was 19 inches, and the other was a 24-inch flatscreen. . . .

Plaintiff claims unauthorized reception of cable services and also conversion, that is, Defendant tortuously obtained possession of the program and wrongfully converted it for her own benefit. Plaintiff alleges that these acts were willful and intentionally designed to harm Plaintiff and subject it to economic distress. . . .

Plaintiff requests $110,000 representing the $10,000 maximum statutory damages and the $100,000 maximum enhancement for a willful violation. Plaintiff also requests $2,200.00, the licensing fee for the program for establishments the size of Restaurant Santa Fe, for the tort of conversion . . .

Under California law, the elements of conversion are: (1) ownership or right to possession of the property; (2) wrongful disposition [by defendant] of that property right; and (3) monetary damages. Because the license fee for an establishment the size of Restaurant Santa Fe would have been $2,200.00, Plaintiff is entitled to $2,200.00 in compensatory damages for the tort of conversion.

Defendants are liable for unauthorized interception and reception of cable television programming. Statutory damages range from $1,000 to no more than $10,000. . . .

The Court has the discretion to increase the damages award by up to $100,000 if the violation was willful and committed for purposes of direct or indirect commercial advantage or gain. . . .

Plaintiff contends that he is entitled to enhanced damages even though he alleges nothing more than that Defendants aired the program. Although Restaurant Santa Fe was almost full (or three-quarters full assuming a 100-person capacity), Defendant did not impose a cover charge. Plaintiff does not contend that food or drink prices were increased. Defendant did not advertise the program. Plaintiff does not allege that any patrons were present primarily to watch the program rather than to patronize the restaurant. . .

Awarding the statutory maximum is inappropriate "in the absence of unusual or particularly egregious circumstances under which a defendant broadcast the fight." Nothing in the record suggests that Defendant experienced any significant "commercial advantage or private financial gain" as a result of airing the program. . . . In light of these facts, imposing the maximum statutory damages and enhancement would be inappropriate.

This Court recommends only basic statutory damages for Defendant's [unauthorized interception and reception of cable television programming].. . . . judgment should be entered in this action against Defendants in the amount of $5,300 for unauthorized interception and $2,200 for the tort of conversion. . . . .

It is so ordered.

QUESTION

1. Do you think the court fairly assessed the issue of enhanced damages? Why or why not?

In a related factual situation, a bar that had not paid a required pay-for-view fee exhibited a videotape of a restricted boxing match that had been made and brought to the bar by a patron who apparently had paid to view the match at home. The tavern was sued for violation of the Communications Act and found liable.[20]

We learn from these cases that companies in the business of selling pay-for-view rights regularly send investigators to bars and restaurants at the time restricted programming is broadcast to determine if the business is illegally exhibiting the limited-access show. A sports bar or like establishment seeking to attract customers by showing restricted events must first obtain the necessary license and pay appropriate fees. Failure to do so will likely result in liability leading to payment of damages, fines, attorney's fees for the opposing party (in addition to one's own), and an injunction.

In numerous cases, an investigator visited a bar during a pay-for-view boxing match, violations were discovered, lawsuits were commenced, and the defendant taverns failed to serve an answer. As we learned in Chapter 2, the result was a default judgment against the bars entitling the plaintiff to damages. It is likely

---

[20] *Kingvision Pay Per View, Ltd., v. 900 Club*, 1996 WL 496600 (Ill. 1996)

that the defendants' default was related to the absence of justification for their actions.[21]

Music Performances

Many restaurants and hotels offer musical entertainment. The music may be live, on a jukebox, or presented by a disc jockey. Live presentations range from a single performer on weekends only, to a band that plays every night of the week. Most music is copyrighted. During any performance, the musicians often play the music of many different copyright owners. Songs played by a disc jockey or on a jukebox likewise are probably copyrighted. The legal responsibility to obtain permission to play copyrighted songs rests with the restaurant or club, not the band or disc jockey. How does the restaurant or hotel know from whom permission must be obtained and how can it manage the many different authorizations that may be required? While at first it may appear that obtaining permissions can be very complicated, a system has been developed that streamlines the process.

ASCAP
American Society of Composers, Authors, and Publishers, an organization that collects and distributes copyright fees.

BMI Broadcast Music, Inc.
An organization that collects and distributes copyright fees for its members.

license
Legal document giving official permission to do something

royalty
A payment made to a composer for the sale of copies or performance of their work.

Most owners of copyrights on musical compositions belong to one of three associations that collect copyright fees for their members. Hotels and restaurants need only deal with these organizations and not with each composer individually. The two main organizations are the American Society of Composers, Authors, and Publishers (**ASCAP**), and Broadcast Music, Inc. (**BMI**). Both **license** (authorize for a fee) the public performance rights of its members' copyrighted works on a nonexclusive basis. A hotel or restaurant must have a license from these organizations to use the works in their collection. Since an establishment cannot easily restrict its musical offerings to the works controlled by one organization only, in most circumstances hotels, restaurants and clubs will need a license from both.

After collecting the license fees, ASCAP and BMI deduct overhead expenses and distribute the balance to their members as royalties for the use of their compositions. A **royalty** is a payment made to a composer for the sale of copies or performance of his or her work. The allocation of the money among members is based on detailed, weighted formulas based in significant part on the popularity of the songs.

---

[21] For example, see *Kingvision Pay-Per-View, Ltd. v. Tito's Bar and Grill*, 2001 WL 682205 (Tex. 2001); *Joe Hand Promotions, Inc. v. Hernandez*, 2004 WL 148810 (N.Y. 2004); *Kingvision Pay-Per-View Ltd.,v. Raimerez*, 2006 WL 2714703 (N.Y. 2006)

ASCAP

The license fees charged to hotels and restaurants, bars, and clubs by ASCAP are not based on the songs actually performed. Rather, they are based on a combination of factors that include the number of nights a week the establishment offers music, seating capacity, and whether admission is charged.

ASCAP controls such a large part of the performance rights of the music industry that it could exercise monopoly power. (See the discussion on antitrust law in this chapter.) To avoid this, the law has imposed restrictions on its ability to dictate fees. The process for determining the license fee a user must pay is as follows: The club or restaurant submits a written application to ASCAP. It responds in writing, advising the business of the proposed fee. A 60-day negotiation period follows during which the facility can object to the fee; the parties can then attempt to reach a mutually agreeable compromise. If they are unsuccessful, the hotel or restaurant can apply to a federal district court for a determination of a reasonable license fee. The mandated negotiation period and the right of the music user to seek a court determination of a reasonable fee substantially lessens ASCAP's ability to wield its potentially controlling bargaining power.

BMI

License fees charged by BMI are determined through negotiations between BMI officials and established trade associations such as the National Restaurant Association. For hotels and restaurants, the fees are determined based on annual expenditures for musicians and entertainers. For concert halls, fees are determined by seating capacity. For other establishments such as ballrooms and clubs, fees are based on a percentage of gross annual income.

Case Example 15-4 examines a case brought by BMI against a hotel that hired bands to play various copyrighted songs, yet the hotel did not have authorization to play copyrighted work. The case illustrates well the elements of copyright infringement.

CASE EXAMPLE 15-4

Broadcast Music, Inc. v. Quality Hotel & Conference Center

2013 WL 2444553 (W.Va., 2013)

This is an action for copyright infringement arising from Defendants' public performance, or Defendants causing the public performance, of copyrighted musical compositions at the Quality Hotel & Conference Center, located in Harpers Ferry, West Virginia. Plaintiff maintains four claims of willful copyright infringement, based upon Defendant's unauthorized public performance of music compositions from the BMI repertoire. . . .

For a plaintiff to prove copyright infringement by an unauthorized public performance, the plaintiff must make sufficient allegations regarding: 1) the originality and authorship of the works involved; 2) compliance with the formalities of federal copyright law; 3) rightful proprietorship of the copyrights at issue; 4) the copyrighted works were performed publicly for profit; and 5) a lack of authorization by the owner or the owner's representative for the alleged infringer to publicly perform the works.

In this case, Plaintiffs have alleged sufficient facts to establish the elements of liability for purposes of default judgment. First, Plaintiffs have alleged that the four songs at issue are original compositions created and written by specified persons. Second, Plaintiffs have alleged the date of registration and registration numbers of the four musical compositions, and that the Plaintiffs have complied in all respects with the requirements of the Copyright Act. Third, Plaintiffs owned the copyrights to the protected works at the time of infringement. Last, Defendant Schultz publicly played these songs and/or caused these songs to be publicly performed without a license or permission. Therefore, these factual allegations are sufficient to satisfy the five elements of Plaintiffs' claims, and Plaintiffs are entitled to entry of default judgment.

Consequence of Performing Music Without a License

If a restaurant or hotel fails to obtain the necessary licenses for musical performances, it will be liable for copyright infringement. Remedies include the following:

- An injunction requiring the infringer to stop

- Damages in an amount equal to the copyright owner's actual loss and the profits the infringer made. In the alternative, the copyright owner can opt for statutory damages, an amount of money determined by the court of not less than $750 or more than $30,000, depending on the circumstances.

- Reimbursement for the plaintiff's attorney's fees

- Reimbursement for other costs associated with the lawsuit

Before bringing a lawsuit, ASCAP or BMI will inform the facility that a license is necessary and encourage its purchase. If the owner refuses to pay and continues to provide musical entertainment, a lawsuit is likely. Both organizations are zealous in pursuing their members' rights. An example of this process is provided in Case Example 15-5.

CASE EXAMPLE 15-5

BMI v. Station House Irish Pub & Steakhouse, Ltd

2014 WL 3943846 (Pa., 2014)

. . . This case arises out of the performance of copyrighted material at The Station House Irish Pub & Steakhouse in Gouldsboro, Pennsylvania. Plaintiffs contend that performances at the restaurant violated their rights under the Copyright Act of 1976.

Plaintiff Broadcast Music, Incorporated (hereinafter "BMI"), is a performing rights society, licensing the right to publicly perform a repertoire of copyrighted musical compositions on behalf of the owners of those copyrights. The remaining plaintiffs own the copyrights to the compositions allegedly played at defendant's establishment.

Defendant Station House Irish Pub & Steakhouse (hereinafter "The Station House") is a limited liability company which operates, maintains and controls an establishment known as Station House Irish Pub & Steakhouse in Gouldsboro, Pennsylvania. Defendant Gary Russo is the President of The Station House with responsibility for its operation and management. Defendant Christopher Benson is the Vice President and Secretary of The Station House with responsibility for its operation and management. The Station House publicly performs musical compositions at the restaurant including performances of live and recorded music.

Beginning in July 2009, BMI learned The Station House was offering musical entertainment without a license from BMI, or without permission from the copyright owners. BMI sent a letter to the defendants stating that defendants required a license to perform music from BMI's repertoire. The letter also contained an information brochure, a BMI license agreement and a licensing fee schedule. BMI received no response from the defendants.

From September 2009 through November 2011, BMI repeatedly sent additional letters to the defendants informing them that they needed permission to offer public performances of BMI's copyrighted music. On September 27, 2010, after receiving no response to any of their advisory letters, BMI sent defendants a cease and desist letter instructing defendants that they should cease public performances of music licensed by BMI.

From September 2011 through July 2013, BMI sent defendants sixteen (16) additional letters notifying them that the cease and desist letter remained in full force and effect. BMI's telephone records indicate that its licensing personnel telephoned defendants on ninety-four (94) occasions and spoke to persons associated with The Station House advising them that they were offering unauthorized public performance of BMI-licensed music and that a license was required. Defendants nevertheless failed to enter into a license agreement with BMI and continued to offer unauthorized public performance of BMI music. BMI then sent an investigator to The Station House who made an audio recording and prepared a written report naming the seventeen songs referenced in this lawsuit as ones played by a band in the restaurant on July 20, 2013.

Plaintiffs filed a complaint on October 2, 2013 alleging copyright infringement for each of the seventeen (17) songs annexed to the complaint. The defendants failed to file a responsive pleading within the time period provided by the [applicable rules]. On February 25, 2014, plaintiffs filed a motion for default judgment. The defendants failed to file any response to the plaintiffs' motion for default judgment and the court determined that a hearing was necessary to determine plaintiffs' relief. . . . .

On August 5, 2014, a hearing regarding the determination of plaintiffs' damages was held and the defendants failed to appear for the hearing. Accordingly, the court heard argument from the plaintiffs, bringing the case to its present posture. . . .

Plaintiff seeks damages against the defendants for copyright violations. Specifically, plaintiffs request the following relief: (1) an injunction preventing the defendants from infringement of any copyrighted material licensed by BMI; (2) statutory damages; and (3) costs and attorney's fees. The court must now determine whether and to what extent plaintiffs are entitled to their requested relief.

A. Injunction

. . . When liability is established and a continuing threat to the copyright exists, courts have usually granted a permanent injunction.

Here, an injunction is warranted. The defendants have not disputed liability. Plaintiffs have demonstrated a threat of continuing infringement. Plaintiffs warned defendants repeatedly over a period of several years of the need to obtain a performance license for the compositions in their repertoire, and defendants refused to do so and continued to publicly perform BMI's copyright music. Further, defendants have failed to obtain a licensing agreement from BMI. The court thus finds that there is a substantial likelihood that defendants will continue to violate plaintiffs' copyrights. The court will, therefore, grant plaintiffs' request for a permanent injunction. . . .

B. Money Damages

Plaintiffs seek monetary damages of $3,000 per copyright violation, arguing that the violation was willful. The copyright act provides that a copyright infringer "is liable for either (1) the copyright owner's actual damages and any additional profits of the infringer, or (2) statutory damages." The copyright act authorizes an award of statutory damages for all infringements involved in the action, with respect to any one work, "in a sum of not less than $750 or more than $30,000 as the court considers just." When the copyright owner proves a willful copyright violation, "the court in its discretion may increase the award of statutory damages to a sum of not more than $150,000. . . ."

Defendants' conduct in failing to secure a license was willful. Plaintiffs wrote to defendants repeatedly to inform them of their infringing activities and to demand that they purchase a license. Plaintiffs provided defendants with an informational brochure by which they could have determined whether songs performed in the restaurant required a BMI agreement. Plaintiffs also sent defendants a "cease and desist" letter informing them that they were violating plaintiffs' copyrights. Moreover, representatives from BMI telephone defendants on 94 separate occasions informing defendants that they were committing copyright infringement by performing BMI's music without a license.

Beyond the question of willfulness, the court must also take into account the purpose of such awards, which is to compensate the plaintiff for lost profit and other injury, as well as to discourage wrongful conduct. Thus, the court's award should be designed to compensate plaintiffs as well as to punish defendant. Recognizing the important deterrent purpose served by statutory damages, courts routinely compute statutory damages in copyright infringement cases between two to six times the license fees defendants "saved" by not obeying the Copyright Act.

The court finds that $1,700 per violation is a more appropriate number by which to calculate damages. Plaintiffs have represented that if the defendants had purchased the proper licenses at the time BMI first contacted them in July 2009, the estimated license fees between April 2009 and February 2014 would have been $20,276.67. A current license would cost the defendants $4,223.33. Thus, if defendants had purchased a license in July 2009, when BMI first contacted them, they would have purchased approximately five licenses before the time of the violation. Such licenses would have cost the defendants at minimum $4,223.33 X 5 or $21,116.65. Awarding plaintiffs damages of $1,700 for each of the seventeen established violations would award plaintiffs a total amount of $28,900. An award of that amount would total the amount of licensing fees defendants would have paid for the period in question plus an addition thirty-five (35) percent. The court finds that such damages significantly exceeds the actual cost of a proper license and thus serves both to punish the defendants' conduct and discourage such future misconduct. As such, we find that plaintiffs are entitled to statutory money damages in the amount of $28,900.

C. Attorney's Fees and Costs

The plaintiffs also seek attorneys' fees and costs. The Copyright Act provides that the court in its discretion may award a reasonable attorney's fee to the prevailing party. . . .

The court will grant the plaintiffs' request for attorneys' fees. The defendants refused to enter into a performance license, willfully infringed on plaintiffs' copyrights, and forced plaintiffs to engage in litigation to protect their property. Defendants have offered no defense in this matter. Awarding attorneys' fees to the plaintiffs is therefore appropriate. . . .

Amplified Radio Music

Not infrequently, a restaurant will mechanically amplify the radio and play it as background music for diners' enjoyment. The music played on the radio is typically copyrighted. Radio stations customarily have a license with BMI and ASCAP to play protected songs. Case Example 15-6 addresses the circumstances in which a restaurant does and does not violate the copyright laws when transmitting radio music in its establishment.

CASE EXAMPLE 15-6

Cass County Music Company v. Port Town Family Restaurant

55 F.3d 263 (Wis. 1995)

The plaintiffs…own copyrights to six songs that are the subject of this suit. The defendant was the owner of the Port Town Family Restaurant located in Racine, Wisconsin. The restaurant is a free-standing building accommodating up to 128 patrons with a public dining area of approximately 1,500 square feet. The restaurant is equipped with a "radio-over-speaker" sound system that provides a consistent level of background music throughout the dining area.

On the night of March 13, 1992, two investigators employed by ASCAP had dinner in the Port Town Family Restaurant. While dining, the investigators heard some of the plaintiffs' songs played over the restaurant's sound system. The source of the music was a radio broadcast of MWYX-FM, a Milwaukee station. The radio station is an ASCAP licensee. The license between ASCAP and WMYX-FM prohibits retransmissions of the station's broadcasts….

The ASCAP licensing fee for establishments that play music four to seven nights a week and seat between 76 and 150 patrons is $327 per year. From May, 1985, until December 1991, ASCAP repeatedly and unsuccessfully approached the Port Town Family Restaurant about the need for the restaurant to obtain an ASCAP license in order to continue legally to play background music.

The plaintiffs subsequently brought this action against the restaurant owner. They allege copyright infringement on the basis of the public performance of the six copyrighted musical compositions. The plaintiffs requested an injunction prohibiting further performances, $1000 damages for each infringement, and costs including reasonable attorneys' fees….

The Copyright Act contains an exemption that allows the use of ordinary ["home-type"] radios and television sets for the incidental entertainment of patrons in small businesses or other professional establishments, such as taverns, lunch counters, hairdressers, dry cleaners, doctors' offices, etc….

There are two ways in which an establishment could fall outside the exemption. First, if any non-home-type components are used, then the entire system must be considered a non-home-type system. Second, if the establishment has configured the home-type equipment in a way not commonly used in a home, the exemption is lost. The critical factors are the type and sophistication of the equipment used, the size of the area in which the broadcast is audible, and whether the equipment has been altered, augmented, or integrated in some fashion….

The Port Town Family Restaurant's music system utilizes, in addition to a Radio Shack receiver, a separate control panel containing five selector switches, nine speakers recessed into the dropped acoustic tile ceiling, and concealed wiring. Each speaker consists of a 12" aluminum grille, an 8" loudspeaker, and a 70-volt (70-V) loudspeaker line matching transformer. Without the addition of the transformers, the receiver is designed to drive only four speakers over moderate lengths of speaker cable. However, with the 70-V transformer attached to each speaker… the receiver effectively can power up to forty speakers wired in parallel, thirty-six speakers more than the receiver was designed to handle without overloading.… The restaurant's nine speakers are evenly spaced within the 1,500 square-foot dining area.… The set up…provides background music that is consistent and evenly audible throughout the public seating area.

The system at issue here cannot be characterized fairly as "homestyle," that is, commonly found in homes. The receiver clearly is used beyond the normal limits of its capabilities. Accordingly, the Port Town Family Restaurant is not exempt from compliance with the Copyright Act.

Artwork

In addition to music, copyright law protects artwork. To merit copyright protection, the work must reflect the artistic creativity of the artist. For example, with photographs such creativity can be reflected in the posing of the subjects, lighting, angle, and other variants.

In a case involving menu design, the defendant, a company that designed and printed restaurant menus, incorporated photographs taken by the plaintiff, a printer specializing in preparing and printing Chinese restaurant menus. The plaintiff sued, claiming copyright infringement. The court noted that the pictures in question depicted Chinese dishes common in takeout menus including sweet and sour chicken, barbecue spare ribs, Pu Pu platter, and Peking duck. The pattern of the food on the plates was "extremely common," reflecting Chinese tradition. Neither the lighting nor the angles were notable. The court concluded the pictures lacked creativity and instead "serve a purely utilitarian purpose; to identify for restaurant customers the appearance and ingredients of certain dishes on the menu." Lacking the necessary inventiveness, the photos were not copyrightable.[22]

The necessary creativity was present in a case where defendant infringed plaintiff's copyright by producing a wallpaper pattern for sale that differed only slightly from plaintiff's copyrighted version. The two patterns were similar in color and design; and both contained elongated diamonds of precisely the same shape (124-degree obtuse angles and 56-degree acute angles). The court described the two designs as "strikingly similar." Marriott International Hotels had purchased a lot of the wallpaper from plaintiff but thereafter had passed over plaintiff's design in favor of defendant's. The court determined that defendant was liable for copyright infringement. Noted the judge, defendant had access to plaintiff's design, defendant's design was created under "highly suspicious" circumstances, and defendant was unable to produce any witnesses who could attest that his pattern was independently created.[23]

---

22 *Oriental Art Printing v. Goldstar Printing*, 175 F. Supp.2d 542 (N.Y. 2001)
23 *Design Tex Group, Inc. v. U.S. Vinyl Manufacturing Corp.*, 2005 WL 1020436 (N.Y. 2005)

The economic system of the United States is based on free and open competition. It seeks to ensure new businesses can enter the market and all businesses can compete on a more or less equal basis. The reason for promoting competition is the belief that it motivates producers both to make better products and to sell them at lower prices, thereby benefiting consumers. Certain laws, called **antitrust laws,** attempt to ensure that open competition is preserved.

An important federal antitrust law is the Sherman Antitrust Act, passed in 1890 and supplemented by a second act in 1914 called the Clayton Act. These remain the two key federal antitrust laws. The U.S. Supreme Court described the objective of the Sherman Act as follows:

> *The Sherman Act was designed to be a comprehensive charter of economic liberty aimed at preserving free and unfettered competition as the rule of trade. It rests on the premise that the unrestrained interaction of competitive forces will yield the best allocation of our economic resources, the lowest prices, the highest quality and the greatest material progress, while at the same time providing an environment conducive to the preservation of our democratic, political, and social institutions. But even were that premise open to question, the policy unequivocally laid down by the act is competition.* [24]

The Sherman Act states the following:

> *Every contract, combination... or conspiracy, in restraint of trade or commerce among the several states... is hereby declared illegal.... Every person who shall monopolize any part of the trade or commerce among the several states... shall be deemed guilty of a felony, and, on conviction thereof, shall be punished by a fine [and/or imprisonment] ...* [25]

The specific activities that restrain competition and are addressed by the antitrust laws are listed below. Some are **per se violations,** which means they are always illegal. Others are subject to the **rule of reason;** that is, they are not always illegal, but sometimes are. Their benefits (such as economic efficiency) are balanced against their anticompetitive effects in each case. If the benefits outweigh the drawbacks, the activity will be permitted. If the anticompetitive impact is too great, the activity will be outlawed.

Penalties

Penalties for violation of antitrust laws are significant and include **dissolution,** which means a business is ordered to terminate its operations; **divestiture,** which means a business is required to terminate *part* of its operations; criminal penalties,

antitrust laws
Laws that attempt to ensure that open competition is preserved, and practices that restrain competition are eliminated.

per se violations (of antitrust laws)
Activities that are always considered illegal under antitrust legislation.

rule of reason (applied to anti-trust laws)
The balancing by the court of the economic benefits and drawbacks in determining the legality of a particular business practice as it affects open competition.

dissolution
The termination of business operations, sometimes applied as a penalty for antitrust violations.

divestiture
The act of giving up part of a business operation, sometimes imposed as a penalty for antitrust violations.

---

[24] *Northern Pacific Railroad v. United States*, 356 U.S. 1, 78 S.Ct. 514, 2 L.Ed.2d 545 (1968)
[25] 15 U.S.C. §§ 1,2

including jail and substantial fines; and **treble damages,** meaning mandated payment of three times the loss suffered by an injured plaintiff.

Application of the Per Se Rule

The following is a list of activities that restrain competition and are per se violations of antitrust laws:

- **Price-fixing agreements**, in which competitors agree among themselves to sell goods at a certain price and not lower

- **Vertical price fixing**, in which a manufacturer establishes minimum prices at which lower-level dealers in a distribution system (for example, retailers) can sell a product

- **Territorial division agreements**, in which competitors assign to each other a territory and agree not to compete in the others' territories, thereby each obtaining a monopoly within a specified geographical area

- **Group boycott**, in which two or more sellers refuse to do business with a particular person or company, intending thereby to eliminate competition or block entry to a market

- **Resale price-maintenance agreements**, in which a manufacturer determines the price at which retailers must sell

- **Price discrimination**, where a seller of goods charges different prices to different buyers for the same product (not applicable to services)

- **Exclusive dealing contracts**, in which a seller (usually a wholesaler) forbids a buyer (usually a retailer) from purchasing the products of the seller's competitors.

An example of the per se violation of price fixing is provided by a case from Hawaii. Four hotel firms and the Hawaii Hotel Association (a trade association of hotel owners) were charged with price fixing relating to the amount charged for a room. All pled no contest, an alternative plea to guilty or not guilty that is allowed in some but not all states. This plea means that the defendant, while not admitting guilt, declines to dispute the charges. Defendants Sheraton Hawaii Corporation and Hilton Hotels were fined $50,000 each, and Cinerama Hawaii Hotels and Flagship International were each ordered to pay $25,000, while the trade group was fined $10,000.

Another example of a per se violation was provided in a case involving the State of Washington's regulatory scheme governing the sale and distribution of beer and wine. State statutes and regulations required distributors to sell beer and wine at a uniform price to all retailers, prohibited volume discounts, required that manufacturers and distributors inform the Washington State Liquor Control Board of their prices, prohibited sales at other than the posted prices for a month, and required a minimum markup of 10 percent on beer and wine prices from manufacturer to

treble damages
Mandated payment of three times the loss suffered by an injured plaintiff.

price-fixing agreements
Agreement among competitors to sell goods at a certain price and not lower.

vertical price fixing
Practice whereby a manufacturer establishes minimum prices at which lower-level dealers in a distribution system can sell a product.

territorial division agreements
Activities in which competitors assign to each other a territory and agree not to compete in the others' territories, thereby creating a territorial monopoly.

group boycott
Circumstance in which two or more sellers refuse to do business with a particular person or company, intending thereby to eliminate competition or block entry to a market.

resale price-maintenance agreeements
Manufacturer sets the price at which retailers must sell.

price discrimination
A seller charges different prices to different buyers for the same product.

exclusive dealing contracts
Situation in which a seller (usually a wholesaler) forbids a buyer (usually a retailer) from purchasing the products of the seller's competitors.

wholesaler, and from wholesaler to retailer. The court found these requirements to be "irreconcilably in conflict with federal antitrust law. Viewed either individually or as an integrated whole, these restraints plainly serve to reduce price competition and to increase the price of beer and wine in Washington."[26]

Case Example 15-7 is an example of the application of the Sherman Act and the per se rule to a group boycott situation. We learn from this case that avoidance of antitrust liability requires a hotel or restaurant to do more than just give detailed directives to its employees about what conduct is unacceptable. The hotel must also conduct follow-up checks to ensure employees are abiding by those orders.

CASE EXAMPLE 15-7

United States v. Hilton Hotels Corporation

467 F.2d 1000 (Ore. 1972)

This is an appeal from a conviction under an indictment charging a violation of section 1 of the Sherman Act.

Operators of hotels, restaurants, hotel and restaurant supply companies, and other businesses in Portland, Oregon, organized an association to attract conventions to their city. To finance the association, members were asked to make contributions in predetermined amounts. Companies selling supplies to hotels were asked to contribute an amount equal to one percent of their sales to hotel members. To aid collections, hotel members, including [Hilton Hotels Corporation] agreed to give preferential treatment to suppliers who paid their assessments, and to curtail purchases from those who did not.

The jury was instructed that such an agreement by the hotel members, if proven, would be a per se violation of the Sherman Act. [Hilton Hotels Corporation] argues that this was error....

[T]he conduct involved here was of the kind long held to be forbidden.... "Throughout the history of the Sherman Act, the courts have had little difficulty in finding unreasonable restraints of trade in agreements among competitors, at any level of distribution, designed to coerce those subject to a boycott to accede to the action or inaction desired by the group or to exclude them from competition."

[T]he necessary and direct consequence of defendants' scheme was to deprive uncooperative suppliers of the opportunity to sell to defendant hotels in free and open competition with other suppliers, and to deprive defendant hotels of the opportunity to buy supplies from such suppliers in accordance with the individual judgment of each hotel, at prices and on terms and conditions of sale determined by free competition....

The primary purpose and direct effect of defendants' agreement was to bring the combined economic power of the hotels to bear upon those suppliers who failed to pay. The exclusion of uncooperative suppliers from the portion of the market represented by the supply requirements of the defendant hotels was the object of the agreement, not merely its incidental consequence. [Hilton Hotel Corpo-

---

[26] *Costco Wholesale Corp., v. Hoen*, 407 F.Supp.2d 1234 (Wash. 2005)

ration's] president testified that it would be contrary to the policy of the corporation for the manager of one of its hotels to condition purchases upon payment of a contribution to a local association by the supplier. The manager of [Hilton's] Portland hotel and his assistant testified that it was the hotel's policy to purchase supplies solely on the basis of price, quality, and service. They also testified that on two occasions they told the hotel's purchasing agent that he was to take no part in the boycott. The purchasing agent confirmed the receipt of these instructions, but admitted that, despite them, he had threatened a supplier with loss of the hotel's business unless the supplier paid the association assessment. He testified that he violated his instructions because of anger and personal pique toward the individual representing the supplier.... The court instructed the jury that a corporation is liable for the acts and statements of its agents "within the scope of their employment," defined to mean "in the corporation's behalf in performance of the agent's general line of work," including "not only that which has been authorized by the corporation, but also that which outsiders could reasonably assume the agent would have authority to do." The court added:

> A corporation is responsible for acts and statements of its agents, done or made within the scope of their employment, even though their conduct may be contrary to their actual instructions or contrary to the corporation's stated policies.

Congress may constitutionally impose criminal liability upon a business entity for acts or omissions of its agents within the scope of their employment. Such liability may attach... even though [the conduct] may have been contrary to express instructions....

In enacting the Sherman Act, Congress was passing drastic legislation to remedy a threatening danger to the public welfare....The statute was designed to be a comprehensive charter of economic liberty aimed at preserving free and unfettered competition as the rule of trade. It rests on the premise that the unrestrained interaction of competitive forces will yield the best allocation of our economic resources, the lowest prices, the highest quality and the greatest material progress, while at the same time providing an environment conducive to the preservation of our democratic, political and social institutions.

With such important public interests at stake, it is reasonable to assume that Congress intended to impose liability upon business entities for the acts of those to whom they choose to delegate the conduct of their affairs, thus stimulating a maximum effort by owners and managers to assure adherence by such agents to the requirements of the Act....

Violations of the Sherman Act are a likely consequence of the pressure to maximize profits that is commonly imposed by corporate owners upon managing agents and, in turn, upon lesser employees. In the face of that pressure, generalized directions to obey the Sherman Act, with the probable effect of foregoing profits, are the least likely to be taken seriously. And if a violation of the Sherman Act occurs, the corporation, and not the individual agents, will have realized the profits from the illegal activity....

For these reasons we conclude that as a general rule a corporation is liable under the Sherman Act for the acts of its agents in the scope of their employment, even though contrary to general corporate policy and express instructions to the agent....

The purchasing agent was authorized to buy all of appellant's supplies. Purchases were made on the basis of specifications, but the purchasing agent exercised complete authority as to source. He was in a unique position to add the corporation's buying power to the force of the boycott. [Hilton] could not gain exculpation [freedom from liability] by issuing general instructions without undertaking to enforce those instructions by means commensurate with the obvious risks....

Ruling of the Court: [Conviction of Hilton for violating the Sherman Act] Affirmed.

CASE QUESTIONS

1. In what way does a group boycott such as the one in this case restrict competition?

2. Why was the hotel liable for the conduct of an employee who was acting contrary to his supervisor's directives?

territorial restrictions
Circumstance in which a manufacturer restricts the territory in which dealers can sell, thereby preventing other dealers from competing in a given territory.

An example of vertical price fixing, another per se violation, is a wholesaler who sells to a distributor chicken-wing sauce intended for restaurants and conditions the sale upon the distributor's agreement not to resell the sauce below a specified price.[27]

Application of the Rule of Reason

monopoly
Instance in which a firm and/or business controls the market for a particular product.

The following is a list of activities that may restrain competition and are judged according to the rule of reason:

- **Territorial restrictions,** in which a manufacturer restricts the territory in which dealers can sell, thereby preventing other dealers from competing in a given territory

tying arrangements
Circumstance in which a seller conditions the sale of a product on the buyer's agreement to also purchase some other product produced or distributed by the seller.

- **Monopoly,** in which one firm controls the market for a particular product with the intent of excluding competitors

- **Tying arrangements,** in which a seller conditions the sale of a product on the buyer's agreement to purchase an additional product produced or distributed by the seller

mergers
A transaction that combines two businesses into one, resulting in a reduction of competition.

- **Mergers,** in which two businesses are combined into one, resulting in a reduction of competition.

---

[27] *Prince Heaton Enterprises, Inc. v. Buffalo's Franchise Concepts, Inc.*, 117 F.Supp.2d 1357 (Ga. 2000)

The rule of reason was applied in a case involving a tying arrangement and McDonald's. The fast-food hamburger operation required its franchisees (owners of individual restaurants; see discussion later in this chapter) to sell Coca-Cola and no other cola drink as a condition of using the McDonald's name. The reason for the requirement was McDonald's interest in a standard menu at all its restaurants for purposes of uniformity, and also the franchisor's interest in a linkage with a product known and popular among consumers. Some franchisees wanted to sell Pepsi because they could buy it for less. They sued McDonald's, seeking to have the Coca-Cola requirement declared an illegal tying arrangement. The court held the restriction was *legal* based on the rule of reason. The court noted that McDonald's is by no means a monopoly in the fast-food industry; McDonald's does not dominate the cola market; competition was not substantially lessened by McDonald's Coca-Cola requirement; McDonald's does not have a financial interest in the profits of the Coca-Cola Company; and its reasons for imposing the restriction (including uniformity among franchises) were reasonable.

In another case a Subway restaurant franchisee complained about being required to purchase a particular computer and POS (point-of-sale) software package to account for food sales. The plaintiff claimed the mandated system constituted an illegal tying arrangement because to purchase a franchise required purchasing the POS system. The court rejected this argument, finding that the franchise and POS system were in reality one purchase and not two because the franchise could not be operated without the POS system. Said the court, "All but the simplest products can be broken down into two or more components that are 'tied together' in the final sale. Unless it is to be illegal to sell cars with engines or cameras with lenses, this analysis (of determining when a product is 'tied' to another), must be guided by some limiting principle. For products to be distinct, the tied product must, at a minimum, be one that some consumers might wish to purchase separately without also purchasing the tying product." The court then determined no one other than a Subway franchisee would want to purchase a Subway-tailored POS system, and so dismissed plaintiff's antitrust claim.[28]

Case Example 15-8 explores restrictions against the formation of monopolies. We discussed in Chapter 10 that a hotel can prohibit from its premises businesses that compete with the services the hotel offers; the resulting exclusive right to sell to hotel guests is not considered an illegal monopoly. Similarly, a sports stadium can prohibit spectators from bringing in food from outside sources. Such a prohibition does not violate the antitrust laws although it gives the stadium the exclusive right during the event to sell food to those in attendance. The reason why these "mini-monopolies" are not illegal is discussed in Case Example 15–8.

---

[28] *Subsolutions, Inc. v. Doctor's Associates, Inc.*, 436 F.Supp.2d 348 (Conn. 2006)

CASE EXAMPLE 15–8

Elliott v. The United Center

126 F.3d 1003 (Ill. 1997)

Millions of spectators have attended games and other events at the United Center, home of the world-famous Chicago Bulls, as well as the Chicago Blackhawks, circuses, ice shows, concerts, and in 1996 the Democratic National Convention. But ever since the United Center opened, it has had a policy that prohibits all patrons of the center from bringing food into the arena. This, according to Thornton Elliott and his co-plaintiffs, has given a "monopoly" on food sales to the Center. Elliott [the plaintiff] and his colleagues are licensed peanut vendors who, up until the time the United Center imposed this policy, turned a respectable profit selling peanuts outside the stadium. They brought this suit under section 2 of the Sherman Act, claiming that the United Center's food policy constitutes an illegal attempt to monopolize food sales inside the arena and in the surrounding geographic area. The district court was unpersuaded and dismissed the case. We agree....

According to the complaint, ever since the United Center implemented its food policy in September 1994, patrons are inspected for food when they enter the stadium, and if any is found, it is confiscated by stadium security. If a fan buys a bag of peanuts from Elliott, therefore, she must consume it before she enters the United Center, unless she wants to risk contributing it to the "illegal food" stash collected by the security personnel. Worse yet, if she has a hankering for peanuts during the Bull's game, her desires will go unfulfilled because the United Center does not offer peanuts for sale in the stadium (except little bags of peanuts for the circus elephants). This policy has cost Elliott dearly...the average sales of peanuts have dropped to approximately one-fifth of sales in previous years. Predictably, some vendors have gone out of business, and the remaining ones are struggling to survive....

[Plaintiffs] conceded that the United Center might have had a legitimate business reason to prohibit certain kinds of food, such as cans, bottles, or alcoholic beverages in general, in the interest of maintaining order in the facility, but plaintiffs claim that no such reason could be advanced for the blanket food ban. The complaint points out the United Center's monopoly over the presentation of live National Basketball Association games and live National Hockey League games in the Chicago market, and implicitly argues that the Center is, through the food policy, attempting to extend its monopoly to the alleged food concession market....Plaintiffs claim the fewer the food concessions, the higher the price the United Center can charge for food its patrons consume, and the more consumers will suffer....

The United Center can recoup the cost of putting on an event in any of a number of ways. It can charge very high ticket prices, and allow unlimited numbers of food concessions in and around the stadium, or it can charge somewhat lower ticket prices and restrict the number of concessions (thereby earning some of its profits from food sales.)...The United Center is obviously not monopolizing the market for peanuts: it is staying strictly out of the peanut business. Prices and output of peanuts in the area are totally unaffected by the United Center's policies.

The logic of Elliott's argument would mean that exclusive restaurants could no longer require customers to purchase their wines only at the establishment, because the restaurant would be "monopolizing" the sale of wine within its interior. Movie theaters, which traditionally (and notoriously) earn a substantial part of their revenue from the sales of candies, popcorn, and soda, would be required by the antitrust laws to allow patrons to bring their own food.…Elliott's principal point is that the customer knows that once he is ready to walk through the entry gate, he may not have with him any "outside" food. The same could be said of any of the establishments we have just mentioned: once inside a restaurant, or a movie theater, the customer is at the mercy of the place he has chosen. The price of the refreshments or the wine is just one part of the price of the evening out.

[The facts here do not present a] violation of the antitrust laws.… We therefore conclude that the district court correctly dismissed Elliott's complaint.… Affirmed.

In another alleged monopoly case, PepsiCo claimed that The Coca-Cola Company monopolized and restrained trade based on "loyalty provisions" Coca-Cola inserted in its contracts with its distributors that prohibit the latter from delivering PepsiCo's products to any customer. Thus the distributors can carry Coca-Cola's products or PepsiCo's, but not both. In deciding the case the court noted that the core element of a monopolization claim is market power. That is, if a company controls a sufficient share of the market it can control prices which is what antitrust laws seeks to prevent. The court determined that Coca-Cola had "only a 64 percent share of the total fountain syrup sales" and said, "A 64 percent market share is insufficient to infer monopoly power." The court thus rejected PepsiCo's claim that Coca-Cola monopolized the market. The latter was thus allowed to continue its use of loyalty provisions in its contracts with distributors.[29]

franchise
An arrangement in which the owner of a trademark, service mark, or copyright, licenses others under specified conditions, to use the mark or copyright in the sale of goods or services.

franchisor
The owner of a trademark, service mark, or copyright who has licensed another to use it in connection with the sale of goods or services.

franchisee
The party who receives the right to use a trademark, service mark, or copyright in connection with the sale of goods or services.

Franchising

Towns and cities look more and more alike as each has hotels, restaurants, and stores with the same names. This phenomenon is based in significant part on franchising. A **franchise** is an arrangement in which the owner of a trademark, service mark, or copyright licenses others to use the mark or copyright in the sale of goods or services. As we have seen, use of another's service mark, trademark, or copyright without permission constitutes infringement.

There are two parties in a franchise arrangement. The **franchisor** is the owner of the mark or copyright; the **franchisee** is the party who receives the right to use it. Examples of franchises include Subway, Dunkin' Donuts, Friday's, Day's Inn, and Super 8 Motels.

alejandro dans neergaard/Shutterstock.com

---

29 *PepsiCo, Inc. v. Coca-Cola Company*, 315 F.3d 101 (N.Y. 2002)

The relationship between the franchisor and the franchisee is contractual. By contract, the franchisor authorizes the franchisee to utilize the trademark, service mark, or copyright. In return, the franchisee customarily agrees to pay the franchisor an initial sum of money plus a percentage of revenue on an ongoing basis, called a royalty. The better known the business name is, the higher will be the royalty paid by the franchisee. Additional fees a franchisee typically pays include mandatory marketing program charges, Internet booking fees, reservation system charges, guest services assessments, interest, and relicense fee. The contract also typically requires the franchisee to maintain certain standards, and the franchisor to provide assistance and advice.

Because the relationship is a contractual one and not an employment relationship or a principal/agent relationship, the franchisor has customarily not been liable for the acts of a franchisee. However, a few recent cases have shed doubt on that previously settled principle of law. Thus, if a fast-food franchisee negligently prepares a meal in such a way that a customer becomes ill, generally the franchisor will not be liable. Instead only the franchisee is legally responsible. The reason is that the franchisee and not the franchisor is the owner and operator of the business and the employer of the negligent employees. This principle is illustrated in a case in which a hotel franchisee was negligent in the maintenance of a balcony railing.

A two-year-old guest fell 70 feet to the ground when deterioration caused a railing to give way while the child was leaning against it. The child's parents sued both the franchisee and the franchisor. The court held the franchisor was not liable.[30] Similarly, a franchisor was not liable to a guest at a franchised hotel who was injured due to the negligence of the franchisee in the maintenance of the elevator. The guest fell while attempting to step out of the elevator into the lobby. The elevator had failed to fully descend so that the floor of the lobby was below the elevator as the guest tried to exit. Liability for any negligence that caused the accident rests with the franchisee and not the franchisor.[31] Nor was the franchisor liable where a fire at a hotel resulted in the death of four guests.[32]

In a restaurant case a McDonald's overnight custodian was attacked by two intruders. The assault was facilitated by deficiencies in the franchisee's security system. The employee sued the franchisor. Consistent with the previous cases, the court dismissed the claim, ruling that the franchisor was not liable for the negligent acts of the franchisee.[33] Until recently, the franchisor would be liable only if the franchisor's agents controlled or participated in the day-to-day operations and management of the business, or, in a case where a patron was injured by a product, if the franchisor made or sold the item that caused the injury.

In typical franchise agreements, franchisors do impose many requirements on franchisees, leading to arguments that the franchisor exercises considerable control over the franchisee. For example, franchisors often dictate the franchisee's choice of com-

---

[30] *Choice Hotels International, Inc. v. Palm-Aire Oceanside, Inc.*, 95 F.3d 41 (Md. 1996)
[31] *Doubletree Hotels v. Person*, 122 S.W.3d 917 (Tex. 2003)
[32] *Allen v. Greenville Hotel Partners, Inc.*, 409 F.Supp.2d 672 (S.C. 2006)
[33] *Vandemark v. McDonald's Corp.*, 904 A.2d 627 (N.H. 2006)

puter system, determine the location, store hours, advertising, the procedure for handling customer complaints, signage, email capabilities, equipment, décor, method and manner of customer payment, pricing of items, book and recordkeeping methods, and insurance requirements. Additionally, the franchisor will insist that its name and logo be prominently displayed on signage, uniforms, products, and packaging.

A few recent cases have raised the specter that the control imposed by these mandates is enough for the court to look anew at the possibility of vicarious liability.[34] Franchisors seeking to avoid such liability should limit controls over franchisees to those that are necessary to maintain brand integrity and promote consistency and uniformity among the franchisees.

Benefits to the Franchisee

The franchisee stands to benefit from a franchise relationship in several ways. The use of the franchised name is usually valuable because it is known to customers and so attracts patronage. In addition, the franchise contract typically requires the franchisor to provide technical help to the franchisee, including the following: market research to decide where to locate the business, advice on layout and design of the building, employee training, recipes, accounting methods, information on suppliers, product preparation, and other assistance that may be needed. Another important benefit is group advertising. Each franchisee contributes a sum of money for promotions. The franchisor accumulates those payments from all the franchisees and uses the money to formulate print and broadcast advertisements. The individual franchisee thus receives the benefit of an expensive advertising campaign for a fraction of the cost.

Hotel franchisors typically offer a reservation system by which incoming calls and online inquiries seeking room reservations are managed. These systems are intended to facilitate the reservation process for customers interested in a hotel within the brand, and to increase occupancy for franchisees. In a case involving the franchisor that owns both the names Crown Plaza and Holiday Inn, a franchisee claimed the franchisor breached its contractual duty to provide promised reservation services. Per the complaint, the franchisor gave preference to a Holiday Inn in a particular geographical location to the disadvantage of the nearby Crown Plaza. In the lawsuit by the owner of the Crown Plaza, the franchisor sought to dismiss the case. The court refused to terminate the case, finding that the franchisor that maintains a reservation system has responsibilities to all its franchisees.[35]

Benefits to the Franchisor

The franchisor benefits financially from the fees paid by franchisees. The franchisor also benefits from the additional exposure of the name resulting from each franchisee's use. The more the name is known and accepted by the public, the more

---

[34] *Patterson v. Domino's Pizza*, 333 P.3d 1777 (Calif., 2014); Fast Food Workers Comm. V. McDonald's USA, LLC, NLRB (2014); Ochoa v. McDonald's Corp., 133 F.Supp.3d 1228 (Calif., 2015); Salazar v. McDonald's, 2016 WL 4394165 (Calif., 2016).
[35] *Lenexa Hotel v. Holiday Hospitality Franchising, Inc.*, 2013 WL 4736245 (Kans, 2013).

valuable it is, and the greater is the franchise fee the franchisor can command from subsequent franchisees. The value of the name is preserved in part by contract provisions requiring the franchisee to maintain certain standards including products sold, size of building, interior and exterior design, and cleanliness. These requirements provide consistency among all the franchisees, which is the foundation for public acceptance of a franchise operation. For example, although each McDonald's restaurant is individually owned, we all have a certain expectation of what we will find if we visit one, and we will likely find what we expect at whichever outlet we choose.

Exclusive Territory

encroachment
Entry onto another's property without right or permission.

An exclusive territory is very valuable to a franchisee because it protects the business from competition from another franchisee opening nearby. If a franchisee receives an exclusive territory, it will be stated in the contract. A franchisee is well advised to attempt to negotiate a provision in the franchise agreement granting an exclusive territory. Without it, the franchisee's patronage may be invaded by a like business opening nearby, called **encroachment**, resulting in a considerable loss of income. In one case a McDonald's franchisee was frustrated when the franchisor authorized two additional restaurants to open within two miles of his eatery. He sued the franchisor for breach of contract. The court stated, "The problem faced by plaintiffs in claiming a breach of contract by McDonald's is their inability to point to any provision in the express and unambiguous agreement between the parties which has been breached by McDonald's." Indeed, a provision in the contract stated, "[N]o exclusive, protected or other territorial rights in the contiguous market area of the restaurant is hereby granted or inferred." The franchisee's case was dismissed.[36] Case Example 15-9 illustrates further the encroachment issue.

CASE EXAMPLE 15-9

Holiday Hospitality Franchising, LLC v. Premier NW Investment Hotels, LLC

2013 WL 2319065 (Ga. 2013)

. . . . Premier NW Investment Hotels, LLC (Premier) entered into a License Agreement with Holiday Hospitality Franchising, LLC (HHFL), dated December 11, 1998, that authorized Premier to operate a Holiday Inn Express Hotel and Suites in Vancouver, Washington. The License Agreement terminated on December 31, 2010 when the license term ended.

On October 16, 2012, Plaintiffs brought the present action alleging that before and since the termination of the License Agreement, Premier has breached its obligations under the License Agreement by failing to (i) pay fees due and owing to HHFL pursuant to the License Agreement, and (ii) cease use of Plaintiffs' Holiday Inn marks in connection with its continued provision of hotel services. . . .

---

36 *Payne v. McDonald's Corp.*, 957 F.Supp. 749 (Md. 1997)

The Court finds that Defendant has failed to offer any meritorious defense to Plaintiffs' claim for damages based upon the failure to pay fees and charges due and owing under the License Agreement. Defendants assert that Plaintiffs caused their own damages by opening a new Holiday Inn Express near Defendant's hotel. However, Defendant was not granted any type of exclusive territory in the License Agreement. Thus, the granting of another license at a location near Defendants' property did not excuse Defendants' obligations under the License Agreement. . . .

In response to the unfair downturn in an existing franchisee's business caused by encroachment, some courts have identified an implied covenant of good faith and fair dealing in franchise contracts and relied upon it to grant a remedy, notwithstanding the absence of an express grant of exclusive territory in the franchise contract. In a California case the court determined that the franchisor breached the implied covenant of good faith and fair dealing by constructing a competing restaurant within a mile and a half from an existing franchisee's restaurant. Said the court, "The franchisee, although not entitled to an exclusive territory, was still entitled to expect that the franchisor would not act to destroy the right of the franchisee to enjoy the fruits of the [franchise] contract."[37] The majority of states take the position that, absent an express grant of an exclusive territory in the franchise contract, the franchisor has the right to authorize new franchise outlets in close proximity to existing ones, and therefore the franchisor is not liable to the franchisee for doing so.

Fraud and Breach of Contract by the Franchisor

If a franchisee pays the franchise fees and the franchisor fails to promote the name, provide assistance, or otherwise comply with its contractual obligations, the franchisee may be the victim of fraud and/or breach of contract. To reduce the chances of this happening, a would-be franchisee should thoroughly investigate a franchisor before investing in a franchise.

Disclosure Requirements for Franchisors

When the concept of franchising first began, unscrupulous franchisors often took money from unsuspecting franchisees and failed to provide the promised services. To protect franchisees against this occurrence, both federal and state laws adopted in the late 1970s require franchisors to disclose detailed information about their business at least 10 days before accepting any money from the franchisee.

The information typically required to be disclosed includes:

- The name and address of the franchisor

- The business experience of persons affiliated with the franchisor

---

[37] *Vylene Enterprises, Inc. v. Naugles, Inc.*, 90 F.3d 1472 (Calif. 1996). See also *Marquis Towers, Inc. v. Highland Group*, 593 S.E.2d 903 (Ga. 2004)

- Whether any such person has been convicted of a felony

- The length of time the franchisor has conducted a business of the type to be operated by the franchisee

- The franchisor's most recent audited financial statement, and information about any material changes in the finances since the statement was prepared

- An explanation of all fees imposed on the franchisee

- A copy of the franchise contract typically used by the franchisor

- A statement of all fees that the franchisee will be required to pay

- The proposed application of the fees by the franchisor

- Whether any franchisees have sued the franchisor and, if so, the nature and status of the lawsuit(s)

- Circumstances under which the franchise agreement can be terminated

- The number of franchises already sold and the number proposed to be sold in the future

- The responsibilities of the franchisor and the franchisee

- Whether or not the franchisee will receive an exclusive territory

prospectus
A disclosure document prepared by franchisors that must be given to potential franchisees before the franchisor can accept any money from a franchisee.

The document in which this information is presented is called a **prospectus.** Recognizing that potential franchisees will rely on the information in the prospectus to make their decisions whether or not to buy into the franchise, a franchisor that provides false information in the prospectus faces both civil and criminal penalties. The punishment includes compensation for damages suffered by the would-be franchisee, jail, and fines.

The required 10-day waiting period between disclosure and acceptance of money by the franchisor from the franchisee is intended to give the franchisee opportunity to review the information and discuss it with advisors such as a lawyer and an accountant.

Tying Arrangements in Franchises as an Antitrust Issue

A franchisor often wants its franchisees to purchase supplies and equipment from the franchisor. This arrangement ensures the franchisor of both a market for its products and the uniformity that is so important to franchise operations. If the trademark is sufficiently valuable, franchisees may be willing to agree to buy from the franchisor exclusively in return for the right to use the name. From an antitrust point of view, this may be a tying arrangement—that is, the obligation to purchase products from the franchisor is tied to the grant of the franchise. As a result, the franchisor is spared from competition by other suppliers and they in turn are denied access to franchisees as potential customers.

As we have seen earlier in this chapter, tying arrangements are not per se violations of antitrust laws, but rather are subject to the rule of reason. In determining whether a particular tying arrangement is legal or not, the court will examine several factors, including the amount of commerce affected and whether some special justification exists for the tying situation. The greater the impact on competition and the less compelling the justification is, the more likely the tying arrangement will be unenforceable. For example, franchisees of Mr. Softee, a soft ice cream seller, objected to a franchise agreement provision requiring that they purchase all of their ice-cream mix from the franchisor. Claiming it was an illegal tying arrangement, the franchisees sued. The court held for the franchisor, ruling that the franchisor's requirements were reasonable for two reasons. First, the mandate ensures that the consumer always receives a consistent product; and second, the particular ice-cream mix sold by the franchisor and the trademark "Mr. Softee" are inseparable.[38] This case notwithstanding, desire by a franchisor to maintain uniformity and quality standards does not always qualify as sufficient justification.

In Case Example 15-10, franchisees of Domino's Pizza alleged that the franchisor violated antitrust laws by requiring that franchisees purchase ingredients and dough from the franchisor. The court disagreed and dismissed the case.

CASE EXAMPLE 15-10

Queens City Pizza, Inc. v. Domino's Pizza, Inc.

124 F.3d 430 (Pa. 1997)

Domino's Pizza, Inc. is a fast-food service company that sells pizza through a national network of over 4,200 stores. Domino's Pizza owns and operates approximately 700 of these stores. Independent franchisees own and operate the remaining 3,500. Domino's Pizza, Inc. is the second largest pizza company in the United States, with revenues in excess of $1.8 billion per year.

A franchisee joins the Domino's System by executing a standard franchise agreement with Domino's Pizza, Inc. Under the franchise agreement, the franchisee receives the right to sell pizza under the "Domino's" name and format. In return, Domino's Pizza receives franchise fees and royalties.

The essence of a successful nationwide fast-food chain is product uniformity and consistency. Uniformity benefits franchisees because customers can purchase pizza from any Domino's store and be certain the pizza will taste exactly like the Domino's Pizza with which they are familiar. This means that individual franchisees need not build up their own goodwill. Uniformity also benefits the franchisor. It ensures the brand name will continue to attract and hold customers, increasing franchise fees and royalties.

---

[38] *Tserpelis v. Mister Softee*, 106 F.Supp.2d 423 (N.Y. 1999)

For these reasons, section 12.2 of the Domino's Pizza standard franchise agreement requires that all pizza ingredients, beverages, and packaging materials used by a Domino's franchisee conform to the standards set by Domino's Pizza Inc. Section 12.2 also provides that Domino's Pizza, Inc. may "in our sole discretion require that ingredients, supplies and materials used in the preparation, packaging and delivery of pizza be purchased exclusively from us or from approved suppliers or distributors." Domino's Pizza reserves the right to "impose reasonable limitations on the number of approved suppliers or distributors of any product." To enforce these rights, Domino's Pizza, Inc. retains the power to inspect franchisee stores and to test materials and ingredients. Section 12.2 is subject to a reasonableness clause providing that Domino's Pizza, Inc. must "exercise reasonable judgment with respect to all determinations to be made by us under the terms of this Agreement." Under the standard franchise agreement, Domino's Pizza, Inc. sells approximately 90% of the $500 million in ingredients and supplies used by Domino's franchisees. These sales, worth some $450 million per year, form a significant part of Domino's Pizza, Inc.'s profits. Franchisees purchase only 10% of their ingredients and supplies from outside sources. With the exception of fresh dough, Domino's Pizza, Inc. does not manufacture the products it sells to franchisees. Instead, it purchases these products from approved suppliers and then resells them to the franchisees at a markup.

The plaintiffs in this case are eleven Domino's franchisees and the International Franchise Advisory Council, Inc. (IFAC), a Michigan corporation consisting of approximately 40% of the Domino's franchisees in the United States, formed to promote their common interests. The plaintiffs contend that Domino's Pizza, Inc. has a monopoly in "the $500 million aftermarket for sales of supplies to Domino's franchisees" and has used its monopoly power to unreasonably restrain trade, limit competition, and extract supra-competitive profits.

First, plaintiffs allege that Domino's Pizza, Inc. has restricted their ability to purchase competitively priced dough. Most franchisees purchase all of their fresh dough from Domino's Pizza, Inc. Plaintiffs here attempted to lower costs by making fresh pizza dough on site. They contend that in response, Domino's Pizza, Inc. increased processing fees and altered quality standards and inspection practices for store-produced dough, which eliminated all potential savings and financial incentives to make their own dough.

Plaintiffs also allege Domino's Pizza, Inc. prohibited stores that produce dough from selling their dough to other franchisees, even though the dough-producing stores were willing to sell dough at a price 25% to 40% below Domino's Pizza, Inc.'s price.

Next, plaintiffs object to efforts by Domino's Pizza, Inc. to block IFAC's attempt to buy less expensive ingredients and supplies from other sources....

Plaintiffs also allege Domino's Pizza entered into exclusive dealing arrangements with several franchisees in order to deny [alternate purveyors] access to a pool of potential buyers sufficiently large to make an alternative purchasing scheme economically feasible. In addition, plaintiffs contend Domino's Pizza, Inc. commenced anti-competitive predatory pricing to shut other suppliers out of the market. For example, they maintain that Domino's Pizza, Inc. lowered prices on many ingredients and supplies to a level competitive with [others'] prices and then recouped lost profits by raising the price on fresh dough, which [competitors] could not supply.

As a result of these and other alleged practices, plaintiffs maintain that each franchisee store now pays between $3,000 and $10,000 more per year for ingredients and supplies than it would in a competitive market. Plaintiffs allege these costs are passed on to consumers....

Courts and legal commentators have long recognized that franchise tying contracts are an essential and important aspect of the franchise form of business organization because they reduce agency costs and prevent franchisees from freeriding—offering products of substandard quality insufficient to maintain the reputational value of the franchise product while benefiting from the quality control efforts of other actors in the franchise system. Franchising is a bedrock of the American economy. More than one-third of all dollars spent in retailing transactions in the United States are paid to franchise outlets. We do not believe the antitrust laws were designed to erect a serious barrier to this form of business organization....

Here, plaintiffs' acceptance of a franchise package that included purchase requirements and contractual restrictions is consistent with the existence of a competitive market in which franchises are valued, in part, according to the terms of the proposed franchise agreement and the availability of alternative franchise opportunities. Plaintiffs need not have become Domino's franchisees. If the contractual restrictions in section 12.2 of the general franchise agreement were viewed as overly burdensome or risky at the time they were proposed, plaintiffs could have purchased a different form of restaurant, or made some alternative investment. They chose not to do so. Plaintiffs must purchase products from Domino's Pizza not because of Domino's market power... but because they are bound by contract to do so. If Domino's Pizza, Inc. acted unreasonably when, under the franchise agreement, it restricted plaintiffs' ability to purchase supplies from other sources, plaintiffs' remedy, if any, is in contract, not under antitrust laws....

CASE QUESTION

1. Explain what the court meant when it said, "Plaintiffs must purchase products from Domino's Pizza not because of Domino's market power... but because they are bound by contract to do so." What effect did this statement have on the decision?

In keeping with the holding in Case Example 15-10, a requirement by a hotel franchisor that franchisees purchase soap and other hotel amenities from designated vendors only, did not violate antitrust laws.[39] Likewise, the franchisor of General Nutrition Corporation ("GNC") stores was able to require its franchisees to purchase inventory only from the franchisor or an approved supplier. The court rejected a claim by franchisees that such mandate constituted an illegal tying arrangement.[40]

---

[39] *Valley Products Co., Inc., v. Landmark, A Division of Hospitality Franchise Systems, Inc.,* 128 F.3d 398 (Tenn. 1997)
[40] *Mumford v. GNC Franchising LLC,* 437 F.Supp.2d 344 (Pa. 2006)

Many abuses have occurred surrounding terminations of franchises. Once a franchisee has invested money, time, and energy in developing the franchise business, courts are reluctant to allow the franchisor to terminate the franchise without good cause. Many states have passed statutes limiting the circumstances under which a franchisor can withdraw the franchise. Typical is the Indiana statute, which bars a franchisor from terminating a franchise "without good cause or in bad faith."[41] Sufficient grounds for termination include repeated failures by a franchisee to pay franchise fees,[42] failure by the franchisee to satisfy the franchisor's operating standards as identified in the contract,[43] and failure to comply with the franchisor's cleanliness standards (dirty restrooms, trash on the floor and "other generally unsanitary conditions") coupled with failure to purchase insurance as required by the contract.[44]

Franchise contracts typically preclude the franchisee from transferring its rights under the contract without prior written consent by the franchisor, and permit the franchisor to withhold consent unless the franchisee and the transferee meet conditions specified in the franchise contract. A Travelodge franchisee that transferred its interests without consent in violation of the contract was liable for breach of contract.[45]

Once a franchise agreement expires or is terminated, the franchisee's right to use the franchisor's trademark terminates. Continued use of the name by the franchisee constitutes trademark infringement. Thus, where a Burger King franchise expired and was not renewed, and the franchisee continued to operate the business under the name Burger King, the franchisee was liable for trademark infringement. The franchisee's claim of wrongful termination was not a defense to the trademark infringement action. The remedy for the alleged wrongful termination was a separate lawsuit seeking money damages based on breach of contract.[46] Where a Dunkin' Donuts franchisee failed to pay franchise and advertising fees, triggering a contractual termination of the franchise agreement, the continued use of the Dunkin' Donuts name constituted trademark infringement.[47] Similarly, where a Ramada franchise was terminated due to the franchisee's failure to upgrade its property and pay franchise fees, continued use of the Ramada name constituted trademark infringement.[48]

More detail of how these termination cases unfold is provided in Case Example 15-11.

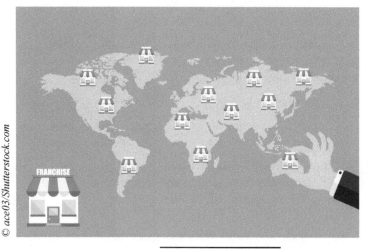

FRANCHISE

---

[41] Ind. Code §§ 23–2-2.7–1(7), (8)

[42] *McDonald's v. Kristina Denise Enterprises*, 189 F.3d 461 (N.Y. 1999); Travelodge Hotels, Inc. v. S.S.B. & Associates, LLC, 2015 WL 4530432 (N.J. 2015).

[43] *Travelodge Hotels, Inc. v. Budget Inns of Defuniak Springs, Inc.*, 2014 WL 1806931 (N.J. 2014); *Pooniwala v. Wyndham Worldwide Corp.*, 2014 WL 1772323 (Minn. 2014).

[44] *Zeidler v. A&W Restaurants*, 2001 WL 62571 (Ill. 2001); aff 'd 301 F.3d 572 (Ill. 2002)

[45] *Travelodge Hotels, Inc. v. Shivmansi, Inc.*, 2015 WL 2354027 (N.J. 2015).

[46] *Burger King Corp. v. Agad*, 911 F.Supp. 1499 (Fla. 1995)

[47] *Dunkin' Donuts, Inc. v. Towns Family, Inc.*, 1996 WL 328018 (Ill. 1996)

[48] *Ramada v. Jacobcart, Inc.*, 2001 WL 540213 (Tex. 2001)

CASE EXAMPLE 15-11

Travelodge Hotels, Inc. v. Budget Inns of Defuniak Sprins, Inc.

2014 WL 1806931 (N.J. 2014).

. . . Plaintiff Travelodge Hotels, Inc. (THI) is a corporation with its principal place of business in Parsippany, New Jersey. Defendant Budget Inns of Defuniak Springs (Defuniak Springs) is a corporation organized under laws of Florida. . . . On June 29, 2007, THI entered into a license agreement (the License Agreement) with Defuniak Springs for the operation of a 57-room Travelodge as a guest lodging facility in Defuniak Springs, Florida (the Facility). . . Defuniak Springs was obligated to operate a Travelodge for a fifteen-year term. . . . Section 3.4 of the License Agreement required Defuniak Springs to operate the Facility in compliance with THI's "System Standards," as defined in the License Agreement, including THI's quality assurance requirements. . . . Under 4.8, THI had the right to conduct unlimited quality assurance inspections of the Facility (and unlimited reinspections if the Facility received a failing score in the inspection) to determine whether the Facility was in compliance with THI's quality assurance requirements.

Section 3.8 of the franchise agreement required Defuniak Springs to prepare and submit monthly reports to THI disclosing among other things, the amount of gross room revenue earned by Defuniak Springs at the Facility in the preceding month for purposes of establishing the amount of royalties and other recurring fees due to THI. Also under that section, Defuniak Springs agreed to maintain at the Facility accurate financial information, including books, records, and accounts relating to the gross room revenue of the Facility, and Defuniak Springs agreed to allow THI to examine, audit, and make copies of the entries in these books, records, and accounts.

Under Section 7, Defuniak Springs was required to make certain periodic payments to THI for royalties, system assessment fees, taxes, interest, reservation system user fees, and other fees. Interest was payable "on any past due amount payable to THI under the agreement at the rate of 1.5% per month or the maximum rate permitted by applicable law, whichever is less." Section 7.3 authorized THI to terminate the License Agreement, with notice to Defuniak Springs, if Defuniak Springs (a) failed to pay any amount due THI under the License Agreement, (b) failed to remedy any other default of its obligations under the License Agreement within 30 days after receipt of written notice from THI specifying one or more defaults under the License Agreement . . .

In the event of termination of the License Agreement [due to Defuniak Spring's default), Defuniak Springs was obligated to pay liquidated damages to THI. Further, the non-prevailing party in a lawsuit was obligated to pay costs and reasonable attorneys' fees incurred by the prevailing party to enforce the agreement.

THI terminated the license agreement after giving proper notice to Defuniak Springs after its failure to pay recurring fees and failure to operate the Facility in accordance with the standards required in the Licensee Agreement. . . .

THI is entitled to damages including unpaid recurring fees in the amount of $174,738.56 plus interest calculated at 15% per month, liquidated damages in the amount of $57,000.00 plus interest, and attorneys' fees in the amount $8,100 and costs in the amount of $1,372.49. . . .

Other cases with similar facts have involved the companies Choice Hotels,[49] Papa John's,[50] and Quizno's.[51]

Regulation of Hotel and Restaurant Internal Affairs

Numerous regulatory laws impact the operation of hospitality establishments. These laws apply to maintenance of guest registers, posting of rates, and recycling.

Guest Register

Most cities and states have passed ordinances that require motels and similar businesses to maintain a register containing guests' names and addresses. One important government interest in a guest register is its use in criminal investigations by both suspects and police. In one case, a defendant charged with a crime sought to use his signature in an out-of-town motel's guest register to substantiate his alibi defense.[52] A register can also aid authorities in locating lost or stolen vehicles and finding wanted persons.

Another example of using the register for police investigations is provided by a case involving a charge of endangering the welfare of a minor. The defendant was 37 years old and developed a sexually explicit online relationship with a 13-year-old. On two occasions he made arrangements to travel from his home to see the girl, staying both times at a hotel. When the relationship was discovered by the girl's mother and reported to the police, the man denied the encounters. The hotel registration documents constituted important evidence to establish his presence in the girl's town on the dates she identified.[53]

A criminal defendant unsuccessfully argued that police access to the guest registry violated his right of privacy. (Recall our discussion of guests' privacy in Chapter 10.) Pursuant to a law-enforcement program called the Lakewood "Crime-Free Hotel Motel Program," the police randomly viewed the registry and compared the names against outstanding warrants. One such check revealed that a guest had outstanding warrants. The police knocked on the guest's room and, when a woman opened the door, the officers entered and arrested defendant. While in the room they observed cocaine on a table and seized it as evidence. The court refused to suppress noting that "checking into the motel was a very public act that anyone could observe, just as walking to his room and any later exits or re-entries were not private."[54]

Privacy rights were determined to be relevant, however, in a case brought by a group of motel operators and a lodging association (a trade association of hotel owners). The statute in question required hoteliers to make their registries available to the police for inspection "at a time and manner that minimizes interference

---

[49] *Choice Hotels v. Frontier Hotels*, 2016 WL 4367993 (Tex. 2016)
[50] *Papa John's International, Inc. V. Rezko*, 446 F. Sup.2d 801 (Ill. 2006)
[51] *The Quizno's Master v. Kadriu*, 2005 WL 948825 (Ill. 2005)
[52] *Norris v. State*, 469 S.E.2d 214 (Ga. 1996)
[53] *Pierce v. State*, 2001 WL 1097728 (Ga. 2001)
[54] *State v. Jorden*, 107 P.3d 130 (Wash. 2005)

with the operation of the business." If the registry is withheld when police ask for it, the hotel is guilty of a misdemeanor. In a case that went to the U.S. Supreme Court, the highest court in the country, the decision held that hotel owners do have privacy interests in the contents of the registry. Therefore, if police come to inspect it and the hotelier objects, the hotel owner is entitled to have a judge conduct a pre-compliance review (prior to revealing the registry to the police) of whether police have sufficient grounds to inspect the book.[55]

Other uses of the register include determining an inn's occupancy rate for purposes of appraising the business,[56] and verifying residence for long-term guests whose ballot in an election is challenged on residency grounds.

Many states have regulations making it unlawful for a hotelkeeper to knowingly accept as a guest a person who has registered under a pseudonym. Falsification of a guest's name frustrates the use of the register as a law enforcement aid. The innkeeper should not permit a guest to register under a name the innkeeper knows is not the guest's true name.

Many states require that the register be retained for a period of several years. The statutes usually specify that the register can be kept using microfilm, electronic imaging, or other like storage process.

Innkeepers should familiarize themselves with locally applicable laws and comply with their mandates.

Room Rates

Many states or localities have statutes requiring hotels to make known the price charged for each room by posting the rates at the hotel. The purpose of these statutes is to eliminate price gouging in the industry. As a court observed in an early Ohio case,

> It is a matter of common knowledge that at times when large numbers of the public meet in cities or towns for conventions, or similar gatherings, the capacity of hotels and places for public accommodation is overtaxed and opportunity is thereby given for the exaction of exorbitant or unfair charges.[57]

The prices are set by the hotel; legislatures do not attempt to fix the price of any room in a hotel, nor do they require that a hotel offer accommodations or services at any particular rate. But when a law has been duly adopted requiring posting of rates, the hotel must post its room charges and abide by the posted prices. Such statutes do not prevent the hotel from raising its rates, but the hotel must post the new rate schedules within specified time limits. Charging more than the posted rate is illegal.[58]

---

55 City of Los Angeles, Ca v. Patel, 192 LE2d 435, 135 S.Ct. 2443 (2015).
56 *Sieger v. Sieger*, 806 N.Y.S.2d 448 (N.Y. 2005)
57 *State v. Norval Hotel Co.*, 133 N.E. 75 (Ohio 1921)
58 See for example New York General Business Law, § 206 et seq.

State laws typically identify where the posting must occur. Customarily the posting must be in a public and conspicuous place in the area where guests register, and also in every guest room.

A hotel can charge different guests different rates provided the different rates are not the result of illegal discrimination. Varying rates would constitute illegal discrimination if based upon gender, race, color, religion, national origin, marital status, or disability. For further discussion on illegal discrimination, see Chapter 3. Issues associated with charging different rates are addressed in Case Example 15-12.

CASE EXAMPLE 15-12

Archibald v. Cinerama Hotels

140 Cal.Rptr. 599 (Calif. 1977)

[Plaintiff is a resident of California who stayed at the defendant's hotel in Hawaii.]

It is alleged in the first cause of action that the rates charged plaintiff and members of her class are higher than those charged to residents of the State of Hawaii. It is not alleged that the rates charged Californians are different than the rates charged any person or class of persons from anywhere else in the world, nor is it alleged that the rates charged plaintiff are unreasonable or excessive. While the complaint categorizes the rate charged her and other nonresidents as a "surcharge" which is "discriminatory," the "preferential treatment" described in the complaint consists of…an unspecified rate presumably lower than the regular rate paid by all nonresidents and is illustrated by advertisement in the yellow pages of the telephone book placed by certain hotels such as "Ask about our [local resident] rates or [local resident] discounts."

Plaintiff has based her case in large part on the common law pertaining to innkeepers. She asserts there was, and is, a duty to charge exactly the same rates to everyone. Reliance is placed by plaintiff principally on textbook authority that innkeepers must provide lodging for all at a reasonable price and that all should be served equally and without discrimination. However, looking at plaintiff's authorities… we observe that the concern of the common law [historically] was and is limited to assuring each traveler freedom from unreasonably high rates. Since travel upon the highway at night was hazardous and there was little choice of lodging for the night, the common law approved restrictions upon innkeepers to [e]nsure a charge of "reasonable value" for services, to prevent them from extorting exorbitant rates.

We have found no authority holding that the offering of a discount to certain clients, patrons or customers based on an attempt to attract their business is unlawful under the common law, whether the discount be for salespeople, clergy, armed services personnel, or local residents. In fact it has been indicated in court decisions that even the common law duty to charge reasonable value for services is inapplicable where the guest is not one who might be stranded on a road in the nighttime or might otherwise be at the mercy of a single innkeeper….

We do not perceive that the common law is concerned with rates as such, except that they not be unreasonable; nor is it concerned with charges lower than reasonable charges, or discounts to induce patronage from certain groups or classes….

Our research has disclosed no California statute, rule or policy which requires a hotel to charge a uniform rate to all its guests.... Insofar as policy or rules are concerned, an innkeeper has a duty to receive and accommodate all persons at a reasonable charge.

The judgment [dismissing the complaint] is affirmed.

CASE QUESTION

1. Can a motel that is the only inn within a 25-mile radius charge whatever rates it chooses? Why or why not?

Price Gouging

When a natural disaster or civil unrest occurs, evacuation of large geographic areas may be necessary. In the process many people typically need a place to stay and flock to hotels. This creates a high demand. Some hotels have responded by raising their room rates significantly.

Approximately 34 states have passed laws that prohibit **price-gouging**, meaning raising prices to excessive levels for essential good and services to take advantage of abnormal market conditions caused by emergencies such as floods, hurricanes, and armed conflicts. Lodging is considered an essential service under these laws. Some states impose civil liability, and some impose both civil and criminal liability. In many states the law is triggered by a formal declaration of a state of emergency by a government official with the authority to make such a declaration. Many states impose specific price limitations, typically ten percent above the price charged immediately prior to the emergency declaration. Other states use a vaguer standard. For example, New York prohibits "unconscionably excessive" increases. Hotel room rates present a tricky proof problem for prosecutors because hotel rates fluctuate frequently, sometimes more than once a day. This is because rates are based on demand for rooms and competitive factors.

price gouging
A pejorative term referring to when a seller spikes the prices of goods, services or commodities to a level much higher than is considered reasonable or fair, and is considered exploitative, potentially to an unethical extent.

Price-gouging statutes typically impose the prohibition for 30 days following the declaration of an emergency. Penalties for violation are substantial. In California hotels are at risk for a fine of up to $10,000; in New York, $25,000; and in Texas, $20,000.

When a crisis occurs, hotels must be vigilant of their room prices to ensure the legal limits are not exceeded.

Mandatory Recycling

Most states and localities have adopted laws requiring businesses and individuals to recycle some of their waste products. The purpose of recycling is to save natural resources, reduce pollution, and decrease the amount of waste that goes into landfills.

Recycling laws vary from state to state and locality to locality, but basically they require that businesses and individuals separate recyclable waste from the rest of the garbage, and waste haulers are required to deliver the recyclable waste to recycling centers. Food service businesses are typically required to separate certain food and beverage containers, such as wine bottles, metal and aluminum containers, and certain types of plastic containers. The law may require that the containers be cleaned, that the glass containers be separated from other recyclables, that each color of glass containers be separated from other colors, and that tops and caps be removed. All businesses are typically required to recycle office paper and corrugated cardboard. Penalties for noncompliance are usually fines ranging in amount from $50 to $1,000 per infraction.

Restaurants and hotels have found a variety of additional ways to further the environment. These include installing water-saving shower heads in guest rooms, offering guests the option of less-than-daily washing of sheets and towels, recycling used fryer oil, and donating used furniture and linens to charitable organizations rather than discarding them.

Licensing and Zoning

Prerequisites to operating a hotel, restaurant, or bar include securing required licenses and permits, and complying with relevant zoning laws. The next sections of this chapter discuss license application, renewal, and revocation processes, and the mandates of zoning laws.

Licensing

The state or government may require that the owner of an inn, hotel, restaurant, or similar establishment obtain various licenses and permits before opening for business. The goal of licensing requirements is to prevent hospitality establishments from becoming menaces to the public welfare by requiring licensed businesses to maintain specified standards for operation, sanitation, construction, compliance with safety rules, and fire protection. The authority of government to license and regulate is based on the power of government to adopt laws that further public health, safety, and welfare. This power is referred to as the **police power**.

police power
The authority of government to license and regulate based on the power of government to adopt laws that further public health, safety, and welfare.

When a government licenses a business or grants a permit, the license or permit confers the right to do something that would otherwise be prohibited. A license is a special privilege rather than a right common to all. For example, you cannot drive a car without a license. Only people who have proven their ability to drive a motor vehicle are entitled to a driver's license. The operation of hotels and restaurants is likewise subject to governmental authority to regulate and license because, like driving, those businesses affect the public welfare.

A considerable body of law has been developed concerning the granting and revoking of licenses. These laws seek to balance the concerns of the government and the interests of the party seeking the license or permit.

Before opening their businesses, hotel and restaurant owners must obtain all necessary licenses and permits. (These terms are used more or less interchangeably; both mean authorization granted by a competent authority to engage in a business.) Those required vary from locality to locality and may include a hotel operator's license, a restaurant operator's license, a liquor license, health and fire code permits, and zoning permits. Determination of what licenses and permits are required and what prerequisites are necessary to qualify for them usually requires considerable research and the aid of an attorney.

Sample Licensing Experience

Every state and county has a health department whose mission is to ensure the health of residents. Included in its domain is the supervision of restaurants. Health departments engage in a multifaceted approach to eliminating foodborne disease. The various components include mandatory plan reviews for all new and remodeled food establishments, mandatory health permits for restaurants, inspections to ensure compliance with health and sanitation rules, prompt investigations of consumer complaints, mandatory food manager training, and litigation against repeat violators of the health code.

Before a restaurant can operate it must obtain a permit from the health department (in addition to other licenses and permits). Prior to issuing the permit, the health department will send an inspector to investigate the premises to determine if it complies with all health and sanitation rules plus any other applicable regulations. If the establishment passes inspection, a permit will be issued. Thereafter, the facility will be subject to periodic announced and unannounced audits. The frequency of these inspections will be accelerated if the health department receives complaints from customers or employees about the health or sanitation conditions at the facility. The purpose of the inspections is to reduce risk factors that contribute to foodborne illness and to avert adulteration of food products.

The health department inspectors are typically trained public-health professionals. They are given various titles depending on the locality, including environmental health specialist, health inspector, and sanitarian.

When they visit an eatery, inspectors will examine the following: how employees receive, process, and store food; the temperatures at which food is cooked, held, and reheated; washing procedures for food and dishes; employee practices such as hair restraints and hand washing; the condition of cooking equipment and how it is shelved; adequacy of the ventilation and heating systems; sewage and waste disposal; whether walls, ceilings, and floors are clean, made of proper materials, and in reasonable condition; the condition of the bathroom facilities; how hazardous materials (e.g., cleaning fluids, insect repellents) are labeled and stored; whether evidence of vermin exists; whether ingredients are properly disclosed to diners (truth-in-menu issues); whether required signs and notices are posted (e.g., mandated warnings about alcohol and pregnancy, poster demonstrating the Heimlich Maneuver, and most localities require restaurants to post their public health permit and business license).

Also, during an inspection the inspector may ask an employee to demonstrate a procedure—such as the use of a sanitizer during dish washing—to determine if it is being done correctly.

As a result of an inspection, the health department may issue to the restaurant citations, which are accusations of health or sanitation code violations. Owners are given the opportunity to promptly correct the problem. If they dispute the alleged violations they have a right to a hearing. If serious or repeated violations are discovered, the health department will suspend or revoke the restaurant's permit, thereby forcing it to close.

Examples of violations restaurants might be cited for include: employees not practicing "good hygiene;" insufficient hand-washing facilities; toxic items improperly stored, labeled, or used; food not meeting temperature requirements during service (or storage); presence of insects or rodents; broken self-closer on back door allowing rodents in; hand-washing facilities not accessible; hand sink missing shields (thereby permitting splashing onto clean dishes); and evidence of cigarette smoking in food preparation areas.

Violations are customarily categorized. The most serious relate directly to the protection of the public from foodborne illness and, if found, must be corrected immediately. A second tier of violations include cleanliness issues and must be remediated within a specified time period.

Many local health departments are now posting inspection results on the Internet to allow consumers to make informed decisions regarding patronage of food establishments. On some sites, to help consumers understand the significance of a violation, the consumer can click on an infraction for which a restaurant was cited and read the public health reasons for the rule.

Compliance with Laws

To qualify for a license, the applicant must prove that he will abide by all applicable laws. In Case Example 15-13, an applicant was denied a hotel license because the government entity charged with issuing the license believed the applicant would permit immoral activity.

CASE EXAMPLE 15-13

Hertenberger v. City of Texarkana

272 S.W.2d 435 (Ark. 1954)

The applicant [E]velyn Hertenberger applied to the City of Texarkana for a license to operate a hotel. The [City] council, after considering the application, refused to issue the license. [She appealed the decision of the City Council.]

Ordinance B-439 of the City of Texarkana pertains to the licensing of rooming houses and hotels, and provides: "such license shall not be granted unless it shall appear probable to the Council that such applicant will not rent rooms for immoral purposes or allow prostitutes or pimps to remain on such premises or permit gambling or the sale, storage or keeping of intoxicating liquor on such premises." ...

Without going into detail as to the evidence, suffice it to say that the council was justified in reaching the conclusion that if Mrs. Hertenberger was granted a license, in all probability the hotel rooms would be rented for immoral purposes; and Ordinance B-439 specifically provides that the license shall not be granted in such circumstances. Although the right to operate a hotel is a property right, this fact does not preclude the city council from refusing to issue a license where the issuance of such license would be in violation of a valid ordinance....

We have reached the conclusion that the ordinance is valid and none of the applicant's constitutional rights were violated in refusing her a license to operate a hotel in Texarkana.

CASE QUESTIONS

1. Why would the City of Texarkana want to ensure that a hotel or boarding house owner would not permit gambling, prostitution, and other illegal activities on the premises?

2. What evidence do you think was presented to convince the city council that Hertenberger would have permitted immoral activity at her hotel?

Grounds for Denial of a License

To deny a license, the licensing body must have a reasonable basis; it cannot deny the license on arbitrary, capricious, or unreasonable grounds. In making its determination, a licensing authority may take into account a wide range of factors such as traffic, noise, size, community sentiment, the type of business conducted by the applicant, and the applicant's reputation. In Case Example 15-13, the court held that the city council's concern about immoral activity was reasonable, probably based on prior incidents in which Hertenberger was found guilty of prostitution, gambling, or illegal sales of alcohol.

Residents in the vicinity of a proposed new restaurant, hotel, or bar may oppose the new establishment for fear of noise, traffic, congestion, or crime. Organized community resistance to the granting of a license is a legitimate consideration when a board is reviewing a license application. In one case, an applicant sought a license to open a liquor store. Fifty-three residents signed a petition urging the town board to deny the application for the following reasons: Two other liquor stores existed within a quarter mile in each direction and the area around the proposed location was across from the community church and "presents the wrong message to children who attend the church." The town board denied the license based in considerable part on the townspeople's resistance. The applicant appealed, claiming that denial of a license based on community opposition is arbitrary and capricious. The court upheld the board's decision, ruling that reliance on residents' opposition is not arbitrary.[59]

Adequate parking is another legitimate concern of a board reviewing a license application. For example, a sports bar applied for a liquor license. A town prerequisite was a specified minimum number of parking spaces. The applicant was able to meet the minimum requirement but only by counting off-site parking that was "remote and not conveniently accessible." This, coupled with a location across the street from homes, schools, and parks, was grounds for denial of the license.[60]

victualler's license
License required to operate a business that sells food.

In an instructive case, McDonald's, the fast-food hamburger company, was denied a **victualer's license** (required for a business that sells food) for a proposed restaurant in a shopping center, in part because of inadequate parking and in part because of concerns about increased traffic endangering students in a nearby high school. McDonald's appealed and the court ruled the denial of the license was arbitrary and capricious, and McDonald's was entitled to the license. The court noted the following: the proposed McDonald's location was in a relatively empty corner of the shopping center, peak hours at the restaurant did not coincide with the arrival and departure of school buses, and police were assigned to traffic duty at times the school buses operate. Further, the shopping center was not close to a major highway, and so the restaurant was likely to attract only those customers already in the immediate area on other business. The court also held the board had incorrectly interpreted a town parking ordinance that required businesses located on a separate lot, as the proposed McDonald's would be, to have adequate parking on that lot, which McDonald's did not. However, according to the terms of the lease, McDonald's was entitled to use the mall's common parking lot, which contained sufficient parking spaces. The court thus held that adequate parking was available.[61]

In Case Example 15-14, also involving a McDonald's location, we learn that the licensing body, when deciding whether to grant a license, can consider not only public sentiment but also the number of similar licenses already granted and the need for another like business. Note the conflict-of-interest issue discussed near the end of the decision.

CASE EXAMPLE 15-14

McDonald's Corp. v. Town of East Longmeadow

506 N.E.2d 172 (Mass. 1987)

[McDonald's Corp. appeals the denial of a victualler's license.]...In denying the license the board [of Selectmen, which is the equivalent of a Town Council] gave the reasons [identified later in this decision].[1] McDonald's claims that the board considered factors which are not connected with the

---

[59] *Thompson v. Lake Edward Township*, 2000 WL 1869565 (Minn. 2000)
[60] *Woods v. Trussville City Council*, 795 So.2d 725 (Ala. 2001)
[61] *McDonald's Corporation v. Board of Selectmen of Randolph*, 399 N.E.2d 38 (Mass. 1980)

preparation and delivery of food, and that the reasons were not supported by evidence. It urges, for example, that the number of twenty-two licenses deemed sufficient was determined arbitrarily and without any studies. We agree with the trial judge that McDonald's has not shown the decision was arbitrary or capricious....

The breadth of discretion which local authorities enjoy in granting or denying licenses varies. In the case of common victualler licenses... for example, town and city boards may exercise judgment about public convenience and public good that is very broad indeed.... There is no question that the board may consider the number of licenses already granted in determining the public good.... The board was not required to make studies to determine the number of licenses to be issued. The board members, local residents of the town, were aware of local patron needs, took a view, and noted that there were fifteen restaurants along route 83. The board also properly considered the proximity of another McDonald's.

In particular, McDonald's challenges the board's consideration of public sentiment, traffic, and litter. There was widespread opposition to the grant of the license at the board's hearing. This was in large part because of the "traffic danger to children in the nearby park."...

While the board's decision appears to be based primarily on the lack of a need for an additional license, the board also took these other considerations into account...These "ancillary and contributing reasons," even if not sufficient in themselves to warrant a denial of license to McDonald's, did not vitiate the action of the [board]....

The licensing authorities are not...required to grant any licenses to common victuallers. Whether any such licenses shall be granted and, if any, the number to be granted, rest in the sound judgment of the licensing board as to the demands of the public welfare in the respective communities....There was here no basis on the record to disturb the board's decision.

One of the selectmen disqualified himself from voting because he was employed by Friendly's Corporation. McDonald's, a competitor of Friendly's, asserts that the selectman's participation in speaking against the application and chairing the board's meetings was a [conflict of interest]. Although such participation may have been inappropriate... the trial judge, on the basis of the testimony of the other two selectmen, concluded that the facts did not warrant a finding that the selectman's affiliation with Friendly Corporation constitutes a conflict of interest which tainted the... decision. That finding was not clearly erroneous and is consonant with applicable law....

Judgment [denying the license] affirmed.

[1] The applicant has offered no evidence of the need for the new establishment on North Main Street, or that the good of the Town of East Longmeadow requires it, and the Board finds that the need does not exist, and the License and Permit would not be for the good of the town.

An expression of protest of the restaurant is reflected in the petition bearing 600 names, and delivered to the Selectmen. The Board finds that with regards to need, there are already 22 Common Victualler's Licenses in this small town. The Springfield McDonald's is but a short distance away.

In making its decision the Selectmen have also considered the potential for increased traffic particularly during peak hours on North Main Street which is the town's main thoroughfare, and the immediacy of the proposed location to the public park and the resulting negative concerns as to pedestrian safety and adequate disposal of waste.

Past Use of the Property

Another factor the licensing body will consider is the prior use of the property. For example, a junior college applied for a license to operate as dormitories certain buildings it owned. Although the buildings had previously been used as dorms by another college, the neighbors staged an intense protest to the proposed use based on fears of congestion, inadequate parking, and noise. The license was initially denied but granted on appeal. The court held the denial was not based on a reasonable basis and noted that the buildings had previously been used as dormitories with no complaints by neighbors. The court also acknowledged that the junior college applicant was an accredited institution and no unfavorable evidence was presented about its capacity to operate the dorms or about the character of its officers.[62]

Administrative Procedure

Licenses are often issued by a government agency—that is, a governmental subdivision managed by directors appointed by elected officials responsible for administering particular laws. When a licensee fails to abide by the applicable rules, the agency is responsible for prosecuting the violation. Until now, most of the cases we have discussed in the book have been pursued in court. When a government agency is involved, the initial forum for the case is usually a hearing officer within the agency rather than a court. If the matter is appealed, the first appeal is often a mandated process housed within the agency and not in court. If the case is appealed again it will be heard by a court.

Before a matter that is within the jurisdiction of a government agency can be heard in a court, the **administrative remedies must be exhausted**. This means all appeals available within the agency must have been utilized before the case is heard.

administrative remedies must be exhausted
Appeals available within an administrative agency must have been utilized and completed before the case is heard in court.

License Fees

Licensees often complain that the cost of a license is high. A municipality can require a reasonable fee to be paid for a license intended to protect the public. Many licenses must be renewed annually with a fee imposed for each renewal. If the fee covers the municipality's costs to administer the license—including the cost to prepare and distribute applications, inspect both licensed and would-be licensed premises, and pursue violators—and does not generate much money beyond the cost to administer the license, the fee is reasonable and valid. Governments cannot use licensing fees as a revenue-raising device. If a license fee produces a significant profit above the costs of administration, the fee will be considered unreasonable and subject to modification. In a ruling more than 100 years old, which remains the law today, a court said,

> *The amount the municipality has a right to demand for [a license] fee depends upon the extent and expense of the municipal supervision made necessary by the business in the city or town that issues the*

---

[62] *Newberry Junior College v. Town of Brookline*, 472 N.E.2d 1373 (Mass. 1985)

licenses. A fee sufficient to cover the expense of issuing the license, and to pay the expenses which may be incurred in the enforcement of such police inspection or superintendence as may be lawfully exercised over the business, may be required. It is obvious that the actual amount necessary to meet such expenses cannot, in all cases, be ascertained in advance, and that it would be futile to require anything of the kind. The result is, if the fee required is not plainly unreasonable, the courts ought not to interfere with the discretion exercised by the [legislature] in fixing it; and, unless the contrary appears on the face of the ordinance requiring it, or is established by proper evidence, they should presume it to be reasonable.[63]

Consequences of Operating Without a License

Failure to obtain a required license can lead to unpleasant consequences, as can failure to obtain a license renewal, which is customarily required at regular intervals, often annually.

Penalties and Fines

If a business fails to qualify for or otherwise obtain a necessary license, the government can bar it from opening or, in the case of an existing business that fails to obtain a renewal, force the business to close. In addition, fines may be imposed. In some states including Florida, the innkeeper or restaurateur may be required to attend "at personal expense, an educational program."[64]

Loss of Protection of Law

Depending on the type of license, another consequence of operating without it may be that the business is unable to enforce its contracts. If the purpose of the license is to protect the public, as is the case of a license to operate a restaurant, the absence of the license will in some states bar the restaurant from enforcing its contracts in court. For example, if a restaurant is not properly licensed and a diner fails to pay, the restaurant may be unable to enforce the guest's contractual duty to resolve the bill. This should be sufficient motivation for restaurateurs and innkeepers to abide by the applicable licensing laws.

In a related case, a tour operator sought to enforce a breach of contract claim in excess of $56,000. The tour operator had failed to comply with a requirement of Florida law necessitating sellers of travel services to register annually with the state. The court stated, "Since plaintiff was not registered as a seller of travel at the time the contracts were made, the contracts are void and unenforceable." Judgment was thus entered for the defendant without regard to the merits of the case.[65]

---

[63] *City of Fayetteville v. Carter*, 12 S.W. 573 (Ark. 1889)
[64] Florida Statutes § 509.261(a)(b)
[65] *Omega Congress, Inc. v. BAF Tour Services, Inc.*, 855 So.2d 113 (Fla. 2003)

Where, however, the purpose of the license is to raise revenue (income for the government) and is unrelated to protection of the public, the ability of a business lacking the license to enforce its contracts will not be affected.

Revocation or Suspension of a License

As we have discussed, a license is a privilege, not a right. A licensee must establish it is worthy of the license; there is no automatic entitlement to it. If a licensee fails to continuously meet the requirements of the license, it can be suspended (withdrawn temporarily) or revoked (withdrawn permanently) by the licensing body, which is usually a government agency.

Cause for Revocation or Suspension

The legislature empowers a licensing board to revoke a license when it is satisfied that the licensee is unfit to engage in a business authorized by the license. For example, licensed innkeepers who allow illegal or objectionable activity on the premises, such as illicit gambling or drinking by minors, may be found unfit to keep the license. A restaurant was warned twice by the Health Department about sanitation violations but the eatery declined to correct the problems. On its third visit to the restaurant the Health Department noted that the violations had not been addressed and more existed, including three "critical" ones. This justified the Health Department forcing closure of the restaurant.[66] Likewise a hotel faced high fines and license termination where it violated various building code mandates including an elevator in disrepair and inoperable for four and a half weeks, lack of functional smoke detectors, cockroach infestation, damaged walls and ceilings, damaged sinks, broken windows, peeling paint on ceilings and walls, and unsanitary carpet on the bathroom floor.[67]

In Case Example 15-15, a restaurant was found to have tolerated numerous safety violations, resulting in a denial of its application for renewal of its liquor license. Take note of the breadth of reasons in the relevant statute that justify denial of a license.

CASE EXAMPLE 15–15

Oronoka Restaurant, Inc. v. Maine State Liquor Commission

532 A.2d 1043 (Maine 1987)

...On January 8, 1986, Oronoka Restaurant (Oronoka) applied for the renewal of its liquor license. On February 10, 1986, the municipal officers of the Town of Orono [in which the restaurant was located] conducted a public hearing on the application and voted unanimously to deny the applica-

---

[66] *Radden v. City of Detroit*, 2006 WL 397945 (Mich. 2006)
[673] *City and County of San Francisco v. Boyd Hotel, LLC*, 2005 WL 958222 (Calif. 2005)

tion for renewal. The Town based its decision on sewage discharge violations, numerous fire code violations, and the failure of the applicant to allow the Town's code enforcement officer access to the premises to inspect for code or ordinance violations. Oronoka filed a timely appeal with the Maine State Liquor Commission (Commission). The Commission ruled that the fire code violations constituted health and safety hazards and thus were valid grounds to deny the application for renewal.... Under the [applicable state statute] the Commission may consider all of the following as grounds to deny a liquor license:

A. Conviction of the applicant of any [of a specified level of crime];

B. Noncompliance of the licensed premise with any local zoning ordinance or other land use ordinance not directly related to liquor control;

C. Conditions of record such as waste disposal violations, health or safety violations, or repeated parking or traffic violations on or in the vicinity of the licensed premises and caused by persons patronizing or employed by the licensed premises; or other such conditions caused by persons patronizing or employed by the licensed premises which unreasonably disturb, interfere with or affect the ability of persons or businesses residing or located in the vicinity of the licensed premises to use their property in a reasonable manner;

D. Repeated incidents of record of breaches of the peace, disorderly conduct, vandalism or other violations of law on or in the vicinity of the licensed premises and caused by persons patronizing or employed by the licensed premises; and

E. A violation of any [of the liquor sales laws]....

The Commission heard extensive and very specific testimony concerning the fire code violations from the Town's fire chief and its code enforcement officer. Of particular concern was an unlicensed, unapproved and illegally installed solid fuel unit or "wood burning boiler." Witnesses testified that the unit lacked appropriate safety systems and could possibly explode. Despite repeated warnings by Town officials that the boiler failed to meet applicable safety standards, Oronoka's owner, as of the time of the Town hearing, had not brought the unit into compliance and had not obtained the necessary approval for its use.

The hazardous solid fuel unit and Oronoka's other fire code violations fall within the grounds specified [by the state statue] upon which a town may deny a liquor license renewal.... We affirm the judgment.

CASE QUESTION

1. Why are safety violations relevant to the renewal of a liquor license?

A license might also be suspended if the licensee provided false information on the application. Thus, where a restaurant obtained a license to operate a family-style eatery, but instead offered nude dancing and the "hottest adult entertainment to hit the Northeast," its license was suspended.[64]

A victualler's license can be revoked where criminal conduct occurs on the premises. Thus, a good cause for nonrenewal of a restaurant license existed where drug dealing was happening in the facility even though neither the owners or employees were involved. "Every business is responsible for illegal activity on its premises."[69]

A victualler's license is needed only when food is served on the premises. A Dunkin Donuts store was directed by the town board to obtain a victualler's license. Dunkin Donuts resisted this requirement claiming it was offering takeout service exclusively and therefore should not need the license. The court concurred, concluding that a victualler is someone who serves food for consumption on the premises.[70]

In Case Example 15-16, a liquor license was suspended because the bar repeatedly served customers who appeared intoxicated.

CASE EXAMPLE 15–16

In Re Cadillac Jacks

2003 WL 1908420 (Minn. 2003)

Cadillac Jacks challenges the three-day suspension of its liquor license, asserting that the Chaska City Council acted arbitrarily and capriciously and employed unlawful procedure when deciding the matter, and that there was insufficient evidence to support its determination.

Cadillac Jacks received two warning letters from the Chaska Police Department (CPD) before these proceedings were instigated and the city council held two hearings on the matter. At the first hearing held June 17, 2002 Police Chief Scott Knight outlined a chronology of police responses to service calls related to Cadillac Jacks. The evidence shows that from February 2001 to mid-June 2002 CPD issued 21 driving-under-the-influence (DWI) citations to intoxicated persons who had just left Cadillac Jacks. Four patrons of Cadillac Jacks were involved in accidents after intoxicated persons left the bar and drove automobiles, and three persons were sent to detox after leaving the bar. In addition, four assault calls were reported for Cadillac Jacks during this time period. Chief Knight testified that, compared to other bars, Cadillac Jacks had received a much higher volume of police calls and has had a greater number of DWI citations, assault charges, detox commits and motor vehicle accidents. Chief Knight indicated that the high number of DWI citations issued to Cadillac Jacks patrons posed a serious safety threat to the public.

Based on this testimony the city council determined that a three-day suspension was appropriate.

---

[68] *D.H.L. Associates, Inc. v. Krussel,* 1996 WL 754910 (Mass. 1996)
[69] *Hard Times Cafe, Inc. v. City of Minneapolis,* 625 S.W.2d 165 (Minn. 2001)
[70] *Town of Wellesley Board of Selectmen v. Javamine, Inc.,* 2006 WL 1345836 (Mass. 2006)

The council had before it overwhelming evidence that Cadillac Jacks was "over-serving" intoxicated persons. These facts amply support the city council's conclusion that Cadillac Jacks's operating procedures posed a significant threat to the health, safety, and welfare of the citizens of Chaska. We conclude that the city acted properly when it decided to suspend Cadillac Jacks's liquor license.

When the town seeks to suspend a license it has the burden of proof to establish that the licensee is unqualified and people's well-being is at risk. Without that proof the license cannot be rescinded. A town sought to invalidate a health department permit for a McDonald's upon discovering that the soil around and beneath the eatery was contaminated with tetrachloroethylene (PCE). Townspeople complained of various health problems, but no evidence was presented at the hearing that connected the illnesses to the presence of the PCE. On appeal the court refused to invalidate the license noting that the residents provided no medical or scientific testimony to support the claim that the illnesses were caused by the PCE.[71]

Due Process

The licensee is entitled to **due process,** the right not to be deprived of property (including a license) without a fair hearing. This means that before a license can be revoked, the licensee is entitled to reasonable notice of the grounds for which revocation is sought, sufficient time before the hearing to prepare a defense, a hearing, the opportunity to obtain an attorney, an impartial decision maker, and a decision based solely on the record, meaning the evidence presented at the hearing.

due process
The right not to be deprived of life, liberty, or property without a fair hearing. With respect to licenses and regulations, this means that proprietors are entitled to reasonable notice of the grounds for any proposed legal action, an opportunity to prepare a defense, and a hearing.

In the notice, the licensee is entitled to information identifying the specific conduct attributable to the licensee that allegedly violates the rules relating to the license. The reason for this requirement is to provide sufficient information to enable the licensee to address the allegations and prepare a response. Clearly, a notice of revocation that does not state the grounds is not sufficiently specific. In a Kentucky case the licensee was charged with operating a hotel improperly. The licensing body gave the following notice:

> *You are herewith advised that...a hearing will be held at 10 A.M. Wednesday, August 24, 1955, 17 Federal Street, on complaints received by the board as regards your operation of the premises known as "Nantucket New Ocean House."*

The court held that this notice did not adequately inform the license holder of the charges she faced, and thus violated her due process rights.[72]

---

[71] *McDonald's Corp. v. Board of License & Inspection Review,* 849 A.2d 1277 (Pa. 2004)
[72] *Manchester v. Selectmen of Nantucket,* 293 S.W.2d 631 (Ky. 1956)

To satisfy due process, not only must the notice of the grounds for revocation be given to the licensee far enough in advance to enable the licensee to prepare a defense, but also the date of the hearing must be provided. In a case involving a lounge, the facility was licensed to provide live entertainment, including exotic dancing. One night it presented male dancers rather than the usual females. The crowd exceeded permissible building capacity. Two days later the town Board of Selectmen, the body that issues and revokes entertainment licenses, notified the owner of the lounge at 5:30 P.M. that a special meeting would be held that evening at 7:00 P.M. to consider revoking his license. This short notice violated the owner's due process rights. He was entitled to have the hearing rescheduled to a later date, thereby enabling him to prepare a defense and attend.[73]

Where a licensee receives a notice to appear before the licensing board and believes the notice is inadequate, the licensee should request additional information concerning the charges or additional time to prepare a defense, as the case may be. Failure to object may result in a waiver of any due process defects in the notice.

Decision Based on Record

Due process requires that decisions concerning a business' license be made based exclusively on evidence presented on the record at the hearing. Due process would be violated if members of a city council, while deciding whether to revoke a restaurant license, considered information not presented at the hearing or if they made up their minds before the hearing was completed. If these circumstances were proven, the due process violation would require a new hearing on the issue of the license revocation.[74]

Zoning

zoning
Restrictions imposed by local governments on the manner in which property owners can use their land.

Zoning is a process by which local governments can restrict the ways property owners can use their land. For example, a zoning ordinance may limit use of property to residential purposes and preclude commercial and industrial uses, or may provide a maximum height for a building—for example, five stories—or may restrict the size, number, and/or type of sign a business can display on its property to advertise its services—for example, flashing neon signs may be prohibited. In a Maine case a restaurant was found to have violated a sign ordinance by erecting more than the permitted two signs.[75]

The purpose of zoning laws is to achieve balanced development, preserve the residential quality of residential neighborhoods, and minimize adverse effects resulting from inappropriate location, use, or design of certain buildings or businesses. A Connecticut case further clarifies these objectives. It involved a zoning district in the town of Stratford in which only single-family residences were permitted.

The owners of one of the homes operated a rooming house with 10 boarders. The zoning enforcement officer ordered the owners to terminate the boardinghouse

---

[73] *Konstantopoulos v. Town of Whately*, 424 N.E.2d 210 (Mass. 1981)
[74] *Hard Times Cafe, Inc. v. City of Minneapolis*, 625 N.W.2d 165 (Minn. 2001)
[75] *B&B Coastal Enterprises, Inc. v. Demers*, 276 F.Supp.2d 155 (Maine 2003)

operation. The owners, wanting to continue, challenged the law. The court upheld it, stating,

> *[Local governments are empowered] to lay out zones where family val-*
> *ues, youth values, and the blessings of quiet seclusion and clean air*
> *make the area a sanctuary for people...[b]oarding houses...present*
> *urban problems. More people occupy a given space; more cars rather*
> *continuously pass by; more cars are parked; noise travels with crowds.*[76]

The rooming house was thus forced to close.

In another case, construction of a 170-room Residence Inn by Marriott (the Marriott) was challenged based on a local zoning ordinance that permitted "hotels" of the size of the proposed project but prohibited "residence hotels." The rule defined a hotel as "a building containing sleeping rooms for resident or transient guests with a provision for serving food in a public dining room, but no cooking in rooms occupied by guests." The Marriott's building plans included a two-burner cooktop in each of the guest rooms. The building inspector and zoning board of appeals determined that the proposed in-room cooking appliance was a limited, occasionally used guest convenience and not a cooking facility. The court concurred and the Marriott was allowed to build the facility as planned.[77]

For the would-be innkeeper or restaurateur, zoning laws may ban development of the business in the desired location. For example, a commercial establishment will not be permitted in an area zoned exclusively residential. Before any resources are committed to a new business, the owner should investigate the applicable zoning restrictions.

Some localities have zoning ordinances that prohibit drive-through sales windows as a means to restrict traffic congestion. These rules effectively bar the utilization of this sales device within the locality to which the ordinance applies. Not surprisingly, these regulations are a bane to fast-food restaurants.[78]

Another zoning ordinance adopted by some municipalities requires that at least 60 percent of a restaurant's total sales be from food rather than alcohol. The city of Fort Worth sent a warning notice to a restaurant believed to be in violation. The eatery was told it needed to rectify the problem or its license to operate would be canceled. The restaurant failed to modify its practices, and a hearing was held following adequate notice to the owner. The city council concluded that although the restaurant claimed to be in compliance, its method for allocating its sales to food or alcohol was a "subterfuge" and in fact it was not complying with the ordinance. The restaurant's license to operate was thus canceled. On appeal, the legality of the ordinance and the revocation of the license were upheld.[79]

A typical zoning ordinance requires a minimum number of parking spaces for various land uses based on factors such as the type of business involved, the number

---

[76] *Dinan v. Board of Zoning Appeals of the Town of Stratford,* 595 A.2d 864 (Conn. 1991)
[77] *Ellis v. Alberghini,* 2016 WL 2986055 (Mass. 2016).
[78] *Renaissance v. Zoning Board,* 2001 WL 770847 (R.I. 2001)
[79] *West End Pink v. City,* 2001 WL 1329242 (Tex. 2001)

of employees, and the square footage of the facility. A license to operate will not be granted without the proper number of parking spots being available. Sometimes, after a license has been issued, the number of parking spaces is reduced perhaps due to development, deterioration, or otherwise. If the number of parking spots remaining is insufficient to satisfy the zoning rules, the business will be required to address the problem or face revocation of its license.[80]

In Case Example 15-17, a bar violated a local zoning ordinance and as a result was required to discontinue its business.

CASE EXAMPLE 15-17

Schleuter v. City of Fort Worth

947 S.W.2d 920 (Tex. 1997)

...In an attempt to mitigate the negative secondary effects of sexually oriented businesses, the City of Fort Worth added sections to its Comprehensive Zoning Ordinance (CZO). A person violates the CZO if he or she operates a "sexually oriented business" within 1000 feet of residentially zoned property. "Sexually oriented business" is defined as "any commercial venture whose operations include the 'providing, featuring or offering of employees or entertainment personnel who appear on the premises while in a state of nudity or simulated nudity....'"

On May 11, 1995, Sports Fantasy opened for business in Fort Worth. Sports Fantasy is a "sports bar"... described by the owner as an "upscale sports bar... catering to gentlemen clientele." Sports Fantasy featured entertainment in the form of "stage dancing" by female entertainers. While dancing, the female entertainers would strip their clothing off to the point where they would only be wearing "T-back" bottoms and latex pasties covering only the areola of their breasts. Sports Fantasy was located within 1000 feet of residentially zoned property.

After a bench trial the trial court entered a permanent injunction against Fantasy Sports [prohibiting it from carrying on a sexually oriented business].

[On appeal, the sports bar raised various arguments seeking to have the zoning ordinance declared invalid and unenforceable. The court rejected these arguments and determined the ordinance was valid and enforceable and affirmed the injunction.][1]

[1]For a similar holding see *Smartt Investments, Inc. d/b/a/ Xoticas v. Martinez*, 2002 WL 31890887 (Tex. 2002)

---

[80] *American Condominium Association v. Benson*, 2001 WL 1452781 (R.I. 2001)

In circumstances where zoning laws prohibit a desired use or development, the land owner can seek a **variance,** which is permission from the local government to deviate from the restrictions. Variances are given sparingly and only when the deviation will not have a significantly negative impact on the goals sought by the zoning law in issue.

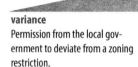

variance
Permission from the local government to deviate from a zoning restriction.

A variance was granted to a hotel seeking relief from a zoning ordinance that limited hotels in a particular district to two stories and 35 feet in height. The hotel seeking the variance wanted to build a five-story, 45-foot-high hotel. The local planning board granted the variance and the town appealed. The court upheld the variance for three reasons: (1) office buildings in the district were permitted to be six stories and 90 feet high; (2) the facade of the proposed hotel was designed to resemble the nearby offices; and (3) the hotel was targeted to commercial travelers and so would complement the surrounding commercial area. The court thus concluded that granting a variance for the hotel's height was consistent with commercial development in the area and had "positive relevance to the town's planned economic development."[81]

A variance was denied to build a Wendy's restaurant where the town zoning law prohibited fast-food establishments throughout the town. The court determined that Wendy's failed to present evidence establishing special reasons to justify the grant of a variance or that the building owner would suffer an undue hardship if the variance was not granted. Absent proof of such circumstances, a variance will be denied. Further, the court noted there were other potential commercial uses for the space earmarked for the Wendy's.[82]

Similarly, a variance was denied to a resort and hotel in Waikiki, Hawaii, that sought to expand its facility 60 feet into an area zoned as a shorefront setback for the purpose of preserving the state's most popular beach. The hotel also wanted to build upward from 8 stories to 26, which would violate the applicable zoning height limitations. A variance was denied for that part of the construction project as well. The resort's adversary was a coalition of environmental groups seeking (successfully) to preserve the coastal protection laws.[83]

In another case a request for a variance from a sign ordinance was denied. The objective of the regulation was to achieve uniformity in shape, size, color, and placement so as not to confuse or mislead vehicular traffic, or obstruct vision. A restaurant sought to erect a sign that was "50 percent taller than permitted; approximately two-and-one-half times larger than the maximum square footage permitted; contains more than two-and-one-half times the items of information permitted; and contains colors other than black and white." The town denied the variance and the court affirmed, stating that the eatery could promote its business and still comply with the ordinance.[84]

---

[81] *Commercial Realty & Resources Corp. v. First Atlantic Properties Co.*, 585 A.2d 928 (N.J. 1991)
[82] *Saddle Brook Realty, LLC v. Township of Saddle Brook Zoning Board of Adjustment,* 906 A.2d 454 (N.J. 2006)
[83] *Surfrider Foundation v. Zoning Board of Appeals*, 358 P.3d 664 (Hawaii 2015).
[84] *The Brick Haus, Inc. v. Board of Adjustment,* 2006 WL 2266299 (Iowa 2006)

Summary

The business of operating a hotel or restaurant is highly regulated. The owner must be aware of applicable laws to avoid liability for violation.

Businesses are prohibited from using another's trademark or service mark, as well as others' copyrighted works, without the permission of the owner. One arrangement where permission is granted to use a trademark or service mark is franchising. The relationship between a franchisor and franchisee is contractual. The parties should include in their agreement all terms relevant to their relationship to help avoid disputes in the operation of the business.

To encourage competition, the law prohibits certain practices that restrain competition. The laws that ban these practices are called antitrust laws.

A hotel is required to maintain a guest register including some or all of the following information, depending on the mandates of the relevant state laws: names; addresses; make and model of car; license number; room assignment; date and hour of arrival; and date of departure. The innkeeper may also be required to post notices of the rates charged for rooms.

Concerns about protecting our environment have engendered laws mandating recycling. While the particular requirements vary from state to state, the purpose of these laws is to save natural resources, reduce pollution, and lower the amount of waste that goes into landfills.

An innkeeper or restaurateur must obtain all necessary licenses and permits. Operating a business without them can result in forced closure, fines, and unenforceable contracts. Zoning laws restrict the permissible uses of land. For example, a business cannot be built in an area that is zoned exclusively residential.

Preventive Law Tips for Managers

- *Do a trademark search before adopting a name for your hotel or restaurant.* Use of another's trademark or service mark can result in forced discontinuance of a name in which you have invested money to advertise and promote. This can be avoided by undertaking a trademark search prior to adopting the name. The search and analysis of the results are customarily done by a trademark attorney. The search reveals the names of any other businesses that are using the same or similar name you propose to adopt. If someone else is already using it for a similar product, you can save promotion money and an infringement lawsuit by selecting an alternative.

- *Do not intercept and transmit copyrighted television programs without the permission of the copyright owner.* Use of a satellite dish to intercept copyrighted programming without the permission of the copyright owners con-

CHAPTER 15: Regulation and Licensing

stitutes copyright infringement and can lead to a lawsuit. If you want to offer your guests the opportunity to watch cable television in their rooms or to view limited-access sports events in a bar or restaurant, make the necessary arrangements with the cable stations to receive cable programming through legal means.

- *Do not offer musical entertainment without first obtaining licenses from AS-CAP and BMI.* Providing music for the enjoyment of a hotel's or restaurant's patrons without purchasing the required copyright licenses constitutes copyright infringement. To comply with the law and avoid a lawsuit, make the necessary arrangements with the organizations that represent the owners of copyrights in musical compositions and recordings.

- *Review the operating practices of your hotel or restaurant to be sure you are not in violation of antitrust laws.* Failure to comply with antitrust laws can result in criminal liability and steep damage awards (treble damages) in civil cases. Initiate regular reviews of the practices of your hotel or restaurant—including pricing, purchasing, selling, advertising, and relationships with other hotels—to ensure your facility is not engaging in antitrust violations. Use for this purpose the checklist of illegal activities contained in this chapter.

- *If you buy a franchise, carefully review the disclosure documents and discuss them with your attorney and accountant before making a decision to buy.* By law, a franchisor is required to disclose in writing detailed information about the franchise operation (the prospectus) at least 10 days prior to accepting any money from a would-be franchisee. Review this information carefully and ask your lawyer and accountant to do the same. The purpose for the disclosure requirement is to give a potential franchisee time to absorb and evaluate all relevant information. Take advantage of the law.

- *If you buy a franchise, be sure all agreements are embodied in the contractual agreement.* The contract between the franchisor and franchisee should be in writing and contain all agreements of the parties. Read the contract carefully before signing to ensure the terms are as expected and all agreements are included.

- *As a manager, keep fully apprised of your employees' actions and practices.* An employer may be liable for the acts of its employees even when the employee is violating the employer's policies. To avoid liability on this ground, keep close tabs on your employees. Inquire often about methods they are using to fulfill job responsibilities, watch them work, review their outgoing mail, and meet with them frequently to discuss the job.

- *Keep a register of guests' names and other information required by law.* Laws in most states require an innkeeper to keep a record of information about all registered guests at the hotel and to preserve the record for a specified period of time. The type of information required varies from state to state, but customarily includes the guest's name and address; make, model, and license number of any car parked at the hotel; date and time of arrival; and room number assigned. Be sure to obtain the necessary information from your guests, preserve the register for the time period required by state law, and provide it to those legally entitled to access.

- *File and post room rates.* Laws in many states require innkeepers to post the rates at the hotel in a place where they will easily be seen. Whenever the rates are changed, the new rates must likewise be posted.

- *Comply with recycling laws applicable in the locality where your business is located.* Laws requiring businesses to recycle parts of their waste have been adopted in most states and localities. These laws typically require a restaurant to recycle glass, metal, aluminum, and some plastic containers. Failure to comply can result in fines plus damage to the environment.

- *Determine the necessary licenses and permits needed for your business and take the appropriate steps to obtain them.* Failure to obtain required licenses and permits can result in the government forcing you to close your business, fines, and refusal by the courts to enforce your contracts. The types of licenses needed for a particular business vary from locality to locality. Check with your lawyer to ensure you are aware of all the licenses and permits you will need. Thereafter, contact the relevant government officials to determine what conditions must be met to qualify for the licenses, and then satisfy those mandates.

- *Determine whether and when your licenses must be renewed and take the necessary steps to extend them.* Failure to renew a license or permit within the allotted time can result in the same penalties applicable to failure to obtain a license when you initially open your business. Check with your lawyer or the governmental entity responsible for administering the licenses to determine when they must be renewed and the process you must follow. Take the necessary steps to ensure your licenses do not expire without obtaining a renewal.

- *Stay current on all requirements contained in the health and sanitation codes, and closely monitor your facility's compliance.* Health department inspectors will make announced and unannounced visits to determine if the establishment is conforming to the mandates in these codes. Violations can result in a variety of consequences, including fines, public embarrassment from Internet or newspaper posting of violations and, for serious infractions, forced closure.

- *When planning to build or expand a hotel or restaurant, comply with the zoning laws or seek a variance.* Zoning laws restrict the ways in which land and buildings can be used. Planning a construction project without verifying that the proposed use and resulting facility comply with applicable zoning laws can result in forced abandonment or scaling down of a project. Advance research of the zoning laws will enable you to plan within zoning restrictions and avoid unwanted and costly surprises.

Review Questions

1. What interest does a city have in requiring a hotel to maintain a register containing guests' names, addresses, type of car, and license plate numbers?

2. What is the objective of the antitrust laws?

3. Name and define three examples of per se violations of the antitrust laws.

4. Name and define three examples of antitrust violations subject to the rule of reason.

5. Must a business register its name to obtain trademark protection? If not, how else is protection obtained?

6. What constitutes a trademark infringement?

7. What is a franchise?

8. What information must a franchisor disclose to a franchisee?

9. What is a copyright? Give three examples of works that can be copyrighted.

10. What are the objectives of recycling laws?

11. What is the purpose of zoning laws?

12. If zoning laws negatively impact you, what remedy can you seek?

13. What is the basis for the government's authority to require hotels and restaurants to obtain a license before opening for business?

14. What penalties can be imposed on a business that operates without necessary licenses?

15. Name five things that a health department will look at when inspecting a restaurant.

16. If the government wants to revoke a liquor license, what rights, if any, does the licensee have?

Discussion Questions

1. What is the policy reason behind the requirement that licensees must be given due process rights before a license can be revoked?

2. What due process rights does a licensee have?

3. Why are some violations of the antitrust laws subject to the rule of reason while others are violations per se?

4. What governmental objective would be fulfilled by a zoning law that limits the size of business signs?

5. Buy a soda and look at the can. How many copyright and trademark notices do you see? What aspect of the soda can is copyrighted?

6. In what ways do the disclosure requirements imposed on franchisors help franchisees to avoid becoming victims of dishonest franchisors?

Application Questions

1. Sharina is a franchisee of Burger King. She has an exclusive territory with a five-mile radius in which Burger King cannot authorize anyone else to open a Burger King restaurant. Why is she fortunate to have this? Does this agreement violate the antitrust laws? Why or why not?

2. You are licensed to operate a hotel in a summer tourist area. You receive a notice from the town council, which has the authority to issue and revoke licenses, that your license may be revoked because of illegal activity occurring at your hotel. What rights do you have concerning the revocation proceeding? What action should you take in response to this notice? What will happen if you take no action?

3. Tamika opened a restaurant in California and named it "The Best in the West." The nationwide hotel chain of Best Western brought a trademark infringement action against Tamika. What factors will the judge consider in deciding whether or not Tamika has violated the Best Western trademark? How would you rule on the issue? Why?

4. Samantha bought a taco at a Mexican food franchise restaurant. When she bit into the food, she discovered a piece of glass in it. The glass injured her gums. What additional information would you need to know to determine if the franchisor is liable to Samantha for her injuries? Why is this information needed?

5. Joshua Sears has decided to develop a franchise chain of bars to be called Sears's Cheers and Beers. The well-known department store is disturbed that its name will be used in conjunction with a bar. Sears Roebuck & Company thus commenced a trademark action against Joshua. What is the department store's likelihood of success and why?

Websites

Websites that will enhance your understanding of the material in this chapter include:

www.copyright.gov This is the official site of the U.S. Copyright Office. It includes information about copyright basics, how to register a copyright, fees, and frequently asked questions.

www.ftc.gov This is the official site of the Federal Trade Commission, a federal agency that monitors consumer safety, including consumers of franchises and business opportunities. The site contains various guides and articles on issues associated with purchasing a franchise.

www.aafd.org This is the site of the American Association of Franchises and Dealers. It provides information about franchises including legal help, franchisee education, purchasing, and new and pending legislation.

www.real-estate-law.freeadvice.com/zoning This site contains helpful information about zoning.

www.franchisee.org This is the official site of the American Franchisee Association, a national trade association of franchisees. The site addresses many relevant issues including problems franchisees face, buying a franchise, the twelve worst franchise agreement provisions, legal resources, and more.

www.ascap.com This is the official site of the American Society of Composers, Authors and Publishers. The site includes information about copyrights, licenses, and the organization's method for distribution of royalties.

CHAPTER 16

Specialized Destinations—Casinos, Theme Parks, Spas, and Condominium Hotels

LEARNING OUTCOMES:

- Learn about the history and current status of legalized gambling in the United States
- Understand legal issues faced by casino operators—both those particular to the gaming industry and also those applicable to all places of public accommodation
- Appreciate the unique legal issues related to Native American casinos
- Ascertain safety precautions that theme parks must address to avoid liability
- Realize the specific legal issues applicable to hotel spas
- Comprehend the concept of condominium hotels and laws specific to them

KEY TERMS

admission discounts	gambling	pari-mutuel betting
assumption of risk	gambling commissions	pathological gambling
card counter	Indian Gaming Regulatory	probable cause
compacts	Act (IGRA)	riverboat casinos
condominium	Jones Act	shoe
condominium hotel	liability waiver	sovereign authority
copyright	maintenance fee	spa
crowd control	maritime laws	
false imprisonment	marker	

Introduction

Exciting developments in the hospitality industry include the increased numbers of casinos, theme parks, spas, and condominium hotels. Just as these facilities present unique management challenges, they also create unique legal issues and applications. While reading the chapter you will reacquaint with some areas of law we have studied in other sections of this book, but the application here will be limited to the four types of referenced facilities. You will also learn about laws we have not yet studied that are applicable exclusively to these specialized destinations.

A Short History of Gambling

gambling
The act of playing a game for stakes in the hope of winning.

Contrary to conventional wisdom, **gambling** is not a recent phenomenon. The Chinese, Japanese, Greeks, Romans, and Egyptians played games of skill and chance for amusement as early as 2300 B.C. In the United States, both European colonists and Native Americans brought a history of gambling from their own cultures. They believed fate and chance were determined by the gods.

British colonization of America was partly financed through lottery proceeds. Lotteries were viewed in England as a popular form of voluntary taxation and became fashionable in America as European settlers arrived here. A half-dozen sweepstakes sponsored by prominent individuals such as Ben Franklin, John Hancock, and George Washington operated in each of the 13 colonies to raise funds for building projects. In the late 1700s, Massachusetts authorized lotteries to help build and equip Harvard College. Many other educational institutions were funded through raffles, including Yale and Columbia. Even the financing for the American Revolution benefited from a lottery.

Attitudes changed, albeit temporarily, and the states outlawed virtually all types of gambling by 1910. Two decades later, the pendulum was swinging back. By 1931 Nevada legalized casinos. In the 1930s, 21 states legalized racetrack gambling, and many states authorized low-stakes charity bingo. During the 1940s and 1950s, most states modified their laws to allow pari-mutuel betting. **Pari-mutuel** means a betting system in which winners share the total stakes minus a percentage paid to the management. Examples of pari-mutuel betting include horse racing and greyhound dog racing. With a pari-mutuel system, the track does not care which horse wins because, unlike other gambling, the money used to pay the winners is not otherwise the track's, but rather that of the people holding the losing tickets.

pari-mutuel
A betting system in which winners share the total stakes minus a percentage paid to the facility hosting the gambling event.

In 1978 the first casino opened in Atlantic City, New Jersey. In 1987 two events occurred that stimulated the proliferation of Indian casinos in this country. These events, discussed in more detail later in this chapter, include the U.S. Supreme Court decision of *California v. Cabazon Band of Mission Indians*, 480 U.S. 202, 107 S.Ct. 1083, 94 L.Ed.2d 244 (1987), which affirmed the right of Indian tribes to self-regulate high-stakes versions of all betting games not prohibited by state law, and the adoption of the Indian Gaming Regulatory Act.

In 1990, riverboat casinos became popular. These are ships carrying casino facilities that take patrons out to sea where state gambling prohibitions are not applicable.

Pari-mutuel betting facilities have suffered with the proliferation of casinos. A phenomenon that is compensating somewhat for pari-mutuel's loss of popularity is simulcast wagering—that is, broadcasting races over a television network enabling bettors at other tracks and locations around the country not only to watch the live races via television and place their bets, but also to cash in their winning tickets locally as if the race were being held at their location.

Gambling Today

Gambling today is a thriving industry in the United States, with about 980 casinos. Most states plus the District of Columbia sponsor lotteries. Pari-mutuel wagering is legal in some form in almost all states, and charitable gaming is legal in virtually all states plus the District of Columbia.

Casinos are second only to lotteries as the most popular form of gaming entertainment in the United States. More than twenty-five percent of the over-age-21 population of this country participate in casino gaming.

Tribal gaming now plays a major role in the gaming industry. There are more than 400 Native American gaming enterprises operating in 28 states, and those numbers continue to grow.

Also popular is online gambling, which includes websites at which players can place their bets. Begun in 1995 with the development of the Internet, this realm of gambling has seen explosive growth.

Gambling is highly regulated by government with the objective of protecting the betting public against potential fraudulent practices and preventing infiltration of the gambling industry by organized crime. State-sponsored gambling commissions oversee casino operations. Among the responsibilities of these commissions are the following: process gambling license applications including financial background checks and criminal history checks; conduct inspections of gambling facilities to ensure compliance with relevant laws; investigate reports of illegal gambling activities; test gambling equipment for compliance and integrity; and in states with tribal casinos, enforce and regulate the tribal-state compacts. This will be discussed later in the chapter.

Gaming Issues

Several legal issues are peculiar to casinos. These include the role of state gaming commissions in the resolution of disputes involving wagering outcomes, blackjack players who are card counters, malfunctioning slot machines, casinos granting credit to players, and compulsive gamblers. These issues are addressed in the next several sections of this chapter.

Resolution of Gaming Issues

gambling commissions
Government agencies created to resolve disputes involving gaming debts and alleged winnings.

States with legalized gambling have created **gambling commissions** for the resolution of disputes involving gaming debts and alleged winnings. These commissions have original jurisdiction to the exclusion of the courts. An example is Mississippi, in which the body is called the Mississippi Gaming Commission. In a case where a casino patron playing mini-baccarat claimed the dealer refused to allow him to increase his "flat" bet although the amount he sought to wager was within the table limits, the only forum with jurisdiction to hear the dispute was the Gaming Commission.[1]

In another case a player claimed advertising material was misleading and untruthful for a game promoted by Harrah's Casino named "Knockout for cash." Again, the court dismissed the case because the forum with jurisdiction was the Gaming Commission.[2]

---

[1] *Grand Casino Tunica v. Shindler*, 772 So.2d 1036 (Miss. 2000) (concerning the final decision, the commission did not believe the gambler attempted to increase the bet)
[2] *Burse v. Harrah's Vickburg Corp.*, 919 So.2d 1014 (Miss. 2005)

CHAPTER 16: Specialized Destinations—Casinos, Theme Parks, Spas, and Condominium Hotels

Casino Owes No Duty to Inform Patrons of Laws Relevant to Gambling

In a number of cases, patrons were arrested for violating gaming laws of which they were unaware. They asserted as a defense a duty on the casino to inform them of the law. The courts have rejected the existence of such a duty. Thus, where a patron was arrested for accepting gaming chips on credit without a **marker** (a written document evidencing the debt and authorizing the casino to take money from the gambler's bank account if payment is not made per terms agreed by the parties), he sued the casino for negligence, claiming it should have warned him that his conduct was illegal. The court dismissed the case, finding no such duty existed.[3]

Similarly, a casino whose employees were aware that a slot machine was out of adjustment, resulting in more frequent payoffs, did not owe a gambler the duty to inform him that use of the machine was illegal. When the player was arrested and thereafter sued the hotel for nondisclosure, the hotel would not be liable.[4] And a casino was not obligated to inform a keno player who found a winning ticket in a wastebasket that redemption of a ticket without having paid for it is illegal. Thus, the casino was not liable for his subsequent arrest.[5]

Exclusion of Card Counters Permissible

A **card counter** is someone who keeps track of the cards played in blackjack, also known as "21," in the course of a **shoe** (a round of play defined by the number of decks of cards included in the round). A card counter has an advantage in blackjack because, as the cards in the shoe decrease, the likelihood of cards not yet played

marker
A written document used by a casino to access money from a gambler's bank account if payment of a loan extended to the player is not made per terms agreed by the parties.

card counter
Someone who keeps track of the cards played in blackjack.

shoe
A round of play of blackjack (or "21") that is defined by the number of decks of cards included in the round.

© pedrosala/Shutterstock.com

---

[3] *Vinci v. Las Vegas Sands, Inc.*, 984 P.2d 750 (Nev. 1999)
[4] *El Dorado Hotel, Inc. v. Brown*, 691 P.2d 436 (Nev. 1984)
[5] *Hazelwood v. Harrah's*, 862 P.2d 1189 (Nev. 1993)

coming up is increased. Thus, the card counter secures an advantage in the odds. Casinos in most states can legally exclude card counters from playing blackjack.[6]

To address the counting advantage, a growing number of casinos utilize a device that, on a continuing basis, automatically shuffles the cards that have been played and uses them to resupply the cards from which the dealer draws. This removes the ability of a counter to anticipate cards not yet played, thereby eliminating the problem of card counters.

Slot Machines

Slot machines are very popular casino gaming devices. Sometimes these machines malfunction, resulting in an apparent but not real win for a customer. This was the circumstance in a Mississippi case that is instructive about several topics including the mechanical aspects of slot machines, preserving evidence, and the role of gambling commissions in payout disputes.

A slot player claimed he was entitled to a $2,700,000 progressive jackpot. He sued the casino when it refused to pay him. He described the circumstances in this way: "I began playing Cool Millions slot machine number 2947 at approximately 11:00 P.M. playing three coins at a time. After playing for a brief period, the machine locked up and began to make noises. Whistles were blowing, bells sounded, and to my left a light flashed white on top and blue on the bottom. At this time 'three animals' were lined up across the pay line." According to [the plaintiff] the three symbols that were lined up on the pay line

© charles taylor/Shutterstock.com

6 *Commonwealth of Pa. v. Hyland, 2014 WL 10575193 (Pa. 2014); Ziglin v. Player's Island Casino,* 36 S.W.3d 786 (Mo. 2001).

looked like frogs, which matched the combination that was indicated on the top of the machine to be the winning combination for the highest jackpot. The casino slot supervisor was called and he investigated.

The casino claimed that the plaintiff was putting coins into the slot before the reels had stopped spinning so that the coins did not register. Therefore, when the plaintiff pulled the handle the reels would not spin and this resulted in the appearance of the three matching frogs. The casino also claimed that the winning combination was three ducks, not frogs. The slot supervisor of the casino testified that he was summoned to the machine in response to plaintiff's claim of winning the jackpot. The supervisor had opened the machine and cleared a coin jam. The assistant slot manager on the night in question testified that he was also called to the machine. He performed a last-game recall test, which indicated the plaintiff had not won the jackpot. The assistant manager also performed a calibration test, which established that, aside from the coin jam, the machine was working properly.

The casino had a policy, presumably like that adopted by many casinos, requiring that when a patron is involved in a disputed claim and the slot supervisor determines the casino should not pay it, the slot surveillance department is notified to focus the cameras on the machine in question. The casino unfortunately failed to follow its policy in this case. Had it been able to capture the circumstance on camera, the pictures would have provided important evidence.

The court ultimately held that the player was not entitled to the jackpot because the slot machine was working properly at the time and did not indicate a jackpot had been won, based on the calibration and recall tests. However, the casino was chastised by the court for failing to initiate contact with the Gambling Commission immediately upon the occurrence of the dispute as required by law. The casino was likely fined for this violation.[7]

In a case with similar facts but a different outcome, plaintiff claimed to have won a jackpot on a progressive slot machine, that is, one linked by computer to similar machines in other casinos. Each networked machine contributes money to a single jackpot, which is called a progressive jackpot. The progressive jackpot is much larger than any jackpot a single machine would pay. In this case, the casino disputed the player's right to the jackpot, explaining with testimony from the responding slot machine technician that the machine had malfunctioned. An independent testing laboratory for gaming equipment examined the microprocessor from the slot machine in issue and concluded that the machine had erred. The case was submitted to a jury and it decided in favor of plaintiff who was then allowed to collect the winnings.[8]

In Case Example 16-1, the plaintiff sued for a slot machine bonus that the casino argued was invalid as a malfunction of the device.

---

[7] *Thomas v. Isle of Capri Casino*, 781 So.2d 125 (Miss. 2001)
[8] *Griggs v. Harrah's Casino*, 929 So.2d 204 (La. 2006)

CASE EXAMPLE 16-1

McKee v. Isle of Capri Casinos, Inc., 864 N.W.2d 518 (Iowa, 2015)

While playing a penny slot machine, a casino patron obtained a win of 185 credits, or $1.85, based on how the symbols had lined up. However, at the same time a message appeared on the screen stating, "Bonus Award - $41,797,550.16." The casino refused to pay the alleged bonus, claiming it was an error and not part of the game. The patron brought suit against the casino, asserting breach of contract, estoppel and consumer fraud. The district court granted summary judgment to the casino. The patron appealed.

On appeal, we conclude the district court's grant of summary judgment was proper. The rules of the game formed a contract between the patron and the casino, and the patron was not entitled to the bonus under those rules.

On July 2, 2011, Pauline McKee, an eighty-seven year old grandmother of thirteen living in Antioch, Illinois, was attending a family reunion. That evening, she and several members of her family gambled at the Isle Casino Hotel. Around nine o'clock, one of McKee's daughters invited McKee to sit down next to her and play a slot machine called "Miss Kitty." McKee had never played this particular game before.

The Miss Kitty game is a penny slot machine that displays five reels and fifty paylines on a video screen. To play the game, a patron selected the number of paylines and the amount bet per line. One cent buys one credit, and one half credit buys one line. A player's total bet is calculated by multiplying the number of credits by the number of lines bet. Therefore, although it is called a penny machine, it is possible to bet more than just one cent per spin. As with other slot machines, a person wins at the Miss Kitty game by lining up different combinations of symbols from left to right on the paylines.

The game includes a button entitled "Touch Game Rules" in the lower left-hand corner of the screen. Tapping this button displays the rules that govern the game and a chart describing potential winning combinations of symbols, known as a paytable. . . . A sign posted on the front of the machine reiterates, "MALFUNCTION VOIDS ALL PAY AND PLAYS."

The parties agree that all the potential ways of winning from lining up various combinations of symbols are accurately listed in the rules and paytable. The rules and paytable do not mention any additional bonuses, jackpots, or prizes available to a patron playing the Miss Kitty game.

McKee did not read the rules of the game or look at the paytable before playing the Miss Kitty game. Around 10:00 p.m., after McKee had been using the machine for a while, she wagered $0.25 on a particular spin. A message appeared indicating she won 185 credits, or $1.85, based on that alignment of symbols. The dispute of course, concerns the "Bonus Award" of $41,797,550.16.

Believing she had won a large bonus, McKee and her daughter summoned a casino attendant to the machine. An employee responded. The senior supervisor/shift manager on duty that night was also called to the machine to investigate. The supervisor photographed the display on the Miss Kitty machine. . . . Eventually a casino manager instructed the supervisor to block off the machine pending further investigation.

The next day, the vice president/general manager of the casino also investigated the incident. She informed the Iowa Racing and Gaming Commission (IRGC) of the situation and that the machine would be secured and studied.

The IRGC conducted an independent investigation. As part of this investigation, it sent the hardware and software from the Miss Kitty machine to a testing Laboratory. The lab's analysis concluded as follows: . . .

> It appears the hardware inside the Miss Kitty machine erroneously determined that it received a legal bonus award from the system and sent it to the game.

The lab was unable to definitively determine the exact cause of the erroneous bonus award. However, it is apparent, based on the reviewed information, that the bonus award was not valid. The lab could not confidently speculate as to how the bonus amount was received and displayed at the gaming machine in question.

The IRGC also requested information from the manufacturer of the machine, Aristocrat. Aristocrat responded to the IRGC with a letter concluding that the bonus displayed on the screen was an error. It noted that the company had previously issued a bulletin regarding the issue. "Aristocrat has been aware of the possibility of an erroneous value being displayed. . . . Aristocrat previously provided a Technical Information Bulletin to the Industry outlining the issue and the course of action Aristocrat was taking in developing a new System Base, as well as ATI's recommendation to casinos for disabling of the bonus option as a preventative action.

Completing the investigation, an IRGC administrator wrote a letter to the casino manager, stating in relevant part:

Based on the information available and received, the jackpot amount displayed on the slot machine game screen is not valid . . . The information pertaining to the maximum award was displayed on the pay table of the slot machine; therefore, the maximum award information was available to the player prior to playing. In addition, the symbols on the slot machine game screen resulting from the spin by the patron demonstrated a combination that should pay out $1.85 as verified by the paytable on the slot machine . . .

Based on the IRGC's determination that the bonus award displayed on the screen was not valid, the casino refused to pay McKee the $41,797.550.16.

McKee filed suit against the casino. She alleged the casino breached a contract to pay her the bonus . . . . The casino moved for summary judgment. The district court granted the casino's motion. With respect to the contract claim, the court stated, . . . The rules of the game constituted the contract between McKee and the casino. These written, approved rules of the Miss Kitty game formed the gambling contract between McKee and the casino. McKee could have read the rules of play had she chosen to do so. Although she did not actually read them, she was nevertheless bound by them when she chose to play the game. It is sufficient that those rules were readily accessible to her and she had an opportunity to read them. Under the contract, McKee promised to pay a certain amount of money and place bets, and the casino promised to give her an award based on what bets she made and the way the "reels" lined up at the end of the game of chance. On the play in question, the alignment of the reels entitled her to a prize of $1.85, and the casino paid it to her, fulfilling its side of the contract. . . .Plaintiff had no reason to believe that by playing the game she might be able to win any money beyond that related to the rules of the game.

A criminal law in Michigan prohibits knowingly playing a malfunctioning slot machine. A case involved a player who was detained by a casino on suspicion of having violated that statute. The player denied knowledge that the machine was not working correctly. Eventually he was released without charges being filed. He sued the casino for false arrest. The jury found the casino had probable cause to make the arrest, which justified the detention. The player's claim against the casino was therefore dismissed.[9]

In an odd set of facts, a casino was sued for misrepresentation by suggesting a particular slot machine "had to hit the jackpot soon." A casino patron sought and received exclusive use for 16 months of that machine. It was part of a progressive jackpot. As the prize money increased, the customer claims a casino manager told him that the machine was probably at a point where a jackpot could be hit. He played 12 to 14 hours a day and spent approximately $500,000. When the jackpot payoff did not occur, he sued for breach of contract. The court dismissed the case, noting that "[a] gaming device is understood by all as a game of chance with random outcomes. . . . casino management could not affect the random outcome of the machine in the customer's favor."[10]

In a case involving the game of baccarat, two players won in excess of $9 million during four visits to a casino. Thereafter the casino sued them claiming fraud (intentional misrepresentation) and conspiracy (two or more people working together to commit illegal conduct). The facility accused the players of using a deceptive scheme called "edge sorting" which surreptitiously manipulates the odds of the game in the players' favor. The players sought unsuccessfully to dismiss the case.[11]

Contracts and Gambling Debts

Many casino patrons who bet large amounts of money will establish credit with the casino. The transaction is a contractual one, not unlike seeking credit on a Visa card or MasterCard. To reacquaint yourself with rules of contract law, see the discussion in Chapter 4. In a credit transaction, the casino agrees to extend credit to the patron to enable her to gamble. In return, the customer agrees to re-

---

[9] *Gazda v. Detroit Entertainment*, 2005 WL 1413207 (Mich. 2005)\
[10] *Master v. Red River Entertainment, LLC*, 188 So.3d 284 (La, 2016).
[11] *Marina District Development Co., LLC v. Ivey*, 93 F.Supp.3d 327 (N.J. 2015).

pay the casino for the amount borrowed plus interest. The patron hopes to make money on gambling, in which case reimbursement to the casino is easy. Unfortunately, gamblers often lose. If the patron fails to repay the casino, it will likely pursue payment in court. The lawsuit is based on contract. As in any contract case, the gambler can assert any applicable contract defenses, including illegality; incapacity (underage, mentally incompetent, or very intoxicated); duress (threats of harm); and unconscionability (gross unfairness resulting from unequal bargaining power).

In one case in which a casino sought payment on a credit contract, the gambler incurred over $165,000 in gambling debts in a 24-hour period. He alleged he was a compulsive gambler and offered as evidence of this condition the following: at various casinos he was abusive, cursed the dealers, accused them of cheating him, threw cards, smashed an ashtray, and made a spectacle of himself. He asserted that because he was a compulsive gambler, it was unconscionable of the casino to have extended him credit. The court rejected the defense of compulsive gambling, stating, "This court finds no support in legislation or case law that the disorder of compulsive gambling should, in and of itself, be recognized as a defense to capacity to contract which will render a contract void."[12] Thus we learn that the circumstance of being a compulsive gambler will not relieve the borrower from liability to repay a gambling debt.

By law, to accommodate problem gamblers, casinos must offer would-be gamblers the opportunity to register themselves on a list of visitors who should be evicted if observed at the casino. Each facility is required to maintain such a list. Casinos do not always notice when someone on the list enters the building and bets. Several players who were allowed access notwithstanding their name was on the list, and who then incurred substantial gambling debts, sought to cancel those obligations by claiming that the casino breached a duty to expel them. The courts have rejected these arguments in opinions to the effect that a casino operator does not owe a duty to protect compulsive gamblers from themselves.[13] Likewise, the casino does not have a duty to evict a known compulsive bettor.[14] While not necessary to avoid liability, many casinos will add a sentence to the written eviction request form stating that the casino will not be liable if it fails to follow its policy to exclude those people who have requested to be on the list.[15]

---

12 *Lomonaco v. Sands Hotel Casino and Country Club*, 614 A.2d 634 (N.J. 1992)
13 See *Rush v. MGM Grand Detroit, LLC*, 705 N.W.2d 135 (Mich. 2005); *Stulajter v. Harrah's Indiana Corp.*, 808 N.E.2d 746 (Ind. 2004)
14 *Merrill v. Trump Indiana, Inc.*, 2002 WL 1307304 (Ind. 2002)
15 For an example of such a provision see *Rush v. MGM Grand Detroit*, LLC, 705 N.W.2d 135 (Mich. 2005)

Another defense asserted by players who were sued for enforcement of gambling debts is that the contract was illegal. As we studied in Chapter 4, if performance of a contract would be illegal, the contract is void and unenforceable. In two cases, efforts to enforce gambling debts were rebuffed by the courts. In one, a player incurred $200,000 in debt on a gambling cruise while the ship was offshore. The company owning the ship attempted to enforce the debt in Florida. The court refused, noting that the state has a strong public policy against enforcing gambling debts, even though the debts were valid and enforceable where incurred.[16]

In the other case, two apparent friends entered a written contract stating they were partners in any betting winnings they received while at Foxwoods Casino or otherwise, and would split the money equally. One won $500,000 on a Powerball lottery ticket and refused to share it with the other. A lawsuit resulted and the Connecticut court cited a state statute: "All contracts of which any part of the consideration is money won or bet at any game shall be void."[17] The court thus refused to enforce the agreement.

Compulsive/Problem Gamblers

pathological gambling
The inability to refrain from gambling, also known as compulsive gambling.

Unfortunately, some people suffer from a recognized disorder called **pathological gambling** or compulsive gambling, which is an inability to refrain from gambling. It is a recognized illness in the field of psychology. Just as some people can become addicted to alcohol or drugs, it is possible for a person to have an uncontrollable urge to gamble. The consequences to the player and his family can be tragic. One court described the phenomenon this way: "David Williams's compulsive desire for the thrill of chance resulted in his loss of every penny he saved from his former career as an auditor, the accumulation of a staggering amount of debt, and untold personal problems. This case documents Williams's long and embarrassing spiral downward through the circles of Hell where an addiction leads."[18] Unfortunately this case does not exist in isolation.[19]

In another case the court described the plaintiff's plight as follows; "As a consequence of his gambling losses, his wife claims they have been unable to make their mortgage payments or their insurance payments, their telephone and water service have been disconnected, and they have been threatened with termination of gas and electric service. At times they have been unable to buy food . . . He had a heart attack and a mild stroke, both of which his wife attributes to the anxiety caused by his gambling losses."[20] In a New Hampshire case a motive for murder was the defendant's escalating gambling loses.[21]

---

[16] *Titan Cruise Lines v. Elliott*, 2006 WL 2848592 (Fla. 2006)
[17] *Sokaitis v. Bakaysa*, 2006 WL 2773552 (Conn. 2006); *Williams v. Aztar Indiana Gaming Corp.*, 351 F.3d 294 (Ind. 2003)
[18] *Burdett v. Harrah's Kansas Casino Corp.*, 311 F.Supp.2d 1166 (Kans. 2004)
[19] For another case involving suicide by a compulsive gambler see *Burdett v. Harrah's Kansas Casino Corp.*, 294 F.Supp.2d 1215 (Kans. 2003)
[20] *Brown v. Argosy Gaming Co.*, 384 F.3d 413 (Ohio 2004)
[21] *State of New Hampshire v. Kim*, 897 A.2d 968 (N.H. 2006)

CHAPTER 16: Specialized Destinations—Casinos, Theme Parks, Spas, and Condominium Hotels

Further insight is provided in a Kansas case involving a gambler who accumulated huge debts. The casino's collection agency used aggressive tactics that became unbearable to the player's wife. His marriage collapsed and he thereafter committed suicide.[22]

In another case a mother was convicted of endangering the welfare of a child for leaving her 9-year-old son alone in a locked minivan in a casino parking lot in summer sun in 94-degree heat while she gambled.[23]

In several of these cases the plaintiffs claimed the casinos, aware of the plaintiffs' compulsive gambling, owed them a duty to prevent them from gambling. According to this theory, failing to stop plaintiffs from accessing the casino floor results in liability for plaintiffs' wagering losses and for the dire effects on plaintiffs' finances and lives. The courts have unanimously rejected this argument, finding that casinos do not owe a duty to prevent compulsive gamblers from betting.[24]

The casino industry has addressed the issue of problem gambling in several ways. For example, as discussed earlier in this chapter, a person who knows he is a compulsive gambler can initiate placement of his name on a list of persons to whom the extension of credit by a casino is prohibited. The list is kept by a state agency, each with a name similar to the Casino Control Commission. These agencies regulate casinos. By law, the agencies are required to provide the list to the credit departments of each casino.[25] Some states maintain a Problem Gamblers Helpline available 24 hours a day, seven days a week, to answer questions and offer confidential assistance. Additionally, the National Council on Problem Gambling serves as a national advocate for programs and services to assist problem gamblers and their families, and also maintains a 24/7 confidential helpline. Its membership consists of states, corporations, and individuals.

Congress created the National Gambling Impact and Policy Commission to conduct a study of the social and economic impact of gambling at all levels of our society. Among the issues the Commission reviewed is, "pathological or problem gambling and its impact on society." The Commission recommended that the government support studies to determine the prevalence of problem and pathological gambling among casino patrons and employees, generally, and also among specific "major subpopulations" including youth, women, elderly, Native American, and other minority group gamblers. Studies examined gambling's effect on divorce, domestic violence, child abuse, suicide, bankruptcies, and crime. An additional topic recommended was "the extent to which the practices of some gambling facilities to provide free alcohol to customers while gambling, the placement of cash advance credit machines close to the gambling area, and the offer of similar inducements" magnify a gambling disorder. The resulting data are used in the development of state and federal legislation dealing with gaming.

---

[22] *Burdett v. Harrah's Kansas Casino Corp.*, 2003 WL 124665 (Kans. 2003)
[23] *State v. Todd*, 183 S.W.3d 273 (Mo. 2006)
[24] See for example *Merrill v. Trump Indiana, Inc.*, 320 F.3d 729 (Ind. 2003)
[25] N.J.S.A. § 5:12–101(j)

Torts Involving Casinos

Negligence

The rules of negligence applicable to hotels and restaurants are also applicable to casinos. See the discussion of negligence in Chapter 5. Like other hospitality facilities, casinos are not insurers of their guests' safety. They are, however, obligated to act reasonably to safeguard the well-being of their patrons and employees.

In one case a plaintiff was playing nickel poker in a slot machine at the Grand Casino in Gulfport, Mississippi. She noticed a chair to her immediate right. While putting money in the machine she reached back to pull the chair to her and began to sit. Unfortunately, in the short interim the chair had been moved. When she started to sit she lost her balance and fell to the floor. She sued the casino claiming it had provided an insufficient number of chairs to accommodate the players. The casino proved that it provided one seat for each slot machine and that virtually all slot machines are designed to be played by only one patron at a time. The court, deciding in favor of the casino, held that the plaintiff was negligent for attempting to sit on the chair before she made certain she had a place to sit. Said the court, "Plaintiff's inattentiveness resulted in her fall, not an unsafe condition of the casino."[26] If the number of chairs in the slot machine area had been less than one per machine, the casino would likely have been at least partially liable. Management should ensure that seating is adequate in the casino playing area.

In another case, the injured party was a change attendant on a riverboat casino who was injured on the job due to the weight of tokens. Her duties included selling customers slot machine tokens, which she carried in a Velcro change belt tied around her waist. Depending on the amount of tokens in the belt, it could weigh as much as 50 pounds. All change attendants had their own storage container known as a change bank, which was stocked with buckets of tokens delivered on a mobile change cart. When the plaintiff's change bank ran low, she ordered additional tokens from a slot attendant who brought the token order to her in buckets on a mobile change cart. The buckets had handles and weighed approximately five to ten pounds. All change attendants were required to lift the buckets from the change cart to their individual change bank. They then replenished the change belt from the change bank. One day, while lifting the buckets, she suffered a back pain for which she sought treatment. It was diagnosed as a dorsal spine sprain and required physical therapy. She was permanently restricted from lifting more than 35 to 40 pounds.

The plaintiff sought compensation from the casino for her back injury, claiming it was negligent for requiring her to carry such heavy loads in the course of her job. The casino moved to dismiss the case on the ground it had done nothing illegal. The court refused to dismiss the case, holding that a reasonable jury could find that the employer failed to use reasonable care in providing the plaintiff with safe equipment to perform the job. For example, the jury might conclude that the

---

[26] *Greco v. Grand Casinos of Mississippi*, 1996 WL 617401 (La. 1996)

employer should have provided the plaintiff with a mobile cart to carry the change rather than wearing a heavy change belt and lifting buckets of tokens.[27]

Note: In most states, lawsuits by employees against employers are controlled by workers' compensation laws, which would have barred the change attendant's lawsuit. However, different rules apply when the employee is injured at sea (remember that this case involved a riverboat casino). See the discussion of the Jones Act later in this chapter.

The rules of negligence we studied in Chapters 5 and 6 apply equally to casinos. The same problems that cause injuries and lawsuits against hotels and restaurants, likewise plague casinos. For example, steps need to be in good repair with railings and adequate lighting.[28] Parking lots need to be well lit; the floors need to be in good repair and not unduly slippery.[29] Plumbing, heating, and electrical systems need to be well maintained and safe. One plaintiff who went to the restroom after gambling for several hours claimed that when he flushed the toilet it rapidly overflowed, startling him and causing him to jump quickly from the toilet stall, resulting in injuries. Like other businesses we have studied, casinos are not insurers against injury. Rather, their duty is to exercise reasonable care to keep the premises in a reasonably safe condition. Here the plaintiff was unable to show that the casino caused the condition, knew about it, or had constructive notice. Therefore, the case was dismissed.[30]

Medical Care

Case Example 16-2 addresses the duty of a casino to a guest who has a medical emergency while gambling. The rules of law reviewed in this decision apply equally to hotels and restaurants. Note the efficient emergency response system in place at the casino.

CASE EXAMPLE 16-2

Lundy v. Adamar of New Jersey, Inc. t/a TropWorld

34 F.3d 1173 (N.J. 1994)

Appellant Sidney Lundy suffered a heart attack while a patron at appellee's casino, TropWorld Casino ("TropWorld"), in Atlantic City, New Jersey. While he survived, Lundy was left with permanent disabilities. . . .

On August 3, 1989, Lundy, a 66-year-old man with a history of coronary artery disease, was patronizing TropWorld Casino. While Lundy was gambling at a blackjack table, he suffered cardiac arrest

---

[27] *Watson v. Hollywood Casino-Aurora, Inc.*, 1996 WL 559960 (Ill. 1996)
[28] See for example *Richardson v. Grand Casinos of Mississippi, Inc.*, 935 So.2d 1146 (Miss. 2006)
[29] *Jacox v. Circus Circus Mississippi, Inc.*, 908 So.2d 181 (Miss. 2005)
[30] *Jacox v. Circus Circus Mississippi, Inc.*, 908 So.2d 181 (Miss. 2005)

and fell to the ground unconscious. Three other patrons [including a critical nurse, a surgeon and a Dr. Greenberg, a pulmonary specialist] quickly ran to Lundy and began to assist him....

Meanwhile, the blackjack dealer at the table where Lundy had been gambling pushed an emergency "call" button at his table which alerted TropWorld's Security Command Post that a problem existed. The Security Command Post is electronically designed to designate the location from which such alarms are triggered and record the time that the alarm is sounded. The alarm was recorded as being received at 10:57 P.M. Noting that the source of the alarm was "Pit 3," a Security Command Post employee notified by phone the security post located on the casino floor near where Lundy had suffered his cardiac arrest. At 10:59 P.M., the Security Command Post employee sent radio directions to all of the guards on the casino floor requesting that they each go to Lundy's location.

A sergeant in TropWorld's security force and a TropWorld security guard arrived at the blackjack table apparently within fifteen seconds of their receiving the radio message from the Security Command Post. [The three patrons] were already assisting Lundy. Upon arriving, the security guard called the Security Command Post on her handheld radio and requested that someone contact the casino medical station, which was located one floor above the casino. Several witnesses agree that Nurse Margaret Slusher ("Nurse Slusher"), the nurse who was on duty at the casino medical station at the time, arrived on the scene within a minute or two of being summoned. As soon as Nurse Slusher arrived, she instructed the security guards to call for an ambulance. TropWorld's records indicate that an ambulance was summoned at 11:00 P.M.

Nurse Slusher brought with her an ambu-bag, oxygen, and an airway. She did not, however, bring an intubation kit [a tube inserted into one's trachea to help restore the ability to breath] to the scene. Dr. Greenberg testified that he asked Nurse Slusher for one and she told him that it was TropWorld's "policy" not to have an intubation kit on the premises. . . . Nurse Slusher testified that some of the equipment normally found in an intubation kit was stocked in TropWorld's medical center, but that she did not bring this equipment with her because she was not qualified to use it.

Nurse Slusher proceeded to assist the three patrons in performing CPR on Lundy. Specifically, Nurse Slusher placed the ambu-bag over Lundy's face while the others took turns doing chest compressions. . . . Dr. Greenberg testified that he was sure that air was entering Lundy's respiratory system and that Lundy was being adequately oxygenated during the period when he was receiving both CPR treatment and air through the ambu-bag. Dr. Greenberg went on to say that the only reason he had requested an intubation kit was "to establish an airway and subsequently provide oxygen in a more efficient manner."

... [A]n Emergency Medical Technician ("EMT") unit arrived at TropWorld by ambulance at approximately 11:03 P.M. A technician, with the help of the two doctor patrons, attempted to intubate Lundy using an intubation kit brought by the EMT unit. Dr. Greenberg claimed that, due to Lundy's stout physique and rigid muscle tone, it was a very difficult intubation, and that there were at least a half dozen failed attempts before the procedure was successfully completed. After intubation, Lundy regained a pulse and his color improved. According to EMT reports, the ambulance departed from TropWorld with Lundy at 11:27 P.M. . . .

TropWorld had a contract with Dr. Carlino providing that he would run an in-house medical station to supply medical services for TropWorld's employees, guests, and patrons in cases of work-related injuries and injuries or sicknesses occurring on the premises. The contract required that Dr. Carlino provide a licensed physician on the casino premises for five hours each day, and a physician "on-call" for the rest of the day. . . . Furthermore, Dr. Carlino was obligated to have a registered nurse present in the medical station during the hours that the casino was open. . . . In August of 1989, Nurse Slusher was a registered, licensed nurse. . . .

The District Court held that TropWorld had fulfilled its duty to Lundy . . .

Generally, a bystander has no duty to provide affirmative aid to an injured person, even if the bystander has the ability to help. New Jersey courts have recognized, however, that the existence of a relationship between the victim and one in a position to render aid may create a duty to render assistance. . . .

The Restatement of Torts [a compilation of rules used for guidance by courts] provides that an innkeeper is under a duty to its guests "to take reasonable action to protect them against unreasonable risk of physical harm and to give them first aid after it knows or has reason to know that they are ill or injured, and to care for them until they can be cared for by others...." The duty does not extend to providing all medical care that the innkeeper could reasonably foresee might be needed by a patron.

Nurse Slusher was a registered, licensed nurse who had been trained in emergency care and who had 15 years of nursing experience. Despite this training and experience, she was not competent to perform an intubation. The Lundys claim the casino was obligated to provide full-time on-site capability to perform intubations. Certainly, maintaining on a full-time basis the capability of performing an intubation goes far beyond any "first aid" contemplated by the Restatement of Torts. . . .

We understand Lundy's contention to be that Nurse Slusher should have returned to the medical center and retrieved the intubation tube for Dr. Greenberg's use, and TropWorld is liable for her failure to do so. We reject the notion that TropWorld, by contracting with Dr. Carlino, voluntarily assumed a duty to Mr. Lundy it would not otherwise have had. . . .

The duty owed to Mr. Lundy was a duty limited to summoning aid and, in the interim, taking reasonable first aid measures. It did not include the duty to provide medical equipment and personnel necessary to perform an intubation. . . .

The judgment of the district court [granting summary judgment to the casino] will be affirmed.

CASE QUESTIONS

1. How big a role did the casino emergency alarm system play in the court's decision?

2. Why do the Restatement of Torts and the courts impose a duty on the casino to provide first aid to a patron in distress?

This decision notwithstanding, if a casino offers medical personnel to administer to injured patrons, a duty exists to provide qualified and appropriate medical care. Cruise ships which often house casinos usually provide a doctor, recognizing that passengers and crew may need medical assistance while at sea. A woman was injured in a ship's casino and sought treatment from the in-house physician. He allegedly committed malpractice, exacerbating her injury. The court denied the ship's motion to dismiss, finding that the ship could be liable for the doctor's error.[31]

Strict Liability

In Chapter 5 we studied strict liability which imposes legal responsibility for injury resulting from ultrahazardous activity on those who engage in such activity. A plaintiff had been sitting on a stool playing slot machines for five hours, taking breaks only to cash in her tickets or to use the restroom. One time when she stood up she tripped over a stool. She sued the casino and urged the court to adopt a new strict liability standard for casinos which would render them liable for injuries suffered by its patrons regardless of fault. The justification plaintiff asserted was that casinos manipulate the physical and psychological environment that surrounds gaming. Plaintiff claimed that casinos are inherently different from other businesses because they "seduce the invitee to get lost in time and space, and they create magical effects and a dream-like state." The court rejected this argument, noting that many other businesses—such as bars, movie theaters, musicals, nightclubs, fairs, amusement parks, and others—"employ flashy attractions designed to keep customers riveted" and are not subject to strict liability.[32]

Criminal Activity at Casinos

The large sums of money that flow in casinos unfortunately attract criminal activity. (See the discussion of crimes in Chapter 10.) One vivid example is the kidnapping of the daughter of Stephen Wynn, a major casino resort developer with properties in Las Vegas, Boston, and China. Mr. Wynn paid $1.45 million in ransom money, after which Ms. Wynn was safely returned. The perpetrators were later arrested and convicted. One was sentenced to 24 years in prison; the other to 19 years.[33]

One scam involves the manufacture and sale of fraudulent slot-machine tokens. When discovered, casinos will alter the machines so that they reject the fraudulent tokens.[34] Another illegal scheme promoted by organized crime involved the game of blackjack and consisted of "capping"—increasing the amount of winning bets after the cards are dealt. The rules of the game forbid players from altering their bets once the dealer begins to distribute the cards. Therefore, this scheme requires the participation of the dealer. In one instance in Massachusetts, dishonest gamblers paid the dealers 25 percent of the proceeds. They all met regularly at a secret location to split the take. Before the conspiracy was caught on surveillance cam-

---

[31] *Huntley v. Carnival Corp.*, 307 F.Supp.2d 1372 (Fla. 2004)
[32] *Ratcliff v. Rainbow Casino*, 914 So.2d 762 (Miss. 2005); see also *Jacox v. Circus Circus Mississippi, Inc.*, 908 So.2d 181 (Miss. 2005)
[33] *United States. v. Sherwood*, 98 F.3d 402 (Nev. 1996)
[34] *United States v. Joost*, 92 F.3d 7 (R.I. 1996)

eras, it went on for five months, five days a week, with an average nightly profit of $10,000.

Casino Patron as Crime Victim

Occasionally casino patrons are robbed, pickpocketed, or drugged. The casino owes its customers the same duty of care owed by hotels and restaurants—use reasonable care to protect patrons' safety. A duty to protect customers from criminal conduct of third persons exists only where such incidents have occurred in the past and are thus foreseeable.

A casino patron on a gambling vessel was attacked in the bathroom. He sued the casino, claiming it was negligent because its security was inadequate. The injured customer argued that "a gambling establishment provides a fertile environment for criminal conduct," and thus the casino should be liable whenever a customer is victimized by crime. The court rejected this argument, saying that "courts have focused on the frequency and similarity of prior criminal acts on the premises, rather than the nature of the [business transacted at the] particular premises in determining foreseeability." In this case, no other incidents of criminal activity had occurred in the casino's restrooms and the casino had experienced virtually no violent criminal activity on its premises. The court refused to find the ship negligent and dismissed the case.[35]

Would-be robbers seeking a target with a lot of money can easily spot the ideal victim in a casino by watching for gamblers with many chips. In a Louisiana case the robbers' target won $20,000 at a blackjack table. He was escorted to his car by casino security. (Note: This is a beneficial and recommended service for casinos to offer their winning patrons.) The robbers followed him on an expressway and, in a remote area, shot his tires, causing a flat that forced him to stop, thereby creating the opportunity for the robbery. Like hotels and restaurants, casinos must exercise reasonable care to protect the safety of their guests. In this case, in addition to the parking-lot escort, the casino provided surveillance cameras at the gambling tables and cashier's stand. These reasonable efforts to protect patrons proved unavailing in this case to stop the criminal act. These precautions will, however, likely protect the casino from civil liability for negligence in the event a crime victim sues the casino for the loss.[36]

Loan sharks (those who lend money at interest rates that exceed legal limits) can often find willing borrowers at casinos. Problem gamblers in particular often need more money to bet.

Duty Owed to Intoxicated Patrons Who Become Crime Victims

Virtually every casino has numerous bars, and free alcohol is frequently provided to gamblers. As a result, overindulgence is a recurrent problem. Intoxication can

---

[35] *Marmer v. Queen of New Orleans at the Hilton,* 787 So.2d 1115 (La. 2001)
[36] *State of Louisiana v. Timon,* 683 So.2d 315 (La. 1996)

lead to disorderly conduct, which may cause the casino to physically evict the person from the premises. Recognizing that inebriated customers may not be able to care for themselves, a legal obligation to exercise reasonable care is imposed on the casino when ejecting a customer. This legal duty applies likewise to hotels, restaurants, and bars.

In one case a patron (the plaintiff) was drinking heavily (the court described her condition as "extremely intoxicated") while her husband was betting. She began talking with another customer (the defendant) and they had numerous drinks together. She then became confrontational with several employees and a guard removed her to the security office. The defendant followed. He informed the guard that he would take care of her and urged the security officer not to arrest her. Ultimately the guard drove the plaintiff and the defendant to the defendant's hotel and left the plaintiff with the defendant. She awoke the next day naked in bed with the defendant and began to scream. The defendant hit her and told her to shut up. He then raped her repeatedly. He later was arrested, pled guilty to rape, and was sentenced to prison.

The plaintiff sued the casino; it claimed it did not have any reason to know an assault was about to occur and therefore did not owe her any duty. The court found that the casino did owe a duty since it voluntarily took charge of the plaintiff, a patron, in an obviously intoxicated state. The casino owed a duty to take reasonable steps to ensure that she was not left in a worse position than when it found her.[37]

The lesson from this case is that a casino must exercise care for the well-being of patrons it takes into custody who are not able to care for themselves due to intoxication or otherwise.

Casino as Crime Victim

The casino is another potential victim of criminal activity. The perpetrator could be someone unknown to the facility or an employee. A cashier was robbed at gunpoint of $42,000 by a team of four who worked in concert. Video cameras led the police to the perpetrators. Casinos use video equipment throughout the facility to record events. The tapes can provide critical evidence in solving crimes.[38]

A dealer was the wrongdoer in a case where large tips were the motive. The dealer rearranged discarded cards and manipulated the deck while shuffling to provide players deuce-rich hands at his "deuces wild" table. Evidence at the trial included the video tapes and an expert to demonstrate the mathematical improbability that the number of deuces dealt on the suspected dealer's shifts was random.[39]

False Imprisonment

false imprisonment
Restraining a person against his will without justification.

False imprisonment occurs when a person is restrained against his will without justification. See the discussion of false imprisonment in Chapter 11. Occasional-

---

[37] *Atkinson v. Stateline Hotel Casino & Resort*, 21 P.3d 667 (Utah 2001)
[38] *Quawrells v. State*, 938 So.2d 370 (Miss. 2006)
[39] *State v. Heffner*, 110 P.3d 219 (Wash. 2005)

CHAPTER 16: Specialized Destinations—Casinos, Theme Parks, Spas, and Condominium Hotels

ly, a casino believes a patron has engaged in criminal activity and wants to detain the person during an investigation. A potential problem exists: If the investigation reveals that the patron has done nothing illegal, the facility may be liable for false imprisonment. For example, in a Missouri case the plaintiff was detained and accused of stealing gaming chips from a roulette table while the owner stepped away temporarily. The basis for the arrest was a surveillance tape that showed the thief was African American and was wearing a sweater. Plaintiff, an African American dressed in a sweater, was seated in a lounge area near the roulette table waiting for a co-worker to finish gambling. Upon questioning, the security officer determined plaintiff was evasive. The day after the arrest casino security viewed more security tapes and plaintiff was seen at the craps table during the time of the theft, prompting the casino to withdraw the charges. The casino was liable for false arrest.[40]

In a Missouri case, a patron found $40 abandoned on the floor of a casino, picked it up, and pocketed it. A security officer accused her of stealing it and directed her to leave the facility. She gave the officer the money, and while she was preparing to leave, the officer accosted her, told her she was under arrest for theft, seized her purse, and handcuffed her. He then paraded her through the casino and took her to a police office. There a second guard, upon hearing what transpired, immediately released her. She sued, the casino sought to dismiss the case before trial, and the court refused to dismiss. Clearly the security officer lacked the necessary evidence to justify an arrest.[41]

To save casinos from this liability, some states have adopted a defense for false imprisonment specifically for gambling establishments. The defense authorizes the casino to detain a person if it has probable cause to believe the patron is engaging in criminal activity. **Probable cause** means sufficient evidence to lead a reasonable person to conclude that the individual detained was committing a crime. Probable cause is to be distinguished from speculation which is a mere whim or guess. The court found the casino had probable cause, and thus dismissed a false arrest case, where the plaintiff gambler knowingly played a malfunctioning slot machine in violation of Michigan gaming statutes.[42] Likewise a casino had probable cause to arrest an employee who was part of a team that retrieves coins from slot machines and then counts them. He found a $100 coin that had failed to fall into the bucket where played coins customarily fall. Instead, the coin had been misdirected to the machine's tray from which winners retrieve their winnings. By statute such misplaced or abandoned coins belong to the casino. Plaintiff was arrested for petit larceny. Eventually the charge was dismissed and plaintiff sued the casino for false arrest. The court determined that the casino had probable cause to make the arrest and thus it was proper. Plaintiff's case was therefore dismissed.[43]

probable cause
Evidence sufficient to form a reasonable basis to believe certain alleged facts are true.

Trademark Infringement

A trademark is a name or logo that identifies the source of a product or service. See the discussion of trademarks in Chapter 15. A well-known trademark has considerable value in attracting customers.

---

[40] *Blue v. Harrah's North Kansas City, LLC*, 170 S.W.3d 466 (Mo. 2005)
[41] *West-Anderson v. Argosy Casino*, 557 Fed. Appx. 620 (Mo., 2014).
[42] *Gazda v. Detroit Entertainment LLC*, 2005 WL 1413207 (Mich. 2005)
[43] *Croft v. Grand Casino Tunica, Inc.*, 910 So.2d 66 (Miss. 2005)

The law makes illegal the use of a trademark that is confusingly similar to another mark when used by a business selling a similar or related product. Remedies include an injunction barring continued use of the name, transfer of an Internet domain name if applicable, damages (actual or statutory), payment of plaintiff's attorney's fees, and dissemination of a corrective advertisement.

A casino in Las Vegas is named New York, New York. Inside and out it portrays the theme of New York City, including the décor, restaurants, and outside façade, which imitates well-known buildings. Its club for frequent gamblers was called "New York-New York $lot Exchange." Sweatshirts, caps, and other souvenirs sold or given free at the casino display the slogan "New York $lot Exchange." Use of these terms was protested by The New York Stock Exchange, which operates and manages one of the foremost national and international facilities for the trading of securities. The court denied the claim, holding that no customer would be confused or misled to patronize the casino in lieu of the stock exchange.[44] See also *The Mashantucket Pequot Tribe v. Redican* in Chapter 15, which addressed issues involving the use of the trademark "Foxwoods."

Copyright Infringement

A **copyright** is the exclusive right to reproduce creative work such as artwork, writings (books, poetry, essays, and stories), music, and software. One who creates such a work is entitled to the exclusive right to reproduce it. See the discussion of copyrights in Chapter 15. If another party wishes to reproduce copyrighted work, such as a restaurant owner who would like to copy a painting onto paper placemats, the restaurateur must first obtain the permission of the artist. Customarily, the artist will charge a fee for that permission. Copying without permission constitutes copyright infringement, a tort. A person whose copyrighted work has been reproduced without permission can sue to force the infringer to "cease and desist" from further copying, and to compensate the copyright owner for any losses resulting from the unauthorized duplication.

We learn from a case involving Harrah's Casino that copyright protection does not extend to designs for costumes or uniforms. The plaintiff was the owner of a company that designs clothing and counsels businesses regarding professional attire. Plaintiff was hired by Harrah's Casino to design uniforms and costumes. The collection included fifty styles of shirts, blouses, vests, jackets, pants, shorts, ensembles, elaborate masquerade-type costumes, and unique headgear. After the designs were completed, the casino terminated its agreement with plaintiff and hired a manufacturer to produce the clothes incorporating plaintiff's designs. Plaintiff sued claiming copyright infringement. The court determined that garment designs are outside the scope of the copyright law even if they contain ornamental features. The reason is that costume designs are embodied in uniforms and do not have a market as a stand-alone piece of artwork. It is the latter that copyright law was created to protect.[45]

44 *New York Stock Exchange, Inc. v. New York, New York Hotel, LLC*, 293 F.3d 550 (N.Y. 2002)
45 *Galiano v. Harrah's Operating Co., Inc.*, 416 F.3d 411 (La. 2005)

Casinos and the Dram Shop Act

A dram shop act is a state statute that imposes liability on establishments that sell alcohol for injuries resulting from certain illegal sales (sales made when the patron was visibly intoxicated when served, was underage, or was a known alcoholic). See the discussion on this topic in Chapter 12. In most states, the liability is imposed when a third party is injured by the illegally served patron but not when the injured party is the patron himself. Thus a gambler who was served six complimentary eight-ounce servings of beer while playing on slot machines could not recover against the casino for injuries she suffered when she passed out and struck her head on the floor.[46]

Some states, including New Jersey, allow the illegally served patron to recover for at least a portion of his damages. An interesting attempt was made to extend dram shop liability to a casino-specific application. Most casinos offer their guests free drinks while they are gambling. The plaintiffs in several lawsuits were given free drinks by a casino after becoming intoxicated. They then incurred significant gambling debts on credit from the casino. They sued the casino claiming that the debt constituted damages resulting from illegal alcohol service and therefore they should be relieved from their obligation to pay.

The complaint in one of these cases described this practice as follows:

> The Casino [Taj Mahal in Atlantic City] continuously provided [plaintiff] with complimentary 4–5 ounce gin martinis during the entire period he was gambling and the casino continued to provide this stream of alcohol to plaintiff beyond the point when he was visibly and substantially intoxicated. Because defendant allowed plaintiff to continue gambling while visibly intoxicated, including extending him additional credit by permitting him to draw markers against his credit account while intoxicated, he allegedly sustained gambling losses in excess of $2,000,000 while visibly intoxicated.[47]

The court rejected this argument and held for the casino. Among the reasons were the following:

1. Dram shop liability had not previously been extended beyond injuries related to driving while intoxicated, barroom accidents, and barroom brawls.

2. The casino industry is very highly regulated. Had New Jersey intended to impose liability on casinos for allowing intoxicated patrons to gamble, the legislature would likely have adopted a statute so stating.

3. Extension of dram shop liability to gambling debts would present difficult questions of proximate cause, as sober gamblers can play well and nonetheless suffer significant losses, intoxicated gamblers can win big, and under the pre-

---

46 *Estate of White v. Rainbow Casino-Vicksburg Partnership*, 910 So.2d 713 (Miss. 2005)
47 *Hakimoglu v. Trump Taj Mahal, Inc.*, 876 F.Supp. 625, 625 (N.J. 1994), aff'd, 70 F.3d 291 (N.J. 1995)

vailing rules and house odds, the house will win and the gamblers will lose in the typical transaction.

4. Even if we assume that alcohol will affect the gambler's judgment, many casino games require no skill and instead are determined by the draw of a card, a throw of the dice, or the random appearance of pictures on a slot machine.

5. Proof of intoxication could be more easily fabricated in a gambling case than in the typical dram shop situation, which is a car accident. In the latter case, the occurrence of the accident is a specific event marked by police and accident reports. Reliable evidence of alcohol in a person's body is usually obtained as part of the accident investigation. None of this occurs in the gambling scenario. A gambler's loss at the gambling table is not cause for investigation, nor is a casino dealer likely to recall it at a later date.[48]

For all of these reasons, the dram shop act does not apply to a gambler who is served alcohol by a casino after becoming visibly intoxicated and who continues to place bets and thereby incurs a gambling debt. The bettor in such situations is not entitled to relief from the loss.

Riverboat Casinos and the Jones Act

riverboat casinos
Casinos located on a water vessel created to circumvent laws that prohibit gambling on shore.

maritime laws
Numerous federal laws which affect events occurring on ships on the waterways of the United States.

Jones Act
A federal statute that addresses the rules under which ships must operate when engaged in commerce in the US.

Many cities bordering on waterways are home to **riverboat casinos.** The proliferation of this type of casino is the result of laws that prohibit gambling on shore but do not apply at sea. In some states, a riverboat located dockside but totally in a body of water can legally house gaming. In other states, a boat must travel a certain distance off shore before it can validly permit gambling.

Numerous federal laws affect events occurring on boats on the waterways of the United States. These laws are referred to as **maritime laws.** Sometimes the outcome of a case can depend on whether maritime law or a state law applies. Litigation has resulted to determine which laws apply to riverboat casinos. One issue that varies greatly depending on which law is determined to apply, is the appropriate remedy when an employee on a riverboat casino is injured while on duty. According to state law, any monetary recovery from the employer in this circumstance will be limited by workers' compensation laws. Such laws produce a relatively prompt resolution of the case outside of court, but restrict the amount of compensation an employee will receive. For example, under workers' compensation laws an employee cannot recover damages for pain and suffering, a measure of damages that reimburses an injured worker for the physical pain and mental anguish that she may have endured because of an injury.

The Jones Act

Contrasted with state workers' compensation laws is a federal maritime law known as the **Jones Act.** It enables employees injured while on a boat to sue in a court for

---

[48] *Annitto v. Trump Marina Hotel Casino*, 2005 WL 4344137 (N.J. 2005)

© *Shutterstock.com*

the full value of their injury, including pain and suffering. For the Jones Act to apply, the boat on which the injury occurred must qualify as a "vessel in navigation." What constitutes such a vessel has been the subject of several cases.

The application of the Jones Act was at issue in a case involving a bartender who stepped on a screw that penetrated his shoe and injured his foot while he was working on a dockside casino in Biloxi, Mississippi. The casino, named the Biloxi Belle, sat on a barge that was moored to shore by lines tied to sunken steel pylons that were filled with concrete. Shoreside utility lines were permanently connected. A continual standby towing contract existed for the barge and casino to tow them to sheltered waters in the event potentially damaging weather was forecast. The Biloxi Belle had no engine, no captain, no navigational aids, no crew quarters, and no lifesaving equipment. For visual effects only, it had a decorative pilot house (an enclosed structure on the deck of a ship from which it can be navigated), which contained no operating parts other than a single light switch. It also had a motorized but nonfunctional paddle wheel, which rested permanently above the water level and served no propulsion function.

The barge had not been built to transport passengers, cargo, or equipment and had never been used for that purpose. The Biloxi Belle did not employ a crew for navigation or nautical purposes. All employees were engaged solely in connection with the casino business.

The court determined, not surprisingly, that the casino and barge were not "vessels in navigation" for purposes of the Jones Act.[49] Therefore, the employee's remedy for his injuries was limited by workers' compensation laws.

Even a boat capable of navigation is not viewed as a vessel if it is moored indefinitely to the shore with intent to be used for gaming purposes only, and not

---

[49] *Pavone v. Mississippi Riverboat Amusement Corporation*, 52 F.3d 560 (La. 1995)

navigation.[50] Forty employees of a riverboat casino sued the owner for injuries they sustained because of exposure to chemicals while working aboard. The boat had been operable as a self-propelled excursion ship that cruised along navigable waters when Illinois state law authorized gambling only on boats "at sea." In 1999, the law changed allowing gaming on permanently moored barges. The casino had thus been docked for more than a year and was not in the business of transporting passengers. It was connected to land-based utilities including electricity, telephone, water, and sewer, but could be disconnected from the dock in 15 to 20 minutes. Further, the boat was licensed and classified as a passenger vessel with the U.S. Coast Guard. It employed a captain and crew qualified to move the casino if necessary. The court determined that the barge's intended use was as a moored dockside casino and not transportation. It therefore held that the Jones Act did not apply[51] and so the employees were limited to the workers' compensation remedy.

Even where the boat is moved on occasion, if its primary purpose is to house a moored casino, the Jones Act will not apply. A cocktail waitress slipped and fell on cooking oil that had leaked from garbage bags on the loading dock of a riverboat casino. She sued, apparently hoping to avoid workers' compensation. Said the judge in ruling that the Jones Act did not apply, "This court inescapably notes that the casino riverboat was built to navigate but ceased its transportation function well before plaintiff's accident and has moved only for maintenance purposes on two occasions. Such limited movement was clearly incidental to the riverboat's primary function as a floating, but stationary, gambling casino."[52]

Rough Waters

Hurricanes and other weather conditions that stir up rough waters can wreak havoc on riverboat casinos and nearby residents. Hurricane Katrina in 2005 brought ferocious winds, and very high, turbulent waters leading to much flooding. A canal barge, the Grand Casino of Mississippi in Biloxi, came loose from its moorings and collided with a nearby beachfront home. The homeowner sought compensation from her insurance company—State Farm, based on her insurance contract—and also from the casino, based on negligence. Concerning State Farm, unfortunately for the homeowner, her policy expressly excluded loss caused by wind or water damage, as well as "loss that would not have occurred in the absence of an excluded event." Because the damage to the home would not have occurred in the absence of an excluded event—the flood caused by the storm surge that broke the casino's barge from its moorings—State Farm was excused from coverage.

In her case against the casino she alleged that it was negligent in the design and maintenance of the barge's mooring system. However, the undisputed evidence showed the safety measures Grand Casino took were designed to withstand a hurricane equaling in severity the worst hurricane then on record. Therefore, the court dismissed that case as well. Unfortunately for the property owner, she will not receive compensation for her loss. This case underscores the need to ensure that adequate insurance coverage exists on valuable property.

---

[50] *De La Rosa v. St. Charles Gaming Company, Inc.*, 474 F.3d 185 (Tex. 2006)
[51] *Howard v. Southern Illinois Riverboat Casino Cruises, Inc.*, 364 F.3d 854 (Ill. 2004)
[52] *Martin v. Boyd Gaming Corp.*, 252 F.Supp.2d 321 (La. 2003)

Casinos on Native American Reservations

In recent times, many casinos have been built on Indian reservations. This phenomenon was a natural outgrowth of two circumstances. First, the laws in most states prohibit gambling. Second, the law accords to Native American reservations sovereign authority, which means the governing bodies of the Native American tribes have the supreme authority to govern the reservation and its inhabitants independent of state and federal laws. Therefore, although the law of the state in which a reservation is located may outlaw gambling, that fact does not preclude the reservation's governing body from determining that gambling will be permitted on the reservation. However, as the following discussion reveals, some limitations do apply.

© SergeBertasiusPhotography/Shutterstock.com

Sovereign Authority

Native American tribes exercise **sovereign authority** over their members and territories. This means tribes are separate from our federal and state governments and have the power to regulate their internal affairs by making their own substantive law. The power to enforce that law rests with their tribal courts and not federal courts. Tribal sovereignty is subordinate only to the federal government. As sovereigns, tribes are immune from lawsuits unless they specifically waive that immunity. These concepts are illustrated in the following discussion.

sovereign authority
The power of self-government.

Application of Tribal Sovereignty to Lawsuits Against Native American Tribes

Indian Gaming Regulatory Act (IGRA)
Federal legislation adopted by Congress in 1988, which to some extent restricts a tribe's ability to conduct gambling activities.

A decisive application of the tribal sovereignty rule occurred in 1987 in a California case. Two Native American tribes in that state were engaging in various forms of gambling. The state sought to force the tribes to comply with state gambling regulations. Resistance by the tribes led to a lawsuit that ultimately was decided by the U.S. Supreme Court. The justices held the state did not have authority to enforce its gambling laws on the Native American reservation.[53] That case led Congress to pass the **Indian Gaming Regulatory Act** (hereinafter "IGRA") in 1988, which imposes some restrictions on a tribe's ability to conduct gambling activities. Before gaming can legally occur on a reservation, the tribe must comply with IGRA. One of IGRA's goals was to balance the states' interest in regulating

---

[53] *California v. Cabazon Band of Mission Indians*, 480 U.S. 202, 107 S.Ct. 1083 (1987)

high stakes gambling within their borders, and the Native Americans' resistance to state intrusions on their sovereignty. IGRA is discussed in more detail in the next section of this chapter.

In another case, a table game operator who had been employed at a Native American casino claimed he was wrongfully terminated. He commenced a lawsuit in federal district court against the casino. The tribe that owned the facility moved to dismiss the case claiming the proper forum was the Tribal Court. The federal court held that, as a sovereign power, the tribe was entitled to sovereign immunity in federal court and it had not waived that entitlement. Accordingly, the court found it lacked jurisdiction and dismissed the case.[54]

Likewise, a claim for sexual harassment asserted against a casino operated by Native Americans was dismissed.[55]

In a Connecticut case a pit cashier at Foxwoods Resort & Casino fell in a nearby parking lot used by casino patrons. Her fall resulted from an accumulation of snow and ice. The lot was not on the reservation but was owned and maintained by the tribe. The cashier sued in federal court the Native American tribe that operates Foxwoods. The court, noting that Native American tribes are independent domestic nations, held that the defendant tribe was immune from lawsuits in federal court involving events occurring on tribal territory. The court case was thus dismissed and the plaintiff was left to pursue her case in the tribal court.[56] Similarly, a plaintiff who fell on a wet, slippery floor at the Mohegan Sun Casino in Connecticut was foreclosed from suing the casino in a state court. Instead, the case was referred to a tribunal created by the tribe to resolve legal disputes arising at the casino. Appropriately, that forum was named the Gaming Disputes Court.[57]

Another plaintiff sued a tribe claiming injuries from being struck by a chair while at a gaming facility. Again the court dismissed based on sovereign immunity.[58]

Case Example 16-3 further illustrates how the courts address the issue of sovereign immunity, and how broad that immunity is.

CASE EXAMPLE 16-3

Buzulis v. Mohegan Sun Casino

2006 WL 2808116 (Mass. 2005)

The plaintiffs, Massachusetts residents, filed this negligence action against the Mohegan Indian Tribe of Connecticut. Because the incident giving rise to this action occurred on the Mohegan reservation

---

[54] *Barker v. Menominee Nation Casino*, 897 F.Supp. 389 (Wis. 1995)
[55] *Tenney v. Iowa Tribe of Kansas*, 243 F.Supp.2d 1196 (Kans. 2003). Note: Title VII of the Civil Rights Act of 1964 specifically exempts Indian tribes from the definition of "employer." 42 U.S.C. Section 2000e(b).
[56] *Paszkowski v. Chapman*, 2001 WL 118765 (Conn. 2001)
[57] *Romanella v. The Mashantucket Pequot Tribal Nation*, 993 F.Supp. 163 (Conn. 1996)
[58] *Seminole Tribe of Florida v. McCor*, 903 So.2d 353 (Fla. 2005)

we conclude that the Connecticut court lacks jurisdiction to adjudicate this action and affirm the trial judge's order of dismissal....

Shortly after midnight on July 7, 2002, plaintiffs Sheila and Michael Buzulis left the gaming area of the Mohegan Sun Casino in Uncasville, Connecticut. They were in the process of retrieving Mrs. Buzulis' coat from the coatroom when a Mohegan Sun security employee, who was responding to an emergency call, negligently ran into and physically injured Mrs. Buzulis.... Monetary relief is sought in this action by Mrs. Buzulis for her personal injuries and by Mr. Buzulis for loss of consortium and economic losses resulting from his wife's injuries.

The United States Supreme Court has held that Indian tribes are distinct, independent political communities...they remain a separate people, with the power of regulating their internal and social relations...They have power to make their own substantive law in internal matters and to enforce that law in their own forums...

The exercise of tribal governing power may preempt state law in areas where state law might otherwise apply. As a matter of federal law, an Indian tribe is subject to suit only where Congress has authorized the suit or the tribe has waived its immunity and the tribe itself has consented to suit in a specified forum....Absent a clear and unequivocal waiver by the tribe or congressional abrogation, the doctrine of sovereign immunity bars suits for damages against the tribe... Such waiver may not be implied, but must be expressed unequivocally. Furthermore, the doctrine of tribal immunity extends to individual tribal officers acting in their representative capacity and within the scope of their authority....

Pursuant to the Indian Gaming Regulatory Act, recognized Indian tribes are permitted to conduct gaming operations in accordance with a gaming compact with a state and approved by the United States Secretary of the Interior. The Mohegan Tribe of Connecticut and the state of Connecticut entered into a Gaming Compact on April 25, 1994. The compact was approved by the Secretary of the Interior. The compact provided that: The tribe shall not be deemed to have waived its sovereign immunity from suit with respect to such claims...but may adopt a remedial system analogous to that available for similar claims arising against the state....

Pursuant to the Constitution of the Mohegan Tribe of Indians, the Tribal Council is the Tribe's governing body. The Tribal Gaming Authority oversees the Tribe's gaming operations, and the Gaming Disputes Court has exclusive jurisdiction over disputes arising out of tribal gaming operations and its customers....

The parties to this action are the Mohegan tribe, its business divisions and others who provided services to and for the tribe on tribal land. These facts lead us to the inevitable conclusion that the Gaming Disputes Court has exclusive subject matter jurisdiction to adjudicate the rights of the parties, and that the trial judge's order dismissing the complaint in this action was legally sound and correct.

Illustrating another application of sovereign immunity, a business that leased space from an Indian casino and operated a restaurant in it sued the tribe alleging various contract and tort claims arising from the tribe's decision not to renew the restaurant's liquor license. This state court lawsuit was dismissed based on sovereign immunity.[59]

Tribes have the option of waiving sovereign immunity and permitting lawsuits against them. In Case Example 16-4, the court held the defendant Native American business had waived immunity, and therefore the plaintiff could continue its lawsuit.

CASE EXAMPLE 16-4

Star Tickets v. Chumash Casino Resort

2015 WL 6438110 (Mich. 2015).

Plaintiff Star Tickets, an entertainment ticketing company, is suing defendant Chumash Casino Resort (CCR) for breach of contract arising out of an alleged agreement making plaintiff the exclusive ticketing agent relative to acts and performances at CCR's establishment in California. The casino is owned and operated by the Santa Ynez Band of Chumash Mission Indians of the Santa Ynez Reservation (the Tribe).

On April 1, 2009, a "USER AGREEMENT" was executed with plaintiff's president signing on behalf of plaintiff and Leah Carrasco ostensibly signing on behalf of CCR. Although the agreement was not executed until April 2009, the parties had actually operated under the terms of the agreement since 2006. . . .

Under the heading of "Applicable Law," the agreement provided: "This Agreement shall be governed by the laws of the State of Michigan. Each party agrees that this Agreement, and each of its terms and provisions, may be enforced against any party hereto in any court of competent jurisdiction within the County of Kent, Michigan. Each party hereto fully consents to and submits to the personal jurisdiction of the State of Michigan for that purpose."

In an affidavit executed by plaintiff's vice-president of finance, she averred that CCR had received—from ticket sales generated under the terms of the agreement—$1,524,371 in 2009; $1,520,787 in 2010; $1,620,249 in 2011; $1,306,161 in 2012; and $1,082,685 in 2013; and that CCR began using someone other than plaintiff as its ticket vendor during 2013. . . .

The Tribe is a federally recognized Indian tribe by the Department of the Interior, occupying a reservation in Santa Barbara County, California.. . .

A tribal ordinance addressed the issues of sovereign immunity and waiver of sovereign immunity. It provides, "the [casino] shall have and enjoy the Tribe's sovereign immunity from unconsented suits and other legal process and claims. No waiver of sovereign immunity will be permitted, recognized or construed unless (i) the waiver is in writing and expressly states that such waiver shall permit recourse and enforcement, and (ii) the waiver is duly approved by the [casino management board of directors]. ..."

---

[59] *R & R Deli, Inc., v. Santa Ana Star Casino*, 128 P.3d 513 (N.M. 2006)

The tribal chairman averred in his affidavit that the Enterprise Board never authorized Carrasco to sign the agreement, the Board never authorized her to waive sovereign immunity, the Board never approved the agreement, and the Enterprise Board never approved or authorized any waiver of sovereign immunity.

CCR notified plaintiff that it did not intend to allow plaintiff to further act as CCR's ticketing agent for performances at the casino. Plaintiff filed suit against CCR, alleging breach of contract. In lieu of filing an answer, CCR filed a motion for summary disposition, arguing that the lawsuit was barred by sovereign immunity. The trial court denied the motion, ruling that the agreement contained language sufficient to constitute a waiver of sovereign immunity, despite the claim that Carrasco lacked authority to execute a waiver of immunity, given that CCR performed and operated under the contract, receiving millions of dollars under its terms. CCR appealed. . . .

We hold that the pertinent language in the agreement constituted a clear and unequivocal waiver of tribal sovereign immunity. . . .

For a tribe to relinquish its immunity, the tribe's waiver must be clear. Likewise, a waiver cannot be implied and must be unequivocally expressed. . . .

Here, the agreement, while not specifically referencing sovereign immunity, indicated that it was enforceable against any party in any court of competent jurisdiction within Kent County, Michigan, that the parties consented and submitted to the personal jurisdiction of Michigan for purposes of enforcing the agreement, and that the agreement was governed by the laws of Michigan. The language clearly, unambiguously, and unequivocally reflected a waiver of sovereign immunity by expressly approving of and allowing litigation in a court of disputes arising from the agreement. The concept of immunity, sovereign or otherwise, is entirely undermined by the agreement's language dictating the enforceability of the agreement in a court of law. . . .

The parties had operated under the agreement for several years, communicating regularly in relation to performances, ticket sales, and fees, that CCR had received at least $7 million dollars in revenue generated by ticket sales handled and managed by plaintiff pursuant to the agreement. CCR's attempt to now disavow the agreement and the waiver of sovereign immunity contained in the agreement borders on the absurd. Under the circumstances, CCR, the Tribe and the various tribal councils and boards were certainly fully aware of the agreement and the relationship with plaintiff, where they had accepted and reaped the benefits of the agreement for several years. . . .And all of CCR's arguments to the contrary are simply unpersuasive and unavailing. . . .

Finally, with respect to Carrasco and her authority to execute the agreement in the first instance, we hold that the doctrine of ratification dictates that CCR is bound by and adopted the agreement and the waiver provision therein, even if Carrasco lacked specific authority to sign the particular agreement. . . . Generally, deliberate and repeated acts of the principal, with knowledge of the facts, that are consistent with an intention to adopt the contract, or inconsistent with a contrary intention, are sufficient evidence of ratification. . . . CCR effectively ratified the agreement on the basis of its conduct over the years in accepting the benefits of the agreement, paying plaintiff for its fees, and regularly interacting with plaintiff with respect to carrying out the agreement.

Accordingly, CCR became bound by the agreement and the waiver of tribal sovereign immunity, and thus the trial court properly denied CCR's motion for summary disposition.

CASE QUESTIONS

1. Why did the court determine the casino had waived its sovereign immunity?

2. Why did the court determine the tribe had adopted the agreement, even though it was signed by someone allegedly without authority to do so?

Lawsuits Against Casino Employees

While tribes are entitled to sovereign immunity from negligence liability, states differ on whether individuals associated with the tribe are immune. Some states hold that individual tribal officers as well as tribal employees acting in their representative capacity and within the scope of their authority are entitled to the immunity. Some states have held otherwise. For example, a casino patron in California suffered a broken hip and shattered elbow when he was knocked down by a participant in a parking lot fight while the plaintiff was en route to his car. He sued various casino employees, claiming they did not exercise sufficient precautions for his safety. The court held that when the casino employees designed the facility's security plan, they were working in their capacities as tribal representatives and were therefore protected by sovereign immunity.[60]

A Connecticut court found otherwise, holding that employees of the tribe, as distinguished from tribal officials, are not entitled to immunity. A woman was injured on the premises of Mohegan Sun Casino, run by the Mohegan tribe. She sued for negligence two employees of the tribe, the director of facilities operations and another "building official." Neither was involved in the operations of the tribal government. The court therefore held they were not entitled to immunity. Said the court, "[T]he mere employment relationship of the defendants with the Mohegan Tribe does not grant them the right to assert the Tribe's sovereign immunity."[61]

Another example of the limitation on Native American sovereignty is provided by a second Connecticut case. The issue was whether a construction company maintained by a Native American tribe and used to construct additions to a casino was subject to the federal Occupational Safety and Health Act ("OSHA"). That act imposes many safety requirements on employers to help ensure the well-being of workers. Federal OSHA inspectors entered the casino and found four safety violations that threatened the health of the construction workers. For these violations, the construction company was fined $4,000. The tribe challenged the imposition of the fine, claiming OSHA did not apply to it due to the tribe's sovereignty. The federal court ruled that the sovereignty of a tribe is limited, not unlike the sovereignty of a state. A tribe's sovereignty applies only to the power needed to control internal matters of the reservation. The construction work, although it occurred

---

[60] *Trudgeon v. Fantasy Springs Casino*, 84 Cal.Rptr.2d 65 (Calif. 1999)
[61] *Kizis v. Morse Diesel International, Inc.*, 2000 WL 1281816 (Conn. 2000)

entirely on the reservation, has a much broader impact than just within the reservation. The company employed non-Native Americans, and the construction project involved a resort and casino that serves a multistate clientele, much broader than just residents of the reservation. For these reasons, the court held that the tribe was bound by OSHA.[62]

Not infrequently, Native American tribes will transfer the management of casinos to a corporate entity separate from the tribe. These entities are normally named as a defendant when a casino patron is injured and sues. The question arises whether these entities are entitled to immunity. Customarily they are.[63]

Dram Shop Act

Tribal immunity is a bar to a lawsuit arising from the wrongful sale of alcohol at a Native American casino.[64] Like other cases against such casinos, claims based on dram shop liability will be referred to tribal courts for resolution to the exclusion of state or federal courts.[65]

Indian Gaming Regulatory Act

The federal government has maintained some oversight of gaming conducted on reservations. Its authority is embodied in the Indian Gaming Regulatory Act (IGRA),[66] which was adopted by Congress in 1988. IGRA provides a comprehensive design for regulating gaming activities on Native American lands. One of IGRA's objectives is "to provide a statutory basis for the operation of gaming by Indian tribes as a means of promoting tribal economic development, self-sufficiency, and strong tribal governments."

IGRA divides gaming into three classifications, each subject to differing degrees of tribal, state, and federal jurisdiction and regulation. The class most highly regulated is known as Class III and includes blackjack, craps and related dice games, wheel games, roulette, electronic games of chance, slot machines, card games in which the players play against the house, and keno. For a casino on a reservation to host these types of games, IGRA mandates the following four requirements: (1) the gaming must be authorized by an ordinance or resolution adopted by the governing body of the Indian tribe having jurisdiction over the land; (2) the type of gaming involved must be permitted by the state for some purpose by some person or organization (such as for charitable purposes); (3) the gaming must be approved by the chairperson of the National Indian Gaming Commission, which was established by Congress to develop and oversee rules and regulations relating to IGRA; and (4) the gaming must be conducted consistent with a tribal-state treaty entered into by the Native American tribe and the state.

---

[62] *Reich v. Mashantucket Sand and Gravel*, 95 F.3d 174 (Conn. 1996)

[63] See, for example, *Trudgeon v. Fantasy Springs Casino*, 84 Cal.Rptr.2d 65 (Calif. 1999)

[64] *Schram v. Ohar*, 1998 WL 811393 (Conn. 1998)

[65] *Filer v. Tohono O'Odham Nation Gaming Enterprise*, 129 P.3d 78 (Ariz. 2006); *Van Etten v. Mashantucket Pequot Gaming Enterprise*, 2005 WL 3112753 (Conn. 2005); *Schram v. Ohar*, 1998 WL 811393 (Conn. 1998)

[66] 25 U.S.C. § 2701 *et seq.*

Such a treaty is initiated by the tribe requesting the state in which the lands are located to negotiate for the purpose of entering into an agreement governing such gaming. These treaties, called **compacts**, are written agreements between a state and an individual tribe, and they govern the operation of casino gaming on Native American lands. Examples of terms that are included in a state-tribal compact are types of games allowed, hours of operation, number of gambling stations authorized, maximum bets, required background investigations of people working in the casino, and minimal standards for internal management and financial controls.

Where tribes have undertaken gaming operations without satisfying these prerequisites, the federal government is authorized to obtain search warrants and seize slot machines and related gambling devices and paraphernalia from the casinos. Further, the managers and operators of a Native American casino operating illegally are subject to federal prosecution. For example, the managers of a Native American casino were prosecuted for providing slot machines without first entering a compact with the state.[67] Additionally, the U.S. government can seek injunctive relief against the casino to prevent it from operating.[68]

Internet Gambling

© Photosani/Shutterstock.com

Since the advent of the Internet in 1995, online gambling has exploded in popularity. The number of gambling websites is in the thousands, and they are very popular. Online casinos, using catchy names such as Virtual Vegas, High Card Casino, and BigCat Internet Casino, feature nearly every game available in a brick-and-mortar facility. These include blackjack, roulette, poker, keno, slot machines, sports wagering, lotteries, and bingo.

To qualify to play, customers open an account with the site by providing certain information. Funds for betting must then be deposited by using a credit card, electronic withdrawal from a bank account, certified check, money order, or wire transfer. Once the account is open the user is able to place bets.

Whereas land-based casinos in the United States are highly regulated, online gambling is much less so. Laws impacting the brick-and-mortar gambling industry address such matters as licensing, fraud, crimes, additional consumer protection measures, and taxation of earnings made by casinos and gamblers. Operators of online casinos based outside this country are not subject to any of these regulations, a matter of considerable concern to federal and state governments and the

[67] *United States v. E.C. Investments, Inc.*, 77 F.3d 327 (Calif. 1996)
[68] *U.S. v. Santee Sioux Tribe of Nebraska*, 174 F.Supp.2d, 1001 (Nebr. 2001); aff'd 324 F.3d 607 (Nebr. 2003)

commercial casino industry. Some states prohibit online gambling within the state. Congress has long considered, but not passed, a law that would ban Internet wagering. The legislation was revived in late 2016. Developments are anticipated in the near future.

Theme Parks

Introduction

Many family travelers spend some of their vacation time at theme or amusement parks. These facilities typically provide various attractions, carnival rides, games of skill, and other entertainment. Issues particular to this type of facility can result in liability if adequate precaution is not exercised by park management.

Crowd Control

Many theme parks attract large numbers of visitors on a daily basis. **Crowd control** requires attention and reasonable care by the park. The facility is not required to tolerate customers who damage property, injure others, or disrupt activities. The park can establish reasonable rules of conduct to ensure that visitors are not exposed to risk of injury by others.

crowd control
Reasonable care to protect against injury required by a facility that attracts large numbers of users.

In a case involving the well-known theme park Magic Mountain, the resort, like most parks, had rules prohibiting line-cutting and guidelines on how park employees should respond to such incidents. The plaintiffs were caught cutting in line and, consistent with park rules, were expelled from the facility. They were African Americans and claimed illegal discrimination. The court dismissed their case, holding that the park was justified in removing them.[69]

Another case implicating crowd control involved a man who was exiting a ride called Autopia at Disneyland. Visitors to the attraction drive miniature cars on a single track in groups of eight vehicles at a time. As the drivers exit the ride, they encounter on the loading area the people next in line. As plaintiff exited his car, the area was crowded with the next riders, causing him to lose his balance, fall, and suffer a fractured hip. The court noted that a cure for the crowding problem could be easily achieved by erecting a small barrier or decorative fence that would separate the exiting patrons from those next in line. The court therefore ruled that Disneyland was negligent and liable for the injuries.[70]

---

[69] *Winbush v. Six Flags Theme Park*, 2004 WL 1551239 (Calif. 2004)
[70] *Stein v. Walt Disney Co.*, 2006 WL 627163 (Calif. 2006)

One of the prime attractions of a theme park is its amusement rides. While they represent fun for many, they also create opportunities for accidents and injuries, and must be carefully managed.

© ChameleonsEye/Shutterstock.com

Warnings About Rides

Theme parks should alert potential riders to anticipated risks. For example, a sign on a roller coaster should include the following warnings: "No smoking, eating, or drinking on the ride. No loose articles. You must be in good health to take this high-speed roller coaster ride. The following should not ride this coaster: those with heart or nervous disorders or weak back or neck or other physical limitation, or who are pregnant."

In a California case, a 20-year-old died from a ruptured cerebral aneurysm while riding a roller coaster. When he boarded the ride he had no idea that he had an aneurysm, a physical condition that is asymptomatic. His family's lawsuit against the park claimed that the facility owed a duty to warn passengers that the roller coaster posed a danger to "apparently healthy persons who suffered from preexisting aneurysms or similar conditions unknown to them." The court declined to impose this requirement, noting that the ride had been operating for almost 30 years and the referenced rider was the only person who had died from an aneurysm on it.[71]

Assumption of Risk

assumption of risk
A doctrine that holds a plaintiff may not recover for injuries received when he voluntarily exposes himself to a known risk.

The rule of **assumption of risk** (see Chapter 5), sometimes called the "no duty" rule, will be applicable in some cases. According to this rule, the participant in an activity impliedly consents to commonly appreciated risks associated with that venture. Thus, a person injured from the usual and expected risks inherent in an activity is not entitled to compensation. For example, a person who rides a roller coaster assumes the risk that he might become dizzy or nauseous. He does not, however, assume the risk of head injury from insufficient cushioning.[72] A spectator at a baseball game was denied recovery for injuries he incurred when a ball in play entered the stands and hit his head because balls at baseball games are known to occasionally enter the spectator area.[73]

---

[71] *Bolla-Shutt v. Cedar Fair*, 2006 WL 401306 (Calif. 2006)
[72] *Beroutsos v. Six Flags Theme Park, Inc.*, 713 N.Y.S.2d 640 (N.Y. 2000)
[73] *Loughran v. The Phillies*, 888 A.2d. 872 (Pa. 2005)

Minimum Height Rules

For safety reasons many rides have minimum height requirements. Park operators should anticipate some disagreements with customers on whether certain young people meet the requirement. If not properly managed, these disputes can escalate to verbal and physical fights, resulting in claims against the park of assault, battery, and false imprisonment.[74] To minimize such confrontations theme parks should develop reasonable rules for security personnel to follow when denying access to a ride.

Ride Safety—Governmental Regulations

Government regulations require that carnival rides be at all times in a safe condition and in conformance with operation and maintenance procedures provided by the manufacturer. All aspects of the ride's operation are implicated—setup, integrity of the structure, inspection schedule, electrical mechanisms and hookup, and more. Violations of these rules can result in serious injury and even death to riders. Some state laws provide that a violation of these regulations that results in death constitutes manslaughter,[75] a serious crime that means recklessly causing a person's death. A conviction can result in a long prison term. Care in all aspects of ride maintenance is imperative.

Ride Safety—Negligence

Freakish accidents can happen if attention to safety is lax. For example, two fingers of a young rider were severed at the second joint when her hand was caught in the spinning portion of a ride.[76]

An incident on the Kingda Ka roller coaster ride at Six Flags Great Adventure in Jackson, New Jersey, led to the crushing of a patron's hand. After she boarded the ride, she placed her hand on the back of the seat in front of her. When the passenger in that seat lowered the safety harness, plaintiff's hand was caught. She sued the park for negligence claiming the amusement park should not have delegated to customers the job of pulling down the safety harness without instructing them how to do it safely. The court denied the park's motion for summary judgment; the case was referred to a jury on the question of whether Six Flags was negligent in these circumstances.[77] In another case, a park maintenance worker was cutting grass and weeds beneath a roller coaster when a mechanic began testing the ride in preparation for the day's business. Unaware that the employee was working in the vicinity, the mechanic sent the coaster on a test run. It struck and killed the worker.[78] To avoid such accidents, parks should establish procedures requiring mechanics to ensure that all employees are clear from dangerous locations before testing rides, and provide appropriate training on the safe testing of rides.

---

[74] *Premier Parks, Inc. v. TIG Insurance Co.*, 2006 WL 2709235 (Del. 2006)
[75] Ohio Statute R.C. 2903.041; *State v. Rock*, 2005 WL 3150176 (Ohio 2005)
[76] *Faulkner v. Darien Lake Theme Park*, 775 N.Y.S.2d 627 (N.Y. 2004)
[77] *Guillen v. Six Flags Great Adventure, LLC*, 2015 WL 9582141 (N.J., 2015).
[78] *Sullivan v. Lake Compounce Theme Park, Inc.*, 889 A.2d 810 (Conn. 2006)

Amusement rides often are transported from fairground to fairground. At the end of each engagement the ride is disassembled, transported to the next location, and reassembled. Proper assembly and adequate training of employees who set up the rides are critical. Additionally, component parts must be adequately affixed to the ride's structure. Otherwise, they can come loose and cause injury.[79]

Fences

Many rides are surrounded by fences. Some act as barriers for protection of passersby and others for demarcation of the area where riders can gather while waiting to board. The fences need to be properly installed and maintained, and of sufficient durability to achieve their purpose. If they are not, liability can result.[80]

Other Attractions

Care of Animals—Negligence

Some theme parks display wild animals of various varieties. These creatures are unpredictable and need to be securely caged so they cannot contact parkgoers. Employees too are at risk. An example includes an incident that occurred at Busch Gardens, a popular theme park in Florida. An employee lost her forearm to a lion while she was feeding the animal. A whale trainer at SeaWorld in Florida was killed by an 11,000-pound, 22-foot-long whale that apparently jumped out of the water, grabbed her by the waist, and drowned her. The criteria that will determine whether the park will be liable in such circumstances include whether it took appropriate precautions and whether it adequately trained the employee.[81]

Advocates for animal rights, including such groups as People for the Ethical Treatment of Animals (PETA), sometimes stage protests at amusement parks and other facilities where they think animals are being abused. The constitutional right of free speech protects protestors from retaliatory action by the government. As a general rule, owners of private property need not tolerate free speech activity, and so private owners, including SeaWorld and like amusements, can direct that demonstrators leave. If they fail to depart, they face prosecution for trespassing, which means entering or remaining unlawfully on the premises.

The Demise of Barnum & Bailey Circus

After 146 years in operation thrilling spectators of all ages, the Ringling Brothers and Barnum & Bailey Circus closed in 2017. Part of the reason for the dissolution was the elimination of the popular elephants from its shows, required by the resolution of a lawsuit brought by PETA.

---

79 *Fabbri v. Superior Court*, 2006 WL 1452105 (Calif. 2006)
80 *Medley v. County of Westchester*, 828 N.Y.S.2d 575 (N.Y. 2007)
81 *Bourassa v. Busch Entertainment Corp.*, 929 So.2d 552 (Fla. 2006)

Parades

Theme parks occasionally provide parades, complete with stunt performers, for the entertainment of patrons. Tricks can be dangerous and cause injury. For example, a 12-year-old parade participant wearing in-line skates was allowed to carry a lit tiki torch. He lost control of it, causing burns to the plaintiff who was marching nearby. The resort sponsoring the parade was found negligent for allowing the young torchbearer to participate on skates and so was liable for the injuries.[82]

© GTS Productions/Shutterstock.com

Skating Rinks

A risk associated with skating rinks is that skaters will collide, causing one or both to fall and suffer injuries. The operator of a rink should develop safety rules for skaters and post signs announcing the rules. Additionally, the operator should provide monitoring to avoid rowdy or inappropriate behavior that might heighten risks.[83]

Other Amusements

Additional attractions that can result in liability if a facility fails to exercise reasonable care in maintenance and operation include rock climbing walls,[84] bicycle paths,[85] go-carts,[86] tube slides,[87] fireworks displays,[88] bleachers for viewing events,[89] and pedestrian walkways.[90]

Admission Discounts

Amusement parks on occasion offer a promotional **admission discount** to residents of the area surrounding the park. The purpose of these discounts is to encourage attendance, particularly during slow periods. Disneyland in Anaheim, California, offered such a discount to people living in several zip codes near the park. This practice was challenged by patrons of Disneyland who lived outside the designated area. The court upheld Disney's varied admission fee structure, determining that the

admission discounts
A promotional rate offered, for example, to residents of the area surrounding an amusement park.

---

82 *Jones v. Lake Hickory R.V. Resort, Inc.*, 606 S.E.2d 119 (N.C. 2004)
83 *Park on Lakeland Drive, Inc. v. Spence*, 941 So.2d 203 (Miss. 2006)
84 *H & H Development Corp., v. N.J. Department of Community Affairs*, 2006 WL 3598427 (N.J. 2006)
85 *State of Utah v. Davis*, 155 P3.d 909 (Utah 2007)
86 *Frost v. Salter Path Fire & Rescue*, 639 S.E.2d 429 (N.C. 2007)
87 *Wilson v. Bilinkas*, 2005 WL 3092893 (N.J. 2005)
88 *Esposito v. New Britain Baseball Club, Inc.*, 895 A.2d 291 (Conn. 2005)
89 *Madelung v. City of New Haven*, 2006 WL 3359744 (Conn. 2006)
90 *Kennedy v. Speedway Motorsports, Inc.*, 631 S.E.2d 212 (N.C. 2006)

park was not required to charge the same admission for all.[91] (Note: If higher fees are imposed due to membership in a protected class—race, color, national origin, religion, gender, marital status, disability, or in some locales sexual orientation—the fee structure would be illegal.)

Season Passes

Theme parks often sell season passes, allowing the holder free admission and access to amusements during specified months. The passes customarily contain written terms and conditions that form part of the contract between the park and the pass holder. Facilities issuing such passes should ensure the terms accurately state the associated rights and restrictions. The wording can determine the outcome of a lawsuit.

A season pass holder at a Six Flags park was unhappy because the park instituted a Fast Lane program, which enabled patrons who paid an additional $10 over the admission fee to access the rides without waiting in the "typical lengthy line." Each day 500 Fast Lane tickets were sold. This program expanded the wait in lines for those not opting to pay the extra money. The plaintiff, angry by the long waits, claimed season pass holders should have the same rights as those paying for the Fast Lane program. The court reviewed the terms and conditions accompanying the season passes. The terms included, in relevant part, "Park capacity and other circumstances may cause Six Flags to limit entry. Your season pass may be used only once each day. Your season pass is good for all rides and attractions except games, arcades, and certain rides and attractions which may require additional charges.... Due to ride maintenance and other circumstances, certain rides and attractions (including new rides) may not be open to the public. Rides subject to availability and/or height and weight restrictions." The court determined that this language did not expressly include Fast Lane privileges, and did not include an implied guarantee to season pass holders of any special treatment regarding access to rides. Summary judgment was granted to Six Flags.[92]

Hotel Spas

spa
A health resort which provides a variety of services intended to promote relaxation, relieve stress, and enhance physical appearance.

Increasingly, upscale hotels have added spas to their offerings. **Spas** provide a variety of services intended to promote relaxation, relieve stress, and enhance physical appearance. The services offered include massages, facials, body wraps (a treatment in which strips of cloth are soaked in herbal teas and swaddled around the body), body scrubs, aromatherapy, manicures and pedicures, makeup lessons and application, exfoliation, cellulite reduction treatments, therapeutic baths, hydrotherapy (moisturizing treatment for dry skin), kurs (a series of body treatments that include mineral water, mud baths, and herbs), salon services (hair treatments), and more. Some spas also offer exercise facilities.

---

[91] *Simon v. Walt Disney World Co.*, 8 Cal. Rptr.3d 459 (Calif. 2004)
[92] *Scales v. Six Flags, Inc.*, 2004 WL 1870499 (Ohio 2004)

© Kurhan/Shutterstock.com

As with virtually all areas of a hotel or restaurant, various aspects of operating a spa can result in liability if reasonable care is overlooked by management. Among the matters of concern in a spa are licensing, sanitation, wet floors, stolen property in lockers, and conduct of service providers.

Licensing

A license evidences authorization from the state for the license holder to offer specified services. In most states the spa itself must be licensed. Additionally, many of the services offered by a spa require that the service-provider be licensed, including manicurists, facialists, masseuses, and cosmetologists (those who provide hair, nail, and skin treatments). Providing services without the license is illegal. Potential penalties for the spa and hotel include fines and negative publicity. For the person who administers the service without the necessary certification, an additional consequence may be jail time. As part of the hiring process, spa management should include verification that workers have the necessary licenses and they are current.

Sanitation and Nails

Most spas offer manicures (treatment of fingernails) and pedicures (treatment of toenails). If sanitation surrounding these treatments is not given high priority, customers can contract a fungus. This will not only reduce repeat business but can also lead to lawsuits. A spa was sued when a customer developed an infection from an alleged dirty foot basin used to give a pedicure.[93] To prevent such occurrences, the spa should ensure the manicure tables and pedicure facilities are scrubbed, all tools are sterilized after each use, emery boards and toe separators are disposed of

---

93 *Sales v. Peabody*, 157 Idaho 195, 335 P.3d 40 (Idaho, 2014).

immediately after use, the manicurist/pedicurist washes her hands between clients, and other sanitary rules are strictly followed.

Wet and Slippery Floors

Spas often include shower facilities, hot tubs, and/or a pool. Customers will inevitably track water onto the floors, having failed to fully dry off after use of the water facilities. To avoid foot fungus, the spa should provide disposable slippers, flip-flops, or shower shoes so that customers are not in bare feet. Absent some form of footwear worn by patrons, the chance they will spread or contract fungus increases significantly. Another issue mandating care is that wet floors are slippery and cause patrons to trip and fall.

Effect of Liability Waivers

liability waiver
An agreement not to sue made by an injured party, usually in exchange for settlement of compensation demands.

To reduce liability, spas often require their customers to sign a **liability waiver,** which is a document stating that customers agree to waive their right to sue the spa and hotel if they are injured while at the facility. As a general rule, the law does not like releases from liability for wrongdoing. However, if the parties genuinely agree to such terms, and the terms are clear and unambiguous, many but not all courts will enforce them. Further, to be enforceable, the activity that caused the injury must be recognizable by the injured party as a potentially dangerous venture. These rules are illustrated in the following spa cases.

A member of a California hotel spa tripped while walking from the pool to the locker room, incurring permanent, disabling injuries. When she sued, the hotel asserted as a defense a provision entitled "Waiver of Liability" included in the spa membership agreement signed by plaintiff. It stated, in relevant part, "MEMBER acknowledges and understands that he/she is using the facilities and services of the HOTEL and SPA at his/her own risk. The SPA and HOTEL and their owners, employees...shall not be liable—and the MEMBER hereby expressly waives any claim of liability—for personal/bodily injury or damages—which occur to any MEMBER...or for any loss of or injury to person or property. This waiver is intended to be a complete release of any responsibility for personal injuries...sustained by any MEMBER...while on the HOTEL and/or SPA premises, whether using exercise equipment or not."

Additionally, the paragraph directly above plaintiff's signature stated in part: "I am aware that this Agreement contains a release of liability and a contract between the SPA and myself." The court determined that the waiver was clear and "easily readable," and granted summary judgment to the spa and the hotel.[94]

In another case, a health club member was injured in a slide aerobics class. The class required the use of an "extremely slippery mat on which participants slide from side to side as an aerobic exercise; special socks are worn to facilitate sliding on the mat." Plaintiff had signed a release waiving all claims "arising out of or connected with the use of the fitness center." Based on the waiver, the court dismissed the case.[95]

---

[94] *Intrilligator v. PLC Santa Monica*, 2002 WL 31424522 (Calif. 2002)
[95] *Sanchez v. Bally's Total Fitness Corp.*, 71 Cal.Rptr.2d 923 (Calif. 1998)

A different outcome resulted where a member of a fitness center was injured while in a sauna when the bench on which he was lying collapsed. He too had signed an unambiguous release agreeing not to sue for any injury he might suffer "of any kind resulting from or related to the use of the facilities...." The court determined that this type of injury was not covered by the release because "No Family Fitness patron can be charged with realistically appreciating the risk of injury from simply reclining on a sauna bench." Therefore the court denied the center's motion for summary judgment.[96]

The lessons for spa managers from these cases is that a waiver of liability may prevent an injured patron from successfully suing the facility provided the wording of the release is clear and the type of injury suffered is foreseeable.

Property Stolen from Lockers

Spa patrons usually change clothes prior to their treatments or before using the sports facilities. They may don a bathrobe or other loose apparel provided by the facility, or their own exercise clothes. In either event the spa customarily provides a locker for the visitor's use. Often the lock for the locker is also provided by the club. On occasion, someone without authority gains access to a locker and steals property inside. The spa customer typically sues the spa seeking compensation for the missing items. The spa may or may not be liable depending on the facts.

A health club member left his expensive Rolex watch, money clip, and $400 cash in a locker while he exercised. The locker was pried open and his valuables stolen. The club had provided a lock and key for his use and kept a master key to permit entry if the patron misplaced the key. The club's written rules provide, "All personal belongings should be stored in your locker. The Health & Wellness Center is not responsible for lost or stolen items...The Wellness Center cannot assure the safety of your valuables and we suggest that you do not bring items of high personal or monetary value to the center." A sign posted at the sign-in desk read, "We cannot assure the safety of your valuables."

The owner of the watch and money sued, claiming the club was liable as a bailee, one to whom goods are entrusted (see Chapter 8). The court disagreed and dismissed the case. To establish a bailment requires that goods be delivered and accepted by the bailor. In the circumstances of this case where the member did not inform the club of the contents of his locker and the member retained the key, the club did not "accept" the expensive watch and considerable sum of money. Indeed, the club had no knowledge of the items stored in the locker and would not be expected to have agreed to a violation of its rules by someone storing unusually valuable property.[97]

If the facts supported the creation of a bailment and the spa failed to exercise reasonable care to prevent the theft, the facility would be responsible to compensate the customer for his loss.

---

[96] *Leon v. Family Fitness Center, Inc.*, 71 Ca. Rptr.2d 923 (Calif. 1998)
[97] *Sisters of Charity v. Meaux*, 122 S.W.3d 428 (Tex. 2003)

Massages

The process of administering a massage necessarily involves close personal contact between the masseur/masseuse and the customer. Often the latter is minimally clothed or draped only in a towel to intensify the benefits of the procedure. This environment can lead to incidents of sexual abuse or rape. In a New Jersey case, a woman was sexually assaulted during her massage at a hotel spa. The patron sued the hotel claiming negligent supervision, management, hiring, and training.[98] To avoid this type of liability, spa management should perform criminal background checks on all its workers and verify credentials including necessary licenses. Ongoing supervision likewise is critical.

Tanning Booths

Spas sometimes include tanning booths. This equipment should be inspected regularly to ensure proper operation. An apparatus that malfunctions due even in part to the fault of the spa can result in injuries and liability. Another issue was illustrated in a California case. A female tanner lay nude in a private tanning booth. A male worker at the salon surreptitiously observed the tanner by opening the doorway to the room and using a reflective compact disc. The patron sued the facility claiming it was liable based on respondeat superior (see Chapter 5), which provides that an employer is liable for the wrongful acts of an employee who is acting within the scope of his employment. The court concluded that the employee's actions were beyond the scope of his employment and so the spa avoided liability.[99] The lesson, however, is that, as with massages, employees must be carefully selected and thoroughly investigated prior to hiring, and thereafter monitored closely.

© Kzenon/Shutterstock.com

Another issue associated with indoor tanning is false claims about alleged health risks and benefits. A national chain of tanning booths was accused by the New York Attorney General (chief state consumer law enforcement officer) of misleading claims about cancer risks from indoor tanning. The company settled the case agreeing to stop making health-related representations, stop offering "unlimited" tanning packages, and stop targeting high school students.[100]

---

98 *Madan-Russo v. Posada*, S.A., 841 A.2d 489 (N.J. 2004)
99 *Sun Lounge Tanning Centers v. Superior Court*, 2004 WL 1194873 (Calif. 2004)
100 See www.ag.ny.gov/press-release/ag-schneiderman-announces

Condominium Hotels

A somewhat new phenomenon in the hotel field is the **condominium hotel**. As the name suggests, this type of facility is a hybrid between a condominium and a hotel. A **condominium** is a multiunit building in which each separate unit is individually owned. Contrast this with an apartment building in which all the units are owned by one party—the landlord. Also contrast the condominium with a hotel in which all the units are customarily owned by the hotel. As with traditional condominiums, each unit of a condominium hotel is individually owned.

Common Areas

The unit owners in condominiums jointly own the common areas of the building such as the lobby, meeting spaces, party rooms, and swimming pools. The owners all have an equal right to use these areas. Each owner is obligated to pay a set amount per month, often called a **maintenance fee**, that is applied to the costs of upkeep of the common areas. A property superintendent is usually hired to perform maintenance work on an ongoing basis.

Unlike condominiums, the common areas of a condominium hotel are typically, but not always, owned by the developer of the condominium hotel project and not by the unit owners. As with condominiums, unit owners pay a monthly maintenance fee. The money is typically used by the developer to hire a brand name hotel company (e.g., the Hyatt) to manage the common areas. Proceeds (e.g., from private parties, weddings, and various other events) accrue to the benefit of the developer and not the unit owners.

Amenities

An additional difference between condominiums and condominium hotels is that the amenities provided to the latter's owners exceed those associated with condominiums, primarily because of the hotel management component.

Unit Rentals

Condominium hotels have become popular in resort areas and are often used by the owners as a second or vacation home. Therefore, the units typically are not owner-occupied year-round. The hotel company that manages the common areas likewise administers rentals of the units for periods when the owner is not in residence. The owners pay a fee for this service. A plaintiff invested in six condominium hotel units in a Four Seasons Hotel in Miami, Florida. The units generated less income than he anticipated. Plaintiff sued the Four Seasons and sale agents claiming fraud. According to the complaint, plaintiff was induced to buy the units by promises that its units would be marketed and rented in the same manner as the Four Seasons regular hotel rooms. Instead, preference was given to renting the hotel rooms. The court denied defendants' motion to dismiss.[101]

> **condominium hotel**
> A building project operated as a commercial hotel even though the units are individually owned.

> **condominium**
> An arrangement where each living unit in a building is separately owned. The common areas (such as the lobby and hallways), plus the structure and land are jointly owned by all of the unit owners.

> **maintenance fee**
> A set amount paid monthly by condominium owners.

---

[101] *Begualg Investment Management, Inc. v. Four Seasons Hotel, Ltd,* 2012 WL 1155128 (Fla. 2012).

Advantages

The appeal to the unit owners of a condominium hotel are many, and include:

- Ownership of a condominium

- Possible receipt of income from renting the room to guests when the owner is not using it

- Avoidance of rental hassles by delegating that task to the hotel company

- Possible appreciation in value of the unit

- Ease in maintenance because repairs are typically handled by the hotel company

- Enjoyment of amenities customarily provided by a hotel

Benefits to the hotel company include:

- Management fees

- Expansion of its brand and affiliated properties

- Wider acceptance of its trademark

Contracts

Among the important contracts involved in the operation of a condominium hotel are the contract between the developer and unit buyer for the sale and purchase of each unit; the contract between the developer and a hotel company for management of the building and of unit rentals; the contract between the unit owner and hotel company for the latter's services in rental of the units when the owner is away; and the rental agreements between the hotel company and guests for occupancy of units when not occupied by the owners.

Future

The advent of condominium hotels is fairly new. How broadly they will penetrate the vacation and hotel markets remains to be determined. To date they have proved to be quite popular.

Summary

The number of casinos, theme parks, and spas has grown rapidly. This phenomenon offers new opportunities for workers in the hospitality field. The legal challenges associated with these specialized entities include some known to hospitality law and others unique to these facilities.

Casinos have venues not normally associated with hotels and restaurants. These include riverboats and Native American reservations. Both of these venues are the subject of laws that are not applicable elsewhere. A thorough study of the law of casinos requires exposure to maritime law and Native American law.

Just as hotels and restaurants need to take appropriate precautions to protect the safety and well-being of their guests, casinos, theme parks, and spas must do the same. Laws dealing with negligence, false imprisonment, trademarks, copyrights, and other areas of law are equally applicable. Dram shop acts and the law of contracts are likewise binding.

Condominium hotels are fairly new. They offer owners enhanced amenities during their stay and the opportunity to lease the unit when the owner is not using it.

Preventive Law Tips for Managers

- *Anticipate circumstances that may cause injury to patrons and take the necessary action to eliminate the risks.* All types of facilities are obligated to use reasonable care to protect their patrons from injury. Failure to do so will result in liability. Managers and employees should always be alert to conditions on the premises that may present risks. Upon discovery of any such conditions, take the necessary action to eliminate them.

- *Aid patrons who evidence signs of physical distress.* While the law does not generally require that people come to the aid of someone in danger, where a special relationship exists—such as a hospitality business and the people it attracts to its premises—a duty does exist to exercise reasonable care to provide first aid to an ill or injured patron. The facility should develop an emergency response system and thoroughly train its employees concerning it.

- *Do not detain a patron without probable cause to believe the customer has engaged in illegal conduct.* Detaining a customer on suspicion of engaging in criminal conduct without having probable cause can lead to liability for false imprisonment. Unfortunately, casinos particularly can be victims of criminal conduct that can cause considerable loss to the casino or its clientele. However, the casino must balance its interest in preventing crime against the interest of its customers who have a right not to be detained without probable cause.

- *Do not adopt a trademark that is confusingly similar to another mark used in the same industry.* If a business uses a name that is confusingly similar to a competitor's, the business may be forced to discontinue use of that name regardless of money spent to advertise and promote it. To avoid this, employ marks that are unique and not likely to be confused with other trademarks already in use.

- *Use only original material in advertising.* If advertising or promotional materials are copied from another's marketing campaign or other source, liability for copyright infringement may result. When designing advertising, use original ideas and elements. If someone else's materials are desirable, obtain authorization for their use.

- *Take precautions to protect customers from criminal activity.* This is particularly important for casinos. Successful gamblers are attractive targets for criminals. Adopt procedures to protect patrons. Such protocols might include providing a security escort to customers' cars; surveillance cameras; a well-trained security force; training all employees to detect and prevent criminal activity; maintaining contact with security personnel in other nearby facilities to learn of illegal conduct reported in the area; and maintaining a close relationship with the local police for ongoing security assistance.

- *Do not sell alcohol illegally.* A casino may be liable when a person is injured by someone who was illegally served alcohol. To avoid dram shop liability, do not sell alcohol to prohibited classes of people; train employees on how to detect a customer who is intoxicated or underage; and reinforce that training regularly.

- *For casinos on Native American reservations, comply fully with the Indian Gaming Regulatory Act (IGRA).* IGRA contains the prerequisites that a casino on a reservation must meet to legally provide gambling on its premises. Failure to comply can result in government seizure of gaming devices and criminal prosecution of the casino's officers and managers. To ensure compliance with this specialized area of law, consult with an attorney knowledgeable about IGRA.

- *Casino and theme park managers should develop procedures for crowd control and train employees frequently on what to do when incidents occur.* Theme parks and casinos attract lots of people, including aggressive and rowdy patrons. They can cause disruptions and fights. The facilities should have rules and protocols for employees to follow to defuse such occurrences and eject the instigators if necessary. Workers whose jobs include quelling combative behavior should be trained frequently and supervised closely to avoid both fights and claims by the aggressor of false imprisonment.

- *Theme park managers should test all rides frequently.* Rides need to be in good order always to avoid various risks of injury. Management should develop rules identifying appropriate frequency of test runs. The resulting regulations should be strictly followed. Management should train those employees who perform the tests on how to execute them effectively and safely.

- *Theme park managers should be sure minimum height restrictions on rides are enforced and sufficient to protect the safety of the shortest permissible riders.* Signage identifying height restrictions should be easily understood and conspicuously displayed without any obstructions. Ride operators should be trained to ensure that would-be riders below the specified minimum are denied access to the ride. The operators should also be trained in procedures to follow if a dispute erupts.

- *Theme park operators should analyze particular risks associated with the facility and develop plans to minimize visitors' exposure to injury.* Theme parks vary greatly in the entertainment they provide. Included might be the presence of skating rinks, rock climbing walls, bike paths, water slides, fireworks, various animals, parades, virtual reality, and more. Each offering needs to be assessed for risks and a plan developed to minimize the danger. Employees should be trained appropriately and supervised well.

- *Spa managers should verify that all service providers have the necessary licenses.* Numerous services offered in spas require licensing. While the requirements vary from state to state, those often needing a license include the spa itself, manicurists, masseuses, and cosmetologists. Penalties if the mandated licenses are missing include fines and possibly jail. Consider also that any associated publicity will not endear patrons to your business.

- *Spa managers should emphasize to workers the importance of sanitation.* Given the inevitable bodily contact between service-providers and customers, the opportunities are ripe to spread diseases, such as fungus, from one patron to another. To avoid this result, cleanliness of workspaces must be given a high priority. Likewise, all tools used in connection with administering services must be sterilized after each use, and products that come in contact with a client's body, such as emery boards and toe separators, should be discarded after one-time use.

- *Spa managers should, if a facility includes showers, hot tubs and/or pools, take precautions to protect patrons from slippery floors and fungus infection.* Some spa users may not fully dry off after using the shower, tub, or pool. Select a material for the floor that is slip-resistant. Develop procedures to ensure the floor is frequently mopped. Offer customers disposable footwear. These efforts should minimize the number of falls from wet and slippery floors and the transmittal of unwanted foot conditions.

- *When using a waiver of liability, ensure it is understandable and easy to read.* In some states an easily understood waiver can result in avoidance or lessening of liability. Waivers should be drafted by an attorney. The finished product should be written in a manner that is readily comprehensible by the facility's customers.

- *Spa managers should verify the integrity of the lockers and the locks, and post signage encouraging patrons to leave their valuables at home.* In many spas, guests will be expected to remove their clothes and don a robe or like garment.

The spa typically provides lockers for temporary storage of patrons' clothing. If the lockers and/or locks are flimsy or broken, a thief's job is made easy. Customers should be encouraged to leave their valuables at home. In the event of a locker failure, liability can be avoided or minimized when the guest's loss is limited in value amount.

■ *Spa managers should recognize that many services are administered while the customer is scantily clad, and take appropriate precautions to prevent rape, assault and peeping.* Such precautions include verifying that the service provider is properly licensed, performing a criminal check on applicants for employment, designing the facility's layout so that rooms in which services are provided are not remotely located, checking latches on doors to verify operability, and more.

■ *Developers and managers of condominium hotels should keep apprised of applicable legal developments.* Those connected with this type of facility should keep current on new laws as they are adopted.

Review Questions

1. What defenses are available to a gambler who has incurred a sizable loss while betting on credit?

2. What is a pathological gambler?

3. What duty of care is owed by a casino to its patrons?

4. What is the Jones Act and what is its relevance to casinos?

5. What is "probable cause" and how does it apply to the tort of false imprisonment?

6. What led to the proliferation of riverboat casinos?

7. What spurred the development of casinos on Native American reservations?

8. What is the Indian Gaming Regulatory Act?

9. What is the meaning of the term *sovereign authority*?

10. What laws regulate online gambling?

11. Identify five amusements at a theme park that can result in liability.

12. Must a theme park charge the same fee for all visitors? Explain your answer.

13. What licenses are needed to operate a spa?

14. What are the consequences for failing to secure the necessary licenses?

15. Why is sanitation particularly important in the operation of a spa?

16. What is assumption of risk?

17. Who owns the living units in a condominium hotel?

18. Who owns the common areas in a condominium hotel?

19. What is a waiver of liability?

Discussion Questions

1. Describe several criminal schemes to which casinos may be vulnerable. How can casinos protect themselves?

2. What determines whether the Jones Act applies to a water-based casino? What attributes of the casino will be considered by a court in determining whether the Jones Act applies?

3. What factors will a court consider when deciding whether the name of a casino constitutes trademark infringement?

4. Why have the courts not applied dram shop liability to gambling debts?

5. What must a Native American tribe, wishing to initiate gambling, do to comply with the Indian Gaming Regulatory Act? What are the consequences if it offers gaming without complying with the act?

6. What do gambling commissions regulate and why?

7. What sanitation precautions should spa management take?

8. What type of injury will be covered by a waiver of liability? What type of injury will a waiver of liability not cover?

9. For spa services during which the patron is partially undressed (massage, various bodily treatments, tanning, etc.), what action can spa management take to reduce the opportunity for sexual abuse?

10. How can theme park managers help ensure that ride operators are enforcing height restrictions?

11. What is the effect of assumption of risk on a theme park visitor's right to sue?

12. Why do some states hold theme park operators liable for the serious crime of manslaughter if they violate regulations applicable to amusement rides and death to a patron results?

13. Identify risks of injury from the following amusements and state how to manage the risks: water parks, parades, go-carts, ice rinks, and animals.

14. Discuss the similarities of, and differences between, a traditional hotel and a condominium hotel.

15. Identify four contracts involved in the development and operation of a condominium hotel. Name two issues for each of the four contracts that would likely be included in the agreement.

Application Questions

1. Eduardo was gambling at a casino. Luck was with him and he won almost $10,000. What security precautions should the casino have in effect to protect Eduardo and other customers from criminal activity?

2. Barry was a security guard at a casino. He took a 15-minute break in the middle of his shift. When he returned, he noticed a player at a blackjack table who had not been there when he left. Barry also noticed the player had a large number of betting chips. Barry suspected foul play and detained the player. When Barry undertook further investigation he learned that the player had done nothing wrong. The player then sued the casino for false imprisonment. Would the casino be able to utilize the defense of probable cause? Why or why not?

3. Sarina was playing the slot machines at a casino for several hours. A waitress periodically approached her and offered her free drinks. After drinking 10 beers she became angry and violent when the player next to her won a major jackpot. Security was called and Sarina was taken to the security office. Security personnel determined that she was very intoxicated. What duty does the casino owe to Sarina under these circumstances?

4. Why is it important for a theme park to state on its season passes all the terms, conditions, and restrictions associated with it?

5. How might theme parks manage the large lines that form at prime times while patrons are waiting to gain admission to the park and access to the attractions?

6. What precautions should spa management take to avoid customers slipping on wet floors?

Websites

Websites that will enhance your understanding of the material in this chapter include:

www.americangaming.org This is the site of the American Gaming Association, a trade association of the "commercial casino entertainment industry." It provides up-to-date information on the gaming industry, including issues associated with responsible gaming.

www.gaming.nv.gov This is the site for the Nevada Gaming Control Board. The Board enforces rules and regulations for the licensing and operation of gaming in the state.

www.ncpgambling.org This is the site of the National Council on Problem Gambling, the national advocate for programs and services to assist problem gamblers and their families.

www.iaapa.org This is the site of the International Association of Amusement Parks and Attractions. It includes information of interest to theme and amusement parks including legislative and regulatory initiatives that impact the industry.

GLOSSARY

absolute liability See *strict liability*.

acceptance Agreement by offeree with terms and conditions of an offer constitutes an acceptance.

act of God A happening not controlled by the power of humans, but rather from the direct, immediate, and exclusive operations of the forces of nature.

administrative agency A governmental subdivision charged with administering legislation that applies to a particular industry.

administrative law Regulations adopted by administrative agencies.

administrative remedies must be exhausted Appeals available within an administrative agency must have been utilized and completed before the case is heard in court.

admission discounts A promotional rate offered, for example, to residents of the area surrounding an amusement park.

affirmative action Employment and education programs designed to remedy past, existing and continuing discrimination and to achieve diversity, by favoring members of disadvantaged groups.

agency A relationship in which one person (the agent) acts for another (the principal) based on authority voluntarily given.

agent A person authorized by a principal to act on the principal's behalf under the principal's direction.

agreement not to compete In the sale of a business, a contractual provision barring the seller from competing with the buyer in the geographical area where the business is located for a specified period of time.

allegation Unproven assertions.

alternative dispute resolution Alternatives to trial. These include, for example, arbitration and mediation.

Americans with Disabilities Act A federal law that bars discrimination against people with disabilities. The scope of the act includes both employment and access to places of public accommodation.

answer The pleading issued by the defendant in response to plaintiff's complaint.

antitrust laws Laws that attempt to ensure that open competition is preserved, and practices that restrain competition are eliminated.

appeal A review by one court of the decision of another court, initiated by the party who lost in the prior court.

appellate court A court with the authority to review the decisions of other courts.

arbitration The process of dispute resolution by an arbitrator chosen by the parties to decide the case.

ASCAP American Society of Composers, Authors, and Publishers, an organization that collects and distributes copyright fees.

assault The tort of intentionally putting someone in fear of harmful physical contact, and the crime of intentionally causing physical injury.

assumption of risk A doctrine that holds a plaintiff may not recover for injuries received when he voluntarily exposes himself to a known risk.

attractive nuisance A potentially dangerous object or condition of exceptional interest to young people.

attrition clause In reference to a room reservation contract between an association hosting a convention and a hotel, a contractual provision obligating the organization to compensate the hotel if less than a specified number of rooms are rented by conventioneers.

at-will employment The rule of law that an employment contract between an employer and an employee is indefinite in duration and can be terminated by either party for any reason or no reason at any time without liability.

back pay An item of damages in an employment discrimination case consisting of pay the plaintiff would have earned but for a wrongful termination.

bailee The person receiving possession of goods or personal property.

bailment A transfer of possession of goods or personal property from a person in possession of the property to another with the understanding that the property will be returned.

bailment for the sole benefit of the bailee The bailor receives no benefit from the bailment.

bailment for the sole benefit of the bailor The bailee receives no benefit from the bailment.

bailor The owner of goods or personal property who transfers such property to a bailee.

battery The tort of causing harmful physical contact to a person, such as punching someone. (Compare assault.)

bench trial A trial in which the judge rather than a jury decides the outcome.

BMI Broadcast Music, Inc. An organization that collects and distributes copyright fees for its members.

bona fide occupational qualification (BFOQ) A job qualification that legally discriminates on the basis of race, religion, national origin, or gender because (1) excluded classes cannot perform the job effectively, (2) such inability is factually supported, and (3) the job classification is reasonably necessary for the normal operation of the business.

breach of contract The failure to perform, without legal excuse, some contracted act.

brief Documents submitted to a court by plaintiff and defendant that contain the arguments in favor of each party's position.

business necessity A criterion for job applicants that has an obvious relationship to the job.

capacity to contract The ability to understand the terms of a contract and to understand also that failure to perform the terms can lead to legal liability.

card counter Someone who keeps track of the cards played in blackjack.

casebooks Books that publish judges' decisions.

case decision An interpretation of the law applied by a judge to a set of facts in a given case.

case-in-chief That part of a trial where each party presents his evidence.

cases Lawsuits; also written decisions by judges.

charge to the jury The procedure at trial where the judge informs the jury of the law applicable to the case. The charge occurs after the summations.

citation A reference to a case containing information on where the case is located in a law library, and how to access the case on a computer database.

civil case A noncriminal case. The remedy sought is typically damages (money).

civil law Law applicable to legal wrongs other than crimes.

civil rights Personal rights that derive primarily from the Constitution, for example, equal protection, free speech, privacy, and due process.

Civil Rights Act of 1964 A federal statute that prohibits discrimination on the basis of race, color, religion, and natural origin.

civil rights laws Laws that protect the rights and privileges of individuals including equal protection, right against unreasonable searches and seizures, due process, and many more.

claim A demand for a remedy, usually money, to compensate for a perceived wrong.

class action A lawsuit brought by a group of persons who are similarly situated.

class action suit A legal device in which many people who have suffered losses from the same cause sue the defendant jointly.

collective bargaining A process where representatives of a union negotiate with representatives of management on terms of employment such as hours, wages, benefits, vacations, and other working conditions.

collective bargaining agreement A contract between workers and management that is a result of collective bargaining.

common law Judges' decisions as opposed to statutory law.

compacts Written agreements between a state and a Native American tribe that govern the operation of casino gaming on Native American lands.

comparable worth The idea that men and women should earn equal pay for jobs requiring comparable skills and responsibility, or are of comparable worth to the employer.

comparative negligence The rule followed in many states apportioning damages according to the comparative contribution of the negligence of the parties. A jury will allocate the liability between the plaintiff and the defendant depending on their degree of culpability based on a total of 100 percent.

compensatory damages Money awarded in a lawsuit to reimburse the plaintiff for expenses incurred from an injury caused by defendant.

complaint The initial pleading filed in court in a civil lawsuit alleging defendant engaged in illegal conduct and seeking compensation.

concessionaire An independent contractor who provides a service to a hotel's guests.

condition An event on which a contractual duty is contingent.

condominium An arrangement where each living unit in a building is separately owned. The common areas (such as the lobby and hallways), plus the structure and land are jointly owned by all of the unit owners.

condominium hotel A building project operated as a commercial hotel even though the units are individually owned.

Congress The primary law-making body of the federal government.

consideration Something of value exchanged for something else of value.

conspicuous Out in the open; easily seen.

constitutional law The law embodied in the federal Constitution, prescribing the organization and powers of the federal government, and defining rights of the people.

constructive bailment Bailment created by law rather than by the parties agreeing.

constructive notice Information or knowledge of a fact imputed to a person by law because he or she could have discovered the fact by proper diligence or because the situation was such as to put upon such person the duty of inquiry.

contract An agreement between two or more parties which creates an obligation that is enforceable in court.

contract (voidable) A contract that may be canceled at the option of one party.

contributory negligence The rule followed in some states that prevents a plaintiff from collecting damages if the plaintiff's negligence contributed to the injury.

copyright The exclusive right of a creator or other copyright owner to reproduce and license (authorize) the reproduction of the following: literature, art, music, drama, sculpture, choreography, motion pictures, computer software, and other audiovisual works including broadcasts of sporting events.

counterclaims Claims the defendant asserts against the plaintiff in an answer.

counteroffer Statement made by offeree to the offeror relating to the same matter as the original offer and proposing a substituted bargain differing from that proposed by the original offer.

court The place where judges work; also refers to the judge.

credit card fraud Use of a credit card that is stolen or otherwise unauthorized by the true cardholder.

criminal case A case involving a legal wrong that can result in jail time for the perpetrator.

criminal law The law applicable to criminal cases.

criminal possession of stolen property Act of knowingly taking possession of stolen property with intent to benefit someone other than the owner.

cross-examination Questioning of a witness called by the opposing side in a case that typically seeks to discredit the witness.

crowd control Reasonable care to protect against injury required by a facility that attracts large numbers of users.

damages The remedy sought by the injured party in a civil case.

decision A judge's determination in a case as to which party should win and which should lose.

defamation The tort of making false written statements about someone to a third person when those statements subject the former to ridicule or scorn.

default judgment A judgment entered in favor of a plaintiff when the defendant fails to appear in court.

defendant The party who is sued by the plaintiff in a lawsuit.

defraud To cheat or trick, intentionally misrepresenting an important fact intending for someone to rely on the misrepresentation and thereby suffer damages.

delegated powers Those powers expressly allocated to the federal government in the Constitution.

deliberations The process undertaken by a jury to examine, review, and weigh the evidence to decide on a verdict.

deposition Pretrial questioning of a witness under oath.

direct examination The questioning of a witness by the attorney who called the witness to the stand.

disability A physical or mental impairment that substantially limits one or more major life activities.

disclaimer A term in a contract that attempts to avoid all liability on the part of one party.

discovery The pretrial process by which each side obtains evidence known to the other side.

discrimination The act of treating some people differently from and less favorably than others.

disparate impact Neutral employment practices that unintentionally result in unequal treatment.

disparate treatment Intentional discrimination based on race, color, religion, gender, or national origin.

dissolution The termination of business operations, sometimes applied as a penalty for antitrust violations.

diversity of citizenship Plaintiff and defendant are residents of different states; one of several criteria for federal court jurisdiction.

divestiture The act of giving up part of a business operation, sometimes imposed as a penalty for antitrust violations.

Dram Shop Act A statute which imposes liability on the seller of alcohol, when a third party is injured as a result of the intoxication of the buyer where the sale has caused or contributed to such intoxication.

due process The right not to be deprived of life, liberty, or property without a fair hearing. With respect to licenses and regulations, this means that proprietors are entitled to reasonable notice of the grounds for any proposed legal action, an opportunity to prepare a defense, and a hearing.

duress Threats of harm if a person does not sign a contract.

easement The privilege of using someone else's land for some limited purpose.

encroachment Entry onto another's property without right or permission.

Equal Employment Opportunity Commission (EEOC) An agency of the federal government that is authorized to both develop policy and enforce Title VII mandates against discrimination.

equal pay for equal work A rule of law that requires that men and women who do virtually the same jobs be paid according to the same pay schedule.

equitable estoppel A legal principle that precludes a person from claiming a right or benefit that might otherwise have existed because that person made a false representation to a person who relied on it to his or her detriment.

errors and omissions Insurance that covers the cost of defending a lawsuit and any adverse judgment resulting from failure to fulfill one's obligation to a client.

essential functions As defined by the Americans with Disabilities Act, the core responsibilities of a job as distinguished from marginal or incidental assignments.

e-tickets (electronic tickets) Paperless tickets representing reservations that are recorded exclusively in computer files. The only paper produced in the transaction is a receipt for payment.

eviction Legal process by which a judge grants the removal of a tenant, by force if necessary, from rental property for a specific reason; for example, nonpayment of rent.

excessive force Unnecessary force; more than is required to defend oneself.

exclusionary rule The rule that holds evidence obtained in consequence of a warrantless search is not admissible in court.

exclusive dealing contracts Situation in which a seller (usually a wholesaler) forbids a buyer (usually a retailer) from purchasing the products of the seller's competitors.

expert witness A witness with superior knowledge about a subject due to education and/or experience.

facts Objective information about circumstances that exist and/or events that have occurred.

Fair Labor Standards Act (FLSA) A federal law adopted in 1938 to eliminate unfair methods of compensation and labor conditions injurious to the health of workers.

false arrest Intentional and unprivileged detention or restraint of another person.

false imprisonment Restraining a person against his will without justification.

forbearance Refraining from doing something you have a legal right to do.

for cause Grounds to remove a potential juror from the jury due to some disqualifying circumstance such as familiarity with the case or the parties, bias, or inability to speak English.

foreign/natural substance test A test that holds that the presence of an object natural to a food product does not breach the warranty implied in its sale. (The presence of a foreign object is a breach of warranty.)

forgery The unauthorized alteration, completion, or making of a written instrument with intent to defraud or deceive.

forum A court or tribunal; a place for resolution of lawsuits.

forum selection clause A clause in a contract preselecting a particular forum, such as a given state, county, court or administrative proceeding, for the resolution of a dispute.

franchise An arrangement in which the owner of a trademark, service mark, or copyright, licenses others under specified conditions, to use the mark or copyright in the sale of goods or services.

franchisee The party who receives the right to use a trademark, service mark, or copyright in connection with the sale of goods or services.

franchisor The owner of a trademark, service mark, or copyright who has licensed others to use it in connection with the sale of goods or services.

fraud The tort of intentionally misleading others resulting in financial loss for those who were deceived.

gambling The act of playing a game for stakes in the hope of winning.

gambling commissions Government agencies created to resolve disputes involving gaming debts and alleged winnings.

genuine assent Concept that the parties involved in a contract must genuinely agree to the contract terms.

glass ceiling Artificial barriers that have held women and minorities back from promotion to management and decision-making positions in business.

Good Samaritan Statutes Laws that protect a person who reacts in an emergency situation by trying to help a sick or injured person or someone in peril.

goodwill A favorable reputation producing an expectation of future business.

group boycott Circumstance in which two or more sellers refuse to do business with a particular person or company, intending thereby to eliminate competition or block entry to a market.

hostile environment sexual harassment Verbal or physical conduct of a sexual nature that creates an intimidating, hostile, or offensive work environment.

hung jury A jury that cannot reach a verdict.

identity theft Obtaining personal financial information about a credit card holder without authority to do so and illegally using that information for the thief's economic gain.

illegal alien One who enters the United States without the necessary authorization.

illusory A contractual term that fails to contain a firm commitment; a promise that is so indefinite that the party making it has not in fact committed to do anything.

immigrant In the United States, a citizen of another country who enters the United States.

independent contractor One who contracts to do work for another, but who maintains control of the method of accomplishing the work. Also, someone hired by another to perform a given task according to methods and procedures that are independent from the control of the hiring party.

Indian Gaming Regulatory Act (IGRA) Federal legislation adopted by Congress in 1988, which to some extent restricts a tribe's ability to conduct gambling activities.

infra hospitium Meaning "within the inn." This doctrine states that under common law, hotels were liable as insurers for guests' property on the hotel premises.

injunction A court order forbidding a party to a lawsuit from engaging in specified acts.

innocent misrepresentation An untruthful statement that the speaker believes is accurate.

insurer One who is generally obligated to compensate another for losses.

in personam jurisdiction The authority of a court to determine a case against a particular defendant.

intentional infliction of emotional distress A tort in which the offending conduct must be outrageous or so extreme as to go beyond all possible bounds of decency, and be regarded as atrocious and utterly intolerable in a civilized community.

interrogatories Formal written questions submitted to the opposing party in a lawsuit as part of the discovery proceedings.

interstate commerce Business affecting more than one state, as opposed to business done between two parties in the same state.

invitation to negotiate Opening discussions that may or may not lead to an offer for a subsequent contract.

invitee Person who is on property of another for the economic benefit of the owner or for the economic benefit of both parties.

issue A legal question that parties to a lawsuit submit to the judge for resolution.

issuing a bad check A check for which the maker has insufficient funds in the bank, or a check written on an account that has been closed. If the bad check is issued knowingly, the business can pursue the patron on criminal charges.

Jones Act A federal statutes that addresses the rules under which ships must operate when engaged in commerce in the US.

judgment The official decision of a judge about the rights and claims of each side in a lawsuit.

jurisdiction The authority of a court to hear a case, as determined by the legislature.

jury trial A case tried by a jury.

kosher A designation referring to food prepared consistent with Jewish religious requirements.

landmark decision A court decision that sets a precedent marking a turning point in the interpretation of law.

larceny Theft of personal property.

Last Clear Chance Doctrine A rule used by plaintiffs in certain negligence cases to support their argument that the defendant should be liable for failing to prevent the injury, even if negligent acts of the plaintiff initially put the plaintiff in peril.

law Rules, enforceable in court, requiring people to meet certain standards of conduct.

legislative process The process by which the federal government, as well as other units of government, adopts laws.

legislators An elected law-maker.

legislature A law-making body whose members are elected to office by the citizenry.

liability waiver An agreement not to sue made by an injured party, usually in exchange for settlement of compensation demands.

libel Written defamation.

license Legal document giving official permission to do something

licensee In cases of negligence, one who does not qualify as an invitee but who has been given permission by the owner or occupier of premises to enter or remain on the property. Also, a person who has been granted a license to engage in certain conduct, such as the sale of alcohol.

lien A security interest in real or personal property that is discharged upon payment of a debt.

limiting liability statutes Laws that restrict an innkeepers' liability for property loss in exchange for strict statutory compliance by the innkeeper. Also called limiting statutes.

liquor liability insurance Insurance purchased by a liquor licensee to cover dram shop liability.

litigants The parties to a lawsuit.

maintenance fee A set amount paid monthly by condominium owners.

maritime laws Numerous federal laws that affect events occurring on ships on the waterways of the United States.

marker A written document used by a casino to access money from a gambler's bank account if payment of a loan extended to the player is not made per terms agreed by the parties.

mediation An alternative dispute resolution method in which litigants settle their dispute out of court by mutual agreement with the aid of a third person called a mediator.

merchandise samples Samples of goods for sale brought to a hotel by a salesperson-guest.

merchantable An implied warranty that goods offered for sale, including food, are at least of average quality and fit for their ordinary purpose.

merger A transaction that combines two businesses into one, resulting in a reduction of competition.

mitigate Lessen; a rule that requires a plaintiff seeking to collect damages for breach of contract to prove an attempt was made to reduce or lessen losses and/or damages.

monopoly Instance in which a firm and/or business controls the market for a particular product.

Montreal Convention An international treaty effective beginning in 2003 that controls many aspects of lawsuits against airlines for injuries and losses caused in the process of international airline travel.

motion A request to a judge for relief that is made while a lawsuit is ongoing.

motion for summary judgment A request to a judge in a lawsuit made by one of the parties, for a judgment without the necessity of a trial.

mutual-benefit bailment Exists when both parties receive some benefit from a bailment.

mutuality All parties to a contract are interested in the terms of the contract and intend to enter an agreement to which they will be legally bound.

mutual mistake A mistake made by both parties to a contract.

national origin The country in which a person was born, or from which their ancestors came.

negligence Breach of a legal duty to act reasonably that is the direct (or proximate) cause of injury to another.

negligence per se When a defendant has violated a law or ordinance designed to protect the safety of the public.

negligent entrustment Providing a product for use by another, knowing that person is likely to use the product in a dangerous manner.

negligent hiring Failure by an employer to investigate the background of a job applicant prior to hiring.

no-cause termination clause A contract term that permits either party to terminate the contract for any or no reason.

nondelegable A duty that cannot be assigned (or delegated) to another.

offer A proposal to do or give something in exchange for something else.

offeree The person to whom an offer is made.

offeror The person who makes an offer.

opening statement A presentation to the jury at the beginning of a trial outlining the proof a lawyer expects to present during the trial.

ordinance A law adopted by a local governmental body.

pain and suffering Compensation for physical pain, mental anguish, stress, or other similar injury.

pari-mutuel betting A betting system in which winners share the total stakes minus a percentage paid to the facility hosting the gambling event.

parol Oral or spoken.

parol evidence rule An evidence rule that seeks to preserve the integrity of written agreements by refusing to permit contracting parties to attempt to alter their contract through use of contemporaneous oral declarations.

parties The individuals in conflict in a lawsuit; the plaintiff and defendant.

pathological gambling The inability to refrain from gambling, also known as compulsive gambling.

peremptory challenges Process during voire dire that allows a limited number of potential jurors to be dismissed by attorneys without a stated reason.

per se violations (of antitrust laws) Activities that are always considered illegal under antitrust legislation.

place of public accommodation A variety of business establishments open to the public including hotels, restaurants, bars, theaters, stores and more.

plaintiff The party who commences a lawsuit seeking a remedy for an injury or loss.

pleadings Documents containing plaintiff's claim and defendant's defense. The pleadings include a complaint, an answer, and if the answer contains a counterclaim, a reply.

police power The authority of government to license and regulate based on the power of government to adopt laws that further public health, safety, and welfare.

precedent A court decision that becomes a basis for deciding future cases.

preexisting condition A prior physical impairment, which may or may not be aggravated, in the event of injuries suffered due to negligence.

pretext An explanation given by an employer why an employee was terminated, intended to disguise the real reason for the termination.

price discrimination A seller charges different prices to different buyers for the same product.

price-fixing agreements Agreement among competitors to sell goods at a certain price and not lower.

prima facie Such evidence as will suffice to establish a cause of action until contradicted and overcome by other evidence.

prima facie liability rule A rule that states that hotelkeepers are liable for property loss only if the loss occurs through their negligence; if the loss results from some other cause, the innkeeper is not liable.

principal A person who authorizes an agent to act on his or her behalf and controls or directs the method used by the agent in performing authorized tasks.

privilege An ability to communicate alleged wrongful acts without fear of a defamation lawsuit for statements believed to be true but ultimately determined to be false.

privity of contract A contractual relationship that exists between two parties.

probable cause Evidence sufficient to form a reasonable basis to believe certain alleged facts are true.

probation A system whereby some criminal offenders remain out of jail but are supervised by a probation officer.

prospectus A disclosure document prepared by franchisors that must be given to potential franchisees ten daysbefore the franchisor can accept any money from a franchisee.

protected classes Groups of people with a common characteristic who are legally protected from discrimination based on that characteristic. A few examples include race, color, religion, and national origin.

proximate cause That which, in a natural and continuous sequence, unbroken by any independent intervening cause, produces injury, and without which the result would not have occurred.

public domain Belonging to the general public and not subject to patent, copyright, or trademark protection.

public enemy An exception to the absolute liability rule applicable when losses are suffered during wartime and/or as a result of terrorist activities.

punitive damages Money awarded to a plaintiff over and above compensatory damages to punish defendant for particularly reprehensible conduct.

quid pro quo sexual harassment Unwelcome sexual advances or requests for sexual favors in return for job benefits.

rape Sexual intercourse that is against the victim's will.

readily achievable Easily accomplishable without great difficulty or expense.

reasonable expectation test A test that examines whether an object found in food ought to have been anticipated by the consumer. If so, its presence in the food does not constitute a breach of warranty.

reasoning The explanation why a judge decides a case.

rebuttal Opportunity at trial for plaintiff to present evidence to contest defendant's evidence.

regulations Laws adopted by administrative agencies.

remittitur A ruling by a judge that the amount of money awarded by the jury is unreasonably high.

reply A pleading issued by plaintiff if and only if defendant's answer contains a counterclaim.

resale price maintenance agreement Manufacturer sets the price at which retailers must sell.

rescue doctrine This rule of law recognizes that "danger invites rescue." The doctrine holds that a person who, through his negligence, jeopardizes the safety of another person, may be liable to a third person (the rescuer) who attempts to save the person at risk and suffers injuries in the process.

res ipsa loquitur "The thing speaks for itself" (Latin). The doctrine that frees the plaintiff from the burden of proving the specific breach of duty committed by the defendant. It applies where an accident would not normally happen without negligence and the instrumentality causing the injury was in the defendant's exclusive control.

respondeat superior "Let the master (employer) answer" (Latin). The rule that imposes liability on the employer for the acts of its employees.

retaliatory discharge Termination of an employee in response to the worker filing a complaint against the employer.

reverse discrimination Discrimination (differential treatment) against members of a dominant or majority group such as Caucasians and males.

riverboat casinos Casinos located on a water vessel created to circumvent laws that prohibit gambling on shore.

royalty Payments made to composers for the sale of copies or performance of their work.

rule of reason A doctrine of anti-trust law that balances economic benefits and drawbacks in determining the legality of a particular business practice as it affects open competition.

search warrant An order from a judge commanding a police officer to search a designated place for evidence of criminal activity.

secondary meaning A doctrine of trademark law that affords protection to an otherwise unprotectable mark when the mark, through advertising and other promotions, has come to be associated in the public's mind with a particular producer.

service mark Any word, name, symbol, or device adopted and used by an organization to identify its services and distinguish them from services provided by others.

service of process Delivery of a complaint (the first pleading in a lawsuit) to the defendant. The method for doing so is prescribed by law, and is designed to ensure defendant receives notice of the lawsuit.

settlement A resolution of a dispute without a trial.

sexual harassment Unwelcome sexual advances, requests for sexual favors, and other verbal or physical annoying actions of a sexual nature occurring in the workplace.

shoe A round of play of blackjack (or "21") that is defined by the number of decks of cards included in the round.

slander The tort of making defamatory statements orally, as opposed to in writing.

small claims court A forum that dispenses with formal rules of evidence and procedure that govern trials in other courts; intended to be user-friendly.

sovereign authority The power of self-government.

spa A health resort that provides a variety of services intended to promote relaxation, relieve stress, and enhance physical appearance.

specific performance A remedy for breach of contract requiring performance of the contract terms.

stare decisis The principal that courts will follow precedents when they are applicable.

statute A law adopted by the federal or state legislature.

Statute of Frauds The law requiring that certain contracts must be written to be enforceable.

statutory law Law passed by legislatures.

strict liability Also called absolute liability; the doctrine that imposes all the risks of an ultra-hazardous activity upon those who engage in it.

strict products liability The doctrine that imposes liability on the seller of a defective product without regard to negligence.

subject matter jurisdiction A court's power to decide cases of a particular category.

summary jury trial A trial heard by a jury without witnesses; sometimes used in federal courts to save time and money. The jury renders a nonbinding decision and the law requires the parties to negotiate their dispute after the jury rules.

summation Closing statements at a trial made by attorneys, that summarize the case for the jury.

summons A document ordering the defendant to appear in a lawsuit and defend the allegations made against him.

tariff A rule or condition of air travel that binds the airline and passengers. Tariffs are developed by airlines and approved by the federal Department of Transportation.

territorial division agreements Activities in which competitors assign to each other a territory and agree not to compete in the others' territories, thereby creating a territorial monopoly.

territorial restrictions Circumstance in which a manufacturer restricts the territory in which dealers can sell, thereby preventing other dealers from competing in a given territory.

theft of services A crime committed by using services, such as a hotel room, without paying for the service.

tort A private or civil wrong or injury for which a court will provide a remedy in a lawsuit for damages; wrongful conduct by one person that causes injury to another.

trademark Any word, name, symbol, or device adopted and used by a manufacturer or merchant to identify its goods and distinguish them from goods sold or manufactured by others.

trademark infringement Use of another company's business name or logo without permission.

trade usage Practices or modes of dealing that are generally adhered to in a particular industry, such that an expectation arises that they will be honored in a given transaction.

transient A person passing through a place for only a brief stay or sojourn.

travel insurance Insurance that may be purchased to protect against financial losses associated with trip cancellations, injuries, and other mishaps that can occur while on a trip.

treble damages Mandated payment of three times the loss suffered by an injured plaintiff.

trespass Entry onto another's property without right or permission.

trespasser One who enters a place without permission of the owner or occupier.

trial The process whereby the parties present evidence, and the judge or jury decides the issues.

tying arrangement Circumstance in which a seller conditions the sale of a product on the buyer's agreement to also purchase some other product produced or distributed by the seller.

undue hardship An accommodation for a disabled employee that would require a significant difficulty or expense for the employer.

Uniform Commercial Code (UCC) A set of rules designed to simplify and modernize the law governing the sale of goods, including food.

unilateral mistake An error made by one party to a contract as to the terms or performance expected.

unitary rule The rule that holds the Civil Rights Act applicable to a facility not otherwise covered by the Act when a covered facility is located within it.

valid Enforceable in court. For a contract to be valid, certain elements must exist. These include contractual capacity, mutuality, legality, consideration, proper form, and genuine assent.

variance Permission from the local government to deviate from a zoning restriction.

verdict A jury's decision in a case.

vertical price-fixing Practice whereby a manufacturer establishes minimum prices at which lower-level dealers in a distribution system can sell a product.

victualler's license License required to operate a business that sells food.

visibly intoxicated A person whose appearance or actions indicate that he is intoxicated. Sale of alcohol to people who are visibly intoxicated is illegal and can result in dram shop liability.

voidable contract A contract that is valid, but which may be legally voided at the option of one of the parties.

void contract A contract that is unenforceable in court.

voir dire Process of questioning randomly selected prospective jurors to determine who will serve as jurors.

Warsaw Convention An international treaty that sets limits of liability for lost, stolen, damaged, or misdelivered baggage.

within the scope of employment In furtherance of duties performed for the employer.

zoning Restrictions imposed by local governments on the manner in which property owners can use their land.

INDEX

A

Abbaa v. Pan Am, 569
Abortion issues, employment and, 694
Abouri v. Florida DOT, 667
Absolute, contracts, 129
Absolute liability, 211–212
    for patron property, 346
Abusive language, 464–466
Accent discrimination, 667–668, 726
Acceptance, 111
Accidents
    alcohol-related, 526
    in rental cars, 624–626
Accommodations
    refusing, 441
    selection by innkeepers, 409–410
Active vigilance, 188–189
Acts of God, as absolute liability exception, 347
ADA cases, pursuing, 714. *See also* Americans with Disabilities Act (ADA) of 1992
Adams v. H&H Meat Products, Inc., 119–120
Adamy v. Friday's, 530
Adamy v. Ziriakus, 532
ADEA. *See* Age Discrimination in Employment Act
Adivtori v. Sky Harbor International Airport, 586
Adjacent premises, liability to, 301
Adler v. Savoy Plaza Inc., 330
Administrative agency, 9–10
Administrative employees, overtime pay and, 643–644
Administrative law, 9–10

Administrative remedies
    must be exhausted, 786
    in granting licenses, 786
Admission discounts, at theme parks, 841–842
Admission policies, 72
Advance notice, guest right to, 474
Advantages, of condominium hotels, 848
Advertisements, under state civil rights laws, 78
Advertising
    obesity and, 514–515
    preventive tips concerning, 850
Affirmative action, 675
Age
    employment and, 695–698
    refusal of service based on, 408–409
Age discrimination, 93
    in car rentals, 630
Age Discrimination in Employment Act (ADEA), 695,
    697, 727
Agency, 557
Agency law, 557–562
Agent, 557, 558
Agreement not to compete, 150
Airbnb, 60–61
Air Carrier Access Act (ACAA) of 1986, 582–585, 632
Airline captains, rights of, 589–595
Airline insurance, 579
airline liability for, 605
Airline passengers, rights of, 592–593
Airlines
    legal issues involving, 603–605
    liability for negligence, 605
    overbooking by, 596–602
    preventive law tips related to, 631–633
    special rights of, 587–589
    websites related to, 635–636
Airline seating, priority rules for, 597–600
Airline tickets, refunds on, 581
Airplane security, 576–578
Airport screenings, interference with, 579
Airport security checkpoints, 574–575
Akiyama v. U.S. Judo, Inc., 67
Alcohol-free teen events, 548
Alcohol inhaling devices, 548
Alcohol-related legalities, by state, 553–554
Alcohol-related websites, 554
Alcohol sale. *See also* Intoxicated casino patrons
    BYOB clubs, 546
    hospitality industry and, 526–532
    in hotel guest rooms, 545
    illegal, 527, 550, 551
    to know habitual drunkards, 532
    liability and, 525–554

    near school or church, 548
    preventive law tips related to, 550–551, 850
    restrictions on, 546
    on Sunday, 546
    to underage patrons, 528–530
    to visibly intoxicated people, 530–531
Alcohol sales promotions, limitations on, 547–548
Alcohol servers, age of, 545–546
Alcohol vendors' liability, 532–541
    apportionment of, 541
    strategies to avoid, 544–545
Alcohol Without Liquid (AWOL) devices, 548
Aldrich v. Waldorf Astoria Hotel, Inc., 396
Alexander v. Northland Inn, 715
*Alexis v. McDonald's Restaurants of Massachusetts,
    Inc.*, 97–98
Allegations, 24
Allen v. Greenville Hotel Partners, Inc., 766
Allen v. Hyatt Regency-Nashville Hotel, 389
Allied Social Science Association (ASSA), 115
Allstate v. MacDonald, 629
Allsup v. McVille, Inc., 225
Al-Qudhai'een v. America West Airlines, Inc, 594–595
Altamuro v. Milner Hotel, Inc., 221
Alternative dispute resolution (ADR), 42
Al-Watan v. Am. Airlines, Inc., 593
Amenities, in condominium hotels, 847
American Condominium Association v. Benson, 794
American Society of Composers, Authors, and Publish-
    ers (ASCAP), 750, 751
Americans with Disabilities Act (ADA) of 1992, 75,
    78–96, 418, 519, 582, 586, 632, 649, 705–716, 727.
    See also ADA cases
    accommodating disabled, 80–81
    auxiliary aids and alternative services, 84
    building modifications under, 85–87
    construction, structural requirements, 88–89
    disabled guests, 80
    impacts on hiring decisions, 710–711
    integrated settings, 79–80
    noncompliance, 89–92
    transportation and telecommunications, 89
Amick v. BN+KM, Inc., 80
Amplified radio music, 755–757
Amusement rides, 287
    at theme parks, 838–840, 850
ANA, Inc. v. Lowery, 432
Anderson v. American Restaurant Group, 269–270
Anderson v. Market Street Developers, Ltd., 258
Anderson v. Turton Development, 284
Andrews v. Marriott Int'l, 455
Animals
    injuries from, 246–250

at theme parks, 840
traveling with, 579–580
Annitto v. Trump Marina Hotel Casino, 826
Answer, 31
response to, 31–32
Antar v. Trans World Airlines, Inc., 581
Antismoking laws, 518–519
Antitrust laws, 113, 758–762, 796, 797
franchisor violations of, 770–773
tying arrangement in franchises and, 770–773
Appeal, 41–42
definition, 41
grounds for, 41
Appellate court, 41–42
A.P. Keller, Inc. Cont'l Airlines, Inc., 589
Aquasviva v. Iberia Lineas Aereas de Espana, 604
Arafi v. Mandarin Oriental, 669
Arbitration, 42
Archibald v. Cinerama Hotels, 778–779
Arenas v. The Cheesecake Factory Restaurants, 489
Armenakis v. Top Notch Family Restaurant, 661, 679
Artwork, copyright protection of, 757
ASCAP. *See* American Society of Composers, Authors, and Publishers
Assault, 13
during eviction, 426
Assigned room, right to occupy, 449
Associated Mills, Inc. v. Drake Hotel, Inc., 362
Assumption of risk, 227–231, 234
at amusement rides, 838
comparative negligence and, 231–233
ignorance of risk and, 233
Atkinson v. Stateline Hotel Casino & Resort, 822
Attack, unpredictable, 304–305
Attorney's fees, 57
Attractive nuisance doctrine, 206–207, 234, 236
Attrition clause, 158–159
At-will employment, 648–649
Auckenthaler v. Grundmeyer, 231
Audi v. Rest-All-Inn, 292–293
Augustine v. Marriott Hotel, 377–378
Automatic doors, 259
Automobile passengers, alcohol vendor's liability to, 538–540
Automotive Gold, Inc., v. Volkswagen of America, Inc., 737
AWOL devices. *See* Alcohol Without Liquid devices

B

Babich v. Hunan Szechwann Inn, Inc., 280
BAC. *See* Blood alcohol content
Bacci Restaurant v. Sunrise Produce Co., 508
Back pay, 651

Baggage claims, 564–576
Baggage control, 631
Baggage, damaged, 571–572
Baggage rooms, property lost in, 361
B&B Coastal Enterprises, Inc. v. Demers, 792
Bailed property, items inside, 386–387
Bailee, 375
bailment for the sole benefit of, 379
reasonable care by, 399
Bailey v. U.S., 622
Bailment(s)
agreement, 376
of cars, 387–391
effect on liability, 377–379
essential elements of, 375–376
law of, 375–396
mutual-benefit, 380–382, 384
for the sole benefit of the bailee, 379
for the sole benefit of the bailor, 379
types, 379–382
Bailment cases, proof of negligence in, 382–386
Bailor, 375
Baker v. Fenneman & Brown Properties, LLC and Southern Bells of Indiana, Inc., all d/b/a Taco Bell, 218–219
Baker v. Solo Nightclub, LLC, 303
Ball v. Hilton Hotels, Inc., 228–229
Baloch v. Norton, 673
Banat v. Pop Restaurants, 647
Bank of New York v. Ansonia Associates, 275
Baptiste v. Cavendish Club, Inc., 69
Barker v. Menominee Nation Casino, 830
Barnes v. Cohen Dry Wall, Inc., 542–543
Barnett v. Network Solutions, 131
Barrier, removal of, 86
Bars, liability for patron property in, 391–394
Bartelli v. O'Brien, 178, 301
Barton v. Wonderful World of Travel, Inc., 610
Bathroom appliances, 250–255
Bathroom doors, defective, 254
Battery, during eviction, 426, 430
Baxley v. Hakiel Industries, Inc., 538
BBB Service Co. v. Glass, 272
BBQ Blues Texas, Ltd. v. Affiliated Business Brokers, Inc., 118
Beach area safety, 317
Beam v. Marriott Corp., 348, 362
Bearley v. Friendly's Ice Cream, 706
Bearse v. Fowler, 251
Beatie v. City of NY, 519
Beds, defective, 243–244
Begualg Investment Management, Inc. v. Four Seasons Hotel, Ltd, 847

Bench trial, 36
Benjamin v. Anderson, 687
Bergeron v. Jazz Seafood & Steakhouse, 497–499, 509
Berger v. State, 463–464
Berlow v. Sheraton Dallas Corp., 478–480
Bermudex Zeonon v. Restaurant Compostela, Inc., 56
Bernath v. People Success, Inc., 501
Beroutsos v. Six Flags Theme Park, Inc., 838
Bertuca v. Martinez, 411, 415, 439, 467
Betancourt v. Manhattan Ford Lincoln Mercury, Inc.,
 626
Beverages, hot, 500–503
BFOQ defense. *See* Bona fide occupational qualification
 defense
Bhattal v. Grand Hyatt-New York, 367–368
Biggs v. City of Birmingham, 527, 548
Bishop v. Hazel & Thomas, 667
Bishop v. KFC National Management Co., Inc., 245
Black Beret Lounge and Restaurant v. Meisnere, 392
Blakemore v. Coleman, 331
Bland v. Scott, 541, 543
Bleiburg Restaurant, Inc. v. NYC Dept. of Health, 518
Blood alcohol content (BAC), 532
"The Blue Note", 26
Blue v. Harrah's North Kansas City, LLC, 823
BMI. *See* Broadcast Music, Inc.
BMI v. Station House Irish Pub & Steakhouse, Ltd,
 753–755
Board review, as grounds for license denial, 784
Bobbitt v. Rage, Inc., 60
Boden v. Friendly's Ice Cream Corp., 699
Boemio v. Love's Restaurant, 90–92
Boisterous conduct, in swimming areas, 295
Boles v. La Quinta Motor Inns, 220
Bolla-Shutt v. Cedar Fair, 838
Bona fide occupational qualification (BFOQ) defense,
 653
Boston v. Paul McNally Realty, 92
Boswell v. Skywest Airlines, Inc., 585
Bottenstein v. Connecticut American Bus Lines, 600
*Bottoms & Tops International, Inc. v. UPS & Marco
 Polo, Inc.*, 478
Bourassa v. Busch Entertainment Corp., 840
Bourque v. Morris, 338
Boyd v. Country Boy Deli Delights, 283
Boyd v. Warren Restaurants, Inc., 190
Boyle v. Jerome Country Club, 67
Bradley v. Domino's Pizza, 650
Bradley v. Radisson Hotel, 191
Brady v. Sam's Town Hotel and Gambling Center, 698,
 699
Bragan v. Symanzik, 203, 207
Brasseaux v. Stand-By Corp. d/b/a Plantation Inn, 249

Breach of contract, 109, 132–140
 by a franchisor, 768–770
 by third-party service suppliers, 616–619
Breach of duty, 178
Brick Haus, Inc. v. Board of Adjustment, 795
Bridge club, 69
Brief, 41
Broadcast Music, Inc. (BMI), 750–752
*Broadcast Music, Inc. v. Quality Hotel & Conference
 Center*, 751–752
Brown Hotel Co. v. Marx, 250
Brown v. Argosy Gaming Co., 814
Brown v. Board of Education, 8
Brown v. Board of Education of Topeka, Kansas, 51
Brown v. City Sam Restaurants, Inc., 504–505
Brown v. Loudoun Golf & Country Club, Inc., 73
Brown v. Mystique Casino, 711
Brown v. Pizza Hut of America, Inc., 645
Buffone v. Rosebud Restaurants, Inc., 690
Building codes, 262
Bullock, Inc. v. Thorpe, 213
Bumped airline passengers, rights of, 596–597
Burden v. Elias Brothers Big Boy Restaurants, 465
Burdett v. Harrah's Kansas Casino Corp., 814, 815
*Burger King Corporation v. Pilgrim's Pride Corpora-
 tion*, 735
Burger King Corp. v. Agad, 774
Burlington Industries v. Ellereth, 684
Burnap v. Tribeca Travel, 606–608
Burnett v. Pizza Hut of America, Inc., 715
Burrows v. Knots, 301
Burse v. Harrah's Vickburg Corp., 806
Business attire, discrimination in, 679
Business competitors, refusing access to, 421–422
Business necessity, 653
 pregnancy and, 691
Business owners, duty to aid invitees in danger, 218–224
Bus transportation, 600
Buzon v. Ballard & Kane, LLC., 540
Buzulis v. Mohegan Sun Casino, 830–831

C

California v. Cabazon Band of Mission Indians, 805,
 829
Callender v. MCO Properties, 197
Callwood v. Dave & Buster's, Inc., 62
Campbell v. Eitak, Inc. T/D/B/A Katana, 222–223
Campbell v. Womack, 451
Cangiano v. Forte Hotels, Inc., 454
Capacity to contract, 110
Capaldo v. Pan American Federal Credit Union, 676
Carballo v. Log Cabin Smokehouse, 680, 690, 699

Card counters, 807
    legal exclusion of, 807–808
Caregivers, ADA protection for, 712
Car keys, transfer of, 389–391
Carley v. Theater Development Fund, 621
Carlo Bay Enterprise, Inc. v. Two Amigo Restaurant, Inc., 738–739
Carlson v. BRGA Associates, LLC, 351–353
Carrasquillo v. Holiday Carpet Service, Inc., 261
Car rentals
    age discrimination and, 630
    preventive law tips related to, 633
Carrero v. New York City Housing Authority, 679
Carroll v. Talman Federal Savings & Loan Association, 679
Cars
    bailment of, 387–391
    procedures for parking, 399
Carter v. Innisfree Hotel, Inc., 453–454
Carter v. Thompson Hotels, 657–658
Casebooks, 14
Case decision, 7
Case-in-chief, 38
Cases, 14
    reading, 14–16
Casey v. Treasure Island Corporation, 294
Casino patrons
    as crime victims, 821
    false imprisonment of, 822–823
    intoxicated, 821–822, 825
Casino Resorts, Inc. v. Monarch Casinos, Inc., 129–130, 133–134
Casinos, 803, 849
    copyright infringement by, 824
    as crime victims, 822
    criminal activity at, 820–822
    detention by, 470–471
    dram shop acts and, 825–826
    false imprisonment by, 822–823
    gaming issues related to, 806–812
    history of, 805
    medical care in, 817–820
    on Native American reservations, 829–836
    negligence by, 816–820
    online, 836
    problem gamblers in, 814–815
    strict liability of, 820
    torts involving, 816–824
    trademark infringement by, 823–824
Cass County Music Company v. Port Town Family Restaurant, 756–757
Castro v. MGM Grand Hotel, Inc., 286
Catering contracts, 162, 163

Ceilings safety, 275
Celebrity alcohol endorsements, 548
Chairs, placement of, 273–274
Chamberlin v. 101 Realty, Inc., 683
Chambley v. Apple Restaurants, Inc., 489
Champie v. Castle Hot Water Springs Co., 421
Chao v. Double JJ Resort Ranch, 640
Charas v. Transworld Airlines, Inc., 605
Charter tour companies, liability of, 605–623
Chase v. Hilton Hotel Corp., 359
Chawla v. Horch d/b/a Master Hotel, 337
Cheaton v. Burger King Corp, 659
Checkin, liability during, 371–372
Check-out
    guest status on, 331
    liability after, 373–375
    theft during, 359
Checkrooms
    bailment related to, 394–396
    procedures in, 398
    property lost in, 361
Chellen v. John Pickle Co. Inc., 652, 664
Cheng Sing Liang v. Chwen Jen Huang, 132
Chesham Auto Supply v. Beresford Hotel, 433
Chessin v. Keystone Resort Management, Inc., 640
Chiang v. Pyro Chemical, Inc., 213
Child labor, restrictions on, 646–647
Children
    duty of care owed to, 234
    facilities used by, 235–236
    reasonable person test and, 203–206
    room furnishings and, 206
Childs v. Extended Stay of America Hotels, 60
Child trespassers, attractive nuisance doctrine and, 206
Chimenti v. Apple Vacations, 621
Choice Hotels International, Inc. v. Palm-Aire Oceanside, Inc., 766
Choice Hotels v. Frontier Hotels, 776
Choice Hotels v. Kaushik, 736
Choice Hotels v. Zeal, 736
Choking laws, 235
Choking rule, 221–222
Chukwu v. British Airways, 604
Cicone v. Cafe Renaissance, Inc., 736
Cigar smoking, 518, 519
Circle-C symbol (©), 747
Circle-R symbol (®), 742
Citation, 43
City and County of San Francisco v. Boyd Hotel, LLC, 789
City of Fayetteville v. Carter, 787
City of Los Angeles, Ca v. Patel, 777
Civil authority, 126

Civil cases, remedies in, 12–13
Civil law, 11, 12
Civil rights, 6
    definition, 52
    hospitality businesses and, 50–101
    laws, 51
    protection, extending, 77–96
    websites related to, 105
Civil Rights Act of 1964, 16, 51, 52, 93, 407, 432, 725
    bed-and-breakfasts under, 68
    dining facilities, 54
    enforcing, 57–68
    establishing jurisdiction under, 57–58
    exempt establishments, 68–77
    interstate commerce, jurisdiction through, 55–56
    lodging for transients, 53–54
    places of entertainment, 54–55
    private clubs under, 68–69
    private-in-name-only clubs under, 70–72
    racial discrimination, 59–64
    remedies, 57
    scope of, 53
    Title VII of, 16, 649–650
Civil Rights Act of 1991, 649, 652, 675
Claim, 23
    basis for, 28
Clark v. Starwood Hotels & Resorts Worldwide, Inc.,
    27–28
Class actions
    against restaurants, 499–500
    suit, 564
    travel-related, 563–564
Clavon, III v. Roscoe BK Restaurant, Inc., 81
Cleanliness of hotel rooms, 243
Clement v. Bojangles' Restaurants, Inc., 715
Clements v. Fitzgerald's Mississippi, Inc., 662–663
Click-on acceptance, 130–131
Clime v. Dewey Beach Enterprises, Inc., 496
Cloakrooms, liability for patron property in, 391–394
Clothes, liability for, 360–363
Cloutier v. Costco Wholesale Corp, 671
Club XS, Inc. v. Pennsylvania Liquor Control Board, 527
Coat rooms, unattended, 399
Cochran v. Burger King Corp., 196
Cohen v. Suburban Sidney-Hill, Inc., 295
Cohen v. Varig Airlines, 571
Coleman v. Ramada Hotel Operating Co., 229
Collective bargaining, 722
    agreement, 722
Colon v. Outback Steakhouse of Florida, Inc., 271
Colterr v. McDonald's Restaurants, 660
*Commercial Realty & Resources Corp. v. First Atlantic
    Properties Co.*, 795

Common areas, in condominium hotels, 847
Common law, 7
    precedents, 7–8
    statutes and Constitution, 8–9
The Commonwealth of Massachusetts v. John Doe, 11
Commonwealth of Pa. v. Hyland, 808
Communications Act, illegal satellite reception and,
    748–749
Community resistance, as grounds for license denial, 783
Compacts, tribal gaming, 836
Comparable worth, 645
Comparative negligence, 225–226, 235, 501
    assumption of risk and, 231–233
    last clear chance doctrine and, 226–227
    property loss and, 368–370
Compensatory damages, 12–13, 132
    in Title VII cases, 651
Competition, antitrust laws and, 758, 759, 796
Complaint, 24, 25
    responses to, 30
Compulsive gambling, 814–815
Conboy v. Studio 54, Inc., 395–396
Concessionaires
    contracts with, 399
    liability of, 396
Conditions, 129–130
Condominium hotels, 803, 847–848, 852
Congress, 6
Conklin v. Hotel Waldorf Astoria, 507
Connolly v. Nicollet Hotel, 411
Connor v. McDonald's Restaurant, 706
Consent to search, 458
Consideration, 113–114
Conspicuous posting, 357
Constitution, 8–9
    statutes and, 8–9
Constitutional law, 6
Constructive bailment, 392
Constructive notice, 269
Consumer Product Safety Commission, 10
Consumer rights movement, impact on travel industry,
    557
Contagiously ill guests, evicting, 418
Contract law, hospitality industry and, 107–164
Contracts, 12, 108–109. *See also* Breach of contract;
    Franchising
    ambiguous terms/trade usage in, 125–130
    breach of, 16, 109, 132–140
    catering, 162, 163
    for condominium hotels, 848
    convention, 163, 164
    elements of, 109–125
    employment, 118

formal, 120
formed on Internet, 130–131
gambling debts as, 812–815
illusory, 114
intention to enter, 326–332
legality of, 113
oral, 116
proper form, 116–121
statute of frauds and, 118–119
term of, 131
websites related to, 170
written, 116, 117
Contractual capacity, 109, 110
Contractual relations, intentional interference with, 160–162
Contributory negligence, 224–225, 235
Convention contracts, 163, 164
Cooke v. Pizza Hut, Inc., 509
Cooking methods, inaccurate, 513
Copeland v. Red Dog Saloon and Café, 532
Copeland v. Tela Corporation, 541
Copeland v. The Lodge Enterprises, Inc., 217, 247–249
Copyright, 6, 824
Copyright infringement, by casinos, 824
Copyright protection, 746–747, 796–797
  of artwork, 757
  in music performances, 750–757
  preventive law tips concerning, 796–798
Corinaldi v. Columbia Courtyard, 309
Costco Wholesale Corp., v. Hoen, 760
Coulter v. American Bakeries Co., 495–496
Counterclaims, 31
Counteroffer, 111–112
Country Road, Inc. v. Witt, 431
Coupe v. Federal Express Corporation, 653
Courtney v. Remler, 566 F. Supp, 309
Court record, license revocation/suspension and, 790
Co-workers, sexual harassment by, 687–688
Cramer v. Tarr, 333
Crawford v. Hertz, 623
Crazy Water Retirement Hotel v. State of Texas, 300
Creators, copyright protection for, 746–747
Credentials fraud, 721
Credit card fraud, 622–623
  protection against, 471–474
Credit cards, 433
Credit transactions, with casinos, 812–813
Creel v. St. Charles Gaming Co, 272
Creteau v. Liberty Travel, Inc., 612, 615
Crill v. WRBF, Inc., 305
Crimes, examples of, 13
Criminal activity, 317
  at casinos, 820–822

foreseeability of, 303–304
investigating, 482
preventive tips concerning, 850
report by innkeeper of, 456
Criminal cases, penalties and remedies in, 13
Criminal charges, pressing, 443
Criminal law, 11
Criminal liability, for fires, 302
Criminal possession of stolen property, 438
Crist v. Dorr to Door Pizza, 692–694
Critical control point (CCP), 512
Croft v. Grand Casino Tunica, Inc., 471, 823
Cross-examination, 38
Crowd control, at theme parks, 837
Crowds, large, 308–309
Cubero Valderama v. Delta Air Lines, Inc., 576
Cuevas v. Royal D'Ibervilee Hotel, 535
Cunningham v. Neil House Hotel Co., 249
Customers
  rowdy/abusive, 303–304
  sexual harassment by, 688–689
Cyberspace, 109, 130
Cybersquatting, as trademark infringement, 746

D

D'Arrigo v. Alitalia, 570
Damages, 12, 132
  allowed by overbooking, 142, 144
  for antitrust law violation, 759
  clauses limiting, 140
  damages limiting, 140
  to goodwill, 147
  punitive, 139–140
  recovery of, 134–136
Dangerous instrument, 9
Dangers, anticipating, 235
Daniels v. Byington, 207
Daniel v. Paul, 56, 70–72
Darby v. Meridien Hotels, Inc., 296
Das v. Royal Jordanian Airlines, 608
David Hanson v. Hyatt Corp., 195
Davidson v. Madison Corp., 363
David v. Prime Hospitality Corp., 366
Davies v. General Tours, Inc., 620
Davis v. Sheraton Society Hill Hotel, 674
Davis v. Valley Hospitality Services LLC, 656, 695
Days Inn v. Tobias Jewelry, Ltd., 358
Day v. Sheehan, 202
Dazo v. Globe Airport Security Services, 575
Deardorff Associations, Inc. v. Brown, 301
Decision, 14, 16
DeCrow v. Hotel Syracuse Corp., 93

Deel v. Metromedia Restaurant Services, 681, 686
Defamation, 428
Default judgment, 30
Defective products, 212, 213
Defective rental cars, 626–627
Defendant(s), 23
    exclusive control by, 200–202
Defibrillators, 312
Defrauding, of hotelkeepers or restaurateurs, 434–438
DeGirolamo v. Alitalia-Linee Aeree Italiano, 585
De La Rosa v. St. Charles Gaming Company, Inc., 828
Delegated powers, 6, 55
DeLema v. Waldorf Astoria Hotel, Inc., 372
Delivery of property, role in contracts, 329–332
Delong v. Commonwealth of Kentucky, 462
Del-Rena, Inc. v. KFM, Inc., 109
Demaille v. Trump Castle Associates, 271
Demarco v. Ouellette, 230–231
Deming Hotel Company v. Prox, 275
Depaemelaere v. Davis, 358
Department of Transportation (DOT), 596
Deposition, 35
Deris v. Finest Foods, Inc., 489
Descriptive terms, in trademark infringement, 741
Design Tex Group, Inc. v. U.S. Vinyl Manufacturing Corp., 757
Desmond v. City of Charlotte, 283
DeWolf v. Ford, 465
D.H.L. Associates, Inc. v. Krussel, 790
DiBiase v. Oasis International, 621
Dille v. Renaissance Hotel Management Co., LLC., 254
Dillon v. United Air Lines, Inc., 572, 580, 587, 589
Dinan v. Board of Zoning Appeals of the Town of Stratford, 793
Diner, refusing, 429–432
Dining rooms
    duty owed guests in, 265–280
    hanging mirrors in, 274–275
DiPilato v. Park Central Hotel, 256
Direct examination, 38
Disabilities
    defined, 705
    past, 712
Disabled, 79
Disabled American Veterans Association, 73
Disabled persons, giving preference to, 709–710
Disabled travelers
    disclosing need for assistance by, 586
    rights of, 582–586
Disaster plan, 310
Disclaimers, travel agent, 621–622
Disclosure requirements, for franchisors, 769–770
Discovery, 34–35

Discrimination, 50, 79
    accent, 667–668
    based on national origin, 663–666
    competency requirement and, 674–675
    disability, 582–586
    gender, 673–676
    hotel room rates and, 778
    illegal, 69
    language, 65–66
    mixed types of, 699–705
    national origin, 64–65
    pretext for, 712
    race-based, 656–662
    religious, 67, 668–669
    reverse, 662–663
    sexual orientation, 95–96
Discriminatory firing, defending against, 657
Disorderly conduct, 415–416, 547
Disparate impact discrimination, 650
Disparate treatment discrimination, 650
Dispeker v. The New Southern Hotel Co., 384
Dissolution, as antitrust law violation penalty, 758
District attorney, 11
Disturbing the peace, 460–461
Diversity of citizenship, 27
Divestiture, as antitrust law violation penalty, 758–759
Diving board regulations, 293
Documentation
    for international travel, 603–604
    wrongful rejection of, 604
Dodge City Saloon, Inc. v. Washington State Liquor Control Board, 528
Doe v. Jameson Inn, 333
Doe v. Regional School Unit, 96
Dog racing, 805
Dold v. Outrigger Hotel, 142–143
Dole v. Papa Gino's of America, Inc., 642
Dollar v. O'Hearn, 531, 537
Domestic baggage claims, 574
Donated foods, risks associated with, 520
Donley v. Dost, Inc., 190
Don-Lin Jewelry Co., Inc. v. The Westin Hotel Co., 376
Door locks, limited liability and, 360
Door service, outside, 280
Doors safety, 258–261
Doorways, crowded, 258–259
Dorkin v. American Express Co., 620
Doubletree Hotels v. Person, 766
Douglas v. Steele, 611
Dowden v. Otis Elevator Company, 256
Dowell v. Gracewood Fruit Co., 541
Doyle v. Walker, 410

Dram shop acts, 849
    alcohol vendor liability under, 533–541
    casinos and, 825–826
    states without, 541
    tribal gaming and, 835
Dram shop insurance, 542–543
Dram shop liability, 550
    of casinos, 825
    on employers, 542–543
Dress code policy, 671
Drew v. Lejay's Sportsmen's Cafe, Inc., 224
Drew v. United States, 430
Drive-through sales windows, zoning laws concerning, 793
Drug tests, in employment, 711–712
Drummond v. Walker, 624–625
Drunkards, sale of alcohol to, 532
Drunken drivers, 533
Duck Dive v. Heydari, 741
Due process, license revocation/suspension and, 791–792
Dumlao v. Atlantic Garage, Inc., 387
Dunbar v. Denny's Restaurant, 190
Dunkin' Donuts, Inc. v. Towns Family, Inc., 774
Durand v. Moore, 430–431
Durandy v. Fairmont Roosevelt Hotel, Inc., 350
Duress, 122
Duties
    balancing rights and, 5
    nondelegable, 216–217
Duties owed, 196–198. *See also* Special duties
    at amusement rides, 838
    by casinos regarding gambling laws, 807
    by casinos to compulsive gamblers, 815
    to children, 203
    to guests, 324, 339
    to guests in hotel rooms, 242–255
    to guests in swimming areas, 288–299
    to guests outside, 280–288
    to intoxicated casino patrons, 821–822
    to invitees, 220
    minority position on, 196
    preventive law tips related to, 339–340
Duty to act reasonably, 176–178
Dwoskin v. Burger King Corp., 270

E

Easement, 117
EEOC v. Beauty Enterprises, Inc., 667
EEOC v. Hacienda Hotel, 700–705
EEOC v. IHOP, 695
EEOC v. Ilona of Hungary, Inc., 672
EEOC v. Joe's Stone Crab, Inc., 673
EEOC v. Johnson & Higgins, 653

EEOC v. Lee's Log Cabin, Inc., 712, 715
EEOC v. Marion Motel Associates, 675, 698
EEOC v. Sage Realty Corp., 689
Eight-factor test, in proving likelihood of confusion, 737
Eisnaugle v. McDonald's, 281–282
Elaine Photography, LLC. v. Willock, 95
El Dorado Hotel, Inc. v. Brown, 807
Eldridge v. Downtowner Hotel, 232–233
Electrical hazards, 246
Electronic signature, 120
Elevator maintenance
    as a nondelegable duty, 256–257
    supervision of, 257
Elevators safety, 210, 255–256
Ellerman v. Atlanta American Motor Hotel Corp., 388
Elliott v. The United Center, 764–765
Ellis v. Adam's Mark Hotel, 687
Ellis v. Alberghini, 793
Ellis v. Luxbury Hotels, Inc., 452
Emergencies, medical, 312
Emergency/disaster plan, 310
Emergency situations
    aiding patrons during, 849
    room entry for, 462
Emotional distress, intentional infliction of, 465–466
Employee action, outside the scope of employment, 214–215
Employee personal data, employer's use of, 723
Employees
    in casinos, 816, 850
    employment status of, 728
    preventive law tips concerning, 797
    retaliatory discharge of, 645–646
Employee training, 235, 236, 317, 398, 482, 550–551
Employer-employee relationship, 638
Employers, dram shop liability on, 542–543
Employment, 637–732. *See also* Illegal job discrimination
    age and, 695–698
    at-will, 648–649
    discrimination in, 649
    drugs and illnesses in, 711–712
    Fair Labor Standards Act, 638–649
    pregnancy and, 689–698
    preventive law tips related to, 725–728
    prohibited and permitted interview questions for, 654–656
    résumé fraud and, 721
    within the scope of, 214
    unions and, 722–723
    websites related to, 731–732
    workplace safety and, 722
Employment Eligibility Verification Form, 717–719

Employment law, 638
    emerging issues in, 723–724
Employment status, mandatory verification of, 716–720
Encroachment, in franchising, 768–769
Endres v. Mingles Restaurant, Ltc., 268
Engle v. State, 456
English, employee fluency in, 664–666
Enstrom v. Garden Place Hotel, 255
Equal Employment Opportunity Commission (EEOC), 650
Equal Employment Opportunity Commission v. Red Robin Gourmet Burgers, Inc., 669–671
Equal Pay Act (EPA) of 1963, 644, 725
Equal pay for equal work practice, 644–645
Equipment, fire safety, 300
Equitable estoppel doctrine, 364–366
Errors and omissions insurance, 622
Escalator safety, 257–258
Esposito v. New Britain Baseball Club, Inc., 841
Essential elements, inability to perform, 715–716
Essential functions, in employment, 705–706
Establishment, reasonable rules of, 98–100
Estate of White v. Rainbow Casino-Vicksburg Partnership, 825
Estoppel, 364–366
Ethnic slurs, 664
E-tickets, 582
Everett v. Peter's La Cuisine, 276
Eviction, process of, 422–429
Excessive force, 405
    during eviction, 426–427
Exclusionary rule, 457
Exclusive dealing contracts, as per se antitrust law violation, 759
Exclusive territory, as franchisee benefit, 768–769
Executive employees, overtime pay and, 642–643
Exemplary damages. *See* Punitive damages
Exempt employees, 641–642
Expert witness fees, in Title VII cases, 652–653

F

Fabbri v. Superior Court, 840
Fabend v. Rosewood Hotels, 297
Facilities, under state civil rights laws, 77
Facsimile correspondence, proper handling of, 477–480
Facts, 14, 16
Fagerhus v. Host Marriott Corp., 286
Failure to pay hotel bill, 412
Fair Labor Standards Act (FLSA) of 1938, 638–649, 725
    enforcement of, 647
False arrest, 439–440, 468
    protection against, 467–471

False food claims, 512–518
False identification, 528
False imprisonment, 822
    by casinos, 822–823, 849
Family and Medical Leave Act (FMLA) of 1993, 647, 725
*Farnham III v. Inland Sea Resort Properties, In*c., 324
Farrenholz v. Mad Crab, Inc., 499, 500
Fasano v. Green-Wood Cemetery, 283
Fast-food operations, relationship with hotels, 515
Fast Food Workers Comm. v. McDonald's USA, 767
Faulkner v. Darien Lake Theme Park, 839
Febesh v. Elcejay Inn Corp., 249–250
Febesh v. Hollow Inn, 178
Federal Aviation Act, 590
Federal Communications Commission, 10
Federal courts, 29
    websites, 19
Federal Insurance Co. v. Waldorf Astoria Hotel, 359
Federal jurisdiction, 27–28
Federal question lawsuits, 27
Federal Tort Claims Act, 575
Fedie v. Travelodge Intern, Inc., 198
Fees
    extraneous, 475–476
    guest rights concerning, 474–477
    license, 786–787
Feldt v. Marriott Corporation, 99–100
Felheimer v. Fairmont Hotels and Resorts, Inc., 286
Feliciano de La Cruz v. El Conquistador Resort, 664
Fences, for amusement rides, 840
Fennema v. Howard Johnson Co., 357, 364–366
Fields v. Robert Chappell Association, Inc., 264–265
Filer v. Tohono O'Odham Nation Gaming Enterprise, 835
Filet Menu, Inc. v. C.C.L. & G., Inc., 122–123
Fines, for operating without license, 787
Fire(s)
    criminal liability for, 302
    injuries caused by, 299–302
    property lost in, 363
Firearms, security personnel and, 310
Firebaugh, W. C., 4
Firefighter's Rule, 301
Fire response training, 300–301
Fire safety, 300, 317
First aid, 221, 222
First-aid procedures, poster showing, 237
First American Bank v. District of Columbia, 380–381
First Overseas Investment Corp. v. Cotton, 208–210
Fisher v. Carrousel Motor Hotel, Inc., 432
Fisher v. Cedar Creek Inn, 80

Fisher v. Kelsey, 362
Fisher v. O'Connor's, Inc., 535
Fish v. Paul, d/b/a Horseshoe Motel, 220
Flagstar Enterprises, Inc. v. Davis, 495
Flambé food safety, 276–278
Floor
    cleaning, 272
    foreign substances on, 266–269
    injury, 272
    matters relating to, 272–274
    slippery, 266
Folkerson v. Circus Circus Hotel & Casino, 688
Fondo v. Delta Airlines, Inc., 604
Fontan-de-Maldonado v. Lineas Aereas Costarricenses, 562–563
Food
    adulterated, 488–512
    inspecting, 521
    in interstate commerce, 56
    merchantable, 489
    objects in, 489–493
Food advertisements, misleading, 513
Food allergies, 509–512
Food and Drug Administration (FDA), 10, 19, 512, 516, 517
Foodborne illnesses, 503–504
Food claims, accurate, 521
Food Code, 512
Food labeling, 515–517
Food merchantability, 493
Food preparation
    negligence in, 509
    safety concerns in, 519–520
    statutory violations in, 509
Food preparers, hand-washing by, 512
Food sale
    adulterated food, 488–512
    false food claims and, 512–518
    food preparation safety concerns and, 519–520
    liability and, 487–524
    preventive law tips related to, 521–522
    smoking restrictions and, 518–519
    websites related to, 524
Foor v. Amici's East Coast Pizzeria, 494
Football games, blackout of, 747
Forbearance, 114
For cause challenges, 37
Foreign/natural substance test, 489
Foreign substances, on the floor, 266–269
Foreseeability, requirement of, 133
Forgery, 438
Forsythe v. Board of Education, Hays, Kansas, 667
Forte v. Hyatt Summerfield Suites, Pleasanton, 416–418

Forum non conveniens, 32–33
Forum selection clause, 131
Foster v. AFC Enterprises, Inc., 505–506
Foster v. State, 405
Foster v. State of Texas, 462
Franchise(s), 765, 796
    benefits to, 767
    breach of contract against, 769
    liabilities of, 765
    preventive law tips concerning, 797
    termination of, 774–776
Franchising, 765–776, 796
    nature of, 766–767
Franchisor(s), 765, 796
    benefits to, 767–768
    disclosure requirements for, 769–770
    fraud and breach of contract by, 769–770
    liabilities of, 765–766
Francis, Connie, 305–306
Francis v. Crawford, 626
Fraud, 12, 122. *See also* Credit card fraud
    credentials, 721
    example of, 122–123
    by franchisors, 769–770
    against hotelkeepers or restaurateurs, 434–438
    misrepresentation and, 122
    résumé, 721
    right to privacy and, 450
Fraudulent payment, 438–439
Freeman v. Kiamesha Concord, Inc., 124, 153–154
Freight elevators, 257
Frelow v. St. Paul Fire & Marine Insurance Co., 204–205
Freudenheim v. Eppley, 331–332
Frigaliment Importing Co., Ltd. v. B.N.S. International Sales Corp., 127
Frost v. Salter Path Fire & Rescue, 841
Fung-Yee Ng v. Barnes and Noble, Inc., 501
Furniture, 244
    hotel room, 243–245
    inspection of, 245, 313–315

G

Gabrielle v. Allegro Resorts Hotel, 615
Gaffney v. EQK Realty Investors, 257
Galiano v. Harrah's Operating Co., Inc., 824
Gambling, 804
    commissions, 806
    history of, 804–806
    illegal, 547
    online, 806
    pathological, 814–815

problem gamblers, 814–815
websites for, 836
Gambling debts, as contracts, 812–815
Gambling laws, duty of casinos to inform patrons of, 807
Gaming Disputes Court, 830
Gaming industry, 806
    casino legal issues, 806–812
Gaming, tribal, 806
Garrett v. Impac Hotels 1, 334, 391
Gary Hotel Courts, Inc. v. Perry, 244
Garza v. Northwest Airlines, Inc., 605
Gas Town, Inc. of Delaware v. Gas Town, 737
Gayer v. Guluch, Inc, 100
Gazda v. Detroit Entertainment, 812, 823
Gender discrimination, 93, 673–676, 726
Gender, grooming standards and, 676–679
General Linen Services, Inc. v. Smirnioudis, 132
Gentile v. Stay Slim, Inc., 500
Genuine assent, 122
Geobel v. United Railways. Co. of St. Louis, 433
Geographic proximity, in trademark infringement, 740–741
Gianocostas v. Rio Hotels, 312
Gingeleskie v. Westin Hotel Co, 312
Glass ceiling, 675–676
Glass Ceiling Commission, 675
Glass, in swimming areas, 295
Glaubius v. YMCA of Norfolk, 295
Gluckman v. American Airlines, 580
GNOC Corp. v. Powers, 359
Golden Shoreline Limited Partnership v. McGowan, 210
Golden Shoreline v. McGowan, 256
Good Samaritan Food Donation Act, 520
Good Samaritan statutes, 221, 235
Goodwill
    agreement not to compete, 150
    damages to, 147
    definition, 147
Goranson v. Trans World Airlines, 597–599
Gordon v. Days Inn, 394
Gordon v. Hotel Seville, Inc., 295
Goss v. Richmond, 539
Government
    gambling regulation by, 806
    licensing by, 780, 786, 787–792
    zoning by, 792–794
Grand Casino Tunica v. Shindler, 806
Grayson Fraternal Order of Eagles v. Claywell, 536
Greco v. Grand Casinos of Mississippi, 816
Green v. Harrah's Casino, 262
Greenville Memorial Auditorium v. Martin, 304, 308
Gregg v. Hay-Adams Hotel, 684–686

Gresham v. Stouffer Corp., 244
Griffin Industries, Inc. v. Foodmaker, Inc., 184
Griffin Motel Co. v. Strickland, 540
Griggs v. Harrah's Casino, 809
Grisby v. O.K. Travel, 610
Grooming standards, gender-differentiated, 676–679
Grounds safety, 281–282
Group boycott, as per se antitrust law violation, 759–762
Guadago v. Diamond Tours and Travel, Inc., 564
Guaranteed reservations, 159–160
Guest accommodations, changing, 410–411
Guest-innkeeper relationship, termination of, 334
Guest negligence, as absolute liability exception, 346
Guest preferences, accommodating, 409
Guest property, selling, 442–443
Guest register, 776–777, 796, 797
    preventive law tips concerning, 797
Guest rights, 447–484
    preventive law tips related to, 481–482
    proper handling of mail, packages, and facsimile correspondence, 477–479
    protection against credit card fraud, 471–474
    protection against false arrest, 467–471
    protection against illegal searches, 455–464
    protection against insults, 464–466
    rights concerning rates and fees, 474–477
    right to occupy assigned room, 449
    right to privacy in guest room, 449–455
    websites related to, 484
Guest rooms
    entering, 410–411
    right to occupy assigned, 449
    right to privacy in, 449–455
Guests
    aiding, 236–237
    breach by, 152
    defined, 324–326
    duty owed in restaurants and dining rooms, 265–280
    evicting, 404, 411–429, 442
    illegal acts by, 332–333
    injuries to, 174
    medical care for, 311–312
    relationships with, 324–340
    search of items mislaid by, 463–464
    versus tenants, 334–338, 340
Guest status, property loss liability and, 371
Guillen v. Six Flags Great Adventure, LLC, 839
Gulf American v. Airco Industrial Gases, 382
Gunning v. Small Feast Caterers, Inc., 212
Guthrie v. Waffle House, Inc., 681
Gutierrez v. Eckert Farm Supply, Inc., 334, 337

H

H & H Development Corp., v. N.J. Department of Community Affairs, 841
Hagan v. Coca-Cola Bottling Co., 490
Hagenet v. Jackson Furniture, 244
Hakimoglu v. Trump Taj Mahal, Inc., 825
Hall v. CAMRAC, LLC., 624
Hallways safety, 261–262
Hand-washing, by food preparers, 512
Hard Times Cafe, Inc. v. City of Minneapolis, 790, 792
Harris v. Laquinta-Redbird Venture, 294
Hart v. Shastri Narayan Swaroop, Inc., 301
Hartzol v. McDonald's Corp., 659
Harvey v. Hart, 410
Harvey v. Sons Rides, Inc., 287
Hashimoto v. Secretary of the Navy, 699
Haynes v. W.C. Caye & Co., 674
Hazard Analysis Critical Control Point (HACCP) system, 512, 522
Hazards, in swimming areas, 293
Hazelwood v. Harrah's, 807
Health claims, by food producers, 515
Health codes, preventive law tips concerning, 798
Health departments, hotel and restaurant permits from, 781–782
Heart of Atlanta Motel, 89
Heart of Atlanta Motel, Inc. v. United States, 57–58
Heating hazards, 246
Heimberger v. Zeal Hotel Grp., Ltd., 344
Heimlich maneuver, 222, 237
Hennig v. Goldberg, 420–421
Henson v. City of Dundee, 679
Hepatitis, 512
Hernandez v. Erlenbusch, 65–66
Hertenberger v. City of Texarkana, 782–783
Hickman v. Cole, 376
Hilton Hotels v. Fleming, 258
Hines v. KMart Corporation, 183
Holiday Inns, Inc. v. Holiday Inn, 742–745, 743–745
Home Box Office, Inc. v. Corinth Motel, Inc., 747
Hooks v. Washington Sheraton Corporation, 294
Hopkins v. Fire Mountain Restaurants, Inc., 273
Hopkins v. Godfather's Pizza, Inc., 705
Hopper v. Colonial Motel Properties, Inc., 305
Hopp v. Thompson, 426–427
Horse racing, 805
Hospitality law, 4, 51
    balancing rights and duties, 5
    harshness of, 5
    history of, 5
    principles of, 4–5
Hospitality practices, negligence and, 241–320

Hostile environment sexual harassment, 679–681
    employer liability in, 684–687
Hostile work environment claim, 673
Hot beverages, 500–503
Hotel bill, failure to pay, 412
Hotel Dempsey Company v. Teel, 245
Hotelkeepers. *See also* Innkeeper entries
    defrauding, 434–438
    statutory protection for, 432–440
Hotel managers, preventive law tips for, 796–798
Hotel negligence, loss of guest property due to, 366–370
Hotel restaurant, theft in, 359–360
Hotels, 4, 55, 58. *See also* Condominium hotels; Places of public accommodation
    canceling reservations, 156
    compliance with laws by, 782–783
    duty owed guests in, 242–255
    guest register for, 776–777, 796
    licensed music performances in, 750–757
    licensing of, 780
    mandatory recycling by, 779–780
    regulation of internal affairs of, 776–780
    relationship with fast-food operations, 515
    room rates for, 777–779
    waterfront risks created by, 297–298
    websites related to, 801
    zoning and, 780, 792–794
Hotels.com L.P. v. Canales, 131
Hotel tenant, evicting, 429
Hotel theft, 344, 345
Hot liquids, serving, 279–280
Hot shower water, 250
Hot tub safety, 254–255
House rules, breaking, 418–421
Howard v. Southern Illinois Riverboat Casino Cruises, Inc., 828
Howell v. Buck Creek State Park, 299
Hubbard v. Pacific Flight Services, Inc., 626
Hubbard v. Rite Aid Corp., 79
Hudechek v. Novi Hotel Fund Limited Partnership, 190–191
Hughes v. Marc's Big Boy, 53
Hung jury, 40
Huntley v. Carnival Corp., 820
Hussein v. Waldorf-Astoria Hotel, 672
Hyatt Regency Hotel, 158
Hyatt Regency v. Women's International Bowling Congress, Inc., 159

I

Iannelli v. Burger King Corp., 304
Ibiza, Inc. v. Samis Foundation, 134–136

Idaho case, 67
Idaho Department of Labor v. Sunset Marts, Inc., 541
Identification cards, fake, 528
Identification documentation, wrongful rejection, 604
Identity theft, 471
Ignorance of risk, 233
Ikepeazu v. Air France, 604
Illegal activity, report by innkeeper of, 456
Illegal acts, by guests, 332–333, 340
Illegal aliens, 716
Illegal discrimination, 60, 69, 726–727
Illegal job discrimination, 649–705
    filing a complaint concerning, 650–651
Illegal satellite reception, 747–750
Illegal searches, guest protection against, 455–464
Illnesses, foodborne, 503–504
Illusory contracts, 114
Immigrants, 716
Immigration Reform and Control Act (IRCA) of 1986,
    716–720, 725, 728
Imminent danger, 411
Immormino v. McDonald's, 279
Inadequate parking, as grounds for license denial, 784
Indemnity and hold harmless clause, 575
Independent contractors, 560
    employer liability for, 216
Indian Gaming Regulatory Act (IGRA) of 1988,
    829–831, 835, 850
Indoor ramps, 265
Information, provided by travel agents, 606–608
Infra hospitium property, 346
Injunction, 57
    in trademark infringement, 737
Injunctive relief, 57
Injuries
    anticipating, 849
    in casinos, 816
    caused by fire, 299–302
    preventing, 175
    proximate cause of, 181
Innkeeper-guest relationship, 329–332, 340
Innkeeper rights, 403–445, 442. *See also* Guest rights
    changing a guest's accommodations, 410–411
    evicting a guest, 411–429
    preventive law tips related to, 441–443
    refusing diners, 429–432
    refusing lodging to a would-be guest, 407–409
    right to exclude nonguests, 404–407
    selecting accommodations, 409–410
    statutory protection for hotelkeepers, 432–440
    websites related to, 445
Innkeeper's lien, 432–434, 442–443

Innocent misrepresentation, 124
Inns, 4
Inns of the Middle Ages, The (Firebaugh, W.C.), 4
In personam jurisdiction, 25
In Re Cadillac Jacks, 790–791
In Re Dixie Restaurants, Inc., 736
In re John Haskin, 415
*In re Online Travel Company Hotel Booking Antitrust
    Litigation*, 131
*In Re The Ground Round, Inc. and Abboud v. The
    Ground Round, Inc.*, 375
Insects, injuries from, 246–250
Inspections, 235, 314–315
    for hotel and restaurant permits, 781–782
Insults, guest protection against, 464–466
Insurance
    errors and omissions, 622
    guest, 345–346
    liquor liability, 542–543
Insurance Co. v. Holiday Inns, Inc., 354
Insurer, 241
Intentional infliction of emotional distress, 465–466
Intentional job discrimination, 651
Intention to enter a contract, 326–332
Intent to defraud, 435–438
International baggage claims, 565–570
International flights
    overbooking on, 602
    personal injury on, 580–581
    punitive damages on, 602
International travel, lack of documentation for, 603–604
International Union v. Michigan, 645
*International Union, United Automobile Workers v.
    Johnson Controls, Inc.*, 674
Internet, 26
    contracts formed on, 130–131
    cybersquatting, as trademark infringement, 746
    gambling, 836–837. *See also* Online gambling
Interrogatories, 35
Interstate commerce, 6, 53
    food moved in, 56
Interstate travelers, 55–56
Intervening occurrence, 183
Interview questions, employment-related, 654–656
Intoxicated casino patrons, 821–822
Intoxication, 415
    detecting, 531
    visible, 530–532
Intrilligator v. PLC Santa Monica, 844
Invitations to negotiate, 111
Invitees
    in danger, duty of business owners to aid, 218–224

duty owed to, 187–190
liability for, 187
limitation on duty to, 220
self-protection by, 189–191
Ippolito v. Hospitality Management Associates, 356
Issue, 14, 16

J

Jack Bowles Services, Inc. v. Stavely, 387
Jackson v. City of Clinton, 283
Jackson v. Nestle-Beich, Inc., 495
Jackson v. PKM Corp., 534
Jackson v. Walker, 538
Jacobson v. Belplaza Corp., 396
Jacox v. Circus Circus Mississippi, Inc., 817, 820
Jacques v. Child's Dining Hall Co., 470
Jai Jalarem Lodging Group, LLC v. Leribeus, 308
J&J Sports Productions, Inc. v. Orellana, 748–749
Jarjoura v. Erikson, Inc., 648
Jason v. Showboat Hotel & Casino, 660
Jaycees, 73
Jefferies v. Clark's Restaurant Enterprises, Inc., 494
Jeffords v. Lesesne, 308
Jeffries v. Gaylord Entertainment, et al., 707
Jenkins v. Kentucky Hotel Co., 465
Jenneh v. Endvest, Inc., 659, 662
Jesperson v. Harrah's Operating Co., Inc., 676–678
Jiminez v. TM Cobb Company, 212
Job discrimination, illegal, 649–705
Joe Garavelli's Restaurant, Inc. v. Colonial Square Associates, 136
Joe Hand Promotions, Inc. v. Hernandez, 750
Jogging paths, 285–286
John Rodgers v. Chevys Restaurants, LLC, 86–87
Johnson Construction Management, Inc., v. Opez, 246
Johnson v. C.F.M., Inc., 495
Johnson v. Houston's Restaurant, Inc., 648
Johnson v. Lone Star Steakhouse & Saloon, 268
Johnson v. Northwest Orient Airlines, 588
Johnson v. Spoetzel Brewery, 80
Johnson v. Unique Vacations, 560
Johnston v. Morrison, Inc, 715
Jones Act, 826
riverboat casinos and, 826–828
Jones v. B.P. Oil, Inc., 529
Jones v. City of Boston, 426
Jones v. GMRI, Inc., 200
Jones v. Lake Hickory R.V. Resort, Inc., 841
Josephs v. Fuller (Club Dominicus), 609–610
Judges, 8
role of, 10
Judgment, 40

Judgment notwithstanding the verdict (judgment NOV), 40
Jurisdiction
definition, 24
in personam, 25
statement of, 24
subject matter, 24
Jury
charging, 39
deliberations, 40
selection, 37–38
trial, 36

K

Kalani v. Castle Village, LLC, 75–77
Kandrach v. Chrisman, 194
Kaplan v. American Multi-Cinema, Inc., 494
Karen Morris v. Mindy Sanders, 11
Katzenbach v. McClung, 56, 58
Kauffmann v. Royal Orleans, Inc., 272
Kellner v. Lowney, 204
Kellogg Co. v. National Biscuit Co., 742
Kelly v. United States, 419–420
Kemp v. Charter House Inn, 291
Kennedy, III v. Sheriff of East Baton Rouge and Jack in the Box, 428
Kennedy v. Speedway Motorsports, Inc., 841
Kessel v. Stansfield Vending, Inc., 501
Keycard system, 345
Khan v. OCB Restaurant Co., 659
Kimbel's Case 168 A., 333
King v. American Airlines, Inc., 565
King v. Club Med, Inc., 564
Kingvision Pay Per View, Ltd., v. 900 Club, 749
Kingvision Pay-Per-View Ltd., v. Raimerez, 750
Kingvision Pay-Per-View, Ltd. v. Tito's Bar and Grill, 750
Kirchner v. Shooters on the Water, Inc., 534–535
Kizis v. Morse Diesel International, Inc., 834
Kladis v. Nick's Patio, Inc., 152
Klonis v. Carroll, 387
Knabe v. Big Boy East, 680
Kodak v. American Airlines, 570
Koehane v. Lakefront Pier Restaurant, Inc., 536
Konstantopoulos v. Town of Whately, 792
Koperwas v. Publix Supermarkets, Inc., 493
Kosher foods, 517–518
Kowavi v. Intercontinental Hotels Group Resources, Inc., 668
Krause v. Sacramento Inn, 673
Krautsack v. Anderson, 606
Kreate v. Disabled American Veterans, 73
Kuchinsky v. Empire Lounge, Inc., 392
Kurzweg v. Hotel St. Regis Corp., 280

L

Lackey v. Disney Vacation Development, 250
Laird v. Eichold, 347
Lake bottom hazards, 298–299
Lakewood Crime-Free Hotel Motel Program, 776
Lamberti v. Positano Ristorante, 740
Landlord-tenant relationship, 334–338
Landmark decision, 51
Landmark Hotel & Casino, Inc. v. Moore, 259
Landrum Mills Hotel Corp. v. Ferhatovic, 298
Laney v. State, 412
Langford v. Vandaveer, 327–328
Lang v. The Red Parrot, Inc., 233
Language discrimination, 65–66
Language, insulting and abusive, 464–466
Lanham Act, 735
LaPlante v. Radisson Hotel Co., 273–274
Laroche v. Denny's Inc., 60
Las Palmeras De Ossining Restaurant, Inc. v. Midway Center Corp., 128
Last clear chance doctrine, 226–227, 234
Lavergne v. America's Pizza Co., 501
Law, 4. *See also* Hospitality law; Regulation; Statutes
    attributes of, 10–14
    sources of, 5–10
Lawson v. Edgewater Hotels, Inc., 295
Lawsuits
    commencing, 24–35
    against Native American tribes, 829–834
    against tribal gaming casino employees, 834–835
Lazar v. Hertz, 630
Ledbetter v. Concord General Corp., 225
Lederman Enterprises, Inc. v. Allied Social Science Associates, 115–116
Lee v. Durow's Restaurant, Inc., 177
Legislative process, 6
Legislators, 7
Legislature, 7
Le Mistral, Inc. v. Columbia Broadcasting System, 416
Lenexa Hotel v. Holiday Hospitality Franchising, Inc., 767
Leonard v. Ryan's Family Steak Houses, Inc., 227
Leon v. Family Fitness Center, Inc., 845
Leo's Partners, LLC v. Ferrari, 151
LeRoy v. Pamax Development, Inc., 716
Less than rule, 226
Levine v. British Overseas Airways Corp., 581
Levin v. Delta Air Lines, Inc., 691
Lewis v. Ritz Carlton Hotel Co., LLC, 468–469
Liability
    absolute/strict, 347
    to adjacent premises, 301
    alcohol sale and, 525–554
    of alcohol vendors, 532–541
    avoiding, 314
    during check-in and check-out, 371–375
    disclaimers and, 621–622
    effect of bailment on, 377–379
    for false imprisonment by casinos, 823
    food sale and, 487–524
    implying greater, 364
    limited, 347–360
    preventive law tips related to, 313–318
    prima facie, 347
    security and, 309–310
    for third-party supplier negligence, 620–621
    of tour operators, 620–621
Liability waivers, for hotel spas, 844–845, 851
Libel, 428
Liberty Mut. Ins. Co. v. Zurich Ins. Co., 346
Licensees, duty owed to, 191–194
License fees, 786–787
    for music performances, 751, 752
Licenses
    failure to renew, 798
    grounds for denying, 783–785
    operating without, 787–788
    preventive law tips concerning, 798
    principles for granting, 781–786
    revocation/suspension of, 788–792
    victualler's, 784
Licensing, 734, 796
    by government, 780, 787–792
    of hotels and restaurants, 780–795
    of hotel spas, 843, 851
    of music performances, 750–757
Liebeck v. McDonald's Restaurants, P.T.S., Inc., 279
Lien, 432
    innkeeper's, 432–434, 442–443
Lienhart v. Caribbean Hospitality Services, Inc., 297
Lighting
    adequate, 262, 316
    outdoor, 287–288
Lightning, 286–287
Likelihood of confusion
    geographic proximity and, 740–741
    in trademark infringement, 736, 737
Limited liability, 347–360
    for clothes and personal property, 360–363
    posting notice of, 357–358
Limiting liability statutes, 348, 363, 397
    in Nevada, 370
    requirements of, 397–398
Lions Club, 73, 94
Liquor liability insurance, 542–543

Liquor licenses, 94, 526–527
    zoning laws concerning, 790
Liquor regulations, miscellaneous, 545–548
Litigants, 23
Liv. Iron Sushi, 639
Lobby inspections, 255
Lockard v. Pizza Hut, Inc., 688
Lockers, for hotel spas, 845, 851–852
Locks, broken, 305
Lodging
    refusing, 407–409
    wrongful refusal of, 408
Loeb v. Tauk Tours, 621
Lomonaco v. Sands Hotel Casino and Country Club, 813
Long v. Coast Resorts, Inc., 80, 92
Lonsdale v. Joseph Horne Co., 250
Lopez v. City of New York, 422
Lopez v. Howth, Inc., 428
Lost baggage tariff, 576
Lost property, unclaimed, 464
Lotteries, 805
Loughran v. The Phillies, 838
Louis v. Commonwealth, 436
Louisiana Department of Health, 497–499
Lourenco v. Trans World Airlines, Inc., 567–569
Love v. Delta Airlines, 585
Loyalty provisions, as rule-of-reason antitrust law violation, 765
Luggage
    airline liability for, 565–569
    lost, 564–576
Lundy v. Adamar of New Jersey, Inc. t/a TropWorld, 817–819
Lundy v. Admar of N.J. Inc., 312
Lupkus v. Otis Elevator Co., 257
Lyons v. Nasby, 536
Lyons v. Red Roof Inns, Inc., 663
Lyttle v. Denny, 243

M

Madan-Russo v. Posada, 846
Madelung v. City of New Haven, 841
Mail, proper handling of, 477–480, 482
Maintenance fee, condominium hotels, 847
Maintenance, of amusement rides, 839
Makousky v. Wing King Three, Inc., 650
Managers, preventive law tips for, 796–798, 849–852
Manchester v. Selectmen of Nantucket, 791
Mandatory recycling, 779–780
Manes v. Coats, 620
Manicures/pedicures, at hotel spas, 842
Mankowski v. Denny's, Inc., 198

Manley v. State, 438
Marina District Development Co., LLC v. Ivey, 812
Maritime laws, riverboat casinos and, 826
Marker, 807
Marketplace, regulation of, 735–762
Mark v. State, 411
Marmer v. Queen of New Orleans at the Hilton, 821
Marquis Towers, Inc. v. Highland Group, 769
Marriott Corp. v. American Academy of Psychotherapists, Inc., 122
Marriott International, Inc. v. Perez-Melendez, 284
Martin v. Boyd Gaming Corp., 828
Martinelli v. Custom Accessories, Inc., 500
Massages, in hotel spas, 846
Master v. Red River Entertainment, LLC, 812
Maurer v. Cerkeunik-Anderson Travel, Inc., 611
McCarley v. West Quality Food Service, 507
McCary v. Commonwealth, 456
McClean v. University Club, 419
McCleod v. Nel-Co Corp., 203
McCoy v. Homestead Studio Suites Hotel, 144
McDonald's Corp. v. Board of License & Inspection Review, 791
McDonald's Corp. v. Town of East Longmeadow, 784–785
McDonald's Corporation v. Board of Selectmen of Randolph, 784
McDonald's food, obesity and, 514
McDonald's v. Kristina Denise Enterprises, 774
McFadden v. Staley, 500
McGee v. Alexander, 543
McGill v. McAninch Corp., 541
McGowan v. St. Antoninus Church, 263
McKeever v. Phoenix Jewish Community Center, 289
McKee v. Isle of Capri Casinos, Inc., 810–812
McLauren v. Waffle House, Inc., 60
Mediation, 42
Medical assistance, 221, 223–224
Medical care, 311–312
    in casinos, 817–820
Medical emergencies, in casinos, 817–820
Medical information, 727
Medical leave, 647–648
Medical services, 318
Medley v. County of Westchester, 840
Mee-Hsiang Lee v. 69 Mott Street Corp., 178
Mejia v. New York Sheraton Hotel, 665–666
Melo-Tone Vending, Inc. v. Sherry, Inc., 161–162
Menu boards safety, 275–276
Menu descriptions, truth in, 513–514
Merchandise samples, liability for, 361–362
Merchantable goods, 489

Mergers, as rule-of-reason antitrust law violation, 762
Meritor Savings Bank v. Vinson, 683
Merrill v. Trump Indiana, Inc., 813, 815
Michalopoulos v. C&D Restaurant, 226, 265
Michigan Restaurant Association v. City of Marquette, 519
Mihill v. Ger-Am Inc., 297–298
Miller v. Warren, 211
Milner Hotels, Inc., v. Brent, 428
Mindykowski v. Olsen & CWB Property Management, Inc. & Alpena Hotels, LLC, 530
Minhas v. Biman Bangladesh Airlines, 601
Mini-monopolies, as rule-of-reason antitrust law violation, 763–765
Minimum height rules, for amusement rides, 839, 851
Minimum-wage requirement, 638–641
    low sales exception to, 639–640
    tips exception to, 640–641
    youth minimum wage exception to, 641
Minkler v. Chumley, 435
Minority rule, 192
Miranda v. Resident and Directors of Georgetown College, 101
Mirrors, hanging in dining rooms, 274–275
Mislaid items, search of, 463–464
Missouri club, 26
Mistake, 124–125
    mutual, 124, 125
    unilateral, 124, 125
Mitchell v. Baker Hotel of Dallas, Inc., 266
Mitchelson v. Sunset Marquis Hotel, 283
Mitigate, 139
Mix v. Ingersoll Candy Co., 490
Mlincek v. CC2 Tree Tenant Corp., 281
Mobile home park, 75
Mohammed v. Air France, 572–573
Monopoly, as rule-of-reason antitrust law violation, 762, 764–765
Montes v. Betcher, 188–189, 299
Montgomery v. McDonald's Corporation, 214
Montreal Convention, 572–573, 581
Moog v. Hilton Hotels Corp., 334
Moog v. Hilton Waldorf-Astoria, 357
Moog v. Waldorf-Astoria, 359
Moose Lodge v. Irvis, 69
Morace v. Melvyn's Restaurant, Inc., 225
Moring v. Arkansas Department of Correction, 681
Morin v. Troymac's, Inc., 499
Morningstar v. Lafayette Hotel Co., 412
Morris v. Players Lake Charles, Inc., 245
Morro v. Resorts Casino Hotel, 648
Morton v. Commonwealth, 435

Motion
    definition, 31
    preliminary, 31
    for summary judgment, 33
Movable steps, 265
Mrs. Murphy's boarding house clause, 68
Mumford v. GNC Franchising LLC, 773
Municipalities
    license fees charged by, 786
    zoning by, 792–794
Munno v. State of New York, 181
Music performances
    licensing of, 750–757
    preventive law tips concerning, 797
Music selection, under the Civil Rights Act of 1964, 64
Musso v. Tourlite International, Inc., 618–619
Mutual-benefit bailment, 380–382, 384
    duty of bailor in, 381–382
Mutuality, 110
Mutual Life Insurance Co. v. Churchwell, 191
Mutual mistake, 124, 125

N

NAACP v. Darcy, Inc., 60
Nashville Clubhouse Inn v. Johnson, 476
National Ass'n of Postmasters of U.S. v. Hyatt Regency Washington, 157–158
National Football League v. McBee and Bruno's, Inc., 747
National Gambling Impact and Policy Commission, 815
National Indian Gaming Commission, 835
National Labor Relations Act (NLRA) of 1935, 722
National Labor Relations Board (NLRB), 723
National Organization of Women (NOW), 93
National origin, 64
    discrimination based on, 64–65, 663–666, 726
Native American reservations
    casinos on, 829–836
    lawsuits against, 829–834
    sovereign authority of, 829, 834–835
Negligence, 12, 174–239
    accidents suggestive of, 199
    in bailment cases, 382–386
    by casinos, 816–820
    concerning theme park animals, 840
    contributory versus comparative, 224–227
    defined, 175
    doctrines favoring defendant, 224–233
    duties owed to guests in swimming areas, 288–299
    duty owed in restaurants and dining rooms, 265–280
    duty owed to guests outside, 280–288
    duty owed to invitees, 187–189

duty owed to licensees, 191–194
duty owed to trespassers, 194–196
elements of, 185–186
in food preparation, 509
hospitality practices and, 241–320
involving amusement rides, 839–840
liability for, 234, 314
nondelegable duties and, 216–217
preventive law tips related to, 235–237
related to medical care, 311–312
within the scope of employment, 214
security and, 302–312
special duties and, 299–302
at theme parks, 839–840
websites related to, 239, 320
Negligence by guest/patron, as absolute liability exception, 347
Negligence cases, elements of, 175–178, 234
Negligence doctrines, favoring plaintiff, 198–224
Negligence, hospitality practices and, 241–312
Negligence per se doctrine, 207–211, 234
proximate cause and, 210–211
Negligent entrustment, 624–626
Negligent hiring, 723
Nelson v. Long Lines, Ltd., 640
Nensen v. Barnett, 468
Nestle Co., Inc. v. Chester's Market, Inc., 742
Nettles v. Forbes Motel, Inc., 243
Nevada case, 127
Nevada, limiting liability statute in, 370
Newberry Junior College v. Town of Brookline, 786
Newman v. Deer Path Inn, 690
Newton v. Standard Candy Co., 489
New York Stock Exchange, Inc. v. New York, New York Hotel, LLC, 824
Ngo v. Reno Hilton Resort Corp., 652
Nichols v. Azteca Restaurant Enterprises, Inc., 683, 687
Nichols v. Frank, 679
Nickel v. Hollywood Casino, 244
Nielson v. Ono and Dollar Rent-A-Car, 626
Nielson v. Ritz Carlton Restaurant and Hotel, 243
Nixon v. Royal Coach Inn of Houston, 409–410
NLRB. See National Labor Relations Board
No-cause termination clause, 159
Noncompetition clause, 150, 152
Nondelegable duty, 216–217
elevator maintenance as, 256–257
Nonguests
duty owed to, 465
right to exclude, 404–407, 408
Nonpayment, right to privacy and, 450
Nordmann v. National Hotel Co., 308

Norman v. Trans World Airlines, Inc., 593
Norris v. Pig'n Whistle Sandwich Shop, Inc., 490
Norris v. State, 776
Northern Pacific Railroad v. United States, 758
North River Insurance Company v. Tisch Management, Inc., 357
Notices, posting in languages other than English, 358
No vacancies, 407
Novak v. Madison Motel Associates, 95
Noveck v. Avis Rent A Car Sys., 627

O

Obeng-Amponsah v. Rorh, Inc., 667
Obesity, advertising and, 514–515
Oby v. Baton Rouge Marriott, 647
Occupancy, disrupting, 481
Occupational Safety and Health Act (OSHA), 10, 721–722
tribal gaming and, 834–835
Oceanfront properties, 296–297
Ochlockonee Banks Restaurant, Inc. v. Colvin, 272
O'Connor v. 11 West 30th Street Restaurant Corp., 61
O'Connor v. Gaspar, 542
Odima v. Westin Tucson Hotel, 664
Odysseys Unlimited, Inc. v. Astrol Travel Service, 616–617
Offer, 110
definite, 111
responses to, 111–112
Offeree, 111
Offeror, 111
Ohio Casualty Insurance Co. v. Todd, 532
Ohio v. Duncan, 456
Okumabuo v. McKinley Community Services, Inc., 664
Olley v. Extended Stay America–Houston, 335–336
Ollie's Barbecue, 89
Olsen v. State, 415
Omega Congress, Inc. v. BAF Tour Services, Inc., 787
Oncale v. Sundowner Offshore Services, Inc., 681
164 Mulberry Street Corp. v. Columbia University, 466
194th St. Hotel Corp. v. Hopf, 266
Online gambling, 806, 836–837
Onyeanusi v. Pan Am, 571
Onyx Acceptance Corporation, 141
Onyx Acceptance Corp. v. Trump Hotel & Casino Resorts, 141
Opening statements, 38
Opryland Hotel v. Millbrook Distribution Services, Inc., 156
Ordinance, 7
Ordonez v. Gillespie, 176–177
Oriental Art Printing v. Goldstar Printing, 757

Orlando Executive Park v. PDR, 308
Orlick v. Grant Hotel and Country Club, 263
Oronoka Restaurant, Inc. v. Maine State Liquor Commission, 788–789
O'Rourke v. Hilton Hotels Corp., 371
OSHA. See Occupational Safety and Health Administration
Otero v. Jordan Restaurant Enterprises, 245
Oubre v. E-Z Serve Corporation, 279, 502–503
Outdoor lighting requirements, 287–288
Outdoor safety, 284
Outdoor sporting facility safety, 284–287
Outside the scope of employment, 214–215
Overbooking, 315
    airline, 596–602, 632
    damages allowed by, 142, 144
    on international flights, 602
    of rental cars, 623
    scope and causes of, 144–147
Overstaying, 412–413
Overtime pay, 641–644

P

Pacello v. Wyndham International, Inc., 217, 312
Pachinger v. MGM Grand Hotel-Las Vegas, Inc., 329, 372
Pacific Diamond Co., Inc. v. Hilton Hotels Corp., 371
Packaged foods, labels on, 516
Packages, proper handling of, 477–480
Padilla v. Manlapaz, Barrio Fiesta Restaurant, et al, 639–640
Pain and suffering, 133
Palace Bar, Inc. v. Fearnot, 182–183
Palagano v. Georgian Terrace Hotel Co., 244
Pancake House, 90
Papa John's International, Inc. v. Rezko, 776
Pappalardo v. NY Health & Racquet Club, 202
Parades, at theme parks, 841
Paradis v. Ghana Airway Ltd., 602
Paraskevaides v. Four Seasons Washington, 355–356
Parianos v. Bruegger's Bagel Bakery, 490
Pari-mutuel betting, 805
Parker v. John Q. Hammons Hotels, Inc., 649
Parker v. Kirkwood, 301
Parking areas
    as grounds for license denial, 784
    zoning laws concerning, 793–794
Parking lots safety, 284
Park on Lakeland Drive, Inc. v. Spence, 841
Parks-Nietzold v. J.C. Penney, Inc., 254
Parks v. Steak & Ale of Texas, Inc., 201–202
Parol, 121
Parol evidence rule, 121

Parris v. Wyndham Vacations Resorts, Inc., 697
Parties, 23
    proof and, 23–24
Past performance, 120–121
Paszkowski v. Chapman, 830
Pathological gambling, 814–815
Patron negligence, as absolute liability exception, 347
Patrons. See also Guests
    alcohol vendor's liability to, 534–536
    duty of business owners to aid, 218–224
    relationships with, 324–340
Patrons' property, 343
    absolute liability for, 347
    appropriate for a safe, 358–359
    liability for, 398
    limited liability for, 347–360
    preventive law tips related to, 397–399
    protecting, 343–402
    in a restaurant, bar, or cloakroom, 391–394
    risk to, 344–347
    websites related to, 402
Patterson v. Domino's Pizza, 767
Paugh v. P.J. Snappers, 689
Pavement problems, 282–284
Pavone v. Mississippi Riverboat Amusement Corporation, 827
Pay-for-view programming, illegal satellite reception of, 748–749
Payment, fraudulent, 438–439
Payne v. Edmonson, 117
Payne v. McDonald's Corp., 768
PDA. See Pregnancy Discrimination Act
Peck v. Rattlesnake Ventures, Inc., 210
Peephole, 305
Peeping toms, 452–455
Peet v. The Sweet Onion, Inc., 499
Pelfrey v. Governor's Inn, 178
Pellegrini v. Landmark Travel Group, 611
Pelman v. McDonald's Corp., 515
People v. Abarrategui, 438
People v. Adams, 438
People v. Alamo Rent-a-Car, 630
People v. D'Antuono, 458
People v. Faureau, 449
People v. Gutierrez, 412, 458
People v. Henning, 460–461
People v. Lerhinan, 412, 458
People v. Love, 411
People v. Ouellette, 459
People v. Perry, 435
People v. Satz, 450
People v. Thorpe, 405–406

People v. Weaver, 415
People v. Zappulla, 462
PepsiCo, Inc. v. Coca-Cola Company, 765
Peremptory challenges, 36
Permits
    failure to renew, 798
    preventive law tips concerning, 798
    principles for granting, 781–786
Perrine v. Paulos, 449
Per se violations, of antitrust laws, 759–762
Personal injury, on international flights, 580–581
Personal property, liability for, 360–363
Person in distress, duty to aid, 217
Persons of ill repute, evicting, 413–414
PGA Tour, Inc. v. Martin, 84
Phillips v. Interstate Hotels, Corp., 64
Phillips v. Taco Bill Corp., 680
Phillips v. West Springfield, 490
Pierce v. State, 776
Pirtle's Administratrix v. Hargis Bank and Trust Co., 300
Places of entertainment, 54–55, 56, 71, 77
Places of public accommodation, 50, 77, 94, 408. *See also* Hotels
    gender discrimination, 93, 95
Plaintiff(s), 23
    legal status of, 187
    negligence doctrines favoring, 198–224
Pleadings, 33
Plessy v. Ferguson, 8
Polesnak v. R.H. Management Systems, Inc., 706
Poleyeff v. Seville Beach Hotel, 296
Police
    alliances with, 345
    reporting illegal activity to, 456
    role in eviction, 425
Police assistance, for trespass, 405–407
Police investigations, guest registers and, 776
Police power, of government, 780
Pollard v. Village of Ovid, 540
Pollock v. Holsa Corp., 466
Pool hazards, guarding against, 295
Pooniwala v. Wyndham Worldwide Corp., 774
Poroznoff v. Alberti, 415
Portanova v. Trump Taj Mahal, 266
Porteous v. St. Ann's Cafe & Deli, 496
Poskos v. Lombardo's of Randolph, Inc., 184
Powell v. Las Vegas Hilton Hotel & Casino, 688
Poythress v. Savannah Airport Commission, 284
Precedents, 7–8
Preexisting condition, 183
Pregnancy
    alcohol risks during, 546

business necessity and, 691
    employment an, 689–698
    reinstatement after, 691–694
Prejudice, national origin, 664
Preliminary Motions, 31
Premier Parks, Inc. v. TIG Insurance Co., 839
Pretrial conference, 35
Pretrial procedure, 34–35
Preventive law tips
    alcohol-related, 550–551
    for casino/theme park managers, 849–852
    employment-related, 725–728
    food-related, 521–522
    for hotel and restaurant managers, 796–798
    liability-related, 313–318
    negligence-related, 235–237
    related to guest rights, 481–482
    related to innkeeper rights, 441–443
    related to patron property, 397–398
    related to travel agents and airlines, 631–633
Price discrimination, as per se antitrust law violation, 759
Price-fixing, 113
Price-fixing agreements, as per se antitrust law violation, 759
Price v. KLM-Royal Dutch Airlines, 580
Price Waterhouse v. Hopkins, 682
Prima facie case, 382
Prima facie evidence, 207
Prima facie liability rule, 347
Prince Heaton Enterprises, Inc. v. Buffalo's Franchise Concepts, Inc., 762
Princess Hotels International, Inc. v. Delaware State Bar Association, 156
Principal, 558
Priority seating rules, airline, 597–600
Prior use of property, as grounds for license denial, 786
Privacy, guest registers and, 776
Privacy rights
    effect of termination of occupancy on, 458
    of hotel guests, 449–455
    in a room registered to another, 462
Private clubs
    under Civil Rights Act of 1964, 68–69
    under state civil rights laws, 68–69
Private-in-name-only clubs, under the Civil Rights Act of 1964, 70–72
Private lawsuit, 89
Privilege, 428
Privity of contract, 507
Probable cause, 457
    for imprisonment by casinos, 823, 849

Probation, 13
Problem gamblers, 814–815
Products liability, strict, 212–213
Professional employees, overtime pay and, 643–644
Professional Golf Association Tours (PGA), 84
Proliance Insurance Co. v. Acura, 384–385
Proof, parties and, 23–24
Property. *See also* Patrons' property
    abandoned, 456, 458
    duty owed on, 198
    innkeeper's lien applicable to, 433
Property damage, privacy rights and, 456
Property in transit, liability for, 363
Property loss liability, bailment and, 375–396
Property past use, as grounds for license denial, 786
Property theft
    from hotel spa lockers, 845
    procedures to limit, 398
Proprietors, rights of, 96–101
    disorderly person, permissible to remove, 96–98
    objectionable persons and trespass, 101
    reasonable rules of establishment, 98–100
    retaliatory exclusion, 100
Prosecutor, 11
    by franchisor, 770
Protected classes, 649
    under state civil rights laws, 78
Proximate cause, 181–184
    negligence per se and, 210–211
Prunty v. Keltie's Bum Steer, 540
Public Citizen, Inc. v. Shalala, 517
Public domain, trademark infringement and, 741–742
Punitive damages, 13, 139–140
    for airline overbooking, 600
    on international flights, 602
    in Title VII cases, 652
Purton v. Marriott International, Inc., 543

Q

Quawrells v. State, 822
Queens City Pizza, Inc. v. Domino's Pizza, Inc., 771–773
Quid pro quo sexual harassment, 679
    employer liability in, 684
Quizno's Master v. Kadriu, 776

R

Racial discrimination, 59–64, 656–662, 726
Racially hostile work environment, 660–662
Radden v. City of Detroit, 788
Radio music, playing amplified, 755–757
Raider v. Dixie Inn, 414, 423

Rainbow Travel Services, Inc. v. Hilton Hotels Corp., 148–150
Ramada v. Jacobcart, Inc., 774
Ramps, safety of, 284
R & R Deli, Inc., v. Santa Ana Star Casino, 832
Rape, 13
Rappaport v. Nichols, 534
Ratcliff v. Rainbow Casino, 820
Rates, guest rights concerning, 474–477
Raymond v. Duffy, 542
Readily achievable, 85
Reasonable accommodation
    for disabilities, 706–707
    for religious holidays and practices, 668–669
Reasonable care, 236
    duty of, 242
    duty to exercise, 211
    in swimming areas, 289–291
    by travel agents, 631
Reasonable certainty, 133
Reasonable expectation test, 490–493
    trend toward, 493–496
Reasonable person standard/test, 178–184
    children and, 203–206
Reasonable protection, duty to provide, 305–308
Reasoning, 14, 16
Rebuttal, 39
Records, maintenance of, 547
Recycling laws, 780, 798
Recycling, mandatory, 779–780
Registration
    role in contracts, 326–328
    of trademarks, 742–745
    using false information, 332–333
Regulation, 10, 734
    of amusement rides, 839
    in franchising, 765–776
    of gambling, 806
    of guest registers, 777
    of hotel/restaurant internal affairs, 776–780
    of hotel room rates, 777–779, 798
    marketplace, 735–762
    obligations beyond, 211
    of recycling, 780
Reich v. Mashantucket Sand and Gravel, 835
Reid v. Her, 246
Reinstatement policies, after pregnancy, 691–694
Relief, claim for, 29
Religious discrimination, 668–669, 726
Religious holidays, reasonable accommodations for, 669–672
Remedies, under state civil rights laws, 78

Remitter, 40
Renaissance v. Zoning Board, 793
Rendon v. Transportation Security Administration, 579
Rene v. MGM Grand Hotel, Inc., 682
Rental cars, 623–630
    accidents in, 624–626
    defective, 626–627
    unauthorized drivers of, 627–630
Reply, 32
Resale price-maintenance agreements, as per se antitrust
    law violation, 759
Rescue doctrine, 221
Reservation contract, breach of, 141–160
Res ipsa loquitur doctrine, 198–203, 234
    elements of, 199–203
Resort hotels, 285
Respondeat superior rule, 213–216, 236
Restaurant, 55, 58
    amplified radio music in, 755–757
    compliance with laws by, 782–783
    detention by, 470
    duty owed guests in, 265–280
    food claims by, 516–517
    food safety in, 487–524
    illegal satellite reception by, 748–749
    liability for patron property in, 391–394
    licensed music performances in, 750–757
    licensing of, 780–795
    managers, preventive law tips for, 796–798
    mandatory recycling by, 779–780
    refusal of service by, 442
    regulation of internal affairs of, 776–780
    right to refuse service, 429–431
    websites related to, 801
    zoning and, 792–794
Restaurateurs, defrauding, 434–438
Résumé fraud, 721
Retaliatory discharge, 645–646, 698–699
Retaliatory exclusion, 100
Reverse discrimination, 662–663
Revocation of a license, 788–792
Reynolds v. L&L Management, Inc., 215
Reynolds v. RIU Resorts & Hotels., 620
Richardson v. Grand Casinos of Mississippi, Inc., 817
Richardson v. N.Y. Dept. of Correctional Services, 662
Richardson v. Sport Shinko, 263
Rights. *See also* Civil rights; Copyright protection;
    Guest rights; Innkeeper rights
    of airline captains, 589–595
    of airline passengers, 592–593
    of airlines, 587–589
    balancing duties and, 5

    of disabled travelers, 582–586
    of proprietors, 96–101
    of travelers, 564–587
Right to equal protection, 8
Right to privacy, in guest room, 449–455
Risk
    anticipating, 849
    assuming at amusement rides, 838
    ignorance of, 233
    misrepresenting, 364–366
Rivera-Aponte v. Restaurant Metropol #3, Inc., 696–697
Riverboat casinos, 805
    Jones Act and, 826–828
Robertson v. Burger King, Inc., 62
Roberts v. Essex Microtex, 439
Roberts v. United States Jaycees, 73
Robinson v. Jacksonville Shipyards, Inc., 680
Robinson v. Jiffy Executive Limousine Co., 216
Rockgate Management Co., v. CGU Insurance, Inc., 429
Rodriquez v. American Airlines, 571
Rodriguez v. Barrita, Inc, 82–83
Rodriguez v. Cardona Travel Agency, 611
Rodriguez v. Goodlin, 537–538
Roe v. Wade, 8
Rogers v. International Association of Lions Clubs, 73,
    94
Rohn v. Wyndham Vacation Resorts, Inc., 695
Romanella v. The Mashantucket Pequot Tribal Nation,
    830
Room-assignment decisions, 410
Room furnishings, children and, 206
Room preferences, 404
Room rates
    for hotels, 777–779, 798
    preventive law tips concerning, 798
Rooms
    cleaning, 314
    contracting for, 141
Room searches, 481
Rosario v. Hilton Hotels Corp., 674
Rosenberg v. State Human Rights Appeal Board, 78, 94
Ross v. Choice Hotels, Inc., 60
Ross v. Kirkeby Hotels, 324
Ross v. Paddy, 276
Roth v. Investment Properties, 357
Rottman v. El Al Israel Airlines, 558–559
Royalties, for music performances, 750
Roy v. Volonino, 530
Rubin v. United Airlines, Inc., 593
Rudloff v. Wendy's Restaurant of Rochester, Inc., 212
Ruggiero v. Perdue Poultry Company, 490
Rule of reason, in antitrust laws, 759–762

Rush v. MGM Grand Detroit, LLC, 813
Ruta v. Delta Airlines, Inc., 593
Rygg v. County of Maui, 296

S

Saachi v. TNT Vacations, 621
Saddle Brook Realty, LLC v. Township of Saddle Brook Zoning Board of Adjustment, 795
Safes
    posting notice of availability of, 353–357
    property appropriate for, 358–359
    providing, 349–353
Safety
    added measures of, 211
    of amusement rides, 839–840, 851
    equipment, swimming-related, 294–295
    in food preparation, 519–522
    workplace, 722
Salazar v. McDonald's, 767
Sales v. Peabody, 843
Salisbury v. St. Regis-Sheraton Hotel, 373–374
Sall v. T.S. Inc., 287
Salte v. YMCA of Metropolitan Chicago Foundation, 312
Salzar v. Giorgio's, 535
Same gender sexual harassment, 681–682
Sams Hotel Group, LLC. v. Environs, Inc., 140
Sanchez v. Bally's Total Fitness Corp., 844
Sanitation, of hotel spas, 843–844, 851
Satellite reception
    illegal, 747–750
    preventive law tips concerning, 796–797
Sawvell v. Gulfside Casino, Inc., 304
Sawyer v. Congress Square Hotel, Co., 412
Sawyer v. Wight, 196 F.Supp.2d, 309
Scale v. American Airlines, 605
Scales v. Six Flags, Inc., 842
Schafer v. JLC Food Systems, Inc., 490
Schatz v. Herco, 283
Scheduled flights, right of airlines to cancel, 587–589
Schlesinger v. Belle of Orleans, LLC, 81
Schleuter v. City of Fort Worth, 794
Schmitz v. M&M MARS, 662
Schneider v. Carlisle Corporation, 121
Schneider v. Suntrips, Inc., 616
Schnuphase v. Storehouse Markets, 270
Schram v. Ohar, 835
Schubert v. Hotel Astor, Inc., 259
Schwapp v. Town of Avon, 661
Schwartz v. Hilton Hotels Corp., 612
Scope of employment, 213
    acting outside, 214–215
Scotti v. W.M. Amusements, 177

Scott v. Salerno and GNOC Corp., d/b/a Bally's Grand Hotel & Casino, 214
Screens, defective, 245–246
Searches, consent to, 458
Search warrant, 457
    exceptions to, 458, 460–461
Searcy v. La Quinta Motor Inns, Inc., 354
Season tickets, at theme parks, 842
Seating
    airline, 597–600
    in casinos, 816
Secondary meaning, in trademark infringement, 741
Secondhand smoke, 518, 522
Security, 317
    at casinos, 821
    liability and, 309–310
    matching to circumstances, 305–308
    responsibility for, 302–312
Security incidents, travel-related, 615
Security measures, basic, 305
Security personnel, firearms and, 310
Security procedures, for cars, 389
Security Services Corp. v. Ramada Inn, Inc., 217
Seelbach, Inc. v. Cadick, 206
Seelbinder v. County of Volusia, 286, 287
Seidenberg v. McSorley's Old Ale House, Inc., 94
Self-service elevators, 256
Seminole Tribe of Florida v. McCor, 830
Service elevators, 315
Service marks, 735–746
    defined, 735
    in franchising, 765–776, 796
Service of process, 29–30
Services, charges for, 482
Settlement, 35
Severn v. Fifth Season Inn, 255
Sexual advances, unwelcome, 683
Sexual harassment, 679–689
    by co-workers, 687–688
    by customers, 688–689
    frequency of, 681
    hostile environment, 679–681, 684–687
    outside the scope of employment, 689
    policies and complaint procedures related to, 689
    quid pro quo, 679, 684
    remedial action for, 687
    same gender, 681–682
    sexual orientation-based, 682
Sexually explicit entertainment, 549
Sexually hostile work environment, 688
Sexually oriented businesses, zoning laws concerning, 794–795

Sexual orientation discrimination, 95–96
Sexual stereotyping, 682–683
Shadburn v. Whitlow, 180
Shaddy v. Omni Hotels Management, Corp., 304
Shamrock Hilton Hotel v. Caranas, 393
Shellfish, raw, 496–499
Sheppard v. Crow-Barker-Paul, 260–261
Sheridan Holiday Inn v. Poletis, 252–253
Sherman Antitrust Act of 1890, 758, 760–762, 764–765
Sherman v. Arno, 282
Sherman v. Marriott Hotel Services, Inc., 62–63
Shiuko v. Good Luck Travel, Inc., 610
Shiv-Ram, Inc. v. McCaleb, 244
Shoe, 807
Showers, malfunctioning, 251
Sidewalks, 282–283
Siegel v. Council of Long Island Educators, Inc., 560
Sieger v. Sieger, 777
Simeon v. The Sweet Pepper Grill, 508
Simmons v. Homatas, 546
Simms v. Prime Hospitality Corp., 303
Simon v. Walt Disney World Co., 842
Singh v. North American Airlines, 605
Sisters of Charity of the Incarnate Word v. Meaux, 376
Sisters of Charity v. Meaux, 845
Sivira v. Midtown Restaurants, Corp., 267
Skating rinks, at theme parks, 841
Ski hills, 285
Slade v. Caesar's Entm't Corp., 405
Slander, 428
Sliding-glass doors, 259
Slight-gross system, 226
Slippery floors, 266
    in hotel spas, 844, 851
Slot machines, malfunctions of, 808–812
Small claims court, 563
Smartt Investments, Inc. d/b/a Xoticas v. Martinez, 794
Smith v. Basin Park Hotel, Inc., 262
Smith v. Blue Mountain Inn, Inc., 530, 536
Smith v. Castaways Family Diner, 650
Smith v. Piedmont Aviation, Inc., 600
Smith v. West Rochelle Travel Agency, Inc., 183–184, 621
Smock v. Peppernill Casinos, Inc., 196
Smoking restrictions, 518–519, 522
Snellgrove v. Hyatt Corp., 181
Sobol v. Continental Airlines, 602
Soggins v. Hillcrest Foods, Inc., 651
Sokaitis v. Bakaysa, 814
Solomon v. Monjuni's Restaurant, 272
Solomon v. Redwood Advisory Co., 691
Soone v. Kyo-Ya Co., Ltd., 707
Soto v. Adam's Mark Hotel, 215

Southern Hospitality, Inc. v. Zurich American Ins. Co., 125–126
Southernmost Affiliates v. Alonzo, 361
Sovereign authority, of Native American reservation, 829, 834–835
Spagnuolo v. McDonald's, 281
Spahn v. Town of Port Royal, 227
Sparks v. HRHH Hotel, 127
Sparks v. Pilot Freight Carriers, Inc., 679
Spas, 803, 842–846, 849, 851–852
Spaude v. Macaroni Grill, 266
Specht v. Netscape Communications, Corp., 131
Special duties, 299–302
Specialized destinations, 803, 849
    websites related to, 855
Specific performance, 132, 140
Spector v. Norwegian Cruise Line, Ltd., 79
Speed v. Northwest Airline, Inc., 466
Spencer v. Red River Lodging, 284
Spiller v. Barclay Hotel, 374–375
Split shifts, 644
Splunge v. Shoney's, Inc., 680
Sporting activities, risks associated with, 229
Sprogis v. United Air Lines, Inc., 674
Staff, fire response training for, 300–301
Stahlin v. Hilton Hotels Corp., 311
Stairway safety, 262–263
Standards, for hotels and restaurants, 780
Starbucks Corp. v. Lundberg, 737
Stare decisis, 7
Starling v. Fisherman's Pier, Inc., 218
Star Tickets v. Chumash Casino Resort, 832–834
State civil rights laws, 77–78
State court system, 28
State Division of Human Rights v. McHarris Gift Center, 77
State Liquor Authority, 94
State of Louisiana v. Timon, 821
State of New Hampshire v. Kim, 814
State of New York v. Waldorf-Astoria, 475–476
State of Utah v. Davis, 841
State of Utah v. Leonard, 436–437
States, alcohol-related legalities in, 553–554
State v. Heffner, 822
State v. Jorden, 776
State v. Lohr, 302
State v. Lowry, 325
State v. Loya, 450
State v. Norval Hotel Co., 777
State v. Perkins, 456
State v. Rock, 839
State v. Todd, 815

State v. Wright, 462

Statute of frauds, 117

Statutes, 7

    common law and, 9

    Constitution and, 8–9

Statutory law, 7

Statutory requirements, for swimming areas, 293–294

Steak & Brew, Inc., v. Beef & Brew Restaurant, Inc., 740

Steak and Ale of Texas, Inc. v. Borneman, 541

Steinberg v. Irwin Operating Co., 192–193

Stein v. Club Med Sales, Inc., 620

Stein v. Walt Disney Co., 837

Stephen v. PGA Sheraton Resort, Ltd., 665

Stephens v. Seven Seventeen HB Philadelphia Corp, 64

Step safety, 261–262

Steps, movable, 265

Sterns v. Baur's Opera House, Inc., 64

Stern v. Four Points by Sheraton Ann Arbor Hotel, 26–27

Stevens v. Spec, Inc., 216

Stevens v. Steak N Shake, Inc., 60

Stolen property

    criminal possession of, 438

    from hotel spa lockers, 845–846

Stonebrook Hillsboro, LLC v. Flavel, 429

Stone v. Courtyard Management Corp., 202

Stouffer Corp. v. Winegardner & Hammons, Inc., 740

Strict liability, 211–212, 234

    of casinos, 820

    for patron property, 346

Strict products liability, 212–213, 236, 508

Stubbs v. McDonald's, 662

Stubbs v. McDonald's Corp, 643

Stulajter v. Harrah's Indiana Corp., 813

Subject matter jurisdiction, 24

Subsequent negligence rule, 226

Subsolutions, Inc. v. Doctor's Associates, Inc., 763

Substantial portion test, 56

Sullivan v. Lake Compounce Theme Park, Inc., 839

Sullivan v. State of New York, 282

Summary judgment, 33

Summary jury trials, 42

Summations, 39

Summer v. Hyatt Corp., 360

Summons, 29, 30

Sun Lounge Tanning Centers v. Superior Court, 846

Superseding occurrence, 183

Supreme Court

    antitrust legislation and, 758

    tribal gaming and, 829–834

    websites, 19

Surfrider Foundation v. Zoning Board of Appeals, 795

Susan Faris Designs, Inc. v. Sheraton New York Corp., 359

Suspension of a license, 788–792

Suspicious circumstances, alertness to, 317

Sweepstakes, 804

Swimming areas, duties owed to guests in, 288–299

Swimming pool safety, 208–210, 316–317

Sysotski v. Air Canada, 580

T

Tables, placement of, 273–274

Taboada v. Daly Seven, Inc., 306–307

Tallarico v. Trans World Airlines, Inc., 583–584

Tandem Properties v. Lawn and Landscape, 127

Tankersley v. New York Brothers Investments, Inc., 538

Tanning booths, in hotel spas, 846

Tariffs, 562–564, 574–576

    disability-related, 585

Tarshis v. Riese Organization, 663

Taverns for Tots, Inc. v. City of Toledo, 518

Tavora v. New York Mercantile Exchange, 676

Taylor v. State, 405

Teen events, alcohol-free, 548

Telephone charges, 476–477, 482

Televisions, hanging, 276

Templeton v. DiPaolo Truck Services, Inc., 386

Tenney v. Iowa Tribe of Kansas, 830

Termination of occupancy, effect on privacy rights, 458–459

Territorial division agreements, as per se antitrust law violation, 759

Territorial restrictions, as rule-of-reason antitrust law violation, 762

Terwillinger v. Kitchen, 540

Theft, 345

    during check-out, 359

    in hotel restaurant, 359–360

    of services, 13, 434–438

Theme parks, 803, 837–842, 849

    admission discounts at, 841–842

    amusement rides at, 838–840

    crowd control at, 837

    negligence at, 839–840

    season tickets at, 842

Thetford v. City of Clanton, 452

Third parties, alcohol vendor's liability to, 536–538

Third-party service suppliers, liability for breach of contract by, 616–619

Third-party supplier negligence, liability for, 620–621

Third-party suppliers, travel agent investigation of, 609–612. *See also* Third-party service suppliers

Thomas v. Duquesne Light Co., 529

Thomas v. HWCC-Tunica, Inc., 489

Thomas v. Isle of Capri Casino, 809

Thomas v. Wyndham Hotel, 294
Thompson v. East Pacific-Enterprises, Inc., 510–511
Thompson v. Lake Edward Township, 784
Thompson v. Pizza Hut, 258
Thompson v. Pizza Hut of America, Inc., 202
Thorough contract, 164
Tiano v. Dillard Department Stores, 672
Time worked, 644
Tips, minimum-wage requirement and, 640–641
Tisch Hotels, Inc., v. Americana Inn, Inc., 736
Titan Cruise Lines v. Elliott, 814
Title VII cases, remedies related to, 651–653
Tobias v. Sports Club, Inc., 534
Torts, 12, 160
 casino-related, 816–824
 guest injuries and, 174
Tournaments, 286
Tour operators, liability of, 620–621
Town of Wellesley Board of Selectmen v. Javamine, Inc.,
 790
Trademark infringement, 12, 735
 after franchise termination, 774–776
 by casinos, 823–824, 850
 descriptive terms in, 741
 geographic proximity in, 740–741
 Internet cybersquatting as, 746
 likelihood of confusion in, 736, 737, 740–741
 penalties for, 737–739
 proving, 736
 public domain and, 741–742
 trademark registration and, 742–745
Trademarks, 735–746, 823
 defined, 735
 in franchising, 765–776
 registration of, 742–745
Trademark search, 738
Trade usage, 127
Training wage, 641
Trans fats, 515
Transients, 53
Transportation Security Administration (TSA), 575
Travel agents, 557
 disclaimers by, 621–622
 duty to disclose, 615–616
 errors and omissions insurance for, 622
 investigation of third-party suppliers, 609–612
 liability for breach of contract by third-party service
 suppliers, 616–619
 liability of, 605–623
 preventive law tips related to, 631–633
 recommendation of travel insurance, 612–616
 third-party supplier negligence and, 620
 websites related to, 635–636

Travelers
 remedies for small damages to, 563–564
 rights of, 564–587
Travelers v. Budget Rent-a-Car Systems, Inc., 627–629
Travel industry, 556–557
 makeup of, 557–563
Travel insurance, 587
 travel agent recommendation of, 612–616
Travelodge Hotels, Inc. v. Budget Inns of Defuniak
 Springs, Inc., 774, 775
Travelodge Hotels, Inc. v. Shivmansi, Inc., 774
Treaties, tribal gaming and, 836
Treble damages, as antitrust law violation penalty, 759
Tremaroli v. Delta Airlines, 574
Trespass, 404
 by overstaying, 413
Trespassers, duty owed to, 194–196
Trial, 36–40
 case-in-chief, 38
 charging jury, 39
 definition, 36
 judgment, 40
 jury deliberations, 40
 jury selection, 37–38
 opening statements, 38
 rebuttal, 39
 summations, 39
 types of, 36–37
 verdict, 40
Tribal Court, 830
Tribal gaming, 806, 830
 casino employees, lawsuits against, 834–835
 dram shop acts and, 835
 Indian Gaming Regulatory Act and, 829–831, 835
 OSHA and, 834–835
Triche v. McDonald's Corporation d/b/a McDonald's
 Restaurant, 501
Trichinosis, 504, 521
Trudgeon v. Fantasy Springs Casino, 834, 835
Truett v. Morgan, 211
Truth-in-menu laws, 513–514
Tserpelis v. Mister Softee, 771
Tucker v. Dixon, 293
Tucson v. Grezafel, 518
Turic v. Holiday Inn, 694
Turner v. Holiday Inn Holidome, 289–291
2625 Building Corp. (Marriott Hotel) v. Deutsch,
 155–156
Tying arrangements
 in franchises, 770–773
 as rule-of-reason antitrust law violation, 762

U

Unauthorized rental car drivers, 627–630
Unclaimed lost property, 464
Underage drinkers, 528–530
Undue hardship, in accommodating disabled persons, 709
Unfair trade practices, 513
Uniform Commercial Code (UCC), 488, 507
Unilateral mistake, 124, 125
Unions, 722–723
Unitary rule, Civil Rights Act of 1964 and, 67–68
United Airlines, Inc. v. Good Taste, Inc., 159
United States Bankruptcy Courts, 24
United States Patent and Trademark Office, 738, 742
United States v. Davies, 458
United States v. E.C. Investments, Inc., 836
United States v. Hilton Hotels Corporation, 760–762
United States v. Joost, 820
United States v. Lansdowne Swim Club, 56
United States v. Marquez, 577–578
United States v. Procknow, 458
United States. v. Sherwood, 820
Unit rentals, of condominium hotels, 847
University Hotel Development, L.L.C. v. Dusterhoft Oil, Inc., 112–113
Unpredictable attack, 304–305
Unreasonable force, 431
Unregistered guests, prohibiting, 419–421
Unwelcome sexual advances, 683
U.S. Attorney General, 89
User Agreement phrase, 131
Uston v. Airport Casino, Inc., 96
U. S. v. Aukai, 578. *See also* United States entries
U.S. v. Davis, 576
U.S. v. Glass Menagerie, Inc., 60
U.S. v. Lansdowne Swim Club, 74–75
U.S. v. Santee Sioux Tribe of Nebraska, 836

V

Valenti v. Great Atlantic & Pacific Tea Company, 507
Valet parking, bailment and, 384
Valets, training, 316
Valid, 109
Valley Products Co., Inc., v. Landmark, A Division of Hospitality Franchise Systems, Inc., 773
Value Rent-A-Car, Inc. v. Collection Chevrolet, Inc., 383–384
Vamos v. Coca-Cola Bottling Company of New York, Inc., 495
Vandemark v. McDonald's Corp., 766
Van de Pol v. Caesars Hotel Casino, 716

Van Etten v. Mashantucket Pequot Gaming Enterprise, 835
Van Rossen v. Penney Travel Services, Inc., 560
Variance
   preventive law tips concerning, 798
   in zoning laws, 795
Vasilios Nicholaides v. University Hotel Associates, 368
Vasil v. Trump Marine Hotel and Casino and Otis Elevator Co., 258
Vaughan v. Amtrak, 695
Vaughn v. Texaco, 657
Vegetarian food, 514
Venetian Casino Resort, LLC v. Venetiangold.com, 746
Verbal abuse, during eviction, 427–429
Verdict, 40
Vermeulen v. Worldwide Holidays, Inc., 561–562
Vern Wells et al. v. Holiday Inns, Inc., 144–146
Vertical price-fixing, as per se antitrust law violation, 759
Victualler's license, 784, 790
Vigilance, active, 188–189
Vinci v. Las Vegas Sands, Inc., 807
Vinson v. Linn-Mar Community School District, 465
Virgo v. Sheraton Ocean Inn, 679
Viscecchia v. Allegria Hotel, 15
Visible intoxication, proving, 531–532
Voidable contract, 110
Void contract, 113
Voir dire, 37
Vylene Enterprises, Inc. v. Naugles, Inc., 769

W

Wackenhut Corp. v. Lippert, 575
Waddell v. Shoney's, Inc., 509
Waiver of liability, for hotel spas, 844–845, 851
Wallace v. Shoreham Hotel Corp., 324–325
Walls v. Cosmopolitan Hotels, Inc., 359
Wal-Mart Stores, Inc. v. Gonzalez, 271
Warfield v. Peninsula Golf & Country Club, 94
Warnings, about amusement rides, 838
Warranty of merchantability, 488–489
   grounds for breach of, 499
Warsaw Convention, 565–569, 580, 602
Warsaw Convention limited liability, grounds for loss of, 570–571
Water faucets, defective, 250
Waterfront risks, created by a hotel, 297–298
Water hazards, 298–299
Waters v. Steak & Ale of Georgia, Inc., 215
Waterton v. Motor Inc., 390–391
Watson v. Enterprise Leasing Company, 630
Watson v. Hollywood Casino-Aurora, Inc., 817

Waugh v. Duke Corporation, 203
Websites, 48
    alcohol-related, 554
    civil-rights-related, 105
    contracts, 170
    employment-related, 731–732
    federal court system, 19
    Food and Drug Administration, 19
    food-related, 524
    for gambling, 836
    negligence, 239
    negligence-related, 320
    patron-property-related, 402
    related to guest rights, 484
    related to hotels and restaurants, 801
    related to innkeeper rights, 445
    related to specialized destinations, 855
    related to travel agents and airlines, 635–636
    Supreme Court, 19
Webster v. Blue Ship Tea Room, Inc., 491–493
Weiss v. El Al Israel Airlines, Ltd., 601–602
Wells v. Burger King Corp., 64
Wenzel v. Marriott International, Inc., 33–34
West-Anderson v. Argosy Casino, 823
West End Pink v. City, 793
Westin Operator, LLC v. Groh, 424–425
Wet floors, in hotel spas, 844, 851
Whirlpools, 254–255
Whitcomb v. El Cajon Ford, 626
White v. Waterbury Lodge, 194
Whites, 61–62
    discrimination against, 663
Wilder v. Nickbert, Inc., 530
Willful misconduct, airline-related, 571
Williams v. Adam's Mark Hotel, 659
Williams v. Arrow Chevrolet, Inc., 673
Williams v. Aztar Indiana Gaming Corp., 814
Williams v. McDonald's of Torrington, 508
Williams v. Milner Hotel Co., 246
Williams v. Northwest Airlines, 603
Williams v. Roche Brothers Supermarkets, Inc., 490
Willig v. Pinnacle Entertainment, 185–186
Wilson v. American Trans Air, Inc., 613–614
Wilson v. Bilinkas, 841
Wilson v. Pier I Imports, 79
Wilson v. Waffle House, 57
Winbush v. Six Flags Theme Park, 837
Window fastenings, limited liability and, 360
Windows/window fixtures
    defective, 245–246
    inspecting, 314

Within the scope of employment, 213
Woeste v. Washington Platform Saloon & Restaurant, 497
Wolfe v. Chateau Renaissance, 251
Women, job discrimination against, 676
Women's International Bowling Conference (WIBC), 158–159
Woods v. Trussville City Council, 784
Wood v. Chalet Susse International, 217
Work environment
    racially hostile, 660–662
    sexually hostile, 679–681, 688
Workplace safety, 722
Would-be guests, refusing lodging to, 407–409
Written contracts, nature of, 120
Wu v. Best Western Lighthouse Hotel, 679
Wyndham International, Inc. v. Ace American Insurance Co., 137–139

X

Xieng v. People's National Bank of Washington, 667

Y

Yearwood v. Club Miami, Inc., 310
Yono v. Coolidge #1, Inc., 215
Young people, discrimination against, 408
Young v. Caribbean Associates, Inc., 276–278
Young v. Delta Airlines, Inc., 579
Young v. Fitzpatrick, 303
Young v. Interstate Hotels and Resorts, 257
Yurchak v. Atkinson and Mullen Travel, Inc., 620

Z

Zabner v. Howard Johnson's, Inc., 494
Zaharavich v. Clingerman, 227
Zaldin v. Concord Hotel, 349–350
Zamora v. Castle Auto Sales, 626
Zeidler v. A&W Restaurants, 774
Zervigon v. Piedmont Aviation, Inc., 590–592
Ziglin v. Player's Island Casino, 808
Zimmerman v. Dominion Hospitality, 434
Zoning
    defined, 792
    hotels and restaurants and, 780, 792–794, 798
    preventive law tips concerning, 798
    variance in, 795

CPSIA information can be obtained
at www.ICGtesting.com
Printed in the USA
LVHW050032091118
596480LV00001B/1/P